BETWEEN RESISTANCE AND MARTYRDOM

Between Resistance and Martyrdom

Jehovah's Witnesses in the Third Reich

Detlef Garbe

Translated by DAGMAR G. GRIMM

THE UNIVERSITY OF WISCONSIN PRESS

Published in association with the
UNITED STATES HOLOCAUST MEMORIAL MUSEUM

The publication of this book was supported by grants from
the ARNOLD-LIEBSTER FOUNDATION,
the UNITED STATES HOLOCAUST MEMORIAL MUSEUM,
and ANDERS 1031 TIC REAL ESTATE.

The assertions, arguments, and conclusions contained herein are those of the author or other contributors. They do not necessarily reflect the opinions of the United States Holocaust Memorial Museum.

The University of Wisconsin Press
1930 Monroe Street, 3rd Floor
Madison, Wisconsin 53711-2059

www.wisc.edu/wisconsinpress/

3 Henrietta Street
London WC2E 8LU, England

Originally published by the Institut für Zeitgeschichte (Munich) as
Zwischen Widerstand und Martyrium: Die Zeugen Jehovas im "Dritten Reich"
© 1993 Oldenbourg Wissenschaftsverlag GmbH, Munich

1   3   5   4   2

Printed in the United States of America

Library of Congress Cataloging-in-Publication Data
Garbe, Detlef, 1956–
[Zwischen Widerstand und Martyrium. English]
Between resistance and martyrdom : Jehovah's Witnesses in the Third Reich / Detlef Garbe ;
translated by Dagmar G. Grimm.
p.   cm.
"Published in association with the United States Holocaust Memorial Museum."
Includes bibliographical references and index.
ISBN 0-299-20790-0 (cloth: alk. paper)
ISBN 0-299-20794-3 (pbk.: alk. paper)
1. Jehovah's Witnesses—Nazi persecution.
2. Jehovah's Witnesses—Germany—History—20th century.
3. National socialism and religion.
I. United States Holocaust Memorial Museum.   II. Title.
BX8525.8.G3G3613   2008
940.53′1808828992—dc22   2007011932

CONTENTS

ILLUSTRATIONS

Figures

Tables

Photos

following page 303

TRANSLATOR'S NOTE

I would like to express my appreciation to all the people who supported the project of translating Dr. Garbe's excellent contribution to scientific literature. The translation is based on the fourth edition of Detlef Garbe's 1999 book *Zwischen Widerstand und Martyrium*, published by Oldenbourg Verlag, Munich, Germany.

First and foremost among these people is my youngest son, Conrad, who showed extraordinary patience and understanding because I had very little time for him, especially during the final period of this translation. Naturally, I also want to thank my dear husband, Eberhard, for his loving support and endurance during this extremely demanding time.

I also want to thank my son Benjamin, at the German branch office of the Watch Tower Society, as well as Jolene Chu at the Watch Tower Society's headquarters in Brooklyn, for their support in helping me with the research of the society's publications. Because of Dr. Garbe's extensive references to the older publications of the Watch Tower Society, it was at times very difficult to locate the corresponding publications in the English language. Therefore, I greatly appreciate their assistance in this regard.

Last but not least, I would like to express my appreciation to Dustin DeGrande, and Edward and Sarah Cobb, in particular, who helped with the polishing of the translated manuscript.

Finally, I would like to express my appreciation and gratitude to my entire family and all my friends without whose loving support and caring assistance I would not have been able to deal with this emotionally distressing material. There were times when, like Dr. Garbe, I was overwhelmed with the tragedies that this persecution brought upon people. At the same time, I find it disturbing to realize what humans in positions of authority are capable of doing to others. Dr. Garbe truly deserves our sincere acknowledgement and recognition for his devoted efforts in making this historical account available to us.

The account touches on an issue at the root of all of mankind's problems: that of power handling. May this piece of German history remind us of the fact that there are two ways of dealing with power. It can be abused, but it can also be used to the benefit of our fellow humans. Despite the fact that the misuse of power was an everyday affair in the Third Reich, with no apparent consequences for those who abused it, there were many people who courageously supported the oppressed, even in the face of serious danger to themselves. Among these were Dr. Kersten, Gustav Ahrend, and Albin Lüdke, to mention just a few. They were only a small minority in this machinery of power-abusing authorities. But they made a difference, even in those darkest of times. May we follow their courageous example and look at our fellow humans with an open mind, and even more importantly, with an open heart. Let us not add to the troubles people have in dealing with their lives; let us bring some sunshine into the lives of people. To do this, we do not need to wait for conditions comparable to those in Nazi Germany. Every day, we have an opportunity to make life a little easier for our neighbors, friends, or family members by giving them a friendly word, supporting them in times of need, and being sensitive enough so as not to hurt them either in word or deed.

In this context, it is probably appropriate to draw again attention to Dr. Garbe's statement in the preface to his book: "May this report serve as a valuable reminder to show a greater appreciation for the past, and to benefit from it, in our effort to shape both our present as well as our future. And may it demonstrate, on the one hand, the consequences that result from practicing inhuman brutality and, on the other hand, the power human conviction and solidarity have in producing perseverance and resistance."

The majority of people will certainly agree that the significance of this statement cannot be overemphasized. Especially at a time when nationalistic emotions run high due to such circumstances as the September 11 attack on the Twin Towers in New York or the anxieties caused by the Iraq war, it is necessary to give careful thought to the question of how we, on an individual basis, respond to such occurrences.

Are we able to put matters in perspective or do we jump to irrational conclusions? Do we, for instance, reject or even persecute certain groups of people only because individuals in this group perform acts of violence? Is our judgment of other people based on sound reasoning or do we blindly follow popular opinion, perhaps out of fear of unpleasant consequences? Do we follow our own conscience or do we blindly accept what the leaders of our country dictate to us?

It is good to think about these questions and ask ourselves what we, on an individual basis, can do to contribute to more peaceful relations with our fellow humans. Therefore, let each one of us be resolved to make a difference, small as it may be.

In conclusion, I would like to direct a word to the people who supported this tremendous task of getting the book ready for publication. Author and translator would be nothing without their support group, such as editor (Sheila Moermond), copy editor (Mary Sutherland), the UW Press publishing house staff, indexer (Tobiah Waldron), and all those working behind the scenes without ever getting recognition. It is therefore appropriate at this place that we express our heartfelt appreciation for the work these people have done to bring this project to a successful end.

The following explanations of recurring terms are intended to help the reader to quickly locate an unfamiliar term and refer back to it. Please also refer to the more extensive list of abbreviations (see pp. xxiii–xxvii).

Bl.	Sheet no. (legal documents are not filed away page by page, but sheet by sheet)
"Deutschland Lied"	Also "Deutschlandlied," German national anthem: "Deutschland, Deutschland über alles" (Germany, Germany above All)
Führerprinzip	Leadership principle
Gestapa	Berlin central office of the Secret State Police
Gestapo	Various regional offices of the Secret State Police throughout Nazi Germany
"Horst Wessel Lied"	Song considered to be second in popularity to "Deutschlandlied," also known as "Die Fahne hoch" (Lift High the Banner)
Kieler Schule	Especially radical part of the legal doctrine in National Socialism that tried to separate dispensation of justice from its affiliation with the written law
legal authorities	Legal system under the Reich Ministry of Justice (Reichsjustizministerium/RJM), including court, judiciary, and penal systems

OKH	Controlled only military forces operating from land, in contrast to the OKW
OKW	Controlled all armed branches (military forces operating from land, naval forces, and air force) and under the direct command of Hitler
police authorities	Law enforcement under the Gestapa, including the Gestapo, various police offices, and political police
Postschutz	Works security and air-raid protection service of the Reich Post Administration along paramilitary lines
PrV office	Special compensation office set up during the early postwar period for the purpose of assisting people who had been politically, racially, and religiously persecuted during National Socialist rule
Reichsführer SS	Reich leader SS
RJM	Reich Ministry/Minister of Justice
SS	Schutzstaffel, a special armed branch of the NSDAP (National Socialist German Worker's Party), consisting of particularly reliable members of the party under leadership of Heinrich Himmler, SS Reich leader
Stürmer	An anti-Semitic weekly newspaper with high circulation in the Third Reich, published by the disreputable Nazi leader F. J. Streicher
völkisch	German exclusivist ethnic nationalism
Volksgemeinschaft	People's community
Volksgenossen	National comrades

DAGMAR G. GRIMM

PREFACE TO THE GERMAN EDITION

In the summer of 1989 the Faculty of the Science of History at Hamburg University approved as a dissertation the following work of research, which I had conducted—with occasional breaks—between 1984 and 1989. For publication purposes, I revised and considerably shortened the study, particularly in the commentary. As far as seemed appropriate, I have also included new findings published on the subject since the completion of my dissertation. Because of its more comprehensive discussion of the sources as well as its extensive literature and subject references, the dissertation may be used for special study purposes. The Munich Institut für Zeitgeschichte, the Hamburg Forschungsstelle für die Geschichte des Nationalsozialismus, and the Neuengamme KZ-Gedenkstätte each have a slightly revised version of this dissertation, which can be examined at those locations.

This dissertation was supervised by Professor Arnold Sywottek, who served as my primary examiner, and Professor Klaus-Jürgen Müller, who served as my second examiner. Their critical suggestions and constructive directions proved to be considerably helpful. I am especially thankful to Professor Sywottek, who represents what is best described by the traditional designation of a "thesis supervisor"—the role of an encouraging associate and counselor. I also want to thank Bruno Knöller, whose report at a meeting of the Evangelical Academy of Bad Boll in the spring of 1984 about his persecution provided the impetus for this work. His confidence, kind support, and especially his encouragement toward me as an "outsider"—encouragement not to lose heart but to continue working on this subject—proved to be a great stimulus to my work. He motivated me to continue despite the reservations of many of those involved, including that of the branch office of the Watch Tower Bible and Tract Society in Selters (Taunus). I am also grateful to all those who helped with the archival research, those who took upon themselves the effort of recollection and thereby became invaluable sources of information, and those who supported my academic studies by entrusting personal documents to me. I am especially thankful to those who showed hospitality toward me. Their candor was invaluable, and their assistance often included board and lodging.

I want to thank the following people for contributing to this work through their testimonies as witnesses or through the supply of important references and pieces of evidence. Among these were Lauritz G. Damgaard, Günther Fahle, Norbert Haase, Karl Hanl, Albrecht Hartmann, Dr. Elke Imberger, Dr. Hermann Kaienburg, Alfred Knegendorf, Dr. Werner Koch, Professor Dietfrid Krause-Vilmar, Elise Kühnle, Hermann Langbein, Helmut Lasarcyk, Willi Lehmbecker, Hubert Mattischek, Reimer Möller, Alois Moser, Dr. Max Oppenheimer, Günther Pape, Marut G. Perle, Richard Rudolph, Günther Schwarberg, Rolf Schwarz, Walter Schwarz, Margot Seidewitz, Josef Ernst Straßer, Charlotte Tetzner, Walter Todt, Ernst Wauer, Norbert Weiss, Joachim Wiechoczek, Johan Wildschut, Rolf Zehender, Karl-Heinz Zietlow, as well as the many people whose names are not listed here.

I also want to acknowledge the assistance that I received from the staff of national, religious, and private archives. The following archives, research institutions, and organizations for victims of persecution, in particular, provided support: Bayerisches Hauptstaatsarchiv; Bundesarchiv in Koblenz; Bundesarchiv–Militärarchiv in Freiburg; the Berlin Document Center; Evangelisches Zentralarchiv in Berlin; Geheimes Staatsarchiv Preußischer Kulturbesitz; Hamburger Landesamt für Wiedergutmachung, Institut für Zeitgeschichte, Kreismuseum Wewelsburg, Concentration Camp Memorial in Dachau; Concentration Camp Memorial in Neuengamme; Landesarchiv in Schleswig-Holstein; Museum Auschwitz (Oswiecim); Staatsanwaltschaft beim Landgericht Hamburg; Staatsarchiv in Hamburg; Staatsarchiv in Munich; the study group for research and communication of the history of German resistance from 1933 to 1945; Vereinigung der Verfolgten des Naziregimes/Bund der Antifaschisten, Landesverband Hamburg.

In addition, I want to thank the Institut für Zeitgeschichte, Dr. Norbert Frei, and Oldenbourg Verlag for publishing my work.

At this point I also want to thank those who supported me in other ways. Primarily, the Evangelical study commission and my parents for their continuous support, my brother Eckart Garbe, and above all my wife, Brigitte Drescher, for their remarkable willingness to listen when the inevitable pressure of dealing with this subject seemed overwhelming.

Much has already been said and written about the people and the powers of the Third Reich, just as many discussions have been held about the victims who suffered and were persecuted. But to this day, the extent to which the National Socialist regime utilized its power has not been completely assessed. This book reports about religious people who refused to conform to the Third Reich but whose faith in God and trust in his biblical promises gave them the strength to preserve their respect for life, even during those difficult times. May this report serve as a valuable reminder to show a greater appreciation for the past, and to benefit from it, in our effort to shape both our present as well as our future. And may it demonstrate, on the one hand, the consequences that result from practicing inhuman brutality and, on the other hand, the power human conviction and solidarity have in producing perseverance and resistance.

DETLEF GARBE

Hamburg
March 1993

PREFACE TO THE ENGLISH EDITION

The victims of National Socialist Germany reach into the millions: people rounded up for forced labor, especially those from Eastern European countries and Soviet prisoners of war, Jews, Sinti and Romanies, the disabled and mentally ill, members of resistance groups and victims of Nazi reprisals in the states under German occupation, Communists and other political opponents of the regime, opposition church groups and labor unions, people who were persecuted because of homosexuality or presumed antisocial behavior, and many more. Members of the religious organization of Jehovah's Witnesses also suffered the full force of persecution. Because of their worldwide prevalence, their missionary activities, and the resulting public exposure, Jehovah's Witnesses are well known to many people. However, few people are familiar with the historical details about this religious organization. This book reports about the ruthless persecution of members of this religious denomination, their nonconformity, their conscientious objection, and the unique situation Jehovah's Witnesses faced in the concentration camps, marked as a separate group by a "purple triangle," or patch.

It is a welcome circumstance that this first, comprehensive scholarly study on this subject, which is considered a standard work and has initiated a number of additional studies, has now also been made available to American readers. The translation is based on the fourth edition of the book *Zwischen Widerstand und Martyrium: Die Zeugen Jehovas im "Dritten Reich,"* which has been revised and amended, and published by R. Oldenbourg Verlag in 1999. In arranging the now-available translation, minor changes have been made and photographs were included. However, it was not possible to incorporate findings of more recent literature. For instance, the new book by M. James Penton, *Jehovah's Witnesses and the Third Reich: Sectarian Politics under Persecution* (University of Toronto Press, 2004), has not been taken into consideration. In this context, however, I would like to refer the reader to my comments about Penton's previous publications, which he also uses as a basis for his new study. His statements, source selection, and interpretation reflect a deep-seated aversion against this religious association, of which he had once been a member. According to Penton's new theory, in 1931/32 the Watch Tower Society's President Rutherford made an adjustment in the teachings of Jehovah's Witnesses with regard to determining its relationship to Judaism because, in Germany, everything pointed to the fact that Hitler would come to power. In this way, Rutherford supposedly wanted to adapt to the anti-Semitic aggression of National Socialism. Contemporary literature does not support such assumptions. In fact, reports in Jehovah's Witnesses' magazine *Golden Age* during that time period show that, in the publications of Jehovah's Witnesses, the Hitler movement was clearly criticized as being ungodly and its anti-Semitism was strongly condemned. Penton does indeed have a right to hold reservations against the religious teachings and practices of Jehovah's Witnesses, but from a historiographic viewpoint Penton's writings perhaps show a lack of scientific objectivity.

Even though my study also includes details about the persecution in neighboring countries, it deals primarily with conditions in Germany during the period between 1933 and 1945. Therefore, it is necessary to provide the American readers with a particular explanation. In the United States, as a result of immigration, a complex religious situation has grown over the centuries, resulting in the coexistence of various denominations. The religious situation in Germany during the first part of the twentieth century, on the other hand, was still marked by a state-church tradition and the predominance of the two major "Volkskirchen" (the Roman-Catholic Church and the Evangelical regional churches, churches to which the majority of people belonged). In southern Germany, religious life was predominated by the Roman Catholic Church, which was also extremely influential in social and political realms. The church developed a complex structure of associations and, prior to 1933, even influenced governmental actions by means of the closely associated denominational parties "Zentrum" and "Bayerische Volkspartei." In northern Germany, the Evangelical churches predominated the religious scene. In 1918, at the end of World War I, as a result of the November Revolution, the German Empire was replaced by a Republic. Prior to that period, this part of Germany was predominantly under territorial rule. Accordingly, the respective *Landesherr* (local ruler) was also in charge of the church in his domain. In this climate, other religious denominations generally faced a difficult struggle, even if they enjoyed state recognition. As a new religious group, the "International Association of Earnest Bible Students" (from 1931 on, Jehovah's Witnesses), with their Watch Tower Bible and Tract Society publishing house, were exposed to this situation in a very special way. The Bible Students Association, which had always displayed anticlerical agitation, was confronted from the outset with a climate of opposition.

The publication of this book would not have been possible without the support of sponsors. I would therefore like to thank every one of them, in particular, Benton Arnovitz, Robert Buckley, and Patricia Heberer from the U. S. Holocaust Memorial Museum (Washington, D.C.); the Arnold-Liebster Foundation (Karben, Germany); as well as the assistance of Jolene Chu from the Jehovah's Witness Holocaust-Era Survivors Fund, Inc. (Patterson, New York). The University of Wisconsin Press deserves credit for diligently supervising the preparations for publication. For many years, Dagmar Grimm carried out the significant work of translation. She performed this task with great professionalism, tireless enthusiasm, and diligent meticulousness. Her commitment for this project, which required overcoming a number of obstacles, proved to be an extraordinary circumstance.

On behalf of all the contemporary witnesses who have provided reports to me and agreed to extensive discussions, this book is dedicated to ninety-five-year-old Richard Rudolph, who—for his faith—suffered nine years of imprisonment in National Socialist concentration camps and subsequently was imprisoned another ten years under Communist rule in prisons of the German Democratic Republic.

DETLEF GARBE

Hamburg
November 2007

ABBREVIATIONS

AfW	Amt für Wiedergutmachung (Office for Compensation)
AG	Amtsgericht (Municipal Court)
B.D.M.	Bund Deutscher Mädel (National Socialist Association for Girls)
BA	Bundesarchiv (Federal Archives)
BA-MA	Bundesarchiv-Militärarchiv (Federal Military Archives)
BBG	Berufsbeamtengesetz (Tenured Civil Servant Law)
BDC	Berlin Document Center
BEG	Bundesentschädigungsgesetz (Federal Compensation Law)
BGB	Bürgerliches Gesetzbuch (German Civil Code)
BGH	Bundesgerichtshof (Federal Court of Justice)
BHStA	Bayerisches Hauptstaatsarchiv (Bavarian Main State Archives)
Bl.	Sheet no.
BPP	Bayerische Politische Polizei (Bavarian Political Police)
DAF	Deutsche Arbeitsfront (German Labor Front)
DDR	Deutsche Demokratische Republik (German Democratic Republic, 1949–89)
DdW	Dokumentationsarchiv des deutschen Widerstandes (Documentation archives of the German resistance)
DhN	Dokumentenhaus der KZ-Gedenkstätte Neuengamme (Document Center of the Neuengamme Concentration Camp Memorial)
DJ	*Deutsche Justiz*
DJZ	*Deutsche Juristenzeitung*
DKBl.	*Deutsches Kriminalpolizeiblatt*
DÖW	Dokumentationsarchiv des österreichischen Widerstandes (Archives of the Austrian Resistance)
DPfar	Deutsches Pfarrarchiv (German parish archives)

DR	Deutsches Recht (German law)
DRiZ	*Deutsche Richterzeitung*
Drs.	Printed matter
DV	*Deutsche Verwaltung*
DVerwBl.	*Deutsche Verwaltungsblätter*
DVO	Durchführungsverordnung (Implementing Regulation)
EKD	Evangelische Kirche in Deutschland (Evangelical churches in Germany)
ETG	Ernst Thälmann Gedenkstätte (Ernst Thälmann Memorial)
EZA	Evangelisches Zentralarchiv in Berlin (Central Berlin Evangelical Archives)
FGN	Forschungstelle für die Geschichte des Nationalsozialismus in Hamburg (Research Office for the History of National Socialism in Hamburg); today called Forschungsstelle für Zeitgeschichte, Hamburg
GBu	Gedenkstätte Buchenwald (Buchenwald Memorial)
Gestapo	Geheime Staatspolizei (Secret State Police)
Gestapa	Geheimes Staatspolizeiamt in Berlin (Secret State Police/ Secret State Police office in Berlin)
GG	Grundgesetz der Bundesrepublik Deutschland (Constitution of the Federal Republic of Germany)
GnH	Gnadenheft (Records of Act of Pardon)
GStAPrK	Geheimes Staatsarchiv Preußischer Kulturbesitz (Secret State Archives of the Prussian Cultural Heritage)
HRGZ	*Hanseatische Rechts- und Gerichts-Zeitschrift*
HRR	*Höchstrichterliche Rechtsprechung*
HSG	Hanseatisches Sondergericht (Hanseatic Special Court)
IBSA	International Bible Students Association
IfZ	Institut für Zeitgeschichte (Institute for Contemporary History)
JW	*Juristische Wochenschrift*
KmW	Kreismuseum Wewelsburg (Wewelsburg District Museum)
KPD	Communist Party of Germany
KSSVO	Kriegssonderstrafrechtsverordnung (Special Penal Regulations during War)
KStVO	Kriegsstrafverfahrensordnung (War Penal Code)
KZGDa	KZ-Gedenkstätte Dachau (Concentration Camp Dachau Memorial)
LA SH	Landesarchiv Schleswig-Holstein (State Archives of Schleswig-Holstein)

MAu	Museum Auschwitz (Auschwitz Memorial)
MBliV	*Ministerialblatt für die Preußische innere Verwaltung*
MD	*Materialdienst*
MdI	Minister/Ministerium des Innern (Ministry/Minister of the Interior)
MfS	Ministerium für Staatssicherheit der DDR (Ministry for State Security)
MGRa	Mahn- und Gedenkstätte Ravensbrück (Ravensbrück Memorial)
MStGB	Militärstrafgesetzbuch (Military Penal Code)
NHS	Nachlaß Hans Schwartz (Unpublished works of Hans Schwarz)
NS	National Socialist
NSDAP	Nationalsozialistische Deutsche Arbeiterpartei (National Socialist German Worker's Party)
NSV	Nationalsozialistische Volkswohlfahrt (National Socialist People's Welfare Organization)
OKH	Oberkommando des Heeres (High Command of the Army)
OKW	Oberkommando der Wehrmacht (Wehrmacht High Command)
OVG	Oberverwaltungsgericht (Higher Administrative Court)
PrGS	*Preußische Gesetzessammlung*
PrMdI	Preußischer Minister/Preußisches Ministerium des Innern (Prussian Ministry/Minister of the Interior)
PrOVG	Preußisches Oberverwaltungsgericht (Prussian Higher Administrative Court)
REG	Rückerstattungsgesetz (Restitution law)
RFSS SS	Reichsführer SS (Reich leader—Heinrich Himmler as head)
RG	Reichsgericht (Reich Court)
RGBl.	*Reichsgesetzblatt*
RJM	Reichsjustizministerium/Reichsjustizminister (Reich Ministry/Minister of Justice)
RJWG	Reichsjugendwohlfahrtsgesetz (Reich Youth Welfare Law)
RKG	Reichskriegsgericht (Reich Military Court)
RKM	Reichskriegsministerium (Reich Ministry of War)
RLB	Reichsluftschutzbund (Reich Federation for Air Raid Protection)
RMBliV	*Ministerialblatt des Reichs- und Preußischen Ministeriums des Innern*

RMdI	Reichsminister des Innern (Reich Ministry of the Interior)
RSHA	Reichssicherheitshauptamt (Reich Security Main Office)
RuPrMdI	Reichs- und Preußischer Minister des Innern (Reich and Prussian Minister of the Interior)
RverwBl.	*Reichsverwaltungsblatt*
RzW	*Rechtsprechung zum Wiedergutmachungsrecht*
SA	Armed and uniformed branch of the NSDAP
SD	Sicherheitsdienst der SS (SS Security Service)
SG	Sondergericht (Special Court)
SH SG	Schleswig-Holsteinisches Sondergericht (Schleswig-Holstein Special Court)
SLG HH	Staatsanwaltschaft beim Landgericht Hamburg (Public prosecutor's office at the Hamburg Regional Court)
SPD	Sopade (German Social Democratic Party)
SS	Schutzstaffel (a special armed branch of the NSDAP)
Sta HH	Staatsarchiv Hamburg (State Archives of Hamburg)
StA M	Staatsarchiv München (State Archives of Munich)
StGB	Strafgesetzbuch (German Penal Code)
StPO	Strafprozeßordnung (Code of Penal Procedure)
USHRI	U. S. Holocaust Research Institute
VB	*Völkischer Beobachter*
VGH	Volksgerichtshof (People's Court)
VOSchdW	Verordnung zur Ergänzung der Strafvorschriften zum Schutz der Wehrkraft des deutschen Volkes (Amendments involving punishment regulations for the protection of military strength of the German nation)
VOSchVuS	Verordnung des Reichspräsidenten zum Schutz von Volk und Staat (Decree of the Reich President for the Protection of People and State)
VVN	Vereinigung der Verfolgten des Naziregimes (Association of Persecution Victims of the National Socialist Regime)
WG	Wehrgesetz (Military Service Law)
WTG	Wachtturm Bibel- und Traktat-Gesellschaft (Watch Tower Society)
WVHA	Wirtschafts-Verwaltungshauptamt (SS Central Office for Economy and Administration)
ZAkDR	*Zeitschrift der Akademie für deutsches Recht* (Journal of the College for German Law)
ZBB	*Zeitschrift für Beamten- und Behördenangestelltenrecht* (Journal for Civil Servants and Office Clerks)

ZJJ	*Zentralblatt für Jugendrecht und Jugendwohlfahrt* (Leading Gazette for Juvenile Justice and Welfare)
ZWR	*Zeitschrift für Wehrrecht* (Journal for the Armed Forces)

BETWEEN RESISTANCE AND MARTYRDOM

Introduction

Jehovah's Witnesses are known to the general public primarily for their doorbell ringing or street-corner sales of the *Watchtower*.[1] What is generally not known is that in Germany, during the infamous Third Reich, this comparatively small denomination was relentlessly persecuted and suppressed. Just a few months after the National Socialist (NS) rise to power, Jehovah's Witnesses—as this Christian denomination has called itself since 1931—were banned. The older designations, Bibelforscher (Bible Students) and Ernste Bibelforscher (Earnest Bible Students), which are abbreviated forms of their official name, Internationale Bibelforscher-Vereinigung (IBV) [International Bible Students Association (IBSA)], remained in use.[2] Consequently, those adhering to the teachings of Jehovah's Witnesses frequently came into conflict with the NS regime due to their defiance of the ban. They steadfastly resisted its demands, including that of giving the obligatory Hitler salute and joining coercive NS associations. As a result thousands of them suffered in prisons and concentration camps, or the NS legal authorities persecuted them as conscientious objectors on the charge of demoralization of the armed forces. Eventually, after the start of the war, large numbers of them were sentenced to death.

Jehovah's Witnesses belong to the group of largely "forgotten victims" of the NS regime.[3] Apparently, the public has not shown much interest in their persecution. In contrast, the request of larger social institutions such as political parties, labor unions, and churches to document their own participation in acts of resistance has initiated a great deal of research and analysis. To a great extent, historiographic studies took into account appeals for legitimacy of these large institutions, which in order to improve their image maintained a "representation theory on acts of resistance."[4] For this purpose, they tried to relate acts of resistance of organizational units, small groups, and individuals (who, at that time, were frequently isolated even within their own ranks) to the overall behavior of large social institutions between 1933 and 1945. This approach categorized acts of resistance against the NS regime according to the respective share that the churches, labor unions, and political parties had in those activities. However, acts of resistance of individuals and groups not belonging to any of these large institutions, especially if they lacked (and in some cases still lack) recognition from society in general, were ignored for years, even decades, to come.

This tendency is particularly apparent in studies on acts of resistance based on religious conviction. Meanwhile, an abundance of publications fill the shelves of specialized libraries featuring the roles of the two major churches in the NS state, their church struggle and clerical answer to NS provocation. Yet, hardly anything is known about the history of the minor denominations between 1933 and 1945.[5] Comprehensive studies on resistance and social refusal, and even separate essays on acts of resistance of Christians in the Third Reich, almost never take into consideration the minor free churches and various other religious denominations.[6] Often this omission may simply indicate a lack of reflection since these smaller religious groups and denominations seem to be beyond the purview of many historians and church chroniclers.

From this point of view, the lack of recognition of Jehovah's Witnesses in historical studies seems understandable considering that, based on their membership, they occupied a rather subordinate place even among the minor denominations.[7] Nevertheless, the lack of interest, even in pertinent literature, is indeed surprising. Friedrich Zipfel, the first historian to manifest an interest in this subject, acknowledges that the persecution of Jehovah's Witnesses is indeed "a very unique phenomenon."[8]

In many ways the history of Jehovah's Witnesses between 1933 and 1945 illustrates some remarkable characteristics in need of explanation:

- The group of Jehovah's Witnesses was the first religious denomination in the Third Reich to be banned.
- No other religious denomination opposed the coercion of the National Socialists with comparable determination.[9] The unity within the group and its missionary spirit prompted a degree of participation in acts of resistance that was otherwise observed only in the KPD (German Communist Party) during the first two years after the NS takeover,[10] in minor political groups like the Internationaler Sozialistischer Kampfbund (ISK [International Socialist Militant Alliance]), or in the KPD Opposition (KPO [Communist Opposition Party]).[11]

- The courageousness and audacity of the members of this numerically insignificant denomination in expressing their convictions had surprising repercussions. At times, the "Bible-Student issue" occupied the highest authorities in the justice administration, the police, and the SS.[12]
- Of all Christian denominations, Jehovah's Witnesses were the most severely and relentlessly persecuted group under NS rule.[13] Hanns Lilje, long-standing bishop of the Hannover National Evangelical-Lutheran Church, asserted in 1947 that "not one of the Christian denominations . . . even came close when compared with their numbers of martyrs."[14]
- During this period, Jehovah's Witnesses were persecuted with such violence and relentlessness that historians compared their fate with that of the Jews.[15]
- In compensation law, because of their indiscriminate persecution, which was based exclusively on a membership in their denomination, the Bible Students, together with the "Jews, including the so-called 'first degree mixed,'" and, "following December 8, 1938, also the gypsies," are placed in among the so-called "group-related victims of persecution."[16]
- Apart from the even smaller group of the Seventh-day Adventist Reform Movement,[17] Jehovah's Witnesses comprised the only Christian group in the Third Reich who propagated, and on a large scale even practiced, conscientious objection. "They can make the claim of having been the only grand scale conscientious objectors in the Third Reich who refused military service openly and based on their conscience."[18]
- In the concentration camps, the SS identified the different groups of prisoners by triangular patches of various colors. Accordingly, political prisoners received red, criminals green, asocials black and homosexuals pink patches. The Bible Students, as a separate category, wore purple patches. However, this classification did not include all those who were persecuted by the National Socialists because of their religiously motivated resistance (for instance, clergymen usually had to wear the red patch), but instead applied specifically and exclusively to the members of this ideological denomination. This exclusive designation denotes, in many ways, the special place Jehovah's Witnesses occupied within the concentration camps. They formed a "separate category of prisoners who clearly distinguished themselves sociologically from all others."[19] Even fellow prisoners viewed the Bible Students as the most "amazing group . . . in the concentration camps."[20]
- Moreover, in pertinent literature, Jehovah's Witnesses are depicted as the only group of prisoners "who could have ended their

imprisonment through actions on their own."[21] However, it is also
acknowledged that Jehovah's Witnesses never, or almost never, used
this possibility.[22] "Only six German or Austrian Bible Students
availed themselves of this option."[23]

In view of the various striking characteristics, each of which requires
a closer examination, and their undeniable historical pertinence, which
despite the numerical marginality of the group cannot easily be dismissed, the evident research deficiencies in this context cannot be ascribed merely to the fact that historical studies in general do not adequately recognize presumed (or real) outsider and marginal groups. As
this study shows, not even the available sources proved to be an insur-
mountable obstacle in approaching this subject. Instead, the reservations of historians seem to be based on the structure of, and unfamiliar-
ity with, the group under consideration. The neglect in approaching
this subject can probably be attributed to certain "peculiarities" of this
controversial denomination: its teachings, which in rational categories
are difficult to understand (especially for those unfamiliar with the Bible),
its intrinsic moral code, and its separation from the outside world. Furthermore, in resistance historiography there is no category for the nonconformist, resistance-oriented, nonsubversive but also radical attitude
of Jehovah's Witnesses, who indeed resisted the NS regime with conscientious determination, even in the face of death, and yet were not active "resistance fighters." They had no intentions of changing the political system. Rather, their acts of resistance were religiously motivated
with the objective of practicing their faith without interference, keeping
true to the commandments of the Bible, and thus fulfilling their responsibility toward God. They regarded their resistance to be an act of confession, a requirement for spiritual self-assertion.

Another possible reason for the lack of recognition can be seen in
the fact that the resistance of this minor group involves a challenge to all
those who claim for themselves to live by Christian moral values and to
have a sense of social responsibility; especially considering that certain
parts of the population regard and reject the views of Jehovah's Witnesses to this day as "doctrinaire," "simple-minded," or plainly "ridicu-
lous."[24] However, it is impossible to ignore that as a group, Jehovah's
Witnesses in NS Germany "took a more courageous stand, prayed
more fervently, believed more cheerfully, and loved more passionately
than many other Christians."[25] Their critics may find it irritating and
difficult to accept that in comparison to the general failure of others,

these "religious fanatics" and "sectarians" were equipped with superior missionary zeal and showed more determination and resistance.

To avoid an obscure and incomprehensible picture, a historical study of Jehovah's Witnesses during the NS period has to examine also their motivations and reason and, consequently, their beliefs as well as their preaching activity. At the same time, the study has to remain free from theological evaluations. As soon as one begins to dispute the teachings of Jehovah's Witnesses, one loses the descriptive purpose of a historical study—that of reporting about historical occurrences based on available sources in an effort to reconstruct past events on an empirical basis.[26] Writing about the past for evaluative purposes is as inappropriate for such a study as confusing the purpose of research studies on resistance with an attempt for public recognition and (as often is the case) the establishment of a literary "memorial" for the group concerned.

In many ways, the conduct of Jehovah's Witnesses in the Third Reich is quite impressive, and their sufferings evoke strong emotions. It is certainly also embarrassing that the churches accepted the martyrdom of Jehovah's Witnesses under the SS state "with the same indifference with which they accepted [the martyrdom] of the political Left."[27] These truths do not exempt us from applying to the history of Jehovah's Witnesses the same critical standards that are applied in historical studies of other groups or individuals in order to determine their actions, failures, and objectives during the NS period or any other period of time. This approach to historical study leaves unaffected the respect for a different ideological or religious conviction. In this regard, this study also takes into account, as far as possible, the different terminology used by this religious group. For example, the denomination of Jehovah's Witnesses is commonly called a sect. But, like any other denomination, Jehovah's Witnesses determinedly reject this designation, claiming to be the only "true faith" and, thus, "God's channel of salvation." The designation "sect" stands for a group that separates itself from the basic church and advocates different teachings. This, however, is more a matter of station than of content, and therefore a matter of personal opinion.[28] Moreover, to designate a group as a sect immediately implies an "unfavorable theological judgment."[29] Sometimes, the designation "sect" carries the stigma of inferiority; it is also used as a synonym for "misconception." Since the objective of this study is not an examination of the teachings of Jehovah's Witnesses, the discriminatory designation "sect" is used only in the context of quotations or in reference to a specific point of view.

The purpose of this study is to describe the history of the denomination of Jehovah's Witnesses, and not only from an external perspective. It is not merely based on publications and documents written about the Bible Students Association, or which explained controversies surrounding this association, but it also takes into consideration an internal perspective, the presentation of events from the viewpoint of Jehovah's Witnesses as well as an examination of their intraorganizational conflicts. Hopefully, this will shed light on previously unknown facts and produce evidence showing that the history of this unique religious denomination is neither an incomprehensible phenomenon nor associated with a specific mystery.

At the same time, this study makes an attempt to explain the question of why Jehovah's Witnesses were persecuted so relentlessly by the NS regime. In this regard, the following questions require consideration:

- Why were Jehovah's Witnesses, who considered themselves apolitical, the first religious denomination that was prohibited and persecuted by the National Socialists?
- Why did Jehovah's Witnesses offer such uncompromising resistance? What methods did they use, and what was the nature of their resistance?
- Why was the NS regime so persistent in its persecution of this numerically insignificant group whose members were interested only in practicing their faith?
- How, and with what methods, did the NS regime try to break the resistance of Jehovah's Witnesses?
- Why did Jehovah's Witnesses refuse to perform even unarmed military service in the Wehrmacht, even though they did not consider themselves pacifists?
- Why were the Bible Students in the concentration camps put into a separate category of prisoners?
- What were the reasons for the significant improvement of conditions for Jehovah's Witnesses in the concentration camps during the last three years of the NS regime?
- Could the efforts of Jehovah's Witnesses to preserve their religious ideas and their attempts to maintain their freedom of action be considered acts of resistance?

Research Results

Comprehensive studies discussing the history of the Third Reich and the majority of essays and anthologies discussing resistance against

National Socialism do not include the struggle of Jehovah's Witnesses for self-assertion, their acts of resistance, or their persecution.[30] During the first two decades after the war, historical studies mention Jehovah's Witnesses only incidentally, if at all. In the German-speaking realm of that period, a detailed examination of that subject simply did not take place. Only former fellow prisoners took Jehovah's Witnesses into consideration. Often, based on common experiences during imprisonment, these prisoners remembered quite vividly their struggle and sufferings.[31] This resulted in a number of recollections, which discussed imprisonment in the concentration camps and which described quite extensively the persecution of the Bible Student prisoners. It seems only natural that resistance-movement historiographers, who themselves were victims of persecution by the NS regime, also include Jehovah's Witnesses in their studies. For instance, in his 1947 book on German resistance, Rudolf Pechel emphasizes the morality and magnitude of the resistance. Even though he considerably idealizes acts of resistance, he also acknowledges the Bible Students as having been exposed to the "most serious kind of persecution."[32] At that time, it was not customary to voice such acknowledgment, regardless of whether in one's home country or elsewhere. Pechel, who met Jehovah's Witnesses in the Sachsenhausen concentration camp, describes them as "good companions" and acknowledges that their loyalty toward their convictions earned them the respect of all other prisoners. In 1953, under the title *Der lautlose Aufstand,* Günther Weisenborn presented his study on the "Resistance Movement of the Germans between 1933 and 1945." Compared to Pechel, he discusses extensively the "resistance of the free religious denominations," and in this context he discusses also Jehovah's Witnesses and their "extremely serious" persecution.[33]

In contrast to Pechel and Weisenborn, Gerhard Ritter, who met the Bible Students during his Gestapo detention in 1944, does not remember them, or more precisely, "their religious fanaticism," favorably.[34] These negative recollections are reflected in the indiscriminate judgments of this renowned historian, which are dominated by his own ideological viewpoints. He describes the Bible Students Association as "a radical, pacifist sect with Socialist-Communist elements" that employed a "very primitive Jewish theology."[35] Ritter considers particularly reprehensible the fact that the members of the IBSA viewed patriotism as "a work of the devil."

In his study involving "the German Opposition against Hitler," which is rightly regarded as a standard work, Hans Rothfels also refers

to the Bible Students. He restricts his reference to the statement that the
Bible Students, just as the Quakers and the Mennonites, put up an "in-
cessantly passive resistance."[36]

In 1965 Friedrich Zipfel presented the first sound scholarly study
concerning the Earnest Bible Students, one based on an extensive
examination of the sources. It is part of his comprehensive study of religious persecution during the NS period and carries the somewhat
misleading title "Kirchenkampf in Deutschland" (Church Struggle in
Germany).[37] Zipfel bases his study primarily on records from the Berlin
Document Center, the Munich Institut für Zeitgeschichte, and on compensation records. In this context, Zipfel analyzes and evaluates data
from statements made by approximately four hundred Jehovah's Witnesses who had applied for recognition as political, racial, and religious
victims of persecution at the PrV-Office of the Berlin Senate.[38] Because
of his extensive references to the Berlin compensation records, Zipfel's
study, rightly regarded as pioneering in this field, is a combination of
comprehensive descriptions and local-historical exemplifications. A concentration on personal statements of the petitioners led Zipfel to focus
on questions in his study of the sources that previously had been neglected or that had not yet been taken into consideration, such as the so-
called extended detention—the Gestapo practice of increasing legally
imposed penalties by sending people to concentration camps *after* they
had served their sentences. Zipfel also discusses the punishment of Jehovah's Witnesses for their refusal to perform military service and their
economic persecution.

In 1969, four years after Zipfel's work, the Canadian historian Michael H. Kater published an essay in the *Vierteljahrshefte für Zeitgeschichte*,
including extensive information about the Earnest Bible Students in the
Third Reich. Kater deserves the credit for being the first historian who
takes into account the publications of Jehovah's Witnesses, a fact that
adds to the integrity and consistency of his descriptions. Furthermore,
in dealing with this subject Kater pursues new methods in his examination of the sources. For instance, he not only conducted interviews with
one of the victims of persecution but also contacted concentration
camp memorials and concentration camp associations (Dachau, Neuengamme). Kater bases his research essentially on records of the American National Archives, which include documents of the central State Police offices in Düsseldorf and Munich, and on records of the Bavarian
Political Police.

Despite the more extensive source basis, the study remains, to a large extent, an external examination. It cannot provide an "insider picture" of the course of events. Kater's lack of familiarity with the religious terminology of Jehovah's Witnesses contributes to the problem, allowing their actions to appear mysterious and peculiar. Consequently, his study does not disclose the reasons for their decisions, which inevitably had an effect on the analytical part of his study. Nevertheless, with this study Kater certainly did original work. By referring to the previous history of the relationship between the NS movement and the Bible Students Association, he is the first historian who attempted to provide an explanation for the extraordinary intensity of the persecution. As this study shows, Kater's approach cannot adequately explain the phenomenon in its entirety because it is based on structural similarities of both ideologies—the Bible Students and the National Socialists—each of which claims exclusivity. Besides statements that can no longer be maintained (based on recent research results), such as the listed number of victims, Kater's study also reveals other deficiencies, especially regarding his description of events involving legal matters. These factors require an updating of his research.[39] Such an updating is also imperative because, apart from the two fundamental studies of Zipfel and Kater, no other monographic studies about the history of Jehovah's Witnesses in NS Germany—at the Reich level—are available.

In 1970, one year after Kater's study, a comprehensive documentation about the Watch Tower Society was published in the DDR. This documentation is part of an assessment of the history of the religious denomination of Jehovah's Witnesses since its founding in the 1870s. Seventy pages of the documentation extensively discuss the conduct of Jehovah's Witnesses between 1933 and 1945.[40] The documentation was published under the name of Manfred Gebhard, even though it had been compiled by a number of unnamed writers under the direction of the Ministry of State Security.[41] In 1971 a licensed edition of this documentation was published in the Federal Republic of Germany. It includes quite a number of details as well as insider information. Because it includes also numerous documents from Gestapo and legal provenance, as well as internal circulars or interoffice memos of the German branch office of the Watch Tower Society, it is a valuable information source. But the material, which had been collected from various sources and put together in the late 1960s, also clearly reflects the ideological standards of that period. The purpose for which this publication had been produced was quite obvious—to justify the ban on the denomination of Jehovah's Witnesses, which the DDR secretary of the interior had issued on August 31, 1950.[42] Moreover, it had to prove that in the DDR Jehovah's Witnesses were not "persecuted for their religious beliefs." Instead, the persecution was directed against "people whose religious zeal had been misused by the Watch Tower Society for the purpose of inciting them to acts of defamation, antidemocratic hate campaigns, foreign intelligence services, and a misuse of the Bible and religion for political purposes, and who are therefore involved in anti-state activities."[43]

From this perspective, the Watch Tower Society was depicted as an organization "in the service of psychological warfare" and "bought by big business." Thus, Jehovah's Witnesses were integrated into the "worldwide conflict between imperialism and socialism."[44] Consequently, the "documentation" primarily served the purpose of "explaining" the unfortunate circumstance that Jehovah's Witnesses were so severely persecuted during the NS period. Carefully selected sources, misrepresented quotations, references to reports in the media from the period after 1933, Gestapo interrogation records, and petitions for pardon from the association's leaders created an image according to which the 1933 ban on Jehovah's Witnesses was a misunderstanding, a "political forgery."[45] In reality, the "Watch Tower Society's leaders" had been exposed as "fascist religious-political speculators" who supposedly tried to gain "the approval of the Nazis" and were later even willing to "betray large numbers of their fellow-believers to the Gestapo."

Even from a general point of view, DDR historiographers had serious difficulties in presenting the persecution of Jehovah's Witnesses during the NS period in Germany.[46] Although Gebhard's documentation was clearly the product of a particular time period, his presentation of the persecution of Jehovah's Witnesses is of great significance today; it is one of the few documentaries on the subject available in libraries, and some of its findings have indeed been uncritically adopted.[47]

During the late 1960s, there was an increasing interest in examining the resistance to NS rule on a more local and regional basis. Historical studies began to include the social-historical perspective, examining the entire spectrum of resistance and overcoming the previous restriction of resistance-movement historiography, which focused on military and religious groups. This resulted in a reconsideration of the current resistance concept. In this context, Jehovah's Witnesses and their religiously motivated resistance also received increased recognition. The first detailed local-historical examination of this kind was Hans-Josef Steinberg's study on resistance and persecution in Essen (*Widerstand und Verfolgung in Essen, 1933–1945*). His analysis of Gestapo records and court records from the Düsseldorf central state archives enabled him to make precise statements about the Bible Students in Essen, thus showing the primary stages and phases in Jehovah's Witnesses' struggle for self-assertion.[48]

Also noteworthy are the studies by Lawrence D. Stokes, conducted in Eutin, that include such previous historical events as the early surveillance of the Bible Students during the 1920s.[49] In their study about the IBSA group in Bremen, Inge Marßolek and René Ott include references to special court (*Sondergericht*) and compensation records. This convincing representation addresses even the question concerning the status of the Bible Students' resistance. The authors conclude that, "because of the character of the regime, the Bible Students' resistance had to have also a political dimension."[50]

While some of these local studies include a few paragraphs about Jehovah's Witnesses, monographic works about local Bible Student groups began to be published in the early 1980s. Some of these studies examine Jehovah's Witnesses in comparison to other groups under persecution, or to groups that had offered resistance. One of the principal works is Gerhard Hetzer's study on the Earnest Bible Students in Augsburg, based on an analysis and evaluation of records from the Munich Special Court and written in the context of the "Bayern Projekt" (Bavarian Project) of the Institut für Zeitgeschichte. Also of importance are Manfred Koch's article on Jehovah's Witnesses in Mannheim, based on an intensive source study, and Monika Minninger's essay on political and religious victims of persecution in the city and district of Bielefeld ("Politisch und religiös Verfolgte in Stadt und Kreis Bielefeld"). Minninger bases her description of the persecution of the Bible Students on compensation records and interviews.[51] An article by Günter Heuzeroth and Sylvia Wille concerning Jehovah's Witnesses in Oldenburg also includes several interviews with victims of persecution. Commendably, this article also discusses the formation and the teachings of Jehovah's Witnesses, even though these passages contain a number of factual errors. In addition, I wrote an essay ("Gott mehr gehorchen") involving the persecution of Christian denominations in NS Hamburg, which focuses primarily on Jehovah's Witnesses. Important articles on a rural and small-town level have also been written. For instance, Reimer Möller conducted a study on the "religious and political resistance of the working class" in the district of Steinburg, in which he compares the methods and consequences of the resistance performed by the SPD, the KPD, and the IBSA. Walter Struve's article on Jehovah's Witnesses in the small industrial town of Osterode am Harz is based on thorough interviews with victims of persecution.[52] Reiner W. Kühl's comprehensive essay "The Earnest Bible Students in Friedrichstadt" discusses extensively the "daily routine" of the persecution, and this in a town especially recognized for its religious tolerance—during pre- and post-NS periods.

Outstanding among the local studies is Elke Imberger's 1991 dissertation on resistance and dissent from members of the Labor Movement and Jehovah's Witnesses in Lübeck and Schleswig-Holstein between 1933 and 1945. While showing consideration for the persecution of Jehovah's Witnesses, Imberger maintains the distance necessary in a scholarly study. She precisely describes the conflicts resulting from the NS demands and from acts of self-assertion and resistance on the part of Jehovah's Witnesses. Imberger categorizes these acts of self-assertion and resistance as "defensive resistance."[53] This extensive and extremely accurate study shows weaknesses in only two areas. The author generally excludes the war years and insufficiently analyzes and evaluates the sources, including court case records from the special courts in Altona and Kiel, which were her primary sources of information. In some aspects, the courts' testimonies require a more critical analysis based on a closer consideration of contemporary literature, publications from the Watch Tower Society, and victims' reports of persecution.

A number of historical studies on a local and regional basis have been published in recent years. These studies include also important information about the persecution and resistance of Jehovah's Witnesses. However, it is not yet customary for German historiographers to address this subject. Neighboring Austria, on the other hand, can offer more favorable research results.[54] This is mainly due to the efforts of members of the Dokumentationsarchiv des österreichischen Widerstandes and their exemplary, historical project on a local basis concerning resistance and persecution in the various federal states of Austria. The previously published documentations, consisting of two and three volumes respectively, extensively describe the resistance of the Bible Students, with only one exception (Burgenland).[55] This demonstrates that in recent Austrian research the positive image of the conduct of Jehovah's Witnesses in the concentration camps, evident in reports of former prisoners, has increasingly gained acceptance, and this even in consideration of a "sect that otherwise is viewed rather skeptically."[56]

In this context, Renate Lichtenegger's 1984 dissertation on the resistance of the Vienna Bible Students against National Socialism between 1938 and 1945 deserves recognition.[57] The author bases her study primarily on information from the records of the Dokumentationsarchiv des österreichischen Widerstandes, as well as on interviews with a number of victims of persecution. Unfortunately, she makes only limited use of these sources, as well as of other reference material, and her study does not go beyond the present state of research. Since the work lacks the conscientiousness required for a critical analysis of the sources and shows almost no terminological selectivity, it includes a number of speculations and misinterpretations.[58]

As in Austria, the subject has been adequately acknowledged in English-speaking countries. This is due primarily to the greater recognition that Jehovah's Witnesses, their teachings, formation, and public activities receive in Great Britain, the United States, and Canada. Some of the numerous studies on the religious denomination of Jehovah's Witnesses within different academic disciplines (social sciences, theology, and jurisprudence) also include discussions of the persecution of Jehovah's Witnesses in NS Germany.[59] References to Jehovah's Witnesses are made also in studies discussing resistance and religious persecution. Of special interest in this regard is the work by Christian Helmreich who draws attention to the efforts of the U.S. Consulate General in 1933/34 to achieve a release of property and alleviation of the ban on the Bible Students. Other works of importance are the study conducted by John S. Conway; and, explicitly contradicting Conway, the study conducted by Barbara Grizzuti Harrison.[60]

The 1982 publication of the British historian Christine Elizabeth King is especially noteworthy. Based on her dissertation, written in the early 1980s, the book describes the history of five minor denominations in the Third Reich (Christian Science, the Church of Jesus Christ of Latter-day Saints [Mormons], the Seventh-day Adventists, the New Apostolic Church, and Jehovah's Witnesses) from the perspective of "nonconformity or resistance."[61] King bases her dissertation on the same sources that Zipfel, Kater, and Hetzer had used previously. Therefore, her work does not produce any significantly new discoveries concerning the reconstruction of historical events, but it does show a comparison of the persecution of Jehovah's Witnesses with that of other minor denominations, which proves to be very informative and pioneering. Her analysis emphasizes the special characteristics that should be attributed to the history of Jehovah's Witnesses in the Third Reich both with regard to the extent of their resistance as well as the nature of the state's persecution. Nevertheless, since her idealization of the conduct of Jehovah's Witnesses at times does not do justice to the actual events, a word of criticism is appropriate.

The same applies to a more recent study concerning the Bible Students and National Socialism published by the French authors Sylvie Graffard and Léo Tristan. Their objective is to produce a popularization of "those lost in history," based on interviews with Jehovah's Witnesses and former fellow prisoners, various branch offices of the Watch Tower Society, and an analysis (regrettably often uncritical) of its publications.[62]

In contrast to the relatively poor recognition this subject received among resistance-movement historiographers, studies about the history of the concentration camps often include accounts of the Bible Student prisoners. In general, these accounts are very brief, focusing only on specific aspects and are almost always based on reports by fellow prisoners from other groups. More extensive descriptions are included in the works by Eugen Kogon, Hermann Langbein, and Falk Pingel.[63] The study by Kirsten John concerning the "prisoners of the Wewelsburg concentration camp," published in 1996, is the first thorough scholarly study of the prisoners with the purple patch. It is based partly on John's master's thesis, which focuses mainly on the Bible Students. Her study is especially important since Jehovah's Witnesses represented the majority of prisoners in the Wewelsburg concentration camp.[64] Even so, a comprehensive monographic study of Bible Student prisoners in the concentration camps is not currently available.

The literature on conscientious objection and military jurisdiction in the Third Reich, which is not very extensive, does not often mention Jehovah's Witnesses. Studies on the legal authorities in the NS state, on the other hand, include some important historical details about the persecution of Jehovah's Witnesses.[65] After 1933, in some fields of law, fundamental decisions were issued with regard to "Bible Student cases." For instance, concerning constitutional law, decisions were made with regard to the continuance of religious freedom guaranteed by the Reich Constitution, called into question by the ban on the Bible Students. Concerning juvenile and family law, decisions were made with regard to the question of whether education contrary to NS ideas justified the withdrawal of custody. Concerning the civil service law, decisions were made with regard to the question as to what extent a refusal to give the Hitler salute was a violation of official duties that would justify dismissal.

Information about legal actions against Jehovah's Witnesses is also included in studies concerning administration of justice at the special courts and the People's Court (*Volksgerichtshof,* a court for the prosecution of political offenses).[66] In this regard, Erika Kalous's study discusses sentences imposed on Bible Students in court cases at the Munich Special Court between 1933 and 1938, and at the Higher Regional Court (*Oberlandesgericht*) in Munich between 1943 and 1945.[67]

The history of Jehovah's Witnesses in the Third Reich is also covered by authors who aim primarily at a theological discussion of the teachings of the Bible Students, or those who are interested in disclosing an alleged difference between claim and reality of the Watch Tower Society. Such studies include discussions about sects and denominations that also report, more or less extensively, significant historical facts.[68] The dissertation about the history of Jehovah's Witnesses between 1870 and 1920, which theologian Dietrich Hellmund presented in 1972, represents a combination of denominational and historical aspects. In its extensive appendix, it discusses the NS period.[69] An especially large number of publications were written by former members of the denomination with the objective of disclosing their own experiences to the public in order to warn people against joining the Watch Tower Society and following the "wrong course" of Jehovah's Witnesses, and trying to persuade former fellow believers to turn away from the denomination.[70] Often, these works make references to the NS period. They were written in the form of recollection accounts, describing either experiences individuals had during their time of being Jehovah's Witnesses or criticizing the direction provided by the Brooklyn headquarters of the Watch Tower Society and its course of "confrontation." These works, which were mainly published by church-owned publishing houses, often reflect the authors' great personal disappointment and bitterness concerning their previous membership with Jehovah's Witnesses, which they subsequently consider as a "wrong course" and therefore oppose. They also reflect these former members' perception of an atmosphere of constraint within the denomination. These are factors that must be taken into consideration when evaluating those works. Details about the history of Jehovah's Witnesses in the Third Reich are mentioned, for example, in the comprehensive documentation *Die Wahrheit über Jehovas Zeugen* by Günther Pape and his autobiography *Ich war ein Zeuge Jehovas;* Hans-Jürgen Twisselmann's essay *Wachtturm-Konzern;* Josy Doyon's report *Hirten ohne Erbarmen;* and Alan Rogerson's report *A Study of Jehovah's Witnesses.*

Sources

Besides scholarly and literary descriptions and contemporary publications, this study is based primarily on documents from the archives of various NS authorities responsible for the persecution of individuals and groups (legal authorities, Gestapo, SS, and concentration camp commandant headquarters). It is also based on documents of other state and clerical administrative offices prior to 1945 as well as individual compensation and retribution offices after 1945. Additionally, it relies on the substantial publications of Jehovah's Witnesses (books, periodicals, and pamphlets written during the period of the ban), and on interviews involving the life stories of formerly persecuted Jehovah's Witnesses and other victims of persecution, primarily former fellow prisoners.[71]

Since Jehovah's Witnesses are a numerically small group, research of the sources proved difficult. For instance, in only a few cases is it possible to attain direct access to archival records. (In several cases, archival handbooks and guides do not even provide the appropriate entry.) Thus, a variety of provenance had to be examined (often unsuccessfully) on supposition. Despite the incompleteness of the records, the general state of the sources can be considered as adequate in comparison to other research studies on resistance-movement historiography.

One of the most important sources proved to be the extensive records from the administration of justice and the judiciary. Given the considerable losses of Gestapo documents, the court records of the special courts, which are based on the results of State Police investigations, are of special importance.[72] Consequently, this study is based on an examination of documents from the Hanseatic Special Court in Hamburg (jurisdictional district of the Hamburg Higher Regional Court), the Schleswig-Holstein Special Court in Altona (jurisdictional district of the Kiel Higher Regional Court), and the Munich Special Court (jurisdictional district of the Munich Higher Regional Court).

The Hanseatic and Schleswig-Holstein special courts were selected in order to obtain further details confirming research hypotheses derived from an extensive data collection of Jehovah's Witnesses in Hamburg. Since the Schleswig-Holstein Special Court had jurisdiction over the Prussian city districts of Altona and Wandsbeck, as well as over several other territories that were later incorporated with Hamburg, the court records of the Schleswig-Holstein Special Court, which are kept mainly at the Schleswig-Holstein state archives and the public prosecutor's office at the Hamburg Regional Court (*Landgericht*), are included in the data collection. (The restructuring of regional jurisdiction took place after the Greater Hamburg Law was issued on January 26, 1937.)[73] A total of forty-three special court cases against Jehovah's Witnesses in Hamburg (total number of defendants: 422, of which 113 were repeatedly accused) could be included in the analysis. Also included are an additional twenty-three preliminary investigations, which for various reasons did not result in condemnation.[74] Other proceedings against IBSA groups in Schleswig-Holstein, Bremen, and Lübeck were examined with regard to the accusations on which the court cases were based. The records of the special court for the jurisdictional district of the Munich Higher Regional Court are included in order to confirm the conclusions derived from an analysis of the court proceedings against the Bible Students in Hamburg. These records also provide information necessary to close the gaps resulting from the absence of a number of execution records and petitions for pardon in the records of the Hanseatic Special Court. Consequently, reliable statements can be made concerning the procedures for the execution of sentences and acts of pardon. With regard to other special courts, the analysis of court proceedings had to be restricted to cases in which sentences were epitomized in legal literature.

During the final two years of the war, jurisdiction for proceedings on the charge of "public demoralization of the armed forces" was transferred from the special courts to the People's Court.[75] Therefore, the Bible Student proceedings that took place at the People's Court have been also examined, provided they were included in the records of the Berlin Document Center and the federal archives. It was even possible to examine a few indictment and judgment records of the Reich Military Court (RKG), at which hundreds of Jehovah's Witnesses were tried on the grounds of conscientious objection during World War II.[76]

Several important procedures are also included in the records of the Reich Ministry of Justice (RJM), especially regarding criminal law, the penal system, and the general political department (*politisches Generalreferat*, which assists the minister with preparatory work). These departments dealt quite extensively with several proceedings against Jehovah's Witnesses. The legal authorities were concerned about the frequent practice by the Gestapo to use protective detention as an instrument to correct unwelcome judicial decisions. This, in turn, resulted in the fear that the judicial authorities would be disposed of their exclusive authority of taking penal actions.

From among the Reich authorities, important information can be derived from the records of the Reich chancellery, which includes several important incidences involving the ban on the denomination. Another important source, even though incomplete, is the records of the Reich Security Main Office (RSHA). However, the research of the records of the Reich Ministry of the Interior, which initiated various actions against Jehovah's Witnesses, has been, to a great extent, unproductive since only a few of these records survived.

Since the German branch office of the IBSA was located in Magdeburg, then under Prussian jurisdiction, in 1933/34, the Prussian Ministry of the Interior played a far more important role than the Reich Ministry of the Interior, especially since the ban was primarily a responsibility of the respective states. Accordingly, important actions and negotiations concerning an elimination of the ban, as well as the confiscation and release of property took place at the Prussian Ministry of the Interior. However, because of the extreme incompleteness of the records of the Berlin secret state archives, any prospect of discovering records relating to those negotiations was eliminated.

However, to a certain extent, the information included in documents of central authorities in other German states compensated for the lack of documents at the above-mentioned authorities. In this regard, the records of the Bavarian Ministry of the Interior as well as the Bavarian Ministry of External Affairs are of special importance. These records include important details about actions taken against the IBSA during the final stages of the Weimar Republic. The undetermined decrees of the (Prussian) Secret State Police office could be compensated by examining the inter- and intraoffice decrees of various regional State Police offices regarding the same circumstances, especially those of the Bavarian Political Police (BPP). A relatively complete collection of the decrees involving the IBSA is included in the archives of the Munich Institut für Zeitgeschichte.[77]

Not very productive, on the other hand, was an examination of the records of party offices, such as the Rosenberg office, which includes extensive records concerning church matters. However, important information is available on matters involving the SS and, in particular, the concentration camps. This information is included in the records of the German federal archives, and especially in the archives of the concentration camp memorials, although generally they include only a few documents concerning Bible Student prisoners.

Important information concerning the subject of conscientious objection of Jehovah's Witnesses is contained in the records of the General

Army Office and the offices of the military legal authorities, which are included in the files of the Freiburg military archives. The main secret decrees (regarding the question of "handling Bible Student cases" issued by the chief of the Wehrmacht High Command [OKW][78] and the commander of the Replacement Army [Ersatzheer]), which are not included in the decree collection at the Army Judge Advocate General's Group (Amtsgruppe Heeresrechtswesen), are included in the records of the Command of Military District VI (Wehrkreiskommando VI).

The records of the Berlin central archives of the Evangelical churches, in particular, provide an explanation of the strained relationship between the Bible Students and the churches.[79] In this regard, important information has been unexpectedly discovered in the records of the Evangelical Higher Church Council of the Old-Prussian Union (Evangelischer Oberkirchenrat der Altpreußischen Union). These records contain details that involve the issuing of the ban on the Bible Students, such as the written report of the decisive meeting with representatives of various ministries. This information is not included in the incomplete records of the Prussian Ministry of the Interior.

The records of the "Hamburg Committee of Former Political Prisoners," which are kept at the Vereinigung der Verfolgten des Naziregimes/Bund der Antifaschisten, Landesverband Hamburg, provide important information involving the data collection of Jehovah's Witnesses in Hamburg. During the years immediately following 1945 approximately 23,000 people "requested papers identifying them as victims of NS political, racial, and religious persecution," or as surviving dependants.[80] These requests, as well as the enclosed evidence, include important information regarding the individual persecution experiences. In specific cases, compensation files have been examined in order to provide additional information. In addition to the special court records, data have been obtained also from prisoner lists of the Fuhlsbüttel police prison. In some cases, information was requested from concentration camp associations and concentration camp memorials in order to clarify previously unresolved questions. In other cases, such information was obtained by means of interviews and correspondence with victims. To substantiate the collected information, the method of record linkage—examination and consolidation of records of various provenance and other sources regarding the same occurrences—was used. This greatly reduced the danger of a distortion in perspective of the analyzed data on the 414 members of the Hamburg group of Jehovah's

Witnesses, on which this study is also based. An exclusive reliance on records of the coercive authorities or compensation records would certainly have increased the possibility of such distortions.[81]

To reconstruct certain facts, resistance-movement historiographers are often forced to draw on information included in the records of legal authorities and the police. However, an examination of such records requires special care, since the truthfulness of Gestapo interrogation records is particularly questionable. For instance, confessions were in many cases extorted by means of coercion and torture.[82] In order to evade the pressure, the victims often confessed to anything the Gestapo would insinuate rather than state the actual facts. It is therefore important to take into consideration that in order to avoid incriminating themselves and their fellow believers, these persecuted ones usually tried to minimize the extent of their acts of resistance. On the other hand, the Gestapo records also show a tendency on the part of their officials to exaggerate the activities of their opponents, probably with the objective of causing superior Gestapo offices to issue a warrant of arrest, or with the objective of causing the courts to increase the punishment.

Particularly important source collections on this subject are situation reports of the State Police offices, the SS, the chief public prosecutor offices, the higher regional court senior judges, and the district presidents. These reports provide a particularly large amount of information about the Bible Student activities between 1935 and 1937. The correspondence of the U.S. State Department, which is included in the records of *Foreign Relations of the United States*, also provides valuable information. Based on this correspondence, it is possible to a certain extent to reconstruct the interventions that the Berlin U.S. Consulate General and the American Embassy made with the Prussian and Reich German government offices on behalf of the Watch Tower Society between the spring of 1933 and early 1934.[83]

Another indispensable source of information for this subject, though previously mostly disregarded, proved to be the large amount of literature from Jehovah's Witnesses themselves. Such information is not only available for the period prior to the ban in 1933. During the period following 1933 the Brooklyn headquarters of the denomination and the central European office in Bern (Switzerland) published extensive material discussing the persecution of Jehovah's Witnesses in Germany. Especially noteworthy in this regard are the yearbooks and semimonthly periodicals, *The Watchtower* and *The Golden Age*. In 1938, in order to draw the attention of the international public to the persecution of Jehovah's

Witnesses, the central European office in Bern published the documentation *Kreuzzug gegen das Christentum*.[84] Other information can be obtained from underground writings of German Bible Student groups. The publications of Joseph Franklin Rutherford, who became president of the denomination in 1917, also provide important information regarding the direction of Jehovah's Witnesses.

In addition to the literature of that period, important information can be derived also from reports about the period of persecution included in publications that Jehovah's Witnesses published after 1945. For instance, between 1971 and 1973 the Watch Tower Society, under the direction of German branch leader Konrad Franke, wrote an especially extensive and thought-provoking report about the history of Jehovah's Witnesses in Germany, which was published in the *Yearbook* in 1974.[85] Other yearbooks include similar country reports; for example, descriptions about the almost unknown situation of Jehovah's Witnesses who lived in countries that were under German occupation during World War II, as well as descriptions about the deportation of non-German members of the denomination into German concentration camps.[86] In several other publications, reports of the persecution, which Jehovah's Witnesses consider to be a religiously motivated persecution, are also used as a means to draw people's attention to their message. These reports bear witness to the strong faith and integrity Jehovah's Witnesses displayed by maintaining their loyalty to Jehovah even under the conditions of NS rule. They also serve the purpose of exalting God for showing loyalty toward His people. However, despite the fact that such reports often tend to present a strongly exaggerated picture, they provide some insight into past events from the perspective of Jehovah's Witnesses.[87] They also provide certain details that contribute to a reconstruction of historical events. These reports include the essay "Jehovah's Witnesses in the Crucible," published in 1946 by Nathan H. Knorr, who became president of the denomination in 1942 after the death of Rutherford, along with *Jehovah's Witnesses in the Divine Purpose*, published in 1959, and *Jehovah's Witnesses—Proclaimers of God's Kingdom*, published in 1993. These comprehensive reports about the history and teachings of the Bible Student movement have been published for educational purposes. To a certain extent, Marley Cole's book *Jehovah's Witnesses: The New World Society* can also be considered a Watch Tower Society report. Cole's generally uncritical approach to this subject indicates a certain familiarity with Jehovah's Witnesses.[88] Cole received the support of the Watch Tower Society, which, based on documents from its central archives, tried to present the history of the religious denomination of Jehovah's Witnesses to "worldly readers."

Several recollections of Jehovah's Witnesses who were persecuted in the Third Reich are also published in the *Watchtower* and *Awake!*. These recollections were published primarily to emphasize the exemplary loyalty of these individuals in order to strengthen the faith of their fellow believers. In the late 1980s, such articles were included in the two principal journals of the Watch Tower Society for the purpose of making the general public aware of the persecution of this "minority group, usually ignored." This is not done with the objective of presenting those Jehovah's Witnesses who were persecuted during the NS period as resistance fighters or victims of persecution. Instead, the Watch Tower Society wants to emphasize the fact that these were martyrs who were persecuted for their religious convictions. "The victim is usually involuntary, while the martyr is voluntary."[89]

Besides the number of recollections published in the literature of Jehovah's Witnesses or in other publications, a large number of unpublished reports have also been examined. These reports are available at concentration camp memorials and, in some cases, other archives, such as the DdW (Dokumentationsarchiv des deutschen Widerstandes), DÖW (Dokumentationsarchiv des österreichischen Widerstandes), FGN (Forschungsstelle für die Geschichte des Nationalsozialismus in Hamburg), IfZ (Institut für Zeitgeschichte), USHMM (U.S. Holocaust Memorial Museum). In addition, an examination was made of fifty-seven reports that were written mainly in 1984 in the context of historical documentation of Jehovah's Witnesses in southern Germany. However, despite encouragement from different sources, up until the completion of this study at the end of 1989, the branch office of the Watch Tower Bible and Tract Society in Selters (Taunus), Germany, has not provided any support for this research project.[90] In recent years, the Watch Tower Society has completely changed its attitude in this regard. Today, it tries to support research projects and exhibitions that are held at concentration camp memorials by providing documents about the persecution of Jehovah's Witnesses.

To complete this study, I conducted a number of interviews. In addition, formerly persecuted Jehovah's Witnesses were requested to provide some information about their persecution in written form. Several of these people declined the request for various, and mostly understandable, reasons. And contrary to initial expectation, there was a generally positive response on the part of the people who had been affected by Nazi persecution. In this context, it was very important to respect the religious convictions of these people. Questions had to be formulated in a way that took into consideration the complete historical background of the people concerned. This includes social, biographical, and religious aspects (such as their conversion to the denomination), as well as other aspects in the lives of these individuals. The discussions could not be restricted to topics such as imprisonment in the concentration camps or religious activities during the period of the ban. Openness and patience were required, especially when the discussions, at times, went beyond the scope of the research topic.

In contrast to other people who belong to the group of "forgotten victims," Jehovah's Witnesses do not view their persecution under National Socialism as something that needs to be concealed in present-day Germany.[91] Rather, they consider the period of persecution as a natural part of their lives. They even view their liberation from NS oppression as an act of salvation by which God rewarded and recognized their faithfulness and loyalty. In the majority of cases, because the interviewees were not interested in a public representation of their persecution, discussions about their experiences were usually restricted to the family circle and members of their denomination. As a result, relatives and friends of these formerly persecuted people lost interest in listening repeatedly to the details of their persecution stories that continued to live on in the minds of the victims. Thus, once the initial apprehension toward a stranger had been overcome and the interviewees became comfortable, they began telling their stories with great enthusiasm. Often, the degree of memory was simply amazing. With regard to contents and clarity, these reports could generally be considered as very good, notwithstanding the problems presented by oral history in general (passage of time, memory deficiencies, various levels of perceiving matters of everyday life or extraordinary events, as well as a psychosocial classification of life experiences).[92] In addition, from a source-critical point of view, consideration must be paid to the extent in which these recollections had been integrated into a religious thought pattern.[93]

As a result of these discussions, it was possible to clarify aspects about the religious teachings and self-conception of Jehovah's Witnesses that had remained unclear even after a study of their literature, and to describe, at least to a certain extent, events that could not have been described otherwise because of the absence, or incompleteness, of written records. This includes, in particular, events and inner-organizational conflicts that are not mentioned in the Watch Tower Society's publications in order to maintain a consistent self-image.

Finally, it is appropriate to mention an additional, especially comprehensive source. A number of published and unpublished reports of former concentration camp prisoners are available that mention the group of Bible Student prisoners and present them from their particular point of view.[94] These reports consistently emphasize how impressed fellow prisoners were with the perseverance of the Bible Students who, regardless of the consequences, maintained their religious conviction. Because their nonconformity was often perceived as stubbornness beyond all rational considerations, admiration easily turned into lack of understanding and rejection. The broad range of feelings that this subject involves is vividly reflected in the reports of fellow prisoners of Jehovah's Witnesses.

- "With an unbelievable steadfastness, these people endured, year after year after year, the most atrocious mistreatment. However, they did not disown or betray their faith. To the contrary, even here in the camp, they persistently tried to persuade other prisoners to accept their ideas. I have to admit that these people commanded my admiration."[95]
- "Their attitude strengthened me. If they can endure, there would be no reason why I as a Christian should not be able to do so? I can only admire their acts of resistance and their strength of character. . . . All of them honest people—even as a Catholic priest I am obliged to acknowledge this with gratitude."[96]
- "Their stubborn attitude certainly did not impart any exemplary strength because it was not built on solid ground. They definitely deserved our respect, but we also felt sorry for them."[97]
- "I will not make any comments regarding the ideology of these people, critical or non-critical. But I can say, for the entire world to hear, the greatness they showed was simply admirable. It was their conduct in the concentration camps that contributed to the fact that I did not lose my faith in humanity, even in those moments of deep darkness."[98]
- "The SS considered these men as lunatics. But in Wöbbelin, when food supplies were exhausted, our eight Bible Students came together and read a Bible verse. These lunatics reflected human dignity."[99]

PART I

THE INTERNATIONAL BIBLE STUDENTS ASSOCIATION

1

The IBSA's Beginnings, 1874–1918

The early beginnings of the Bible Student movement, which now has a membership of about 6.7 million, reach back into the 1870s.[1] Its founder, Charles Taze Russell, was born on February 16, 1852, the son of a prosperous family of textile merchants. He was raised in the Presbyterian faith from which he later turned away. Afterwards he was sympathetic toward Adventist theology. In 1872 in Allegheny, Pennsylvania, near Pittsburgh, he gathered around himself a group of people who shared his convictions. When, in 1874, the predictions of the Adventists concerning a visible return of Christ in the flesh failed to come true, the majority of the group around Russell withdrew from the Adventist church in disappointment. In that same year, Russell announced that Christ's return had indeed taken place, a conclusion he had reached after extensive personal Bible study. Even though he did not have any formal theological education, he had acquired considerable biblical knowledge on his own. Based on this knowledge, he announced that Christ had truly returned in spirit, invisible to human eyes. Russell associated this interpretation of Christ's return (the so-called second presence of the Lord) as an entirely spiritual event, as it were, with the announcement of a new date of historical significance for the salvation of mankind. During a forty-year harvest period, the invisible Christ would be gathering the faithful followers of the Lord. At the end of this period, in 1914, God's Kingdom would rule over the earth, marking the beginning of the thousand-year reign, as promised by John in the book of Revelation.[2] This message, which Russell proclaimed in 50,000 copies of his publication *The Object and Manner of Our Lord's Return* (1877), met with great response. Even outside of Pittsburgh, more and more groups of Christians began to follow his teachings.[3]

Russell then became very active. Besides public discourses and missionary tours, his attention was directed primarily toward an extensive publishing campaign.[4] In July 1879 he began to publish the journal *Zion's Watch Tower and Herald of Christ's Presence* (later called *The Watchtower Announcing Jehovah's Kingdom*), which became the principal journal of this new religious denomination. Two years later, under the name "Zion's Watch Tower Tract Society," Russell established his own publishing house for the distribution of his publications. In 1884 he had his company legally registered in the state of Pennsylvania. In 1896 he changed the name of his publishing house to Watch Tower Bible and Tract Society. As a result, a first official corporation of this new religious denomination was instituted, with Russell as president. In 1909 the headquarters of the Watch Tower Bible and Tract Society were transferred from Pittsburgh to Brooklyn, New York. To satisfy legal requirements of the state of New York, an associate society was established, the "Peoples Pulpit Association." Five years later, another association was added to these two publishing houses: in order to unify the group's membership, the "International Bible Students Association," (or "International Association of Earnest Bible Students") was established in London.[5] This was the final step in the formal constitution of the denomination. From that time on, the followers of Russell adopted the name "Bible Students." Previously, they simply called themselves "Christians," and outsiders—to distinguish them from other groups—referred to them as "Russellites" or "Millennial Dawners." This action also changed the character of the denomination; until then, the members of this religious movement had regarded themselves as an ecumenical movement. Often, the followers of Russell remained nominal members of the churches or religious groups they had previously attended. Now, they formed a separate denomination.

In the early 1890s, Russell also made an effort to propagate his teachings on the European continent. Initially he was not very successful, but he persistently followed his missionary course. The Watch Tower Bible and Tract Society published translations of a number of Russell's writings and established its own distribution network in Europe. Beginning in the spring of 1897 its principal journal *Zion's Watch Tower and Herald of Christ's Presence* was also published in German, even though initially it was still printed in the United States. As a result, the denomination achieved its first responses in Germany. Shortly after the turn of the century, subscribers to the *Watchtower* in the Black Forest, Bergisches Land (now, the state of North Rhine-Westphalia), and Westphalia started to form small groups that distributed the teachings of Russell. In 1902 the Watch Tower Society established its first, very modest branch office in a rented place in Elberfeld (now, Wuppertal). In October of the following year, Russell appointed Otto Albert Kötitz, who until then had been editing the German issue of the *Watchtower* in the United States, to be the leader of the German branch. Kötitz was originally from Kranichfeld in Thuringia (Germany) and came to know Russell and his teachings after his immigration to the United States. He strengthened the organizational structure of the German branch and introduced his German fellow-believers to the successful methods of the parent society in the "land of opportunity." Less than two years after Kötitz arrived in Germany, around 1905, 1.5 million pamphlets were circulated among the German people. The majority of these pamphlets were distributed in an expensive campaign as a newspaper insert. The "Russellites" were now beginning to be noticed in other places. In his 1905 handbook *Kirchen und Sekten der Gegenwart*, the Stuttgart garrison curate Geiges informed his readership of theologians about the teachings of the Watch Tower Bible and Tract Society. His action was prompted primarily by the Watch Tower Society's "active publicity campaign," for which, according to the clergyman, they even made use of the "most popular church magazines."[6]

As early as 1905 the number of *Watchtower* subscriptions had reached one thousand. Russell and his staff in the United States continued to write the articles for the *Watchtower*, which, beginning in 1904, was printed in Germany. With satisfaction, the Brooklyn headquarters took note of the good results that the "harvest time of the Lord" produced in Germany, and there was a continuous increase in subscriptions. In 1914, the year for which Russell had predicted that the establishment of God's Kingdom would be visible on earth, approximately three thousand to four thousand Christians in Germany had accepted the teachings of the Bible Students.[7]

At the beginning of 1914 the Bible Students were certain that the end of the world had arrived. Several of them even began distributing their material belongings, abandoning their places of employment, and eagerly anticipating the future. To observers, such behavior seemed quite unusual, but not even public ridicule could diminish the faith of the Bible Students. Based on their study of the Bible, they were convinced that it was possible to determine the date of historical significance for the salvation of mankind—1914—directly from the Holy Scriptures.[8]

When, one month after the gunshots of Sarajevo, the European nations engaged in World War I, the Bible Students viewed this event as a sign from God. They considered it to be the turning point in history, introducing the destruction of the world and establishing Christ's Kingdom that would bring peace to the earth. In their opinion, the outbreak of the war was a fulfillment of Bible prophecy. Jesus's prophecy concerning the time of the End, recorded in the Gospel accounts, seemed to unfold before their very eyes. "Nation will fight against nation, and kingdom against kingdom. There will be great earthquakes and plagues and famines in various places; there will be terrifying events and great signs from heaven."[9]

However, those signs from heaven did not introduce the Thousand-Year Reign of Christ, as predicted by Russell. The expectations of the Bible Students concerning the year 1914 were not fulfilled, and disappointment set in. The Bible Student movement experienced its first major setback. While its members were still struggling with the consequences of their misinterpretation, the next setback occurred. On October 31, 1916, at the age of sixty-four, Russell died before he had been able to provide new explanations for the fact that his predictions concerning the end of the world had not come true. Consequently, the movement lost its founder and most outstanding personality of that period.

Now the denomination was confronted with yet another problem. In addition to eschatological uncertainties, there were also ethical concerns. In other words, besides the unresolved questions regarding "the end of the world," the Bible Students were faced with the reality of war in a world that had not yet perished. Since the Bible Students had lived with the expectation of an imminent end, they had not given much consideration to the question of which position to take on military service.

The Watch Tower Society recommended that the members of the International Bible Students Association should make use of their legal right of conscientious objection for religious reasons in countries that provided this possibility.[10] However, the majority of countries (which included the German Reich) did not provide for any exemption from military service. Regarding these countries, Russell did not promote the refusal of military service or insubordination. He did emphasize that in principle, a Christian was not allowed to kill. Therefore, in countries that did not allow for conscientious objection, his followers should, in the event of war, try to perform military service without arms. "In such event, we would consider it not amiss . . . to request a transference to the medical or hospital department, . . . but even if compelled to service in the ranks and to fire our guns, we need not feel compelled to shoot a fellow creature."[11]

Hundreds of German Bible Students obeyed the command for military service, but they did not join in the general war hysteria.[12] In the second year of the war, 350 of them went "into the battle field," but it cannot be determined to what extent they were able to follow Russell's instructions.[13] A considerable number succeeded in performing service in the "army medical corps" or army offices. According to reports, the military authorities and superiors often were quite willing to cooperate with the Bible Students in this regard.[14]

During the middle of the war, the question of whether Christians were allowed to perform military service at all, or whether they should follow "a course of strict Christian neutrality," resulted in controversies among the members of the IBSA. More and more Bible Students refused to participate in military service.[15] They not only refused to submit to the draft order but many of them left their units even after they had served for a considerable period of time. Among these was Hero von Ahlften, who later became leader of the Bible Students Association in northern Germany. He was drafted into the German Imperial Army in 1915, but two years later he refused "to do the Devil's business any longer."[16] The conscientious objectors were either sentenced to periods of imprisonment or placed in mental institutions as religious "lunatics."[17]

Toward the end of World War I, as a result of these conscientious objections, clerical as well as secular authorities became increasingly aware of the activities of the Bible Students.[18] At the same time, they took note of antiwar tendencies in the publications and at conventions of the Watch Tower Society. In the autumn of 1917 the *Pommersche Tagespost* published an article that criticized the Bible Students' agitation "against state authority." With reference to a convention that the Bible Students held in Munich, the *Tagespost* reported that the speaker there had even made an attempt to "discredit the war loans."[19] This prompted the Royal War Ministry and the Higher Church Council of the Evangelical churches to pay closer attention to the activities of the IBSA.[20]

The War Ministry requested the church authorities to provide some information about the IBSA, which was practically unknown to them. They also requested the church authorities to put the Bible Students under surveillance. The churches were only too willing to accept this request. Consequently, the Kiel consistory gave instructions to their pastors to report "any harmful activities of this sect." It even suggested, "if possible, to take action against [the Bible Students]."[21] On March 20, 1918, the royal consistory of the state of Westphalia sent a letter, which included the reports that the pastors had submitted, to the Evangelical church council in Berlin.[22] In these reports, the pastors were offended that the Bible Students had stated publicly that it was a religious duty "as a soldier in war not to shoot at humans."[23]

Various military authorities now began to take administrative actions against such tendencies. Consequently, in October 1917 the deputy corps headquarters of the Second Army Corps prohibited in its jurisdictional area the distribution of Bible Student publications. It also prohibited any other public IBSA activities.[24] The Kiel military authorities even issued an order that soldiers were not allowed to attend Bible Student meetings.[25]

The religious denomination was accused of pursuing pacifist ideas, demoralizing military ambitions, propagating conscientious objection, and hiding deserters.[26] As a result, national-minded groups categorized the Bible Students as "state-endangering forces."

2

Teachings of the Denomination

About three months after the death of Russell, the association's former legal counsel, Joseph Franklin Rutherford, became the new president of the Watch Tower Bible and Tract Society. The January 6, 1917, nomination of forty-seven-year-old Rutherford was not without controversy. Six months after Rutherford became president, he published Russell's incomplete seventh volume of the *Studies in the Scriptures* under the title *The Finished Mystery*. The publication of this volume caused a rift among the organization's leaders.[27] Four of the seven members of the board of directors accused Rutherford of having fundamentally changed and adulterated the teachings of the founder of the denomination by editing Russell's literary remains. Rutherford defended Russell's work and accused his critics of closing their minds to new biblical enlightenment. By making use of a technicality involving the election of the board members, Rutherford dismissed the opposing board members and replaced them with four of his most loyal followers. However, the controversy affected not only the board members but resulted also in a series of divisions. During the next three years, about four thousand people withdrew from the association, forming new, independent Bible Student groups.[28]

Over the next twenty-five years, Rutherford considerably influenced the affairs of the Watch Tower Society. Under his leadership, the Bible Student teachings underwent a number of changes.[29] First, Rutherford tried to reinterpret the events surrounding the year 1914. But even according to this newly proclaimed version, the year 1914 was the date that determined mankind's salvation. The outbreak of World War I confirmed the fact that 1914 was indeed a turning point in history. As predicted, the "times of the nations" ended when Christ received Kingdom power. He received this Kingdom power from Jehovah and began ruling in Heaven, still invisible to human eyes. From then on, the Watch Tower Society announced that the Thousand-Year Reign had begun in

1914. In the near future (that is, during the lifetimes of many people living today) it would be established also on the earth.[30] Thus, the Bible Students had basically received a fulfillment of their expectations.

This interpretation emphasized a continuity of Russell's teachings and, based on other premises, transformed the actual nonrealization of anticipated events into a fulfillment of his predictions. It involved several changes resulting from the conflict between the proclaimed presence of Christ's Kingdom and the fact that the world around them was still in existence. Besides imminent expectations of future events and historical determinism, such dualistic contrasts between the Old and the New World had always characterized the teachings of the Bible Students. Rutherford now increasingly emphasized the antagonism between a "people whom God had set aside for salvation" and "pagan" powers of a world that was doomed for destruction. According to his interpretation, the worldly nations had lost their right to rule in 1914 as soon as Christ ascended to the heavenly throne of the New World. Now the Bible Students had to submit directly under God's authority. Thus, Rutherford reinterpreted the fact that God's Kingdom had not started to rule over the earth in 1914, which would have resulted in the destruction of all earthly governments, into the fact that the earthly governments had lost their claim to power in that year.

To understand the far-reaching consequences that this interpretation had on the relationship between the Bible Students and the secular authorities, it is necessary to examine some of their basic teachings.[31]

The Bible Students, or Jehovah's Witnesses, believe that God's acts of salvation have a direct effect on the unfolding of historical events. To this end they take the scriptures, which they examine to the letter, as literally as possible.[32] They accept the Bible in its entirety as the revealed Word of God.[33] In doing so they try to harmonize, by means of allegoric-typological interpretations, the various and sometimes conflicting concepts within the canon of the Bible. Rather than leaving a text in its respective context, they often relate it to other parts of the Bible, resulting in a new, dogmatically oriented, interpretation. According to Jehovah's Witnesses, it is possible in this way to dispose the Bible of some of its conflicting statements and thus directly determine the will of God. Each believer has the responsibility to adjust his life according to the biblical directives that have unconditional validity. Considering themselves to be followers of Christ, Jehovah's Witnesses try to live up to this claim with all seriousness and godliness. Their religious service is based primarily on two elements: First, a study of the Bible during which Bible texts are read and examined with the help of the *Watchtower*, and second, participation in the preaching activity.[34] Jehovah's Witnesses view their faith and their preaching activity as two inseparable elements. As a group of preachers, they cannot imagine themselves to be merely passive members or to restrict their religious activities to the privacy of their homes. They expect each individual "to 'exert [himself] vigorously' in the work of the Lord."[35]

Jehovah's Witnesses belong to the group of chiliastic denominations that have appeared repeatedly throughout the history of Christendom.[36] It is their belief that God's thousand-year Kingdom, the "Millennium," will soon bring an end to world history and will extend its rule over all the earth that associates them with chiliasm, which has its roots in the apocalyptic Jewish expectations of an imminent end.[37] According to Christian millennialism with its completely earth-oriented concept, this thousand-year Kingdom, in which only righteous people will live, will soon manifest itself on earth. Jehovah's Witnesses, whose expectations of an imminent end are based primarily on the symbolic descriptions in the book of Revelation, teach that prior to this imminent Golden Age a decisive battle, the War of Armageddon, will take place on earth in which Jehovah God will destroy the forces of the Devil.[38] Only on the ruins of this world order will it be possible to establish under God's leadership a new order. In their opinion, only people who have accepted Jehovah and subsequently submit to his requirements will survive Armageddon and enter into the New World. Those who do not conform to God's requirements will be destroyed. Every person now living therefore faces the choice of deciding in favor of everlasting life or departing into everlasting death. This is also the background against which the missionary zeal of Jehovah's Witnesses needs to be seen, considering that they want to reach as many people as possible with the message of God's Kingdom before Armageddon, so that they can take a stand on the side of Jehovah before it is too late. At the same time, unbelievers are warned about the impending destruction.

In this respect, there are no, or only insignificant, differences between the teachings of the Bible Students and those of other chiliastic denominations that consider, or considered, the time of their appearance as the time in which the Bible's promises would be fulfilled.[39] However, Jehovah's Witnesses also believe that a person confessing to worship God has to be associated with the true Christian denomination. Since they claim to be the true religious denomination, they also claim to have the only means for salvation. After the day of Jehovah's anger,

God's people—those who have been gathered into His organization—will form the nucleus of a new human society. The 144,000 chosen ones, or spirit-anointed ones, will be raised into Heaven to become co-rulers of Christ.[40] Under the rule of God, the earth will be transformed into a wonderful paradise. The conditions in the New World are described in the most beautiful colors: no longer will there be war or famine, neither crime nor sickness; there will also be no more wickedness and no more death.

According to the teachings of Jehovah's Witnesses, God's Kingdom is composed of two groups, the heavenly one, a "little flock" of 144,000 "spirit-anointed ones," and the earthly one, which consists of a "great crowd." Initially, the Bible Students believed that the purpose of their preaching activity was to gather, within the "Harvest period," the remnant of the "spirit-anointed ones of the Lord." The gathering of these anointed ones who will rule with Christ during his "Thousand-Year Reign" began at the early Christian festival of Pentecost and has continued through the centuries. Under the leadership of Rutherford, this concept received a new perspective, mostly to make the message of the denomination more effective. Now, the preaching activity also involved the ingathering of a "great, unnumbered crowd of people."[41] During the mid-1930s, the "heavenly calling" ceased because the number of 144,000 "spirit-anointed ones" had been completed.

In the opinion of Jehovah's Witnesses, there is a close relationship between an individual's responsibility to make a personal decision and Satan's challenge of God's universal sovereignty. At the time when the Kingdom was established, Christ began his final battle against his opponent, Satan the Devil. This battle took place in heaven, resulting in the fact that Satan was cast down to the earth. Being confined to the earth, Satan is now trying to gather his forces. Since he disputes the fact that humans would remain loyal, even under the most serious circumstances, God gave him a last chance to put humans to the test before God's War of Armageddon. Faithful Christians are now under obligation to prove Satan wrong. For this very reason, Jehovah did not extend his Kingdom rule over the earth in 1914. By means of the trials that believers would have to endure during the remaining period, God "is training men to faithfulness in their devotion to Him that He might put them into positions of honor and trust in the ages to come to carry out his purposes."[42] Only those who remain loyal to God under all circumstances will receive everlasting life as a reward for their faithfulness.

The publications of the Watch Tower Society announced that Satan was furious about the fact that he had not been able to cause true Christians to abandon their faith in God. Consequently, he mobilized his forces for an attack against God's organization. Based on these facts, the Bible Students considered the growing resistance to their activities and the increasing seriousness of persecution as evidence that the end was drawing near. These occurrences proved that Satan had become very active because he knew that his destruction was near at hand.

While, in view of the preceding explanations, the reservations against the Bible Student teachings (including ridicule and religious opposition on the part of the general public) may seem understandable, a completely different aspect of their religious teachings caused secular and clerical authorities to launch an even more serious attack against the Bible Students.

Even under Russell's leadership, the Bible Students had already announced that all human powers that were under the influence of Satan would be destroyed before God's Kingdom would rule over the earth. Rutherford, however, further expanded this view and presented it as the focal point of the Bible Student teachings. He proclaimed that Satan used the commercial, political, and religious powers of this world to accomplish his goals. Big business, politics, and the churches were the tools by means of which he dominated the world. In the Watch Tower Society's publications, Rutherford now began to expose the activities of this satanic alliance. Even though his attacks were only verbal, leaving the actual overthrow completely in the hands of God, without any action on the part of humans,[43] the Bible Student teachings now radically challenged the supporting pillars of contemporary society. From the mid-1920s on, Rutherford increased his public campaign against the commercial, political, and religious powers. Initially, he accused "unfaithful preachers, conscienceless profiteers, and unscrupulous politicians" of having joined the conspiracy of Satan.[44] Now, however, he declared that "the Devil's organization visible [is] made up of the commercial, political, and ecclesiastical factors."[45] In 1927 he proclaimed "Freedom for the Peoples" and explained in the book published under the same title that the human family now living in bondage was forced into silence by its respective governments. The presidents and kings of this world, in turn, were merely puppets in the hands of the Devil.[46] One year later, in his book *Government*, Rutherford announced that the increasing economic crises, intrapolitical unrests, international conflicts, and resulting wars clearly showed that the governments throughout the world had failed.[47] Everywhere in the world, it could be observed that the nations were, in fact, "suffering under the burdens of unrighteous governments."[48] This emphasized the fact that a new and righteous government was needed that only Jehovah was able to provide.

These explanations were based exclusively on religious reasoning and on the assumption that future glory would seem all the more brilliant, the gloomier the present was portrayed. After all, every salvation-oriented religion proclaims that humans would be delivered from current hardships. But for certain groups of people, such statements practically proved the allegedly state-endangering and revolutionary character of the Bible Student teachings.

The rejection of this Old World as being under the power of Satan had repercussions that affected not only the Bible Students' relationship to the outside world; it had a direct effect also on the denomination itself. Based on the premise that only the coming of God's Kingdom would be able to solve the world's problems and that human society was not able to rule itself, any effort to improve the present political system seemed unnecessary. Instead, such efforts could be considered as presumptuous on the part of humans.[49] The Bible Students were therefore requested to refrain from any political activity and, instead, remain strictly neutral. This meant refusing any activities in political parties and labor unions, as well as refusing any participation in elections.

The issue of neutrality is based on the conception that Christ's faithful followers would become part of the coming New World as soon as he began his rule. In this regard, the Bible Students related their situation after Christ's return to that of Jesus's early followers during his first presence, referring to a statement Jesus made to his followers: "They do not belong to the world any more than I belong to the world" (John 17:16). The German issue of the *Watchtower* instructed its readers, "Our citizenship is in the land of our King in the heavens. We abide in this country only as His representatives."[50] As subjects of a heavenly government, announced Rutherford, the Bible Students "now on earth are ambassadors of God and his King."[51] An ambassador, however, would not be allowed to interfere with the political activities of his host country. In a similar way, the neutrality teaching would leave no room for any participation in the political conflicts between nations.

This concept of statehood, according to which God had scattered the Bible Students (as strangers) in among the nations of a vanishing world, completely affected their relationship to the secular authorities.

Nevertheless, the Watch Tower Society allowed the various states to fulfill their function of managing the affairs of the Old World (upholding legal order, collecting taxes, and the like). In accordance with the Bible's command, "pay Caesar what belongs to Caesar" (Matt. 22:21), the Watch Tower Society requested its members to obey carefully the secular laws, as long as these did not conflict with their responsibilities as citizens of the New World and with their obligation to maintain neutrality. Consequently, the Bible Students did not come in conflict with the interests of the state as long as the state did not (explicitly) require of them to get involved in any of its political affairs.

In 1929 Rutherford presented a new interpretation of a certain Bible text, which had far-reaching consequences on this latent conflict between the Bible Students and the secular authorities. It involved Paul's letter to the Romans (Rom. 13), which deals with the subjection of Christians under the governing authorities and which significantly affected the development of future events. The chapter opens with the words: "Everyone is to obey the governing authorities, because there is no authority except from God." Based on this text, the Watch Tower Society previously taught regarding the present worldly government that Christians "should render to them due respect and obedience, because God has permitted them to rule."[52] Now, the society proclaimed "that Jehovah God and Jesus Christ, rather than worldly rulers and governments are 'The Higher Powers'" to which Paul referred in his *Letter to the Romans*.[53] These, and only these, were the "higher powers" a Christian had to obey.[54]

This clear change in the use of the term "governing authorities" was part of a process during which Rutherford, at the beginning of his presidency, gradually started to ascribe prophetic and priestly dignity to himself. The revival movement was turned into a hierarchically structured, strictly centralized, organization whose leaders professed to be representatives of God, thus placing themselves at the third position of a so-called theocratic order, after Jehovah God and Jesus Christ. Consequently, these theocratic "governing authorities" were closely connected to the Watch Tower Bible and Tract Society, which was raised to the status of God's organization, and its membership, which was declared to be God's people. The claim is exclusive: The Watch Tower Society considers itself as the only true and authentic representative of all Christians professing to follow Christ—it represents the only truth. No other religious group and denomination can make this claim. Rutherford declared the Watch Tower Society to be "the faithful servant of the Lord, speaking by inspiration and authority from the Most High."[55] Since this organization has its authority from God, each member has to submit to all aspects of authority. To a certain extent, this provided the president of the Watch Tower Bible and Tract Society with dictatorial authority. With reference to the theocratic rule, he used his position to gradually eliminate any democratic elements.[56]

He was the only one to decide which truths should be proclaimed in the *Watchtower*. This same authority he had regarding matters of teaching, Rutherford had also with organizational matters. For instance, he alone appointed the leaders of the various branch offices. Even though he was just a brother among brothers (and sisters), the denomination's president had the power of an absolute ruler. The believers were expected to obey him faithfully and without questioning.

As a result of this change in the use of the term "governing authorities," the people of the "New World Society"[57] had to ask themselves the following question in countries where they were denied their right to remain neutral and follow the Bible's instructions: Would they submit to the authority of Satan, the god of this world, or to theocratic authority? In other words, would they remain loyal to Jehovah God and Jesus Christ and be obedient to God's organization? This was the challenging situation to which the Bible Students were exposed when, after the victory of the NS party in Germany, a regime was established that proclaimed its own Thousand-Year Reich of salvation, following its *own* conception of chiliasm.

The increasing opposition that the Bible Students encountered in many countries during Rutherford's era did not come unexpectedly. Had not even Jesus Christ and his early followers experienced opposition from the world? Therefore, the Bible Students considered the beginning persecution as a fulfillment of the predicted trials by means of which they could prove their loyalty. They saw this development as further evidence that they were the chosen people of God. The opposition they experienced was a confirmation of Jesus's words: "But because you do not belong to the world, because my choice of you has drawn you out of the world, that is why the world hates you."[58] The Bible Students considered themselves, even prior to 1933, as victims of a persecution against Christians who had to suffer because of their loyalty to the commandments of the Bible in the same way in which the early Christians had suffered.[59]

Moreover, the seriousness of the persecution in this context almost seemed to indicate the nearness of the end. According to their beliefs, it could be expected that Satan, during this most difficult period since 1914, "was intensifying his campaign of terror against the defenders of truth on earth" before the end would come at Armageddon.[60] However, not even they could anticipate the extent of persecution that Jehovah's Witnesses were about to experience after 1933 in Germany. Reality by far exceeded the myth.

3

Development and Expansion in the German Reich, 1918–33

After accepting the denomination's presidency, Joseph Franklin Ruther-ford arranged also for a reorganization of the IBSA in Europe. The rea-son for this reorganization was a dispute between Rutherford and F. L. Alexandre Freytag, the leader of the branch office in Geneva, respon-sible for the French-speaking part of Switzerland. It involved the ques-tion of whether Freytag was permitted to publish articles that had not been authorized by the association's leadership, that is, by Rutherford himself. As a result, in 1919 Rutherford dissolved the branch office in Geneva.[61] During the following year, on his inspection tour through Europe, he restructured the association. Under leadership of Conrad C. Binkele, Rutherford established the central European office in Zurich for the purpose of supervising the branches in France, Belgium, the Nether-lands, Italy, Switzerland, Austria, and Germany (later the central office also supervised Poland and Czechoslovakia). While this central Euro-pean office was responsible for the Bible Student movement in western and central Europe, a northern European office primarily supervised the activities of the Bible Students in Scandinavia and the Baltic countries.

On his inspection tour, Rutherford addressed also the problems of the IBSA branch in Germany. The German branch was still suffering the effects from differences that arose regarding the question of con-scientious objection and the repercussions associated with the develop-ments involving the year 1914. In the course of 1914 the German branch leader Otto Albert Kötitz had been removed from office, which ended a period of mutual understanding. Accusations and counteraccusations were the order of the day. The controversies resulted in several changes in leadership in short succession. At times, leadership was even carried out by a group of people rather than only one chosen leader. Finally,

Table 1. Membership of local IBSA groups, 1906–26

	1906	1909	1916	1919	1924	1925	1926
Dresden	17	?	111	230	1104	1309	1430
Berlin	5	50-60	130	260	749	915	964
Hamburg	?	16	87	136	453	470	480

Rutherford arranged that the position of leadership would be once again in the hands of a person with a strong personality who was also equipped with appropriate authority. In November 1920 a specially appointed committee elected thirty-four-year-old Paul Balzereit to be leader of the German branch office.[62] Prior to becoming the responsible leader of the Watch Tower Society's German branch office, Balzereit had been an ironworker at the Germania Werft (dockyard) in Kiel. Apparently, he also had notable qualifications as a public speaker because, among other things, he was active as a writer and lyricist (pseudonym Paul Gerhard). During the following years, under the leadership of Balzereit, the preaching activity became quite successful.

By the end of World War I, the religious denomination in the German Reich had a total of 3,868 "publishers" or "Kingdom proclaimers" organized in approximately one hundred groups.[63] During the three years following World War I, the denomination had a considerable increase in the number of believers. As early as 1919 the number of believers amounted to 5,545.[64] However, beginning in 1921/22 this increase was even more remarkable. Within a short period of time, the number of Bible Students as well as their popularity increased significantly.[65] Between 1918 and 1926 more than ten million tracts and other publications of the Watch Tower Society were distributed in Germany.[66] During this period an almost sixfold increase in the number of Bible Students took place. In 1926 a total of 22,535 proclaimers of the Kingdom were organized in 316 groups.[67] In the cities, the Bible Student teachings met with even greater response than in rural areas.[68] A consideration of the data of the local groups in Dresden, Berlin, and Hamburg demonstrates this numerical increase (see table 1).

During this period, the group of Bible Students in Dresden represented the largest local IBSA group in the world.[69] It outnumbered by almost two hundred believers[70] the group in New York, the location of "the earthly headquarters of the work of the Lord."[71]

Because of the tremendous increase in believers between 1922 and 1926, Germany had become an important center of the International Bible Student movement. Only in the United States did God's people have a larger following. On a worldwide scale, more than one in four Bible Students came from Germany.[72]

This development can be attributed first and foremost to after-effects of World War I, notwithstanding the fact that during the 1920s there was apparently, particularly fruitful ground for religious activities in Germany. The experience of this first modern war with its deployment of poison gas and drumfire, loss of family members, economic hardship, as well as the general spirit of upheaval after 1918, had many people question traditional values and perceptions, looking for new directions. The people who had been directly affected by the terrors of the war responded especially favorably to the message of the Bible Students. In visits to homes, and by means of public discourses and publications, the Bible Students announced that Christ's Kingdom would soon extend its rule over the earth, bringing love, righteousness, and peace, everlasting life, and a resurrection of the dead. Disabled war veterans, widows whose husbands had bled to death on the battlefield, soldiers who had been crushed by their experiences in the trenches, and church members who felt that God had been betrayed by the fact that their army chaplains had blessed the weapons—these were the people who turned to the comforting teachings of the *Watchtower.*[73] In addition, the denomination also gained a substantial number of followers from among the poorest of society.[74] It was unemployment, inflation, and hunger that drew these people to the promises of salvation. They longed for the time when God would radically change conditions. The Bible Students provided them with teachings that gave them not only a better outlook for the future but also a community that supplied the recognition and warmth they were denied from society in general. Their newfound faith did not merely provide them with a promise of peaceful conditions in a future Kingdom of God, which He was going to establish after Armageddon. These newly converted ones had become part of God's people. The Bible Student teachings had transformed their state of rejection into a state of acceptance by God. In the majority of cases, one conversion resulted in more conversions, as the newly converted tried to persuade family members and relatives into accepting their newfound beliefs.[75]

To a certain extent, this increase was also related to the fact that the Bible Student teachings were given a new direction. In his booklet with the promising title *Millions Now Living Will Never Die,* which had a high circulation in Germany during the early 1920s, Rutherford presented a new calculation regarding the anticipated date for the End. The president of the Watch Tower Society announced to oppressed mankind that in the very near future the Old Order of Things, or Old World, would be ending, and he even mentioned a specific year for this event. According to his predictions, "1925 shall mark the resurrection of the faithful worthies of old and the beginning of reconstruction."[76]

The prospect of being relieved from material and emotional hardship within a very short period of time, and for people to enter God's Kingdom without ever having to die, proved to be very effective. At conventions of the Watch Tower Society, at which a lecture campaign based on Rutherford's publication had been started, there were record attendances. On four special days in 1922, on which this discourse was given in hundreds of German cities, the organizers counted a total attendance of almost 250,000 people.[77] During his extensive tour through Europe in 1922 Rutherford even gave some of the discourses himself at big conventions in German cities. When he spoke to an audience of more than 7,000 people in Zirkus Krone, in Munich, it sent church authorities into a state of agitation. Just prior to the convention, on February 18, 1922, Cardinal Faulhaber, the archbishop of Munich and Freising, had issued a decree for his diocese according to which "it was prohibited to attend meetings of anti-Catholic sects." In this regard, he addressed especially the Earnest Bible Students. He also threatened to "excommunicate any person who read their publications."[78]

The increasing preaching activity, accompanied by an upswing in donations and proceeds from the distribution of their publications, allowed the Watch Tower Society to consolidate its structure. In 1923, on the Magdeburg premises, new publishing facilities were put into operation. Two years later, after the purchase of more property, a larger complex was erected that included printing facilities with modern rotary presses. The complex included an assembly hall seating about 8,000 people and accommodations for the approximately 200 people working at the Magdeburg Bible House. In 1930 the construction of a new and larger residential complex followed. The Magdeburg Bible House, also called Bethel, reflected the meaningful increase the Watch Tower Society had achieved during the period of the 1920s.

The Bible Students Association also expanded their publishing program with regard to contents. This resulted in the fact that they found recognition even among people on the European continent. In October 1922 the Bible Students began to publish a German edition of their journal by the name of *The Golden Age,* which had already been published in English three years earlier. In contrast to the *Watchtower,* the *Golden Age* was not addressed primarily to people who had already accepted the Bible Student teachings. According to the editors, the *Golden Age* was supposed to introduce and advocate the Bible Students Association to the general public. The purpose of this semimonthly journal was to present the "earthly hope and the magnificence of the Messianic Kingdom in a generally comprehensible way to a larger readership."[79] For this reason, it included not only Bible-based subjects or cultural information but also articles informing readers about current events and discussions from the Bible Students' perspective.[80] Soon, the journal had a large number of subscribers: at the beginning of the 1930s, it had a circulation of more than 400,000 copies, and before long, the journal attracted the special hatred of the ideological opponents of the IBSA.

Legally, the Bible Students initiated measures that were of significance for the future confrontation. Until 1921, no efforts had been made to protect legally the activities of the German IBSA branch. However, the requirements associated with printing and distributing publications made it seem appropriate to make adjustments in this area, even before Armageddon. At the same time, it was also important to protect the interests of the Brooklyn headquarters. According to the Introductory Law of the German Civil Code (Bürgerliches Gesetzbuch, BGB), Article 10, it was possible under certain conditions to give legal status to an association if it was legally recognized in another country. With reference to this law, by means of the December 1, 1921, decision by the Reichsrat (State Council), the Wachtturm-Gesellschaft (WTG, German branch of the Watch Tower Society) obtained permission to function as a branch of the American publishing house, Watch Tower Bible and Tract Society.[81] This provided the WTG with the legal status of being the subsidiary association of an American corporation. In 1926, as a further legal entity, the Internationale Bibelforscher-Vereinigung, deutscher Zweig (International Bible Students Association, German Branch) was established, and in 1927 this association was entered into the Register of Associations at the municipal court (*Amtsgericht*) in Magdeburg.[82]

The Bible Students as Objects of Aggression

State and church authorities had already become aware of the antiwar attitude of the Bible Students during World War I. It was now the

enormous growth of the religious denomination and the uncompromising manner of appearance of its adherents that caused quite a stir. At
the same time, it seems that during the postwar period the number of
opponents grew even faster than the number of believers. This growing
opposition, however, involved not only the harsh rejection of large parts
of the population against the Bible Students' missionary spirit and zeal-
ous preaching activity; it involved also active countermeasures coming
from various directions. It is the background of this controversy against
which the IBSA ban in the Third Reich needs to be viewed. Even
though in principle the defense took on different forms, the motives for
the later persecution were one and all devised during the period of the
1920s: the slogans to "justify the later persecution of the Bible Students"[83] were given out as early as the beginning of the Weimar Republic in 1918.

Because of their neutrality teaching, the Bible Students did not participate in the political controversies and revolutionary activities of the
postwar period. And since the secular authorities during the Weimar
Republic (1918–33) did not require anything that conflicted with their religious beliefs, they also conscientiously obeyed the laws. Despite these
facts, the Bible Students were increasingly accused of being "agitators"
and "supporters of the subversion." In this regard, it was not only the
rapid growth of the IBSA and its missionary spirit that gave reason for
concern but rather the Bible Students' predictions of an imminent destruction of all worldly governments by the hand of Jehovah that was
seen as a threat, and this, in particular, was interpreted to be a dangerous
and deliberate act of subversion on the part of the IBSA. The authorities did not recognize that the anticipated change of conditions would
be realized by Jehovah's saving power, according to the Bible Student
teachings. Accordingly, as long as God did not decide to take action, the
rulers of this world actually had nothing to fear from the Bible Students.
All the authorities heard was, "establishment of a Kingdom that would
bring peace on earth without any class and race distinctions," and "destruction of the powers of this world." This sounded familiar in the era
of the Russian Revolution and its resulting upheavals.[84] Strange as it
might seem, the opponents accused the Bible Students quite simply of
being pioneers of Bolshevism. Doubting skeptics were told: "As absurd
as it may sound, it is the truth! It is a known fact that Bolshevism has unmistakable characteristics of apocalyptic chiliasm, albeit misinterpreted
in a physical, earthly way. . . . Therefore, it is not surprising that Germany, in particular, the last stronghold of European culture against

Oriental barbarism, has been literally flooded with the pioneers of Bolshevism, namely the Bible Students."[85]

The struggle against the Bible Students, who had thus been classified as enemies of the Fatherland, began by means of a publicity campaign. *Völkisch* groups (German exclusivist ethnic nationalism) provoked intense counterpropaganda. At first, their protagonists tried to establish an affinity between the Bible Student teachings and Communist ideology. To this end, a certain August Fetz discredited the Bible Student teachings as "nothing but Bolshevism in disguise of religion."[86] In the fourth edition of his work *Der grosse Volks- und Weltbetrug durch die Ernsten Bibelforscher,* published in 1924 by Deutschvölkische Verlagsanstalt in Hamburg, Fetz states:

> As already explained, this opinion is based on a total agreement between the Bible Student teachings and the objectives of international Talmudic Judaism, international Freemasonry, and international Social Democracy, including their most recent subsidiary organization, Russian Bolshevism. Their mutual concept: Subversion of all governmental, religious, and economical systems, complete destruction of all national, *völkisch,* and Christian-minded opponents, as well as unrestricted world domination of Judaism after previous world revolution, anarchy, and world subjugation.[87]

According to Fetz, the Bible Students participation in world revolution was restricted not only to intellectual involvement. Fetz paints a horrifying picture describing the IBSA as "fanatical combat patrols and storm troopers that will take action against State, church, and civil order:

> Bible Student troops will tear down altars, destroy churches, storm schools and universities, stone religious and university teachers, and—as in Russia—nail clergymen to church doors. All the while, they will imagine that, with these acts of destruction, they are rendering an especially pleasing and loyal service to God.[88]

In his 164-page work *Weltvernichtung durch Bibelforscher und Juden,* published in 1925 by Deutscher Volksverlag, Fetz changes his argumentation. At the center of his contemplations are now the alleged similarities between the Bible Students and Judaism. For this purpose, Fetz states that the Bible Student teachings are not based on Christian beliefs. In his opinion, these teachings "have a pre-Christian, Jewish origin and are based on pagan ideas."[89] He no longer upholds his previous accusation that the Bible Students were merely instruments exploited by Judaism.

The controversy now centers on an alleged "Jewish character" of the "Brooklyn sect." As a result, the most serious anti-Semitic hatred hails down on the IBSA, which, according to Fetz, is in reality a "Jewish organization."

Actually, the Bible Students did not repudiate the Jewish origin of the Christian faith. This gave anti-Semitic groups ammunition for their hate campaigns. For instance, they resented the Bible Students' use of the name Jehovah.[90] They also took offense at the fact that the Bible Students placed special importance on the Old Testament, emphasizing that the Israelites were God's chosen people, acknowledging the patriarchy of Abraham, Isaac, and Jacob, and showing respect for the Mosaic Law. But most of all, the anti-Semites resented the Bible Students' adherence to Bible prophecies involving Zion (Ezek. 38–39; Zech. 8). The publications of the Watch Tower Bible and Tract Society explained that the Zionist movement gave clear evidence that the time of the End had arrived, the time when Jehovah God would gather his covenant people in Palestine, and Zion would once again become home to Israel.[91] For the anti-Semites such explanations amounted to collaboration with their most hated enemy, Zionism. The majority of the Christian churches who rejected their Jewish origin (or were at least not aware of it) had long forgotten their biblical heritage and did not acknowledge Jesus' words according to which "salvation comes from the Jews" (John 4:22). That the Bible Students accepted their biblical heritage provoked the relentless hatred and opposition of anti-Semitic groups.

The Bible Student teachings in the 1920s were completely free from any anti-Judaism of the Christian churches.[92] In 1925 the Watch Tower Society's president, Rutherford, as the highest earthly spokesman of the present people of God, stated that it was important to acknowledge the nation of Israel for the very fact that "for a long time [it] was the visible part of God's organization on earth."[93] He then added: "The persecution of the Jews by so-called Christians is one of the blackest things upon the world's escutcheon."[94]

Even a few years prior to Fetz, Hans Lienhardt selected the Bible Students as an object of his insolent anti-Semitic attacks. He considered the IBSA activities to be a "gigantic crime against the German nation." Lienhardt announced that the IBSA intended to destroy the churches, overthrow the governments, and strive for world revolution to confer world domination to a future Jewish Messiah. For this reason alone the Bible Students propagated the destruction of the nations in the War of Armageddon. The whole matter supposedly was a "criminal act on the part of the Jews, wrapped up in Bible texts, with the objective of securing world domination and subjugating the German nation."[95]

Lienhardt states that the Bible Students with German heritage had been mislead without recognizing the background of the teachings of the denomination's founder, whom Lienhardt describes, in his 1921 publication, as "Russell, the Jew."[96] In Lienhardt's opinion, these German Bible Students were not completely lost, especially since they had within their ranks "very decent, morally and religiously upright, people." He continued his explanations with a complaint that clearly reflected the inconsistency in his *völkisch* National Socialist judgment about the Bible Students: "How great it would be if such high morals could be found in the entire German nation!"[97]

During the following years, the ideological patrons of the German National Socialist Workers' Party (NSDAP) also joined in the campaign against the Bible Students. In 1923 Alfred Rosenberg, who later represented the Führer in supervising the entire intellectual and ideological education of the NSDAP, declared that the Jews had commissioned the Bible Students to "hypnotize" the masses in order to "cause complete confusion." This increasing confusion, in turn, would set the mental stage for Jewish world domination. Finally, Rosenberg came to the conclusion: "What democracy and Marxism accomplished in the political arena, the Bible Students do in the field of church and religion."[98]

The party-ideologist Dietrich Eckart who, right from the beginning, gave the NSDAP its theoretical structure, and who was regarded also as the political mentor of Hitler, characterized the Bible Students as an organization equipped with large sums of money, which was moving "in the Jewish current toward the Soviet."[99] In his work, posthumously published in 1924, Eckart states that Adolf Hitler perceived in the Bible Students *den jüdischen Wurm* — that is, they were supposedly deeply infiltrated with Jewish ideas.[100]

In January 1923, after stating that nothing in the Holy Scriptures indicates that God had ultimately rejected his chosen people, the Jews, one of the first German issues of the *Golden Age* predicted: "Anyone who dares today to speak in favor of God's chosen people will soon be accused of being paid by the Jews."[101] How true this statement proved to be.

Especially during the period of 1924/25, efforts were made to discredit the Bible Students for supposedly receiving financial support from Jewish or Freemason groups. Thus, at the beginning of 1924, proceedings at the district court (*Bezirksgericht*) in St. Gallen gained great importance, especially with regard to their outcome. The events leading up to these proceedings were not unusual for that particular time period. On January 21, 1924, in collaboration with the Theological Faculty of the Zurich University in St. Gallen, a church protest meeting took place against the rapidly increasing Bible Student activities in Switzerland. In his speech, the primary speaker Professor Köhler stated that he had a problem understanding from where the Bible Students received the financial resources for their enormous publicity campaign. However, he strongly rejected the opinion held among *völkisch* groups that these resources were "Jewish money." During the following discussion, Dr. Fehrmann, a well-known physician in St. Gallen, contradicted his opinion. According to the press report, Dr. Fehrmann asserted (with reference to alleged evidence) that "International Judaism provided the so-called 'Earnest Bible Students' with substantial amounts of money for the purpose of causing confusion within western European Christendom."[102]

The authorized IBSA representative Conrad Binkele, leader of the central European office, instituted legal proceedings against this accusation on the charge of defamation. In court, Dr. Fehrmann presented as evidence a December 27, 1922, "letter from highest Freemason groups." Supposedly, this letter was written by a "high-ranking thirty-third degree Freemason " and there was "no question" regarding its authenticity. The ominous letter, which was repeatedly cited by the NS press, stated in part, "in our usual indirect way, we provide them [the Bible Students] with large amounts of money through a number of our brothers who made a lot of money during the war. This does not hurt their considerable portfolios! They are associated with the Jews."[103]

The St. Gallen District Court rejected the IBSA defamation suit. It sentenced the association to pay a compensation of 450 Swiss francs to Dr. Fehrmann. As a result, the IBSA opponents had their longed for "evidence" to which they henceforth repeatedly made reference. They did not mention the fact that the court decision was basically made for reasons of formality. The court had never entered the hearing of evidence. The IBSA opponents also did not mention that according to the judges, the Freemason letter was a completely unsuitable piece of evidence.[104] With considerable effort, the IBSA tried to defend itself against these insinuations and defamation. However, not even pamphlet campaigns and newspaper reports, in which the Watch Tower Society offered to pay one thousand German marks to anybody who could prove that the Bible Students Association had received money or other benefits "from the Jews," were able to stop the defamation campaign against the Bible Students.[105]

With reference to the St. Gallen court proceedings, numerous articles and pamphlets spread the rumor that international Judaism supported the extremely expensive publicity campaign of the Bible Students.[106] Certain parts of society were now convinced that they knew who were the manipulators of the entire movement. This was the breeding ground on which absurd conspiracy theories began to grow. They culminated in the conception that the IBSA was a "subsidiary organization of a secret Jewish government."[107]

Confrontation Between the Churches and the Bible Students

Not only propagandists from *völkisch* and NS groups accused the Bible Students of having formed an alliance with the Freemasons, Jews, and Marxists. German national-minded groups of the Evangelical churches and certain parts of the Roman Catholic clergy also joined in these accusations, and they incited each other in their defamatory slogans.

Before taking a closer look at the churches' defense struggle, it is important to provide some background information that would contribute to a better understanding of the charged relationship between the churches and the Bible Students Association.

The controversy involved not just the churches' concern that the Bible Student activities would cause them heavy losses in membership — a concern they had also toward other competing denominations. It centered on the Bible Students' antichurch polemics, which increased considerably over the years, on the one hand, because of the churches' counterattacks and, on the other hand, because of Rutherford's more radical approach and his anti-Satanic campaign.

The Bible Students measured the churches against Bible standards and then declared them to be false religions (or so-called nominal Christians) against whom people had to be warned. In their opinion, an apostasy took place in the second and third centuries, during which Christians had deviated from Bible principles. This apostasy culminated in the fact that Christendom was raised to the status of a Roman state religion. This, in turn, resulted in a network of "large church systems that did not maintain the purity of the early Christian congregation."[108] The Bible Students claimed that Satan used the clergy of Christendom as his instrument to keep people away from "true Christianity" and, consequently, from "God's organization." Religious organizations that unconditionally supported the governments were therefore actually misleading the people. Such deceiving religious organizations are described in Revelation as Babylon, "the great prostitute . . . with whom all the kings of the earth have prostituted themselves."[109] "Babylon the Great, the mother of all the prostitutes and all the filthy practices on the earth" is therefore a "symbol for Satan's world empire of false religion."[110]

The interpretation that Satan dominates humans by means of an entire religious system was—and still is—a fundamental characteristic of the Bible Student teachings.[111] The Bible Students, therefore, did not consider themselves as a religious group in the strict sense of the word, but rather as the only religious denomination carrying out the will of God.

Even prior to the expansion of the Bible Student movement, the clergy had complained that the sect caused confusion among church members.[112] For this reason, the Catholic and Evangelical clergy warned their members to beware of the Bible Students even more than any other sect. The church members were told to turn the Bible Students away whenever they came to visit.[113] In sermons, pastoral care, and other religious education, clergymen admonished their adherents not to listen to the proclaimers of the teachings of Russell and Rutherford. They organized public counterevents and series of discussions to warn people about the danger emanating from sectarian groups. Even during Bible Student conventions, the clergy tried to take the platform and force a discussion, which, according to a report from the Saxony consistory, the Bible Students "refused with every means at their disposal."[114] From the Bible Students perspective, however, the situation was seen as completely different. They complained about provocations and that religious groups deliberately disrupted their conventions, preventing their speakers from delivering their messages.[115]

The church authorities "desperately tried" finding "effective ways to resist" the Bible Students. They called upon their clergy to take appropriate measures and requested support from secular authorities.[116] According to the June 1920 report of the Evangelical Higher Church Council in Baden, the German Evangelical church committee proposed to ban the "most disturbing of the so-called 'Earnest Bible Student publications.'"[117]

In 1921 the "central committee of the Evangelical Association for the Internal Mission in Germany" founded the Apologetische Centrale. This office "collected evidence of the activities of every religious, ideological, and sectarian movement."[118] It carefully recorded the IBSA activities and analyzed pamphlets, booklets, press reports, and a number of articles that clergymen had written after attending IBSA conventions in order to launch a religious counterattack.[119] Based on the information obtained, literature and training programs were provided to equip the eager clergy for their assignment. For the same purpose, the Catholic Church also formed an "apologetic" department. Konrad Algermissen, the director of this department, published several books and essays in which he made the Bible Students his special target, describing them as "a true menace and a nationwide spiritual epidemic."[120]

Especially between 1921 and 1925, a large number of informational pamphlets were published about the Bible Students Association.[121] However, the apologetic literature presented not merely the viewpoint of the churches against these false teachings, restricting the discussion mainly to a religious controversy. It even included a number of works that could be viewed as religious variations of *völkisch*, anti-Semitic lampoons.[122] The counterpropaganda of the Evangelical churches was even more extensive than that of the Catholic Church. Interestingly, the pamphlets based on *völkisch* Christian thinking clearly outnumbered the standard studies on sectarian groups.[123]

In 1918 Secret Consistory Counsel Friedrich Loofs considered the Bible Students Association as an American growth detrimental to German national pride.[124] Four years later, with the approval of the archepiscopal ordinariate in Freiburg, Fritz Schlegel published a book in which he called the Bible Students a "Bolshevik association and shock squads of International Judaism."[125] As early as 1922, Fritz Schlegel took the liberty of publishing disclosures (which subsequently were further disseminated by *völkisch* authors) concerning the alleged financial sources of the IBSA: "The tracks led us to the Jewish bank Hirsch in New York." This bank supposedly provided the IBSA "with substantial amounts of money."[126] In a second volume, published by Abwehrverlag, Schlegel increased his anti-Semitic polemics and produced the distorted image of a Christian community surrounded by enemy forces. At the same time as August Fetz, Schlegel proclaimed that the Bible Student movement and Judaism were similar in nature. Schlegel included even Freemasonry and stated that these three were entities like "peas in a pod."[127]

In contrast to Catholic author Fritz Schlegel, Paul Braeunlich, the secretary general of the Evangelical Federation and holding a doctorate in theology, mentioned in his 1925 book that not the Jews but the Bolsheviks were the financial supporters of the IBSA. According to Braeunlich, this was their way of investing in preparations for world revolution.[128] Braeunlich, who allegedly examined the political background of the Bible Student movement, did not agree with the theory of a Jewish source of financial support. He clearly considered the Bible Student movement as a Bolshevik instrument of achieving world domination. According to Braeunlich, the Communists used the Bible Students primarily for the purpose of weakening the churches by "depriving them of their most religious members." This, in turn, would "to a great extent impede the resistance, which a nonreligious 'Soviet regime' had to fear especially from the religious people of the lower classes of society."[129]

Obsessed with this idea, Braeunlich reached ever more absurd conclusions. For instance, he considered Russell, the founder of the sect, as the possible schemer in the assassination at Sarajevo. This was supposedly his way of engaging the nations in World War I. Braeunlich also did not consider it a coincidence that the general insubordination, including the entire revolution," came from exactly the same city that the Bible Students had used as one of the principal centers of their activities during the previous years.[130] Finally, the whole idea escalated in his reference to the birthplace and profession of Paul Balzereit, the leader of their German branch office. As a former dockworker from Kiel, Balzereit could not deny that he had been there "at the crucial time."[131]

The anti-Semites objected to Braeunlich's statement that the Jews did not provide financial support for the Bible Students. In reply to the statement of the secretary general of the Evangelical Federation, Julius Kuptsch, an Evangelical pastor from Riesenburg, Eastern Prussia, stated: "At times, Bolshevism could be the intermediary of the money but never its source. Bolshevism, or communism, is only a poor proletarian. Only the power that produced Bolshevism could also give financial support to the Bible Students, namely Judaism."[132]

In Kuptsch's study, the particular point on which all accusations of world revolution and world domination were based is succinctly tangible: the earthly view of the eschatological announcements of the Bible Students. A religion that promises its followers better conditions in the hereafter projects its predictions into another sphere—one that is unworldly or transcendent. The announcement that God's Kingdom would extend its rule over the earth, however, was perceived as a threat. If the old powers were to be removed and replaced with a new power, this promised Kingdom of peace had to be, according to the critics of the Bible Student teachings, an earthly, political power of significant dimensions. This concept reflected the age-old Jewish expectation of a messianic ruler who was equipped with the insignia of earthly political power. According to the critics, the Bible Student teachings did not announce the Christian expectation of God's Kingdom. Instead, according to Kuptsch, they proclaimed the "thousand-year world government under the control of a Jewish council."[133] Kuptsch's representation of the Bible Student teachings clearly demonstrates how, by inserting specific concepts and ideas, eschatological predictions can be transformed into revolutionary and state-endangering program statements. The following excerpt from an article in *Völkischer Beobachter* (a NS party paper), published in 1931, clearly shows what such "manipulations" did to the Bible Student teachings. After explaining to the readers of the party paper that the IBSA believed that the Earnest Bible Students, the Jews, the anarchists, and the revolutionary masses are the visible representatives of Christ on earth, Pastor Kuptsch made the following statement:

> Through them, as his instruments, the invisible Christ has acted even as early as 1789, that is, as early as the French revolution. By means of them, he is going to destroy the works and organizations of Satan, including all states, all Christian churches and all of Christianity, as well as the instruments and servants of Satan, that is, the clergy, the militarists and capitalists. When this has been accomplished in the great, imminent "War of Armageddon," that is, in the world revolution, all Jewish people will go to Palestine. At that time, Abraham, Isaac, Jacob, and other worthy people from the Old Testament will rise from the dead. As visible representatives of Christ, they will extend world domination from Jerusalem to the ends of the earth. The Jewish people will lead the nations and will rule over them with an iron rod according to the divine law of the Old Testament. Any rebellious elements among them will be destroyed. This will bring about the Kingdom of peace, the Golden Age on earth.[134]

Such interpretation of the Bible Student teachings soon gained acceptance with the ideological cartel of *völkisch* NS groups. After the National Socialists took power, this interpretation was used to inform the population of the "danger" emanating from the IBSA. Among the opponents of the Bible Students who disseminated these ideas were ideological outsiders of the most obscure kind, especially in the undefined area between the German Christian Movement and the German Faith Movement (an anti-Semitic movement).[135] During the Weimar Republic, these outsiders certainly did not keep their ideas confined to their own groups. Many of their ideas found their way into official church reports and theological studies. For instance, the *Kirchliche Jahrbuch für die evangelischen Landeskirchen Deutschlands* readily accepted the assertion that the Bible Students Association was involved in a Communist-oriented agitation.[136] Cardinal Michael von Faulhaber, the archbishop of Munich and Freising, accused the Bible Students even of performing "American [!] Communist activities."[137] Ultimately, only a small minority within the churches maintained an untarnished judgment. Among those who did not succumb to the agitators of the campaign against the IBSA was (certainly not by coincidence) the theologian Gerhard Jacobi, one of the leading personalities of the "Bekennende Kirche" in the Third Reich.[138]

Both in and out of the churches, there were almost no differences in the right-wing positions; the Bible Student issue was thus a matter of mutual interest, and early efforts were made to combine forces against the IBSA. In September 1923 the Evangelical Reich Committee of the German National People's Party considered it necessary to form an association of "Christian and national-minded groups for the purpose of resisting this sect" in view of its not to be underestimated subversive effects on broad sections of the population.[139]

Alternating Pamphlet Campaigns

During the mid-1920s, in an effort to defend themselves against the accusations, the IBSA (who also sought a dialogue with the churches by distributing tracts in front of church buildings and cemeteries), took on an increasingly brazen tone. In this regard, two actions in particular intensified the confrontation, which resulted in the fact that the churches determinedly demanded state intervention.

In 1924 the Watch Tower Society made a counterattack by means of a book, published by Stern-Verlag in Leipzig, with a circulation of 200,000 copies. The book, *Die grösste Geheimmacht der Welt*, was written by the German IBSA leader Paul Balzereit, under the pseudonym P. B. Gotthilf. The book, which was not identified to outsiders as a Bible Student publication, asserted that pontifical Rome was only mistakenly viewed as a religious institution. In reality it was a power-hungry institution using religion as a disguise.[140] Its objective was "absolute subjugation of the whole world and the suppression of any national [!] autonomy."[141]

In a manner akin to the Kulturkampf (the struggle between the Evangelical state of Prussia and the Catholic Church, 1871–87) and the powers employed at that time against Ultramontanism (the faction in the Roman Catholic Church advocating the doctrine of papal supremacy), Balzereit criticized the supranational attitude of Catholicism. A Catholic would first of all have to be a Catholic, in line with the motto "First comes Rome, then the fatherland." Balzereit asserted that, by means of its church apparatus, the curia determinedly exerted an increasing influence over all the nations, thus engaging them in World War I. This was a "positive achievement" for Catholicism, which, during the phase of secularization, was in danger of decline. As a result, Germany became one of the "most deplorable victims of this huge secret world power."

In his conclusion, in which Balzereit shows his concern for the nations and especially for Germany, he emphasizes that there was an "enemy, dreaded by Rome," who, by means of his "campaign . . . rendered humankind an invaluable service." This enemy was the Bible Students Association, which was contending solely with explanations from the Bible. That the IBSA was carrying out a "propaganda campaign in favor of Jewish world domination" was an accusation that in reality originated with "religious opponents of the Bible Students who sought world domination for themselves."

Thus, the circle had been closed, and it was no longer difficult for the accused to identify who was behind those agitating assumptions. Because of the "lies and insults against the Catholic Church" included in the book, the Dresden Higher Regional Court ordered the confiscation of the remaining copies of its first edition, and under application of the penal regulations for blasphemy and religious offenses, a fine was imposed on the publisher, Stern-Verlag.[142]

Employing the same type of argumentation used by the opponents, Balzereit's book indicates that for the sake of the attack, or counterattack, against the Catholic Church, at least he, the German IBSA leader, was willing to pay tribute to the national atmosphere prevalent in large parts of the German population. At the same time, he distanced himself from Rutherford's propagated rejection of the nations. The IBSA, however, in its second campaign, placed its emphasis on other charges.

At the turn of the year 1924/25 the Bible Students started an extensive pamphlet campaign.[143] They distributed millions of copies of "Ecclesiastics Indicted," even in the smallest villages.[144] The message was directed against both the Catholic and Evangelical clergy. The IBSA list of transgressions directed against the clergymen included the following offenses: "The clergy had exalted themselves"; they refused "to nourish the people with God's Word of truth"; they misused their spiritual powers "to gratify their own selfish desires"; the church dignitaries clothed themselves in "gaudy apparel," and had formed an "alliance with the devil, the god of all evil"; in every country, the clergy had made themselves the "spokesmen of militarism and war and had preached the soldiers into the trenches"; their church buildings had been turned into "recruiting places"; these "unfaithful preachers" even accepted payments for their services from the governments;and finally, because of these offenses, the clergy now received their judgment because "God's day of anger over Christendom" had arrived.

The distribution of this indictment caused quite some agitation among the church leaders.[145] There was mention of an "onslaught on the part of the Bible Students."[146] At the beginning of March, the *Deutsche Pfarrerblatt* (a church paper) prepared for a counterattack. A large number of pamphlets were provided for distribution in the parishes. In these pamphlets, the "accusations" of the Bible Students were compared with the "facts." With reference to the St. Gallen proceedings, the journal of the German Evangelical Pastors Associations went even so far as to suggest that, in reality, the Bible Student propaganda was initiated by Judaism and Zionism. The counterpamphlet *Deutsche Pfarrerblatt* made the concluding remark: "It is certainly not the Evangelical clergy who are in the dock; instead it is the leaders of the so-called 'Bible Students' who are inciting, seducing, and misleading our people!"[147]

In previous years, the church offices had repeatedly tried to "draw the attention of the state authorities . . . to this matter."[148] But, in contrast to the period of 1917/18, the state authorities reacted rather reserved, trying to resolve the differences. They agreed to keep the Bible Students under observation with regard to Communist infiltration but were not willing to take extensive administrative action against them. Now, however, after this pamphlet campaign, the churches desperately demanded state intervention. On March 20, 1935, Hermann Kapler, the president of the German Evangelical church committee, requested the Reich Minister of the Interior (RMdI) to order an immediate "police confiscation of the pamphlet and the plates for its production." It was expected that the minister would "protect the clergy from the attacks directed at them because of the fact that they had fulfilled their duties for their fatherland during the war and postwar period."[149] However, those efforts remained unsuccessful. The churches continued to have to resort to legal action.[150]

The IBSA and the Theocratic Rule

Legally, there were not many possibilities to take action against the Bible Students. There was, for instance, the law punishing insults directed against recognized religious organizations (StGB [Strafgesetzbuch, German Penal Code], articles 166, 167). The only other option was to make use of the regulations of the Reich Industrial Code (Reichsgewerbegesetz), by means of which action could be taken against the Bible Students' preaching activity at people's homes. Based on these regulations, police offices in various places had already taken action against IBSA members in previous years. However, in the mid-1920s there was a considerable increase in the number of complaints concerning the IBSA activities. In 1926, 897 legal proceedings were instituted against the Bible Students on the charge of unauthorized peddling or violations against the Reich Industrial Code. Two years later, this number almost doubled (1,660). In only a few cases the courts imposed fines. In the majority of cases, the Bible Students were acquitted.[151] But IBSA members were increasingly confronted with difficulties. In 1927 as many as 1,169 cases were registered in which Bible Students were temporarily arrested and had to appear at police offices. Therefore, to support the arrested Bible Students, the Magdeburg branch office established its own legal department. In some cases, this department took matters to higher authorities. At least at the Prussian Ministry of the Interior, such actions indeed met with success. On April 19, 1930, the ministry issued a decree instructing its subordinate offices to refrain subsequently "from instituting such legal action."[152]

During the second half of the 1920s, the Bible Students Association had to deal not only with difficulties from the outside. First of all, they had to cope with another disappointment involving their expectations concerning the end of the world. When "the apocalyptic War of Armageddon, which they had expected in the autumn of 1925, and the subsequent restoration of all things under the righteous rule of Christ and his faithful followers" failed to come about, further divisions took place.[153] About two thousand people left the Bible Students Association.[154] The most serious effects of these disappointing developments were experienced in neighboring Switzerland, affecting even the central European office. In February 1926 the Watch Tower Society in Brooklyn appointed the German-American Martin C. Harbeck to be the new leader of its central European office in Bern to replace Conrad C. Binkele who had become apostate.[155]

Figure 1. Increasing membership of the Hamburg Bible Student community, 1909–32

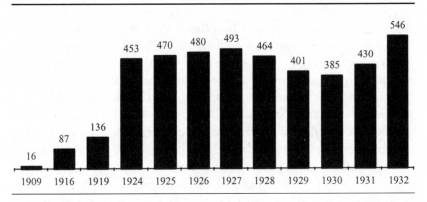

In the beginning, it was still possible to compensate the numerical losses with new conversions, but the growth rate continued to decline rapidly. By 1928 the number of believers even began to decrease. This decline of the Bible Student movement noted toward the end of the 1920s continued until 1930–31.[156] During the next two years, the period just prior to NS takeover, the IBSA membership began to increase again, with numbers comparable to those between 1922 and 1925. In 1930 the Watch Tower Bible and Tract Society reported a 150 percent increase in their book and booklet distribution. In the following year Germany reported a maximum distribution of 5.6 million Bible Student publications. In the course of 1931 a total of eighty new congregations, or local IBSA groups, could be established.[157] Apart from the increasing preaching activity of the Bible Students, this development can be attributed also to the great poverty and unemployment caused by the economic crisis in Germany.[158] The timely message about "Jehovah God, the Friend of the Poor and Oppressed" corresponded to the situation and gave reason to expect increasing reception.[159] In this respect, the fluctuating numbers of believers also reflected socioeconomic trends. During the period of crisis in the Republic, high increases in membership were recorded; during periods of relative prosperity, the number of IBSA members stagnated or even declined. Based on the membership numbers that are available for the IBSA group in Hamburg, the fluctuations are represented in figure 1.[160]

During the mid-1920s, because of the fluctuations, the total number of Bible Students in Germany changed only insignificantly. In 1926 the denomination had a membership of 22,535 organized in 316 groups; in 1931 this number had increased to a total of 24,135 believers organized in approximately 395 groups.[161] In view of the numbers of Bible Students at the beginning of the Third Reich, the following statements can be made: 24,843 people attended their memorial celebration of Christ's death on April 9, 1933. During the same month, 19,268 Jehovah's Witnesses participated in the preaching activity during their eight-day "testimony period."[162] In addition to these approximately 20,000 Kingdom proclaimers or about 25,000 members, there was a group of 10,000 people that could be described as interested or newly associated, but these were not considered to be members of the Bible Students Association and did not consider themselves as such.[163] Accordingly, it can be estimated that at the beginning of the NS regime, the IBSA, or Jehovah's Witnesses, had a membership of between 25,000 and 30,000 representing a ratio of 0.38 per thousand of the total population in the German Reich.[164] This proportion clearly indicates the contrast that existed between the alleged "danger" the IBSA presented according to its opponents and the insignificant social position the Bible Students really occupied.

The period between 1931 and 1932 brought an influx of members that compensated for the losses of 1931. This was the year in which the denomination adopted the name "Jehovah's Witnesses" by accepting a resolution at the general assembly in Columbus, Ohio. The name was based on a Bible text from the Old Testament (Isa. 43:10, 11), which states: "You are my witnesses, quoth Jehovah." Thereafter, the IBSA groups in the various countries were asked to "joyfully receive and bear the name which the mouth of Jehovah God has named and given" them.[165] At about the same time that the Bible Students accepted their new name, they were also introduced to the new theocratic rule. Previously, the Bible Student groups had been supervised by elders who were democratically elected into office in each individual congregation. Now the leaders or service committees for the local congregations were appointed directly at the IBSA branch office. This theocratic method took the place of all elections (which from then on were considered unbiblical) and became manifest in the IBSA leaders' claim for unconditional subordination of the local groups. In the *Watchtower*, critics were told that there were no "matters that would apply only to a particular group and in which the organization was not allowed to be involved. Whoever did not know this should quickly learn it."[166] In this "large congregation" of

Jehovah's Witnesses that replaced the Bible Student movement there was no longer any room for individualism.[167]

In several Bible Student groups, these new arrangements involving the leadership resulted in serious controversies. Even though the majority of Bible Students accepted the restructuring willingly, many Witnesses, in some cases even entire congregations, disassociated from the Watch Tower Society. Some of these groups continued to use the name Bible Students.[168] Besides Jehovah's Witnesses, who continued to be known as Bible Students or Earnest Bible Students and whose persecution in the Third Reich was closely related to this name, there were now *other* groups in Germany who called themselves Bible Students. By using the supplementary phrase "Free Association," some of these groups indicated that they were not associated with the original organization. Since, during the NS period, these groups played only a secondary role, the term "Bible Students," as it is used in this study, will refer to those believers who were associated with the Watch Tower Society. This is also in agreement with Jehovah's Witnesses' viewpoint as they continue to use the term "Bible Students" even today.

From 1930 onward, demands for state intervention against the Bible Students increased, even though these demands were often made in the context of requests to repress freethinking and atheist movements.[169] With increasing determination, the churches demanded that efforts should be made to prohibit the propaganda of "freethinking and skepticism" as well as "sectarian heresy." As a result, on March 28, 1931, the Reich president issued the Decree for the Resistance of Political Acts of Violence (Verordnung des Reichspräsidenten zur Bekämpfung politischer Ausschreitungen). Although issued primarily with the objective of increasing the authority of the police to take action against extreme political forces, the decree provided a legal handle to take action in cases in which "a publicly recognized religious organization, its institutions, customs or objects of religious veneration were abused or maliciously disparaged."[170]

With reference to this clause, Bavaria was the first German state that issued bans on the Bible Student activities. In addition to prohibiting their meetings, the police began to confiscate several of their publications. On November 18, 1931, the Munich police authorities issued a decree expanding this practice, which resulted in the prohibition and confiscation of all Bible Student publications throughout the Free State of Bavaria.[171] The Watch Tower Society appealed on a point of law against this decree. However, on February 10, 1932, the government of Upper Bavaria and, one month later, the Bavarian Department of the Interior rejected this appeal. Consequently, the Watch Tower Society took legal action against the state of Bavaria. But even this action remained unsuccessful. The Bavarian Highest National Court pronounced the decree to be legal.[172]

In his actions against the IBSA, Minister of the Interior Karl Stützel (a member of the Bavarian People's Party) received the support of the parliamentary faction of the NSDAP, which otherwise was in strict opposition to the Bavarian government.[173] Then again, with reference to the determined actions the National Socialists were taking against the Bible Students, Cardinal Faulhaber had earlier found words of approval for the NSDAP. He actually deemed the NSDAP position against the "terrible agitation of the Bible Students" to be a well-meaning gesture of the Hitler party, with the obvious objective "of minimizing the sharp contrast between the national-socialist ideology and Christianity."[174] Once more it became evident that it was possible to unite even the strongest of opponents if they had a mutual enemy. In their resistance against the Bible Students, they had a common goal, which, even after January 30, 1933, would form one of the puzzle pieces in their course toward an agreement.

In *Klerusblatt*, the journal of the Bavarian Association of Diocesan Priests, the decree of the Munich police authorities was emphatically welcomed and the active support of the clergy was requested: "As soon as these pamphlet distributors appear, the appropriate constabularies or police offices should be informed so that they can proceed with the confiscation of the publications."[175] Thus, the IBSA attributed the rigorous actions of the state authorities to the fact "that in Bavaria everything is under clerical control."[176] Consequently, the IBSA considered its anticlerical attitude to be justified: It was clearly the Bavarian episcopacy that was manipulating matters from behind the scenes and, in its struggle against the Bible Students, it had the full support of the Bavarian People's Party, which, "on the one hand, was under the control of the clergy and, on the other hand, provided the ministry with most of its civil servants."

In 1932, with reference to the March 28, 1931, Decree of the Reich President for the Protection of People and State (emergency decree), Bible Student publications were confiscated in other German states such as Württemberg and Baden.[177] At least in Baden, the Watch Tower Society was able to achieve a withdrawal of the confiscation orders. In response to the society's complaint, the Baden Administrative Court, in its June 15, 1932, decision, stated that the authorities could not base the confiscations on the Decree of the Reich President since the contents of the Bible Student publications could not "cause such agitation in a large group of people that this agitation would endanger public law and order."[178]

Even the request made to the Reich government to "dissolve the sect" remained unsuccessful even though members of the Zentrumsfraktion had repeatedly asked Reich Chancellor Brüning, who himself used to be a member of that party, to take resolute actions against anti-church movements.[179] The opponents of the Bible Students who complained "When will the holy anger of Christendom finally break forth?" could only hope for a change in government.[180]

As this *other* Thousand-Year Reich began, the one that the National Socialists had proclaimed, it was obvious that Jehovah's Witnesses would face serious persecution in the country in which they had their second-largest membership. The development was predetermined: on the one hand, there were bans and persecution; on the other hand, there was an absolute determination for self-assertion. On January 15, 1933, in the German issue of the *Golden Age*, the issue just prior to the change in government, the Magdeburg branch office of the Watch Tower Bible and Tract Society made the following "solemn statement," which was part of a declaration:

> We will never stop looking for ways to continue our activities. As long as our feet will carry us, as long as we can move and speak, and as long as we are free, we will proclaim Jehovah's name, and we will tell the people that Satan is the ruler of this world and that his kingdom, and thus, all wickedness on earth, will come to an end and that Jehovah's Kingdom alone is the only hope for the future and for salvation of all mankind.[181]

PART 2

JEHOVAH'S WITNESSES IN THE THIRD REICH, 1933–34

4

Efforts to Adapt to National Circumstances, 1933

On January 30, 1933, when Adolf Hitler became Reich chancellor of Germany and the National Socialists had succeeded in consolidating their power, Jehovah's Witnesses knew that the propaganda against them would intensify, and the authorities would take more serious actions against them.

In response to this situation, the leaders of the Bible Students Association attempted to invalidate the opponents' attacks by emphasizing the completely religious and nonpolitical nature of their association, and by demonstrating their loyalty toward State and government.

However, *völkisch* propaganda considered even the association's name, Internationale Bibelforscher Vereinigung, to be evidence that the Bible Students were involved in political activities in terms of the despised Internationale.[1] Also the Bible Students subordination to the Watch Tower Society's headquarters in New York and its president Joseph Franklin Rutherford supposedly proved that the Bible Students supported a foreign power. Therefore, the Bible Students made efforts to counteract these accusations. In the German issue of the journal *Golden Age*, published immediately after the appointment of the national coalition government, the WTG leaders provided an explanation to the question "How do Jehovah's enemies understand the term 'international'?" This article repudiated accusations made in certain press reports according to which the IBSA associated the expression "international" with a political program.[2] The article emphasized that the international and transnational attitude of Jehovah's Witnesses was based entirely on religious reasoning because Jehovah is not a God restricted to national boundaries and his message is directed to all people, regardless of whether they are "German, French, Jewish, Christian, free man or slave."

However, considering the contemporary spirit of national uprising in Germany, there was not much hope that these efforts of clarifying matters would produce any positive results. They were not going to satisfy chauvinistic forces that despised international concepts and implications of impartiality among humans, even if they were based on religious reasoning.

The primary purpose of the statement in the *Golden Age* was to explain the Watch Tower Society's position to its members and the considerable number of readers of its journal, people whom Jehovah's Witnesses consider as "men of good will."[3] At the same time, the Watch Tower Society's leaders did not inform these people of their intention to institute organizational changes. Without informing the local congregations, the leaders of the association substituted the "International Bible Students Association (German Branch)," which continued to function as a corporate body even after the association had accepted the name Jehovah's Witnesses, with two new legal entities: The "Northern German Bible Students Association," which had its branch office in Hamburg, and the "Southern German Bible Students Association," which had its branch office in Stuttgart. In this way, the IBSA leaders tried to "adapt to political circumstances in Germany," and anticipated reducing the confrontations with their opponents in addition to being better equipped to deal with expected administrative interventions.[4] The reorganization was motivated by a concern for the future existence of the association and was, from that perspective, a preventive defense measure. However, the IBSA leaders conceded to external circumstances and abandoned, at least to a certain extent, their own identity. Balzereit and the other leaders thought that they would be able to restrict the adaptation to external measures and leave the religious contents unaffected, but this idea soon proved to be an illusion. Since the IBSA claimed to be the epitome of truth, it was inevitable that concessions would lead to conflicts with their religious self-conception.

Both of the German Bible Student Associations were founded in February/March 1933. There were no differences in structure and thus the following explanations about the Northern German Bible Students Association apply also to the Southern German Bible Students Association.[5] The Northern German Bible Students Association was founded on March 1 by ten leading IBSA functionaries, including the leader of the Magdeburg branch office, its authorized signatory, and its bookkeeper.[6]

Paul Balzereit, the German IBSA leader and director of the German branch office of the Watch Tower Society, accepted the position as president of the Northern German Bible Students Association. According to its statutes, the president had the right to appoint the other board members at his own discretion.[7] Accordingly, Balzereit appointed the Hamburg IBSA district overseer, the merchant Hero von Ahften, as chairman; the Kiel IBSA district overseer, Police Surveyor Dr. Max Karl, as treasurer; and the Dresden IBSA district overseer, Municipal Court Counsel Dr. Alfred Mütze (retired), as secretary.

Since the situation in the German Reich presented an increasing danger for the future existence of the Bible Students Association, the IBSA leaders placed special emphasis on the reputation and social status of its prospective board members. For the same reason, the statutes of the newly formed association also included specific regulations emphasizing the conformity of the denomination to secular laws and its absolute restriction to religious matters. For instance, one of the statutes required that public events being organized by the association or its representatives would "always follow legal regulations" and "never violate the regulations implemented for such events." The IBSA leaders particularly emphasized that such public events must "never be misused for political agitation." In all other aspects, the statutes indicated that the new associations would continue to function in the same way as the original Bible Students Association. Accordingly, besides other regulations, the statements specifying the association's objectives corresponded exactly with the original IBSA statutes.

The authorities did not pay much attention to the establishment of this Northern German Bible Students Association. Apparently, they did not even have a clear concept about the nature of this group. While other German states had already started to ban the International Bible Students Association,[8] NSDAP Reichstag representative Dr. Hans Nieland, the recently appointed Hamburg chief of police, stated that the establishment of this association did not give any cause for concern. On March 24, 1933, he informed the municipal court in Hamburg that the authorities "had no objections against the registration of the 'Northern German Bible Students Association.'"[9]

When, on April 10, 1933, the Schwerin Ministry of the Interior banned the Bible Students Association for the state of Mecklenburg-Schwerin, it became obvious that the measures the Bible Students had taken in their own defense could no longer keep the situation under control.[10] Such concessions, if they were acknowledged at all, proved ineffective as far as impressing authorities who, for a considerable period of time, had already been convinced that the IBSA was a pacifist association subject to uncontrollable foreign influences. According to these authorities, the IBSA was even paving the way for Jewry and should therefore be eliminated at the next possible opportunity.

Three days after the ban had been issued in the state of Mecklenburg-Schwerin, a second ban was issued in the state of Bavaria. Based on article 4 of the February 28, 1933, Decree of the Reich President for the Protection of People and State (Verordnung des Reichspräsidenten zum Schutz von Volk und Staat), the Bavarian Ministry of the Interior decreed the dissolution of the "Associations of 'Earnest Bible Students.'" It prohibited also any kind of advertisement of the Bible Students and placed any defiance of the ban under threat of punishment.[11] The Reich Ministry for Education and Cultural Affairs took matters a step further. For example, it requested the dioceses to continue using the methods that had already been successfully used in 1931 in prohibiting the group's publications. In response, the dioceses instructed their parish offices "to report immediately any further activities of the Bible Students Association, which had been dissolved and banned since April 13, 1933, to the nearest police offices (local police offices, constabularies, district offices, etc.)."[12] The Reich Ministry for Education and Cultural Affairs also requested the school administrators to inform the police authorities immediately of "any defiance of the ban within the schools."[13]

During the period following the enactment of those two bans, twenty thousand Jehovah's Witnesses participated in an international testimony period that the Watch Tower Society had organized.[14] During this special campaign, they distributed a booklet with the appropriate title *Crisis* from village to village and house to house. In many places, even outside the states of Mecklenburg and Bavaria, their missionary campaign resulted in serious opposition. Many people equipped with "a healthy opinion" resented these doomsday prophets who preached a different "Thousand-Year Reign," one that was based on righteousness. The police offices were flooded with complaints, publications were confiscated, houses searched. People began to be arrested. In a few cases, particularly nationalistic-minded countrymen, national comrades (*Volksgenossen*) and especially the SA (armed and uniformed branch of the NSDAP), which served as an auxiliary police force for the purpose of enforcing state authority, took the law into their own hands, using methods that had already been successfully used to stop the resistance of the political Left.[15] Subordinate police offices also recognized the need to act.

For instance, on April 19, 1933, a police office in the state of Schleswig-Holstein gave the following report to the Itzehoe district administrator's office:

> The national public is complaining about the distribution of certain publications from an American sect with strong Communist elements. They demand that the distribution of the above-mentioned publications should be prohibited. In view of the national uprising in Germany, it has therefore become necessary to examine whether the Earnest Bible Students Association should be allowed to continue.[16]

For Jehovah's Witnesses this united missionary campaign provided the necessary reassurance and encouragement to continue preaching the Word of God, despite increasing opposition. However, until that point, hardly any preparations had been made for the possibility of a ban. Therefore, the local Bible Student groups now began to make arrangements to adapt to the new situation. At the beginning of April 1933 the IBSA district overseers discussed the matter at the Magdeburg Bible House. They decided that in the event of a ban, the district overseers should maintain close contact with the local Bible Student groups and thus encourage these groups to continue conducting their meetings.[17] At first, the Watch Tower Society's leaders did not directly mention the possibility of a ban and the resulting consequences on its membership in the Watch Tower publications. However, in the April 15, 1933, issue of the *Golden Age*, they published an article involving Judean king Hezekiah who resisted the Assyrian superpower between 705 BCE and 701 BCE by putting his trust in Jehovah. The various Bible Student groups certainly understood the message of the article, which basically called for: "obedience in the face of danger."[18]

On April 18, 1933, two days after the testimony, the IBSA in Germany received its worst blow. In the state of Saxony, the stronghold of the Bible Students, the association was dissolved with immediate consequences. For instance, its publications were confiscated throughout the state. In contrast to the ban in the state of Bavaria, the ban issued by Saxony's State Ministry of the Interior placed not only the preaching activity, or any kind of advertisement of the Bible Students, under threat of punishment, but even any efforts of upholding the association or providing support "in other ways."[19]

On April 19 the Bible Students were banned in the state of Hessen. At first, this state prohibited only their preaching activity; the Bible

Students Association itself was not dissolved. The instructions that the state commissioner for the police authorities in Hessen sent to the district offices explained that the actions against the IBSA were based on the fact that their "propaganda . . . had repeatedly resulted in disruption of public law and order." The association was also under suspicion "of maintaining contact with Marxist parties."[20]

Bad news kept arriving at the Magdeburg Bible House on a daily basis. Apparently, the WTG leaders had not expected such rapid and severe actions that were so different from the pressures of the previous years, which had already been considered as persecution. On April 24, 1933, during this tense situation, police officials arrived at the WTG premises, occupied offices and printing facilities, and began searching the whole area belonging to the Magdeburg Bible House.[21] Finally, the WTG leaders came to realize that the National Socialists were determined to carry out their threats to the fullest extent. As a result, the continuation of the entire preaching activity of the Bible Students in Germany was at risk.

Occupation of the Magdeburg Branch Office

The WTG leaders immediately approached the Magdeburg district president and other authorities to obtain a withdrawal of the occupation. In this regard, the WTG benefited from its legal status as German branch of an American association. For example, in contrast to the occupations of the KPD party offices throughout the German Reich, in this case the Prussian police had taken possession of foreign property. Immediately, the Watch Tower Society's headquarters in Brooklyn, New York, was informed, which, in turn, intervened by utilizing various American authorities, requesting them to secure their rights in Germany.

On April 26, 1933, while these negotiations continued, Hans Dollinger, the legal counsel of the WTG, traveled to Berlin. On behalf of the Northern and the Southern German Bible Students Association, that is, by using the names of the two newly formed corporations, he submitted a petition to the Reich chancellor.[22] Dollinger requested the Reich chancellor to receive a delegation that could explain that the actions taken against the Bible Students were based on a "deliberate misrepresentation" of the objectives of the Bible Students Association. Since the denomination had always been "completely nonpolitical" and in their struggle against unbelief and a decline of moral and traditional values was actually working "in the same direction" as the Reich government, the ban could only be a result of "intolerant clerical influences, which had already been active for a considerable period of time." In a memo of the "German Bible Students Associations," enclosed in the petition, the leaders of the denomination indicated that in view of the situation, they were definitely willing to adapt to the spirit of the times.[23] For instance, they considered it to be opportune to mention that, "because of the changed political situation," they would allow "only German citizens to become members or hold positions of responsibility" in the two newly formed associations. And, in view of the fact that the bans had been issued in connection with the Reichstag Fire Decree (Reichstagsbrandverordnung), which served as a "protection against Communist state-endangering acts of violence," the leaders of the denomination tried to emphasize especially the untenability of an asserted connection with Communism, which this reference to the Reichstag Fire Decree implied. While this was still permissible, the writers of the memo believed they could underscore their distance to Communism by emphasizing that they approved of the actions the government took against atheism and freethinking movements, and by stating that the Bible Students were enemies of Communism. The fact that such a position did not really harmonize with their postulated political neutrality did not trouble the writers of the memo. They even emphasized the following passage by putting it in italics: "*As previously indicated . . . our association is completely nonpolitical and rejects communism, in particular, as being ungodly and subversive.*" The leaders of the WTG had become so preoccupied with their efforts to secure a continuation of their association that they were even willing to pay a high price to achieve this goal.

Despite such efforts, the petition was not very successful. More than one month later, the secretary of state at the Reich chancellery informed the WTG that, "as a result of an inordinate amount of urgent official duties," the chancellor was unable to receive the delegation.[24] However, the interventions of the Brooklyn headquarters of the Watch Tower Society did have an effect. On April 27, 1933, the third day of the occupation of the Magdeburg branch office, the U.S. Department of State instructed its Berlin embassy to "investigate . . . and submit a telegraphic report on the situation." Only five days later, the American consul general, George S. Messersmith, was able to inform the Department of State that, as a result of his efforts, the property of the Watch Tower Society had been released.[25] The *Magdeburger Tageszeitung* reported on April 29, 1933, that the police occupation was withdrawn because "no incriminating evidence for allegedly Communist activities had been found."[26]

One day prior to the release of the Magdeburg branch office, the order (issued by the Berlin police headquarters on April 25, 1933, for the territory of the Free State of Prussia) to confiscate all published IBSA literature was withdrawn.[27] The Bible Students also received permission to resume the publication of *Das Goldene Zeitalter*, which also had been prohibited.[28] The Prussian Ministry of the Interior, which apparently up to that point had not been completely informed about the actual ownership rights, feared diplomatic complications. In the consolidation phase of the NS regime, the ministry did not want to jeopardize unnecessarily its self-image of a Reich maintaining moderate foreign policies. Since there was no imminent danger, it discontinued its actions against the IBSA. Instead, the ministry began preparing actions against the IBSA in a way that allowed them to keep up appearances.

At the beginning of May, the Magdeburg branch office resumed its work, but its leaders were aware of the fact that the withdrawal of the bans was no guarantee for an undisturbed continuation of their activities, especially since the bans remained effective outside of Prussia. The leading members under Balzereit decided to continue following the adopted course of compromise. They gave instructions to avoid everything that could be misinterpreted by the state authorities as an affront. They even encouraged the IBSA membership to take this same course of action. In the May 15, 1933, issue of *Das Goldene Zeitalter*, the German leaders included a public statement explaining their viewpoint about the events involving the occupation of the Magdeburg branch office, which had previously been published in the Magdeburg newspapers.[29] In this statement, the withdrawal of the occupation of the Magdeburg branch office was used as evidence that the accusations against the Bible Students Association were completely unfounded. To confirm this point, the WTG emphasized that it never maintained "any direct or indirect political alliances" with any party, "be it Communist, Social Democrat, or any other atheist faction." At the same time, by pointing to the party membership of their legal counsel in the very next paragraph of that statement, the WTG acknowledged that they understood which way the wind was now blowing in Germany. "For many years now, Justizrat [Counselor of Justice] Karl Kohl, defense attorney in Munich and a member of the German National Party, has been representing the 'Wachtturm Bibel- und Traktat-Gesellschaft' as legal counsel. For about four years, Horst Kohl, defense attorney in Munich and a member of the National Socialist German Workers' Party, has also been representing the 'Wachtturm Bibel- und Traktat-Gesellschaft' as legal counsel."

To prove beyond any doubt that the association was not lacking the required reliability, its leaders promised to inform the foreign "sister associations" about the "absolute decent manner" in which the German officials had performed the occupation and search of the Magdeburg branch office. As they had done previously, they would also in the future do "everything to repudiate misrepresentations (known as atrocity propaganda) about conditions in Germany."

The Magdeburg branch office requested all service leaders of the local Bible Student groups to submit an affirmation in lieu of oath to counteract the accusations of alleged Communist connections. By means of these preformulated statements, the service leaders of the respective local Bible Student groups had to confirm "that, at no time, now or previously, members of the Communist Party, or any other political party . . . had been accepted [into this association]. They had also never accepted any group, large or small, of a dissolved political party or any other political party."[30]

The German edition of the *Golden Age*, which the German IBSA leaders were able to edit extensively, now included only uncontroversial articles.[31] At the same time, members of the immediate group of German IBSA leaders complained that publications written at the Brooklyn headquarters of the Watch Tower Society did not take into consideration the exceptional circumstances in Germany. The German IBSA leaders in Magdeburg considered it necessary that the *Watchtower* (written by an editorial committee under Rutherford) should, at least temporarily, refrain from including any polemics about an impending destruction of the governing authorities. Even the U.S. Consulate General was able to perceive these differences. A report to the U.S. Department of State regarding discussions conducted with Balzereit and Dollinger at the consulate stated that Rutherford's "representatives in Germany had complained that the pamphlets prepared in New York for this country were not in accordance with the ideas that have come about with the so-called national resurgence." To which Consul General Messersmith, who submitted this report, added: "These men being Germans, understood thoroughly the disrepute into which the Watch Tower Bible and Tract Society had fallen in this country."[32]

However, the withdrawal of the confiscations, which the Prussian Ministry of the Interior had issued on April 28, 1933, did not mean that the considerable number of publications confiscated at the local Bible Student groups were actually always returned to its rightful owners. For example, the Steinburg district administrator sent the May 12, 1933, withdrawal notice to the subordinate police offices, with the notation that they would receive "further instructions about the release of the confiscated publications."[33] This indicated that for the time being the confiscated publications should not be returned. The district administrator defended his unauthorized action by informing the Schleswig district president that a release of the Bible Student publications was not in the "interest of the state." Instead, he made the suggestion that "the secured publications should first be examined by a competent authority. . . . If the contents of the publications proved to be unobjectionable, it would still be possible to release them." Consequently, the Kiel State Police office, which shared the concerns of the district administrator, investigated the matter and classified the confiscated publications as "subversive material." In the meantime, the Gestapa office that had been formed at the end of April 1933 from the former Department 1A of the Berlin police headquarters, had issued additional decrees concerning an examination of the Bible Student publications.[34] Consequently, the delay brought about by the district administrator resulted in the fact that a complete return of the confiscated publications did not occur. After a period of seven weeks, the Bible Students in the district of Steinburg received only those publications that were considered to be unobjectionable.

From the middle of May on, the Bible Students were also banned in other German states, regardless of the efforts of the WTG leaders to find common ground. For instance, bans were issued in Lippe and Thuringia, thereafter in Baden (on May 15), in Oldenburg (on May 17), and in Braunschweig (on May 19).[35] Once again, the U.S. Department of State, which the Watch Tower Society had asked for support, turned to the Consulate General in Berlin. Finally, Consul Raymond H. Geist arranged to discuss matters of the Bible Student bans with the minister of the interior.[36] During the first intervention, the discussion had centered on the question of protecting the property of an American organization and, consequently, affected the immediate interests of the United States. But the dissolution orders, which the highest German state authorities had issued against the German Bible Students Associations with reference to the Reichstag Fire Decree, did not have an effect on the interests of the United States.

Agreement between State and Churches

Beside the Jews, Jehovah's Witnesses were the first religious denomination in the Third Reich exposed to serious persecution. These quick and

massive actions against Jehovah's Witnesses did not only have the objective of resisting a group that the National Socialists had considered
to be subversive for quite a long time. They also reflected an effort on
the part of the state to reach an agreement with the two predominant
churches in Germany. In the same way that the churches applauded the
actions the NS state took against godless propaganda, Communist organizations, and Social Democratic freethinking associations, they now
considered the actions taken against the Bible Students as evidence that
the new state took seriously the promises that the Reich chancellor had
made in his March 23, 1933, government declaration regarding his protection of the two Christian confessions.[37]

The state authorities considered such a signal for cooperation especially important with regard to the Catholic Church. Already, during
the weeks after January 1933, the Catholic Church deviated from its
former course of opposition against National Socialism and was now
looking for a modus vivendi with the Hitler government. The Catholic
Church acknowledged—with satisfaction—that finally the state initiated
the steps that the church had already unsuccessfully pursued in the Weimar Republic. Even though in his letter to the Bavarian ministers of
state, Cardinal Faulhaber determinedly protested against the "severe
and cruel" actions against political Catholicism, he expressed appreciation for the fact "that, under the new government, many things in
public life had improved: The godless movement has been restricted,
the freethinkers can no longer openly accuse Christianity and church,
and the Bible Students are no longer able to perform their American-
Communist activities."[38]

In contrast to the Catholics, the Evangelical Churches in Germany
did not have a strained relationship with National Socialism during the
initial period of the Third Reich. Even in previous years, the highest
church leaders had observed with anticipation the increasing popularity
of the NS movement and were now showing their willingness for support. A memo of the Evangelical National Union even described the
governmental bans against "anti-Christian movements," among which
the Bible Students were counted, as an expression of an "alliance" between state and church.[39]

Some of the official statements explaining the reasons for the Bible
Student bans issued in the various German states clearly reflect this
agreement between state and church. For example, in a decree to the
police authorities explaining the June 14, 1933, ban by the Württemberg
Ministry of the Interior on the IBSA activities,[40] the actions against the

Bible Students are almost exclusively represented as a protective measure for the Christian denominations:

> Particularly on Sundays and Christian holidays, people sent by the "Earnest Bible Students" go from house to house and bother people by imposing upon them the journals of the Magdeburg Watch Tower Bible and Tract Society, which contain malicious attacks on the major Christian churches and their institutions. . . . This demoralizing activity, which represents a misuse of the right of freedom of expression, causes dissension not only in individual families but also in entire communities. It is incompatible with the idea of a Christian people's community [*Volksgemeinschaft*] in Germany and can therefore no longer be permitted.[41]

The religious movement of the German Christians offered their services to the state authorities with particular eagerness. In Württemberg, the NS-Pfarrerbund (ministers' federation) and the religious movement of German Christians established an "office for the purpose of collecting information for people-demoralizing, sectarian activities."[42] Two weeks after the IBSA ban had been issued, the district overseers of the NS-Pfarrerbund and the German Christians were requested "to observe closely throughout their districts the activities of the sects. They should immediately report to the state authorities any offense against the new governmental regulations, providing detailed and irrefutable pieces of evidence."[43]

By the middle of June 1933 the Bible Students Association was banned in almost every state of the German Reich[44] or was restricted in ways similar to a ban.[45] However, in Prussia, the largest state, a ban had not yet been issued. The question of a possible ban for Prussia was especially significant since the IBSA branch office was located on Prussian ground.

In Berlin, the Ministry of the Interior, as well as the Ministry for Science, Art, and National Education, were occupied with the necessary preparations. To this end, they tried to harmonize their decision with other governmental and religious authorities. On May 29, 1933, a small number of officials came together for a first preliminary discussion at the police headquarters.[46] Then, on June 1, 1933, the Prussian Minister for Science, Art, and National Education invited the representatives of the RMdI, the Prussian Ministry of Justice, the Ministry of Foreign Affairs, the Secret State Police office, the Breslau Archepiscopal Ordinariate (office of the chairman of the Fulda bishops' conference), the Berlin

Episcopal Ordinariate, the Higher Church Council of the Evangelical churches, and the Apologetic Office for a discussion, which was scheduled for June 9, 1933. The meeting had the objective of discussing whether, and to what extent, it would be necessary for the state to take actions against the Bible Students and the Tannenbergbund (a small religious group in Germany).[47] The letter briefly commented that the activities of the two associations would "increasingly cause concern and opposition among the members of other Christian denominations."

During this discussion, which took place on the second Friday of June 1933, at 5 p.m., the various representatives (twenty-one men and one woman) who had assembled in the small conference room of the ministry agreed that it was necessary to find a solution.[48] However, the representative of the Secret State Police office did not consider the presented material, which came primarily from religious sources, to be sufficient to justify a ban. It would be especially "difficult to provide clear evidence that the 'Earnest Bible Students' were involved in subversive activities." The representative of the Interior Ministry's police department, Ministerialdirigent (Ministerial Section Head) Fischer determinedly contradicted this opinion. He not only considered the ban necessary for "reasons of national policy" he also recommended the ban especially because of the "strong leanings of the 'Earnest Bible Students' toward the ideas of Judaism and its expectations for the future." Oberregierungsrat (Higher Senior Civil Servant) Dr. Rudolf Diels, who had become chief of the Secret State Police office six weeks earlier, also scolded his representative and emphasized that there were "obvious political, in fact, subversive tendencies." To confirm his statement, he added that "the 'Earnest Bible Students' and the Socialist Freethinkers maintained a close connection for special purposes." This revealed the Gestapa chief's complete lack of knowledge about the Bible Student activities. As far as Diels was concerned, the only obstacle speaking against a ban would be, at best, certain foreign policies, since the consul general of the United States had repeatedly argued in favor of "protecting" the Bible Students. Diels believed, however, that he could dispel the concerns of the consulate regarding ownership rights by simply refraining from confiscating the property of the Bible Students Association and offering the possibility of transferring its offices to neighboring countries.

Diels's vote in this matter gave the direction for further actions. During the following discussion, not one of the attendees challenged the legitimacy of a ban. Not even the representatives of the churches considered the ban to be interfering with the right of religious freedom. The representative of the Breslau Archiepiscopal Ordinariate, Domkapitular (Vicar Capitular) Piontek, reported extensively about the "demoralizing activities" of the Bible Students in the Breslau diocese. It would not be sufficient "just to give warnings." This situation required "strict official measures." Oberkonsistorialrat (Senior Consistory Counsel) Fischer, the representative of the Higher Church Council of the Evangelical churches, on the other hand, was much more diplomatic. Strictly separating the church political domain from the state political domain, he concluded that the churches should resist the danger that the Bible Students presented for church life with "their own methods." Since, however, the Bible Students also presented a threat to "German tradition," a ban would certainly be appreciated.[49]

The representative of the Ministry of Foreign Affairs stated that there would be no objections to the ban as long as "it was emphasized that the 'Earnest Bible Students' had strong Communist leanings." Consequently, the officials of the Ministry of the Interior knew what they had to do.

Two weeks later, the ban was issued. An extensive statement explained the reasons for the ban. This statement gave clear evidence that an effort had been made to take into account all of the above-mentioned suggestions. Secretary of State Grauert was authorized to sign the decree in representation of the Prussian minister of the interior. This decree, issued on June 24, 1933, stated:

> On the basis of Article 1 of the February 28, 1933, Decree of the Reich President for the Protection of People and State (RGB1. I, page 83), and Article 14 of the PVG [police administrative law],[50] the International Bible Students Association, including all of its subordinate associations (Wachtturm-, Bibel- und Traktatgesellschaft Lünen-Magdeburg der Neuapostolischen Sekte) has been dissolved and banned in the territory of the Free State of Prussia. The property of the association will be confiscated and withdrawn. On the basis of Article 4 of the above-mentioned February 28, 1933, decree, defiance of this ban is subject to punishment.
>
> Reasons for the ban: Under the pretense of supposedly educational Bible studies, the International Bible Students Association and its subordinate associations are obviously involved in agitation against political and religious institutions in word and written form. By declaring both institutions as agencies of Satan, they undermine the very foundation of life in the people's community. In their numerous publications . . . they deliberately and maliciously

misrepresent Bible accounts for the purpose of ridiculing State and church institutions.

One of the characteristics of their struggle is a fanatical manipulation of their followers. Through considerable financial resources, they gain the necessary momentum to perform their demoralizing, cultural-Bolshevik activities. To a certain extent, the influence they exert on considerable numbers of people is based on strange ceremonies, which cause their followers to become fanatical and, consequently, emotionally disturbed.

It is therefore obvious that the above-mentioned association tend to be in complete opposition to the present state and its cultural and moral structures. Naturally, in harmony with their goals, the 'International Bible Students' consider the Christian-national state that emerged from the political uprising [in Germany] as an especially distinctive opponent and have accordingly radically increased their resistance. This is evident from various malicious attacks that their leading functionaries recently made against National Socialism and its representatives in word and written form. (See the May 31, 1933, report by the Wuppertal chief of police—I Ad. I 60001.) This completely contradicts [the Bible Students'] claim of a strictly religiously based ideological struggle.

The increasing danger that the activities of the above-mentioned religious associations present for our present state can be seen from the fact that most recently large numbers of former members of Communist and Marxist parties and organizations have joined their ranks. These people hope to find a secure hiding place in these supposedly strictly religious associations to perform their secret struggle against the present governmental systems. Thus, the Bible Students Association and its subsidiary associations promote communism even in a political way and are about to become an organization accepting all kinds of subversive elements. The Communist members of this movement are ambitiously involved in organizing Communist actions. To resist Communist activities and maintain public law and order, it is therefore necessary to dissolve [this association] for the protection of people and state.[51]

By means of clever wordings, the officials of the Prussian Ministry of the Interior tried to present the ban in a way that appeared to be logical, well documented, and irrefutable. The last paragraph construed the connection to communism, which was required to base the ban on the decree of the Reich president. The thesis of an organization that accepts members of the political Left was made up only for the above-mentioned purpose and was completely unfounded. According to a report of the WTG's legal counsel after his discussion with Ministerial-dirigent Fischer, the officials obtained an expert opinion of the Reich leader of the German Christians, Rev. Joachim Hossenfelder, and of the military district chaplain and later Reich bishop, Ludwig Müller, before they put the ban in writing.[52]

However, a closer look at the meticulousness that had been put into preparing this ban, which exceeds preparations for any other bans, soon proved to be the work of an amateur and showed a lack of knowledge of the facts. Some of the errors were of great significance in the later controversy regarding the legality of the IBSA ban:

The first error occurred already in the context of addressing the recipient of the decree.[53] There was no association by the name of Wachtturm-, Bibel- und Traktatgesellschaft Lünen-Magdeburg der Neuapostolischen Sekte. It also made no sense to associate the independent groups of the New Apostolic Church with the WTG.[54] Moreover, the Magdeburg WTG branch office was unable to understand why the town of Lünen was included in the address.[55] Based on the May 31, 1933, report by the Wuppertal chief of police, and cited as evidence, the WTG leaders were able to prove that the accusations mentioned in the decree did not apply to them or to the IBSA. Rather they applied to a small group of former Bible Students who called themselves Wahrheitsfreunde and who had separated from the Watch Tower Society as early as 1923. On the one hand, this occurrence proves the "lack of knowledge regarding the various sects" on the part of the officials responsible for putting the ban in writing. On the other hand, it showed that possibly these officials deliberately drew attention to the resistance activities of members of the Wahrheitsfreunde to support their assertion that the IBSA was "maliciously attacking National Socialism."[56]

The Prussian State Police offices and the district administrator's offices were not immediately informed about the ban but received a radio message almost three days later, on June 27, 1933.[57] The WTG was informed as late as July 3, 1933.[58] However, during the previous days, newspapers and radio stations throughout the German Reich had already reported on the Prussian IBSA ban.[59] In its July 9, 1933, issue, the Sunday paper *Evangelium im Dritten Reich,* published by Hossenfelder, expressed its approval of the fact that the "Marxist 'Bible Students'" in Prussia had now been banned.[60] The ban, however, was not published in the Prussian law collection as was required for a decree issued by the police according to the Police Administrative Law.[61]

Efforts to Adapt

On short notice, the Magdeburg branch office of the Watch Tower Society invited the IBSA members to a large convention that was scheduled for June 25, 1933. When, on this particular Sunday, about seven thousand Jehovah's Witnesses from all parts of Germany assembled in the Wilmensdorfer Tennishalle in Berlin, they did not know that Prussia had banned the IBSA on the previous day.[62]

The Watch Tower Society's president, J. F. Rutherford, was personally involved in the preparations for this convention, which had been planned on his initiative.[63] Together with his future successor, Nathan H. Knorr, he had traveled to Berlin in June to negotiate the possibilities of continuing the preaching activity in Germany. Rutherford, who had expressed his concern about the critical situation of Jehovah's Witnesses in Germany in his discussion with American Consul Geist, still had confidence in a positive outcome of the matter.[64] In the course of the preparations for the convention, he discussed with Balzereit and a few other leading members the actions that needed to be taken in the future. Rutherford had also prepared a Declaration of Facts in which he mentioned the false accusations made against Jehovah's Witnesses, and by means of which he hoped to change the minds of the NS rulers.[65]

At the Wilmersdorf convention (which Rutherford did not attend), by means of this Declaration of Facts, the IBSA members were encouraged to follow the same course of loyalty that their leaders had manifested in the previous months.[66] In an effort to make a good impression on the outside world, the WTG leaders began the convention with the song "Zions herrliche Hoffnung" (Zion's Glorious Hope), based on a 1797 composition by Joseph Haydn.[67] In 1841 Hoffmann von Fallersleben wrote "Lied der Deutschen" based on this same melody, and the selection of this song, which resulted in opening the convention with the melody for the German national anthem, was probably not a coincidence.[68] In this regard, Konrad Franke, who later became leader of the German branch office of the Watch Tower Society, reported that the Bible Students who attended this convention reacted with surprise to these circumstances.[69]

After finishing his discourse, in which he asked for understanding, Balzereit presented to his audience the Declaration of Facts with a request for approval. The declaration requested the appropriate authorities to reexamine "the real facts" since wrong accusations on the Bible

Students Association had been made to the governmental authorities. These accusations had been made at the instigation of—as was now unmistakably stated—"a political clergy, priests, and Jesuits." This group of people had pursued certain interests in accusing Jehovah's Witnesses of an allegedly subversive attitude. In an effort to prove that such accusations were completely unsubstantiated, the IBSA presented itself as an organization that had a positive attitude toward the present state: "Instead of our organization's being a menace to the peace and safety of the government, it is the one organization standing for the peace and safety of this land."[70] It was further stated that it was important to respect the powers supporting the state, emphasizing areas of common interests with the new rulers.

> A careful examination of our books and literature will disclose the fact that the very high ideals held and promulgated by the present national government are set forth and endorsed and strongly emphasized in our publications . . . Instead, therefore of our literature and our work's being a menace to the principles of the present government we are the strongest supporters of such high ideals. For this reason Satan, the enemy of all men who desire righteousness, has sought to misrepresent our work and prevent us from carrying it on in this land.

In the context of repudiating a further accusation against Jehovah's Witnesses, the association clearly distanced itself from another group under oppression:

> It is falsely charged by our enemies that we have received financial support for our work from the Jews. Nothing is farther from the truth. Up to this hour, there never has been the slightest bit of money contributed to our work by Jews. We are the faithful followers of Jesus Christ and believe upon Him as the Savior of the world, whereas the Jews entirely reject Jesus Christ and emphatically deny that he is the Savior of the world sent of God for man's good. This of itself should be sufficient proof to show that we receive no support from Jews and that therefore the charges against us are maliciously false and could proceed only from Satan, our great enemy.[71]

Until this point, the passage still reflected an effort to correct the situation. However, the following passage indicates the extent to which they were willing to accommodate the terminology prevalent at that period:

> The greatest and the most oppressive empire on earth is the Anglo-American empire . . . It has been the commercial Jews of the British-American empire that have built up and carried on Big Business as a means of exploiting and oppressing the peoples of many nations.[72]

Now it became apparent that their efforts to adapt to the situation had not left undamaged their former religious self-conception. Instead, it affected its very substance: Anyone who tried to improve his standing with the authorities of the Old World by making such statements had left far behind the position of neutrality he had accepted for himself. Political calculation, and nothing else, determined the diction, when, less than three months after the boycott of Jewish stores in Germany, anti-Jewish slogans were included in the declaration.

Two years earlier, in his three-volume publication, *Vindication,* Rutherford had already introduced a new orientation of the Watch Tower Society's assessment of Judaism.[73] In contrast to his previous pro-Zionist viewpoint, he now announced that the restoration prophecies of the Bible did not apply to the "old covenant people" of God, that is, the Jews, but rather applied to "God's new covenant people," Jehovah's Witnesses.[74] From then on, certain religious tendencies toward anti-Judaism became apparent even in the publications of Jehovah's Witnesses.[75] In Rutherford's discourses and publications, this anti-Judaism was often associated with religious rejections. His reasoning regarding this issue showed similarities with the anti-Jewish viewpoint, which was prevalent in the major churches during that period of time. For instance, in his 1929 publication *Vindication* he explained that the Jews were forced to leave Palestine because they "rejected Christ Jesus, the beloved and anointed King of Jehovah." He further stated: "To this day, the Jews have not repented of this wrongful act committed by their forefathers."[76] Rutherford's strong rejection of the Jews had, however, predominantly religious characteristics.[77] This is indicated by his proclamation that even though the Jews "have been unfaithful, especially during the time of their covenant," Jehovah would "extend His mercy to them." Therefore, during the period of the Millennium, Jehovah would give them the opportunity to be "fully reconciled to Him."[78]

The Wilmersdorf declaration proves that during the circumstances of 1933 the leaders of the Watch Tower Society were primarily concerned about two matters of existential importance: the possibility of keeping their association in operation, and the possibility of maintaining their freedom to preach.[79] Therefore, they would not show any submissiveness in areas that affected these matters. "Our organization is not political in any sense. We only insist on teaching the Word of Jehovah God to the people, and that without hindrance." The declaration did not allow for any ambiguity in matters that concerned one's obligation to preach God's Word.

Later publications of the Watch Tower Society tried to misrepresent the declaration as a "resolution of protest"[80] or claimed that Balzereit "had watered down the clear and unmistakable language of the Society's publications" without authorization.[81] As is customary at all IBSA conventions, the audience, which represented members from almost every Bible Student group in Germany, "unanimously adopted" the declaration. Even so, quite a number of Jehovah's Witnesses present at the Wilmersdorf convention "could not wholeheartedly agree to its adoption," as is indicated by the 1974 Watch Tower Society's history report.[82] They "were disappointed in the 'declaration,' since in many points it failed to be as strong as the brothers had hoped."[83] Occasionally, there was even some criticism.[84]

According to the records of the Watch Tower Society, 2.5 million copies of the declaration were distributed publicly in a four-page pamphlet. One day after the convention, the declaration was sent to Reich Chancellor Hitler, together with a seven-page cover letter.[85] In contrast to the April 26, 1933, petition of the Northern and Southern German Bible Students Associations, the Bible Students now apparently anticipated leaving an impression on the authorities. They stated in the cover letter that the Wilmersdorf "convention was attended by seven thousand delegates of German Bible Students (Jehovah's Witnesses) who represented several million German people." In this letter, which Balzereit had signed and apparently also written, the IBSA was described as an "association that was firmly established in positive Christianity."[86] Balzereit evidently used this formulation with reference to the NSDAP party program. He took matters even a step further by stating that the association "was not in opposition to the national government of the German Reich."[87] To the contrary, "the entirely religious, nonpolitical objectives and efforts of the Bible Students" were "completely in agreement with the corresponding goals of the national government." By using subtle forms of wording, Balzereit allowed for the possibility of interpreting the letter in terms of the Bible Student teachings and, at the same time, anticipating a misconception on the part of the opponents. Balzereit guaranteed that the regulations for the bans in the various states would be observed since he was convinced that, "in consideration of the facts, the Reich chancellor and his government officials would withdraw the bans, because otherwise tens of thousands of Christian men and women would be exposed to a martyrdom comparable to that of the early Christians."[88] However, the anticipation that Hitler and his government officials would change their attitude merely on the basis of the declaration and its explanations proved to be an illusion.

Only a few days after the letter had been sent to the Reich chancellery, the IBSA leader, Paul Balzereit, who had anticipated the authorities concerned to be understanding, left Germany and emigrated to Prague.

5

The Watch Tower Society, 1933–35

Along with the announcement of the IBSA ban, the Secret State Police office also issued a search and confiscation warrant throughout the whole state of Prussia. On June 28 approximately thirty SA storm troopers occupied the Magdeburg branch office for the second time.[89] They hoisted the swastika over the Bible House, closed down the factory, sealed the printing presses, and locked the premises. The leader of the Watch Tower Society's branch office and IBSA in Germany, Paul Balzereit, and a few other leading members had already escaped to Prague. This seemed to end the era of the Watch Tower Bible and Tract Society in Germany.

The headquarters of the Watch Tower Society in Brooklyn again consulted U.S. government offices and sent the leader of the IBSA central European office, Martin Christian Harbeck, as authorized representative to Magdeburg. Consul Geist immediately consulted the Prussian Ministry of the Interior. He was able to receive confirmation from Secretary of State Grauert that the Prussian decree concerning the confiscation of the society's property would be withdrawn. However, the Ministry of the Interior demanded that the Magdeburg branch office should be completely abandoned and dissolved, and offered to dismantle its printing presses and transfer them to another country. The Ministry told Consul Geist that the Prussian government did not intend to appropriate American property. The purpose of the ban and confiscation decree was rather to prohibit any future activities of the Watch Tower Bible and Tract Society in Germany.[90] Thus, the Ministry of the Interior followed the suggestion of Gestapa chief Rudolf Diels that he had made during the June 9, 1933, discussions in anticipation of consular complaints.

On July 12, 1933, Consul General Messersmith informed Washington about previous efforts and discussions. Messersmith advised the U.S.

secretary of state also that, in his opinion, the efforts of the U.S. administration should be strictly limited to property rights and added that, after he "read some of the pamphlets which have been distributed . . . [he could] see that objection could reasonably be raised to them by the German government."[91]

At the same time, the Consulate General informed the Watch Tower Society that it had not been able to persuade the Prussian government to withdraw the ban. However, the consulate hoped to be able to protect the property of the Watch Tower Society, with the exception of the publications that the State Police office had already confiscated. The officials at the consulate were confident that they would be able not only to keep the financial losses at a minimum but also ensure the transfer of the property to another country. For the New York headquarters of the Watch Tower Society, it was unacceptable to agree to an abandonment of the German branch office. In this regard, the Watch Tower Society was not so much concerned about protecting its significant property holdings in Germany, which amounted to five million Reichsmark in premises and factories. The main objective of the Watch Tower Society and its negotiators was to find ways to continue their activities in Germany. With this objective, they continued negotiating with the U.S. Department of State and the Berlin Consulate General.

Not just the U.S. authorities tried to find a solution to this problems; there were also efforts made by the legal counsel of the German branch office of the Watch Tower Society, Hans Dollinger, and the authorized representative of the headquarters of the Watch Tower Society, Harbeck, whose American citizenship proved to be of benefit for the negotiations.[92] Dollinger had several discussions at the Ministry of the Interior with Ministerialdirigent Dr. Fischer. On at least one occasion, he also met with Gerichtsassessor (title of new entrant into the administrative grade of the civil service after passing his second state examination) Dr. Richter-Brohm, the leader of the appropriate Gestapa department. During these discussions, Dollinger presented evidence to try to convince these officials that there was no basis for supporting the accusation that the Bible Students Association was under Communist influence. Dollinger was also able to persuade several attorneys established in public law, whom he knew from the time when he was leader of the legal department of the German branch office of the Watch Tower Society, to represent the interests of the society. These attorneys not only examined the legal possibilities, they also acted as advocates of the Bible Students Association. Of special support in this regard was Justizrat Karl Kohl from Munich. In previous years, Kohl had already represented a number of Bible Students in court cases involving violations of the Industrial Code, and the like. Kohl was also one of the legal counsels of General Erich Ludendorf and Adolf Hitler in the proceedings against the insurgents of November 9, 1923, that took place at the People's Court in Munich between February 24 and April 1, 1924.[93] He was one of the defense attorneys in the Hitler trial and, according to his own statements, even defended "a number of prominent National Socialists" in subsequent years. As a long-standing member of the DNVP (German National People's Party), he emphasized that he would have never defended the Bible Students if there had been the "slightest evidence that the IBSA had connections with the SPD and the KPD."[94]

The German branch office of the Watch Tower Society even tried to dispute the ban by means of proceedings in contentious administrative matters, but these efforts were hopeless right from the beginning. On July 15, 1933, the Magdeburg Higher Administrative Court (Oberverwaltungsgericht) refused to accept the group's complaint because the court could not examine a ban that was based on the Decree of the Reich President for the Protection of People and State.[95]

Toward the end of July 1933 Consul Geist urged the Prussian Ministry of the Interior to immediately release the Magdeburg branch office, which was still under SA occupation. He told Ministerialdirigent Dr. Fischer that Secretary of State Grauert had already promised the release of the branch office and that the IBSA had already satisfied the interests of the German state by discontinuing its activities. In his response, Fischer stated another reason for the confiscation. According to this statement, the property was to "remain in Government's possession as a guarantee that no propaganda will be made by this society abroad against the German government." This provided the American Consulate General with a completely new perspective. Consequently, Consul General Messersmith informed the U.S. Department of State about the situation and emphasized that this was "tantamount to confiscation, and if such confiscation is made without due process of law in the courts, it certainly renders insecure the existence of all American property in Germany."[96] Far more than the request for protection of a religious publishing house, this aspect gave an incentive to intensify the diplomatic efforts.

In the meantime, the occupants destroyed the publications that had been stored in the warehouse. On August 21, 23, and 24, 1933, twenty-five truckloads of books were brought to the outskirts of the city and publicly burned.[97] Three months earlier, publications of Marxist, pacifist, and Jewish authors had already been "consigned to the flames." The 130,000–140,000 pounds (65,000–70,000 kilograms) of publications of the Watch Tower Society that were publicly burned even included a large number of Bibles. In a complaint to the Reich chancellor, Harbeck protested against this act of vandalism, reflecting his deep indignation: "How inconsiderate this burning was could be seen from the fact that . . . even sheets of paper with pictures of Christ but no written information were consigned to the flames. Not even the request to have the books and pamphlets pulped and to give the proceeds of the pulping to the unemployed was being granted."[98]

As soon as the Brooklyn headquarters of the Watch Tower Society was informed about the burning, it turned to the U.S. Department of State in amazement and requested support. This attracted high-level attention. On September 9, 1933, Secretary of State Cordell Hull sent a telegram to Ambassador William A. Dodd. In view of the "drastic consequences "taken by the German authorities, he requested Dodd to take immediate steps to secure the release of the Watch Tower Society's property.[99] Hull expressed his surprise about the fact that the German authorities had refused the accused Watch Tower Society an opportunity to legally defend itself against this strictly administrative order. This action on the part of the German authorities violated the 1923 Treaty of Friendship, Commerce, and Diplomacy between the German Reich and the United States. This treaty granted an association operating in a different country the opportunity of having recourse to law.[100] Consequently, Hull instructed Ambassador Dodd to file a complaint with the German Ministry of Foreign Affairs on behalf of the government of the United States. It should also be examined to what extent the question of resuming the activities of the Watch Tower Society could be included in the complaint. The efforts on the part of the American secretary of state therefore exceeded the requests of the Consulate General, which tried to restrict the matter to property rights. Apparently, Washington showed more concern for the immediate affairs of the religious denomination than the representatives of the U.S. Department of State in Berlin.

Only three days later, Ambassador Dodd was able to report his accomplishments to the secretary of state: The release of the property had been guaranteed.[101] On September 26 the ministry authorized the Magdeburg district president to introduce the appropriate steps, and on October 7 the Magdeburg branch office was returned to the WTG. But the return involved certain restrictions. The WTG was not allowed to print or to conduct meetings on the premises. They could, however, resume their office work. This resulted in a situation of coexistence of legalized WTG and prohibited Bible Student activities.

This situation came about through the September 28, 1933, decree of the Prussian minister of the interior, which released the confiscated property of the Watch Tower Society. The release included the statement that the "association's production of books and pamphlets, as well as its preaching and congregational activities would continue to be prohibited."[102] This regulation implied that *all* nonprohibited activities would be permitted again. Based on that fact, the German branch of the Watch Tower Society was actually officially recognized, even though the ban had not been officially withdrawn. On October 13 the Secret State Police office distributed an interoffice decree to its subordinate State Police offices, informing them of the decree by the minister of the interior and giving instructions to keep the association under surveillance to guarantee that the restrictions would be observed.[103]

Consequently, the diplomatic interventions and the efforts of Harbeck and Dollinger had accomplished more than merely a return of the Watch Tower Society's property. One important achievement of the Gestapa decree of September 28 was that it also ordered "the release of all Bible Students who had been taken into protective detention by the police action."[104]

During the previous weeks, the Prussian IBSA ban and the resulting dissolution of the Magdeburg branch office had considerably affected the confidence of the local Bible Student groups. The members of the denomination had no unified conception of how to deal with the new situation.[105] The fact that, at least temporarily, communication with their leaders was interrupted and the supply of regular "spiritual food" (a term Jehovah's Witnesses use in reference to the *Watchtower* and other publications of the Watch Tower Society) was cut off began to show effect.

In some places, the Bible Students continued their preaching activity despite the ban. Other Bible Student groups merely came together for their religious meetings or Bible studies. Even though these meetings were held in private homes with only few people present, it always involved the danger of an intervention by the Gestapo. The Gestapo considered even these Bible studies in private homes to be a punishable offense against the Bible Student ban. Because of this danger, many believers completely withdrew from the association.[106] These Bible Students had accepted the viewpoint of waiting to see how things would turn out; some were of the opinion that Jehovah would step in and bring about a change, but others simply refused to participate in secret meetings because Jehovah "also does not [do] anything in secret."

In several places, all activities came to a standstill. For example, the service leader in Mannheim dissolved the local group.[107] According to reports, only four of the eighty-two Jehovah's Witnesses of the group in Freiburg (Breisgau) continued their preaching activity under the ban.[108] And especially in Saxony, which had been the stronghold of the IBSA with the most active groups during the 1920s, the Bible Students became disheartened and completely discontinued their activities. In many cases, they stopped having close relationships with one another. Another setback for their preaching activity occurred in the spring when the Gestapo discovered several of the storage places used for hiding literature that the Bible Students had established in different areas.[109]

On August 28—at the critical time of repeated occupation of the Magdeburg branch office—Harbeck wrote a memo to the various local groups. This letter contributed considerably to a measure of uncertainty among the still active Bible Students. In order not to jeopardize the negotiations about the release of the property and withdrawal of the bans, Harbeck made a request to the local groups, basing this request on special authorization by the Watch Tower Bible and Tract Society and, "particularly, its president, Judge Rutherford." He requested the groups to discontinue temporarily their activities and submit to the measures of the authorities, unless they had explicit permission from the police: "In particular, I would like to ask you to stop distributing any prohibited publications and to stop conducting meetings or giving discourses without permission from the police."[110] In practical terms, the leaders requested the groups to discontinue their preaching activity, which until then had been presented as an absolute necessity. The active ones from among them were especially disappointed about the fact that nonparticipation in the preaching activity was actually represented as something that was pleasing to God: "We want to be good citizens of this country, and want to honor God and vindicate his name and his Word also through our actions and our conduct."[111]

The German branch office of the Watch Tower Society immediately informed the local groups about the September 28 Gestapa decree, which had issued the release of their property. Consequently, the Bible Students now approached the police offices in various places to request the confiscated publications. To this end, they told the police officers that the confiscated publications were part of the released property of the Watch Tower Society.[112] This actually resulted in the return of a number of publications, and in some cases, complete stocks of publications were returned.[113] However, these police actions did not always meet with approval. When the Schleswig provost was informed that the confiscated publications were being returned to the Bible Students, he immediately approached the regional church office in Kiel. The clergyman was unable to understand this police action since these Kingdom proclaimers could now continue to spread "their teachings among the people" and proclaim "their subversive and anti-clerical propaganda throughout the country." To counteract this development, he requested that the "church authorities should try to persuade the secular authorities to put a stop to the resumed propaganda of this dangerous sect."[114]

Although completely unrelated to the requests by the provost from Schleswig, two days later the Berlin Secret State Police office issued a decree that took the complaints into account. On December 9, 1933, the Secret State Police office ordered that the release of the Bible Student publications should be discontinued and that the confiscated publications should be destroyed.[115]

Preaching despite the Ban

During the second half of 1933 numerous efforts were made to guarantee the distribution of "spiritual food." Since the German branch office in Magdeburg had to discontinue its operations (the July 1, 1933, issue of the *Golden Age* was the last journal printed in Magdeburg, and it was distributed shortly before the occupation), arrangements were made to receive the publications from neighboring countries. Initially, this was done by way of ordinary mail. Inconspicuously wrapped, the *Watchtower* and the *Golden Age* were sent to Germany from abroad. Although some of the journals were printed in Bern, the printing of the German journals was mainly done in Prague. There, the IBSA leader of Czechoslovakia, Karl Kopetzky, and the IBSA functionaries of Germany, Paul Balzereit and Dr. Alfred Mütze, were responsible for editing the *Golden Age*, which had been banned in Germany.

The police authorities soon discovered that the Bible Students received these journals by mail. Consequently, they were completely convinced that this was the way in which "the Earnest Bible Students in Czechoslovakia tried to reestablish and strengthen their relationship with their fellow believers in Germany." And, on February 12, 1934, the Bavarian Political Police ordered "the confiscation of mail of all known members of the Earnest Bible Students so that they would be able to resist successfully the importation of the prohibited publications."[116]

This did not mean that the Bible Students were no longer able to receive these publications. With ingenious methods, they continued, in some cases for years, to receive the publications by mail. This required the use of cover addresses. Even more so, it required the use of alternative names for the *Watchtower*. For instance, for quite some time, the *Watchtower* was published under the title *The Jonadab: The Journal for People of Good Will*, using a Zurich publishing house. When the Gestapo discovered this method, the title and packaging of the *Watchtower* were changed with almost every issue. Some of the titles of these alternative journals were *Obadiah, The Three Feasts, The Time,* or *Temple Singers,* and they were sent to Germany under the name of different publishing houses. The addresses on the parcels were written by hand and sent from post offices in different areas. Before the Gestapo could even be informed and was able to issue a confiscation order for the journal concerned, the post offices had usually already distributed the parcels.[117]

The postal distribution of the journals involved many risks and often resulted in confiscation, followed by police repression. The Bible Students started to mimeograph *Watchtower* articles at various places, such as Schwarzenberg (Saxony), Munich, and Altona.[118] Those who participated in the work of mimeographing were Jehovah's Witnesses who no longer were willing to follow the request of discontinuing their preaching activity. Their religious conviction did not allow them to stop for "tactical reasons" proclaiming publicly the establishment of Christ's Kingdom rule over the earth. Moreover, despite minor achievements in negotiation, the problems of Jehovah's Witnesses resulting from the NS state's demand for ideological conformity (that is, the Hitler salute, and the like) had actually increased.[119] They doubted that there was any possibility at all of settling "these questions at a conference table" and decided "to fight for the truth."[120] Consequently, they obtained mimeograph machines and organized a courier system; at the end of 1933 a small number of Jehovah's Witnesses took the initiative of reorganizing their religious association under the conditions of the ban and continuing their preaching activity.

The authorities responsible for the persecution soon took note of this development. "In the beginning," they had actually assumed "that the adherents of the IBSA would submit to the ban."[121] Now, however, the authorities noticed "an increase in activity." In his December 27, 1933, interoffice decree, Reinhard Heydrich, the leader of the Bavarian

Political Police, stated that an increased "distribution of prohibited publications and typewritten handbills had been observed in various places." Heydrich instructed the subordinate police offices "to take immediate actions against the people responsible for these activities and, if necessary, impose protective detention."[122] The Prussian Secret State Police office in Berlin had instructed its various subordinate State Police offices already at the beginning of December to monitor "carefully" the Bible Students' activities.[123] In the middle of February 1934 the Secret State Police office even requested "an intensification of the surveillance of the prohibited IBSA activities that could be still observed in various places." In contrast to the interoffice decree in Munich, the Prussian State Police office held the view (at least in the beginning) that defiance of the bans should be punished by the legal authorities: "People who are involved in [IBSA] activities must be referred to the prosecuting authorities."[124]

Only one month later, the Gestapa reviewed the reports it had received from the local police offices.[125] According to these reports, there was "consistent evidence" that the "banned International Bible Students Association continued their prohibited activities, being extremely active at several places in the [German] Reich." As evidence, reference was made to the Bible Students' refusal to give the Hitler salute and to an increasing distribution of IBSA publications: "It has also been observed that a considerable number of prohibited publications of this sect are being sent into the German Reich, particularly from Czechoslovakia. Quite a number of pamphlets, some of which are entitled 'For how long will Hitler rule?' were even mailed in at post offices in Leipzig. Typewritten handbills of the Bible Students were also found in trains between Plauen and Dresden." The Gestapa considered these reports by the Political Police as evidence "that, in its prohibited state this sect had, as expected, increasingly drifted into the political minefield of communism." In the concluding paragraph of its March 10, 1934, situation report, the Berlin Gestapo headquarters made the following statement: "These observations prove that the ban imposed on this sect is completely justified."

After Jehovah's Witnesses had been the first Christian denomination banned in the Third Reich, measures were taken around the turn of 1933/34 to ban those groups that had disassociated from the Watch Tower Society in previous years. Accordingly, in November 1933 the Freie Bibelforscher-Vereinigung was dissolved.[126] On December 16 the property of the Freie Vereinigung der Bibelforscher Augsburgs was confiscated in favor of the state of Bavaria.[127] And on January 13, 1934,

Prussia banned the Menschenfreundliche Versammlung (Engel Jehovas) that the former IBSA functionary, F. L. Alexandre Freytag from Geneva, had founded in 1920.[128]

The NS authorities increasingly took action against other Christian and non-Christian denominations.[129] According to NS opinion, the regime resisted religious minorities merely for the fact that they, in its opinion, "contributed to the ideological fragmentation of the German people," preventing the forming of a united German community.[130] There was no room for religious diversity in the NS ideological claim for absolutism.

Religious associations whose activities were restricted to the immediate group of their members and who did not preach or perform other public activities, and especially whose beliefs and activities did not conflict with NS ideologies, experienced fewer difficulties. As soon as there were doubts regarding the loyalty toward the NS state, however, persecution would set in. The major denominations enjoyed a certain measure of freedom of action as a result of their large representation in society and their general preservation of organizational structure, even in the "totalitarian state." But the minor denominations were relatively unprotected against the coercion from the state. Those sects that had not yet been dissolved were constantly confronted with the alternative of accepting the possibility of a ban or completely conforming to the expectations of the state, which often involved abandoning their identity. As a result, many of those religious groups succumbed to the pressure and accepted the inevitable.[131] Reports from the SS mentioned that, "out of fear of being dissolved, the sects often [displayed] a neutral, or even especially loyal attitude. At times, they anxiously tried to prove their National Socialist attitude at every opportunity."[132]

The Gestapo and the SS certainly made a distinction between associations that were considered to be "extremely subversive" and those that did "not pose an immediate threat to the state," and as a result of the increasing confrontation with the churches, or church factions, changed their ideological policy.[133] For instance, from then on the presence of "harmless sects" was accepted, because the SS had now decided that "they certainly were not interested in somehow eliminating religious diversity."[134] At the same time, though, the measures of resisting the troublemaking sects were intensified, year after year.[135] Gestapo and legal authorities prosecuted believers who did not observe the ban on their religious association. The majority received prison sentences of several months. In a number of cases, they were sent to the concentration camps for years. In this respect, the persecution of Jehovah's Witnesses was part of a development that also included other Christian denominations. However, since they were the first and most extensively persecuted Christian denomination, their persecution also set a certain precedent.[136]

Interaction between State and Churches

After the ban had been imposed on the Bible Students, state and church authorities demanded that the same measures also be taken against other Christian denominations. To this end, the Bavarian Ministry for Education and Cultural Affairs had already contemplated the necessity of dealing with the troublemaking sects. Only a few weeks after the IBSA ban had been issued in Bavaria, the ministry discussed the question of "whether the actions taken against the Earnest Bible Students could also be taken against the sect of Seventh-day Adventists."[137] Even in the church press, demands were made not to let matters rest with just this one step. For example, in a report regarding the Prussian Bible Student ban, *Das Evangelische Deutschland,* a leading Evangelical paper, stated: "The church certainly appreciates that, by means of this ban, one kind of religious corruption has been removed. . . . However, this does not completely solve the problem associated with sectarian groups, only to mention the New Apostolic Church."[138] Various other church committees and authorities acted immediately and substantiated these suggestions. And in August 1933 the Waldenburg (Silesia) District Synod mentioned several denominations to be considered for a possible ban, such as the Mormons, the Adventists, and the Evangelisch-Johannische Kirche (Weißenberg-Sekte, a sect founded in 1926 by Joseph Weißenberg). The synod requested the church authorities "to approach the appropriate secular authorities with this matter."[139]

Until at least the mid-1930s, the major churches and the state closely worked together in taking actions against various sects. To this end, the church authorities supported the secular authorities by providing them with the necessary background information concerning the respective religious denominations.[140] The Secret State Police office, in turn, promised in January 1934 to "inform the higher church authorities of any ban they would subsequently impose on a religious sect."[141]

It is indeed surprising how willingly some church officials in higher positions, and even a number of those in subordinate positions, supported the "struggle of resistance" against Jehovah's Witnesses. They had, for instance, no scruples to serve as informers for the authorities responsible for the persecution. In its October 1934 issue, the bulletin of the *Apologetische Centrale* merely requested its readers "to be cautious" about the activities of the Bible Students[142] whereas in August 1937 the representative of the bishop of the Evangelical churches in Bremen openly called on the leaders of the various Evangelical parishes to report any IBSA propaganda to the Gestapo.[143] Consequently, when on October 22, 1939, a curate from Münsterland found the Bible Student pamphlet "War or Peace?" in front of his door, he immediately informed the police about the incident and disclosed the name of the person he thought to be responsible for the offense.[144]

On the other hand, there were also church officials who showed solidarity with Jehovah's Witnesses who were persecuted for their faith. This is reflected in the following report published in April 1937 in the *Deutschland-Berichte* of the exiled SPD (Sopade):

> In Stollberg and Lugau, where recently quite a number of Bible Students had been arrested, pastors took a stand for them in their churches. For instance, the pastor in Lugau discussed the adherence of the Bible Students to the Holy Scriptures and presented them to his parishioners as an example worth following. Despite persecution and special court proceedings, these Bible Students fanatically advocate the Holy Scriptures. This certainly demands our respect and calls for support.[145]

During the same year, upon request by the central European office of the Watch Tower Society, leading theologians confirmed that the accusations made by the National Socialists against Jehovah's Witnesses were not substantiated. To this end, Professor Karl Barth, who was exiled in Switzerland and who was the Spiritus Rector behind the Bruderrat faction (an association of prominent Evangelical theologians founded in 1934) of the "Bekennende Kirche," stated that "Jehovah's Witnesses are a religious movement that is particularly concerned with the prophecies of the Bible." The accusation that they perform pro-Communist activities could therefore be based on "unintended, possibly even intended misunderstandings."[146]

Professor Ernst Staehelin also defended the Bible Students, even though he described the Bible Students from a reformational point of view in his 1925 pamphlet, as "a very controversial group."[147] He stated that, in his opinion, the Bible Students are "part of the Christian churches." But he also wrote that they are not involved in any political activities: "Their criticism of governmental and religious conditions is Bible-based and is supposed to promote the interests of God's Kingdom."[148]

The Balancing Act

The September 28, 1933, decree by the Prussian minister of the interior allowed the WTG to resume its activities—at least to a certain extent. The leaders of the Magdeburg branch office, who had resumed their work, made efforts to reduce the limitations of the ban even more. With patience and determination, they tried to convince the authorities that the accusations against the Bible Students Association could not be substantiated. Thus, they continued following the course of concessions that they had adopted since the beginning of 1933, and at the same time, they used the freedom they had been granted to the fullest extent. For instance, they reestablished contact with the local groups and admonished them to remain faithful but also to be patient. In this regard, the leaders were confronted with two problems. First, they had to counteract the dissolution of groups, and they had to encourage those who had left the association to return. Second, the leaders were concerned about those Bible Students who had resumed their prohibited activities, which was considered to be a threat and an obstacle to their course of compromise. The leaders of the German branch of the Watch Tower Society were confronted with problems involving their own membership, problems to an extent that this theocratic organization had not known before.

During the following months, a large number of Jehovah's Witnesses became increasingly indignant with the negotiating efforts of the Magdeburg branch office. Many of the active Bible Students in the IBSA groups became impatient because they did not believe that the negotiations would be successful, and locally, there was also no evidence for any positive results. This presented a crucial test for the association: On the one hand, there were the leaders who followed the motto "Let's make the best out of the situation." Several Bible Student groups supported these efforts of their leaders and, consequently, admonished their fellow believers not to provoke the authorities unnecessarily. On the other hand, some Bible Students were determined to confront the "powers of Satan" without making any compromises. In several local IBSA groups, the confrontation between those that supported their leaders' course of compromise with those that rejected this course resulted in divisions.

This was the case, for instance, in the local groups in Flensburg, Kiel, and Neumünster.[149]

Initially, the Watch Tower Society's headquarters in Brooklyn apparently approved of the actions of the leaders of its German branch office. In his petition to the Reich president, the Reich chancellor, and the Prussian prime minister, Rutherford's authorized representative Harbeck adopted the same tone that the German leaders and their intermediaries had used in their petitions.[150] For instance, Harbeck asserted, "We have never accepted Communists or Marxists in our religious denomination. And the denomination certainly does not include any Jews. Even so, all IBSA members appreciate the National Socialist government because of the fact that Hitler and his State profess to be Christians."[151]

Neither the efforts of the German branch office of the Watch Tower Society nor the continuous diplomatic negotiations brought any positive results.[152] There were no indications that the bans would be withdrawn. Therefore, at the end of 1933 the Watch Tower Society's leaders in Brooklyn and Harbeck came to the conclusion that it was unrealistic to expect any improvement of the situation in Germany. Their negotiations had failed.[153] Even their good conduct had not produced any noteworthy improvement. They also realized that something needed to be done if they did not want to run the risk of losing more members. Now, the Brooklyn headquarters tried using protests and threats from abroad to persuade the Hitler government to withdraw the bans against the IBSA.[154]

On February 9, 1934, Joseph Franklin Rutherford sent a letter to the Reich chancellor. In this letter, Rutherford requested the chancellor "to instruct all administrative authorities and government officials to allow Jehovah's Witnesses in Germany (that is, [members of] the Bible Students Association and the [German branch of the] Watch Tower Bible and Tract Society) to assemble quietly, to worship God without hindrance, and to follow His commandments."[155] Rutherford concluded his letter with the following ultimatum: "If you do not respond to this request by March 24, 1934, and your government does not take steps to improve the situation of Jehovah's Witnesses in Germany, God's people in other countries will publish the facts about Germany's unjust treatment of Christians among all the nations of the earth."[156] Rutherford added strongly that the matter would also be "brought to the attention of Jehovah God, and, through Jesus Christ, He would punish in His own way those responsible for the mistreatment." This statement, as well as Rutherford's unconcealed warning that "the Lord would destroy in Armageddon all those opposing God and His Kingdom," indicated the completely different perspectives and positions of both opponents. Rutherford based his actions on the authority of God, which, of course, did not provide him with real power. Hitler acted of his own accord, presuming to have almost unlimited secular power at his disposal. For this reason, Rutherford's warning probably did not make any lasting impression on the governmental authorities in Berlin.

Rutherford now closed this chapter of petitioning. But the German leaders under Balzereit, who, in the meantime, had returned from Prague to Magdeburg, continued to place their confidence in the negotiations. This did not cause any conflict between the Brooklyn headquarters and its Magdeburg branch office, because Brooklyn did not stop supporting the leaders of its second largest branch office in Magdeburg. The Magdeburg leaders, on the other hand, indicated their willingness to increase their efforts of reactivating the preaching activity, irrespective of continued efforts of negotiating. At the beginning of 1934, for example, Balzereit instructed the district overseers to continue meeting in small groups of three to five people, or resume these meetings if they had been discontinued.[157] Any public activities, however, should not be resumed. The preaching activity should be restricted to people who were already considered to be "interested ones." With the necessary caution, the distribution of the *Watchtower* and other publications should be resumed.

The Magdeburg leaders approached the matter by using special strategic methods. The local IBSA groups as well as independently acting groups were encouraged to follow the directions of the IBSA leadership. But, to those on the outside, the leaders carefully tried to present the activities of the Watch Tower Bible and Tract Society to be unrelated to the activities of the banned IBSA. In their negotiations with the secular authorities, they had been able to secure for the Watch Tower Society the status as a solely religious publishing house, a status that they tried not to endanger. This legalization of the society provided the Magdeburg branch office with a limited amount of freedom, which they used for the purpose of distributing biblical publications, such as Bibles and concordances from the British Bible Association. For this purpose, they employed so-called sales representatives who established and maintained communication with the believers in the various areas. The society provided these sales representatives with special photo ID cards so they could prove that they were authorized to distribute the religious publications. The sales representatives were asked to sign an agreement, which in turn protected the Magdeburg branch office against any future complications. According to this agreement, the sales representatives took full responsibility for everything that occurred after they had obtained the Bibles and other publications from the Watch Tower Society. Consequently, "the Watch Tower Bible and Tract Society was no longer responsible, not even indirectly, should any legal consequences arise."[158]

This development did not escape the notice of the Secret State Police office. On January 20, 1934, this office informed the subordinate State Police offices about the situation and demanded increased attention.[159] Two months later, in its report regarding the results of the previous observations, the Gestapa stated that "in various places" the sales representatives "used their customer calls for 'group Bible discussions.'" The report emphasized those investigation results according to which the legal department of the Watch Tower Society had instructed its sales representatives "to avoid the impression that their activities were in any way related to the activities of the organization."[160]

The Berlin Gestapo headquarters carefully recorded the activities of the WTG. However, probably in consideration of foreign policy, it did not take action against the Magdeburg branch office but restricted State Police measures to further observations. During the following months, Gestapo officials increasingly focused on the activities of the WTG legal department. The Watch Tower Society used this department for the purpose of collecting reports about police actions such as arrests, house searches, and confiscations, as well as other infringements, and as a result, the legal department now had a clear picture of the persecution methods that the Reich authorities had instituted against Jehovah's Witnesses and kept "an account of all items that had been confiscated including those that were not yet released."[161] The legal department also provided legal advice for fellow believers who had to appear in court and tried to obtain details about cases in which fellow believers were taken into protective detention. For this purpose, the department stayed in close contact with the local groups, inquiring about the whereabouts of the people concerned.[162] Increasingly, the Magdeburg branch office was used as an office for legal support. It even provided a "pamphlet including legal advice and information about prosecution,"[163] which apparently was distributed to the local groups by the sales representatives.

Throughout 1934 the German IBSA leaders were confident that their efforts could still be successful and that ultimately their adherence to the negotiations would produce the anticipated results. This was indicated by the fact that Jehovah's Witnesses were able to obtain acquittals in court, and by the fact that, from the middle of 1934 on, the authorities seemed to be more accommodating.[164] In the June 9, 1934, decree by the Prussian Ministry of Justice, for instance, brief reference was made to the decree that the minister of the interior had issued in September of the previous year (1933). Because this decree had also been published in the official paper of the Ministry of Justice, the WTG was able to use it to prove toward a third party that the Ministry of Justice had confirmed its legality.[165] Moreover, the WTG found ways to use this somewhat late announcement in such a way that some authorities were under the impression that the release of the confiscated Bible Student property had been repeated.

On June 22, 1934, Ministerialdirektor (head of a ministerial department) Dr. Crohne informed the Magdeburg branch office about the decree by the Prussian Ministry of Justice. Magdeburg immediately gave instructions to the leaders of the various IBSA groups to appear at the local police offices and, with reference to the decree by the Prussian Minister of Justice, request the publications that had been confiscated in the meantime. For this purpose, the group leaders were asked to submit at the police offices a copy of the decree as it appeared in the "official paper of the Ministry of Justice, *Deutsche Justiz*," as well as a cover letter. The letter requested to return to the "person submitting this letter the entire confiscated property of the Bible Students Association, its subsidiary associations, and of the 'Watch Tower Bible and Tract Society.' The person submitting this letter has been authorized to accept, on our behalf, the confiscated sums of money and objects of value, pieces of furniture, publications, factory equipment, and material assets."[166]

In some cases, the Bible Students appearing at the local police offices were quite successful. To counteract the confusion the Bible Students caused with their actions, the higher police authorities considered it necessary to issue new decrees in order to confirm that the Bible Student bans were still in effect. Accordingly, on July 14, 1934, the Bavarian Political Police issued an interoffice decree, which stated that there was no reason "to return the confiscated property."[167] The Secret State Police office in Berlin also referred to the fact that "no new decision had been made but rather the announcement had been delayed." It also stated that "the confiscated publications and pamphlets did not come under the decree." However, "if the Magdeburg branch office of the 'Watch Tower Bible and Tract Society' submitted an appropriate application, [the publications] could be released for use in other countries."[168]

A real improvement of the situation, according to the expectations of the Watch Tower Society, was achieved by the September 13, 1934, decree of the Reich and Prussian minister of the interior. This decree regulated, for the first time, the affairs of the IBSA at the Reich level. Even in this case, the decree was issued as a result of previous efforts by the American Consulate General.[169] On the same day, Dr. Helmut Nicolai, expert for constitutional questions at the RMdI, sent a letter to the Berlin Consulate informing it about the contents of the decree. From his previous position as Magdeburg district president, he was most likely familiar with the subject. According to Nicolai, the governments of the various German states had been instructed "to release the property of the International Bible Students Association and its subsidiary associations and not to interfere with the printing and distribution of Bibles and other unobjectionable publications," but "all other activities of the Earnest Bible Students, such as their preaching and meeting activities, the printing and distribution of tracts, pamphlets, advertisements, etc., would continue to be prohibited."[170]

The actual wording of the decree significantly deviated from the promise made to the consulate: "The printing and distribution of *commonly used* Bibles as well as the printing of journals with *unobjectionable contents that is unrelated to the activities of the 'Earnest Bible Students Association'* . . . would not be objectionable."[171] This Reich-ministerial decree now represented a protection of the distribution activities, a permission to resume the printing work, and consequently the prospect of continuing, on a legal basis, the preaching activity of the Watch Tower Bible and Tract Society, even under the difficult circumstances and restrictions in the Third Reich. The interoffice decree issued by the Secret State Police office on September 28, 1934, took the recent developments into account but further restricted the term "commonly used Bibles (*Luther Bible*)."[172] The Munich colleagues of the Bavarian Political Police even considered it necessary to emphasize again that "the ban on the 'Earnest Bible Students' . . . remained unaffected."[173]

Based on this property release at the Reich level, the Magdeburg leaders now hoped to have the authority required to request the return of the considerable number of Bible Student publications that had been confiscated by the police. On October 5, 1934, the Magdeburg leaders sent a letter to local Bible Student groups. In this letter they requested the group leaders "to appear again" at the local police authorities and request, under reference to the Reich-ministerial decree, "the return" of the confiscated publications.[174] At the same time, preparations were made to take advantage of the fact that they were allowed to distribute Bibles and "publications with unobjectionable contents." On October 17, 1934, by way of regular mail, the WTG sent a memo to the various Bible Student groups informing them that the Watch Tower Society planned, as in previous years, to publish a tear-off calendar that would include encouraging Bible texts. The local groups were then asked to submit their orders to the Magdeburg branch office within the next two weeks.[175]

Resumption of the Preaching Activity

In the autumn of 1934, when the negotiations of the German IBSA leaders slowly began to produce positive results, the Brooklyn headquarters and others who were determined to remain active had already decided on a further course of action. Since October 7, 1934, ten days prior to the Magdeburg branch office memo, several thousand Jehovah's Witnesses in Germany had been involved in the preaching activity, regardless of the ban and other official restrictions. They also did not restrict their activities to the distribution of Bibles and approved calendars but used the publications of Rutherford and other pamphlets of the Watch Tower Society to proclaim their faith. These developments completely disregarded the actions taken by Magdeburg. The leaders of the Brooklyn headquarters then took matters into their own hands.

The Watch Tower Society had invited delegates from various Bible Student groups to attend an international convention in Basel between September 7 and September 9, 1934.[176] Among the thirty-five hundred attendees from ten different nations, there were approximately one thousand German Jehovah's Witnesses. For some of them it had been extremely difficult to attend this convention. The convention had the motto "Fear Them Not" and focused mainly on the questions of how to respond to the persecution of Jehovah's Witnesses and how to continue the preaching activity in NS Germany. In this regard, Rutherford requested the German Jehovah's Witnesses, among whom various opinions prevailed, to resume completely their preaching activity. According to one report, he addressed the German attendees with the words: "Brothers, do not only focus on the fiery furnace—also focus on your deliverance."[177]

Three decisions made at the Basel convention proved to be of special significance: (1) the adoption of a public resolution of protest; (2) the decision to resume the preaching activity in Germany with a collective start on October 7, 1934, regardless of the ban; and (3) arrangements regarding a continuation of the prohibited activities and the manner in which to deal with cases of arrest and other police interventions.

The resolution of protest, which was transmitted to the Swiss press, requested "all righteously inclined people around the earth" to show solidarity.[178] Enclosed in a letter dated September 15, this resolution of protest was also sent to the Reich chancellor. The letter included "the repeated request" that, "based on Article 137 of the German Reich Constitution, the Reich chancellor should restore to peaceable people in Germany the right to worship their living God, a right that they had been denied by the German government." The letter also included the unmistakable warning: "Your ill-treatment of Jehovah's Witnesses shocks all good people on earth and dishonors God's name. Refrain from further persecution of Jehovah's Witnesses; otherwise God will destroy you and your national party."[179]

At the Basel convention, it was decided to set up meetings in as many places as possible for the purpose of simultaneously resuming the preaching activity. Consequently, the Bible Students began making the necessary preparations as soon as they returned from the convention. The Magdeburg leaders accepted this decision and instructed the district overseers accordingly; they tried very carefully, to the fullest extent possible, to keep the German branch office of the society out of this action. In the local congregations, which had not held any meetings or met for Bible discussions in homes during the previous year, small subordinate groups of six to twelve people were formed. Not all of the people who were approached with the request to resume their preaching activity were also willing to participate. Nonetheless, a total of more than ten thousand Bible Students expressed their willingness to participate.[180]

On Sunday, October 7, 1934, at 9 a.m., the small groups came together, most of them in the homes of their group leaders. Specific arrangements had been made for these meetings. After a short prayer, the respective leaders informed their group about the decisions made at the Basel convention and read the following letter from Rutherford:

> You have heretofore made a covenant to do the will of God. He has taken you at your word, begotten you as His own, and called you to his Kingdom. Christ Jesus at the temple of God has gathered unto himself the faithful and taken them into the covenant for God's kingdom. . . . Contrary to and in violation of the foregoing positive commandments from Jehovah God the government of Germany has forbidden you to meet together and worship Jehovah

and serve him. Whom will you obey: God or men? The faithful apostles were placed in a similar position, and to the worldly rulers they said: "Whether it be right in the sight of God to hearken unto you more than unto God, judge ye. We ought to obey God rather than men." (Acts 4:13–20, 5:29)[181]

Following this request to acknowledge Jehovah and to submit to His authority, another letter was read. This letter, which each group was expected to send to the Reich government, informed the government that the Bible Students were determined to act on the advice of the faithful apostles: "Therefore this is to advise you that at any cost we will obey God's commandments, will meet together for the study of his Word."[182]

The meeting was concluded by reflecting on Matthew 10:16–24, a Bible text in which Jesus told his followers that they would be persecuted. What would happen next, Rutherford's letter describes as follows: "Then [you should] adjourn the meeting and . . . go out among your neighbors and bear testimony to the name of Jehovah God and his Kingdom under Christ Jesus."

To show their solidarity with their fellow believers in Germany, the Bible Student groups abroad also came together at this specific time. Afterwards, they sent protest telegrams to the Reich government in Germany with the following request: "Your ill-treatment of Jehovah's Witnesses shocks all good people on earth and dishonors God's name. Refrain from further persecution of Jehovah's Witnesses; otherwise God will destroy you and your national party."[183]

The post offices were literally flooded with telegrams. As early as October 8, 1934, a senior official of the Reich post administration asked the appropriate higher senior civil servant at the Reich chancellery what they should do with the telegrams. As a result, the Berlin main telegraph office combined large numbers of telegrams for collective shipments. The first shipment of five hundred protest telegrams was sent to the Reich chancellery that very same day.[184] During the next two days, telegrams from all parts of the world arrived in Berlin, the majority of which came from the United States, Great Britain, France, Switzerland, and the Netherlands. The foreign post offices were informed to stop transmitting the telegrams, since the recipient refused to accept them. On October 10, 1934, the Berlin main telegraph office arranged with the telegraph offices in Bern, Krakow, Göteburg, London, and Brussels to destroy all telegrams that had not yet been delivered or transmitted.[185]

Even the presidential office received large amounts of letters. On October 9 the office informed the Reich bishop that it had received, "yesterday and today, from all parts of Germany, 1,032 letters with almost the same wording, signed 'Jehovah's Witnesses.'"[186] Apparently, in this case, it was not possible to find out from where these letters had been sent. Therefore, an inquiry was made with the church authorities, and on November 20, 1934, they informed the presidential office that "Jehovah's Witnesses" represent the former "International Association of Earnest Bible Students," which had been banned.[187]

On November 17, 1934, Hitler's private office requested the Reich chancellery to "submit to us all previously received, as well as all anticipated, letters of the sect of 'Jehovah's Witnesses.' We will handle the matter at our office."[188] The Reich chancellery, in turn, inquired as to "how the matter would be handled there."[189] On November 24, 1934, Hitler's private office responded that, "upon request by the 'Department for Cultural Peace,' all material had been transferred to the Secret State Police office for further examination."[190]

Aware that they disregarded the ban, and accepting the open conflict with the state authorities, the majority of Bible Student groups followed the instructions of the Watch Tower Society's headquarters and began resuming their religious activities. At the same time, the German IBSA leaders still expected to be able to gradually create the prerequisites so that the preaching activity could be continued under legal conditions, even if this would be possible only to a limited extent.

These different approaches resulted in alienation between the leadership of the WTG under Balzereit and some parts of the Bible Student movement. The extent of this alienation becomes apparent by reflecting on the conflict that arose regarding the leadership of the Northern German IBSA groups.

In June 1934 the leader of the Hamburg IBSA youth group was arrested because of a letter he had written to the central European office in Bern. In this letter, he had "criticized the election methods of the National Socialists." The letter was intercepted at the censor's office in Frankfurt am Main.[191] Since the leader of the Hamburg IBSA youth group had used the initials H. v. A. in his letter, the Gestapo detained for seven weeks Hero von Ahlften, the head of the Northern German Bible Students Association, which had been banned on July 15 of the previous year. The leaders of the Magdeburg branch office were not pleased when they learned about the imprisonment of a member of their immediate group of leaders. Balzereit and Dollinger were concerned that this incident could have detrimental effects on their negotiations. Even though the Magdeburg leaders did not know all the circumstances, they attributed the unauthorized action to Ahlften, and he incurred their disfavor. As a result, Balzereit removed Ahlften, as well as the previous service committee, from office.[192] In place of Ahlften, he appointed the Lübeck IBSA leader, Arno Thümmler, to be responsible for the areas of Hamburg and Schleswig-Holstein.[193] This action naturally offended Ahlften who had been a long-standing service leader in Hamburg. Since this decision was not merely a matter of personal differences, it resulted in serious tension between the local groups concerned and the Magdeburg branch office. It even involved the Brooklyn headquarters.

On October 15, 1934, Ahlften wrote a letter to J. F. Rutherford. In this letter, he complained about the decisions that the Magdeburg branch office had made during the previous weeks and months and informed Rutherford that in agreement with the decisions made in Basel and *Watchtower* articles to the same end, a number of Bible Students were determined to move forward with the preaching activity. Thümmler, the new district service overseer, held the view that the statements of the *Watchtower* were not that important. In Ahlften's opinion, this was more proof that the leadership members around "Balzereit disobeyed the clear and precise orders from the Brooklyn headquarter [*sic*]."[194]

As a result, two members of the German leadership wrote a letter in which they repudiated the accusations made by Ahlften. This letter was distributed to a considerable number of Jehovah's Witnesses in leading positions. It also explained that the previous service committee, under the leadership of Ahlften, was "no longer in any position of authority" since it "did not fulfill the requirements for dealing with the present situation of the work." Therefore, the committee was no longer in charge and had been removed. Like their opponents [the group around Ahlften], the members of the German leadership also claimed to have the support of Rutherford: He "fully approves of the measures taken by the German leadership and condemns the actions of these brothers."[195]

At the beginning of December, Rutherford requested Paul Balzereit to clarify the matter. If there was evidence that Thümmler had made that statement, he should be immediately removed from office. "Any man who regards the *Watchtower*, which the Lord uses to feed his people, as unimportant has no business in the Lord's service."[196] At the same time, Rutherford indicated that it was "not possible for him to judge between Ahlften and Balzereit." Thus, the president of the Watch Tower Society refused to take a clear stand against Balzereit, a stand that several people had expected him to take.

Toward the end of 1934 the local groups became increasingly critical of the actions of the leaders of the German branch office. On December 10, 1934, Jehovah's Witnesses in Emden made the following statement that reflected the spirit among the active ones in the groups: "Since October 7 of this year, through His mercy and loving kindness, Jehovah has set us completely free from the powers of the devil. We actually had anticipated that the brothers that took the lead in this work before the ban would take a clear stand for the truth and take sides with Jehovah. . . . We are, however, surprised that these brothers are more interested in publishing calendars and Bibles than in proclaiming the truth in the way that has been approved by our Lord since many years."[197] Instead, the active groups "are urged to consider the negotiations being made with regard to the publication of the *Golden Age.*" The leaders further complained "that our determined actions are considered to be detrimental to the moderate progress they were making in their negotiations." It hardly came as a surprise that "quite a few of our brothers are confused by the course of the Magdeburg leaders," and they requested Rutherford to take a clear stand, again, for those believers who refused to compromise.

After October 7 the groups engaged in the dangerous act of resuming the preaching activity and attending their weekly religious meetings. But the Gestapo soon discovered this resumption of the preaching activity. In its November 4, 1934, situation report, the Hannover State Police office stated about the events of the previous month: "Recently, it has been observed that the prohibited 'International Bible Students Association' has considerably increased its activities. An increasing number of men and women are going from house to house trying to inform people about their religious viewpoints."[198]

During the following weeks and months, a number of people were arrested. Now it was merely a question of time when the "concessions" that had been made toward the WTG would be withdrawn and a new, final ban would be issued.[199] Besides withdrawing the concessions made in the autumn of 1933, the authorities issued a ban at the Reich level, replacing the former bans in the various German states. One of the reasons for this prohibition was that in previous court cases against the Bible Students, a large number of Bible Students had been acquitted, which prevented further prosecution in case of defiance of the IBSA bans. Furthermore, serious formal errors had been made involving the issuing of the bans. For example, in at least three German states (Prussia,

Mecklenburg-Schwerin, and Hessen), the legally required publication in the ministerial papers or in the legal digest had been neglected.[200] A ban at the Reich level would finally remove any legal difficulties regarding the question of legality of certain state-related bans. In a letter, the Oldenburg minister of the interior summarized this motive by stating that a ban at the Reich level would make it possible "to take legal action against any defiance [of the ban]."[201]

On April 1, 1935, the Reich and Prussian minister of the interior instructed the Magdeburg district president to dissolve the German branch of the Watch Tower Bible and Tract Society, and to give its leaders an official notification of the ban.[202] Consequently, on April 27, 1935, the Magdeburg district president issued the dissolution order. Probably out of concern for the reputation the German Reich might leave with the American Consulate General, the order included a particular statement indicating the possibility that the Watch Tower Society could appeal this decision:

> Based on article 1 of the Decree of the Reich President for the Protection of People and State (*RGBl.* I, 83), and article 14 of the June 1, 1931, Police Administrative Law (GS., 77), the Wachtturm, Bibel und Traktat Gesellschaft in Magdeburg has been dissolved and banned. According to Article 4 of the February 28, 1933, decree, defiance of this ban is subject to punishment. Within a period of two weeks after receipt, an appeal can be filed against this decision at the Magdeburg District Administrative Court [*Bezirksverwaltungs-gericht*], according to Article 49 of the PVG. Thereafter, according to Article 51 of the PVG, a second appeal can be filed in the form of an administrative procedure at the Prussian Higher Administrative Court. In that event, two copies of the complaint must be submitted to the Magdeburg District Administrative Court.[203]

In his effort to give the ban an appearance of legality, the Magdeburg district president took great pains in explaining the reasons for the ban. In a two-page statement, he explained that the Watch Tower Society did not comply with the conditions of the ban. Instead, its leaders requested "former members of the banned IBSA" to obtain "books and journals, possibly for further distribution." These also "deliberately made it appear as if the activities of the allegedly subversive IBSA were again permitted." In this way, the "Bible and Tract Society, which is a former branch of the IBSA," attempted to circumvent the ban on the IBSA: "This means that the above-mentioned society is directly associated with the prohibited IBSA and therefore has to be considered as a subversive organization that obviously opposes our present State and its cultural and moral structure. Consequently, the ban is completely justified."

On July 13, 1935, the Reich and Prussian minister of the interior issued an interoffice decree in which he informed the governments of the various German states about the confiscation of the property of the German branch of the Watch Tower Bible and Tract Society.[204] Consequently, the Bavarian Political Police instructed the State Police offices to confiscate "all publications of the Watch Tower Society, including commonly used Bibles and other unobjectionable publications."[205] The action was no longer restricted to supposedly "subversive Bible Student publications." Even the Bible itself seemed to pose a threat to the state. Six months later, on January 30, 1936, the Reich minister of the interior gave instructions to the police "to take action against the distribution of Bibles and religious publications, though unobjectionable, by former members of the prohibited International Bible Students Association."[206]

In December and January 1934/35 all efforts of the German leadership of the Watch Tower Society to stop this development proved to be ineffective.[207] On January 5, 1935, Legal Counsel Hans Dollinger made a final personal petition to the Führer and Reich chancellor in which he appealed to the fundamental right of freedom of religion. At last, the struggle to legalize the Bible Students Association had turned into an entreaty to end this persecution of Christians: "But the fact that the Bible Students Association has been dissolved in the various [German] states cannot possibly mean that we Christians are no longer allowed to assemble with other Christians for prayer and worship of our God."[208]

In May 1935, possibly in the context of the repeated occupation of the Magdeburg branch office, Paul Balzereit and Hans Dollinger were arrested. Seven months later, on December 17, 1935, nine members of the group of WTG leaders were tried at the Saxony Special Court in Halle. Balzereit was sentenced to two and a half years of imprisonment, Dollinger to two years, even though both had denied any defiance of the bans.[209] During the following year, Balzereit and a number of other former leaders were expelled from the organization of Jehovah's Witnesses. In his letter "To Jehovah's Faithful People in Germany," Rutherford severely criticized "the action taken by the one who formerly was the manager of the Society in Germany."[210] In reference to the court proceedings at the special court in Halle, the president of the Brooklyn headquarters expressed his surprise that "not one of those on trial at that time gave a faithful and true testimony to the name of Jehovah." While several thousand of Jehovah's Witnesses in Germany fearlessly supported the work of proclaiming the Kingdom, Balzereit did not say anything "showing his complete reliance upon Jehovah." Therefore, "the Society will henceforth have nothing to do with him." The Society would also "put forth no effort in seeking to release them from prison, even if it had the power to do anything." Subsequently, Jehovah's Witnesses viewed the compromises that the German leaders of the IBSA had made at the beginning of the Third Reich to be a wrong course. According to a 1942 underground publication, the Magdeburg branch office in 1935 had completely refrained from any efforts to "secure the interests of God's people in Germany."[211]

The era of Balzereit had come to a disreputable end. From then on, Jehovah's Witnesses no longer needed people who would go to extremes in "fighting for a probable cause." They needed people who would be consistently "fighting for the truth."

6

Judicial Conflict and Freedom of Religion

In mid-1933 the courts began to institute legal proceedings against Bible Students who had defied the IBSA ban. These proceedings resulted in a judicial conflict of such extent that it far exceeded its original cause. This first ban of a religious denomination in the Third Reich called into question the constitutional right of freedom of religion, which ultimately called into question the continuation of the Reich Constitution.

The governmental authorities for the various German states based their dissolution orders on the February 28, 1933, "Decree of the Reich President for the Protection of People and State" (*RGBl.*).[212] According to article 1 of this "Emergency Decree" (Notverordnung), which had been issued following the Decree of the Reich President, seven fundamental rights of the Reich Constitution were repealed for "the resistance of Communist state-endangering acts of violence." These rights included the right of free expression of opinion, freedom of the press, the association and meeting right, the inviolability of personal freedom, interferences in private letters, post office privacy, and rights of privacy in telegraph and telephone correspondence. Article 4 determined that defiance of any orders issued by the highest state authorities on the basis of this decree would be punished with fines or prison sentences. By means of this Decree of the Reich President, which was based on Reich Constitution, article 48, and validated through the signature of Reich president Hindenburg, the coalition government of the "National Union" had acquired extensive authority. Four weeks after its rise to power, with reference to a state of emergency, the government was in a position to continue its persecution of opponents of the regime. Consequently, the so-called Reichstag Fire Decree formed the legal basis of the Third Reich, and thus, as it has frequently been called, the "constitution of the dictatorship."[213]

According to the preamble of the Decree of the Reich President, its use was restricted to "the resistance of Communist state-endangering acts of violence." Despite this specific restriction, it was intended *from the beginning* to use this decree beyond its immediate purpose. Even the implementing regulations issued on March 3, 1933, by Hermann Göring, the acting Prussian minister of the interior, extended the original application of the decree, that of resisting "Communist state-endangering acts of violence," to a resistance of all "opponents of people and State": "To avoid mistakes, I want to emphasize that measures taken against members or institutions of organizations other than Communist and anarchist organizations, or other than Social Democratic parties, can only be based on the February 28, 1933, Decree of the Reich President for the Protection of People and State if they serve the purpose of resisting such Communist endeavors in the broadest sense."[214] In the case of the dissolution orders that had been issued against the IBSA, the courts first of all had to clarify whether it was permissible to ban a religious denomination with reference to this Emergency Decree.

In the initial court proceedings held with reference to the Decree of the Reich President, Jehovah's Witnesses were usually punished with fines of between 150 and 300 Reichsmark.[215] As a result, several people, in some cases with the support of the Watch Tower Society's legal department, filed an appeal, or even subsequent appeals, against the decision.[216] Their appeals were based on the fundamental right of freedom of religion, which was guaranteed in articles 135 through 137 of the Reich Constitution.[217] These articles had not been repealed by the Decree of the Reich President, especially since, according to constitutional law, it was not even permissible to repeal these articles on the basis of Article 48 (Emergency Decree). Moreover, since the IBSA was by no means a state-endangering or Communist association, this particular decree that had been issued for "the resistance of Communist state-endangering acts of violence" did not even provide a legal basis to take action against the Bible Students Association. In their complaints, Jehovah's Witnesses also included appropriate quotations according to which even National Socialism proclaimed freedom of religion.

As early as 1933 there was also a decision by the highest court regarding the legality of the, in this case, Bavarian ban on the Bible Students. On May 21, 1933, five weeks after the Bavarian Ministry of the Interior had issued the ban, the complainant had visited a farmer, leaving him with an issue of the *Golden Age*. Since he thus became involved in the prohibited act of distributing Bible Student publications, the man was punished because of an offense against article 4 of the Decree of the Reich President. Consequently, he filed an appeal at the Bavarian Highest National Court; on December 7, 1933, the court, which had always held freedom of religion in high regard, rejected his appeal.[218] The Bavarian judges had no problem applying the Decree of the Reich President to the Bible Student ban, which, according to the preamble of the decree, had been issued for "the resistance of Communist state-endangering acts of violence." Even during the period prior to the NS takeover, the Munich authorities had considered the Bible Students as "Communists in disguise." For instance, in 1932 this same court pronounced the November 18, 1931, decree by the Munich police authorities regarding a general confiscation of Bible Student publications to be legal.[219]

In their December 1933 decision the judges explained that "because of their attacks on state-approved Christian churches and on State measures for the purpose of protecting these churches, the Bible Students present a danger to the continuance of public law and order that is comparable to the danger presented by the anti-religious and anti-clerical activities of the Communist Party." Therefore, the penal instrument, which had been issued for "the resistance of Communist state-endangering acts of violence," was declared to be applicable to these "anti-clerical sectarians," and the state was declared as *advocatus ecclesiae.*[220]

Three months later, in a decision involving the same issue, the Bavarian Highest National Court used, with slightly adjusted argumentation, the same strategy of legalizing the IBSA ban and, at the same time, upholding the constitutional articles guaranteeing freedom of religion.[221] According to this argumentation, the Bible Student ban "did not affect in any way" the constitutional articles that guaranteed freedom of religion. It did not affect freedom of religion, which was guaranteed according to articles 135 and 136, because the Bible Students could continue to adhere to their religious teachings. It also did not affect the protection of an association, which was guaranteed according to article 137, since the IBSA could not be considered as a religious association. Consequently, the ban issued on the IBSA "was merely a restriction of the right to form an association." It was not at all a governmental interference on one's right to practice religion. This, however, was not specifically mentioned.

At the beginning of 1934 the Reich Court (*Reichsgericht*) in Leipzig, the highest German court dealing with civil and criminal matters, also concerned itself with the question of the IBSA ban.[222] In this particular case, the senior Reich attorney had filed an appeal in which he disputed an acquittal from a subordinate court. Even though this subordinate regional court had confirmed the legality of the ban, it refused to view the actions of the two defendants as acts of defiance of the (in this case Saxony) ban. The court considered the distribution of the Wilmersdorf declaration, in which the defendants had been involved, merely as an expression of protest against the issued ban and not as advertisement for the banned association. The senior Reich attorney, however, considered the distribution of this protest declaration as an action that had the objective "of reuniting the members of the association and, consequently, of reorganizing the association." This, in turn, was clearly an act of defiance of the ban and was therefore subject to punishment.

On the one hand, the Reich Court dismissed the appeal for reasons of procedural law.[223] On the other hand, the legal counsels of the Reich Court found it "difficult to understand how the defendants could have become guilty of maintaining the organizational structure of their dissolved association" by distributing the declaration "to people who had never been members of their association."

This January 21, 1934, Reich Court decision gained importance that far exceeded this particular case. Even though this was not the immediate subject matter of the case, the proceedings raised the question of whether the ban on the Bible Students Association, which the Saxony minister of the interior had issued on April 18, 1933, could actually be viewed as a violation of the Reich Constitution. In this regard, the Reich Court stated that it was not permissible to dissolve a religious association with reference to the February 28, 1933, decree of the Reich president since Reich Constitution, article 137, was still in effect. This law had not been repealed by the Reich president. In fact, according to article 48, it was one of the laws he was not even authorized to repeal. Therefore, to resolve the question of legality of the Bible Student ban, it first had to be clarified whether the IBSA was a religious association or whether it was an association used for religious purposes according to laws outlining the right of association. The Reich Court stated: "If this association is a religious association, the ban by the Saxony minister of the interior would be . . . unconstitutional." And since the regional court had not made specific statements in this regard, the crucial question of whether the IBSA was a religious association remained unanswered.

In various respects, these explanations had far-reaching consequences. Administration of justice at the Reich Court still generally followed the legal precepts of the previous years.[224] One year after the NS takeover, the Reich Court still acknowledged the Reich Constitution to be the established law. It recognized, in particular, that certain laws could not be repealed by an Emergency Decree and therefore were inviolable. With regard to the legality of the IBSA ban, the subordinate courts now had to resolve the question of whether the IBSA was a religious association, the question the Reich Court had left unanswered. Now, however, the legal authorities complained that "the dispute has unfortunately been moved to the complicated area of theological and religious issues."[225]

But this does not mean that the Reich Court would have had any problems in using the February 28, 1933, Decree of the Reich President, since the introductory statements regarding "the resistance of Communist state-endangering acts of violence" merely defined "the immediate purpose of the decree."[226] In the administration of justice, the general viewpoint accepted that the statements of the preamble did not literally restrict the area of application but merely gave the reasons for which the decree had been issued.[227] To form a legal basis for extending an application of the decree, the theory of "an indirect Communist threat" was developed.[228] As a result, the permissibility of basing the Bible Student ban on the decree was generally undisputed.

To the regret of the National Socialists, it was one of these legal institutions that had been formed as a "Special Penal Division for the purpose of resolving political issues," which based its court proceedings on this Leipzig Reich Court decision. In its March 26, 1934, decision, the Hessen Special Court in Darmstadt pronounced the IBSA ban to be unconstitutional and legally ineffective. On the one hand, the court based this decision on the fact that the February 28, 1933, Decree of the Reich President repealed only seven specifically mentioned articles of the Reich Constitution. The other articles, including the article guaranteeing freedom of religion, were still in effect. On the other hand, after extensive hearing of evidence, the court granted the IBSA the status of a religious association, thus placing it under the protection of the unrepealed Reich Constitution, article 137. As a result, the twenty-nine defendants, Bible Students from Offenbach, were acquitted.[229]

According to a press report, the accused Jehovah's Witnesses determinedly denied in court any relationship between the Bible Student teachings and the Jewish religion or Communist ideologies. "What distinguishes them from the Jews is the fact that they believe in the life and death of Christ. And the fact that they reject principally the use of violence distinguishes them from the Communists."[230]

Professor Carl Schmitt, who, during the initial period of the Third Reich, was regarded as an undisputed NS authority in the field of constitutional law, asserted that "the Weimar Constitution, in whole or in part, was no longer legally binding."[231] However, the decision of the Darmstadt judges explicitly contradicted this viewpoint.[232] In the same way as the Reich Court previously, the Hessen Special Court also took a stand against Schmitt by adhering to the so-called theory of inviolability, which constitutionalists had developed during the 1920s. According to this theory, fundamental rights other than the seven constitution articles that the Reich president was authorized to repeal according to Reich Constitution, article 48, paragraph 2, would continue to be "binding, even during a dictatorship." They could not even be repealed during a state of emergency.[233] Therefore, the constitutional right of freedom of religion was also principally inviolable.

This decision of the Darmstadt Special Court provoked the most serious opposition on the part of the NS judges.[234] Professor Ernst Rudolf Huber, an exponent of the "Kieler Schule" and its most radically advocated "new legal thinking," was one of the promoters of NS jurisprudence.[235] Huber spoke of "errors in law" and "unsustainable results." Since the basic principles of the Weimar period had been replaced with the principles of a NS view of state, such as "national-oriented thinking," the "Führer principle," and "political totality," it was imperative "to break completely free from the image of a written formal constitution." A few of the regulations of the Weimar constitutional law were certainly still in effect: "But they are not binding because the Weimar Constitution 'in whole or in part' is still in effect. They are binding because they are now part of the constitutional law of National Socialism."[236] Huber discredited the Darmstadt Special Court for still adhering to the normative standards of the Weimar Constitution, which should have been abandoned, and for persisting in positivistic thinking. His criticism escalated in the statement: "The liberal principle *nulla poena sine lege*, to which this court refers, should not be applied to protect lawbreakers from punishments administered by the highest legal authority. . . . The formal legal thinking of the former state has in my opinion clearly resulted in a judicial error."[237]

At the legal department of the Watch Tower Society and among Jehovah's Witnesses, this decision of the Darmstadt Special Court decision had raised great anticipations. The evidence for the unlawfulness of the dissolution orders that the Administrative Court proceedings had not been able to provide was finally provided by a criminal court. The Watch

Tower Society provided the legal counsels of accused Jehovah's Witnesses with copies of this court decision and also published it in its literature. Based on this decision, quite a number of acquittals were obtained throughout 1934. For example, on July 20, 1934, seven Bible Students were acquitted at the court (*Schöffengericht*) in Peine.[238] On November 15, 1934, the Bielefeld *Schöffengericht* refused to sentence nine Jehovah's Witnesses, since there was no evidence that they had been involved in "subversive, political activities in the disguise of religion." The fact that they assembled for religious services in the privacy of their homes was not an offence punishable on the basis of the Decree of the Reich President.[239]

The Gestapo greatly resented this development. In its situation report for the month of July 1934 the Hannover State Police office stated that "the majority of Bible Student court cases" resulted in acquittals.[240] During the court proceedings, the defendants would repeatedly refer to, and read excerpts of, acquittals from other courts. Shortly afterwards, the State Police office reported that "the public prosecutor's office, without exception, had dismissed the Bible Student cases or . . . had pronounced an acquittal." The report added the following explanation: "The proceedings are usually dismissed because, in consideration of the March 26, 1934, decision of the Darmstadt Special Court, it is unlikely that a sentence will be pronounced."[241] According to the Hannover Gestapo, such practices on the part of the legal authorities would "only confirm the Bible Students' opinion that the ban was unlawful."[242]

At the beginning of 1935 a change in the administration of justice took place. On March 30, 1935, the Hamm Higher Regional Court overruled the acquittals of the Bielefeld *Schöffengericht* that had been issued in November of the previous year, but the reasoning the court used in this regard was not very convincing. It was not the IBSA ban that violated the freedom of religion of the Bible Students; they could not be granted freedom of religion because they were involved in "subversive activities."[243] According to the special court in Halle, which dealt with the Prussian IBSA ban in its January 29, 1935, proceedings, the dissolution order that the Prussian Ministry of the Interior had issued on June 24, 1933, did not violate the established law of the Reich Constitution. But Reich Constitution, article 137, was valid only to the extent that it did not contradict the principles of NS ideology.[244] If an association such as the IBSA tried to counteract the declared objective of the Führer to form a united people's community, it should be prepared to encounter opposition from the NS state. In such a case, not even a religious association could expect to be granted the constitutionally guaranteed freedom of religion.

This legal conception expressed in the court decision clearly restricted the constitutional right of freedom of religion. Even though
from the aspect of administration of justice and jurisprudence, the articles guaranteeing freedom of religion remained formally unaffected,
they had been deprived of their substantial meaning. Religious freedom
in the NS state was no longer based on the constitutional articles guaranteeing freedom of religion. They were based on the statements of the
NSDAP and the Führer.[245]

Despite its obvious political compliance with the NS program
clauses, the Halle Special Court assumed, with reservations, that the articles guaranteeing freedom of religion continued to be valid. Six weeks
later, the Hanseatic Special Court used these very NS program clauses
to legitimize the ban on the Bible Students. At the beginning of December 1934, after the preaching activity had been resumed (starting with
the mutual October 7, 1934, campaign), a considerable number of Bible
Students were arrested in Hamburg.[246] The legal authorities in Hamburg instructed public prosecutors who specialized in "offenses with political leanings" to institute court proceedings against a total of 170 Bible
Students. On February 21, 1935, even before the investigations had been
completed, the public prosecutor's office at the Hanseatic Special Court
brought charges against thirty local "functionaries" of the banned
IBSA.[247] The legal authorities apparently reasoned that an early judgment would have a long-lasting effect on the controversial administration of justice in "Bible Student matters."

The Watch Tower Society, which was in danger of being "prohibited throughout the German Reich," knew about the significance of
these proceedings. During the previous year, the Watch Tower Society
had been able to employ the services of Hamburg legal counsel Dr.
Walter Buchholz, an expert in his field, to represent its interests in court.
In a seventeen-page memo, Buchholz provided a detailed list of reasons
for the unlawfulness of the ban on the Bible Students: The February 28,
1933, decree could not be applied in this case because its stated purpose
was "the resistance of Communist state-endangering acts of violence,"
or similar political activities. The ban was unconstitutional because
Reich Constitution, article 137, which had not been repealed, protected
the "freedom of religious associations." Even in its wording the ban obviously had unsubstantiated and incorrectly worded statements. In addition, the ban did not directly prohibit the IBSA members from carrying
out their activities. If anything, the dissolution order was directed against
the legal entity of the religious association. Finally, even the legally

required publication of the ban had been neglected. The memo concluded: "The Bible Students do not possess any subversive characteristics. The activities viewed as subversive by the prosecution are in reality a religiously motivated natural response to an intentional destruction of faith and a prohibition of religious activities."[248]

On March 14 and 15, 1935, the public proceedings against the thirty members of the Hamburg Bible Student groups (those who were mainly responsible for the October 7 campaign of the previous year) took place at the Hanseatic Special Court. Those proceedings, however, could hardly be called a legal procedure in the true sense of the word. To the contrary, the judges performed the role they had been assigned by the Reich government—sentencing all defendants "in especially expedited proceedings, without a possibility of filing an appeal."[249] All motions for admission of evidence by the defense were denied as "nonessential." The judges indeed allowed the prosecution to use them as instruments. The following excerpts from the proceedings clearly demonstrate the methods used in court:

> Defendant A requested his Bible, which he would need to defend himself. The public prosecutor objected and asked for his request to be denied. Decided and pronounced: The motion of defendant A to use his Bible during the proceedings has been denied since, particularly in this case, it would undermine the authority of the special court.[250]

The defendants received prison sentences from between six months and one year. The explanations supporting the judgment indicated that they were not punished for any "actions" on their part but for their "subversive attitudes." To this end, the following statement was made with regard to the Bible Student teachings:

> They speak against patriotic devotion. Because of their pacifist attitude, they also discourage people, more or less openly, from performing military service. . . . According to the court, such an attitude is completely contrary to German honor, one of the most fundamental elements of National Socialist thinking. German patriotism is closely associated with heroism. Germans never accepted a position of servitude. The teachings of the Bible Students violate these fundamental truths.[251]

In summary, the special court stated that, "through their teachings and activities," the Bible Students endangered "the continued existence of the state" and violated "the sense of morality and ethics of the

German race."[252] Consequently, their viewpoints completely contradicted point 24 of the NSDAP party program.[253]

At the same time, the Hamburg judges "apparently considered the Earnest Bible Students as a religious association in the sense of article 137 of the Weimar Constitution." This did not mean that the ban was illegal because, at the time of the ban, article 137 of the constitution was "no longer in effect." Since the Hanseatic Special Court evidently declared the NSDAP party program to be the basis for current constitutional law and considered the former Reich Constitution "to be ineffective once and for all, beginning on March 5, 1933," any reference to article 137 of the Reich Constitution had become pointless.[254]

The court decision clearly demonstrated that NS judges were prepared to abandon any kind of commitment to legal norms and laws; just as the party program was declared to be the basis for the current constitution, "popular opinion . . . became the recognized tutor for all law in the Third Reich."[255]

With this decision, the Hanseatic Special Court took a firm stand in favor of the Bible Student ban, and at the same time, it tried to affect the controversy regarding a continuance of the Reich Constitution. The court decision supported the interpreters of an NS constitutional law who not only strongly opposed a continuation of the Reich Constitution but who also stated that it had plainly lost its significance in the Third Reich. In jurisprudential discussion, however, the opinion prevailed that the upheaval had outdated the Reich Constitution as a whole, but some of its regulations, such as basic laws, could certainly continue to be effective, as long as they did not conflict with NS principles. A small number of judges even supported the idea of allowing a parallel existence of new NS constitutional laws and certain laws of the Weimar Constitution, at least during the initial time frame.[256]

The higher authorities must have highly appreciated the Hamburg judges' reasoning, which made the IBSA bans irrefutable because of the de facto repeal of the constitutional articles guaranteeing freedom of religion. Excerpts of this court decision were published in the Reich administration gazette as well as in other journals.[257] The Reich Court also used this decision as a principal ruling on which to base the legality of the IBSA bans.[258]

The literature of Third Reich jurisprudence emphasized that "fortunately" the Hamburg judges "clearly" abandoned the considerations and conclusions made in the decision of the Darmstadt Special Court. To this end, it was anticipated "that the legal conception of the

Hanseatic Special Court would ultimately be recognized as the only acceptable application of law."[259]

The Dispute Regarding the Legacy of the Constitution

During the following period, quite a number of courts,[260] and by no means only special courts,[261] adopted the decision of those Hamburg judges. However, not all judges were willing to accept such obvious NS arguments. Frequently, instead of radically rejecting the Reich Constitution as a whole, these judges tried to preserve those parts of the constitution they considered worthy of upholding. They also tried to reach the same conclusions regarding the specific question of the Bible Student bans. For instance, at the end of April 1935, in its decision regarding the Prussian Bible Student ban, the Breslau Special Court explicitly contradicted the opinion of the Hanseatic Special Court, according to which the Weimar Constitution, as a whole, was no longer legally binding. The Breslau judges were not willing to accept such indiscriminate rejection; however, even they changed the Weimar Constitution to an arbitrary rule of convenience. They accepted as effective *only* those constitutional articles "that had not been quietly or openly replaced with articles contradicting the constitution or that did not directly contradict the spirit of the National Socialist movement."[262]

Although the Breslau Special Court agreed that Reich Constitution, article 137, should remain effective, following the opinion of the Darmstadt Special Court and the Reich Court, it considered the IBSA ban to be legally binding. In this regard, it called into question the status of the Bible Students Association as a religious association in the sense of those articles of the constitution. Basically, the court objected that the IBSA did not have a "specific statement of belief" that was a fundamental element of a religious association. To this end, the court referred to earlier statements on the part of the IBSA that it did not intend to form a "church." The court also referred to the fact that the IBSA based its religious beliefs exclusively on the Bible. In this regard, the Breslau judges stated: "Since all Christian associations base their religious beliefs on the Bible, it is not possible to consider the Bible as a specific statement of belief. Because of the difference in character of its various writings, the Bible requires interpretation to such an extent that it cannot, in itself, be considered as a specific statement of belief."

In this debate, the court described the IBSA as an organization that simply did not have the distinctive characteristics required for a religious association. Since the IBSA could be considered only as an association that was used for religious purposes, the Breslau judges stated that it could not refer to the constitutional rights reserved for religious associations. By describing the IBSA as an association that was used for religious purposes, the authorities had the opportunity to use the Decree of the Reich President to intervene, since the suspension of Reich Constitution, article 124, opened the way to place restrictions on the freedom of associations.

The IBSA was not, like other religious associations, equipped with the rights of a corporation under public law in any of the states of the German Reich.[263] According to constitutional law, however, a religious association is determined by its mutual practice of religious beliefs and not its legal concept and legal capacity. According to Reich Constitution, article 137, paragraph 4, religious associations under public law enjoyed the same legal standing as associations under civil, or private, law. This also included the IBSA, which was a membership association. If such associations constituted themselves as independent religious denominations, they could not be denied the protection of the constitutional articles guaranteeing freedom of religion.[264] From this point of view, even though the Breslau Special Court claimed to support a continuance of the articles guaranteeing freedom of religion, it actually deprived these articles of their very substance.

Some of the courts accepted the position of the Breslau Special Court and considered the IBSA to be a religious association in the sense of the—repealed—Reich Constitution, article 124.[265] Other courts solved the legal problems in radical ways by simply refusing to accept the legal effect of these constitutional articles. In the end, both opinions confirmed the IBSA bans. Then, in April 1935, a previously disregarded aspect entered the controversy. On April 3, 1935, the Schleswig-Holstein Special Court in Altona had acquitted six Jehovah's Witnesses from Elmshorn who, since October of the previous year, had come together on a weekly basis to conduct their study of the Bible and the *Watchtower*. According to the court, "the defendants had not committed any acts deserving punishment."[266] The court acknowledged that there was no doubt that the defendants came together on a regular basis to read and discuss the Bible Student publications. But when looking at the actual wording of the Prussian Bible Student ban, "the decree by the Prussian minister of the interior was directed against a specific entity, the membership association, and against a specific group of people, the legal members of the association."[267] Since the defendants did not belong to this group of legal members of the association but were merely a "group of people who came together because of their mutual religious beliefs," they did not feel that the ban on the "International Bible Students Association, German Branch, Inc." applied to them.

Legally, the debate centered around the fact that the June 24, 1933, ban by the Ministry of the Interior was not only based on the Decree of the Reich President but also on the Prussian Police Administrative Law.[268] Thus, the Altona Special Court made reference to a fact that had previously been disregarded: in order to direct a decree to an unspecified number of people, such as the adherents of the Bible Student teachings, "a legally binding police order" was required. Even though the June 24, 1933, Prussian ban on the Bible Students Association was a police decree in nature, it had not been published in the Prussian law collection as required according to Police Administrative Law, article 35. The police decree had also not been officially announced as required according to Police Administrative Law, article 32. According to the public prosecutor's criticism of the judgment, this meant that "a punishable offense can be committed only by those people to whom the police decree was directed, in this case, the twelve former legal members of the association."[269]

The senior public prosecutor was not willing to accept this decision. He considered it to be "incorrect and the explanations supporting the judgment to be an error in law." He therefore submitted the following detailed report about the court proceedings to the superior office: "From the situation itself, as well as from the second decree issued on September 28, 1933, it is obvious that the minister of the interior did not intend to ban merely the twelve legal members of the association. He wanted to prohibit all activity, in word and written form, of the Earnest Bible Students throughout Prussia."[270] To prevent further court decisions that would be "detrimental" to the reputation of the legal authorities, and "to avoid the pronouncement of further acquittals," the Altona public prosecutor's office withdrew all actions dealing "with the same matter" for the time being.

This court decision caused a great deal of concern among legal and police authorities. During the previous months, despite the continuing controversy about a continuance of the constitutional articles guaranteeing freedom of religion, it appeared that the question of legality of the IBSA bans had been resolved. Moreover, the Prussian Ministry of the Interior had made serious undeniable errors in the context of issuing the ban and thus provided the basis for the acquittals. As a result, the

Reich Ministry of Justice (RJM) instructed all Prussian senior public prosecutors "to avoid preferring charges and to cancel all scheduled court proceedings" until this issue had been settled.[271] An examination of the matter revealed that the RMdI had actually forgotten to publish the ban at that time.[272]

In the meantime, Dr. Geschke, chief of the Kiel State Police office, had strongly criticized the decision of the Altona judges. He informed Berlin that because of the "incomprehensible position of the Altona Special Court," it had to be expected that "the accused Bible Students would not be sentenced," which could, in turn, "result in" increasing Bible Student activities.[273] Also at the Ministry of Justice, the officials were shocked about the "formalistic" approach of the chief judge of the Altona Regional Court and the two legal counsels who had been appointed as his assistants during the special court proceedings. The head of the criminal department, Ministerialdirektor Dr. Wilhelm Crohne, published his criticism of the judgment in the *Deutsche Justiz* (a directive of German courts, public prosecutors' offices, penal institutions, and the Ministry of Justice). In his introduction, he gave a general description of objections that other courts had previously raised against the legality of the Bible Student bans. This included, for example, the question of whether the February 28, 1933, Decree of the Reich President could be applied to the IBSA ban and the issue of the significance of constitutional articles in the NS state. Crohne then addressed the concerns regarding the formal aspect of the IBSA ban. Without mentioning its name, he severely reprimanded the court: "First of all, the court should have answered the basic question of whether it is in agreement with our current opinion that judges pronounce acquittals on such formal grounds."[274] According to Crohne, the judges failed to contemplate whether formal requirements would also be taken into consideration "if it means that observing them would contradict the explicit will of the National Socialist leaders."

Crohne could not deny the formal errors made by the Prussian Ministry of the Interior. However, in view of the fact that the February 28, 1933, decree authorized the "resistance of opponents of the State," he considered these facts to be of secondary importance: "At least the highest state authority should not be requested to base their regulations on the formal requirements of the Prussian Police Administrative Law." Moreover, in the two years following the upheaval, the new legal concept of "State Police regulations" had been established, which did not correspond to any "traditional pattern of 'police regulations' or 'police decrees.'"[275] In his concluding remarks, Crohne reminded the judges of their (in his opinion) only obligation:

> All reservations against the validity of the ban on the International Bible Students are therefore invalid. In discharging their important and honorable assignment of protecting and supporting the continued existence of our people and our state, the courts have to appreciate that they cannot stumble on supposedly formal difficulties. They have to look for ways to discharge this serious assignment despite these apparent difficulties.

Crohne's criticism produced the anticipated results; as far as can be determined, the courts no longer questioned the legality of the IBSA ban.[276] But they also refused to handle cases involving this issue. On November 29, 1935, for example, the Dresden Higher Regional Court refused to accept responsibility for examining a sentence that had been passed on the charge of defiance of the Saxony Bible Student ban, if the ban was based on the February 28, 1933, Decree of the Reich President.[277] The court explained that decisions involving concern for the continuance of public law and order should be handled strictly by the executive authorities.

In view of the legal problems involving the IBSA bans in the various German states, the Dresden Regional Court had tried as early as March 18, 1935, to find "new ways to solve" the question of legality of these bans.[278] To solve once and for all the legal problems that were caused by the IBSA bans being based on the Decree of the Reich President, the Dresden Regional Court based the legality of the IBSA bans not on decrees issued by the various state authorities but on the September 13, 1934, decree issued by the RMdI.[279] Even though this decree actually had the objective of easing the restrictions, it included a statement according to which the Bible Students Association "continued to be prohibited" from preaching and assembling. This, in turn, provided the Dresden judges with a new basis for a legal justification of the Bible Student ban. Therefore, according to the judges, Reich Constitution, article 137, which had not been repealed by the February 28, 1933, decree of the Reich president, could no longer impede the ban. The September 13, 1934, decree of the RMdI had introduced "new constitutional law." Thus, with regard to the Bible Students, the fundamental right of freedom of religion had lost its validity. In addition, the decree of the RMdI, which had been elevated to the status of constitutional law, had been applied retroactively. Consequently, the court defied even the

Retroactive Prohibition Law (Rückwirkungsverbot), according to which an offense could be punished only according to the laws that were in effect at the time of the offense.

In support of this new interpretation of law, the Dresden Regional Court explained that the government was able to amend constitutional law by issuing "administrative orders and taking any kind of measures." In reality, this meant that the formal act of implementing laws was no longer of any significance in the NS state. To this end, a judgment included the statement that henceforth it was not important whether it was a law or merely a decree that was issued. To be legally effective, it was only important that it had the backing of the Führer.[280] This attitude totally abandoned the concept of law. Ultimately, any statement made by government officials of NS agencies could be used to amend the constitution. Certainly, the Dresden Regional Court had taken matters one step too far. Such a radical disruption with the basic principles of the "legal system" had the same effect even for the protagonists of NS legal thinking. Now they cautioned against a "complete confusion of the concepts of the new constitutional law."[281] The Dresden judges had already anticipated that "some of the more conservative lawyers would consider their opinion too audacious, if not even completely absurd."[282] But this unanimous negative response of both administration of justice as well as jurisprudence quickly put a stop to the "solution" the Dresden Regional Court had suggested.

Because of the confusion with regard to administration of justice in Bible Student proceedings, in September 1935 the Reich Court was requested to set a precedent. In its September 24, 1935, decision regarding the Baden IBSA ban, the Reich Court stated that the Decree of the Reich President could not be "applied completely indiscriminately."[283] It would not be appropriate to simply ignore that the decree had been "issued for the resistance of Communist state-endangering acts of violence, as was indicated in its preamble." According to the Reich Court, though, the decree also had the objective of resisting efforts to prepare the ground for "Communist state-endangering acts of violence, even if this was done unintentionally." The court considered it appropriate to base measures against the IBSA on the decree even if its range of application was restricted.

The legal counsels of the Reich Court carefully avoided making any statement regarding the question of whether the Reich Constitution (and consequently also the constitutional articles that had not been repealed by the February 28, 1933, decree), which, according to Reich

Constitution, article 48, could not even be repealed, were still in effect. For the conservative lawyers, this was a very critical legal question. The legal counsels explained that "even though basically" Constitution article 137 "was still in effect, with the *correct* interpretation, it would be possible to use it for the purpose of restricting the continuation and activities of a religious association by means of police actions, if these activities conflict with the order of the political system."[284] Then, in contrast to the Sixth Penal Division at the Reich Court and its January 23, 1934, decision, the First Penal Division determined that Reich Constitution, article 137, did not necessarily impede the imposition of a ban. It was not even important whether the IBSA was considered to be a "religious association" or an "association that was used for religious purposes." This leading decision signified that the highest German court had approved of the legality of the Bible Student bans.[285]

The September 24, 1935, decision of the First Penal Division gained acceptance and also determined future decisions regarding the IBSA bans. Only two weeks later, without giving any specific reasons, the Penal Division that had been overruled by this recent judgment agreed to this "legal conception."[286] But this did not end the controversy. On several other occasions, the Reich Court itself had to deal with the subject. For instance, in its March 1936 decision, the Leipzig Reich Court dismissed the formal objections against the Prussian Bible Student ban by disregarding the definition of the Police Administrative Law and explaining that the regulations of the highest state authorities can be viewed as being issued in an appropriate form "if they have been announced to the people concerned and have been explained in writing."[287] In this particular case, it was handled by means of notification of the people concerned and by means of publication in the daily newspapers.

In February 1939 the Reich Court abandoned even its last reservations and adopted the NS opinion that "the upheaval of 1933 had outdated the Reich Constitution as a whole."[288]

Thus, the constitutional barriers were eliminated, and the "will of the Führer" became the law. Freedom of religion and freedom of conscience in the Third Reich had long been a thing of the past. The results of judicial investigations in 1936 show the extent to which values had been reversed: "The IBSA ban does not repeal the right of freedom of religion. In reality, the ban brings out the inherent dignity of this 'majestic human right.'"[289]

PART 3

NONCONFORMIST BEHAVIOR AND STATE REPRESSION OF JEHOVAH'S WITNESSES

7

Intensification of the Conflict

The authorities not only took action against the Bible Students Association as a whole but took repressive measures also against individual
members of the association from the beginning. In all areas of public
life, the new state and its supporting party made demands that were incompatible with the religious convictions of Jehovah's Witnesses and
their obligation to follow unconditionally and without exception the instructions of the Bible.

The first open confrontations occurred on March 5, 1933, during
the Reichstag elections. Previously, elections had been noncompulsory.
Therefore, it was not difficult for Jehovah's Witnesses to refuse to vote,
in accordance with their religious conviction of maintaining neutrality
in political matters. However, the March 5, 1933, elections fundamentally changed the character of elections in Germany. The National Socialists were determined to achieve an absolute majority for their Reich
chancellor and Führer, who had been appointed five weeks earlier as
head of a coalition government. Therefore, SA troopers and members
of other party factions tried to coerce the people to vote for "List Number One" (NSDAP). Canvassers appeared at people's homes, requesting
their participation in the elections, and they were determined to bring
as many people as possible to the polling booths. Those who refused to
follow these requests were accused of not acknowledging the new state
and its Reich chancellor. In this way, opponents of the regime were
identified, even if those people did not consider themselves to be opponents. The National Socialists also considered the religiously based nonparticipation of Jehovah's Witnesses in the elections as evidence for
their supposed opposition to the Hitler state and, consequently, considered them to be untrustworthy.

Jehovah's Witnesses had completely different reasons for their nonparticipation. Their decision not to participate in the elections was

139

based entirely on religious considerations: "We do not go to the polls because we have already chosen Christ as our king, once and for all. We
will follow him wherever he goes. We fight for him and together with
him because we love, respect, and recognize him! Why would we have
to go to the polls?"[1]

The idea of voting for somebody other than Adolf Hitler, even if it
was for the King Christ Jesus, completely conflicted with the fundamental NS conception, whose ideology demanded total exclusivity. This in
itself presented a significant reason for the persecution of Jehovah's
Witnesses in the Third Reich.

Acts of terror against Jehovah's Witnesses began with the March 5,
1933, Reichstag elections, even though in the majority of cases, the oppression was still limited to psychological pressure. During the November
12, 1933, plebiscite regarding the withdrawal of the German Reich from
the League of Nations, which took place in the context of the Reichstag
elections, serious attacks against Jehovah's Witnesses occurred. Such attacks also took place at the subsequent staged elections of this one-party
state. SA officers raided the homes of Jehovah's Witnesses as well as the
homes of other people who did not participate in the elections for political reasons, insulting and threatening them. The SA officers then forced
people to go to the polls. Those who continued to refuse to vote exposed
themselves to the danger of serious mistreatment.

Even in NS Germany, de jure, there was no compulsory voting.[2]
However, de facto, voting was enforced without exception. It was useless
for Jehovah's Witnesses to refer to the law, according to which voting
was a matter of choice. The representatives of the Political Police considered voting to be a duty of all national comrades, even if there was
no legal basis. In a report of the Secret State Police office about the conduct of Jehovah's Witnesses during the November 12, 1933, plebiscite,
the following statement was made: "Former members of this sect who
had been requested by canvassers to go to the polls determinedly refused to fulfill their duty. They based this refusal on the fact that, according to their understanding, the Bible prohibited any participation in the
act of voting."[3] The Gestapo, however, considered this refusal to vote as
evidence for the fact "that the supposedly religious convictions of the
International Bible Students could simply not be harmonized . . . with
the civil duties in the National Socialist state."[4] In this regard, Reinhard
Heydrich, chief of the Bavarian Political Police, thought that the Bible
Students' nonparticipation in the November plebiscite was the result
of certain instructions they had received. Therefore, Heydrich even

suggested that their leading members should be placed in protective detention. In his December 27, 1933, interoffice decree, he stated that such behavior could "agitate the public and disrupt law and order."[5]

In some places, after the November plebiscite, Jehovah's Witnesses were exposed to public anger and the anger of the NS party. For example, SA troopers had Jehovah's Witnesses walk around with placards that stated, "We betrayed our fatherland because we did not vote."[6] In Oschatz, a small town in Saxony, a Bible Student had to drive through the streets on a horse-drawn cart for two-and-a-half hours. The cart was escorted by SA drummers who chanted: "Villains, betrayers of the Fatherland."[7] In Pölitz, just outside of Stettin, a billboard was placed in the market place for three weeks. On a traitor list, it stated the names of the local Bible Students who had not participated in the plebiscite.[8]

In other cases, the matter did not end with such harassment. A few days after the November plebiscite, strangers set fire to the Uhlmann farm, located outside of Schwäbisch-Gmünd, because the Uhlmanns had not followed repeated requests to participate in the plebiscite. Stables, barns, and a house were completely destroyed, depriving the family of their livelihood. During the preliminary investigations, Karl Uhlmann himself was accused of arson and was taken into pretrial detention. The accusation of insurance fraud was dropped only after it became evident that the farm was not insured. No further investigations were made, and the proceedings were dismissed.[9] An incident that occurred in Bochum on the day of the plebiscite had even more serious consequences. SA troopers forced Rudolf Nicolaus, a fifty-two-year-old disabled mineworker, from his home and took him to SA quarters, located at Johanniterstrasse 8. There he was beaten with rubber clubs. Rudolf Nicolaus, who suffered from occupational lung disease, never recovered from this abuse and died several months later.[10]

Similar incidents took place during the plebiscites and elections of the following years. Often, on Election Day eve, large groups of party followers would march to the houses and apartments of Jehovah's Witnesses. A Jehovah's Witness who lived in Leutenbach (district of Waiblingen) remembers such a crowd gathering in front of her house: "During the night following the election, a mob gathered in front of our house and chanted that we betrayers of the people should come out. But we simply stayed behind our locked doors and closed shutters and remained quiet, even though they were throwing stones against our shutters. Then they painted across the house wall: 'We betrayed our people and betrayed Germany!'"[11]

To the greatest extent possible, Jehovah's Witnesses tried to avoid any confrontations on Election Day.[12] Many left their homes early in the morning, stayed away from villages and towns during the day, and returned home only after dark, when the polling stations were closed. Others, especially those who had discontinued their preaching activity during the period of the ban, succumbed to the pressure and participated in the elections. However, according to reports, some of these invalidated their ballots with statements such as, "to choose you is an outrage" (Isa. 41:24). Some of Jehovah's Witnesses, even though only a very small minority, completely abandoned their position of resistance. They reasoned that participation in a vote, such as took place on April 10, 1938, on the annexation of Austria to Germany, did not really require a political decision that would conflict with the biblical principle of neutrality.

Jehovah's Witnesses were often the only ones in their neighborhood who did not go to the polls. Especially in small villages, this exposed them to serious coercion since their refusal to vote, in and of itself, could destroy the objective of the local party leaders to reach a 100 percent participation ratio. Especially in cases in which Jehovah's Witnesses had been integrated in the social environment for a long time and had already been accepted members of their communities during pre-NS periods, some people, even party members, tried to avoid possible confrontations. Such people suggested that Jehovah's Witnesses might participate in the elections pro forma, simply submitting an empty ballot and leaving the matter of the 100 percent participation ratio up to the local party leaders. Jehovah's Witnesses, who were determined to make a sincere declaration of their faith before God and the world, were not willing to accept tactics that would satisfy the religious convictions of Jehovah's Witnesses and at the same time produce the desired election results.

The authorities responsible for the persecution did not make any allowances for the refusal of Jehovah's Witnesses to vote. They viewed the refusal as a "political element," which emphasized the danger this religious group supposedly represented. For instance, on the August 19, 1934, plebiscite, when Hitler assumed the office of Reich presidency after Hindenburg's death, the Kassel State Police office reported that, "in various places, it was not possible to persuade the Bible Students to participate in the elections."[13] In later years, though, such euphemism gave way to more prosaic terms. In this regard, the 1938 annual situation report of the Reich Security Main Office (RSHA) of the Reich leader SS mentions that, among the seven hundred Bible Students who were taken into protective detention, several people "publicly refused to participate in the April 10, 1938, elections and were involved in acts of agitation against the Führer."[14]

Even more than the issue of voting, it was the refusal of Jehovah's Witnesses to give the Hitler salute that resulted in serious confrontations with the NS state. To attribute "Heil" (salvation) to a human being, which, according to the Bible knowledge of Jehovah's Witnesses, was exclusively reserved for God, affected a central question of Christian identity. For Jehovah's Witnesses, it was impossible to use the word Heil in reference to any person other than God. On the one hand, this belief was based on their solemn promise toward the one and only God to keep "your name . . . holy," as stated in the Lord's Prayer. On the other hand, it was based on the fact that Heil could be attributed only to the savior and redeemer mentioned in the book of Acts: "Only in him [Christ] is there salvation; for of all the names in the world given to men, this is the only one by which we can be saved."[15] The Hitler salute, however, ascribed this power of salvation to a human being. Consequently, Jehovah's Witnesses considered this salutation in acknowledgement of the Führer as an act of blasphemy and glorification of a human being, an act that the Bible prohibited. They viewed the phrase "Heil Hitler" not only as a political acknowledgement of the NS regime and an act of worshiping a human being but also considered the Hitler salute as an act of denying Christ.

The National Socialists were not at all willing to respect such religious reasoning, and they demanded that every national comrade must give the Hitler salute in the proper form. The National Socialists also considered the Hitler salute to be more than a mere formality, even more than a ritualization of the leadership principle (*Führerprinzip*). The Hitler salute had been deliberately introduced as a means of conscience control, an instrument of securing power. It reassured the followers of the regime while, at the same time, it often undermined the integrity of opponents.[16]

The uncompromising attitude of many Jehovah's Witnesses regarding the issue of the Hitler salute had serious consequences. Even as early as 1933, besides arbitrary mistreatment and provocations, the refusal to give the Hitler salute also resulted in arrests. During a ceremony in Hamburg, for example, a Bible Student refused to raise his arm for the Hitler salute. He was arrested by State Police officers and taken to the city hall, the Hamburg Gestapo quarters. There, when it became obvious that he was not going to give in, he was beaten.[17] During the initial period of the Third Reich, those arrested were usually released from police detention after several hours or a few days.[18] But from 1934/35 on, as the persecution of Jehovah's Witnesses increased, this practice also changed. At times Jehovah's Witnesses were even sent to concentration camps, merely based on a refusal to give the Hitler salute. A 1936 order for protective detention simply states: "His conduct considerably aggravated the public."[19] In 1937 the Gestapo arrested a couple at their wedding ceremony because they did not follow the request of the Görlitz registrar to give the Hitler salute.[20] In mid-1939 the Gestapo arrested a Jehovah's Witness who was a member of the Düsseldorf symphony orchestra. At the beginning of an opera performance, he had refused to return the Hitler salute to the concertmaster. As a result, he spent more than five years of imprisonment in the Sachsenhausen and Neuengamme concentration camps.[21]

Despite such consequences, it was not possible to deter the majority of Jehovah's Witnesses from following their religious convictions. For example, the commanding officer of the Moringen concentration camp for women stated in his March 7, 1935, review of a detention order (regarding Bible Student Rosina G.) that she had to be considered as incorrigible because she stated "that she would rather spend ten years in forced labor than attribute 'Heil' to the name of Hitler."[22]

In this ideological state, which demanded public confession of its principles and goals, there was no room for neutrality. Increasingly, the entire population was integrated into parties and mass organizations. A block warden system was established that monitored the people and tried to record any attitude that was not in agreement with the regime. Actions such as nonparticipation at NS events and processions, refusal to contribute to any of the numerous house and street collections, or refusal to display the swastika were monitored closely. These appointed, or self-appointed, overseers showed a special eagerness in the case of Jehovah's Witnesses because they openly demonstrated their position. Regardless of the consequences, they were not afraid to express freely their opinions. In Wewelsfleth, near Glückstadt, during the launching of a ship that was accompanied by the singing of the first stanza of the "Deutschlandlied" and the "Horst Wessel Song," a Bible Student buried his hands in his pockets instead of raising his arm for the Hitler salute, like the other workers.[23] When he was questioned about his behavior, he provocatively stated: " . . . you would probably not dare to sing the second [actually, the third] stanza, because it speaks of unity, justice and freedom."[24]

Just like the Hitler salute, Jehovah's Witnesses also considered the flag salute as an act of worship, and thus a form of pagan idolatry. They could not imagine bowing to an emblem of the state. Here, they referred to the example of the early Christians who refused to salute the image of Caesar, pointing to the fact that they did "not violate the law" with their actions.[25] However, for the legal authorities not even owning a swastika was sufficient evidence to prove an existing opposition against National Socialism, which could seriously affect the judgment in court proceedings.[26] In addition to being exposed to arbitrary acts of persecution and mistreatment (often in the context of specific provocations, such as situations in which Jehovah's Witnesses were rounded up by SA troopers and ordered to salute the flag that they carried along), Jehovah's Witnesses also suffered legal consequences.[27] For instance, toward the end of the 1930s a Bible Student from Knittelfeld (Steiermark) received a court order evicting her from her apartment because she had persistently refused to display the swastika from her window, which faced the street.[28]

If the legal authorities could find a plausible reason on which to base an accusation, even acts such as the refusal to give the Hitler salute could result in penal actions. For example, on November 21, 1940, the St. Pölten Special Court sentenced a Bible Student from Hofstaat (Lower Austria) to fifteen months of imprisonment because he had refused to contribute to the Winter Welfare organization (Winterhilfswerk). The court based its decision on the Law against Insidious Attacks since Leopold Höflinger had told the SA officers with the collection box: "No, I will not give anything that would contribute to the killing of people."[29] If there was no legal handle, the Gestapo settled matters in their own way. In the summer of 1940 the merchant Martin Heinel from Eickhorst (Westphalia) agreed to contribute to the Winter Welfare organization "if he could be certain that the money would not be used for the purchase of weapons." He was subsequently arrested and sent for almost five years to the concentration camps in Dachau, Buchenwald, and Natzweiler.[30]

By means of various methods, such as shopping with two bags, so as to have an excuse for not lifting their arm for the salutation, the Bible Students tried to protect themselves against police actions. Sometimes they would cover their mouth with a handkerchief if somebody on the street approached them with a collection box.[31] However, these methods were not able to protect them from all situations in which they had to take a stand. This was the case if Jehovah's Witnesses were questioned as to why they had not yet joined any of the mass organizations into which the National Socialists tried to organize all citizens. For Bible Students who had already refused to cooperate with such worldly organizations during the Weimar Republic, this presented another problem: the intended integration of the various groups of people into such organizations as the Hitler Youth (Hitler Jugend, HJ) or the German Labor Front (Deutsche Arbeitsfront) actually involved mandatory membership. However, these dedicated and baptized Jehovah's Witnesses were obligated to keep the Christian principle of neutrality; they did not even send their unbaptized children to the Hitler Youth. To this end, a certain Bible Student pamphlet states regarding the three reasons for this decision: (1) "The Hitler Youth is an organization that discusses and performs political actions," (2) "In the Hitler Youth organization the Hitler salute is required," and (3) "There are also pre-military exercises . . ."[32]

By far, the majority of Jehovah's Witnesses resisted the coercion to join and participate in organizations such as the NS Peoples' Welfare organization (NSV) or the Reich Federation for Air Raid Protection (Reichsluftschutzbund). The NSV, the NS Women's Association (NS-Frauenschaft), or other associations that were connected to the party did not demand compulsory membership.[33] Therefore, a refusal to join these associations did not immediately result in administrative measures; however, the National Socialists considered these refusals as unwillingness on the part of the Bible Students to renounce their "false teachings" and become an integral part of the people's community.

If Bible Students refused to accept positions as air-raid wardens, they could expect more serious consequences. The National Socialists considered the air-raid protection campaign as an important element in the militarization of the population. The 1935 air-raid protection guidelines (*Luftschutzleitfaden*) stated: "The air-raid protection is a useful service for the people's community. There is no exemption from this service."[34] In that same year, the Bavarian Political Police instructed its subordinate police offices "to report immediately any cases in which members of the 'International Association of Earnest Bible Students' refused to perform military service, air-raid protection service, NSV, etc."[35] Two years later, the central State Police office in Munich ordered that Bible Students who refused to follow the request of performing service in the Reich Federation for Air Raid Protection should be taken into protective detention.[36] After the beginning of the war, liability for such refusals was based on the Decree for the Protection of Military Strength (Wehrkraftschutzverordnung).[37] The ministerial commentary

to this decree especially emphasized that the term "anti-military attitude" also included the refusal "to fulfill air-raid protection duties."[38]

Besides protective detention or imprisonment in penal institutions,
such refusals could also result in other forms of punishment. In September 1936, for instance, the *Deutschland-Berichte*, a journal published on behalf of the exiled board members of the German SPD, reported about
two Bible Students who had been dismissed from a company in Silesia.
The Bible Students had refused to join the air-raid protection program
of the company: "This [refusal] was regarded as an act of subversion
and sabotage."[39]

Besides the principle of neutrality, the refusal of Jehovah's Witnesses to perform air-raid duties involved another area of their religious
beliefs: with regard to the issue of air-raid protection, they would put
their full trust in Jehovah God who was the only one able to protect mankind: "In the case of war, a Christian would not get involved with an air-
protection organization since such an organization is actually associated
with military institutions. In reality, such involvement would indicate
that the Christian expected this organization to bring salvation and
deliverance."[40]

The most serious problems involved the question of membership in
the German Labor Front (Deutsche Arbeitsfront, DAF), which had
been established as an "organization for the entire working class of the
German people."[41] Initially, the members of the DAF included former
members of the dissolved labor unions. Later, members of craftsmanship unions and industrial federations also joined the DAF. Soon, membership in the DAF became a requirement for employment, and some
businesses automatically registered all workers and employees as members. The membership fees were deducted from the wages. Even though
the German Labor Front was legally an independent association with
an analogous structure, it was associated with the political organization
of the NSDAP under the leadership of Dr. Robert Ley, the staff leader
of the NSDAP and later (from 1936 on) Reich association leader. Thus,
Jehovah's Witnesses also refused membership in the DAF because they
adhered to the principle of neutrality. Even a nominal membership
through their places of employment was out of the question. In a number of cases, such refusal to join the DAF resulted in dismissal, and without evidence of membership it was almost impossible to find other employment. Besides these occupational and social difficulties, refusal to
join the DAF could also cause other problems. For instance, on October
13, 1936, the Hamburg Gestapo arrested Bible Student Franz P. because

Table 2. Memberships of Hamburg Jehovah's Witnesses in NS associations

	Number	Percent
No membership	146	86.4
NSDAP	0	0.0
National Socialist Welfare organization	1	0.6
Reich Federation for Air-Raid Protection	2	1.2
German Worker's Front	20	11.8
Total	**169**	**100.0**

he responded to the request to join the DAF by submitting a statement that his refusal to join the DAF was based on his religious beliefs.[42] He was sent to a concentration camp for more than two years, from which he was not released until December 12, 1938.

Out of fear that the loss of their jobs would cause economic hardships for their families, some Jehovah's Witnesses were willing to join the DAF. Even though it bothered their consciences, a DAF membership represented the least objectionable concession to the NS state. Only a very small number of Bible Students joined party factions or other associations associated with the NSDAP,[43] such as the NSV, the NS Women's Association, or the NS war-victims welfare service (NS-Kriegsopferversorgung).[44] The number of Bible Students who joined the DAF was higher, even though generally speaking it was comparatively small. This can be demonstrated using data on Jehovah's Witnesses in Hamburg.[45] Information about membership in NS associations during the Third Reich is available for a total of 169 people (see table 2).

This considerably high degree of consistent refusal to conform to the requirements of the ideological NS state and the uncompromising attitude of many Jehovah's Witnesses were reason enough for the NS authorities to persecute them with such severity. (Other reasons for the severe persecution were the ideological rejection of the Bible Student teachings and the NS's response to the fact that the IBSA continued their activities even during the period of the ban.)

8

Instruments of Persecution

In their struggle against Jehovah's Witnesses, Gestapo and criminal courts used the "classical" means of eliminating actual or supposed opponents of the regime: concentration camps and prisons. Another instrument of persecution used by the NS regime was the destruction of Jehovah's Witnesses' economic basis of existence.[46]

Most obvious were the efforts to remove Jehovah's Witnesses from the civil service. Jehovah's Witnesses employed in post offices, railroad stations, and municipal or state administrations were dismissed, almost without exception. In most cases, their colleagues and superiors acknowledged them to be especially diligent workers, equipped with the "qualifications required for civil servants." Generally, they were considered to be industrious, honest, and obedient. Despite these facts, the NS authorities took severe actions against them. Usually, the dismissals were pronounced because of the refusal to give the Hitler salute or to take the oath required for civil servants.[47] In most cases, the legal basis for such dismissals was the Law for the Reestablishment of the Civil Service with Tenure (Gesetz zur Wiederherstellung des Berufsbeamtentums), which the National Socialists had established for the purpose of legalizing mass dismissals of opponents of the regime and Jewish citizens.

The first difficulty involved the compulsory order to give the Hitler salute. On July 20, 1933, the minister of the interior issued a decree for Prussia that during working hours and inside official buildings the Hitler salute had to be given by raising the right arm.[48] Consequently, the salute became mandatory for *all* officials in the civil service, and failure to give the Hitler salute was considered a violation of official duties. Even though the act of raising one's right arm had become the visible sign of subordination and conformity to the new political situation, a large number of Jehovah's Witnesses did not strictly refuse to perform this act. In their understanding, the act of silently raising one's arm in itself

149

did not specifically attribute to the Führer of the National Socialist movement the power of bringing Heil (salvation), a power that can be attributed only to God.

In addition to the salute decree, no instructions had been issued with regard to the manner in which the Hitler salute had to be given. Apparently, the leading administrative authorities could not reach an agreement regarding the question of "whether the words 'Heil Hitler' should accompany the Hitler salute under any circumstances."[49] On December 18, 1933, the Prussian minister of finance stated in behalf of the Prussian prime minister and the ministers of state of all other German states that it was "optional to say 'Heil Hitler,' or 'Heil,' or even nothing at all when raising one's arm for the Hitler salute. However, it is not appropriate to say anything else along with the Hitler salute."[50]

Legislatively, this regulation was effective until the beginning of 1935. (The heads of various administrative authorities had already previously given their own, in some cases very specific, instructions for their administrative districts.) On January 22, 1935, the Reich and Prussian minister of the interior withdrew this previous liberty in performing the Hitler salute and decreed "that, subsequently, during working hours and inside of official buildings and facilities, civil servants, employees of public authorities, and workers have to give the Hitler salute by raising their right arm. In cases of disability, they have to perform the salutation by raising their left arm. This act of raising their arm has to be accompanied by the clear statement, 'Heil Hitler.'"[51]

This reversal deprived Jehovah's Witnesses employed in the civil service of their last possibility in dealing with the salutation problem. Now, even those who had formerly performed the Hitler salute by silently raising their arm committed a disciplinary offense: the National Socialist state demanded the unmistakable recognition of its Führer.

Civil service managers confronted Jehovah's Witnesses with the alternative of giving the Hitler salute in the required form or being dismissed from their jobs. In several cases, these managers even requested Jehovah's Witnesses to submit a written statement explaining their position on the Hitler salute. At the end of 1934, at least in Magdeburg, a written statement circulated among the Bible Students that included information arguing against a compulsory giving of the Hitler salute. In its opening paragraph, it stated: "I would like to inform the municipal authority (civil service) that I will not give the Hitler salute, neither today nor in the future, regardless of whether inside or outside of the official buildings. For a true Christian it is inappropriate to render homage to a human being."[52]

The refusal of Jehovah's Witnesses to give the Hitler salute was, again, based on their religious beliefs. These same beliefs also prevented them from taking the official oath introduced on August 20, 1934, in the context of the Law Regarding the Swearing in of Civil Servants and Soldiers of the Wehrmacht (Gesetz über die Vereidigung der Beamten und der Soldaten der Wehrmacht). The oath had the following wording: "I swear: I shall be loyal and obedient to Adolf Hitler, the Führer of the German Reich and people, respect the laws, and fulfill my official duties conscientiously, so help me God."[53] Noncompliance also in this case resulted in dismissal. Article 57 of the relatively recent amendment of the Tenured Civil Servant Law (Berufsbeamtengesetz, BBG) clearly stated: "Anyone refusing to take the oath required for civil servants will be dismissed."[54]

In the majority of cases, the April 7, 1933, Law for the Re-establishment of the Civil Service with Tenure formed the legal basis for the dismissal of civil servants who were members of the Bible Students Association.[55] On June 11, 1934, with reference to this law, which was used as a legal basis for the politically based mass dismissals at the beginning of the Third Reich, the RMdI issued basic regulations for the purpose of applying this law to Jehovah's Witnesses. Hans Pfundtner, the secretary of state at the Ministry of the Interior, stated that even though the Bible Students were no "party book officials" and were also not involved in Communist activities, as mentioned in the law or its implementing regulations, their IBSA membership was a violation of official duties that required dismissal from the civil service:[56]

> The fact that the Bible Students accept former members of communist and Marxist parties and groups in their organization and, by means of their anti-state tendencies, encourage communism, even if unintentionally, does not mean that they can be considered as an "organization supporting communism," in terms of the BBG. On the other hand, the Bible Students certainly belong to the group of anti-state associations. If therefore a civil servant who is a member of the International Bible Students Association violates his official duties and his oath of allegiance, he deserves to be subjected to disciplinary proceedings with the objective of being dismissed, especially if he persistently refuses to give the Hitler salute. Such civil servants do not show that they would support the [German] state under all circumstances without reservations.[57]

Secretary of State Pfundtner instructed the governments of the various German states and the highest Reich authorities "to take the necessary steps." He also requested to be informed about "any disciplinary measures" that would be taken in this matter. As a result, in the various states, the appropriate examinations were instituted. On August 31, 1934, the Hildesheim district president issued a decree according to which all teachers of the *Volksschule* (a combination of elementary and secondary school) and *Mittelschule* (secondary school or high school) in his district had to sign a statement, within the following three weeks, confirming that they did not belong to the International Bible Students Association, or any of its subsidiary associations.[58] After a considerable number of workers and employees in administrative offices had already been dismissed from their places of employment as early as 1933 because they refused to give the Hitler salute and were members of the IBSA, this ministerial decree now resulted also in the dismissal of even more civil servants who belonged to the Bible Students Association.[59]

The people concerned tried to appeal these decisions. Quite a number of disciplinary proceedings took place at the Leipzig Reich Court of Disciplinary Hearings, which was used as an appellate court for the various subordinate Disciplinary Divisions. Reich senior judge Dr. Edwin Bumke stated in a discussion that took place at the RJM in June 1937 that "in almost every hearing, at least one or two Bible Students appeared in court."[60] Bumke summarized his impression of the accused with the following words: "It is always the same picture: an older civil servant who has never caused any problem. These people just accept their dismissal." Bumke generally viewed the Bible Students to be rather "naive" and knew of only one case in which the proceedings resulted in the fact that the person concerned abandoned his position and was now willing to take the oath in acknowledgement of the Führer.

In the opinion of the disciplinary judges, only people who subsequently agreed to submit to the requirements of the NS state without making concessions could remain in the civil service. This was the opinion on which they based their judgments against Jehovah's Witnesses. For instance, in the case of a post office official from Warmbrunn (Silesia) who had tenure since May 1, 1927, disciplinary proceedings were instituted based on the October 25, 1934, decree of the Reich postmaster general. As a result, in its December 21, 1934, decision, the Reich Disciplinary Division in Liegnitz ordered the dismissal of this official because he had refused to take "the new oath for officials in its requested form, despite repeated admonitions."[61] At the Disciplinary Division, the post office official referred to the fact that he had already fulfilled his duties as a civil servant by taking the oath when he entered postal service in 1922. Because of religious reasons, he stated that he was not able to take the oath in its current "religious form." The court, however, considered it "obvious" that, "because of its new political foundation," this state required a new stating of the oath since the civil servants had to fulfill their duties "under different circumstances." Therefore, by refusing to give the oath, the post office official placed himself "in deliberate opposition to the current state." According to the judges, even his statement of not being able to take the oath because of religious reasons made a difference in the matter. The judges considered the nonperformance of the oath to be evidence for his refusal to accept the "basic foundation of the new state: "The National Socialist state is based on the leadership principle and on allegiance to the Führer and his following. Therefore, by refusing to give his allegiance to the Führer, the accused is actually rejecting what the new state has to require from all national comrades and from its civil servants in particular."

Even though the Disciplinary Division acknowledged that the post office official "was a quiet and reliable civil servant who had always fulfilled his duties," it refused to grant the payment of his pension, even for a transitional period.[62] According to the court, a civil servant could not expect a "state and people whom he rejected to pay him a pension."

The Jehovah's Witness, who had expressly stated that he would give a written statement in lieu of oath, filed an appeal at the Reich Court. On May 6, 1935, the Reich Court confirmed the previous decision, since the Disciplinary Division in Liegnitz had rightly assessed that his refusal to take the oath was a "serious violation of his official duties." The Reich Court considered his religious reservations to be "individual concerns based on personal account." Such reservations, however, could not be taken into consideration since civil servants were obligated "to become an integral part of the community as a whole regardless of their personal considerations."[63] Only because of his exemplary conduct as a civil servant, his previous participation in military service, and in consideration of his three children, the Reich Court of Disciplinary Hearings changed the decision of the subordinate court to the extent that he was permitted to receive three-quarters of his pension for the following two years.

Six months later, in a similar case, the same court clearly understood the argument of a tax auditor of the Internal Revenue Service, stating that "his refusal to take the oath was based on religious reasons."[64] This assessment did not affect the court decision. To the contrary, the court upheld the August 27, 1934, dismissal of the tax auditor from the Tuttlingen tax office, because he had rejected several requests on that day to take the oath.

On February 22, 1935, a post office official in Hamburg was dismissed after forty-three years of service during which he had not given cause for any complaint. Also in this case, the Reich Court considered the dismissal lawful even though in August of the previous year, the post office official had taken the oath and had even raised his right arm for the salute.[65] Since his salutation was not accompanied by "Heil Hitler" because of his religious beliefs, the Leipzig Reich Court viewed his behavior to be a "serious violation of official duties."

A post office clerk, who had been an IBSA member since 1922, made concessions to the state's requirements even to the extent that he performed the salute by raising his arm and saying "Heil."[66] However, to the Reich Court, this statement gave no evidence that the post office clerk gave "recognition to the Führer." According to the judges, such recognition was one of the "most distinguished duties of a civil servant in the Third Reich." Since the refusal to give the Hitler salute in its required form inevitably "raised the suspicion" that the official did "not completely accept the basic requirements of the Third Reich," it was "impossible to leave him in the civil service."

The proceedings against a senior secretary at the Internal Revenue Service resulted in a different, rather exceptional, judgment. In its June 4, 1935, decision, the Reich Court stated that an IBSA membership *prior* to the period of the ban could not be considered to be a violation of official duties. Even during the period of the ban, the court did not view mere adherence to the religious convictions of the Bible Students in itself as a violation of official duties. A violation of official duties would occur only if a Bible Student manifested his convictions to the general public by means of certain actions or a failure to perform certain actions. Therefore, the explanations supporting the judgment stated that "under the prevailing circumstances, the accused did not violate his official duties by continuing to adhere to the teachings of the banned International Bible Students Association. He merely exercised his right to examine each secular law in the light of Bible teachings."[67]

By arguing that an adherence to a certain ideology did not justify a dismissal from the civil service, the Reich Court still maintained legal principles from the period prior to National Socialism. (The NS-minded judges, however, did not agree with this reasoning. In their opinion it was important to consider a person's personal convictions as well as his actual behavior to determine whether he had violated his official duties.) The Leipzig Reich Court, however, emphasized that an inappropriate giving of the Hitler salute, that of restricting the salutation to raising one's right arm of which the senior secretary had been accused, was actually a serious violation of official duties, just as a refusal to join the NSV and nonparticipation in special trade association events were serious violations of official duties. This was especially so here, since such refusals did not help to eliminate the suspicion that the person concerned was "generally opposed to the arrangements of the new state and the closely connected NSDAP." Since, however, during the proceedings, the senior secretary of the Internal Revenue Service promised to improve and to fulfill his assigned official duties—the wording of the judgment stated in this regard that the accused "adapted to the different circumstances and tried to become a National Socialist"—the Reich Court withdrew the decision of the subordinate court. By mentioning his "previous exemplary conduct in fulfilling his official duties," the court considered it sufficient to give a warning to the accused.

Only a very small number of court decisions ruled in favor of leaving civil servants in the civil service. In some cases the disciplinary judges (as well as judges from the majority of other law courts dealing with Bible Student issues) did use an area of discretion they enjoyed even in the NS state to allow mitigating circumstances. Such a decision was made in the case of a thirty-five-year-old post office official from Altona who had refused to join the Postschutz (works security and air-raid protection service of the Reich Post Administration along paramilitary lines).[68] As a result, on March 24, 1936, the Reich Post Administration instituted disciplinary proceedings against him, arguing that the post office official advocated the teachings of the International Bible Students and even promoted these at his place of employment." However, in its June 8, 1938, decision, the Schleswig Reich Disciplinary Division did not rule in favor of a dismissal. Instead, the court decided in favor of leaving him in the civil service. Consequently, on behalf of the Reich postmaster general, the office of chief public prosecutor filed an appeal against this decision. What is more, additional disciplinary proceedings were instituted "because, on March 29, 1936, M. did not fulfill his duty of voting." These efforts on the part of the Reich Post Administration also failed, and this despite the fact that the accused was held in Gestapo detention for one month during the period of the proceedings and other legal proceedings against him were in progress on the charge of defiance of the IBSA ban.[69] However, even though the post office official was denied any occupational advancement, at the end of November 1937, after eighteen months of suspension, the Altona Jehovah's Witness was able to resume work in his former delivery area.

Nevertheless, in most cases, the disciplinary judges in the NS state did not make allowances for Jehovah's Witnesses. To this end, they even requested evidence for "national reliability," in addition to the evidence of allegiance required by NS Civil Service Law (NS-Beamtenrecht). For example, in November 1936 the Prussian Higher Administrative Court confirmed the dismissal of a police officer who had been a Bible Student since 1931 because, in his statements, he demonstrated lack of interest in the objectives of the NS leadership.[70] Also in this case, the Higher Administrative Court did not consider the personal attitude of a person, in itself, to be a violation of official duties as long as it did not become apparent to the general public. According to the court, however, the lack of interest toward the affairs of the state displayed in this case had to be considered as "neglect contrary to duty." The police officer had intentionally neglected "to acquaint himself at least with the most important principles of the National Socialist state and the NSDAP." In support of their debate, the judges referred to a statement of the accused, in which, probably in response to questions he was asked in this regard, he stated: "I do not subscribe to a newspaper since I do not consider it necessary to concern myself with worldly affairs. I read the Bible on a daily basis. This is my spiritual food. I also do not concern myself with the affairs of this state and the National Socialist movement. I heard that compulsory military service had been introduced . . . I did not know that Mussolini had intentions of occupying Abyssinia. I also do not know what kind of government rules Austria, nor do I have any idea of whether this government has friendly relations with the German Reich."[71] According to the judges of the Higher Administrative Court, such "low level of knowledge" was incompatible with official duties.[72] Therefore, the Prussian Higher Administrative Court considered the dismissal of this civil servant from the civil service to be justified.

The same tendency was shown in a court decision that was made regarding a midwife who was employed in the civil service. In this case, in its December 4, 1936, decision, the Saxony Higher Administrative Court considered her dismissal lawful, even though the court acknowledged that previously the Bible Student had "not shown any hostility toward people and state."[73] According to the judges, though, the midwife also did not support people and state in any way. To the contrary, she even refused "without exception, to participate in any activities and events of the state." Her reservation, in this regard, gave reason for concern that she would actually not hesitate to take a stand against the German people and their leaders, "if she was confronted with a situation in which state measures conflicted with her beliefs about the 'Bible' or the 'commandments of Jehovah.'" Consequently, the Saxony Higher Administrative Court judges' opinions, based on a prediction of the midwife's future behavior, had a negative legal consequence. This is a perfect example demonstrating that even in the area of civil law, legal structures of National Socialist thinking were applied.

The judges did not criticize the performance of the midwife's occupational duties. The specific accusation was that she had principally refused any participation in elections and plebiscites for at least ten years. In this regard, the court stated (which emphasizes the characteristics of a politically oriented administration of justice) that, prior to the NS takeover, "such behavior was certainly acceptable." But "since 1933" circumstances had changed. The woman obviously did not understand "the meaning of the takeover and the necessity of taking a political stand." Instead, she demonstrated an "incorrigible attitude" and "stubbornly" adhered to her conceptions, "which, under certain circumstances, could result in a clear opposition to the current nationalist way of life." Under the circumstances, the court considered it imperative that the midwife be dismissed from the civil service.

Layoffs, Dismissals, and Occupational Prohibitions

Even in the private sector of the economy, Jehovah's Witnesses were dismissed for the same or similar reasons and were thus deprived of their livelihood. Protection against unfair dismissal applied to them, as well as to other "opponents of the state" only to a very limited extent. As early as April 1933 the legal right to object, which was guaranteed to labor unions in case of dismissals, was revoked if the dismissal was based on a "suspicion of anti-state attitude."[74] After the labor unions were dissolved and the German Labor Front (DAF) had been established, its officials insisted on the dismissals of the Bible Students in many cases. To this end, the letter of dismissal of a department store clearly states: "Because of your anti-state attitude, the German Labor Front requested us to submit to you a notice of dismissal. Under the prevailing circumstances, we are forced to follow this request. We inform you therefore of your instant dismissal."[75] Especially in cases of nonmembership in the DAF, its representatives were concerned that the Bible Students would "disturb the peace" in the company.[76] However, company owners did not always follow such requests for dismissal. In April 1936 the manager of a company in Chemnitz refused to submit to this coercion on the part of the DAF: "The manager explained that he would not be able to find another man for his warehouse who would be just as capable, knowing everything by heart. In response, the works council's representative stated that, because of this one man the company would not be able to display the sign of the German Labor Front: 'This whole company belongs to the Worker's Front.' However, not even this remark could persuade the manager to dismiss the Bible Student."[77]

In such cases, NS party members tried to exert pressure on the management of the companies from the outside. At the same time, they also tried within the companies to incite fellow employees against the Bible Students. In a Rhineland mining company, for example, signatures were collected for a statement indicating that the fellow workers no longer wanted to work with these "traitors of the German people." This resulted in the dismissal of the four Jehovah's Witnesses who were working in this mine.[78] In other cases, the majority of employees refused to take a position against their colleagues.[79] Even after dismissals were pronounced, there were expressions of solidarity. In a company in Silesia, for example, the employees collected money to bridge the period for which the two dismissed Bible Students were refused financial assistance.[80]

In the private sector of the economy, besides the refusal to join the DAF, dismissals could also be based on the refusal to give the Hitler salute or on refusals to respond to "company roll calls." On February 28, 1934, the Hamburg dockyard Blohm u. Voss dismissed two of the company's firemen who were Jehovah's Witnesses because they refused to raise their arm to give the Hitler salute when entering the company complex.[81] On a regular basis, Jehovah's Witnesses experienced difficulties in the context of ceremonies involving the "day of the national work" (*Tag der nationalen Arbeit*), which took place annually on May 1. Companies were requested to attend these ceremonies collectively. According to a labor court (*Arbeitsgericht*) decision, the failure to attend these ceremonies constituted a "serious violation of the duty to obey, required in the work contract."[82] Eventually, in 1936, the NS press requested that the Bible Students should be removed from all German companies.[83]

However, because of the increasing demand for employees such plans were not put into practice. In quite a few cases, the employers intervened on behalf of Jehovah's Witnesses who worked with them. These employers even hired Jehovah's Witnesses who had been dismissed from other companies. Moreover, they used them in areas where they would not so easily be discovered.[84] Such commitment on the part of the employers can be attributed primarily to the fact that they did not want to miss out on the work capacity of Jehovah's Witnesses who were known to be industrious and diligent workers. In some instances, though, employers even wanted to support those who were persecuted for their faith. The manager of a Weißenfels paper factory, while respecting their religious principles, employed a number of Jehovah's Witnesses who had been dismissed from their previous workplaces. Even the industrial magnate Robert Bosch protected a Bible Student who had been dismissed from the Heilbronn municipality on May 3, 1935. Four years later, this Bible Student was hired at the Bosch Company in the field of measuring technology. During his employment, he encountered difficulties because of his refusal to give the Hitler salute. And so to make things easier for the Bible Student, Bosch took him out of his company and gave him work at his private house.[85]

Many Jehovah's Witnesses who had been dismissed and had unsuccessfully looked for other work tried to become self-employed. But even in this area, they were subjected to a number of restrictions. In many cases, they were completely deprived of the opportunity to establish a new basis of existence. This is what happened in the case of the tax auditor mentioned earlier (see p. 153). In its October 29, 1935, decision, the Reich Court of Disciplinary Hearings had ruled his dismissal to be lawful.[86] On January 27, 1936, the Tuttlingen tax office informed him that he was not allowed to work as a tax consultant "because he was politically unreliable."[87] Another case involved the leader of the Hamburg IBSA youth group, a commercial employee, who was dismissed from his place of employment as early as 1933. Despite sincere efforts, he could not open a commercial business because he was not able to obtain a business license.[88] An electrician from Dresden was not even allowed to work after his dismissal as a rag-and-bone man. In this case, on January 9, 1937, the Leipzig trade office notified the man that "there is evidence indicating that you intend to use your business for anti-state purposes." With regard to the type of "evidence," the notice stated: "You do not show any interest in the affairs of the state and refuse to become a member of any of its associations. You even refuse to become a member of the DAF. . . . Because of these facts you have to be considered politically unreliable."[89]

The "legal basis" for such decisions was the July 3, 1934, Amendment to the Reich Industrial Code. The revision of article 57 of this amendment allowed for a refusal of a business license if there was evidence indicating that the applicant intended to use his business for anti-state purposes.[90] According to the January 28, 1936, decree by the Bavarian Political Police, such assumptions could generally be made with regard to the Bible Students:

> It has been repeatedly observed that, especially in the disguise of the itinerant trade, the Earnest Bible Students are spreading their ideas in spoken and written form. If such cases become known, it is extremely difficult to determine the culprits of such activities. Therefore, the respective authorities have been asked to reject applications from members of the Earnest Bible Students who request itinerant trade or business licenses.[91]

In some cases, even previously issued business licenses were withdrawn again.[92] On May 8, 1936, the Bavarian Administrative Court rejected the complaint of a Bible Student whose itinerant trade license had been confiscated. According to the court, the complainant "was deeply involved with the teachings of this association" and had refused "to submit a statement" confirming that she would no longer perform any activities of the sect of the Bible Students."[93] It could therefore be assumed that she would "use her itinerant trade for the purpose of disseminating her convictions among her customers and other countrymen." The court was unable to produce any evidence that the woman had actually used her itinerant trade for the purpose of influencing others. But the assumption of such activities was reason enough for the court to withdraw the license on the charge of suspicion of a "misuse for anti-state purposes."

In contrast to the Bavarian Administrative Court, the Prussian Higher Administrative Court did not see an immediate relationship between belonging to the group of Jehovah's Witnesses and commercial unreliability. In its January 16, 1936, decision, the court stated that such a presumption "required more evidence."[94] Six months later, the court confirmed this opinion by stating that punishment because of involvement in Bible Student activities did not necessarily justify the rejection of a trading license.[95] In its April 1938 decision, the Prussian Higher Administrative Court reminded the administrative authorities of their obligation to provide evidence: "According to the concept of the ban, it is not the religious beliefs that have to be considered but the associated outward manifestation of such beliefs. According to the principles of Administrative Court procedures, activities in defiance of the ban have to be substantiated by evidence."[96] The administrative authorities, however, considered merely a lack of interest in the affairs of the State and nonparticipation in elections to be "evidence for an outward manifestation of one's beliefs." Therefore, the argumentation of the Prussian Higher Administrative Court was only of sophistic value.

The authorities did not just refuse and withdraw trade licenses; they even withdrew operating licenses for businesses. For example, after not participating in the March 29, 1936, Reichstag elections, a businessman who was a member of the Bible Students received the following notice:

> By means of this notice, you are prohibited from producing and selling *Fleischsalat* [a meat salad] and mayonnaise. According to Article 20 of the July 13, 1923, Regulations of Trade Restrictions [Verordnung über Handelsbeschränkungen], you do not have the required political reliability for operating your business. Based on our investigations, you participated in activities of the prohibited International Bible Students Association as late as 1936.[97]

The businessman took legal action against this decision but without success. In its February 18, 1938, decision, the Saxony Higher Administrative Court declared the ruling by the administrative authorities to be lawful. According to the judges promoting the interests of the National Socialist state, based on the 1923 Regulations of Trade Restrictions, the term "reliability" referred not only to commercial reliability but also to political reliability.[98]

On May 12, 1941, the Bible Students Marie and Rolf Appel from Süderbrarup (Schleswig) were informed that they were not allowed to operate a printing business within Reich territory. At that time, Rolf Appel had served already two months in pretrial detention because of his refusal to perform military service at the Alt Moabit Wehrmacht Prison in Berlin. As a result, Marie Appel was forced to sell their printing business, far below market value, to the news agency Schleswiger Nachrichten.[99] Even farmers were deprived of their livelihood. In its January 4, 1939, decision, the *Landeserbhofgericht* (regional probate court) in Celle pronounced a Jehovah's Witness who had managed his own farm since 1907 to be "incapable of farming" because he had repeatedly refused to participate in the elections. In this regard, the court also referred to a prison sentence of nine months, which the farmer had received during the previous year because of his participation in IBSA activities.[100]

Not all were completely restricted from operating businesses; some received only partial restrictions. In 1935, after six months of imprisonment on the charge of his IBSA activities, a fifty-year-old master tailor was prohibited from training apprentices.[101] Often, self-employed

Jehovah's Witnesses also experienced economic losses because their businesses were boycotted.[102] This was the case with a Bible Student in Hamburg who had, together with her husband, a flourishing barbershop with four employees. This couple also actively supported the local IBSA group. She reports: "As early as 1933, the Nazis repeatedly boycotted our business. Consequently, our customers were afraid even to enter our shop, which resulted in loss of income. Until the second arrest of my husband, on December 15, 1936, we had a monthly deficit of approximately two hundred Reichsmark. Since both of us were repeatedly imprisoned and our shop continued to be boycotted, our business was eventually completely ruined.[103]

However, the consequences were not always that disastrous. The general public was rather reluctant to support the boycotts encouraged by the local National Socialist Women's Association and the SA. Therefore, in some cases, major losses could be avoided. In this regard, Bruno Knöller had the following recollections of events that took place at his parents' grocery store in Simmozheim, near Pforzheim:

> On the morning of Election Day, armed SA officials came to intimidate my parents. However, the elections were "free" and our parents had decided not to go. . . . Consequently, the party decided to boycott our grocery store: If the Knöllers do not go to the elections, we will boycott them. This usually lasted three or four weeks. In the end, however, the one or the other person started coming back by night. Before long, even some of the party members started coming back. Finally, people said: "Well, if you shop here, I might as well come back during the day." And so, things returned to normal, until the next election.[104]

Confiscation, Withdrawal of Pensions, and Pecuniary Losses

With reference to the July 14, 1933, Law on the Reversion of Property Inimical to Nation and State (Gesetz über die Einziehung volks- und staatsfeindlichen Vermögens), it was also possible to confiscate property belonging to the Bible Students.[105] Primarily, these confiscations concerned the property of the IBSA groups, such as proceeds from the distribution of books and booklets, as well as contributions.[106] In a number of cases, however, even private property of the Bible Students was confiscated. As a result, several Bible Students were prevented from continuing to work in their former occupation. This was the case if the State Police ordered the confiscation of cars, trucks, or motorcycles belonging to salesmen.[107] In a few cases, even bicycles were confiscated to restrict Jehovah's Witnesses in their freedom of movement.[108] Often, other measures were taken along with these confiscations. For instance, the State Police confiscated not only the motorbike of a salesman but also withdrew his driver's license "since it has to be assumed that this [license] is used for prohibited activities."[109] In the case of a professional truck driver, the Gestapo withdrew his driver's license, which resulted in the fact that the fifty-year-old man had to "use horse and cart."[110]

Such interferences into the private domain involved almost all areas of life of the Bible Students. On June 1, 1933, Reinhard Lemke, a Bible Student from Pölitz (Pomerania), received a letter from the local magistrate, informing him that his request for a piece of property for the purpose of building a home in a small suburban district had been approved. However, toward the end of 1933, the mayor of this town took steps to withdraw this approval, since Lemke had not participated in the November 12, 1933, plebiscite.[111] The mayor based his rejection of the magistrate's decision on the May 16, 1933, decree of the district president of Stettin. According to this decree, permission for obtaining such property was granted only to people whose political attitude indicated "that they would always be willing to support the National Socialist state."[112]

Lemke determinedly fought for his rights. He sent two letters to the Reich minister of the interior, "firmly objecting" to this measure, "which was completely unfounded."[113] At the same time—and probably not (only) for tactical reasons but rather based on his conviction, a conviction that he shared with the majority of Jehovah's Witnesses—he indicated that his nonparticipation in the elections did not "reflect any opposition against the state." His religious beliefs did not allow him to participate in any kind of political activity. For this very reason he had also "not been involved in political activities during the fourteen years of Marxist rule in the period following the war." To show his loyalty to his Lord and Savior, he had to adhere to these standards "under all circumstances."

Initially, it even seemed as if Lemke's complaints would produce results. On January 22, 1934, Hans Pfundtner, the secretary of state at the RmdI, requested the Prussian prime minister to see to it "that the measures taken against the petitioner because of his nonparticipation in the Reichstag elections and the November 12, 1933, plebiscite would be immediately revoked."[114] In the meantime, the mayor had sent an extensive report to the Prussian prime minister informing him about the state-endangering activities of this "malicious nonvoter," who supposedly had discussed his actions with other local Bible Students two days prior to the elections. Consequently, on April 10, 1934, the prime minister accepted the explanations of the mayor and rejected Lemke's complaint.

The authorities not only withdrew previously granted approvals. In some cases, they even evicted entire families of Jehovah's Witnesses from their homes. This happened to three families in Miesbach, a town in Upper Bavaria, in 1937.[115] In the spring of 1936 the local NSDAP district office requested that the Steppes should be evicted from their home. The NSDAP district office stated that Mr. Steppe's "anti-state activities for the prohibited sect of the Bible Students indicated that he was basically opposed to the ideas of the Führer."[116] The Miesbach municipality did not comply with this request at the time. Therefore, on April 23, 1937, the district homestead office of the DAF sent a formal request to the municipality stating that "all authorities concerned were in agreement" that the three Bible Student families "should be evicted from their homes, because of their conduct." Now, the Miesbach municipality took immediate action. Five days later, the three families were given notice that their leases had been terminated, requesting them to vacate their homes by June 1, 1937. In case of a refusal to comply with this request, they would be evicted. The homes were then given to "reliable members" of the people's community. The "district group leader of the German settler federation" received one of the homes.

In many cases, even the pensions of Jehovah's Witnesses were curtailed or completely withdrawn.[117] The Hamburg sailor Alfred Knegendorf who became permanently unable to work because of an occupational accident had his accident annuity withdrawn.[118] The Gestapo introduced this procedure after it discovered that Knegendorf, who had moved in the meantime to another country and against whom court proceedings were pending because of his Bible Student activities, still received his pension. On August 30, 1937, the Hamburg State Police office requested the Seamen's Accident Prevention and Insurance Association "to stop the payments of the pension for Knegendorf." The request was based on a memorandum that the Reich minister of the interior had sent to all insurance companies on July 2, 1937.[119] On April 27, 1938, the Reich and Prussian secretary of labor ordered that the payments of the accident annuity "will be suspended until further notice" because Alfred Knegendorf had become "involved in anti-state activities against Germany since January 30, 1933."[120]

Another case involved a railroad worker who was in line for retirement on November 1, 1934, and had been granted leave of absence until that date. When he refused to take the new oath of allegiance of the civil servants that was introduced on August 20, 1934, and which required acknowledgment of Hitler, his pension was withdrawn. During the disciplinary proceedings, he was sentenced to dismissal without temporary allowance.[121] The Reich Court of Disciplinary Hearings for civil servants (*Reichsdienststrafhof*, another court dealing with violations of official duties) even withdrew the pension from pensioners who retired before the "Law Regarding the Swearing in of Civil Servants" had been issued and, consequently, were no longer required to take the oath of allegiance in acknowledgement of Hitler. In one case, the court withdrew the pension because the pensioner had subscribed to the *Watchtower*.[122] A pensioner from Bad Lippspringe had his pension curtailed because he refused to return the Hitler salute.[123] In the case of a dismissed civil servant even the support payment that he had been granted upon dismissal was withdrawn because he had continued to participate in IBSA activities.[124]

However, at least in its November 29, 1939, decision, the Reich Labor Court (*Reichsarbeitsgericht*) did not follow the course of the Reich Court of Disciplinary Hearings. In this decision, the judges of the Reich Labor Court obligated the Reich Association of German Civil Servants, a professional organization associated with the NSDAP, to continue—as legal successor—paying the pension to a Bible Student who had been employed with the German Association of Civil Servants until 1933. Since this particular Bible Student had been sentenced to twenty-one months of imprisonment because of defiance against the Bible Student ban, his pension was withdrawn. The Reich Association of German Civil Servants had asserted that, as a subsidiary organization of the NSDAP, it could not be expected to make payments to a person who had been punished on the charge of anti-national and anti-state activities. However, contrary to the two subordinate courts, the Reich Labor Court stated that, in this case, the Reich Association of German Civil Servants had no right to refuse the payment of the pension since a participation in the prohibited Bible Student activities did not violate the "duty of allegiance" toward the association. The complainant had therefore the legal right to make the pecuniary claim based on the previous pension arrangement. This decision, which clearly distinguished itself from other judicial decisions, reflected the language of the normative state: "Those having been punished because of an offense against nation, State, and party are not outside of civil law."[125]

For Jehovah's Witnesses who had been dismissed or who had otherwise been deprived of their livelihoods, the search for other employment or source of income proved to be very difficult. What is more, the authorities went so far as severely restricting the support to which they were legally entitled. First of all, those dismissed were subjected to a waiting period of six weeks during which they did not receive any financial support. If they appeared at employment offices, they were accused, for instance, of being responsible for the loss of their employment because of their "stubborn attitude."[126] They were told that before they could request anything, they would have to join the DAF.[127] Some of them were even told that indeed there was work, but "this work is not available to you."[128] Others were rudely informed that "our party members are the first ones we take care of. But even then, it will be a long time before we will do anything for you."[129]

One Jehovah's Witness reported that the manager of an employment office gave him a one-hour lecture. Then the manager told him that he could give him neither a registration form nor grant him financial support. He should, instead, ask his God Jehovah to give him something to eat. The man, however, did not accept such treatment. With reference to the fact that it was not forbidden to refuse participation in the elections, on the charge of which he had been dismissed, and that he had therefore not committed an offense deserving punishment, the man insisted on his rights. Consequently, the employment office manager had him arrested by the Gestapo.[130] If Jehovah's Witnesses were given any work at all, they received only inferior jobs with low wages. Those who depended on social welfare assistance were used for compulsory duties. (In those areas, people had no objections to using the work capacity of Jehovah's Witnesses.) From 1936/37 on, the employment offices were generally instructed that the Bible Students, because of their refusal to give the Hitler salute, should be considered as nonplaceable labor. Therefore, they would also be denied any financial support.[131]

This arrangement had been made between the Ministry for Labor, the Ministry of the Interior, and the Gestapo. On February 2, 1936, the Reich and Prussian minister of the interior had ordered that members of the IBSA should not be granted recognition for unemployment support.[132] During the next year, Jehovah's Witnesses were generally denied unemployment support, to which, according to the Law of Employment Placement and Unemployment Insurance (Arbeitsvermittlungs-und Arbeitslosenversicherungsgesetz, AVAVG), they were legally entitled. In this regard, it is stated in the August 8, 1937, memo of the president of the employment office in the Rhineland:

According to the May 14, 1937, letter of the Reich and Prussian Minister of the Interior . . . which has been approved by the Reich and Prussian Minister for employment, the members of the "Earnest Bible Students" have to be considered as asocial. Consequently, they cannot be used in employment of labor. Therefore, they are basically also not entitled to receive unemployment support. For the same reason, they cannot even be considered as unemployed according to AVAVG, article 89a, because a person who is not available for employment of labor can also not be considered as unemployed. According to AVAVG, article 89a, any requests from members of the "Earnest Bible Students" to receive unemployment support will therefore have to be rejected with a right to objection.[133]

As a result, the managers of employment offices requested from the Gestapo the names of Jehovah's Witnesses in their districts, in order to exclude them from employment placement. In its February 7, 1938, memo, the Regensburg State Police office instructed the Upper Palatinate police authorities "to disclose" to the employment offices the names of Jehovah's Witnesses "for confidential official purposes." The State Police office admonished the police authorities to use discretion with regard to the disclosure of names: "I request that only those people will be included in the list whose previous activities clearly show that they are especially active Bible Students."[134]

For the carriers of welfare institutions, in most cases the municipalities, this development did not come at the right time. Instructions to refuse to give unemployment support to the Bible Students resulted in additional expenses for the municipalities, and in response to this dilemma, the Reichsführer SS gave the following instructions:

I do not deny that a refusal to grant unemployment support would initially put a special burden on the welfare institutions. On the other hand, the welfare institutions can reduce their expenses by curtailing the support to the legally required minimum payments on the charge of an anti-state attitude of the people requesting the support. However, from a political perspective, such minimum payments have to be made. These minimum payments are considerably lower than the funds that have to be raised to keep this military organization economically under control.[135]

Even the Reich and Prussian minister of the interior stated that the welfare institutions would probably not be able to avoid making these additional payments for reasons of state. But he also suggested that the welfare institutions could lower these expenses by exhausting "all possible means" provided by the regulations for social welfare assistance. In practical terms this meant that they should try to avoid, to the extent possible, making any support payments.[136]

While the welfare institutions and municipal administrations tried to minimize their expenditures, these administrative measures brought serious hardships on Jehovah's Witnesses. Only with the beginning of the war did the situation of Jehovah's Witnesses still living in "freedom" improve a little; because of the general labor shortage, the authorities withdrew the restrictions with regard to employment placement.

Summary

The measures taken by the authorities had the objective of exhausting the financial resources of the people concerned. As a result, they were confronted with the alternative of giving up their resistance and, consequently, their faith, or ultimately facing financial ruin. In most cases, those who were dismissed did not receive other employment. Finding employment in other occupations was almost impossible. In many cases, they were not allowed to start their own businesses. Itinerant trade licenses were no longer issued to Bible Students. They did not receive any unemployment support and were also not allowed to receive payments, to which they were legally entitled, from unemployment insurances. Therefore, Jehovah's Witnesses depended on the meager minimum allowances from the welfare institutions. If they had no savings, no items they could sell, or no relatives who were able and willing to support them, Jehovah's Witnesses were condemned to a life of extreme poverty.

After the war, the Watch Tower Bible and Tract Society tried to record the measures that were used in the Third Reich to destroy the economic livelihood of Jehovah's Witnesses. The incomplete records show the following results:

> During Hitler's rule, 1687 of them [Jehovah's Witnesses] had lost their jobs, 284 their businesses, 735 their homes and 457 were not allowed to carry on their trade. In 129 cases their property had been confiscated, 826 pensioners had been refused their pensions and 329 others suffered other personal loss.[137]

9

Escalating Persecution

The problems that Jehovah's Witnesses experienced in the ideological National Socialist state as a result of continuing to practice their religious beliefs were not just restricted to conflicts involving the requirements of the state and to material hardships. They also involved the very survival of their families, including difficulties for their children and the breakdown of marriages. Especially in religiously divided households, in which one of the partners was not a Jehovah's Witness and rejected the religious beliefs of the Bible Students, the IBSA activities caused serious conflicts. These conflicts involved the problem of accepting the high risk of persecution and the difficulties this persecution would bring for the whole family. Therefore, in many cases, party offices and administrative authorities, and even relatives, exerted pressure on these non-Witness partners to dissolve their marriages.[138] If the non-Witness partners succumbed to this coercion, such marriages were actually dissolved even if the Witness partner did not consent to the divorce.

The January 11, 1937, decision of the Rudolstadt Regional Court is of fundamental importance here. In these proceedings, the court granted a civil servant the right to divorce his wife, based on the German Civil Code, article 1568, because she had attended Bible Student meetings against his will. In this regard, the decision stated that "it is incompatible with the character of marriage in Germany if the wife of a civil servant, contrary to the wishes and convictions of her husband, adheres to political ideas that are in opposition to the state and to the National Socialist ideology. With such an attitude, she causes her husband unacceptable economic and emotional difficulties, completely undermines his position in public life, and causes him great distress."[139] By accepting the Bible Student teachings, "this woman has excluded herself from the people's community. Through her conduct, she has also become responsible for the serious marital breakdown." A wife who conducted herself in this way disrupted the unity of the marriage to such an extent that "her husband cannot be expected to continue the marriage." The party offices publicized this decision because it was considered, beyond this individual case, to be a policy-making decision with regard to marriages in NS Germany. According to an NSDAP public statement, this decision included "guidelines for every marriage of national comrades."[140]

Even the children of Jehovah's Witnesses were exposed to a number of difficulties. In NS Germany, not only were they affected by the repression directed against their parents but they often became objects of coercive measures by the state. These difficulties began soon after the National Socialist rise to power when the political changes affected daily life at school. In addition to the educational content and restructuring of the subject matter, the increasing orientation toward NS principles also involved external aspects of school education.[141] Foremost importance was attributed to the so-called community spirit. The main focus was no longer directed toward the "person as an individual." The objective of school education was rather an integration of the student into the people's community. Besides conveying knowledge and skills, the schools also imparted strict militaristic training. The students were "formed" into useful members of the "Führer state." Thus, education was transformed into "training" according to NS ideology.

Integration into the people's community, propagation of the superiority of the German race, or military training found their ways into the classroom not only by means of lectures from teachers and textbooks but also through specifically introduced actions, especially through politically symbolic rituals. The most obvious expression, and actually the basis of the NS cult, even in the schools, was the Hitler salute. To this end, the school authorities ordered that the Hitler salute had to be given at the beginning and end of the school day, as well as every time a different teacher entered the classroom.[142] To perform this ritual in the requested militaristic manner, the authorities issued the following instructions: "To guarantee the appropriate performance of the Hitler salute, it should be practiced during physical education."[143]

On July 1, 1933, the Hamburg school authorities decreed that every Monday morning before school a flag salute roll call should take place in the presence of all teachers and students to teach the youths "to take pride in their country."[144] During the hoisting of the swastika, the students were requested to sing the first stanza of the "Deutschlandlied" and the "Horst Wessel Song." At the beginning of 1934 this ceremony was restricted to the day before and after school vacations.[145] Additionally, a number of other celebrations were included in the school program. Annually, on specific days, elaborate school ceremonies took place. Such ceremonies were held, for instance, on the occasion of Hitler's birthday. Another ceremony involved the anniversary of the 1923 Hitler putsch that was celebrated in remembrance of "those who died for the cause" on that occasion. For these ceremonies, the school auditoriums were decorated with swastikas and Hitler portraits. A political program and speeches followed. In addition to attending the program and listening to the speeches, the students were expected to play an active part in those ceremonies. They were required to acknowledge the NS state and its Führer through various forms of proclamations (such as songs, mass recitations of poetry, pledges, the Hitler salute, and other forms of adulation).[146] Attendance at these school ceremonies was mandatory. The students were also required to participate in other activities, such as the numerous street and house collections for the Winter Welfare organization. Frequently, the students also had to listen to speeches by Hitler and other prominent NS politicians that the schools received on the radio.

For children raised according to Bible Student teachings, this ideologizing and ritualizing inevitably had to result in a conflict of interests. In their family environment, they were confronted with the requirement of observing divine commandments unconditionally. Now, they were exposed to a school system that demanded a public acknowledgment of worldly institutions. Many of the older students did not require the direct intervention of their parents to meet these challenges. They had been taught that salvation depended on their faithfulness to the commandments of the Bible. They were also admonished to avoid performing acts of idolatry. Therefore, they considered the NS rituals of conformity, which, at times, resembled religious ceremonies, to be acts of blasphemy and apostasy. Besides being solidly based in their religious beliefs, these older students followed the example of their parents in an effort to please them and get their approval. For the younger children, on the other hand, this conflict was difficult to understand, even though they could certainly feel it. They were caught in the crossfire between the school authorities and the authority of their parents. Nevertheless, by observing the difference between the reproach and beatings they received from their teachers and the loving care and protection they experienced at home, these children soon began to follow the examples of their older siblings.

The following reports clearly show the pressures to which the children of Jehovah's Witnesses were exposed at school on a daily basis. Helmut Knöller, who attended a business school in Stuttgart, made the following statement: "When the teacher entered the room, the students were required to stand up, greet with the words 'Heil Hitler' and raise their right hand. This I did not do. The teacher naturally directed his attention only to me and there were often scenes like: 'Knöller, come here! Why don't you greet with "Heil Hitler?"' 'It is against my conscience, sir.' 'What? You pig! Get away from me—you stink—farther away. Shame! A traitor!'"[147] Karl-Heinz Zietlow, born in 1922, had the following recollections of his school years in Hamburg: "I started the *Volksschule* in 1929. Everything went well until the proclamation of the 'Thousand-Year Reich,' when the daily ritual at school was no longer 'Good morning,' but 'Heil Hitler.' My father had impressed upon me not to raise my arm in school, and not to say 'Heil Hitler.' . . . Whenever my class teacher had the duty of supervision during breaks, and I walked passed him, saying 'Good morning,' he sent me back. I had to walk past him again and he watched me to see what I would say. If, also this time, I simply replied 'Good morning,' he started screaming at me. Sometimes he even hit me on my head."[148]

In many cases, the recollections indicate that teachers would try, time and again, to put the children of Jehovah's Witnesses to the test. Elise Kühnle, who attended school in a small Swabian village, reports that she was called to the principal's office specifically for the purpose of embarrassing her upon entry. If she entered the office without giving the Hitler salute, the teacher would have an outburst of anger. She states: "He was a big screamer. This was terrible. I was only seven years old at the time. And if a teacher screams at you like that . . ."[149] In many cases, the mistreatment was not restricted to verbal outbursts of anger. In such cases, the records include the following statements: "Despite repeated admonitions and punishments by the principal, the children Alfred and Friedrich . . . refused to give the Hitler salute and refused to sing patriotic songs."[150] At times, punishment included serious physical mistreatment.[151]

In addition to these problems, psychological pressure was exerted in the form of serious threats. This happened, for instance, in the case of a ten-year-old boy who refused to recite a poem in class that glorified the NS state. His mother stated that because of his refusal, the teacher ordered two classmates to lead the boy away "like a prisoner."[152] He was taken to the principal. Since the boy even refused to recite the poem before the principal, he threatened to beat his fingers "black and blue."

The principal then asked the boy whether he would also refuse military service, which the boy answered in the affirmative. Consequently, the principal instructed his class teacher to punish him "in the usual way." He also threatened the boy that if he did not change his attitude, he would never again see his father who, at that time, was serving a three-year prison sentence for being involved in IBSA activities. The boy who had been mistreated in this way was dismissed with the remark that the school authorities would now consider informing the police, so that he could immediately be sent to a reformatory.

In many cases, the teachers even instigated fellow students to take action against classmates who refused to give the Hitler salute. One particular case reported by Elise Kühnle about her sister's treatment stated: "The whole class went off on her. They surrounded her and beat her up. The teachers said, 'This is unbelievable. If the entire school is willing to say "Heil Hitler," these two children can certainly not be exempted!'"[153]

The feelings of hatred were further intensified by the fact that the children of Jehovah's Witnesses were almost always completely isolated.[154] Even outside of school, they had hardly any contacts with children of other religions. To be treated by their classmates as "oddballs" often hurt the Bible Student children more than the beatings of their teachers.

These sentiments are reflected in a contemporary report from 1937. Twelve-year-old Willi Seitz from Karlsruhe summarizes his school experiences in the following words: "It is almost impossible to describe what I had to endure until now. At school, my classmates would beat me. On field trips, provided I went, I had to walk alone. I was not even allowed to speak with classmates who liked me. In other words, I was hated and ridiculed and treated like the plague."[155]

Under these circumstances, school attendance became a continuous struggle, a never-ending humiliation. "With butterflies in our stomachs, the youngest of us went to school each day. The teachers demanded that we salute the flag, sing Nazi songs, and raise our arms while saying 'Heil Hitler.' Because we refused, we were made objects of derision."[156] Such situations could easily exceed the strength of the children. They realized that they could diminish the pressure if they agreed to give the Hitler salute. In contrast to the Jewish students, they certainly were able to change their precarious situation through actions on their own. When the teacher entered the classroom in the morning, they could avoid various problems by simply raising their arm and silently moving their lips. In this regard, the report by Horst Henschel helps us understand the inner turmoil these repeated challenges provoked in the children:

"When I refused to give the Hitler greeting, which was daily required at school, I would be struck, but I rejoiced to know, strengthened by my parents, that I had remained faithful. But there were times when either because of physical punishment or out of fear of the situation I would say 'Heil Hitler.' I remember how I would then go home, my eyes filled with tears, and how we would pray together to Jehovah and how I would once again take courage to resist the enemy's attacks the next time. Then the same thing would happen again."[157]

Ceremonies, flag salute roll calls, and parades were particular challenging for the children of Jehovah's Witnesses.[158] The NS slogan "With every ceremony we demonstrate our commitment" was a bad omen for the children.[159] Previously, it was the teacher who determined what he wanted to see, or overlook, in the classroom. Now that the celebrations took place in front of the entire panel of teachers and the school management, it affected even those children whose teachers were not devoted Nazis. The anticipation to be able to hide in the last rows or to be overlooked in the large crowd proved to be deceptive. On the contrary, what the "little Bible Students" would do was painstakingly monitored. "The occasion of Hitler's birthday always included that the flag was hoisted and patriotic songs were sung. All students had to be present. Then the principal walked through the rows until he found me."[160] If the student persisted in his refusal, he was called to the front. He was forced to stand beside the flagpole so that all students could see the "traitor."[161]

The Bible Students certainly did not seek an open confrontation with the NS cult from the outset. To the contrary, as far as possible, the children of Jehovah's Witnesses tried to avoid conflicts. The following report by Bruno Knöller, born in 1922, illustrates this point: "Finally, during one flag salute at school I was caught. The hoisting of the flag was considered to be a serious ceremony. All students had to line up and raise their arm for the flag salute. They also had to sing the national anthem and the 'Horst Wessel Song.' Several times, I had been able to avoid this ceremony. I would just leave or go to the bathroom. But somehow, this must have been observed. As a result, one of the teachers forced me to come out with him. Now, all the attention was on me. This resulted in a teachers' conference to which I was summoned and asked why I refused to salute the flag."[162] Bruno Knöller was well prepared for this situation. His family had often discussed the question of "why Jehovah's Witnesses do not salute the flag. We cannot salute the flag because, according to the Bible, this is an act of veneration of a lifeless piece of cloth, that is, it is idolatry. . . . This is simply part of our religious conviction. If we accept God as our ruler, we cannot, at the same time, bow down to the emblems of National Socialism. But even in this regard, our father admonished us to be cautious. If we were able to avoid a confrontation, we were told to do so. We followed his advice. However, at school, it was no longer possible to avoid those confrontations."[163]

Expulsions from the Schools

The conduct of these Bible Students also had consequences on an administrative level. As early as 1933, a number of children were expelled from the schools. In September 1933 a fourteen-year-old student was expelled from the Hamburg-Eilbeck *Oberrealschule* (secondary school) because he "refused to follow the order of the school management to give the Hitler salute."[164] His admission into another school also depended on his willingness to give the Hitler salute.

An expulsion from school almost always ended the prospect of further education. Only in exceptional cases was it possible to be accepted at another school. Often, the financial situation did not allow Bible Students to send their children to any of the private schools, which, at least during the initial period of the NS regime, were not completely under the control of the NSDAP.[165] In March 1935 the Reich Ministry of Education issued guidelines involving the "selection of students for secondary schools." Under point 4, 2, the guidelines state: "Students who, by means of their conduct inside and outside of school, repeatedly endanger the people's community and the state have to be expelled from school."[166] According to available reports, these students were sometimes even refused a final certificate.

Such compulsory termination of school education could result in a refusal to receive occupational training. In the case of Helmut Knöller, who was expelled from a business school in 1934, the principal instructed the DAF to inquire at his place of apprenticeship whether he was giving the Hitler salute. As a result, Knöller was expelled from his apprenticeship. However, Knöller's father was a former member of the SPD municipal council and, therefore, used to dealing with the authorities. He did not merely accept this situation but objected to these actions against his son and instituted legal proceedings at the labor court. He was supported by a defense attorney who had heard about the case and had offered to represent Knöller in court. But all his efforts remained unsuccessful: "[Helmut Knöller] has been completely denied the right to receive an apprenticeship, or a place of employment, in Germany. The decision states that he has excluded himself from the people's community by his own actions."[167]

These denunciations from teachers and relevant information provided by the school authorities resulted in the Gestapo learning of these refusals to give the Hitler salute at the schools. Consequently, the Secret State Police office sent a directive to its subordinate State Police offices. For this purpose, on August 8, 1934, the Gestapa made the following announcement: "Recently, in an increasing number of cases, situations involving the prohibited 'International Bible Students' have been observed. They have an especially high influence on the school children. In one case, a thirteen-year-old student refused to sing the 'Horst Wessel Song' and give the Hitler salute. He justified his refusal by stating that the Bible Students were an international organization and that he recognized only one leader, 'Jehovah.' The parents of this boy are devoted adherents of the Bible Student sect."[168] The State Police offices were requested to report, within a period of two weeks, any cases in their districts in which "members of the 'International Bible Students Association' are involved in anti-state activities, or in which they present a danger to the youth with regard to aspects of morality and national policy."

This memo reflects a general lack of knowledge about the Bible Students in the Gestapa, the highest Gestapo office of the German Reich: During the previous months, hundreds of such occurrences had taken place at the schools. Yet, this letter refers to merely one case—and not even a very spectacular one. The letter further indicates the IBSA did not restrict its influence only to members of its own religious denomination but intended to influence the "school children in general."

Based on information subsequently received by the Berlin State Police office, the officials responsible for dealing with sectarian affairs were finally able to realistically assess the situation. They came to realize that the refusal to give the Hitler salute in the schools was not primarily the result of a specific IBSA campaign but resulted from the instruction the children received in their homes. The source of the problem was considered to be that the children were caught between requests by their parents, on the one hand, and the school authorities, on the other. Principally, this was correct. An internal Gestapo memo stated: "The Bible Students try to corrupt even their children with their false teachings. Repeatedly, children refuse to give the Hitler salute, stating that 'our parents do not allow us to do so because the Bible prohibits such actions.' It is certainly not necessary to provide any further explanation to see the moral conflict in which these children find themselves if they are educated according to the National Socialist ideology at school and are taught international pro-Jewish slogans at home."[169]

At this point in time, the children were not yet the focus of attack by the Gestapo. This is also indicated by the March 21, 1936, protective detention order: "In an increasing number of cases involving the arrest of Bible Students, both parents are taken into protective detention at the same time. In the majority of these cases, the children become a burden to the social welfare services. Therefore, in order to protect these children from serious emotional and economic harm, I request that a simultaneous arrest of both parents should be avoided."[170]

The truthfulness of this statement, according to which "in the majority of cases, the children [had] become a burden to the social welfare services," can perhaps be called into question. According to reports from Jehovah's Witnesses, grandparents, other relatives, or fellow believers usually accepted the responsibility of supporting and caring for the children if both parents were arrested at the same time.[171] However, if the children had to be accommodated with relatives who did not belong to this religious denomination, serious problems often resulted.

Custody Withdrawals

By means of its protective detention order, the Gestapo formed a basis for leaving the children of Jehovah's Witnesses in the care of their parental homes and, at the same time, saving public funds. During that same period, however, other authorities started to separate the children from their families, an action that could be more precisely described as "state-controlled child robbery."[172] As a result, Jehovah's Witnesses were confronted with yet another form of persecution. For many of them, this form of persecution presented even greater hardships than the destruction of their economic life, surveillance by the Gestapo, or imprisonment. An increasing number of representatives of public authorities held the view that the state had to use compulsory measures if children, "because of parental influence, displayed a negative attitude toward the state and passively resisted all efforts to change this attitude."[173] The school authorities and youth welfare offices expected, by means of social welfare measures, to be able to reduce, if not even eliminate, the influence of the parents. Only then would it be possible to liberate the children from the ideas of the Bible Students and reclaim them again for the people's community.

In their actions against Jehovah's Witnesses, the authorities used the usual instruments of social welfare institutions and legal measures. At first, they made use of the Regulation of Protective Supervision (Anordnung zur Schutzaufsicht): According to the 1922 Youth Welfare Law, article 56, in cases of anticipated danger of minors, the youth welfare office could make use of protective supervision as a measure of prevention.[174] This regulation had the objective of supervising and supporting the educational work of the persons having child custody. In practical terms, this protective supervision was a surveillance of parental education on the part of the youth welfare offices or their social workers. At the same time, this regulation allowed also for an extensive social and political control.[175] However, during the NS period, the youth welfare offices did not restrict measures of protective supervision and public education to endangered children from broken homes. These measures were used as means of punishment for children who did not conform to, or even rejected, National Socialism.[176]

Jehovah's Witnesses generally resisted the efforts of youth welfare offices to subject their children to protective supervision.[177] If parents refused to give their approval, the youth welfare offices were able to file a request for an imposition of protective supervision at the guardianship court (*Vormundschaftsgericht*). If the youth welfare offices decided to take legal action, they not only thought of it as an imposition of protective supervision. In those cases, they also requested the withdrawal of custody and an order for guardianship by the youth welfare office. According to German Civil Code regulations, parents could be deprived of child custody, by means of a court order, if the "welfare of the child is endangered (BGB, article 1666)." Based on this regulation, the youth welfare offices stated that an education according to Bible Student teachings would expose the children to the danger of "spiritual and moral neglect." The guardianship courts based their administration of justice on this argument. Consequently, an orientation toward NS state objectives did not require new legal regulations with regard to family and juvenile law. It was also possible to interpret the current German Civil Code according to NS legal conceptions and achieve the desired results.

As far as can be determined, the first court decisions regarding child custody withdrawals for Bible Students were made in the spring of 1936. On March 12, 1936, by request of the Hamburg youth welfare office, the

Hamburg Municipal Court deprived the married couple Z——— of the custody of their children, including the power of representation. The court appointed the youth welfare office as guardian for the twelve- and thirteen-year-old sons. Consequently, the father filed an appeal against this decision. The appeal proceedings took place at the Hamburg Regional Court on June 5, 1936. Apparently, a great deal of significance was attributed to this court decision, because it was published in the legal press.[178]

During the regional court proceedings, the representative of the youth welfare office was the driving force behind the action. He insisted on upholding the custody withdrawal, referring to the evidence that had been collected in the meantime. To this end, he stated "that even at the orphanage, all efforts to persuade Alfred to give the Hitler salute had failed. Since the children already had such deep-rooted convictions, it was absolutely necessary to remove them from their parents to teach them to become useful members of the people's community."[179]

With reference to a statement by the previous court, the decision briefly mentions the reasoning of the parents: "During the regional court proceedings, the father explained that he taught his children the principles of the Holy Scriptures. For this reason, he cannot encourage his children to give the Hitler salute, since 'Heil' will only be brought about by God and not by humans. He did not answer the question of whether he is prejudiced against National Socialism."[180]

During the regional court proceedings, the father took a courageous stand. He described the custody withdrawal of his children as "kidnapping and persecution of Christians." The decision further states: "Regarding the question of whether he would be willing to raise his children according to the standards currently accepted in Germany, he responded that his children were taught by Jehovah God. He refused to give any further comments in this regard."[181]

The Hamburg judges were not at all impressed by the statements of this Jehovah's Witness. The regional court confirmed the decision of the previous court. Since the parents "are involved with the ideology of an international religious denomination" and refuse to educate their children "according to the ideology of the present state, the spiritual welfare of the children is most seriously endangered. For many years, these parents have exposed their children to strange ideas that prevent them from being integrated into the people's community of our present German state." Thus, the criterion for the custody withdrawal was clearly and exclusively the National Socialist concern for "integration into the ideology of the national state," not the alleged interest in the "welfare of the children." The *Hanseatische Rechts- und Gerichts-Zeitschrift* summarized the tenor of this decision with the following statement: "Parents have to be deprived of custody if they alienate their children from the National Socialist ideology by teaching them religious fanaticism."[182]

The youth welfare offices and school authorities were not the only authorities that instigated custody withdrawals, at times even non-Witness parents made such efforts. This is demonstrated by the following case, which also shows that youth welfare office caseworkers were able to use their authority in various ways.

At the beginning of February 1936 a father submitted a request at the Hamburg Guardianship Court according to which his former wife should be deprived of custody of his two children. She had received custody after the couple's divorce in 1931. The father based his request on the fact that his former wife did not educate the children according to the ideas of the Third Reich. As a result, the youth welfare office started to investigate matters. These investigations revealed that the mother was a member of the prohibited IBSA. Initially, the youth welfare office did not consider it necessary to order custody withdrawal, stating that, "in other respects, the woman had high moral and ethical standards. She took good care of her two children and had a very warm relationship with them."[183]

On March 10, 1936, based on the opinion of the youth welfare office, the guardianship court deferred the request of the father for the following six months. During this probationary period, the youth welfare office repeatedly examined whether the mother started to adopt a "more positive attitude toward the state." The thirty-one-year-old woman could not be discouraged from her course of action. She continued refusing to enroll her ten- and eleven-year-old boys in the Jungvolk (a National Socialist youth organization for children between the ages of ten and fourteen). Before long, the youth welfare office realized that their anticipation of "being able to have a favorable influence on the mother" proved to be mistaken. As a result, on September 18, 1936, protective supervision for the children was ordered. Six months later, instructions were given to withdraw custody. The municipal court stated that the mother was "completely partial toward the ideas of 'Jehovah's Witnesses.'" Since she persistently refused "to integrate her children into the Hitler Youth," the court was convinced "that it was in the best interest of the children to remove them from the custody of their mother."[184]

The municipal court decision also included the assessment by the youth welfare office regarding the respectability of the mother.[185] Therefore, this decision is a noteworthy document: The court particularly emphasized the fact that the mother faithfully cared for her children. At the same time, however, it states "that the mother is unqualified to educate her children according to the requirements of the present state."[186]

Quite frequently, the reasoning used by the judges of guardianship courts in Bible Student cases resulted in embarrassing situations. In general, they were confronted with family situations that were considered by the public as perfectly acceptable. It was therefore difficult to associate these situations with the commonly accepted picture of an environment that posed a danger to the well-being of a child. A guardianship court decision made on March 7, 1937, stated: "All youth welfare office caseworkers agree that . . . [the girl] is well behaved. Even from the school and the reformatory we received . . . only the most favorable reports."[187] But despite these facts, custody withdrawal was considered to be necessary since the NS state could not allow parents "who oppose the policy of the country in which they live to educate German children, not even if these children are their own."

Even though in a court decision from the second half of 1937, the judge speaks of "religious fanaticism" and "an abnormal disposition," he gives a particularly positive assessment about the personality of the child: "Apart from her refusal to give the Hitler salute, her behavior in school can only be described to be excellent. Her intellectual capacity is above average. With regard to her achievements, she is at the top of her class. In school, she distinguishes herself through her diligence, attentiveness, and perseverance. She has a creative mind and a special gift with regard to artistic activities. Even the outward appearance of the child is very pleasant. . . . The child shows a level of maturity that is far above average compared to other children her age."[188] He further states that in comparison to the 1920s, "the legal opinion had changed fundamentally." Therefore, it has to be taken into consideration that a child "who refuses to give outward recognition to the state, generally [must be] considered as neglected, despite her moral characteristics." It is certainly not difficult to notice that in these statements, the judge of the municipal court quite obviously got involved in a contradiction. His personal opinion and the actions he was supposed to take were poles apart.

During the middle of 1937 the Gestapo looked into the matter of official measures taken against the children of Jehovah's Witnesses. Previously, the local youth welfare offices were able to separate children from their parents only in isolated cases, but now the Berlin Secret State Police office was seeking a nationwide solution. By means of its June 21, 1937, interoffice decree, the subordinate State Police offices were requested to support these actions:

> To prevent the IBSA teachings from being distributed among our young people, it is necessary to remove the children of Bible Students from the influence of their parents. For this purpose, I request to obtain custody withdrawals, based on BGB, Article 1666, at the respective municipal courts, for IBSA members who endanger the welfare of their children by means of their prohibited activities and their adherence to IBSA teachings.[189]

To be specific, the Gestapa referred to a court decision made during the previous month:

> On May 4, 1937, based on BGB, article 1666, the Zwickau Municipal Court withdrew custody from a father whose son's welfare was endangered because he was educated according to the teachings of the Bible Students. On March 13, 1937, based on RJWG [Reich Youth Welfare Law], article 63, paragraph 1, clause 2, the court ordered corrective training for the boy, because these teachings were already influencing him. (Zwickau Municipal Court, reference no. 56 XII, S 226/36.) This decision has to be brought to the attention of the respective courts. Every case of custody withdrawal based on article 1666 must be reported, as well as corrective training ordered because of involvement in prohibited IBSA activities.

During the following weeks the Gestapo offices became quite busy. On July 2, 1937, the central State Police office in Munich gave the appropriate instructions for its districts.[190] Four days later, the central State Police office in Stuttgart instructed the district administrators to introduce the necessary steps, specifically emphasizing that "the local police offices should not be informed" about the decree.[191] However, Dr. Geschke, the chief of the Kiel State Police office, was not inclined to pay attention to the worries of his Württemberg colleagues. Apparently, he did not consider it necessary to keep the subordinate police offices uninformed about the obvious attempt on the part of the Gestapo to interfere with civil court jurisdiction. Therefore, in the administrative district of Schleswig, the decree was distributed also to the local police offices.[192]

As a result, the local police offices examined which of the Jehovah's Witnesses under surveillance had minor children, and to what extent these children were raised according to the Bible Student teachings. On July 30, 1937, the municipal police office in Eutin reported that Elfriede O., born in 1920, "was completely raised according to IBSA teachings." The report concludes with the statement: "To what extent it will be necessary to take actions against Elfriede O. cannot be determined at our office."[193]

Educational Requirements

The decision of the Zwickau Municipal Court to which the June 21, 1937, Gestapa interoffice decree referred is noteworthy in that it marks the next step in taking legal action against the Bible Students: it ordered the most serious means of coercion permitted by law. In addition to protective supervision and custody withdrawal, the authorities now ordered corrective training. According to Youth Welfare Law, article 62, "corrective training" has been provided as an ultimate public means of correction for the purpose of "preventing and eliminating neglect."[194]

At the Zwickau Regional Court, an appeal was filed against this Zwickau Municipal Court decision requesting corrective training. Since the decision of these appeal proceedings was recorded in the *Juristische Wochenschrift*, it is possible to provide more extensive information about the case mentioned in the Gestapa interoffice decree.

The Zwickau court had imposed "curative" corrective training for so-called restoration purposes on seventeen-year-old Herbert S. in order to "eliminate mental and moral neglect." The youth was considered to be "neglected" because he had accepted the teachings of Jehovah's Witnesses without reservation. According to the court, this attitude could only be attributed to the fact that his parents had "not given him the right direction in life." At home, he was "completely involved with the views of these 'Earnest Bible Students'":

> The mother and her circle of friends have blindly accepted these ideas to the extent that it does not even concern them if they come in conflict with the authorities. The mother adheres to principles of the "Earnest Bible Students," as, for instance, "we have to obey God rather than humans," even "if this involves ending up behind bars." One of Herbert S.'s stepbrothers was already punished because of his refusal to perform military service. This is a frequently observed result of the anti-state attitude of the Bible Students. Now, the mother has also raised her youngest son, Herbert, in this unrealistic and anti-state spirit. With reference to his

Bible knowledge and despite repeated admonitions and punishment, the boy stubbornly refuses to give the Hitler salute. Following the example of his older stepbrother, he is already now determined to refuse military and labor service. . . . Without a doubt, the boy has been formed by his environment as well as by the wrong and inadequate education of his mother. Since there is no basis to anticipate any improvement, it is absolutely necessary to protect him from this environment. Consequently, the requirements of article 63, paragraph 1, clause 2 of the RJWG for ordering corrective training for restoration purposes have been fulfilled.[195]

Beyond this individual case, which the court apparently considered to be especially suitable for ordering corrective training (it reflected the "radical" nature of the Bible Student teachings), it would first of all be important to examine the general legal argument. According to this decision, signs of neglect were already evident if a "developing situation was observed that was contrary to the generally-accepted objectives of education." (See RJugWohlfG, article 1, as well as the Dec. 1, 1936, Hitler Youth Law [Hitlerjugendgesetz].) Thus, the assumption was made again that the state's educational claim had priority over the parents' educational rights. What is more, with reference to the Hitler Youth Law, the NS principles of educating youth were elevated to the status of "generally accepted objectives of education."[196] Consequently, in every case in which parental education contradicted the objectives of the Hitler Youth Law, the authorities could impose compulsory educational measures.

With the December 1, 1936, promulgation of the Hitler Youth Law, the Hitler Youth organization, in cooperation with school and the parental home, was declared to be the responsible body for educating the German youth. To this end, article 2 of the Hitler Youth Law determined: "Aside from the parental home and school, the entire German youth must be educated in the Hitler Youth physically, mentally, and morally in the spirit of National Socialism to be equipped for service to the people and to become a part of the people's community."[197] At the same time, this law elevated the former party youth organization to a youth organization on state level. All children and youths between the ages of ten and eighteen were then, de facto, under obligation to join the Hitler Youth, even though the legal requirements for such "compulsory service of the youth" were not established until 1939.[198] However, as early as the end of 1936, coercive measures to join the Hitler Youth increased significantly. As a result, at the beginning of 1939, the time of the official introduction of compulsory youth service, 98 percent of ten- to eighteen-year-old youths had already been organized in the Hitler Youth.[199]

The refusal of Jehovah's Witnesses to enroll their children in the Hitler Youth increasingly became the focus of custody proceedings. According to the courts, in every case in which parents did not educate their children according to the principles of the NS state it was necessary to restrict the parents' educational rights, even though these rights were legally established in the German Civil Code.[200] Thus, by transferring the power of definition of all substantial questions of education to this ideological state, the legal authorities allowed the parents to occupy merely a subordinate educational role.[201] Ministerialrat (Ministerial Counsel) Dr. Rudolf Benze, head of the German Central Institute for Education and Instruction, summarizes the facts:

> All educational work within the family has to be recognized as part of the overall National Socialist education of the German people and is accountable to those to whom the German people have been entrusted, the NSDAP and the State. Generally, both [institutions] do not interfere with family education. They will do so, however, if parents violate their duties as educators and fellow countrymen and seriously endanger the political, social, and physical welfare of their children.[202]

Thus, Jehovah's Witnesses were not accused of inadequately caring for their children. The accusation involved their failure to fulfill their duties toward the state. The refusal to give the Hitler salute, to participate in flag salute roll calls, or, at least until 1939, nonmembership in the Hitler Youth, were not even offenses subject to prosecution. In Bible Student proceedings, the guardianship courts were rather judging an (negative) "attitude" or (oppositional) "disposition" toward the State. Consequently, these proceedings gave evidence of the extent to which NS legal thinking in the Third Reich was applied, even outside of penal jurisdiction.

On February 26, 1938, the Wilster (Schleswig-Holstein) Municipal Court withdrew custody from the married couple B., even though "according to statements by the teachers, . . . [their children] had not manifested an attitude of resistance at school. To the contrary, they [had] participated in the singing of patriotic songs and always given the Hitler salute." Consequently, there was no evidence of "neglect." But even in this case, the parents were found guilty of having violated their educational duties because they refused to enroll their children in the Hitler Youth. In this regard, the parents disregarded the regulation that, "aside from the parental home and school," the youth in the NS state "must be educated in the Hitler Youth organization." With reference to the Hitler Youth Law, the municipal court stated: "The objectives of National Socialist education can only be achieved if all three educational institutions cooperate according to plan. If the parents refuse to cooperate in working toward this educational goal, or try to impede or interfere with the education of the other two institutions, these institutions would be required to increase their influence on the youth."[203] However, because of the parents' refusal, the children could not be "supervised and educated by the Hitler Youth organization." As a result, they were completely subjected to the influence of their parents, especially during periods away from school. Consequently, there was "a substantial danger for the state to lose these children to the ideas of the IBSA." The court considered this to be a "serious mental endangerment for the children" which justified custody withdrawal, according to BGB, Article 1666.[204]

However, not all guardianship courts came to such conclusions in Bible Student cases. Even during the period of the war, there were individual cases in which the courts refused to order custody withdrawals. In 1938, the Calw Municipal Court was not willing to impose coercive measures on a thirteen-year-old boy who had refused to join the Hitler Youth.[205] In another case involving a thirteen-year-old girl, the court considered an order for corrective training to be "neither appropriate nor acceptable" since there was no "potential for success," which was required according to article 63 of the Youth Welfare Law.[206] According to the municipal court expert opinion, the girl had such strong inner convictions that it was unlikely that "corrective training would change her attitude."[207]

In 1937 the Schwäbisch-Gmünd Municipal Court also refused to order corrective training for the children of Bible Students. Since this case resulted in a leading decision, it is appropriate to discuss it in more detail. The court proceedings involved the farmer, Karl Uhlmann, and his wife, Christine, who had been baptized as Jehovah's Witnesses in 1932. They were confronted with custody withdrawal of their daughters Ida and Elise. The principal of the *Volksschule* in Alfdorf was responsible for instituting the proceedings because he was not willing to accept the fact that the girls persistently refused to give the Hitler salute. Even beatings could not persuade them to change their behavior. Consequently, on April 22, 1937, by way of the youth welfare office, an urgent request was submitted to the Schwäbisch Gmünd court for the imposition of temporary corrective training because there was "imminent danger," according to article 67 of the Youth Welfare Law.

Elise Kühnle, née Uhlmann, who was eight years old at the time, only vaguely remembers the court proceedings: "The judge of the municipal court, an older man, remained very neutral. He questioned us children—one at a time. Of course, I do not remember what he asked. However, he gave a favorable judgment about us. He wrote that there was no reason why we should be subjected to compulsory corrective training because we were well-behaved children. But the teachers did not leave us alone. They continued to harass us."[208]

Immediately, the youth welfare office filed an appeal against this decision of the municipal court. Consequently, the Ellwangen Regional Court withdrew the decision of the municipal court and ordered preventive corrective training. Then, Mr. Uhlmann intervened and immediately filed a subsequent appeal. As a result, the court of appeals temporarily suspended the imposition of "corrective training." Jehovah's Witnesses considered it to be a "God-given duty to educate their children to honor God's commandments, a responsibility, from which no political or public institution [could] release them."[209]

The December 3, 1937, appeal proceedings took place at the Munich Higher Regional Court. At first, the judges of the Eighth Division for civil matters examined whether there was any evidence of misuse of parental authority. It was confirmed that the parents had neglected their custodial rights. This neglect was apparent in the parents' adherence to Bible Student teachings, because these teachings were "extremely demoralizing to the German people and presented a danger to the state." In this regard, the court provided the following details:

> In consideration of these facts, the mental (moral) welfare of a German child would be undoubtedly in serious danger if the child were raised according to the views of the Earnest Bible Students. Education according to these principles will result in the fact that the child is alienated from his home country and his people. It will also incline the child to disrespect and disobey official orders and measures. This will make the child incapable of becoming a useful member of the people's community, and of fulfilling its duties toward the state and the community. . . . Education that brings an immature and unbiased child into conflict with the state and the people's community by means of anti-state

teachings would seriously endanger the child's future development and welfare. If a person having educational rights takes his responsibility seriously, he has to realize that such education so obviously infringes upon common sense and public order that he cannot overlook these facts, despite his religious reservations. If this person persists in his wrong course of action despite admonishment and instruction, it has to be assumed that he acts contrary to all reason and is guilty of misusing his parental authority. Such a parent cannot even dispel his guiltiness by referring to his religious convictions. The question is not whether the parents are allowed to adhere to any religiously perceived teachings. What needs to be considered is the question of what educational duties parents have toward their minor children, and whether these duties are carried out in the best interest of their children. . . . Children whose education shows the above-mentioned results are considerably deprived of the moral characteristics that can be observed in children who, in otherwise similar circumstances, benefit from an appropriate education. Therefore, such children must be considered to be morally neglected. Based on these principles, and in consideration of the facts that the regional court considers as proven, it can be assumed . . . that both children are exposed to the danger of being morally neglected in their parental home.[210]

The appeal was dismissed on principle since the regional court could "assume, without infringement of a right, that in order to prevent the anticipated neglect, both children had to be removed from their parental home and accommodated elsewhere." The only objection to the decision was the question of whether the removal of the children required an official order for preventive corrective training.

So much for the legal considerations of the higher regional court. They are consistent and, in this respect, differ from various other court decisions. However, how exactly did the lack of moral characteristics manifest itself? How was the alleged neglect shown in the conduct of the children? These questions can be answered by considering the further explanations of the court because, in addition to the question of law, the judges also made an extensive statement regarding the point of fact. With regard to the conduct of the children at school, they stated the following:

Accordingly, the two children did not attend the celebrations of the Day of the National Work but were absent without valid excuse, even though all students were required to participate in the celebrations. Furthermore, for quite some time they also refuse to give the Hitler salute at school by referring to a Bible text, according to Bible Student practice. Ida gave a clear negative answer to the teacher's question of whether she would support the Führer. Elise repeatedly refused to sing the "Horst Wessel Song." She also refused to draw a picture of the swastika during art lessons. The children did not respond to admonition and punishment.[211]

Several legal journals reported on this higher regional court decision.[212] The journal *Kriminalistik*, published by Reinhard Heydrich, chief of the Security Police, emphasized the "general importance" of this decision.[213] Because of its "fundamental importance," the Reich minister of the interior had an excerpt of the decision published even in the daily press.[214]

The higher regional court requested the regional court to examine the question of whether in this case it was possible, instead of putting the children in corrective training, to place them elsewhere, without using public funds. As a result, after repeated court proceedings, there were no further legal obstacles preventing the children from being removed from their parental home. On May 5, 1938, Ida and Elise were taken away from their home.[215] At first, the youth welfare office placed the two children into the care of two farmers' families. There, the girls did not only suffer the grief of separation and homesickness; they were also confronted with additional pressure. In this regard, Elise Kühnle reports that the "foster parents" with whom she was placed were "very fanatical Nazis." "It was a most difficult time for me. Every evening, the woman gave me a lecture about Hitler. She was totally absorbed in her duty. She was determined to persuade me to say 'Heil Hitler.' She felt obligated to do this." At the local school, Elise was confronted with a similar situation. The teachers tried by all possible means to force her to change her behavior. Because of her stubbornness, she was made to do extra work every day. This situation became completely unbearable for the nine-year-old girl. After a period of about six weeks, Elise ran away, first walking to her aunt's home some ten miles (approximately fifteen kilometers) away. From there, she returned to her parents. Her sister also escaped from the care of her "foster parents." She took a bicycle to get home to her parents' house. "We knew, of course, that this would not work."

Soon, the children were picked up again. This time they were sent to a children's home near Crailsheim, primarily used to accommodate "difficult children." In this regard, Elise Kühnle reports: "The principal was not ill disposed toward us. About every six to eight weeks, he asked us into his office to give us a lecture on National Socialism. He even told us that we would have the potential to become good National Socialists. We were the kind of children the Führer was looking for. If only we would agree to say 'Heil Hitler.'" The children's home was a Protestant institution, which also included a church. Elise's recollections of the pastor were quite distinct from her other impressions: "But the pastor there was a very nice man. He was particularly well disposed toward us. He told my mother that he did not feel sorry for us. To the contrary, he really admired our steadfastness. He even came and took special interest in me. . . . He did not put us under pressure. Quite to the contrary, he offered us protection."

In January 1942 Elise was released from the children's home. Retrospectively, she states about her three and a half years in the home: "Fortunately, children forget. We were in a group with many other children and had our daily routine. The teachers treated us better than these other children, because we were not difficult to educate. Therefore, they did not have a lot of problems with us. It was not too difficult to deal with the situation. But our mother, who was at home and had to manage the entire farm on her own, and our father, who was in the concentration camp, constantly dealing with loneliness, for them the situation was extremely difficult."[216]

Decisions such as the previously described Munich Higher Regional Court decision clearly outlined the kind of administration of justice the subordinate courts were expected to use in Bible Student cases. Thus, the legal stage had been set for extensive child abduction. In this way, the NS authorities had found a most effective way to take legal action against a minority group in its entirety, which, unlike the Jews and the Sinti and the Roma, did not come under a statutory exemption: After 1937/38, anyone who was still involved in Bible Student activities not only faced the possibility of being legally prosecuted and imprisoned, or being sent to a concentration camp by the State Police authorities, but was also confronted with the possibility of being deprived of his or her children.

Subsequently, the municipal courts were able to substantiate custody withdrawals with only a few sentences. To this end, they used the following standardized document:

- The parents adhere to Bible Student teachings that deny all governmental authority.
- By educating their children in accordance with these teachings, the parents bring them into serious conflicts with the people's

community and, consequently, endanger the welfare of their children.

- Therefore, according to BGB, article 1666, it has become necessary to withdraw custody and order foster care for the children.[217]

In the Third Reich, custody withdrawals were pronounced also against other opponents of the regime, even though these cases were not handled as routinely as the cases against Jehovah's Witnesses: "Bible Student was equal to endangering a child's welfare." In its 1935 decision, the Berlin-Lichterfelde Municipal Court stated that "Communist and atheist education" could be a reason on which to base a custody withdrawal. In this case, it was actually the *lack* of religious education that served as evidence for the violation of the parents' educational responsibilities: "According to his [the father's] own statements, he is a nonconformist and refuses to have his child baptized or religiously educated. This, however, is a serious violation of his educational duty. It is a generally accepted principle that a parent is not entitled to leave his children without any religious instruction and education. . . . Such a parent who, contrary to German viewpoints, refuses to provide religious education for his children and raises them according to atheist ideas neglects his child and endangers his moral development."[218]

In another case, the guardianship court proceedings involved a woman who was considered "unworthy" of educating her children because of her "extramarital relationship with a Jew."[219] Other court proceedings were instituted against a mother who wanted her children to be educated in a Catholic monastery.[220]

There are no records indicating that these decisions resulted in general actions against groups of opponents in their entirety, as, for instance, against Communists, the Social Democrats, the "Katholische Aktion," or the "Bekennende Kirche." In the case of the relatively small group of Bible Students, custody withdrawals were a significant instrument in the arsenal of oppressive measures. According to investigations by the Watch Tower Bible and Tract Society, there were "860 known cases of children being taken from their parents," and this number may be considerably higher.[221]

Means of Exerting Pressure and Controlled Administration of Justice

Kidnapping was used as a means of exerting pressure to break the resistance of Jehovah's Witnesses. In quite a few cases, the threat of custody withdrawal proved to be an extremely effective method. Even those Jehovah's Witnesses who continued their IBSA activities despite repeated imprisonment yielded to this pressure. Out of concern for their children and to be able to keep their family together, they completely discontinued their activities, or at least made concessions with regard to their children. In such cases, the reports include statements, such as: "We were threatened that our youngest daughter would be taken away if she did not join the B.D.M. So we had no choice. She rarely ever went. But, in this way, she could stay with us."[222]

On the other hand, there were also cases in which children who had been subjected to corrective training were returned to their parents if they were able to convince the authorities that they had separated from the Bible Students Association. In 1940 a Jehovah's Witness was released from prison after he had signed a declaration renouncing his faith at the Wolfenbüttel prison. Subsequently, he no longer participated in Bible Student activities. As a result, after a certain period of time, his child was returned to him.[223]

Often such efforts to exert pressure were ineffective, as in the case of Rolf Appel, the printer from Süderbrarup in Schleswig (see p. 161). On March 3, 1941, Appel had received his draft notice for the German Wehrmacht. Appel did not comply with the draft but sent a written statement to the respective military unit in Lübeck, where he was supposed to begin his duties, informing them that his religious beliefs did not allow him to perform military service. A few days later, the military police appeared in the small Schleswig-Holstein village and arrested Rolf Appel. They brought him to Lübeck where, according to his wife, "a high-ranking officer had an extensive fatherly talk with him and asked him, first of all, to put on the uniform."[224] On June 30, 1941, Appel's wife received an order from the mayor requesting her to bring her four children to the local authorities on July 3, 1941, at ten o'clock.[225]

With the support of police officers, the children, aged nine, ten, fourteen, and fifteen, were sent to two different reformatories. At the same time, Marie Appel was forbidden to continue the family's business; she was forced to sell their small printing business and their home, far below value. Even the family car was confiscated.

In the meantime, at the order of the Berlin Reich Military Court (*Kriegsgericht*), Rolf Appel was held in pretrial detention. There, he was regularly informed about any official measures taken against his family. Marie Appel, who was allowed to visit her husband a few times at the prison in Berlin, concluded: "They hoped that this would soften him up. He was accused of being dishonest and unscrupulous in having left his family in the lurch."[226]

Not even the measures taken against his family were able to change Rolf Appel's mind. As a result, on August 29, 1941, the Reich Military Court sentenced the thirty-nine-year-old to death "on the charge of demoralizing the armed forces (conscientious objection)." Six weeks later, he was executed at the Brandenburg-Görden penitentiary.[227]

At least once, the question of legality of the guardianship court proceedings against Jehovah's Witnesses was also discussed at the RJM. The topic was included in the third issue of the *Richterbriefe* (law letters), published in December 1942. Since October 1942, these *Richterbriefe* were published by the RJM for the purpose of providing direction for the judiciary and giving instructions to the legal authorities.[228]

In August 1942 Otto Georg Thierack became the new RJM. Immediately, he tried by all possible means to get the "judicial crisis" under control, which resulted from Hitler's April 26, 1942, Reichstag speech. In this speech, the "Führer and highest judicial authority" severely scolded the German judiciary for their alleged leniency.[229] The *Richterbriefe* were part of the measures by means of which Thierack tried to increase his influence on matters of jurisdiction. In this way, he tried to push through court decisions that would convince the NSDAP party leaders of a "decisive" and "effective" administration of justice.

Richterbriefe that were marked "confidential" criticized particular court decisions that the state and the NSDAP party leadership considered to be miscarriages of justice. Thierack particularly emphasized that, by means of these statements, the judges were expected to get an "idea of how the legal authorities anticipated to apply National Socialist law."[230] In this regard, the RJM expected that the judges would "no longer tediously cling to the letter of the law." Consequently, the judges were requested to pervert justice, thus separating administration of justice from its attachment to the law.

In its third issue the *Richterbriefe* also included a rejection of custody withdrawal pronounced in a Bible Student case, which apparently indicates that the Ministry of Justice considered it necessary to influence even these court proceedings.[231] The case described is based on the following incident: An eleven year-old girl attracted attention at school for repeatedly refusing to give the Hitler salute because of her religious convictions. When asked particular "questions regarding the Führer, she showed herself . . . completely uninterested." The parents obviously approved of their daughter's behavior and "stubbornly" refused, despite "admonitions" by the school management, "to influence her into changing her view." Consequently, the youth welfare office requested custody withdrawal for the girl. At the same time, as a "preventive" measure, they also requested custody withdrawal for her six-year-old sister, who did not even go to school. However, in its March 21, 1942, decision, the Oberhausen Municipal Court rejected this request, ordering, instead, "merely" protective supervision.[232]

Even though this decision was revoked in appellate court proceedings, resulting in the fact that the NS authorities achieved their goal of withdrawing custody for both children, the case was included in the *Richterbriefe*.[233] Apparently, it was the reason that the Oberhausen court used to reject the request of the youth welfare office that prompted the highest legal authorities to use this case for the purpose of influencing the judges.

On the one hand, the guardianship court judge had based his decision on the fact that the parents could not directly be considered as opponents of the NS state. According to the judge's statements, the parents were simply "not favorably disposed toward" the NS movement "and had "no intentions of promoting it." As long as the parents did not violate any laws requiring punishment by the legal authorities, however, their attitude did not, in itself, provide sufficient reason for custody withdrawal. On the other hand, the judge had reached the conclusion that the children's conduct, apart from the complaints at school, did not provide any reason for interfering with the parental education. Since it could be expected that the parents would at least "not oppose the National Socialist instruction at school," the judge considered it necessary to continue observing the children. For this reason, he ordered protective supervision, but at that point he was not willing to order custody withdrawal. That decision was also based on the fact that the judge considered the parents to be "absolutely reliable people."

According to the highest judicial authorities, such reasoning certainly required severe public criticism. By means of the *Richterbriefe*, the RJM informed the entire panel of judges about his opinion of the court decision. He accused the guardianship court judge of "misconceiving the principles of National Socialist education of the youth." As emphasized in the official statement, educational duties included also "conveying respect and reverence for the symbols of the state and the [National Socialist] movement." In this regard, the state required active involvement on the part of parents. With reference to the incriminating decision, the statement continues: "Passive neutrality is as dangerous as opposition to the National Socialist idea." To this end, the guardianship court judge failed to recognize that even "indifference [to the matter of training children] to become patriotic Germans" has to be considered as a serious "violation" of parents' educational duties.

In particular, the Ministry of Justice objected to the fact that the court had made a distinction between an opponent and a nonsupporter of the National Socialist movement. Therefore, the ministry clearly stated: "Any person who persistently refuses to give the Hitler salute based on religious misconceptions, who, without valid reasons, refuses to support the great social work of establishing the NSV, and who deliberately forbids his children to join the Hitler Youth and follow its instructions, cannot be considered merely as having an 'unfavorable attitude to' or being 'nonsupportive of' the National Socialist movement. Such a person offers resistance to the National Socialist movement and is therefore an enemy." The RJM had absolutely no sympathy for the different view of the guardianship court judge even though he had based his decision also on other aspects of the parental training. A German municipal court judge was not supposed to make such contemplations. His duty was to judge. For this purpose he received the *Richterbriefe* from the RJM, which clearly stated: "Therefore, the guardianship court judge would have been required to withdraw custody, based on the simple argument that parents who openly adhere to the ideas of the 'Bible Students' are not capable of educating their children according to National Socialist ideology."

In December 1943 a high-ranking official of the RJM became secretary of state. In previous years, this ambitious official had suggested taking more drastic legal action in cases in which "parents misused their education rights." He had based this suggestion on a particular Reich Court decision. On February 17, 1938, the court had stated that even coming together for family prayer had to be considered a prohibited activity, since it involved the danger that the close relationship among the former members of this denomination was continued within the family circle; and this, in turn, could result in the fact that the family was used as a "center for the future reestablishment of this sect."[234]

Dr. Herbert Klemm, the senior public prosecutor who, at that time, was still head of the general political department and mediator between the highest SA leaders and the RJM, commented on this court decision and took matters a step further. In his opinion, a prohibited activity was already performed if Bible Students tried to exert an influence on other members of their family not belonging to this sect to win them over to their prohibited denomination. This was specifically the case "if sectarian parents educated their children according to the ideas of the prohibited sect." Previously, education contrary to the requirements of the state was punished according to family and juvenile law. Klemm now requested an application of criminal law: "Such education according to the teachings of this prohibited sect is an activity subject to punishment because it involves the high danger of contributing to the fact that a new 'nucleus for future activities [of the sect]' is formed."[235] Klemm requested legal action and subsequent imprisonment for parents who educated their children according to Bible Student teachings.[236]

"Foster Parents," Homes, and Other "Reformatory Institutions"

What happened to the children after custody withdrawal was ordered? Generally, the courts assigned guardianship to the youth welfare offices. Sometimes, the courts would also assign guardianship to specific people. People to whom guardianship and, consequently, custody, was assigned were first of all required to support NS educational goals.

The youth welfare offices placed the children either with "foster families" or in homes. Among the authorities, however, there was no agreement regarding the question of where to place "children from politically unreliable families." In its December 27, 1938, interoffice decree, the RMdI ordered that corrective training in an institution "should be considered only if, apart from, or as a result of, the political unreliability of the families, the children were in danger of being neglected, or such neglect was already evident." In the majority of cases, it was sufficient "if the youth welfare office obtained an order from the guardianship court indicating that the children should be placed with another suitable, politically reliable family."[237]

These politically reliable families included, primarily, the families of state and party officials. As a result, children of Jehovah's Witnesses came into custody of families of managing directors of employment offices, *Studienräte* (graduate high school teachers with tenure), municipal administrative officers, court officials, and local group leaders of the NSDAP.

It is almost impossible to describe the personal tragedies that resulted from the removal of the children from their parents and the years of separation, at times without the possibility of contacting their parents.

Especially difficult for the children were the drastic educational measures that were used in the homes and, even more so, in NS families, for the purpose of integrating the children into the "National Socialist people's community."

The children for whom foster care and corrective training was ordered included all age groups of minors, from first grade on.[238] In many cases the children were too young to understand why they had been forcibly separated from their parents. This was the experience of Hans Neumann. In 1937, at the age of seven, he was removed from his home. At first he was taken to a youth camp. Later he was brought to a farm. He reports: "All this time I had no idea why these things were happening to me. My parents had been careful about what they told me. . . . Hence, I did not understand why I had been separated from them. Nor did I understand why the farmer who was responsible for me used to scold me and shout at me that I was a criminal, or why other children would have nothing to do with me."[239]

Even though the children often were not able to understand their situation, the emotional pain of being separated from their parents caused them to become introverted and stubborn in their new environment. Older children and youths alike resisted their foster parents or the teachers in the homes if they, often by employing physical violence, tried to persuade them to accept National Socialism.[240] In many cases, such conflicts resulted in the fact that the youth welfare offices had to find other accommodation for the children. For example, a seventeen-year-old boy who had been placed with a "very National Socialist–minded family" was admitted to a youth center because of "homelessness." In this regard, the official report states that the NS family "did not want to keep [the boy] under any circumstances, because he adhered to the ideas of the 'Earnest Bible Students' and refused to give the Hitler salute."[241]

In the majority of cases involving Bible Student children, the NS authorities, the homes, and the foster families were not able to produce any positive results by using coercive measures. Perhaps with the exception of the very little children, their families and personal Bible study at home had strengthened them sufficiently so that they resisted any efforts to influence them otherwise. The calculations of the National Socialists, according to which all that was necessary was to remove the children from the " dangerous influence of their parents" in order to mold them to become "useful members of the people's community," did not succeed. On the contrary: For the majority of children and youths, the experience of being separated from their parents resulted in even stronger resistance. Not only did they consider a weakening of their faith to be apostasy (according to what they had learned), they also considered it to be a betrayal of their parents.

Almost all recollections mention the fact that the tremendous pressure exhausted the children emotionally. A fifteen-year-old girl who was sent to the regional youth center in Selent (Holstein) in 1941 reports that she cried for days on end and initially refused even to eat.[242]

However, if the pressure decreased or if, after months or years of separation, the memory of the instruction received at home diminished, it could happen that the children abandoned their attitude of resistance. In this regard, the Watch Tower Society's history report states: "There were cases where children who were separated from their parents became weak in faith for a time and actually stood in danger of being drawn into the Nazi camp, just as the movement's leaders figured they would be."[243] The fact that these children agreed to participate in activities of the Hitler Youth or perform community and military service could hardly be viewed as an active recognition of National Socialism. And yet, often a slowly developing change of mind took place that affected the relationship between parents and children even beyond 1945.

If the educational efforts of the NS authorities did not produce the anticipated results, corrective training merely turned into a matter of institutional custodianship. Such custodianship no longer had the objective of achieving the intended "re-education." It rather served the purpose of "protecting" the community from the "incorrigible" children of Jehovah's Witnesses. In most cases, the children were not taken out of corrective training programs, even though the regulations of the Youth Welfare Law (JWG, article 63, paragraph 2) required evidence for the prospect of success. One of the reasons for keeping the children in the homes could be the fact that the management of these institutions valued the working capacity of the Bible Student children in domestic and agricultural areas.

To a large extent, the youth welfare offices tried to eliminate any contact between parents and children. The children often did not even receive permission to write their parents. Visits of the parents required permission from the home management or the youth welfare office. In many cases, such visits were denied. In 1942 a mother whose husband had been executed in January of that year because of his refusal to perform military service requested leaves of absence for her ten- and eleven-year-old children during summer vacation and Christmas time. However, the Württemberg Association of Welfare Services rejected categorically several requests of the mother "because of educational reasons."[244]

According to several reports, quite a number of parents were not told at all, or at least not initially, where their children had been housed. At times, the removal of the children took place even without any prior notice to the parents.[245]

This was the experience of a mother from Striegau (Silesia) who waited in vain for her ten-and-a-half-year-old son to return from school. When she finally started looking for him, the authorities refused to give her any information about the place to which he had been taken. Only after a considerable period of time was she able to find out that the boy had been sent to an orphanage.[246] The authorities proceeded in a similar way with a Bible Student from Bad Lippspringe. In this case, without notice to the parents, three of the children, aged seven, nine, and thirteen, were picked up from school. One of the daughters reports: "Mother tried to find out where the children had been taken. At last, after some weeks, she located them in a reform school in Dorsten."[247]

To maintain the relationship with their children, parents made all kinds of efforts to work around the prohibitions placed on contacting their children. They devised secret arrangements to meet their children or smuggled letters in and out of the home, sometimes even with the support of employees working at the institution.[248]

In some cases, children and youths tried to avoid being placed in corrective training, or their parents tried to protect them from the grasp of the authorities. In the spring of 1937 Franz Josef Seitz from Karlsruhe took his twelve-year-old son Willi (see p. 173) abroad because he was afraid that his son would be sent to a reformatory. Court proceedings for this purpose had already been scheduled at the municipal court. At first, Seitz was able to house his son in neighboring Alsace. Later, he took him to Switzerland.[249] Also in 1937, a Jehovah's Witness who was released from prison for a few days to attend the funeral of his wife took his child and "made a dramatic escape across the border into Switzerland." After the death of his wife, he had to consider the possibility that the authorities would now also take away his child.[250]

Youths who resisted instructions at the reformatories were promptly categorized as extremely difficult or incorrigible.[251] On October 3, 1941, the RMdI issued a decree stating that children could be transferred to the police authorities for further placement if "the treatment provided by the youth welfare services, especially protective supervision and corrective training, had failed or did not promise any prospect of success."[252] Some

Bible Student children were even sent to special youth concentration camps, which were under the direct supervision of the Reich Police Office of Criminal Investigation.[253] However, whether the Gestapo sent these youth to the so-called protective detention camps for the youth because they were involved in anti-state activities or because they resisted corrective training remains unknown.

There are only a few reports that provide us with information about the fate of the young Bible Students who were sent to these camps. At the Moringen youth concentration camp, the Bible Students refused to work in the ammunition factory. Two reports of former fellow prisoners include descriptions of such acts of refusal. According to one report, a Bible Student newly assigned to work in the underground ammunition factory stopped at the entrance of the shaft and flatly refused ever to touch any arms or ammunition.[254] Several SS men grabbed him and put several hand grenades into his shirt. The young Bible Student tried to offer resistance and threw the grenades away. "Then they beat him until he was no longer able to get up. We thought he was dead. But he was tough. . . . Later, he even came back to the ammunition factory. However, they let him sweep the floors of the workshop. He was never again forced to handle any ammunition."[255]

The other report describes the uncompromising attitude of a Bible Student who strictly refused to work in the ammunition factory. Consequently, the SS-Kommandoführer (commanding officer) incited fellow prisoners to beat the "uncooperative prisoner." According to the statements of a fellow prisoner, other prisoners followed this request "because his refusal meant that they had to work more. This made them angry because they said, 'Why should he dodge the work and we are supposed to let him get away with it!' They had absolutely no idea what it meant to be a Bible Student. . . . I remember that they beat him to a pulp. He just lay there and did not even make a sound."[256]

Bible Student children who had no German citizenship were exposed to even more serious conditions. On July 13, 1943, the district administrator of Teschen submitted a request to the Kattowitz youth welfare office to send a seven-year-old boy to the "Litzmannstadt concentration-camp for Polish youths."[257] The administrator was concerned that the boy, who had also been expelled from school, would have a "subversive influence on other children."[258] The boy's parents, who were Bible Students, had refused to have their names included in the *Deutsche Volksliste*. (This list included the names of people who were of German ethnicity. To have one's name entered on the list signified a person's approval of National Socialism in Germany.) Consequently, the German authorities took ruthless actions: The twenty-eight-year-old mother of the boy was "resettled." The father had already "died" during the previous year at the age of thirty-two. Then, the boy was sent to the disreputable Litzmannstadt (Lodz) youth concentration camp. It is not known if he survived.[259]

There were also cases in which children were not removed from their homes. This was the case if parents no longer participated publicly in Bible Student activities, if the Gestapo did not have any knowledge of such activities, if the children did not attract attention at school for refusing to give the Hitler salute, or if they agreed to participate in "compulsory duties of the youth." Even in such cases, the families were exposed to innumerable discriminations. A classic example involved the authorities refusing to pay the parents the children's allowance (government subsidy) to which they were legally entitled.[260]

The January 30, 1941, interoffice decree by the Reich minister of financial affairs stipulated that children's allowance should not be granted if it was "used for purposes contrary to the objectives of the children's allowance." Its purpose was to "assist healthy German families who are worthy of the [people's] community."[261] The guidelines issued three months later listed various groups of people who were generally excluded from receiving these benefits. According to these guidelines, the children's allowance would not be paid to "family heads whom the NSDAP district overseer considered unwilling or unsuitable to render loyal services to the German Reich and nation, or who discouraged his children from participating in activities of the NSDAP, or any of its factions."[262]

Sometimes such regulations were even used to coerce people into becoming members of the NSDAP, as is shown by the report of the son of a Jehovah's Witness from Hamburg: "We were seven children in our family and were supposed to receive the children's allowance, based on the fact that we were a large family. For one month we received the benefits. But already by the second month, [my parents] were handed a form, stating: If you want to continue receiving the benefits, you have to join the party. Or you have to relinquish any further claims. It did not take my parents very long to choose the latter. . . . They even returned the money they had received for the first month."[263]

In one particularly informative case, for which the documents are available, the parents objected to the denial of the children's allowance at the Reich governor's office in Hamburg.[264] This complaint was made in 1942. The working-class family of five was in financial straits and depended on the children's allowance.

The Reich governor's office responsible for dealing with complaints obtained statements from the various authorities and party factions regarding the question of whether the children "were educated according to current viewpoints of state policy."[265] The school authorities had "no reason for complaint." Even the Secret State Police office had "no reservations" against granting the requested children's allowance since the parents were no longer involved in IBSA activities:

> At their recent release from prison, they signed a declaration indicating that they would no longer participate in Bible Student activities. Subsequently, the married couple H. was placed under surveillance. So far, there has been no evidence of involvement in [IBSA] activities contrary to their declaration. . . . According to local experience, as soon as the Bible Students completely abandon their false teachings, they actually become quite useful and reliable citizens. According to the recent behavior of the couple H., it has to be assumed that they are in the process of completely abandoning the Bible Student teachings.[266]

The officials at the Reich governor's office were surprised at the Gestapo's unreserved approval for granting the children's allowance, because only two months earlier, the NSDAP district overseer concerned had stated that the father who was requesting the children's allowance rejected the NS movement. Consequently, another letter was sent to the NSDAP district overseer. With reference to the enclosed Gestapo statement, the NSDAP district overseer was asked whether his observations had been made "recently."[267] In his reply, the NSDAP overseer of district Hamburg 1 stated that he would not deviate from his statement regarding his observations. To prove the father's opposition to National Socialism, he informed the Reich governor about the following occurrence:

> On Feb. 13, when Mrs. H. appeared in my office in response to a summons, she stated that God condemned war and that all the governments were responsible for this war. When asked whether she and her husband would support the fatherland, Mrs. H. replied that she would not do so because her God would not allow that. If her husband were asked to go to war, he would refuse to go even if he was killed for that.[268]

The NSDAP district overseer stated that, based on such an attitude, he could "not support the approval of the children's allowance."

The Reich governor and *Gauleiter* (Nazi Party provincial chief), who was the highest official of the state administration, followed the decision of his NSDAP district overseer. He rejected the complaint because the parents refused "to render loyal service to the German Reich and people."[269] Furthermore, by enclosing the NSDAP district overseer's statement, Privy Councillor Dr. Becker, the head of the Reich governor's office, decided to inform the Gestapo of the "real" attitude of the Bible Student couple.[270] Consequently, instead of the anticipated children's allowance, the family was again exposed to problems with the Gestapo.

PART 4

SELF-ASSERTION OF JEHOVAH'S WITNESSES UNTIL 1939

10

Courageous Conviction and Covert Measures

On October 7, 1934, Jehovah's Witnesses made a united effort to resume their preaching activity despite the ban in Germany. For this purpose, the Bible Students had formed smaller groups, in which they now came together for about one hour each week to study the Bible and the *Watchtower*. They opened and closed each meeting with prayer and singing of "Kingdom songs." These meetings, which took place in the private homes of fellow believers, were often concealed as casual gatherings of friends or family members, and as groups meeting to play cards or do crafts. Since these small groups often consisted of neighbors, close friends, or relatives, the meetings actually reflected a certain atmosphere of familiarity. Therefore, as long as the Gestapo did not take any special surveillance measures, there was only a slight danger of being discovered. For this reason, outsiders or newly interested people were not immediately invited to these religious meetings. They first had to prove, through an extended period of personal Bible study with one of the Bible Students, that they could be considered reliable.

In the beginning, the Gestapo's lack of knowledge about the religious practices of the Bible Students contributed to the fact that these meetings were discovered in only a few cases.[1] In such cases, the Gestapo first searched for evidence indicating that the group had discussed "prohibited literature." The gathering of several Jehovah's Witnesses in itself did not necessarily cause them to take immediate action. On October 7, 1934, when the Gestapo raided a meeting of Jehovah's Witnesses in Magdeburg, they left empty-handed. All they found in the room was a group of people singing along to piano music. Otherwise, they could not find anything objectionable.[2] After the police left, Jehovah's Witnesses continued their meeting. They discussed how to proceed

207

with the resolution of protest to Hitler and how to continue their preaching activity.

Not only in Magdeburg, the October 7, 1934, meeting (the meeting for "simultaneously resuming the preaching activity" referred to on p. 111) and subsequent IBSA reorganization was hidden from the Gestapo. In Hamburg, the city with the largest number of arrests, it took the State Police offices two weeks to learn of that meeting and reorganization. The matter was brought to their attention by the Dresden police headquarters, which requested official assistance in a different matter (investigations regarding the illegal smuggling of Bible Student publications into Germany by way of the Czechoslovakian border).[3] As a result of the increased mail surveillance, from October 25, 1934, on, the Hamburg State Police discovered the place and time of a weekly meeting in one of the Hamburg districts, even though the intercepted letter of November 28, 1934, included a coded message: "If you can arrange it, please come to our family gathering on Thursday evening. Dinner starts at 7:30."[4]

On Thursday, December 6, 1934, the State Police struck. They surprised the group during their mutual *Watchtower* study. During the house search and interrogations, the three Gestapo officers were able to obtain more details. The next day Max Grote, the primary leader of the Hamburg IBSA group, was arrested. State Police officials found a notebook in Grote's home, which included the names of twenty-two leaders of the twenty-four subordinate groups in the various districts. These records provided the State Police with sufficient information for further investigation. Consequently, a number of arrests took place in Hamburg. This, in turn, resulted in court cases against 170 people who had attended the October 7, 1934, meeting. The State Police also discovered a storage place of publications and confiscated "approximately 30,000 kilograms [60,000 pounds] of Bible Student booklets."

On the one hand, the Hamburg incident shows that the IBSA groups were not yet adequately prepared to work under the conditions of a ban. Later on, they carefully avoided including any names in their written records. On the other hand, it also shows that they were prepared for the possibility of being arrested and had made appropriate arrangements. According to State Police records, the IBSA members had prepared a statement for use in cases of arrest, which had the following wording: "On October 7, 1934, I was in the home of X and attended a meeting of Jehovah's Witnesses. We were approximately ten people but I do not remember any names."[5] The statement did not require Jehovah's

Witnesses to lie and, at the same time, did not reveal any names and details that could have presented a danger for fellow believers.

During interrogations, Jehovah's Witnesses generally remained steadfast. They provided the requested personal data. But otherwise they pretended to be completely uninformed. On February 7, 1935, the official in charge at the Hamburg State Police office recorded that the police investigations were very difficult, despite the large number of arrests: "It is not possible to persuade the Bible Students to provide the required information."[6]

On October 24, 1934, the outpost of the State Police office for the administrative district of Schleswig, in neighboring Altona, also gave instructions "to pay close attention to the propaganda of the Bible Students and to take action against them."[7] On January 12, 1935, however, the State Police office had to acknowledge that "the police actions for the purpose of enforcing the ban against the Association of Earnest Bible Students . . . was not really successful."[8] During 1934/35, approximately forty Jehovah's Witnesses were in protective detention in Dresden, twenty were imprisoned in Berlin, and another twenty in Halle.[9]

During the following months, the number of arrests increased significantly. The increasing cases of arrest could not primarily be attributed to more efficient methods of investigation on the part of the police authorities but rather to the high risk associated with the resumption of the preaching activity.[10] In contrast to their religious gatherings, the preaching activity involved a much greater danger of discovery. Therefore, Jehovah's Witnesses tried to take certain precautionary measures. In most cases, in their house-to-house or door-to-door activity, they did not take anything along except their Bibles. Only on their "return visits" with people who had shown interest would they also take along the Watch Tower Society's publications.[11] On an initial visit, they started the conversation with a few general statements. By means of the reaction of the householder, they were then able to determine whether they were speaking to a "follower of the Hitler party" or to somebody to whom they could bring the Kingdom message. Only in this case did they continue the conversation. However, as soon as something seemed suspicious, they stopped the conversation under a certain pretense and immediately left the house. Then, they continued preaching in a different street.

Many Jehovah's Witnesses also avoided preaching in their immediate neighborhoods. Instead, they went to a neighboring village or district of town where nobody knew them. Sometimes they traveled to a specific area with a larger group in order to cover several places simultaneously with their preaching activity. The advantage of such arrangements is described in the following report:

> But we did not leave out any opportunity to outsmart the Gestapo. For this purpose, we distributed the territory among us and then we began. We began preaching in any street in the various villages and towns, all at the same time. But everyone visited only a few houses. We distributed our journals and disappeared again. In the meantime, the police offices were flooded with telephone calls from all the surrounding villages, informing them that Jehovah's Witnesses were there. The Gestapo did not know where to start. And by the time the flying squads arrived we were long gone.[12]

During this time of increasing numbers of informers, the preaching activity was extremely dangerous.[13] Numerous complaints were made to the police offices. In quite a number of cases, the "Kingdom preachers" were stopped in the hallways or on the street, and the tenants quickly called the police to have them arrested. A senior police officer from the Hamburg police office describes the following incident:

> On December 5, 1934, at 3:30 p.m., when I was walking through the Elligersweg, the landlord Carl S—— informed me that a stranger had sold a book with the title *Government* for 0.20 [Reichsmark] at the home of Sch., who lived in Elligersweg, No. 53, on the first floor. The book was published by the International Bible Students Association, Wachtturm Bibel- und Traktat-Gesellschaft, Magdeburg. I took the man immediately to the police office . . . and took the precaution of informing the State Police office.[14]

Even children were persuaded to make a statement. For example, a thirteen-year-old schoolgirl informed the police that a stranger had visited her parents: "The man talked about God and the Bible, and about war and killing. I cannot tell you what exactly they talked about. I saw that the man gave three books to my parents. What kind of books these were I do not know. I did not look at them. I also do not know what the man really wanted from us. But I would recognize him, if I saw him again."[15] As a result, the police presented the girl with five people. Among them, she recognized the man who had spoken with her parents.

Fearlessness despite Arrests

Neither the increasing number of arrests nor the resulting punishment discouraged these active Jehovah's Witnesses from participating in their preaching activity. From the beginning of 1935 on, hundreds of Jehovah's Witnesses were sent to the concentration camps at Esterwegen, Moringen, and especially Sachsenburg.[16] In some cases, the criminal courts were already imposing severe penalties.[17] At the beginning of November 1935, at the Silesia Special Court, legal proceedings were instituted against a Jehovah's Witness whom the same court had already sentenced to three months of imprisonment six weeks earlier, on September 17. He was arrested again only one day after the initial judgment because he had been involved yet again in "advertising activities for the sect."[18]

This fearless involvement in religious activities on the part of Jehovah's Witnesses was primarily based on a solid faith in God and on their conviction that Christ's Kingdom rule would soon be extended over the earth. However, it was also based on certain expectations included in the publications coming from the Brooklyn headquarters of the Watch Tower Society. The first *Watchtower* published after the October 7, 1934, meetings requested Jehovah's Witnesses in Germany to remain faithful as the "little flock" that God had chosen "to give [them] the kingdom," and to stand firm even in the face of danger: "The Lord Jesus admonished his followers to fear none of these things, and then gave them this assurance: 'Be thou faithful unto death, and I will give thee a crown of life.' Rev. 2:10."[19] While these words confirmed that God would save those who remained faithful in the "service of the Lord," they also emphasized that those faithful ones had now entered a period of trial that required them to remain loyal to God and, consequently, prove Satan a liar. To this end, the 1935 *Yearbook* of Jehovah's Witnesses, which was probably written in October/November 1934, states: "Many of these faithful followers of Christ Jesus have been put in concentration camps or other prisons and woefully ill-treated because they refuse to vote for Hitler or refuse to hail him as the savior of mankind. The faithful ones have determined to remain true and loyal to Jehovah God and take whatever punishment God permits to be inflicted upon them. This is the only way whereby the final test can be put upon any people in maintaining their integrity towards Jehovah."[20] Regarding Jehovah's Witnesses in Germany, the *Watchtower* and other Bible Student publications emphasized that Christians were under obligation to be obedient to the theocratic "higher powers" (see p. 41). They were, however, *not* obligated to follow the "ungodly" requirements of Hitler's government. This government was "undoubtedly under the control of the invisible power of Satan and his wicked cohorts who were waging war against Jehovah's Witnesses." Therefore, it was clearly stated: "For righteous people no laws are required (1 Tim. 1:9). Any law that contradicts the special laws of Jehovah or opposes divine laws is unjust."[21]

The faithful ones were strengthened and reassured by the fact that their loyalty to God's requirements and their active declaration of the Kingdom message would result in everlasting life. They would also be richly blessed with becoming co-rulers in Christ's Kingdom. Conversely, there was the pain of penalty: "and if they fail to keep God's law their disobedience will result in everlasting destruction."[22]

This psychological pressure of having no choice was accompanied by the fear that unfaithful Jehovah's Witnesses would be avoided by their fellow believers, excluded from their religious association, and expelled as an apostate. Several of Jehovah's Witnesses participated in the religious activities out of fear of these consequences. Others courageously took a stand for their conviction. There were also those who actively participated in the preaching activity but, at the same time, admonished their fellow believers to use good judgment. Often, fellow believers interpreted such reservations against a certain action because of the high risks involved, as "indecisiveness" and a "lack of trust in Jehovah." And this, despite the fact that these more cautious Jehovah's Witnesses showed the same uncompromising attitude as their fellow believers on questions involving matters of conscience, such as the question of giving the Hitler salute. They were mainly concerned about not provoking" their enemies unnecessarily and adapting to the situation wherever possible. However, if it were required they would stand up for their convictions, "Then it is necessary to show resistance. There cannot be any compromise."[23]

Some among Jehovah's Witnesses, on the other hand, took the Watch Tower Society's request of adopting a fearless attitude very literally. They were not afraid of giving a "witness" in public, even deliberately seeking the confrontation with the "satanic" enemy. In July 1935 a Bible Student from Itzehoe approached a stranger on the street and quite frankly told her that he disapproved of the badge of the National Socialist Women's Association she was wearing.[24] He also told her that he considered the Wehrmacht a tool of the devil. In reference to the NS leadership, he even proclaimed that "everybody making derogatory remarks about the Old Testament will be done away with." His frankness toward the woman, who viewed this as an insult on her "privilege of wearing the badge," earned the man three months of imprisonment.

The arrests in connection with the preaching activity made the few principal celebrations of Jehovah's Witnesses even more important. Of particular importance is the ceremony of the Memorial of Christ's Death, which Jehovah's Witnesses observe annually, in remembrance of Jesus's last evening meal with his disciples. According to the gospel accounts, this last evening meal took place on Nisan 14 of the Jewish calendar, after sundown, which was the evening before the Passover. This meant that on a fixed date, which Jehovah's Witnesses consider to be unchangeable, all Bible Student groups tried to come together in order to commemorate this special occasion. At first, the Gestapo was apparently not familiar with all the details. But at the beginning of March 1935, by means of mail surveillance, they discovered the date for the 1935 Memorial celebration and recognized their chance for an attack. On March 5, 1935, the Kiel State Police office sent the following report to Berlin: "The Bible and Tract Society is still sending the familiar publications from Switzerland to known Bible Students in Germany. Recently, they even sent a journal, titled, 'Jehovah's Battle' [*Die Schlacht Gottes*], dated March 1, 1935. In this journal, they are requested to celebrate the Passover on April 17, 1935."[25] Two weeks later, on March 20, 1935, the Secret State Police office sent an interoffice decree to all Prussian State Police offices.[26] The main Gestapo offices of the other German states also adopted this decree. On April 8, 1935, the Bavarian Political Police informed the local police offices that, according to a confiscated Bible Student publication, "the 'groups of the anointed' are planning to meet on April 17, 1935, at 6 p.m., for a celebration of the name Jehovah and of the sacrifice of Jesus Christ. A surprise attack on the known leading members of the Earnest Bible Students at the above-mentioned date seems very promising and should therefore be initiated."[27]

At this point, the IBSA received a warning informing them about the preparations of the Gestapo. Consequently, the district overseers were able to instruct the groups about the need to take extensive precautionary measures. Even though numerous IBSA groups had gathered for their Memorial celebrations, it was possible to keep the number of arrests within limits.[28] The Bible Students had changed their meeting places so that the Dortmund Gestapo, for instance, "was able to report only that the homes of those believed to be leaders of the Bible Students Association had been placed under surveillance but that in no case were meetings held."[29] A few State Police offices did indeed report "positive results." In Hannover, the city on the Leine River, thirteen people who had attended the Memorial celebrations were arrested. In Hildesheim twelve people were arrested.[30] The Gestapo in Kiel took action even before the Memorial celebrations; they reported that the Bible Student leadership in their administrative district "had been arrested when they were observed purchasing matzos [unleavened bread] in preparation for their celebration."[31]

After Paul Balzereit and other German leaders of the Watch Tower Society were arrested in May 1935, Martin C. Harbeck, the leader responsible for the IBSA central European office in Bern, temporarily accepted the leadership in Germany. After an initial assessment of the situation, Harbeck traveled to the Brooklyn headquarters in order to discuss the arrangements for a new leadership of the German IBSA branch. In July 1935, after his return from Brooklyn, Harbeck appointed the former district overseer of Berlin, thirty-six-year-old Fritz Winkler (a former employee of an insurance company), to supervise the preaching activity of Jehovah's Witnesses in Germany in exchange for Balzereit.[32] The leadership of the German branch office closely cooperated with Harbeck, who was the link to the Brooklyn headquarters. Apparently, even the American Consulate General in Berlin was instrumental in maintaining communication, because Winkler supposedly used the consulate to forward his reports to Bern.[33] Under the leadership of Winkler, who supervised the preaching activity during the period of the ban, the German Reich was divided into thirteen districts. During the restructuring, new district overseers were appointed to replace the IBSA functionaries who were imprisoned. These new appointments, as well as the appointment of Winkler, also represented a younger age group in the leadership of the Bible Students Association. In the district of Palatinate-Baden, twenty-six-year-old Konrad Franke replaced Dr. Franz Merk, who was thirty years older. In Schleswig-Holstein, forty-four-year-old Hermann Schlömer accepted the responsibilities of Arno Thümmler and Alfred Zimmer, who belonged to the leadership group around Balzereit. And in Bavaria, thirty-year-old Otto Lehmann replaced the aged and experienced IBSA functionary Konrad Glamann. This development continued in the years following; primarily, the younger ones (both regarding their age as well as the duration of their IBSA membership) were the managers during the period of the ban. Several former functionaries withdrew and were no longer involved in the organization's activities, often after having served many months of imprisonment imposed on them in 1935.

Winkler periodically met with the respective district overseers to discuss activities and accept the service reports that had been compiled based on the reports submitted by the various local groups.[34] For instance, every four weeks at 4 o'clock in the afternoon he had a meeting at the Stuttgart Hindenburgbau with the leaders responsible for the area of southern Germany. The meetings with the district overseers of northern and eastern Germany took place at a chair-rental facility at the "Berlin zoological gardens," which were managed by a fellow believer.[35] Eventually, as a precautionary measure, these monthly meetings were usually held on a train. One week in advance Winkler would provide the coded information about the ever-changing dates and railroad routes to be used. The district overseer concerned would then board the train at a prearranged train station. After a few stations, one of them would leave the train. Because of the high risk involved in postal correspondence, the district overseers also maintained contact with the local group leaders by means of these travel arrangements. Therefore, all of them, including Winkler, had regional rail passes on the German Reichsbahn.

Precautionary Measures and Shrewdness

Increasingly, the prohibited organization used conspiratorial techniques, ranging from a permanent courier service to "dead drops" to code names. In a 1936 memo "about the prohibited Bible Student activities," the Gestapo stated, almost in admiration, that everything was "handled in complete secrecy and with all possible precautionary measures."[36] Even at the lower level, the Bible Students had developed methods of avoiding the increasing mail surveillance, which had been ordered for all "officially known Bible Students" at the end of 1934.[37] Jehovah's Witnesses arranged well-thought-out secret codes for their written correspondence, in addition to a terminology that was anyway difficult for outsiders to understand, such as calling the *Watchtower* "brown bread."[38] They worked with cover addresses, using them as collecting places for their mail. In general, these were the addresses of acquaintances or relatives who were not Jehovah's Witnesses themselves or who were not publicly acknowledged as such, and this is where the mail was sent because the Witnesses assumed that these people, who were not suspected of being involved in a prohibited activity, would be protected from mail censorship. The fact that now the Bible Students no longer received any mail also raised suspicion, as is indicated in a letter written by the mayor of Friedrichstadt on August 23, 1935: "The Schleswig district administrator had instructed the local post office to keep the mail of the local Bible Students under surveillance. However, somehow the Bible Students found this out and, since quite some time, no longer receive any mail from the local post office. It has now been observed that the Bible Student Buchholz, a baker from Drage, drives during the night to Eiderstedt and picks up mail, apparently for the local Bible Students, in Witzwort at the home of Mrs. Bove . . . who seems to receive quite a lot of mail. I request, therefore, that mail surveillance should be ordered for the incoming and outgoing mail of Mrs. Bove in Witzwort."[39]

The extent to which the underground organization of Jehovah's Witnesses was able to adapt to the conditions of the ban is manifested especially in the methods they used to supply the groups with Bible Student publications. For a considerable period of time, they were still able to use for their preaching activity an adequate amount of older books and booklets, which were deposited in concealed places and had escaped the grasp of the Gestapo. Moreover, Jehovah's Witnesses in Germany still received publications of the Watch Tower Society by regular mail, but this did not cover the personal requirements of the groups for more recent Bible Student publications. In the autumn of 1934 Jehovah's Witnesses began to smuggle publications over the German-Czechoslovakian border. Right at the start, however, these efforts resulted in a setback: at the beginning of October 1934, the Saxony police office arrested ten Jehovah's Witnesses who had smuggled between 1,500 and 2,000 books into Germany during the previous month.[40] Later on, for a period of almost two years, they were able to smuggle a considerable number of Bible Student publications over the border into Germany. The district overseer of western Silesia and Saxony, August Fehst, arranged the coordination of the smuggling and subsequent distribution of the publications. The publications, which were printed in Prague or Bern, were transported from Prague by train to Hohenelbe (Riesengebirge), located about ten miles away from the border. The publications were then brought to Spindlermühle, a summer resort close to the border.[41] In this little village, the hayloft of a farmhouse served as a temporary storage place. From there, usually twice a week around midnight, small groups of Bible Students carried the publications in knapsacks—in winter, on skis and sleds—over the border. During the early hours of the day, the publications were brought on bicycles to Hirschberg, from where they were distributed to places of storage in Breslau, Halle, Berlin, and other locations.

Similar methods as those used at the Spindler mountain pass were also used for smuggling publications from Warnstorf (Zittau mountains). Other publications were carried into Germany over the French and Dutch borders. Until March 1935 they were also smuggled in from the Saarland. For a while, couriers from Switzerland even brought publications over the regular checkpoints. They concealed these publications "either in their shoes, between double soles, or under their clothing."[42] In Germany, the home of a Bible Student from Konstanz served as a temporary place of storage. Her home formed the connection between the Bern IBSA central European office and the district overseers of southern Germany.[43]

The books and booklets were smuggled into Germany almost entirely from abroad by these methods. *Watchtower* publications that were smuggled in were also duplicated or reprinted in several locations within the German Reich. The *Watchtower*, which was originally written at the Brooklyn headquarters, was mimeographed by making several typescripts, each of which was used to produce a large number of copies. The copying was also performed by using stencils on a reprint machine (*Umdruckapparat*) and a contact-print machine (*Abzugsgerät*). These substitute journals did not always include the entire contents of the original issues. Often, as a result of an inadequate paper supply, deletions had to be made. Every issue of these prohibited *Watchtowers* usually consisted of six or seven tightly typed double pages. Initially, these journals did not include any articles originally written in Germany. They were generally produced twice a month and, therefore, at the same time interval as the original *Watchtower*. The distribution took place approximately four to eight weeks later. The number of issues produced was calculated in a way that every small IBSA group or unit received at least one copy of the respective *Watchtower*. At first, the Altona service leader copied the *Watchtowers* during the night in a laborious manual (*Handroller*) procedure. Finally, in the spring of 1936, the Bible Students were able to obtain a mimeograph machine (*Trommelvervielfältiger*). And so, during 1935/36, it was possible to produce, per issue, a total of two hundred to three hundred copies of the *Watchtower*. These were produced primarily for the Schleswig-Holstein Bible Student groups.[44] An additional one hundred copies were printed in Kiel to supply the villages along the coast of the Baltic Sea. Bremen supplied the *Watchtowers* for the northwestern area of Germany. But in August 1936 a wave of arrests by the Bremen Gestapo put an end to the prohibited printing activities there.[45] During the summer of 1936 Hamburg's main IBSA group, which previously had received a certain number from the 350 copies produced in Bremen, was able to purchase a contact-print machine. They were now in the position, at least to a certain extent, to make up for the losses. Two hundred and fifty copies of the *Watchtower* were produced in Hamburg. Through the mail and by means of a well-arranged network system, 150 of these copies were distributed to locations outside of Hamburg. Additionally, in Altona, the production increased so that in 1936/37, approximately 500 copies of the *Watchtower* were printed there. Two hundred of these copies were sent to Hannover, 70 to Bremen, and 140 to Bielefeld for the purpose of further distribution.[46]

Other areas in the German Reich used methods similar to those used in northern Germany in order to organize the printing of the *Watchtower*. The journal was also printed in Berlin (in 1936/37, about 240 copies), in Munich (about 500 copies), and (until May 1936) in Karlsruhe. Sometimes, instead of Karlsruhe, printing took place in Mannheim (until August 1936, about 400 copies).[47] During the first months of 1936, up to 3,000 copies of every issue of the *Watchtower* were produced and distributed in underground activities.[48]

Even though quite a few people participated in these underground activities of printing and distributing the *Watchtower*, it was very difficult for the Gestapo to receive knowledge about these activities. In order to reduce the danger of discovery, the mimeograph machines were frequently taken to different places. Jehovah's Witnesses made sure not to place the machines with anyone the Gestapo already knew to be Bible Students. Usually even the couriers knew only the name of the person from whom they received the publications so that, in case of arrest, they would not be able to provide any further information.

The courier services were generally carried out by male Bible Students, whereas production of the *Watchtower* was increasingly performed by female Bible Students. They were the ones who usually prepared the stencils and, in many cases, also operated the mimeograph machines. Because of the responsibilities these women accepted during the period of the ban, they were required to occupy leading positions within the IBSA organization, even though previously they had occupied only subordinate positions.[49]

The expenses that were required for the purchase of mimeograph machines and typewriters, as well as the continuous demand for ink, paper, and packaging material, were covered by the proceeds from the distribution of books and booklets, and from contributions. The group leaders and district overseers collected the money and deposited it in a

"Good Hope Fund." In addition to supporting the production of the *Watchtower*, this fund not only provided the means to supply the necessities of life for those Bible Students who had to live underground during the period of the ban but covered also the considerable travel expenses of the couriers and district overseers and supported fellow believers in difficult circumstances. This fund provided regular assistance for Bible Students whose husbands were in prison. Therefore, the various IBSA groups retained a certain amount of money required for such purposes. In each group, the service overseer responsible for the "Good Hope Fund" supervised the distribution of the money. Even though many Jehovah's Witnesses had lost their jobs and the majority of them already lived in modest circumstances, the groups were at times able to accumulate considerable sums of money because they were willing to share and show solidarity. In addition to supporting one another by means of the fund, they also provided personal support, sharing food and clothing. The mutual experience of suffering oppression and persecution strengthened their relationships with one another. They suffered the fate of the others as if it were their own. To the fullest extent possible, the members of this religious denomination tried to support each other.

Other Initiatives and Activities

In 1935 Jehovah's Witnesses introduced a new method of preaching in Germany, one that the Watch Tower Society had already started to use in other countries during the previous year. In those other countries, although under legal conditions, the methods had increased the success of their religious preaching activity. The new method involved the use of portable phonographs. By providing the prospect of listening to a record, Jehovah's Witnesses hoped to increase people's interest. They also hoped to be able to return and be invited into their homes. The records included short five- to ten-minute discourses of Rutherford, which had been translated into German. These talks provided basic information about the message of the imminent Kingdom of Christ and the Bible Students' viewpoint of world events.[50] Jehovah's Witnesses used various methods in order to conceal the phonographs. For example, a Jehovah's Witness from Burg in Dithmarschen had the phonograph in an inconspicuous brown cardboard box, which carried the label "Der selbsttätige Waschmittel-Kappus" (roughly, automatic soap machine).[51]

Initially, the records were smuggled into Germany from abroad, but starting in 1935, records began to be produced in Hennigsdorf, near Berlin. Georg Klohe, who was employed with AEG (General Electricity Company), provided cutting tools, wax discs, and other materials from a radio wholesale dealer. In a small shed in his backyard, Klohe and his son recorded *Watchtower* articles on untempered, unfinished records. Since Klohe had a supply of several cutting tools and recording equipment, they were able to make five recordings at one time. Afterwards, the untempered wax discs were hardened in a small electric heater. By July 1936 more than 1,000 records were supposedly produced in this way.[52] The required phonographs were produced in Erfurt. For the NS authorities, this use of phonographs was an indication that "the Bible Students were involved in a very powerful advertising activity." Thus, in November 1936, the Reich minister of finance issued the following instructions to the customs offices:

> For propaganda purposes, [the Bible Students] frequently use recordings containing discourses of the notorious leader of their association, Rutherford, which mainly consist of attacks against the Third Reich and National Socialism. Some of these agitating recordings are produced in Germany. However, the majority of them are illegally imported from abroad. The State Police offices consider it necessary to prevent, by all possible means, that these recordings are imported into Germany. Therefore, in agreement with the Reichsführer SS and German chief of police at the Reich Ministry of the Interior, I am ordering the confiscation of any recordings that are sent by mail and freight and that are not addressed to music shops. It is also important to inform the nearest Secret State Police office, even by telephone, so that further appropriate actions can be taken.[53]

Despite these difficulties, Jehovah's Witnesses were able to consolidate their preaching activity during 1935/36. With great ingenuity, they found ways to conduct their religious meetings, even in larger groups. In the summer of 1935, thirty Bible Students from Itzehoe and surrounding areas rented a steamboat and conducted their Bible study during their journey on the Stör River.[54] During the summer months, many Jehovah's Witnesses held their meetings at concealed places in the forests. These meetings were conducted under the pretense of having a picnic or a meeting of the local garden club.

Many new people joined the Bible Students Association. Quite a number of these people had formerly been associated with left-wing parties. They were impressed with the determined position Jehovah's Witnesses took against the NS regime.[55] Among these people was a thirty-one-year-old construction worker from Nesse (district of Oldenburg). Even though he had sympathized with the German Social Democratic Party, the party's attitude toward the construction of tank cruisers made him join the German Communist Party instead. The worker had his first contact with Jehovah's Witnesses in 1933/34 and permanently joined them in 1935.[56] At around the same time, a thirty-three-year-old SPD sailor from Hamburg joined the IBSA because the Bible Students shared his attitude of "refusing military service."[57] In 1934, in Breslau, a thirty-three-year-old warehouseman, who was working with several Jewish colleagues in a hardware store, also became acquainted with the Bible Students. His wife stated that it all began with his reception of a *Watchtower:* "A man came to our door who was associated with the group of Jehovah's Witnesses, which was already banned at that time. The man persuaded [my husband] to join Jehovah's Witnesses. In the course of several discussions, my husband found out that Jehovah's Witnesses believed that the Jews also had a right to live, an opinion he had always expressed in the family circle."[58]

During this time, the house-to-house activity of Jehovah's Witnesses had become dangerous, and the IBSA leaders warned their fellow believers against indiscriminately addressing strangers but to be selective in their approach. Consequently, Jehovah's Witnesses began looking for people who did not support National Socialism. They were encouraged to concentrate on people who did not display "the swastika during ceremonies and special events," and to try to persuade these people to become believers.[59]

In mid-1936 even the *Deutschland-Berichte* published by the exiled SPD recorded that an increasing number of people were joining the IBSA, especially in Saxony and the Rhineland.[60] According to one report, these were people who "were struggling emotionally" and were trying to find support with the Bible Students. Reports from the small villages in eastern Saxony stated that this religious movement had "devastating effects" even "on party members." In this regard, the SPD editorial department stated: "It seems that the mental distress of this time period causes people who previously supported political movements to join religious sectarianism."

Even though the preaching activity of Jehovah's Witnesses was very successful, despite the persecution they had to endure, the general increase was rather modest. As far as can be determined, in Hamburg a total of thirty people who had joined the religious association after 1933 participated in the preaching activity of Jehovah's Witnesses.[61] Of these thirty, about eighteen to twenty-two were baptized according to the custom of Jehovah's Witnesses in 1936/37. In Hamburg every tenth Bible Student who participated in the preaching activity during the period of the ban was probably a newly converted person, but based on the general growth rate of the previous years, there was not a significant increase.[62]

The reports of the authorities responsible for the persecution quite clearly show the extent of the IBSA activities during this period. The February/March 1935 report of the Reichsführer SS registered "increasing agitation" and mentioned that "great quantities of propaganda material" had been smuggled into Germany from abroad.[63] Three months later, the Frankfurt Gestapo stated: "Despite the fact that countless measures have been taken against members of the prohibited Bible Students Associations it seems that not even a ban is able to discourage them. . . . In many ways, they use the same methods as the Communists, in particular, in their distribution of literature, during police interrogations, and during court proceedings."[64] In early 1936 the Hannover State Police office complained that it was "difficult" to keep Jehovah's Witnesses under surveillance.[65] At the same time, the police offices in Munich reported about an "unbelievable religious fanaticism," which resulted in the fact that it was "not even possible to discourage Jehovah's Witnesses with measures of protective detention and police actions." In its February 1, 1936, interoffice decree, the Bavarian Political Police administration reprimanded its subordinate police offices that "they did not use the necessary ruthlessness in their actions against the Earnest Bible Students, who were known to be dangerous opponents of the State." The law enforcement authorities "were again put under obligation . . . to strictly observe the Earnest Bible Students."[66] This increasing observation on the part of the Gestapo resulted in quite a number of arrests, but the anticipated "destruction" of the prohibited IBSA could not be achieved. The Gestapo memo summarized the period from the resumption of the preaching activity until the middle of 1936: "The Secret State Police offices and the courts punished each attempt on their part to become active. However, month after month, the members of this sect continued to increase their prohibited activities."[67]

In Berlin, preparations were now made to launch a major attack against the Bible Students Association. On June 24, 1936, the Secret State Police formed a special unit (*Sonderkommando*). Two weeks later, on behalf of the Prussian Secret State Police and the Political Police Commander of the German states, Chief Officer Heinrich Müller instructed the State Police offices throughout the German Reich "to take action against the International Bible Students Association by using all available means of resistance."[68]

11

Organized Resistance Activities

In mid-1936 a new chapter began in the relationship between the Bible Students and the NS regime: Jehovah's Witnesses proceeded to launch a counterattack against the state that had refused to grant them the elementary human right of practicing their religious beliefs. In the meantime, Jehovah's Witnesses in the Third Reich were not allowed to perform any religious activities because the legal authorities considered even a nonpublic, mutual performance of religious rituals as a continuation of the banned Bible Students Association, requiring punishment. During the October 1935 proceedings against seventeen Jehovah's Witnesses at the Breslau Special Court, the senior public prosecutor stated that there was actually only one charge against them—their attendance at a meeting that took place on April 26, 1935: "At this meeting, the Bible was read and Bible texts compared, Bible texts relating to this period of time. Also prayers were said and the accused . . . was leading those prayers."[69] The special courts concerned sentenced a number of Jehovah's Witnesses to several months of imprisonments on the charge of such "offenses" or similar ones. However, as early as 1935, several special courts imposed even higher penalties. In July 1935 the Weimar Special Court sentenced a forty-five-year-old nursemaid from Hohenleuben, near Gera, to two years and five months of imprisonment on the charge of continued attendance of Bible Student meetings. One month later a seventy-one-year-old woman was sentenced for the same reason to one year and two months of imprisonment.[70] As far as can be determined, in 1935 alone, 198 of Jehovah's Witnesses in Hamburg were taken into protective detention or were legally punished. In five cases the State Police offices sent people to concentration camps outside of Hamburg.[71] During the same period, 197 Jehovah's Witnesses were punished by special courts in the state of Baden.[72] In almost all cases, the verdicts were pronounced on the charge of defiance of the IBSA ban, punishable according to the February 28, 1933, Decree of the Reich President for the Protection of People and State. Some verdicts were also based on "disparaging statements about the Reich government," "distribution of propaganda about acts of atrocity," and other offenses that were punishable according to the Law against Insidious Attacks on State and Party and for the Protection of the Party Uniform.[73] Consequently, until a new "legal foundation" was established based on military law, court proceedings against Bible Students completely fell under special court jurisdiction.[74]

Characteristic for legal prosecution with the objective of punishing unpopular opinions is the following incident: On August 2, 1935, four Jehovah's Witnesses from Hamburg were sentenced to imprisonment of between four and six months on the charge of their continued participation in the preaching activity.[75] During a recess period, one of the observers mentioned to a friend, in a private discussion outside the courtroom, that it would be terrible if the defendants were punished.[76] A woman who had been summoned as a witness overheard this remark. Immediately, she informed some court officials about it and, after the recess, also submitted the information to the court.

Because of this accusation, the man had to appear before the judges and was asked to give an explanation. He told the judges about his previous period of protective detention because of being a Jehovah's Witness and stated that his wife and his twenty-four-year-old son were among the defendants. Immediately, the court handed the fifty-year-old man over to the State Police authorities. Once again, he was placed in protective detention. On the following day, an arrest warrant was issued according to which the man was strongly suspected of "criticizing the measures of the court against the 'International Bible Students Association' and, in this way, publicly damaging the reputation of the State."[77]

The incident was also published in the *Hamburger Tageblatt*, where it stated in very cynical terms:

> Recently, a person who could not handle freedom stood outside a courtroom and thought he had to make a philippic statement against the state and its juridical institutions. It would be a disgrace to God if these religious martyrs were to be punished. In front of the judge he was asked to repeat his statements. He squirms. Then he is confronted with a witness and becomes sassy. But he has to admit: He said it. The court decides to put this "weird saint" behind bars. Apparently, the concentration camp [sentence] that had been imposed on this "champion of all persecuted Bible Students"

did not bring the anticipated results. However, let us not give up hope. Perhaps his next imprisonment will be more successful.[78]

The authorities also gave detailed explanations as to how to interpret what constituted activities for the banned IBSA. At funerals of Jehovah's Witnesses, Gestapo officials who were present (for the purpose of surveillance) immediately took action against the group of mourners if the speaker even used the name Jehovah or if he tried to mention the hope for God's future peaceful kingdom. Reading words of comfort directly from the Bible could also prove to be dangerous if the Gestapo considered the selected verses to have "subversive character."[79] As early as the spring of 1934, preliminary investigations were instituted against Jehovah's Witnesses in Hamburg because they supposedly had advocated IBSA ideas at three funerals.[80] In another case, accusations were made against a fifty-seven-year-old Bible Student whose wife had died on April 27, 1934. When, five days later, he gave the funeral sermon at his wife's grave, the State Police officials were especially attentive because, indirectly, the deceased was the very first victim of NS persecution from among Jehovah's Witnesses in Hamburg. Since repeated house searches had put the woman under extreme "emotional distress," she subsequently died of heart failure.[81]

In 1936 the Gestapo realized that it could not stop the activities of this small religious denomination. Therefore, it began persecuting Jehovah's Witnesses with renewed brutality. Increasingly, the Gestapo used methods of interrogation that were used to question political opponents of the regime, such as acts of brutality and torture.[82] As a result, mistreatment of Bible Students became the rule of the day at the Dortmund Gestapo office, nicknamed "Steinwache" (stone guard). To throw a blanket over the head of the victim, or to muzzle him so as to suppress his screams gave the interrogations "more force." The torture arsenal included horsewhips and other brutal torture instruments. In June 1936 an arrested Jehovah's Witness made his "acquaintance" with Criminal Investigator Theiß, the disreputable Gestapo examiner for "sectarian affairs." In his report, which was smuggled out of Germany, he describes his experiences as follows:

> Before even starting interrogations, Theiß began beating me. For this purpose, he used a horsewhip and a rubber truncheon. After this procedure, they tried to force me to betray my fellow believers. I refused to give them any information and also told them I was not like Judas, betraying people. As a result, he used the horsewhip to

beat me on the head and all over my body. . . . The constant beatings made me lose consciousness. When I opened my eyes, dirty
soap water was poured over me. Some of it was also poured into
my mouth. Their scornful laughs told me they were happy to see
me awake.[83]

During the following week, three to four times a day, this man was
summoned for "interrogations." Even though Theiß and his accom-
plices were not able to persuade him to betray his fellow believers, their
"efforts" did not remain entirely unsuccessful. Finally, they held a "confession" of the accused in their hands:

> Since they could not extract any information from me, a police of-
> ficer wrote an incriminating report about me. Unfortunately, I
> signed it so that I would no longer be exposed to their tortures. I
> felt relieved when they brought me back to my prison cell.[84]

Along with such mistreatments of the defenseless victims came the
use of ridicule. These inconspicuous but religiously steadfast "sectarians," whom the Gestapo officials considered to be "lunatics" or "idealists," gave the Gestapo the possibility to show their "almightiness:"
"Where is this Jehovah who said he would save you? Did he not promise
to help you? But he gives a sh—— about you. I am the one who has
power over you. I am the executioner of Dortmund. You will all learn to
say 'Heil Hitler!'"[85]

Besides physical torture, there were also threats and repressive
measures against family members along with other efforts to break the
psychological resistance of the victims. According to reports from Jehovah's Witnesses, Gestapo officials would place a revolver to their heads
and threaten to shoot them if they refused to give up their resistance and
provide the required information or requested names.[86] In a few cases,
the Gestapo even took relatives hostage. At the beginning of 1936 the
sister of the Bible Student Rudolf Meißner, who had fled the German
Reich in the previous year in order to avoid further persecution, was
taken hostage because of her brother's activities abroad.[87] The same
happened to Gertrud Franke, the wife of the Palatinate-Baden IBSA
district overseer Konrad Franke, when the authorities searched for her
husband. She was imprisoned in the spring of 1936 and released five
months later, but only after her husband had been arrested.[88]

Several Jehovah's Witnesses tried to make the authorities aware of
these Gestapo practices and sent petitions to administrative offices, ministries, or even the Reich chancellor. However, all these efforts remained

unsuccessful and resulted at best in investigations about the people who made the petitions. This is what happened to the wife of a Jehovah's Witness when she sent a letter of complaint to the government after she had been informed about the mistreatment of her husband in the Sachsenburg concentration camp. After the authorities had received her letter, she was imprisoned for six months on the charge of distributing "propaganda about acts of atrocity."[89]

Stubbornness, Fanaticism, and Paranoia

In some cases, the special courts requested that Jehovah's Witnesses should be subjected to psychiatric evaluations in order to establish diminished criminal responsibility, according to StGB, art. 51. Therefore, during the mid-1930s, in addition to legal authorities and police authorities, even psychiatric experts studied the uncompromising attitude and "stubbornness" of the Bible Students. These experts, however, were more interested in supporting the welfare of the state during the Third Reich than they were in supporting the welfare of the people. Frequently, they assessed the behavior of the accused as "persecution mania," being caused by "religious fanaticism," or "religious paranoia."[90] Sometimes, they even supported court decisions for admission into a "psychiatric clinic."[91] As a result, a number of Bible Students were sent to mental institutions. According to a 1938 publication of the Watch Tower Society, "mentally completely healthy Jehovah's Witnesses were committed to mental institutions, where they were left to die."[92]

The example of Richard P., a forty-six-year-old invalid, shows what kind of circumstances and dispositions could lead to a Bible Student's admission to an institution. At the end of 1936 Richard P. was arrested because of his refusal to participate in air-raid protection duties. During the police interrogations, he did not yield. The Munich police officer wrote in the interrogation records:

> In response to my objection that the Bible Student activities are banned, he bluntly told me that nobody could prohibit these activities, neither the Third Reich nor Hitler himself. Terrible times will come upon the people in Germany. The world is going downhill because it does not believe in Jehovah.[93]

Because of these statements, the police officer of Munich Police District 5 made the following unambiguous entry in the interrogation records:

> I consider P. as a very bad and dangerous person. . . . P. is an extremely fanatical adherent of his sect and is completely incorrigible. I consider it to be disastrous and irresponsible to allow such individuals to walk about freely among decent people. He has no scruples to advocate his fanatical views even before the police authorities. He will therefore propagate his viewpoints even more in public.

Six weeks later, Richard P. was transferred from protective detention to the psychiatric clinic at the Munich prison. The psychiatrist attested "schizophrenic behavior" and considered it appropriate to assign him StGB, art. 51 (diminished responsibility) status: because of an apparent "morbid dysfunction of his mental capacity," the Bible Student lacked the ability to recognize the inappropriateness of his actions.[94] As a result, the director of public prosecutions at the Munich Special Court abandoned the court proceedings and, instead, approved of an admission into a mental institution.

During the Third Reich there was an increasing tendency to diagnose any deviant behavior and ideological divergence from National Socialism as abnormal and, consequently, according to generally accepted standards, as "insane," or as a "psychic defect." Despite this tendency, legal and medical authorities became increasingly apprehensive about awarding defendants StGB, art. 51, status. Apparently, in this "authoritarian state," it did not seem opportune to take into consideration mitigating circumstances or grounds for exemption from punishment.

During the twenty-fifth conference of the "German Association for Legal and Social Medicine" that took place in Dresden on September 17–19, 1936, two professors of the psychiatric hospital at Breslau University advocated the "diminished responsibility" viewpoint. These professors considered the "Bible Student issue" to be primarily a responsibility of the prosecuting authorities and not of psychiatric hospitals. Under the supervision of Professor Johannes Lange, the director of the Breslau psychiatric clinic, these two physicians, Sollmann and Wagner, examined eleven Jehovah's Witnesses for an extended period of time and conducted a series of specific medical studies with them.[95] Reporting on the results of their studies, they stated that there was not one mentally deranged person among the eleven Bible Students, even though the majority of them were rather "peculiar people," which, in turn, could be grouped as quiet ones and active ones. Among these examined people was a twenty-two-year-old Bible Student who, when he was drafted to perform Reich Labor Service, refused to take the required oath in acknowledgement of the Führer but "always carefully" fulfilled his duties. Therefore, Sollmann and Wagner considered him as one of the "most valuable of these sectarians." The following statement, however, provides some insight into the motives of psychiatrists involved in this issue and shows their examination practices: "Because of his high intelligence and good Bible knowledge, it was difficult to corner him."[96]

Sollmann and Wagner considered "sectarianism" to be in contradiction to "the ideology of the National Socialist State" and, therefore, requested the "leaders of the state to take determined actions against sectarian groups that previously [had been] simply tolerated." At the same time, they acknowledged that, "basically, the majority of Jehovah's Witnesses were quite useful people." In order to avoid "that people searching for true religious values would come into conflicts that are unprofitable and destructive, the state [has to] take severe disciplinary actions against these incorrigible active [Bible Students] who are essentially only seeking a controversy."[97] During the following years even the prosecuting authorities accepted the view that uncompromising Jehovah's Witnesses should not be placed in a mental institution. Other "corrective institutions" would be more appropriate for them.

Besides those Jehovah's Witnesses who, based on StGB, art. 51, were sent to mental institutions, mostly during the mid-1930s, a small number of Jehovah's Witnesses were also subjected to psychiatric treatment in connection with the Nazi persecution of *Ballastexistenzen* (people whom the Nazis considered to be dispensable), according to the ideology of eugenics. Based on the July 14, 1933, Law Regarding Prevention of Hereditarily Ill Generations (Gesetz zur Verhütung erbkranken Nachwuchses), the hereditary health courts (*Erbgesundheitsgerichte*) ordered compulsory sterilization on a small number of Jehovah's Witnesses. In 1936 a twenty-four-year-old barber refused to follow the order for a medical examination before army enlistment. Even after he was forced to appear before the examining physician, he resisted the medical examination. Consequently, the district medical officer in charge of the medical examination ordered his sterilization, based on his diagnosis of "schizophrenia."[98] In Hamburg the hereditary health court ordered the sterilization of a twenty-seven-year-old laborer who was a Jehovah's Witness. In this case, the February 4, 1936, medical report of the Langenhorn Hospital specifically refuted the presence of "mental deficiency." However, because of his "stubborn attitude" that centered on a few "superior ideas," the medical report attested the onset of schizophrenia.[99] The sterilization was performed in 1937 at the Wandsbek Hospital.

First Wave of Arrests at the Reich Level

In view of the massive wave of repression against their fellow believers in Germany, the Watch Tower Society decided to provide the public, inside and outside of Germany, with increasing information about this "persecution of Christians" and to intensify their previous campaigns of protest. They scheduled an international general assembly in Lucerne (Switzerland) for September 4–7, 1936. For this general assembly, Jehovah's Witnesses from Germany were asked to provide a large number of reports about the religious persecution, arrests, and mistreatments. As far as possible, the respective group leaders collected the reports and submitted them to the district overseers. The district overseers, in turn, forwarded the reports to Wilhelm Ruhnau, a Bible Student from Danzig. Ruhnau accepted the responsibility of coordinating this action and taking the reports out of Germany via the city-state of Danzig.[100]

The action was carried out using the greatest possible precautionary measures. As a result, quite a number of the reports actually reached Switzerland. However, the Gestapo Special Command, which had been formed only two months earlier, and the SS Security Service were able to deal a serious blow to the banned IBSA organization. On August 24, 1936, Fritz Winkler, Balzereit's successor, as well as several other members of the Berlin IBSA group, were arrested. Based on the information acquired in connection with Winkler's arrest, the Gestapo officials now recognized their chance to destroy the entire banned IBSA organization "by means of an extensive action."[101] Throughout the Reich, a large-scale search was introduced and the various police offices were equipped with an increased number of policemen. On August 28, 1936, the Secret State Police office sent a letter that included the interrogation records of Winkler to the subordinate State Police offices, instructing them "to introduce a united action," on August 31, 1936, against all functionaries mentioned.[102] As a result, on the last day of August 1936, a considerable number of the IBSA functionaries were arrested. In Dresden the police arrested the district overseer of Schleswig-Holstein, the technician Georg Bär.[103] In Munich they arrested Johann Köbl, the post office clerk who supervised the Bavarian district, along with Josef Zissler, who was arrested on the following day. And in the State Police district of Mainz they arrested the district overseer of Palatinate-Baden, Konrad Franke.

On September 1, 1936, expedited instructions were given to the subordinate police offices to "immediately perform thorough searches and interrogations of all people there that were known as Bible Students," since "it was possible to dissolve the entire group of IBSA leaders."[104] These measures were to be taken immediately because the IBSA had scheduled their general assembly in Lucerne four days later. In addition, German IBSA functionaries had made plans to attend this general assembly. The State Police offices received a questionnaire whereby they were to determine "the structure of the banned organization down to the lowest level."

A wave of arrests took place, and many local IBSA groups were dissolved. These included groups in Berlin, Bremen, and Munich. In some districts, such as Schleswig-Holstein and Bavaria, the majority of the Bible Student groups were disbanded. Moreover, the police also dissolved several prohibited printing places of the *Watchtower*. This included the "shed for record production" in Hennigsdorf. In the course of this action, the Gestapo was able to arrest more than half of the number of district overseers. On the other hand, the Gestapo certainly did not dissolve the "entire group of IBSA leaders" as the Gestapa Department for Sectarian Affairs had initially claimed on August 28, 1936.[105] The district overseer of Thuringia and Hannover, the baker Walter Friese, was one of those who escaped his pursuers. Like a number of other IBSA functionaries, he was on the most-wanted list of the German journal of the Criminal Investigation Department (*Deutsches Kriminalpolizeiblatt*) to be hunted throughout the German Reich: "Code name: businessman 'Karl Rössler,' April 27, 1898, Halle. It is possible that Friese performs his prohibited activities in the disguise of a traveling tradesman selling motor oil. He has been put on the most-wanted list on August 29, 1936, and is searched because of his prohibited activities for the 'International Bible Students Association.'"[106] Four other district overseers wanted by the police managed to cross the border to Switzerland in order to attend the Lucerne general assembly. In the next few years, these district overseers, namely, Georg Rabe (eastern Prussia), Albert Wandres (Rhineland, Southern Hessen), Heinrich Dietschi (Northwestern Germany), and Erich Frost (Saxony), carried the main responsibility for the IBSA organization in Germany.

A total of three hundred Jehovah's Witnesses from Germany had been able to cross the border and get to Lucerne for the general assembly. And this despite the fact that only a few days before the wave of arrests, on August 20, 1936, the Bavarian Political Police had informed the subordinate police authorities about the anticipated IBSA assembly in Switzerland and had instructed them "to confiscate the passports of the persons concerned in order to prevent them from leaving the country."[107] As a result, the local police offices not only confiscated the passports, they even arrested all Bible Students who had recently requested a passport.

At the general assembly, disapproval was expressed for the bans that had been issued during the previous year in Danzig and Austria.[108] The recent mass arrests in Germany added another hostile reaction: a resolution was then adopted that exposed the leaders of the Catholic Church as being greatly responsible for the persecution of Jehovah's Witnesses. The resolution also included a request for solidarity:

> We request all like-minded people to take notice that Jehovah's Witnesses in Germany, Austria, and other places are terribly persecuted, punished with prison sentences, and horribly mistreated. Some of them are even killed. . . . We raise strong objections to the cruel treatment of Jehovah's Witnesses by the Roman Catholic hierarchy and their allies in Germany as well as in all other parts of the world. But we leave the outcome of the matter completely in the hands of the Lord, our God who, according to his Word, will recompense in full. . . . We send heartfelt greetings to our persecuted brethren in Germany and ask them to remain courageous and to trust completely in the promises of the Almighty God, Jehovah, and Christ.[109]

Two thousand to three thousand copies of this resolution were sent to governmental, public, and clerical authorities. In particular, it was sent to Hitler and Pope Pius XI.[110] By means of the resolution, the Watch Tower Society's leaders increased its anti-Catholic attacks. They accused the higher Catholic clergy to be the conspirators of the persecution campaign against Jehovah's Witnesses, for which it was possible to produce some significant evidence.[111] Even more so, in misconceiving the nature of NS rule, they stated that the Hitler government was "aided and incited by the Jesuits of the Roman Catholic Hierarchy and, therefore, a form of agency of the Roman Catholic Curia." Subsequently, the Watch Tower Society's publications described the Secret State Police officials as "the sleuths of the Hierarchy," or simply as the "Roman Gestapo," comparing the methods of the NS regime to the "actions that the Jesuits used during the Inquisition."[112] This development is most obviously reflected in Rutherford's book *Enemies*, published a few months later, in which Rutherford almost exclusively identifies the enemies to be the "religious leaders." The powers of "capitalism" and "politics," which, according to Rutherford's teachings, were also influenced by Satan, were pushed into the background. In his dichotomous world-view and the conception that the decisive War of God had already begun, the Watch Tower Society's president gave world affairs a subordinate place: The whole issue involved only one major controversy, the conflict between Jehovah's organization and Satan's organization in which the "Roman Catholic Hierarchy" occupied a leading position. In this conflict, "the people of earth [were] subjected to one or the other of these two organizations."[113] Based on this premise, other aberrations followed. According to Rutherford, not only National Socialism but also "Communism had been encouraged by the Jesuits . . . and then used as a camouflage or scarecrow" to draw the masses to Hitler. The reason for the persecution of Jehovah's Witnesses was the fact that "the Nazis of Germany, with Hitler as the leader, were organized and now carry on a ruthless, cruel and murderous rule in that land; and . . . persecute those who faithfully represent God and Christ." During this same period the NS state had also restricted the movements of the Catholic Church in various ways and priests had to appear before the same special courts as Jehovah's Witnesses, based on the Law against Insidious Attacks, but this fact did not hinder Rutherford to view "the Hitler government in full accord with the Vatican of Rome."[114]

Pamphlet Campaigns

Besides escalating verbal attacks and addressing Hitler as an "arbitrary dictator" who supposedly had made an alliance with the pope, it was specifically a decision made at the Lucerne general assembly that introduced the open counterattack against the NS regime.[115] This was the decision to distribute the Lucerne resolution by means of an extensive campaign throughout Germany. Several other important decisions regarding the prohibited activities in Germany were also made in Lucerne, apart from the general assembly events, and thus also hidden from Gestapo surveillance.[116] Now Rutherford met with the district overseers present and several other German IBSA functionaries. Balzereit's expulsion and the arrests of Winkler and the majority of district overseers made it necessary to reorganize the German IBSA leadership. Consequently, Erich Frost, a thirty-five-year-old musical director from Leipzig, was appointed to supervise the preaching activity in Germany in close cooperation with Heinrich Dwenger, the former leader and authorized officer of the service department at the Magdeburg branch office of the Watch Tower Society, who was now in exile managing the Prague branch office. At the same time, Rutherford appointed Heinrich Dietschi, a forty-six-year-old locksmith from Bochum, to be Erich Frost's successor in the event of Frost's arrest. In the course of the replacement of the district overseers, Rutherford had also implemented a complete restructuring of Germany's IBSA organization. (Based on the new understanding that all of Jehovah's Witnesses would be considered as "servants of the Word of God," the term "district overseer" was changed to "regional service director.") The objective of this restructuring was to achieve greater flexibility by means of clearer arrangements and a distribution of responsibilities. This would enable the IBSA to respond better to conditions of the ban. The Reich territory was divided into thirteen districts. The larger districts were subdivided into smaller districts with corresponding subordinate regional service directors. Each district or subordinate district was divided into main groups and subordinate groups. These subordinate groups, in turn, were divided into even smaller groups, which again were divided into cells.[117] The cells generally consisted of three to six people. One of these people was appointed to be the cell leader, or the contact person to the superior small group leader. If groups were not subdivided in smaller cells, the cell leader was the contact person to the superior group leader. The arrangement of such extensive subdivisions had the objective of preventing or impeding a destruction of the association if functionaries in key positions were arrested. Communication took place only from one group to the next. The individual IBSA members had contact only with two or three functionaries. In this way, it was hoped that the danger of discovery would be reduced, especially as a result of informers who had infiltrated the IBSA. By means of this restructuring, the small groups in the rural areas were also more closely connected to the nationwide structure of the organization.[118]

After their return from the Lucerne general assembly, several of the three hundred German attendees were arrested. In many cases, the Gestapo awaited them at their homes. As a precautionary measure, many of Jehovah's Witnesses who were in possession of a passport "lost" their passport in order to avoid being convicted on the basis of the visa. The Gestapo was apparently well informed about the people who had attended the assembly.[119] Later, the NS Press rejoiced that they had been able to arrest "a number of these travel-crazy 'Bible Students' who crossed the border in all kinds of secret ways in order to attend the agitating Lucerne general assembly."[120] According to *Völkischer Beobachter*, other groups supported the Bible Students in Lucerne in their "subversive activities against National Socialist Germany": "In cooperation with Communists and emigrants, they disgraced and criticized Germany verbally and graphically."[121]

During the following days and weeks, far more people were arrested than the number that had attended the Lucerne general assembly. The Gestapo had mobilized a large number of officials just for the persecution of this minor denomination.[122] And since the Bible Student affairs occupied an extensive part of State Police actions, the Gestapo had even increased its number of departments for sectarian affairs.[123] Therefore, the Gestapo was able to arrest far more than one thousand IBSA members between August and September 1936. Two weeks after the Lucerne general assembly, on September 25, 1936, Wilhelm Ruhnau, who was responsible for sending the reports to the IBSA central European office in Bern, was arrested in Danzig-Zoppot. Apparently the local police authorities acted on orders from the German Gestapo. Four days later, Ruhnau was extradited, possibly via the border into eastern Prussia. There, he was handed over to the Reich German authorities.[124] This secret extradition was a serious violation of the constitution of the Free City of Danzig, guaranteed by the League of Nations.[125] In the following months, the Watch Tower Society sent several requests to the Polish Commissar General of Danzig and the High Commissioner of the League of Nations, but all these efforts were in vain.[126] Ruhnau remained missing. Most probably, the Gestapo had murdered him.

The repeated arrests of active Jehovah's Witnesses following the Lucerne general assembly resulted in serious losses to the organization.[127] Despite these losses, most of the districts could be restructured in just a few weeks as had been planned at the general assembly. As far as can be determined, in October 1936 the Bavaria IBSA was divided into seventeen main groups and subordinate groups; Munich had twenty-three IBSA cells, and Hamburg had four subordinate groups supervised by group leader Max Grote and those were subdivided into twenty-five cells (see figure 2).[128]

Gestapo officials, who at this point imagined the IBSA to be virtually destroyed, were surprised at the ability of the Bible Students Association to reorganize. A memo of the Secret State Police office, written at the end of 1936, complained that their methods had not been able to act as a deterrent: "For instance, in one district it was observed that, while the discovery of the banned organization was being investigated, the IBSA was already establishing a substitute organization."[129]

Figure 2. Structure of the IBSA main groups in Hamburg and Altona, 1936

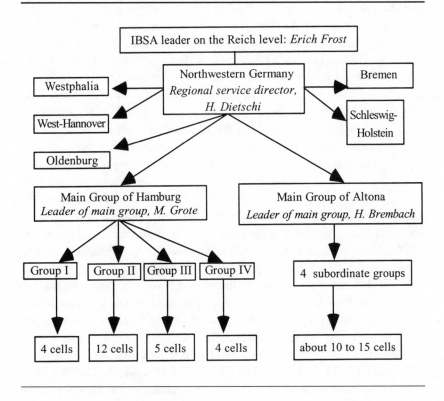

During the period of restructuring, plans were also made to start the pamphlet campaign that had been decided on in Lucerne. In Hamburg such planning began as early as September 1936. During an initial meeting at a Wellingsbüttel beer garden, the regional service director Heinrich Dietschi informed approximately fifteen Jehovah's Witnesses about the decisions that had been made at the Lucerne general assembly. These Jehovah's Witnesses were, in turn, responsible for the main groups in Hamburg and Altona, as well as for a few groups in Schleswig-Holstein. Dietschi also read to them the resolution that had been adopted at the assembly and that was intended to be distributed. A few days later, under the leadership of main group leader Grote, a total of sixty to seventy Hamburg Jehovah's Witnesses, including the leaders of all subordinate groups, met outside of the city at a water tower. There, they made specific arrangements for the distribution. Each group was assigned a specific area in Hamburg outside of their respective home districts. The distribution was to take place simultaneously, within a period of no more than thirty minutes. At every house, only one or two copies of the pamphlet were to be put into a mailbox or slipped under the door. Afterwards, the Bible Students were to go quickly to a different street and proceed in the same way, a method that had already been successfully used in their house-to-house activity. In the remaining time until the beginning of the pamphlet campaign, the group leaders should discuss appropriate details and precautionary measures with the members of their respective group or cell. In other locations, similar preparations were made.

Throughout the German Reich, the pamphlet campaign was scheduled to take place in the late afternoon of December 12, 1936, between the hours of five and seven. Jehovah's Witnesses intended to distribute a total of 300,000 copies of the resolution that had been printed in Switzerland. However, only the resolutions that were smuggled in via the Czechoslovakian border reached Germany. Smuggling the 100,000 copies via the Dutch border, intended for distribution in northern Germany and Berlin, was not successful, so that Jehovah's Witnesses tried to compensate these losses by printing an additional number of resolutions and redistributing the pamphlets smuggled into Germany via the Riesengebirge (Czechoslovakian border).

After the various groups and cells had received their respective packages, the resolutions were folded—with gloves—and put into blank envelopes. No addresses were written on the envelopes intended for distribution in mailboxes. Other resolutions were sent anonymously by mail, primarily to government officials, functionaries of the NSDAP, judges, and public prosecutors, as well as to the religious leaders of various churches, and these were appropriately addressed. Everything was well organized. Up until the last minute, there was the danger that the Gestapo would discover this secret campaign. On December 10, 1936, in Augsburg (in the northern part of the city), Gestapo officials raided an IBSA cell during its preparations for the pamphlet campaign, just two days before the date of distribution. The arrested women remained silent, and the Augsburg Gestapo could not draw any further conclusions from this discovery.[130]

On the second Saturday of December, according to plan, at exactly five in the afternoon, and in almost all of Germany, more than three thousand Jehovah's Witnesses began to distribute the resolution.[131] They dropped envelopes with copies of the resolution into mailboxes, attached them with thumbtacks to entrances or gates, and put them under doormats. They also left resolutions in phone booths, on park benches, or on parked cars. In this way, tens of thousands of resolutions were distributed.[132]

The police authorities were not prepared to deal with such a rapid and well-organized pamphlet campaign. After only a few minutes into the campaign, the police offices received the first complaints. Before they were even able to get an idea of the extent of the campaign in order to introduce countermeasures, the action had already ended. During the distribution, a very small number of arrests took place.[133] In Munich the police were able to arrest the group leader Martin Pötzinger, whom they caught "in the act." An SS officer began his pursuit immediately after the resolution had been dropped into his mailbox. Even though Pötzinger tried to escape, he was overpowered by an SA officer who had been called. At exactly 6:20 p.m., the two "eager" party members handed Martin Pötzinger over to the police officers at Police Station 1 of Munich police district 9.[134] Not long after, a radio warning was transmitted to all police offices in the "center of the [National Socialist] movement," stating that "pamphlets with malicious content against the government [were] distributed in various parts of the city."[135] At half-past midnight, the Würzburg Secret State Police office sent out a telex, alerting the police offices to this "pamphlet campaign that was conducted by the banned Bible Students and carried the title 'Resolution.'" "The police patrols are instructed, even tonight, to keep an eye on this pamphlet campaign. The distributors are to be arrested and the evidence confiscated. The Bible Student homes are also to be searched."[136]

Shortly thereafter, at one of his visits to Prague, IBSA leader on the Reich level Erich Frost reported to the branch office there that the distribution of the resolution in Germany "proved to be a tremendous blow to the government and the Gestapo."[137] Even the public prosecutor's office at the Schleswig-Holstein Special Court stated that this campaign had been "carried out with so much skill that it was possible in only a few cases to determine the persons responsible."[138] The following report regarding the police measures introduced, which reflects the great satisfaction of Jehovah's Witnesses about their success, states: "The police thoroughly combed whole blocks of houses and demanded at each door the immediate delivery of the tract. As only a very few people had one and most of them did not even know about the matter, the impression was created that the whole citizenry was in league with the Bible Students, granting them by their denial a kind of solidarity and protection. This impression . . . had a destructive effect."[139]

"Quite a number of loyal Germans" even went to the police offices and delivered the "resolutions," or they sent them directly to the State Police offices. According to the evidence included in the public prosecutor's court exhibits, at least twenty-three letters arrived at the Flensburg outpost of the Kiel State Police office alone.[140] The people sending the letters had generally received the resolution by mail. These people were officials of the Flensburg city council, the mayor, members of the local NSDAP group, representatives of a company, and administrative officers of the Allgemeine Ortskrankenkasse (general health insurance company). Some resolutions had also been sent to private citizens such as a *Studienrat* (a permanent teacher at a higher school), a specialist in orthopedic surgery, several police officers, and the district veterinarian. Immediately, on that same Saturday evening, the veterinarian typed a letter to the police authorities: "Enclosed you will find a letter that has been dropped into my mailbox by a stranger this afternoon at about 5:30. Because of its treasonous contents I am submitting it to the appropriate authorities."[141]

Two days later the Secret State Police office made preparations for a counterattack. On the evening of December 14, 1936, the State Police offices sent a telegram to the subordinate police offices, as well as the superior administrative authorities, with the following information:

> Attention—to be observed promptly. The means by which this campaign has been performed shows that the IBSA is still in existence, despite the August 28, 1936 [police] action. Consequently, the Secret State Police—Secret State Police Office in Berlin—has given instructions to perform house searches in all State Police districts in which this pamphlet was distributed. The searches should take place on December 15, 1936, at four in the morning, and should be performed in the homes of all people who are suspected of being involved in IBSA activities or who are members of the IBSA. All people suspected of involvement in prohibited IBSA activities, and especially participation in the December 12, 1936, IBSA pamphlet distribution, should be taken into protective detention. . . . It is anticipated that this newly performed [police] action will help to arrest the remaining leaders of the banned IBSA.[142]

An enormous police force went into action and at several places people were arrested. On December 15, 1936, a total of thirty-three Jehovah's Witnesses were arrested in Kassel.[143] But this time the Gestapo action throughout the German Reich turned out to be a failure. According to a report by the Munich State Police office, Jehovah's

Witnesses were prepared for this one: "Due to the fact that the members of the International Earnest Bible Students followed certain tactics, the house searches remained unsuccessful. There was not a single piece of incriminating material in the homes of the members of this association. According to our experience, these materials have been either burned or stored at locations outside of their homes."[144]

After the pamphlet distribution, the legal authorities and the Gestapo increased their efforts to thwart the IBSA. On December 20, 1936, the Karlsruhe chief public prosecutor reported to the RJM, in response to the IBSA campaign, that he had given instructions "to enforce immediately punishment on the few 'Earnest Bible Students' who had been sentenced but not yet put in prison."[145] During the following spring, the special courts sentenced the pamphlet distributors to imprisonment of between six and twelve months. In some cases, they even imposed prison sentences of up to two years.[146] In its decision of February 27, 1937, the Schleswig-Holstein Special Court considered the distribution of the resolution even as an offense against the Law against Insidious Attacks on State and a Party. According to the judges, the assertion that people were persecuted in Germany had to be considered as untruth: "The resolution contains inaccurate statements that can severely damage the welfare and reputation of the [German] Reich and the Reich government."[147]

At the end of 1936 a Gestapa memo made a similar statement: "In Germany information is being collected and sent abroad to 'fellow believers' according to which Bible Students allegedly are exposed to occupational or other discriminations. Based on these reports, these people distribute the most serious propaganda about acts of atrocity. They even report that true Christians in Germany are being persecuted and Jehovah's Witnesses are thrown into concentration camps and prisons solely on the basis of their faith, where they are supposedly tortured and even killed."[148] At this same time, the Gestapo methods of persecution became increasingly brutal.[149] This was reflected by the fact that an increasing number of Jehovah's Witnesses died as a result of these methods of persecution. For example, by mid-1936 three Jehovah's Witnesses had lost their lives. Only one year later, the number of deaths had increased to at least seventeen. The Gestapo usually declared or covered up these cases as "suicides committed by hanging." Based on the reports that had been sent to Switzerland, by mid-1937 the IBSA central European office in Bern had knowledge of the following "deaths from unnatural causes:"[150]

- Eleven Jehovah's Witnesses died as a result of Gestapo interrogations (mistreatment) and during police detention (death by hanging, slashing of wrists). Four of these deaths occurred in the second half of 1936 and seven in the first half of 1937.
- A fifty-two-year-old invalid died in July 1934 as a result of the mistreatment inflicted upon him by SA storm troopers.
- One Jehovah's Witness was shot in mid-1935 at the Esterwegen concentration camp while passing through the guards' line.
- An approximately thirty-five-year-old Jehovah's Witness supposedly committed suicide on December 5, 1935, during his imprisonment in the Ichtershausen penal institution.
- One Jehovah's Witness died at a psychiatric clinic three weeks after his arrest in August 1936.
- A Jehovah's Witness suffering from diabetes died a few days after his arrest because of his refusal to take lifesaving injections.
- A thirty-one-year-old Jehovah's Witness died in 1937 as a result of the mistreatment inflicted in the Dachau concentration camp.

Most likely, these statements reflect the real situation only to a certain extent and do not represent the complete picture.[151] They do however provide some insight into the escalation of terror against Jehovah's Witnesses during 1936/37.

During February and March 1937 Jehovah's Witnesses repeated their distribution campaign in several other places, but apparently not on a nationwide level. On February 11, 1937, Jehovah's Witnesses in Augsburg distributed 1,200 to 1,400 "resolutions."[152] On the same day, proceedings against a number of their fellow believers took place at the Augsburg Special Court. On February 20, 1937, the pamphlet campaign was repeated in the Ruhrgebiet. A number of Jehovah's Witnesses were subsequently arrested in Essen because, prior to the distribution, an "absolutely reliable contact person" from among the Bible Students had provided the State Police office with information about this distribution.[153] In the district of Rottenburg, some resolutions were even placed on billboards.[154] During February, under the leadership of regional service director Dietschi, another distribution took place in Hamburg. This action was supported by Jehovah's Witnesses from Lübeck because some fellow believers in Hamburg hesitated to participate in this repeated campaign.[155]

At this time, the Gestapo investigations in other locations resulted in a number of arrests. Now, the Gestapo finally achieved the "results" that they had anticipated after the first pamphlet campaign of December 12, 1936. In mid-February 1937 the Munich police authorities imprisoned a total of sixty pamphlet distributors. In its February 19, 1937, report, the State Police office reported that they had been able "to destroy this prohibited association in Munich, on the right side of the Isar."[156]

About one or two weeks later Georg Rabe was arrested. He was the regional service director responsible for the then-enlarged districts of eastern and western Prussia, Pomerania, and Mecklenburg. On March 4, 1937, the regional service director of Bavaria was arrested. And probably around the same time, the two regional service directors responsible for eastern Silesia, Berlin, and the Brandenburg district were also arrested. On March 21, 1937, IBSA leader on the Reich level Erich Frost, who traveled under the code name "Meindl," fell into the hands of the Gestapo.[157] At the Security Service of the Reichsführer SS, these arrests marked the beginning of a "second action against the IBSA." In order to be able to "thwart the IBSA successfully," a total department "special command" (*Sonderkommando*) was formed. This special command was to include "knowledgeable officials from the various State Police offices" and "experts from the superior Security Service departments who were familiar with these matters" because "experiences from both actions" had shown "that officials with no experience in this field are unsuitable for such actions."[158] "Every possible means and all energy" were to be employed to conclude this second action. By now, the authorities knew about the Bible Students Association's innerorganizational recruiting power: "As long as we have not caught every single one of the main functionaries of the banned IBSA, there is the danger that the IBSA will be reorganized."

In the following months the number of arrests continued to increase. In a discussion that took place on June 18, 1937, at the RJM, the Dresden chief public prosecutor mentioned that between 1,300 and 1,500 people had been arrested in his district.[159] In comparison to Saxony, fewer arrests were made in Pomerania due to the smaller population. However, the five hundred to six hundred Witness arrests presented a serious organizational problem for the Stettin chief public prosecutor. Since there was no concentration camp in Pomerania, the Gestapo had to put so many people into the local prisons that they were "completely overcrowded."[160]

Despite the great number of arrests, the Gestapo and the Security Service had not achieved its anticipated destruction of the IBSA. Even though the names of the top-level functionaries were known and the most diligent searches were performed, the Gestapo was not able to track them down.[161] According to the decision made in Lucerne, Heinrich

Dietschi assumed responsibility as IBSA leader on the Reich level after Erich Frost had been arrested. Apart from general arrangements, Dietschi once again reorganized the distribution of the various districts. For the first time, he even appointed women as "regional service directors."[162] Previously, only men had occupied leading positions in the Bible Students Association. Jehovah's Witnesses base this arrangement on the statements of the apostle Paul regarding the subordinate position of women in the Christian congregation (1 Cor. 11:3; 14:34). From mid-1936 on, an increasing number of women occupied positions of leadership as, for example, group or cell leaders. These women performed their responsibilities with great determination, and in this regard, they certainly did not lack the courage and fearlessness of the men. On the contrary, they administered their assignments even more radically because of their strong conviction.[163] After the wave of arrests during the spring of 1937, the following arrangements were made: Auguste Schneider from Bad Kreuznach (code name "Paula") was appointed to supervise the districts of Baden, Saarland, and Palatinate. Frieda Christiansen from Flensburg (code name "Hermine Friedrichs," or "Minchen") accepted responsibility for the district of Schleswig-Holstein. Elfriede Löhr from Munich was responsible for Silesia, and Gertrud Pötzinger (code name "Gertrud" or "Nelly") for Bavaria. Besides those women supervising larger districts as regional service directors, quite a number of women now also supervised the smaller groups.

"Barbarian Acts in a 'Christian' Country"

The ranks of the IBSA members had now been considerably diminished. But once again, the Bible Students were able to undertake a major campaign. Besides Heinrich Dietschi, the new IBSA leader on the Reich level, and Albert Wandres, the regional service director of western Germany, the female regional service directors played a principal role in the preparations for this campaign. They prepared an "open letter" in which they intended to criticize strongly the Gestapo's methods and the conditions in prisons and concentration camps, even more extensively and in more detail than the Lucerne resolution, which was written in a somewhat moderate tone. In preparation for this letter, they first of all contacted the IBSA central European office in Bern and suggested using a selection of the reports about the persecution of Jehovah's Witnesses, which the regional service directors had collected and sent to Bern for the purpose of compiling these into an informational pamphlet.[164] After

Rutherford had given his approval to this campaign, Martin Harbeck, the leader of the Bern IBSA central European office, wrote the text for the letter based on those reports. He even cited extensive excerpts from Nazi sources such as an April 5, 1937, letter of the NSDAP administration of Walsenburg (Silesia)[165] and an article on "Bible Students in Penal Institutions," published in the journal *Der Deutsche Justizbeamte*.[166] The pamphlet compared the persecution of Jehovah's Witnesses in the Third Reich to the torture methods used during the Inquisition. With reference to specific locations and names of the Gestapo officials concerned, the pamphlet reported on mistreatment with clubs and truncheons, as well as violent killings. The following sentence was italicized for emphasis: "*Particularly brutal were the mistreatments administered by Criminal Investigator Theiß from Dortmund, as well as Tennhoff and Heimann from the Secret State Police office in Gelsenkirchen and Bochum.*"[167] Regarding a Jehovah's Witness by the name of Peter Heinen, the pamphlet stated that "Secret State Police officials beat him to death in the city hall of Gelsenkirchen."[168]

The pamphlet also pointed out that Jehovah's Witnesses considered themselves to be Christian martyrs and would not surrender even in the face of NS persecution:

> For many years, we, Jehovah's Witnesses, formerly known as Bible Students, have taught people in Germany the Bible and its comforting message. Unselfishly, we have also invested millions in order to help people in times of material and spiritual difficulties. In return, thousands of Jehovah's Witnesses in Germany have been severely persecuted, mistreated, and put into prisons and concentration camps. However, despite extreme emotional pressure and sadistic physical mistreatment, which has been committed against German women, mothers, and even small children, it was not possible, during the previous four years, to eliminate Jehovah's Witnesses. We will not be intimidated but will continue to obey God rather than men just as the apostles of Christ did when they were told to stop preaching the Gospel.

Two hundred thousand copies of this two-page pamphlet, compactly written on DIN-A3 format (12.2" x 16.8"), were printed in Bern. This time, however, all attempts to smuggle the copies over the border into Germany failed. Consequently, the printing had to be organized in Germany. After the matrices for the printing plates were smuggled into Germany, a Jehovah's Witness from Lemgo (Lippe) printed on a rapid press a total of 69,000 copies of the pamphlet titled "Open Letter—To the German people who believe in the Bible and have respect for Christ."

On Sunday, June 20, 1937, between noon and one o'clock in the afternoon, the open letter was distributed simultaneously in a number of German cities.[169] Like the distribution six months earlier, the Gestapo did not have any knowledge about the specific arrangements for this campaign—the distribution could be carried out in the same way as the distribution of the Lucerne resolution. In Hamburg, approximately seventy people distributed several thousand pamphlets. As in the previous campaign, a large number of pamphlets were mailed. Besides government officials, the attention of this campaign was specifically directed toward people "who were expected to read the pamphlet and think about its contents, instead of carelessly throwing it away."[170]

Even in this pamphlet campaign, the primary objective of Jehovah's Witnesses was to demonstrate publicly their faith in Jehovah God and to expose the "barbarian acts in a 'Christian' country."[171] As with the previous resolution, this pamphlet might say to the general public, "See for yourselves who really are God's people and who are their enemies!" Inasmuch as the pamphlet campaign of Jehovah's Witnesses informed people about the atrocities of the NS regime, it did not have the objective of mobilizing the German people to take up arms against fascism. One of its aims was to persuade people in Germany to withdraw their allegiance from the barbarian Hitler state. But the primary purpose of this action was to encourage people to submit to the authority of God, especially in consideration of the imminent War of Armageddon. Consequently, the open letter requested people to use the remaining time in order to "wholeheartedly [take] sides with God and Christ Jesus." The resistance of Jehovah's Witnesses supported God's Kingdom and did not have the objective of overthrowing the NS rulers. This action was something that would be accomplished only by Jehovah God; of that, Jehovah's Witnesses were certain.

The National Socialists considered the open letter as an "act of sedition such as otherwise could be seen only in Jewish emigrant papers or in libelous Communist press reports written abroad."[172] As a result, after the pamphlet campaign, the Gestapo intensified its actions against the IBSA even more. It was able to prevent almost all German Jehovah's Witnesses from attending the general assembly held at the "Maison de la Mutualité" in Paris from August 21 to 23, 1937, which Rutherford also attended. Similar to the Lucerne assembly in 1936, this assembly also had the objective of discussing the further approach to the situation in

Germany in the presence of as many German fellow believers as possible.[173] As early as five weeks before the general assembly, the Secret State Police offices had given appropriate instructions to the police authorities and had requested to be informed about "any members of the IBSA who applied for a passport."[174] One week before the assembly, the local State Police office in Munich gave instructions to take all Bible Students who they suspected would attempt to attend the assembly despite the withdrawal of their passports "temporarily into protective detention, as a precautionary measure."[175]

Under these circumstances, only five Jehovah's Witnesses were able to cross the border and attend the general assembly in Paris. Among these was IBSA leader on the Reich level Heinrich Dietschi. When he returned to his secret living quarters, the Gestapo was there waiting for him. One week later, on September 3, 1937, they also arrested Albert Wandres in Dresden.[176] Because Wandres had accepted temporary responsibility for the districts of other regional service directors who had been arrested (in addition to his own area of activity in the western and southwestern parts of Germany),[177] the Gestapo also considered him to be the substitute IBSA leader on the Reich level.[178]

As a result of the investigations that led to the arrest of the IBSA leader Dietschi and his representative Wandres, the Gestapo was able to arrest almost all IBSA functionaries in leading positions in a very short period of time. At the end of August, even before the arrest of Dietschi, the Bavarian regional service director, Elfriede Löhr, was arrested in Berlin. A few days later, Gertrud Pötzinger, who was responsible for the activities in Silesia, was arrested in Dresden. On September 13, 1937, at 9 a.m., Gestapo officials arrested regional service director Frieda Christiansen when she arrived at a meeting that Wandres had arranged for the regional service directors in northern Germany.[179] Regional service director Auguste Schneider was arrested at a train station in Bingen.[180] During that same period, Walter Friese, the regional service director of Thuringia and Hannover, Ludwig Stickel, the subordinate regional service director of Württemberg, and a number of other regional service directors were also placed under arrest. Following those arrests, several IBSA groups were destroyed, such as the groups in Freiburg, Baden-Baden, and Karlsruhe.

Even the IBSA groups in Hamburg that had survived almost unscathed both waves of arrests at the end of August 1936—and also the distribution of the resolution in the spring of 1937—were now affected by this latest Gestapo action. Initially, the Gestapo had only limited success.

Two days after the especially extensive open-letter campaign in the Hanseatic city of Hamburg, the Gestapo was able to arrest one of the distributors. At the end of June other arrests followed. According to a Gestapo note, the interrogations were "complicated and slow, because some of the arrested people denied the accusations or completely refused to make any statements."[181] As late as August 29, 1937, Jehovah's Witnesses were able to arrange in Rönneburg (near Harburg) a larger meeting of group and cell leaders from Hamburg and Schleswig-Holstein. They concealed this meeting, held at the Rönneburger Park restaurant, as a social gathering of the local "garden club." After everybody present confirmed that they had not been followed, they started taking a walk. They went to a small clearing in the forest. There, a non-local Jehovah's Witness gave the fifty-two "gardeners" a report about the Paris general assembly, which had been held during the previous week. Afterwards, they discussed their plans of action.

Two weeks after this meeting, the Gestapo was successful in destroying the Hamburg groups of the IBSA. On September 11, 1937, they arrested main group leader Max Grote. Two days later the regional service director Frieda Christiansen was arrested. Subsequently, the various IBSA groups were systematically destroyed, from the top down to the smallest cells.[182] After the leaders had been arrested in mid-September, more than one hundred members of the various groups were arrested during the months of October and November. Until the time of their transfer to the legal authorities, these Jehovah's Witnesses were kept at the Fuhlsbüttel Police Prison. (From 1936 on, this was the official name of the Fuhlsbüttel concentration camp established for the "resistance of sedition and atrocity propaganda.") For several months, Jehovah's Witnesses were the largest group of prisoners in this concentration camp from among all people taken into protective detention by the Gestapo. In October 1937 at least 122 of a total of 234 prisoners at Fuhlsbüttel were Jehovah's Witnesses. In January 1938 at least 132 of a total of 258 prisoners were Jehovah's Witnesses.[183] In the spring of 1938 eight court cases involving a total of 187 Jehovah's Witnesses from Hamburg (77 men and 110 women) took place at the Hanseatic Special Court. Fifty-five of these people were sentenced to imprisonment ranging from more than one year to four years.[184] Consequently, in November 1938 the local State Police office in Hamburg stated with satisfaction that "it had been able, since its action in 1937, to destroy completely the IBSA in the local special court district."[185]

For a considerable period of time, the IBSA was unable to recover from this wave of arrests in 1937. In some locations, it did not recover at all.[186] The majority of active believers were in prison or in concentration camps. Those who had not been arrested discontinued their activities because of fear or lack of leadership. After September 1937 there was no longer any nationwide structure of the organization. The remaining groups no longer participated in any public activities.[187] To the greatest extent possible, the reduced number of faithful ones tried to continue their religious meetings in small groups. Often, they could use only their Bibles because the supply of the *Watchtowers* had temporarily been almost completely stopped.

As a result, the authorities responsible for the persecution considered their struggle against the Bible Students Association to be over. On October 18, 1937, the Karlsruhe chief public prosecutor reported to Berlin that in his jurisdictional district "the activities of the Bible Students . . . [had] decreased."[188] Three months later, the SS Central Security Office (SS-Sicherheitshauptamt), made the following statement regarding the IBSA in one of their situation reports: "The International Bible Students have not made a significant appearance."[189] Even though, during 1938, Security Service informers noticed increasing IBSA activities, and the State Police offices made a considerable number of arrests, the authorities did not attach as much importance to this development as they had during the previous two years. In this regard, the annual situation report of 1938 of the Reich Security Main Office gave the following summary:

> From all prohibited sectarian groups, only the "International Bible Students Association" (IBSA) has made again a significant appearance. However, because of firm actions on the part of the authorities, it has been possible to destroy this organization completely. Therefore, the recent IBSA activities will not have any significant effect. It has also been possible to stop almost completely the smuggling of IBSA publications over the border of Switzerland and France. In 1938 approximately seven hundred Bible Students were taken into protective detention throughout the Reich. This number includes several people who publicly refused to participate in the April 4, 1938, elections and who were involved in acts of sedition against the Führer.[190]

In the first quarterly situation report for 1939, the SS Security Service recorded: "There have been only a few instances in which 'Bible

Students' have made an appearance. The fact that they continue to perform their prohibited propaganda and prohibited magazine distribution from Switzerland clearly shows that presently they do not have a uniform leadership in the Reich."[191]

The three waves of arrest in August/September 1936, March/April 1937, and August/September 1937 had destroyed the nationwide structure of the Bible Students Association. However, it had not been possible to suppress the courageous conviction and determination of Jehovah's Witnesses. They were still strong enough to make another attempt at reestablishing their organization.

12

Jurisdictional Conflicts between the Legal Authorities and Police

In the Third Reich the question of taking legal action against Jehovah's Witnesses sparked conflicts between the legal authorities and the police. In 1934 a considerable number of Bible Student cases resulted in acquittals because the courts declared the IBSA bans, which had been issued in the various states, to be legally invalid. These judicial decisions greatly restricted the Gestapo's possibilities of persecuting Jehovah's Witnesses. The Gestapo quickly decided to use their own methods in punishing the defiance of Jehovah's Witnesses against the ban. For this purpose, they used the "protective detention" clause, which had been made available for the executive body of the police authorities by means of the February 28, 1933, Decree of the Reich President for the Protection of People and State. This decree enabled the police authorities to impose protective detention for an unlimited period of time, at their own discretion, in all cases in which they considered "public law and order to be endangered."[192] In practical terms, such protective detention orders amounted to orders for imprisonment at one of the concentration camps, which had been in use since March 1933. However, in contrast to a judicial arrest warrant, a warrant for protective detention from the police authorities could *not* be appealed. This particular warrant had primarily been introduced so that immediate action could be taken against political opponents. It provided the police authorities with the right to take action against all groups of opponents without involving the legal authorities.

In the regulations outlining the warrant's objectives, it was specifically emphasized that protective detention should be used exclusively for prevention purposes. Consequently, it should leave unaffected the legal authorities' function of punishing offenses. However, the State Police authorities as well as the criminal police made excessive use of this warrant. In practice, it was from the beginning an artificial, problematic procedure to try to differentiate the various functions of imprisonment between the legal and the police authorities. Any coexistence of normative and non-normative powers involved areas of friction that inevitably led to conflicts. Soon, there were complaints about inappropriate uses of protective detention.

At the beginning of 1934 the RMdI reminded the police authorities that protective detention had been introduced for the purpose of combating dangerous developments. He also emphasized, once again, that it should be used exclusively as a means of prevention. To this end, on January 9, 1934, Minister Frick gave the following clarifying instructions to the governments of the various German states: "Therefore, protective detention may not be imposed as a form of 'punishment,' that is, as an alternative for punishment imposed by the legal or police authorities, especially not with a predetermined period of detention. In principle, it is not permissible to use protective detention in order to replace legal proceedings.[193]

In 1934, and at least during the first half of 1935, the Gestapo took a number of Jehovah's Witnesses into custody and brought them before a custodial judge in order to institute proceedings on the charge of defiance of the Bible Student ban. In many cases, however, the custodial judges refused to take Jehovah's Witnesses into pretrial detention. In other cases, they based their decision on a lack of evidence. Contrary to the Gestapo methods, the custodial judges did not consider the attendance at religious meetings as a continuance of prohibited IBSA activities. In other cases, they based their decision on the opinion of the Darmstadt Special Court and other courts, according to which the IBSA ban was legally ineffective because the constitutional articles guaranteeing freedom of religion had not been repealed and were still valid (see pp. 119–35). Accordingly, the custodial judge stated that under the prevailing circumstances, the accused would probably not be convicted. The Gestapo was already displeased that quite a few court cases involving Jehovah's Witnesses resulted in acquittals. Even more so, they refused to accept that they had to release Bible Students from under their authority because a custodial judge refused to issue a warrant for arrest. According to State Police investigations, these Bible Students, who had displayed an "incorrigible attitude" during the interrogations, had already been convicted of a punishable offense against "state and people." They had been released from protective detention and handed over to the legal authorities for further punishment.

As a result, the State Police offices established the practice of issuing protective detention, a practice that clearly contradicted the ministerial regulations with regard to the purpose of protective detention. With its interoffice decree of January 12, 1935, the State Police office for the jurisdictional district of Schleswig (Altona) informed the local police authorities about an increase in Bible Student activities. In the decree the chief of the local Gestapo office had to acknowledge: "However, there is not enough evidence to institute legal proceedings against the offenders and obtain arrest warrants."[194] Since the results of the police investigations did not allow for an institution of legal proceedings, the Gestapo used a method that went beyond the control of the legal authorities: "I decided to stop the anti-state activities of the Bible Students by imposing protective detention. Therefore, I request to carefully investigate and locate immediately the people who present an imminent danger to the National Socialist State because of their activities for the Bible Students Association. These people have to be reported to me together with a detailed report."

For those concerned, this new action meant that they would not be handed over to a court for punishment but would be sent directly to a concentration camp, even though during 1935/36 incarceration was generally not for an extended period. For example, from the Altona IBSA group alone, three members were sent to the Esterwegen concentration camp: a thirty-year-old brewery worker between February 19 and October 20, 1935; a thirty-one-year-old factory worker between March 12 and June 9, 1935; and a forty-nine-year-old cigar manufacturer between May 10 and October 22, 1935.[195]

In the spring of 1935 State Police offices in other districts followed Altona. The procedure was always the same: After the conclusion of the police investigations, Jehovah's Witnesses were first brought before a custodial judge. If the custodial judge issued an arrest warrant, the prisoners were handed over to the legal authorities for further prosecution. If, because of insufficient evidence or other reasons, the judge did not issue an arrest warrant, the police authorities could either keep the prisoners in protective detention or send them to a concentration camp.[196] Thus, the police authorities used protective detention as a form of "preliminary pretrial detention" during which they would decide the next step to be taken.[197] Cases liable for trial in a court of justice were handed over to the legal authorities. The other cases remained under the authority of the Gestapo and were handled according to their own methods. As a result, protective detention became a corrective measure of unwelcome legal decisions.

According to a report that the district president of Hildesheim sent to the Reich minister of the interior in April 1935, the State Police office took twelve Bible Students from Hildesheim "into protective detention after, as was frequently the case, the municipal court had refused to issue an arrest warrant."[198] In September 1935 the Bavarian Political Police gave the following instructions to the police authorities regarding protective detention for Bible Students: "First-time offenders charged with involvement in activities for the 'International Bible Students Association' have to be taken into protective detention for up to seven days if no judicial arrest warrant has been issued. After they have been severely warned and possibly required to report to the police, they should be released. In cases that involve IBSA leaders, protective detention can be extended to up to two months."[199] Such instructions emphasize that protective detention was used as a substitute for legal punishment. Accordingly, the Gestapo established a system of "administering justice" in which the police authorities determined the respective punishment in their own range of competence.

Sometimes a Jehovah's Witness was turned over to the legal authorities, but the custodial judge might withdraw the arrest warrant and order a release from pretrial detention because the preliminary investigations of the public prosecutor had produced exonerating evidence, or because the judge did not expect the offender to escape. If this was the case, the Gestapo took action again. According to an interoffice decree, which the Bavarian Political Police issued on June 26, 1935, "an arrest warrant for protective detention shall be ordered for members of the 'International Bible Students Association' in cases in which a judicial arrest warrant has been withdrawn."[200] This decree even stated that the practice had the approval of the RMdI and the RJM.

In cases in which the legal authorities considered the available evidence insufficient to issue an arrest warrant, the Gestapo not only ordered protective detention or punished offenses with its own methods of punishment but also tried to persuade the legal authorities to take more serious action. According to the Gestapo, the legal authorities generally lacked the necessary determination to punish the various opponents of the regime. To this end, in its interoffice decree of April 26, 1935, the Secret State Police office in Berlin complained "that particular courts did not handle or punish opponents of the state with the necessary severity." It requested the subordinate State Police offices to monitor the legal authorities' administration of justice in the future, and "to make sure that the measures taken by the courts are actually suitable for the suppression of opponents of the state."[201]

Especially in court proceedings involving Jehovah's Witnesses, the imposed punishments were considerably lower than the Gestapo expected. Granted, during the second half of 1935, the judges no longer questioned the legality of the IBSA bans because of the reproof they had received from the RJM. As a result, they generally considered any substantiated involvement in Bible Student activities to be subject to punishment. However, in quite a few Bible Student cases, the imposed penalties were still remarkably lenient. In August 1935 court proceedings were instituted against forty-three Jehovah's Witnesses from the district of Göppingen on the charge of repeated attendance at "meetings with their fellow believers." During these proceedings the principal defendant was sentenced to a fine of 300 Reichsmark, two defendants were sentenced to a fine of 200 Reichsmark, and thirty defendants were sentenced to the legal minimum punishment of 150 Reichsmark each. Because of lack of evidence, all other defendants were acquitted, with all costs incurred for the court proceedings being borne by the state.[202] Such court decisions did not meet with Gestapo approval or the approval of the superior courts. Consequently, in November 1935 the State Police office in Frankfurt am Main stated: "The dangerousness of the Bible Student activities is generally underestimated, especially by the courts."[203]

According to State Police situation reports and National Socialist press reports, the Bible Students had to be considered as "dangerous opponents of the state." Based on the personal appearances of the various defendants and the nature of their offenses, such as participation in Bible discussions or the distribution of Bible Student publications for missionary purposes, many courts refused to accept the opinion reflected in these reports. On January 16, 1935, for example, during appeal proceedings at the Dortmund Regional Court, the judges stated that it would be appropriate if the penalties imposed by the previous judge would be "considerably reduced, especially since the overall impression of the defendants during trial at the previous court did not give any indication that the defendants were law-breakers in the usual sense."[204] During proceedings against members of the Bad Dürkheim IBSA group, the Frankenthal Special Court described all defendants as "ordinary people" who "certainly did not have evil intentions."[205] During the court proceedings against the Göppingen Bible Students (August 1935), even the public prosecutor acknowledged that the defendants were "innocent, respectable people."

In most cases, it was not at all possible to associate the accused Jehovah's Witnesses with the commonly accepted picture of "insidious opponents of the state." Even the superior courts were at times concerned that the special courts would lose their authority. For example, in his March 1937 report, the Karlsruhe chief public prosecutor stated: "Quite frequently, sometimes even after long travels, aged and infirm members of the 'Earnest Bible Students' have to appear before the special courts. At times this diminishes the real objective of this institution." According to the chief public prosecutor, these cases undermined the credibility of the special courts as institutions for the resistance of dangerous opponents of the state. Out of concern for the reputation of the special courts, the highest prosecuting attorney in Baden suggested that in the future the special courts should no longer be burdened with such cases: "Preferably, court proceedings in which the defendants can be clearly identified as followers should be handed over for due process of law."[206]

Other state officials, and apparently even some Gestapo officials, also considered Jehovah's Witnesses as "harmless sectarians" instead of viewing them as an oppositional group. Some Gestapo decrees warned against this complacency, which only increased the danger to which the activities of the Bible Students exposed the state. In its interoffice decree of February 1, 1936, the Bavarian Political Police complained that "the struggle against the Earnest Bible Students, who were known to be dangerous opponents of the state, is not performed with the necessary severity." The decree warned not to underestimate the "danger" emanating from the IBSA.[207] The State Police office in Munich stated that the Bible Students "are not simply harmless sectarians. Rather, they are dangerous opponents of the state who quietly and persistently try to persuade German national comrades to accept their international anti-state opinions and objectives. Under the pretense of religion, they teach them to become opponents of the state."[208] A confidential Gestapa memo sent to the police offices at the end of 1936 stated: "Even today, among large parts of the population, including governmental authorities and the [National Socialist] movement, the opinion prevails that the IBSA is merely a harmless sect and its adherents are simply misdirected people 'in search of God.'"[209]

Campaign of NS Propagandists to Inform
the General Public

In order to extricate themselves from this deplorable state of affairs, the Gestapo departments for sectarian affairs and the SS Security Service increased their efforts to provide information about the political objectives of the IBSA. They prepared internal background information and memos, which they sent confidentially to the authorities involved in taking action against the Bible Students.[210] To this end, the Gestapa memo carefully "instructed the officials concerned."[211] In addition to such information and training materials, the subordinate police offices were also provided with personal statements from Bible Students that supposedly proved "that the Earnest Bible Students really were malicious and absolutely subversive elements."[212] The State Police office in Munich transmitted an article taken from the February 1, 1937, issue of *Das Goldene Zeitalter.* According to the Bavarian Gestapo officials, the article shows "an incomparable degree of maliciousness and brazenness. Not only does it portray the Führer as a 'predator'; the remaining explanations also reflect the same agitating tendencies and call to mind Bolshevik aggressiveness. This excerpt is to be distributed to subordinate [police] officials, reminding them of their duty to pay special attention to these opponents of the state."[213]

As a further measure, the various party factions were increasingly mobilized for the struggle against the Bible Students. The October 1936 issue of the *Mitteilungen zur weltanschaulichen Lage,* published by the "representative of the Führer for monitoring the entire mental and ideological education of the NSDAP," discussed the "political backgrounds" of the Bible Students Association. Based on the "research" of Hans Jonak von Freyenwald, a known anti-Semite, this Rosenberg training paper (see p. 52) focused on the Jewish origin of the Bible Student teachings. Looking at the matter from this point of view, it supposedly had now become possible "to provide incontestable evidence for a direct line of connection between the 'Earnest Bible Students,' on the one hand, and Marxism and Freemasonry, on the other hand."[214] The paper then included several passages regarding the eschatological expectations of the Bible Students that focused on the belief that the future Kingdom of God would extend its rule over the earth, comprising all peoples, "regardless of their present national differences." In summary, the paper stated:

These ideas clearly describe a situation that has already become
a terrible reality in global Bolshevism, do they not? Subjugation
of all nations under Jewish dictatorship—violent destruction—
elimination of all national differences, just as it is proclaimed in the
above-mentioned statements of the Bible Students. What else can
this mean other than global Jewish Bolshevism? Therefore, there
cannot be any doubt that the "Earnest Bible Students" are spiritual
forerunners of global Bolshevism.

The Rosenberg information paper thus supported a thesis exclusively used by NS propagandists, that of a global "Jewish–Bolshevik
conspiracy." In this context, it viewed the Bible Students to be the spiritual and tangible partners in this "alliance." Since Judaism made use of
"the incredibly well-structured organization of the Bible Students Association," the effects on world events were perhaps already noticeable.
For instance, considering the situation in Spain, where the Bible Students were especially active, "it is not difficult . . . to see these connections."[215] In conclusion, the article in the information paper stated that
therefore "the Bible served the interests of World Revolution."

Even the background reports, published by Robert Ley, the Reich
organizational leader of the NSDAP, in the official journal *Der Hoheitsträger*, extensively discussed the subject of the Bible Students Association
and the dangers that the IBSA supposedly presented to the NS state.[216]
In this journal, which provided confidential information and training
for its dignitaries and political leaders, the party was urged to take up a
ruthless fight against the Bible Students. Apparently, the previous support of the various party factions in persecuting Jehovah's Witnesses did
not completely meet the expectations of the superior authorities. Therefore, the journal continued to instruct the party members that this attack against Jehovah's Witnesses could not be performed by the police
alone. According to the *Hoheitsträger*, "everybody had to support this elimination of the members of the Bible Students Association who did not
have any constructive share in establishing the state. In doing so he helps
to destroy an opponent of the people and the state."[217]

Besides instructing officials who were officially required to persecute
IBSA members and mobilizing the party factions, a third measure involved a campaign to inform the general public to accept the ruthless actions against Jehovah's Witnesses. SS-Hauptsturmführer (Captain) Kolrep, who provided specific training material for this purpose, stated that
such a campaign had to be executed in close cooperation with State Police defense measures: "If, by means of newspaper articles, the national

comrades can be repeatedly informed about the deceitfulness of sectarian groups, and if they can be persuaded to accept the appropriateness of official measures against these groups, our work will be successful."[218]

In press reports that informed people about special court proceedings involving IBSA members an increasingly stronger tone was adopted.[219] And in order to "expose" the Bible Students, the same methods of defamation were used that had already been successfully employed in anti-Semitic propaganda campaigns. Jehovah's Witnesses were now no longer merely accused of supposedly having connections with Communism or even of being agents in the service of American perpetrators. Rather, beyond this propagandistic struggle against IBSA teachings and activities, the NS editors now even stirred up hatred on a personal basis: individual Jehovah's Witnesses were exposed to criticism, ridicule, and racial prejudice. They were even considered to be inferior people. In the same way in which the *Hoheitsträger* persuaded party officials, the NS editors used every means of journalistic dissemination to present to the general public the horror story of a criminal organization that operated "in the disguise of religion."[220] To this end, the SS paper *Das Schwarze Korps* stated that "people in general could not even comprehend the danger this organization presented to the state."[221] Under the title "Die Ernsten Bibelforscher: Sendboten des jüdischen Bolschewismus," the *Westdeutsche Beobachter* published a full-page illustrated report, which presented the founders of the Bible Student teachings as "malicious perpetrators who should be ruthlessly eliminated."[222] Skeptical and disbelieving people were told: "The persecution of the 'Earnest Bible Students' is not a matter of persecuting a religious denomination or preventing people from following their religious beliefs. It rather is a very important struggle against dangerous opponents of the state and humanity." For this struggle, the NS propagandists employed notorious *Stürmer* fashion. In the *Westdeutsche Beobachter,* the caption text under the picture portraying fifteen Jehovah's Witnesses reads: "These 'Bible Student' leaders clearly demonstrate the efforts of this association to organize an inferior human race on behalf of Jewish Bolshevism. Accordingly, they try to replace a national and moral world order with the chaos of a bastard race under Jewish leadership." Such viewpoints were not only published in party press reports. Even the renowned *Meyer's Lexikon* stated that the International Bible Students Association was an "especially dangerous" organization because "it addressed racially, morally, and mentally inferior people with their fantastic ideas and encouraged them to commit acts of sabotage against state and people."[223]

In order to add credibility to their public defamation of Jehovah's Witnesses, the NS editors cited specific "evidence." For instance, a number of articles and reports referred to a certain letter, dated September 5, 1936, that had been confiscated during mail surveillance. The letter came from Winnipeg, Canada, and was addressed to the German branch office of the Watch Tower Bible and Tract Society in Magdeburg.[224] According to press reports, this ominous letter was sent by an "American Bible Student" by the name of Hope Slipachuk, and the following passage was usually quoted: "The present wicked governments have now come to an end. Soon, an honest, legitimate government will be established for the benefit of humanity under the leadership of the Great Messiah, our Holy Father, Joseph Stalin of New Russia—Union of the Soviet Republics."[225] Not only was this letter accepted by the NS press as adequate evidence that the Bible Students "acknowledged Stalin as the representative of Jehovah," it was even used as admissible evidence during special court proceedings in Berlin.[226] This is especially indicative of the methods in finding justice used in the Third Reich.[227]

In their campaign to inform the general public, the National Socialist propagandists even used "scientific papers."[228] For instance, they used an "expert opinion" from Oberstleutnant a. D. (1st Lt., ret.) Ulrich Fleischhauer, the publisher of the anti-Semitic periodical *Welt-Dienst*. In 1935 Fleischhauer submitted this expert opinion to the Court of Justice in Bern regarding the question of authenticity of the "Protocols of the Learned Elders of Zion." (These "protocols," first published in Russia, in 1901, involve secret sessions of "the innermost circle of the rulers of Zion" who are striving to obtain world domination.[229]) The eleventh paragraph of this four-hundred-page polemic states: "The world domination plans of the 'International Bible Students Association' prove the authenticity of the protocols."[230] Its objective was to expose "plans" supposedly made by the Bible Students by means of which the "true intentions" of Judaism are revealed: "Never before have the world domination plans of the chosen people become so clear: Denationalization of all people, elimination of all states, dividing of all people into twelve administrative areas according to the model of the twelve tribes of Israel, which will be ruled by a completely Jewish government. These are the plans of the Earnest Bible Students. They base their plans on divine prophecies given to the Jewish people and advocate them under the pretense of trying to save corrupted Christendom."[231] Fleischhauer considered Jehovah's Witnesses as nothing but a militant organization "in the service of Judas," which only outwardly appeared as a Christian denomination.

Of great importance in the NS struggle against Jehovah's Witnesses was the 1936 work of Dr. Hans Jonak von Freyenwald, the infamous Viennese anti-Semite. The Gestapo were well aware that Freyenwald was an "expert on the Bible Student issue."[232] Freyenwald's work *Die Zeugen Jehovas—Pioniere für ein jüdisches Weltreich* was published with the approval of the Catholic Church. In his work, this "expert" demonstrated the methods of defamation: quotations from Bible Student publications were taken out of context, concepts changed, and obscure letters from some "American Freemasons" (according to which the Bible Students supposedly were under Jewish control) used for reference. Elaborately, Jonak von Freyenwald interpreted Jehovah's Witnesses' proclamations of world destruction as an appeal for a complete overthrow of the current social order, and consequently, an appeal for World Revolution: "Consequently, the program of the Earnest Bible Students involves the destruction of all state governments, and this is a political program. This cannot be changed by the fact that Rutherford, by blatantly misinterpreting Bible texts, tries to represent his program as God's plan, thus shifting the responsibility for his subversive ideas to Jehovah. People with such ideas, depending on their mental condition, belong either in a psychiatric hospital because of religious madness, or into a penal institution because of agitation against the state and the churches."[233] Jonak von Freyenwald's work had also an effect on adjudication. In their judgments, the special courts often used the book to represent and assess the Bible Student teachings.[234]

Controversial Court Decisions and Courts of Justice

The campaign to inform the general public, which increased incentives to persecute "dissidents," was not the only measure taken. The Gestapo even tried to directly influence judicial decisions in Bible Student proceedings. To this end, the Gestapo underlined court decisions that they considered to be especially exemplary. For example, in its interoffice decree of December 17, 1935, the Bavarian Political Police sent a copy of the August 27, 1935, decision of the Weimar Special Court in Thuringia to the police authorities, the State Police offices, and the district authorities, emphasizing that the explanations of the Weimar judges were "applicable in all points." The Bavarian Political Police also ordered "to contact the local offices of public prosecutors persuading them to accept the opinion of the Weimar Special Court."[235] On April 1, 1936, the Political Police Commander of the German states sent a copy of the special court judgment of January 24, 1936, to the subordinate State Police offices in all non-Prussian states. Once again, as in the case of the previous interoffice decree by the Bavarian Political Police, the police offices were requested to contact the offices of public prosecutors to persuade them to accept "these same viewpoints."[236] In this particular decision of the Weimar Special Court it was emphasized that it would be necessary to impose "strict punishment" on the "offenders." At the same time, the court decision underscored the necessity to warn those who were "in danger of following the teachings of the International Bible Students Association."[237] The court's conclusion that in Bible Student cases the "deterrent purpose and deterrent effect of the punishment . . . would be important factors in determining the penalty" undoubtedly contributed to the fact that the Gestapo placed special emphasis on this judgment. At the same time, the judges stated that in the NS state, everything was subject to the will of the Führer, and he did not allow anybody to "interfere with his plans, not even the International Bible Students Association."

The Secret State Police office repeatedly complained to the RJM about the leniency apparent in many court proceedings involving Bible Students and demanded an increase in punishment. Even the RJM was obviously not satisfied with the administration of justice in the "area of resisting the Bible Students." In a discussion with the senior Reich attorney and the chief public prosecutors held on September 23, 1935, the ministry complained especially about the "obvious differences in the amount of punishment."[238] For offenses of the same kind and seriousness, the courts imposed "completely different degrees" of penalty. The ministry presented the chief public prosecutors with a comparison of the punishment imposed by three different courts: the average sentences imposed on IBSA leaders varied between four months and three weeks of imprisonment and three years and three months of imprisonment. One court imposed on people who were considered to be mere "followers" fines of between 150 and 300 Reichsmark and, as the ministry complained, pronounced prison sentences averaging two months and three weeks in "only" 23 percent of the cases. The other two courts, on the other hand, pronounced prison sentences only (one court an average of four months and one week, the other court an average of fifteen months).[239] Since these sentences generally followed the public prosecutors' requests, the RJM instructed the chief public prosecutors to use their influence on the subordinate public prosecutors. In the future, they should "examine the demands for penalty and avoid such unacceptable differences."

During this discussion in September 1935, an increase in punishment for Jehovah's Witnesses was not yet explicitly requested. Instead, it was consistency in administering punishment that was asked for. Subsequently, the obligation of the public prosecutors to follow instructions was often used to achieve the more serious punishments in court cases involving Jehovah's Witnesses. On December 5, 1936, the RJM issued a decree to the public prosecutors requesting the special courts to impose "the most serious punishments" on the Bible Students.[240] In view of the "state-endangering" nature of the Bible Students Association, it would be generally inappropriate to impose fines, even if the people were merely followers. In cases involving IBSA functionaries, the court should "make full use of the legally permissible amount of punishment."[241] To emphasize the necessity for more serious legal punishment, the RJM also confidentially provided the public prosecutors with a memo discussing the prohibited activities of the IBSA prepared by the Secret State Police office in the autumn of 1936.[242] Three months later, on March 2, 1937, the ministry needed to remind the public prosecutors of the December 1936 decree because "several courts still did not proceed with the necessary severity."[243] With these efforts of exerting influence, the ministry seriously violated its obligations of instructing the public prosecutors. Instead, the ministry tried to dictate on these legal institutions the amount of punishment they were supposed to impose. Thus, they restricted the independence of the courts, which, according to procedural law, was protected—even in the Third Reich.

The Altona Special Court, in particular, demonstrates the reluctance that several courts showed about following the ministerial instructions in court cases involving Jehovah's Witnesses. In cases involving other opponents of the state, this court displayed no leniency at all.[244] On April 3, 1935, this court, the appropriate higher regional court for the jurisdictional district of Kiel, pronounced an acquittal based on formal errors made in the context of the Prussian IBSA ban and its subsequent legal ineffectiveness. As a result, the Gestapo and the RJM severely reprimanded the court.[245] However, even subsequently, in court proceedings involving Bible Students, the judges of the Altona Special Court did not "pronounce sentences meeting the expectations" of the Berlin authorities.[246] The same thing happened in the Schleswig-Holstein Special Court. Because of public criticism and various admonitions by the superior courts, this court also no longer questioned the legality of the IBSA ban and liability for punishment resulting from involvement in Bible Student activities. However, the judgments pronounced by this court were generally still comparatively lenient.[247] At the Kiel State Police office, which was responsible for this particular administrative district of Schleswig, this state of affairs was recorded with obvious disapproval. In its January 1936 situation report, the Kiel State Police office once more complained: "During the previous weeks, repeated court cases involving Bible Students took place. However, the imposed punishments were completely inappropriate considering the terrible actions of these fanatics who are contaminated with Communist ideas and who undermine the military strength of the [German] nation."[248]

On November 11, 1935, the Altona Special Court handed down comparatively mild penalties on the leaders of the local IBSA groups of Wandsbeck and Bad Oldesloe, punishing them with only one and two months of imprisonment.[249] The usual punishment for followers was still just a fine.[250] Frequently, the court pronounced acquittals, "because of lack of evidence."[251] At times the penalties imposed on Bible Students by the Schleswig-Holstein Special Court were considerably lower than those requested by the public prosecutor.[252] In 1935, in Hanseatic Special Court proceedings involving Jehovah's Witnesses from Hamburg, the average punishment amounted to 3.1 months of imprisonment. In 1936 the average punishment imposed by this same court amounted to 10 months of imprisonment. At the same time though, the judges at the Altona Special Court still pronounced more lenient punishment on IBSA members from the neighboring cities of Altona and Wandsbeck, only about two miles (three kilometers) away. On average, the imposed penalties amounted to 2.2 months (1935) and 2.5 months (1936) of imprisonment.[253]

On September 3, 1936, court proceedings involving nine members of the Altona IBSA group took place at the Schleswig-Holstein Special Court. During these court proceedings, one of the defendants openly criticized the Gestapo interrogation methods. The Bible Student stated that Criminal Investigator Willy T., who was present as a witness, had put him under pressure during the interrogation and had beaten him with a club.[254] The court then questioned the twenty-three-year-old Gestapo official from the Altona outpost of the Kiel Gestapo office; he completely denied the incident. As a result, the court complained about the inaccuracy of the police reports written during the preliminary investigations and questioned in two cases the trustworthiness of these reports. This, in turn, resulted in one case in an acquittal, and in the other case in a discontinuation of the court proceedings. The judges did not have the courage to punish the Gestapo interrogator for the threats and coercive acts with which he obviously had forced the confessions. Nevertheless, it was specifically recorded that the criminal investigator had been put under oath to make his statement.

Three weeks later, on September 24, 1936, court proceedings involving another Bible Student case took place at the Division of the Schleswig-Holstein Special Court, under presidency of Landgerichtsdirektor (senior judge at a regional court) Dr. Gohlke-Kasten. With the exception of one judge, the court had the same makeup. This time, the court proceedings involved six members from the Altona-Stellingen IBSA cell who were accused of attending "prohibited meetings." The court proceedings seemed to follow the usual procedure—the Gestapo report had already predetermined the judgment. But according to this report, the defendants were, without exception, "fanatical" and "incorrigible" members of the Earnest Bible Students and should, therefore, receive an "exemplary punishment."[255] The proceedings did not take the turn that had been anticipated by the Gestapo investigator, who, it turned out, was once again the Altona Criminal Investigator Willy T.

During the proceedings, the defendants stated that the Gestapo interrogation records did not correspond to the facts since they had been forced into confession. To this end, a thirty-six-year-old defendant, Annemarie B., explained to the judges the methods that had been used to pressure her into signing the statement, which had been drafted by the Gestapo official. As noted in the judgment, the Gestapo official had "threatened to beat her and to take her into the basement. . . . There, she would have to undress herself completely and would be beaten. Then, looking at her bruises she could go and complain."[256] Her husband stated that this same Gestapo official had also threatened him with beatings. Moreover, the Gestapo official had even told him that if he did not sign the interrogation records, he could pick up a shovel and start digging his own grave.

Based on these statements, the judges interrogated Willy T., who was summoned as a witness. At first, he denied the accusations. But when asked to confirm his statements under oath, he stated, "he could not exactly remember [the incident]." Upon further questioning he said that it was "possible he had said those things." Under these circumstances, the court was unable to base its judgment on "the statements made during the preliminary investigations. As a result, all six defendants were acquitted "because of lack of evidence."

Willy T. also had personal reasons for his eagerness in tormenting these individuals.[257] He knew the majority of members of the Stellingen

IBSA group because they lived in his neighborhood. With one of them, a thirty-five-year-old mailman, Willy T. had had a serious argument because the mailman had to deliver a bill to him. Willy T. considered the mailman responsible for the fee he was charged for the bill. Therefore, he threatened the man, telling him that he would find ways to pay him back. This background information clearly shows why the judges considered this otherwise ordinary case as an opportunity to turn the tables and demonstrate their strength toward the State Police authorities. Not only were they able to prove that the Gestapo official abused his authority by extorting a confession through use of force; the hot-tempered official had indeed abused his authority for personal reasons, acting on very base vindictiveness. Consequently, apart from acquitting all six defendants on that and the following day, the court initiated several measures that caused quite an outrage among the Kiel Gestapo's highest officials.

The September 24, 1936, court proceedings raised the suspicion that the Gestapo official concerned had performed his investigations with the "use of inadmissible methods." Therefore, the public prosecutor's office ordered an examination of other Bible Student cases, which were still pending at this court. In order to produce evidence that the court could use, arrangements were made for a judicial review, during which a specially assigned special court judge would interrogate all the accused again.[258] In one case involving six members of the Wandsbek IBSA group, for whom the trial was scheduled for October 1, 1936, the accused were released from prison on September 25, 1936, and the date of the trial was cancelled.[259] In addition, on the day following those court proceedings, the leader of the IBSA group in Itzehoe was released from pretrial detention, even though he was under investigation for other court proceedings.

This particular action especially aggravated the Kiel State Police office. At the end of October 1936 the office sent a formal letter of complaint to the Kiel public prosecutor's office objecting to the fact that the Altona Special Court had ordered the withdrawal of the arrest warrant without informing the Gestapo of the release from prison of the twenty-nine-year-old functionary of the Itzehoe IBSA group. In the letter of complaint, the Kiel Gestapo requested that the chief public prosecutor "see to it that the State Police office would be immediately informed of any withdrawals of arrest warrants against Bible Students."[260]

At the same time, the Kiel State Police office also sent an extensive letter of complaint to the senior public prosecutor at the Altona Special Court. This letter stated that "the special court's methods of interrogating Criminal Investigator T. and its reasons for the judgment gave cause for serious concern. The methods used could damage the reputation of a public authority. . . . I am therefore forced to take further action in this matter."[261]

This "further action" resulted in the Secret State Police office submitting a complaint to the RJM, which, in turn, corresponded with the Reichsführer SS. Then, as stated in a report of the Hanseatic Higher Regional Court, "the Reichsführer SS was impelled to reprimand the actions of the court."[262]

There was yet another reason why this Altona Special Court decision was discussed on a higher level. The public prosecutor's office at the Altona Regional Court had instituted preliminary investigations against the criminal investigator "on the charge of offense against StGB, article 343" (extortion of testimony by duress).[263] Because of the serious accusations and the suspicion of abuse of authority for personal reasons, even the Kiel State Police office was now forced to take action. In October the Gestapo official Willy T. was "temporarily suspended from his official duties." Three months later, probably as a result of certain interventions, the public prosecutor's preliminary investigations were simply abandoned. During the middle of January 1937 the Altona criminal investigator Willy T. was able to resume his duties. But now, it was considered appropriate to transfer him to the Kiel State Police office.

Since, in the context of various offenses, other public prosecutor's offices also instituted preliminary investigations against Gestapo officials who were suspected of abusing their authority through use of force, it seemed necessary to investigate. Consequently, on June 4, 1937, leading officials of the Secret State Police office and the RJM came together for the purpose of discussing how to "eliminate these developing problems."[264] The RJM requested regulations describing precisely the degree to which methods of police interrogations were permissible. With these regulations, the public prosecutors could determine whether testimonies had been exerted with permissible methods. The representative of the RJM stated that it would actually be "counterproductive" to prosecute Gestapo officials for their abuse of authority if, at the same time, it was officially "required and important" to "intensify the methods of interrogation."

During this discussion, the officials of the RJM voted in favor of "intensifying the methods of interrogation" in cases "in which the interests of the state are directly affected." While the representatives of the legal authorities had in mind primarily acts of treason and high treason, the records show that the Gestapo officials "indicated that it would possibly be necessary to intensify the methods of interrogation in Bible Student cases and cases that involve the use of explosives and acts of sabotage." The officials did not decide what kind of offenses and groups of people should be included in this regulation at that time. The representatives of the Gestapo requested a consultation with the Reichsführer SS. Subsequently, the details for the officially ordered mistreatments were discussed: "During 'intensified interrogations,' it is generally permissible to perform beatings only with a club on the buttocks, twenty-five at the most. [The] Gestapo will determine beforehand the number of strokes. From the tenth stroke onward, a doctor has to be present. Only 'one kind of club' is allowed in order to avoid arbitrariness."

Subsequently issued decrees indicate that it was allowed to use "corporal punishment in the appropriate form" during interrogations of Jehovah's Witnesses.[265] And so, as long as the Gestapo officials administered the punishment in the appropriate form, they did not have to worry about any preliminary investigations instituted by the public prosecutor's office. Thus, they now were officially ordered to administer corporal punishment.[266] On June 12, 1942, the chief of the Security Police and Security Service issued new regulations that extended the group of people concerned to include "Communists, Marxists, Bible Students, saboteurs, terrorists, members of resistance movements, parachute agents, asocials, Polish and Soviet Russian people refusing to work, as well as lazy people." As additional forms of punishment, besides beatings with a club, the regulations mentioned, "basic food (water and bread), plank beds, dark prison cells, sleep deprivation, and physical regiments to the point of exhaustion."[267]

Persistent Silence, Ineffective Punishments

Since, in the autumn of 1936, the IBSA became increasingly active, the Berlin Secret State Police office became more and more dissatisfied with the results the legal authorities achieved with regard to the Bible Students. It complained not only about the insufficient amount of punishment but the ineffectiveness as well. In view of the increasing activities of Jehovah's Witnesses, the Gestapa came to the conclusion that the previously imposed punishments did not produce any deterrent effect: "When the Bible Students were released from prison usually after only a few months of imprisonment, most of them had not changed their attitudes. On the contrary, they now considered themselves to be martyrs and adhered even more to the 'work of the Lord.'"[268]

It is totally ineffective to use conventional measures of prosecution in taking actions against people who consider their fates to be trials that have God's approval, trials that require maintaining one's faith without compromising, despite opposition and endangerment. This ineffectiveness is clearly illustrated by means of the following example: On March 24, 1937, after a search of several weeks, a Bible Student from Hamburg was arrested in Glückstadt. On the day of his arrest, during his first interrogation, he made only one statement: "When Jesus was brought before his judges, he kept silent. Therefore, I will also keep silent."[269] In the following five months, during which this Jehovah's Witness was imprisoned, first at the Fuhlsbüttel police prison and later for pretrial detention at a different penal institution, he literally refused to make any statement during Gestapo interrogations. Therefore, only the following note could be made in the interrogation records: "Also this time, he did not respond to any question, neither regarding the facts nor regarding personal data."[270] On his personal record of identification, he signed "Jehovah's Witness." Whatever might have taken place until he finally signed the document with his personal name can only be left to our imagination.

On August 17, 1937, subsequent proceedings took place at the Hanseatic Special Court, and the man was sentenced to one year of imprisonment. He remained silent throughout the entire proceedings. Instead of speaking, he wrote notes on small pieces of paper. On one piece of paper he wrote: "Since, according to Isaiah 43:10–12, I am a Jehovah's Witness, I am bound by my conscience to follow the instructions of my Lord and Savior in the Holy Scriptures. And if I get ten years, so be it. May Jehovah God help me." On another piece of paper he wrote the words of the prophet Amos: "Amos 5:13, 'This is what Jehovah says—That is why anyone prudent keeps silent now, since the time is evil.'"

The court decision stated that the defendant did not speak a single word: "By means of written notes, which he submitted to be read in court, he indicated that Jehovah had given him the command to be silent on March 24, 1937." The defense attorney assigned by the court tried to achieve a more lenient sentence by suggesting diminished mental capacities. However, the court considered any doubts with regard to the mental capacities of the defendant as unsubstantiated since he was "able to follow the procedures of the trial without difficulties. He also immediately responded to any questions the court would direct at him by writing Bible texts on a piece of paper." At the same time, the court did not become aggravated by the actions of the defendant. In clear contrast to the Gestapo officials during the preliminary investigations, the court even described his attitude as "harmless." One written statement of the defendant, however, did not find the approval of the court: "He made the dangerous statement that he would refuse to perform military service in case of an emergency and would, instead, restrict his activities to prayer. Like all fanatical Bible Students, he completely fails to recognize the true sense of the commandment 'You shall not kill.'"[271]

In many cases, the legal authorities and especially the prison administrators had to acknowledge the failure of their efforts. In most cases, they were not able to break the steadfastness of Jehovah's Witnesses. The chief public prosecutor in Zweibrücken even stated that "imprisonment [proved to be] ineffective" in almost all Bible Student cases.[272] The prison wardens in penal institutions shared this acquiescent viewpoint. In an article that the journal *Der Deutsche Justizbeamte* published in March 1937 regarding "Bible Students in penal institutions," a prison warden stated that in only a few cases "imprisonment brought them to their senses."[273] The Eisenach prison warden Dr. Brandstätter stated that even though "every punishment available at penal institutions has been used," the "purpose of punishment" has only been achieved with a small number of Jehovah's Witnesses.[274] In Eisenach a "special educational program" for Bible Students was introduced with the objective of "convincing these prisoners of the wrongness of their teachings by providing them with proper education and treatment. This program was also supposed to teach them National Socialist ideas and persuade them to [become an integral part of] the Third Reich."[275] The majority of these "students" resisted such indoctrinations and could not at all be persuaded to "approve of the Third Reich." The instructors had to acknowledge: "To these people, the totalitarian state, the desired correct and ideal form of government, is the utopia of the Thousand-Year Reign."[276]

As early as 1935 the presiding judge at the Jena Special Court suggested that the RJM issue instructions that imprisoned Jehovah's Witnesses should no longer be provided with a Bible, as prisoners usually were. In this way, Jehovah's Witnesses would be deprived of the equipment that gave them the strength to maintain their resistance, because they supposedly derived their subversive ideas from a "collection of Bible texts that they carefully pieced together."[277] Initially, the minister of justice did not consider it necessary to issue such instructions. In his reply of November 21, 1935, he stated that it was the "responsibility of the penal institutions to prevent the prisoner from using the Bible to take notes for subversive purposes." He also believed that the whole problem "could be avoided by giving the Earnest Bible Students not the whole Bible, but only the New Testament."[278] The prison wardens were not satisfied with these suggestions, however. They cautioned against giving Jehovah's Witnesses even portions of the Bible since it would conflict with the purpose of punishment "to supply Jehovah's Witnesses with publications (Bible and New Testament) that gave them continuous nourishment and encouragement to strengthen their emotional attachment to this prohibited sect."[279]

The instructors complained about the "extreme difficulties" they encountered in trying to perform an "ideological transformation" with the imprisoned Bible Students. A senior instructor at the Ichtershausen penal institution reported that he tried, by means of lessons and visits to the prison cells, to "expose gradually the IBSA teachings for what they really were, namely, false teachings and a misuse of religiousness." But his efforts were persistently refused. Based on his experiences, he came to the conclusion "that, of all ideological education provided for political prisoners, the instruction of Bible Students was the most difficult, most time consuming, and most unrewarding."[280]

In addition to this indoctrination, the prison wardens tried to change the attitude of the Bible Students by coercion—solitary confinement. Not only should this particular punishment deprive Jehovah's Witnesses of mutual encouragement, it also had the objective of preventing them from actively proselytizing among their fellow prisoners. Thus, a decree by the RJM in 1940 stated that "prisoners with a tendency to discuss their anti-state viewpoints or other wrong ideas with fellow prisoners, i.e., the Earnest Bible Students, should be strictly separated from other prisoners."[281] This practice had already been used previously, provided the prison had an adequate number of cells.

Imposters and New Believers

Since the law enforcement authorities tried to stop the distribution of Bible Student teachings completely, they considered it necessary to take the most serious actions against their preaching activity. This was not merely an ordinary matter of concern. In many cases, the prison wardens had reason to worry because the preaching activity of the imprisoned Jehovah's Witnesses often met with a positive response among fellow prisoners. Some of them even became believers.[282] Even though these responses caused problems for the law enforcement authorities, they sometimes created serious issues for Jehovah's Witnesses themselves.

This is demonstrated by the following example: In 1936 a woman who had been repeatedly convicted on the charge of theft and fraud shared her prison cell at the Hamburg remand prison with a Bible Student. The Bible Student had several discussions with this woman about the coming of God's Kingdom and future conditions of a paradise on earth. The woman finally indicated that she had accepted the Bible Student teachings. As a result, the Bible Student offered this woman, who was without money and a home, the option to move into her spacious apartment after both of them were released from prison; later, this actually happened after their release. This new believer was immediately involved in resistance activities. At the end of 1936 she also participated in the distribution of the resolution pamphlets.[283]

It soon became apparent that the acceptance of this "new believer" was a rather unfortunate catch for the Hamburg IBSA group. When the Bible Student learned that the woman tried, under false pretenses, to defraud sums of money from her, the Bible Student abruptly discontinued the relationship. Shortly thereafter, the unsuccessful defrauder reported to the Hamburg police that her former fellow prisoner was again involved in Bible Student activities. But obviously the woman misjudged the situation. When the police learned of her own participation in the pamphlet campaign, she was also sentenced for her involvement in Bible Student activities.

In many cases, the Gestapo used such methods to infiltrate police informers into IBSA groups.[284] Informers were put into prison cells with Bible Students. After a short period of time, these paid informers of the Gestapo pretended to be interested in the Bible Student teachings. Eventually, they began pretending to be "converted to the truth." In most cases, though, the Bible Student prisoners were more careful than the members of the IBSA group in Wandsbek-Bramfeld. They carefully examined the state of conversion and the trustworthiness of the new believer. Eventually, the efforts of infiltrating police informers from the outside into IBSA groups proved to be unproductive for the departments of sectarian affairs at the State Police offices. Apparently, these people did not have the necessary intuition required for religious matters. Therefore, the method was changed: police informers were recruited from the very ranks of the Bible Students.[285]

This method used by the Gestapo is very well illustrated by the example of the Hamburg IBSA cell leader Mr. X, who was arrested during the middle of 1937.[286] After being sentenced to two years of imprisonment, Mr. X was sent to a convict camp in the Emsland. The nearly fifty-year-old man was not able to deal with the harsh working conditions in the camp. His health rapidly deteriorated. Since the prisoners had to work even under adverse weather conditions "until they were drenched," Mr. X constantly suffered from a cold and fever. Soon, he began to have gastro-intestinal bleeding. Six months later, he had a complete physical breakdown and spent several months in a military hospital. Several months earlier, Mrs. X had submitted a petition for pardon because of her husband's poor health. The Department for Sectarian Affairs II B 1 of the Hamburg State Police office considered the question of using Mr. X as a police informer. The department informed the public prosecutor's office that "they would approve of an immediate release of Mr. X from prison for State Police purposes" because they "intended to use him as future police informer for IBSA affairs in Hamburg." In contrast to the petition Mrs. X had submitted, the request on the part of the State Police office immediately found the approval of the legal authorities. Only five days later, the public prosecutor's office informed the prison warden that the imprisonment of Mr. X would be temporarily interrupted. The prison warden was also informed that the prisoner, who had been recently relocated from the military hospital to the prison, should not be simply released because he would be "picked up by the Secret State Police." As reasons for the release, his papers should mention his poor health.

Six months later, the Gestapo made a statement regarding Mr. X's pardon, which was still pending even though a temporary interruption of the penalty had been granted. The Hamburg State Police office stated that Mr. X was considered "worthy" of receiving pardon because he had maintained "close contact with the local police office as a police informer after his temporary release from prison": "He is grateful for the confidence shown to him and, in this respect, has rendered valuable services to this police office." In mid-1939 his remaining sentence of eleven months was suspended on the terms of a three-year probation.

Apart from occasional denunciations and the employment of police informers as in Mr. X's case, the official resistance against the IBSA generally remained ineffective. At the end of 1936 the Gestapo looked for more effective ways to obstruct the Bible Students. To this end, the Gestapa memo, which was supposed to substantiate the need for more serious actions, stated that it was "imperative for the state to punish any activity promoting the unlawful objectives of the International Bible Students Association. This punishment would involve that the people concerned would be kept away from society for long periods of time in order to prevent them from continuing their activities."[287] Thus it would be necessary to employ every available means against the IBSA in order "to eliminate it forever, at least in Germany."

The fact that "in most cases, the Bible Students resumed their objectionable activities even more fanatically after being released from prison," served as clear evidence for the Secret State Police "that the previously imposed punishments on the charge of involvement in prohibited activities for the International Bible Students Association had failed to accomplish their purpose."[288] For this reason, the Gestapo requested the legal authorities to considerably increase the generally imposed punishments. Since the February 28, 1933, Decree of the Reich President (as legal basis) restricted punishment to a maximum of five years of imprisonment, the Secret State Police office requested that the RJM change the penal regulations for Bible Student proceedings. The Gestapa suggested the use of penal regulations for punishing acts of high treason (StGB, articles 80–84) because "the activities of the Bible Students [could be] compared to the subversive activities of the Communists and the Marxists." As an alternative, it suggested issuing new penal regulations "according to which the functionaries of the prohibited IBSA would be punished with a severe prison sentence and mere followers with imprisonment of at least six months."[289]

In addition to requests made to the legal authorities by the Gestapo, the Gestapo itself also increased its measures of protective detention for IBSA members. Previously, protective detention was imposed on Bible Students for limited periods of time as a substitute in cases where legal punishment was not administered. Now, it was imposed *in addition to* legal castigation and became an instrument of intensified punishment with the objective of "permanently detaining" all nonconforming Jehovah's Witnesses. As early as 1936 the Gestapo had already sent a number of Jehovah's Witnesses to concentration camps immediately after their release from prison. This became a general practice in the spring of 1937. Jehovah's Witnesses who refused to renounce their faith were inevitably sent to a concentration camp, as a police measure of supplementary detention. The April 22, 1937, Gestapa decree concerning this matter stated: "All IBSA members who have been released from prison after serving their sentences should immediately be taken into protective detention. On the request for transfer, the reasons for admission into a concentration camp have to be stated."[290]

Three weeks later, the State Police office in Stettin informed the local chief public prosecutor about the April 22, 1937, interoffice decree by the Secret State Police office. The chief public prosecutor was asked for his assistance and requested "not to release" IBSA members from prison after they had served their sentences. Instead, he should "transfer them to the local State Police office and arrange for their admission into the local police prison."[291] The chief public prosecutor, in turn, contacted the RJM, which only then learned about the existence of the April 22 Gestapa decree. The ministry kept a low profile. It did not offer any ministerial regulations regarding procedures of imminent releases of Bible Students from prison.[292] As a result, the Stettin chief public prosecutor acted on his own authority and gave the respective instructions for his area of jurisdiction.[293]

Often, the Gestapo did not even wait for the release date from prison but issued subsequent protective detention months before this date. For example, on June 4, 1937, the Flensburg outpost of the Schleswig State Police office sent a letter to the senior public prosecutor in Kiel informing him that "protective detention had been ordered" for four Jehovah's Witnesses from Flensburg. Three months earlier, the Schleswig-Holstein Special Court had sentenced the four Jehovah's Witnesses to imprisonments of between ten and eighteen months, while making allowance for the time they had previously spent in protective and pretrial detention. Consequently, the dates for their releases were still in the distant future. Without being concerned that this order would foresee that the purpose of punishment had not been fulfilled, the State Police office requested the senior public prosecutor who had sentenced these Bible Students for his assistance: "Protective detention begins on the day of their release from prison. Therefore, we request you to inform us of the date of release from prison of the following persons. . . . We further request that you inform the prison administrations concerned so that we can initiate the appropriate steps to pick up the prisoners."[294]

Protective Detention of Jehovah's Witnesses

The practice, by the highest Gestapo officials, of imposing protective detention on Jehovah's Witnesses immediately after release from prison and then ordering routinely supplementary detention was greatly criticized by the legal authorities. They considered the imposition of protective detention for the purpose of increasing legally imposed penalties as an open discrimination of due process of law.[295] Such practices were a further infringement on the legal authorities' area of competence in meting out penal actions. De facto, this meant that in the future it would no longer be the judges who determined the period of imprisonment, or who actually set the real amount of punishment for "offenders" who were sentenced on the charge of "defiance of the IBSA ban." Quite the contrary, this decision was now in the hands of the Gestapo officials who were dealing with the respective cases. From that time on, the Secret State Police often imposed supplementary protective detention, completely independent from the legal authorities.

The prison wardens especially criticized these actions on the part of the Gestapo. They immediately saw through this procedure when, at times, Bible Students, after having served their sentences, remained in the same penal institution, often even in the same prison cell, until their ultimate transfer to a concentration camp. Now, however, they were the prisoners of the Gestapo. Furthermore, there were also typical reservations. The prison warden of the Freiburg penal institutions, for example, was concerned that "indiscriminately imposed protective detention" after a sentence had been served "called into question the deterrent purpose and deterrent effect of punishment for Earnest Bible Students."[296] The Eisenach prison warden emphasized that the period of imprisonment gave ample opportunity to determine "who was still an opponent of the state at the time of his release from prison." However, even he considered it appropriate "to show no consideration" to people who had not "abandoned the Bible Student ideas" during their imprisonment. Such "incorrigible Bible Students" should indeed be sent to a concentration camp. On the other hand, for "people who had changed their attitude," the warden strongly suggested a different procedure: These people should be "released to give them an opportunity to become part of the Third Reich. If they are refused to do this right at the point when they finished serving their sentence, every effort of imprisonment would have been in vain."[297]

Because of such indiscriminate measures, those who tried to "ideologically reform" the Bible Students and who adhered to the idea of "special crime prevention" saw the success of their determined efforts endangered. They refused to leave the decision of when to release people from prison to the discretion of the police. According to a senior instructor, the penal institutions could be trusted that they would "suggest only people for release from prison whose release would also be in the interest of the state."[298] Such words reflect the general opinion of the prison wardens whose hard work had been destroyed by the Gestapo, which left them without recourse, because the Gestapo transferred people to concentration camps after they had already served their sentences.

Not only did the Gestapo send members of the IBSA to concentration camps after they had completed their prison term, they also sent people to the camps who had been acquitted by the special courts or who were exempted from further punishment by making allowance for the time they had already spent in protective and pretrial detention. In such cases, "accused" could usually leave the courtroom as "free people." But as soon as they left the courthouse, or shortly thereafter, the Gestapo took them into custody by an arrest warrant.

These procedures provoked serious opposition on the part of the legal authorities. Consequently, on May 21, 1937, "in consideration of the general significance of the matter," the senior judge of the Frankfurt (am Main) Higher Regional Court sent a letter to the Reich minister of justice, including a report from the presiding judge at the Frankfurt Special Court. In this report, the presiding judge complained about the circumstances of three specific trials at the local special court, which involved a total of sixty-two defendants who had participated in IBSA activities. For some of the defendants, the court had considered imprisonment of between two and seven months to be sufficient. Since the defendants had already undergone protective and pretrial detention, the judges considered their sentences to be alleviated. Therefore, the judges withdrew the arrest warrants and ordered the Bible Students' release from prison. The presiding judge at the Frankfurt Special Court reported with obvious anger:

> Every time a court decision was pronounced, the officer commissioned by the Secret State Police immediately gave orders to arrest the defendant again, right there in the courthouse, even though the special court had . . . ordered a release from prison. The special court considers such actions to be damaging to the reputation of the legal authorities and to be detrimental to the confidence people place in administration of justice. In this way, the impression is given that a previously pronounced court decision needs to be corrected immediately. What is more, such actions invalidate the process of evaluating and assessing the amount of punishment that was based on careful considerations. Therefore, the special court considers it imperative to inform the legal authorities of these occurrences and to emphasize the dangers involved.[299]

The special court judges considered the blatant disregard the police showed for court decisions by reversing previously made judgments as an invalidation of their position as judges.[300] It hurt their pride because they regarded themselves to be the elite of NS "protectors of justice," convinced that they alone resisted opponents of the state with the appropriate severity.

The Reich Ministry of Justice and the "Bible Student Issue"

Because of the fact that the legal authorities resented the Gestapo's measures of protective detention, the RJM placed the subject of "protective detention and the Bible Students" on the agenda of a ministerial discussion scheduled for June 18, 1937. As in previous so-called discussions with the leading judges, the RJM had invited the higher regional court senior judges, the chief public prosecutors, the senior judge of the Reich Court, the senior Reich attorney, the senior judge of the People's Court, and the Reich attorney at the People's Court.[301]

The discussion took place on Friday, June 18, 1937, at ten o'clock in the morning at the Wilhelmstrasse in Berlin. During this meeting the heads of the ministry and the judges extensively deliberated over the difficulties that the Gestapo measures presented to the legal authorities along with the consequences these measures would have on future legal actions against Jehovah's Witnesses.[302] In his introduction to this item on the agenda, Dr. Franz Gürtner, the Reich minister of justice, indicated that in general he shared the reservations mentioned in the reports of several higher regional court senior judges and chief public prosecutors. He also regretted the fact that the issue of protective detention frequently presented difficulties for the legal authorities. In this context, he mentioned "certain applications that would be difficult to maintain." In many cases, protective detention was no longer imposed for the purpose of prevention. Instead, it was used for other purposes such as persuading a person to compromise, or to keep a person in custody after he was acquitted or was given "inadequate punishment." Since, "this aspect [had] led to an awkward situation with regard to the International Bible Students," the minister of justice considered it a matter of priority to come to an agreement on this matter.

Ministerialdirektor Dr. Wilhelm Crohne, the head of the ministerial department concerning questions on criminal justice and administrative measures of punishment, stated that the RJM learned about the increasing number of people that had been taken into protective detention after having been acquitted from reports submitted by the chief public prosecutors. As a result, Crohne assured his listeners, the ministry "had immediately contacted the Gestapo." Crohne began his report by presenting his listeners with the contents of the April 22, 1937, decree that the Secret State Police office had issued to its subordinate State Police offices throughout the Reich, requesting them to keep this information confidential. According to this decree, all IBSA members should be taken into protective detention immediately after they had served their sentences. Since this general decree had already been issued, the legal authorities could do nothing but accept it: "In view of the fact that the decree is specifically directed to the police authorities, we cannot do anything about it. We were particularly told that the police measures do not have the objective of criticizing previously made court decisions." The RJM simply accepted this mollifying statement from the highest police authorities, whose main office was located at Prinz-Albrecht-Strasse in Berlin. Consequently, the ministry openly admitted that it had no freedom of action in the matter and then announced that the representatives of the RJM had been promised by the Gestapa that a few small cosmetic corrections would be made. Here, the Gestapa gave the assurance that the State Police offices would be informed that they should refrain from arresting people who had been acquitted directly in the courtroom.

All things considered, even these few introductory statements made it clear that the ministry and Dr. Crohne had arranged this discussion with the judges only for the purpose of informing them about an agreement that had already been made between the RJM and the Secret State Police office.

According to the records, Crohne made the following statements regarding the significance of the IBSA: "The Bible Students shall no longer be considered as a religious sect. They have developed into an absolutely subversive association, which, to a certain extent, is directed from abroad. They refuse, for instance, to perform military service. Moreover, they also refuse to work in factories that support the Wehrmacht. This is especially important because, in the event of war, they would even refuse to work for the railroad and the post offices."[303] Besides its demoralizing effect on the armed forces, Bible Students supposedly presented an even greater danger: "We have information from the Gestapo according to which communism has a powerful influence on the IBSA."[304] Because of its size, the IBSA "is clearly able to launch a massive attack against the National Socialist state": "The Gestapo has informed me that the International Bible Students in Germany have a membership of between five and six million. Personally, I estimate this number to be between one and two million."[305]

In order to emphasize the increasing significance of this association, Crohne referred to the "extensive pamphlet campaigns that the Bible Students" had previously carried out. He then explained the legal authorities' function in the fight to repress Jehovah's Witnesses: "Time and again, it has been observed that only inadequate use is made of the possibility of increasing prison sentences to a maximum of five years. In a recent interoffice decree, Secretary of State Freisler emphasized that these cases require strict measures. . . . Therefore, I request, in court proceedings, that the International Bible Students are no longer treated with leniency."[306] Not only did Crohne reprimand the judges for their previous practice of handing out judgment because they did not adequately use the amount of punishment provided by the Decree of the Reich President for the Protection of People and State, he even announced *by name* the jurisdictional districts in which the respective special courts did not meet the recommended requirements but had made considerably more lenient court decisions. The RJM informed the higher regional court senior judges that the districts rendering lenient judgments included Breslau, Celle, Düsseldorf, Naumburg, Stettin, and Zweibrücken. At the same time, they were informed that in Darmstadt, Dresden, Jena, and Königsberg such leniency was unheard of.[307]

Crohne further informed the judges that, according to the Reichsführer SS, the legal punishment provided for special court proceedings against Bible Students was not even high enough. Therefore, the Reichsführer SS had suggested to the RJM that an amendment be prepared threatening to impose more severe prison penalties. However, the ministry replied that, for the time being, it was not able to comply with this request. At the same time, Crohne pointed out that a new German Penal Code[308] was in preparation, the draft of which already included such possibilities.[309] Therefore, it would be possible "in the future to punish the Bible Students with imprisonment . . . simply on the charge of involvement in an anti-military association." However, until this new law became effective, it was important to make use of the current legal possibilities to the limit. Crohne went on to say: "I probably do not have to emphasize that an imposition of a fine is no longer appropriate." Then, the Ministerialdirektor and later vice president of the People's Court gave his listeners the directive he had received from the Gestapo:

"The struggle against the International Bible Students must be performed with increasing severity."

However, during the discussion, various substantially differing opinions were expressed. For instance, Chief Public Prosecutor Schnöring from the Düsseldorf Higher Regional Court, one of the districts criticized for being too lenient, was willing to view the Bible Students *only to a certain extent* as dangerous opponents of the state. According to his opinion, "the majority of them [were] . . . rather naive people." Even their outward appearance would sometimes indicate that these people were mentally "not quite normal." However, Windhausen, Schnöring's colleague from the neighboring jurisdictional district of Cologne, contradicted this viewpoint. He stated that the growth-rate of the Bible Students in the Saarland had to be attributed to "political factors." He pointed out that the IBSA, prior to the elections in the Saarland, had advocated not voting for an annexation to the German Reich.

The Stettin chief public prosecutor, Staecker, directed attention to the motives why people joined the Bible Student movement. According to Staecker's opinion, the matter was, to a certain extent, an aftereffect of World War I: "A considerable number of people who had been left disillusioned no longer found any fulfillment of their religious needs. Therefore, they became interested in this sectarian group." Despite this fact, the IBSA needed to be considered an "extremely dangerous" organization. Specifically, the pacifist ideas of its members could easily be misused for "Communist purposes." Since Bible Student groups included people from a variety of backgrounds, Chief Public Prosecutor Staecker also considered it necessary to use some discernment during the court proceedings. "Quite a number of people were merely followers of the Bible Students and showed such naiveté that it only seemed appropriate to impose lenient sentences."

Chief Public Prosecutor Jantzen from Marienwerder stated that Elbing (within his jurisdictional district) might be considered a stronghold of the IBSA. There, the sect was "quite extensively represented" and also reflected "considerable Communist influence." Recently, however, "a significant decline" could be seen. According to Jantzen, this decline was certainly a result of the "draconian measures of punishment" that were imposed in his district—punishments of up to three or four years of imprisonment. On the other hand, Dr. Sturm, chief public prosecutor in Breslau, did not agree with the viewpoint that the IBSA activities were decreasing. In his opinion, the Bible Student activities were "on an increase rather than a decrease." In order to break the

IBSA's resistance, Chief Public Prosecutor Jung from Dresden suggested making adjustments in the treatment of Bible Students in the penal institutions. For example, their functionaries should, without exception, be put into solitary confinement. By means of this isolation, Jung anticipated protecting a number of Jehovah's Witnesses from the influence of their mouthpieces: "Several of their adherents do not have very strong connections with the IBSA. Efforts should be directed toward these people in order to remove them from this movement during the period of their imprisonment."

In conclusion, the secretary of state, Dr. Roland Freisler, gave a brief summary of the discussion: Obviously, it had not been possible to come to an agreement "regarding the appropriate amount and kind of punishment." This was especially reflected by the fact that the higher regional courts of the various jurisdictional districts had different viewpoints about the maximum amount of punishment to be imposed. Freisler once again urgently admonished his listeners not to minimize the danger that the IBSA presented to the Reich: "Often, one views the Bible Students as members of a sect with a rather peculiar spiritual basis to which one does not want to respond with prison sentences." However, people with such reasoning do not fully understand the situation: "The rejection of military service and the basis for legal regulations regarding racial policies present an extremely dangerous situation for the [German] nation. This danger must be taken into account in every district."

If the legal authorities were not able to implement measures of punishment that complied with the expectations of all authorities concerned, they should also not be surprised "if these other authorities responsible for maintaining security were to take matters into their own hands," Freisler further stated. Lack of determination in this regard could have the undesirable effect that "the duty of the legal authorities, that of administering justice, would be assumed by other authorities." Thus, Freisler directed the attention of those leading officials to the actual problem of the legal authorities in NS Germany. To the extent that the Gestapo—and Freisler was not referring to anyone else by saying the "other authorities"—considered it necessary to correct court decisions by means of police measures, that is, by exceeding the authority of the legal institutions and establishing "their own legal system," the impression would also be that the legal institutions were increasingly unable to meet the requirements "of the totalitarian State" and, consequently, do their part in resisting opponents of the state. Ultimately, it was not only the monopoly of the administration of justice that was at stake. Rather, the legal authorities, as an institution, were also losing their rightful powers.

Freisler's final speech, in which he advocated a clear differentiation of the areas of responsibility, should be seen in this context. On the one hand, the Gestapo had to be made aware of the fact that the administration of justice would "always [be] the responsibility of the legal authorities." Therefore, any situation causing confusion had to be avoided: "It is not a good idea if people who have been condemned remain in prison after having served their sentence, even though they have not committed another offense, thereby causing the impression that the period of imprisonment has been increased. Furthermore, it is unthinkable that such occurrences take place in our penal institutions. . . . It is completely out of the question that the penal institutions tolerate or support situations in which people who served a legally imposed penalty remain in the same cell, but now under protective detention by the police." Freisler went on to state that "the respective authorities that ordered protective detention" in addition to a legally imposed penalty should also provide the appropriate detention centers. He clearly emphasized that in the future the RJM was no longer willing to allow the police authorities to use the penal institutions, which were under the jurisdiction of the legal authorities, for protective detention, at least not if the police used these facilities for the purpose of so-called subsequent detention. As a result, the secretary of state requested the Gestapo to transfer these prisoners only to institutions that were under their jurisdiction, that is, to the concentration camps of the SS.

On the other hand, the legal authorities also had to take decisive actions against the prevailing impression that, "to a certain extent, agencies other than the legal authorities dictated the reasons for punishment." Freisler's final remarks once again requested these leading judicial officials to bear in mind what was at stake if the resistance of the Bible Students was left entirely in the hands of the Gestapo: "We could not, and should not, cause the impression that we consider ourselves incapable of representing the state in speaking and executing the final judgment against criminality."

Thus, the higher regional court senior judges and the chief public prosecutors were finally informed about the agreement that the Secret State Police office had already made, in principle, with the RJM. They were also informed that they could do nothing but accept this arrangement. In quick succession, they were now given the necessary instructions. On July 2, 1937, the Reich minister of justice issued an interoffice decree stating that the legal authorities had to inform the appropriate State Police offices about any anticipated releases of Bible Students from prison and had "to place them at the disposal" of the Gestapo, after they served their legally imposed penalty. The senior public prosecutors and the administrations of the penal institutions should also be informed about the fact that they had to provide official assistance to the State Police authorities.[310] Four days later, on July 6, 1937, the minister of justice sent a letter to the Reichsführer SS and chief of the German Police. In this letter, the minister expressed his general agreement with an imposition of protective detention on Bible Students who had served their legally imposed penalty and had not convincingly separated from the IBSA.[311] On the following day, a decree was issued that took into account the most important concerns of the legal authorities: "Protective detention imposed on Bible Students after they have served their legally imposed penalty, or pretrial detention, on the charge of their [religious] activities cannot be carried out in a penal institution, not even temporarily."[312] On July 8, 1937, the RJM concluded their series of decrees with another interoffice decree specifying the "arrangements of executing punishment against the Earnest Bible Students."[313]

On August 5, 1937, the Secret State Police office, on their part, informed the subordinate State Police offices about these arrangements. They explained to the local Gestapo officials that there was no reason to become disturbed about the criticism by the legal authorities. In this regard, Kriminalrat (criminal counsel, major) Heinrich Müller, the chief of the national Political Police department, emphasized that the "Reich minister of justice " had informed him "that he did not share the opinion expressed by subordinate authorities on various occasions, that the practice of taking Bible Students into protective detention after they had served their sentence would jeopardize the authority of the courts." The minister "certainly realized . . . the necessity of State Police measures, even after a sentence had been served." However, the minister also requested that the Gestapo should make sure that "the transfer of the Bible Students into protective detention did not take place under circumstances that would jeopardize the reputation of the courts." Therefore, in the Gestapa decree of August 5, 1937, Müller gave the State Police offices the following rules of procedure:

> (1) If court proceedings involving Bible Students result in an acquittal or allowance is made for the time the individual had already spent in pretrial detention, the arrest for protective detention (which might be required according to the April 22, 1937, interoffice

decree—II B 2/326/37 S) should not take place immediately in the courtroom. (2) In cases in which penal institutions announce an impending release of Bible Students, I will have to be immediately informed in order to give appropriate instructions regarding State Police measures according to the above-mentioned April 22, 1937, interoffice decree. In this way, [the prisoner] could be sent to a concentration camp immediately after he had served his sentence. In cases in which it is not possible to transfer Bible Students to a concentration camp immediately after they served their sentence, they should be placed into police prisons.[314]

Since Jehovah's Witnesses could no longer be kept in the penal institutions used by the legal authorities after they had served their legally imposed penalties, they were temporarily (in most cases for several weeks) placed into police prisons, other institutions of custody, or workhouses until the Secret State Police offices announced their decision regarding protective detention.[315] When the August 5, 1937, decree was put into operation, the Gestapo followed a specific pattern that can be illustrated by the actions taken by the State Police office in Karlsruhe against a leather worker from Heidelberg. This particular Jehovah's Witness served a prison sentence of eight months at the penal institution for the district of Wiesloch. The sentence had been imposed by the Mannheim Special Court; it ended on October 21, 1937. Two weeks prior to his release from prison, the Karlsruhe Gestapo ordered protective detention against him. On the day of his release from prison, he was "temporarily transferred to the Kislau detention camp," as had been previously ordered and arranged.[316] On November 4, 1937, after the confirmation of the arrest warrant by the Secret State Police office, the leather worker was transferred from the Kislau detention camp in Baden to the Munich Police headquarters in order to be "sent to the Dachau concentration camp."

In reality, protective detention was nothing but a continuation of imprisonment after a sentence had been served. However, as a result of the regulation, the prisoners were always removed from the penal institutions of the legal authorities on the day of the supposed release from prison. In this way, the RJM was content that they could at least keep up appearances. On the "day of their release from prison," the only thing that changed for the prisoners was the authority of persecution under which they were placed. They exchanged the harsh conditions of "regular imprisonment" with an uncertain future in the concentration camps.

The Function of the "Reverse Statement"

By no means did the Gestapo transfer all Bible Students immediately to concentration camps after they had served their sentences.[317] Before it issued an arrest warrant, the Gestapo examined, within its own range of competence, whether the prisoner still professed to be a Jehovah's Witness or whether he had completely disassociated from the IBSA. The Gestapo had prepared a certain "reverse statement," or declaration, for this specific purpose. Evidently, during some reviews of detention orders, various Gestapo offices presented such reverse statements (or declarations) for signature to imprisoned Bible Students as early as 1935.[318] Initially, the statements that were used in the various concentration camps and police prisons differed in wording. These statements requested the formal confirmation that the person concerned would no longer participate in IBSA activities.[319] Jehovah's Witnesses who signed the declaration were allowed to go home. However, the Gestapo associated such releases from protective detention with the admonition that in the case of a second offense, they could no longer expect to be shown leniency.

During the first days of National Socialism, these statements, which at times were also presented during police interrogations, did not ask Jehovah's Witnesses to openly renounce their faith.[320] During 1937/38, the Hamburg State Police office used a statement with the following wording:

> I . . . hereby certify that, subsequently, I will refrain from any association with members of or adherents to the "International Bible Students Association" (Jehovah's Witnesses) for the purpose of studying the Bible, the *Watchtower* and other Bible Student publications. I will also refrain from participating in any activities of Jehovah's Witnesses.
>
> I have been informed that any gatherings with other Jehovah's Witnesses, even if such gatherings take place in the form of social or family get-togethers, come under the prohibition of continuing the Bible Students Association.
>
> I am going to submit all Bible Student publications that I will receive in the future to the State Police office. I will also report to the State Police office any observations indicating that people are gathering for the purpose of continuing the organizational structure of Jehovah's Witnesses.[321]

Even in cases in which court proceedings were pending, provided the cases involved only insignificant offenses, IBSA members were immediately released from protective detention if they signed the statement, or one with similar wording. Thus, the accused were exempt from further periods of imprisonment until the date for the court proceedings.

Among Jehovah's Witnesses, the question of whether it was appropriate to sign such statements was controversial. Since these statements did not require a denial of their faith, and in view of the fact that they were also requested to use practical strategies, quite a few Jehovah's Witnesses gave their signature, even though they had their reservations.[322] They considered the statement as a coercive measure that did not involve an active decision of one's conscience. They reasoned that it was possible to sign such a statement because "it was not wrong to deceive the enemy if this would result in being set free so that [they] might better serve Jehovah outside."[323] Some families even discussed the question of who would give up the resistance and sign the statement, so that one parent could remain with the children in order to protect them from the grasp of the NS authorities. In some cases, the IBSA members also considered it possible to sign the statement because the wording might mention only the "Bible Students," but did not specifically refer to Jehovah's Witnesses.[324] Others who signed the statements were actually willing to discontinue their IBSA activities, but they were certainly not willing to give up their faith.[325]

The case of forty-nine IBSA members from the IBSA group Hamburg II, who were arrested and taken to the Fuhlsbüttel police prison in the autumn of 1937, illustrates this maneuver.[326] Between January 28 and February 4, 1938, at the conclusion of the preliminary investigations, the Gestapo official concerned presented the statement for signature to those who were considered to be "mere followers." Those who signed the statement were generally released from protective detention on that same day. These people remained free until the date of the court proceedings. However, those who refused to sign the statement were kept in protective detention. After a few days, they were brought before a custodial judge in order to apply for an arrest warrant. If the case involved a functionary (group and cell leader), and there were serious accusations, such arrest warrants were usually obtained, presenting the general picture outlined in table 3.

Compared to later developments, a relatively high number of people signed the statement.[327] Apparently, during the period prior to the war a comparably high number of people also signed the statement after they had served their sentences.[328] Thus, there was a significant difference when compared to the extremely low numbers of Bible Student

Table 3. Reverse statements, Hamburg IBSA, Gestapo records, 1938

	Number	Percent
Statement signed/resulting release from protective detention	19	39.0
Arrest warrants issued	23	47.0
Release from protective detention prior to the conclusion of the preliminary investigations because of sickness or old age	6	12.0
Deceased during the period of preliminary investigations	1	2.0
Total	**49**	**100.0**

prisoners who signed the statements in the concentration camps during the following years. This can be attributed to a number of reasons: The Bible Students who were imprisoned in the concentration camps were usually active members who had already demonstrated their steadfastness through repeated refusals to sign the statement. However, for many of the Bible Students who were imprisoned in penal institutions or who served short-term periods of protective detention, this was their first experience of imprisonment and, consequently, they were still in shock. They also experienced social isolation within the penal institutions. In solitary confinement or in association with people of different religious beliefs, these Bible Students lacked the support that those in the concentration camps received from their fellow believers.[329]

Probably the most important reason was a decree issued at the end of 1938 establishing a uniform version of the statement, which considerably changed its character. Formerly, the people signing the statement had promised to display good behavior, to refrain from certain activities, and to be willing to provide information to, and cooperate with, the police authorities. These were matters relating to actions of an external nature. With the new wording, however, the statement came to reflect one's conviction and represented a request to renounce one's faith. This shift in emphasis made it impossible for Jehovah's Witnesses to provide the required signature.

The statement, which, according to the May 4, 1938, Secret State Police decree, had to be presented for signature to Bible Students covered by the April 30, 1938, amnesty decree, still required "merely" a confirmation that the person concerned would "no longer participate in IBSA activities or give any testimony for the IBSA."[330] To this end, the Gestapa issued the following instructions: "Bible Students who sign this statement should be released. Those who refuse to sign should be temporarily taken into custody. Their arrest should be carried out in the usual manner."[331] The State Police office in Munich, which forwarded the Gestapa decree ten days later, was not willing to handle the matter in such a way and was also not willing to merely accept an assurance of nonparticipation in IBSA activities; it intensified the order by stating that "in most cases, Bible Students covered by the amnesty will be released only if they have appropriately adjusted their attitude so that, at the time of their release, they no longer present a danger to public law and order. This is going to be the case if, in addition to signing the above-mentioned statement, the Bible Students have come to realize that they must become an integral part of the people's community and accept the responsibility of fulfilling their civil duties such as participating in elections, performing military service, participating in air-raid protection services, etc."[332]

By requesting Jehovah's Witnesses to acknowledge and accept their "civil duties" (which they could not fulfill because of their religious convictions) in addition to signing the "customary statement" the Munich Gestapo already introduced the approaching change.

In its interoffice decree dated December 24, 1938, the Secret State Police office transmitted an order from the Reichsführer SS and chief of the German Police that the various versions of the former statements, to which the Gestapa "objected because of their differences in contents and style," should be replaced with only one uniform version. And this should also be the only version to be used in the concentration camps. This "uniform statement," which was to be presented to Bible Students who were in line for a release from prison, was supposed to have the following wording:

> Statement. I acknowledge that the International Bible Students Association distributes false teachings and, in the disguise of religious activities, pursues only subversive objectives. Therefore, I have completely disassociated from this organization and have also inwardly rejected the teachings of this sect. I hereby confirm that I will never again participate in any activities of the International Bible Students Association. I will immediately report anybody who approaches me with the false teachings of the Bible Students. I will also immediately submit to the nearest police office any Bible Student publications that I receive by mail. In the future, I will obey the laws of the State and will become a completely integrated part of the people's community. I have been informed

that I will be immediately arrested again if I perform any activities in defiance of this statement.[333]

In transmitting this version, the State Police office in Munich emphasized that "Bible Students suggested or considered to be set free" could be released *only* if "they signed the statement."[334] Their refusal to sign the statement would indicate "that these Bible Students had not yet changed their attitude."[335]

Now, even a refusal to sign the statement was sufficient reason for the Gestapo to send a person to a concentration camp. On April 15, 1941, for example, the Secret State Police office issued an arrest warrant for protective detention based on the following reasoning: "Emma S. has been taken into protective detention. Reasons: Through her conduct . . . she endangers the continuation and security of the state and the people. Her refusal to sign the statement clearly proves that she fanatically adheres to the IBSA. This, in turn, gives cause for concern that she will again use her freedom to support the false teachings of the IBSA, even after she has served her sentence."[336]

The request to deny the Bible Student teachings as "false teachings" left Jehovah's Witnesses with no alternative. Signing such a statement would have amounted to "a betrayal" of their declaration of loyalty to God and, consequently, was entirely impossible for them. Many Jehovah's Witnesses would rather have died than agree to such a request.

In the Third Reich, the Gestapo officials were not the only ones who used such declarations for the purpose of "examining the convictions" of people. On a local level, there were also some party officials who acted on their own initiatives. In the spring of 1937 the NSDAP district overseer of Waldenburg sent a letter to all members of the IBSA, including those who were known to have associated with this organization in the past, or who just "sympathized" with the association.[337] The recipients were requested, within a period of two weeks, to sign and return an enclosed statement officially renouncing the tenets of the Bible Students. Hypocritically, the district overseer declared that he considered this measure to be appropriate because he wanted to protect "generally innocent and honest fellow Germans from being punished." With regard to people who refused to sign this statement, the overseer stated that he had to assume that they obviously took a stand against state and party. Therefore, they would have to accept the resulting consequences. The wording of the statement was quite harsh, forcing the people who signed to make serious concessions. The statement not only requested a confirmation that the signee would carefully follow the laws and instructions of state and party in the future, it also requested them to instill the "spirit of the Führer" in their families, but "especially in the hearts" of their children.

Initially, the Gestapo presented the statement only if Jehovah's Witnesses were directly under their authority and jurisdiction (interrogations, protective detention, and concentration camps). However, from 1938 on, the arrangements the legal authorities had previously made with the Gestapo leaders had an impact on the situation (see pp. 277–84). In an increasing number of cases, the statements were presented to a prisoner several weeks prior to his release, or on the day of his release before he could leave the prison. In this way, the Gestapo avoided the impression that the prisoner had been released and, subsequently, was again taken into custody by the police. Increasingly, this procedure took on the character of an organized transfer of prisoners. Even though two Gestapo officials appeared at the penal institution to present the statement to the prisoner for signing, officials of the legal authorities, at least indirectly, assisted in examining the conviction of Jehovah's Witnesses in order to undermine their self-esteem.[338]

The Gestapo generally considered the Bible Students to be "incorrigible" elements that needed to be ruthlessly eliminated. Prison wardens and other judicial officers, however, still believed in the concept of reforming prisoners and thus fulfilling the purpose of punishment. If, therefore, they considered a Jehovah's Witness to be reformed, they tried to persuade the prisoner to sign the statement. (On the other hand, for the "incorrigible" ones they suggested admission in a concentration camp, just as the Gestapo did.[339]) Still, they could not understand why Jehovah's Witnesses maintained their uncompromising attitude: How could somebody who is given the opportunity to be released choose to go to a concentration camp? Consequently, even though the judicial officers tried to act in the "best" interest of "their" prisoners, they presented a greater threat to Jehovah's Witnesses than the request of signing the statement. The report of a Jehovah's Witness from Hamburg who had served a sentence of two and a half years in Fuhlsbüttel, Wolfenbüttel, and the convict camps in the Emsland illustrates this point:

> Finally, the end of my imprisonment was nearing. It was April 19, 1940. I was supposed to be released at 9 a.m. However, the Gestapo officials were already waiting for me. In the presence of a judicial officer, they asked me what kind of attitude I currently had about

my faith and whether I still wanted to be a Bible Student, or a Jehovah's Witness. . . . They told me that I would be immediately released if I agreed that I would no longer participate in any IBSA activities. I was also requested to speak to no one in my hometown about my imprisonment and about my religious convictions. I had expected this. I was not surprised that they would deal with us in this way. The Gestapo officials were quite reasonable. However, I still had to deal with the judicial officer who would handle my release. He gave me a speech for about fifteen minutes and praised my good behavior during the period of my imprisonment. He told me that, during the entire period, I had been an exemplary [prisoner]. However, now it was time for me to think about my family and my future. There was really nothing wrong with accepting this offer, and then I would be free again. . . . I replied that I knew the contents [of the statement] and that I perceived from the discussion that I would be put under pressure to deny my faith. Therefore, I would never sign such a statement. The judicial officer became white as a sheet and was angry. He began to threaten me. He said that I was crazy. Had the Gestapo officials not been there, I don't know what he would have done in his rage.[340]

After his refusal to sign the statement, he was transferred from the Neusustrum convict camp to temporary imprisonment in Lingen. The three days he spent in that penal institution presented a serious trial for the thirty-six-year-old coppersmith. The psychological pressure to which the situation exposed him is reflected in his recollections:

I was treated very kindly and was told that, if I made concessions, I would be taken to Hamburg in order to be released. I was also admonished to think of my family. However, I was already doing this. But I also thought of my fellow [believers]. All day long, I tried to remain calm, but my thoughts kept racing. I thought about the possibility of being released or being sent to the concentration camp. . . . All afternoon I tried to keep my feelings under control, but at night I was unable to sleep. And then, it just happened. I was overtaken by homesickness for my family and cried profusely all night long. I entreated Jehovah to remove this feeling of homesickness from me and to let everything take place according to his will. But he should protect me from compromising at this crucial moment. . . . Anxiously I awaited the next day, a day that I will never forget. It was April 20, the birthday of the greatest enemy of our faith who was determined to also undermine my faith as he had tried with many others before. I thought of the October 7, 1934,

> resolution and told myself, we will see who is stronger: Our God, Jehovah, or this god, Hitler.

For Jehovah's Witnesses, the statement renouncing their faith became a symbol of the trial that had been imposed on them. They had to prove their "loyalty toward Jehovah and his organization" and maintain their "integrity." Therefore, they also considered the interrogations as "tests of loyalty."[341]

Frequently, the emotional pressure was increased by the fact that family members tried to persuade individuals to sign the statement. The Gestapo took advantage of this and, shortly before or after a sentence had been served, arranged for a meeting between the uncompromising Jehovah's Witnesses and their spouses, children, or parents. The Gestapo often successfully calculated that these Jehovah's Witnesses would yield to the entreaties of their family members. In these cases, the Gestapo was not primarily concerned with establishing a basis for release. Their objective was, rather, to undermine the self-esteem of the believers. The Gestapo was also aware of the fact that, in many cases, signing the statement resulted in a serious spiritual crisis.[342]

Legal Authorities Protest against "Inappropriate Measures of Protective Detention"

During the June 18, 1937, discussion with the chief senior judges, an agreement had been reached with regard to the question of taking IBSA members into protective detention after they had served their sentences. However, the issue of imposing protective detention after an acquittal had been pronounced—a practice that the judges severely criticized—had not been resolved. This issue, which caused even greater conflicts between the Gestapo and the legal authorities, resulted in increased confrontations in the following years. In Hamburg, the Gestapo increasingly issued arrest warrants after acquittals had been pronounced or allowances had been made for pretrial detention. Consequently, in the spring of 1938 Dr. Curt Rothenberger, senior judge at the Hanseatic Higher Regional Court, decided to protest against such forms of judgment reversals. Rothenberger was a protagonist of the NS legal reform that tried to guarantee a rightful place for administration of justice by means of a firm and severe handling of penal power, even in the totalitarian state.[343] The cases of two Jehovah's Witnesses provided him with a concrete opportunity for his argument. In one case, the Hanseatic

Special Court sentenced a Jehovah's Witness to the relatively lenient eight months of imprisonment (in contrast to, by that time, considerably more serious punishments pronounced against Bible Students) because he had apparently changed his attitude. By making allowances for the time spent in protective and pretrial detention, the court considered his sentence completed. Moreover, the court emphasized that the decision to release the defendant had the objective of giving him an opportunity "to prove that his apparent acceptance of National Socialism was trustworthy."[344]

However, the State Police saw this matter in a different light: After the conclusion of the proceedings, the man was arrested again and taken to the Fuhlsbüttel police prison.[345] By taking the defendant into custody, which assumed that he continued to present a danger to public security, the Gestapo had deliberately counteracted the decision of the court.

The judges were offended. Such police interventions were perceived as an outright challenge of their area of jurisdiction, and they submitted the following report to Rothenberger:

> Under these circumstances, it is difficult to see the point in determining and substantiating a sentence. . . . Eventually, the judges must have the feeling that their work is useless if, as is indicated by the extreme case of P., their carefully substantiated considerations regarding the amount of punishment actually become meaningless, because the amount of punishment is determined by a subordinate official of the State Police office who does not show any regard for the reasons stated in the judgment.[346]

In his April 25, 1938, letter to Higher Senior Civil Servant Bruno Streckenbach, the chief of the central State Police office in Hamburg, Rothenberger protested the procedures of the Gestapo. Initially, with the remark that protective detention had been ordered elsewhere, Rothenberger received only an evasive response. Finally, on October 7, 1938, that is, almost six months later, Streckenbach simply rejected the protest (with reference to the April 22, 1937, Gestapa decree) without mentioning any details about the above-mentioned case. Rothenberger was surprised about the manner in which the Gestapo rejected his carefully presented objections; five days later, he sent a letter of complaint to the RJM.

Then, in his December 13, 1938, letter, Dr. Herbert Klemm, the head of the local *Generalreferat* (department) for political criminal cases, requested a statement from the chief of the Security Police regarding Rothenberger's complaints,[347] asking him to take into consideration that the general practice of taking Jehovah's Witnesses into protective detention after they had served their sentence could have just the opposite effect. He based his reasoning on the other case about which Rothenberger had complained. In this case, protective detention was imposed on the Bible Student, Johanna F., a mother of two children. In January 1938, after serving a sentence of fifteen months, she was sent to a concentration camp, even though the legal authorities had considered her earlier imprisonment to be "severe enough." Klemm objected that such action involved the danger that non–Bible Student family members "could become so resentful that they would develop an anti-state attitude." Therefore, the ministry considered it appropriate that Bible Students who had been imprisoned because of their IBSA activities would be released after serving their sentences *if* they abandoned the Bible Student teachings: "In this way, they are able to undermine the faith of their former fellow sectarians, by their example alone."

On January 24, 1939, all higher regional court senior judges met in Berlin to again discuss protective detention measures. For this meeting, Rothenberger had compiled records that listed twenty-three cases in the Hamburg Higher Regional Court district in which the police had pronounced judgment reversals by imposing protective detention after people had been acquitted or a sentence had been served. Some of these cases also involved Jehovah's Witnesses. During the discussion, based on the reasons (of imprisonment) the Gestapo had included in the court records, Rothenberger was able to show that the Gestapo considered itself authorized to make judgment reversals of previously imposed court decisions. In one case, for example, a detective ordered protective detention in order to "make the previously served sentence more effective."[348]

After his return from Berlin, Rothenberger informed the Hamburg senior judges that the ministry "did not object to measures of protective detention as long as it was obvious that they were imposed exclusively for the purpose of prevention. However, judgment reversals, such as had become known in particular cases, should not become the norm."[349] In order to emphasize that he would no longer accept such presumptuous actions on the part of the police authorities, Rothenberger asked to be immediately informed of all cases in which "it could be assumed that the police authorities would try to make judgment reversals by imposing protective detention." He also asked to be notified as soon as the police tried to arrest a person directly in the courtroom.

In the beginning of February 1939 the RJM received from the Gestapo leaders the requested statement regarding the two Hamburg cases, which, beyond the individual case, has to be considered as a basic ruling regarding the question of imposing protective detention on Bible Students. This statement by the Reichsführer SS and chief of the German police was signed by Kriminalrat (criminal lawyer) Heinrich Müller and indicated that Bible Students, "after having served their sentences, are taken into protective detention or sent to a concentration camp *only* if they stubbornly continue to adhere to the false teachings of this sect, despite their previous imprisonment."[350] In such cases, "subsequent detention is absolutely necessary since, according to our experience, it can be expected that the IBSA members would resume their activities for this prohibited sect because of their fanatical attitude." According to these explanations, not all Jehovah's Witnesses should be transferred to a concentration camp after having served their time. This should be done only in cases in which the Gestapo was uncertain of whether the particular person had completely changed his oppositional attitude and, consequently, could not determine his future actions. Even though these measures had been a Gestapo practice for more than one year, they were quite contrary to the April 22, 1937, Gestapa decree.

The statement further mentions that the Gestapo would "carefully examine" every individual case to determine "whether an IBSA member had actually abandoned the false teachings of this sect":

> Therefore, it is not possible to use a Bible Student's statement as a basis for determining whether he has abandoned these false teachings. Our experience in conducting such examinations has shown that such statements are often made only in order to obtain freedom. In several cases, Bible Students became involved again in prohibited IBSA activities shortly after they were released on the basis of such a statement. Therefore, it is necessary to examine carefully the trustworthiness of the statements of these Bible Students.

This confirmed that the Gestapo did not consider a signature under the statement renouncing one's faith to be sufficient evidence for the required change in attitude. The signing of the reverse statement, in itself, was no guarantee that a person was exempt from further imprisonment. It certainly did not automatically result in a release from prison. Even after submitting the required statement, a person was subjected to an extensive "examination of trustworthiness."[351]

With regard to the particular cases on which Rothenberger had based his complaints, the Gestapo stated that in the first case, an imposition of protective detention was justified. Even after the proceedings, the Jehovah's Witness "did not desist from the false teachings of his sect" although the judges indicated by their lenient judgment that they considered further imprisonment unnecessary. And in the second case, it was "absolutely necessary" to send the Bible Student to a concentration camp because this was a case of a "very dangerous and extremely fanatical IBSA member." Since the woman was a "stubborn Bible Student," it had to be expected that she would continue "pursuing the subversive activities of the IBSA, probably immediately after her release." This statement was supposed to emphasize the *preventive* function of protective detention as opposed to the *punishing* objective of legally imposed penalties. In this way, the Gestapo assured the RJM that it was not criticizing the legally imposed penalties and was also not unlawfully extending the sentence. It further emphasized that in this case as well as in all other Bible Student cases, a release from the concentration camp would not be considered until the "purpose [of protective detention] with regard to the policy of State security" was fulfilled.

Based on these statements, the Ministry of Justice decided to inform the senior judge of the Hanseatic Higher Regional Court that "in consideration of the explanations of the Reichsführer SS," the cases he had complained about "did not require any further actions."[352]

The subsequent reply to Rothenberger, dated March 27, 1939, and signed by Ministerialdirektor Crohne, is a typical example of the attitude adopted by the legal authorities in response to the Gestapo's infringement on legal decisions. They simply withdrew into the respective areas of jurisdiction to which the Gestapo had confined them and, therefore, contributed to the "legalizing" of the Gestapo practices. Crohne's statement to Rothenberger could hardly be seen as anything else but a surrender of jurisdiction on the part of the legal authorities: he noted that it therefore had to be left to the "discretion of these authorities, who are entrusted with handling preventive measures, whether they will use these measures in order to resist offenses against the law."[353]

Finally, in a quibbling tone, the letter lists those cases in which the Gestapo considered it to be appropriate to impose protective detention as a "preventive measure," even after the legal authorities had instituted and concluded legal proceedings, and contrasts them with cases in which an imposition of protective detention would have to be considered as inappropriate. Referring to the agreement that had been made with the Reichsführer SS regarding these questions, the RJM informed the senior judge of the Hanseatic Higher Regional Court that "it would even be appropriate to impose protective detention on Bible Students after they had served a sentence if they persistently adhered to their false teachings and, therefore, continued to endanger the welfare of the state." In some cases, "it would even be appropriate" to impose protective detention "on opponents of the state who had been acquitted because of lack of evidence." On the one hand, the ministry gave its approval to an imposition of protective detention in cases in which a legally imposed penalty had been served and in cases in which a defendant had been acquitted.[354] On the other hand, it raised objections against the practice of imposing protective detention in cases in which the legal authorities had granted a pardon, because exemption from punishment by way of pardon involving a period of probation required that the legal authorities had "ruled out the possibility of subsequent offenses." Since the Gestapo issued orders for protective detention in cases in which they considered "public law and order to be endangered," the ministry was concerned, particularly with regard to the case of the "extremely fanatical IBSA member," that there would be a possible discrepancy between legal measures and measures of the police authorities. Therefore, it requested the Reichsführer SS to provide clear guidelines for these particular instances. This was certainly not an insignificant matter since the issue directly involved the interests of the Ministry of Justice as an authority possessing the power of granting acts of pardon.

In the other case in which the ministry considered protective detention possibly "not to be appropriate," such decisiveness could not be observed. This involved court proceedings in which "there was sufficient evidence" to prove that the "purpose of punishment had been achieved by means of legally imposed penalties." By stating that "this would involve only a few cases," Crohne indicated that the ministry did not consider it to be a very significant problem. He even pointed out that in most cases the courts were not able to make a competent judgment anyway, since "the peculiarity of the Bible Students generally required a longer period of observation." It is therefore not surprising that Crohne finally informed the senior judge of the Hamburg Higher Regional Court that—all facts considered—he was "not able to prevent" the imposition of protective detention, not even in the particular cases Rothenberger had presented to him.

Since 1933, when the RJM had accepted the viewpoint that there was no reason to object to an imposition of protective detention as "a police measure of prevention," the legal authorities deprived themselves, right from the start, of the opportunity to criticize the increasing infringement of the Gestapo on matters relating to court proceedings.[355]

By taking this viewpoint, the Ministry of Justice had also turned over to the Gestapo all authority of defining the requirements for protective detention. All the Gestapo needed to do was refer to some knowledge the police had supposedly received about prevailing or anticipated danger to the state and it could present an imposition of protective detention as a preventive measure.

The Police Enforce Judgment Reversals

Since the Gestapo practice of imposing protective detention on Bible Students had been approved in principle, even at the highest authority, the courts now tried to maintain their authority by increasing the duration of penalties. In this way, they expected to prevent possible Gestapo interventions and to avoid disparaging judgment reversals. In 1938 the Hanseatic Special Court established detailed "guidelines for the punishment of defendants in Bible Student proceedings." These guidelines determined minimum penalties of four years of imprisonment for "higher IBSA functionaries with a previous conviction" (group leaders, main group leaders). They determined a minimum penalty of three years of imprisonment for "higher functionaries without a previous conviction." The penalty for cell leaders was set at two years and six months of imprisonment (with a previous conviction), and two years (without a previous conviction). Bible Students who had been convicted of distributing publications were to be punished with either one year or one year and three months of imprisonment. "Mere members, who had not participated in any distributions, that is, who merely received and read the *Watchtower*," should be punished with six or nine months of imprisonment.[356]

At the end of 1938 the Security Service of the SS stated with satisfaction that the special courts had adopted an increasingly "consistent and strict" administration of justice. Consequently, there was no longer any reason for complaint.[357] However, the stricter application of legal authority was reflected not only in more serious penalties imposed by the courts but also in an increase of the scope of offenses.[358] As a result, even religious family discussions or reading of Bible-related literature was considered as involvement in Bible Student activities.[359]

In May 1940 the Hanseatic Special Court considered the friendship of two Jehovah's Witnesses as "defiance against the IBSA ban" by stating that they "deliberately maintained their friendship" and "continued to talk about the Bible despite the IBSA ban."[360] According to the court, this required serious punishment because the defendants "had formed a new center for the prohibited IBSA, even if it was only a small one."[361] The court decision was based primarily on the fact that the defendants, both of whom had previously served long prison sentences, still displayed an uncompromising attitude and openly adhered to their religious beliefs. Apart from their private Bible discussions, there was no evidence that they maintained any connections with groups who were involved in prohibited IBSA activities, or that they tried to exert an influence on people in any other way. For their mutual Bible discussions, they were each sentenced to three years of imprisonment. During the next year, the same court also sentenced a forty-nine-year-old Bible Student from Hamburg to three years of imprisonment on the charge of "disparagement of the Reich government" (Law against Insidious Attacks on State and Party and for the Protection of the Party Uniform). The Hamburg Bible Student had once stated in a private conversation that Hitler was "a devil that had been put into office by the pope in Rome," and had thus been betrayed by his former fiancée.[362]

Some legal authorities even followed the Gestapo's suggestion to sentence the Bible Students on the charge of "organizing high treason." On this basis, the chief public prosecutor at the Hanseatic Higher Regional Court took action against Jehovah's Witnesses who had been involved in the June 1937 pamphlet campaign in Hamburg. Since high treason was a charge that came under the jurisdiction of the senior Reich attorney, the Chief Public Prosecutor General Erich Drescher submitted to the attorney the investigation records for cases against 127 defendants, in order to examine them. In the accompanying letter, dated January 5, 1938, Drescher made the following statements: "Previously, the members of the Bible Students Association were sentenced for their prohibited activities based on article 4 of the February 28, 1933, Decree of the Reich President for the Protection of People and State. However, since according to their . . . objectives the IBSA is gradually drifting into the political minefield of communism, there is reason to suspect that they are involved in acts of high treason. Therefore, the records are being [submitted] for the purpose of determining whether, and to what extent, the activities of the defendants can be regarded as involvement in acts of high treason and should be prosecuted accordingly."[363] In order to be able to count the activities of Jehovah's Witnesses as acts of high treason for a seditious organization, Drescher made reference to the "subversive" objectives (in his opinion) of this religious denomination, objectives "consisting of the destruction of all governments—supposedly predetermined by God—and, consequently, also the National Socialist government."

However, the highest representative of prosecution in the German Reich was not willing to adopt such a perspective. Only two weeks later, Berlin sent the 139 individual files and folders regarding the above-mentioned cases back to the Hamburg senior public prosecutor. In his corresponding January 19, 1938, court order, the senior Reich attorney at the People's Court stated that from his perspective, there was no sufficient evidence that this was an offense that would come under his jurisdiction: "In particular, the investigations did not provide any evidence indicating that the accused were personally involved in activities with the objective of overthrowing the National Socialist government. There is also no evidence that they had any knowledge of, or were involved in, such endeavors performed by the foreign organization of the IBSA supposedly in collaboration with communism."[364] The attorney then requested the Hanseatic Higher Regional Court to take "the required actions" in its own jurisdiction, as had been done previously.

For the accused Jehovah's Witnesses, this meant that they would also subsequently be punished "merely" to a maximum of five years of imprisonment, according to articles 1 and 4 of the Decree of the Reich President for the Protection of People and State. In proceedings on the charge of involvement in high treason, on the other hand, punishment could have even included the death penalty.

When, three months after this decision by the senior Reich attorney, court proceedings took place at the Hanseatic Special Court in Hamburg, this issue was addressed in the judgment: "And merely the fact that the Bible Students are not personally involved in this destruction but leave it in the hands of their master, Christ, distinguishes them from traitors."[365]

Thus, according to the court, the activities—but not the objectives—of Jehovah's Witnesses differed from revolutionists and traitors. The judges, who supposedly had "carefully examined" the teachings of Jehovah's Witnesses, substantiated their accusation by referring to the concept of a future world order of a thousand-year duration proclaimed by Jehovah's Witnesses. To this end, the judges stated that "the entire economic life . . . [would be] arranged according to a religious-Communist community." The Bible Students believed that God's Kingdom would be established on the basis of the conditions that existed among the early Christians. "Everything they owned was equally distributed (Acts 4:32)."[366] Evidently, the NS judges connected such early Christian ideals to the objectives of revolutionists and traitors.

Other public prosecutors also submitted records of Bible Student cases to the senior Reich attorney in order to press charges based on "involvement in high treason." However, according to this attorney, in none of these cases could the accusation of high treason be sustained. In January 1940 the same attorney returned the records of three court cases against members from IBSA groups in the Sudetenland and Austria to the local public prosecutor's offices with the remark that in none of these cases was there "any evidence of treasonable intent."[367] During the entire twelve-year period of the NS regime, it appeared that not a single Bible Student was sentenced on the basis of penal regulations for high treason (StGB, arts. 80–84). If at all, these were cases with extremely exceptional circumstances.[368] Since these particular penal regulations could not be applied to the activities of the Bible Students, new legal regulations were required in order to impose penalties that would exceed the punishment provided by the Decree of the Reich President for the Protection of People and State. This took place after the beginning of the war, when legal regulations were established that introduced two new categories of offenses, "involvement in an anti-military association" and "demoralization of the armed forces," and these new legal regulations resulted in the most serious penalties.

In the same way that the legal authorities yielded to the police requests for more severe penalties, they also made extensive concessions to the Gestapo with regard to acts of pardon.[369] Now, before granting pardon, the judges first consulted with the Gestapo to determine whether the Gestapo would object to a suspension of the sentence, and whether the Gestapo intended to take the people concerned into protective detention. Then, the judges would base their consequent actions on the respective decisions made by the Gestapo. This is how the petition for pardon was handled in the case of a sixty-three-year-old prisoner who had been sentenced to two and a half years of imprisonment on the charge of involvement in IBSA activities during the previous year. Four weeks after the legal authorities had received the man's petition for pardon, they requested a statement from the central State Police office in Hamburg. In its November 11, 1939, letter, the central State Police office in Hamburg replied that it had no objections to an act of pardon as long as the person concerned signed the enclosed statement. Protective detention would be taken into "consideration only if he refused to sign this particular statement."[370]

In this respect, the proceedings corresponded with the method established by the legal authorities in order to avoid a pronouncement of pardon that would conflict with a possible imposition of protective detention. Even before these proceedings could be concluded, however, the Gestapo changed its previous attitude. On March 16, 1940, the central State Police office in Hamburg informed the public prosecutor's office about a generally binding decision that had been made in Berlin regarding such cases: "The Reich Security Main Office has informed us that it principally cannot approve of acts of pardon for Bible Students, especially during wartime."[371]

The court then dropped the subject, especially since the petition for pardon had prolonged the court proceedings, which resulted in the fact that most of the penalty had already been served. Since this Berlin ruling apparently caused certain insecurity among the judges, they took the precautionary measure of asking the Gestapo whether the police intended to take further action. The Gestapo put them at ease and stated: "We do not intend to impose protective detention after the sentence has been served because F. has signed the statement prepared for the Bible Students."[372]

Thus, the Gestapo was actively involved in determining the outcome of acts of pardon as well as the actual amount of punishment. These are powerful examples of a development that ultimately resulted in the fact that the police, as an institution, was no longer a viable one that supported the legal authorities. On the contrary, the legal authorities themselves eventually carried out the instructions coming from the highest police authorities at the Prinz-Albrecht Strasse in Berlin—to some extent under compulsion or because of overzealous compliance— but based on their own initiative. In other words: The manner in which these especially obvious conflicts and questions of competence regarding court proceedings against Jehovah's Witnesses were handled and resolved gave evidence of the fact that, ultimately, the legal authorities surrendered almost completely to the Reichsführer SS.

Top at right: Members of the Hamburg congregation of Jehovah's Witnesses attending the Berlin convention, June 25, 1933. No swastika flags are visible in the interior of the "Wilmersdorf Sporthalle," which can be seen in the background. *Arrow in the middle:* Hero von Alften, leader of Hamburg group. *Arrow on the right:* Erwin Zimmermann, leader of youth group. (Courtesy of M. Renner, Oldendorf)

Bottom at right: A few months after the National Socialists took power, Jehovah's Witnesses were banned in all German states. In Hamburg, the ban was imposed on July 15, 1933, and published in the *Amtlicher Anzeiger* (official gazette) on July 18, 1933. (Hamburg State Archives)

Amtlicher Anzeiger.

Beiblatt zum Hamburgischen Gesetz= und Verordnungsblatt.

Nr. 165   **Dienstag, den 18. Juli**   **1933**

22381

Bekanntmachung.

Auf Grund des § 1 der Verordnung des Reichspräsidenten zum Schutze von Volk und Staat vom 28. Februar 1933 (Reichsgesetzblatt Teil I Seite 83) wird die Norddeutsche Bibel= forscher=Vereinigung e. V. für das gesamte hamburgische Staats= gebiet verboten und aufgelöst.

Hamburg, den 15. Juli 1933.

Die Polizeibehörde.

Demonstrations against Jehovah's Witnesses who refused to participate in the elections. Place unknown. Poster translates as "We are traitors, we did not go to the polls." (Franz Zürcher, *Kreuzzug gegen das Christentum. Moderne Christenverfolgung. Eine Dokumentensammlung* [Crusade against Christianity. Modern Persecution of Christians]. Document collection. Zurich, 1938, 126)

Offener Brief

An das bibelgläubige und Christus liebende Volk Deutschlands!

Als Dank dafür sind Tausende von Zeugen Jehovas in Deutschland aufs grausamste verfolgt, mißhandelt und in Gefängnisse und Konzentrationslager eingesperrt worden. Trotz größtem seelischem Druck und trotz sadistischer körperlicher Mißhandlung, auch an deutschen Frauen, Müttern und an Kindern im zarten Alter, hat man in vier Jahren nicht vermocht die Zeugen Jehovas auszurotten; denn sie lassen sich nicht einschüchtern, sondern fahren fort, *Gott mehr zu gehorchen als den Menschen,* wie es seinerzeit die Apostel Christi auch taten, als man ihnen verbot, das Evangelium zu verkündigen.

Die gegenwärtige unchristliche und bibelfeindliche Regierung maßt sich ferner an zu erklären, daß nur die römisch-katholische Kirche und die Staatskirche eine Art Religionsfreiheit ausüben kann, daß aber allen anderen wahrhaft bibelgläubigen Christen *keine Glaubens- und Gewissensfreiheit* gewährt wird.

Der Hoheitsträger, a Nazi journal published by Robert Ley, the Reich organization leader of the NSDAP. This and other journals incited the "political leaders" of the National Socialist Party to fight relentlessly against Jehovah's Witnesses. The bottom image shows a "rogue's gallery" of Jehovah's Witnesses. (*Der Hoheitsträger*, Series 8, August 1938)

Bottom left: "Open Letter" (excerpts), a pamphlet distributed throughout Germany by Jehovah's Witnesses on June 20, 1937. (Archive Detlef Garbe)

Richard Rudolph *(left)*, with fellow believer Walter Grunz and his family in Landeshut, Silesia, 1935. Both men were arrested one year later and met again in 1939 in the Sachsenhausen concentration camp. They remained in camp detention until liberation in 1945. (Courtesy of Richard Rudolph, Husum)

Faschismus oder Freiheit (Fascism or Freedom). Title of a Jehovah's Witness booklet published in Switzerland in 1939 and illegally distributed in Germany. (Watch Tower Bible and Tract Society, Brooklyn, 1939)

Geheime Staatspolizei

Staatspolizeileitstelle Hamburg

B.Nr. II B 1 - 2052 /3.7

Hamburg 36, den 10.Mai 1939.
Stadthausbrücke 8

Annahmestelle

An der Staatsan... Und der U...

11. MAI 1939

Kal. ..... Nr. ......

An die

    Gnadenabteilung beim Landgericht ~~Eisenach~~

    z.Hd.des Herrn Ersten Staatsanwalts Dr.Schwarz

           H a m b u r g

Betrifft: Gnadenerweis für den Strafgefangenen ████████,
         geb.23.11.1891 in Tillendorf.

Vorgang: Strafsache gegen Grote u.A. - Bibelforscher -
         Aktenzeichen 11 Js. Sond. 298/38.

       Unter Bezugnahme auf mein Schreiben vom 21.11.38
teile ich mit,daß ██████ seit seiner vorläufigen Entlas-
sung aus der Strafhaft am 28.11.38 mit der hiesigen Dienststelle als Vertrauensmann in engster Fühlungnahme gestanden
hat. Er weiß das ihm geschenkte Vertrauen zu schätzen und
hat der Dienststelle in dieser Zeit gute Dienste geleistet.
Z. ist ein äusserst bescheidener und ehrlicher Charakter,
der jetzt gänzlich von der Irrlehre der I.B.V. frei ist.
Daß er jemals rückfällig werden könnte, ist nach seinem
jetzigen Verhalten nicht zu befürchten.

           ██████ ist eines Gnadenerweises würdig. Es be-
steht ausserdem ein erheblich dienstliches Interesse daran, daß
dem ██████ die Reststrafe auf dem Gnadenwege erlassen wird.

        I.A.

       [signature]

Gestapo 7a

Pardon granted to an informer by the Hamburg Regional Office of the Gestapo, May 10, 1939. (Hamburg State Archives)

Geheime Staatspolizei
Staatspolizeileitstelle Hamburg

Hamburg 36, den 16.3.40.
Stadthausbrücke 8

B. Nr. II D 109 /40

Annahmestelle

19. MRZ 1940

An den
Oberstaatsanwalt bei dem Landgericht

H a m b u r g .

Betrifft: Gnadenanfrage Friedrich ███
-11 Js Sond 298/38.-

Vorgang: Gns 138/40 -Schreiben v.7.2.40.

Anlagen: 3.

Anliegend sende ich die Gnadenvorgänge
in der Sache ███ zurück. Das Reichssicherheitshauptamt hat hier mitgeteilt, dass es aus
grundsätzlichen Erwägungen-insbesondere während
der Kriegszeit-Begnadigungen bei Bibelforschern
nicht zu befürworten vermag.

In 1940 the Reich Security Main Office refused to pardon Bible Students "out of fundamental considerations," especially because it was during wartime. (Hamburg State Archives)

The photo, taken in the early 1930s, shows Erich Golly with his employees in front of his Hamburg beauty salon on Eppendorferweg 168. The SS sent Golly from one concentration camp to the next. In March 1938, after he had served several prison terms, he was transferred to Sachsenhausen; in February 1940 to the Wewelsburg camp; in April 1943 to the Buchenwald camp; one month later to the Bergen-Belsen camp; and at the beginning of 1944 back to the Sachsenhausen camp. From there, in June 1944, he was brought to Dachau and the Sudelfeld labor detail. On February 16, 1945, he died at the Dachau main camp. (Courtesy of Erich Kraushaar, Buchholz)

Erich Golly's wife, Dorothea, seen here (on the left) several days after her return home, was also imprisoned in September 1937. She was held in Ravensbrück from October 1941 until liberation in 1945. She returned to Hamburg completely blind and with other serious health problems. (Courtesy of Erich Kraushaar, Buchholz)

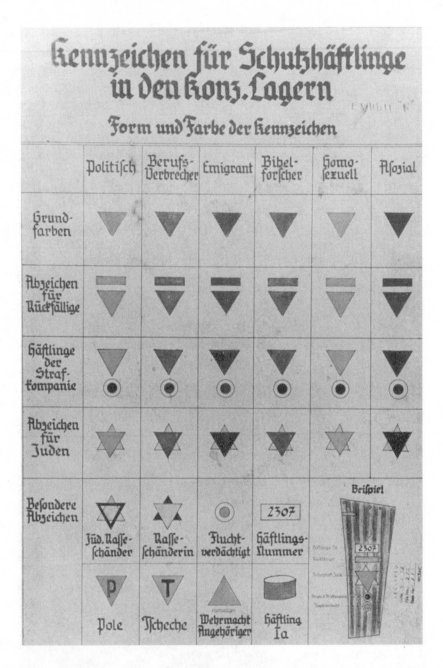

Chart with identification patches from the Dachau concentration camp. Prisoners had to wear triangles of various colors on their uniforms: red ("political"); green ("habitual criminals"); black ("asocials"); pink ("homosexuals"); purple ("Bible Students"). (International Tracing Service, Bad Arolsen)

Jehovah's Witnesses at the Wewelsburg concentration camp, which was liberated 1945. (Wachtturm Bibel- und Traktat-Gesellschaft [WTG], historical archives)

Max Liebster, who was persecuted as a Jew, had his first encounter with Jehovah's Witnesses during his imprisonment. Later, he shared the same barracks at Neuengamme with them. In October 1942 Liebster was transferred to the extermination camp Auschwitz-Birkenau but survived the selection and harsh work at the IG Farben construction site in Monowitz. In Buchenwald, right after his liberation, he was baptized as one of Jehovah's Witnesses along with his Jewish fellow prisoner Fritz Heikorn. (WTG, historical archives)

Portrait of Otto Keil. Keil was thirty-five years old when he was sentenced to death on April 18, 1941, by the RKG in Brandenburg on the grounds of conscientious objection. He was guillotined on May 24, 1941, in Brandenburg.

Der Oberreichskriegsanwalt
St.P.L.(RKA) II 13/41

Berlin-Charlottenburg 5, den 24. 5. 194 1
Wilzlebenstraße 4−10
Fernruf: 30 06 81

An

Frau Hedwig K e i l, geb. Schlägel
in L e i p z i g N 22,
Werder Str. 9.III r.

Ihr Ehemann, der Schütze Otto K e i l, ist durch Feld=
urteil des Reichskriegsgerichts vom 18.4.1941, bestätigt am
5.5.1941, wegen Zersetzung der Wehrkraft zum Tode verurteilt
worden.

Das Urteil wurde heute vollstreckt.

Im Auftrage

Tschima

Confirmation of Keil's execution, May 24, 1941. (Courtesy of Traudel Milbach, Steinhude)

On September 18, 1999, a plaque memorializing August Dickmann was unveiled at the Sachsenhausen concentration camp. On September 15, 1939, because of Dickmann's conscientious objection, the SS executed him in front of the other prisoners lined up in the roll call area. (Archive Detlef Garbe)

PART 5

JEHOVAH'S WITNESSES DURING THE WAR YEARS

13

Reorganization of Regional Resistance

After the series of arrests in 1937, IBSA activities throughout the Third Reich generally came to a standstill. During 1938/39, there was also no longer any organized resistance activity. However, the still extant groups, consisting mostly of women, were gradually able to reestablish contact and strengthen their network of communication. Even though the authorities had destroyed their organizational structure to a great extent, they had not been able to diminish the courage of many Jehovah's Witnesses in standing up for their convictions. They were not dependent on the encouragement and instructions of district overseers or other functionaries of their religious denomination to show their religious conviction with decisiveness and determination. This has been confirmed through the actions of many individual Jehovah's Witnesses. Left on their own, they now tried to resume the former activities of the IBSA leaders. According to a search warrant of the Würzburg State Police office, August Drda, a twenty-nine-year-old Jehovah's Witness from Homberg, had "repeatedly distributed large numbers of the IBSA pamphlets 'Justification' and 'Government' in various German cities.[1] His last distribution took place during the night of February 22, 1938." He had removed the front page of the pamphlets and had covered them with black paper.

At that time, organized activities of any extent were recorded only in those areas that had been annexed to the German Reich. In Austria, Jehovah's Witnesses had been banned in mid-1935 and were therefore already under ban when the German troops invaded the country on March 12, 1938.[2] Consequently, they had been able to prepare for the anticipated repression and persecution under NS rule.[3] This was also the purpose of a convention that Jehovah's Witnesses had organized in Prague at the end of August 1937.[4] Approximately two hundred members from the Austrian IBSA group, which in comparison to the German group was considerably smaller, attended this convention.[5] Because several arrests took place in Germany as a result of inadequate precautionary measures, the Austrian fellow believers received specific instructions and direction for their prohibited activities at this convention from members of the Prague branch office and the central European office in Bern. They were instructed to divide the organization into small groups and cells, a pattern that had been introduced in Germany in September 1936 (see p. 235). Consequently, the decision was made to divide the Bible Student organization in Austria in a similar way. Specific rules of conduct were also arranged for the purpose of reducing the danger of discovery.

At the beginning of March 1938, the Watch Tower Society sold the building at Pouthongasse 12 in Vienna that had served as its branch office since 1923. Then, apparently based on instructions by the Watch Tower Society's headquarters, the leader of the Austrian branch office left the country and went to Switzerland.[6] After the branch leader's escape, another member of the Vienna branch office, the fifty-two-year-old sales representative August Kraft, assumed leadership of the Austrian IBSA branch office during the period of the ban. Kraft carried out with great determination the underground activities according to the instructions received at the convention held in 1937 in Prague. He organized the formation of smaller groups and established locations for the distribution of publications. Special precautionary measures were taken in order to conduct meetings, and the locations for the meetings were repeatedly changed. Meetings were even held in places such as park areas. As far as possible, August Kraft avoided using intermediaries but instead tried to maintain personal contact with the leaders responsible for the various districts. He frequently traveled between Klagenfurt, Innsbruck, and Vienna; he even personally organized the smuggling of literature. During the initial period of Austria's annexation to Germany, fellow believers from Switzerland smuggled the *Watchtower* and other Bible Student publications over the border to Vorarlberg. There, Kraft accepted the publications and brought them via several intermediate distribution points—at which couriers from other Austrian states accepted the publications designated for their districts—all the way to Vienna. At this same time, Jehovah's Witnesses began copying the *Watchtower* by means of a simple reprint machine. This was necessary because the Bible Student group in Vienna included almost three-quarters of the total number of Austrian Bible Students and could not be sufficiently supplied with the number of publications being smuggled into

Austria. As was the case in Germany, the women played an especially important part in the production of these publications in Austria.[7]

The *Watchtower* was printed in the basement of a gardener's home on the outskirts of Vienna, at Grinzinger Allee 54. Extensive precautionary measures were taken: particular measures were taken to secure the room; special provisions were made to shield it from outside surveillance, and the basement was also disguised as a workshop. After each use, typewriters and mimeograph machines were carefully stored away. In one section of the basement, the floor was covered with cobblestones. Removing these stones and a layer of dirt revealed several wooden planks. These planks, in turn, concealed a storage space at the side of the house that could be used for hiding the printing equipment. In addition to the onerous task of mimeographing, the Bible Students involved in the printing had to perform the hard manual work of opening and closing this storage space.

The Austrian Jehovah's Witnesses became quite active. In comparison to their fellow believers in Germany (of whom every second Jehovah's Witness was involved in religious resistance activities after the National Socialists took power), the degree of participation in these activities among the Austrian Jehovah's Witnesses was considerably higher. To a certain extent, this was probably due to the smaller membership, which resulted in a closer relationship among the Austrian Jehovah's Witnesses. It can also be attributed to the fact that in that Catholic country, Jehovah's Witnesses had already been exposed to difficulties and an associated exclusion from society in general since the early 1920s. As a result, the membership of Jehovah's Witnesses in Austria had already accumulated experiences in discrimination and persecution.[8]

On April 4, 1939, many Jehovah's Witnesses were arrested.[9] These arrests took place on the date of their Memorial celebrations. In its March 21, 1939, interoffice decree, the Berlin Secret State Police office had informed the State Police offices of this date and had given instructions to keep all the homes of IBSA members living in the respective districts under surveillance.[10] This surveillance was to be carried out in "consultation with the respective branch offices of the Security Service."[11]

On May 25, 1939, August Kraft, the leader of the Austrian branch office, was arrested in Vienna. Even though he had been in charge of quite a few of the prohibited activities, the Austrian IBSA branch recovered relatively quickly from this blow. Kraft had arranged with the Bern central European office that in the event of his arrest, Peter Gölles, a forty-seven-year-old manager of a grocery store, should be entrusted with the leadership of the Austrian IBSA branch. Consequently, Gölles's grocery store became a place of literature distribution and center of activities during the period of the ban in Austria. At night, the *Watchtower* was printed in hidden areas of the basement. During the day, concealed in paper bags for meat products or vegetables, the *Watchtowers* were handed over to "customers" who served as couriers. In contrast to Kraft, who had carried out his responsibilities of leadership from the underground by means of traveling, Gölles continued to run his grocery store and fulfilled these responsibilities simultaneously. Ernst Bojanowski, a businessman from Berlin who had fled from Germany to Austria in 1938, accepted the assignment of traveling. Bojanowski supplied the groups in the various parts of Austria with the publications printed in Vienna. He also recommended that the organization, which had been weakened as a result of the arrests, should be restructured. He encouraged the Bible Students to support this restructuring and assisted the formation of new groups. Bojanowski supposedly advised the Austrian Bible Students to refrain from conducting group Bible discussions on a regular basis in order to avoid chain reactions in case of arrests.[12] Besides Bojanowski, Ludwig Cyranek, another Jehovah's Witness from Germany, offered strong support for the underground activities of the Austrian IBSA branch. While Bojanowski was responsible for the distribution of the publications, Ludwig Cyranek, together with Anna Voll, a Bible Student from Vienna, accepted responsibility for the printing of the *Watchtower* and other Bible Student publications. They also produced copies of the book *Fascism or Freedom*, based on a public lecture that J. F. Rutherford, the president of the Watch Tower Society, had given in New York, on October 2, 1938.[13]

In October 1939, though, the Gestapo arrested a certain Jehovah's Witness who, according to the daily report of the Vienna Gestapo, disclosed "the names of the leading brothers of almost all of Vienna's districts."[14] As a result, the Gestapo was able to arrest a considerable number of people. In the context of this wave of arrests, the Gestapo also learned about the duplicating of the *Watchtower* in the basement of the gardener's home. As a precautionary measure, however, Jehovah's Witnesses had already taken the mimeograph machines to a different location. During the following weeks and months, the locations for the printing equipment were repeatedly changed. Finally, a new hiding place was established in a garden plot shed. In the meantime, the Gestapo had activated a tremendous police force in order to search for the prohibited printing place. According to a Vienna Special Court decision involving those who had produced these publications, it was possible only after detailed investigations to find "the place where the printed material was produced, discover the shaft, and seize the duplicating machine together with the typewriter and other material."[15]

During these times, it became increasingly difficult to maintain communication with the central European office in Bern. It also became impossible to smuggle *Watchtower* publications into Austria by way of Bratislava (Slovakia). After all possibilities of bringing publications into the country had been exhausted, though, Jehovah's Witnesses were able to smuggle film slides with *Watchtower* articles over the Italian border into Austria. Later, the film slides were enlarged, and a female Jehovah's Witness from western Tirol prepared the matrixes for mimeographing. The copies were then taken to a place in the Alps for distribution to other locations.

Two months after the wave of arrests, around the turn of 1939/40, Ernst Bojanowski, Anna Voll, and Ludwig Cyranek left Vienna to coordinate the resistance activities of the IBSA in Germany. The Reich Security Main Office (RSHA) had ordered a State Police action on June 12, 1940; according to the decree the pogrom was to include "the whole territory of the German state," and should be "executed all of a sudden."[16] During this raid, the Austrian IBSA leader, Peter Gölles, and forty-four other Bible Students were arrested.[17] After the two waves of arrests in October 1939 and June 1940, the underground organization of Jehovah's Witnesses in Austria was almost completely destroyed. As in Germany, only a few small groups survived. These groups conducted their meetings only on an irregular basis and were no longer able to perform any significant activities.

The authorities responsible for the persecution took serious actions against the people who had been arrested. Based on the recently issued military laws, the majority of Jehovah's Witnesses were sentenced to several years of imprisonment on either the charge of "involvement in an anti-military association" or "demoralization of the armed forces." In the majority of cases, the amount of punishment ranged between two and three years of imprisonment.[18] After serving their sentences, the prisoners were usually transferred to a concentration camp. However, the Gestapo even sent quite a number of Jehovah's Witnesses immediately to the concentration camps without first instituting legal proceedings. A considerable number of them were sent to the Mauthausen concentration camp. The terrible conditions at this concentration camp between 1939 and 1942 resulted in an extremely high death rate.[19] As far as can be determined, a total of 445 members of the Austrian IBSA branch (which, prior to annexation to the German Reich in 1937, included 549 Kingdom proclaimers) were imprisoned for several months or even years in various penal institutions and concentration camps. At least 142 Austrian Jehovah's Witnesses died as a result of NS persecution. A total of ninety-four of these were killed in concentration camps and penal institutions. Forty-eight were sentenced to death by the legal authorities or military courts and were executed. The Reich Military Court (RKG) sentenced the majority of them to death as conscientious objectors.[20]

As in Austria and in the German-speaking areas of Czechoslovakia, such as the *Reichsgau* (Nazi party province) Sudetenland that was annexed to the NS state in October 1938, the IBSA groups became quite active. Even before the Anschluss (annexation), the Sudeten-German party, which was indeed pro-NS-minded, had already collected information about the IBSA members. Therefore, several Jehovah's Witnesses were arrested immediately after the invasion of the Wehrmacht.[21] In addition, during the following spring, the police authorities took a number of actions against the IBSA in the Sudetenland.[22]

Because Czechoslovakia borders on Germany, a number of German Jehovah's Witnesses had previously been able to escape the German authorities by fleeing to Czechoslovakia. After the Anschluss of the Sudetenland, the Watch Tower Society's branch office in Czechoslovakia also took into consideration the possibility that NS Germany would eventually occupy the remaining part of Czechoslovakia, and they took certain precautionary measures. On March 30, 1939, two weeks after the Anschluss, the Gestapo appeared at the Prague branch office. Jehovah's Witnesses had already taken most of the machinery and equipment out of the country and had sent three of the printing presses to the Netherlands. There, they were used to produce Bible Student publications for their fellow believers in Germany.[23] Heinrich Dwenger from Hamburg, who formerly had been the head and authorized officer of the Watch Tower Society's service department at the Magdeburg Bible House, became the leader of the Czechoslovakian IBSA branch office in 1936. He also temporarily supervised the IBSA activities in Hungary. Before the occupation of the remaining part of Czechoslovakia, he fled to Switzerland, "as instructed by the society."[24] In the following weeks, as a result of the March 16, 1939, Führer decree (Decree of the Führer and Reich Chancellor Regarding the Protectorates Böhmen and

Mähren), the Gestapo specifically searched for German IBSA members in the areas of Czechoslovakia that had come under German occupation as the protectorates of Bohemia and Moravia. Initially, the Gestapo did not pursue Jehovah's Witnesses of Czechoslovakian nationality. But at the beginning of 1940, they also began to arrest Czechoslovakian Jehovah's Witnesses as well as other foreign Jehovah's Witnesses.[25]

More Radical Tendencies

Around the middle of 1939, Jehovah's Witnesses began to reorganize their resistance activities in Germany. Since the German IBSA branch had lost all its leading functionaries, Ludwig Cyranek occupied a major role in these activities. Cyranek, who was born in 1907, was one of the younger dynamic leaders, and he also had a measure of experience in various fields of activity of the Watch Tower Society. Since the end of the 1920s, he had held a permanent position at the Magdeburg branch office. In October 1931 he had accepted the Watch Tower Society's request to become a missionary in neighboring countries, and in the next three years, he established contacts in the Netherlands, France, Yugoslavia, Austria, and Switzerland. In 1934 he returned to Germany and participated in the IBSA activities, which, at that time, had already been prohibited. As a result, in 1936 he was arrested in Mannheim and sentenced to two years of imprisonment. Immediately after his release from prison, Cyranek began to reestablish the prohibited organization that had been destroyed in 1937/38, and in the spring of 1939 he visited fellow believers in several places to request their support for this project.

Among those whom Cyranek visited was Julius Engelhard, a roofer from Karlsruhe.[26] From June 1939 on, Engelhard, after work, printed Bible Student publications (for which a retired female teacher from Bruchsal made the matrices) on his employer's mimeograph machine. In the autumn of 1939 the Gestapo almost succeeded in catching Engelhard because his hiding place had been betrayed. As soon as Engelhard had entered the house, a Gestapo official grabbed hold of him. He was able to break free and disappear into the crowd on the street, and the search for him remained unsuccessful. Engelhard then went underground, first in Bruchsal and, from March 1940 on, in Essen. There, Paul Noernheim, whom Cyranek had persuaded in April of the previous year to support these activities, directed a group of very active IBSA members. At the end of 1939, after six months of supporting his fellow believers in Vienna, Cyranek returned to Germany. On his return, he found a network of groups of devoted IBSA members in the southwestern and western parts of Germany. In 1940, in the Ruhr district alone, about 240 Jehovah's Witnesses, organized in various groups, were involved in reestablishing IBSA activities.[27] From Stuttgart, Cyranek coordinated the distribution of the *Watchtower* and other Bible Student publications. He also compiled reports about the preaching activity in Germany, as had previous IBSA leaders on the Reich level. These reports were then sent to the Netherlands. Maria Hombach, who did secretarial work for Cyranek, wrote the reports with lemon juice on pages that otherwise contained information of no importance. At the branch office in the Netherlands, located in Heemstede, near Haarlem, the pages were ironed, disclosing the reports. Jehovah's Witnesses even used several other conspiratorial methods such as adopting assumed names and using concealed language (for instance, they called the Watch Tower Society "Mother"). On two different occasions Cyranek was even able to travel to the Netherlands by using a counterfeit passport. There, he discussed future plans of activity with Robert Arthur Winkler, the IBSA branch leader of the Netherlands who had escaped from Prague via Switzerland to the Netherlands in 1939, and Heinrich Dwenger, the former authorized officer of the Magdeburg Bible House.[28]

After the dissolution of the Prague branch office, which had temporarily supervised the activities in Germany and Austria, the Watch Tower Society transferred the responsibility for the German and Austrian branches to Winkler, the branch leader of the Netherlands.[29] In the autumn of 1937, after the arrest of Heinrich Dietschi and the general destruction of the IBSA organization in Germany, the position of IBSA leader on the Reich level was no longer occupied until the end of the war.[30] The groups in the German Reich that were under the leadership of Ludwig Cyranek (southwestern and western parts of Germany) and Peter Gölles (Austria) received their instructions from the Netherlands.[31] Subsequently, after the execution of Cyranek in March 1941 and the arrest of Winkler at the end of October 1941, Narciso Riet and Julius Engelhard (southern and western parts of Germany, Austria and the protectorates of Bohemia and Moravia) as well as Wilhelm Schumann and Franz Fritsche (Magdeburg, Berlin) supervised the activities of the organization. As far as communication could be maintained, they received their instructions directly from Bern.

Even the SS took note of the IBSA restructuring in the various parts of Germany. (However, during the war in the northern and eastern parts of the German Reich it was not possible to organize activities of nationwide significance.[32]) On February 19, 1940, the Security Service reported that the Bible Students had "appeared again with their anti-state propaganda in various parts of the [German] Reich": For example, "members of the International Bible Students were arrested in Salzburg, Berlin, Plauen, Würzburg, and Stuttgart. It has been noted that several of the arrested people received instructions from the Netherlands."[33] During this period, the informers of the Security Service also reported increased IBSA activities in Berlin, Dortmund, Dresden, Graz, Karlsbad, Küstrin, Niederdonau, and Northern Schleswig.[34] With the outbreak of the war, the refusal of Jehovah's Witnesses to perform military service gained importance and increasingly attracted the attention of the SS. In his October 20, 1939, report to Reich Minister Hans-Heinrich Lammers, the head of the Reich chancellery, Reinhard Heydrich, the chief of the Secret State Police office and SS, informed the Reich minister of "the attitude of the political churches and sectarian groups toward the current situation." With reference to the conscientious objection propagated and practiced by Jehovah's Witnesses, he stated that the Bible Students now resorted to unconcealed acts of "sabotage and resistance." In an effort to support this statement, he referred to the case of Berthold Mewes, a radio operator from Paderborn. This "fanatical Bible Student" had informed the commanding officer of his military unit that "his conscience did not allow him to perform military service in the Wehrmacht."[35]

In the spring of 1940, after the occupation of the Netherlands, Belgium, and northern France, it became increasingly difficult to smuggle the *Watchtower* and other publications into Germany. Almost all states bordering Germany were now under the authority of the NS government or were ruled by governments in alliance with Hitler's Germany. In other European states not under NS rule (such as the Balkan states), with the exception of Switzerland, the Watch Tower Society did not have any adequate organizational structures. In some of these states (Portugal, Spain, and the Soviet Union), the Watch Tower Society was also banned or under restrictions similar to a ban. It thus became increasingly difficult to smuggle publications over the border between Switzerland and Germany. Instead, IBSA couriers smuggled single copies of the *Watchtower* or the corresponding typescripts of the particular journals from Switzerland via France or Italy, into the German Reich.[36] But even with these new methods, they could not prevent the complete, though temporary, interruption of the supply of publications. As a result, the Brooklyn headquarters of the Watch Tower Society was no longer, or only infrequently, able to provide instructions for the remaining IBSA groups involved in underground activities. Increasingly, Jehovah's Witnesses in Germany had to make their own decisions.

During the war, some IBSA groups were able to print Bible Student publications even under the conditions of the ban. Small numbers of these publications were distributed among the various groups. They served the purpose of fortifying the members of the denomination. During those years, though, it was possible to mimeograph and distribute the *Watchtower* only if the couriers were able to smuggle the appropriate material into the country. As far as possible, Jehovah's Witnesses copied the articles that appeared in the German issues of the *Watchtower* in Switzerland. Sometimes, if available, they translated *Watchtower* articles from other languages. They even began writing their own articles and commentaries and including them in the journal. They also included excerpts from copies of farewell letters. These were letters that Jehovah's Witnesses who had been sentenced on the charge of conscientious objection wrote to their relatives prior to execution. ("Letters of brothers who were murdered by Satan's agents for the sake of truth and righteousness.")[37]

Articles in the *Watchtower* provided explanations about Bible texts discussing the persecution of righteous people (such as 1 Pet., Heb. 10:32–34, 1. Cor. 4:12, and Matt. 5:10) and about the Book of Revelation, which formed an essential part of the Bible Student teachings. Increasingly, these articles also included the apocalyptic explanations in the book of Daniel, which contains visions about the struggle of the King of the South (Egypt) and the King of the North (Syria, Babylon) during the time of the end.[38] In *Watchtower* articles, these "visions of the prophecies of Daniel," which theologically reflected the power struggles of the Hellenistic period, were projected to the current wartime situation.[39] Accordingly, Hitler and his alliance (the King of the North) were diametrically opposed to the alliance of the confronting states (the King of the South). In their desperate struggle for world domination, the King of the North would first perish and be destroyed forever. Thereafter, even the King of the South would face the same fate. After this decisive battle, for the benefit of all mankind, a righteous government would be established under the rulership of Christ. By means of these and similar explanations regarding the subject of "Armageddon and the coming Kingdom of God," the Bible Students interpreted World War II as part of a divine plan, which clearly demonstrated the imminent end of this world.[40]

The German branch office of the Watch Tower Society also occasionally provided at this time the publication *Mitteilungsblatt der deutschen Verbreitungsstelle des W.T. [Watchtower] an alle treuen Zeugen Jehovas in Deutschland*. Like the *Watchtowers* during this period, the *Mitteilungsblatt* was a typewritten document and generally included six to ten pages.[41] It discussed issues that were of immediate concern for Jehovah's Witnesses in Germany. For example, the paper included practical applications of *Watchtower* articles discussing specific biblical subjects and thus provided its readers with realistic instructions and rules of conduct. In this regard, a *Mitteilungsblatt* distributed at the beginning of 1942 requested its readers to refrain from supporting collections of NS organizations. At the same time, it also gave instructions to refuse making any contributions to the Red Cross: "To support the Red Cross means supporting the 'war.' If the National Socialists want to assist their wounded soldiers, they should end the war and not produce more wounded soldiers."[42] In September 1942 the *Mitteilungsblatt* reported wartime atrocities committed by the SS in the Soviet Union. Even though it was not possible to guarantee the accuracy of these reports, the SS was "certainly capable of committing such crimes. People who set fire to the Reichstag and put the blame on others can also be expected to commit other offenses."[43] In view of such atrocities, the destruction of Germany was practically predestined. Three months before the battle of Stalingrad, the *Mitteilungsblatt* stated: "Hitler and his Nazis are the ones to be blamed for the ruination of this prosperous country. Starvation, desolation, and destruction have left their marks in Germany."

The political and economic situation in the German Reich was compared to the conditions in the Soviet Union, used by the NS propagandists for the purpose of deterrence, in order to prove that the NS slogan of "protecting Germany from Bolshevism" was in reality only used to justify this war of aggression:

> Suppose Bolshevism would have flooded Germany, what would have changed? Nothing at all! The Nazi press always tried to expose certain aspects that supposedly are typical and characteristic for Bolshevik Russia. However, in exactly these aspects, Russia and National Socialist Germany are like two peas in a pod. Russia has a cruel dictator. So do we. That country is ruled by bloodshed and terror. So is ours. Russia has the GPU [Soviet Secret Police]. We have the Gestapo [Secret State Police]. They have labor camps in Siberia and GPU prisons. We have concentration camps and Gestapo bunkers.

Even though such descriptions bring to mind theories of totalitarianism, they can certainly not be considered as an attempt to interpret the political situation. From the viewpoint of the writers of the *Mitteilungsblatt*, current world events were still the result of an attack by Satan and the "Roman Catholic Church," which was under his control. However, the choice in terminology alone made the article appear even more radical. The pope was now depicted as the "top gangster of religion" or "gangster chief." He was the one "mainly responsible for this war." Hitler in Germany, Mussolini in Italy, and Franco in Spain were all in the service of this "totalitarian god."

Compared with the *Watchtower*, which reflected the opinion of the Watch Tower Society's leaders abroad, the *Mitteilungsblatt* written in Germany made some bold statements. It almost seems that extreme opinions were at work among the Bible Students involved in the underground operations and those in the concentration camps. These Bible Students asked their fellow believers to intensify their resistance activities and to take a determined stand in the face of the enemy. Consideration for personal circumstances was regarded as religious weakness. The intensifying struggle against the powers of Satan did not allow for any half-hearted actions. The message of the *Mitteilungsblatt* was clear: Do not shrink back.

This was especially obvious in the July 1942 *Mitteilungsblatt*, titled "Answers to Frequently Asked Questions," which dealt with subjects that had resulted in controversies and differences in opinion. Such controversies involved questions of performing military service without arms and taking the military oath. They also involved the issue of how to deal with people who had been expelled from the religious denomination or who had withdrawn from the association in order to "wait and see." People who had adopted a radical position were seriously criticizing those among them who were indecisive and fearful. At least those who considered military service without arms as a possible alternative took into account the Christian commandment not to kill, as opposed to an uncompromising refusal to perform military service that definitely resulted in a death penalty. These Bible Students were viewed as having been lured into Satan's trap and having violated Jehovah's laws, even if they refused to take the military oath.[44] The issue not only involved "the oath and the act of shooting, it involved the question of serving, or not serving, Satan's organization." Quite appropriately, the *Mitteilungsblatt* added: "The act of shooting is the last link in a series of actions that are obviously required to make shooting possible. Everyone contributing to this series of actions is *as important and as responsible* as the soldier performing the act of shooting."[45] Each sincere person was therefore required to adopt an uncompromising attitude and to avoid succumbing to temptations: "We know of several preliminary investigations and court proceedings involving Jehovah's Witnesses who refused to perform military service in which the judges almost always tried, and will continue to try, using this wrong reasoning in order to lure faithful Jehovah's Witnesses into a trap."[46]

On the other hand, those whose actions were not in harmony with God's requirements were still able "to correct their mistake," but only if they "turned around immediately." In order to demonstrate what was involved in turning around, the *Mitteilungsblatt* included a letter from a Jehovah's Witness, who "had been persuaded to perform military service" after he had received a death penalty and who now reported about his change of mind. When he finally saw the terrible slaughter on the eastern front, he came to realize that it was against God's will to have any part in these actions. Consequently, he decided to take off his uniform. Now, he was determined not to "look back but, instead, move forward": "Even if I received another death penalty, [it] would not matter. I would rather die for the Lord than for an organization that is nearing its end . . . death to Satan's organization, long live Theocracy!" The *Mitteilungsblatt* commented: "*Only* his present attitude can save him from destruction." Nobody can serve two masters: " There is no kind of military service that a person could perform and, at the same time, submit to Theocracy."

By means of such written reminders, Jehovah's Witnesses were constantly admonished to keep a strong faith, despite all opposition. Along with such admonitions not to become weak during those trials and not to compromise, the faithful ones were given promises, whereas the unfaithful ones were rejected. This is clearly shown in a *Watchtower* titled "Trost für die Verfolgten" (Defeat of Persecution), which was distributed among Jehovah's Witnesses in 1942/43. Accordingly, there was only one question that should determine all actions of Jehovah's Witnesses: Which government should be allowed to rule, "the government of Jehovah or that of the oppressor?" There was no room for compromising. Every person had to make a clear decision and be aware of the consequences of his choice, which simply stated would be either "a blessing or condemnation":

> Those who endure the persecution unto the end and keep integrity have a part in the vindication of God's name. Everlasting blessings go along with that privilege. . . . Those who do not maintain their integrity lend support to the persecutor's argument and shall share

a like fate with him, that is, everlasting destruction. . . . The reward which he bestows is sure and unfading and infinitely greater than any selfish rewards that all the enemy organization on earth could bestow upon anyone yielding to its persecution. Those who hate "iniquity" or lawlessness toward God and who come out for the righteousness of Jehovah's Theocratic Government are anointed to be fellows with his God-like Son in that kingdom.[47]

Underground Activities

In the countries under German occupation, Jehovah's Witnesses were subjected to serious and ruthless persecution.[48] Only a few weeks or months after the occupation, the German authorities banned the IBSA branch offices in the respective countries.[49] Great losses resulted from the persecution in the Netherlands. On May 10, 1940, the German Wehrmacht invaded that country. As in Czechoslovakia in 1939, the Gestapo immediately began to search for Jehovah's Witnesses who had fled to the Netherlands.[50] Three weeks later, on May 29, 1940, Reich commissioner Arthur Seyß-Inquart issued a decree banning the association. Despite these circumstances, the approximately five hundred IBSA members in the Netherlands continued their preaching activity and actively participated in resistance activities with great public response. As a result of their uncompromising attitude and pamphlet campaigns, many people became interested in the activities of Jehovah's Witnesses. Even though the considerable number of arrests during the period following the autumn of 1940 had weakened the association, their preaching activity was deemed successful. In the five-year period between August 1940 and August 1945, the number of Kingdom proclaimers "soared from about 500 . . . to a new peak of 3,125."[51] During the German occupation, 426 Jehovah's Witnesses were arrested in the Netherlands. Probably 200 to 250 of those were sent to concentration camps in Germany. A total of 117 of them died as a result of the extreme working conditions, starvation, and mistreatment.[52]

Without exception, Jehovah's Witnesses were banned in the countries that had an alliance with Germany, although the seriousness of repression differed from one country to the next.[53] In Slovakia, the Hlinka-Guards under Josef Tiso also severely persecuted Jehovah's Witnesses.[54] In Italy, on the other hand, the most serious acts of persecution were committed only after NS Germany occupied the country in the autumn of 1943.

The Italian government had closed the Watch Tower Society's branch office in Italy as early as 1932. About three years later, an increasing wave of repression forced the Italian Jehovah's Witnesses to go underground in order to continue their activities. On August 22, 1939, orders were given to confiscate all Bible Student publications. However, the Italian Ministry of the Interior did not issue the official IBSA ban until March 13, 1940. Nevertheless, these measures of persecution did not, in any way, compare to the intensity and brutality of those committed by the National Socialists. After Mussolini was removed from office in July 1943, Jehovah's Witnesses were released from the penal institutions. However, in the Fascist Republic of Italy, they were subjected to a new wave of persecution.[55]

In Hungary, on the other hand, Jehovah's Witnesses were persecuted as seriously as in the German Reich. As early as 1937/38, the police took extensive actions against local IBSA members. In order to justify these police actions, press reports stated, just like in Germany, that "the advocators of this sect" acted on "orders by the International Communist Movement." As a result, after the official IBSA ban had been issued on December 13, 1939, many IBSA members were sent to prison camps.[56] As in the NS concentration camps, Bible Students were requested to sign a statement indicating that they would renounce their faith. Jehovah's Witnesses who refused to sign this statement were subjected to serious mistreatment. In the summer of 1943, after unsuccessful attempts to draft them for military service, 160 imprisoned Jehovah's Witnesses were deported to Bor, the concentration camp in Serbia. In October 1944, with the support of Germany, the fascist Pfeilkreuzler government (members of this party terrorized the Budapest ghetto and killed several thousand Jews until liberation by the Soviet army in 1945) seized power under leadership of Ferenc Szálasi. Subsequently, Jehovah's Witnesses who refused to perform military service under arms were executed according to martial law. A total of sixteen Jehovah's Witnesses were reportedly executed on that particular charge. Another twenty-six Hungarian Jehovah's Witnesses died as a result of mistreatment.[57]

Jehovah's Witnesses were also persecuted in several other European countries: in Portugal, under Antonio de Oliveira Salazar, who ruled Portugal from 1932 on; in Spain, under Caudillo Francisco Franco; and in the USSR, under Joseph Vissarionovich Stalin, secretary general of the Communist Party of the Soviet Union.[58] During World War II, the activities of Jehovah's Witnesses were even restricted in a number of free countries.[59] They were exposed to serious persecution if military service was compulsory, or compulsory military service was introduced. Because they refused to perform military service, they were subjected to imprisonment. However, the situation in the United States and Great Britain shows that "democratic states allowed for compromises in their dealings with people of different opinion, even during periods of extreme difficulty."[60]

During the war in Germany, not even the increasing police actions of the Gestapo could completely stop the underground activities of Jehovah's Witnesses, which, according to the Gestapo, were performed with renewed strength. And this despite the fact that from 1937/38 on, the Secret State Police authorities had at their disposal an important police informer in their struggle against the Bible Students Association. Hans Müller, an IBSA member from Dresden, worked at the central European office in Bern. He provided the Gestapo with crucial information about the prohibited IBSA activities. Numerous arrests, such as those of Ludwig Cyranek, Ernst Bojanowski, Anna Voll, and Paul Noernheim (the leader of the IBSA group in Essen), all of which took place around the turn of 1940/41, were probably the result of his betrayals.[61] On March 18, 1941, Special Court I at the Dresden Regional Court sentenced Ludwig Cyranek to death "on the charge of demoralization of the armed forces in concurrence of involvement with an anti-military association and defiance against the ban of the International Association of Earnest Bible Students." Three months later, the thirty-three-year-old IBSA leader was executed.[62]

Despite these setbacks, the IBSA organizations in the western and southwestern parts of Germany were able to consolidate again. Julius Engelhard accepted the responsibilities of Ludwig Cyranek. After the arrest of Noernheim, Engelhard left Essen in order to join the small but very active IBSA group in Oberhausen-Sterkrade. From the beginning of 1941 until March 1943, in cooperation with the members of this group, Engelhard organized the printing of twenty-seven different issues of the *Watchtower*. In the beginning, a total of 240 copies were printed. The production was later increased to a total of 360 copies. In addition, the sporadic *Mitteilungsblätter,* as well as other Bible Student publications, were also reprinted. From Oberhausen small numbers of publications were distributed to several IBSA groups throughout the German Reich by a courier system. In this way, contacts were established to IBSA groups in Munich, Mannheim, Mainz, Speyer, Berlin, Dresden, and Vienna. Beginning in December 1942, at first infrequently, but later on a regular basis, Bible Student prisoners at the Niederhagen concentration camp were also supplied with issues of the *Watchtower*.[63] The SS used these Bible Student prisoners for the reconstruction of Wewelsburg castle, which was located approximately thirteen miles (twenty kilometers) to the southwest of Paderborn, into a central SS-Ordensburg, a training school for future NS leaders. Female Bible Students from surrounding areas established contacts between the banned IBSA organization in the district of Oberhausen-Essen and the Wewelsburg prisoners. To this end, they placed *Watchtower* issues, which included secret private letters, under gravestones at the Wewelsburg cemetery or at other "dead drops." The Bible Students positioned these mailboxes in areas where labor details would be working during the day.[64]

Julius Engelhard frequently visited the local groups to make arrangements for the underground activities and collect the "service reports." Sixty-year-old Auguste Hetkamp generally maintained contacts with the IBSA leaders in the Netherlands and in Switzerland. Together with the families of her children, she greatly supported the Sterkrade IBSA group. The expenses involved in carrying out these extensive activities, such as rent and living expenses of the underground functionaries, were covered by means of contributions from fellow believers ("Good Hope Fund"; see pp. 218–19).

On April 3, 1943, shortly after the Essen IBSA group had been dissolved, the police arrested Julius Engelhard.[65] During an extensive police action, further arrests took place, resulting in the dissolution of the IBSA groups in Oberhausen and other locations in the Rhineland. In September 1944 the Hamm Higher Regional Court instituted mass proceedings against eighty-three Bible Students after they had spent more than one year in protective detention and pretrial detention. Most were sentenced to several years of imprisonment.[66] On June 2, 1944, the sixth division of the People's Court instituted proceedings on the charge of "demoralization of the armed forces" against eight "ringleaders" of the Oberhausen, Mülheim, and Essen IBSA groups, including Julius Engelhard and Auguste Hetkamp (KSSVO, article 5, paragraph 1, clause 1). The charges also included "treasonable favoritism of the enemy" (StGB, article 91) since the Bible Student publications supposedly had "weakened the military strength of the [German] Reich." In consideration of the "seriousness of their offenses" and the "dangerousness of their actions," all eight defendants were sentenced to death.[67]

As a result of the destruction of the groups around Julius Engelhard and Auguste Hetkamp in the spring of 1943, it was no longer possible to provide the Niederhagen (Wewelsburg) concentration camp with publications. Between the end of April and the beginning of May 1943, almost all prisoners in Wewelsburg were transferred to other penal institutions. (This transfer was based on orders to discontinue all building projects that did not directly support the war.) The remaining command left at the Wewelsburg concentration camp included only forty-seven Bible Student prisoners and two political prisoners. As a result, the Bible Students enjoyed relative freedom at the concentration camp.[68] This small Wewelsburg Bible Student group decided to turn matters around. Among the rubble of a building that had been destroyed by fire, they found a typewriter. They were also able to construct a simple mimeograph machine, and as a result, these prisoners began printing the *Watchtower*, under the very eyes of the SS-Ordensburg, as it were. The female Bible Students, who were responsible for the courier services, obtained paper and ink for the printing and also carried out the distribution. Consequently, Jehovah's Witnesses were able to supply their fellow believers in various locations in the northwestern parts of Germany with "spiritual food" until the end of the war.[69]

In a way similar to the efforts of Cyranek and Engelhard, Narciso Riet, Wilhelm Schumann, and Franz Fritsche directed the underground activities of their groups. Born in Mülheim (Ruhr), Germany, Riet had Italian parents; he was also called "Franzl" and tried, in close cooperation with the Oberhausen group, to reestablish the underground activities in Austria that had not been resumed since the wave of arrests in June 1940.[70] The considerable number of arrests had seriously weakened the Austrian IBSA branch so that these efforts were not very successful. But at the beginning of 1942, Narciso Riet was able to resume the IBSA activities in Czechoslovakia, which had also been, for the most part, discontinued in 1940. Together with Marie Teubel, a thirty-year-old Bible Student from Prague, he reorganized the Bible Student groups in Prague, Pilsen, and several other locations. These groups then began resuming their preaching activity, conducting religious meetings, distributing Bible Student publications in the German and Czech languages, and even started going from house to house again. With tireless determination, Narciso Riet traveled between the various parts of the German Reich and was even able to reactivate the IBSA groups in the southern and western parts of Germany. He also organized and coordinated the increasingly growing network of smuggling publications to the Bible Student prisoners in the various concentration camps.[71] Eventually, Riet became aware of the fact that the Gestapo was watching him, and he escaped to Italy in order to avoid being arrested. From his new home in Cernobbio on Lake Como, near the Swiss border, Riet again became very active. By arrangement with the branch office in Switzerland, he translated the *Watchtower* that had been smuggled over the Swiss border. He then distributed the mimeographed copies to fellow believers in northern and central Italy who worked as intermediaries. He even maintained contacts with the IBSA groups in Austria. At the end of December 1943 the Gestapo discovered Riet's hiding place in Cernobbio. After a long search, the RSHA finally reported that it had arrested the "contact person between the Bern Bible House and the prohibited IBSA in Germany and the areas of the protectorates." Thus, it had been able to eliminate the person responsible for the "organizational structure of the prohibited IBSA."[72]

Riet's efforts of reorganizing the IBSA groups in the southern parts of Germany, as well as Engelhard's activities in the western parts of Germany, served as motivation for other Jehovah's Witnesses. In December 1941 Georg Halder from Augsburg was released after almost six years of imprisonment in various penal institutions and concentration camps. Encouraged through these and other examples, he made arrangements for a reorganization of the Augsburg IBSA group.[73] Halder enthusiastically tried to arrange that his fellow believers in the concentration camps would be supported. At the end of 1942 he also organized an extensive campaign to collect money and food, or food-ration stamps. These arrangements were made to provide support for family members of imprisoned Jehovah's Witnesses or for family members of those who had died. The provisions were also used to send packages to their fellow believers in the concentration camps.

From Augsburg, Georg Halder extended his area of activity throughout Swabia and the western parts of Württemberg. However, at the beginning of 1943 Halder was arrested with approximately fifteen other Jehovah's Witnesses from Augsburg.[74] At the end of January/beginning of February 1943, a large number of Jehovah's Witnesses were also arrested in Munich and other locations in southern Germany. The senior Reich attorney at the People's Court conducted preliminary investigations of sixty-six people who were arrested on the charge of distributing "IBSA publications with controversial contents." The attorney also considered levying charges on the grounds of "demoralization of the armed forces."[75] One year later, the central State Police office in Munich took a major step against the IBSA groups in the border area of Middle Franconia-Württemberg. According to the April 21, 1944, report by the RSHA, the Gestapo had already arrested 254 people during this continuing police action. In this regard, the RSHA report stated: "An increasing number of people who are accused on the charge of demoralization of the armed forces or attempts at high treason are being transferred to the People's Court. . . . During the initial court proceedings, forty-nine of the accused were sentenced to severe imprisonment of between two and five years. One of the functionaries was sentenced to death."[76] During that same year, twenty-five Jehovah's Witnesses who had provided hiding places and food for a young fellow believer were arrested in the area of Swabia. This particular Jehovah's Witness was up for military service and had just been drafted. The prisoners were accused of "assisting in desertion."[77]

Jehovah's Witnesses protected fellow believers who evaded military service in other ways as well.[78] For example, three conscientious objectors were allowed to use the home of the newspaper deliverer, Emmi Zehden from Berlin Hohengatow, and the greenhouse of the Bible Students Otto and Jasmine Muß from Berlin Spandau as hiding places.[79] One of the conscientious objectors was Horst Günther Schmidt (a foster son of Emmi Zehden), who had gone underground in 1940 and was on the most-wanted list of the police. In September 1941 Schmidt's nineteen-year-old friend, Gerhard Liebold from Plauen, received his draft notice. He too went underground and joined Schmidt in October 1941. With a new identity and under the assumed name Kurt Vogel, Liebold, who was a gardener, worked at the Spandau greenhouse. From their hiding place, both young men participated in the activities of the Berlin IBSA groups. They were involved in the activities of duplicating the *Watchtower* and other Bible Student publications. At the beginning of December 1942 Schmidt brought Werner Gaßner, a twenty-two-year-old *Obergefreiter* (Senior Corporal) who had deserted the Wehrmacht, into the home of Otto and Jasmine Muß. In September 1942 Gaßner had been released from the Niort (France) military hospital, but he did not report back to his military unit. Instead, he withdrew from military service and escaped to Berlin. Not long afterwards, on December 28, 1942, Werner Gaßner, Gerhard Liebold, Otto and Jasmine Muß, and five other people were arrested. Gaßner, Liebold, and Schmidt—those who had evaded military service—were sentenced to death.[80] Those who had provided support and protection were subjected to court proceedings at the (Berlin) Court of Appeals. There, the chief public prosecutor charged them with an attempt at "preventing others from fulfilling their duty to perform military service."

The Bible Students at that time had been part of a large Berlin IBSA group under the leadership of Franz Fritsche. After the IBSA groups that Engelhard had coordinated in the western parts of Germany were destroyed in the spring of 1943, the Spree River Bible Students were responsible for producing the prohibited Bible Student publications. Between June and August 1943 they printed nearly one thousand copies of each issue of the *Watchtower* in Berlin, in a garden shed. These *Watchtowers* were distributed to various groups and individuals throughout the entire territory of the German Reich. From August 1943 on, the Berlin IBSA group also organized the distribution of the publications that Wilhelm and Gerhard Schumann printed in Magdeburg. During the previous years, Wilhelm Schumann, a forty-three-year-old chiropractor from Magdeburg, had used his office as a center for the underground activities of Jehovah's Witnesses, and between 1924 and 1933, Schumann had supervised the printing department at the German branch office.[81]

The group around Franz Fritsche maintained close contact with their fellow believers at the Ravensbrück and Sachsenhausen concentration camps. Over a period of about eighteen months, they regularly provided these fellow believers with the latest *Watchtowers* and other publications by way of prisoners who worked in outside labor details and other places outside of the concentration camps. One report states: "The organization operated so well that Brother Fritsche was able to forward letters to the brothers' relatives, or letters into other camps or to foreign branches. Thus it was possible within one and a half years to smuggle out 150 and nearly as many into the camp. . . . Some were even mimeographed and served as an encouragement to the brothers outside and especially for the relatives of those who were imprisoned."[82]

During January and February 1944 the Gestapo discovered the IBSA groups under leadership of Fritsche and Schumann. In November 1944 the chief public prosecutor at the Berlin Court of Justice (*Kammergericht*) levied charges on the grounds of "involvement in an anti-military association" and "demoralization of the armed forces" against seventy-six Bible Students who had distributed and received publications.[83] Almost all of the accused were older people, and the majority were women. During these proceedings, which were concluded before the end of the war, long prison sentences were imposed.

In October 1944 the People's Court instituted proceedings against "the main offenders, the writers of the recent publications, the functionaries and their collaborators," including Franz Fritsche and Wilhelm

Schumann. Fritsche, Schumann, and Johannes Schindler,[84] a forty-three-year-old factory inspector who had performed courier services for the IBSA, were sentenced to death. The sentences were not carried out.[85]

During 1944/45 the Bible Students were no longer able to organize their activities in an effective way throughout Germany. There is no evidence of Bible Student activities during the final years of the war. But at the same time, there is no reason to doubt the history report of Jehovah's Witnesses in this regard, which states: "It was no longer possible to determine for sure where the *Watchtowers* were being mimeographed, *but they were being produced.*"[86]

In some areas, the membership of the various groups decreased due to the arrests of several active ones and the withdrawal of people who did not want to expose themselves to further persecution. As a result, the groups no longer came together for religious meetings and had only infrequent communication with one another. Even under these circumstances, though, resistance was shown on an individual basis, and people openly expressed their convictions.[87] Such acts of courage included "bearing witness for Jehovah" in air-raid shelters as well as listening to foreign radio stations and passing along received information.

Besides showing solidarity for their fellow believers, the Bible Students also showed Christian love by supporting people who were persecuted for other reasons.[88] For example, after his release from the Wewelsburg concentration camp where he had been imprisoned for more than two years, the Swabian farmer Karl Uhlmann provided a hiding place for Friedrich Schlotterbeck, his former fellow prisoner and workmate at the concentration camp carpentry. During the middle years of the war, Schlotterbeck, a former chairman of the Württemberg KJVD (Communist Youth Association of Germany) and active resistance fighter, had to go underground.[89] For ten months, Hamburg Bible Student Pauline Matschke hid the Communist Jonny Stüve, a leader of the "Bästlein-Jacob-Abshagen-Group." In October 1942 Stüve was able to escape "the clutches of the police at the last moment."[90]

In some cases, Jehovah's Witnesses also provided support for persecuted Jews. (Since they did not make any distinction between people from different backgrounds but "considered all people to be equal," the National Socialists also accused them of "undermining the anti-Jewish tendencies of our ideology."[91]) The Witnesses established friendly relationships with Jews, sharing food-ration stamps with them as well as providing hiding places for those who were in danger of being deported.[92] The printer Lothar Schirmacher, a son of Bible Students from Kassel, became involved in such organized acts of assistance. His resistance activities had religious as well as political motivations. In 1932, at the age of sixteen, Schirmacher joined the International Socialist Combat Federation. Two years later, he was dismissed from his place of employment because of his refusal to give the Hitler salute. He also participated in the activities of the Kassel IBSA group. On December 15, 1936, after the distribution of the "Resolution" pamphlet, he was arrested and sentenced to two years of imprisonment on the charge of participation in IBSA activities. In 1939, after his release from prison, he resumed contact with his socialist friends in Berlin. Together with these friends, he provided counterfeit passports for Jewish citizens and helped them to flee to other countries or to go underground.[93]

Martial Laws

As early as 1937/38, penalties for Jehovah's Witnesses increased considerably. During the war, however, the authorities imposed even more serious punishments on the IBSA members. The legal authorities could no longer be accused of neglecting their duties and being too lenient with the Bible Students. In order to establish a legal basis for drastically increasing the punishment, two new decrees were issued and became effective at the beginning of the war.

On August 26, 1939, the day of mobilization, a decree was enacted that seriously increased penal regulations during periods of war and states of emergency. This decree was called Special Penal Regulations during War and a State of Emergency (KSSVO).[94] Article 5 of this decree introduced the offense of "demoralization of the armed forces," which was used extensively to prosecute opponents of the regime and had serious consequences. It stated that any refusal to perform military service, any public inducement to this effect, and any efforts of demoralizing "the armed forces" would be punishable by death. The death penalty was now considered as "standard punishment."[95] Only in "less serious cases" should the penalty *not* be imposed. The new penal regulation had the objective of suppressing "any anti-military agitation," regardless of the source.[96] According to the committee for Military Law at the Academy for German Legislation (Wehrrecht in der Akademie für Deutsches Recht), the new regulations satisfied "a long-standing National Socialist request."[97]

As early as 1930, the NSDAP faction had requested the Reichstag to pass a Law for the Protection of the German Nation (Gesetz zum

Schutz der deutschen Nation), according to which demoralization of the armed forces, participation in anti-military endeavors, and the refusal to perform military service should be punished with death on the charge of "treasonable acts against the armed forces."[98] At the latest, at the beginning of 1934, the RJM and the Reich Ministry of War (RKM) began to establish a basis for special martial law regulations. Consequently, the groundwork for the infamous and serious martial law regulations had already been laid at that time. For example, a ministerial draft prepared during the spring of 1934 even included regulations involving "demoralization of a person's willingness to perform military service." According to these regulations, death penalties or lifelong prison sentences would be imposed upon anyone who publicly requested or incited people to refuse military service, or who criticized Germans for agreeing to perform military service during periods of war.[99]

In June 1934 a regulation protecting "people's willingness to perform military service" was included in this draft. As a result, this draft already contained the very terminology for which the judicial decisions of the NS special courts later acquired their unsavory reputation. The draft stated that punishment would be imposed even upon people who "publicly weakened or demoralized the willingness of the German people to perform military service in other ways."[100] Consequently, it was not only military deployment plans that were prepared long before Hitler and his top military leaders invaded Poland initiating World War II, but the German Reich had also prepared to mobilize the legal system.

On November 25, 1939, the Nazis issued another legal regulation that was used in all court cases against Jehovah's Witnesses during the war.[101] This was the "amendment of penal regulations for the protection of military strength of the German people." Article 3 of this regulation decreed that people who "supported, or were involved in, an anti-military association" would be "punished with a prison sentence, in less serious cases with jail." This decree took into account demands for increased punishment in Bible Student cases. As a result, it became possible to impose prison penalties simply on the charge of an IBSA membership, a demand that had been made as early as the mid-1930s. Consequently, in legal proceedings against Jehovah's Witnesses, the Decree for the Protection of Military Strength replaced the February 28, 1933, Decree of the Reich President for the Protection of People and State. This new legal regulation not only extended the statutory amount of punishment for "*participation* in prohibited Bible Student activities," it even threatened punishment for an "anti-military *attitude*," which was expressed through

IBSA membership. To this end, the legal commentaries emphasized that punishment on the charge of involvement in an anti-military association could be based merely on a "display of an anti military attitude": "Any person associating with this association was also a part of it."[102]

The ministerial commentary clearly shows that the struggle against the IBSA was a decisive factor in drafting this regulation.[103] The Ministerialräte of the RJM—Grau, Krug, and Rietzsch, who had drafted and signed the new regulation—also provided a definition as to what could be considered as an anti-military association. They explained that anti-military associations would include groups of people "who based their anti-military attitude on a sectarian-religious source without forming an association." To illustrate they added: "Such an anti-military association would be, for example, the International Bible Students."[104] Consequently, according to article 3 of the Decree for the Protection of Military Strength, professing to be a Bible Student became a punishable offense. This regulation clearly reflects the legal concepts of NS thinking.

Subsequently, the special courts sentenced "mere" IBSA members on the charge of "involvement in an anti-military association." The functionaries, or people "who practiced their anti-military attitude," were punished on the charge of "demoralization of the armed forces" according to KSSVO, article 5.[105]

At the beginning of 1943 jurisdiction for proceedings according to KSSVO, article 5, paragraph 1, clause 1, was transferred from the special courts to the People's Court or, in appropriate cases, to the higher regional courts. This resulted in further intensification of judicial decisions against IBSA members.[106] Previously, special court proceedings against Jehovah's Witnesses were based in only a few cases on the charge of "public demoralization of the armed forces." Also death penalties were imposed in only a few cases. However, under the jurisdiction of the People's Court, the number of death penalties increased considerably. The senior Reich attorney at the People's Court had the authority to decide whether he would transfer such proceedings to the chief public prosecutor's offices and, consequently, to the higher regional courts. In cases involving "demoralization of the armed forces," he placed the Bible Students in the category of "people acting on deliberate intent," along with former Marxists, "reactionary elements," pacifists, and religious people (mostly Catholics). He clearly distinguished these people from those who acted on personal motivation, "people without ideological conviction."[107]

In the opinion of the People's Court, for example, thirty-nine-year-old Helene Delacher had to be considered as a "dangerous person." This Bible Student from Innsbruck was charged with "demoralization of the armed forces in conjunction with an attempt of treasonable defamation" (StGB, article 90ff.). The charge was based on the fact that she had tried "to smuggle anti-military pamphlets of the International Bible Students Association . . . into Italy."[108] In June 1943 an officer of the border police arrested Helene Delacher at a place in the Austrian Alps near the Italian border, just as she was about to give several copies of the *Watchtower* to her fiancé, who lived in northern Italy. The People's Court refused to accept her statement that the publications were intended only as personal reading material for her fiancé. The court thus considered the defendant as a courier who took publications over the border for the purpose of further distribution. On October 4, 1943, Delacher was sentenced to death and "a permanent loss of civil rights." The execution was carried out on November 12, 1943, at the Berlin-Plötzensee prison.

Eight weeks later, on November 30, 1943, under presiding Judge Freisler, the People's Court also sentenced Martha Hopp, a fifty-three-year-old housekeeper from Lübeck, to death and "a permanent loss of civil rights" on the charge of "demoralization of the armed forces."[109] According to Freisler, the sentence was justified because she had indicated to a fellow worker and acquaintance that Germany would lose the war and that the loss in lives would surpass our imagination. According to the court, a person who made such pessimistic statements to other German women was "undermining our military strength."

On August 4, 1944, legal proceedings against nine Jehovah's Witnesses from Neuß, Herne, Rheydt, and Düsseldorf took place at the sixth division of the People's Court.[110] The six women and three men were found guilty of "demoralizing the armed forces in conjunction with treasonable favoritism of the enemy" because they had been "involved in activities of the International Bible Students Association, up until December 1943." Seven of the defendants were sentenced to death. Two of them were each sentenced to six years of imprisonment. All death penalties were carried out: On December 8, 1944, Helene Gotthold, Henriette Meyer, Luise Pakull, and Else Woiecziech were executed in Berlin-Plötzensee. Three days later, Wilhelm Hengeveld and Ernst Meyer were beheaded in Brandenburg-Görden. On January 12, 1945, the last of the defendants, Mathilde Hengeveld, was executed on the scaffold.[111]

Sometimes the People's Court judges reached different verdicts in cases involving "demoralization of the armed forces." On August 30, 1944, a sixty-eight-year-old woman had to appear before the People's Court because she had stated that even though Satan was presently still ruling, he would soon be destroyed and then God's Kingdom would be established and bring peace to this earth. The senior Reich attorney accused her of having undermined "the military strength of the German people" by spreading Bible Student ideas. The People's Court judges, however, considered this accusation to be exaggerated. They also refused to sentence the woman on the charge of "involvement in an anti-military association" and, instead, granted an acquittal. In view of the fact that the courts generally applied legal concepts of National Socialist thinking, the explanations supporting the judgment are quite remarkable. The judges acknowledged "that the defendant still bases her religious convictions on the teachings of the International Bible Students Association."[112] However, according to the judges "this in itself is not a punishable offense." In order to punish a person on the basis of the Decree for the Protection of Military Strength, the defendant would have had to "act on [her] religious convictions, and, consequently, promote the anti-military attitude of the Bible Students Association." There was no conclusive evidence that her incriminating statements were "actually promoting ideas of the Bible Students Association." According to the first division at the People's Court, even the fact that the defendant occasionally expressed the opinion that a Christian should not take up arms against another Christian "merely reflects her religious convictions, without pursuing a specific purpose." This decision clearly differed from the general administration of justice in Bible Student proceedings at the People's Court. However, this certainly does not mean that the judges miraculously returned to the legal concept of taking into consideration the facts of a case. It rather shows that, even in this case, legal concepts of NS thinking had been applied. According to the court, an acquittal was necessary because punishment would have adversely affected "popular opinion." Three of this woman's sons "were German soldiers involved in battle against Bolshevism." It would have certainly "thwarted their enthusiasm" if they found out that legal actions had been taken against "their aged mother."

Even in some cases involving non-German Jehovah's Witnesses, the People's Court pronounced judgments that differed from the standard punishment. On November 9, 1944, the court took legal actions against eight Jehovah's Witnesses from the protectorates of Bohemia and Moravia. In principal, the court agreed with the charge of "demoralization of the armed forces": "Because of the fact that [the accused] encouraged each other to continue adhering to their false religious ideas and advocated [these ideas] even toward outsiders, they became guilty of demoralizing the armed forces among the Czech protectorate population (KSSVO, article 5, paragraph 1, clause 1)."[113] Apparently the judges of the People's Court, as well as the party officials acting as lay judges, wondered about the question as to what extent an advertising of Bible Student teachings among the Czech population would undermine the military strength of the German people. It seems, at least, that this was one of the questions asked during the discussion regarding the amount of punishment. As a result, the first division of the People's Court granted mitigation of punishment because the activities of the accused "did not immediately undermine our military strength since the Czech people were exempt from compulsory military service." In view of these considerations, the court did not pronounce death penalties even though—compared to other cases—the accused had been extensively involved in IBSA activities. Instead, they were punished with a prison sentence and, in three cases, with jail.[114]

On November 19, 1943, the Berlin newspaper deliverer Emmi Zehden had to appear before the judges of the People's Court. The foster mother of Horst-Günther Schmidt (who had gone underground with two of his friends and evaded compulsory military service) was accused of "treasonable favoritism toward the enemy and evasion of compulsory military service." Between 1940 and 1942, "Zehden had provided in Berlin a hiding place and food for three people of her association eligible for military service and thus helped them to evade compulsory military service."[115] The court sentenced the forty-three-year-old woman to death and "permanent loss of civil rights."

Three days after the court decision, Emmi Zehden submitted a petition for an act of pardon to the Senior Reich Attorney at the People's Court: "I have always been a hard-working and decent person and [have] always supported other people." On the same day, the women's prison in Berlin also commented on the petition: "Emmy Zehden, who has been sentenced to death, conducts herself well. Even though she has been chained, she works in the sock-repairing section. She is displaying considerable self-discipline. Since I have not been informed about the reasons of her judgment, I am not exactly able to approve of her petition." Emmi Zehden continued to submit petitions and hoped to be granted a pardon. But after more than six months, Dr. Herbert Klemm, who in the meantime had been promoted to the position of secretary of state at the RJM, ordered her execution, "with the authorization of the Führer."[116] Then, with a precision tried and tested countless times, the wheels of that murderous legal system were mercilessly set in motion. On Friday, June 9, 1944, Emmi Zehden was transferred to the Plötzensee prison. At one o'clock in the afternoon, ninety minutes after she had been officially informed of her execution, she was taken away. With her hands tied behind her back, she was handed over to the executioner and his three assistants. Regarding the following twelve seconds, the execution records state: "After confirming the identity of the prisoner, the official in charge ordered the execution. The prisoner was calm and composed and did not resist being placed on the guillotine. Then, the executioner beheaded the prisoner and announced that the penalty had been carried out." The execution expenses of 122.18 Reichsmark were charged to the Reich attorney's office at the People's Court.

Because of incomplete available written records, it is not possible to provide a full report of the extent of court proceedings against Jehovah's Witnesses held at the People's Court.[117] In only eleven cases, judgment records and other documents are available. These eleven People's Court proceedings involved a total of thirty-seven defendants. Twenty-five of these people (thirteen men and twelve women) were sentenced to death.[118] Eleven people were sentenced to certain periods of imprisonment (average penalty: 4.2 years). In one case, an acquittal was pronounced. However, the incomplete records show a considerable increase in punishment when the court cases were transferred to People's Court jurisdiction during the last two years of the declining NS regime. And so, punitive justice against Jehovah's Witnesses was at its peak exactly at the time when living conditions and prospects for survival for the concentration camp prisoners with the purple patch began to improve.[119] The tables had been turned—in the beginning, the legal system had still protected Jehovah's Witnesses from the rigorous actions of the Gestapo. During the final stages of the war, however, it was less dangerous for actively preaching Jehovah's Witnesses to be exposed to the SS in the concentration camps than it was for them to be exposed to the legal authorities outside of the camps.

On April 12, 1946, during the International Military Court proceedings in Nuremberg against Ernst Kaltenbrunner, the successor of Reinhard Heydrich as leader of the RSHA, the issue of unrelenting penal actions against Jehovah's Witnesses during the war was also raised.

When questioned by Dr. Kurt Kauffmann, his defense attorney, about the actions taken against the Bible Students, Kaltenbrunner used the opportunity to present himself as the one who came to the rescue of these people who were persecuted for their religious beliefs. He first explained that military and civil courts pronounced death penalties against the Bible Students. But the Secret State Police offices "certainly did not impose" death penalties. Trying to leave an impression by means of such elaborate statements, he said that "these sectarians had been subjected to excessive hardships only because of their religious beliefs."[120] Then he implied that these rigorous court proceedings had greatly concerned him: "I mentioned this issue to the party office, the Ministry of Justice, Himmler, even in my situation reports to Hitler. I also requested in several discussions with Thierack that this kind of administration of justice should be discontinued."

Kaltenbrunner did not stop at this attempt of excusing his actions. He explained to his audience, which was apparently not particularly well informed, that his efforts finally produced "results." He boasted about an order he had given to the senior public prosecutors that "previously pronounced judgments should be withdrawn." Because of his interference, he claimed, the "Bible Students were no longer taken to court." Finally Kaltenbrunner stated: "I consider it to be my personal achievement that the interventions with Thierack . . . completely ended this particular form of administration of justice against these sectarian groups."[121]

The fact that such an impertinent attempt in clearing oneself from guilt could be made during the Nuremberg trials, only one year after the NS regime had ended, shows that Jehovah's Witnesses continued to be a largely unrecognized group, even after 1945. This lack of recognition and the general lack of knowledge about the religious denomination provide actually the perfect breeding-ground for misrepresentation and manipulation.

14

Conscientious Objection

On March 16, 1935, Adolf Hitler reintroduced compulsory military service. As a result, Jehovah's Witnesses were exposed to further serious difficulties. Following the end of World War I, a refusal of military service did not have any consequences. However, when on May 21, 1935, the Military Penal Code (MStGB) was decreed, every German man between the ages of eighteen and forty-five was liable for military service.[122] Consequently, the members of the Bible Students Association were now directly confronted with the question of being drafted for military service. Regulations for exemption from military service for religious or other reasons were not provided. Such regulations were not in agreement with NS thinking.[123] In the Third Reich, it was considered to be an honor to do military service for the German people.[124] According to NS conception, the fact that compulsory military service had been reintroduced provided fellow Germans with an opportunity to "show their allegiance to their nation."[125]

Jehovah's Witnesses had to fulfill a different kind of allegiance— that of being loyal to God and the commandments of the Bible. This loyalty toward the one and only Lord for Christians, as well as their obligation to maintain "neutrality with regard to the affairs of this perishing world,"[126] prevented them from getting involved in any kind of military service.[127] As "soldiers of Christ," they had to keep away from all political and nationalistic endeavors. Moreover, according to their religious conviction, any war gave evidence of the devil's invisible rule over this world. The fact that the New Testament prohibited violence and the Old Testament commanded "you shall not kill" prevented them from taking up arms against fellow men or people from other nations. Military service completely contradicted their Christian beliefs. Regarding their motives, the following report states: "Our conscience was trained by the Bible and gave us an international outlook. It was unthinkable for us to take up arms and fight against other people only because the state considered them to be enemies. We did not consider them to be enemies. . . . We did not even consider ourselves to be Germans. Therefore we were also not concerned about German honor, German glory, or the German fatherland. We simply consider one another as brothers. Even an enemy is worthy to be loved."[128]

The oath of allegiance, required upon entering military service in the Wehrmacht, presented another problem for Jehovah's Witnesses. This oath of allegiance, which had to be taken in acknowledgement of Hitler, associated the vow of fulfilling one's duties as a soldier with a petition to God. It stated: "I swear to God this sacred oath that I will be obedient to Adolf Hitler, the Führer of the German Reich and nation and highest commander of the Wehrmacht. As a brave soldier, I will give my life for this oath at any time.[129]

The refusal to take the military oath, and even more so statements toward military registration officers and military commanders not to comply with the draft, resulted in Jehovah's Witnesses' coming in conflict with the Military Penal Code (MStGB). Article 48 of the MStGB specified that a person was liable even for actions performed out of religious motives.[130] This regulation, which according to this prominent legal commentary was directed "especially against members of sectarian groups and pacifists," gave military duty to obey "absolute priority" over "the duty to follow one's conscience" or personal considerations.[131] The legal commentary by Ministerialrat Georg Dörken and military court senior legal counsel Dr. Werner Scherer made the following significant statement regarding this article: "The regulation that religious or conscientious considerations do not exempt [a person] from following the laws of the state is included merely for informational purposes. In view of the totalitarian claim to power of the state, this goes without saying."[132]

In the Third Reich, offenses against the MStGB came under the jurisdiction of the military courts. After World War I, military jurisdiction had been withdrawn. On May 12, 1933, only a few months after NS takeover, it was reintroduced.[133] On January 1, 1934, jurisdiction of first instance was given to the military courts, and jurisdiction of second instance to the higher military courts. On September 5, 1936, the RKG was introduced as the highest military court of the NS armed forces.[134]

With regard to military law, the amendments of November 23, 1934, and May 12, 1935, adapted the 1872 MStGB to the "new requirements."[135] These amendments eliminated the majority of mitigations of punishment that had been included in the military penal code following World War I. Even after the amendment, the code[136] did not include any provisions for "conscientious objection"[137] or any special penal sanction for a "refusal to take the military oath." However, the October 14, 1936, decree by the RKM determined that the refusal to take the military oath was illegal and subject to disciplinary and criminal prosecution on the charge of "military disobedience" (MStGB, article 92). Every person refusing to take the military oath "in its required form" was taking a stand against the Führer.[138] The refusal to perform military service was punished according to the penal regulations for "desertion" (MStGB, articles 69, 70), because such refusal would indicate a person's intention to "evade military service in the Wehrmacht on a permanent basis."[139] Prior to the beginning of World War II, the military courts punished the majority of Jehovah's Witnesses who refused to perform military service on the charge of both offenses, insubordination and desertion. Generally, the penalties for these offenses ranged between one and two years of imprisonment.

In cases in which people who evaded military service were not, or not yet, subject to military court jurisdiction, they were prosecuted according to the regulations of the (general) penal code (StGB, articles 140–43). After the introduction of compulsory military service, by means of the "Amendment to the Penal Code" of June 28, 1935, these regulations were amended with a view that evasion of military service now had to be taken into consideration.[140] In this regard, Dr. Karl Schäfer, the legal counsel of the higher regional court, told his professional legal audience that "all of these regulations included serious punishments."[141] This resulted in the fact that people liable for military service who intended to evade military service permanently, for instance, by leaving the Reich territory before they received the draft, could be punished with several years of imprisonment on the charge of evading military service, based on article 140 of the Penal Code.[142] People who incited soldiers to desertion or who assisted in desertion could be punished, in "especially serious cases," with imprisonment for up to ten years, based on article 141 of the Penal Code.[143]

Removing Niches, Preventing Escape

Only a few weeks after the introduction of compulsory military service, the police authorities received instructions to report any cases in which "members of the 'International Bible Students Association' had refused to perform military service."[144] Now, the Gestapo focused especially on the refusal of Jehovah's Witnesses to take up arms. At the beginning of 1936 the Bavarian Political Police (BPP) informed its subordinate police offices "that, in addition to their propaganda against military service and active service during periods of war," members of the Earnest Bible Students had even "tried to propagate [their] ideas among members of the armed forces." This supposedly emphasized "the dangerousness of the Earnest Bible Students."[145]

Even the military leaders cautioned against the advertisements of Jehovah's Witnesses and requested the military offices to be increasingly aware of the danger. To this end, the Reich minister of war provided the January 18, 1937, memo in which he listed "a number of especially informative cases of Communist attempts of demoralization." These cases should be used during military instructions for the purpose of "providing direction for commanding officers and sergeants." "In an appropriate form," this material should also be made available to "soldiers."[146] The memo included seven cases for which "appropriate behavior toward attempts of demoralization by means of people from outside of the Wehrmacht" should be demonstrated. One of these cases involved the activities of the IBSA: "On January 2, 1936, the soldier T. received on the street a publication of the International Bible Students Association with demoralizing contents. He immediately reported the incident and gave a personal description of the person concerned. Consequently, the police could identify Otto M. from Munich as perpetrator. As a result, he was sentenced to one year and nine months of imprisonment."

A 1936 Gestapo memo even reported that the Bible Students Association tried "to persuade all people liable for military service to refuse military service."[147] For this purpose, forms were distributed that supposedly stated the following: "Unfortunately, I have to inform you that my conscience and my religious convictions as a Jehovah's Witness do not allow me to participate in military exercises. I have dedicated my life to the Supreme God, Jehovah."[148] Statements with this or similar wording were actually submitted. However, the request of refusing military service was restricted to members of their own denomination and did not present a danger to the general public, as the Gestapo had indicated.

The Gestapo memo further reported that the Bible Students, in some cases, deliberately distributed their prohibited publications in the street in order to be noticed, arrested, and legally punished: "After their release from prison, they would then state that they are no longer in a position to perform military service. According to the law, they are now unworthy of serving in the armed forces because they had been imprisoned on the charge of involvement in anti-state activities."[149]

By means of this argument, Jehovah's Witnesses tried to take advantage of a regulation in the MStGB,[150] according to which people who had been "punished because of involvement in subversive activities" were restricted from performing military service since they were considered "unworthy of serving in the armed forces."[151] Soon, the NS and military leaders realized the "twofold character" of a regulation that decreed that opponents of the regime should *not* be given the honor of performing military service, one introduced for ideological and pragmatic reasons. Therefore, they subsequently considerably reduced the possibility of evading military service on the basis of previous political conviction.[152] As early as May 6, 1936, the "guidelines of the RKM concerning the question of unworthiness of serving in the armed forces due to legal punishment on the charge of anti-state activities" determined that "unworthiness of serving in the armed forces" applied only in cases in which the penalty involved a minimum of nine months of imprisonment.[153] In April 1937 official explanations were issued that defined the concept of "anti-state activities." According to these specified explanations, anti-state activities involved only actions "that were capable of, and according to the offender's objectives intended to, undermine and endanger the existence and security of the National Socialist state."[154] Consequently, people who were sentenced according to article 4 of the February 28, 1933, "Decree of the Reich President for the Protection of People and State" (that is, the penal regulations that had generally been used to sentence Jehovah's Witnesses during the prewar period) would no longer automatically be considered as "unworthy of serving in the armed forces," not even if the punishment exceeded nine months of imprisonment."[155] As a result, IBSA members were no longer able to evade the draft for military service on a "legal basis." Exemption from military service was granted only in exceptional cases.[156]

The respective age groups drafted for military service generally included only a small number of Jehovah's Witnesses. The first age group drafted for compulsory military service in the autumn of 1935 consisted of people born in 1914 (those who were twenty-one years old). However, due to the fact that even older age groups were drafted for reserve duty training and short-term military training courses, a continually increasing number of Jehovah's Witnesses had to deal with this issue.[157] The majority of these people did not take any steps until they were drafted, at which time they submitted a written statement to the appropriate military district headquarters explaining their intentions of refusing military service. Others reported, as ordered, on the date of their conscription to the appropriate military unit or meeting place and informed the officer on duty of their intention to refuse military service. Several IBSA members even refused to fill out the registration forms for military service that were sent to them. Others informed the military authorities on the date of their medical examination before enlistment about their decision not to comply with the draft because of religious reasons. These conscientious objectors were not yet under military court jurisdiction and also had not "evaded military service" in the sense of articles 140–43 of the Penal Code. However, as soon as the Gestapo knew about such steps, they immediately went into action. In March 1937 two Bible Students were taken into protective detention in Bad Kissingen because they had refused to sign the registration forms for military service.[158] In such cases, they were sent to the concentration camps from which they could hope to be released *only* if they agreed without reservation to fulfill their military duty or perform military service.

On the other hand, the Gestapo also had to accept the fact that conscientious objectors were exclusively under legal jurisdiction of the Wehrmacht, following the date of their conscription. On November 14, 1935, the Political Police commander of the German states issued a decree that took this restriction of jurisdiction into account:

> Since the new Law for Military Penal Jurisdiction [Militärstrafgerichtsordnung] and the new Disciplinary Regulations [Disziplinarordnung] for the Wehrmacht have been issued, it is no longer appropriate to impose protective detention on people liable for military service who refuse to comply with the draft. . . . From now on, it is the exclusive responsibility of the military authorities to take disciplinary actions or institute military court proceedings against people who stubbornly refuse to comply with the draft. Naturally, this does not affect cases in which people liable for military service participated in subversive activities before they were drafted. In such cases, it is still the responsibility of the Political Police to use the means for resisting opponents of the state at their disposal, particularly the measure of protective detention.[159]

The regulations issued by the Gestapo chief Heydrich six months later emphasize yet again the Gestapo's presumption of entitlement of taking legal actions against people who refused to perform military service and other forms of compulsory service. To this end, Heydrich informed the State Police offices that these people could be "subjected to any necessary police measures," since they were not under military jurisdiction until the date of their draft.[160] Gestapo offices tried to use every opportunity to take actions against potential conscientious objectors, apparently in the opinion that the sentences imposed by the military courts for the anticipated refusal of military service of these "incorrigible" Jehovah's Witnesses (during the prewar period!) would not be serious enough.

The following examples will show the consequences Jehovah's Witnesses faced if they refused military service from the draft: In spring 1937 thirty-eight-year-old Johannes Rauthe from Bad Warmbronn (Silesia) was drafted to participate in a four-week military training course.[161] After he informed the captain of his military unit that he could not participate in this military training because of religious reasons, he was arrested. At the end of April 1937 court proceedings against him took place at the Liegnitz Military Court (of division no. 18). As a result, Rauthe was sentenced to six months of imprisonment. After several weeks of imprisonment in a detention cell at the Liegnitz *Funkerkaserne* (military garrison), he was transferred in June 1937 to the Torgau military prison where he joined another small group of imprisoned Jehovah's Witnesses. After he had served his prison sentence, which had been imposed upon him by a military court, he was not released to go home. Instead, the Gestapo took him into their so-called protective detention. The Gestapo asked that he be sent back with the argument that, because of the short period of imprisonment, he could certainly not have changed his mind. On November 4, 1937, the conscientious objector was sent to the Buchenwald concentration camp.[162]

In the case of thirty-two-year-old Ernst Wilhelm Zehender, the military judges took more serious actions. Zehender and two fellow believers from his hometown of Gemmrigheim (near Heilbronn) had refused to report for military training of the territorial reserve that took place at an engineering battalion in Rosenheim between February 7 and March 6, 1938.[163] As a result, on March 29, 1938, the Stuttgart Military Court of the Fifth Army Corps sentenced him to one year of imprisonment on the charge of "desertion." During his imprisonment, Zehender refused to participate in a military drill. Consequently, three months later, this time by the Mannheim Military Court (division no. 33), he was sentenced to two years of imprisonment on the charge of "insubordination before the entire group of enlisted men" (MStGB, article 95).[164]

The amount of punishment imposed on conscientious objectors did not differ from the punishment of Jehovah's Witnesses who agreed to perform military service during the prewar period but refused to take the military oath. This minority among the IBSA members included a twenty-three-year-old commercial clerk who had to report for basic military training on September 1, 1936. The training was part of an eight-week military training course that took place in Neustettin.[165] Even though this Hamburg Jehovah's Witness participated in the military training course until it ended on October 24, the Wandsbeck Military Court sentenced him to six months of imprisonment. The public prosecutor suggested appealing this decision. The appeal proceedings took place at the higher military court of the Tenth Army Corps, on December 4, 1936. This time, the court accepted the public prosecutor's request and sentenced the Jehovah's Witness to two years of imprisonment on the charge of "serious insubordination with adverse consequences" (MStGB, articles 92 and 95). He had to serve his sentence at the Wolfenbüttel prison and the Emsland prison camps Oberlangen and Neusustrum.[166]

In cases of refusal to perform military service, those Jehovah's Witnesses who were drafted into the Wehrmacht (which included primarily older age groups called for military training purposes), had to appear before a military court. This was different from the procedure taken with Jehovah's Witnesses who belonged to age groups that also had to fulfill duties of labor service prior to their draft for compulsory military service.[167] Some of these generally eighteen- to-twenty-year-olds drafted to the Reich Labor Service did not consider fulfilling this duty to be a violation of "Christian neutrality." Therefore, they agreed to perform strictly labor service related activities.[168] But even at the Reich Labor Service, Jehovah's Witnesses were required to take the (military) oath, which they refused with the same uncompromising attitude as those Jehovah's Witnesses who principally refused any participation in the pre-military activities of the Reich Labor Service.[169] Now, if Jehovah's Witnesses reported for labor service and refused to take the oath, which they were unable to take because of religious reasons, they were first of all locked up in a detention cell at the Reich Labor Service. If it was not possible to adjust their attitude, they were expelled from the Reich Labor Service and handed over to the Gestapo. The Gestapo, in turn, sent them to a concentration camp.

In November 1937 a Jehovah's Witness from Leutenbach (district of Waiblingen), born in 1915, reported to Labor Service but refused to take the oath in acknowledgement of Hitler and to put on a uniform. As a result, he was detained for twenty-one days.[170] After serving his sentence, he was admitted into a hospital for psychiatric examinations, probably on orders from a medical officer at the labor service. After two weeks of examination, the twenty-two-year-old was "declared completely 'normal.'" Then, the Gestapo arrested him. At the beginning of 1938, because of his refusal to sign a statement renouncing his faith, he was sent to the Dachau concentration camp.

Another twenty-two-year-old Jehovah's Witness, who refused to take the oath when he was drafted to the Reich Labor Service in 1936, "fulfilled his labor service related duties . . . very carefully."[171] According to the experts at the Breslau University Hospital for mental and psychiatric disorders, the Reich Labor Service officials tried "with kindness and harshness to change his mind, but to no avail." His sincerity had "prompted the officials to try even harder to persuade him." The psychiatric report further states: "Not even detention could discourage him from following his course of action."[172]

The case of a twenty-one-year-old plumber from Hamburg had a different outcome. On April 1, 1936, he was drafted in Elmshorn. The local leader of Reich Labor Service Department 5/71, General von Bonin, tried to persuade him to take the oath and to salute Hitler, using "all possible forms of drill exercises" as well as repeated periods of detention.[173] On December 24, 1936, he was transferred to the prison at the Altona courthouse to serve a 150-day detention. On May 4, 1937, three weeks before he completed his prison sentence, his prison term was suspended because he agreed to take the oath, after he had been repeatedly threatened. The Gestapo did not get involved since the young man finished his remaining period of labor service and later even performed military service.

Even during the war, the Gestapo imposed protective detention on Jehovah's Witnesses who were liable for compulsory labor or military service.[174] In 1940 a-nineteen year-old Jehovah's Witness was sent to Dachau because he refused to take the oath required for Reich Labor Service.[175] For the same reason, a not-yet-eighteen-year-old Jehovah's Witness was sent to the Schirmeck concentration camp in 1943.[176] Also in 1943, seventeen-year-old Jonathan Stark from Ulm was sent to the Sachsenhausen camp because of his refusal to take the oath. There, he was assigned to a punishment battalion. After repeated interrogations at the concentration camp commanding office, he was executed by hanging because he refused to change his mind.[177]

Penalties were not just imposed on people liable for compulsory service who refused to take the required oath or perform military service, or who expressed their resolve to refuse these actions in advance. From 1935 on, Jehovah's Witnesses liable for military service were questioned principally about their attitude toward military service during Gestapo or custodial judge interrogations. In the majority of cases, they were even asked directly whether they would comply with the draft if they were conscripted. If they stated that they would refuse military service, not only could the State Police impose protective detention but such statements might also seriously affect the *amount* of punishment.

Efforts to prevent people from refusing military service were even made toward Jehovah's Witnesses who were no longer involved in IBSA activities. They were also made toward sons of Bible Student families. In one example, Hans Joachim H. from Kassel, born in 1918, was repeatedly summoned to the Gestapo office for interrogations after his parents had been imprisoned in 1936 because of defiance of the Bible Student ban. There, he was beaten and forced to submit a statement indicating that he agreed to perform military service: "After I had been forced to sign a statement according to which I would fulfill my military duty, they left me alone. However, after the beginning of the war, the Gestapo came back to admonish me to comply with the draft."[178]

Punished with Death

With the war beginning, the situation of Jehovah's Witnesses who refused to perform military service changed drastically. On the day of mobilization, the KSSVO became effective. Under the newly introduced penal offense of "demoralization of the armed forces," this decree also included the refusal of military service.[179] It also determined that anyone "who attempted to evade military service completely, partially, or for certain periods of time by means of self-mutilation or mutilation of other people, by means of methods intended for deception or by any other means" would be sentenced to death on the charge of "demoralization of the armed forces." In this regard, the official explanations for the KSSVO stated:

> This article includes in the group of offenders also those who try to evade military service 'in other ways': It is supposed to cover any form of evasion of military service . . . According to article 5, paragraph 1, clause 3, punishment will be imposed even on people who base their conscientious objection on reasons mentioned in MStGB, article 48.[180]

The RKG judges even further defined the laws regulating "demoralization of the armed forces." In order to apply this penal law, it was irrelevant whether a particular action actually adversely affected the armed forces or even if such adverse effect had been intended. Consequently, culpability was not dependent on intent of "demoralization":

> In all offenses involving paragraph 1, clause 3, it is not required that the offense itself was motivated by intent of demoralizing the armed forces. The action of the offender can be restricted to the consequences of the offense on himself. It is not required that his action affect others, especially the spirit of the Wehrmacht. . . . Paragraph 1, clause 3 includes especially offenders who acted on their conviction (Bible Students and others like them).[181]

This penal law, based on KSSVO, article 5, paragraph 1, clause 3, determined the death penalty to be the standard punishment for conscientious objection. Paragraph 2 did provide the possibility of assuming a "less serious case," and, consequently, resulting in a prison sentence or jail. But, according to the "principles" of the RKG judges, in general there was no basis for reducing the punishment in cases of conscientious objection: "With regard to people who stubbornly act on their conviction (Bible Students), it is generally required to impose the death penalty because of the propagandistic effect of their actions."[182]

The military courts rigorously applied this punitive measure against Jehovah's Witnesses and other conscientious objectors. Anyone who did not comply with the draft after August 26, 1939—the day on which the KSSVO was enacted—could expect to be sentenced to death and subsequently executed if he did not withdraw his conscientious objection. The crucial factor was the day of the draft: according to military law regulations, a person who received his draft *before* August 26, 1939, did not commit his offense "on the battle field." Therefore, he was not subject to the more serious punitive measures during the state of mobilization and war. On November 1, 1939, a military court, the Gericht der 2. Admiral der Ostseestation, still sentenced a conscientious objector who had been drafted to the Navy on August 22, 1939, to one year of imprisonment on the charge of "desertion." The sentence was based on the "peace regulations" of the Military Penal Code.[183] The forty-year-old Jehovah's Witness Paul Frick, on the other hand, received his draft four days later. On reporting for duty, he immediately declared his refusal to perform military service, and on October 23, 1939, the RKG sentenced him to death on the basis of KSSVO, article 5. Two weeks later, this father of four children was beheaded in Berlin-Plötzensee.[184]

After the beginning of the war, court proceedings against Jehovah's Witnesses who refused military service took place at the highest military court of the Wehrmacht, the RKG in Berlin-Charlottenburg.[185] According to the War Penal Code,[186] which was enacted at the same time as the KSSVO, initially all cases regarding "demoralization of the armed forces" came under the jurisdiction of this RKG, regardless of whether the accused were members of the Wehrmacht or civilians. On September 12, 1939, Admiral Max Bastian became senior judge and judicial convening authority of this court.[187]

On May 18, 1940, the seventh implementing regulation was adopted, which terminated exclusive military court jurisdiction for proceedings according to KSSVO, article 5. As a result, these disreputable penal standards could now be applied by the general court system as well. At the same time, this implementing regulation rearranged jurisdiction for cases involving "demoralization of the armed forces" in the field of military administration of justice.[188] Accordingly, the RKG continued to handle cases of "public demoralization of the willingness to perform military service" (article 5, clause 1). However, the offense categories "undermining military discipline" (article 5, clause 2) and "evading performance of military service" (article 5, clause 3) were handled at the (subordinate) military courts. However, differing from this general regulation of the seventh implementing regulation, proceedings against Jehovah's Witnesses and other conscientious objectors remained principally under the jurisdiction of the highest military court of the Wehrmacht. For this purpose, the Wehrmacht High Command decreed, on that same day (May 18, 1940), that the judicial convening authorities of the respective courts had to transfer court cases on the charge of "demoralization of the armed forces" according to KSSVO, article 5, paragraph 1, clauses 2 and 3, to the senior judge of the RKG for examination and punishment in all cases in which "the offender based his actions on reasons of conscience or on instructions received from his religious denomination (MStGB, article 48, for instance, Earnest Bible Students, Jünger Jehovas [disciples of Jehovah], Adventists, etc.).[189]

The total number of proceedings on the charge of "demoralization of the armed forces" that took place at the RKG during the early period of the war included quite a few proceedings against Jehovah's Witnesses who refused military service. At least one in four defendants was a Bible

Student.[190] These cases of conscientious objectors for religious reasons confronted the legal counsels of the RKG with a phenomenon that they had not encountered in previous court cases. As a general rule, the KSSVO, desperately longed for by the military judges to be able to impose serious sentences and "legal deterrent effect" on a broad range of offenses, required the death penalty for these religiously devoted people.[191] During the first weeks of the war, the various RKG divisions made decisions that sentenced Jehovah's Witnesses "to death, permanent loss of civil rights, and loss of the right of serving in the armed forces."[192] Generally, two to four weeks after the judgment was pronounced and confirmed by the judicial convening authority of the RKG, the execution in the form of beheading was carried out at a place specified by the Reich Administration of Justice.[193] (Initially, these executions were carried out only at the Berlin-Plötzensee prison.[194]) On September 13, 1939, thirty-seven-year-old Adolf Bultmeyer from Rethorn (near Delmenhorst) was sentenced to death on the charge of conscientious objection. On October 13, 1939, he was executed in Berlin-Plötzensee.[195] On the same day, a forty-two-year-old Jehovah's Witness from Boizenburg, whom the RKG had sentenced to death on September 26, 1939, was also beheaded.[196]

In general, the Wehrmacht judges made sure that court decisions, once carried out, were publicly announced in order to get the anticipated deterrent effect. By constant propagation and exposure to these punishments, the military judges expected to be able to force the general public into giving their allegiance to the state.[197] They soon began to doubt the appropriateness and practicality of such announcements in cases in which people were punished for conscientious objection based on religious convictions. In this regard, the senior judge of the RKG pointed out that an announcement of such court decisions would only benefit the "propaganda of the opponents." What is more, it would strengthen these conscientious objectors "in their fanatical martyrdom."[198] On October 17, 1939, the High Command of the Army/Commander of the Reserve Army (OKH) issued a secret decree according to which the highest Wehrmacht leaders shared these reservations:

> With regard to the question of announcing death penalties imposed on "Earnest Bible Students" who refused to take the oath of allegiance and to perform any kind of military service, the High Command of the Army, as well as the General Staff of the Army, take the following position: Executions of such death penalties

should not be publicly announced. They should also not be reported on in the newspapers. Relatives of those sentenced to death may [!] be informed about the execution.[199]

During the following weeks, the number of Bible Student cases continued to increase. During November 1939 alone, the RKG imposed almost as many death penalties on Jehovah's Witnesses on the charge of conscientious objection based on religious convictions as had been pronounced in all court cases held at this court during the entire previous year.[200] As a result, the military judges became increasingly concerned. Quite a number of the RKG legal counsels adhered to a rather conservative legal tradition. Often, because of this adherence to a fundamental German position, they kept a certain distance from the NS ideology.[201] Now, these judges were confronted with the consequences of their own legal opinion.

During the prewar period, on January 20, 1939, the RKG decreed a principal ruling that the refusal to perform military service by even one person could demoralize the military strength of the entire German Reich: "The undisturbed process of mobilization requires that every person liable for military service follows orders without opposition. . . . This means that the refusal to perform military service of even one person can impede the military strength and the security of the Reich. Consequently, the military strength and the security of the Reich are already endangered if there is only the possibility that a person liable for military service would evade his responsibility in this regard."[202] Thus, the military judges were primarily concerned with satisfying the interests of the state, that is, first and foremost they tried to meet military "requirements." These military judges had accepted the credo that, "in times of governmental and national crisis, it is not important to focus on the welfare of an individual but, rather, on the welfare of the community."[203] They perverted the course of justice in order to make it suitable for militaristic purposes. In turn, they became the executioners of a murderous administration of justice after the KSSVO and other NS military laws had been enacted.[204]

Even though the killing of people whose only "offense" was conscientious objection based on religious convictions proved to be a consequence of their own "legal conceptions," the RKG legal counsels were shocked about the result of their actions. The Bible Student proceedings raised a problem that could "not easily be disregarded." In this regard, Admiral Max Bastian, the senior judge of the RKG, later stated that the death penalties against Jehovah's Witnesses made him feel "very uncomfortable."[205] Even during the initial days of the war, this problem had been brought to the attention of the Führer. On September 11, 1939, senior Reich military attorney Dr. Walter Rehdans informed the confused group of judges about the decision of the highest military commander. According to Bastian's account, Rehdans reported that Hitler had refused to grant Jehovah's Witnesses "special status." He was of the opinion that, "in the event of war, that is, in a national crisis of the fatherland, these sectarians should put aside their personal convictions for higher ethical purposes."[206]

According to a letter of Generaloberst (Colonel General) Wilhelm Keitel, the chief of the High Command of the Armed Forces (OKW), similar approaches to the Führer were made even during the following weeks and months. On December 1, 1939, under the subject "handling of Bible Students," with the remark "confidential," Keitel informed the OKW:

> Based on the Special Penal Regulations during War, article 5, clause 3, the Reich Military Court has imposed death penalties on a considerable number of so-called Earnest Bible Students who refused to perform military service. The executions have been carried out. Several recent court decisions prompted me to present this urgent problem of handling the Earnest Bible Students again to the Führer.
>
> The Führer has made the following decision:
>
> In Poland alone, more than ten thousand decent soldiers have been killed. Thousands of soldiers have been seriously wounded. If he requires such sacrifices from every German man fit for military service, he is unable to grant a pardon to people who persistently refuse military service. In this regard, it does not make any difference for what reasons a person refuses military service. Even otherwise mitigating circumstances, or circumstances that would have a bearing on an act of pardon, could not be taken into consideration in this case. Therefore, if it is not possible to destroy the will of a man who refuses military service, the sentence has to be carried out.
>
> The judicial convening authorities and the various courts should be informed about this decision of the Führer.[207]

With this *Führerwort* (final decision of the Führer), the stage was set for "handling" cases of refusal of military service. In January 1940 the RKG senior judge had a discussion with the various court division senior judges, informing them about the attitude of the political and military leaders with regard to the problem of the Earnest Bible Students. In the following years, the RKG carefully followed these basic instructions, although several judges probably did so with certain reluctance. The RKG most likely adopted the fatal "logic" that these "stubborn" conscientious objectors were actually the ones to blame for the executions, not the least because in this way they could sooth their own consciences, as it were: if the defendants refused to change their attitude, despite all efforts of persuasion, they were also fully responsible for the consequences, at least in the opinion of the judges.

With reference to the "importance of meeting state requirements" and the "written law," the legal counsels of the RKG used every official and legal means at their disposal to send Jehovah's Witnesses and other conscientious objectors to their death, without showing any compassion. But the opinion of their highest judicial convening authority, Hitler, was not necessary based merely on the reasoning that conscientious objectors could not be shown special consideration because the soldiers on the battlefield were exposed to dangers and were expected to give their lives. At least during the later years, he was motivated by a rather violent hatred. On June 7, 1942, in one of his endless after-dinner monologues at the Wolfsschanze (one of Hitler's headquarters) in which he repeatedly complained about the lack of initiative and decisiveness of the legal authorities, Hitler also addressed the subject of the Bible Students. Acts of treason were not done on the basis of idealistic convictions. Time and again, he had used this argument to persuade the legal authorities to take more drastic actions against traitors. If treasonable offenses could be attributed to idealistic convictions at all, it would be conscientious objection based on religious convictions. Thereafter, Hitler supposedly continued his speech as follows:

> These elements, however, who refuse to go to war because of their religious convictions, should be reminded of the fact that they obviously have no problem to take the food for which others have fought. However, for the sake of justice, this is not acceptable. Therefore, let them starve to death. The fact that they—the so-called Bible Students, 130 in number—were not left to die, but instead, were shot to death, should be considered a special act of mercy on his part. Incidentally, these 130 executions had quite a sobering effect. On hearing of these executions, thousands of like-minded ones lost courage and no longer tried to evade military service by quoting some Bible texts. If someone wants to be successful in warfare and, particularly, if he wants to lead a people through

difficult periods of time, he should make sure of one fact: in this time period, anybody who excludes himself from the people's community, actively or passively, will be eliminated by the people's community.[208]

Eight weeks later, on August 1, 1942, the Führer addressed the subject of Jehovah's Witnesses again. According to the records of Heinrich Heim, the adjutant of Reich leader Martin Bormann, Hitler stated that these Bible Students had to be exterminated. And once again, he referred to the social concepts of Darwin: Any society that surrenders to such "antisocial tendencies," actually gives up its struggle. Even in the animal world, "antisocial elements are eliminated."[209]

Condemned by the RKG

In subsequent RKG decisions, these relentless actions demanded in the *Führerwort* are clearly reflected. There are no indications that the reservations previously raised had any effect on the military court proceedings. Around the turn of 1939/40, the SS had already included several of these RKG decisions against Jehovah's Witnesses in the *Meldungen aus dem Reich,* an official paper for keeping the immediate group of leaders (Reichsführer SS, state leadership, party leadership) informed.[210] On February 7, 1940, the paper reported that "more than fifty-five Bible Students had already been sentenced to death on the charge of conscientious objection" since the beginning of the war.[211] On May 30, 1940, Admiral Bastian sent an activity report to the chief of the OKW stating that "large numbers of Bible Students refused to perform military service" since the beginning of the war, primarily older age groups.[212] In a special paper for internal use of the Wehrmacht High Command (OKW), which included confidential information about the criminological statistics of the first year of the war, it stated regarding the offense category of "demoralization of the armed forces" that there was a "serious increase" in these offenses. Not even "the most serious penalties" could "effectively prevent" this increase. However, these "enormously increasing offenses of demoralization of the armed forces according to KSSVO, article 5," did not occur within the military ranks: "The increase in cases of demoralization of the armed forces is primarily based on the fact that, after their conscription, growing numbers of Earnest Bible Students refuse to perform military service under arms. For instance, between August 26, 1939, and September 30, 1940, in Germany alone, a total of 152 court cases against Earnest Bible Students on the charge of demoralization of the armed forces took place at the Reich Military Court."[213] The statistics further indicate that 112 death penalties had been "imposed on Earnest Bible Students in Germany."

An analysis of the numerical data shows the magnitude these court proceedings against Jehovah's Witnesses who refused to perform military service had at the highest military court of the Wehrmacht, even during the first year of the war. Of the 1,087 cases held on the charge of "demoralization of the armed forces" (KSSVO, article 5), a total of 152 were cases involving Bible Students (14%). Of the 117 death penalties that were pronounced on the charge of "demoralization of the armed forces," a total of 112 (95.7%) were pronounced against Jehovah's Witnesses.[214] This shows that only 40 of the 152 Bible Student cases did not result in a death penalty (26.3%). In 73.7 percent of the cases, death penalties were pronounced: Consequently, during the first year of the war, in three out of four cases held at the RKG, Jehovah's Witnesses were sentenced to death.

According to the activity report by Admiral Bastian, in the course of 1940 the RKG took even more serious measures. Previously, the military courts had offered the Bible Students an opportunity to withdraw their refusal to perform military service even after the judgment was pronounced. In many cases, though, even if they withdrew their refusals, the Bible Students later returned to their initial stand. Therefore, in such cases of repeated change of mind, the various RKG divisions no longer accepted the withdrawals and refused to reopen the cases.[215]

In his June 10, 1940, statement, Generaloberst Keitel showed sympathy for the emotional pressure to which the Reich Court judges were exposed. At the same time, he voiced his appreciation for the court decisions made with regard to the Bible Students. With reference to the general decrease in court proceedings against conscientious objectors, he stated with satisfaction "that the instructions of the Führer had produced also in these cases the anticipated results." Then, the chief of the OKW commended the judges and showed his approval for their unyielding attitude, stating: "Because of its determined actions, the court has protected many other people liable for military service from committing such serious offenses. Consequently, the RKG has greatly contributed to the preservation of military strength of the [German] people. At the same time, it has performed a great service for the people, in protecting [the armed forces] and preventing [them from being harmed]."[216]

At the end of 1940 the OKW gave orders to draft immediately all people liable for military service "who had indicated their refusal to perform military service during the examination before enlistment, during meetings for military instruction, or in other communication with offices for alternative military service," and who based their decision—as stated in the November 8, 1940, decree concerning this matter—"on their conscience or the requirements of their religious association (for instance, Earnest Bible Students, Jünger Jehovas, Adventists, etc.)."[217] In the years following these special drafts, the number of Bible Student proceedings held at the RKG decreased.[218] At the same time, in comparison to the first year of the war, a slight increase could be noted in the number of cases in which prison sentences were imposed.[219] The death penalty continued to be the standard punishment. Even later, the death penalty was imposed in considerably more than 50 percent of the Bible Student cases held at the RKG.[220] Only approximately one in five pronounced death penalties was not confirmed or was withdrawn by means of an act of pardon.[221] It can be assumed that, during World War II, a total of approximately 250 (German and Austrian) Jehovah's Witnesses were executed as a result of military court decisions.[222] Consequently, the majority of people[223] who were condemned as conscientious objectors by the military courts of the Wehrmacht in the Third Reich were Jehovah's Witnesses,[224] even though compared to other offenses of refusal (such as desertion, self-mutilation, etc.), their number was relatively small.[225]

These cases involving people who refused compulsory military service based on religious convictions clearly show that the judges were concerned mainly with the supposed "welfare of the state." They certainly did not show any compassion for the conscientious objectors, as they had often claimed.[226] Instead, all legal considerations were dominated by meeting the "requirements of the war." As early as the very onset of the war, the legal counsels of the RKG and the officers acting as lay judges declared that because of its "struggle for existence," the German Reich was entitled to a "right of self-defense": "The present situation of Germany" required that every soldier fulfill his duties and be prepared to make sacrifices. Therefore, on May 3, 1940, the highest military court of the Wehrmacht decreed that the "requirements of the war" had priority over "all other considerations": "However, this means that a German who refuses military service during periods of serious adversity for the nation and the Reich and who upholds this attitude even after serious admonitions cannot expect to be shown mercy, regardless of the reasons for his refusal. Only the death penalty will have a deterrent effect in this case. During Germany's struggle, it is an act of self-defense."[227]

Aspects of general prevention determined the operative provisions of a judgment. The motives of the individual were not taken into consideration: "The fact that his actions are based on his religious convictions does not have any bearing on his penal liability." Granted, the defendant did "not act in cowardice. However, because of his stubbornness and incorrigibility, it is impossible to allow extenuating circumstances. Such stubborn conscientious objection involves the danger that others are encouraged to follow this example and, thus, undermine their willingness to perform military service. Therefore, it is necessary to impose the death penalty."[228]

This was the judgment pronounced against Ernst Wilhelm Zehender (see p. 355), who had been sentenced to three years of imprisonment on the charge of "desertion" and "insubordination" as early as 1938. Less than three months after his release from prison on March 15, 1941, he was again drafted into the Wehrmacht by the Stuttgart military district headquarters. On June 5, his first day of military service at the Fifth Company of the L.S. Rekrutenausbildungskommando II (Fliegerhorst Mühldorf), the thirty-six-year-old man refused "to put on his uniform and to bear arms" because, as stated in the July 31, 1941, indictment, "the Bible prohibited such actions."[229] The captain in charge of the company gave him a "serious lecture," but to no avail. The next day, "his company commander asked him again." But the involuntary soldier stated that "he will not perform military service." He was arrested and taken to the Berlin Alt Moabit military prison for pretrial detention. Zehender faithfully adhered to his religious conviction of refusing military service, "even though, in repeated interrogations and even during the main proceedings, he was fully informed about the consequences of his actions." On December 10, 1942, the RKG sentenced "Airman Zehender" to death. On January 17, 1942, he was beheaded at the Brandenburg-Görden prison.

The RKG made excessive use of the "Special Penal Regulations during War." It adopted the view that, even prior to the draft into the Wehrmacht, punishment according to KSSVO, article 5, paragraph 1, clause 3, would be appropriate in all cases in which the person concerned stated his refusal to perform military service in advance. For example, at his examination before enlistment, an eighteen-year-old man refused to sign the military identification card because he considered this signature to confirm his agreement to perform military service. As a result, in its December 6, 1939, decision, the RKG regarded his refusal as "an act of evading military service," although he had not even been considered for draft by the military district headquarters.[230]

According to the administration of justice of the RKG, not even a possible disability for service due to illness protected a person against punishment. On February 20, 1940, the military judges rendered judgment in a case in which the defendant had told the recruiting board that he would refuse to comply with the draft. Even though the examination before enlistment revealed that the man was "unfit for military service," the RKG considered it appropriate to impose a judgment: "In order to determine whether the defendant has committed an offense of refusing military service according to KSSVO, article 5, paragraph 1, clause 3, it is insignificant that he is unfit for military service, as was established by means of the examination before enlistment. It is also insignificant that in this case, according to the MStGB, article 14, clause 1, he is not even allowed to perform military service. Even the 'attempt' of evading military service is already subject to punishment."[231] Consequently, the highest military court announced that "people liable for military service who are found to be unfit for military service . . . [can be] punished on the charge of an (unfit) attempt of evading military service, according to KSSVO, article 5, paragraph 1, clause 3."[232]

The increasing seriousness of the RKG decisions in cases involving people who refused compulsory military service based on religious convictions and, consequently, the gradual removal from previously raised reservations became especially obvious in the context of the question as to what extent extenuating circumstances should be allowed. Legally, the judges had the possibility of deviating from the standard punishment of imposing a death penalty by taking into account the regulations for "less serious cases" (KSSVO, article 5, paragraph 2), which they could do at their own discretion.[233] They could also make use of the German Penal Code (StGB), article 51, paragraph 1 (unsoundness of mind), and StGB, article 51, paragraph 2 (diminished responsibility), with the objective of granting exemption from punishment or mitigation of punishment. In cases involving the refusal of military service based on religious convictions, these possibilities played a significant role. This was the case since the defense attorneys frequently requested the consultation of a psychiatric expert's report in order to prove that the actions resulted from a moral dilemma and, consequently, restricted the person's ability to "determine his decisions." In this way, the defense attorneys tried to protect their clients from impending execution."[234]

From the viewpoint of the judges and psychiatrists, religious convictions that depict warfare as disgusting and profoundly reprehensible originated from a deranged mind, and "people who refused compulsory military service for religious reasons" were to be placed in the same category with "unrealistic and peculiar psychopaths," such as "peace talkers and freedom-crazy enthusiasts."[235] Despite this fact, they rarely pleaded for mitigation of punishment because of insanity, based on article 51. To this end, Professor Johannes Lange, director of the psychiatric and neurological department at Breslau University and recognized specialist in the field of psychiatry, conducted a clinical series of examinations of IBSA members in the prewar period. As a result of these examinations, Lange stated that they could generally not be considered as mentally deranged people in medical terms.[236] He further explained that the question of "how to handle this kind of refusal of compulsory military service" was primarily the responsibility of judges who would have to address this problem with serious legal measures. At the same time, Professor Lange acknowledged that among these people who refused compulsory military service for religious reasons, there were some whose refusal was based on "sincere faith." However, this was only a minority. In the majority of cases, the religious conviction was merely a pretense concealing "the fear of not being strong enough to face death, a pretense for cowardice hidden behind a façade of sincere convictions, or it was a craving for attention and recognition at all cost."[237] Based on these assumptions, Lange reached the following conclusion: "It seems that we have no possibility to handle this kind of refusal of compulsory military service different from the way other forms of refusal of compulsory military service are handled. However, the probably very small number of true martyrs will consider themselves honored by their God through any kind of punishment."

Generally, Jehovah's Witnesses who refused military service and participation in war were declared to be "fully responsible under penal law." Accordingly, the military courts of the Wehrmacht took the most serious actions against them. Gradually and with increasing forcefulness, the RKG restricted the possibilities of allowing for mitigation of punishment because of insanity, based on article 51. In contrast to the situation in World War I, in World War II only a very small number of people who refused military service for religious reasons were sent to institutions that were euphemistically called *Heilanstalten* (mental homes). The German word carries the meaning of healing or curative hospitals.[238]

In Principle, No "Less Serious Cases"

One after another, the last possibilities of allowing extenuating circumstances were restricted. Of some importance were Bible Student proceedings that took place at the second division of the RKG, on January 24, 1940.[239] The defendant in this case came from a family with a history of "serious hereditary diseases" as well as other "obvious defects." The psychiatric expert whom the court had consulted considered "the defendant's extraordinary stubbornness and determination with which he adhered to his refusal [to perform military service] and the conceptions and convictions on which he based his refusal" as evidence for the presence of such obvious defects. Therefore, the court assumed "in favor of the defendant," that his actions resulted from a diminished responsibility according to StGB, article 51, paragraph 2.

The court also emphasized "that the special circumstances of the Wehrmacht and the requirements of the war demanded that people with diminished responsibility should not be treated differently from people with full penal responsibility. Therefore, the mitigation of punishment for which StGB, article 51, paragraph 2, allowed should be restricted to exceptional cases." Since, however, this case could be considered to be exceptional, the RKG decided to impose a penalty of three years of imprisonment.

At the same time, the second division of the RKG emphasized— probably in order to avoid raising the impression that conscientious objectors were judged with "leniency"—that the court had deviated from standard punishment only because of the exceptional circumstances in this particular case. In general, such stubborn offenders were not considered to be "less serious cases." Accordingly, the judges explained "that, principally, conscientious objection cannot be considered to be less serious as long as the offender has not seriously and without reservations declared his willingness to perform military service." Consequently, the decision of the highest court declared the will of Führer to be the binding guideline for administration of justice in military court proceedings. According to him, the death penalty would *not* be imposed in cases in which the defendant withdrew his refusal to perform military service.

Three months later, the highest military court of the Wehrmacht confirmed its position that in cases of stubborn conscientious objection, "only an imposition of the most serious punishment would achieve the purpose of punishment."[240] Extenuating causes would generally not be indicated in such cases. But at the same time, the court's reasoning completely deprived the mitigation clause of its meaning: "The question of when to assume a less serious case is not to be determined from the standpoint of the individual offender. It has to be determined primarily from the standpoint of the general public, in particular, from the standpoint of the requirements of the war." Even if "StGB, article 51, paragraph 2, would apply to a defendant," the judges would "not use this legal possibility of reducing punishment according to this regulation."

These explanations of the RKG initiated a controversy in the pertinent literature of jurisprudence regarding the question of what constituted a "less serious case." They also raised the question of whether every conscientious objector had to expect the death penalty, regardless of the circumstances of his particular case. In this regard, Eberhard Schmidt, professor of criminal law and military court senior legal counsel of the reserve army, criticized the opinion of the RKG, which contradicted the established administration of justice of the previous RKG. Accordingly, legal examination of mitigating circumstances would have to be made only on the basis of objective considerations, such as requirements of the war mentioned in the RKG decision. Thus, it should not be based on subjective aspects involving personal circumstances of the offender. If it is possible to determine the "seriousness of a case" on the basis of objective (evading of military service) as well as subjective (stubbornness of the offender) circumstances, it should certainly be possible to apply these same principles in determining a "less serious case." According to Schmidt, it was certainly possible "to judge this issue 'from the standpoint of the individual offender.'"[241] If, therefore, it was important to take into consideration the personal question of guilt, or more precisely, the subjective guilt factor, it would be completely inappropriate to consider StGB, article 51, paragraph 2, to be inconsequential. With his objections to the administration of justice of the RKG, Schmidt adhered to the traditional concept of penal law. According to this concept, the amount of punishment could not be determined only on the basis of the committed offense. It also depended on the degree of guilt.

The RKG rejected such conservative objections to a practice of rendering judgment that was willing to relinquish a basic rule of reaching a verdict. With determination, Dr. Karl Schmauser, senior judge of one of the RKG divisions, opposed the "misconceptions and misinterpretations of Schmidt." However, in his reply, Schmauser did make the restrictive statement that the explanations supporting the judgment were not supposed to have general application. Thus, the explanations of the RKG regarding the issue of "less serious cases" should be applied only to "similar cases of non-revoked refusals to perform military service."[242] The question of "whether the rule of diminished responsibility according to StGB, article 51, paragraph 2, can be applied to a conscientious objector . . . requires an approach that is completely different from that taken in usual cases." Since the refusal of military service was not a one-time offense but, rather, a so-called continuous offense, it was not possible to take into consideration a person's accountability at the time of the offense. To the contrary, the conscientious objector was able to consider the consequences of his refusal. Between the time of his arrest and the trial, he was "even repeatedly reminded" of these consequences. If, despite repeated admonitions, he continued to refuse military service, he was fully aware of the unlawfulness of his actions. Moreover, he was also aware of the "kind and extent of punishment." It could, of course, be possible that "offenders of this kind" had a diminished capacity in "understanding *why* the state required obedience, or rather, in this case, military service from every person, regardless of his personal ideology or similar reasons (MStGB, article 48), and *why* the refusal to perform military service would be punished." It would be difficult to believe that these people did not understand "*that* the refusal of military service was prohibited by law." From a legal standpoint, "full comprehension" required "that the people concerned had the mental capacity to understand completely *this* fact and its significance."[243] In the majority of cases, the mental capacity of comprehension could be presumed. Consequently, it could be presumed also with regard to decision-making. If, therefore, a conscientious objector "persisted in his refusal, possibly for several months, despite the fact that he will possibly be sentenced to death," he demonstrated such "extraordinary determination" that the rule of diminished responsibility could certainly not be applied to him. If a person had the mental capacity to understand that the refusal of military service would endanger his life, but decided to maintain his position, he committed a deliberate offense. According to the senior judge of this RKG division, such a person voluntarily decided to die on the guillotine, as it were.

However, according to Schmauser, the court should not even allow for extenuating circumstances in cases in which the psychiatric experts certified that the rule of diminished responsibility applied to a conscientious objector and, consequently, the requirements for applying StGB, article 51, paragraph 2, were fulfilled. In explaining his viewpoint,

Schmauser referred to the fact that such refusals to perform military service involved the danger that others might be encouraged to follow this example. In harmony with the legal thinking prevalent at the military courts of the Wehrmacht, Schmauser stated that the motives of the individual conscientious objector were completely insignificant for the court decision:

> In particular cases, the reasons for conscientious objection can certainly be respectable. However, quite a number of people act on reasons that are not respectable, anticipating to be granted a pardon or hoping for the end of the war. They would rather accept the most serious prison sentences than put their lives at risk in fighting for the fatherland. *This* is the danger that needs to be prevented with all possible means.[244]

According to Schmauser's explanations, conscientious objectors actually came under a statutory exemption—an actual suspension of the legal possibilities for mitigation of punishment. Accordingly, on March 10, 1942, the RKG issued a principal ruling, emphasizing its determination to base its judicial decisions entirely on this view.[245] The court proceedings concerned involved a Jehovah's Witness who was drafted into the Wehrmacht on May 14, 1941. Initially, he complied with the draft. After three weeks in the armed forces, he refused to put on the gas mask. Two days later, he informed the *Hauptfeldwebel* (senior sergeant) of his military unit that he would refuse to take the military oath. He was consequently arrested. During repeated interrogations, the man stated that his conscience prohibited him from continuing to perform military service. On August 23, 1941, the highest military court of the Wehrmacht sentenced him to death on the charge of "demoralization of the armed forces." Before the judgment was confirmed, he was asked again whether he was willing to reconsider his decision, in view of the penalty. The Jehovah's Witness explained that he was "willing to accept some work, even in the medical department. But he would not be willing to take the military oath or perform service under arms."

The willingness of this Jehovah's Witness to perform unarmed service did not change the mind of the RKG senior judge.[246] The execution was scheduled to take place on the morning of September 27, 1941: "A few hours before [the execution], the defendant stated that he was now willing to accept without reservation any kind of military service. As a result, the execution was withdrawn. Upon request by the defendant, the legal proceedings were resumed in accordance with the usual

RKG procedure in such cases." Three weeks later, on October 16, 1941, another trial took place. As mentioned later in the judgment, the defendant stated during trial "that he was willing to perform military service but he was not able to do so because his conscience bothered him." As a result, the court division suspended the proceedings. In order to determine the question of accountability, the court ordered the "defendant to be admitted into a psychiatric hospital to monitor his mental condition." On March 10, 1942, legal proceedings against this thirty-nine-year-old man were resumed for the third time at the Lietzensee courthouse.[247] Now the defendant stated that, as a result of careful consideration, he had come to the conclusion that he was no longer able to perform military service. As stated in the judgment, he maintained this attitude "despite being given the most serious admonitions."

During the initial trial, Oberfeldarzt (Lieutenant Colonel) Dr. X.,[248] who, according to the court records, was an "expert in assessing such cases," did not think that StGB, article 51, paragraph 2, applied to the defendant. But based on the results of the six-week period of examinations at the mental hospital, a psychiatrist indicated that the defendant had "an inadequate degree of intelligence resulting from a mild form of congenital mental deficiency. Because of this mental deficiency, the defendant has uncritically accepted fanatical viewpoints, which, in turn, greatly reduced his accountability. As a result, his ability to understand the unlawfulness of his actions and his ability to act on this understanding are considerably diminished."

Based on the results of the medical examinations, the psychiatrist submitted a report in which he pleaded for StGB, article 51, paragraph 2, to be applied in this case, which would have provided a possibility of mitigating punishment. However, the third division of the RKG "decided to maintain the August 23, 1941, decision of the initial court division, requesting execution, loss of right to serve in the armed forces, and permanent loss of civil rights." The judges of the third court division (of which Dr. Schmauser was the senior judge) explained their decision by stating that, during war, "it is not the personality of the offender that is taken into account, but it is rather the dangerous effect the action has on the people": "However, this dangerous effect is not determined by the question of whether the offender can be made fully responsible for his actions or whether his accountability is diminished. Possibly, the actions of a person with diminished responsibility can be even more detrimental in the situation of war than the actions of a person with full penal responsibility." Consequently, even in this case it would be necessary to "maintain the Reich Military Court's position according to which the refusal of military service cannot be considered to be less serious as long as the offender does not indicate his willingness to fulfill his duties toward the German people seriously and without reservation."

No Mitigation of Punishment

Only in cases in which Jehovah's Witnesses completely abandoned their position of refusal and agreed to perform military service without reservation could they expect to be granted a pardon from the judges of the RKG. To this end, the judges persistently tried to persuade the defendants in this direction, having various reasons to do so. Some judges were motivated by a desire to "protect the defendants from the death penalty." For others it was an effort to sooth their consciences so that they could pronounce the sentence in the knowledge that they had tried everything to change the attitude of the defendants. In other words, it was also necessary to "gain control over the emotional side of the problem."[249]

In August 1942 the RKG senior judge informed the senior judges of the various court divisions that he considered relaxing the legal regulations so as to provide Jehovah's Witnesses with a remedy. He also stated that this action should under no circumstances minimize, from the viewpoint of war, the unlawful behavior of conscientious objectors. Apparently, to avoid misunderstandings, Admiral Bastian emphasized that his viewpoint was certainly not based on sentimentality. Instead, he was looking for a possibility "to provide the Wehrmacht with *useful* soldiers or keep them in their service, even in this most critical final period of the war."[250]

Even after the trials were completed and the court decisions pronounced, the judges offered conscientious objectors an opportunity to withdraw their refusal to perform military service.[251] Often, they delayed the date of execution so that the defendant could withdraw his refusal and, in this way, reopen the case. This revealed the Janus-faced attitude of a judiciary that did not consider it repugnant to impose unscrupulously Draconian sentences and, at the same time, try to "bring" these victims "to their senses." However, many Jehovah's Witnesses confronted with the option of choosing between death and military service did not view this as an alternative.[252] And many judges failed to comprehend this steadfast attitude of Jehovah's Witnesses. Amazingly, these judges actively supported the fact that these people, in order to uphold their faith, "rushed to their own ruin," as it was termed.

To persuade conscientious objectors to change their mind, the RKG judges used several methods. According to senior judge Bastian, the custodial judges "did everything in their power to convince" these people. Military officers also instructed Jehovah's Witnesses about "the obligation of every German fit for military service to serve his people, his own family, in a word, his fatherland." Even prison chaplains of Catholic and Protestant denominations were asked to provide pastoral care for Jehovah's Witnesses and "convince them that the performance of military service did not conflict with the commandments, instructions, and statements of the Bible."[253] Several Jehovah's Witnesses promptly rejected these offers for a discussion—they "did not trust" these prison chaplains.[254]

The Protestant prison chaplain at the Berlin-Plötzensee prison, Dr. Harald Poelchau, who had connections to resistance groups, was one of the prison chaplains requested to persuade Jehovah's Witnesses. He also viewed "military service in a war, and particularly in this war, as an offense against the fifth commandment." Therefore, he considered the RKG request "to persuade these people to perform military service with theological reasoning in order to save them to be an impossible task."[255] According to Poelchau's recollections, the efforts of the prison chaplains produced not "a single 'positive' result."[256] Judged by the intentions of the RKG, these efforts accomplished just the opposite. These discussions made Jehovah's Witnesses even more determined "to follow their difficult course."[257]

These discussions—in many cases the first personal contacts with the Bible Students—left a deep impression on the theologians. Even though they did not share their convictions, the chaplains began to respect the faithful and God-fearing attitude of Jehovah's Witnesses.[258] The report of the Stuttgart chaplain, Rudolf Daur, provides some remarkable evidence. At the beginning of 1942 he repeatedly visited the shoemaker Gustav Stange, a Jehovah's Witness from Stammheim (near Stuttgart), in prison. After Stange's execution on February 20, 1942, Daur also tried to comfort Stange's widow, even though this was somewhat unusual. In his letter to the widow written on the day of Stange's execution, Daur acknowledged that although he could "not completely share" the viewpoints of her husband, he had "heartfelt sympathy" for him, one who had now "escaped the darkness and turmoil of this wicked world and [was] in the presence of God."[259] Regarding his discussions with Stange, Daur states:

> He strictly refused military service because it did not harmonize with his conscience. He also clearly refused to take the military oath in acknowledgement of Adolf Hitler. I tried everything to persuade him to take a different position. I truly wanted . . . to save the life of this exceptional man. But he was completely convinced that he did the right thing. During the military court proceedings, the Hauptmann [captain] asked him: "What would be the case if all people were like you?" He responded: "This would be the end of the war."[260]

The assignment of these prison chaplains was especially tragic considering the fact that they could save the lives of the imprisoned Bible Students only if they were able to undermine their religious convictions. The discussions took place under the most nerve-wracking circumstances. The report of prison chaplain Dr. Werner Jentsch tells about his encounter with a nineteen-year-old youth (Bernhard Grimm) awaiting execution at the Brandenburg-Görden prison. Jentsch visited the young Jehovah's Witness in his prison cell during the night before his execution, which was scheduled for August 21, 1942:[261]

> According to military court regulations, he was allowed, even as late as his last night, to write a note and indicate his willingness to perform military service and take the military oath. This could have saved his life. Our discussion was practically my last opportunity to persuade him. We earnestly discussed one Bible scripture after another. He wanted to think about it again. Then I left him alone with the Lord. When I came back early the next morning, he was determined and composed. He did not sign the paper. What choice did I have but to respect his decision in the face of Jesus and to prepare him for his final journey.[262]

In September 1940 RKG counsel Dr. Hans-Ulrich Rottka was transferred to the Reich military attorney's office because he was not wanted as judge of a court division.[263] Rottka, a close friend of Jentsch, requested Kraell, senior judge of one of the court divisions, to arrange for a discussion between Jentsch and Admiral Bastian. Jentsch, shortly after his moving encounter with Bernhard Grimm, the condemned youth, was able to present the problem of conscientious objection from a theological viewpoint to the RKG senior judge.[264] Jentsch made the suggestion that he could write an essay about Bible text on the subject of war and peace from a theological point of view, which could be used not only by the people who refused military service for religious reasons but also by the judges who had to sentence these people. Bastian approved of this suggestion. In 1943, on the explicit request of Dr. Alexander Kraell, who had recently been appointed to the position of senior Reich military attorney, Jentsch prepared the draft for a brochure providing theological instruction for "people who refuse to perform military service and to take the military oath."[265] The brochure was written in the form of a letter. In 1944 a second draft of the brochure was distributed after it "had been 'officially' read and approved" by RKG officials.[266] It had the objective of "assisting the accused to examine carefully his viewpoint based on a study of the Bible."[267] However, in his recollections, Admiral Bastian states that not even this brochure "could change the difficult situation."[268]

The authorities used various methods of persuasion, such as emotional torture (extended periods of confinement in a "death cell")[269] and threats, such as imposing legal measures on family members of the accused (taking children away by means of custody withdrawals).[270] They even used subtle forms of "persuasion." For instance, to persuade already condemned people into changing their minds, family members were recruited to put pressure on them.[271] In this way, the authorities hoped that the direct confrontation with wives, children, and other relatives (situations that were almost like final farewell visits) would cause the prisoners to become "weak." To a certain extent, this strategy was successful, especially with regard to non-Witness relatives. Often, on their own initiative, relatives tried to influence the prisoners by means of serious requests and pleas, sometimes even by means of accusations. In some cases, the "condemned" succumbed to this pressure. According to senior judge Bastian, there were also some "strange occurrences": "In many cases, relatives admonished the accused to remain steadfast under all circumstances, not to become weak, and to die rather than 'surrender.'"[272]

This situation resulted from the fact that there is something that Jehovah's Witnesses fear more than ordinary death: suffering "real" death because of unfaithfulness. Elise Harms, whose husband was beheaded at the Brandenburg-Görden prison on January 8, 1941, at the age of thirty, remembers her thoughts when the news of his death reached her. She states: "I knew the difficult times he had gone through. There was little I could do to help him. So when I was notified that he had been executed, I was relieved to know it was over. For the moment, I [was] . . . just thinking: 'Now they cannot make him compromise.

There is no danger any longer of his being unfaithful. He has endured faithful unto death.'"[273]

In some cases, right up to the point before the judgment was confirmed, the military judges offered those sentenced to death an opportunity to perform unarmed military service if they withdrew their refusal to perform military service.[274] However, Jehovah's Witnesses considered it to be a victory over the powers of Satan if they maintained their position of refusal and refused to make "compromises." By keeping their integrity even during the most difficult times, they tried to prove that the powers of Satan were not able to undermine the power of faith.[275] Their main concern was to "contribute to the vindication of Jehovah's name" by remaining steadfast. The efforts of the judges to persuade them into participating in the war were therefore considered to be an attempt to lure these faithful Jehovah's Witnesses into a trap.[276]

The letters that faithful Jehovah's Witnesses wrote to their families in the face of death demonstrate the seriousness of the inner struggles to which they were exposed. Johannes Harms states in his farewell letter to his father, who was imprisoned at the Sachsenhausen concentration camp:

> And now I, too, have been given an opportunity to prove my faithfulness to the Lord unto death, yes, in faithfulness not only up unto death, but even into death. My death penalty has already been announced and I am chained both day and night . . . but I still have not conquered to the full. Remaining faithful is not made easy for one of Jehovah's Witnesses. I still have an opportunity to save my earthly life, but only thereby to lose the real life. Yes, one of Jehovah's Witnesses is given an opportunity to break his covenant even when in view of the gallows. Therefore, I am still in the midst of the fight and I still have many victories to win before I can say that "I have fought the good fight, I have observed the faith, there is reserved for me the crown of righteousness which God, the righteous judge, will give me." The fight is doubtless difficult, but I am wholeheartedly grateful to the Lord that he not only has given me the necessary strength to stand up until now in the face of death, but has given me a joy I would like to share with all my loved ones. . . . My dear father, in spirit I call to you, remain faithful, as I have attempted to remain faithful, and then we will see one another again.[277]

For many Jehovah's Witnesses who refused to perform military service, the execution proved to be a relief from the tremendous emotional pressure. They were no longer confronted with the question of remaining steadfast and withstanding the "trial." Finally, they were released from the inner struggles and confrontations, which especially resulted from concerns for their families and the suffering they would have to endure. In this regard, on December 1, 1939, a few hours before his execution early the next morning, twenty-four-year-old Franz Mattischek from Wolfsegg (Upper Austria) wrote the following letter to his family: "You will certainly be relieved that I am now resting in peace. On the one hand, I have been longing for this moment, because I have experienced difficult times, especially during the recent months. If, now, I have found favor with Jehovah, everything will be good."[278] A fellow believer summarizes his feelings with the following words: "Could I ever be happy again in this world after having disowned our Lord Jesus Christ? Certainly not! However, in this way you can be certain that I died content and in peace. . . . I have made my decision. All struggle, all suffering, have come to an end!"[279]

The fact that their struggle had ended and the sure hope in the resurrection gave Jehovah's Witnesses the strength to maintain a positive attitude. This attitude left a deep impression on fellow prisoners and military judges. It is even mentioned in the reports of the prison chaplains who accompanied those Jehovah's Witnesses on their last journey.[280] They died with the conviction that death would soon be conquered and that they would be reunited with their loved ones during the millennial rule of God's Kingdom, which they could already envision.

Jehovah's Witnesses who succumbed to the pressure and finally agreed to perform military service were considered as "less serious cases" of "demoralization of the armed forces" and usually sentenced "only" to imprisonment of between one and three years. In these cases, the execution of these sentences was suspended until the end of the war. A prison sentence gave the military judges the opportunity to suspend the sentence so that the conscientious objector could "prove his adjusted attitude in direct contact with the enemy." These conscientious objectors were thus sent to a Wehrmacht punishment battalion at the front lines so that they could "actively show remorse for their offense."[281] The harsh conditions in these punishment-and-probation battalions (*Bewährungbataillon*), as well as the dangerous military operations, resulted in high numbers of casualties even among those Jehovah's Witnesses who, under the pressure of the military courts, had given up their position of refusal and agreed to perform military service.

The imposition of prison sentences, on the other hand, would have resulted in an expulsion from the Wehrmacht on the charge of "unworthiness of serving in the armed forces." People who were imprisoned by the military courts of the Wehrmacht were handed over for "indefinite periods of imprisonment" to the Reich administration of justice.[282] Most were sent to the Emsland penal camps.[283] Since this more serious form of punishment also exempted one from performing military service,[284] it was generally not imposed on people who "withdrew their refusal to perform military service" because it was considered to run contrary to the "purpose of punishment."

As a result, only in a few cases did the RKG impose prison sentences on Jehovah's Witnesses. At first, this applied to the small number of conscientious objectors who, for instance, based on StGB, article 51, paragraph 2, received mitigation of punishment even without a withdrawal of their refusal to perform military service. In some particular cases, conscientious objectors were also granted clemency without being required to withdraw their refusal to perform military service. In these cases, the death penalties were changed into prison life sentences.

Because of these reasons, the military courts of the Wehrmacht sentenced only a very small number of Jehovah's Witnesses to imprisonment at the Emsland penal camps. But those conscientious objectors who were sent to harsh penal camps as a result of a military court decision received especially harsh and cruel mistreatment from the guards.[285]

Sentences, Desertion, and Military Service in the Wehrmacht

Toward the end of the war, exclusive jurisdiction over proceedings against Jehovah's Witnesses and other people refusing military service for religious reasons was withdrawn from the RKG. In this regard, on June 7, 1944, the RKG senior judge sent a report to the chief of the OKW. He stated that the highest military court of the Wehrmacht had established a definite procedure of administration of justice regarding the question of court proceedings against Earnest Bible Students. As a result, the RKG would subsequently be relieved from such cases. Two months later, the senior judge sent a detailed list of rules according to which the RKG had previously handled these cases.[286] On August 15, 1944, the chief of the OKW sent a letter, which included a copy of these RKG rules, to the three Wehrmacht subdivisions (Army, Navy, and Air Force). He also sent a copy of this letter to the chief of the Central Office of the SS Court and to the SS judges at the Reichsführer SS. In this letter, the OKW chief requested a statement indicating whether these departments had any reservations against a transfer of cases involving Bible Students and other people refusing military service for religious reasons to the field military courts under the requirement that these courts based their judgments on the RKG regulations. The letter further states that the OKW tended to accept the request of the RKG and to "relieve the highest military court of the Wehrmacht from further prosecuting and sentencing of Bible Students," especially since this transfer would also result in a simplification of administrative procedures.[287]

At the beginning of September 1944, after no reservations had been expressed up to the deadline (August 31, 1944)[288] and even the RSHA had approved of the rules of procedure without objections,[289] the OKW made the appropriate arrangements. The decree of May 18, 1940, that had determined that the RKG had exclusive jurisdiction over conscientious objectors who based their actions on reasons of conscience or on instructions received from their religious denomination was cancelled. As a result, the field military courts at the Wehrmacht commandant's headquarters or its appropriate subdivisions would now judge all cases of refusal to perform military service. In order to guarantee legal consistency, the courts received an instruction leaflet titled "Regulations regarding Court Proceedings involving Earnest Bible Students, etc." The wording of this instruction leaflet differed only slightly from the regulations of the RKG. It divided the proceedings into eight different case categories and made a clear distinction between the methods of proceedings, for instance, in cases of withdrawal (of the refusal to perform military service) before the trial, withdrawal before the confirmation of the sentence, and withdrawal before the execution of the sentence. Among other things, it stated:

> (1) A person liable for military service who complied with the draft but refuses to take the military oath and to perform military service, and does not withdraw this refusal despite repeated admonitions, will be sentenced to death according to KSSVO, article 5, paragraph 1, clause 3. He will also be sentenced to loss of the right of serving in the armed forces as well as permanent loss of civil rights. . . . (7) In cases in which a person liable for military service convincingly withdraws his refusal of performing military service before the period to finalize the death penalty has expired, and subsequently agrees to perform military service without reservations, the death penalty will be withdrawn. Generally, before such a sentence will be withdrawn, an examination by a judge will take place in order to determine whether his withdrawal resulted from a

sincere adjustment of his attitude or whether it resulted only from
fear of the death penalty. The subsequent sentence will generally
be imprisonment of between one and three years.[290]

By means of these RKG regulations, the field military court judges
had received clear instructions for their actions. Their legal finding was
basically restricted to the question of the case category to which the particular defendant belonged. Even the reasons for the judgment had already been preformulated for them:

> The imposition of the death penalty is generally substantiated by
> the fact that a person liable for military service who persistently up-
> holds his position of refusal seriously violates his obligation of loy-
> alty toward his fellow countrymen. In this way, he excludes himself
> from the [national] community. Moreover, his behavior could en-
> courage others to follow his example and, thus, have a demoraliz-
> ing effect on other people.

Even the comparatively small number of Jehovah's Witnesses who
were excluded from "the privilege of serving" in the Wehrmacht as a result of being considered "unworthy of serving in the armed forces" was
not exempt from the draft. Because of a serious need for reserves, the
Wehrmacht leaders even considered drafting people for military service
who were regarded as "unworthy of serving in the armed forces," at the
latest toward the beginning of 1942. With its October 2, 1942, decree,
the Wehrmacht ordered the establishment of the Probation Battalion
999. People who were drafted to serve in this unit were informed that
they would be considered—during the war—"worthy of serving in the
armed forces (worthy for the time being)." The authorities took the
"paper documenting their exclusion" and issued them a military identification card instead.[291] Thus, in October 1942 the first draftees were
sent to the Reserve and Training Battalion 999 at the Heuberg military
training area near Stetten (the Swabian Mountains).

The Austrian Jehovah's Witness Franz Oswald, who had been sentenced by the St. Pölten Special Court on September 26, 1940, to two
years of imprisonment on the charge of his "involvement in an anti-
military association," was sent to the penal camp Elberegulierung located in Griebo (near Coswig). There, he was again awarded the "right
to serve in the armed forces" and received his draft to a probation battalion on November 15, 1942.[292] At the Heuberg military training area, Oswald explained that "he was not able to perform military service because

of religious reasons." Consequently, Oswald was brought before the court of the Africa Brigade 999 (military court), where he persisted in his refusal to perform military service. As a result, the custodial judge transferred the case to the RKG. On April 6, 1943, this court sentenced the thirty-four-year-old Jehovah's Witness to death on the charge of "demoralization of the armed forces."

Executions of Jehovah's Witnesses who, after being drafted to the probation battalion, refused to perform military service under arms usually did not take place at the designated places. Instead, probably for the purpose of deterrence, they were carried out at the Heuberg military training area "in the presence of the troops."[293] Herbert Baade, a Communist from Hamburg considered "unworthy of serving in the armed forces" after he had been sentenced because of an "attempt to commit high treason," was drafted at the end of 1942. He arrived at the military training area in Heuberg/Stetten with a group of new recruits that also included a Jehovah's Witness. This Jehovah's Witness even refused to accept his military uniform. He stated that as a "Christian" he was not able to wear such a uniform, and was soon transferred to a different location. After a short while, this Jehovah's Witness, together with two fellow believers, was sentenced to death because he had refused to wear "the uniform in honor of the nation." Baade reports about the execution: "The three Bible Students were shot to death. We had to look on as they were shot. And they even sang a song: 'To Kapernaum We Shall Go.'"[294]

Not all Jehovah's Witnesses liable for military service but still in "freedom" openly declared their refusals to the military authorities; a persistent conscientious objection definitely resulted in a "death penalty." Understandably, they tried to find ways in which they could maintain their faith, evade military service, and also avoid the "certainty of the death penalty." Unquestionably, their conduct also required great courage and involved immense risk. Within the IBSA, this conduct was not without controversy. At least according to the more radical ones, a Jehovah's Witness was required to declare openly and publicly his refusal to submit to the requirements of "Caesar."[295] Other forms of evading military service were rejected as "indecisive" and "fearful."[296] At the same time, though, many fellow believers supported those who went underground to the best of their ability.

From the very day on which the draft was issued, a Jehovah's Witness who evaded military service by not reporting to his unit was considered to be a "deserter." Anyone who supported such a person became guilty of "assisting in desertion." For example, for a certain period of time, Heinrich Finke from Wulferdingsen (Westphalia) provided a hiding place for his fellow believer Hans Baumgart. However, when Finke tried to take Baumgart to a different location, he was discovered. The Bielefeld Special Court punished Finke with three years of imprisonment on the charge of assisting in desertion.[297] The Austrian Bible Student Andrea Haas tried to protect her husband, who was drafted at the end of May 1940, by giving the military registration office the wrong information about his place of residence. For this reason, and because she hid him in a garden shed, the Vienna Special Court sentenced Andrea Haas, in December 1941, on the charge of assisting her husband's evasion of military service. Unfortunately, all Haas's efforts were in vain. On March 5, 1942, the RKG sentenced her husband to death.[298] Harm Buß, who lived on the North Sea island of Norderney and who had joined the denomination of Jehovah's Witnesses in 1935 at the age of thirty-one, had spent several months of imprisonment at the Esterwegen concentration camp. In 1939 he was drafted.[299] He returned the draft notice stating that he was under the assumption that former concentration camp prisoners would be unworthy of serving in the armed forces. However, he later complied with the draft but explained that he could not and would not take the military oath in acknowledgement of Hitler. Before the procedure of taking the military oath took place, his engineering unit was transferred to the Weichsel, a river to the south of Warsaw. There, on his eighth day of being in the Wehrmacht, he was asked to take the military oath. A few hours before taking the oath, however, Harm Buß escaped over the fence surrounding the barracks. From Poland, he walked all the way to his Oldenburg homeland. On the way, a few Polish people gave him civilian clothes. He walked at night, but during the day he looked for places to hide. Finally, he arrived in his hometown Nesse (district of Oldenburg). For five years, he hid in the attic of his parents' home. The police and military police searched for Harm Buß at his home on Norderney. But in Nesse, he was safe.

A number of those who had gone underground were drafted into the Wehrmacht after they had been released from the concentration camps.[300] For instance, the IBSA group leader Albert Trey, a thirty-six-year-old truck driver from Bremen, had been sentenced to two years of imprisonment in a penal institution and subsequent imprisonment at Sachsenhausen, Neuengamme, and Dachau. In July 1941, immediately after his release from the concentration camps, he evaded the draft by hiding, mostly in various garden sheds of fellow believers in Bremen.[301]

Toward the end of the war, an increasing number of Jehovah's Witnesses went underground to evade the draft. After repeated examinations before enlistment, Bruno Knöller was deferred as unfit for military service until December 31, 1944, because of illness. At the end of 1944, without a repeated medical examination, he was drafted again.[302] Then, upon the advice of his physician, he went to the Heilbronn military district office to apply for another medical examination. A friendly Wehrmacht military officer showed him a letter from the *Ortsgruppenleiter* (local group leader) of his hometown Simmozheim (near Pforzheim). The letter indicated that the people of Simmozheim were outraged that this twenty-two-year-old Bible Student "was still at home while other people were fighting and dying for the Fatherland." However, the military officer did give orders for a repeated examination before enlistment. He also gave Knöller the following advice: eight days after receiving the order for an examination before enlistment, Knöller should notify the authorities in Heilbronn that he was moving away. Then he should wait a few days before he registered at a different place of residence, as requested on the form of notice for change of address. After another two weeks, he should again register in Heilbronn. Bruno Knöller followed this advice. In this way, he played for time until this method was no longer effective: "Then I went underground. I kept myself hidden, either in Heilbronn or at the home of my parents. I was not able to stay at the same place for an extended period of time because somehow people always found out and were extremely angry. The war was at its critical point." Bruno Knöller repeatedly changed his hiding places. In the spring of 1945 he was able to hide with a factory owner in Heilbronn. This man protected Knöller, even though he himself was not a Jehovah's Witness.

Another Jehovah's Witness also tried to play for time by repeatedly reporting a change of address and filing petitions (his father, who was born in the Ukraine, was a "stateless person"). Finally, in March 1945, he decided to go underground and escape "to the forest." There, he lived in a cave and went into the village only to get food. He remained in this hiding place until the end of the war.[303]

As a last resort, the NS regime formed the Volkssturm (German Home Guard) units to bring about a change in the war's outcome. These units consisted of old men, young men barely out of childhood, and disabled people. Jehovah's Witnesses also objected to joining the Volkssturm. As examples, two Jehovah's Witnesses in East Friesland went into hiding in barns and haylofts; one Jehovah's Witness hid in Berlin for a period of four months.[304] During the final months of the war, seven Bible Students were sent to Buchenwald because they refused to join a Volkssturm unit.[305] On October 22, 1944, a fifty-five-year-old auto mechanic from Hamburg received his draft for the Volkssturm. Immediately, he sent a letter to the leader of the operation informing him: "Enclosed, I am returning the uncompleted forms. I am not able to join the Hamburg Volkssturm unit. I am a practicing Christian and a free person. My religious beliefs do not allow me to participate in political or military activities. I also want to mention that, because of being a Bible Student, I have had two previous convictions."[306] A few days later, this Jehovah's Witness was summoned to the Gestapo. There, he was accused of conduct that revealed an "unpatriotic attitude." In response, he stated: "I am accused of not submitting to the authorities. However, I do not think that I have to be obedient to a worldly authority. I rather have to obey the authority of God who requires of us to keep His commandments."[307] The Gestapo immediately arrested him.

As early as November 25, 1944, the senior public prosecutor at the Hanseatic Special Court charged this Jehovah's Witness with an "offense against the KSSVO, article 5, paragraph 1, clause 3." However, the senior public prosecutor had some uncertainties regarding the legal situation and regarding matters of jurisdiction, especially since this was "the first case of refusal to perform compulsory service in the Volkssturm in this district." Consequently, he sent a copy of the indictment to the RJM. In the accompanying letter, the senior public prosecutor stated that, in his opinion, this case should come under the "special court jurisdiction instead of military court jurisdiction since the actions of the accused were not performed during service in the Volkssturm."[308] As a result, the RJM requested the records and cancelled the court proceedings that were scheduled for January 26, 1945. The Jehovah's Witness was kept at the Hamburg prison for another three months without being taken to court. On April 25, 1945, he was released from pretrial detention.[309]

The "special court for the operation zone Alpenvorland," on the other hand, sentenced Johann Haslinger, an Austrian Bible Student from Straßwalchen (near Salzburg), to death as late as April 9, 1945. Haslinger had been released from Sachsenhausen and Wewelsburg on September 24, 1941. When he was later drafted to join the Volkssturm on March 11, 1945, he responded that he would "not agree to military service under any circumstances."[310]

Besides those Jehovah's Witnesses who refused military service or tried to evade military service in other ways (by escaping to other countries, for example),[311] there were also some IBSA members who complied with the draft, even though it caused them pangs of conscience.[312] In April 1940 a thirty-one-year-old Bible Student from Hamburg and father of four children reported for duty in the Wehrmacht. He had previously refused to join the military service. His reports indicate the great stress he experienced as a result of his decision to join, which he had made "out of consideration for his family." As far as possible, he tried to avoid abandoning his principles, to remain humane and decent even during the war. Because he refused to comply with orders in his unit on the eastern front, he was taken into custody. He relates: "I was requested to set houses on fire that were occupied with women and children. [Because of my refusal], I was supposed to be shot to death. I don't know why this did not happen. . . . During the entire period of the war, I did not kill a single person."[313]

In other cases, well-meaning military officers deployed Jehovah's Witnesses for services that did not require the use of weapons. The leader of the Itzehoe IBSA group who performed military service from February 10, 1940, on, reports that he informed the commander of his unit of his refusal to use weapons against human beings. His commander told him that he would be allowed to "perform his military service without being required to kill anybody."[314] Some of the active IBSA members also served in the Wehrmacht. An older leader of a smaller district who had gained the rank of an officer during World War I now served as a captain, despite his reservations. However, he did not serve on the frontline but at a Wehrmacht office in his hometown.[315] One Jehovah's Witness (who had actively supported the smuggling of IBSA publications over the German-Czechoslovakian border between 1934 and 1936) was pressured by prison guards into performing military service. According to the report of a fellow believer, "the prison guards repeatedly admonished him to think of his family. Finally, he became so distressed that he agreed to become a soldier."[316] There were even a few cases in which Bible Students who were imprisoned in concentration camps agreed to military service. If the Gestapo was convinced that their statements were "trustworthy," they withdrew the order of protective detention,[317] released the Bible Students from the concentration camps, and transferred them to the Wehrmacht.

In quite a number of cases, the sons of Bible Students or other people who were associated with the Bible Students but were not yet baptized also joined the Wehrmacht.[318] According to the opinion of many Bible Students, their situation was different. They should not have been expected to make the same decision as would those Jehovah's Witnesses who had completely dedicated their lives to God through baptism. This was, for instance, the case with a young man whose father was imprisoned at the Neuengamme concentration camp. When the mother of the nineteen-year-old informed her husband that their son had decided to refuse military service, the father discussed this matter with the leaders of the Bible Student group at the Neuengamme concentration camp. These leaders, in turn, discouraged the young man from refusing military service for the following reasons: The mother needed the support of her only son. He was not yet strong enough in faith and was also not baptized and would therefore not be breaking his word toward Jehovah. Instead, to the greatest extent possible, he should try to avoid military service under arms and, instead, try to report to a technical unit. Mother and son received this answer through a letter that was smuggled out of the concentration camp.[319]

Jehovah's Witnesses who agreed to military service had serious pangs of conscience. This can be illustrated by a report about an IBSA member who was drafted to the Probation Battalion 999 at the beginning of 1943. Karl Schild, a regime opponent (and member of the Socialist Labor Youth Organization), met the Jehovah's Witness at the Heuberg military training area. Because of his opposition to the regime, Schild had previously been excluded from military service in the armed forces. He was later reconsidered as "worthy of serving in the armed forces" and on February 4, 1943, drafted to the Probation Battalion 999. Regarding this Jehovah's Witness, Schild states:

> We had an older roommate by the name of Fuchs who attracted our attention. He was difficult to judge because he was very shy and reserved. Only gradually did he open up and we learned that he was going through a serious crisis of conscience because of his religious beliefs. He was a Bible Student and, as a result, had been subjected to legal punishment. Now, he wanted to refuse being trained in the use of weapons. He also did not want to take the military oath. We immediately realized: This was his death penalty. We three had several discussions with him. He came from Palatinate and had three or four children. Repeatedly, we tried to explain to him that this was not only a matter of going to prison. Now, it was a matter of life and death. Continuously we told him to think of his family. We also told him that, during a military operation, he could shoot past the target. After a considerable period of time he began to understand. Finally he participated in the training, but

he was still struggling. He was, however, able to keep himself under control. Then, a certain *Hauptwachtmeister* [technical sergeant] was looking for an orderly, and we persuaded him to apply for this position. It worked out. As a result, his situation improved a little, especially in consideration of the fact that, during the military training, he was viewed by his superiors as "useless" and as a "coward."

After a while, there was a second conflict. The time had arrived for taking the oath. He did not want to participate. His "highest leader" was God and he would only be obedient to him. He would not take an oath in acknowledgement of the Führer. . . . Finally, Emil Schäfer and I got the idea of suggesting to him that he should act the way the Sinti did when they were requested to take an oath: While they raised the right hand to the oath with three of their fingers spread, they put the left hand with three of their fingers spread on their back. According to an old superstitious belief, in this way, the oath "went right through the body" and would, therefore, be ineffective. When we had to repeat the words of the oath, he should just move his lips. To this day, I can picture him as he stood there during the ceremony of swearing in with his hand on his back. . . . After these two serious tests of endurance, our friend came with us to the island of Rhodes. Until the end [of the war], he was a good comrade. As an orderly of the *Oberleutnant* [first lieutenant] of the Staff Battery, he could give our resistance group some quite valuable information that he picked up from the conversations of the officers.[320]

Prior to the war, administration of justice by the military courts against conscientious objectors was still relatively lenient. Persecution by the Gestapo during that period presented a considerably higher danger, but with the beginning of the war the situation changed dramatically. After August 26, 1939, the day of mobilization, Jehovah's Witnesses who were liable for military service and received their draft but refused to comply with the draft were in danger of being sentenced to death by the military courts and executed. On the other hand, those whom the Gestapo had already sent to the concentration camps during previous years were not subject to military jurisdiction. In retrospect, compared to the danger of legal prosecution in the case of a refusal to perform military service, the transport of these Jehovah's Witnesses to the concentration camps proved to be "the lesser of the two evils," as it were. For example, after his release from prison, Paul Marszałek refused to sign the reverse statement. As a result, he was sent to Buchenwald before the beginning of the war. He considers this as a circumstance "that saved [his] life": "If

I had remained free, I would have faced more serious consequences. My refusal would have resulted in the fact that I would have been sentenced to death!"[321] Alois Moser, who was arrested on April 4, 1939, because of his refusal to sign the statement and was sent to Dachau by the Gestapo, states: "If I had compromised, my supposed freedom would have lasted five months. Why? Because on September 1, 1939, the war broke out. Once again, I would have had to make the decision: military service or death for Christ's sake. . . . Only four months later, I would have no longer been punished with 'protective detention' but, under martial law, I would have been sentenced to 'death' by firing squad."[322]

The basis for nondeployment for military service of concentration camp prisoners decreed that people liable for military service had to be "deferred from compulsory labor service and active military service until they would have been released from protective detention." The decree had been issued by the RKM in cooperation with the Gestapo. [323] However, these people who had been taken into protective detention remained under the supervision of the military registration office that had administrative jurisdiction over concentration camp prisoners as well as over other people liable for military service who had been deferred from military service.[324] Therefore, even prisoners in protective detention had to report to a recruiting board or were subjected to examinations before enlistment, even at the concentration camps.[325] After the beginning of the war, the military district commands sent recruiting boards to the prisons and concentration camps to examine the fitness for military service of people who had not previously been examined.[326] The Bible Students, however, were exempt from military service only if they had convincingly and without reservations declared their willingness to perform military service. Those Jehovah's Witnesses who refused military service remained under the authority of the Gestapo. Attempts to transfer Bible Student prisoners to the Wehrmacht, even without their declared consent, only proved the ineffectiveness of the endeavor: because of their adherence to an uncompromising attitude of refusal, the Wehrmacht received cases for their military jurisdiction, but no soldiers.

This was also the case when, in February 1941, twenty-seven Bible Student prisoners from the Niederhagen concentration camp were drafted into the Wehrmacht, even though they had not agreed to perform military service.[327] Their examination before enlistment had already taken place in November 1940. In January 1941 they received their notices. Thereafter, they were transferred to various military units, the garrisons in Paderborn and Gütersloh (military airfield), Minden (infantry regiment), and Iserlohn (medical corps). With the exception of one Bible Student, all of them refused military service for religious reasons. Even though they were now under military jurisdiction because they had been drafted, military court proceedings were not carried out. Courts-martial would have resulted in condemnation on the charge of "demoralization of the armed forces." Instead, the twenty-six conscientious objectors were returned to the Gestapo, and the attempt to draft Bible Students to the Wehrmacht without their prior consent proved to be a complete failure.[328]

As a result of such experiences, the Gestapo no longer transferred Bible Student prisoners to the Wehrmacht unless the Bible Students decided on their own to report for military service. Apparently, the Wehrmacht as well as the Gestapo and the SS were not interested in a procedure that simply transferred concentration camp prisoners to military jurisdiction. In the meantime, the SS also had come to appreciate the working capacity of the Bible Student prisoners. Toward the end of the war, an increasing number of German concentration camp prisoners were drafted for military service and thousands of prisoners were integrated into combat units such as the disreputable SS unit of General Dirlewanger, first on a voluntary basis, later by force.[329] The Bible Student prisoners, however, remained in the concentration camps. As strange as this may seem, from their subjective point of view, many Bible Students considered the concentration camp as a relatively secure place, a place that at least offered the prospect of survival. Despite the suffering, barbaric tortures, and deprivations, the Bible Students preferred to accept the uncertain future of the concentration camps than the predictable future outside of the concentration camps.[330]

15

Prisoners with the "Purple Patch"

In 1935 the authorities started sending several hundred Jehovah's Witnesses to the concentration camps on a grand scale. Besides groups of Communists, Socialists, union members, members of the Center Party[331] and other non-Socialist Democratic parties, as well as the initially relatively small number of "nonpolitical" prisoners, the Bible Students formed a separate group of prisoners within the concentration camp community. They distinguished themselves by means of a strong spirit of solidarity, a distinctive moral code, and, in particular, an ideological separation from the "political prisoners." As a result, they formed a community that differed considerably from the other prisoner groups.[332] During the prewar period, the total number of concentration camp prisoners was still relatively small. For instance, during the winter of 1936/37, there were approximately 7,500 concentration camp prisoners in "protective detention," the lowest number on record.[333] During this time, numerically the Bible Students represented a considerable group of prisoners. In general, their proportion of the total number of concentration camp prisoners corresponded to between 5 percent and 10 percent. In May 1938 the number of Jehovah's Witnesses at the Buchenwald concentration camp even amounted to as much as 12 percent of the prisoners. And in May 1939 the Bible Students represented 40 percent of the total number of prisoners at Schloß Lichtenburg, which was the central concentration camp for women between December 1937 and May 1939, as was later the Ravensbrück concentration camp.[334] Thus, the number of Bible Student prisoners at Schloß Lichtenburg significantly exceeded the total number of Communists and Social Democratic prisoners (together slightly above 10 percent).

After the beginning of the war,[335] the number of prisoners increased rapidly as a result of hundreds of thousands of non-Germans who were sent to the concentration camps.[336] Consequently, in comparison to the

Figure 3. Proportion of Bible Students to the total number of prisoners, Buchenwald

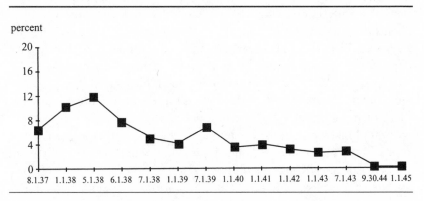

percent

Note: Date line corresponds to month/day/year.

total number of prisoners, Jehovah's Witnesses came to represent only a very small minority: For instance, in December 1939 the Bible Students in Mauthausen represented 5.2 percent of the total number of prisoners. At the same time, they made up 3.3 percent of the prisoners in Buchenwald. At the end of 1944 the statistical records of Mauthausen listed a total of 0.12 percent Bible Student prisoners and the records of Buchenwald, a total of 0.3 percent (see figure 3).[337]

The SS began to isolate the Bible Students from other prisoners in the concentration camps early on by placing them in separate barracks and labor details. With these measures, the SS tried to stop the enthusiastic preaching activity of the Bible Students and restrict their possibilities of communicating with other prisoners.[338] On December 9, 1935, the commanding officer of the Sachsenburg (near Chemnitz) concentration camp gave the following instructions: "The guards have to watch that the Bible Students do not involve other prisoners in conversations during their free time in order to prevent a distribution of the Bible Student teachings."[339]

In 1935/36 the SS began to mark the various prisoner groups through specific patches on their clothing. In the beginning, patches of different colors were used that varied from camp to camp. For example, at the Sachsenburg concentration camp, asocials were identified with black patches, criminals with green patches, and the Bible Students with blue patches. At the Lichtenburg concentration camp, which was still occupied with male prisoners during the middle of the 1930s, Jehovah's

Witnesses were identified with a blue circle on their chest. Jewish prisoners were marked with a yellow circle. The other prisoner groups were identified with different forms of patches.[340] At Sachsenhausen and Buchenwald, established in mid-1937, Jehovah's Witnesses were also initially identified with blue patches.[341] In 1938 a unified system of specific color codes was introduced for all concentration camps. From then on, each prisoner had to wear a triangular patch of a specific color on the left side of the chest. Below this patch, there was a white rectangular piece of material on which the number of the respective prisoner was written in black numerals. For Jehovah's Witnesses, the purple triangle replaced the blue patch.[342] Political prisoners, who, as a group, had not yet been specifically identified, received a red triangle.

Now it was possible to distinguish the various prisoner groups. There were political prisoners (red), the group of asocials (black), and homosexuals (pink). There was also the group of *Sicherungsverwahrte* (convicts transferred from the judicial system to the concentration camps) and the group of *befristete Vorbeugungshäftlinge* (prisoners in protective detention with limited duration, whom the SS branded as "habitual criminals"); both groups were identified with green triangles. The Bible Students were a completely separate category.[343] The fact that the SS separated them in that way made Jehovah's Witnesses easily discernable among the other prisoner groups. At the same time, this separation reflected the actual "special status" of these prisoners whose behavior differed considerably from that of the other groups.[344] With the category "Bible Students," the SS had selected a classification that applied specifically and exclusively to members of this ideological religious denomination. The category of the "political" prisoners marked with the red triangle included a variety of prisoners, such as Communists and Social Democrats, anarchists and members of non-Socialist Democratic parties, clergymen, and resistance fighters of the major Christian denominations. It also included oppositional National Socialists or those who had incurred the disfavor of the National Socialists (as, for instance, members of the Schwarze Front of Otto Strasser). It also included people who were "discontents" but did not consider themselves to be opponents of the regime ("complainers and critics"). The Bible Student prisoners, however, had received their own, exclusive mark of identification. Besides the IBSA members, the category with the purple triangle included only some members from Bible Student groups that had separated from the Watch Tower Society[345] and members of the Adventists.[346] However, the

Adventists represented only a very small number, and the SS did not consider them to be at all different from the Bible Students.

This special status occupied by Jehovah's Witnesses within the concentration camp community was based on their almost unshakable faith, a spirit of solidarity, and courage in expressing their religious beliefs. In May 1937 the *Deutschland-Berichte,* published by the exiled SPD in Prague, included a report about the conditions at the Sachsenburg concentration camp. This report, which was smuggled out of Germany, provided an explanation for this "special characteristic" that caused the SS to place the Bible Students into a separate category:

> The behavior of these Earnest Bible Students is truly amazing. These . . . people demonstrate an unyielding spirit of resistance. They manifest the courage of martyrs and display a steadfastness that is without equal within the concentration camp. From the beginning, we political prisoners have made an agreement among ourselves not to rebel and submit to all instructions coming from the concentration camp administration. We know that the SS officers just wait for an opportunity and would not hesitate to take action against us. Therefore, we give the required Hitler salute, etc. However, there is absolutely nothing that would move the Earnest Bible Students [to give the Hitler salute]. Their faith in Jehovah prohibits them from doing so and they act in harmony with their faith. Several of them even refuse to accept the offer of being released from the concentration camp. Some of them state that they will stay in the camp until they will be again allowed to perform their religious activities.[347]

Regarding the group of female IBSA members imprisoned at the Moringen concentration camp, the same issue of the *Deutschland-Berichte* stated: "The elderly Bible Students are causing considerable trouble for the prison guards. They refuse to give the Hitler salute and nothing can stop them from conducting their religious meetings."[348] The SS records included many reports that provided evidence of such an unyielding attitude of resistance. However, this attitude was by no means based on any tactical calculations on the part of Jehovah's Witnesses; they displayed it for the sake of their religious conviction, and not even the power of the SS was strong enough to undermine their beliefs. There are numerous examples to support this fact. On April 24, 1935, an SS-Oberscharführer (staff sergeant) submitted a report to the commanding officer of the Sachsenburg concentration camp in which he requested severe punishment and eight days of detention for a thirty-six-year-old Bible Student prisoner. In addition, he should also be punished with twenty-five strokes with a club before and after his detention.[349] In order to substantiate this request for punishment, the sergeant stated that the Jehovah's Witness had deliberately refused to give the required Hitler salute. By this action, he indicated "that he was not willing to submit to authority." The sergeant further complained that the Bible Student also refused to join in the songs that the marching columns would sing during their return to the barracks. Repeated admonitions had not been able to persuade him to give up his position of refusal: "In response to my admonitions, he stated impudently that 'he does not know these songs,' even though he has been in the camp since March 5, 1935. He also refused to follow my orders to stand at attention." The indignant SS officer continued his report by stating that the Bible Student "also did not consider it necessary to stand at attention" as he was passing the guard when he was taken to the military police station. The guard called him back and ordered him to stand at attention. The Bible Student impudently replied: "As a Jehovah's Witness, I would not be required to perform such acts!"

The concentration camp commanding officer immediately sent a letter to the inspection office of the concentration camps in Berlin. In this letter, he requested permission to punish this Bible Student prisoner, as well as another Jehovah's Witness who refused to follow "the usual orders" of the concentration camp "according to article 6, paragraph 1, of the Disziplinar- und Lagerordnung [Disciplinary Regulations of the Concentration Camp]."[350] The commanding officer explained: "By stating that they are Jehovah's Witnesses, they refuse to perform any military action. They also state that they are not required to show respect to any person except God. They refuse to stand at attention before overseers and superior guards and to give the Hitler salute. They also refuse to join the other prisoners in singing the customary songs when they leave and return to the barracks."

Special Objects of Hatred by the SS

Otherwise, Jehovah's Witnesses carefully observed the concentration camp regulations, especially when they received specific assignments, but they did not make any concessions in matters contradicting their conscience. And yet, there were differences in opinion among the Bible Student prisoners regarding the question of which requirements of the

SS they were *not* supposed to follow as Jehovah's Witnesses. For instance, a few of them refused to greet the SS officers "in the required form."[351] The majority, however, took off their hats, according to instructions, and stood at attention. The small group who refused to greet the SS officers in this way considered it to be an act of idolatry and, consequently, an act of worship of one of Satan's servants. In his recollections, Rudolf Höß describes the effect that such behavior had on the SS officers. Höß was first the adjutant of the Sachsenhausen concentration camp commanding officer between August 1938 and May 1940, and later became its commanding officer. He reports that, during his time of duty, he had an encounter with two especially fanatical Bible Students: "They would not stand at attention, or drill in time with the rest, or lay their hands along the seam of the trousers, or remove their caps. They said that such marks of respect were due only to Jehovah and not to man. They recognized only one lord and master, Jehovah. Both of them had to be taken from the block set aside for Jehovah's Witnesses and put in the cells, since they constantly urged the other Witnesses to behave in a similar manner."[352]

The two Bible Students, Weiß and Zibold, were kept in detention for a long period of time. According to the statement of SS-Hauptscharführer (Master Sergeant) Kurt Eccarius, the prison warden of the Sachsenhausen concentration camp, "Himmler personally ordered" the execution of these two Bible Students "because they also refused to greet Himmler in the required form when he visited the prison. Instead, they kept kneeling and continued with their prayer."[353]

On the other hand, the vast majority of Bible Student prisoners greeted the SS guards in the required form and did not consider this to be an act prohibited by their religious beliefs. They rather considered it as part of the concentration camp regulations and thus a necessary requirement that they had to follow—and were also able to follow—without denying their faith.[354] In general, Jehovah's Witnesses also profited from the fact that, contrary to previous conditions in the concentration camps, the SS had accepted the view that concentration camp prisoners were notorious "enemies of the people" and should therefore not have the "right" to give the Hitler salute.[355] And so these prisoners in protective detention were even prohibited from performing this salutation and shouting "Heil Hitler."

The Bible Student prisoners still had to deal with the NS songs, and as a result, Jehovah's Witnesses were exposed to conflicts, as can be seen from the following report from the Dachau concentration camp:

> Like all the other prisoners, the Bible Student Edelmann was also expected to sing. He did not sing. Other prisoners tried to persuade him to sing. He replied, "If it is the will of Jehovah, I will die." — One day, a guard said to him: "You foolish Jehovah's Witness! You know all about the Bible. Why are you so stupid that you cannot even sing?" — "Who says I cannot sing? I can sing." The battalion had to stop and he was asked: "What? You can sing? You swine, why did you lie to us?" — "I only sing Christian songs!" he said. He sang a Christian battle song. The battalion continued marching. Edelmann had to sing alone. We had our peace. The SS officers roared with laughter.[356]

Usually though, such instances did not turn out that well. Instead, they often resulted in beatings, in most cases, without particularly reporting the punishment. Moreover, their genuine display of faith in Jehovah made the Bible Student prisoners special objects of hatred of the SS.

Humiliating remarks and mockeries of their faith were the order of the day. The SS officers adopted a whole arsenal of insults for the prisoners with the purple triangle. They called them comedians of heaven and Bible worms, but also *Paradiesvögel* (birds of paradise), *Jordanscheiche* (Arab sheiks), and *Gethsemane-Soldaten* (Gethsemane soldiers). In Dachau, the Bible Student prisoners had to stand on a large pile of sand and shout: "I am the greatest idiot of the twentieth century."[357] Time and time again, the SS officers ridiculed the faith that the IBSA members held in the power of Almighty God. In a secret report written by the journalist and political prisoner Edgar Kupfer-Koberwitz during his imprisonment at Dachau, such an incident of an SS officer ridiculing a Bible Student is described: "You and your God! Why does he not come and help you? Because he is a fool, your God! Because he is not able to, this piece of shit!" While hurling these abuses at the Bible Student, the SS officer was laughing and shaking his fist heavenward: "God — God — I am your God, do you understand me, you comedian of heaven?"[358] And with those words he punched the man, just for the sake of reinforcement, as it were.

Particularly serious consequences could result if several prisoners shared in acts of refusal. This occurred on October 6, 1938, at the Lichtenburg concentration camp, six days after the Wehrmacht had occupied the Sudetenland. The SS had ordered all prisoners of the concentration camp to appear in the courtyard to listen to a radio speech from the Führer.[359] The political prisoners wanted to attend the ceremony because they expected to get information about the political situation.

However, the female Bible Students had decided not to attend but, instead, remain in their dormitories. The political prisoners tried to persuade the Bible Students to attend the speech. Hamburg Communist Charlotte Groß remembers the discussions with the Bible Students: "We tried to make them realize that their refusal was unwise and useless. They would be forced to attend. However, they declared they had only one Führer and that was Jehovah. Listening to the speech of another Führer would be like a betrayal. At the same time, they were certainly interested . . . in getting information about the political situation."[360]

The speech was supposed to be broadcast in the evening, but the Bible Students did not appear in the courtyard. Male and female SS officers went to the dormitories and began beating the Bible Students so that they would come to the courtyard. When this proved to be impossible, the SS officers connected a fireman's hose to a hydrant. They directed the jet of ice-cold water on the Bible Students and washed them down the stone staircase into the courtyard. The statements of Communist Gertrud Geßmann give a glimpse of what the situation must have been like: "Panic broke out, women running in terror, human bodies falling, screams of pain, drowned out by the shouts of command of SS officers and prison guards."[361] Fellow prisoners remember the Bible Students screaming "Bible words against the war," and, "There will be war!" Outside, the SS officers continued beating the Bible Students with clubs. The completely drenched women were made to stand outside for over an hour and endure the Hitler speech.

The SS had warned the Bible Students that their refusal would have serious consequences, and they followed through with the warning that those who had caught colds were not allowed to see a doctor. For the next two or three days, they did not receive any food. They were not even allowed to receive mail or write letters. The "ringleaders" were confined in a darkened cell. Because of the cold and damp conditions in the dungeon of the fortress bunker, this turned out to be terrible torture. According to the Communist Maria Zeh, many of these Bible Students "never recovered" from this torture, despite the assistance they received from the political prisoners.[362]

In an effort to undermine the unusual resistance of the Bible Students, the SS continued to increase the terror. However, they were dealing with the most active ones from among the IBSA members, the majority of whom had already demonstrated their firm determination and resistance during previous imprisonment and the Gestapo reviews that followed the imprisonment. On the outside, the Gestapo and the legal authorities had been able to put quite a number of Jehovah's Witnesses under so much pressure that they discontinued their Bible Student activities. But within the barbed-wire confines of the concentration camps, the SS was able to achieve such results only in exceptional cases.

In 1937, at the concentration camps for men, the SS began to apply to the Bible Students the regulations (forming "special battalions") that had been issued during the previous year for prisoners who had been sent a second time to the concentration camp (second-offenders).[363] In these special battalions, the prisoners had to do particularly heavy work. They could receive and send letters only every three months. They were not allowed to receive any packages at all.

At Buchenwald, the first Jehovah's Witnesses were sent to the infamous punishment battalions in August 1937. Besides second-offense political prisoners, other prisoners were also sent to punishment battalions for certain periods of time. Subsequently, all newly arriving Bible Students at the concentration camp were sent first to a punishment battalion by the SS. Generally, they had to stay there for three months, in some cases up to nine months.[364] Because of the long periods of detention, Jehovah's Witnesses represented a considerable group of prisoners within the punishment battalions.[365] The prisoners had to do the dirtiest and most laborious work (carrying stones and other heavy loads, excavating, disposing of liquid manure, etc.). They had to work between ten and twelve hours per day, and had to work even on Sundays. A few days after his release from Buchenwald, the IBSA district overseer Karl Siebeneichler stated that the "political prisoners and habitual criminals," acting as overseers, "did whatever they could to make life miserable" for the Bible Students.[366] The prisoners did not receive "the least of privileges."[367] They were not allowed to wear sweaters or warm underwear. If there was no work on Sunday afternoons, all of them had to stand at the gate.

During October 1937 a total of 144 Bible Students from Dachau were sent to a punishment battalion.[368] All of them were housed in isolation blocks separated by barbed-wire fences from the remaining camp. Even those Jehovah's Witnesses who had completed their term in the punishment battalion and were assigned to different labor details had to stay in the isolation blocks.

This Dachau model of establishing isolation blocks was also put into practice at Sachsenhausen. It was introduced by SS-Standartenführer (Colonel) Hermann Baranowski, who had previously been the commanding officer at the Dachau concentration camp from the autumn of

1936 on.[369] On March 20, 1938, Baranowski, who was now the concentration camp commanding officer of Sachsenhausen, gave instructions to confine the Bible Students, political second-offenders, and the punishment battalion in a separate camp.[370] For this purpose, barracks 11 and 12 of the first block and barracks 35 and 36 of the second block were separated from the rest of the camp with barbed-wire fences. Those confined in these isolation blocks had no access to the remaining camp and their fellow prisoners. They could leave these small areas only for their work assignments in the labor details. Erich Mundt, whom the Stettin Gestapo sent to the Sachsenhausen concentration camp in August 1937 after he completed an eighteen-month prison sentence, gave the following description about the working conditions for these prisoners: "Being at this place meant hard physical labor. It was strenuous excavation work. The dirt had to be transported double-quick in cars three-quarters of a cubic yard in size over a distance of more than one kilometer [approximately two-thirds of one mile]. During this work, the block wardens were standing on the cars or riding on bicycles alongside the cars. They continuously beat the prisoners with clubs in order to increase their speed."[371]

All prisoners at the isolation blocks were subjected to these harsh conditions. But for the Bible Student prisoners, the regulations were even intensified. Increasingly, they were subjected to more serious conditions and persecution. In March 1938, when Baranowski established the isolation blocks, he completely prohibited the Bible Students from writing any letters. This absolute correspondence ban, which the SS also issued in other concentration camps, lasted in Sachsenhausen for a period of nine months.[372] At the beginning of 1939 the prohibition was withdrawn. Even though the prisoners could now write one letter per month to their families, the Bible Students were not allowed more than twenty-five words per letter.[373] These special regulations for Jehovah's Witnesses applied in all concentration camps and were in effect for three and a half years. In Buchenwald, they lasted until the end of the war. In order to indicate that correspondence was restricted so that inquiries from relatives would not have to be answered individually, the SS instructed the censorship office to stamp the following note on the letters: "The prisoner continues to be a stubborn Bible Student and refuses to reject the Bible Students' false teachings. For this reason, he has been denied the usual privileges of correspondence."[374] The families of Jehovah's Witnesses outside of the camps considered this stamp as evidence that the writers had remained faithful. In this regard, one Jehovah's

Witness reminisces: "We were less interested in the contents of the letter—for what could one say in five lines?—but that stamp always brought us joy."[375]

In their effort to undermine the resistance of Jehovah's Witnesses, the SS restricted them from purchasing items, temporarily excluded them from medical treatment in the concentration camp infirmary, and continued to subject them to acts of persecution and mistreatment.[376] One of their main methods of persecution was food deprivation. At Dachau, for example, the Bible Student prisoners received even smaller food rations than the other prisoners for an extended period of time. Then, they were told that they would immediately receive the normal food rations if they renounced their faith.

In 1940 the bread rations for Jehovah's Witnesses were also cancelled at the Neuengamme concentration camp. The deprivation of even this meager two hundred grams (approximately seven ounces) of bread per day was extremely painful. In the evening, the camp senior, or one of the prisoners assigned for the job, would not distribute to the Bible Students their portion of bread from the breadbox. The formidable SS-Hauptscharführer Franz Xaver Trenkle was usually stationed beside the box. When a prisoner with the purple triangle approached the bread-box, Trenkle would ask, "Are you still a Bible Student?" If the answer was "Yes," he received a stroke with a horsewhip instead of a piece of bread.[377]

Terrorized by the SS

The worst acts of terror the SS committed against the Bible Student prisoners occurred between 1939 and 1940. The following example from Sachsenhausen well demonstrates the methods by means of which the SS tried to undermine the resistance of Jehovah's Witnesses. SS-Hauptscharführer Richard Bugdalle was the responsible commanding officer for the local *SK-Isolierung* (special command isolation blocks). Under his leadership, the block leaders Fritz Fickert, Martin Knittler, Wilhelm Schubert, and Gustav Sorge held their reign of terror. Their special hatred was directed against Jehovah's Witnesses who refused to renounce their faith.

The torture began on the day of arrival at the concentration camp. For new arrivals, the SS had prepared a special "welcome." All new prisoners were asked to announce what kind of "crime" they had committed. If Jehovah's Witnesses responded to this question by explaining their faith in the Bible and in Jesus Christ, matters just took their course. In some cases, they were immediately beaten. In other cases, the "strange person" was subjected to further cross-examinations. On April 20, 1940, Willi Lehmbecker was admitted into the concentration camp. He reports: "I tried to answer all their questions with the Bible. When they asked me who the Führer was, they wanted to hear 'Adolf Hitler.' But I remained silent."[378] As a result, the thirty-six-year-old Jehovah's Witness was beaten to a pulp.

The SS officers indulged in their "sadistic thirst" to torment the "stubborn Bible-worms."[379] The torture continued throughout the entire day. At every place that the Bible Students had to go past, such as the clothing distribution, they were exposed to the same dreadful scene. On January 27, 1940, Gerhard Oltmanns was sent to Sachsenhausen after having served an eighteen-month prison sentence. He remembers the day of his arrival: "Among 101 prisoners coming from Berlin, I was the only Jehovah's Witness. As soon as we arrived at the camp, the question was asked, 'Bible Students, step forward.' Immediately, there was a hail of punches and kicks. Surrounded by twenty SS officers, I was asked, 'Would you sign the draft card?' I said, 'No.' I ducked before them like a chicken. Immediately, I was engulfed in a flood of abuses and screaming. For several minutes, I was kicked around like a soccer ball. Suddenly, someone pointed a gun at me, shouting, 'We should kill that scoundrel!' Immediately, the SS officers mimicked summary court proceedings, stating, 'Death by firing squad!'"[380] At the special command isolation blocks of the Sachsenhausen concentration camp, the psychological torture arsenal also included the threat of execution. All newly arriving prisoners were told that everything would be set in motion to make sure that they would not remain Jehovah's Witnesses. In many cases, these trials resulted in the most horrible mistreatments, even on the first day. In September 1939 Alexander Joseph was sent to Sachsenhausen on the charge of a "broadcasting offense" (listening to foreign radio stations). He describes such a scene as follows: "One Bible Student collapsed under Schubert's mistreatment. At the same time, an SS officer asked him, 'Do you still believe in Jehovah?' When the Bible Student replied, 'Yes,' Schubert continued to kick him and repeated his question. This occurred four or five times until, in the end, the Bible Student could only moan, 'Yes.'"[381]

In order to undermine the steadfastness of the Bible Students, the SS henchmen picked out individual members from among them and used them to establish a precedent. For instance, in the spring of 1939 one of the SS block leaders in Sachsenhausen announced that he would show the Bible Students and their God Jehovah who really had the power. To this end, he told his SS comrades who shared his way of thinking that he would be able to persuade two twenty-year-old Bible Students to renounce their faith within ten days.[382] In the concentration camp, this particular SS block leader was considered to be a *Windhund* (a good-for-nothing). From day to day, with increasing intensity, he persecuted and tormented the two Bible Students. The fact that they survived the ten days was due only to a strategy that had been arranged by their fellow prisoners. These fellow prisoners cleverly maneuvered things so that the concentration camp administration found out that the block leader, who occasionally ordered certain items from the camp carpentry for private purposes, was actually involved in black-marketing.[383]

In one case, such a trial continued for several years and caused quite a stir throughout the Sachsenhausen concentration camp. Dr. Werner Koch, a Protestant pastor, who was imprisoned at Sachsenhausen between February 13, 1937, and December 1, 1938, reports about this case in his autobiography: "One of them, Rachuba by name, refused to take off his hat and stand at attention as the swastika was hoisted. 'This is idolatry,' he said, and he was right! Repeatedly, they strapped him on the rack and confined him to a darkened cell. However, he did not compromise. His physical capacity of resistance was a phenomenon that we admired as much as the SS did."[384] In this regard, former fellow prisoner Willy Henschel reports that "Sorge continued to torment the Bible Student Rachuba" until he was finally no longer able even to crawl. However, despite his condition, he "stood head and shoulders above his tormentors."[385]

The miner Johann Ludwig Rachuba was considered to be the "heart of the resistance" of the imprisoned Bible Students. On June 28, 1935, at the age of thirty-nine, he was arrested. The Gestapo immediately sent him to the Esterwegen concentration camp.[386] After that camp in the Emsland was dissolved in September 1936, Rachuba and the other prisoners were transferred to Sachsenhausen. The father of three children, who had already been seriously mistreated at the Esterwegen concentration camp, obviously had such extraordinary determination and courage that he presented a special challenge for the SS. At the special command isolation blocks in Sachsenhausen, Rachuba stubbornly refused to take off his hat when the "Horst Wessel Song" was played. The SS henchmen did everything possible to persuade this man to renounce his faith. In this regard, the court records of Sorge and

Schubert, whose court case took place at the Bonn Regional Court in 1958/59, make the following statement: "The concentration camp administration was convinced that quite a number of Bible Students would have reported for military service if Rachuba had signed the statement indicating his willingness to perform military service or if he had been killed. In this case, his example of resistance would no longer serve to be of encouragement for his fellow believers. The concentration camp administration did not appreciate the fact that only a few Bible Students agreed to perform military service because Himmler asked every time he visited the concentration camp for the number of people who had signed the statement."[387]

In order to destroy the willpower of Rachuba (and this—not his murder—was what would bring the desired results, according to the SS), the SS exposed him to a series of tortures. Rachuba's punishment record listed a total of twelve "official concentration camp penalties."[388] In addition, he was subjected to arbitrary acts of torture. For example, Johann Rachuba was forced to push a wooden wheelbarrow, fully loaded with sand, with his neck through the sand, while he was crawling on hands and knees. During this procedure, according to the report of his fellow believer Paul Buder, "he was kicked with boots wherever they landed."[389] In spite of it all, the miner remained steadfast and maintained his willpower. His determination demonstrated to all other prisoners that even the power of the SS had its limits. Nothing was able to destroy his unwavering faith. This made a deep impression, even on people of other prisoner groups: "After he had accepted twenty-five strokes with a club without groaning, Rachuba got up and walked to his block. This happened only in exceptional cases."[390]

An incident from 1938 demonstrates the brutal acts to which the SS henchmen resorted in some cases. When the former prisoner Otto Gede had to testify before the Soviet military tribunal that took place in Berlin-Pankow between October 23 and November 1, 1947, he stated, regarding the atrocities committed at the Sachsenhausen concentration camp:

> During the autumn of 1938 I worked as a bricklayer on the construction site of a sawmill. The crew of workers also included prisoners, some of whom were sectarians. One day, Sorge and the block leader Bugdalle came to the construction site. They ordered a group of prisoners to dig a hole in the ground as deep as a human being. After the prisoners had finished their job, Sorge and Bugdalle put a prisoner by the name of Rachuba into the hole. Thereafter, they filled it with dirt up to the neck of the man. When

only Rachuba's head was protruding, Sorge and Bugdalle began to ridicule him. With cruel amusement, they relieved themselves on the head and in the face of the prisoner. After this, Rachuba had to stay in the hole for about another hour. When they dug him out, he was still alive, but he could hardly keep himself on his feet.[391]

In 1940 Johann Rachuba was transferred to the subcamp in Wewelsburg. The mistreatments he had received in Sachsenhausen had left their marks: "His body was full of scars. He was no longer able to walk normally. He could only drag his legs. His muscles had been destroyed. But he was always happy. . . ."[392] On September 3, 1942, at the age of forty-two, Johann Rachuba died as a result of "physical weakness." The SS had finally succeeded in killing him, but they could not destroy his willpower.

The numerous persecutions of the SS proved to be especially difficult for older Bible Students and those in poor health. Prisoners who were not able to work and were not assigned to a labor detail were not allowed to stay in the prisoners' barracks or in the block. In Sachsenhausen, as in other concentration camps, prisoners who could not be used for work were put into so-called *Stehkommandos* (punishment by standing). Sometimes, these *Stehkommandos* included about 2,000 prisoners.[393] The prisoners were forced to stand the whole day outside of the barracks. Among the Bible Students at the Sachsenhausen concentration camp, quite a few were disabled war veterans from World War I. Some of them had artificial limbs. For these veterans, the *Stehkommandos* were a terrible torture: "Standing in one spot for an entire day, the entire day in the cold and in the heat, in the wind and in the rain. People dropped like flies."[394] Even though all prisoners were subjected to torture, the SS used the *Stehkommandos* especially for the purpose of ridiculing the Bible Students. They had to hold posters reading, "We are the idiots of Jehovah," "We are comedians of heaven," and the like. The Bible Students were ordered to march around in circles with these signs. SS officers and sometimes even the prisoner functionaries observed these scenes, sneering and poking fun at these aged, handicapped characters.[395]

This terrorizing of the Bible Students also occurred within the blocks. Very often, block leaders came in the middle of the night, mostly under the influence of alcohol, in order to "prove their courage" toward these "comedians of heaven." In such cases, the prisoners had to leave their three-story bunk beds and run several times around the barracks. Or they had to crawl under the few tables. In that case, the prisoners had to make sure that no hands or feet were sticking out because otherwise the SS henchmen would have stepped on them. The SS, not satisfied with this, made the prisoners, who were squeezed together, sing.[396] In the isolation blocks, Jehovah's Witnesses were also repeatedly tormented with regard to locker and bed arrangements. Even the prisoner functionaries joined in these acts of persecution, sometimes at the command of the SS, sometimes at their own initiative.[397] Punishment drills that the SS specified as "sports" were ordered for only minor offenses: "[These were] not sports in the proper sense. It rather amounted to murder, for many a prisoner, if he suffered from a heart ailment, remained dead on the ground. Three SS men commandeered: 'Up! Down! Roll!' till we had to vomit, and all that on ground that consisted of dusty, black coal cinder."[398]

During the especially harsh winter of 1939/40, with temperatures of 30 degrees below zero Celsius (almost 25 degrees below zero Fahrenheit), a considerable number of the prisoners in Sachsenhausen died. Between January and May 1940 alone, a total of 2,184 deaths were recorded.[399] During this period, Jehovah's Witnesses in the isolation blocks experienced the worst suffering. Many of them were literally destroyed. Dozens died of starvation and deprivation, and also because of complete exhaustion from hours of standing during roll call and *Stehkommandos.*

At the beginning of 1940, at least once (but according to other sources perhaps three or four times) the SS in Sachsenhausen tried to kill Bible Student prisoners by suffocation. For this purpose, they locked about twenty-five prisoners into a broom closet. These were tiny rooms of approximately 3 feet by 10.5 feet (about 1 meter by 3.5 meters). Near the top of the room was only a small window. The SS plugged the keyholes from the outside with paper. They sealed the window and the door with blankets. The door was kept closed for twelve hours. According to a statement by Paul Wauer, fifteen Jehovah's Witnesses did not survive this torture.[400] Willi Lehmbecker, a fellow believer, stated in this regard: "We could hear the people scream, but there was nothing we could do to help them."[401]

In order to force the Bible Student prisoners to renounce their religious beliefs and deny their faith in Jehovah, Bugdalle, Sorge, and the other SS henchmen performed acts of a most unimaginable brutality.[402] Their torture arsenal included drowning, running the gauntlet, forcing a prisoner to climb a tree and then shaking him down. It also included directing a water jet at a prisoner's heart until he died, inserting a water hose into body openings, and letting drenched prisoners stand outside until they froze to death.

As far as can be determined, a total of 130 Jehovah's Witnesses lost their lives during the winter of 1939/40 alone, that is, about one in four Bible Student prisoners.[403] During the same period, efforts at destroying Jehovah's Witnesses were also made at the Mauthausen concentration camp.[404] But the atrocities committed at the Sachsenhausen isolation blocks claimed the highest number of victims from among the Bible Student prisoners. Not only petty SS henchmen arbitrarily terrorized IBSA members; even the highest political leaders in the Third Reich considered it appropriate to take rigorous actions against people who refused military service, including Jehovah's Witnesses.

Gestapo Executions

At the beginning of the war, the SS—following orders—increased its efforts of persuading Jehovah's Witnesses liable for military service to sign statements indicating their willingness to perform military service. This was at a time when Reinhard Heydrich, the chief of the Security Police, had already seriously interfered with legal procedures of penal prosecution. As a final step in equipping the police with corresponding judicial authority, Heydrich decreed that executions could be carried out without prior court proceedings. As a result, the order of the Reichsführer SS took the place of legally imposed death penalties.

On September 3, 1939, Heydrich issued a secret interoffice decree that provided the leaders of all regional State Police offices with Regulations for Internal State Security during War (Grundsätze der inneren Staatssicherung während des Krieges). The first regulation stated: "Every attempt to undermine the unity and military strength of the German nation has to be ruthlessly suppressed."[405] Arrangements were made to take rapid police actions against "tendencies of defeatism": this called for immediate arrest, and prompt notification of the chief of the Security Police so that, "if necessary, the superior authorities can give appropriate instructions to eliminate such elements ruthlessly." By means of these regulations, the Gestapo had established its own method of resisting "demoralizing statements" and so-called war offenses, above and beyond the KSSVO. Subsequently, the Sachsenhausen concentration camp, located near Berlin, served as the Gestapo's place of execution.

On September 15, 1939, preparations were made for Sachsenhausen's first public execution.[406] The camp administration had "quietly" instructed the carpentry shop to build double walls from thick wooden planks.[407] The space between the walls was filled with sandbags serving as backstop. At the roll-call area, a dirt mound was made. On that Friday, the prisoners were dismissed from work earlier than usual. After evening roll call, which was done "in a great hurry," the prisoners were not allowed to leave. The Bible Students were called to the front. They were stationed in the first row right next to the execution wall. Two columns of SS guard detachments took position around the parade grounds. They uncovered their machine guns and brought them into a firing position.

The SS intended to use this opportunity to establish a precedent and put on a "big show." From the punishment block, a prisoner with his hands tied was brought forward. It was thirty-nine-year-old August Dickmann from Dinslaken. He had been sent to the Sachsenhausen concentration camp in October 1937 after having served his prison sentence, even though he had signed the statement.[408] In the concentration camp, Dickmann later requested to withdraw his signature. At the beginning of September, three days after the beginning of the war, he was summoned to the Gestapo political office, probably because of this withdrawal.[409] His wife had forwarded his military identification card, which had been sent to his home address, to the concentration camp. The Gestapo asked this Jehovah's Witness to agree to perform military service. Dickmann refused, just as he had told his fellow believers before he went to the political office that he "would not compromise again," no matter what the SS would do to him. But the SS did not end matters with merely beating him. He was not simply sent back to his block, according to the way such cases of interrogation were handled prior to the war. Instead, the SS sent this Jehovah's Witness to the punishment block and put him in solitary confinement. Considering the sequence of events, it can be assumed that the Gestapo reported this case to Berlin. There, the officials came to the conclusion that Dickmann's case was particularly suitable to carry out the "special action" outlined in the regulations for resisting war offenses. On September 15, 1939, this special action was supposed to be carried out at the Sachsenhausen concentration camp.

Dickmann was led to the wooden wall. Even in the face of death, the SS tried to discourage him. In front of the wall, he was repeatedly ordered back and forth, one step to the right, one step to the left. Then, the loudspeakers were turned on. Over the microphone, the concentration camp commanding officer, Hermann Baranowski, who meanwhile had been promoted to SS-Oberführer (Senior Leader) and, consequently, to the rank of general, read the execution order stating that

August Dickmann was to be executed on the charge of refusal to perform military service, upon orders by the Reichsführer SS. Thereafter, Baranowski commanded the condemned man: "Turn around." Harry Naujoks, a Communist from Hamburg and, at that time, senior block leader at Sachsenhausen, describes the following minute: "Then, the firing squad stepped forward. Upon command, they fired! August Dickmann collapsed. Baranowski gave his adjutant, Hauptsturmführer Höß, a sign. Höß hurried to the prisoner who was lying on the ground, pulled his pistol, and shot him in the head. Dickmann's body made one more move. Then it was over."[410] Four Bible Students, among them Heinrich Dickmann, the brother of the executed, had to put the dead body into the available coffin. Heinrich Dickmann had to nail the coffin shut.

After the execution, the majority of the prisoners were ordered to go to their barracks. The concentration camp community was horrified, despite the fact that death had long become part of life for the prisoners in Sachsenhausen. Perhaps for the first time there was a feeling of solidarity with Jehovah's Witnesses, even among the fellow prisoners who previously had regarded them only with a pitiful smile. The Bavarian physician and revolutionary Arthur Schinnagel reports about this event: "After they returned to the barracks, the prisoners stood together in groups, deeply moved. In simple terms, they showed their recognition for a fellow prisoner who had died for his religious convictions."[411]

The Bible Student prisoners had to stay at the roll-call area. Commanding officer Baranowski gave them a lecture and stated that they would experience the same fate if they refused to sign the statement and renounce their refusal to perform military service. According to Gustav Auschner, a fellow Jehovah's Witness, Baranowski threatened that they would be taken to the sandpit in groups of thirty or forty at a time and would be shot.[412] Then he gave orders that those who did not want to be executed should step forward. Silence followed. Finally, two Jehovah's Witnesses stepped forward—but not to sign. They informed the commanding officer that this experience had moved them to correct their mistake. They would like to withdraw their signature from the statement that they had signed during the previous year. Apparently, the precedent the SS had tried to establish accomplished just the opposite. According to several reports, Baranowski left the area roaring with rage.[413] Afterwards, these two Jehovah's Witnesses, as well as two of their fellow believers who were serving a long-term bunker penalty on the charge of refusal to give the Hitler salute, were strapped on the rack and flogged. On this day and the following days, all Bible Student prisoners "were hounded back and forth on the parade ground, kicked and beaten with sticks until we couldn't move anymore."[414] During the following days, one by one, they had to report to the political office. According to Heinrich Dickmann, the brother of the executed prisoner, two Gestapo officials came from Berlin specifically for the purpose of examining the "results" of this public execution. In response to his statement that he was a "Jehovah's Witness and would remain a Jehovah's Witness," these two Gestapo officials told Dickmann that he would be the next in line to be executed.[415]

Several Jehovah's Witnesses succumbed to the pressure of the interrogations and ultimately signed the statement.[416] But after this unsuccessful demonstration, the SS refrained from public executions of Jehovah's Witnesses who refused to perform military service.[417] In the following months and years, the Reichsführer SS occasionally ordered executions of IBSA members. The exact number of these executions cannot be determined. Most likely, about ten executions took place in Sachsenhausen.[418] However, these were executions of Jehovah's Witnesses who refused to follow the camp regulations (such as refusal to greet the SS officers in the required form, refusal to work in the armaments industry, etc.), or who refused to fulfill their labor service duties. The SS usually carried out these executions in a secluded area at the Sachsenhausen industrial court where they had special execution equipment.

The execution of August Dickmann was also announced through press reports and radio transmission. The press report by the Reichsführer SS and chief of the German police, which was transmitted through the German news agency, included the following statement: "Executions: . . . (2) August Dickmann from Dinslaken, born on Jan. 7, 1919, executed on Sep. 15, 1939, because of his refusal to fulfill his military duties. D. justified his refusal by stating that he was a 'Jehovah's Witness.' He was a fanatical adherent of the international sect of the Earnest Bible Students."[419]

The RJM also learned only through press reports that the SS and Gestapo had started to punish "military offenses" by means of out-of-court executions.[420] The first report about such an execution ordered by the Reichsführer SS was published in the newspapers on September 8, 1939. Immediately, the RJM requested information and an explanation from the leading police officials. These officials responded by stating that Hitler had personally provided the Reichsführer SS with the appropriate authorization. SS-Gruppenführer Reinhard Heydrich refused to give any further explanations in this regard. Instead, he suggested to the

RJM that he should "directly approach the Führer."[421] On the following day, the chief of the Wehrmacht requested an explanation from Hermann Göring, the Prussian prime minister and commander in chief of the air force, who stated that "death penalties can never be carried out without a verdict."[422] Now the legal authorities began to suspect that the SS and the leading police officials had arbitrarily extended their authority. A few days later, a press report announced the execution of Dickmann. This report included also information about a man who had been executed "on the charge of intentional arson and sabotage." As a result, Reich Minister of Justice Dr. Gürtner requested the head of the Reich chancellery to ask Hitler for an explanation. Gürtner had principally objected to the "rivalry for judicial authority" between the legal authorities and the police in cases involving the punishment of people from "nonoccupied territories of the German Reich" who had violated military laws. He had tacitly agreed to SS executions in Poland without prior court proceedings. Gürtner based his reconsideration mainly on the argument that the police did not need such special authorization since the legal authorities were certainly able to fulfill their responsibility by making use of the means at their disposal, particularly the special courts.[423] On October 14, 1939, Hitler instructed Reich Minister Hans-Heinrich Lammers, the head of the Reich chancellery, to inform the RJM that he had not provided the SS with a general authorization. The three executions to which Gürtner had objected, including the execution of August Dickmann, had been carried out on his personal orders. Even in the future, in particular cases, it would "be necessary for him to give such orders, since the courts (military and civil) were not able to meet the special requirements of war."[424]

Most certainly, in the RJM, this reproof from Hitler was considered to be unfounded and unjust. After all, the court proceedings against conscientious objectors produced the same results. Up until this point alone, that is, within the first six weeks of the war, the military courts had sentenced at least six Jehovah's Witnesses to death on the charge of "demoralization of the armed forces."[425]

Refusal to Produce Military Equipment

Despite these ruthless actions carried out with the approval of the Third Reich's highest leadership, despite the power demonstrations of the concentration camp commandant's headquarters and the cruel acts of SS terror, it was impossible to undermine the resistance of Jehovah's

Witnesses. As in Sachsenhausen, Bible Student prisoners were threatened during "special roll calls" at other concentration camps that they would be executed if they did not abandon their steadfast refusals. A few days after the beginning of the war, during roll call, the concentration camp commanding officer in Buchenwald, SS-Obersturmbannführer Arthur Rödl, asked Jehovah's Witnesses to agree to perform military service. Even though guards with machine guns had lined up and, according to reports, everything seemed to be prepared "for a mass execution," nobody responded.[426] The SS did not carry out their threat, but this uncompromising attitude resulted in sending the Bible Student prisoners to the quarry labor detail for disciplinary reasons. For a certain period of time, they were even excluded from receiving any medical treatment at the concentration camp infirmary.[427]

Such "special roll calls" took place repeatedly, and the SS always imposed severe punishments and deprivation of food.[428] In spite of these tortures, and even though the SS used subtle methods to persuade Jehovah's Witnesses to renounce their faith and to show by their signature that they would agree to join the Wehrmacht, only "very, very few [declarations] were ever signed."[429] For example, Jehovah's Witnesses had to read aloud, in front of everybody, letters from relatives that asked them to sign the statement. A chair, on which the particular prisoner had to stand, was brought to the roll-call area. After he finished reading, he was asked whether he was now willing to sign. Generally, the answer was no, and it was followed by insults and beatings. At the Mauthausen concentration camp, the camp administration even tried to persuade the assembled Bible Student prisoners with other methods. Hubert Mattischek reports:

> Bible texts were taken out of context and we had to read them. For instance, Matthew 22:21, where it states that we have to "pay Caesar what belongs to Caesar." Then the commanding officer accused us of violating the instructions of the Bible if we refused to submit to the requirements of Caesar (he referred to Hitler and the German authorities).[430]

On the occasion of "detention order reviews," inquiries from military registration offices, or any other reasons, the Bible Student prisoners were repeatedly called to the concentration camp commandant's office or the political office and requested to sign the statement.[431] Such requests were made at intervals of several months, sometimes after one or two years, and were viewed by Jehovah's Witnesses as "loyalty tests."

The interrogations accompanying these requests had the objective of persuading Jehovah's Witnesses to reject their religious beliefs as false teachings, which made it impossible for them to sign the statement. During the war, there was an additional factor that prohibited them from signing. The prisoners knew that, as soon as they were released, they could be drafted into the Wehrmacht if they were eligible for military service. Since they would not take up arms, they were aware of the fact that the signature could possibly be their death warrant.[432] From this aspect alone, they realized that signing the statement would not bring them "freedom." In the concentration camp, on the other hand, they had the comfort of knowing that their God Jehovah would ultimately deliver them from pain and suffering if they remained faithful. In addition, peer pressure, social environment, fear of losing the close association with their fellow believers, and the fear of losing their heavenly reward greatly contributed to the decision not to sign the statement. One Jehovah's Witness put his feelings of that time into the following words: "If I have to die, well, then I must die: But I will not sign. I thought of Queen Esther, who said, 'If I perish, I perish.' I realized that, if I signed, I would have lost all my happiness."[433]

In the majority of cases, the SS efforts to persuade Jehovah's Witnesses to renounce their faith failed almost completely. This was also due to the fact that the Gestapo subjected Jehovah's Witnesses to a considerable period of surveillance to confirm the "reliability" of their statements before they would issue a release from imprisonment.[434] According to the recollections of Rudolf Höß, the Reichsführer SS "kept people imprisoned" to "determine whether they had sincerely and truly renounced their religious convictions."[435] And this surveillance greatly reduced the willingness of the prisoners to sign. In this regard, the Jewish Buchenwald prisoner Benedikt Kautsky states in his report about the "interrogation sessions" of Jehovah's Witnesses: "On one occasion during the war, the SS made a special effort to persuade [Jehovah's Witnesses]. As a result, a considerable number, I think about thirty of the more than four hundred, of especially younger ones signed [the statement]. Immediately, the others rejected these disloyal ones. Soon, it became apparent that the denial of their convictions was not even worth it: only a small number of those who had signed were released. With this action, the SS condemned any future attempts in this regard to failure."[436]

Those Bible Student prisoners who signed the statements, even with guilty consciences, usually did so under extreme pressure. Consequently, they remained insecure and were also later exposed to great psychological pressure. The SS officers took advantage of this situation and used these Bible Students as "examples" for their fellow believers. In the roll-call area, for example, they had to announce publicly that they had actually given their signature.

Those who had signed the statement were viewed by their fellow believers as apostate and disloyal. Consequently, they faced "disfellowshipment," a term used by Jehovah's Witnesses for expelling a person from their group. But if they were able to explain their actions and showed repentance by withdrawing their signature, they were also accepted back into the community of Jehovah's Witnesses. And so, according to reports, many of those who had signed the statement decided after a short period of time to withdraw their signatures at the political office.[437] Rudolf Höß made the following statement: "The abjurers were berated by their brother and sister Witnesses for their disloyalty to Jehovah. Many of the abjurers, especially among the women, later felt remorse and repudiated their signatures. The constant moral pressure was too great. It was quite impossible to shake their faith, and even those who had abjured still wished to remain completely loyal to their beliefs, even though they had broken away from their spiritual community."[438]

The refusal of Jehovah's Witnesses to renounce their faith also included a principal refusal of all actions that were prohibited according to their religious beliefs. Therefore, when, from 1942 on, the concentration camps became increasingly involved in the production of armaments, Jehovah's Witnesses were exposed to further serious difficulties.[439] The SS interpreted their refusal to support the war effort as refusal to work. For such refusals, concentration camp prisoners received serious penalties, including the death penalty. In March 1943 the Buchenwald camp was involved in the production of the automatic assault weapon "K 43" and gun carriages for anti-aircraft weapons. The production took place at the Gustloff Factory, which had been in the process of construction since the previous summer. However, the Bible Student prisoners deployed for this duty refused to take up work. The SS imposed on them various camp punishments, such as twenty-five strokes strapped on the rack or work in a punishment battalion. But despite these punishments, by far the majority of Jehovah's Witnesses could not be forced to do this kind of work. The strictly organized Bible Student group in Buchenwald carefully tried to avoid, even to the smallest degree, weakening their unity and resistance to the armament production. In 1945, after their liberation from Buchenwald, Jehovah's Witnesses made a declaration that states: "A few among us, who feared being beaten or killed by the willing henchmen of the devil, accepted the work. As a result, they were immediately expelled from the community of this neutral people."[440]

The group members were expected to show unreserved obedience to the commandments of the Bible. A Jehovah's Witness who was sent to Buchenwald in November 1942 after he had served a prison sentence of several years states that he was initially assigned to work at a labor detail for sewage disposal. Later, he was assigned to the Gustloff Factory to do welding work. However, the Bible Student group admonished him to refuse categorically any work related to armament production. The prisoner, who was not yet familiar with concentration camp conditions, was apparently not aware of the consequences of such a step. He reports: "Since I was a Bible Student, the group required of me to refuse this work, regardless of the consequences . . . I was not aware of the danger. Since all of them were long-term prisoners I trusted their judgment."[441] Upon arrival at the factory, this Jehovah's Witness refused to take up the assigned work. Consequently, he was sent back to the concentration camp with the comment, "refused work in armament production." At the camp, he was handed over to the commanding officer in charge of the labor details with the remark, "this is the lazy dog that refused to work at the Gustloff Factory." In response, he was simply told that he would be hanged. At first, he had to stand at the camp gate. While he stood there completely panic-stricken, another Bible Student, used as a messenger, delivered orders to him that he should report to the "work statistics" department to receive his next work assignment. Describing his feelings, this Jehovah's Witness later stated: "I thought I was dreaming. I still heard the messenger say, we all have been watching you—you made it."

Finally, the SS had no choice but to accept the refusal of Jehovah's Witnesses to work in armament production. They assigned these prisoners to other labor details, generally to the craftsmen labor details in the concentration camp workshops.[442] While the Bible Student prisoners generally agreed that the Bible prohibited a Christian from producing weapons and ammunition, the question of where to draw the line in their refusal of "war-related services" caused a serious controversy among them.[443] Those from among them who were more "moderate" in their viewpoints considered only the immediate production of war equipment designed for killing as "work supporting the war." For the more radical ones such work also included other activities that had to be refused for religious reasons. Such a conflict arose, for instance, when the Bible Students learned that the skiing boards that were produced in one of the workshops at the Buchenwald concentration camp were to be sent to the soldiers of the Wehrmacht divisions that had been stranded in the Russian winter. Consequently, Willi Töllner, the leader of the Bible Student group in Buchenwald, declared that Jehovah's Witnesses assigned to the workshops also had to refuse this kind of work, since the skis belonged to the equipment of the troops and, consequently, had to be considered as war equipment.

The majority of Jehovah's Witnesses willingly accepted this decision. However, a small group from among them did not agree with Willi Töllner's viewpoint. They reasoned that nobody could kill people with skis. To them there was a difference between producing skis or being involved in the production of grenades. To refuse this kind of work would unnecessarily provoke punitive action from the SS that should be avoided, especially for the sake of their sick and weak fellow believers. Moreover, they argued that they should be allowed to follow their own consciences and not those of others. The small group of Jehovah's Witnesses who supported this viewpoint accepted the work of producing skis. But, when the group of Jehovah's Witnesses who had adopted this minority viewpoint refused to stop working in this workshop, they were immediately expelled from the Buchenwald Bible Student group, based on their "unbiblical" attitude. Another reason for this severe response might have been that the behavior of this minority indicated that they no longer "submitted to the leadership of Brother Töllner," which was required according to the "theocratic rule."

As in no other concentration camp, Brother Willi Töllner, a persuasive leadership figure, determined the lives of the Buchenwald Bible Student group. Even prisoners from other prisoner groups were amazed about his "speaking skills."[444] From the end of 1937 on, Töllner secretly delivered discourses and sermons in the concentration camp. For many Jehovah's Witnesses he became an idol, "the wonder of Buchenwald."[445] Based on the conception that Jehovah's Witnesses had to form a united front against Satan's world, Töllner gave the Bible Student group a strictly hierarchical structure. He required compliance from the various members. Under concentration camp conditions, this internal structure certainly had its advantages. By building a united front, the Buchenwald Bible Student group was relatively successful in holding its ground. It was also able to organize underground activities (such as conducting secret meetings and producing copies of Bible Student publications). However, this group of almost 400 Jehovah's Witnesses who supported

Töllner strictly excluded the disfellowshipped minority from any of their activities. They were considered as "enemies of the Kingdom" who had to be avoided by the "faithful ones." This small group of Jehovah's Witnesses, which also included several IBSA functionaries, was completely excluded from the solidarity of the Bible Student group—and this action represented a serious test for them. One of them describes his feelings during that period as follows: "When I realized that I too had been disfellowshipped I was so spiritually shaken and depressed that I asked myself how such a thing was possible. . . . I often got down on my knees and prayed to Jehovah that he should give me a sign. I asked myself if I were to blame for the situation and whether he too had disfellowshipped me. I had a Bible and I would read in it in the dim light and I found a great deal of comfort in the thought that this was coming upon me as a test, otherwise I would have already been destroyed, for this being cut off from the brothers was a tremendous pain."[446] This division within the Bible Student group at the Buchenwald concentration camp lasted until the end of the war, and no other concentration camp was exposed to such an extreme situation. The groups at the other concentration camps also had their tensions and controversies involving the question of what kind of work they had to refuse because it supported the war. But these controversies did not result in open and lasting divisions.

A similar radical position was adopted by the female Bible Students at the Ravensbrück concentration camp. They too refused to perform any kind of work that, in their opinion, supported the war. The women who were assigned to work in the sewing room determinedly refused to sew uniforms for the Waffen SS (armed divisions of the SS).[447] On another occasion, they were told to sew pouches according to a certain pattern. Consequently, they assembled with their fellow believers in their dormitory and discussed what position they should take in the matter. As a result, the almost four hundred Bible Students occupying Block 17 at the Ravensbrück concentration camp unanimously decided to refuse the work. They assumed, not without good reason, that these pouches would not be used to store sewing materials but were actually made for military purposes, to store ammunition supplies.[448] The SS responded to their refusal by imposing the most serious punishments. They confined several women in a single cell in the bunker of the punishment block. For three weeks, they were subjected to conditions of so-called intensified detention. Only once every four days did they receive a bowl of soup. The Ravensbrück Bible Students also refused to unload bales of straw for the Wehrmacht horses, just as they refused to put together first-aid boxes.[449] Nanda Herbersmann, who was arrested and sent to Ravensbrück because of her collaboration with a dissident Jesuit priest, reports about a different refusal action and its consequences:

> Reflecting on one particular day in the camp puts me into a rage, even to this day. I clench my fists in indignation. It all happened during the summer. The whole block was assigned . . . to build an air-raid shelter. The dreadful commanding officer Kögel deliberately assigned the Bible Students for this work because he knew that their teachings prohibit any kind of work that supported the war. He was determined to force them to do this work. However, all of them firmly refused to follow his orders. The commanding officer was furious. Consequently, he ordered that each Bible Student should be punished with ten strokes with a club. All of them had to line up to receive their punishment. I can still picture this procession of mostly dear old women. . . . They were driven like cattle to the slaughter—in this case, to the rack. They were strapped on the rack. . . . Then it happened, one by one. . . . They, however, prayed, silently and faithfully. Courageously they stood their ground, bravely accepting the ten strokes in reflection of their "faith." When they afterwards returned from the bunker of the punishment block, they tried to keep posture, as much as they could. Many of them could move only slowly, their maltreated old bodies bent and aching with pain. Several of these women were sixty years and older. . . . Some of these old women did not survive the beatings.[450]

From 1940 on, the political prisoner Margarete Buber-Neumann was block leader in one of the Bible Student barracks in Ravensbrück. She reports that one day there were "heated discussions in the block" involving the refusal to do work that would support the war.[451] The *Angora-Zucht* (rabbit tending) labor detail stopped working because the Bible Students assigned to this labor detail had found out that the wool of the rabbits was used for military purposes (lining of the jackets for the aircraft pilots).[452] On the same day, the *Kellerbruch* (horticultural work crew) labor detail also discontinued their work, since the harvested vegetables were sent to the SS military hospital. A total of approximately ninety Jehovah's Witnesses stopped working. As a punishment, the SS forced them to stand for three days and three nights in the courtyard of the prison wing. Then they were brought to the bunker of the punishment block and confined in darkened cells for forty days. In addition, they were punished with three times twenty-five strokes with a club. Despite this harsh punishment, the women did not abandon their refusal to work.[453]

At the other concentration camps as well, Jehovah's Witnesses withstood the most serious punishments rather than perform "any kind of work that would support the war." In Hohenlychen, a subcamp of Ravensbrück, a group of Bible Students had been assigned to cut down trees. When they learned from the guards that the wood was used to "support the war," they stopped working. Consequently, the SS commanding officer gave them the alternative of resuming their work or being shot to death. According to a report by Alois Moser, "all the brothers stood there as one 'solid front,'" and the Jehovah's Witness who was supervising this labor detail was sent back to the main camp.[454] The SS did not carry out the threatened penalty. Instead, the labor detail received a new assignment on a farm. Besides these united refusal actions, there were also several individuals who performed similar acts of refusal. For instance, in the Schirmeck (Alsace) concentration camp, which included only a small number of prisoners who were Jehovah's Witnesses, one female Bible Student refused to repair military clothing. In order to undermine her resistance, she was put into a prison cell. And again in this case, the SS was not able to achieve its goals. After seven months of solitary confinement, the woman was brought back into the camp.[455] In Sachsenhausen, one Jehovah's Witness was assigned to work in the painter's shop of the SS company Deutsche Ausrüstungswerke. According to a report by Wolfgang Szepansky, a former political prisoner, this Jehovah's Witness even "refused to paint war toys."[456]

Besides refusing certain kinds of work, fundamentalist Bible Students also refused other actions they considered to be incompatible with their consciences. At the beginning of 1942 the German prisoners at the Buchenwald concentration camp were told to donate their woolen materials to the German troops on the eastern front. Prisoners who possessed an additional sweater besides the one provided by the concentration camp were expected to give it up. The Bible Student prisoners refused to follow this request.[457] According to a report by Viktor Bruch, a Jehovah's Witness from Luxemburg, all of them, as one united group, refused "to give even a handkerchief in support of the war."[458] And so, on January 15, 1942, an extremely cold winter day, the Bible Student prisoners were punished with standing for hours in the roll-call area. The SS took away their sweaters, gloves, earmuffs, and even underwear. Leather shoes were confiscated. In return, the prisoners received heavy half-open clogs. In addition, these prisoners, who were now dressed only in drilling material uniforms (a coarse linen or cotton cloth with a diagonal weave), were forced to perform extra work: "Under flood lights we had to level a hilly area into a playing field. This was hard work after quitting time, with the soil frozen hard and with a temperature of minus 20 degrees Centigrade (minus 4 degrees Fahrenheit)."[459] After three weeks, the torture finally ended.

In Ravensbrück, several of the Bible Students responded to the serious punishments they had received because of their "refusal to work" at the *Angora-Zucht* and *Kellerbruch* labor details by refusing to report to roll call after their release from detention.[460] Margarete Buber-Neumann gives the following description about the consequences:

> They were distributed amongst all the blocks and the Block Seniors received orders to have them present at the roll-call under all circumstances. The more humane Block Leaders had their recalcitrants carried out, but many of these poor old women were dragged along the ground. They all refused to stand; many of them could not have stood even if they had wanted to. And there they sat hunched up like bundles of rags. The S.S. Camp Leader Redwitz seemed to take a delight in bullying and mocking these wretched women. He ordered them to stand up, and when they paid no attention, he began to bellow. It still had no effect, so then he ordered the "camp police" to fetch buckets of water and pour them over the squatting women.[461]

Demonstrations, such as the refusal to report to roll call, were extremely controversial among Jehovah's Witnesses.[462] This was especially the case with regard to actions that really worked to their disadvantage. Even though letter writing had become almost a mere farce for Jehovah's Witnesses because they were allowed to write only twenty-five words, some of the female Bible Students at Ravensbrück rejected this opportunity. They explained this rejection by stating that they would not put a stamp with a picture of the Führer on their letters.[463] One group of approximately twenty-five radical Bible Students under the leadership of Ilse Unterdörfer, a close fellow worker of former IBSA leader on the Reich level Erich Frost, refused to accept the blood sausage that was part of their daily food rations. With reference to the Mosaic Law ("none of you will consume blood"), they "drew up a list of the names of all those who refused to eat blood sausage and presented it in the office."[464] According to Margarete Buber-Neumann, "at first, the SS only laughed."[465] As a result, the SS not only withdrew the blood sausage but also refused to give these women any margarine. Blood sausage was generally served only once a week, on Sundays. But according to the Socialist Herta Brünen-Niederhellmann, because of the generally inadequate food rations, this "strange food strike" of those Bible Students who strictly followed this "biblical commandment" turned "into a catastrophe."[466]

The majority of Jehovah's Witnesses imprisoned at the concentration camps did not participate in such demonstrations. Even though almost all Bible Student prisoners steadfastly refused to work in armament production involving weapons or other war equipment, they generally considered any other actions of refusal as too "radical" and refused to participate in such actions. While the Bible Students at Ravensbrück refused to tend the rabbits because the wool was delivered to the Wehrmacht, their fellow believers at the Neuengamme concentration camp did not have any objection to this kind of work. For about three years, fifteen Bible Students there worked at the *Angora-Zucht* labor detail. They even used this location as a center for the "IBSA resistance activities" in Neuengamme. This particular detail was very secluded and supervised by a relatively reasonable SS-Scharführer. Moreover, only Bible Students were assigned to this labor detail at first. These were ideal conditions for conducting secret meetings and for hiding Bible Student publications. And since the 3,800 rabbits at this labor detail were fed with leftovers from the SS kitchen, Jehovah's Witnesses assigned to the detail were even able to find food for themselves that exceeded the quality of the food generally provided for the prisoners. Thus, they were able to support fellow believers who were in desperate need of nourishment.[467] A small group of Jehovah's Witnesses from the Neuengamme concentration camp also worked at the Carl Jastram engineering company. Since they refused to work in production (such as the assembly of submarine parts and aircraft construction, repair of motorboat engines), they received other job assignments (janitorial work, cleaning services, warehouse keepers).[468]

In addition to controversies involving Bible-based conduct, divisions sometimes resulted from differences in interpretation and understanding of various prophecies. In most cases, however, such divisions were only temporary. In mid-1937 speculations regarding the date for the beginning of the decisive battle of Armageddon resulted in splitting the Bible Student group at the Sachsenhausen concentration camp in various factions. For instance, one Jehovah's Witness believed that he could determine from the Bible the date for the destruction of Satan's forces and for the deliverance of the Bible Students from the concentration camps. Understandably, predictions about the destruction of the Hitler regime and the end of their persecution were of special interest for the concentration camp prisoners. The Protestant pastor and former concentration camp prisoner Dr. Werner Koch, who specifically emphasizes his rejection of the religious conceptions of Jehovah's Witnesses, reports his recollections of a specific day in June, on which "the Lord . . . [would] destroy the governments of the Third Reich and of all other nations":

> Over and over again, the Bible Students look to the sky, eagerly anticipating the coming events. Around noon, there are a few clouds—but nothing happens! During the afternoon, their enthusiasm begins to wane. In the evening, under the usual screams and shouts of the SS, they despondently march back to the camp. After evening roll call, their elders can be seen sitting together in heated discussions. The next morning, the problem is solved: Some figures from the Old and the New Testaments had been incorrectly combined. A mathematical error was to blame for miscalculating the date for the return of the Lord.[469]

Supported by Faith

An unwavering confidence in their religious beliefs, a unique community spirit, and a mutual spirit of solidarity provided Jehovah's Witnesses with the inner strength to remain true to their convictions even in the concentration camps. On this basis, they were able to continue in their struggle for self-assertion, despite SS torture. Fellow prisoners who later reported about Jehovah's Witnesses almost always emphasized the spirit of solidarity within this group.[470] To this end, the former Buchenwald prisoner Moritz Zahnwetzer states that the Bible Students at the concentration camp embraced one another in "a Christian bond of brotherly love. . . . this brotherly love was shown on a daily, even hourly, basis through acts of mutual support. And, in turn, it explains that only a relatively small number of people from among them lost their lives, lives which the inhumane circumstances in Buchenwald otherwise claimed."[471] Margarete Buber-Neumann generally makes rather critical comments about Jehovah's Witnesses, their religious beliefs, and their adherence to the Bible, which resulted in the fact that their actions did not always reflect what was sensible from a human standpoint (for instance, their relentless refusal "to sign the Bible-Student Declaration," even in the case of a seriously ill fellow believer). However, she recognizes that the behavior of the female Bible Students contributed to their survival in the concentration camp. To this end, Buber-Neumann acknowledges that "nothing was ever stolen on Block 3. There was no lying and no tale-bearing. Each of the women was not only highly conscientious personally, but held herself responsible for the well-being of the group as a whole.[472]

The spirit of solidarity among the Bible Student prisoners enabled them to develop collective strategies of survival, which, in turn, reduced the stresses of daily life in the concentration camps. The means by which the SS initially intended to isolate the Bible Students from other prisoners ultimately proved to be of advantage. Subsequent efforts to undermine this spirit of solidarity by intermingling them with other prisoners were no longer successful.

Jehovah's Witnesses took particularly good care of their sick and weak fellow believers, even sharing their food rations with them. As a result, they were able to restore people with serious illnesses back to health, even those who would not have survived had they been left to regular hospital treatment at the concentration camp. This spirit of solidarity proved to be especially vital during periods in which Jehovah's Witnesses were excluded from treatment at the concentration camp infirmary, for disciplinary reasons, and were denied access to any medical assistance: within the blocks, Jehovah's Witnesses organized their own medical assistance programs.[473]

The Bible Student groups developed very precise structures of solidarity. For instance, Jehovah's Witnesses formed "funds for the collection of money and packages." Once a month at the concentration camps, the Reich German prisoners and sometimes also the foreigners were allowed to receive a maximum amount of money (e.g., thirty Reichsmark) with which they could increase their meager food rations by buying additional food at the camp dining hall. However, most of the few food items available at the dining hall were of inferior quality and extremely overpriced by the SS. Moreover, some Jehovah's Witnesses came from poor families and, consequently, did not receive any money from home (or only very limited amounts), especially in cases where other family members were also imprisoned. Other Jehovah's Witnesses, on the other hand, received considerable financial support. Therefore, they formed community funds in the various blocks where they collected the incoming money.[474] The money was put into a box and entrusted to the care of a fellow believer. Equal amounts of money were distributed to the individual Bible Student prisoners. The amounts were kept small so that they would last for an extended period of time until more money came in. Apparently, this method of dividing and distributing the money worked well. Everybody always had as much or as little as the others. In this way, the Bible Student prisoners also protected themselves from the possible development of envy and resentment. Only an exceptionally small number from among Jehovah's Witnesses refused to contribute to this community fund because they belonged to the group of financially more affluent prisoners. But, after a while, even these people generally joined the arrangement. The loss of companionship with their fellow believers was more difficult to bear than the loss of their (relative) financial advantages.

From the autumn of 1942 on, the prisoners were allowed to receive food packages from their relatives.[475] In some concentration camps, Jehovah's Witnesses formed funds for the collection of these packages according to the model of the money funds. This required the forming of well-arranged structures of solidarity, as was the case with the Bible Student group at the Neuengamme concentration camp. Jehovah's Witnesses there who received packages did not keep them to themselves. They also did not hand them over for storage to the block leader (in which cases the block leader requested a percentage of the contents of the package in exchange for his services). Rather, the people who received the packages immediately submitted them to their fellow believers who carefully weighed each package and equally distributed the contents among those who "participated in the arrangement." Then, the goods were consumed. Jehovah's Witnesses in Neuengamme had "on almost every evening a piece of sausage, sometimes even a little butter, a small amount of jam, or a piece of cake."[476] The advantage of such arrangements was obvious. Since the goods were immediately distributed among the group, the poor ones had no reason to be envious and resentful toward those who received the packages. There was also no need to protect the goods against possible theft. And it was not necessary to make special arrangements to keep the foods from spoiling.

Jehovah's Witnesses also benefited from the fact that they attach great importance to orderliness and cleanliness, virtues that, under the difficult hygienic circumstances in the concentration camps, provided the only protection against infectious diseases and the much-dreaded fear of lice. Well-organized cleaning assignments and strict rules of hygiene contributed to the highest possible degree of cleanliness in their dormitories.[477] In this regard, Margarete Buber-Neumann, block leader for the Bible Students in Ravensbrück, states that, in this model of

cleanliness and neatness, everything "went like clockwork . . . the distribution of food, lights out, and all the rest of the prisoners' day."[478] Because of their meticulous observance of the camp regulations, the SS
used Jehovah's Witnesses as "model prisoners" per se, much to the surprise of fellow prisoners. In Ravensbrück, the SS used the Bible Student
barracks as "inspection blocks" when they showed the concentration
camp to various commissions of visitors.[479] In this respect, the SS sometimes even misused the orderliness and sincerity of Jehovah's Witnesses
in order to present a distorted picture of the actual conditions in NS
concentration camps. With the same determination with which Jehovah's Witnesses tried to observe the camp regulations (provided they did
not violate their religious principles), they resisted and objected to anything that contradicted their beliefs.

Jehovah's Witnesses did not collaborate with any other prisoner
group at the concentration camps. They refused to participate in, or cooperate with, the camp resistance initiated by the political prisoners.
Their religious beliefs also did not allow them to get involved in acts of
sabotage and politically motivated actions against the SS. Even in the
camps, the Bible Students tried to keep their Christian "neutrality."[480]
Moreover, the political prisoners who were involved in the camp resistance felt threatened by the Bible Students' determination to always
speak the truth. Nevertheless, individual contacts did come about.[481]
For instance, a Bible Student who was assigned as a housekeeper for the
family of an SS officer smuggled news about the war situation from a
foreign radio station into the Ravensbrück concentration camp.[482]

Despite the fact that many fellow prisoners rejected the religious
teachings of Jehovah's Witnesses, did not understand these teachings, or
viewed them with skepticism, they admired the spirit of unity and solidarity among them. The good example that the Bible Student groups
were setting sometimes had a powerful effect on other prisoners. Edgar
Kupfer-Koberwitz reports on a discussion he had with a young Jewish
fellow prisoner at the Neuengamme concentration camp, in 1940/41.
The Jewish prisoner had been recently transferred from Dachau and
had been assigned to the block the Jews shared with the Bible Students.[483] He expressed his admiration for their God-fearing attitude and
spirit of solidarity. The prisoner acknowledged their inner strength, the
harmony among them, and the spiritual richness that was reflected in
their eyes despite the physical deprivations. He describes his first encounter with Jehovah's Witnesses after his arrival in Neuengamme as
follows:

As soon as we Jews from Dachau came into the block, the other Jews began to hide everything they had so that they would not have to share with us. You are shaking your head, but it is true. Outside [of the concentration camp], we had been there for one another. But here, in a situation of life and death, everybody's first concern is to save himself, forgetting about the others. But imagine what the Bible Students were doing. At that time, they had to work very hard, repairing some water pipes. The weather was cold and they were standing all day long in ice-cold water. Nobody understood how they could endure this. They said Jehovah gives them the strength. They needed their bread desperately, just like we, because they were hungry. But what were they doing? They collected all the bread they had, took half of it for themselves, and the other half they gave to their fellow believers who had just arrived from Dachau. And they welcomed them and kissed them. Before they ate, they prayed. Afterwards, they all were satisfied and happy. They said that they were no longer hungry. You see, that is when I thought: These are the true Christians. This is how I had always imagined them.[484]

Even within the concentration camps, Jehovah's Witnesses spared no effort to win new adherents to their faith. Quite a few fellow prisoners—often, to their own dismay—became objects of these efforts of conversion.[485] Even in the face of death, the Bible Students still gave witness and proclaimed the message of the Bible to their fellow prisoners. For example, the SS had crowded together almost 5,000 "evacuated" prisoners from the Neuengamme concentration camp under the most terrible conditions on the *Cap Arcona*, a ship anchored in the Bay of Neustadt. When, on May 3, 1945, this ship went up in flames after being attacked by a British fighter-bomber, only a few hundred prisoners were able to escape. Among them was a thirty-three-year-old Jehovah's Witness from Düsseldorf, Ernst Schneider, a professional musician. For two hours, Schneider and two Russian prisoners held on to each other in the ice-cold water. Finally, by means of a rope, Alfred Knegendorf, a sailor from Hamburg and a fellow concentration camp prisoner and also a Jehovah's Witness, was able to pull the exhausted men onto the wreck of the ship that had meanwhile capsized and was protruding approximately twenty-one feet (about seven meters) out of the water.[486] After a short recovery period, Ernst Schneider began to talk to the two Russians who, like himself, had just escaped death, about the teachings of Jehovah's Witnesses and the hope of the peaceful Kingdom of God. A few days later, this enthusiastic Kingdom proclaimer wrote in his diary about the disaster: "As far as I could, despite my condition, I told them that they should submit to the Theocracy, the Kingdom of God, which is going to be established on this earth, if they wanted to receive the blessings of everlasting life on earth under perfect conditions of righteousness, prosperity, and happiness."[487]

The undeterred preaching activity of Jehovah's Witnesses was not without response. In the hopelessness of imprisonment at the concentration camps, the active proclamation of the coming of God's Kingdom was favorably received. Members of other prisoner groups began to join them. Quite a number of them, however, were motivated by the prospect of receiving the "advantages" of participating in the Bible Student community rather than being converted to the knowledge of the "true faith." Jehovah's Witnesses, on the other hand, did not simply accept verbal expressions of conversion. They were aware that participating in their community was appealing for others and that conversions for opportunistic purposes could cause problems. Therefore, they would observe these newly converted people for extended periods of time. As a result, many of these conversions did not last very long. Those who joined the Bible Students out of an inner conviction generally continued to be Jehovah's Witnesses even after the concentration camp gates opened in 1945.

The majority of people who were open-minded toward the Bible Student teachings were foreign prisoners, primarily Russians, and members of nonpolitical groups.[488] In a few cases, even a few Jewish prisoners converted to the religious beliefs of Jehovah's Witnesses.[489] Also, prisoners with Communist and atheist backgrounds, who usually distanced themselves from any religious ideologies, were so deeply impressed by the faith and community spirit of Jehovah's Witnesses that they felt drawn to them. Some of them ultimately even embraced the Bible Student teachings. The following report might illustrate the reasons for taking such a step, as well as the obstacles this involved.

On April 15, 1941, a few days after the German attack on Yugoslavia, Charlotte Tetzner, née Decker, the daughter of a Croatian Communist living in Germany, was arrested by the Gestapo, together with her parents.[490] Her father was sent to the Dachau concentration camp, and Charlotte and her mother were taken to Ravensbrück. There, she had her first encounter with Jehovah's Witnesses. Since Charlotte Tetzner had been raised in an atheistic household, she was not interested in "listening to any subjects related to religion." "Like the majority of concentration camp prisoners," she also initially scoffed at the Bible Student beliefs. In July 1941 Charlotte was informed that her father had been killed in Dachau. This drastically changed her attitude.[491] Her mother had a nervous breakdown; Charlotte Tetzner fell into a serious spiritual and mental crisis. She began to feel a need for religious direction. She reports: "Then, a change began to take place within me. I became open to serious discussions with the Witnesses. . . . Increasingly, I was overcome and filled with a faith that had nothing to do with sentimentality. I also realized the determination with which, particularly, this religious group (the only religious organization that was actually represented as a group because the churches and other sectarian groups were represented by only a few individual members) refused, even in the concentration camp, to perform any kind of work in support of the war, even work that was in some way related to military activities and the war."

As a political prisoner, Charlotte Tetzner had to wear the red patch. However, her relationship with the Bible Students continued to grow and, finally, she joined them. On December 15, 1941, Charlotte Tetzner and her mother were to be released. But to her surprise, senior supervisor Langefeld at the concentration camp administration asked her to sign the "statement of the Bible Students."[492] Spontaneously, twenty-one-year-old Charlotte Tetzner refused to sign the statement. As a result, she had to return her civilian clothing that had already been given to her in anticipation of her release, and she had to go back to the concentration camp. Her mother, on the other hand, was released.

The courageous act of determination of this young woman caused the SS camp administration to be caught between feelings of anger and a complete lack of understanding. This case presented a particular challenge to them. They did not expect such manifestation of faith from a prisoner in line for a release who was not even a nominal member of the Bible Students. During the following months, this young woman was repeatedly called to the commandant's headquarters, the political office (Gestapo), the senior supervisor, and the administrator for the labor details: "They tried to persuade me with special offers, threats, and mockeries." She was "continuously put under emotional pressure," but her newly acquired faith gave her the necessary strength. On one of Himmler's visits, she was personally taken to the Reichsführer SS. "They probably expected that this encounter would change my mind. However, I simply told him that, as long as he could not offer me anything better, I would stick to my faith."

Charlotte Tetzner had to remain in the concentration camp. She was assigned to work as a typist for the senior supervisor Maria Mandel.

At the beginning of 1942 Maria Mandel was transferred to the Auschwitz-Birkenau concentration camp for women where she was promoted to the position of concentration camp commanding officer. Charlotte Tetzner was also transferred to this camp. She arrived in Auschwitz with the first transport of prisoners, on March 26, 1942.[493] Tetzner was again put into the category of "political prisoners." However, she no longer considered this categorization as appropriate. She made a purple triangle for herself and put it on her prisoner's clothing.[494] By doing this, Charlotte Tetzner openly declared her solidarity with the Bible Students and her confession of being a Jehovah's Witness. This resulted in severe problems with the SS supervisors, but they finally gave up and allowed her to keep the purple triangle.[495]

The Bible Students' preaching efforts did not stop with the concentration camp guards and SS officers.[496] Such attempts often had grave consequences for the "Kingdom proclaimers": One Bible Student was assigned to do personal services for Karl Koch, the commanding officer of the Buchenwald concentration camp. When the Bible Student tried to share his religious beliefs with the family of the commanding officer, Ilse Koch asked her husband to have him punished "because of his misbehavior."[497] In some cases, though, Jehovah's Witnesses also came across people who showed interest. There were even cases in which SS officers agreed to read the Bible with them.[498] The following episode, which occurred at the Neuengamme concentration camp, shows that sometimes circumstances offered an opportunity for religious discussions with members of the SS. It also shows how important it was to take advantage of such situations. In the spring of 1943 Richard Rudolph was assigned as cook in the SS kitchen and developed a friendly relationship with an SS officer, Gustav Ahrend, who was in charge of the food supplies.[499] This relationship was not solely based on the daily contact between the two men and the respect the SS officer had developed for this reliable prisoner because he did not have to worry about any embezzlement. Apart from the fact that both men were bakers by profession, their friendship was based primarily on the fact that the SS officer showed an interest in the religious convictions of the Bible Student. Every morning, the Bible Student prisoner preached, in the privacy of the food-supply repository, to the former SS-Rottenführer (squad leader); Gustav Ahrend had recently returned from deployment on the Eastern Front and was now assigned as a guard at Neuengamme. Because of his previous war experiences, which had left a deep impression on him, Ahrend was receptive to the Bible's message of the coming Kingdom of God. Both men had to be very careful because "these discussions had to be kept secret from both SS officers as well as fellow prisoners."

One year later, this friendship protected Richard Rudolph from the most dire consequences. In the late summer of 1944 he was transferred for disciplinary reasons to the subcamp Salzgitter-Watenstedt. There, Rudolph, a long-term concentration camp prisoner and Jehovah's Witness, was assigned to supervise a labor detail of Soviet prisoners at the bomb-foundry of the Stahlwerke Braunschweig ("Reich Steelworks of Hermann Göring"). He categorically refused to accept the assignment, explaining to the SS officers that his religious convictions prohibited him from doing any work associated with ammunition production. The commanding officer of the subcamp, SS-Obersturmführer (senior Storm leader) Arnold Strippel, informed Rudolph that as soon as permission was granted, he would be executed on the charge of his refusal to work. For the time being, Rudolph was assigned to a punishment battalion. In the meantime, SS-Rottenführer Ahrend was also transferred from Neuengamme to the subcamp Salzgitter-Watenstedt and was put in charge of supervising the prisoners' kitchen. Somehow, he learned of the incident with Richard Rudolph. After a week or so, he was able to withdraw Rudolph from the punishment battalion and use him in the prisoners' kitchen. Several months later, Ahrend learned from the rapport officer that orders had been received to carry out the execution.[500] Ahrend then hid his protégé in the basement and arranged for incorrect information to be included in the work statistics stating that the prisoner had already left the camp in one of the transports. Some time later, he was able to hide Rudolph in a food-supply truck, and in this truck Rudolph finally did leave the camp. In retrospect, Rudolph emphasized that this SS officer risked his life for him and stated: "All I can say is that I have personally experienced that the name of Jehovah is indeed a strong tower."[501]

Jehovah's Witnesses considered the fact that people from other religions accepted the Bible Student teachings to be evidence of the fact that God had not abandoned this religious denomination, even in the concentration camps. He was still allowing "the Kingdom work to increase." Strong faith and community spirit gave Jehovah's Witnesses the needed strength to resist SS persecution and endure the hardships of the concentration camp. In 1942 conditions of daily life in the camps began to change. Jehovah's Witnesses consistently used these changes for the purpose of increasing their Bible Student activities.

Smuggling Publications and Gestapo Actions

Toward the middle years of the war, the conditions for Jehovah's Witnesses in the camps began to improve, and in many cases the Bible Students were given "special positions."[502] This, in turn, provided them with various opportunities to produce and distribute publications. They were able to organize their "preaching activity" even within the confines of the camps. Particularly in small labor details that had "special duties" and consisted only of Bible Students, such as the "sculptor's workshop" in Buchenwald[503] and the remaining command in the Wewelsburg concentration camp,[504] they were able to take up the prohibited production and duplication of Bible Student publications. At least temporarily, Jehovah's Witnesses were even able to establish a network of courier services between the different concentration camps.[505] To this end, Bible Students who were assigned to labor details outside of the camp forwarded not only personal letters but also biblical explanations and reports about the situation in the concentration camps to fellow believers via intermediaries, dead drops, and the like. Some of these writings were smuggled out for the purpose of strengthening relatives on the outside and informing them about the conditions inside the camps. Other writings, not intended for personal use, were copied, by hand or typewriter, and distributed by Jehovah's Witnesses who were at liberty. Subsequently, these writings were brought into other concentration camps by means of the same underground operations, only in reversed direction.[506]

Prior to that time, the groups in the various concentration camps had been, for the most part, isolated. A certain information flow took place only through the transfer of prisoners from one camp to another. As a result, the groups had developed their own viewpoints regarding a number of different issues. The information exchange resulted in clashes of those varying opinions, and this, in turn, resulted in controversies about religious issues, which were carried on between the concentration camps. This situation was probably one of the most unusual occurrences in the history of Jehovah's Witnesses, which certainly had its share of unusual situations. It might even be said that this was a "dispute about the truth" between the "radical" viewpoints of the Buchenwald Bible Student group under the leadership of Willi Töllner, on the one hand, and the predominantly "moderate" position of the Sachsenhausen Bible Student group under leadership of Erich Frost and the Neuengamme Bible Student group under leadership of Ernst Wauer, on the other hand.[507] The Buchenwald Bible Students were of the opinion that the "moderate" groups had abandoned their fearless confession of complete reliance on Jehovah in favor of an inappropriate willingness to compromise. The moderate groups in the Sachsenhausen and Neuengamme camps, on the other hand, held the viewpoint that their fellow believers in Buchenwald had a stubborn attitude and tried to elevate themselves above the *Watchtower*. They had made Töllner into an "idol" and worshiped him "like a saint."[508]

In 1943 the female Bible Students at Ravensbrück wrote information for Jehovah's Witnesses and their companions under the title "Briefe. Nachrichten für die Zeugen Jehovas und ihre Gefährten." "Associates of the theocratic organization" who were not imprisoned included supplementary explanations at the beginning and end of these letters. After mimeographing the letters, they distributed them, as well as possible, throughout the entire territory of the German Reich. The letters are a most remarkable testimony because they describe extensively the controversies involving religious issues that developed between different factions of the Bible Student group at the Ravensbrück concentration camp. Four different "categories" are mentioned: the "very extreme ones" who categorically refused to submit to any of the concentration camp regulations ("truly insane," is the commentary); those who thought that their radical actions could expedite the "coming of Armageddon" and whose concern of "not eating blood sausage became a principal issue"; those who thought that "their main problems were things of the past" because, in their opinion, the war raging in Europe was an "execution" of divine "judgment against the nations"; and, finally, those who confidently looked into the future, who "vigilantly and objectively" trusted, through all trials, "that Jehovah [would] not leave his people," in accordance with his promise, "God is faithful if we *are faithful*."[509] The Bible Students who belonged to this fourth category considered the disagreements as a work of Satan who had not left a stone unturned to lead "God's people" in the concentration camps away from true worship by means of hunger and persecution ("tribulation of the flesh") as well as temptations of the spirit. To a certain extent, they attributed these divisions to a lack of "spiritual food." Therefore, in view of the fact that they had been able to receive *Watchtower* issues through underground ways since the end of 1942, they were confident that Jehovah God would direct them again onto the right path and would reestablish their unity.

The activities of the Bible Student prisoners, their increasing contacts with the outside world, and their smuggling of publications did not remain completely unnoticed. Therefore, in September 1943, after several attempts by the Gestapo, the chief of the SS Central Office for Economy and Administration (WVHA), SS-Obergruppenführer (senior group leader) Oswald Pohl, reprimanded the concentration camp administrations that they had allowed the good work performance of Jehovah's Witnesses to neglect their primary responsibility of keeping Jehovah's Witnesses under surveillance. On September 10, 1943, the WVHA issued a central interoffice decree regarding the "anti-state propaganda of the Bible Students in the concentration camps and at their places of work." In this decree, Pohl summarized the current state of affairs as follows:

> Recently, we confiscated propaganda pamphlets of the sect of the International Bible Students that indicate that Bible Student prisoners at the concentration camps are able (1) to conduct, during the night, unsupervised meetings in the camps (the washing-rooms, etc.) (2) to carry on prohibited correspondence with Bible Student prisoners at other concentration camps, and (3) even to smuggle letters out of the camps to Bible Students who are still living in freedom and smuggle their replies back into the camps. These letters describe events inside the camps and the sufferings of the Bible Students that are full of lies and hatred against the [German] Reich. Apparently, the Bible Students can lie if it is to the advantage of their Jehovah-teachings. In the publications that have been forwarded to the appropriate department of the Central Office for Reich Security, the names of several concentration camps are listed in which this kind of letter smuggling has been possible. Regardless of whether or not these statements are true, the fact remains that the supervision of the Bible Students in the concentration camps has been neglected. This negligence in supervision and surveillance has certainly resulted from the fact that the Bible Students perform reliable and outstanding work wherever they are assigned. Therefore, I give instructions, as an experiment, to change this impossible situation by immediately separating the Bible Student prisoners at the concentration camps from one another. This separation should be performed in the way that two or three Bible Student prisoners are put into every block of other prisoners. By means of appropriate surveillance (police informers, etc.), it should be determined whether the Bible Student prisoners try to talk to other prisoners about their teachings or whether they try to continue their IBSA activities in any other ways. The first results in this regard should be submitted on October 15, 1943. Thereafter, reports should be made every three months.[510]

As a result of this decree, the Bible Student prisoners were now separated from one another in concentration camps where they had formerly been grouped together.[511] Jehovah's Witnesses at Neuengamme, one of the camps in which the Bible Students had increased their prohibited activities, were dispersed to various barracks at the end of 1943.[512] There were also other restrictions: The five or six Jehovah's Witnesses assigned to the same block were not allowed to sit together at one table; on Sundays, the only day where they did not have to work, the Bible Student prisoners had to be careful not to be seen together outside of their barracks. However, the Neuengamme concentration camp administration was not able, even with these measures, to counteract the development and successfully stop the Bible Student activities, as had been required by the superior authorities.

At Buchenwald, Jehovah's Witnesses were dispersed throughout the barracks of other prisoners in the middle of November 1943. Only forty of them remained in their former block, into which the SS also placed French prisoners. The new occupancy proved to be a failure for the SS because it had "undesirable" side effects: because of their "friendly relationships with these new arrivals," six Jehovah's Witnesses were immediately "reported on the charge of agitation" and were transferred for disciplinary reasons.[513] Neither the efforts of the SS to weaken the spirit of resistance and bond of union between the Bible Students by separating them at their workplaces nor isolation from fellow prisoners in the barracks produced the anticipated results. To the contrary, such situations only strengthened their bonds. Such separation and isolation had the objective of undermining the structures of their community and demoralizing the spirit of each individual member, but the Bible Students used this trial to gain new adherents to their beliefs and act as strangers who are "dispersed among other people."[514]

In reality, the SS officers in the concentration camps were not unfamiliar with this phenomenon. As early as 1939/40, the SS at the Dachau concentration camp realized that the communal housing of the Bible Students served as a tremendous strengthening aid for them. According to the report of one Jehovah's Witness, the SS made an "experiment by transferring some of the brothers to the barracks of the political prisoners."[515] The SS soon noticed that quite a few of the political prisoners "began to accept the truth." As a result, those Bible Student prisoners who had been housed with the political prisoners were again transferred back to their fellow believers (in the barracks 15, 17, and 19). One Jehovah's Witness reports: "What next? For several

months, an experiment was made by placing some political prisoners . . .
into our barracks. Then, they were removed again. Next, they tried to
put 'church leaders' into our barracks. And these were replaced with
habitual criminals . . . to see how we would deal with them."[516]

The whole experiment was a complete failure. In Dachau, Jehovah's
Witnesses conducted their Bible discussions almost every evening.[517] In
Gusen, they performed baptisms and celebrated the Lord's Supper in a
washing room, by candlelight.[518] In Ravensbrück, they made use of the
Christmas period and held a three-day "assembly" with Bible Students
from six different nations, comparable to the assemblies held when they
were free.[519] In Neuengamme, they formed Bible study groups with
interested people from different blocks.[520] Even in Buchenwald, Jehovah's Witnesses regularly held secret religious meetings. Two hundred
and fifty gathered at midnight to celebrate their Memorial. They even
used a rain barrel to perform secret baptisms.[521] The countermeasures
by the SS had not been able to prevent Jehovah's Witnesses from distributing their religious teachings even within the confines of the concentration camps. In some camps, the preaching activity was organized so
well that they were able to send out monthly service reports reporting
the "total amount of time they had spent evangelizing." In these reports,
the Bible Students even made a distinction between the amount of time
spent in witnessing to fellow prisoners and the "amount of time spent
preaching to members of the SS."[522]

The higher authorities considered it necessary to counteract the persistent preaching activity and various other underground activities with
more lasting measures. At the end of April/beginning of May 1944, the
Gestapo performed a large-scale police search of Jehovah's Witnesses in
the camps in order to put an end to these "prohibited activities," which
resulted in confiscations and punishment.

In these instances, Gestapo officials came "from Berlin, particularly
for the purpose of dealing the Bible Students in Neuengamme a major
blow."[523] They appeared suddenly, early in the morning. All Jehovah's
Witnesses were driven out to the roll-call area. They had to take off all
their clothes. Everything was searched. At the same time, a thorough
search was made of their living quarters and workplaces. The Gestapo
discovered Bible texts, *Watchtowers*, and articles from their journal *Consolation*. They piled up everything they found in front of the respective
prisoner in the roll-call area: Almost every prisoner had "a small pile."
The Gestapo officials put the evidence in large envelopes and identified
the envelopes with the name of the respective prisoner. Then, some

Jehovah's Witnesses were beaten "black and blue" with whips of steel. "Gate-restrictions" were imposed.[524] They were sent to punishment battalions, and two Bible Students were subsequently transferred to a subcamp for disciplinary reasons.

Gestapo actions like the one in Neuengamme were also performed at other concentration camps. At times, they were observed by prisoners from other prisoner groups. For instance, on April 28, 1944, Odd Nansen, a Sachsenhausen concentration camp prisoner from Norway, made the following entry in his diary: "It seems that something is going on with the Bible Students. There are quite a few of them in the camp. Apparently, they sent out a pamphlet indicating a particular date on which the Führer is supposed to die. Some of these pamphlets are suspected to be at this camp. The [Gestapo] is supposed to find them. Last night, as we marched into the camp, all Bible Students had to line up in the roll-call area and were searched. They had to take off all their clothes and everything was turned inside out." The Gestapo found several publications and the Bible Students "were beaten," but nothing else happened to them.[525]

In Buchenwald, the Gestapo action took place at the beginning of May 1944. In the roll-call area, "all Jehovah's Witnesses were thoroughly searched for anti-Nazi literature. Their work areas were likewise turned inside out. The results after days of waiting: "nothing."[526] At the Ravensbrück camp for women, the Gestapo action took place on May 3 and 4, 1944. Again, here the Gestapo took drastic measures. Fifteen of the "ringleaders" were sent to the dreaded punishment block.[527] According to reports from Jehovah's Witnesses, "before long the sisters were put back on their old jobs . . . after requests had been made by the responsible heads of the departments."[528] Ultimately, the SS's interest in making use of the "good qualities" of Jehovah's Witnesses, their excellent work performance, and the economic requirements of daily life in the camps predominated: eventually, concentration camp life went back to its normal routine.

Privileged Positions, Improved Conditions

In 1942 the situation of Jehovah's Witnesses in the concentration camps improved. Previously, they had been extensively exposed to SS terror, just like the Jews and homosexuals. Now, conditions became noticeably easier.[529] This change was part of a general development: Increasingly, the concentration camps became occupied with foreign prisoners. As a result, the status of non-Jewish German prisoners within the camp structure gained importance.[530] The Bible Students were a group of primarily (Reich) German prisoners. For the organization of their constantly expanding concentration camps, the SS required, quickly and increasingly, the support of experienced prisoners. Initially, they almost exclusively used German prisoners for positions of responsibility, such as the "prisoners' self administration" and "camp management." The camps were also more and more involved in the war economy and armament production, and the SS recognized the considerable potential of the working capacity of prisoners.[531] For prisoners with special skills that the SS could use, chances of survival improved tremendously.[532] For hundreds of thousands of concentration camp prisoners, on the other hand, who worked under the most extreme conditions with completely insufficient food supplies, this extensive labor meant their certain death.

The improved living conditions of the Bible Students were also based on specific characteristics involving the behavior patterns of this group. The majority of Jehovah's Witnesses were craftsmen and businessmen by occupation, and diligently and meticulously performed their assignments, provided these did not conflict with their religious principles.[533] As a result, the SS commanders of the various labor details highly valued the work performance of Jehovah's Witnesses. They considered them as accurate, reliable, and, most importantly, trustworthy workers.[534] In general, the SS did not need to fear that the Bible Students would become involved in dubious transactions or would plot against them.

Moreover, they had two traits that practically predestined them to be used for work in small outside labor details: They worked diligently without force and also without constant supervision. And, because of their religious convictions, they did not make any attempt to escape from the concentration camp.

Since Jehovah's Witnesses had completely subjected their lives under the authority of their God, Jehovah, they considered an escape from the concentration camp an act of rebellion against divine providence. This was closely related to their strong conviction that Jehovah permitted the serious persecution and difficulties in the concentration camps for a reason—in order to test his people. God's chosen people could not merely avoid this test; rather, they had to view it as a challenge they were supposed to meet. They were also confident that Jehovah God would soon establish his Kingdom over all the earth, open the gates of concentration camps and prisons, and lead his people into freedom.[535]

If, therefore, someone took matters into his own hands or attempted to flee, he actually demonstrated, in the opinion of the majority of Jehovah's Witnesses, a lack of trust in Jehovah. Moreover, the escape of one individual would jeopardize the well-being of the entire group of Bible Student prisoners, especially since they had been able to improve their status within the concentration camp by loyally fulfilling their work assignments.

And so there was no reason to fear that Bible Student prisoners would make an attempt to flee.[536] The SS used them frequently to work in outside labor details that were difficult to supervise (such as farming, transportation, loading and unloading, etc.).[537] In many cases, such labor details included only Jehovah's Witnesses, particularly since the SS tried to separate Jehovah's Witnesses from the rest of the prisoners even in their work assignments. In this way, they could restrict Jehovah's Witnesses from preaching to their fellow prisoners. Gradually, the SS reduced the number of guards for "labor details consisting of Bible Students." At Neuengamme, the number of guards supervising Bible Student labor details assigned to mow grass outside of the camp was reduced to one guard for every five prisoners. At the same time, the SS assigned one guard for every two prisoners in labor details consisting of non-Witness prisoners.[538]

In most cases, the work at these small labor details was very difficult, and the prisoners were exposed to the varying moods of their guards. But such deployments often provided opportunities to bring in some additional food.[539]

At Neuengamme, for example, Jehovah's Witnesses assigned to the *Entkrautungskommando* (drainage ditch cleaning detail) took advantage of the fact that fish got caught in the accumulating sludge when they cleaned the ditches with rakes and hooks. The prisoners knew how to use the fish in order to improve their food rations: "At noon, a cart with thermos containers full of watery soup was brought to our workplaces. We put some pieces of fish on our plates before we accepted the warm soup. We thanked God for this [provision]. Even though the fish was not fully cooked, the cabbage or rutabaga soup gave us at least some strength."[540]

These smaller labor details were especially interested in achieving good results; particularly in those that did preliminary work for small farms and industrial businesses, it was not uncommon for good work to be rewarded. Such cases included situations where the commanding officers used prisoner labor for private purposes (such as chopping wood or building garden sheds).[541] A labor detail consisting of twenty Bible Student prisoners, who were assigned to mow grass, had to build a shed for their commanding officer. After they were finished, the SS officer showed his appreciation by giving them, once a week, a sack of potatoes to supplement their food ration.[542]

Even SS officers in higher positions used Bible Student prisoners for special assignments. As early as 1938, Hans Loritz, the commanding officer of the Dachau concentration camp, had Jehovah's Witnesses work for him privately. One day, they were unexpectedly called to the roll-call area, and nine people were selected for a special work assignment.[543] Together with a political prisoner who was assigned as supervisor and several SS officers, these nine Bible Students were taken on a truck to Lake Wolfgang in Salzkammergut (Austria). There, close to St. Gilden, Loritz had bought a plot of land. He wanted to build a mansion there with a boathouse and landing pier. The prisoners had to do the preparatory work (clearing the area, excavating dirt, transporting stone blocks, laying a concrete foundation) under very difficult conditions. They were housed in a nearby prison. In January 1940 Loritz became the commanding officer of the Sachsenhausen concentration camp, replacing Hermann Baranowski. However, this did not stop him from continuing the construction work on his mansion. He now also used Bible Student prisoners from the Sachsenhausen concentration camp, increasing the labor detail at Lake Wolfgang to about twenty-five prisoners.[544]

SS-Obersturmbannführer Arthur Liebehenschel, the leader of Department D at the WVHA, also had a building project at Lake Wolfgang. According to Paul Wauer, a Bible Student prisoner from Sachsenhausen, he used a group of fifteen prisoners at this building site.[545]

Even the SS organization, as a whole, took advantage of the fact that it was safe to use Bible Student prisoners. From 1940 on, Jehovah's Witnesses worked at the Bayrischzell SS Mountain Hotel and Holiday Resort in Sudelfeld am Wendelstein, improving the parks and gardens of the facility.[546] In 1940/41 this detail consisted of between thirty and fifty Jehovah's Witnesses, as well as several political prisoners. For housing, they were cramped together in a small garage complex. On the other hand, the food provisions at this labor detail were described to be adequate. Until 1945, various groups of Bible Students were used to work there, and later on, even the living quarters improved. Willi Lehmbecker, who was transferred from Sachsenhausen to Obersudelfeld during the second half of 1943, reports: "Even though we brothers were in captivity, we were housed in a small hut at the mountainside, with only a few guards. We had considerable freedom of movement. But all the brothers had to work extremely hard. . . . Before I arrived the brothers had built the road leading up the mountain to the hotel. It is beyond imagination to picture the sorrow and streams of tears that must have flowed during that period."[547]

A total of between thirty and fifty Jehovah's Witnesses had to work for a while at the SS Sanatorium Hohenlychen. During the final days of the war, the highest leaders of NSDAP and SS—Oswald Pohl, Albert Speer, Josef Goebbels, Himmler, and several times even Hitler himself— regularly visited this health resort, which was situated in a secluded area of the Uckermark, at Great Lychensee. They sought the peace and quiet of Hohenlychen in order to have contemplative conversations. The Bible Student prisoners were dressed in civilian clothing.[548]

Jehovah's Witnesses were also used at other SS facilities and party offices. Several IBSA prisoners from the Sachsenhausen concentration camp were assigned to a labor detail at the RSHA in Berlin-Lichterfelde, doing construction and craftsman work. A number of Jehovah's Witnesses from the Dachau concentration camp were also assigned to the labor detail working at the "Munich Reich chancellery."[549] In the spring of 1944, fifteen female Bible Students were assigned to the Hedin Institution for Inner-Asia, a Reich institution that was part of the SS department of *Ahnenerbe* (genealogical heritage) located at the Mittersill Fortress in the Pinzgau.[550]

Compared to conditions in the concentration camps in general, the Bible Student prisoners assigned to labor details at agricultural estates during the final days of the war had quite favorable conditions. They were primarily assigned to NS leaders and people who had special connections. As early as 1942, ten female Bible Students were assigned as housekeepers for the kitchen and greenhouse at the Hartzwalde estate of Dr. Felix Kersten, Himmler's personal physician.[551] In February 1944, fifteen Bible Student prisoners were assigned to the Jungfern-Breschan estate of Lina Heydrich, the widow of RSHA Chief Reinhard Heydrich, who had died in 1942.[552] At times, up to fifty Jehovah's Witnesses worked at the Comthurey estate in the immediate neighborhood of Ravensbrück. Comthurey was the country estate of Oswald Pohl, the chief of the SS and WVHA. When, in 1943/44, Alois Moser, together with a group of fellow believers, had to build a pigsty at Comthurey, only one SS officer was assigned to this labor detail as a guard: "Eventually, this single SS officer placed so much trust in the Bible Students that he allowed us on Sundays to go 'unguarded' into the forest to pick blueberries and blackberries. We each brought home our aluminum bowl filled with berries."[553]

In some cases, Bible Student prisoners were also sent individually to various farms. One Jehovah's Witness was assigned to work on a farm in Fridolfing (Upper Bavaria). In June 1943 Himmler had offered a farmer from Tristenau in Upper Bavaria a Bible Student prisoner to help him bring in the harvest.[554] Some agricultural estates and farms even requested Jehovah's Witnesses from the concentration camps for specific assignments. On June 2, 1943, the WVHA sent a telex to all concentration camp commanding officers, instructing them to report whether any of the "Bible Student prisoners had the skills to manage a farm."[555]

A number of Bible Students were assigned to the agricultural estates (concentration camp subcamps) under the management of the Deutsche Versuchsanstalt für Ernährung und Verpflegung GmbH, an institution that the SS had established in 1939.[556] Here, Jehovah's Witnesses generally worked together with prisoners from other prisoner groups. Only on smaller farms did labor details consist "only" of Bible Students. Farms connected to the research institute that deployed Jehovah's Witnesses included the Ravensbrück estate, the Werderhof estate (near the Stutthof concentration camp), and the fish-farming facilities at Unterfahlheim (near Munich). A total of approximately three thousand prisoners were assigned to the larger agricultural estates connected to the Auschwitz concentration camp.[557] There, Jehovah's Witnesses worked at the Raisko estate (department of plant cultivation at the Kaiser Wilhelm Institute) and at the Harmense poultry farm.[558] Even Jehovah's Witnesses from Mauthausen worked at agricultural estates located outside the concentration camp. These included the Rumbler, Fechter, Fuchsberger, and Preller farms. At St. Lambrecht, a large agricultural estate that until 1942 was under supervision of the Dachau concentration camp, female Bible Students were used "to cook for the farm workers."[559]

Even for the Bible Students who were not deployed at special labor details outside of the camp, conditions increasingly improved, although, inside the camps, they were still exposed to the arbitrariness of the SS. Numerous Jehovah's Witnesses were given "privileged positions" and so-called trust positions.[560] Such positions were especially desired. Prisoners in these positions worked as specialized craftsmen, clerks for SS officers, and even as SS servants (barbers, caretakers, and cooks).[561] As barbers for SS officers, Jehovah's Witnesses were already being used as early as the mid-1930s. A Bible Student reports: "The commanding officer and other high-ranking officials assigned . . . a Jehovah's Witness to shave them because they believed that Jehovah's Witnesses would not use such occasions to cut their throats."[562]

Increasingly, the SS used Jehovah's Witnesses for other sensitive special assignments. At Buchenwald, for example, Bible Students worked at the photographic laboratory.[563] They also worked in the "sculptor's workshop," under special supervision of Karl Koch, the concentration camp commanding officer.[564] At the punishment block (camp prison) of the Ravensbrück concentration camp, the SS deployed female Bible Students as caretakers.[565] In 1943 one Bible Student from Ravensbrück was transferred for a special assignment to Buchenwald. She was assigned to see to the needs of Princess Mafalda of Hessen, the daughter of the Italian King Victor Emmanuel III, who was under arrest in Buchenwald.[566] For prominent prisoners (so-called special prisoners), Buchenwald, like other concentration camps, provided special living quarters outside of the camp. At this particular living quarter, officially called "Fichtenhain Settlement," other Jehovah's Witnesses also worked as caretakers or servants. At the "Falkenhof Settlement," the Gestapo detained the former French prime minister, Léon Blum, and the former minister of the interior, Georg Mandel. There, the Bible Student prisoner Joachim Escher was assigned to care for the needs of these special prisoners—cleaning house, serving meals, and doing dishes.[567]

According to Rudolf Höß, the SS officers said female Jehovah's Witnesses "were very much in demand as servants in the homes of SS men with large families."[568] In the households of SS families, Jehovah's Witnesses not only performed cleaning jobs, which they were known to carry out with particular care, but they were also entrusted with meal preparation and childcare. With regard to the assignment of these highly esteemed housekeepers, the SS followed a strict hierarchical order of leadership. According to the "plan for the deployment of labor,"[569] in the autumn of 1944, fifteen Bible Students from Auschwitz were assigned to households of SS officers, including the Auschwitz medical doctor, Dr. Eduard Wirths, as well as Josef Kramer, the commanding officer of Auschwitz II (Birkenau). These SS officers, as well as nine other SS leaders, each had "only" one housekeeper. Concentration camp commanding officer Rudolf Höß and SS-Obersturmbannführer Dr. Joachim Caesar, the leader of the agricultural estates of the Auschwitz concentration camp (who had the same rank as Höß), each had two Bible Students as housekeepers. The commanding officer, Rudolf Höß, had only words of commendation for Jehovah's Witnesses assigned to

his household. To this end, his memoirs include the following statements: "My wife often said that she herself could not have seen to everything better than did these two women. The care that they bestowed on
the children, both big and small, was particularly touching. The children loved them as though they were members of the family. At first we
were afraid that they might try to save the children for Jehovah. But we
were wrong. They never talked to the children about religion. This was
really remarkable, considering their fanatical attitude."[570] Not all housekeepers fulfilled their assignments to full satisfaction: "There were other
wonderful beings among them. One of them worked for an SS officer,
doing everything that had to be done without needing to be told, but she
absolutely refused to clean his uniform, cap, or boots, or indeed even to
touch anything that had any connection with the military life."[571]

Officials from areas other than camp administrations also highly
esteemed the Bible Students as housekeepers. In 1943 selected prisoners
from Ravensbrück were assigned to families of SS leaders to serve as
nursemaids or cleaning ladies.[572] It almost seems as if, within a certain
salary bracket, the usual package of bonuses for the SS officers included, besides the necessary connections, the provision of a maid.[573]
Female Bible Students were assigned, for instance, to the households of
Oswald Pohl, the chief of the WVHA; SS-Obergruppenführer Dr.
Hans Kammler, the leader of Department C (building department) at
the WVHA; and SS-Sturmbannführer (Storm Battalion Leader) Karl
Mummenthey, the leader of Department W I (building materials) at the
WVHA.[574]

During the final years of the war, Jehovah's Witnesses were also often
entrusted with positions involving the "prisoners' self-administration."
These were primarily positions as "foremen" and "supervisors." In
only a few cases, Jehovah's Witnesses also occupied positions as "block
leaders."[575]

Members of other prisoner groups report that Jehovah's Witnesses
generally handled positions of authority in an "exemplary" manner.[576]
Lauritz G. Damgaard, who was imprisoned at Neuengamme, worked in
a greenhouse labor detail under the supervision of a Jehovah's Witness
and had pleasant memories of him: "August, the Bible Student, was one
of the older ones in the camp. This seniority, as well as the fact that he
was German, entitled him to the position of foreman. From an NS
viewpoint, he was a miserable foreman. However, in all other respects,
he was an excellent foreman and a great person. He did not beat us and
did not use any force. He even protected us from the SS and superior

foremen from among the prisoners, with whom he, however, had a good relationship."[577] Such individual experiences can be substantiated through the observations of Bruno Bettelheim, a psychoanalyst and prisoner at Dachau and Auschwitz. His report also mentions the reasons for which the SS preferred the Bible Students even as supervisors: "When they were appointed as supervisors, and the SS officers gave them a certain order, they insisted that the prisoners do a good job and also did the work in the allotted time. Granted, [the Bible Students] were the only group of prisoners that never insulted or abused other prisoners (to the contrary, they generally treated their fellow prisoners very respectfully). Still, the SS officers preferred them as supervisors because they were diligent workers, skillful, and reserved."[578]

Observations and Ideas of the Reichsführer SS

On January 6, 1943, after he had personally given this subject much thought, the Reichsführer SS gave orders to assign female Bible Student prisoners to SS households.[579] According to his own statements, Himmler had "an opportunity to study the matter of the Earnest Bible Students from all angles" on his frequent visits to the Hartzwalde agricultural estate, which he had given to his personal physician and masseur, the Finnish medical officer Dr. Felix Kersten. The estate was located approximately sixteen miles (twenty-five kilometers) north of Oranienburg and included ten Bible Students who worked there as agricultural assistants and housekeepers.[580] Himmler sent an extensive report to the two top leaders of the appropriate SS authorities—SS-Obergruppenführer Oswald Pohl, the chief of the WVHA; and SS-Gruppenführer Heinrich Müller, the Gestapo chief of the RSHA—informing them about his observations.[581] This report clearly reflects the beginning of a change in Himmler's attitude toward Jehovah's Witnesses.[582] Himmler first reports the statements of Mrs. Kersten, who had told him "that she had never had such good, willing, faithful, and obedient personnel as these ten women." The women were willing to accept any kind of work; they even worked in the evenings and on Sundays. Himmler showed honest admiration as he related the following episode: "One of the women once received 5.00 RM as a tip from a guest. She accepted the money since she did not want to cast aspersions upon the home, and later gave it to Mrs. Kersten, since it was prohibited to have money in the camp." In view of such honesty and conscientiousness, it is understandable that the highest leader of the SS was overcome with feelings of envy, because even though the SS considered themselves as the "elite of the German nation," this could not conceal the fact that in reality they were a group of corrupt people: "This completes my picture of the Bible Students. They are incredibly fanatical, willing people, ready to make sacrifices. If it were possible to put their fanaticism to work for Germany, or instill such fanaticism into our people during this period of war, then we would be stronger than ever before!" However, Himmler quickly added: "Of course, since they reject the war, we are not able to permit their teachings without running the risk of causing serious harm to Germany."

For Himmler it was "impossible to accept a refusal to perform military service during the present state of the [German] Reich" because this would "have unforeseeable consequences." Therefore, he informed Alfred Rosenberg (whom "the Führer had entrusted with the supervision of the mental and ideological education of the NSDAP"), with whom he had discussed the problem of the Bible Students, that he often sought personal discussion with these prisoners "in order to understand them better and possibly be able to persuade them."[583] His efforts remained ineffective since they responded "to all questions with memorized quotations, Bible quotations" which, in turn, were "of no use" to him.

As a result of these observations, Himmler realized that it required completely different strategies to handle the Bible Student issue: "Nothing is accomplished by punishing them, since they only talk about it afterward with enthusiasm. . . . Each punishment serves as a merit for the other world. That is why every true Bible Student will let himself be executed without hesitation. . . . Every confinement in the dungeon, every pang of hunger, every period of freezing, every punishment, every blow is a merit with Jehovah."[584] It seems that Himmler recognized that not even acts of terror could undermine the religious resistance of this group of active ones from among Jehovah's Witnesses in the concentration camps. Therefore, he gave the instruction "that all of the Bible Students be put to work—for example, farm work, which has nothing to do with war and all its madness. One can leave them unguarded if properly assigned; they will not run away. They can be given unsupervised jobs, they will prove to be the best administrators and workers." Himmler also suggested deploying the Bible Students in the "'Lebensborn homes' (homes assisting unmarried and married Nazi women to give birth anonymously), not as nurses, but as cooks, housekeepers, or in other capacities, such as the laundry."[585] Himmler also pointed to the possibility of assigning the Bible Students to private homes of families with several children. The women assigned to such homes should by no means wear prison garb. In these cases, even their prisoner status should actually be withdrawn. In this context, Himmler also addressed the issue of the reverse statements, which had been discussed for several months at the RSHA, apparently on his initiative. Most certainly, some of his remarks on this subject caused the officials at the Department for Sectarian Affairs to look at him in disbelief: "In all these cases where prisoners are partially free and have been assigned to such work we want to avoid written records or signatures and make such agreements with just a handshake."[586]

At outside labor details of the concentration camps and in positions of trust, Himmler's suggestions had, to a certain extent, already been put into practice. SS officers had long recognized the considerable practical value of Jehovah's Witnesses. Himmler's idea, however, did not originate from sentimental enthusiasm or humanitarian viewpoints. Instead, the proposed concessions (no punishment, no work in armament production, work assignments to privileged positions, concentration camp releases without the requirement to sign the statement) were the result of matter-of-fact calculations on how to get the greatest possible benefits for the SS and the German Reich. The objective was to utilize the positive characteristics of Jehovah's Witnesses for the interests of the state. Thus, Himmler began to consider the Bible Student issue more from a "practical" rather than an ideological standpoint.

At the Gestapo offices, however, these ideas were not accepted very positively. At the same time as the highest leader of the police in the German Reich contemplated the possibility of partially releasing Jehovah's Witnesses, the Gestapo officials made every effort (often unsuccessfully) to locate and arrest all active members of the IBSA groups, who had become especially active in the western and southern parts of Germany. They wanted to dispose of Jehovah's Witnesses by locking them up in prisons or detaining them behind the barbed-wire fences of the concentration camps.

It still took almost six months until Himmler finally received a response regarding a realization of his suggestions. On July 15, 1943, Ernst Kaltenbrunner, who had become the leader of the RSHA on January 30, 1943, replacing Reinhard Heydrich, who had been killed on June 5, 1942, by Czech patriots in Prague, sent his report to Himmler. Himmler received the report while he was staying at the *Feldkommandantur* (district military administrative headquarters). Kaltenbrunner stated that "the Bible Student prisoners were already used in SS households and

Lebensborn homes. However, a release of the prisoners had 'not yet taken place.'" About the concept of his office as to how to carry out Himmler's suggestions, Kaltenbrunner replied:

> In a few isolated cases, female Bible Students have been released merely on the basis of a handshake. These were cases in which both the concentration camp administration and the employer of the particular Bible Student could be certain that the prisoner would fulfill her promise that she had confirmed with a handshake. This promise involved that, irrespective of her religious convictions, she would no longer publicly talk about her religious beliefs or the teachings of the IBSA. . . . The decision of whether or not a Bible Student will be released merely on the basis of a handshake is made by the RSHA. The RSHA, in turn, receives an assessment of the concentration camp commanding officer and the employer after they carefully examined the environment in which the prisoner intends to live after her release.[587]

As is indicated by the restrictive wording, the new leader of the RSHA had some reservations about the suggestions of his Reichsführer.[588] The RSHA had observed that the current situation of war made the general public increasingly receptive for religious teachings and predictions of an imminent end of the world, "especially in rural areas." Kaltenbrunner did not want to take the concessions too far. If the released IBSA members would, contrary to their promise, make such proclamations, this could have serious consequences for the German Reich. After all, predictions about duration and end of the present world order were "the main activity of the IBSA," which they pursued "more fanatically than any other religious group." Kaltenbrunner then requested that more concern be shown for the policy of state security. He suggested that "the prisoners should not immediately be informed about a possible release. A release should take place only if the Bible Student makes such a request on her own."[589]

As far as can be determined, the RSHA continued to handle releases in a very restrictive manner. Apparently, in 1943/44, a release of Bible Students who had not signed the statement occurred only in the "few exceptional cases" that Kaltenbrunner had mentioned. Nevertheless, the Bible Students who were assigned as housekeepers in families of SS leaders actually had the status of being "partially released." For example, those Bible Students from Auschwitz and Ravensbrück who worked in the "houses of SS leaders" were even given special passes permitting them to leave and enter the camp for their work."[590] The SS families welcomed this regulation because it enabled them to use the Bible Students to do their shopping and run errands for them.

In 1943 the SS also assigned a labor detail consisting of male Bible Student prisoners to the Hartzwalde estate of Dr. Kersten. According to Franz Birk, one of the prisoners of this labor detail, this operation had the objective of "examining, for the first time, whether it was possible to put Jehovah's Witnesses to work without supervision."[591] During the final year of the war, such increasing freedom of movement was also given to Jehovah's Witnesses who worked at other agricultural estates and at several outside labor details with special assignments. In some cases, they were even no longer considered to be in protective detention. Still, they were obligated to fulfill their assignments with the same conscientiousness.

Heinrich Himmler was also personally involved in this arrangement. This can be seen from the way he cared for the interests of the widow of his subordinate official, Reinhard Heydrich. In October 1944 Heydrich's widow received a letter requesting her to assess the performance and conduct of the fifteen Bible Students working at her estate. She was also asked to give her opinion with regard to the possibility of releasing these prisoners. Such releases could take place if the Bible Students confirmed, by means of their signature, that they would no longer be involved in "propagating" their religious beliefs. Mrs. Heydrich's response to this request is reflected in the following statements from her autobiography, provided one can believe her explanations: "I thought about this question for a long time. Then, I said: 'What if you could be released *without* having to sign.' They were all excited. Consequently, I sent a letter to Himmler and requested the release of my prisoners who were even willing to stay with me after their release. Himmler agreed with my suggestion. He understood that Jehovah's Witnesses, conscientious objectors, were the best guarantee for a peaceful life in occupied territory."[592] Three months later, Himmler gave orders that the Bible Students from Jungfern-Breschan should be released without the requirement of having to sign the statement, an action, which, as Mrs. Heydrich claimed, was done on her initiative. On January 14, 1945, Himmler sent a letter to the chief of the Security Police and the Security Service, as well as the chief of the WVHA, in which he gave the following instructions:

> In the context of the action of giving complete freedom to Bible Students who are held in isolation at various estates, particularly in

favor of a positive political policy abroad, I request that the Bible Students assigned to the Jungfern-Breschan estate of Mrs. Heydrich should be released under the same conditions as those who are released with areal restrictions. . . . They will therefore no longer have to be supervised. The releases should take place in the usual formal setting.[593]

Not all of the fifteen Jehovah's Witnesses working at the Jungfern-Breschan estate got this privilege. It was granted only to the ten German and three Dutch Jehovah's Witnesses. For the other two prisoners, Himmler had other plans. His letter states: "The two Czech Bible Students who were working for Mrs. Heydrich should not be released. They should be transferred." The German and Dutch Jehovah's Witnesses actually were released. According to Lina Heydrich, the former supervisor got himself a dog "and now walked the fields pretending to be grand seigneur."[594]

Heinrich Himmler, a certified farmer, was deeply impressed with the proverbial diligence he had observed with the Bible Students. Even though he described them as "belonging to a crazy sect," he was fascinated by the power of their faith.[595] If the statements of Rudolf Höß, the commanding officer of the Auschwitz concentration camp, can be considered to be reliable (and, in this context, there should be no reason not to believe him), Himmler and Theodor Eicke, the inspector of the concentration camps, used "on many occasions . . . the fanatical faith of Jehovah's Witnesses as an example" for his troops: "SS men must have the same fanatical and unshakable faith in the National Socialist ideal and in Adolf Hitler that the Witnesses had in Jehovah. Only when all SS men believed as fanatically in their own philosophy would Adolf Hitler's state be permanently secure. A *Weltanschauung* (worldview, philosophy of life) could only be established and permanently maintained by fanatics utterly prepared to sacrifice their egos for their ideas."[596]

Finally, Himmler had the idea of including Jehovah's Witnesses also in his geopolitical postwar plans. On July 21, 1944, he sent a letter to Kaltenbrunner describing his various ideas and considerations with regard to the questions of "how [to] control and pacify Russia" if, during the following years, Germany would be able to recapture "large areas of Russian ground" (of which the highest SS leader did not seem to have any doubt.) Besides reestablishing a "new Cossack community" at the border line (here, Himmler envisioned a concept of *Wehrbauern* [militarized farmers] who determinedly defended their land against the threat of collectivization),[597] it was necessary to populate the interior with people

who were "peace-loving and would not take up arms against us."
Himmler continued:

> Any idea of introducing some kind of National Socialism would be
> insane. However, people need a religion or an ideology. To support
> and restore the Orthodox Church would be unwise since it would
> again be an organization of national assembly. It would be just as
> unwise to give the Catholic Church a chance to establish itself.
> Nothing more needs to be said in this regard. . . . We need to sup-
> port forms of religion and sectarian groups that have a pacifying
> effect. For all Turk-peoples,[598] this would be the Buddhist religion.
> For all other people, it is the Bible Student teachings. As you are
> probably aware, the Bible Students have the following characteris-
> tics, incredibly favorable for us: Despite the fact that they refuse
> military service and any work in support of the war, a work which
> they consider to be "destructive," they are strongly opposed to the
> Jews as well as the Catholic Church and the pope. They are also re-
> markably realistic, do not drink and smoke, are very diligent and
> honest, and always keep their promises. Furthermore, they are ex-
> cellent livestock breeders and farm workers. They do not pursue
> riches and possessions. It destroys their outlook on everlasting life.
> All of these are ideal characteristics, as can be generally stated that
> these truly convinced, idealistic Bible Students, like the Mennon-
> ites, have greatly desirable characteristics. . . . Therefore, I request
> that a committee be formed to examine all Bible Students in the
> concentration camps who are known to be genuine so that we can
> separate them from those who joined the Bible Students during
> their imprisonment or shortly before being arrested for their own
> advantage. In this way, we can also avoid that the Bible Student
> groups are exploited for Communist purposes. We also avoid that
> people pretend to be Bible Students who, in reality, lack the char-
> acteristic of diligence and are lazy, as I have observed at some
> places, such as Fridolfing/Upper Bavaria. This [examination] will
> also afford us the opportunity to use, in the concentration camps,
> the real Bible Students in positions of trust that involve the danger
> of embezzling money or other material assets. These Bible Stu-
> dents have to be treated particularly well. This, in turn, will lay the
> foundation for using these German Bible Students in the future in
> Russia. As a result, we have the missionaries by means of whom we
> will be able to appease the Russian people with the teachings of the
> Bible Students.[599]

These "apparently fantastic plans" of Himmler are consistent in
that they persistently follow the idea of using the characteristics of

Jehovah's Witnesses for specific purposes.[600] To this end, Himmler wanted to take advantage of a circumstance that he had come to realize in the meantime. The fact that Jehovah's Witnesses took a position of neutrality meant not only that they refrained from fulfilling certain requirements of the NS state but also that they would not become involved in any subversive activity and, consequently, any activity representing a substantial threat to the state. This perfidious idea of misusing the missionary zeal of Jehovah's Witnesses in order to spread an antimilitary attitude among the people of the Soviet Union and thus paralyze the political threat these people could present revealed a peculiar combination of plain pragmatism and ideological insanity. It was an expression of a "hybrid instrumentalism of ideas, according to which it would be possible to exploit religion and humans simply for personal political purposes."[601] Himmler's conception of a great Germanic Reich, one that would make use of the Bible Student teachings in order to secure its future eastern border, was a truly grotesque flight of fancy. What is more, it was penned during the decline of NS rule and, incidentally, on the day after the assassination attempt on Hitler.

Death Marches into Freedom

When, during the final weeks of the war, the concentration camps were evacuated, tens of thousands of concentration camp prisoners were shot to death by the SS, starved, or eliminated in other ways. Among these were also several Jehovah's Witnesses. For instance, on May 3, 1945, when the *Cap Arcona* and the *Thielbek* sank in the Bay of Neustadt, at least ten members of the small Bible Student group from Neuengamme died together with seven thousand fellow prisoners.[602] During the evacuation marches, all prisoners who were no longer able to walk were simply shot to death at the roadside. The "memo explaining the evacuation march of Jehovah's Witnesses from the Sachsenhausen concentration camp," written in May 1945 by people who were involved in these horrible marches, describes in an impressive way what Jehovah's Witnesses had to endure.[603]

On the morning of April 25, 1945, the prisoners from the Sachsenhausen concentration camp were "evacuated." In marching columns, the 33,000 inmates of the camp were driven in the direction of the Baltic Sea. Included in this number were 230 Jehovah's Witnesses. Seventeen of these—according to other sources eighteen—were female prisoners. The memo states that the SS allowed Jehovah's Witnesses to form a separate marching block, even though it did not include the required number of 500 prisoners. It also did not meet the requirement of separation according to nationality. Before they moved out, they had been able to gather up their sick fellow believers from the camp infirmary. On no account did they want to leave these sick ones to the uncertainty of the camp. Several female Bible Students were also among the thousands of female prisoners who had been brought to Sachsenhausen at the beginning of 1945. Some of them were in the small camp, others were in the isolation blocks. A seriously ill Polish Jehovah's Witness was in the camp infirmary of the women's section. Regarding the help that she received, the memo states: "To take her along, was our foremost concern. Therefore, we decided, if necessary, we would take this sister by force from the women's section of the concentration camp. The next morning, a brother was able to accomplish this. She was brought to us in men's clothing and entrusted into our tender care."

During the march, Jehovah's Witnesses maintained strict unity within their marching block. They shared the meager food rations and supported each other: "We did not even lose one of the very weak and sick from among us, even though we had quite a few brothers between the ages of sixty-five and seventy-two." Even during the march, Jehovah's Witnesses would try to talk with the people from the various villages through which they passed about the good news of the Kingdom. The SS guards for the purple column, under the command of an SS-Unterscharführer (sergeant), did not object to these efforts. In this way, the Bible Students were able to obtain additional food as well as barns for shelter during the night. After several days of strenuous marching, the columns made a stop in the forest of Below (near Wittstock).[604] Between April 26 and 29, more than 30,000 prisoners were confined in this small beech forest. They were surrounded by vast forces of guards. Under these difficult circumstances, severe lack of water, insufficient food, and the like, a united and well-disciplined group of prisoners proved to be especially beneficial. On the northern edge of the forest and apart from the other prisoners, Jehovah's Witnesses immediately began building temporary shelters. They made a fireplace and dug a hole for a latrine. Other fellow believers gathered everything they could find to eat, especially nettles and roots. Despite the enormous labor and the uncertainty of the length of stay, they even decided to dig a well. With combined effort, they were able to accomplish this task with their food bowls, the only tools they had. At a depth of fifteen to eighteen feet (five to six meters), they found ground water. According to the memo, this successful search for water also had some disadvantages: "Of course, this 'miracle' quickly made the rounds and later caused several conflicts with our envious neighbors."

Even during the period of their stay in the Below forest, Jehovah's Witnesses formed strict organizational structures. To a certain extent, this was already the beginning of the restructuring of the preaching activity during the postwar period. They divided their entire group into nine, later ten, subordinate groups. Each group was supervised by a group leader. The group leaders, in turn, formed a leadership board. To this end, the memo mentions that these clear assignments tremendously improved this difficult situation: "Since now everyone knew to which group he belonged, it was easier to distribute food, make announcements, and even conduct uninterrupted meetings."

After three days, on April 29, 1945, at nine o'clock in the morning, the camp in the Below forest was dissolved and the departure began. Hundreds of prisoners had died from starvation, but Jehovah's Witnesses had survived this terrible period of deprivation unharmed. On May 2, 1945, the marching columns reached a forest near Schwerin. Jehovah's Witnesses noticed that the SS officers became increasingly nervous: "Suddenly our 'heroes' started to tremble. They began addressing us with 'comrades.'" The SS started to withdraw. In view of the approaching Soviet troops, one SS officer indicated to the prisoners that they should try to make their way to the American units that were also only a few miles away. Because of the general chaos, Jehovah's Witnesses hesitated to follow this advice and, for the time being, stayed where they were: "We wanted to put our complete trust in Jehovah who had provided so much evidence of his guidance, nearness, and power during the previous eleven days." As soon became evident, in this way, they escaped the absurd shooting by dispersed SS officers that claimed the lives of many prisoners who frantically tried to flee toward the American units.

On May 3, 1945, at about eleven o'clock in the morning, the band of Jehovah's Witnesses set off toward Schwerin. A few hours later, they passed the first American guard forces. The years of imprisonment had come to an end; the hour of liberation had finally come. Approximately six thousand fellow prisoners had died on this death march. They had been shot or beaten to death along the wayside, had died from starvation or exhaustion. All 230 Bible Student prisoners who had left the Sachsenhausen concentration camp survived this torture without exception. Jehovah's Witnesses attributed this fact to the close relationships among one another and the manifestation of "Christian love." Their "wonderful deliverance" gave evidence of "Jehovah's protection."[605]

At first, Jehovah's Witnesses were brought into a temporary reception camp at Zippendorf, a suburb of Schwerin. They remained there until May 5, 1945. During this time, they wrote the "memo regarding the evacuation march of Jehovah's Witnesses from the Sachsenhausen concentration camp" on a typewriter that had been part of the Wehrmacht supply. They also decided to send a resolution to their fellow believers throughout the world. This "resolution of 230 Jehovah's Witnesses from 10 different nationalities gathered in a forest near Schwerin in Mecklenburg" states in part:

> We witnesses of Jehovah gathered here send heartfelt greetings to the faithful covenant people of Jehovah and their companions throughout the entire world. . . . Let it be known that our great God, whose name is Jehovah, has fulfilled his word to his people. . . . A long hard period of testing is behind us. . . . Thanks to the Lord's assistance and his gracious support, the enemy's designs to cause us to undermine our integrity have failed, even though he attempted this by employing innumerable violent, devilish schemes as well as thousands of inquisitional practices right out of the Middle Ages, both physical and mental, and many flatteries and enticements. . . . The great issue has been decided again in Jehovah's favor to his honor.[606]

They also made sure to mention that "the Lord, Jehovah, has blessed us with rich spoils, thirty-six men of goodwill, who upon our leaving Sachsenhausen . . . voluntarily declared: 'We will go with you people, for we have heard that God is with you.'"

The breakdown of the Hitler regime did not bring the Thousand-Year Reign, as they had firmly expected during the previous years, but it did not diminish confidence in their religious beliefs. Their liberation was evidence of divine acts of salvation and a sign of Jehovah's loyalty toward his people. These people who had been delivered from years of imprisonment in concentration camps had the same feelings as the Israelites of old. They interpreted the experiences of the death march as the Exodus experience of biblical dimensions: in the same way Jehovah God guided his people out of Egypt and later delivered them from Babylonian captivity, he now had delivered his people from bondage in the concentration camps.[607] Therefore, they introduced their "memo regarding the evacuation march of Jehovah's Witnesses from the Sachsenhausen concentration camp" with the first verses of Psalms 126: "When

Jehovah gathered back the captive ones of Zion, we became like those who were dreaming. At that time our mouth came to be filled with laughter, and our tongue with a joyful cry."[608]

16

Jehovah's Witnesses at the Neuengamme Concentration Camp

Studies about prisoner groups in NS concentration camps are based almost exclusively on testimony from former prisoners, or statements by SS officers or officials from other authorities responsible for the persecution. They are also based on central orders or decrees from concentration camp commandant's headquarters and superior authorities (RSHA, WVHA, RFSS, etc.). In only a few cases are analyses made by means of empirical methods based on statistics of the various camps and data from personal records.[609] A principal reason for the lack of research studies is the insufficient availability of concentration camp records. Immediately before the concentration camps were dissolved, the SS destroyed a large number of records to cover up the traces of their crimes. Consequently, it was often not possible to provide such simple data as, for example, the exact number of prisoners. In this context, the following study regarding the Bible Student prisoners at the Neuengamme concentration camp remains only an attempt in shedding more light on the subject. At the same time, such an attempt seems appropriate in order to be able to base the analysis on more than vague presumptions and estimations.

There are also no records to *substantiate* the exact number of Bible Students who were imprisoned at the Neuengamme concentration camp.[610] Publications about this camp, provided they at all quantified Jehovah's Witnesses as a group of prisoners, mention the following numbers: "Several hundred,"[611] "between 300 and 500,"[612] "at the end of the war, approximately 200."[613] The numbers included in recollections and the numbers mentioned by former prisoners who belong to the group of Bible Students at Neuengamme are, without exception, smaller. Independent from one another, these people mention numbers of between 70 and 80 Bible Student prisoners.[614] Because of the close relationship and, at times, shared lodgings as a group, they are certainly able to estimate the number of people belonging to their religious denomination. Even after more than four decades, former prisoners remember quite a few of the names of their fellow sufferers. However, the total number of Jehovah's Witnesses who were imprisoned in Neuengamme is probably higher. Based on the research made in the context of this study, this number can be estimated to be between 150 and 160. This discrepancy is due primarily to the fact that recollection is a relative point of reference; that is, it always refers only to the number of prisoners who were imprisoned at the same time. It does not take into consideration the changing of prisoners over time, of which the individual prisoner might not have been directly aware but which is imperative to estimate the total number of prisoners.

The following description of the group of Bible Student prisoners can be based on an analysis of available information[615] regarding 116 people.[616] In view of a total number of 140 to 150 Jehovah's Witnesses imprisoned at the Neuengamme concentration camp, this number seems to be a methodologically acceptable basis.

In December 1938 a first detachment of 100 prisoners, identified with the green patch (habitual criminals), was transferred from Sachsenhausen to Hamburg-Neuengamme. They had been assigned to put a closed-down brickyard back into operation. Fourteen months later, on February 29/March 1, 1940, a second command of prisoners arrived to increase the size of the concentration camp. This transport of between 100 and 120 prisoners included, besides political prisoners, 40 Bible Students. At this point, every fifth or sixth prisoner in Neuengamme was a Jehovah's Witness. Since the Bible Students never made any attempts to escape, they seemed especially suitable for deployment at this construction site because it was not yet fenced in.

On June 4, 1940, another transport of 520 prisoners from Sachsenhausen arrived at Neuengamme and included a small group of Bible Students. The exact number cannot be determined. Since in the spring of 1940 this former outside labor detail was turned into an independent concentration camp, more prisoners were transferred to this concentration camp in short succession. While the number of prisoners from other groups increased considerably, the number of Bible Student prisoners rose only slowly. During the winter of 1940/41, the majority of prisoners arriving at Neuengamme were foreigners. Soon, the foreign prisoners considerably exceeded the number of German prisoners. Within this camp community of several thousand prisoners, the Bible Students ultimately became only a small minority.[617] On January 23, 1941, a transport of 484 prisoners from Dachau arrived at this camp, including 30 Jehovah's Witnesses. During the next few years, the number of Bible Student prisoners increased only insignificantly.

By far the majority of the Neuengamme Bible Student prisoners (86 percent) were transferred from other concentration camps. The number of people admitted directly by the Gestapo was small and remained small. Based on the established dates of arrest, the majority of these people had already served long periods of imprisonment in penal institutions and concentration camps before they were sent to Neuengamme. In 58.9 percent of the cases, they had been arrested prior to the beginning of 1938.[618] The earliest date of arrest that can be established is December 7, 1934, involving a Jehovah's Witness who was sent to Sachsenhausen in 1936, after a two-year period of imprisonment in a penal institution. Four years later, he was transferred to Neuengamme, where he remained until the end of the war. Consequently, this Bible Student spent ten and a half years in various penal institutions in the Third Reich.[619] On average, Jehovah's Witnesses imprisoned at Neuengamme spent a total of 6.9 years in various penal institutions. A number of them spent the major part of this imprisonment in Neuengamme. There, the long duration of shared imprisonment and, during the initial period, the communal living quarters strengthened the homogeneity and solidarity among this group.

In ninety-nine cases, the admission dates of Bible Student prisoners into the Neuengamme concentration camp can be determined (see table 4). Almost 50 percent of the Bible Student prisoners at the Neuengamme concentration camp belonged to the age group of people born between 1895 and 1905 (see table 5). At the time of admission into the Neuengamme concentration camp, on average, the Bible Student prisoners were 40.8 years old.[620] One out of five was older than 50. However, only 7.5 percent were younger than 30 years of age.[621]

A comparison of the ages of the concentration camp prisoners as a whole shows that the Bible Student prisoners had relatively high ages. However, for Neuengamme, it is not possible to determine the age structure of other prison communities. For Buchenwald, on the other hand, these numbers are available. There, based on statistics, the SS periodically provided an overview about the age brackets of the prisoners.

Table 4. Admissions of Jehovah's Witnesses to Neuengamme

Date	Number	Transferred from
Feb. 2–Mar. 3, 1940	40	Sachsenhausen
June 4, 1940	10	Sachsenhausen
Aug. 17, 1940	1	Wolfenbüttel Prison
Sep. 15, 1940	1	Wolfenbüttel Prison
Dec. 10, 1940	1	Buchenwald
Jan. 23, 1941	30	Dachau
Jan. 29, 1941	1	Vechta Prison
Feb. 1941	1	unknown
Oct. 23, 1941	1	Fuhlsbüttel Police Prison
July 1942	1	Netherlands
Nov. 2, 1942	3	Dachau
Sept. 1942	6	Netherlands
June 1944	1	Fuhlsbüttel Police Prison
Oct. 1944	1	Amersfoort/ Netherlands
Jan. 1945	1	Sachsenhausen
Total	**99**	

Table 5. Birth years of Bible Students imprisoned at Neuengamme

Years	Number
1881–1885	7
1886–1890	9
1891–1895	13
1896–1900	15
1901–1905	24
1906–1910	9
1911–1915	5
1916–1920	2
1921–1925	2
Total	**86**

Table 6. Age brackets of Bible Students, Buchenwald, Jan. 30, 1941

	Bible Students		Total prisoners	
	Number	Percent	Number	Percent
Up to 20 years	—	0.0	139	1.9
20–30 years	10	3.3	1124	15.3
30–40 years	69	23.0	2400	32.6
40–50 years	136	45.4	2314	31.4
50–60 years	70	23.3	1134	15.4
60–70 years	15	5.0	246	3.3
70–80 years	—	0.0	5	0.1
Total	**300**	**100.0**	**7362**	**100.0**

Consequently, based on the "January 30, 1941, division into age brackets of the Buchenwald concentration camp prisoners," it is possible to calculate the percentages shown in table 6.[622]

The age structure of other prisoner groups deviates only insignificantly from the structure of the prisoners as a whole. However, with regard to the Bible Students, there are significant differences. Figure 4 demonstrates the difference in age structure between the Bible Students and the prisoners as a whole.

The majority of the Bible Student prisoners in Neuengamme were married (almost 90 percent). Apparently, they had only a relatively small

Figure 4. Division into age brackets, Buchenwald, Jan. 30, 1941

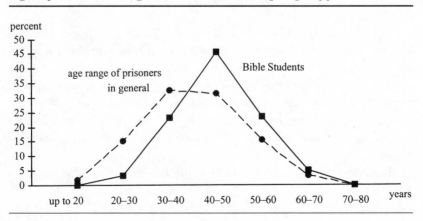

Table 7. Occupations of Bible Students, Neuengamme

Occupation	Number
Factory, agricultural, and day laborers	15
Skilled craftsmen	11
Craftsmen	10
Employees	4
Farmers	3
Sailors	3
Self-employed	3
Lower and higher civil servants	3
Others (two musicians and one artist)	3
Total	**55**

number of children (an average of 1.6). However, only fragmentary information is available regarding the social status of Jehovah's Witnesses at Neuengamme. The majority belonged to the lower middle class and lower class; only a very small number belonged to the upper middle class. In fifty-five cases, it is also possible to determine the occupation of the people (see table 7).

Before their imprisonments, the majority of IBSA members performed manual work. This familiarity with manual work and the ability to deal with hard labor were important factors for survival within the camps. Knowledge and skilled craftsmanship often gave the Bible Students access to relatively tolerable labor details. Because of their eagerness to work, the Bible Student prisoners soon acquired a reputation as reliable laborers.

During construction of the camp, the forty Bible Students who had been transferred from the Sachsenhausen concentration camp, on February 29/March 1, 1940, were housed in one of the buildings of the brickworks, along with the 180 prisoners from other categories who were deployed at the Neuengamme outside labor detail. The attic of the drying plant served as their living space. On June 4, 1940, after the completion of the first three barracks, they were moved into the actual concentration camp.

From the second half of 1940 on, the Bible Students and the Jews were isolated from the rest of the prisoners in separate quarters.[623] A Communist from Mönchengladbach became their block leader. He had already spent time in various concentration camps since March 1, 1933. The IBSA members knew this man from his position as a functionary prisoner at the isolation blocks in Sachsenhausen. However, they did not remember him very favorably. The Bible Student Heinrich Heine from Neuß had been assigned to be room senior for the sleeping quarters for the section of the block in which Jehovah's Witnesses were housed. While they were all housed together, Jehovah's Witnesses were able to form a strict system of mutual assistance (distribution of food items, collective deposits of money, and so forth).

Because of their assignments to special labor details, several Jehovah's Witnesses had already been transferred to other quarters.[624] In 1943, probably as a result of the September 10, 1943, interoffice decree by the WVHA, which had ordered the "immediate" separation of "all Bible Student prisoners in the concentration camps," housing Bible Students together was completely discontinued.[625] In groups of five or six, Jehovah's Witnesses were dispersed to various other blocks. It was only toward the end of the war that the SS in Neuengamme no longer strictly dispersed small numbers of Bible Students among the barracks.

Usually, Jehovah's Witnesses in the camps refused to accept assignments in the context of the "prisoners' self-administration."[626] At Neuengamme, however, the SS assigned positions of camp organization more frequently to Bible Students than to prisoners of other groups. Not that the Bible Student prisoners made any special efforts to receive such positions, or participated in the "fight" for predominance in the "prisoners' self-administration." But especially in cases in which the labor details and communities of the barracks consisted entirely or primarily of Bible Students, they were willing to accept such positions of leadership. In view of this evidence, it is no longer possible to maintain the general assertion that Jehovah's Witnesses did "not have any access . . . to functionary positions" within the concentration camp community.[627]

According to available information, at least 10 percent of the IBSA members in Neuengamme occupied positions as functionary prisoners. In the majority of cases, such positions were occupied in labor details. For instance, Jehovah's Witnesses were assigned as foremen in the following labor details: *Angora-Zucht*, *Betonplattenfertigung* (concrete manufacture), *Gärtnerei* (gardening), *Kartoffelkeller* (potato cellar), *Richtkolonnen* no. 2 and no. 3 (labor detail repairing roof constructions), construction of the "Ley-Haus-Siedlung" Lohbrügger Landstrasse (German housing welfare organization to provide people affected by air raids with provisional housing after autumn 1943) outside labor details at the Bergedorf

Figure 5. Nationality of Jehovah's Witnesses, Neuengamme

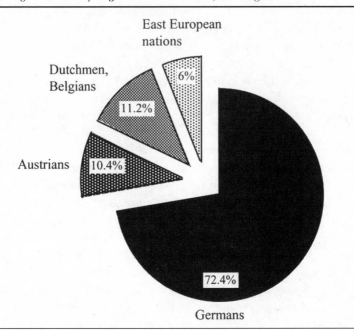

East European
nations

Dutchmen,
Belgians

6%

11.2%

Austrians   10.4%

72.4%

Germans

Note: N = 116: Reichs Germany, 96; Netherlands, 12; Czechoslovakia, 3; Poland, 2; Belgium, 1; Yugoslavia, 1; and Soviet Union, 1.

companies Behr (timber processing industry) and Glunz (iron factory), *Bahnhofskommando* (loading and unloading of freight), *Entkrautungskommando,* and *Gleisträger* (rail or track carrier). These five labor details consisted only of Bible Students; the other labor details also included prisoners from other prisoner groups.

At least one Bible Student from Neuengamme held a position as supervisor: the architect Eduard Lauterbach, who was deployed at the "Central Construction Management of the Waffen SS" for the construction of the *Deutsche Ausrüstungswerke* (Reich armament works) in Neuengamme.[628] Two Bible Students also held positions as room seniors as part of the "prisoners' self-administration" in Neuengamme. In 1944 one Jehovah's Witness was assigned to be block leader at the subcamp Schwesing, and later in Meppen-Dalum.

By far the majority of imprisoned IBSA members in Neuengamme were Germans and Austrians (a total of 82.8 percent). Only a small number came from non-German language areas (see figure 5). The group of Bible Students even differed in their national composition

Table 8. Whereabouts of Bible Students, Neuengamme

	Number	Percent
Releases from concentration camp imprisonment	48[1]	41.4
Releases from prison	2	1.7
Transfers to other concentration camps	4	34.0
Deceased prisoners	37	31.9[2]
"Invalid transports"	10	8.6
People unaccounted for	15	13.0
Total	**116**	**100.0**

[1]Included in this number are seven people who survived the sinking of the *Cap Arcona* on May 3, 1945.

[2]Accordingly, the death rate determined for Neuengamme, 31.9% (without taking into consideration the number of people who died shortly before the liberation of *Cap Arcona*, 23.3%), is lower than the death rate mentioned in the study by Lautmann, Grikschat, and Schmidt, 35% (by way of comparison: death rate of political prisoners 41%, homosexuals 60% [see *Der rosa Winkel*, 350]). This difference is probably due to the fact that the first Jehovah's Witnesses were sent to the Neuengamme concentration camp when the specific humiliations and mistreatments/tortures of Bible Students were already on a decline. In Neuengamme, for example, the Bible Students were never placed in punishment battalions for certain periods of time.

from the other prison groups at the concentration camp.[629] As more and more foreigners were sent to the camps, the characteristic of being a prisoner group consisting of primarily (Reich) Germans increasingly determined the "place value" of a prisoner group within the camp structure, which was set up by the SS.

In the concentration camps located on Reich German territory, the number of foreign Jehovah's Witnesses was very small in comparison to the number of their German fellow believers. Only at the Mauthausen concentration camp was the percentage of foreign Bible Student prisoners higher. Here, at the end of 1944, the number of Polish and Czechoslovakian IBSA members almost equaled the number of Reich German IBSA members (46 German and Austrian Bible Students, 36 Polish and Czech Bible Students).[630]

Of the 116 Jehovah's Witnesses whose data has been examined, 26 died at the main camp in Neuengamme,[631] one person died at the subcamp Drütte, and at least ten died during the "evacuation" of the prisoners, on May 3, 1945, as the ships *Cap Arcona* and *Thielbek* sank in the Bay of Neustadt.[632] According to the corresponding transfer lists, another ten Bible Student prisoners were sent on an "invalid transport" as people "unfit for work" or as "TB patients." Three of these prisoners died a few days or weeks later. The fate of the other seven who were transferred to Majdanek and Dachau cannot be determined. Only 54

Figure 6. Deaths and invalid transports in relation to the number of Bible Student prisoners, Neuengamme

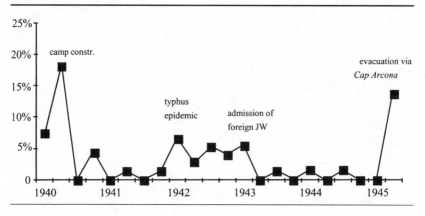

Note: Percentages determined at intervals of three months.

Neuengamme Bible Student prisoners evidently survived the concentration camp imprisonment.

These numbers probably do not provide a very meaningful picture. However, a more precise and, with regard to time, more differentiated consideration clearly shows a relationship to the respective work and living conditions.

As early as three months after the first forty Jehovah's Witnesses arrived in Neuengamme (transport from Sachsenhausen on Feb. 29/ March 1, 1940), one out of every five died as a result of the dreadful conditions during the construction of the camp. As "causes for death" of these eight Jehovah's Witnesses between the ages of thirty-five and fifty-six years, the death register lists pneumonia, heart failure, circulatory collapse, enteritis, pleurisy, and general physical weakness.[633]

During 1940, three more Bible Student prisoners died. It is possible that one of them committed suicide.[634] During the same period, three Jehovah's Witnesses were transferred to Dachau as "prisoners unfit for work."

Between November 1940 and January 1942, with only one exception, no additional deaths are recorded among Jehovah's Witnesses in Neuengamme.[635] The exception involves Johann Trausner, who was executed on October 24, 1941, "upon direct orders by the Führer and Reich chancellor," on the charge of his refusal to work and to give the Hitler salute.[636] The fact that no other deaths are recorded indicates that during this period the Bible Students' chances of survival increased. As the following explanations show, these increasing chances of survival resulted especially from improved working conditions and also from the communal housing quarters during this period that provided more possibilities for solidarity within the group of Jehovah's Witnesses. However, conditions changed drastically when a typhus epidemic raged throughout the Neuengamme concentration camp at the beginning of 1942. The epidemic claimed more than one thousand lives from among the prisoners. To a large extent, this was due to the disastrous undersupply of medication for which the SS was responsible. The camp was put under quarantine until the end of March 1942. Among the victims were five Jehovah's Witnesses.[637]

During the following months, four Bible Students were transferred to Dachau in one of the "invalid transports." Several prisoners died during the following winter of 1942/43. These deaths can be attributed primarily to the fact that an increasing number of foreign Jehovah's Witnesses were sent to Neuengamme. For instance, between December 18, 1942, and March 29, 1943, six Dutch IBSA members, who had been at the Neuengamme concentration camp only between three and six months, died.[638] On the other hand, among the German prisoners who had been at the camp since 1940/41, a completely different development can be seen. According to the available information, with only one exception, no deaths were registered among the German Bible Students at Neuengamme between December 1942 and the evacuation in May 1945.[639]

In general, there was an increasing death rate among the concentration camp prisoners in Neuengamme. However, with regard to the Bible Student prisoners, just the opposite took place.[640] Because of the small number of Bible Students at this concentration camp, an attempt to interpret the situation requires a measure of caution. At the same time, it can be established that this was not an incidental occurrence, or a specific characteristic of the Neuengamme concentration camp. This remarkable decrease of deaths among the Bible Student prisoners between 1942 and 1945 has been noted in previous publications.[641]

The decrease of deaths resulted from the following factors:

1. As a result of the continuously increasing number of foreign prisoners admitted to the concentration camps, the general situation of non-Jewish German prisoners improved (relatively) during the war. This numerical increase of foreign prisoners also resulted in the fact that, in comparison to the total number of prisoners, the number of Jehovah's Witnesses decreased.

2. The majority of Jehovah's Witnesses had long-term experience "as concentration camp prisoners" whose resistance had already been put to the test.

3. Because of relatively insignificant fluctuations, the Bible Student prisoners had been able to build strong relationships.

4. The SS had put an increasing number of IBSA members into privileged positions.

Besides the "invalid transports," there were only four cases of Bible Students transferred from Neuengamme to other concentration camps. In general, transfers were a common practice within the concentration camp system, and so this is indeed a remarkable occurrence. An exceptionally small number of Bible Students was also transferred from the main camp to a subcamp. As far as can be determined, such transfers took place in only eight cases. Three of the prisoners concerned had been admitted into the Neuengamme concentration camp only during the second half of 1944. After just a few weeks at the main camp, they were transferred to the subcamps in Bremen-Farge, Husum-Schwesing, and Meppen-Versen.[642]

The small number of transfers indicates that the SS tried to keep the Bible Students in the main camp because they were reliable workers and could be used in positions of trust. During the first year of its existence, eighty-five Bible Students (the "nucleus of the camp community") had been admitted to the Neuengamme concentration camp. Fifty-five of these prisoners (65 percent) remained in the main camp in Neuengamme until evacuation, without being employed anywhere else. These inmates had already experienced many years of imprisonment. Because of their low prisoners' numbers, they were easily recognized within the "camp community." From 1942 on, almost all of them occupied privileged workplaces that provided relatively good and secure conditions for survival (if at all conditions in a concentration camp can be considered "good"). Since they carried out all work assigned to them with conscientiousness, they made themselves almost indispensable at their various workplaces. Often, the immediate patronage of their SS superiors protected them from being deployed at labor details with less favorable conditions or from being transferred to a subcamp.[643]

The working conditions were of central importance for survival within the camp. In Neuengamme, Jehovah's Witnesses were deployed at several work places. A total of 215 records include information about deployment at 38 different labor details or work fields. Since prisoners generally were not deployed at the same labor detail during the entire period of their imprisonment at the camps, in the majority of cases the name of a particular prisoner appears in several reports. In other cases, however, there is not a single record indicating to which labor detail the prisoner was assigned. It is necessary to emphasize again that due to the incompleteness of the data, it is possible to show only a general development of the situation.

To be able to categorize the working conditions of the various assignments according to seriousness, they have been grouped according to the following classification:[644]

1. *Work with (relatively) good conditions for survival:*
   Assignments at the SS camp (dining hall, SS kitchen, stable), skilled labor, and (construction) specialists (construction office);
2. *Work with relatively acceptable conditions for survival:*
   Activities within the concentration camp area (kitchen, orderly room), assignments at small outside labor details such as commercial businesses, farms (*Angora-Zucht*, greenhouse, etc.), craftsman columns, skilled labor in production;
3. *Work with difficult conditions for survival:*
   Construction work or work related to construction work, production of concrete slabs, bomb-clearing commands, burial commands;
4. *Work with poor or difficult conditions for survival:*
   Mass deployments for the purpose of dirt moving, excavations, and transports ("Elbe" Command, work at the clay mines, excavation work for the construction of the concentration camp and brickworks), carrying or laying tracks, cutting reed on the Baltic Peninsula Darß, punishment battalion.

The analysis of these assignments according to these classifications regarding the deployment of Jehovah's Witnesses at the Neuengamme concentration camp is shown in table 9.

Almost half of the work assignments were at labor details inside of the concentration camp (45.4 percent). With 54.6 percent, an extremely high number of assignments were located at labor details outside of the fenced-in camps. For these assignments, small groups consisting entirely of Jehovah's Witnesses were formed that generally worked under reduced supervision. Such commands consisting entirely of Bible Students were, for instance, the so-called *Bahnhofskommando*, the *Entkrautungskommando*, as well as the commands of the Bergedorf companies Behr and Glunz.

Highly significant results can be obtained by breaking down the information about the deployment at various labor details according to the time period in which the respective activities were performed. For

Table 9. Deployment in labor details, Neuengamme

Work with	Percent
Good conditions for survival	6.5
Relatively acceptable conditions for survival	32.5
Difficult conditions for survival	27.0
Poor or terrible conditions for survival	34.0
Total	**100.0**

Note: N = 215.

this analysis, a comparison of the periods of 1940 to 1942, as well as 1943 to 1945, proved to be very informative.

This obvious positive development certainly contributed to increasingly improved living conditions.[645] Even though from 1942/43 on, non-Jewish German prisoners generally had a better chance of survival in the NS concentration camps because of the increasing importance of prisoner labor,[646] the degree of improvement of the Bible Students' situation is still remarkable.

Various factors also contributed to the fact that the Bible Students at the Neuengamme concentration camp were able to increase their religious activities. These factors included, for instance, the relatively small size of the prisoner group, its homogeneity, the commonly shared religious beliefs, and the close relationship that had developed during years of communal housing, as well as the improvement of their material situation, and their access to privileged workplaces.[647] The Neuengamme Bible Student group, which from 1943 onward had been dispersed to the barracks of various other prisoner groups, was subdivided into seven study groups. Each study group was under the supervision of a group leader. Each group tried to gather for their book study at least once a week. For book studies, Ernst Wauer secretly prepared and duplicated carbon copies of the *Watchtower* at the office of the commanding officer, SS-Obersturmführer Albert Lütkemeyer, for whom he worked as a clerk. The Bible Students were also able to use a Bible, which they circulated throughout the camp.[648] At times, they even managed to provide the groups during roll call in the morning with a copy of the daily text (a booklet including a scripture for the day).

At the beginning of 1943 the Bible Students organized a special missionary campaign. For this purpose, they divided the concentration camp into territories and formed special "missionary groups." To reach

Table 10. Assignments to labor details, 1940–42 and 1943–45

Work with	1940–42 [Percent]	1943–45 [Percent]
Good conditions for survival	2.0	15.0
Relatively acceptable conditions for survival	13.5	54.0
Difficult conditions for survival	27.0	18.0
Poor or dreadful conditions for survival	57.5	13.0
Total	**100.0**	**100.0**

Note: N = 111 for 1940–42; N = 78 for 1943–45.

as many prisoners as possible, small groups of Jehovah's Witnesses went from block to block and gave "a witness" of their faith. They prepared "testimony cards" that held a brief passage from the Bible as well as an offer for a discussion about the Kingdom message in different languages.[649] Even discourses that were interpreted for the Russian and Polish prisoners were given. When fellow prisoners manifested an interest, the Witnesses made return visits and conducted Bible studies.

They were even able to smuggle publications, which, despite the circumstances, was at times quite a flourishing activity. A connection to the outside was made through the outside labor detail in Bergedorf.[650] Every day, under strict surveillance, between four and ten Jehovah's Witnesses marched the four miles (six kilometers) from the concentration camp to the village where they had to sort screws and other metal pieces for the Glunz iron factory. The sister of a fellow believer, who worked at this labor detail, learned about this working assignment and courageously established contact with these Jehovah's Witnesses. Subsequently, she became the intermediary for the contacts between the Bible Students who were imprisoned at the Neuengamme concentration camp and various IBSA groups who were active in the underground. The publications she brought to Bergedorf were at first hidden in the basement of the Glunz factory. From there, little by little, they were brought into the camp. Letters to relatives and biblical explanations about the situation of the prisoners were brought out of the camp. During 1943/44, these reports even reached the central European office of the Watch Tower Society in Switzerland.

Former Bible Student prisoners from Neuengamme also report about celebrations of the Lord's Supper. On several occasions, even baptisms were performed in the camp. Persons who wanted to be baptized, as was reportedly the case with a Russian and a young Polish prisoner, were smuggled into the *Entkrautungskommando,* which was in charge of digging out drainage ditches. There, they pretended that they had inadvertently slipped. Then, a Bible Student elder working at the labor detail said to the person concerned, "now that you are already in the water, at least let's do it right." Then, he would grab his head and dunk him completely under water. The SS guards, who took the whole thing as a joke, roared with laughter. Jehovah's Witnesses, however, attended the scene with silent prayers.[651]

For Jehovah's Witnesses, such occasions demonstrated, once again, how their faith prevailed over the "dullness of the worldly powers."

PART 6

CONCLUSION

17

Intensity of the Persecution

A variety of statements have been published regarding the extent of the persecution of members of the religious denomination of Jehovah's Witnesses in the Third Reich. During the sixties, Friedrich Zipfel was the first historian who made a determined effort to examine this subject. He bases his study on two cases, which Annedore Leber mentions in her 1956 biographical collection, *Das Gewissen steht auf.* In the context of describing sixty-four life stories, she discusses the persecution of seventeen-year-old Jonathan Stark, who was executed at the end of 1943 because of his refusal to take an oath required for labor service in the Sachsenhausen concentration camp. Annedore Leber states that Stark was "one of 6,034 'Jehovah's Witnesses,' who [were] in Germany at that time: In the period between 1933 and 1945, a total of 5,911 of them were arrested. More than two thousand were executed. Others lost their lives through acts of violence, hunger, illness, or compulsory labor."[1] Based on this considerably underestimated total number of Jehovah's Witnesses,[2] Zipfel concludes that "97% of the members of this minor religious denomination, that is, almost all of them, became victims of NS persecution."[3] He further states that one out of every three Jehovah's Witnesses were killed.[4] Subsequently, other authors began to use these figures, as well as Zipfel's statement about the high level of persecution.[5] In 1969 Michael H. Kater corrected the statements of Leber and Zipfel. Since then, the statements in Kater's study have been considered as reliable. Until today, they have been accepted in almost all scholarly studies.

Kater believed that in April 1933 a total of 19,268 Jehovah's Witnesses were living in the German Reich.[6] Therefore, in his study, he states that the number of victims was "much higher" than "previously" assumed. He mentions new estimates, according to which approximately

10,000 Jehovah's Witnesses had been imprisoned. Four to five thousand of these allegedly lost their lives in the concentration camps. Consequently, Kater concludes:

> Assuming that, in the period between 1933 and 1945, this sect had a steady membership of twenty thousand, it can be estimated that one out of every two Bible Students was imprisoned in the Third Reich. One out of every four [Bible Students] lost their lives. This means that, during the Hitler regime, besides the Jews, there was hardly another group that was persecuted as severely as the Earnest Bible Students.[7]

Otherwise, Kater's study is well documented. Even though Kater clearly states that these figures are estimates, they have been accepted by other authors as established facts.[8] For instance, in her 1982 book *The Nazi State and the New Religions* Christine Elizabeth King confirms the magnitude of figures estimated by Kater and states: "One out of every two German Witnesses was imprisoned, one in four lost their lives."[9] Two years later, under the title "Impressed by the Integrity of Jehovah's Witnesses," the *Watchtower* published a report about King's book. The article states, "most outstanding among Dr. King's findings are the figures of deaths and imprisonment of Jehovah's Witnesses." The article further states that "Dr. King's source for these statistics was a volume published . . . by Michael Kater." The *Watchtower* quotes King: "My own perusal of court and Gestapo records would certainly support these higher figures."[10]

Without supplying any additional information, the Watch Tower Society published these "higher figures," provided by a "worldly historian," even though the inaccuracy of these figures must have been obvious. For many years, the German branch office of the Watch Tower Society (in a special department for historical research) had compiled its own figures. After a first publication in 1974, these figures repeatedly appeared in the literature of Jehovah's Witnesses.

The Watch Tower Society's *Yearbook* of 1974 includes an extensive history report about the Bible Student movement in Germany, which is based on a careful analysis of statistically recorded cases known to the Watch Tower Society. The society emphasizes that the report includes only a minimum of cases, those that can be substantiated with supporting evidence.[11] The report concludes with the following statements about the number of persecuted Jehovah's Witnesses:

A total of 6,019 had been arrested, several two, three, or even more times, so that, all together, 8,917 arrests were registered. All together they had been sentenced to serve 13,924 years and two months in prison, two and a quarter times as long as the period since Adam's creation. A total of 2,000 brothers and sisters had been put into concentration camps, where they had spent 8,078 years and six months, an average of four years. A total of 635 had died in prison, 253 had been sentenced to death, and 203 of these had actually been executed. What a record of integrity![12]

We can assume that the actual number of victims is considerably higher than the figures mentioned by the Watch Tower Society. However, the disproportion between the 838 deaths the Watch Tower Society recorded and the four thousand to five thousand assumed in research studies indicates that the "estimates" (made by Kater) or the "findings" (of King) are more than questionable. The confusion is further increased by statements that one out of every three (according to Zipfel) or one out of every four (according to Kater) Jehovah's Witnesses lost their lives.[13] At the same time, scholarly literature speaks of the "secret of the high number of survivors" (Hellmund).[14]

Consequently, in the interest of scholarly honesty, it is necessary to adjust the figures previously mentioned in research studies regarding Jehovah's Witnesses who were killed during the NS period. Especially in studies discussing persecution and resistance during NS dictatorship, it can frequently be observed that the use of figures is handled in a careless way.[15] However, anyone who thinks that an exaggeration of the victim numbers increases sensitivity and consequently increases interest in this subject does a disservice to the objective of historical studies. These numbers are sad, as it is, and the atrocities enormous. What is more, sadness cannot be measured in numbers.

In view of the complexity of this subject, even the following statements can be regarded only as an attempt at estimation. It is almost impossible to make precise statements about the total number of Jehovah's Witnesses persecuted. If the meaning of the term "persecution" is used more extensively to also include situations of "endangering a person's life, inflicting damage to body, health, freedom, property, and other possessions," as well as preventing a person from "advancing occupationally and economically" (BEG, article 1, paragraph 1), it would be appropriate to assume that every Jehovah's Witness who did not abandon his faith as early as 1933/34 became a victim of NS persecution.[16]

Especially high was the number of Jehovah's Witnesses who were taken into custody for various periods of time. The published numbers vary between 5,911 (Leber and Zipfel) and 10,000 (Kater). The Watch Tower Society mentions the number of 6,262 Jehovah's Witnesses who were imprisoned an average of 2.3 years, considering the fact that several individuals were arrested repeatedly.[17] The same report states that a total of 2,074 German Bible Students were sent to concentration camps.[18]

With regard to the main camps during the war, the following figures have been determined. However, these figures always represent the highest number of Bible Student prisoners in the respective concentration camps and not the total number of IBSA members imprisoned there: Auschwitz (approx. 150),[19] Buchenwald (477),[20] Dachau (approx. 150),[21] Flossenbürg (205),[22] Mauthausen (approx. 150),[23] Neuengamme (approx. 100),[24] Ravensbrück (almost 600),[25] Sachsenhausen (500–600),[26] and Wewelsburg (306).[27] Smaller groups were imprisoned at the main camps of Majdanek, Natzweiler, Stutthof, and Vught (Herzogenbusch).[28] These figures do not include transfers and death rates ("admissions and releases"). Based on these figures it can be estimated that more than 3,000 "prisoners with the purple patch" were imprisoned in the concentration camps. This figure also includes the non-German Bible Student prisoners. More recent estimates based primarily on information from concentration camp memorials and the respective branches of the Watch Tower Society[29] suggest that a total of 1,000 foreign Jehovah's Witnesses were imprisoned in the NS concentration camps.[30] For the following nationalities, it is possible to determine the number of Bible Student prisoners. Some of these figures also include imprisonment in penal institutions other than the concentration camps: Austria (445), Poland (282), Netherlands (approx. 250), France (60), Belgium (7), Italy and Luxemburg (2 each). It is not possible to determine any exact numbers for the countries of Yugoslavia, the Soviet Union, Czechoslovakia, and Hungary. However, the number of Bible Student prisoners from these countries was small; about one-third of the Bible Student prisoners were from other countries. The number of German Jehovah's Witnesses, who represented the majority of those "prisoners with the purple patch" in the concentration camps, was probably around, or slightly above, 2,200.

Even more difficult than determining the number of concentration camp prisoners is determining the total number of the imprisoned. The incomplete records do not provide an accurate basis for the collection of data regarding Bible Student cases, even though attempts have been made. Moreover, it is not possible to reconstruct the number of people who were taken into protective detention by the police authorities. It is generally not even possible to use previous analyses based on individual Bible Student groups since they provide only a small data basis or do not provide the respective number of believers in 1933. Instead, as a basis for calculation, only the number of people is available from prosecution records of the legal authorities and the Gestapo.[31] For the Hamburg group of Jehovah's Witnesses, which was examined in the context of this study, it is also not possible to find an accurate basis for examination, not even on the basis of different sources. Since Jehovah's Witnesses do not have a formal membership and there are no internal records, or these records cannot be accessed, only a partial analysis could be made. The relatively high number of people who can be included in the examination (414, in comparison to a total number of 500 to 800 believers) provides the possibility for making indicative statements. There is evidence that 328 of the Hamburg Jehovah's Witnesses were in police detention or were imprisoned by the legal authorities. According to this estimation, one in every two Jehovah's Witnesses was imprisoned. At the beginning of NS rule, an estimated 25,000 to 30,000 people were members of the IBSA, or Jehovah's Witnesses. A comparison of the total number of prisoners recorded by the Watch Tower Society with the IBSA membership indicates that the actual number of Jehovah's Witnesses who were imprisoned in the Third Reich for various periods of time is probably considerably higher than the minimum number of 6,019 (or 6,262 for which supportive evidence is available).[32] Therefore, the number of approximately 10,000 prisoners mentioned in the Watch Tower Society's publications is by no means an overestimation. It is, rather, more than likely accurate. At the same time, these results establish the fact that probably not more than 50 percent of Jehovah's Witnesses were imprisoned or prosecuted. This also indicates that in the period from 1933 to 1934, a considerable number of Jehovah's Witnesses withdrew from the IBSA and were practicing their faith only in private, or had completely turned away from this faith.[33] On the other hand, it has to be taken into consideration that not every Jehovah's Witness who participated in the preaching activity during the period of the ban, or who actively participated in the resistance activities, was also arrested or otherwise on record with the NS persecuting authorities.[34]

Zipfel and authors who base their research on his study evidently make incorrect statements with regard to the degree of the persecution. Apart from these inaccurate statements, the figures used in previous research studies regarding the number of people arrested can generally be considered as correct. However, incorrect statements have obviously been made regarding the number of deaths. After the publication of Kater's study, it was generally assumed that four to five thousand people were killed, or 25 percent of the IBSA members ("one out of four Jehovah's Witnesses"). The history report of the Watch Tower Society, on the other hand, mentions a number of 838 recorded deaths. Compared to a membership of 25,000 Jehovah's Witnesses in the Third Reich in 1933, this would represent 3.35 percent. The figures determined for individual Bible Student congregations confirm these results, even though local deviations and special circumstances have to be taken into account. For instance, fourteen Jehovah's Witnesses from Hamburg were killed as a result of NS persecution. In consideration of the membership of 1933, this amounts to a maximum death rate of 2.8 percent. Similar results can be obtained regarding two other places for which it is possible to determine the membership of 1933: in Freiburg, the death rate was 2 percent[35] and in Bielefeld 3 percent.[36] Mannheim, on the other hand, represents an exception. There, the death rate was approximately 10 percent.[37] In other local studies, in which the calculations cannot be based on the membership but on the number of Jehovah's Witnesses who were arrested and legally punished, the percentages are considerably higher. For instance, Augsburg had a ratio of 5.1 percent,[38] Berlin 5.2 percent,[39] Karsruhe 10.6 percent,[40] and Duisburg 15.6 percent.[41] Oberhausen, a center of Bible Student resistance during the war, had a ratio of 14.6 percent.[42] Even though, because of their reference figures, the latter figures in particular provide a distorted picture, these percentages show that the assumption that one out of four German Jehovah's Witnesses lost their lives during the NS dictatorship is considerably overestimated, a misconception that has generally been supported in the literature since Kater's study.[43]

An examination of the number of deaths in the various concentration camps produces similar results. As far as can be determined, approximately 100 to 120 Jehovah's Witnesses died in Mauthausen,[44] at least 37 in Neuengamme, and more than 200 in Sachsenhausen.[45] About 30 percent of the total number of Bible Student prisoners were probably imprisoned in these three main camps. Other sources determine that (based on the total number of Bible Student prisoners) there was a death rate of 35 percent.[46] Consequently, it can be assumed that an estimated 1,100 to 1,200 Jehovah's Witnesses were killed in the concentration camps. This figure also includes the number of foreign Bible Student prisoners. To determine the number of foreign Bible Students who were killed during their imprisonment presents some difficulties. For Austria there is evidence that at least 94 Jehovah's Witnesses died during imprisonment and 117 Dutch Witnesses were killed.[47] Presumably, the death rate for Jehovah's Witnesses from Eastern European countries is much higher.[48] Therefore, it can be assumed that approximately 400 foreign Jehovah's Witnesses died during their imprisonment in the concentration camps. That would mean that about 700 to 800 German IBSA members lost their lives in the concentration camps.[49] In addition, several Jehovah's Witnesses died during their imprisonment in penal institutions, during Gestapo interrogations, and as a result of their imprisonment. Based on these calculations, the total number of Jehovah's Witnesses who were killed *without* due process of law can, therefore, be estimated at almost 1,000. According to the records of the Watch Tower Society, a total of 635 German Jehovah's Witnesses died during their imprisonment.[50]

The Watch Tower Society's history report also includes the figure of 203 people who were sentenced to death and executed, emphasizing the incomplete statistics.[51] With regard to the rulings of the Reich Military Court and other Wehrmacht courts, the People's Court, special courts, and courts of appeal, as well as other jurisdictions, quantifiable statements can be provided only to a very limited extent. However, even these few statements essentially confirm the numbers mentioned by the Watch Tower Society. At the same time, it can be assumed that the actual number of executions would probably be one-fourth, or even one-third, higher than the numbers included in the statistical records of the Watch Tower Society.[52]

In summary, the numerical data in the Watch Tower Society's 1974 report about the Bible Students Association in Germany is a remarkably reliable source. Taking into consideration the uncertainties associated with these estimations, the following conclusion can be made regarding Jehovah's Witnesses who were killed during the National Socialist period: The total numbers assumed in each case exceed (more or less) the numbers documented by the Watch Tower Society. Completely different numbers cannot be established. However, it has been confirmed that the statements of previous research studies, especially regarding the extent of the persecution and the number of deaths, must be considered as incorrect: It was not *every* fourth Jehovah's Witness who lost his life during the NS period, and the number of those killed did not nearly amount to four thousand or five thousand. Instead, future calculations can be based on the following statements: At the beginning of the Third Reich (1933), the religious denomination of Jehovah's Witnesses in Germany had a membership of between 25,000 and 30,000 people. Ten thousand of these were imprisoned for various periods of time. Of these imprisoned people, a total of two thousand were sent to concentration camps. From among the German Jehovah's Witnesses, a total of 1,200 lost their lives. Approximately 250 of them were executed, in most cases as a result of a military court sentence, on the charge of conscientious objection.

Even though the numbers previously mentioned in the literature had to be corrected, the evidence still indicates that—after the Jews—Jehovah's Witnesses were, percentage-wise, the most severely persecuted religious denomination during the NS regime.

18

Case Study: The IBSA in Hamburg

In order to make precise statements about the social structure, the degree of participation in resistance activities, and the intensity of persecution, it is necessary to substantiate and scrutinize the assertions made in the descriptions throughout this study. For this purpose, a data analysis has been made regarding the Hamburg IBSA group. However, the validity of this empirical study is limited in that only data could be used for the assessment for which records are available or which could be reconstructed on the basis of other sources.

In 1932 a total of 546 people belonged to the Hamburg group of Bible Students (people attending their Memorial celebrations).[53] However, at the time of the national census, June 16, 1933, which already showed signs of the beginning NS persecution, only 355 people (162 men and 193 women) disclosed their Bible Student membership.[54] It has to be taken into consideration that the Prussian districts of Altona, Wandsbek, Harburg-Wilhelmsburg, and some other small villages were not yet incorporated with Hamburg. The incorporation took place only in the context of the "Greater Hamburg Law" of January 26, 1937. It is not possible to determine the exact number of Jehovah's Witnesses who lived in these towns and villages at that time.[55] Since, for the period of the persecution, no data is available for the individual districts of Hamburg, it is necessary to project the (previous) Hamburg figures according to the population increase in order to have a basis for a data analysis. The population figures of Hamburg in 1933 correspond almost exactly to two-thirds of the population figures of the Greater Hamburg. Consequently, based on the results of the national census in June 16, 1933, it can be assumed that at the beginning of the Third Reich, in the total area of the later Greater Hamburg, about 500 people openly professed to be Bible Students. Furthermore, based on the number of people who

Figure 7. Age structrue (year of birth), Hamburg IBSA, 1933–45

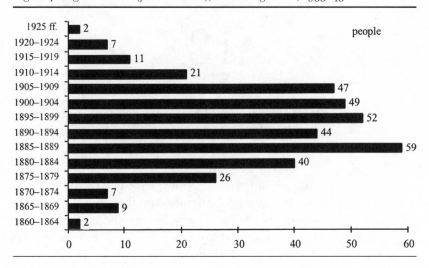

attended the 1932 Memorial celebration, an additional 300 people in Hamburg were loosely associated with the Bible Students.

On the basis of compensation files and court records, records of various archives, and extensive questioning of contemporary witnesses, it was possible to collect data regarding a total of 414 Jehovah's Witnesses in Hamburg who were active during the NS period.[56] (Subsequently, the term "Hamburg" will always refer to the total area of the Hanseatic city, in the context of the Greater Hamburg Law of January 26, 1937.) Consequently, against the background of the statements regarding the total number of Bible Students in Hamburg at the beginning of the Third Reich, we can assume (based on the analysis of the Hamburg IBSA group) that there is an adequate basis for a data analysis about Jehovah's Witnesses between 1933 and 1945.[57]

Age Structure

The year of birth could be determined for 376 Jehovah's Witnesses in Hamburg (see fig. 7). People born between 1890 and 1909 (51.1%) are well represented. At the point of NS takeover, these people were between twenty-three and forty-three years old. The small number of young people (born in 1910 and later: 10.9%) and the relatively high number of older people (born in 1889 and earlier: 38.0%) indicates that,

Figure 8. Gender representation, Hamburg IBSA, 1933–45

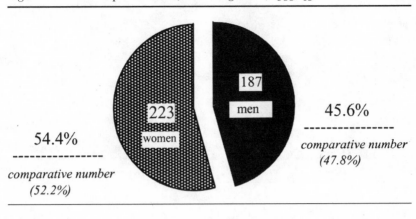

223
women

54.4%
----
comparative number
(52.2%)

187
men

45.6%
----
comparative number
(47.8%)

Note: N = 410.

on average, the IBSA members who practiced their faith during the period of the ban were older people.[58] This corresponds to the average age structure of any other religious association. It does not correspond to the average age structure of groups involved in resistance activities, which generally had a stronger participation of younger people.[59]

Representation of Men and Women

Until March 31, 1947, a total of 12,119 people in Hamburg received recognition as opponents to the NS regime, 8,813 men (72.7%) and 3,306 women (27.3%).[60] It can be assumed that this represents the distribution between the sexes during the actual period of resistance. Consequently, the total number of resistance fighters in Hamburg included a little more than one quarter women and almost three quarters men. By way of contrast, the majority of Jehovah's Witnesses persecuted because of their IBSA activities (54.4%) were women.[61] This clearly different distribution between the sexes allows for the conclusion that Jehovah's Witnesses had considerably more women participating in resistance activities than other religious, social, and political groups, including the prohibited parties.[62]

The distribution between the sexes from among the persecuted Hamburg members of the IBSA corresponds exactly to their proportions at the beginning of the Third Reich. According to the national census on June 16, 1933, the Hamburg Bible Students (not including the

Figure 9. Marital status, Hamburg IBSA, 1933–45

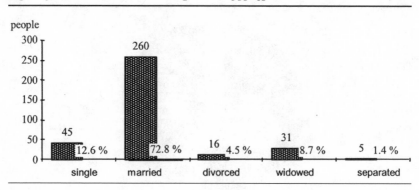

districts of Altona, Wandsbek, and Harburg-Wilhelmsburg) had a membership of 193 women (54.37%) and 162 men (45.63%).[63] Therefore, it can be assumed that during the period of the ban, male and female Jehovah's Witnesses had an equal share in the prohibited IBSA activities.

Marital Status

A total of 72.8 percent Jehovah's Witnesses participating in IBSA activities during the National Socialist period were married, 8.7 percent of them were widowed, 4.5 percent were divorced, 1.4 percent were separated, and 12.6 percent were single.

By way of comparison, according to the 1933 national census, the population figures for the city-state of Hamburg are as follows: 62.1 percent were married, 8.9 percent widowed, 2.9 percent divorced, and 26.1 percent single.[64] According to these statistics, the proportion of married people from among Jehovah's Witnesses was above average and the number of single people comparatively low.[65] This reflects the generally accepted high regard for marriage and family within this denomination. Single fellow believers within the denomination were encouraged to marry. In this context, it should also be mentioned that there were only seven Jehovah's Witnesses who were not married to a fellow believer. Interestingly, compared to the general population of Hamburg, the divorce rate was comparatively high. It is, however, not known to what extent the difference in faith contributed to these divorces. This can perhaps also explain why, among the 230 married Bible Students, 23 were married a second, or even a third time.

Figure 10. Number of children, Hamburg IBSA, 1933–45

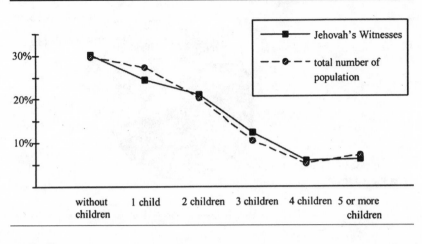

Note: N = 299.

Number of Children

Of the 299 Jehovah's Witnesses, a total of 90 (30.1%) had no children. This is similar to the ratio in the Hamburg population as a whole (29.6%).[66] Also, all other statements regarding the number of children did not significantly deviate from comparative numbers in the population as a whole: A total of 21 percent of Jehovah's Witnesses had two children; in the general population, the ratio was 20.4 percent. A total of 6 percent of Jehovah's Witnesses had four children; in the general population, this ratio was 5.2 percent.

As a result, it can be established that the Bible Student families had about the same number of children as the Hamburg population in general.[67]

Mobility

During the NS period, a total of 355 members of the Hamburg Bible Student group participated in prohibited IBSA activities. A total of 30.1 percent of these were born in the Hanseatic city of Hamburg. The others had moved to Hamburg during the course of their life.

During the period of industrial growth and the far-reaching economic crises, large numbers of people moved to the cities. Therefore,

Figure 11. Mobility, Hamburg IBSA, 1933–45

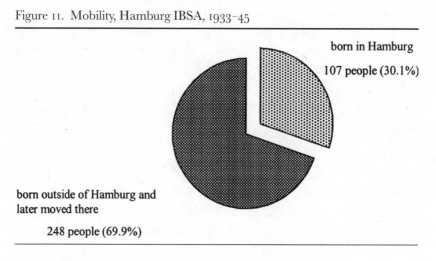

born in Hamburg

107 people (30.1%)

born outside of Hamburg and
later moved there

248 people (69.9%)

Note: N = 355.

the number of Jehovah's Witnesses who had moved to Hamburg during later periods in their lives does not seem to be unusually high.[68]

Status/Social Structure

For a total of 322 Jehovah's Witnesses, information is available about their occupational activities. According to this information, the majority of these Jehovah's Witnesses came from a social background of lower or lower middle class. However, a considerable number of Hamburg Bible Students also belonged to the middle class. Only two families of Hamburg Jehovah's Witnesses belonged to the upper middle class and upper class. The same results can be determined regarding school education. Accordingly, 88.1 percent of the Hamburg IBSA members attended the *Volksschule*. A total of 5.9 percent attended the *Mittelschule* (secondary school) and other secondary schools. Only a few Jehovah's Witnesses (1.0%) acquired a certificate after attending the *Gymnasium* (college preparatory high school). Approximately 5 percent left school without graduating.

The fact that 15.5 percent of Bible Students worked in factories, on farms, or had casual jobs and another 11.2 percent worked as maidservants and cleaning women indicates that quite a number of them were socially affiliated with the lower class. Moreover, the high number of

Table 11. Hamburg IBSA occupational groups, 1933–45

Area of employment[1]	Number	Percent
Factory, farm, and day laborers	50	15.5
Skilled craftsmen/women	46	14.3
Craftsmen	37	11.5
Professionals	29	9.0
Self-employed people (Shopkeeper, businessmen/women, tradesmen/women, etc.)	17	5.3
Lower and upper levels of civil service	8	2.5
Higher occupational levels (executive clerks)	1	0.3
Housewives	77	23.9
Domestic helpers (maids, cleaning ladies, etc.)	36	11.2
Pensioners	11	3.4
Others	10	3.1
Total	**322**	**100.0**

[1]In cases in which Bible Students worked at different occupations during the NS period, the analysis is based on the occupation they held at the beginning of the Third Reich. Generally, such changes in occupation were made because of political circumstances (disbarment for civil servants, dismissals because of nonmembership in the DAF, etc.).

employed women (52.5%) suggests that many women among the Bible Students had to support their families with an additional income. It is also noteworthy that quite a number of Jehovah's Witnesses worked in the trades. In analyzing these numbers, it should be taken into account that the occupational structure of the group under consideration was typical for a big city. (For this reason, no farmers are mentioned.)

Of special interest is a comparison with the social structure of the Hamburg population of 1933. For a comparison of the percentages, it was necessary to analyze the disparate groups of occupation according to employment status.

The number of workers among Jehovah's Witnesses was 7 percent higher than the number of workers among the general population in Hamburg (55.6% compared to 48.5%). However, there were only half as many employees and civil servants among the IBSA members than among the Hamburg population in general (employees, 12.6% compared to 24.5%; civil servants, 3.3% compared to 6.8%).

Consequently, the majority of the Hamburg IBSA members belonged to the working and underprivileged classes of the population.

Table 12. Analyses of Hamburg IBSA members' occupations, 1933–45

Employed people	IBSA members [Percent]	Hamburg (without rural districts) [Percent]
Workers	55.6	48.5
Employees	12.6	24.5
Civil servants	3.3	6.8
Self-employed	11.3	15.7
Family members	2.1	1.4
Domestic workers	15.1	3.1

Note: N = 239. These figures refer to employed as well as unemployed people. For comparison, the numbers of family members without a primary occupation (housewives, pensioners, people with secondary occupations, etc.) are left out of consideration. See *Die Volks-, Berufs- und Betriebszählung in Hamburg/1933*, 22, chart 14, "Employed people and their dependants in Hamburg according to their occupational status in 1933."

However, since almost 30 percent belonged to the middle and lower middle class, the indiscriminate characterization of Jehovah's Witnesses as a "religion of the poor" can no longer be maintained.[69]

Former Memberships in Parties and Trade Unions

Only a small number of Jehovah's Witnesses in Hamburg had been members of political parties or trade unions before they joined the Bible Students Association. Information about former party memberships can be determined only in the cases of left-wing parties. The available data regarding 127 Jehovah's Witnesses included in this analysis does

Table 13. Former memberships in political parties and trade unions of the Hamburg IBSA, 1933–45

	Number	Percent
SPD	11	8.7
KPD	5	3.9
Trade unions	24[1]	18.9
Without membership in unions or parties	94	74.0

Note: N = 127.
[1]Seven of the twenty-four members of trade unions were also members of the SPD or KPD.

not indicate a former membership in any other party. According to this data, 8.7 percent of the Hamburg IBSA members had previously been members of the SPD. A total of 3.9 percent had previously been members of the KPD.[70] A considerable number of Jehovah's Witnesses used to be members of trade unions. About one-third of them continued this membership in trade unions even after becoming Jehovah's Witnesses.

Number of Years within the Denomination

A total of 49.3 percent of the Hamburg Bible Students who participated in the prohibited preaching activity during the NS period had joined the denomination during the 1920s. Only a small number of Jehovah's Witnesses who were persecuted during that period had been associated with this religious denomination for more than twenty years. A total of 3.7 percent had become Jehovah's Witnesses before World War I. An exceptionally high number became Bible Students during the two years prior to the National Socialist seizure of power (82 people, or 27.3%).

Of the three hundred ban-defying Jehovah's Witnesses whose date of baptism and date of joining the association is available, one out of ten joined the IBSA during the Third Reich. This means that in Hamburg, as far as can be determined, at least thirty people joined Jehovah's Witnesses during the period of persecution. In an empirical study, it is not possible to establish to what extent the decision of those who became Jehovah's Witnesses after 1933 was based on opposition to National

Figure 12. Years of conversion, Hamburg IBSA, 1933–45

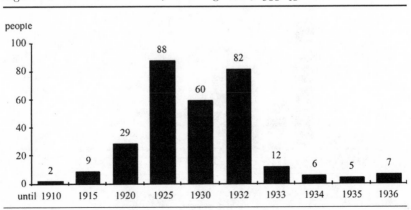

Note: N = 300.

Socialism. However, based on statements of contemporary witnesses, as well as statements made in retrospect, it can be assumed that this aspect had a certain effect on a person's decision to join the Bible Students Association, just as sympathy and solidarity for the persecuted fellow believers were decisive factors in this decision.[71] These new members also showed that even during the NS period the preaching activity of Jehovah's Witnesses was not without success.

Persecution

The NS measures of persecution against Jehovah's Witnesses had, indeed, assumed horrifying dimensions. This is emphasized by means of an analysis of data concerning the numbers and dates of arrests and court decisions, the number of imprisonments per year between 1933 and 1945, the total number of years of imprisonment, as well as data about the people who lost their lives because of their religious steadfastness.

Number of Convictions / Orders of Protective Detention per Year

The analysis of court decisions indicates that there were two waves of repression during 1935 and 1937. In some cases, people were put into

Figure 13. Judgments/measures of protective detention, Hamburg IBSA, 1933–45

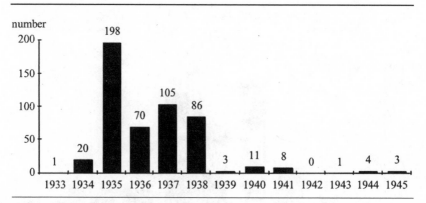

Note: N = 510. Over the years, many Jehovah's Witnesses were sentenced more than once. For instance, 87 people were sentenced twice, 20 people three times, and 6 people four times, resulting in a total of 510 cases in which sentences were pronounced. In 49 cases no information is available, since no sentences were pronounced. If the Gestapo ordered protective detention, it is not on record. Temporary detention in police custody and Gestapo summons are not recorded.

protective detention or sent to concentration camps without first under-going court proceedings. In these cases, the date of arrest was used as a basis for the analysis. The waves of repression mentioned above show how the persecuting authorities reacted to the periods of increased IBSA activities (resumption of preaching activity after October 7, 1934;

Table 14. Special Court proceedings against Hamburg Jehovah's Witnesses

	1935	1936	1937	1938	1940	1941	**Total**	**Percent**
Acquittals		9	1	7		1	**18**	**4.3**
Discontinuance of proceedings								
(amnesties, etc.)	10	3		11	1		**25**	**5.9**
Fines		11					**11**	**2.6**
Prison sentences							**368**	**87.2**
1 month	4							
2 months	121	9		4				
3 months	7			3				
4 months	2	2	3	7				
5 months	1	2		1				
6 months	31	8	3	12		1		
7 months		2	2					
8 months	2			6				
9 months	4	1	2	19				
10 months				8				
1 year	1		4	24	1			
14 months				1				
15 months				11				
18 months		2	3	4				
20 months				3				
21 months				5				
2 years		2	1	4				
27 months				2				
30 months				15				
32 months				1				
33 months				1				
34 months				2				
3 years				5	2	1		
3.5 years				4	1			
4 years				1				
Total number of defendants	**183**	**51**	**19**	**161**	**5**	**3**	**422**	**100.0**

pamphlet campaigns of December 1936 and June 1937 at the Reich level). Between 1939 and 1945, on the other hand, there were merely 30 cases (5.9%) in which sentences were pronounced or in which the Gestapo ordered "protective detention."

According to available records, 43 special court proceedings took place against Hamburg Jehovah's Witnesses (total number of defendants: 422; of this number, a total of 113 people were repeatedly accused). In 1935 the average prison sentence amounted to 3.1 months. As table 14 indicates, these prison sentences greatly increased during the subsequent years.

Number of Jehovah's Witnesses Imprisoned per Year

The large number of proceedings between 1935 and 1938 had seriously weakened the Hamburg IBSA group. Since the functionaries and active members of the group had received long prison sentences and, after serving their sentences, were sent to the concentration camps, the group was left without appropriate leadership. Deprived of these motivating people, it was very difficult to reorganize the group and resume its preaching activity. During the war, the Hamburg IBSA group and its subordinate groups did not perform any significant organized activities. The majority of Jehovah's Witnesses discontinued their preaching activity. They tried to maintain and uphold their religious activities in the

Figure 14. Number of imprisoned Jehovah's Witnesses, Hamburg IBSA, 1933–45

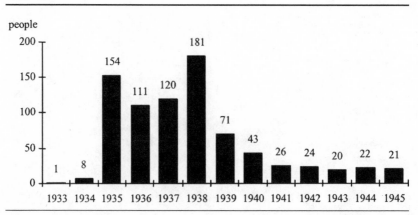

Note: N = 802.

privacy of their homes. In view of the totalitarian demands of National Socialism, this endeavor in itself involved many hardships.

An analysis and representation of the data according to the number of people imprisoned per year shows that the nucleus of the Hamburg group of approximately twenty Jehovah's Witnesses remained in prison, or were kept imprisoned (or killed) behind the barbed-wire fences of the concentration camps, until 1945. The majority of people belonging to this religious denomination, on the other hand, were released from imprisonment between 1938 and 1939.

Periods of Imprisonment

In 400 cases (based on 414 data sheets), the periods of imprisonment of the Hamburg Jehovah's Witnesses could be determined. A total of 328 people were imprisoned for more than seven days. Of this number, a total of 103 people spent more than one year in prisons, concentration camps, or other penal institutions. A total of 35 Jehovah's Witnesses from Hamburg were imprisoned for more than three years. Ten Jehovah's Witnesses served prison sentences of eight to ten years in various prisons and concentration camps. The average period of imprisonment amounted to one and a half years.

If an analysis of the periods of imprisonment is divided according to the sexes, it becomes evident that more female Bible Students than male Bible Students (a ratio of 170 to 158) received a prison sentence of more than seven days. However, on average, the periods of imprisonment for

Figure 15. Periods of imprisonment, Hamburg IBSA, 1933–45

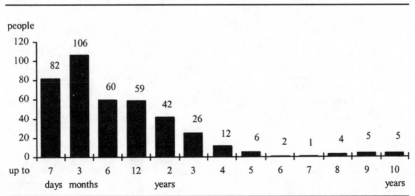

Note: N = 410.

Figure 16. Periods of imprisonment (women), Hamburg IBSA, 1933–45

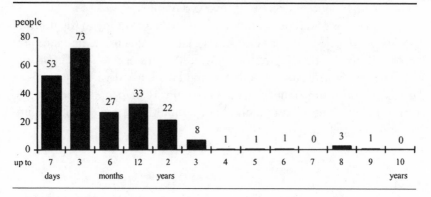

Figure 17. Periods of imprisonmnet (men), Hamburg IBSA, 1933–45

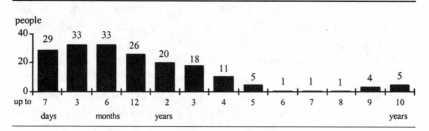

Table 15. Periods of imprisonment for Hamburg IBSA members, 1933–45

	No imprisonment or fewer than 7 days amnesty granted	Up to 3 months	Up to 1 year	Up to 3 years	Up to 6 years	More than 6 years
Women	23.8%	32.8%	26.9%	13.6%	1.2%	1.7%
Men	15.6%	17.6%	31.5%	20.4%	9.1%	5.8%

Note: for women, N = 223; for men, N = 187.

men were twice as long as the periods of imprisonment for women (men, an average of two years; women, an average of one year).

Victims of National Socialist Persecution

During the National Socialist regime, a total of fourteen IBSA members in Hamburg lost their lives because of NS persecution:

> Deceased in penal institutions or during pretrial detention: 4
> Deceased in concentration camps: 7
> Deceased as a result of their imprisonment: 3

19

Social Refusal and Resistance

In conclusion, after this discussion about the extent of the persecution and its exemplification based on records of the Hamburg IBSA group, it is important to discuss the question of how the activities of Jehovah's Witnesses in the Third Reich can be assessed from a historical perspective. This assessment should also consider the question of whether these activities can be integrated into resistance-historiographic categories. In this regard, special consideration shall be given to the question of whether it would be appropriate and justified to consider the attitude and actions of the IBSA members as acts of "resistance."

In contemporary historiographic studies regarding National Socialism, the concept of resistance has been extensively and controversially discussed. However, to this day, historiographers have been unable to offer a generally acceptable definition of the term "resistance." In this regard, neither the diversity of oppositional groups and their objectives nor the aspect of disruption of governmental authority through other actions and forms of resistance has been taken into consideration. However, during the 1970s and 1980s, special emphasis began to be placed on an examination of this issue. As a result, the former viewpoint of categorically minimizing resistance activities as attempts toward subversion was replaced with the concept of an extensive range of various degrees in the behavior patterns of opposition against the objectives of the NS regime.[72]

In early studies of resistance, an attempt was made to minimize the idea of "collective guilt" toward the outside world. Therefore, the picture of a "different Germany" was created. Such studies even had to make large numbers of the German population aware of the fact that offering resistance could actually be a choice of action. With regard to motives and objectives, measures employed, and social supporters of resistance, these studies greatly restricted the concept of resistance, which corresponded to a monolithic picture of the NS regime as a total-itarian system of rule (akin to the Stalinist system). During the 1950s, and, to a certain extent, even during the 1960s, resistance was seen as an action that was solely restricted to the civil, religious, and military elite (in the truest sense of the word), having its roots in distress and patriot-ism. It had the purpose of reestablishing freedom and rights, using con-spiracy and subversion to achieve these goals, and had its most visible expression in the attempted assassination of Hitler and coup d'état of July 20, 1944. Acts of resistance were therefore described as "appropri-ate actions with the objective of changing the political system." "With regard to a totalitarian system," however, this objective was achieved only if a "considerable change, better yet, a complete and successful re-moval of the regime was accomplished, or any efforts to this end would not be doomed to failure right from the start."[73] In consideration of a concept of resistance that is measured according to its degree of suc-cess, that of overthrowing a government, Gerhard Schulz stated that such actions could logically be performed only by groups "that have the possibility of long-term advance planning, groups with . . . influential functions or offices within the hierarchical structure of the totalitarian regime, and that, ultimately, also have the required instruments of power. People who are persecuted in a totalitarian state are no longer in any position to offer political resistance."[74]

From the middle of the 1960s on, studies concerning the history of the labor movement also resulted in the fact that the concept of resist-ance was reevaluated. Groundbreaking in this regard are the studies on Dortmund, Duisburg, and Essen (Klotzbach, Bludau, Steinberg), pub-lished in a series by the Friedrich-Ebert-Stiftung. By also taking the so-cial environment into consideration, these studies, which focus on the worker's opposition, that is, social democratic, Socialist, and Commu-nist resistance, overcame the previous view of restricting acts of resist-ance to certain circles. They try to include the entire spectrum of resist-ance activities within a respective local area. By including all groups that offered resistance, which also drew attention to Jehovah's Witnesses, it was possible to perform a comparative analysis and to describe the vari-ous possibilities and perspectives of actions according to their social and political background. The restriction of the research study to a specific locality resulted therefore in an "expansion of the perspective."[75] How-ever, the concept of resistance continued to be divided into a dualistic model, in which the one side represents the persecuting (to a large extent monolithic) governmental authorities, and the other side shows groups offering resistance.

Toward the end of the 1970s, historians began to take an interest in the social aspects of everyday life in the Third Reich. They also began to place the issue of "resistance and persecution" into a setting of "sociopolitical behavior."[76] This resulted in the recognition of the various forms of "unusual behavior," which did not necessarily reflect political resistance but represented resistance attitudes and actions that concerned the very question of survival. These individual and, to a large extent, unorganized acts of resistance included spontaneous expressions of disapproval, the dissemination of anti-NS rumors, and listening in on prohibited foreign radio stations. These acts of resistance even included the refusal to perform certain actions at the workplace as well as providing support for persecuted people. The concept of resistance was no longer restricted to organized groups and deliberate political actions. This new social-historical perception of the study of resistance realized that even nonpolitically motivated social refusal or opposition could disrupt, at times even jeopardize, the execution of NS authority. Consequently, resistance certainly could have political consequences.

This aspect of the degree to which a particular action would affect the interaction, or interdependence, between the general public and the governmental authority also shaped the reevaluated concept of resistance. According to Peter Hüttenberger, who modeled the concept of resistance on socio-scientific theories, resistance includes "all actions that prevent a government from making demands on certain social groups. This includes any refusal to perform a certain action, as well as any action that could result in such refusal."[77]

By extending the field of research to practically all areas of social life, historians were able to introduce more differentiated definitions of the concept of resistance. To this end, they replaced the dichotomous use of the concept of resistance with a system of graduated and differentiated relational single concepts. These efforts to achieve conceptual differentiation resulted for the various graduations in a number of vocabularies, described and applied by authors in a variety of ways. The most common concepts in this regard are: selective discontentment, dissent, social protest, *Resistenz*, partial insubordination, nonconformity, social refusal, opposition, resistance, antagonism, conspiracy, and scheming.[78]

By means of typologies, several authors established an analytical framework by means of which they could determine the scope of certain attitudes and actions. These categorizing attempts generally make a distinction between organized and spontaneous actions, between private, nonpublic actions and anti-state actions intended to draw the greatest possible publicity, and regarding the extent of criticism, between fundamental and partial opposition.

Very significant in this regard is Richard Löwenthal's model. He uses "resistance" as a generic term that includes the whole spectrum of nonconformist actions, and he makes a distinction between "political opposition," "social refusal," and "ideological dissent," and describes these characteristics as the "three basic forms of anti-totalitarian resistance."[79] Concerning the term "social refusal," Löwenthal emphasizes that "the factual political effect of such resistance . . . [is] independent from its primarily nonpolitical intentions: Even partial resistance because of religious or moral reasons, because of adherence to traditional, social ties and ways of life . . . or even partially because of material interests restricted the totalitarian exercise of power."[80]

In other typological studies, the concept of "resistance" was mostly restricted to political actions, actions that were directed at overthrowing or permanently damaging the NS regime, or rejecting National Socialism on principle. A good example is Detlev Peukert's model. He introduced a "flowing scale" of terms describing deviant behavior in the Third Reich, which range from "actions of nonconformity" (individual violations of standards that did not call into question the whole system) to "social refusal" (contumacies against official instructions) to "protest" (more serious rejection of the regime), and culminating in "resistance" (rejection of the NS regime as a whole, as well as participation in subversive actions against the regime, within the scope of a person's opportunities).[81] Günther van Norden subsumes the role of church opposition during the Third Reich by the term "partial resistance."[82] He subdivides this term into "defensive *Resistenz,* offensive protest, active confession, proclamation of natural human rights—defense of rights and humanity, and active political resistance."

In the discussion of resistance typologies presented during the 1980s, various factions cautioned against "weakening the concept of resistance." For example, Hans Mommsen emphasizes that "basically active resistance also denoted political action and therefore was subject to criteria such as feasibility, balancing of interests, and the necessity of securing power. These are characteristics that could not be applied to mere opposition to Hitler, which, in itself, could not be considered as an act of resistance."[83] For the same reason, Ian Kershaw argued in favor of "restricting" the concept of resistance to "deliberate political actions of fundamental opposition to the regime."[84] In order to be able to make terminological distinctions, Kershaw suggests using the word "dissent" as a generic term for all forms of deviant behavior and attitudes.

Of special interest is a radical re-determination of the conceptual field and its propositions made in the context of the comprehensive research study "Bavaria during the National Socialist period." This unique study has had a lasting effect on resistance movement historiography. By means of this study, the Munich Institute for Contemporary History definitely eliminates the unfounded picture of the Third Reich as a monolithic system of absolute power and replaces it with the analysis of a state order that was implemented as a result of a continuous conflict between the ruling powers and society. The study examines the wide range of unusual behavior patterns and reactions to situations other than resistance and persecution.[85] It also introduces into the scholarly discussion the term *Resistenz* in order to describe the various forms of oppositional and nonconformist behavior. In contrast to the moral-political concept of "resistance," which focuses on subjective actions, the concept of *Resistenz* does not center on the intentions, motives, and objectives of the people involved. It focuses exclusively on the actual results of their actions. Therefore, Martin Broszat, the director of the institute, defines this concept of *Resistenz* as "effective defense, restriction, eradication of the National Socialist rule and its demands, regardless of the motives, reasons, and forces involved."[86] Since the issue "solely" involves the question of actual eradication of NS rule and ideology, scholars maintain that this definition provides research studies with an impartial category.[87] Accordingly, all forms of attitude and reaction in the Third Reich that were directed against certain ideological, disciplinary, or organizational measures, and against unreasonable demands of the National Socialist regime and that, consequently, had a restricting effect on an exercising of power, are subsumed under the term *Resistenz*.[88] This includes active opposition in the same way as it does civil insubordination. Among other things, Broszat mentions, for instance, nonparticipation in NS events and refusal to give the Hitler salute.[89] He even mentions the act of "merely" upholding anti–National Socialist principles.

In contrast to resistance movement historiography, a historical examination based on the concept of *Resistenz* uses a completely different approach: Historical studies that examine motives and behavior patterns almost exclusively concentrate on the actions and the people offering resistance. Frequently, such studies succumb to the danger of mythologizing and heroicizing. Historical studies based on the concept of *Resistenz*, however, focus on the effects and social aspects of resistance. By involving comprehensive correlations of group phenomena and problems of everyday life, these historical studies examine the conditions that caused attitudes and acts of resistance. The examination focuses especially on the ability of social milieus or certain organizations, particularly the churches, to show perseverance or relative resistance. The concept of *Resistenz*, which increased the field of examination, certainly resulted in a more appropriate inclusion of the social groups that opposed the ideas of the NS government. Initially, however, a comparison between "*Resistenz*" and "resistance" presents some difficulties. In comparing the often martyrlike resistance activities that provoked "unnecessary risks and sacrifices" and aimed at subversion, Martin Broszat ascribes more efficiency, a suitable purpose-method-relation, and greater rationality to the strategy of "pragmatically oriented passive *Resistenz*." According to Broszat, the restriction to "a less dangerous *Resistenz* that was especially directed toward self-protection and the survival of non–National Socialist forces and values" demonstrated a "more realistic view of the governmental powers." Consequently, it can "be considered as the most effective and, typologically, most appropriate form of opposition against totalitarian rule."[90]

Against this concept of *Resistenz* the objection has been made that it involves the danger of overextending its use by including even partial and merely insignificant manifestations of nonconformity. And because of a lack of clear categorization, it could, therefore, possibly involve any form of behavior that did not expressly declare one's approval of National Socialism. According to historians, resistance had to involve more than someone's determination to survive. It had to be more comprehensive than nonperformance of demonstrations of loyalty or refusal to submit completely to the standards of NS leadership.[91] Consequently, there is the danger of placing diverse actions on the same level, as well as the danger of classifying too many acts of dissent as resistance. Far more serious is the problem that the term *Resistenz* cannot be translated.[92] In view of its linguistic affinity with the terms *resistance, résistance,* and *resistenza,* which correspond to the German term *Widerstand,* the possibility for differentiation involves some terminological difficulties. Moreover, since in natural science and in the medical field the term *Resistenz* has a rather negative connotation, the objection has been made that a use of this term is not the best choice. In these fields, *Resistenz* is used to characterize a condition that inhibits the recovery from an ailment. Also in view of the fact that *Resistenz* is passive with regard to cause and effect, the choice has been considered rather unfortunate.[93] Other criticism involves the exclusive reservation of the concept of *Resistenz* for intentional political acts of opposition (which, however, applies only during the initial period of the Bavarian research study[94]) because it restricts "the customary resistance concept" so that it fails to "give consideration to nonpolitical forms of resistance."[95]

"Silent Refusal"

For many decades, historiography restricted the concept of resistance to political actions that aimed at subversion. This is probably another reason why the history of Jehovah's Witnesses in the Third Reich found only little response in historical studies. But even the relatively few historical studies that discuss the attitudes of Jehovah's Witnesses in the Third Reich provide a variety of interpretative models for assessing Bible Student activities. These models can be divided into five main groups: passive resistance, religiously motivated resistance, nonpolitical revolt of an underprivileged group, futile martyrdom, and acts of social refusal with political objectives or (at least) political consequences.

With reference to the willingness to compromise of the major churches who initially seem to have been unaware of the "irreconcilable contradictions in principle matters," Hans Rothfels wrote in 1958: "Only sectarian groups such as the Quakers, the Mennonites, or the 'Earnest Bible Students' were not subject to fluctuations. They continuously offered passive resistance. But they were insignificant in number."[96] Falk Pingel, who placed the activities of Jehovah's Witnesses also in the category of "passive resistance," additionally depicted the "fundamental pattern of their social actions" as "passive *Resistenz*."[97] Jehovah's Witnesses were not explicitly accredited with a quietistic mentality, even though at least Wolfgang Benz makes reference to that effect by presenting their resistance as even more passive. He describes their behavior during the NS period as "silent refusal" and as "resistance without action."[98]

The refusal and consistent rejection of requirements of the NS regime that, according to their conviction, were incompatible with biblical principles, certainly made the Bible Students stand out in the Third Reich. "In a world where 'Yes' had become the obligatory response, they, like other opponents of the regime, determinedly said 'No.'"[99]

Not only did they refuse to obey and evade the NS coercive measures to force the entire people into line, they also refused to display an attitude of ideological opposition. Furthermore, they did not simply accept suppression and persecution or occupy a defensive position. Viewed as a group, their response was not exclusively and predominantly passive. They certainly did perform actions. As is documented by the various forms of offensive resistance, Jehovah's Witnesses did not only think differently, they also acted differently. Even Manfred Koch states that the description of their behavior as passive "underestimates the degree of resistance of Jehovah's Witnesses."[100]

The majority of authors describe the actions of the Bible Students Association from a motive-historical perspective as acts of resistance based on their religious beliefs. In his 1965 study, Friedrich Zipfel mentions as primary reasons for the opposition of IBSA members against National Socialism: "their rejection of any authority that contradicted biblical principles," "their preaching activity, warning unbelievers of an impending divine punishment," and "the strict requirement not to kill."[101] Michael H. Kater also views the "unshakable religious devotion" of Jehovah's Witnesses "as fundamental reasons for their opposition against the National Socialist regime."[102] In the *Handbuch der deutschen Geschichte* (Gebhardt), Karl Dietrich Erdmann emphasizes: "It was a small minority that consistently followed their religious conviction, free from the social-political involvement and considerations of the major churches."[103] Manfred Koch states that "their resistance was ultimately based on their religious teachings, according to which the day would come when Jehovah, in his Holy War, would destroy all worldly governments by means of His Kingdom, which was established in 1914."[104] Koch further states that the history of Jehovah's Witnesses has become "paradigmatic for religiously motivated resistance without the use of violence."[105]

Different aspects determine the classification if, besides their motivation, the position of *Resistenz* and the resistance-disposed behavior of Jehovah's Witnesses were based on their social structure. Kater, for example, also described in 1970 the "resistance" of Jehovah's Witnesses as "opposition of socially and economically underprivileged circles."[106] At about the same time, Eberhard Aleff depicted the behavior of Jehovah's Witnesses as "nonpolitical escape of the underprivileged."[107] According to the American historian Walter Struve, Jehovah's Witnesses, whose social structure had a specifically "proletarian composition," were also "class-conscious workers." In his 1990 study, Struve states that they resisted National Socialism because they were "servants of Jehovah" and not because they belonged to the working class. Yet, the National Socialists also persecuted them because any "autonomous activity of the lower classes" represented a threat to the NS regime.[108] Accordingly, Struve concludes that the seriousness of the measures of persecution against Jehovah's Witnesses could have resulted, "to a certain extent, from their affiliation with the working class."[109]

In his 1981 research study, "Bavaria during the National Socialist Period," Martin Broszat also focuses more closely on the social backgrounds of people showing resistance. Taking an effect-historical approach, Broszat associates the Bible Students with a "resistance type that is at the very end of the scale of oppositional behavior." Within this form of resistance an "extremely high price in the severity of persecution and number of victims is 'paid' for activities that were almost inconsequential with regard to an actual restriction of National Socialist rule. Commitment and willingness to take risks obviously stood in sharp contrast to the results of the resistance activities."[110] Under the aspect of rationality and a suitable purpose-method-relation, Broszat classifies the behavior of the IBSA members as "futile martyrdom."[111] It is appropriate, however, to raise objections to both aspects that Martin Broszat uses to describe the IBSA activities—"martyrlike" and "futile."

Contemporary witnesses, as well as people of later periods, often describe the attitude the Bible Students displayed in the Third Reich as martyrdom. For example, a contemporary report about the conditions in the Sachsenburg concentration camp states: "The behavior of the Earnest Bible Students is truly amazing. These . . . people displayed an unshakable spirit of opposition. They had a martyr's disposition and were uncompromising as no other group."[112] However, this was not a matter of martyrdom in the true sense of the word. Jehovah's Witnesses did not consider death primarily as a public testimony to the world. They did not even consider it as a silent protest against arbitrary political actions and the NS regime of terror. By no means did they see themselves in the role of martyrs. The majority of them tried everything in their power to avoid persecution for as long as possible. The spiritually strong IBSA members also tried hard to stick to their principles, even under the most difficult circumstances. On September 9, 1944, the Reich Military Court (RKG) sentenced a Jehovah's Witness to death on the charge of conscientious objection. In his farewell letter, he wrote that he had "done everything possible to prolong the process." In view of the fact that he was requested to take up arms, there was "actually nothing else he could do."[113]

Jehovah's Witnesses were not seeking to die. But if it became a life-and-death matter, they would choose death rather than deny their faith. This does not mean that they idealized death, as did their ideological opponents who, by means of necrophilous mysticism, called upon their subjects to "sacrifice their lives for people and Führer." But at the same time, Jehovah's Witnesses did not overemphasize the value of their present life. For "God's people" this life merely represented an interme-diate stage to the "true life." Therefore, at least with regard to their reli-gious convictions, death had long lost its sting. Those who accepted the possibility of dying a "martyr's death" lived with the certainty that they would soon be resurrected and reunited with their loved ones. Rudi Auschner's farewell letter concludes with the statement: "I will conclude this letter in the anticipation of seeing you and all my dear brothers and sisters soon in the Kingdom of God."[114]

Considering the empirical evidence from the standpoint of an out-sider, it would certainly be justified to assess the Bible Student activities as "futile" with regard to their effectiveness and overall success. Such an assessment judges the activities of Jehovah's Witnesses on the premise that the resistance of oppositional forces has the objective of damaging, in the broadest sense, the NS regime and changing the political situa-tion. (Such oppositional forces had to be concerned with success.) It also judges these activities on premises that could be used to describe the "intended," actually achieved interference with NS rule. Under these premises, it is very difficult to understand the actions of Jehovah's Wit-nesses because they did not determine their actions according to fea-sibility or prospects of enforceability. With the exception of the 1933/34 struggle of the Watch Tower Society's leadership to withdraw the ban, Jehovah's Witnesses, who were anticipating the imminent end of the world, were not at all concerned with "success" in this world. They had no doubt that the NS regime would be overthrown, but not by means of any "successes" they had to achieve. This overthrow would be accom-plished by the "successful actions of the Lord during the apocalyptic battle of Armageddon." The actions of Jehovah's Witnesses were there-fore not based on power scheming. They could hardly be measured on a scale of political effectiveness. These acts of resistance demonstrated faithful adherence to their religious beliefs.

Because of these different levels of resistance, an effect-historical ap-proach can explain the resistance of the Bible Students only to a limited extent. In the discussion about Jehovah's Witnesses in the Third Reich, it must be considered that their actions were never, or only to some degree, subject to tactical calculations. Manfred Koch, for instance, misjudges

their intentions when he states that the "provocative radical nature of
the position of Jehovah's Witnesses . . . [stood in] serious disproportion
to the external opportunities of the sect to assert themselves under the
changed political conditions."[115] This statement about the nonconformity to totalitarian rule of this religious denomination does not take into
consideration that Jehovah's Witnesses did not consider the protection
of their organization and property to be of primary importance. They
did not weigh matters to determine "the lesser of two evils." The IBSA
members did not try to maintain their organization and, if possible, preserve it even under the changed political conditions, regardless of the
cost involved. In 1934 it became obvious that they were not willing and
not able to pay the corresponding price in concessions and identity loss.
Instead, Jehovah's Witnesses were concerned about continuing their
preaching activity and remaining strong in faith and thus upholding
their relationship (with their God). Consequently, Jehovah's Witnesses
did not consider their sufferings in the Third Reich as "futile," an opinion they still hold today.

Several authors emphasize that Jehovah's Witnesses in the Third
Reich took a "firm stand against the National Socialist State" (Erdmann),[116] showed "unreserved opposition" (Kammler),[117] and offered
"determined resistance" (Halle).[118] This unquestionably oppositional
behavior has been attributed to the fact that the Bible Student beliefs
condemned any secular authority that contradicted "the standards of
the Bible." Therefore, because of the totalitarian claim to power of the
NS regime, the Bible Student beliefs received "a political component"
(Marßolek and Ott).[119] Kater even considers the Bible Students' refusal
to give the Hitler salute and to participate in elections as actions "that
give clear evidence of political resistance."[120]

Authors who ascribe political dimensions or properties to Jehovah's Witnesses' acts of refusal and resistance find support for their opinion even with contemporary assessments. For example, in July 1936 the
Deutschland-Berichte, published on behalf of the exile executive committee of the German SPD, stated with regard to the IBSA activities: "First
of all, this is certainly a matter of religious fanaticism [on the part of
people] who adhere to their faith, despite serious persecution, and who
consider martyrdom more like a spiritual blessing and an 'act of godly
grace.' However, in time, even this resistance type brings about political
opposition against the regime, which the Bible Students increasingly describe as a form of 'anti-Christ.'"[121]

There are certainly indications that the IBSA resistance (indirectly)
affected the political situation and, therefore, can be considered as part

of the "silent revolt"[122] against the tyranny of National Socialism that was collectively carried out by various anti-fascist forces. Consequently, it is appropriate to subsume the Bible Students' activities under the concept of "resistance" in the stricter sense of the word. After all, a considerable number of IBSA members did not submit to the ban. To the contrary, by means of diverse conspiratorial procedures, they persistently offered resistance to the NS regime. They looked for ways that they could adapt to the conditions of the ban. They also used couriers to maintain communications abroad and to support an extensive system of smuggling literature. Their underground activities involved printing and distributing publications, as well as organizing pamphlet campaigns in order to inform the public about the criminal nature of the NS regime.[123] In summation, from an outward appearance, the activities they used resembled very closely the methods political opponents of the regime adopted in their struggle of resistance. As those political opponents of the regime, Jehovah's Witnesses also contested the totalitarian claim of National Socialism to form an ideologically monolithic "national community" in which the Führer had the final say and in which, from that perspective, there was no room for other (politically, as well as religiously conflicting) views. Besides this partial consistency in their objectives and methods, one must consider that for the National Socialists everything that resisted their ideas became a political issue. Therefore, Inge Marßolek and René Ott came to the conclusion that, unlike other minor religious denominations, Jehovah's Witnesses employed "illegal acts of resistance that, due to the nature of the regime, inevitably had to take on political momentum, as well."[124]

Jehovah's Witnesses performed these acts of resistance primarily in order to continue their God-assigned preaching activity, even during a "period of severe trials." They used conspiratorial procedures and methods of (political) resistance. If, however, their underground activities were exposed, they also boldly defended their religious principles before the Gestapo, such as their refusal to perform military service. At times, they engaged in these methods, even if they had been able to give an evasive answer.

Apart from a very few exceptions, the fact that Jehovah's Witnesses engaged in conspiratorial underground activities and, at the same time, boldly expressed their convictions indicates that they did not have the objective of leading some kind of anti-fascist, and therefore political, resistance against the National Socialist regime. They did not intend to weaken and eventually overthrow the regime. To accomplish this goal of overthrowing the regime would have required keeping their forces together and using everything at their disposal to mislead the opponent, possibly even by means of renunciation, in order to continue the struggle of resistance. It might have even required putting tactical considerations ahead of moral viewpoints. However, the resistance of the IBSA members, in word and deed, was based on religious principles. It was a demonstration of "Christian integrity" and of "loyalty" of every individual Jehovah's Witness toward Jehovah God. Their "resistance" was an expression of faith, an essential requirement of Christian testimony and spiritual self-assertion.

Despite differing viewpoints, the various studies about Jehovah's Witnesses in the Third Reich agree that Jehovah's Witnesses certainly were not merely victims and objects of NS persecution. The previous discussion has also demonstrated that the various models of interpretation used to describe the course of action of the IBSA are certainly able to identify individual aspects. In order to explain adequately the phenomenon as a whole, it is necessary to consider even more aspects.

NS Persecution and Resistance of Jehovah's Witnesses

The complexity and, to some extent, ambiguity of the various models of interpretation attempting to explain and "categorize" the behavior of Jehovah's Witnesses in the Third Reich is also a result of the fact that the IBSA members manifested a broad spectrum of behavior patterns, such as dissent, nonconformity, social refusal, protest, resistance, and conspiratorial procedures. The fact that Jehovah's Witnesses performed such a persistent struggle of self-assertion can by no means be attributed only to an adherence to their religious teachings. It cannot even be attributed entirely to the Watch Tower Society's teaching about a test through which the Bible Students had to pass during the "final apocalyptic battle" between Jehovah and the anti-Christ, Hitler, who had an alliance with the powers of Satan, and for which those who remained faithful would receive an abundant reward. This determined willingness to offer resistance was just as much a reaction to the unrelenting severity with which the NS regime persecuted Jehovah's Witnesses.

From this perspective, some authors consider the opposition that the National Socialists brought against the IBSA from the very beginning as a decisive, if not even *the* decisive, factor in the development of the Bible Students' resistance. In an effort to explain why the NS leadership considered it imperative to oppose this minor denomination with such brutality and why they denied its right to exist,[125] these same authors often mention the refusal of Jehovah's Witnesses to perform military service and other military-related activities, based on the biblical prohibition to kill.[126] They also mention the uncompromising refusal of Jehovah's Witnesses to obey secular orders that contradicted their conception of the Bible, which ultimately amounted to their refusal to accept the National Socialists' claim to power.[127] As an additional reason, the authors point to the "supranational structure" of the denomination and the associated accusation of maintaining treasonous connections. From this point of view, it is certainly possible that the National Socialists could have viewed the Bible Students as "political-ideological opponents," even though their actions were based entirely on religious reasoning.[128] Therefore, in his 1968 study concerning "the National Socialist policy toward the churches," John S. Conway suggests that the persecution of Jehovah's Witnesses was not based primarily on their refusal to follow secular orders (the obligation to give the Hitler salute, compulsory membership in NS associations, performance of military service). It "rather stemmed from the Nazi belief that this tiny sect presented a real political danger."[129] This assessment of the NS leadership, so Conway further explains, draws attention to a reason for the confrontation with the Bible Students that has been previously, to a large extent, disregarded: "But even more significantly, in the Witnesses' 'petit bourgeois' milieu, their messianic message, their fanaticism and readiness to make ultimate sacrifices, and their skilful manipulation of propaganda, the Nazis believed they saw a new form of their own Party organization."[130]

The same year in which Conway published his work, Michael Kater also mentions similar correlations between "sect" and "National Socialist Party" to be the decisive reason for the severe persecution administered by the rulers of the Third Reich.

> The deeper reason for the serious animosity between National Socialism and the Bible Student teachings can be found in the similarities in structure of both ideologies. Just as the National Socialist ideology, so were also the teachings of Jehovah's Witnesses dominated not by a democratically but an authoritarian policy. Both systems were totalitarian in that they strictly integrated national comrades as well as fellow believers into the respective authoritarian structure and requested them to give up their own personal identity for the objectives of the system. While the National Socialists accepted the "Führer State," the "Earnest Bible Students" submitted to the "Theocracy," in which not the Führer, but Jehovah, was the dictatorial ruler. Since both groups claimed exclusiveness,

this inevitably had to result in conflicts. A Bible Student who had
devoted himself to Jehovah was in no way able to carry out the
duties that the National Socialist State demanded of him as a national comrade.[131]

Kater's thesis of the "similarities in structure of both ideologies,"
which has influenced a number of studies about Jehovah's Witnesses
in the Third Reich, suggests extensive analogies in both ideological
systems. Both systems have in common an authoritarian basis, a totalitarian orientation, the claim of exclusiveness, and a dichotomous conception of the world. In comparison to other religious denominations
that the NS regime rejected and opposed, the Bible Students were persecuted with an extraordinary intensity. At the same time, the IBSA
members also showed a remarkable consistency of refusal and willingness to offer resistance. According to Kater, this NS persecution and the
resistance of the Bible Students were provoked by the conflict that
resulted from two "totalitarian" and "authoritarian" ideologies. Subsequently, various aspects of Kater's interpretation have been discussed in
other historical studies.[132] The Austrian historian Wolfgang Neugebauer even went beyond the phrasing of "similarities in structure." He
mentions as primary reasons for the opposition between National Socialism and the Bible Student teachings the "same claim of both ideologies, both of which were based on authoritarianism and totalitarianism,
that is, both involved a hierarchical system of rule and complete control
over a human being."[133] This kind of cause-and-effect explanation may
tend, even unintentionally, to place almost all blame on the victim. This
is shown in the statement of Hans-Rainer Sandvoß: "Ultimately, the violent oppression of Jehovah's Witnesses resulted from the fact that this
denomination demanded the 'person as a whole' and did not allow for
any compromises."[134]

In order to determine the motives for the persecution and the
causes for the resistance, it is certainly of significance to look at the self-
conception of both ideologies and their mutual exclusiveness. In this
context, the statement that both ideologies claimed to represent the
"epitome of truth" and demanded the person as a whole seems appropriate. No tolerance was shown with regard to ideological questions.
However, it would not be appropriate to conclude that this ideological
disposition or rigid religious doctrinarism gave the National Socialists
a reason for their particularly hateful opposition and thus caused the
suppression. It would also not be germane to say that the structural

similarities between NS ideology and Bible Student teachings were the deeper reasons for the persecution of Jehovah's Witnesses. Before making such assumptions, a number of questions need to be answered.

Was the fierce ideological enmity that *völkisch* reactionary circles showed toward the Bible Students Association since the end of World War I merely a reaction to their hierarchical structure, which was not at that point "theocratically" structured? Or was this enmity based on the Bible Students' demand for unreserved loyalty and unselfish dedication to Jehovah? Was it not rather a reaction to the fact that the Bible Students Association radically challenged "Christian-occidental" and German national virtues, as well as those of patriotism and military enthusiasm?

Did the National Socialists take action against Jehovah's Witnesses immediately after their takeover because they feared their uncompromising attitude, which was, at the time, rather cooperative? Did they consider the conflict between two similar ideologies (which were exclusive as regards content) to be unavoidable? Or were their actions in 1933 not somewhat characterized by their proclaimed struggle against "un-German" ideas and those ideas that were "contaminated with Jewish thinking?" Was it not also a proposal to the church leaders who were striving for a modus vivendi with the new rulers?

Was this adamant frontline position of both opponents already obvious at the beginning of the Third Reich, that is, was it an antagonism par excellence? Or did the situation escalate gradually with progressively increasing repression on the one side and a corresponding offensive resistance on the other side?

This also raises a hypothetical question: Would the NS regime have reacted differently toward Jehovah's Witnesses if their actions of opposition—their refusal to give the Hitler salute, their rejection to be coerced into membership of NS organizations (DAF, HJ, RLB, etc.), the continuation of their preaching activity and regular religious meetings despite the ban, their pamphlet campaigns, as well as their refusal to take oaths and to perform military service—were based not on a rigid doctrinairism and an authoritarian hierarchical system of rule, but on other ideological premises instead?

Was it merely an "unfortunate" circumstance that Jehovah's Witnesses, half a century after their association had been formed, met with a counterpart that had organizational similarities but was considerably more powerful? Or, taking matters a step further (even if this is provocative), was it merely the unequal power situation of two otherwise similar

opponents that was the decisive factor for the fact that the National Socialists persecuted Jehovah's Witnesses, and not the other way around?

Despite the problematic nature of a structural comparison, in referring to the mutual claim of exclusiveness, Kater provides an important
reason for the serious confrontation between the NS "Führer state" and
the "theocratic structure" of the Watch Tower Society. In response to
Kater's theses, some authors extend the list of structural similarities in
both ideologies to a similarity, or uniformity, of even the *ideologeme* (the
smallest element of the ideological concept). Kater in no way assumes
that the structural similarities between National Socialism and the Bible
Student teachings also included convergence in content, however strong
or weak it might be reflected.

Gerhard Hetzer, who argues in favor of such supposed convergence
in content, states in his 1981 study that Kater's interpretation that the
"serious enmity" between the NS regime and Jehovah's Witnesses was
based on "structural similarities of both ideologies" does not sufficiently
explain the phenomena. This interpretation would be limited to "a reference to the authoritarian aspect of both systems, that is, the Führer
state and the Bible Students' concept of theocratic structure."[135] Therefore, Hetzer supplements this structural comparison by examining the
ideological basis and history of ideas within each doctrine. In his comparison of National Socialism and Bible Student teachings, Hetzer
refers to the existence of a "mutual magic philosophy" and of "mutual
roots in illiberal, even culture-critical, and life-reforming ideas" from
the period following World War I. Consequently, it was the "similarities
between the predictions of the 'Third Reich' and those of the 'Golden
Age'" that prompted the mutual rejection.[136] However, Hetzer compared NS propaganda against the Bible Students from a period long before the NS takeover in 1933 with (supposedly) early statements of the
Brooklyn headquarters of the Watch Tower Society "against the European forms of fascism."[137]

From this aspect of interpretation,[138] it seems possible to derive certain similarities between National Socialism and Bible Student teachings. (There are, however, valid reasons to dispute the assumption that
both ideologies are based on the same ideas. At best, both ideologies originate from the viewpoints prevalent during one specific time period. In
one sense, National Socialism, which is based on social-Darwinist, anti-
Semitic ideas, and the Bible Student teachings, which developed from
Christian millennialism and the North American revivalist movement,
both provided answers, albeit different ones, to the increasing crises and

disorientation of large population circles. These crises resulted from the extensive modernization processes that took place at the beginning of the twentieth century.) But there is no substantial evidence for these supposed convergences. It only *appears* that way. Although both ideologies have in common the magic philosophy of salvation utopias for certain parts of humankind and the vision of a Thousand-Year Reign (or Reich), the one side relied on Jehovah God to establish His Kingdom so that righteous people can live in peace while the other side expected the National Socialists to bring about a domain for the racially superior.[139] Therefore, the fact that the National Socialists, as well as Jehovah's Witnesses, each based their future prospects on idealistic promises of salvation and a supernatural worldview cannot be used as evidence for spiritual affinity, or as a basis to explain the serious confrontation. The apparent distortions of reality inherent in both ideologies were based on the respective dichotomous worldview, which, in turn, resulted from a holistic world explanation. These distortions of reality have noteworthy parallels since they were unable to explain the phenomenon of the other but were only able to see it as an instrument of the opponent. The Watch Tower Society, on the one hand, viewed National Socialism as an "anti-Christ" venture under the control of the "Jesuits" and the "Roman Papal Church." The NS ideologists, on the other hand, subsumed the Bible Students under the label "Jewish Bolshevik world conspiracy."[140]

In summary, it can be asserted that the reference to the analogy in structure, that is, to similarities of the (inner and outer) structures of both ideologies, explains this unrelenting confrontation only to a very limited extent and cannot be compared to the general categories of political antagonism. Probably for this reason, Friedrich Zipfel considers the history of the persecution of Jehovah's Witnesses as "a unique phenomenon."[141] However, in some important aspects with regard to their structure (in the case of Jehovah's Witnesses, their conversion based on an inner acceptance of their beliefs; in the case of the NS state, compulsory membership in their organizations), and particularly with regard to their objectives, both ideologies differ almost diametrically. The National Socialists pursued the realization of worldly pleasures; Jehovah's Witnesses completely trusted in Jehovah God and pursued a Kingdom that would bring peace according to "heavenly law." These "spirit-anointed ones" leave the solution to the problems of the world in God's hands. They remain completely neutral regarding political affairs on earth. In anticipation of the fact that God will soon begin to rule, Jehovah's Witnesses refrain from participating in the worldly struggle for rulership. Because of this completely unambitious attitude with regard to earthly affairs, those striving for earthly authority should have realized that the Bible Student teachings represented absolutely no threat in the power struggle. Even though Jehovah's Witnesses are very mission-oriented (their preaching activity), the means they use for this purpose are strictly in harmony with their comprehensive Bible understanding. They never consider using violence and military force to expand their religious beliefs. During the NS period, Jehovah's Witnesses tried to convince people of the truth of their religious beliefs exclusively by means of persuasion, but the NS powers pressured skeptics and opponents of the regime with threats and violence to join the national community. In the Third Reich, "totality" was synonymous with an "exclusive acceptance of the National Socialist concept of the State and this concept was expected to pervade all areas of German life."[142] Such totalitarian characteristics were also evident in the claim to leadership of the Watch Tower Society's leaders. According to the "theocratic rule," these leaders claimed to be the intermediaries of the perfect "will of God" and required complete obedience from the believers. They also declared their own convictions to be the only means for salvation. Even though exclusiveness is one of the characteristics of these "chosen ones," Jehovah's Witnesses certainly do not use actual instruments of power or physical force to affect the lives of all people, let alone the lives of all German people.

Previously, only a few historical studies expressed reservations against Kater's explanations, which are based on a comparison of the structure of these two ideologies. For example, Falk Pingel fittingly argues that "the ideological competition" of the two, to a certain extent, structurally similar systems certainly increased the mutual alertness. But this is not as significant as some historical studies make it appear. It certainly was not the real reason for the seriousness of the conflict: "In considering the various stages of the persecution, it becomes apparent that it was not merely the structure of the ideology but the actions on both sides that primarily determined extent and character of the persecution."[143] Particularly with regard to Jehovah's Witnesses, Pingel states "their determination to continue their religious activities despite restrictions—that was the actual controversy between them and the National Socialists."[144]

To explain the confrontation, that is, the NS violence in their dealings with the Bible Students, as well as the determined resistance on the part of the Bible Students, it is extremely important to consider the sequence of events and the historical background of this gradually increasing conflict. National Socialist ideologists had always considered the Bible Student teachings as a "monstrosity" that needed to be opposed. Even during the early 1920s, they insisted on a ruthless resistance of the IBSA that, supposedly in association with the Freemasons, the Jews, and the Marxists, propagated the overthrow of current conditions and was striving for "absolute world domination of the Jews."[145] The determination to take actions against the IBSA was even increased by the fact that the NS state, in its efforts for uniformity after 1933, did not want to tolerate any exceptions. Still, Jehovah's Witnesses were only an outsider group and insignificant minority that, from the political viewpoint of power, did not present any serious danger to the authority of the NS regime and, therefore, could have been ignored. But the NS rulers were convinced that an "eradication of the Bible Student teachings" was necessary. In this regard, the claim of exclusiveness dominated all other considerations. It excluded the possibility of permitting the IBSA members to live and act according to their own principles and rules. Another factor to consider is that Jehovah's Witnesses contradicted, in their publications, the religious misrepresentation of the National Socialists that "the Führer had been sent for the purpose of restoring the German people." In this regard, an SA report from the period of the upheaval remarks with annoyance that "a member of this sect [predicted] by means of the Holy Scriptures that the Third Reich would soon disappear to make room for Jehovah's Kingdom."[146]

As an insignificant outsider group, the Bible Students could hardly expect to be shown solidarity, which resulted in the fact that the NS system could take quick and unrestricted actions against them. These actions were, at times, emboldened by the fact that the major churches (which, during the period of stabilization of the regime, were not significantly exposed to persecution) provided the NS state with the necessary protection. Initially, the German IBSA headquarters in Magdeburg had expected to be able to make an arrangement with the authorities and rulers of the Third Reich. They soon realized that they were fighting a losing battle. It soon became apparent that it was not possible for the Bible Students to achieve a state of tolerance between their activities and specific actions by the various levels of state authorities without giving up their identity. For Jehovah's Witnesses, the confrontation became unavoidable when they faced the exclusive demands of a different power, which also claimed to possess the absolute truth.[147] This power made it impossible for them to exercise their faith. In essential areas, it was diametrically opposed to their concept of life. As a result, Jehovah's

Witnesses eventually had no choice but to perform their preaching activity using conspiratorial methods.

Regarding the question of the onset of this controversy, it should be emphasized again that it is not possible to ignore the time factor, the dynamic, and its development. Without a doubt, the National Socialists were the ones who put in motion the escalation of persecution and resistance against it. They were the ones who imposed bans on the Bible Student activities and, consequently, caused Jehovah's Witnesses to defend themselves. The increasing repression also provoked their determination to go underground. Without bans and persecution, there would probably not have been such a response. The IBSA members did not even explicitly oppose the National Socialists from the outset. Despite particularly serious attacks by *völkisch* and NS groups during the early 1920s, the Watch Tower Society hardly made any mention of them in their publications. Their fomenting campaign was directed almost exclusively to the representatives of "false religion," the clergy, and the papacy. Therefore, Jehovah's Witnesses were "placed" into an oppositional situation through the actions forced upon them by the National Socialists in 1933 and through the persecution against them. Their actions were a response to the repression and persecution to which they had been exposed. It was a response to the suppression of their faith. By their opposition to the regime, Jehovah's Witnesses tried to resist NS coercion and to maintain their religious identity.

From this perspective, it would be wrong to transfer the discussion about the deeper reasons for the unrelenting mutual enmity to an ideological or structural level of the historical events that ignores the actual power struggle and the empirically verifiable events. To speak of the similarities of both ideologies involves the danger of placing the religious teachings of Jehovah's Witnesses on the same level as the ideologies of their opponents, at least if such ideas are thoughtlessly circulated in public. It substitutes cause with effect. It presents the persecution of Jehovah's Witnesses in a way that gives the impression that they *provoked the persecution through their own actions*. In other words, it implies the idea that the deeper reasons for the persecution can be found with the groups of victims.

Even in view of the fact that opponents in the Third Reich were in general persecuted inexorably, the extraordinary severity with which Jehovah's Witnesses were persecuted resulted from a conflict that gradually escalated in an interaction of action and reaction. In this conflict, the authorities responsible for the persecution always responded with increasing severity to the continuous stubbornness of the IBSA members, which reflected the lack of success of the NS measures of suppression.

The declared intention of the NS rulers was to completely eliminate the Bible Students from German history. This required taking ruthless actions against the large number of IBSA members who absolutely refused to give up their religious activities. As a result, several Jehovah's Witnesses found themselves in a predicament in which they succumbed to the pressure or were no longer able to offer resistance and, consequently, withdrew from the IBSA. In these cases, the National Socialists refrained from further suppression if they were convinced about the seriousness of a withdrawal from the religious association.[148] This fact reveals a significant difference between the persecution of Jehovah's Witnesses and persecution for racial reasons: if Jehovah's Witnesses renounced their faith and became part of the German society, they were able to avoid further persecution. The Jews did not have this possibility. They were not persecuted because of their religious conceptions. They were persecuted simply because they were Jews.

A number of Bible Students had already discontinued their preaching activity at the beginning of the Third Reich because they were either afraid of defying the ban, or they no longer believed in Bible Student teachings. The regime generally offered such Bible Students, as well as those who abandoned their religious ideas in later periods, a "normal" life if they provided evidence for their ideological adjustment or, at least, behaved in an acceptable way: prohibitions on their occupation, custody withdrawals, and other discriminating measures were then revoked. However, the authorities and the police continued to keep them under surveillance.

In this way, the National Socialists suppressed the activities of quite a number of IBSA members through coercive measures. For instance, during the period following the ban in 1933, as a result of various official actions, a certain number of believers withdrew from the Bible Students Association or at least no longer participated in its activities. These official actions included the first major wave of repressions following the resumption of their preaching activity in 1934/35, the severe Gestapo action after their pamphlet campaign in 1936/37, and the destruction of the IBSA organization in 1937/38. The remaining believers, however, were always able to reorganize their underground activities, even though after the wave of arrests in 1937/38, the reorganization took some time and they resumed their activities only to a limited extent.

Despite the large membership losses due to arrests, noncontinuation of religious activities, and apostasy, this remaining group of IBSA members undauntedly carried on their religious activities.

The coercive NS authorities tried various methods to break the spirit of resistance of these nonconforming Jehovah's Witnesses, those who were strong in faith and willing to make sacrifices. However, their efforts to suppress this group of spiritually strong Jehovah's Witnesses remained unsuccessful. As a result, apart from their adherence to Bible Student teachings, some high party officials and SS functionaries certainly appreciated the high moral standards of Jehovah's Witnesses. In cases in which Jehovah's Witnesses abandoned their faith, the National Socialists not only allowed them to return to the national community, they even made special efforts to reintegrate them. However, only in exceptional cases was the regime able to truly reintegrate devoted Jehovah's Witnesses. Often, Gestapo reports state that their measures of suppression produced no, or only limited, results in cases involving IBSA members. On January 28, 1936, the Bavarian Political Police (BPP) reported: "Despite protective detention and legal prosecution, it is not possible to discourage the Bible Students from distributing 'Jehovah's word' in spoken and written form, in order to gain new adherents, and to discourage them from keeping close relationships with each other."[149]

The number of active Bible Students in the concentration camps, in particular, could not be persuaded to deny or renounce their faith, regardless of the methods used. These methods included continuous ridicule, terrible mistreatment, isolation, or permanent assignment in punishment battalions. Not even the temptations associated with the privileged treatment of the Bible Student prisoners who were placed in special labor details could persuade them to deny or renounce the Bible Student teachings. They persistently refused to sign the statement especially prepared for IBSA members so that they would renounce their faith. They refused to sign the statement even though it offered them the prospect of release from the concentration camp. Finally, Heinrich Himmler, the Reichsführer SS and highest authority of the concentration camps, realized that it was impossible to deter Jehovah's Witnesses even with continued acts of terror: "Even punishment has no effect on them." Consequently, in 1943, based on consideration for what would be most practical for the SS and the Reich, he gave instructions that the Bible Students should no longer be assigned to work in armament production. They should "all . . . be put to work—on farms, for instance, where they have nothing to do with the war and all its madness."[150]

The majority of Jehovah's Witnesses drafted for military service to defend "the people and the Führer" showed a similar steadfastness. This touched on an area of their religious convictions that was of central importance. As a result, in order to remain faithful to the Old Testament commandment to not kill, the New Testament commandment of refusing to use violence, and the Watch Tower Society's requirement for Christian neutrality, these Jehovah's Witnesses refused to perform military service. For these very same reasons, even a number of Bible Students who were no longer involved in IBSA underground activities for various reasons, also refused to perform military service. They were certainly aware of the inevitable consequences of their actions, but they took the course of martyrdom rather than renounce their faith. Ultimately, the instruments of National Socialism had no authority over the dictates of conscience, the sincerity of true convictions, and the power of faith.[151] The legal authorities were not able to control the undeterred missionary spirit of Jehovah's Witnesses. In many cases, the Gestapo was powerless against the courageous expression of conviction of Jehovah's Witnesses. According to Eugen Kogon, "psychologically speaking the SS were never quite equal to the challenge offered by Jehovah's Witnesses."[152] They could impose bans to suppress these godly people, but in general, no matter what means the regime employed, it was unable to break the stubborn, uncompromising behavior of Jehovah's Witnesses.

The National Socialists were confronted with an opponent whom they could not understand. Despite increasing intensity of the persecution, this opponent did not respond in a way that the coercive authorities expected.[153] The unconcealed, demonstrative attitude of active IBSA members, which was deeply rooted in a strong faith, and which made believers, if necessary, even willing to make sacrifices, often frustrated the NS functionaries. There was nothing that could deter the Bible Students from their course. These factors could have contributed to the fact that, on the lower levels of the NS organization, efforts to break their resolve were intensified and even more brutal. From this point of view, the IBSA members contributed to a certain extent to the severity of the NS actions but this certainly does not mean that they intentionally provoked these measures. Therefore, without a doubt, it would be more than questionable to place some of the responsibility for the intensity of the persecution on the determined and uncompromising attitude of Jehovah's Witnesses. The evidence points to the fact that the NS claim of exclusiveness can be considered as the cause for the persecution of Jehovah's Witnesses in the Third Reich. Even though the

totalitarian characteristics in organization and ideology of the IBSA increased the conflict, they certainly did not cause the "serious animosity"
of the NS.

Between Resistance and Martyrdom

After this discussion of various theories concerning persecution and
resistance of Jehovah's Witnesses (as they are represented in historical
studies as well as in legal records) it is appropriate to revisit the question
of whether the resistance activities and the uncompromising attitude of
Jehovah's Witnesses can be placed into the category of political resistance, or whether it would be suitable, in a broader sense, to describe the
fundamental resistance and unconcealed and conspiratorial counterac-
tions in a different way.

Jehovah's Witnesses viewed the fact that they strictly followed Christian principles and commandments according to their understanding
as the only way in which they could please God and would be able to
receive the promises of the New World. Their religious requirements
clearly conflicted in important areas with requirements of the NS state
(the "politicization" of public life, taking oaths and giving other expressions of allegiance, youth education, liability of compulsory service,
etc.). Therefore, these uncompromising IBSA members who loyally adhered to their principles almost inevitably came in serious conflict with
National Socialism, which itself also demanded absolute subordination,
required total allegiance, and rejected any worldview that deviated from
its ideology.

The IBSA members offered organized resistance against the efforts
of the NS regime to achieve uniformity. Even though they opposed the
regime in word and written form, their actions of opposition cannot
be considered as a politically directed resistance that had the objective
of overthrowing the fascist Hitler government. And although they also
longed for a change in government, they placed the removal of the NS
government completely into the hands of God. According to the Bible
Students, the Hitler government was not to be replaced by another political power. It was to be replaced by a ruler that would be appointed
by God. In their underground activities, especially in their pamphlet
campaigns of 1936/37 (resolution and the open letter), Jehovah's Witnesses made efforts to inform the public about the "persecution of
Christians" (in reference to the persecution of members of their religious
denomination) that was raging in Hitler's Germany. At least from this

perspective, the earlier Bible Students' campaigns can be considered as information campaigns that exposed the atrocities of the NS regime. These efforts were not intended to mobilize the people for an anti-fascist struggle. If, in this context, Jehovah's Witnesses tried to persuade the German people to withdraw their loyalty from the "barbarian Hitler state," it was done with the objective of encouraging people to give their loyalty to Jehovah God instead. The resistance of Jehovah's Witnesses had the intention of helping people to put faith in the future Kingdom of God. They had no intention of changing political conditions.[154]

Jehovah's Witnesses did not pursue an overthrow of government from a literal point of view. In their conception, success of their organized resistance did not depend on their ability to undermine the NS regime. They were successful if they demonstrated their loyalty to their religious beliefs. Their primary concerns involved an endeavor to remain steadfast in faith, to endure the trials imposed upon them and, consequently, present themselves as true witnesses of their God, Jehovah.

In 1933 many Jehovah's Witnesses determinedly refused to accept, without resistance, the ban on their preaching activity and other religious activities, as well as the destruction of the Bible Students Association. Had they neglected the interests of God's organization and submitted to the orders of the state, they would have abandoned their faith. Because of their mutual religious convictions, their integration into a group that was secluded from society in general, their adherence to the same principles, and their deep sense of unity and solidarity, they had a relatively favorable starting position for their prohibited activities. But the fact that the Watch Tower Society's leaders depicted the Hitler regime *until the end* as an instrument of a Roman Catholic conspiracy, and thus completely failed to recognize its true characteristics, did not reduce the seriousness of this radical confrontation in any way.

The continuous resistance of these determined Jehovah's Witnesses certainly disrupted the NS rule, which was intent on achieving an uncontested integration of all national comrades into the national community. To a certain extent, this resistance did indeed weaken the regime, although, in view of the numerically completely different relation of the two opponents, it did not have any significant consequences. Jehovah's Witnesses certainly did not intend to destabilize the government, overthrow Hitler and the NSDAP, or reestablish a democratic government. Therefore, even in this regard, it would not be appropriate to subsume the resistance of Jehovah's Witnesses under a concept of resistance for political purposes. The National Socialists, on the other hand, increasingly considered the Christian neutrality of Jehovah's Witnesses, that is, their political refusal (nonparticipation in parades, ceremonies, and elections; nonmembership in NS organizations; refusal to give the Hitler salute, and rejection of all national symbolism) to be detrimental to the community, subversive, and state endangering. They viewed the resistance of Jehovah's Witnesses as political opposition.

Especially during the late 1970s and the 1980s, new definitions were introduced that extended the range of behavior patterns in order to explain the concept of resistance. Also according to these definitions, the concept of resistance did not require political motivations and objectives to be essential basic elements. In the context of these definitions, it is indeed possible to include the activities of Jehovah's Witnesses in the concept of resistance "in a broader sense." Without a doubt, they meet Peter Hüttenberger's terms of definition that resistance activities are "acts of refusal, or actions that result in acts of refusal."[155] The IBSA activities fulfill even the criteria of the concept of *Resistenz* that had been developed in the context of the "Bavarian Project" of the Institut für Zeitgeschichte. According to this concept, *Resistenz* includes those "forms of refusal, of individual and collective protest, or of dissent and nonconformity that are directed against certain ideological, disciplinary, or organizational measures and impositions of the NS state."[156] The various classifications and gradations for the concept of *Resistenz* suggested in these typological studies also cannot adequately describe the attitudes and actions of members of the Bible Students Association. Terminological expressions such as nonconformity, dissent, refusal, opposition, and conspiracy certainly apply to the actions of Jehovah's Witnesses. But each of these expressions explains only particular aspects of the IBSA activities and not the phenomenon as a whole. The resistance activities of Jehovah's Witnesses in the Third Reich do not seem to fit into any currently used pattern of interpretation. These resistance activities were more than "merely" acts of nonconformity. They were more profound than dissent and more active than refusal. To classify them as enmity, however, the actions of Jehovah's Witnesses lack oppositional objectives. To classify them as conspiracy, they lack subsequent conspiratorial and subversive plans. In view of the empirical evidence, it is impossible to establish one particular, and possibly exclusive, concept for the purpose of describing the behavior of Jehovah's Witnesses "between resistance and martyrdom." Ultimately, not even the more appropriate gradations and descriptions, such as active religious *Resistenz*, steadfast resistance for the purpose of protecting one's faith, or radical struggle for conviction and self-assertion can adequately explain these acts of resistance of Jehovah's Witnesses. Even the attempt to provide a new concept would not contribute to a clarification but would rather complicate matters further. In this regard, the various phases of persecution of Jehovah's Witnesses in the Third Reich have resulted in quite a number of different reactions. In order to provide a specific situation with a definite concept, it is necessary to modify currently used concepts or to provide a combination of various concepts. It is not even possible to integrate the IBSA activities into the currently used resistance typologies because the resistance activities of Jehovah's Witnesses differ completely from any other resistance activities. The concepts of resistance describe the relationship of more or less large parts of society toward NS rule, an interaction of concessions and repressions on the one side, and conformity and *Resistenz* on the other side, and therefore a political controversy. The resistance of Jehovah's Witnesses is a religious phenomenon that cannot be subsumed under the patterns of political actions and does not comply with rational calculations of protecting one's interests.

In the context of describing this specific characteristic of the IBSA resistance, it is important to emphasize that Jehovah's Witnesses' activities in the Third Reich did not merely question certain aspects of the regime—even though the Bible Students did not pursue a change in political conditions. Their actions represented "fundamental opposition" in the truest sense of the word. In this context, the attempt to reduce resistance to actions with deliberate political objectives certainly fails to recognize that even nonpolitical resistance, that is, resistance for other reasons, could result in disruption, even endangerment, of rule in the NS state. It could, therefore, certainly have political consequences. Even though Jehovah's Witnesses never presented a serious danger to the totalitarian NS regime, they definitely undermined the demands of this political system. In other words, they put obstacles into the NS machinery of destruction rather than support it.

Jehovah's Witnesses belong to the only Christian group that as a whole resisted the various coercions of the NS regime. Their resistance was based on acts of self-assertion. Initially, they resisted the fact that their religious association was banned and they were prohibited from carrying out their religious activities—from proclaiming the message of the imminent establishment of the Kingdom of God. Jehovah's Witnesses considered these measures as a prohibition to exercise their faith. They stood up against this massive form of state interference. They directed their resistance against the NS restrictions on carrying out their religious activities. In this regard, they requested no more and no less from the Third Reich than that they be granted a small area to carry out their form of worship and way of life in this world, which—according to their conviction—was about to end. Their struggle did not have the objective of changing the actual political system or supporting others outside of the close circle of their religious denomination. They were concerned primarily about maintaining their religious stance against interventions by the state or the party; they were concerned about maintaining their religious, social, and humanly identity against efforts of indoctrination and moral constraint.

From that perspective, the concept of *Resistenz* describes the behavior of Jehovah's Witnesses in the Third Reich as a complete rejection of the NS ideological claim for absolute power. At the same time, their *Resistenz* was an active struggle to defend the realm of their religious activities against state interventions that claimed omnipotence.

Certainly, in their religiously motivated *Resistenz,* Jehovah's Witnesses made use of active forms of conspiracy that also had the objective of reaching the public. Also, their radical questioning of the NS claim for absolute power definitely had political consequences, even though they did not have any political objectives. Basically, with their actions, their acts of resistance, Jehovah's Witnesses did not endeavor to point the way or "light a torch" for others. Their intention was to give "witness." In the end, their efforts were reduced to preserving their faith, which they had no intentions of renouncing. Beyond the endeavor to maintain or restore the possibility of performing their religious activities, they had no ambitions to change the political conditions of this "Old World." They struggled for their religious objectives with great determination and unparalleled courage. For them, submitting "to a demon" amounted to forfeiting the "real life." They did not allow themselves to just surrender to the circumstances: giving up their integrity would have amounted to self-denial. Accordingly, the NS regime had absolutely no place for people who lived in harmony with the teachings of the Bible Students. As a totalitarian state, it required that people give their full devotion to the regime. The Hitler government had placed itself in the position of God and demanded that the entire "national community" be in harmony with the Führer. And thus, resistance became a mandatory dictate of self-esteem and self-assertion for the religious denomination of Jehovah's Witnesses.

Epilogue

Since the first German edition of this book was published in 1993, several important changes have taken place regarding public acceptance of the persecution of Jehovah's Witnesses in the Third Reich.

For decades, Jehovah's Witnesses were denied public recognition as a group of victims of National Socialism. In the social sciences, there was also a general lack of interest in the history of their persecution. Jehovah's Witnesses shared this fate of nonrecognition with other victims of NS persecution, such as the Sinti and the Roma, whose outsider status continued even after 1945.

In the eastern part of Germany, the population has considered themselves to be acquitted or exculpated from the responsibility of the past because of the revolutionary tradition of the ruling party and the fact that they allegedly paid for their anti-fascist legacy. Jehovah's Witnesses, who were again exposed to persecution after the ban in the German Democratic Republic in August 1950, were at best a subject of state security. They were accused of anti-state espionage and anti-state actions. To counter the embarrassing fact that Jehovah's Witnesses had been victims of persecution under NS rule, the DDR authorities resorted to defamation: leaders of Jehovah's Witnesses were supposedly "religious-political adventurers, bought by big business, who had been exposed as fascists." They had supposedly tried to gain the "approval of the Nazis" and were later willing to "betray large numbers of their fellow-believers to the Gestapo."[1]

In western Germany, the initial two postwar decades were marked by a general refusal of the population to acknowledge the events of the past and thus accept responsibility. Far more attention was given to the reintegration of those in responsible positions of administration, wartime economy, and the Wehrmacht than to the rehabilitation of victims of NS persecution. For a long time, the subject of persecution and resistance was restricted to the events of July 20, the "White Rose," as well as those involving the "Bekennende Kirche" and the Catholic Church. Toward the end of the 1970s, though, a change took place: attention was now directed to local and regional histories. Efforts were also made to represent the events between 1933 and 1945 in their respective environments and to view them from the perspective of everyday life. As a result, the resistance of the working classes—resistant milieus, for example, in Catholic Bavaria—and the fate of victims of persecution who previously had been excluded from examination were brought to public attention. Even during this time, Jehovah's Witnesses remained unrecognized in historical studies, documentaries on television, or commemorative addresses.

In the introduction to the first German edition, I mentioned that the long years of nonrecognition by the social sciences and the public toward this subject cannot be entirely attributed to the general disregard of outsider groups. Neither can it be attributed only to the prejudice that society, in general, shows toward Jehovah's Witnesses. It would not be appropriate to attribute this nonrecognition merely to the fact that the churches, in particular, forced an "informational campaign" against sectarian groups. At least to a certain extent, the lack of interest and rejection of this subject can also be based on the structure and peculiarities of the Watch Tower Bible and Tract Society. In my opinion, the claim of this controversial denomination to be the "only true religion," the claim of their governing body to be the only true and authentic representative of the divine will, as well as the isolation of this group from the outside world certainly contribute to lack of consideration and recognition. For a very long time, the German branch office of the Watch Tower Society treated efforts to examine this subject, if such efforts were made at all, with reservation. For example, the Watch Tower Society and its branch offices denied outsiders access to their archives. This uncooperative attitude was largely a result of fear and negative experiences. Journalists, in particular, were interested primarily in providing ominous "exposés."[2] And too, Jehovah's Witnesses also preferred to provide their own interpretation of their history.

In the meantime, an extensive change took place in this regard. Since 1993/94, the Watch Tower Society became increasingly receptive toward questions of historical representations.[3] In line with this increasing receptiveness, they also carry out costly public relations work. Several years ago, the Watch Tower Society did not consider such work to be beneficial.[4] Now, however, they acknowledge the value of such historical studies and, by means of them, seek recognition.

They first asserted in their publications that consideration of the atrocities of the NS regime required special recognition of the persecution of Jehovah's Witnesses because their persecution represents a unique testimony of faith. In this regard, the May 8, 1993, issue of their semimonthly journal *Awake!* states under the title "Victims or Martyrs: What Is the Difference?":

> Thousands were sent to the dreaded concentration camps, where many were executed and others died from mistreatment. Yet, they did not have to suffer and die. They had a choice. They were offered a way out. If they would just sign a paper renouncing their faith, they could walk away free. The vast majority chose not to sign and became not only victims of the Nazi terror but also martyrs. Thus, while all martyrs are victims, only a few victims could and did choose to become martyrs. They were victorious in the face of death.[5]

Following the commemoration of the fiftieth anniversary of concentration camp liberation, which received considerable public response in Europe and North America, *Awake!* published a series of articles addressing the question "The Holocaust—Who Spoke Out?"[6] This journal includes information concerning the persecution of Jehovah's Witnesses in NS Germany, as well as excerpts from reports of contemporary witnesses and from articles of Watch Tower publications from that time period. It also discusses the part the churches played in the Hitler state. The editors of *Awake!* make the following profound statement: "Unlike the churches, Jehovah's Witnesses spoke out against Nazism."[7] This description suggests that Jehovah's Witnesses were the only ones who, at an early stage, steadfastly "exposed the murderous intent of the Third Reich" and the "atrocities [committed] against Jews, Poles, the handicapped, and others." Under the title "From Our Readers," a subsequent issue of *Awake!* published a letter from an American who responded to this series of articles. He expressed his feelings with the following statement: "I have always wondered why no one ever spoke up regarding the Holocaust. The series 'The Holocaust—Who Spoke Out?' (Aug. 22, 1995) has answered my question. Jehovah's Witnesses spoke out, and I am very proud of my fellow Witnesses!"[8]

In special publications, which do not focus entirely on religious subjects, the Watch Tower Society also turns its attention to people who have a rather reserved attitude toward Jehovah's Witnesses. In 1995 they published the booklet *Jehovas Zeugen, Menschen aus der Nachbarschaft: Wer sind sie?* (Jehovah's Witnesses, People in Your Neighborhood: Who Are

They?). Besides a general description of this denomination, the booklet also emphasizes the persecution of Jehovah's Witnesses during National Socialism. To this end, it mentions that the uncompromising attitude of Jehovah's Witnesses, which is described as "a passive resistance," increasingly finds recognition with the public.[9] In response to the fact that "recently . . . Jehovah's Witnesses have become the focus of public attention," in January 1996 the German branch office of the Watch Tower Society established an information service of Jehovah's Witnesses in order to support the press coverage.[10] This service's objective is aimed at improving the public's image of Jehovah's Witnesses. Among other things, it has been organizing events that direct attention to Jehovah's Witnesses as a group of generally "forgotten victims of persecution of the National Socialist regime." At the same time, it has arranged exhibitions, which present the concentration camp prisoners with the purple patch by means of impressive photos and documents. In 1995 the European group of formerly deported and imprisoned Jehovah's Witnesses (Cercle Européen des Témoins de Jéhovah anciens déportés et internés, with its headquarters in Boulogne-Billancourt), which was founded on the initiative of the Watch Tower Society's branch office in France, organized a touring exhibition. In the meantime, the exhibition traveled to a number of cities throughout France and had a considerable public response.[11]

An extensive use of film presentations is just one of the ways in which the information service of the German branch office of the Watch Tower Society tries to make the general public aware of Jehovah's Witnesses as a group of victims of persecution. The Watch Tower Society bought the rights to the documentary *Purple Triangles*, which was broadcast by British television in the series *The Human Factor*. The U.S. Holocaust Memorial Museum has recommended this documentary film, which the Watch Tower Society distributes in the form of videotapes, for use in schools.[12] The twenty-five-minute film reports on the persecution of the thirteen members of the Kusserow family from Bad Lippspringe who suffered especially drastic persecution during the NS period. (The father was sentenced to prison terms; the mother was imprisoned at the Ravensbrück concentration camp; the couple lost custody of three children; five of their children were imprisoned in penal institutions or concentration camps; two sons were executed for their refusal to perform military service.)

The documentary *Jehovah's Witnesses Stand Firm against Nazi Assault*, which the Watch Tower Society produced in 1996, is even more significant. This seventy-eight-minute film describes, in chronological sequence, the history of their persecution. Besides more than twenty contemporary witnesses, it includes statements from ten historians from Europe and North America, including Sybil Milton and Michael Berenbaum of the U.S. Holocaust Memorial Museum in Washington, D.C.; professors John Conway, Susannah Heschel, and Christine King; as well as representatives of the memorials in Brandenburg, Neuengamme, Ravensbrück, and Wewelsburg.

On November 6, 1996, the film was first shown at the Ravensbrück Memorial. Several public representatives attended the presentation. Dr. Manfred Stolpe, the prime minister of the state of Brandenburg, sent a special message to this event in which he expressed his respect for Jehovah's Witnesses, "who courageously resisted National Socialism and unselfishly supported fellow prisoners."[13] He further stated that the Brandenburg government was interested in a "comprehensive exhibition on the persecution of Jehovah's Witnesses in the concentration camps." For this purpose, he suggested using this film to inform people visiting the memorials of Ravensbrück and Sachsenhausen.

During the following weeks and months, the Watch Tower Society's information service had public premieres of this film in various cities throughout Germany. In many cases, the regional press covered these presentations extensively. The film was often followed by discussions with surviving witnesses and lectures by historians. It was also shown in cooperation with other organizers (e.g., on Nov. 7, 1996, in Berlin, in cooperation with the Zentrum für Antisemitismusforschung [Center for Research on Anti-Semitism]). On occasion, other groups of victims of persecution joined these presentations (e.g., on Jan. 25, 1997, in Bad Nauheim, the Dokumentations- und Kulturzentrum Deutscher Sinti und Roma [Documentation and Cultural Center of German Sinti and Roma]). In other cases, the presentation was supported by government funds (e.g., on Feb. 26, 1997, in Kiel, with funds from the Schleswig-Holstein Ministerium für Bildung, Wissenschaft, Forschung und Kultur [Schleswig-Holstein Ministry for Education, Sciences, Research, and Culture]). In this way, the information service expects to address people who, for various reasons, would generally not respond to the invitations of Jehovah's Witnesses. For the March 19, 1997, premiere in Karlsruhe, which included a lecture by the Karlsruhe historian Dr. Manfred Koch, the invitation stated: "This event does not include any religious discussions!"

Within a few months, a total of 500,000 German and English copies of the video *Jehovah's Witnesses Stand Firm against Nazi Assault* were distributed. This video has been translated into an additional twenty-four languages. The Watch Tower Society has also provided, free of charge, an abbreviated version of the video that includes a textbook for teachers, universities, and other educational institutions.[14] Furthermore, the Watch Tower Society encouraged the concentration camp memorials to include this video in their educational work, presenting it "in the context of the Memorial Day for Victims of Persecution of National Socialism, which had been announced by President Dr. Roman Herzog." To this end, the Watch Tower Society supplies written materials and photos from its historical archives so that, "in future exhibitions and publications, the prisoners with the purple patch will receive more recognition than in the past."[15]

On April 26, 1997, at the Urania theater in Berlin, another film about the "Persecution and Resistance of Jehovah's Witnesses under the Nazi Regime" had its premiere (under the title *Fear Not*).[16] This documentary was produced by a private association and was supported by the U.S. Holocaust Memorial Museum. It received public funds from the Kuratorium junger deutscher Film (a foundation benefitting German film projects) and the Kulturelle Filmförderung in Niedersachsen (Cultural Film Promotion in Lower Saxony). The film, based on extensive interviews with surviving witnesses, describes in an impressive way the motives for the persecution of Jehovah's Witnesses in the Third Reich. It thus contributes to a better understanding of the background for their religiously based resistance.

However, both *Fear Not* and *Stand Firm* call for some criticism. Although these films are important contributions for an introduction to this subject through the media, from a scientific standpoint they do not, or do to a limited extent, meet the requirements for film documentaries. In the one case, the self-representation is overwhelming. In the other case, considerable emphasis is placed on empathy for the victims, which, though certainly necessary, may impede objectivity. Both films lack an equally required critical distance: apparently no significant importance was attached to the question of validity of the recollections by the contemporary witnesses and aspects that might conflict with the intended objective of the film were not included.[17]

From a historical perspective, the increasing openness of the Watch Tower Society with regard to questions of historical review is a very welcome development. After decades of reserve toward the public, Jehovah's Witnesses are now investing much time and effort in order to gain recognition from the society as a group of victims of NS persecution. The motives of the Watch Tower Society in this regard are of a complex nature. As is the case with other groups of so-called forgotten victims of persecution, their quest for recognition is not primarily a matter of dealing with the past. During the last ten to fifteen years, many of these groups have been included, at least to a certain extent, in public remembrances. (These groups include, for instance, the Sinti and the Roma, euthanasia victims, people who had been subjected to forced sterilization, and homosexuals.) Jehovah's Witnesses have a very real concern: In a statement made during the November 6, 1996, press conference regarding the Ravensbrück film premiere, the Watch Tower Society's information service indicated that "the present-day stigmatization of Jehovah's Witnesses among the general public can be compared to the way people discriminated against them during the period of the purple triangle."[18] The information service further stated that there is a recurring wave of "defensive polemics" on the part of "religious competitors," which probably addresses primarily the Protestant churches and the Catholic Church. The religious scholar Dr. Gabriele Yonan is quoted as saying: "Such discrimination of Jehovah's Witnesses should never be allowed again."[19]

Since the early 1990s (with reference to the secular recognition the Council of Ministers of the former GDR—then in its transitional stage—granted Jehovah's Witnesses on March 14, 1990, in the context of withdrawing the ban on their association), the "Religious Denomination of Jehovah's Witnesses in Germany,"[20] which has been legally established in the new federal states, is trying to obtain the legal status of a "corporation under public law." (This status provides the association with special concessions in tax law and with the same legal rights that other recognized churches and denominations have in Germany.) When this request was rejected by the Land Berlin (which includes all districts falling under Berlin administration), Jehovah's Witnesses instituted legal proceedings. As a result, they were able to win the 1993 Administrative Court proceedings, as well as the 1995 Higher Administrative Court proceedings to the extent that the courts affirmed that Jehovah's Witnesses could not be denied legal status since this religious denomination fulfills all constitutional requirements for a corporation under public law.[21] To this end, the court stated that the objections raised by the Land Berlin against Jehovah's Witnesses were of no legal importance, since the Land Berlin had to remain neutral in matters regarding religion and ideology. After further proceedings before the highest German courts— the Federal Administrative Court and Constitutional Court—the religious organization of Jehovah's Witnesses finally prevailed. On February

1, 2006, the Leipzig Federal Administrative Court obligated the Land Berlin to grant the religious organization the legal status of a "corporation under public law." Since then, Jehovah's Witnesses in Germany enjoy the same rights as the churches and other recognized religious denominations.

The efforts of Jehovah's Witnesses to receive recognition as victims of NS persecution must be viewed against this background. In this regard, another aspect should also be taken into consideration—that of an adjustment concerning the expectations for the end of this world proclaimed in a 1995 *Watchtower.* Previously, Jehovah's Witnesses believed that God would establish a New World "during the lifetime of the generation that experienced the events of the year 1914."[22] Today, the more than six million Jehovah's Witnesses worldwide who share in the preaching activity still put their trust in the fact that God will fulfill this promise of the New World "shortly." However, he will do so at a time that cannot be determined by men and that must, therefore, be left completely in God's hands.[23] Religious history has taught the lesson that as soon as the religious thinking of a group is no longer exclusively based on expectations of the future, its history will take on greater importance for the religious identity of its members.

In recent years, a considerable change took place regarding the public reception of the subject of NS persecution of Jehovah's Witnesses.[24] To a large extent, this development was promoted through the U.S. Holocaust Memorial Museum in Washington, D.C., established in 1993. In the exhibition of this museum, Jehovah's Witnesses receive extensive recognition as a group of victims of NS persecution. Even during its foundation, besides the central subject of the Shoah, the Holocaust Museum also gave considerable attention to "other victims."[25] It included Jehovah's Witnesses among the groups that experienced the worst persecution after the Jews, the Soviet prisoners of war, and the Sinti and the Roma. In its exhibits and publications, Jehovah's Witnesses receive similar recognition as do persecuted homosexuals.[26] In September 1994, in cooperation with the Watch Tower Society, the Holocaust Memorial Museum organized a conference at which historians and surviving witnesses presented reports about the persecution of Jehovah's Witnesses in the Third Reich.[27] For the exhibition, the museum also published an accompanying booklet on the subject. The archives of the Holocaust Museum include a comprehensive collection of evidence regarding the persecution of Jehovah's Witnesses, as well as more than 100 oral history video interviews with survivors of the NS period from among the group of this denomination.

Even in Germany, Jehovah's Witnesses are no longer excluded from the reorganization of memorials. This is the case with regard to the 1995 reorganization of the Buchenwald and Neuengamme memorials on the occasion of the fiftieth anniversary of the liberation from the concentration camps. In 1989 a new permanent exhibition was organized at the Berlin Memorial "Deutscher Widerstand" (German Resistance). The fifth (of a total of twenty-six) part of this exhibition analyzes the issue of "resistance on the basis of Christian faith until 1939." This part not only discusses the religious resistance from the aspect of Protestant and Catholic people but also devotes its third section to the minor denominations, including an extensive representation of Jehovah's Witnesses.

To a certain extent, Jehovah's Witnesses are now recognized even outside of the memorials. Since 1992, in the immediate neighborhood of the Plötzensee Memorial of Berlin-Charlottenburg, the Emmy-Zehden-Weg serves as a reminder of a Jehovah's Witness who was executed on June 9, 1944, as a result of a People's Court decision for hiding three other Jehovah's Witnesses who had been called for military service.[28] In 1993, in the Baden village of Baltmannsweiler, a street was named after Bernhard Grimm, who was sentenced to death by the RKG on the charge of conscientious objection. On August 21, 1942, the nineteen-year-old Jehovah's Witness was guillotined at the Brandenburg prison.[29]

The extensive acceptance of this present book also indicates an increasing interest in this subject. It came quite unexpectedly that a scholarly discussion of a subject previously largely disregarded would reach a fourth German edition. Reviews of the book are included in relevant domestic as well as foreign literature.[30] Moreover, such reviews are also included in publications that address the general public.[31]

Certain groups, including those who had survived NS persecution and their family members, particularly approved of this book, irrespective of whether these people are still closely associated with the denomination of Jehovah's Witnesses or later disassociated themselves from it. At times, however, the response is determined by the strong controversy about the true faith and the "sectarian characteristics" of this denomination carried on between those Jehovah's Witnesses who are completely convinced that their religious activities represent the truth and their critics (which include former Jehovah's Witnesses and members of mostly religious groups and information centers). For example, Jehovah's

Witnesses objected to the fact that I included in this study certain literary evidence from "apostates," stating that I had fallen victim to their efforts of discrediting the organization. Critics, on the other hand, charged that I had been persuaded by the Watch Tower Society to promote their goals, imputing even dubious motives.

On both sides, the majority of people acknowledged my efforts to review history based strictly on the sources and appropriate facts. In 1995 the religiously nonaligned Bruderdienst, which employs a number of former Jehovah's Witnesses, published a special journal under the title *Das Ende einer Legende: Die Wachtturm-Gesellschaft und das "Dritte Reich." Vom Anpassungskurs zur Konfrontation* (The End of a Legend: The Watch Tower Society and the Third Reich. From a Course of Adaptation to Confrontation). To a great extent, this journal readily accepted the results of my research study. The Watch Tower Society initially expressed "some reservations toward the publication of this study."[32] However, on November 6, in the context of the 1996 premiere of the video documentary, its representative stated that it is, "not the least, due [to this work] that, especially among specialized historians, Jehovah's Witnesses receive the status they deserve."[33]

Unfortunately, ongoing controversies are often carried out on the basis of an interpretation of past events. Reference to the sufferings experienced by Jehovah's Witnesses in Hitler Germany due to their faithful adherence to their conviction and the intrepidness with which they confronted the regime is also made (among a German population that has been sensitized to the subject of NS persecution) because it influences the way Jehovah's Witnesses are viewed today, which often is somewhat negative. The Watch Tower Society is not unfamiliar with the tendency to use the history of resistance for the purpose of self-representation, a practice also used by other groups. (This tendency is, for instance, reflected in the early apologetic historiography of the "church struggle."[34])

Some critics of Jehovah's Witnesses even show a tendency to use the past, not for a critical analysis of historical evidence but for the purpose of giving, in advance, a derogatory judgment in order to stimulate the present controversy involving the activities of Jehovah's Witnesses. With regard to such approaches, let me emphasize that the objective of historiography is that of reconstructing previous events from the various sources on an empirical basis. An assessment of the actions of Jehovah's Witnesses in the Third Reich should not be based on the pros and cons of the controversial activities of the Watch Tower Society today. Research results regarding the persecution of Jehovah's Witnesses in the Third Reich, based on an analysis of extensive empirical material and which confirm the exceptional intensity of the persecution, do not become invalid only because the Watch Tower Society, for various reasons, did an about-face and, with reference to the persecution of Jehovah's Witnesses in the Third Reich, now tries to improve its public reputation.

Especially controversial is the question of how to assess the efforts of the denomination's leaders at the beginning of the NS government to utilize available legal and other means of negotiation in order to form a legal basis for a continuation of IBSA activities. In this regard, the June 25, 1933, Berlin-Wilmersdorf convention is of special significance. The seven thousand Jehovah's Witnesses who attended this convention accepted a resolution written by Rutherford, the Watch Tower Society's president. This resolution emphasized the completely religious and nonpolitical purpose of the denomination and had the objective of convincing government officials that the accusations of an "anti-state attitude" of Jehovah's Witnesses, as well as other accusations against them, were untenable. It was even emphasized that the objectives of the denomination were, to a certain extent, similar to the "high ideals" of the NS state. To this end, the writers of the resolution went even as far as using anti-Jewish language.

Even though the Watch Tower Society is now more open toward the outside, it has not yet distanced itself from its efforts to adapt to national circumstances in 1933. Requests to do so were made not just from people outside of the organization. Within the denomination, quite a large number of Jehovah's Witnesses apparently also expect a clarification of the situation. Today, the Wilmersdorf declaration is no longer presented as a "resolution of protest." However, the Watch Tower Society continues to justify the concessions made by the Magdeburg and, initially, even the Brooklyn leadership during this period of great difficulties in order to achieve a withdrawal of the bans on the Bible Students Association. It seems that the Watch Tower Society is generally unable to admit that during the initial months of the Third Reich, the "visible organization of Jehovah," like other groups, adopted a course of adaptation with the secular authorities in order to guarantee its survival, at times even requesting its members to discontinue their preaching activity. Consequently, in the beginning, the Watch Tower Society did not act with the same determination that later characterized the actions of Jehovah's Witnesses under NS rule. To admit such a course would also raise questions involving the authority of the governing body, or "faithful and discreet slave," of the religious denomination of Jehovah's Witnesses.[35]

For the fourth German edition of this present book, the paragraph regarding the Wilmersdorf convention has been revised as a result of an examination of additional sources.[36] Two statements about the circumstances of the convention have been corrected or put in perspective. I had based my statements on the tape recording of a 1976 lecture (parts of which were also published) by Konrad Franke, the former branch leader of the Watch Tower Society in Germany. But I have been assured that the convention was not introduced with the "Deutschlandlied." Rather, the convention began with a Bible Student song based on the same melody of Haydn for which Hoffmann von Fallersleben wrote the "Deutschlandlied" in the nineteenth century. In 1922 this particular song was declared to be the national anthem of Germany. It is also not possible to find additional proof that the convention center was decorated with swastikas. Only two reports and some photos of the interior are available, which seem to present a different picture. Since it is not possible to resolve this issue beyond all doubt, the assertion that the place was decorated with swastikas can no longer be upheld according to currently available information. Because of the meaningful symbolism, much significance has been attached to these two statements. Regretfully, based on the available sources, it has not been possible to clarify this issue and such clarification can also not be expected in the future.

Two further points require an explanation. First, because of absolute adherence to their religious convictions, Jehovah's Witnesses refused to give their allegiance to the NS regime. They did not pay tribute to the Führer, nor did they allow the authorities to integrate them into NS organizations. They generally did not comply with the draft into the German Wehrmacht. They also did not submit to the bans imposed on their religious denomination. And all of this despite the fact that their attitude of resistance resulted in imprisonment for thousands of Jehovah's Witnesses in the concentration camps. For hundreds of them, this attitude even resulted in a death penalty. Appropriately, this attitude deserves highest respect and public recognition. Regardless of how people might view the motives and actions of Jehovah's Witnesses, undoubtedly, in contrast to the majority of Germans, Jehovah's Witnesses did not support the NS government at any time. According to Klaus Drobisch, this was a course that would have been "equally appropriate" for the majority of the German population.[37] At the same time, we should take into consideration that Jehovah's Witnesses struggled for their (own) organizational and religious freedom in this conflict with the NS regime. They certainly did not fight for freedom in a more comprehensive and political sense; their resistance of this dictatorship was not based on a democratic disposition.[38] From that perspective, their courageous attitude in the Third Reich merits respect and recognition. However, it cannot be used as a model for a democratically oriented society. The same would apply to many other victims of the NS regime, including quite a few political resistance fighters (Stalinists, NS renegades, monarchists, and even the reactionary wing of "July 20" [1944, the assassination attempt on Hitler and failed coup d'état]). Today, the martyrs from among Jehovah's Witnesses receive the respect they deserve by being included in exhibitions, publications, and commemorative events. From a pedagogical point of view, however, they do not occupy a role model position. This position should be reserved for Herbert Baum, Dietrich Bonhoeffer, Mildred and Arvid Harnack, Helmuth Hübener, Julius Leber, Max Josef Metzger, Carl von Ossietzky, Sophie and Hans Scholl, Claus Schenk Graf von Stauffenberg, Hilda Monte, and others.

Second, I should also emphasize again that the resistance of Jehovah's Witnesses was not directed solely against the NS dictatorship—it was not only the NS state that they exposed and condemned as an instrument of Satan. Even in other countries and during all periods of time, actions such as the refusal to salute the flag or to become (compulsory) members of political organizations—and especially the refusal to perform military service—brought Jehovah's Witnesses into conflict with the authorities.[39] And in reference to Rutherford's satanic trilogy of "big business, politics, and the churches," the Watch Tower Society considers governments in general as instruments under the authority of the devil. This, in turn, explains why the Watch Tower Society's publications also show a negative attitude toward nondictatorial states.[40] In 1962 the Watch Tower Society changed its viewpoint and abandoned Rutherford's concept of the "higher powers." From then on, the governing authorities—stated in Romans 13—were again identified to be the worldly governments. Consequently, the Watch Tower Society attributes to these worldly governments a God-given function for the purpose of keeping order in this "Old World."[41]

Since the first publication of my book, various people have provided me with important additional information and documents. The majority of these documents are from relatives of persecuted Jehovah's Witnesses, and they provide information about the persecution to which these individuals had been subjected. During the process of revising the book for its fourth German edition, I took into consideration all information that brought to my attention incorrect or unsupported statements. However, it is not possible to include all the information and documents I received. To include them would have resulted in a diversification of certain aspects, which, in turn, would have adversely affected the character of this work as a comprehensive study of this subject. These documents will be taken into consideration in the context of individual studies. In recent years, several of these studies have already been written; others are in the process of planning or nearing completion.

In conclusion, I would like to express special appreciation for the critical and explanatory comments provided by the following people: Dr. Franz Graf-Stuhlhofer, Kirsten John, Gerhard Kaiser, Addi Klohe, Erich Kraushaar, Helmut Milde, Dieter Obele, Willi Seitz, Dr. Richard Singelenberg, Bernhard Strebel, Kurt Willy Triller, Karlo Vegelahn, as well as Johannes Wrobel and Willi K. Pohl from the Watch Tower Bible and Tract Society in Selters/Taunus. In addition, I would like to express my appreciation to all who helped with this book and who are not mentioned here by name.

DETLEF GARBE

Hamburg
April 1997

NOTES

Introduction

1. In this work, the designation "Watch Tower" will refer to the corporate entities of Jehovah's Witnesses, for instance, "Watch Tower Society," whereas *Watchtower* will refer to the journal published by Jehovah's Witnesses from 1879 to the present.

2. The names "Bible Students" and "Jehovah's Witnesses" apply to the denomination as a group as well as to its individual members. For the period after 1931, both terms are used interchangeably. This is appropriate, since the old name "Bible Students" has continued to be in use by the public, the NS authorities, as well as the members of the denomination. The name "International Bible Students Association" (IBSA) stands for the denomination or the Bible Students (Jehovah's Witnesses) as an organization. The name "Watch Tower Bible and Tract Society," or "Wachtturm Bibel- und Traktat-Gesellschaft" (WTG), represents the legal entity and publishing corporation of Jehovah's Witnesses, and is used to identify either the American leadership of the denomination or the leadership of its German branch office.

3. I had my first encounter with Jehovah's Witnesses while preparing for a project involving the history of persecuted minorities in NS-controlled Hamburg. On this research and exhibition project, which was encouraged and supported by various sources, including the Hamburg Kulturbehörde (since the end of 1983), see Garbe, "Die 'vergessenen' Opfer," 5–13.

4. Hüttenberger, "Vorüberlegungen," 118.

5. On literature discussing the free churches, minor religious denominations, and religious sects in the Third Reich, see this book, p. 584, n.129.

6. In the chapter "Christen im Widerstand," in their otherwise outstanding collection *Widerstand und Verweigerung in Deutschland 1933 bis 1945*, Richard Löwenthal and Patrick von zur Mühlen do not mention the minor denominations or the struggle for self-assertion of some of their members against the NS regime.

7. According to a 1933 population census, the "members of other evangelical religious denominations," including the Bible Students, represented 0.9 percent of the population (see *Die Bevölkerung des Deutschen Reichs 1933*, 11.) The Reich Office of Statistics does not include a detailed membership list of religious denominations. Therefore, a comparison has to be based on the 1925 population census. Accordingly (apart from orthodox churches and the Old Catholics), the membership of the minor Christian religious denominations is divided as follows: New Apostolic Church, 138,000; Baptists, 70,000; Methodists, 49,000; Adventists, 30,000; Mennonites, 13,000; other evangelical groups, 39,000; and members of other Christian denominations, 36,000 (*Die Bevölkerung des Deutschen Reichs 1925*, 356–57). According to subsequent statements (see this book, pt. 1, ch. 3, p. 45), the number of Bible Students in 1925 probably amounted to approximately 20,000.

8. See, e.g., M. Koch, "Die kleinen Glaubensgemeinschaften," 434; Mitterrutnzer, "Internationale Bibelforscher-Vereinigung," 275; Neugebauer, "'Ernste Bibelforscher,'" 161; Zipfel, *Kirchenkampf*, 176.

9. In his study *The Dual State*, first published in 1941 in New York, Ernst Fraenkel, former legal counsel of the German Metalworkers' Union, applied this statement even beyond the immediate circle of religious denominations. "These sectarians, whose absolute pacifism requires them to eschew all compromise and whose exclusive worship of Jehovah involves the negation of every kind of secular authority, must be considered as the embodiment of behavior exclusively in accordance with norms derived from absolute Natural Law. No illegal group in Germany is more uncompromisingly opposed to National-Socialism than this obstinate sect." Fraenkel, *Dual State*, 117.

10. In 1933/34 about 60,000 of the approximately 300,000 KPD members registered in 1932 were arrested and detained in prisons or concentration camps. See H. Weber, "Widerstandsstrategie," 79. Based on available documents about KPD resistance groups in western Germany, Detlef Peukert estimates that "the number of Communists actively involved in illegal organizations at some point between 1933 and 1935 . . . amounted to more than one fourth, probably between one third and one half of the total number of members at the turn of 1932/33." Peukert, *KPD*, 166.

11. On participation in acts of resistance of small politically Leftist groups, see Foitzik, *Zwischen den Fronten*, esp. 241ff. Jan Foitzik assumes that during the mid-1930s about half of the membership of small politically Leftist groups were still involved in acts of resistance (total membership in 1933: 22,000.) The IBSA showed an almost identical ratio—even considering its membership numbers.

12. The Schutzstaffel was a special armed branch of the NSDAP, consisting of particularly reliable members of the party under leadership of Heinrich Himmler, Reichsführer SS (Reich leader).

13. See Conway, *Nazi Persecution of the Churches*, 196; Garbe, "'Gott mehr gehorchen als den Menschen,'" 180.

14. Lilje, *Im finstern Tal*, 59.

15. This comparison was made by Friedman, *Das andere Deutschland*, 23; Kühl, "Friedrichstadt," 165; and Zipfel, *Kirchenkampf*, 203.

16. See the commentary in *Verhandlungen des Bundestages*, vol. 341, Oct. 31, 1986, report of the federal government concerning compensation and retributions for National Socialist injustices (Drs. [printed matter] 10/6287, 11). In compensation and retribution law, for many years, there was a controversy of whether the Bible Students should be listed among those who were victims of group-related persecution whom the NS regime "tried to exclude from cultural and economic life in Germany" (BEG, art. 51, para. 4). See *RzW* [*Rechtsprechung zum Wiedergutmachungsrecht*] 9 (1958): 29, BGH, IV ZB 154/57, decision of Oct. 9, 1957; Blessin, *Bundesentschädigungsgesetze*, 483; Schwarz, *Rückerstattung*, 130–31. The legal authorities generally denied compensation for Jehovah's Witnesses who had refused military service in the German Wehrmacht (Armed Forces) for religious reasons. They also denied compensation for family members of Jehovah's Witnesses because they did not consider punishment on the charge of conscientious objection as NS persecution. They also disputed that Jehovah's Witnesses were persecuted for religious reasons, which would have resulted in the fact that they would have to be recognized as victims of persecution by National Socialism according to BEG, art. 1. According to the legal authorities, Jehovah's Witnesses were not persecuted for their religious beliefs but for their refusal to perform the "legally required military service." See Garbe, "Im Namen des Volkes," 116–22.

17. See Heinz, "Kriegsdienstverweigerer"; Fleschutz, *Siebenten-Tags-Adventisten Reformationsbewegung*.

18. Lilje, *Im finstern Tal*, 59. Apart from non-Germans whom the National Socialists tried to force into service in the German Wehrmacht (people from Lorraine, Alsace, Luxembourg, and Poland from group 3 of the *Deutsche Volksliste*, the German People's List, or list of "discovered" ethnic Germans), Jehovah's Witnesses in the Third Reich represented by far the largest number of conscientious objectors. For more details, see this book, pt. 5, ch. 14, pp. 366–68.

19. Kater, "Bibelforscher," 208. Kater rightly emphasizes that in previous research this fact has not been adequately taken into consideration.

20. Meier, *Neuengamme*, 31–32.

21. Pingel, *Häftlinge*, 87. In his publication *Mauthausen*, 273, Maršálek uses the same wording. In her book *Milena* (170), Buber-Neumann even states that "in a sense, the Jehovah's Witnesses were voluntary prisoners." See this book, pt. 4, ch. 12, p. 296.

22. See Grünewald, *Kriegsdienstverweigerung*, 29. Report by Björn Hallström, a Swedish journalist, who conducted interviews in Buchenwald after the liberation in Apr./May 1945.

23. Maislinger, "Die Zeugen Jehovas" (Tirol), 370. With reference to Langbein, Andreas Maislinger generalizes his statements, i.e., he does not restrict

them to a certain location. Langbein, on the other hand (as the context shows), refers only to the "small numbers" of Jehovah's Witnesses imprisoned at the Mauthausen concentration camp. See Langbein, *Against All Hope*, 179.

24. With reference to their "religious fanaticism," the resistance of Jehovah's Witnesses was usually played down completely, even in scholarly literature. See Kater, "Bibelforscher," 182; Neugebauer, "'Ernste Bibelforscher,'" 161. For instance, with regard to the persecution of Jehovah's Witnesses, Konrad Algermissen, professor of Catholic theology and expert on denomination and sect-related issues, considered it necessary to point out that a historical study about the IBSA in the Third Reich also bears in mind the "difference between martyrdom on account of the truth and determined intolerance of nonsense." Algermissen, *Zeugen Jehovas*, 10.

25. Angela Genger and Bernd Rusinek, "Gedenkstätten-Rundbrief," cited in *Aktion Sühnezeichen/Friedensdienste*, no. 29 (Mar. 1989): 9. The wording is based on the "Stuttgarter Schulderklärung" (Stuttgart Confession) made on Aug. 18 and 19, 1945, by the council of the Evangelical churches in Germany in front of ecumenical representatives.

26. In his dissertation about the history of Jehovah's Witnesses in the United States, William Cumberland appropriately emphasizes that it is not, and should not be, the purpose of a historical study "to judge" the validity of the teachings of Jehovah's Witnesses. This is a responsibility reserved for religious scholars and theologians. See Cumberland, "History of Jehovah's Witnesses," 3.

27. Prolingheuer, *Kirchengeschichte*, 10.

28. On the difficulties of defining the term "sect," and on theological and sociological criteria that characterize a religious denomination as a "sect," see Köppl, *Zeugen Jehovas*, 7–28. Because of the terminological difficulties and the customary (de)valuating use of the term in denominational discussions, important factors speak against applying the term "sect" to a religious denomination, especially in scholarly studies. However, according to Köppl, it is empirically verifiable that Jehovah's Witnesses fulfill several of the attributes that characterize a religious denomination as a "sect." These attributes include, for instance, the claim that only they have a universally acceptable or absolute concept of reality, their perception of belonging to a specially selected group of people and, closely related, the request for specific performances in order to be accepted into this group secluded from society in general, as well as their uncompromising moral and ethical lifestyle.

29. Kortzfleisch, "Sekten," col. 2279.

30. In the few cases in which Jehovah's Witnesses are mentioned in comprehensive studies, they are mentioned only in the context of explanations involving the different categories of concentration camp prisoners, or they are used as a group to exemplify the Gestapo practice of imposing "sentencing reversals" by ordering protective detention. However, in chapters discussing resistance Jehovah's Witnesses are generally disregarded.

31. During the period immediately following World War II, the Association of Persecution Victims of the National Socialist Regime (VVN, Vereinigung der Verfolgten des Naziregimes), which included almost all groups of victims of NS persecution, made an effort to include also the Bible Students. For instance, on May 9, 1948, at the delegate conference of the VVN for the British zone, Carl Dominik, a Bible Student from Schleswig, was elected to the board of directors consisting of thirty-five members (see Stobwasser, *VVN,* 42–43). During 1949, however, many Jehovah's Witnesses decided to withdraw from the VVN. On the one hand, these withdrawals were based on the fact that the VVN had adopted a party-political agenda, which made it impossible for Jehovah's Witnesses to continue their membership for reasons of Christian neutrality. On the other hand, the withdrawals were based on the measures of repression being initiated against Jehovah's Witnesses in 1949 in the SBZ (Soviet Occupied Zone), or DDR (German Democratic Republic).

32. Pechel, *Widerstand,* 107.

33. Weisenborn, *Aufstand,* 87–92.

34. Ritter, "Wunschträume Heinrich Himmlers," 166.

35. Ibid., 165.

36. Rothfels, *Opposition,* 44. Despite the fact that it is still necessary to examine the question of whether their resistance could be classified as "passive resistance," it is completely justified to mention the Quakers in this context. See Oleschinski, "Religiöse Gemeinschaften," 198ff.; Otto, *Quäkertum,* 297–373. However, the Mennonites, as a group, can hardly be associated with resistance movements. See Lichdi, *Mennoniten.* Only a few Mennonites offered resistance to the regime, while their leaders and the majority of believers largely adapted to the circumstances. In 1934, in the course of this adaptation, the Mennonite groups completely abandoned their position of conscientious objection. Even though their initial approval of National Socialism later gave way to an increasingly reserved attitude, this was not expressed publicly.

37. Zipfel, *Kirchenkampf,* 175–203.

38. This special compensation office was set up during the early postwar period for the purpose of assisting people who had been politically, racially, and religiously persecuted during NS rule.

39. This criticism applies especially to statements involving special court and military court proceedings. For instance, Kater incorrectly states that the "various offenses of the Bible Students" were punished according to the Heimtückegesetz (Law against Insidious Attacks on State and Party and for the Protection of the Party Uniform). Kater, "Bibelforscher," 197; see also this book, pt. 4, ch. 11, pp. 224–25, and esp. p. 624, n.73. Kater is also incorrect in stating that, after the initiation of compulsory military service, the special courts "sentenced Jehovah's Witnesses on the charge of conscientious objection." (See Kater, "Bibelforscher," 198; cases on the charge of conscientious objection were not under special court jurisdiction. The considerably increasing number

of condemnations of Jehovah's Witnesses after 1935 was not directly related to the initiation of compulsory military service; see this book, p. 618, n.10.) Because of his lack of familiarity with the subject, Kater arrived, for instance, at the conclusion that, prior to the beginning of the war, the judges "were still reluctant" to impose death penalties (Kater, 198). This, in turn, prompted him to speculate on the reasons for this "reluctance of the civil courts to impose death penalties until 1939" (Kater, 199). Had Kater been aware of the fact that, until Aug. 26, 1939, the day of mobilization, there was no law in the Third Reich on which to base death penalties for Bible Student activities, he would not have made such statements. In fact, contrary to Kater's assumption, death penalties on Jehovah's Witnesses were not pronounced until the beginning of the war. The fact that during the NS period dozens of Jehovah's Witnesses were tortured to death during Gestapo interrogations and in the concentration camps involves a different problem.

40. Gebhard, *Zeugen Jehovas*, 134–42, 153–213.

41. The documentation was originally based on Gebhard's manuscript, which he wrote at the end of the 1960s after his separation from Jehovah's Witnesses. He was not personally involved in preparing the documentation for publication. Therefore, Gebhard clearly distances himself from its exaggerations and misrepresentations. To this end, he stated to the secretary of state for church matters in the DDR that he considered it a mistake to have agreed on the use of his name because he was unaware of the final result of this documentation. See the May 29, 1994, recollections by Manfred Gebhard; private documents of Willi K. Pohl. On the support the book project received from the Main Department 20 of the MfS (Ministry for State Security), see Besier and Wolf, *Ministerium für Staatssicherheit*, 84.

42. The decree issued by Secretary of the Interior Steinhoff gave the following reasons for the ban: involvement in activities supporting "unconstitutional purposes," performance of a "systematic hate campaign against existing democratic law and order in the disguise of a religious denomination," as well as introduction of "prohibited publications." The main accusation was that, supposedly, "'Jehovah's Witnesses' work for the intelligence service of an imperialistic power" (see Menter, "Himmlers Auferstehung"; the prohibition order is published in Nobel, *Falschspieler Gottes*, 101). After the ban had been issued, Jehovah's Witnesses in the DDR were subjected to a massive repression wave, which also affected quite a number of former concentration camp prisoners. DDR courts imposed heavy penalties on Jehovah's Witnesses on the charge of "espionage and war-mongering." In some cases, the courts considered the fact that Jehovah's Witnesses refused to sign the "Stockholm Appeal for peace" as evidence of "warmongering" (see *Partei-Justiz*, 64–70). According to available records, between 1950 and 1955 a total of 2,891 Jehovah's Witnesses were arrested in the DDR, 2,202 (674 were women) of whom were condemned. In fourteen cases, lifelong prison sentences were imposed. A total of sixty-two

Jehovah's Witnesses died during their imprisonment or as an immediate result of their imprisonment (see Cole, *Jehovah's Witnesses*, 188 [German edition, 209]; Dirksen, "German Democratic Republic," 215ff.). Twenty-nine of these people had already been imprisoned during the NS regime (Jehovas Zeugen, Nov. 1, 2002, press release no. 15/02). The status as "victims of Fascism" that Jehovah's Witnesses were granted during the initial postwar period was usually withdrawn. They were also excluded from receiving the "honor pension" that victims of NS persecution were granted in the DDR. This practice of social exclusion ended only with the social upheaval that took place in the autumn of 1989. On Mar. 14, 1990, after a forty-year ban, Jehovah's Witnesses were again formally recognized as a religious denomination.

43. Gebhard, *Zeugen Jehovas*, 255.

44. Ibid., 67–68, 75–76. It is actually more than surprising that the writers of this "documentation" base their assertion of an alleged interaction between the U.S. State Department and the Watch Tower Society on Gestapo situation reports, reports in which the international connections of the denomination were used as evidence for its opposition to the NS regime.

45. Especially questionable are references to petitions for pardon in which some of Jehovah's Witnesses who had been sentenced to death pleaded for their life. Naturally, these pleas were not presented in the "heroic voice of resistance" but instead reflect the compliant tone of a petitioner expressing regrets for his "acts of defiance" against "the Führer and the people." However, it would be easy to produce such "evidence" for any other resistance group. The fact that these statements of despair are used to discredit a group of people and are depicted as "disgraceful courting for the favor of Fascist executioners" (Gebhard, *Zeugen Jehovas*, 203) characterizes the more than questionable style of this documentation.

46. In the majority of cases, until the mid-1970s, Jehovah's Witnesses were simply disregarded or ignored in DDR historiography. Because it is almost impossible to avoid mentioning this group in historical studies about the concentration camps, the writers simply changed the terminology. For instance, when referring to Jehovah's Witnesses, they used terms such as "prisoners from religious groups," "clergymen, or "sectarians" (*Die Frauen von Ravensbrück*, 146–47; *Todeslager Sachsenhausen*, 42–43, 206).

47. See Knaut, *Propheten;* Nobel, *Falschspieler Gottes*.

48. Steinberg, *Essen*, 159–66, 278–84.

49. Stokes, *Eutin*, 697–716.

50. Marßolek and Ott, *Bremen*, 303–12 (308).

51. Minninger, "Bielefeld." For specific information on the IBSA, see 65–75.

52. See also the slightly revised chapter "Widerstand und Verfolgung der Zeugen Jehovas: Arbeiter und religiöses Märtyrertum" in Struve's comprehensive 1992 study *Aufstieg und Herrschaft des Nationalsozialismus in einer industriellen Kleinstadt*, originally published in 1990.

53. Imberger, *Widerstand*, 243–376.

54. In Austrian studies, without any reservations, conscientious objectors (*Eidesverweigerer*) from among Jehovah's Witnesses are included with the "resistance fighters within the Wehrmacht" (see Vogl, *Widerstand*, 160–73). However, it is certainly fitting to question the appropriateness of including, in this context, the religiously motivated conscientious objection of Jehovah's Witnesses in the overall picture of "Austrian resistance," which was carried out for patriotic reasons and with the objective of national autonomy, and of including them in the number of victims of National Socialism "who considered their homeland Austria to be more valuable than their lives" (Steiner, *Österreich*, 27).

55. Maislinger, "Die Zeugen Jehovas" (Tirol); Maislinger, "Andere religiöse Gruppen" (Salzburg); Mitterrutzner, "Internationale Bibelforscher-Vereinigung"; Neugebauer, "'Ernste Bibelforscher'"; Zinnhobler, "Zeugen Jehovas."

56. Maislinger, "Die Zeugen Jehovas," 370; see also Mitterrutzner, "Internationale Bibelforscher-Vereinigung," 274. Erika Weinzierl points in the same direction by stating that "the conduct of Jehovah's Witnesses during the National Socialist period is truly admirable" (Weinzierl, "Österreichische Frauen," 182).

57. In 1986, though with a topical extension, a short summary of Renate Lichtenegger's dissertation was published in the journal *Zeitgeschichte*. See Lichtenegger, "Die Bibelforscher im Widerstand gegen das NS-Regime."

58. On the different points of criticism and evidence of factual deficiencies, see the explanations in the respective notes of this work: p. 590, n.199; p. 602, n.57; p. 618, n.10; pp. 632–33, n.163; p. 650, n.329; and p. 739, n.43.

59. See Bergman's extensive bibliography, *Jehovah's Witnesses*. Most of the titles involve popular scholarly works, but even the sheer number of scholarly studies is remarkable. In addition to several master's theses, the biography mentions eighteen dissertations (eight social scientific, six theological, three legal dissertations, and one historical dissertation). Eight of these were written at universities in the United States, seven in Great Britain, two in Germany, and one in Canada.

60. Helmreich, *German Churches*, 91–92, 392–97. Conway, *Nazi Persecution of the Churches*, 195–99; Harrison, *Visions of Glory*, 208–307. The work of Barbara Grizzuti Harrison contradicts Conway's explanations because, in her opinion, Conway's approach in presenting the behavior of Jehovah's Witnesses in the Third Reich is uncritical and too positive. Her study is a typical example of historiography written with the objective of exposing Jehovah's Witnesses.

61. King, *The Nazi State and the New Religions*. In 1979 Christine E. King published a preliminary study. See King, "Strategies for Survival."

62. Graffard and Tristan, *Les Bibelforscher et le nazisme, 1933–1945: Ces oubliés de l'Histoire*, was published in 1990. In the meantime, the book has been reprinted five times and has been translated into Italian.

63. Kogon, *The Theory and Practice of Hell,* 41–43. To a great extent, Kogon's study is based on a statement that Jehovah's Witnesses wrote after their liberation from Buchenwald. This statement was first published in the Watch Tower Society's journal *Comfort* on Aug. 15, 1945, 6–7. (Reprinted in Grünewald, *Kriegsdienstverweigerung,* 30–33. A shortened and revised edition of this statement is included in the so-called *Buchenwald-Report;* see Hackett, 212–14.) Kogon's explanations about Buchenwald are based on personal experiences and the above-mentioned statement. However, in the chapter discussing the Bible Students, his study contains factual errors wherever the author had to rely on reports he received from other concentration camps (see this book, pp. 704–5, n.418). Langbein, *Against All Hope,* 178–91; Pingel, *Häftlinge,* 87–91.

64. See this book, pt. 5, ch. 13, pp. 334–36, and p. 721, n.575.

65. See, for instance, Volkmann, *Rechtsprechung,* 23–50. For additional literary references, see the corresponding notes in this book: p. 592, n.220; p. 593, n.245; p. 595, n.256; p. 603, n.72.

66. See, for instance, Wagner, *Volksgerichtshof,* 306ff. For additional literary references, see corresponding notes in this book: p. 667, n.114; pp. 667–68, n.118.

67. The Munich Special Court records illustrate the large number of Bible Student court cases. In 1937, of the 571 defendants recorded by name, 158 (27.7 percent) were IBSA members. See Hüttenberger, "Heimtückefälle," 446–47.

68. Of special interest in this regard is Hutten's revised standard work, *Seher, Grübler, Enthusiasten.* It discusses "traditional sects and special religious movements" and includes extensive footnotes on the history of Jehovah's Witnesses (80–135, esp. 116ff.).

69. See Hellmund, "Zeugen Jehovas," chap. 4.

70. Throughout the Federal Republic of Germany, there are a number of institutions and associations that seek a critical examination of the activities and teachings of the Watch Tower Society and offer support for Jehovah's Witnesses who are contemplating disassociation (from the denomination). Such institutions are, for instance, the Evangelische Zentralstelle für Weltanschauungsfragen (Hölderlinplatz 2a, 70193 Stuttgart), the Initiative für Glaubensfreiheit (Postfach 101 202, 44712 Bochum), and the Bruderdienst (Hans-Jürgen Twisselmann, Postfach 30, 25764 Wesselburen). The Bruderdienst publishes a periodical titled *Brücke zum Menschen* (Bruderdienst-Missionsverlag, Kremper Weg 38b, 25524 Itzehoe).

71. In source quotations, orthographic inaccuracies and mistakes in punctuation were generally corrected, unless they indicate a particular reasoning on the part of the author(s) and are therefore of a certain significance. Style and diction, however, have been left unchanged—even with incorrect sentence structures—in order not to reduce the authenticity of reports and documents.

72. See Bästlein, "Erkenntniswert von Justizakten," 85ff.

73. See *DJ* [*Deutsche Justiz*] 99 (1937): 415, RJM, general decree of Mar. 18, 1937, concerning district changes in the Greater Hamburg area and other

regions. On Mar. 31, 1937, the Altona Special Court was dissolved. At the same time, the seat of the Schleswig-Holstein Special Court was transferred to Kiel. Pending cases at the Altona Special Court against people from Altona and Wandsbeck, urban districts that were later incorporated with Hamburg (as was Harburg-Wilhelmsburg), were transferred to the Hanseatic Special Court in Hamburg. See Bästlein, "Sondergericht Kiel," 159–60.

74. The records of the Hanseatic Special Court, which are stored in the archives of the public prosecutor's office at the Hamburg Regional Court, include a total of fifty "Bible Student proceedings" (twenty of which are preliminary proceedings that did not result in condemnation).

75. See the Jan. 29, 1943, Verordnung und Ergänzung der Zuständigkeitsverordnung (*RGBl.* 1943, 1:76) by means of which jurisdiction of cases based on the KSSVO, art. 5, para. 1, cl. 1 (Demoralizing Statements) was transferred to the People's Court and, if appropriate, to the higher regional court.

76. The majority of case records from the RKG were destroyed. In the Freiburg military archives, only 122 case records from the RKG (only two of which involve Jehovah's Witnesses) include documents, such as indictments and statements of court decisions. Other records are included in the Vienna documentation archives of the Austrian resistance. Also a number of private documents have been analyzed. The eighty-nine boxes of incomplete records included in the Archives of Military History in Prague could not be used for this work. In Germany, these records became known as late as 1990 through the research performed by Norbert Haase (see Haase, *Reichskriegsgericht,* 383–84; *Inventar archivalischer Quellen des NS-Staates,* 235).

77. The completeness of central interoffice decrees concerning the IBSA can be confirmed because of two available lists in which these decrees are mentioned. The first list includes a "summary of decrees on sectarian affairs," which the RSHA compiled until the end of 1942 (BA, R 58/1074, Bl. 28–35). The second list includes the "Aug. 1, 1936 collection of the Bavarian current protective detention regulations" compiled by the BPP. (BA, R 58/264, Bl. 239ff.).

78. OKW controlled all armed branches: military forces operating from land, naval forces, and air force. It was under the direct command of Hitler.

79. Prior to 1933, the church authorities sometimes monitored the Bible Students by infiltrating informers into their meetings. The subsequently written reports include interesting details, especially since they are relatively factual, in contrast to ecclesiastic defense literature, counterpamphlets, and public statements. Besides literature compiled by church authorities, these records include also Bible Student declarations, pamphlets, and announcements of IBSA events, particularly involving the period around 1925 and in 1928/29.

80. For more information on these applications and the committee, see Asmussen, *Der kurze Traum,* 34–40; W-D Schmidt, "Verfolgten," 329ff.; Romey, "Entschädigung," 223ff.

81. On the method of record linkage, see Mann, *Protest,* 85ff. (especially regarding the difference in perspective of Gestapo records and compensation records, 99–100).

82. On the critical assessment of sources involving files being compiled on the part of the persecutors, see Mann, *Protest,* 97–99; Steinberg, *Essen,* 21–23. On the special difficulties involving legal records, see Bästlein, "Sondergericht Kiel," 188–90; Hüttenberger, "Heimtückefälle," 458–64. On the tendency of overemphasizing the extent of the IBSA underground activities prevalent in reports written by the coercive authorities, see this book, p. 737, n.33.

83. See *Foreign Relations of the United States,* 2:406–17.

84. A German edition of *Kreuzzug gegen das Christentum* (for more information see this book, p. 633, n.164) was published in 1938 (Europa-Verlag: Zurich, New York) by Franz Zürcher, the managing editor of the German edition of the journal *Golden Age.* In the following year, a French edition was published by Éditions Rieder (Paris). Even though the book, published by a "worldly" publishing house, reflects the ideas of Jehovah's Witnesses, it is written in a moderate manner compared with other contemporary writings of the Watch Tower Society. It recognizes the stand of the Confessional Church (Bekennende Kirche) against the NS ideological claim for absolutism. In consideration of the general anti-clerical attitude of Jehovah's Witnesses, this is noteworthy. See Zürcher, *Kreuzzug,* 28–29, 169.

85. See the report on the situation in Germany, published in the 1974 *Yearbook* of Jehovah's Witnesses, 65–253. Regarding the persecution of Jehovah's Witnesses under NS rule, see 108–212.

86. Pertinent information is included in the following reports: Italy (*Yearbook* 1982, 113–256); Luxembourg (*Yearbook* 1976, 34–47); the Netherlands (*Yearbook* 1986, 110–85); Austria (*Yearbook* 1989, 66–147); Poland (*Yearbook* 1994, 171–252); Czechoslovakia (*Yearbook* 1972, 125–31); Hungary (*Yearbook* 1996, 67–115).

87. According to the Watch Tower Society, the persecution Jehovah's Witnesses suffered because of their obedience to the Bible's commandments provides evidence that they are the only true followers of Christ on earth. In this regard, the churches of Christendom, in particular, proved to be a failure: "Who have really responded to God's command 'not to learn war anymore'? Who have spent a total of thousands of years in prisons and concentration camps in our time rather than kill their neighbors? . . . The answer can only be, Jehovah's Witnesses" (*Watchtower,* Mar. 15, 1984, 13).

88. Cole, *Jehovah's Witnesses;* in *Crisis of Conscience,* Raymond Franz indicates that Cole was in reality a Jehovah's Witness. However, for tactical reasons, Cole tried to give the impression that he was an outsider. In this way, that is, by writing under the pretense of being an outsider, the Watch Tower Society supposedly intended to reach also people who would not normally read its publications. For this reason, Cole's book was published by a different publishing

house. As a former member of the governing body of the Watch Tower Society and nephew of its former president Frederik W. Franz, who died in 1992 at the age of ninety-nine, Raymond Franz had extensive knowledge of the internal circumstances in the leadership of this denomination. He is probably the most prominent dropout from among Jehovah's Witnesses.

89. "The Holocaust—Victims or Martyrs?" *Awake!,* Apr. 8, 1989, 12.

90. In 1983, in response to a request by the author, the German branch office of the Watch Tower Society stated that it cannot support his research project because, according to its statutes, its activities are restricted to "the religious service of informing people about the Good News" (letter of Apr. 15, 1983). Several letters addressed to the German branch office of the Watch Tower Society in the following years remained unanswered. Only after the publication of an anthology on the "forgotten victims," which included an essay involving the persecution of Jehovah's Witnesses in NS Hamburg, the author finally received a response. However, even then he was informed that, unfortunately, it was not possible to support his research project. The Watch Tower Society's secretary for public affairs apologized for the previous lack of response on the part of the society, indicating that in the past similar requests had "been received from different sides." However, a response to such requests had "always resulted in disappointment." Therefore, it was decided "no longer to respond to such requests" (WTG, Willi K. Pohl, letter of Feb. 14, 1987).

91. See Garbe, "Die 'vergessenen' Opfer," 8–9.

92. For general information on the concept of oral history, see Niethammer, *Kollektives Gedächtnis;* Botz and Weidenholzer, *Mündliche Geschichte.*

93. To the greatest extent possible, the objectivity of the recollections cited in this study was examined on the basis of other sources. These examinations show only in exceptional cases a subjective misrepresentation of the facts. Generally, these reports can be considered to be reliable sources.

94. It is certainly appropriate to emphasize Zipfel's statement: "there is almost no study or recollection record about the concentration camps that does not describe the religious views, industriousness, cooperativeness, and fanatical martyrdom of the Earnest Bible Students" (Zipfel, *Kirchenkampf,* 175). The report of Margarete Buber-Neumann is of special interest here: it is characterized by a high degree of authenticity and information density. In 1933 the Communist Margarete Buber-Neumann and her husband, KPD politburo member Heinz Neumann, were sent into exile. Two years later, they went to the USSR where Heinz Neumann was arrested during the Great Purge. After three years of imprisonment in the Siberian forced-labor camp of Karaganda, Margarete Buber-Neumann was deported to the German Reich by the NKVD (Russian Secret Service). In July 1940 she was sent to the Ravensbrück concentration camp. From Oct. 1940 until the summer of 1942, she was a block leader (a prisoner in charge of a block or barracks of other prisoners) and was put in charge

of about three hundred Bible Students, first in Block No. 3, and later in Block No. 17. In her autobiography *Als Gefangene bei Stalin und Hitler,* Buber-Neumann gives a detailed report about her association with the Bible Students. Jehovah's Witnesses affirmed the correctness of her explanations. See "Faith is Practical! Testimony from the Concentration Camps," *Watchtower,* June 15, 1981, 6–12.

95. DhN (Document Center of the Neuengamme Concentration Camp Memorial), Ng. 2.8, Hans Flatterich, "Die Hölle von Neuengamme," unpublished manuscripts, Schleswig (1945?), 16–17.

96. A discussion between Karl Klinkhammer and Paul Karalus, cited in *Es gab nicht nur den 20. Juli,* 107.

97. Wiechert, "Totenwald," 151.

98. Zahnwetzer, *Buchenwald,* 27.

99. Albert Rohmer, FGN, NHS (unpublished works of Hans Schwarz) 13-7-0-3, 15. Albert Rohmer's report "Herren, 'Befreite,' Sklaven," first published in France in 1947, has been partially translated and is cited in Ernst and Jensen, *Als letztes starb die Hoffnung,* 141–45.

Part 1. The International Bible Students Association

1. According to the service report for the year 2006 (*Yearbook* 2007, 31ff.), a total of 6,491,775 people participate in the preaching activity of Jehovah's Witnesses. They are organized in 99,770 congregations in 236 countries. An additional ten million unbaptized people attended the Memorial of Christ's death, which Jehovah's Witnesses consider to be the most important event of the service year. Statistically, the Federal Republic of Germany had a peak of 163,904 Kingdom proclaimers, and a total of 277,102 people attended their memorial celebrations. The denomination does not have a nominal membership. Every member is expected to be a proclaimer of God's Word. Consequently, membership is exclusively based on baptism and participation in the preaching activity.

2. See Rev. 20:1ff.

3. See Penton, *Apocalypse Delayed,* 13–46; Hutten, *Seher, Grübler, Enthusiasten,* 80–84; Twisselmann, *Vom "Zeugen Jehovas,"* 88–92. On the perspective of Jehovah's Witnesses, see *"Let God be True,"* 219ff.

4. In 1886 Russell began to publish his six volumes of the *Studies in the Scriptures,* which are considered his principal works. After his death, under the leadership of J. F. Rutherford, members of the Watch Tower Bible and Tract Society finished his seventh volume. This volume introduced far-reaching changes in the Bible Student teachings (see this book, pt. 1, ch. 2, pp. 35–43).

5. On the different corporations of the denomination, see Cole, *Jehovah's Witnesses,* 173–74. The three corporations are similar in structure. They are connected to a central office, or headquarters. In all three corporations, Russell—like his successors—held the position of presidency.

6. Garrison vicar Geiges, "Ch. T. Russell," in Kalb, *Kirchen,* 516–18 (516). This seems to be the first mention of the Watch Tower Society's activities in Germany in a church study on denominations.

7. It is difficult to establish exact numbers for this period. Until World War I, the Bible Students were only a small, almost unrecognized religious movement in Germany. Therefore, official statistics, as well as the records of the Watch Tower Society, do not include any specific information. For the year 1918, one source mentions the number of 3,868 "Kingdom proclaimers." See Siedenschnur, *Zeugen Jehovas,* 5.

8. One of the basic teachings of the Bible Students is their conviction that God, in his inspired Word, prearranged the chronological sequence of events in world history as well as the time for salvation. This study is not intended to provide a detailed explanation of the chronological calculations of Jehovah's Witnesses and any corrections of these calculations that have been made during the more than 100 years of their existence. For better understanding, the following simplified explanations are provided. In reference to the book of Revelation, Jehovah's Witnesses base their reasoning on the conception that, analogous to the "week of creating the world," one of the seven-day periods of God's creation was 7,000 years long. The final period of the seventh day, God's day of rest, consists of the Thousand-Year Reign of Christ. The preceding 6,000 years of that final day involve the history of mankind. By combining several biblical statements, Russell calculated that the first human was created in 4128 BCE. Russell concluded that the fall of mankind took place after a period of two years in paradise. Consequently, the 6,000 years of human history include the period between man's expulsion from paradise and the beginning of the Thousand-Year Reign of Christ. Russell then subtracted 4,126 years from the 6,000 years and arrived at the year 1874 as the date of Christ's return. Accordingly, the forty-year period of the "harvest time" ended in 1914.

9. Luke 21:10b, 11 (all Bible references, if not indicated otherwise, are taken from the New Jerusalem Bible [NJB]).

10. The following countries granted exemption from military service because of conscientious objection, mostly restricted to religious reasons. Denmark, the Netherlands (in 1917, because of an army order), Great Britain (after the introduction of general compulsory military service in 1916), and the United States (after the introduction of general compulsory military service in 1916–17). See Hecker, *Kriegsdienstverweigerung,* 8ff.

11. Russell, *New Creation,* 559.

12. See Gebhard, *Zeugen Jehovas,* 107; Stuhlhofer, *Russell,* 183–91. During the war, the German issue of the *Watchtower* included the section "From our Brothers in the Battlefield," which contained excerpts from letters of Bible Students who served as soldiers.

13. *Der Wachtturm,* 1915, 162.

14. See *Yearbook* 1974, 82–83; June 2, 1984, recollections by Gertrud Semmler; recollections by Johannes Rauthe, "Geschichtsbericht," 6–20. In 1917, at the age of eighteen, Johannes Rauthe was drafted into the German Imperial Army. In a letter to the Hirschberg Wehrbezirkskommando (district headquarters of the armed forces), he explained the religious reasons for his refusal to perform military service under arms and requested to be transferred to a unit where he did not have to take up arms. In response to his letter, he was informed that, "if possible," his request would be taken into consideration. As a result, he was placed in a railroad battalion where he did not have to perform that particular military service.

15. See *Yearbook* 1974, 82–83; *Watchtower,* Mar. 1, 1972, 143; Hartmann, "Kriegsdienstverweigerung" (1982), 85. It is difficult to estimate the number of Bible Students who completely refused to perform military service. This number was probably not higher than the number of conscientious objectors from among the Seventh-day Adventists Reformation Movement, which was the only religious denomination besides the Bible Students that refused military service as a group. A publication from the year 1932 mentions the figure of fifty refusees; twenty of these were each sentenced to five years of imprisonment. See Ohrtmann, *Kriegsdienstgegnerbewegung,* 9.

16. Hero von Ahlften, *Watchtower,* Feb. 15, 1931, 63.

17. Contemporary medical and psychiatric publications discuss extensively the conscientious objection of the Bible Students and the Adventists. In contrast to other offenses of evasion (such as desertion, false pretenses, and self-mutilation), the military psychiatrists considered religiously motivated conscientious objection as a phenomenon that did not belong under the jurisdiction of military judges but was rather within their field of competence. Between 1917 and 1919, the following principal studies involving psychiatric assessment of conscientious objection for religious reasons were published: Gaupp, "Dienstverweigerung"; Hoppe, "Ungehorsam"; Horstmann, "Religiosität oder Wahn."

18. See Loofs, *Die "Internationale Vereinigung Ernster Bibelforscher,"* 3ff.

19. These were credits that the German government demanded from state and citizens to be able to finance World War I. "Pommersche Tagespost," Sept. 15, 1917, cited in Loofs, *"Bibelforscher,"* 4.

20. EZA, 14/809, "Königliches Kriegsministerium," memorandum of Oct. 8, 1917; EZA, 7/Generalia 12, no. 161, "Evangelischer Oberkirchenrat," letter of Dec. 19, 1917.

21. Cited in Hellmund, "Zeugen Jehovas," no page numbers, pt. 4, ch. 1, "Die Anfänge in Deutschland."

22. EZA, 7/Generalia 12, no. 161, "Königliches Konsistorium der Provinz Westfalen," Mar. 20, 1918, letter to the Higher Church Council of the Evangelical churches. The letter includes copies of the reports submitted by the pastors.

23. Ibid., Jan. 18, 1918, letter by a parish priest from Datteln.

24. Ibid., cited in the Jan. 22, 1924, letter of the Evangelical Consistory of the state of Pomerania.

25. See Braeunlich, *Bibelforscher,* 26–27.

26. See Hutten, *Seher, Grübler, Enthusiasten,* 116; see also the numerous documents in the EZA, 7/Generalia 12, no. 161.

27. For background information on the above-mentioned controversy, see Hutten, *Seher, Grübler, Enthusiasten,* 84–87; Gebhard, *Zeugen Jehovas,* 103–6. On the viewpoint of the Watch Tower Society, see Cole, *Jehovah's Witnesses,* 86ff.; *Jehovah's Witnesses: Proclaimers of God's Kingdom,* 623–24.

28. Those new groups considered themselves as keepers of Russell's theological legacy. They claimed that the Watch Tower Society under Rutherford's leadership had deviated from the original teachings of the Bible Student movement. A number of independent groups of Bible students, which were formed between 1917 and 1920 as a result of the controversies, are still in existence today. Foremost among them are the Laien-Heim-Missionsbewegung and the Menschenfreundliche Versammlung/Engel Jehovas. Other groups are the Tagesanbruch-Bibelstudien-Vereinigung, an association of smaller groups formed in 1931, as well as the Freie Bibelgemeinde, an alliance of local groups that maintain their independence, also formed in 1931.

29. During the further development of the denomination, or as a result of increased Bible knowledge, the teachings of Jehovah's Witnesses, as they appeared under the presidency of Rutherford, have been repeatedly modified. It is not the purpose of this study to give detailed explanations of any of the changes in these teachings (e.g., their adjustment of the date for Christ's return from 1874 to 1914, which they made during 1943–44). If not mentioned otherwise, explanations involving the Bible Student teachings refer to the understanding that was prevalent during the period under discussion.

30. The predictions regarding the year 1914 were made with reference to Jesus's prophecy of the time of the End that he gave to his disciples on the Mount of Olives. "So with you when you see all these things: Know that he is near, right at the gates. In truth I tell you, before this generation has passed away, all these things will have taken place" (Matt. 24:33, 34).

31. James Penton rightly pointed out that only an understanding of Jehovah's Witnesses' conception of, and relationship to, the secular authorities can explain the fact that they have been persecuted in the twentieth century with an intensity and frequency that was not displayed toward any other Christian denomination. They were persecuted under Fascist regimes, Communist states, states of the Third World (e.g., Burundi, Malawi, and Zaire), and at times, even in democratic states such as the United States and Great Britain. See Penton, "Jehovah's Witnesses and the Secular State," 55ff.

32. Subsequently, the teachings of the Bible Students, or Jehovah's Witnesses, are explained only to the extent necessary to understand their actions in the Third Reich. More information can be obtained from the numerous

publications that deal with the teachings of Jehovah's Witnesses and discuss them more from a religious point of view. Basic works in this regard are the studies by Friedrich-Wilhelm Haack, Eckhard von Süsskind, Hans-Jürgen Twisselmann, and Christian Weis. Most informative is Kurt Hutten's revised 1982 handbook discussing special religious movements because it is written in an objective and well-founded way. See Hutten, *Seher, Grübler, Enthusiasten,* 80–135.

33. In contrast to religious viewpoints that make a difference between the Old and the New Testaments of the Bible, Jehovah's Witnesses show high regard for the Old Testament. Their propensity for the Hebrew Scriptures immediately provoked the suspicions of anti-Semitic groups.

34. Jehovah's Witnesses do not accept any other religious traditions and activities. They also consider cults, ceremonies, and celebrations (e.g., Christmas) to be pagan forms of idolatry. The only symbolic performances they observe are (adult) baptism and the annual celebration of the Memorial of Christ's death. At this celebration, however, the symbols of bread and wine are exclusively reserved for the remnant of 144,000 "anointed ones" (see this book, pt. 1, ch. 2, p. 37–38). Moreover, the Watch Tower Society does not consider charitable activities on a social basis to be part of their responsibilities. Material assistance is restricted to members of their denomination. In his book discussing the New World Society, which Marley Cole published in cooperation with the Watch Tower Society during the mid-1950s, he states: "The contributions were for the brothers, not for promiscuous charity" (Cole, *Jehovah's Witnesses,* 194).

35. See *Yearbook* 1988, 255.

36. See, for instance, the Montanists of the second century CE (Montanism is the teaching of the imminent return of Christ). See also the Albigenses of the Middle Ages (religious sect in the South of France from 1020–1250 CE); and the Taborites toward the end of the Middle Ages (a radical group that branched off from the Hussites in about 1420 CE. They were named after their main city, Tabor, in the south of Bohemia). During the Reformation, there were various Baptist groups, and in modern times there are groups like the Adventists, the Mormons, and the New Apostolic Church. In 1993 Norman Cohn presented his informative historical study, *The Pursuit of the Millennium.* It discusses numerous millennial movements of the Middle Ages that dealt with expectations of an imminent end and religious reformation.

37. The majority of historical studies about Jehovah's Witnesses misrepresent their concept of eschatology. It should be noted that the millennium does not refer to the ultimate Kingdom of God; instead, it is an intermediate Kingdom in the hands of the Messiah that will culminate in the Last Judgment. This conception corresponds to the description given in the book of Revelation (Rev. 20:7ff.). See Lohse, *Offenbarung,* 104ff.

38. See Rev. 16:16.

39. See Obst, "Reich-Gottes-Erwartungen," 357–69.

40. The number of 144,000 is also taken from the book of Revelation (Rev. 14:1–5).

41. See *Jehovah's Witnesses: Unitedly Doing God's Will Worldwide*, 10; Twisselmann, *Vom "Zeugen Jehovas,"* 11.

42. *Yearbook* 1927, 18.

43. In this respect, Jehovah's Witnesses principally differ from other "enthusiastic" followers of chiliasm, e.g., the Anabaptists during the period of the Reformation. Jehovah's Witnesses leave the actual change of conditions exclusively in the hands of God. They do not consider themselves as "kingdom builders, because God builds His Kingdom" (Rutherford, *Fascism or Freedom*, 25).

44. EZA, 14/809, "Ecclesiastics Indicted," resolution passed at the general assembly of the IBSA in Columbus (Ohio), on July 27, 1924.

45. See Rutherford, *Deliverance*, 264.

46. See Rutherford, *Freedom*, 23.

47. This does not mean, however, that Rutherford did not accept the fact that there were different forms of government. But although he recognized these differences, he always emphasized that even the best democratic government was not able to offer a permanent solution for the problems of the nations. See Rutherford, *Government*, 13ff.

48. Ibid., 222.

49. This is also the reason for the strict rejection of the League of Nations, which Rutherford also exposed as an "instrument of Satan." See Rutherford, *Peoples Friend*, 56–57. He describes the League of Nations as a community of states that tried to prevent ultimate destruction, and that was doomed to failure. At the same time, it revealed the "blasphemous" ambition of humans to set up their own universal government.

50. *Der Wachtturm*, July 1922, 110, cited in Twisselmann, *Wachtturm-Konzern*, 139.

51. Rutherford, *Government*, 229–30.

52. Charles Taze Russell, *Studies in the Scriptures*, 2:81, cited in Twisselmann, *Vom "Zeugen Jehovas,"* 105.

53. *The Truth Shall Make You Free*, 312.

54. At the end of 1962, the Watch Tower Society returned to its original interpretation of Rom. 13. Once again, it considered the worldly governments as "authorities . . . appointed by God." In sharp contrast to a conviction held for more than thirty years, the *Watchtower*, under the headline "Conscience and Subjection to Authorities," now acknowledged the benefits of public order because it permitted "Christians to lead a calm and quiet life" (*Watchtower*, Dec. 1, 1962, 721). Even though today, the Watch Tower Society emphasizes its appreciation for the human governments and requests its followers to obey carefully the laws of these governments as long as they do not conflict with God's laws, it tries to justify Rutherford's position concerning the governing authorities and his condemnation of the nations. In this regard, the Watch Tower Society states

that, from a historical point of view, it had great significance "during the crucial period before and during World War II": "Looking back, it must be said that this view of things, exalting as it did the supremacy of Jehovah and his Christ, helped God's people to maintain an uncompromisingly neutral stand throughout this difficult period" (*Watchtower*, May 1, 1996, 14).

55. Rutherford, *Enemies*, 73.

56. On the inner-organizational aspect of putting this theocratic rule into practice, see Stevenson, *Inside Story*, 141ff.; Schnell, *Thirty Years a Watch Tower Slave*, 37–38; Twisselmann, *Wachtturm-Konzern*, 19ff.

57. During the 1950s, this was another name that the Watch Tower Society accepted for their denomination.

58. John 15:19b. The text of John 15:18–27, in which John tries to explain the persecution of the Christians, probably the one under Emperor Domitian, and in which he comforts and encourages the Christian community to endure, is regarded by Jehovah's Witnesses as a rule of causality. Accordingly, in retrospect, they state: "So this hatred simply proved that we were right" (*Awake!*, Apr. 22, 1986, 16; see also *Awake!*, May 8, 1993, 12; *Jehovah's Witnesses: Proclaimers of God's Kingdom*, 677.)

59. See the article "Jehovah's Witnesses: Why Persecuted?" *Golden Age*, May 15, 1932, 516–22 [*Das Goldene Zeitalter*, Aug. 15, 1932, 247–53].

60. According to Beckford (*Trumpet of Prophecy*, 33), based on their belief "that Satan was intensifying his campaign of terror against the defenders of truth on earth," the Watch Tower Society's members in other countries were not the least surprised when they learned about the serious persecution of Jehovah's Witnesses in Germany by the NS regime.

61. Freytag left the association with a large following. (As many as four out of five Bible Students in the French speaking part of Switzerland followed him.) In 1920, under the name "Engel Jehovas," also known as "Menschenfreundliche Versammlung," he established his own Bible and Tract Society, known today as "Kirche des Reiches Gottes."

62. In 1920 the theocratic rule was not yet in operation. At that time, the various groups were still supervised by so-called elected elders who were voted into office through democratic methods.

63. See Siedenschnur, *Zeugen Jehovas*, 5. At this place, some basic comments should be made regarding the numerical data: The IBSA did not have any formal membership. People adhering to their teachings were not members in a legal sense. The group of legal members of the association included only a small group of its functionaries. Even though (adult) baptism is considered to be a symbol for joining the association, this is not a membership based on legal criteria. For this reason, it is not possible to provide actual membership numbers analogous to those of a church membership. According to their own perception, the Bible Students consider their association a spiritual community. They do not even have other typical characteristics of an association in the

stricter sense of the word, such as contribution lists, for example. Concerning the question of membership, it is stated in the Watch Tower publications: "The International Bible Students Association has no membership roll and is not seeking membership. All who believe in the truth taught by Jesus and the apostles, and who now believe in the presence of the Lord and that the time has come for him to set up His Kingdom, and who desire to participate and, to the best of their ability and opportunity, do participate in giving witness to the name of Jehovah, are counted in as members of the association or society" (*Yearbook* 1929, 16). Consequently, every person who adheres to the teachings of the Bible Students and participates in their activities is considered to be a member. Any numbers of membership mentioned in this chapter and in the following chapters are therefore based on the results of governmental censuses (the question of membership in a religious organization). They are also based on the numbers of Kingdom proclaimers mentioned in the publications of the Watch Tower Society, which generally can be considered reliable. See Rogerson, *Millions Now Living Will Never Die*, 73.

64. See Algermissen, *Zeugen Jehovas*, 7.

65. See, for instance, the explanations of Karl Heinz Debus concerning the Bible Students in Speyer. Debus probably overemphasizes their activities when he states that they "presented a threat to the two major churches, which could only be compared to the wave of church withdrawals during the 1920s" (Debus, "Speyer," 471).

66. See *Yearbook* 1927, 68. This yearbook mentions the exact number of 10,108,502 books and booklets. Even though the yearbooks of Jehovah's Witnesses during the 1920s list the exact numbers of distributed publications, they generally do not include membership numbers. In contrast to the yearbooks published after 1945, these earlier publications fail to include information about the expansion of the denomination including statements about the average number of Kingdom proclaimers.

67. See *Die Religion in Geschichte und Gegenwart* (1962), col. 1019. This publication also includes the membership numbers of the local groups in Dresden, Berlin, and Hamburg that are mentioned in the chart.

68. According to the Oct. 31, 1923, report (EZA, 7/Generalia 12, no. 161) of the Evangelical consistory of the state of Saxony, which is based on a survey by the superintendent of the church district, the IBSA had gained ground particularly in big cities, such as, Magdeburg, Halle, and other industrial centers. In the rural areas, its preaching activity did not produce any "noteworthy" results.

69. In contrast to other parts of the German Reich, the Bible Student movement had an especially favorable response in the entire state of Saxony, including its capital, Dresden. Therefore, at least during the 1920s, Saxony could certainly be considered to be a stronghold of the IBSA. The 1974 history report about Jehovah's Witnesses mentions that in Saxony "congregations now began springing up like sprouting mushrooms after a gentle rain" (*Yearbook* 1974, 87).

70. Algermissen, *Zeugen Jehovas*, 8.

71. See *Yearbook* 1934, 11.

72. In Germany, the Bible Student movement had by far the second largest membership. In 1926 the worldwide membership amounted to 89,278. Of these, 31,328 were living in the United States and were organized in 372 local groups. At the same time, a total of 22,535 members, organized in 316 local groups, lived in Germany. Great Britain had a membership of 9,640, organized in 114 local groups. See *Die Religion in Geschichte und Gegenwart* (1962), col. 1019.

73. Recollections and personal data in legal records show that the conversion, in many cases, was closely related to the wartime experiences of the individuals. Even an examination of the Watch Tower Society's publications of that period demonstrates the strong influence these experiences had on the religious orientation of these people. Accordingly, during the early 1920s, this subject was especially emphasized in the IBSA campaigns (e.g., in the discourse series "Where Are the Dead?"). See also Zipfel, *Kirchenkampf*, 176–77; *Yearbook* 1974, 86–87.

74. Superficially, Zipfel's asssessment of the IBSA as a "religion of the poor" (Zipfel, *Kirchenkampf*, 203) may seem convincing. However, in my opinion, this represents merely part of the aspect. Upon closer examination, Zipfel's assessment proves to be problematic. On the one hand, it is evident that during the 1920s and 1930s, the IBSA undoubtedly also included members of the middle class. (An examination of available data involving the social status of the Bible Students in Hamburg shows that close to 30 percent belonged to the middle or lower middle class; see Zipfel, 507–8.) On the other hand, such classifying can result in the misconception that a certain social disposition was characteristic for a membership in this denomination. For this reason, Zipfel probably reached the conclusion that the Bible Student teachings had "a considerable potential of future followers at their disposal." Even recent empirical studies concerning the social structure of Jehovah's Witnesses do not produce any results that would justify a certain classification. In this regard, the study of Elmar Köppl clearly emphasizes that Jehovah's Witnesses are not a group of people "with a predominantly marginal social status" nor are they, as Werner Cohn put it, a typical example of a "proletarian movement." See Cohn, "Jehovah's Witnesses," 281ff. To the contrary, the data analysis concerning their social status indicates rather that "Jehovah's Witnesses have a wide range of occupational qualifications" and, at least today, "Jehovah's Witnesses occupy primarily the social status of the middle class" (Köppl, *Zeugen Jehovas*, 199).

75. To a certain extent, the family is the center of religious activities for Jehovah's Witnesses. In most cases, all family members participate in the preaching activity. Religiously divided marriages are uncommon. In the various congregations, many Jehovah's Witnesses are related to each other, which can, to a certain extent, be attributed to the appropriate choice of a marriage mate.

76. Rutherford, *Millions Now Living Will Never Die*, 97.

77. See *Yearbook* 1974, 90–91. Evidence of the high attendance numbers at the four specific convention days in 1922 (Feb. 26, June 25, Oct. 29, and Dec. 12) is included in press and police reports. These numbers are even included in the reports that the pastors who had been sent to the conventions as observers submitted to their church authorities. Therefore, there is no reason to doubt the numbers provided by the Watch Tower Society.

78. Cited in Algermissen, *Christliche Sekten,* 26.

79. "Purpose for the journal, as stated in *Watchtower* of 1919," cited in Loofs, *"Bibelforscher,"* 46.

80. Principally, the journals of the Watch Tower Society are still dichotomous in nature. However, in contrast to *Awake!,* published since 1946–47, the former journal (*Golden Age*) includes more nonreligious subjects. To a certain extent, this was due to the different circumstances of that particular time period. The following articles from 1932 (German) editions of the *Golden Age* serve as an example in this regard: "In the Grip of Unemployment," "Accusations!," "At the Limit of Civilization," "Militaristic Nonsense," "Fascist Creed," "The Good Samaritan or: The Christendom of High Society."

81. See *Yearbook* 1934, 129–30; Zürcher, *Kreuzzug,* 81. This legal status, which later was even supported through article 12 of the Treaty of Friendship, Commerce, and Diplomacy between the German Reich and the United States (*RGBl.* 1925 II, 795, concluded in 1923, ratified in 1925), is of great importance in the controversy involving the IBSA ban in the NS period. See this book, pt. 2, ch. 5, p. 95, and p. 586, n.152.

82. The association was not formed for the purpose of legally registering all members of the Bible Students living in Germany. Rather, it was established exclusively for the purpose of providing legal representation of the association. In accordance with the statutes, membership was restricted to nine, and later, twelve people. See BA, R 43 II/179, Bl. 102; Stödter, "Verfassungsproblematik," 166, 210.

83. Stokes, *Eutin,* 697.

84. In view of their religious teachings, there is no particular need to emphasize that the Bible Students did not give any cause for the accusation of supporting the Soviet Union. It is noteworthy that in their publications they apply the same standard of judgment not only to the Soviet Union but to any other country, as well. They do not leave any room for the distorted image of a Bolshevik underling. Even though they explain that "Bolshevism is doomed to certain and complete failure" (Rutherford, *Government,* 13), there is no evidence to support the accusation of an anti-Soviet hate campaign. For instance, the *Golden Age* points out that "Soviet Russia has two faces: A good one in the social and economic field, which deserves acknowledgement, and a dreadfully cruel one in the ideological field since communism is ridiculing Jehovah" (*Das Goldene Zeitalter,* Dec. 15, 1929).

85. *Neue Pfälzische Landeszeitung,* Mar. 12, 1925 ("Die 'ernsten Bibelforscher': Eine nationale Gefahr").

86. Fetz, *Volks- und Weltbetrug,* 4.

87. Ibid., 34–35.

88. Ibid., 37.

89. Fetz, *Weltvernichtung,* 6.

90. Following are some explanations regarding the divine name, Jehovah: In Hebrew, the language of ancient Israel, the divine name, as it was revealed to Moses (Exod. 3:14–15), was "JHWH." (In written form, Hebrew consists only of consonants.) Out of respect, the faithful Jews did not pronounce this God-given name, since they considered it to be sacred. Instead, whenever JHWH appeared in the biblical text, the Hebrew word for Lord was read. Beginning in the fifth century CE, Jewish scholars provided the biblical text with phonetic symbols for the missing vowels, because by then the Hebrew language had been replaced with the Aramaic language. As a result, the Hebrew pronunciation was in danger of being forgotten. Therefore, the divine name, JHWH, was provided with the vocal points of the Hebrew word for Lord, which was to be read in place of JHWH. In the eleventh century, Christian theologians who were ignorant of these facts began to combine these two elements. They joined the consonants JHWH in the Hebrew text with the vowels for the word Lord, which resulted in the reading of J(e)H(o)W(a)H = Jehovah. During the Reformation, in which the original Hebrew text of the Old Testament was used as the basis for translations of the Bible instead of the Latin Bible (Vulgate), this form of reading became the established practice. To this day, it is used in a number of church hymns. Modern Bible scholars have tried to reconstruct the original pronunciation and thus encourage the reading of J(a)HW(e)H = Yahweh. The major churches and most Christian denominations have adopted this form of reading. Therefore, there are currently two variations of the divine name, Jehovah and Yahweh.

91. See especially Rutherford, *Comfort for the Jews.* In 1911, during his missionary tour through Europe, Russell, who was credited with writing the booklet "The Approaching Restoration of the Nation of Israel," gave discourses on the subject "Zionism in Prophecy." See Stuhlhofer, *Russell,* 238.

92. On the new explanation of Judaism in the religious teachings of the IBSA since the beginning of the 1930s, see this book, pt. 2, ch. 4, p. 89.

93. Rutherford, *Comfort for the Jews,* 34. The foreword to this book mentions that Rutherford "is known throughout the world as an unselfish friend of the Jews" who rejects the "so-called conversion of the Jews" as unbiblical and who actively supports the "proprietary claims of the Jews to the Promised Land."

94. Rutherford, *Comfort for the Jews,* 111.

95. Lienhardt, *Riesenverbrechen,* 13.

96. With regard to calling the first president of the Bible Students "Russell the Jew," see the revealing statements made by the known anti-Semite Hans Jonak von Freyenwald in 1941: "Charles Taze Russell, who most likely is of Jewish descent, even though this has not been confirmed, was the founder and first president [of the Bible Student movement] until 1916. His teachings definitely

indicate that he was of the same mind as the Jews" (Jonak von Freyenwald, *Jüdische Bekenntnisse*, 6). Not surprisingly, similar statements were made regarding Rutherford. In Apr. 1937 the Württemberg Evangelische Presseverband published an article in its journal *Materialdienst* on the subject: "Sektenwesen— Der Wirrwar der Sekten." This article includes the following statement: "Assertions have been made that Rutherford is of Jewish descent" (*MD* 9 [1937]: col. 62 [Apr. 16, 1937]). However, Jonak von Freyenwald, who also published under the pseudonym Dr. Hans von Jonak during the NS period, did not want to take matters to that extreme. Yet, even he used this most effective argument of that particular time period: "Even though their current president, J. F. Rutherford, is not a Jew, he uses his Jewish vice president, C. A. Wiese, to publish various agitating articles in his name" (Jonak von Freyenwald, *Jüdische Bekenntnisse*, 6).

97. Lienhardt, *Riesenverbrechen*, 43.

98. Rosenberg, "Protokolle," 409.

99. Mosse, *Rassismus*, 169. The playwright Dietrich Eckart, one of the pioneers of the German Workers' Party, was a close friend of Adolf Hitler and Alfred Rosenberg. Eckart influenced considerably the thinking of both men. He died in 1923. Eckart, *Bolschewismus*, 56. On Eckart's work and its status as ideological reference for National Socialism, see Nolte, *Three Faces of Fascism*, 325–29.

100. Eckart, *Bolschewismus*, 39.

101. *Das Goldene Zeitalter*, Jan. 15, 1923, 127.

102. Quotation from F. R. von Lama, "Die Entlarvung der ernsten Bibelforscher," cited in *Neue Pfälzische Landeszeitung*, Apr. 1, 1924.

103. Cited in Miksch, *Bibelforscher*, 36.

104. On Mar. 9, 1925, in its *Berichtigungsdienst*, the Evangelischer Presseverband for Germany published the authentic statement from the St. Gallen District Court presidency. According to this statement, the court did not enter the proceedings because it denied the Bible Students Association legal entity. The rejected complainant was punished with an out-of-court compensation payment of 450 Swiss francs to the defendant, Dr. Fehrmann. The court was unable to consider the statements of the defendant as an offense against the International Association of Earnest Bible Students, since he had discussed the objectives of Judaism. However, the *Berichtigungsdienst* clearly emphasized that this did not confirm the truthfulness of the accusations made by Feldmann. The court stated "that the documents presented do not prove that the International Association of Earnest Bible Students received money from the Jews."

105. See EZA, 7/Generalia 12, no. 161; *Das Goldene Zeitalter*, May 15, 1933, 148–49. Efforts on the part of the IBSA to repeat the court proceedings were not successful. The document in question ("the Freemason letter") completely disappeared after the St. Gallen court proceedings. See Zürcher, *Kreuzzug*, 66. In his work *Zeugen Jehovas*, 93, Gebhard accuses the Watch Tower Society of having removed the letter to dispose of the evidence.

106. See Algermissen, *Christliche Sekten*, 282ff.; Braeunlich, *Bibelforscher*, 36–37; Jonak von Freyenwald, *Zeugen Jehovas*, 9–10; Miksch, *Bibelforscher*, 35ff.; Paffrath, *Bibelforscher*, 11ff.

107. Miksch, *Bibelforscher*, 31.

108. *Jehovah's Witnesses: Unitedly Doing God's Will Worldwide*, 7.

109. The term "Babylon the Great" appears only in the book of Revelation. According to traditional theological interpretation, John, who wrote about the time of the Christian persecution under Domitian or shortly thereafter, used this term as a code name for hostile Rome. See Lohse, *Offenbarung*, 85 and 94.

110. Text references in the sequence of quotation, Rev. 17:1; 18:3; 17:5.

111. The anti-church, or anti-religious (including all other religious groups) attitude of the Watch Tower Society is still apparent in its publications today. However, this uncompromising rejection of all other denominations is directed against the respective "religious systems" and not against any of their individual members. Because Jehovah's Witnesses consider their religion to be the only true religion, they do not collaborate with other denominations. The Watch Tower Society does not support any tendencies toward ecumenical group efforts. Consequently, Jehovah's Witnesses are completely separate from all other religious groups.

112. See Lasch, *Bibelforscher*, foreword, unpaginated.

113. For instance, in a pamphlet published in 1927, the Evangelical pastor Julius Kuptsch gives the following advice to Christians concerning their response toward the Bible Students: "Dismiss them ruthlessly and chase them away from your homes, these dogmatic and insolent people, these messengers of the devil who are mocking the Son of God and the Gospel" (Kuptsch, *Aufklärung*, 45).

114. EZA, 7/Generalia 12, no. 161, Evangelical Consistory of the state of Saxony, report of Oct. 31, 1923. This report is based on a survey among the superintendents in the Saxony church district.

115. See *Yearbook* 1974, 90–91; *Jehovah's Witnesses in the Divine Purpose*, 81ff.

116. EZA, 7/Generalia 12, no. 161, "Das Evangelische Konsistorium der Provinz Pommern," Jan. 22, 1924, letter to the Higher Church Council of the Evangelical churches.

117. See *Zeitschrift für badische Verwaltung und Verwaltungsrechtspflege*, Sept. 1932, 137.

118. Carl Schweitzer, *Handbuch der neuen Apologetik*, 291. In contrast to the *völkisch*-Christian groups, the Apologetische Centrale saw its function entirely in the religious arena. Despite extensive examinations, they were not able to assess the Bible Student teachings. This is also indicated by the fact that in the so-called guide, the IBSA is associated with Communist ideas (249).

119. These archives for sectarian affairs contained records that included data about the IBSA as well as a number of other sects and ideological groups.

However, the archives came to a rather tragic end. Toward the end of 1937, the Apologetische Centrale, which had been under the direction of Walter Künneth since 1927, was dissolved and banned. (In his 1935 work *Antwort auf den Mythus*, Künneth gave a spectacular response to Rosenberg's publication *Mythus des 20. Jahrhunderts*.) During the occupation of the Apologetische Centrale, archives and files fell into the hands of the Gestapo. The Gestapo Department for Sectarian Affairs certainly welcomed this finding because it enabled them to complete their records. See Gerhardt, *Innere Mission*, 407; H. Schmid, *Wetterleuchten*, 169.

120. Algermissen, *Christliche Sekten*, 284. Konrad Algermissen illustrates the aberration that had entered the theological assessments of the Bible Students. To a far greater extent than Carl Schweitzer and Walter Künneth, the directors of the Evangelical Apostolische Centrale, Konrad Algermissen accepted the interpretations of *völkisch*, anti-Semitic "experts" on questions concerning the Bible Students. For instance, he speaks of the "anti-Christian and anti-State actions of this Jewish-Freemason-Bolshevik sect." He also reports of "actual fraternization demonstrations between the 'Earnest Bible Students' and the Bolsheviks" (284). Later, however, Professor Algermissen, whose subsequent studies concerning denominations and sects are still regarded as standard works in Roman Catholic groups, abandoned such positions. This change became evident even prior to the NS period. See Algermissen, "Bibelforscher." However, in 1949, four years after the end of the Third Reich, Algermissen attacked the IBSA again because of their "defamation of the Christian churches," and again he requested their "punishment." Algermissen, *Zeugen Jehovas*, 9.

121. In his publication *Zeugen Jehovas*, 102ff., Jonak von Freyenwald lists forty-one works of defense literature (eleven from Catholic, twenty-five from Evangelical sources). I can add another fourteen works (four from Catholic, seven from Evangelical sources).

122. On the part of the Catholic Church, the "guidelines for clergy and parish" that discuss the Bible Student teachings during the 1920s are primarily the books of Dr. Max Heimbucher, professor of theology in Munich; Monsignor A. Meyenberg, director of the Apologetic Institute of Switzerland; and pontifical prelate Dr. Franz Meffert. Even though not completely free from distortion and bias, these works generally do not include malicious, polemic, and anti-Semitic statements.

123. The most important Evangelical "defense literature" that can generally be considered as traditional studies of sectarian groups, are the works of Fiebig, *Bibelauslegung;* Herrmann, *Bibelforscher;* Lasch, *Bibelforscher;* Petrich, *Sekten*, 238–51.

124. Loofs, *"Bibelforscher,"* 5, 31.

125. Schlegel, *Wahrheit*, 269, 273.

126. Ibid., 269.

127. Schlegel, *Teufelsmaske*, 203.

128. Braeunlich, *Bibelforscher*, 35.

129. Ibid., 3.

130. Ibid., 25.

131. Ibid., 39.

132. Kuptsch, *Aufklärung*, 41.

133. Ibid., 22.

134. Julius Kuptsch, "Die Wahrheit über die 'Ernsten Bibelforscher'. Im Grunde Bundesgenossen der Marxisten," cited in *VB* [*Völkischer Beobachter*], Mar. 11, 1931.

135. The writings of Pastor Karl Gerecke belong in this gray area. They can certainly be considered as the worst and most peculiar works about the IBSA. Gerecke belonged to those groups in Protestantism that supported the idea of a connection between Germanic faith and Aryan Christian faith. With reference to the Bible Students, he speaks about an "all-consuming, anticlerical cancer of Jewish sedition," calling them "messengers of the plague of an oriental mammon religion" (Gerecke, *Gotteslästerungen*, 159–60). In the summer of 1933, in a statement he had prepared for the Reich chancellor, Gerecke increased his hate campaign to persuade the chancellor to take serious actions against the IBSA. At this time, he even accused the IBSA of having already made specific arrangements for a "Bolshevik Armageddon": "The assassination lists with the names of those doomed for destruction in bloody Armageddon were already prepared at the outbreak of the National Socialist revolution (even at this place!)." However, owing to "God's mercy, the incredible revolution" that took place on Jan. 30 protected the human race against this "kind of secret Bolshevik murder" (BA, R 43 II/179, Bl. 152–66).

136. See the statements of Senior Consistory Counsel Johannes Schneider, cited in *Kirchliches Jahrbuch für die evangelischen Landeskirchen Deutschlands* 56 (1929): 388.

137. *Akten Deutscher Bischöfe*, 1:259.

138. See Jacobi, "Sekten." The studies of Ernst Staehelin from Basel and his colleague Walther Köhler from Heidelberg, published in 1925 and 1930, respectively, also provide an objective discussion on a biblical-theological basis. Staehelin reminds his parishioners to bear in mind "that the legacy of the gospels is not an exclusive possession and that the 'Bible Students' are accountable to God and not to us for the blessing or curse they are causing with their message" (Staehelin, *Was haben wir von den "ernsten Bibelforschern" zu halten?*, 27). During the NS period, Staehelin belonged to the small group of theologians who spoke up in defense of the persecuted Jehovah's Witnesses. See Zürcher, *Kreuzzug*, 32.

139. EZA, 7/Generalia 12, no. 161, Evangelischer Reichsausschuß der Deutschnationalen Volkspartei, confidential report, no. 5, Sept. 1923.

140. See Gotthilf, *Geheimmacht*, 5ff.

141. Ibid., foreword.

142. See *Neue Pfälzische Landeszeitung*, Aug. 7, 1926 ("Die 'Ernsten Bibelforscher' gerichtlich verurteilt").

143. On the pamphlet campaign and its consequences, see Algermissen, *Christliche Sekten*, 270–71; Deutsch, *Sekte der Ernsten Bibelforscher*, 38–43. According to the theologian Dr. Braeunlich, in this pamphlet "the whole flood of insults included in the hate campaign against revolutionaries and deserters during the period of the closing years of World War I was poured out upon the official representatives of the churches" (Braeunlich, *Bibelforscher*, 27).

144. EZA, 14/809, pamphlet, "Ecclesiastics Indicted."

145. This agitation was reflected in numerous complaints, requests, and articles published in the church press. See EZA, 1/A2 No. 465, Bl. 92; EZA, 7/Generalia 12, no. 161; EZA, 14/809.

146. *Das Evangelische Deutschland* (church paper of the Evangelical churches in Germany), Mar. 8, 1925, 75 ("Der Ansturm der Bibelforscher").

147. EZA, 7/Generalia 12, no. 161.

148. Ibid., "Evangelisches Konsistorium der Mark Brandenburg," letter of May 12, 1921.

149. Ibid., "Deutscher Evangelischer Kirchenausschuß," Mar. 20, 1935, letter to the RMdI.

150. On May 16, 1925, the Evangelical Consistory of the state of Pomerania filed a complaint against Paul Balzereit, the editor responsible, on the charge of libel. At the beginning of the following year, the Magdeburg Schöffengericht (a court consisting of one judge and two lay judges) acquitted Balzereit because he had not directed his attacks against individual clergymen or against the complaining consistory, but against the clergy in the whole world. See EZA, 7/Generalia 12, no. 161.

151. In 1928 thirty-three of the judicial cases were sentenced. A total of 729 proceedings resulted in acquittal. See *Yearbook* 1929, 85.

152. *MbliV* [*Ministerialblatt für die Preußische innere Verwaltung*] 91 (1930): 400–401, PrMdI, interoffice decree of Apr. 19, 1930. This decree also provided the IBSA with a confirmation that its work was unobjectionable. For instance, it includes the statement: "At present, the association is only involved in religious activities and does not engage in any political actions."

153. *Das Goldene Zeitalter*, Mar. 15, 1924.

154. See *Handbuch religiöse Gemeinschaften*, 448; *Evangelischer Pressedienst*, no. 25, June 17, 1925 ("Schwere Zerwürfnisse in der Bibelforscherbewegung").

155. See *Yearbook* 1987, 131ff. On Apr. 1, 1925, the central European office was moved from Zurich to Bern.

156. See Algermissen, *Konfessionskunde* (1930), 777; *Kirchliches Jahrbuch für die evangelischen Landeskirchen Deutschlands* 56 (1929): 388.

157. See *Yearbook* 1931, 127; *Yearbook* 1932, 123.

158. By using new methods and media, the Bible Students were able to address a great number of people to bring them the Kingdom message. In this regard, the "Photo Drama of Creation" resulted in extensive publicity. It was an artistic presentation of the creation of the earth over a period of 49,000 years. It covered the period from the beginning of the earth in its original gaseous state until the time of the Messianic Kingdom. Initially, it was a slide presentation. Later, it was presented as a silent movie, accompanied with music played by the Watch Tower Society's band. Over the years, in Germany, the presentations of this eight-hour work, which were given in rented halls and auditoriums (e.g., the Berlin Sportpalast), drew audiences of several hundred thousand. The free admission and the attraction of modern film technology greatly contributed to the large attendances. See Hutten, *Seher, Grübler, Enthusiasten,* 83.

159. *Watchtower,* Mar. 1, 1930, 75–79 [*Der Wachtturm,* Apr. 1, 1930, 107–11].

160. These numbers are based on information from *Statistisches Jahrbuch für die Freie und Hansestadt Hamburg* (1925ff.); *Die Religion in Geschichte und Gegenwart* (1962), col. 1019; *Yearbook* 1974, 74. Figure 1 indicates that the greatest percentage increase of believers occurred during the first five years after the end of World War I and that the decline in membership toward the end of the 1920s was quite significant. (Compared to 1927, the number for 1930 is lower by 108 people, or 21.9%.) However, only within the next two years, a large increase of 41.8 percent is recorded (from 1930 to 1932, an increase by 161 members). The records of baptisms performed by the Hamburg group of Bible Students also show the tendency in the development of membership numbers: 1924 (47 baptisms), 1926 (56 baptisms), 1927 (35 baptisms), 1928 (14 baptisms), 1929 (no baptism), 1930 (no baptism), 1931 (54 baptisms), 1932 (112 baptisms). At the Reich level, only the numbers for the years 1926 (22,535), 1928 (23,988), and 1931 (24,135) are available. Since it is not possible to determine the membership numbers between 1929 and 1930—the period that probably include the losses—the record indicates a continuous increase. Membership numbers at the Reich level according to Algermissen, "Bibelforscher," col. 279; Algermissen, *Zeugen Jehovas,* 8; Siedenschnur, *Zeugen Jehovas,* 5.

161. See Algermissen, "Bibelforscher," col. 279.

162. See *Yearbook* 1934, 145; *Yearbook* 1974, 109. The numbers of people who attended the memorial celebrations and those who participated in the testimony period are based on the service reports that the Magdeburg branch office sent to the Watch Tower Society's headquarters. During this testimony period, which was carried out on an international basis between Apr. 8 and 16, 1933, the so-called thanksgiving period of the remnant, Jehovah's Witnesses increased their preaching activity. During this special campaign, they also distributed the booklet *The Crisis,* with two million copies supposedly being distributed in Germany.

163. See Hutten, *Seher, Grübler, Enthusiasten,* 117. Contrary to Hutten's statement, it is incorrect to speak of 35,000 Jehovah's Witnesses since interested

people who occasionally attended the meetings of the Bible Students only had a casual relationship with the Bible Students Association. They had not, or not yet, made a decision to become Jehovah's Witnesses. Objective criteria indicating that a person professes to be one of Jehovah's Witnesses or has joined this religious group are (1) conversion and (2) baptism.

164. Previous research studies basically mention two numbers, both of which have to be corrected. On the one hand, there is the considerably underestimated number of 6,034 Jehovah's Witnesses who supposedly lived in Germany "at that time" based on the studies of Annedore Leber and Friedrich Zipfel. On the other hand, there is the number of 19,268 Bible Students who supposedly lived in the German Reich in Apr. of 1933 mentioned by Michael H. Kater (and subsequently in almost all literature). The fact that both numbers are based on a misconception of the numbers mentioned in the Watch Tower publications is not the main reason for concern. (The first number is based on the number of Jehovah's Witnesses who were active during the period of the ban and who were affected by the coercive measures. The second number is based on the number of participants during their special missionary campaign.) Extensive theories about the intensity of their persecution are based on these numbers. See this book, pt. 6, ch. 17, pp. 477–79 (these pages also include the respective references).

165. Byington, *Bible in Living English; Watchtower,* Oct. 1, 1931, 296–303 ("A New Name") [*Der Wachtturm,* Nov. 1, 1931, 323–30].

166. *Der Wachtturm,* June 1, 1931, 175.

167. *Watchtower,* Mar. 15, 1931, 88 [*Der Wachtturm,* Nov. 15, 1931, 344]. This development toward an authoritarian administration of the organization was completed in 1938, when every group had to sign a statement according to which the leaders of the Watch Tower Society would be "the visible representative of the Lord on earth." See Reimer, *Stichwort "Sekten,"* 45.

168. See *Brücke zum Menschen,* book 29/30, 13; Eggenberger, *Kirchen,* 112. Some congregations formed the group Freie Bibelgemeinde. Their center of worship was the congregation in Kirchlenglern, near Herford. Even Bible Students who had disassociated from the IBSA in previous years joined the Freie Bibelgemeinde.

169. These requests have to be considered in the context of high membership losses from among the ranks of the working class. However, the churches did not attribute these losses to a failure on their part with regard to social issues. They rather attributed them to the godless propaganda of the Communists. The rate of resignations escalated to an extent that was more than alarming for the churches. In the ten-year period between 1919 and 1929, a total of 1,903,755 people left the Evangelical churches, and 318,915 people left the Catholic Church. About 50 percent of those who had resigned from the churches organized in freethinking groups (the majority of them in the German Association of Freethinkers. See Künneth and Schweitzer, *Freidenkertum,*

49ff.). A considerably smaller number of church members, on the other hand, joined sectarian groups and other religious denominations. For example, in 1929, a total of 153,037 people resigned from the Evangelical churches. However, only 8,117 of these people joined another religious denomination or sectarian group. See *Kirchliches Jahrbuch für die evangelischen Landeskirchen Deutschlands* 59 (1932): 245.

170. Art. 1, para. 1, no. 3, of the Mar. 28, 1931, Verordnung des Reichspräsidenten zur Bekämpfung politischer Ausschreitungen, *RGBl.* 1932, pt. 1, 79.

171. The Bavarian Department of State of the exterior submitted monthly reports to the Reich Ministry of the Interior (RMdI) "concerning the measures that the Bavarian police authorities took to enforce the Decree of the Reich President for the Resistance of Political Acts of Violence" (BHStA, MA 100397). According to these reports, between Dec. 1931 and May 1932, the Bavarian police banned or otherwise restricted twenty-seven Bible Student publications.

172. See *Das Goldene Zeitalter*, Aug. 15, 1932, 254 ("Bibelforscher verklagen den bayrischen Staat"); *Bayrische Zeitschrift für Rechtspflege*, 1932, 202.

173. In his study concerning the ban on the Bible Students, published in 1936, Rolf Stödter emphasizes that the Bavarian state government took action against the IBSA at the instigation of the NSDAP state parliamentary faction. However, this has to be considered as an overstatement, probably with the intention of giving the impression that the NSDAP perceived the impending "danger" at an early stage. See Stödter, "Verfassungsproblematik," 169.

174. Cardinal Faulhaber, Dec. 6, 1930, letter to the Bavarian episcopacy, *Akten Deutscher Bischöfe*, 1:790. In his letter to the Bavarian bishops, in which he discusses the pastoral consequences of the position of the Catholic Church concerning the incompatibility of church membership and NSDAP membership, Cardinal Faulhaber approves of the opposition that the Hitler movement showed toward the IBSA.

175. *Klerusblatt*, Dec. 23, 1931, col. "Aus der Praxis für die Praxis."

176. *Das Goldene Zeitalter*, Aug. 15, 1932, 254.

177. Ibid., 247; *Yearbook 1933*, 125.

178. Administrative Court in Baden, 25/32, decision of June 15, 1932, cited in Zürcher, *Kreuzzug*, 79. See also *Das Goldene Zeitalter*, Jan. 1, 1933, 15.

179. See Gebhard, *Zeugen Jehovas*, 132–34; *Der Deutsche Weg* (Lodz), May 29, 1938, 4. Brüning's memoirs indicate that the Catholic politician basically refused to counteract antichurch tendencies with legal actions and bans. He recommended that the churches counteract these tendencies rather with convincing and powerful proclamations. He did not think that "antireligious tendencies" could be counteracted "with a policeman's club." Brüning, *Memoiren*, 571.

180. Gerecke, *Gotteslästerungen*, 159.

181. *Das Goldene Zeitalter*, Jan. 15, 1933, 22.

Part 2. Jehovah's Witnesses in the Third Reich, 1933–34

1. See, for instance, Fetz, *Volks- und Weltbetrug*, 34. ("Internationale" is a revolutionary socialist hymn written in 1871 by Eugène Pottier.)

2. *Das Goldene Zeitalter*, Feb. 15, 1933, 50–53.

3. In 1932/33 between 400,000 and 450,000 copies of the *Golden Age* were printed. This, in itself, does not indicate the number of subscribers. However, based on the fact that about 20,000 Jehovah's Witnesses participated in the house-to-house activity, it certainly can be assumed that usually all of these journals were distributed.

4. BA, R 43 II/179, Bl. 102–12 (103), Apr. 26, 1933, memo of the Northern and Southern German Bible Students Associations.

5. Besides Prussia, the Northern German Bible Students Association included all other twelve states of northern and central Germany. The Southern German Bible Students Association, on the other hand, was responsible for the states of Bavaria, Württemberg, Baden, and Hessen, which had a considerably smaller population. Up until that time, the IBSA experienced more problems in this part of the German Reich.

6. AG [municipal court] HH, Dept. 69 VR, Index no. 2846.

7. Sta HH [state archives of Hamburg], Hamburg Municipal Court, register of associations B 1965-3, Bl. 5–16, Statutes of the Northern German Bible Students Association, membership association. In this regard, the statutes of the association corresponded completely with the principles of the theocratic leadership. Democratic elements were restricted to the minimum of legal requirements. Consequently, the president, who was elected for an indefinite period, was able at any time to dismiss and replace at his own discretion the board of directors or individual board members (article 13). Membership was restricted to an exclusively selected group of people. According to the statutes, it was restricted to the "founders of the association" (article 16). New appointments were made only for the purpose of replacing a member who had resigned or who had been expelled (article 23). The detailed instructions with regard to the possibility of an expulsion from the association clearly emphasized the importance that was attached to a structure of uniformity and strict leadership According to these instructions, among other factors, such exclusion could take place if the member no longer agreed with important ideological viewpoints and objectives of the association (article 18).

8. For instance, in Württemberg, at the initiative of a NS pastor, the question of a Bible Student ban was discussed at the Ministry for Education and Cultural Affairs as early as Mar. 1933. However, the Higher Church Council of the Evangelical churches in Stuttgart, from whom the ministry had requested a statement in this regard, gave a rather reserved response. On Mar. 30, 1933, church president Theophil Wurm informed the German Evangelical church committee (the principal authority of the Evangelical churches in the German

Reich) about the response of the higher church council. According to Wurm's explanations, he had stated "that he was not able to give his opinion about any actions the state should take in this matter. It would certainly not be beneficial if the impression were given that the churches had requested any measures of suppression. In his opinion, a ban on a religious denomination had to be issued by the Reich's authorities, in which case, however, it would be appropriate to take the opinion of the church committee into consideration" (Schäfer, *Die Evangelische Landeskirche in Württemberg*, 2:30).

9. Sta HH, Hamburg Municipal Court, register of associations B 1965–3, Bl. 18, Hamburg police authorities, letter of Mar. 24, 1933.

10. *JW* [*Juristische Wochenschrift*] 64 (1935): 2082. This circular decree that the Mecklenburg Schwerin Ministry of the Interior sent to the police offices has never been published.

11. *Bayerischer Staatsanzeiger* 88 (Apr. 14/15, 1933), Bavarian Ministry of the Interior, announcement of Apr. 13, 1933.

12. Oberhirtliches Verordnungsblatt (Bishopric Gazette) for the diocese of Passau, no. 10, May 6, 1933, 50–51.

13. *Bayerischer Staatsanzeiger* 109 (May 12, 1933), Bavarian Ministry for Education and Cultural Affairs, decree of May 9, 1933.

14. See this book, pt. 1, ch. 3, p. 64.

15. During the National Socialist period, *Volksgenosse(n)* referred to those who directly belonged to the German people or race and were especially attached to their German heritage.

16. "Der Oberlandjäger in St. Margarethen," report of Apr. 19, 1933, cited in Möller, "Steinburg," 163.

17. See Imberger, *Widerstand*, 257, 266.

18. See *Golden Age*, Nov. 22, 1932, 122–22 [*Das Goldene Zeitalter*, Apr. 15, 1933, 116].

19. *Sächsisches Verwaltungsblatt* 34 (1933): 251, Saxony's Ministry of the Interior, decree of Apr. 18, 1933.

20. DdW [Document archives of the German resistance] AN 788, state commissioner for the police authorities in Hessen, Apr. 19, 1933 instructions to the police authorities.

21. See *Yearbook* 1974, 110.

22. BA, R 43 II/179, Bl. 98–101, "Norddeutsche Bibelforschervereinigung und Süddeutsche Bibelforschervereinigung," letter of Apr. 26, 1933.

23. BA, R 43 II/179, Bl. 102–12, memo as encl. to the letter of Apr. 26, 1933.

24. BA, R 43 II/179, Bl. 113, "Der Staatssekretär in der Reichskanzlei," letter of May 30, 1933.

25. See *Foreign Relations of the United States*, 2:406.

26. BA, R 43 II/179, Bl. 121, *Magdeburger Tageszeitung*, May 5, 1933.

27. See Möller, "Steinburg," 164.

28. See *Golden Age*, Apr. 25, 1934, 456 [*Das Goldene Zeitalter*, May 15, 1933, 148].

29. Ibid., 456–57.

30. Cited in Zürcher, *Kreuzzug*, 84. On Nov. 17, 1933, Legal Counsel Hans Dollinger presented 1,900 statements for notarization to the U.S. Consulate General in Berlin.

31. Beginning on May 15, 1933, the German edition of the *Golden Age* included the following statement: "Please note! This is a completely nonpolitical journal. It has been nonpolitical in the past and will continue to be nonpolitical. Therefore, it will not make any statements regarding current political issues. It is politically neutral."

32. *Foreign Relations of the United States*, 2:408, Consul General Messersmith, letter of July 12, 1933.

33. The subsequent explanations are based on the extensive description of the events, in Möller, "Steinburg," 163–65.

34. Gestapa refers to the Berlin headquarters of the Secret State Police office, whereas Gestapo refers to the various Secret State Police offices throughout the country. Between May 5 and 26, 1933, the Gestapa banned a total of nineteen publications, including the booklets *The Crisis; The Final War; The Kingdom, the Hope of the World; Who Is God?;* and *What Is Truth?* The Gestapa also banned Rutherford's previously mentioned book, *Government*.

35. The ban in Thuringia coincided with the occupation of the Magdeburg branch office. The Thuringia Ministry of the Interior issued the ban on Apr. 26, 1933 (cited in BA, R 58/405, Bl. 25–38, SG [Special Court] Weimar, So. G. 4/36, decision of Jan. 24, 1936); decree by the Baden minister of the interior, cited in *Entscheidungen des Reichsgerichts in Strafsachen* 69 (1936): 341, RG [Reich Court], 1 D 235/35, decision of Sept. 24, 1935; Stokes, *Eutin*, 705n2; *Braunschweigische Gesetz- und Verordnungssammlung* 120 (1933): 91 (no. 61).

36. See *Foreign Relations of the United States*, 2:407.

37. See Helmreich, *German Churches*, 129.

38. Cardinal Faulhaber, letter of May 5, 1933, *Akten Deutscher Bischöfe*, 1:259.

39. Apr. 24, 1933, memo "Die Neuorganisation des Evangelischen Volksbundes," in Schäfer, *Die Evangelische Landeskirche in Württemberg*, 1:515.

40. With its June 14, 1933, ban (*Regierungsblatt für Württemberg*, 1933, 191), the Württemberg Ministry of the Interior did not yet order the dissolution of the various IBSA groups. It "merely" prohibited them (as also the sect of the New Apostolic Church) from performing their preaching activity or any other activities in public. Therefore, for some time, the Bible Students in Württemberg were legally still able to conduct their religious meetings. According to personal recollections, the authorities did not take action against their religious meetings until several months later. See BA, R 43 II/179; June 1984 recollections by Gustav Widmaier.

41. *Württembergischer Staatsanzeiger* 139 (June 19, 1933), cited in *MD* 7 (1935): col. 72.

42. "NS-Pfarrerbund," district of Württemberg, memo of June 1, 1933, cited in Schäfer, *Die Evangelische Landeskirche in Württemberg*, 2:153.

43. Ibid., 2:448–49, memo of June 30, 1933.

44. In Lübeck, the IBSA ban was issued on June 6, 1933 (see Imberger, *Widerstand*, 258). After the ban in Prussia, the IBSA was prohibited in Bremen on June 28, 1933 (see Marßolek and Ott, *Bremen*, 303–4), and in Hamburg on July 15, 1933 (*Amtlicher Anzeiger*, insert of the *Hamburgisches Gesetz- und Verordnungsblatt*, no. 165, July 18, 1933, 705). It is not possible to determine when the bans in Anhalt, Mecklenburg-Strelitz, and Schaumburg-Lippe were issued.

45. On Oct. 18, 1933, the Hessen Ministry of State issued a dissolution order, replacing the assembly and missionary ban issued on Apr. 19 (DdW, AN 788). In Württemberg, the Ministry of the Interior issued the final ban on Feb. 1, 1934 (see this book, p. 000, n.40).

46. EZA, 7/Generalia 12, no. 161, Secret State Police office, letter of May 26, 1933. No information is available regarding the contents of the May 29, 1933, discussions; only the invitation to this meeting is available.

47. EZA, 7/Generalia 12, no. 161, "Der Preußische Minister für Wissenschaft, Kunst und Volksbildung," June 1, 1933, express letter. However, the minister refrained from banning the Tannenbergbund.

48. EZA, 7/Generalia 12, no. 161, memo regarding the June 9, 1933, discussion at the Ministry for Science, Art, and National Education.

49. A statement submitted during the preliminary discussion clearly shows the position of the Higher Church Council: "I responded to the question that the chief senior civil servant Diels raised in this regard during the meeting by explaining that the Evangelical churches would basically never initiate the use of governmental instruments of power against the Earnest Bible Students. However, in view of the clearly destructive tendencies of this movement, which threaten both the authority of the churches and the state, I would have no objections if the state decided in favor of a ban" (EZA, 7/Generalia 12, no. 161, no page numbers, handwritten statement).

50. The Prussian Police Administrative Law [Polizeiverwaltungsgesetz] of June 1, 1931, article 14, decreed: "Within the scope of current laws, the police authorities have to take the necessary actions according to their best judgment, to protect the general public and individuals against dangers that threaten public law and order." *PrGS* [*Preußische Gesetzessammlung*, Prussian Law Collection] 1931, 77.

51. The Prussian minister of the interior, decree of June 24, 1933 (II G 1316a); in Zürcher, *Kreuzzug*, 75–77; abridged edition of the decree published in Stödter, "Verfassungsproblematik," 169–70.

52. See SLG HH, HSG [public prosecutor's office of at the Hamburg Regional Court, Hanseatic Special Court] 11 Js. Sond. 1617/34, vol. 3, Bl. 452. It is not possible to find this report in the archives.

53. This error might be attributed to the fact that the Württemberg decree, issued ten days earlier, mentions both the Bible Students Association and the New Apostolic Sect, prohibiting the advertising activities of both groups. See BA, R 43 II/179, Bl. 141–46; *MD* 7 (1935): col. 72.

54. See Zürcher, *Kreuzzug*, 78. Some Prussian authorities immediately corrected the error, as, for instance, the Kiel State Police office in its July 11, 1933, memo (see Möller, "Steinburg," 166). For a number of years, however, this incorrect name remained in use. As late as 1936, the Reich Court had not even noticed this error and came up with other names, such as Neu-Apostolische Sekte der Internationalen Bibelforschervereinigung e. V. Magdeburg. See RG, 4 D 58/36, decision of Mar. 3, 1936, *JW* 65 (1936): 2237.

55. See SLG HH, HSG 11 Js. Sond. 1617/34, vol. 3, Bl. 451.

56. See Zürcher, *Kreuzzug*, 77; Gebhard, *Zeugen Jehovas*, 135, 153–58. This occurrence is of certain significance because it is used in the documentation, published under the name of Gebhard, to prove the theory that the ban on the Bible Students was *not* directed against the IBSA. In other words, the NS persecution of the Bible Students was actually not justified. The DDR publication needed this theory to be able to explain to its readers why it was possible that an association that was "serving the interests of capitalism" and that had "anti-Soviet" views could become victim to NS persecution. Therefore, the "documentation" also had to conceal the fact that measures of persecution had already been instituted before the Prussian ban.

57. Secret State Police office, June 27, 1933, radio message to all State Police offices, "Die Lageberichte der Geheimen Staatspolizei über die Provinz Hessen-Nassau," 612. The radio message announced that the Bible Students Association "has been banned today throughout the district of Prussia." This statement caused quite some confusion concerning the date of the ban. For instance, Hetzer incorrectly states that the ban was issued at the end of June 1933 in response to the Wilmersdorf convention. See Hetzer, "Augsburg," 624.

58. See *DJ* 98 (1936): 690.

59. See *VB*, June 30, 1933; *Süddeutsche Zeitung*, June 30, 1933.

60. *Evangelium im Dritten Reich* 2 (July 9, 1933): 262.

61. Officially, the legal authorities were informed about the ban more than six months later by means of a general decree of the Prussian Ministry of Justice. See *DJ* 96 (1934): 177, general decree of Feb. 5, 1934.

62. The Magdeburg branch office expected 5,000 delegates to attend the convention. (This is also the number mentioned on the cover letters that had already been prepared for mailing out the declarations. However, on the original copy of the letter that was sent to Hitler on June 26, 1933, this number was subsequently changed by hand to 7,000. See BA, R 43 II/179, Bl. 119.) The actual number of attendees is also 7,000 (see *Yearbook* 1934, 131).

63. See *The Spirit and the Sword*, 4; Wrobel, "Anbiederung oder Glaubenszeugnis?: Die Petition der Zeugen Jehovas vom 25. Juni 1933 und der Kongressbericht an den Reichskanzler," private document, ch. 3.4.1.

64. See *Foreign Relations of the United States*, 2:407–8.

65. There is no doubt that Rutherford is the author, even though *Yearbook* 1974 puts his authorship in question (see this book, p. 580, n.81). Presently, the

Watch Tower Society no longer denies this fact. This is, for instance, indicated by the predominant American diction that clearly identifies the style of the Watch Tower Society's president. The English version, which is published in its complete wording in *Yearbook* 1934 (131–43), does not significantly differ from its German version, published in *Yearbook* 1934 (89–100). If, as indicated in the German *Yearbook* 1974, Balzereit had actually based the declaration on a different text than the one he had received from Rutherford, the president would certainly not have given his approval for its publication. On Rutherford's share in preparing the Wilmersdorf convention and in writing the declaration, see also Penton, *Apocalypse Delayed*, 36ff.

66. Rutherford left Germany a few days before the start of the convention. On June 25 he attended the convention of Jehovah's Witnesses in The Hague, Netherlands, which took place at the same time.

67. According to Konrad Franke's report (see the following note), Jehovah's Witnesses in Germany tried to avoid using that hymn (song 64 from the Watch Tower Society's 1928 songbook, *Songs of Praise to Jehovah*) because of its melody. However, it was used on occasion, for instance, at the IBSA convention in Leipzig on May 20, 1929 (Wrobel).

68. The statement made in the first two German editions of this book, according to which the convention "was introduced with the 'Deutschlandlied,'" is based on a misconception. Also the assertion "that the place for the convention was decorated with swastikas" can and should no longer be maintained. The statement is based on a tape recording of a discourse given by the former IBSA branch leader Konrad Franke. Excerpts of this discourse are published in the journal *Christian Quest* 3, no. 1 (1990): 46–47. However, since there are doubts that this is a correct representation, it would not be appropriate to maintain this assertion. Photos from the Wilmersdorfer Tennishalle [tennis court], taken during the IBSA convention, do not show any swastika decorations, at least not in the interior of the hall. This is also confirmed by eyewitness reports (Wrobel). One day prior to the IBSA convention, the SA, SS, and other NS factions held summer solstice celebrations in the immediate neighborhood of the Wilmersdorfer Tennishalle, and it is certainly possible that the outside of the Tennishalle was decorated with swastikas (see Christoffel, *Wilmersdorf*, 269).

69. Helmut Lasarcyk, personal documents: Konrad Franke, "Geschichte der Zeugen Jehovas in Deutschland," discourse [transcript], Bad Hersfeld, 1976, 28; excerpts published in *Christian Quest 3* (1990): 49.

70. *Yearbook* 1934, 142; the following statement, ibid., 137. The declaration is also published in Pape, *Wahrheit*, 141–46. The typewritten original document is included in BA, R 43 II/179, Bl. 126–40, encl. to the June 26, 1933, letter by the Watch Tower Society.

71. *Yearbook* 1934, 134.

72. Ibid.

73. See Hutten, *Seher, Grübler, Enthusiasten*, 88; Penton, *Apocalypse Delayed*, 34–36.

74. See this book, pt. 1, ch. 3, p. 51.

75. See, for instance, *"Let God Be True,"* 211–26.

76. Rutherford, *Vindication*, 2:257–58, cited in Wrobel, "Anbiederung oder Glaubenszeugnis?," ch. 19.4.6. (See this book, p. 578, n.63.)

77. Some literary works include the statement that Jehovah's Witnesses support a "religiously based" (Kater, "Bibelforscher," 187), or "outright" (Penton, *Apocalypse Delayed*, 42) anti-Semitism. However, such statements fail to recognize the real characteristics of this controversy. Even though the controversy is not completely free from polemics and verbal lapses, it would not be appropriate to subsume it under a term of anti-Semitism that implies racial hatred. The general membership of the denomination anyway continued to show the high regard for the Jews that their leaders had proclaimed up until the early 1930s. Moreover, being exposed to the same kind of persecution in the Third Reich, it was more likely that Jehovah's Witnesses expressed compassion for their situation, which manifested itself in the fact that they continued to shop at Jewish stores, despite the boycott. See Struve, "Zeugen Jehovas," 287. On the assistance that individual Jehovah's Witnesses rendered toward Jews in dangerous situations, see this book, pt. 5, ch. 13, pp. 340–41.

78. Rutherford, *Vindication*, 3:300, cited in Wrobel, "Anbiederung oder Glaubenszeugnis?," ch. 19.4.8. (See this book, p. 578, n.63.)

79. Much of the criticism that has been made in literature with reference to the Wilmersdorf declaration does not do justice to its contents and to the situation. For instance, it is not appropriate to conclude that Jehovah's Witnesses declared themselves to be anti-Semites and offered their potential alliance (M. Koch, "Die kleinen Glaubensgemeinschaften," 418; M. Koch, "Engelhard," 99). Statements to the effect that this "convention displayed sympathy for National Socialism" (Knaut, *Propheten*, 128), or the assertion that the Watch Tower Society's leaders tried to "make a pact with Hitler" (Nobel, *Falschspieler Gottes*, 71), were deliberate efforts to discredit Jehovah's Witnesses. The same holds true regarding the statement made in Gebhard's publication, the DDR "documentation" of 1970, which indicates that Jehovah's Witnesses supposedly provided "criminal support for the anti-Semitic policy of Hitler" (Gebhard, *Zeugen Jehovas*, 166.)

80. *Jehovah's Witnesses in the Divine Purpose*, 141. This 1959 publication provides an overall view about the history of Jehovah's Witnesses. In the historical report (1993), it is factually more correctly stated that the Wilmersdorf declaration describes "their ministry [preaching activity] and its objectives." Even in this report, Jehovah's Witnesses do not deny the fact that they tried to adapt to circumstances in 1933 (*Jehovah's Witnesses: Proclaimers of God's Kingdom*, 693).

81. This is the explanation given in the historical report of Jehovah's Witnesses, *Yearbook 1974*, 111. In the meantime, the Watch Tower Society changed

its viewpoint regarding this representation. It had the objective of subsequently placing the responsibility for the efforts to adapt to circumstances in 1933 entirely on Balzereit and other members of the German leadership See Twisselmann, *Wachtturm-Konzern,* 147.

82. See *Yearbook* 1974, 111.

83. Hutten, *Seher, Grübler, Enthusiasten,* 118.

84. June 24, 1984, recollections by Alfred Skoda.

85. *Jehovah's Witnesses in the Divine Purpose,* 130.

86. A comparison (Wrobel) of this letter with an English version that the Magdeburg branch office sent to the central European office in Bern indicates that, in contrast to the Declaration of Facts, this letter was translated from German into English and not vice versa. Quite contrary to the declaration written by Rutherford, the cover letter was probably written by Balzereit, possibly in cooperation with his legal counsel Dollinger and other leading members.

87. BA, R 43 II/179, Bl. 119–25, "Watch Tower Bible and Tract Society, German Branch," letter of June 26, 1933. A copy of this letter is published in Pape, *Wahrheit,* 137–40.

88. Ibid.

89. See *Yearbook* 1934, 129; *VB,* June 30, 1933.

90. See *Foreign Relations of the United States,* 2:409.

91. Ibid.

92. On the following explanations, see SLG HH, HSG 11 Js. Sond. 1617/34, vol. 4, Bl. 447–63, Mar. 12, 1935, memo of Defense Attorney Dr. Walter B.; BA, R 43 II/179, Bl. 203–18, Sept. 26, 1933, memo of M. C. Harbeck.

93. On Kohl's activities as defense attorney in the 1923 Hitler trial, see Hannover and Hannover-Drück, *Politische Justiz,* 149.

94. BA, R 43 II/179, Bl. 219–22, Oct. 11, 1933, memo of Counselor of Justice Karl Kohl.

95. See Gebhard, *Zeugen Jehovas,* 135. On the elimination of the possibility of legally examining State Police orders, see Kirchberg, "Verwaltungsgerichte," 141ff.

96. See *Foreign Relations of the United Sates,* 2:410–11.

97. See *Yearbook* 1974, 112; Zürcher, *Kreuzzug,* 85.

98. BA, R 43 II/179, Bl. 203–18 (205–6), M. C. Harbeck, petition of Sept. 26, 1933. This Magdeburg action was later repeated in other parts of this German state. For instance, probably in the spring of 1935, Bible Student publications were also burned in the marketplace of Eutin. See Stokes, *Eutin,* 698n6.

99. See *Foreign Relations of the United States,* 2:412–13.

100. See this book, p. 564, n.81; p. 586, n.152.

101. See *Foreign Relations of the United States,* 2:412–13.

102. BHStA [Bayerisches Hauptarchiv, Bavarian main state archives], Reichsstatthalter [Reich governor] 638, PrMdI, decree of Sept. 28, 1933. Cited in the Apr. 27, 1935, dissolution order of the Magdeburg district president. A

copy of this decree is included in the June 21, 1935, BPP memo. The decree was never published. However, an indirect publication took place through the June 9, 1934, general decree by the Prussian Ministry of Justice, which includes a quotation of this decree by the minister of the interior. See *DJ* 96 (1934): 757.

103. Reimer Möller, Secret State Police office, copy of the Oct. 13, 1933, interoffice decree, local authorities of Kellinghusen, Bestand [stock] II 340 b.

104. Ibid.

105. In her instructive discussion about the different conceptions that existed among Jehovah's Witnesses regarding the question of what behavior patterns the new circumstances required, Elke Imberger makes a distinction between unconditional adaptation or partial adaptation, dissent while maintaining casual connections, and defensive resistance. See Imberger, *Widerstand*, 262–68, 273–77, 285.

106. See Ziebold et al., "Das Schicksal der Freiburger Zeugen Jehovas," 74; Pape, *Zeuge Jehovas*, 8; *Yearbook* 1974, 129–30.

107. See M. Koch, "Die kleinen Glaubensgemeinschaften," 420.

108. See Ziebold et al., "Das Schicksal der Freiburger Zeugen Jehovas," 74.

109. After the first occupation of the Magdeburg branch office at the end of Apr., the Bible Students moved large amounts of publications to other places. In the summer of 1933 extensive confiscations took place, for instance, in Hamburg (see Garbe, "'Gott mehr gehorchen als den Menschen,'" 185); in Cologne (see *Yearbook* 1974, 112); in Bremen (see F. Peters, *Bremen*, 31), as well as in other places throughout the state (see Kühl, "Friedrichstadt," 166).

110. SLG HH, HSG 11 Js. Sond. 1617/34, vol. 1, encl. to Bl. 36, "Watch Tower Bible and Tract Society, Brooklyn, New York," letter of Aug. 28, 1933.

111. Ibid. On the reaction of Jehovah's Witnesses to this letter, see *Yearbook* 1974, 131–32.

112. See Kühl, "Friedrichstadt," 169.

113. See Möller, "Steinburg," 167; SLG HH, HSG 11 Js. Sond. 1617/34, vol. 1, encl. to Bl. 26.

114. EZA, 1/C3 No. 309, "Der Propst in Schleswig," Dec. 7, 1933, letter to the regional church office of the Evangelical-Lutheran church. The regional church office in Kiel sent the request to the Reich clerical authorities. They, in turn, asked the RMdI for advice. With reference to the Sept. 28, 1933, decree by the Prussian Minister of the Interior (PrMdI), the RMdI explained that property had been released because "it belonged to an American association, as it were" (EZA, 1/C3 No. 309, RMdI, Apr. 7, 1934, letter to the Reich church authorities).

115. It is not possible to find this particular Gestapa decree. However, a reference to this decree is included in an available subsequent memo. See BA, R 58/405, Bl. 5, Secret State Police office, interoffice decree of Sept. 15, 1934. A copy of this Gestapa decree is included in the Sept. 22, 1934, interoffice decree by the Cologne State Police office.

116. BA, Sammlung [collection] Schumacher/267 I, BPP, interoffice decree of Feb. 12, 1934.

117. See *Yearbook* 1974, 114ff.; IfZ, Fa 119/2, Bl. 266–67, BPP, decree of May 28, 1936. In the spring of 1936 the Secret State Police office was tired of the frequent confiscation orders. On Apr. 16, 1936, the subordinate police offices were informed that "in the future, no formal distribution ban" would be issued at the appearance of IBSA publications. See BA, R 58/1074, Bl. 29.

118. See Imberger, *Widerstand*, 320ff.; *Yearbook* 1974, 113ff.; Garbe, "'Gott mehr gehorchen als den Menschen,'" 186; M. Koch, "Die kleinen Glaubensgemeinschaften," 425.

119. See this book, pt. 3, ch. 7, pp. 139–48.

120. *Yearbook* 1974, 113.

121. SLG HH, SG Kiel, 11 Son KMs 149/36, Bl. 76.

122. IfZ, MA 554, 936374, BPP, interoffice decree of Dec. 27, 1933.

123. See Secret State Police office, interoffice decree of Dec. 8, 1933, "Die Lageberichte der Geheimen Staatspolizei über die Provinz Hessen-Nassau," 626–27.

124. See the RSHA "collection of decrees regarding sectarian affairs" that was compiled until the end of 1942. This collection also includes the Feb. 16, 1934, Gestapa decree under serial no. 4/IBSA. BA, R 58/1074, Bl. 28–35 (28). From the spring of 1934 on, the Secret State Police office also reported regularly on the activities of the Bible Students Association in its internal "Mitteilungen über die politische Lage" [Reports about the Political Situation]. (See BA, R 58/1068; the first report about the IBSA was included in report no. 4, dated Oct. 3, 1934.) These extensive secret reports were based on an analysis of the information received from the various State Police offices. In different subordinate sections, they provided information about the current state of acts of opposition. Until 1938 the IBSA activities were recorded in a separate section, which also included the activities of KPD, SPD and other Socialist organizations, the Schwarze Front, the "church-political situation," and the like. On a local basis, a special section for the "Bible Students" or for "sectarian affairs" had already been established in Jan. 1934. See Minninger, "Bielefeld," 54.

125. BA, R 58/1068, Bl. 172, Secret State Police office, report no. 4, Mar. 10, 1934.

126. See BA, R 58/405, Bl. 83.

127. See Hetzer, "Augsburg," 624.

128. On the persecution of members of the Menschenfreundliche Versammlung/Engel Jehovas, see Bludau, *Gestapo-geheim!*, 291, 295; M. Koch, "Die kleinen Glaubensgemeinschaften," 431–32; Minninger, "Bielefeld," 65. According to Koch, the religious denomination Engel Jehovas did not experience such intense persecution because they did not promote the refusal of military service, did not refuse to give the Hitler salute, and, generally, were not involved

in anti-state activities. They also restricted their activities to their immediate group of members. However, local State and party authorities often did not differentiate between the various groups of Bible Students. For instance, at the beginning of 1938, the senior public prosecutor in Mannheim considered "the religious sect of Engel Jehovas to be as dangerous as the 'Earnest Bible Students,' especially in view of their refusal to perform military service, their rejection of marriage and reproduction, and their refusal to support the major charitable activities of the NSDA" (BA, R 22/3136, Bl. 190, cited in the Apr. 7, 1938, situation report of the chief public prosecutor in Karlsruh).

129. For the following explanations, see Zipfel, *Kirchenkampf,* 203–10. There is a general lack of publications discussing the persecution of the minor denominations in the Third Reich. Until now, a comprehensive study based on sound historical information has not been written. However, in recent years, several studies have been published that include important details on this matter. Foremost among these studies is the 1982 book by Christine E. King (*The Nazi State and the New Religions*). King makes a comparison between five religious denominations: Christian Science, the Church of Jesus Christ of Latter-day Saints (Mormons), the Seventh-day Adventists, the New Apostolic Church, and Jehovah's Witnesses. Anne Sabine Halle, representative of the Quakers in the Federal Republic of Germany on questions regarding resistance, also wrote a shorter report about five religious groups: Apostelamt Simeon, Johannische Kirche, Mormons, Quakers, and Jehovah's Witnesses (see Halle, "'Alle Menschen sind unsere Brüder'"). Also noteworthy are three additional informative monographic studies. As a group, however, these religious associations or free churches cannot be included in the religious denominations that were persecuted. Their respective leaders as well as the majority of their members chose to conform to the circumstances. Kösling, "Baptisten"; Lichdi, *Mennoniten;* and Zehrer, *Evangelische Freikirchen.*

130. BA, Sammlung Schumacher/267 II, Amt Lehrwesen des Hauptschulungsamtes der NSDAP, "Kampf gegen okkultes Sektierertum und sogenannte Geheimwissenschaften in Deutschland," Munich, n.d., 19.

131. In Mar. 1938 the "Mitteilungen zur weltanschaulichen Lage" made the following statement regarding the Mennonites, whose sect belongs to the historic peace churches: "The chairman of the 'Association of German Mennonites' repeated in a public declaration that, based on the June 11, 1934, statutes of the Mennonite communities, the principle of defenselessness has been completely abandoned. This means that, fortunately, the German Mennonites renounced their previous dogmatic viewpoint of conscientious objection" (IfZ, MA 603, 20198, report no. 8, Mar. 11, 1938). It should be noted, however, that this statement was not undisputed. During World War II, several Mennonites tried to serve in the medical corps or technical departments of the Wehrmacht. See Lichdi, *Mennoniten,* 135ff.

132. BA, R 58/1094, Bl. 75, 1938, situation report of the RSHA.

133. See, for instance, BA, R 58/233, RFSS, special report, "Die Lage in der protestantischen Kirche und in den verschiedenen Sekten und deren staatsfeindliche Auswirkung," Feb./Mar. 1935, 18ff.

134. Instructions of the SS for resisting religious opponents, published in Neuhäusler, *Kreuz und Hakenkreuz,* 1:361ff. (364). These instructions were issued at the July 18, 1937, conference of the SS. On Feb. 15, 1938, they were distributed to the subordinate SS offices.

135. According to a list (incomplete) of "bans on sectarian groups" that the Secret State Police office compiled until Dec. 31, 1938, a total of thirty-nine religious denominations were banned up until this point. Four bans were issued in 1933, three bans in 1934, five bans in 1935, seven bans in 1936, thirteen bans in 1937, and seven bans in 1938. See BA, R 58/405, Bl. 80–84, Secret State Police office, letter of June 7, 1939, regarding the "list of banned sects."

136. See King, *Nazi State and the New Religions,* 181ff.

137. BHStA, MA 107297, "Bayerisches Staatsministerium für Unterricht und Kultus," May 26, 1933, letter to the Bavarian Ministry of the Interior. The Seventh-day Adventists were not banned at that time because, even though their teachings were "not necessarily according to standard," the ministry did not see a need for "a complete ban." For the time being, the religious movement of the Adventists was in no danger of being dissolved. During World War I, several members of the Adventists separated from the original association and formed the "Seventh-day Adventists Reformation Movement" because the Adventist leaders requested their members to perform military service. This association was banned on Apr. 29, 1936 (GstAPrK [Secret State Archives of the Prussian Cultural Heritage], Re 90 P/57, Bl. 10). The "Seventh-day Adventists, Third Division" were banned on Apr. 19, 1937 (BA, R 58/405, Bl. 82), and the "Tabernacle Seventh-day Adventist Church" was banned on Dec. 18, 1941 (BA, R 58/405, Bl. 64).

138. *Das Evangelische Deutschland,* no. 37, Sept. 10, 1933.

139. EZA, 14/810, no page numbers.

140. See the respective records in the EZA, 1/C3 No. 298ff.; 14/810 and 811.

141. EZA, 14/811, statement in the Mar. 7, 1934, letter of the bishop of the Evangelical churches in the Old Prussian Union.

142. *Wort und Tat. Zeitschrift für volksmissionarische Arbeit* 10, no. 10 (1934): 323.

143. See Marßolek and Ott, *Bremen,* 495n105.

144. See BA, R 60 II/33, Bl. 2–5.

145. *Deutschland Berichte* 4 (1937): 501. During subsequent years, individual pastors and members of the major churches provided support for persecuted Jehovah's Witnesses, provided they came in contact with them, as for instance, during periods of imprisonment. However, this does not mean that they formed an "alliance of resistance" with the "Bekennende Kirche," as was

stated by Heinz Brunotte, long-standing president of the EKD [Evangelical churches in Germany] church office (see Brunotte, *Bekenntnis*, 158).

146. Karl Barth, letter of Feb. 2, 1937, cited in Zürcher, *Kreuzzug*, 32 (following photo section).

147. Staehelin, *Was haben wir von den "ernsten Bibelforschern" zu halten?*, 32.

148. Ernst Staehelin, letter of Feb. 2, 1937, cited in Zürcher, *Kreuzzug*, 32 (following photo section).

149. See Imberger, *Widerstand*, 262–63, 274–77.

150. The following petitions are available: petitions of Legal Counsel Hans Dollinger (BA, R 43 II/179, Bl. 268–72; Gebhard, *Zeugen Jehovas*, 120–22, 156–57); petitions of the IBSA district overseer of Palatinate-Baden, Dr. Franz Merk (see *Verfolgung und Widerstand unter dem Nationalsozialismus in Baden*, 65); and petitions of Karl Kohl, Munich Counselor of Justice (BA, R 43 II/179, Bl. 219–22, petition of Oct. 11, 1933).

151. BA, R 43 II/179, Bl. 203–18 (214–15), M. C. Harbeck, petition of Sept. 26, 1933.

152. In the meantime, the negotiations focused on the question of whether the refusal to provide legal recourse was a violation of article 12 of the German-American Treaty of Friendship, Commerce, and Diplomacy. With its verbal "note" of Nov. 13, 1933, the German Ministry of Foreign Affairs rejected the protest of the American government in this regard. At the beginning of 1934 Ambassador William E. Dodd reported to the U.S. Department of State that the request for an examination by the Administrative Court had been rejected. Consequently, the American authorities considered the possibility of filing a complaint at the International Court of Justice in The Hague. At the same time, they discussed with the RMdI the possibility of an out-of-court settlement, that is, an agreement to withdraw the prohibitions against the German branch office of the Watch Tower Society (publishing ban and assembly ban). See *Foreign Relations of the United States*, 2:415–17; Gebhard, *Zeugen Jehovas*, 135–37.

153. On Dec. 4, 1933, Ambassador Dodd reported that Harbeck had "expressed grave doubt whether the remedy suggested by the German Government would afford any relief." See *Foreign Relations of the United States*, 2:414. On Jan. 12, 1934, Rutherford informed Harbeck that he also had "little hope that we will get anything at all from the German government" (*Yearbook* 1974, 132).

154. In the Watch Tower publications, this change of tendency during 1933/34 is clearly evident. For instance, in the Nov. 1, 1933, *Watchtower*, published under the headline "Fear Them Not," the readers were requested to take a firm stand. It was not directly indicated that this article was written for the believers in Germany. However, the active ones among Jehovah's Witnesses in Germany considered this particular issue of the *Watchtower* to be a confirmation of their course of action by the Brooklyn headquarters. The yearbooks published by the Watch Tower Society also reflected the change that had been made in assessing the situation. For instance, in *Yearbook* 1934 (Oct./Nov. 1933), complaints were

made about the restrictions Germany had placed on religious freedom. However, these accusations focused on the actions that the Secret State Police took against the Bible Students. See *Yearbook* 1934, 127–46. In *Yearbook* 1935, on the other hand, without tactical considerations, the accusations were clearly directed at the government as the entity responsible for the actions. Concerning Hitler, it states: "Manifestly, that man is under the direct supervision of the Devil and is his special representative on the earth" (*Yearbook* 1935, 116).

155. Joseph Franklin Rutherford, letter of Feb. 9, 1934, cited in Cole, *Jehovah's Witnesses* [German edition], 194–96.

156. Ibid., 196. In mid-1934 the Watch Tower Society began to publish specific reports about the situation of their persecuted fellow believers in Germany. See, for instance, *Golden Age*, Apr. 25, 1934, "Persecution in Germany."

157. See M. Koch, "Die kleinen Glaubensgemeinschaften," 418–20.

158. SLG HH, HSG 11 Js. Sond. 1617/34, vol. 3, encl., no page numbers.

159. See BA, R 58/1074, Bl. 28.

160. BA, R 58/1068, Bl. 172, Secret State Police office, report no. 4, Mar. 10, 1934.

161. Rolf Schwarz, "Watch Tower Bible and Tract Society, German Branch," letter of Oct. 5, 1984.

162. See SLG HH HSG 11 Js. Sond. 1617/34, vol. 3, encl., no page numbers, "Legal department of the Wachtturm Gesellschaft," Sept. 11, 1934, letter to the leader of the Hamburg IBSA group, Max Grote.

163. See BHStA, Reichsstatthalter 638, "Der Regierungspräsident in Magdeburg," Apr. 27, 1935, dissolution order, copy included in the June 21, 1935, memo by the BBP.

164. See this book, pt. 2, ch. 6, pp. 123–29.

165. *DJ* 96 (1934): 757, Prussian Ministry of Justice, general decree of June 9, 1934. This late announcement of the Sept. 28, 1933, decree by the minister of the interior, which took place on June 9, 1934, through a general decree by the Ministry of Justice, caused considerable confusion at the subordinate administration offices. It also resulted in misconceptions among historians. For instance, Zipfel mistakenly states that "the Prussian minister of the interior had issued a new decree for the release [of the Watch Tower Society's publications]" (Zipfel, *Kirchenkampf,* 181–82). Möller, on the other hand, incorrectly questions the existence of the June 9, 1934, decree (Möller, "Steinburg," 168).

166. BA, Sammlung Schumacher/267 I, "Watch Tower Bible and Tract Society, German Branch," letter of June 25, 1934; copy included in the July 14, 1934, interoffice decree by the BBP.

167. IfZ, MA 554, 936366, BPP, interoffice decree of July 14, 1934.

168. BA, R 58/405, Bl. 5, Secret State Police office, interoffice decree of Sept. 15, 1934. On Sept. 22, 1934, the Cologne State Police office sent a copy of this decree in the form of an interoffice decree to the Gummersbach district administrator's office.

169. See Gebhard, *Zeugen Jehovas*, 136; Stödter, "Verfassungsproblematik," 170–71.

170. BA, R 43 II/179, Bl. 273, RMdI, letter of Sept. 13, 1934; copy enclosed in the Jan. 5, 1935, petition by Hans Dollinger.

171. IfZ, MA 554, 936364, RMdI, decree of Sept. 13, 1934 (my emphasis). Copy in the form of the Oct. 2, 1934 interoffice decree by the BBP.

172. Rolf Schwarz, Secret State Police office; interoffice decree of Sept. 28, 1934 (my emphasis). On Oct. 3, 1934, the Rendsburg district administrator's office sent a copy of this decree in the form of an interoffice decree to the local district police offices.

173. IfZ, MA 554, 936365, BPP, interoffice decree of Oct. 2, 1934.

174. SLG HH, HSG 11 Js. Sond. 1617/34, vol. 1, encl. to Bl. 26, "Watch Tower Bible and Tract Society, German Branch," letter of Oct. 5, 1934.

175. SLG HH, HSG 11 Js. Sond. 1617/34, vol. 3, encl., no page numbers, "Watch Tower Bible and Tract Society, German Branch," letter of Oct. 17, 1934.

176. See *Yearbook* 1935, 116; *Yearbook* 1974, 132–33; Zipfel, *Kirchenkampf*, 182. Apparently the Gestapo heard about the Basel convention only weeks later. Not until Oct. 12 (Gestapa) and Oct. 31, 1934 (BPP), were the State Police offices alerted to the situation and informed that "the leaders of the 'International Bible Students Association' had conducted in Basel a secret convention." At this meeting, as was vaguely indicated, they had supposedly decided to carry out a new intensive propaganda campaign in Germany to promote the interests of the Bible Students (BHStA, Reichsstatthalter 638, interoffice decree of Oct. 31, 1934).

177. June 6, 1984, recollections by B. Maurer. The term "fiery furnace" is taken from the book of Daniel, chap. 3, which discusses the account of the three God-fearing Hebrews who refused to bow down before the image of the Babylonian King Nebuchadnezzar. According to the Bible account, when they were threatened to be thrown into the fiery furnace, they stated: "Our God, the one we serve, is able to save us from the burning fiery furnace and from your power, Your Majesty, he will save us" (Dan. 3:17). The deliverance of these God-fearing men is an account that is frequently used in the publications of the Bible Students.

178. BA, R 43/179, Bl. 255, "protest manifestation," encl. to the Sept. 15, 1934, letter of the Watch Tower Bible and Tract Society.

179. Ibid., Bl. 253–54, Watch Tower Bible and Tract Society, central European office, letter of Sept. 15, 1934. Reich Constitution, article 137, guaranteed religious associations freedom of assembly. See this book, p. 591, n.217.

180. It is not possible to provide even approximate numbers here. The numbers of Kingdom proclaimers that were active during the period of the ban mentioned in the IBSA publications vary between 6,000 (for the year 1936, see *Yearbook* 1937, 152) and 20,000 (*Jehovah's Witnesses in the Divine Purpose*, 163).

The historical account in *Yearbook* 1974, 141, mentions the number of "at least 10,000." In 1976 Konrad Franke, German branch leader of the Watch Tower Society between 1955 and 1969, estimated that about "fifty percent" of IBSA members "remained faithful" and participated in the prohibited activities. The others withdrew and, if they did not completely abandon their faith, limited their activities to their private realm (see Lasarcyk, peronsal documents: Konrad Franke, "Geschichte der Zeugen Jehovas in Deutschland," *Christian Quest 3* [1990]: 31). In Hamburg, based on the membership numbers for 1932, far more than 50 percent of the believers participated in the preaching activity, even during the period of the ban. See this book, pt. 6, ch. 18, p. 485 and pp. 494–99.

181. *Yearbook* 1935, 117.

182. Ibid., 118.

183. *Yearbook* 1935, 119; "Ablichtung eines Telegramms," cited in Hildebrandt and Hoffmann, *Streiflichter*, 41. According to the records of the Watch Tower Society, a total of 20,000 telegrams were sent to the Reich government. See Zürcher, *Kreuzzug*, 189.

184. See BA, R 43 II/179, Bl. 257, main telegraph office, letter of Oct. 8, 1934.

185. Ibid., Bl. 258, main telegraph office, letter of Oct. 10, 1934.

186. EZA, 1/C3 No. 309, presidential chancellery, Oct. 9, 1934, letter to the Reich bishop.

187. Ibid., church authorities, Nov. 20, 1934, letter to the presidential chancellery.

188. BA, R 43 II/179, Bl. 264, private office, Nov. 17, 1934, letter to the Reich chancellery.

189. Ibid., Bl. 265, Reich chancellery, Nov. 23, 1934, letter to the private office.

190. Ibid., Bl. 266, private office, Nov. 24, 1934, letter to the Reich chancellery.

191. AfW [Amt für Wiedergutmachung, Office for Compensation] HH [Hamburg], 310300, Bl. 10, statutory declaration of Dec. 27, 1945. Records about the preliminary investigations are not available. However, detailed information about this event is included in the records about court proceedings against the leaders of the Hamburg IBSA group that took place in the following year. See SLG HH, HSG 11 Js. Sond. 1617/34.

192. A service overseer, who was responsible for a city or a certain district, was generally assisted by a committee of five people. This committee included a treasurer, bookkeeper, secretary, and assistants.

193. See SLG HH, HSG 11 Js. Sond. 1617/34, vol. 2, Bl. 181–82.

194. Hero von Ahlften, letter of Oct. 15, 1934, SLG HH, HSG 11 Js. Sond. 1617/34, vol. 1, encl. to Bl. 12a. Von Ahlften gave Rutherford a detailed report about the methods Balzereit used to exclude the Watch Tower Society's branch office in Magdeburg from the Oct. 7, 1934, activities. Von Ahlften concluded

his explanations with a question that reveals the motives of his opponents: "Is it a wonder that a great hurly-burly broke out? Who will prepare himself to the battle, if the trumpet gives an uncertain sound?"

195. SLG HH, HSG 11 Js. Sond. 1617/34, vol. 1, encl. to Bl. 26a, Arno Thümmler and Alfred Zimmer, letter, n.d.

196. Ibid., J. F. Rutherford, letter of Dec. 8, 1934.

197. Ibid., Dec. 10, 1934, letter by Jehovah's Witnesses in Emden.

198. Hannover State Police office, Nov. 4, 1934, situation report for the month of Oct. 1934, in *Gestapo Hannover*, 260.

199. The different publication dates, partial withdrawals and negotiations resulted in the fact that it is extremely difficult to reconstruct the sequence in which the decrees were issued. Literature therefore often includes incorrect, even contradicting, statements regarding the date(s) of the Bible Student ban(s). For instance, several people consider the June 27, 1933, radio message by the Gestapa to be a ban at the Reich level (see, for instance, Hetzer, "Augsburg," 624; Mammach, *Widerstand 1933–1939*, 146.) The statement in Renate Lichtenegger's dissertation, according to which the "IBSA in Germany" had been banned as early as Apr. 13, 1933, erroneously refers to the ban that was issued in the Free State of Bavaria (Lichtenegger, "Wiens Bibelforscherinnen," 66). Between 1987 and 1989, Reimer Möller made an attempt "to explain the administrative tactics of the central authorities" (Möller, "Steinburg," 224). However, even his efforts have to be considered as a failure because he could not adequately re-establish the sequence of the decrees, their backgrounds, as well as the various State authorities and authorities at the Reich level.

200. The neglected publication of the bans in the state of Mecklenburg-Schwerin (Apr. 10, 1933) and in the state of Hessen (Apr. 19, 1933) was compensated by new decrees being issued in each state. See *JW* 64 (1935): 2082, decree of the Mecklenburg-Schwerin minister of the interior issued on Aug. 5, 1933 (published in the official government paper); *JW* 63 (1934): 1745, decree of the Hessen ministry of state issued on Oct. 18, 1933 (published in the official paper of the Hessen government, the *Darmstädter Zeitung*).

201. MdI, "announcement of Apr. 10, 1935," cited in Stokes, *Eutin*, 708.

202. See Zipfel, *Kirchenkampf*, 182. On May 21, 1935, by means of a special memo, the RuPrMdI pronounced the Sept. 13, 1934, decree to be invalid. See BA, R 58/405, Bl. 2.

203. BHStA, Reichsstatthalter 638, "Der Regierungspräsident in Magdeburg," dissolution order of Apr. 27, 1935, copy included in the June 21, 1935 memo by the BBP.

204. IfZ, MA 554, 936352, cited in BPP, July 26, 1935.

205. Ibid.

206. BA, R 58/405, Bl. 2, RuPrMdI, interoffice decree of Jan. 30, 1936.

207. See "Watch Tower Bible and Tract Society, German branch," petition of Dec. 19, 1934, excerpts published in Gebhard, *Zeugen Jehovas*, 120–22.

208. BA, R 43 II/179, Bl. 268–72 (270), Hans Dollinger, petition of Jan. 5, 1935.

209. See *Yearbook* 1974, 148–50

210. Ibid., 149.

211. "Beantwortung einiger Fragen: Mitteilungsblatt der deutschen Verbreitungsstelle des W. T.," July 1942 (copy in my possession). After his release from prison in Dec. 1937, Balzereit was sent to the Sachsenhausen concentration camp in 1939; after more than one year of imprisonment, he was released. In 1945 he immediately began to reorganize the German branch of the Watch Tower Society in Magdeburg and insisted on being reinstated to his former positions. This resulted in serious conflicts with those members of the Bible Students who had been in the concentration camps until the end of the war. Because of their steadfastness, they also claimed positions of leadership in the association. In Oct. 1945 Nathan H. Knorr, who succeeded Rutherford as president, settled this conflict. Erich Frost became the leader of the German branch office (he was the IBSA "leader on the Reich level" from Sept. 1936 until his arrest on Mar. 21, 1937). In 1955 Konrad Franke succeeded him as branch leader (he was the district overseer of Palatinate-Baden from June 1935 to Aug. 1936).

212. *RGBl.* 1933 I, 83 (also known as Reichstag Fire Decree).

213. See Bracher, "Stufen der Machtergreifung," 82–88.

214. *MBliV* 94 (1933): pt. 1, 233, MdI, interoffice decree of Mar. 3, 1933.

215. See Kalous, "Bibelforscher," 35; Warmbrunn, "Strafgerichtsbarkeit," 373–74.

216. At first, not all of the cases dealing with offenses against the Feb. 28, 1933, Decree of the Reich President were handled at the special courts. On Mar. 21, 1933, the Reich government gave instructions to establish special courts in every jurisdictional district of a higher regional court (*RGBl.* 1933 I, 136). Prior to this date, in some cases even as late as 1935, offenses against the Decree of the Reich President were still handled at the usual criminal courts. At these criminal courts, the defendants had the possibility to file an appeal and, if necessary, even subsequent appeals. Special court proceedings, on the other hand, could not be appealed.

217. Reich Constitution, article 135, guaranteed "complete freedom of religion and freedom of conscience" and placed this freedom under the protection of the State. In addition, Reich Constitution, article 137, paragraph 2, guaranteed "the freedom to form religious associations." This article also determined that, within the German Reich, the forming of religious associations was not subject to any restrictions (German Constitution of Aug. 11, 1919, *RGBl.* 1919 II, 1383).

218. *DVerwBl.* [*Deutsche Verwaltungsblätter*], 1934, 60, Bavarian Highest National Court, 275/33, decision of Dec. 7, 1933; judgment excerpt published in *DJZ* [*Deutsche Juristenzeitung*] 39 (1934): col. 416.

219. See this book, pt. i, ch. 3, pp. 65–66.

220. Volkmann, *Rechtsprechung*, 47.

221. DPfar 23 (1935): 135–38, Bavarian Highest National Court, 298/33, decision of Feb. 22, 1934; judgment excerpt published in *DverwBl.*, 1934, 445. In this particular case, the court did not regard the actions of the defendants as an offense against the Feb. 28, 1933, VOSchVuS Decree of the Reich President for the Protection of People and State, article 4. According to the court, there was no evidence to prove that the defendants had been involved in activities of the prohibited Bible Students Association. Contrary to later judicial decisions, the court did not take a restrictive position: "Gatherings for the exclusive purpose of upholding social and personal relationships do not fall into the category of prohibited activities."

222. *JW* 63 (1934): 767–69, RG, 4 D 244/33, decision of Jan. 21, 1934.

223. The statements of the senior public prosecutor at the Reich Court contradicted the fact assessment of the regional court. However, in this regard, he unduly defied the restrictions of appeal proceedings.

224. On administration of justice at the Reich Court, see the critical study by Friedrich Karl Kaul and the biographical study by Dieter Kolbe about Reich Court president Dr. Bumke. See also the apologetic dissertation ("Höchstrichterliche Strafgerichtsbarkeit unter der Herrschaft des Nationalsozialismus") by Rolf Lengemann about "criminal jurisdiction of the Highest Court under National Socialist rule," which may be considered as extremely questionable.

225. *JW* 64 (1935): 1949, Gerichtsassessor Dr. Dreher, annotations to the judgment.

226. *JW* 63 (1934): 767–69 (768), RG, 4 D 244/33, decision of Jan. 21, 1934.

227. See Schäfer and von Dohnanyi, *Die Strafgesetzgebung*, 252.

228. See Fraenkel, *Dual State*, 18ff.; I. Müller, *Juristen*, 55ff.

229. *JW* 63 (1934): 1744–47, SG Darmstadt, S M 26/34, decision of Mar. 26, 1934.

230. *Frankfurter Zeitung*, Mar. 28, 1934. The article, published under the headline "Freedom of Religion and the Constitution," also discusses the position of the defendants very objectively. Since the *Frankfurter Zeitung* was not yet completely censored, its reports are completely different from the NS press reports.

231. Schmitt considered the Weimar Constitution to be part of the previous state system, a system that had been conquered by means of the "upheaval." The normative constitution was replaced with a "real" constitution, which received its authority from the legal sources of specific arrangements (family, community, army, etc.). See Neumann, "Ordnungsdenken."

232. *JW* 63 (1934): 1744–47, SG Darmstadt, S M 26/34, decision of Mar. 26, 1934.

233. See Anschütz, *Verfassung*, 289. The opponents of this theory of inviolability, on the other hand, among whom Carl Schmitt was the most prominent,

accepted the viewpoint that the listing of the seven fundamental rights in Reich Constitution, article 48, had exemplifying character, not a restrictive one.

234. Details about the NS criticism of the decision of the Darmstadt Special Court in Hessen are included in Stödter, "Verfassungsproblematik," 175–88. Even Ministerialdirektor Dr. Wilhelm Crohne, a high-ranking official of the RJM, publicly criticized those Darmstadt judges (see Crohne, "Verbote," 1144–45). One year later, the Darmstadt Special Court abandoned its "formerly contrary administration of justice." See SG Darmstadt, S M 20/35, decision of Apr. 29, 1935, cited in *DJ* 97 (1935): 1145.

235. See Marxen, *Antiliberalismus,* 167ff. The Kieler School was an especially radical part of the legal doctrine in National Socialism that tried to seperate dispensation of justice from its affiliation with the written law.

236. Ernst Rudolf Huber, explanations to the judgment, *JW* 63 (1934): 1745–47 (1745). Huber's attitude in this regard is also reflected in his explanatory commentary about the (NS) constitution. In this commentary, with obvious reference to the IBSA, he states: "Religious teachings that reject, for instance, any state authority to be a 'work of the devil' and that disapprove of military service cannot demand freedom of religion" (Huber, *Verfassungsrecht,* 496).

237. Huber, explanations to the judgment, *JW* 63 (1934): 1747.

238. See *Gestapo Hannover,* 188.

239. *Westfälische Neueste Nachrichten,* Nov. 15, 1934. On Mar. 30, 1935, the Hamm Higher Regional Court ordered that the judgment should be repealed. On Sept. 13, 1935, the Bielefeld Schöffengericht reopened the proceedings. Also this time, the nine defendants were acquitted on the charge that they were not registered members of the dissolved association and therefore could not have defied the ban. However, in its Feb. 10, 1936, decision, the Hamm Higher Regional Court cancelled these acquittals again, which means that they were not of long duration. See Minninger, "Bielefeld," 69; Minninger, "Staatsfeind Bibelforscher," 61–63.

240. Hannover State Police office, Aug. 4, 1934, situation report for the month of July 1934, *Gestapo Hannover,* 188.

241. Ibid., Nov. 4, 1934, situation report for the month of Oct. 1934, *Gestapo Hannover,* 260–61.

242. Ibid., Aug. 4, 1934, situation report for the month of July 1934, *Gestapo Hannover,* 188.

243. See Minninger, "Staatsfeind Bibelforscher," 63.

244. *DRiZ* 27 (1935): pt. 2 (Rechtsprechung), no. 312, Halle Special Court, GSM 72/34, decision of Jan. 29, 1935.

245. See Huber, *Verfassungsrecht,* 494ff.; Klöckner, "Grundrecht," passim; Volkmann, *Rechtsprechung,* 6–15 (with additional references of contemporary publications).

246. The historical report of the Watch Tower Society states that "hardest hit was Hamburg where, just a few days after Oct. 7, the Gestapo arrested 142

brothers" (*Yearbook* 1974, 139). However, the report incorrectly states that the wave of arrests took place "just a few days" after Oct. 7, 1934. Actually, the arrests took place between Dec. 1934 and the beginning of Feb. 1935. See Garbe, "'Gott mehr gehorchen als den Menschen,'" 189, 201–2.

247. A condemnation of mere attendees at the Oct. 7, 1934, IBSA meetings began in autumn of 1935. In seven proceedings at the Hanseatic Special Court, a total of 134 men and women were sentenced to an average of two months of imprisonment on the charge of being "followers." In six cases, the proceedings were discontinued or acquittals were pronounced. See SLG HH, HSG 11 Js. Sond. 1617/34.

248. SLG HH, HSG 11 Js. Sond. 1617/34, vol. 3, Bl. 447–63 (459), Mar. 12, 1935, memo of Defense Attorney Dr. Walter Buchholz. The Hanseatic Special Court rejected the reasoning of Buchholz. However, three weeks later, in proceedings at the neighboring Altona Special Court, in which Buchholz also represented the defense, his explanations were accepted. On the significance of the Mar. 4, 1935, decision, see 148ff. If a defense attorney became too involved in the defense of his client, he was in danger of being prosecuted himself, as is evident from the following example: On May 13, 1936, a defense attorney had to appear before the disciplinary court [Ehrengerichtshof] at the Reich Bar Association [Reichs-Rechtsanwalts-Kammer] to account for his legal activities with regard to the Bible Students. A board of representatives of his profession reprimanded the attorney and imposed a fine on him because, in defending the "'Earnest Bible Students,' he had disregarded the interests of the German people." The disciplinary court rejected his appeal against this decision. He was accused of sending a report to the Watch Tower Society's branch office in Magdeburg, in the context of discharging his responsibilities as defense attorney. According to the disciplinary court, his report included disparaging remarks about the "authorities in charge of imposing and implementing protective detention. Such criticism was disreputable for a German defense attorney" (*Entscheidungen des Ehrengerichtshofs*, 30:106–9, *Ehrengerichtshof*, 1. Senat G 184/35–47/36, decision of May 13, 1936).

249. Article 1, paragraph 1, of the Mar. 21, 1933, decree of the Reich government regarding the forming of special courts, *RGBl.* 1933 I, 136. These special courts, which had been established in every jurisdictional district of a higher regional court for the purpose of expediting the sentencing of opponents of the regime, were not familiar with several of the procedural laws that applied to criminal justice. To strengthen the position of the public prosecutor's office, no preliminary investigations and indictments were performed. At the same time, the legal rights of the defense attorneys had been considerably restricted. The most serious infringement was the abolition of the possibility of filing an appeal and subsequent appeals: As soon as a decision was pronounced it was legally binding. The convicted person did not have any legal means to file an appeal. On procedural restrictions in the context of special court proceedings, see Johe, *Justiz*, 81–108; Schimmler, *Sondergerichte*, 9–22.

250. SLG HH, HSG 11 Js. Sond. 161/34, vol. 3, Bl. 467, Mar. 14, 1935, records of public proceedings.

251. Ibid., 471–502 (492, 497), decision of Mar. 15, 1935.

252. Ibid., 496.

253. In Point 24 of the Feb. 24, 1920, NSDAP party program: "We demand freedom of religion for all religious denominations in our state, as long as these do not endanger the continued existence of the state or violate the moral or ethical convictions of the German race. The party takes the position of positive Christianity without showing preference toward any specific denomination" (*Der Nationalsozialismus*, 144).

254. SLG HH, HSG 11 Js. Sond. 1617/34, vol. 3, Bl. 494, decision of Mar. 15, 1935. The phrase "once and for all" was later added to the original text— probably for the purpose of publication. Mar. 5, 1933, was the date of the Reichstag election on which the Coalition Government of the "National Union" received the absolute majority of votes and seats in the Reichstag.

255. Wilhelm Weimar, "Reichsfachgruppe Richter und Staatsanwälte," *DRiZ* 27 (1935): 342.

256. See Volkmann, *Rechtsprechung*, 7–15; Echterhölter, *Recht*, 156–66.

257. See *RverwBl.* [*Reichsverwaltungsblatt*] 56 (1935): 700–701; the judgment is published in legal journals (for instance, in *JW* 64 [1935]: 2988–89), in the Hamburg daily press, and in other German papers.

258. Reich Court, 5 D 416/1935; see in this regard SLG HH, HSG 11 Js. Sond. 1617/34, vol. 3.

259. Stödter, "Verfassungsproblematik," 186, 188.

260. See, for instance, *JW* 64 (1935): 2082, Schwerin Special Court, KMs 31/35, decision of May 13, 1935.

261. In its May 29, 1935, decision, the Braunschweig Higher Regional Court confirmed the legality of the IBSA ban. In this regard, the court stated that, even though the Emergency Decree did not repeal Reich Constitution, article 137, it would still be invalid since it "no longer" corresponded "with the present constitutional principles." The Reich Constitution had lost its validity as "the basic constitutional law of the German Reich," since it "no longer corresponded with the present Führer state." The Braunschweig judges also stated that the established legal uniformity and the desire for conformity reflected in this way did not leave any room for examining "whether a 'state law' or 'state decree' effective in the Third Reich would violate the constitutional laws of the 'German Reich'" (*HRR* [*Höchstrichterliche Rechtsprechung*] 12 [1936]: no. 98, Braunschweig Higher Regional Court, SS 5/35, decision of May 29, 1935).

262. *DRiZ* 27 (1935): pt. 2 (Rechtsprechung), no. 432, Breslau Special Court, 42 Sg. 10 KMs 19/35, decision of Apr. 27, 1935.

263. See Reintjes, "Glaubensgemeinschaften," 70–73 (a list of religious associations in the German states that were equipped with the right of a corporation under public law). The IBSA had never requested to be given this right in accordance with Constitution article 137, paragraph 5. However, in all

probability, the IBSA would have been denied this right. In similar cases, as, for instance, in the case of the New Apostolic Church, this request had also been denied. See GStAPrK, Re 84a/612, 46.

264. According to the administration of justice, the following characteristics were required to be considered as a religious association: A well-founded, comprehensive organization of its followers; a specific statement of belief; and the mutual practice of religious beliefs. Viewed objectively, the Bible Students Association fulfilled all three of these characteristics. On the difference in legal status of "religious associations" and "associations used for religious purposes" in the Third Reich, see Klöckner, "Grundrecht," 42ff.

265. See BA, R 58/405, 25–38, Weimar Special Court, So. G. 4/36, decision of Jan. 24, 1936. The wording of the judgment is almost completely published in Zipfel, *Kirchenkampf,* 332–58; as well as Imberger, *Widerstand,* 286 (with reference to the May 28, 1934, decision of the Dresden Regional Court).

266. LA SH [state archives of Schleswig Holstein], Abt. 352 Altona no. 8869, 57, SH SG [Schleswig Holstein Special Court], 11 Son KM 10/35, decision of Apr. 3, 1935.

267. Ibid., 58.

268. See this book, p. 000, n.50.

269. LA SH, Abt. 352 Altona No. 8869, "Der Oberstaatsanwalt bei dem SG in Altona," May 8, 1935, letter to the chief public prosecutor in Kiel.

270. Ibid. The Sept. 28, 1933, decree ordered the release of the confiscated property; see this book, pt. 2, ch. 5, p. 96.

271. June 5, 1935, instructions by Ministerialdirektor Crohne, cited in Gruchmann, *Justiz,* 541n28.

272. See Gruchmann, *Justiz,* 541.

273. BA, R 58/480, 53, Kiel State Police office for the administrative district of Schleswig, general assessment of the political situation in May 1935.

274. Crohne, "Verbote," 1145.

275. With the "new legal concept," Crohne expressed an idea that originated from the Ministry of the Interior. See Gruchmann, *Justiz,* 541–42.

276. Subsequently, the Altona Special Court no longer questioned the legality of the IBSA ban. However, in other respects, the court continued to have a remarkably stubborn attitude regarding Bible Student proceedings. See this book, pt. 4, ch. 12, pp. 264–68.

277. See *HRR* 12 (1936): no. 937, Dresden Higher Regional Court, 48/35, decision of Nov. 29, 1935.

278. *JW* 64 (1935): 1949, explanations to the judgment by Gerichtsassessor Dr. Dreher.

279. See ibid., Dresden Regional Court, 16 StA 4666/34, decision of Mar. 18, 1935.

280. *JW* 64 (1935): 1949, explanations to the judgment by Gerichtsassessor Dr. Dreher.

281. Stödter, "Verfassungsproblematik," 190.

282. *JW* 64 (1935): 1950, explanations to the judgment by Gerichtsassessor Dr. Dreher.

283. *Entscheidungen des Reichsgerichts in Strafsachen* 69 (1936): 341–48, RG, 1 D 235/35, decision of Sept. 24, 1935.

284. Ibid., 345–46 (italics in original).

285. Even in another area, which, in subsequent special court proceedings had serious consequences for the people concerned, this decision set the course. To this end, the Reich Court stated that "even a person who continues to display a measure of friendship toward his fellow believers would be involved in the prohibited 'activities.' This includes words of encouragement about a 'future improvement of conditions' or provisions of assistance which could have a positive effect on the persons concerned" (*Entscheidungen des Reichsgerichts in Strafsachen* 69 [1936]: 348). As a result, all gatherings of Jehovah's Witnesses became offenses subject to punishment, even those in which religious subjects were not the main topic of discussion. With reference to these statements, the special courts could regard even visits to sick people, funeral services, mutual walks, or group performances of craftsmanship as activities for the purpose of continuing a prohibited association. People were actually sentenced based on these examples.

286. *JW* 64 (1935): 3379, RG, 4 D 805/35, decision of Oct. 4, 1935.

287. *DJ* 98 (1936): 689–90, RG, 4 D 58/36, decision of Mar. 3, 1936; excerpt of judgment published in *JW* 65 (1936): 2237. Cited in the guidelines published in the *Juristische Wochenzeitschrift*.

288. *Entscheidungen des Reichsgerichts in Zivilsachen*, 160:195.

289. Stödter, "Verfassungsproblematik," 226.

Part 3. Jehovah's Witnesses' Nonconformist Behavior and State Repression

1. Excerpt from an underground publication that circulated among the Bible Students in the Third Reich titled "Unser Kampf und Hitlers 'Mein Kampf.'" Cited in Steinberg, *Essen*, 162.

2. In 1935 Werner Weber, an expert in jurisprudence, stated that the question of participation in elections was a "most significant national requirement." However, according to Weber, "the recognition of Führer and people" expressed in the act of voting would fulfill its purpose only if it was "voluntary" (Weber, *Dienst- und Leistungspflichten*, 5ff.)

3. BA, R 58/1068, Bl. 172, Secret State Police office, report no. 4, Mar. 10, 1934.

4. Ibid.

5. IfZ, MA 554, 936374, BPP, interoffice decree of Dec. 27, 1933.

6. See Zürcher, *Kreuzzug*, 126ff.

7. See *Yearbook* 1974, 115–16.

8. See Thévoz et al., *Pommern 1934/35*, 2:410–13.

9. Nov. 23, 1987, recollections by Elise Kühnle. Even the resistance fighter Friedrich Schlotterbeck, former chairman of the Württemberg Communist Youth Association of Germany, referred to this occurrence in his memoirs, which he wrote immediately after the end of the war. His personal account is titled: "Je dunkler die Nacht—: Erinnerungen eines deutschen Arbeiters 1933–1945" (see Schlotterbeck, *Erinnerungen*, 297–99). Schlotterbeck was first arrested in 1933. When he had to go underground again during the war, he remembered Karl Uhlmann, the Bible Student with whom he had been imprisoned in the Welzheim concentration camp. He visited Uhlmann's farm, which was located in a secluded forest valley near the Swabian village Haselbach, to hide there: "SA men had set fire to his house. The fire department was not permitted to extinguish the fire. He was also not allowed to rebuild his house and had to live in the ruins" (ibid., 298).

10. See Zürcher, *Kreuzzug*, 114, 171.

11. June 8, 1984, recollections by Minna Knöller.

12. The following descriptions are based on the June 8, 1984, recollections by Liesel Baroni; the June 1984 recollections by Hanna Bläse; the May 3, 1984, recollections by Hedwig Ehmann; the Nov. 23, 1987, recollections by Bruno Knöller; the June 1984 recollections by Gustav Widmaier; and the Jan. 25, 1986, recollections by Karl-Heinz Zielow.

13. Kassel State Police office, Sept. 5, 1934, situation report for the month of Aug. 1934, "Die Lageberichte der Geheimen Staatspolizei über die Provinz Hessen-Nassau," 154.

14. 1938 annual situation report of the RSHA, BA, R 58/1094, Bl. 76.

15. Acts 4:12.

16. Psychologist Bruno Bettelheim indicates that the mandatory Hitler salute was not merely a perpetual public demonstration of allegiance of every individual German citizen toward the new state. It also served the purpose of undermining the integrity of opponents of the regime. By means of day-to-day coercion to act against their own convictions, opponents of the regime should be deprived of their self-esteem: "Every time he had to greet somebody in public he had an experience that shook and weakened his integration. More specifically, if the situation forced him to salute, he immediately felt as traitor to his deepest convictions. . . . Thus, many times a day the anti-Nazi had either to become a martyr or abandon self-respect" (Bettelheim, *The Informed Heart*, 291; for more details see Bettelheim, "Die psychische Korruption," 332ff.).

17. Jan. 29, 1985, recollections by Alfred Knegendorf; VVN, Komiteeakten K 14.

18. During 1933/34 people were usually released from police detention after only a few days. In assessing these releases, it has to be taken into consideration that the initially mostly improvised coercive measures were mainly aimed at intimidating the people concerned and adjusting their attitude. It was

hoped that a brief and rigorous period of imprisonment would accomplish this purpose. A longer period of imprisonment or isolation from the rest of the community was not yet intended.

19. BDC, Schongau district office, Feb. 7, 1936, order for protective detention.

20. June 6, 1984, recollections by Paul Scholz.

21. Personal documents of Günther Schwarberg, diary of Ernst Schneider.

22. Cited in Zipfel, *Kirchenkampf,* 185.

23. "Das Deutschlandlied" is the German national anthem ("Deutschland, Deutschland über alles" [Germany, Germany Above All]). The "Horst Wessel Song" is considered to be a second *Deutschlandlied* (Germany song), known as "Die Fahne hoch" (Lift High the Banner).

24. Cited in Möller, "Steinburg," 214.

25. See the Bible Student publication, "Unser Kampf und Hitlers 'Mein Kampf,'" as represented in Steinberg, *Essen,* 162.

26. See *Richterbriefe,* 48.

27. See Zürcher, *Kreuzzug,* 112; VVN HH, Komiteeakten F 9 und L 6.

28. See *Yearbook* 1989, 100–101.

29. Dec. 12, 1934, Law against Insidious Attacks on State and Party and for the Protection of the Party Uniform, *RGBl.* 1934 I, 1269. According to article 2, anyone "who publicly made spiteful, agitating, or disparaging remarks undermining the confidence people place in their political leaders" would be punished with imprisonment. Gestapo Vienna, daily report no. 4 of Jan. 10 and 12, 1941, in Mitterrutzner, "Internationale Bibelforscher-Vereinigung," 293; see also ibid., 276. After serving his sentence, Höflinger was transferred to Dachau.

30. See Struckmeier, "Heinel," 162–63.

31. See Kühl, "Friedrichstadt," 183–84.

32. Cited in the 1940/41 Bible Student pamphlet (distributed in Austria), "Meine Gründe, weshalb ich mich weigere, den H.J.-Dienst mitzumachen." The quotations are published in Neugebauer, "'Ernste Bibelforscher,'" 176–77.

33. Toward the end of the 1930s, over ten million members were registered in the NSV. See J. F. Zimmermann, *NS-Volkswohlfahrt.*

34. Teetzmann, *Luftschutz-Leitfaden,* 98. In 1939 the Reich Federation for Air Raid Protection had a membership of 13.5 million, that is, one quarter of the German adult population.

35. BHStA, Reichsstatthalter 638, BPP, interoffice decree of May 24, 1935.

36. BA, R 58/264, Bl. 306, central State Police office in Munich, interoffice decree of May 19, 1937. In her study *Widerstand,* 368, Imberger reports of several cases of Jehovah's Witnesses from Schleswig Holstein who were taken into protective detention and sent to concentration camps for several months, immediately after the May 26, 1935, Law for Air-Raid Protection [Luftschutzgesetz] had been issued.

37. VOSchdW of Nov. 25, 1939, *RGBl.* 1939 I, 2319; see also 345–46.

38. *Deutsches Strafrecht*, 1:172. According to Zipfel, in one case involving the refusal to join the Reich Federation for Air Raid Protection, the Berlin Special Court imposed a prison sentence of six months on the charge of disparagement of the provision of air-raid protection (see Zipfel, *Kirchenkampf*, 196n48). This decision made in 1936/37 indicates that even before the beginning of the war, a refusal to participate in activities of the RLB resulted in legal proceedings, based on the Law against Insidious Attacks.

39. *Deutschland-Berichte* 3 (1936): 1177.

40. BDC, Aug. 3, 1943, "Mitteilungsblatt der deutschen Verbreitungsstelle des W. T.," Sept. 1942, cited in the Aug. 3, 1943, indictment of the Senior Reich Attorney of the VGH, 8 J 131/43.

41. Officially, membership in the DAF was voluntary. In 1938, 20 million employees had joined the DAF. See Mason, *Sozialpolitik*, 100ff.; Mai, "Warum steht der deutsche Arbeiter zu Hitler?," 212ff.

42. See BA, R 22/1467, Bl. 326.

43. In his study regarding Augsburg, Gerhard Hetzer reports about a small number of Jehovah's Witnesses who showed a certain affinity for National Socialism. Some even gave their unconcealed support to the NS movement. In 1922 a foreman became a member of the IBSA. Three years later he was one of the elders of the Augsburg Bible Student group. In the summer of 1927, however, he joined the NSDAP. Hetzer also indicates that, according to some Gestapo interrogation records, it was popular in Bible Student groups to read the *Stürmer* (an anti-Semitic weekly newspaper with high circulation in the Third Reich published by the Nazi leader F. J. Streicher). Some Bible Students even allowed their children, at an early age, to join the Hitler Youth (Hetzer, "Augsburg," 639). These were only infrequent and isolated cases, which do not have any significance with regard to the phenomenon as a whole. What is more, considering their source, these statements need to be regarded as extremely questionable.

44. Some of the petitions for pardon (StA M, SLG HH) examined in this context include references to memberships in NS organizations, as, for instance, the NS Betriebszellenorganisation (operating cell organization), or the NS Women's Association. The petitioners even specifically mentioned the membership of their own children in the Hitler Youth or memberships of relatives in the NSDAP. However, with regard to these records, it has to be taken into consideration that these petitions for pardon were written under extreme circumstances. They reflect the desperation and determination of the petitioners in search of possibilities for relief.

45. For supporting evidence, see this book, pt. 6, ch. 17, pp. 485–92.

46. In view of the severity of the measures, Friedrich Zipfel states that "within the unique National Socialist state," Jehovah's Witnesses were "under special statutory exemption with the objective of destroying their livelihood" (Zipfel, *Kirchenkampf*, 192). However, in court cases dealing with compensation, the situation was sometimes viewed completely differently. For instance, on

June 28, 1950, the Bielefeld court dealing with compensation for wrongs perpetrated under National Socialism refused to acknowledge that the Bible Students, as a "group," had been "exposed to persecution in terms of Article 1 of the REG." The decision states that, even though their religious activities were prohibited by the NS government and any defiance against this prohibition was also subject to punishment, "the government of that time" did not try "to exclude the Earnest Bible Students from economic life in Germany." Finally, in its concluding statement, the Bielefeld court completely misrepresented the actual state of affairs: "The Bible Students did not have to suffer any economic hardships" (*RzW* 1 [1949/50]: 409).

47. In his study regarding the IBSA in Mannheim, Manfred Koch makes the statement that Jehovah's Witnesses were exposed to disciplinary proceedings or dismissals "only in cases in which they were taken into custody" (M. Koch, "Die kleinen Glaubensgemeinschaften," 428). Even though this applied in a number of cases, the statement cannot be maintained with regard to the group as a whole. In the majority of cases, the dismissal was the beginning of persecution. It is, however, correct that, for civil servants who were (still) employed in the civil service, punishment for involvement in IBSA activities always resulted in dismissal.

48. MAu 94 (1933): 859, PrMdI, interoffice decree of July 20, 1933.

49. *ZBB* [*Zeitschrift für Beamten- und Behördenangestelltenrecht*] 7 (1936/37): 259, Reich Court of Disciplinary Hearings [Reichsdisziplinarhof, a court of appeals examining decisions of the various subordinate Disciplinary Divisions], F 47/35, decision of June 4, 1935. According to the court, in 1933 not even the highest Reich authorities were able to reach an agreement on this issue.

50. *MBliV* 94 (1933): 1487, Dec. 18, 1933, interoffice decree that the Prussian Minister of Finance issued also on behalf of the Prussian prime minister and the ministers of state of the other German states. Eleven days later, the RMdI issued a decree with the same wording "in view of the confusion that arose with regard to the way in which the Hitler salute was supposed to be given." See Lehberger, "'Umbau' der Hamburger Volksschule," 20.

51. *DJ* 97 (1935): 213, RuPrMdI, decree of Jan. 22, 1935.

52. SLG HH, HSG 11 Js. Sond 1617/34, vol. 2, Bl. 193, "Zur Ehre Jehovas," written statement, enclosed in the Jan. 16, 1935, letter of the Magdeburg State Police office.

53. *RGBl.* 1934 I, 785. For the oath required for civil servants, that is, the swearing in of civil servants in the Third Reich in acknowledgement of Hitler, see Bauernfeind, *Eid und Frieden,* 38–43.

54. Jan. 26, 1937, Tenured Civil Servant Law, *RGBl.* 1937 I, 41. Even before the revision of the Tenured Civil Servant Law had been issued such actions were taken, based on ministerial decrees and specific interpretation of the current Civil Service Law [Beamtenrecht]. According to article 4, paragraph 2, of the Civil Service Law, members of certain religious associations were legally

permitted to use a statement different from the oath to be sworn in. However, such permission was given only to the religious denomination of the Mennonites whose religious objection to the act of taking an oath (the biblical commandment not to swear, see Matt. 5:33, 34) had been taken into account even during pre-NS periods. However, this "concession" was made only for a short period of time. With his Dec. 15, 1938, letter, Martin Bormann ordered that "in the future . . . the Mennonites will be no longer exempt from taking the oath" (BA, Sammlung Schumacher/267 II, "Der Stellvertreter des Führers," Dec. 15, 1938, memorandum, no. 2/1939).

55. *RGBl.* 1933 I, 175.

56. The third DVO for the May 6, 1933, Law for the Re-establishment of the Civil Service with Tenure (*RGBl.* 1933 I, 245) determined that, apart from the "party book officials" and civil servants of "non-Aryan descent," "politically unreliable civil servants" should also be considered for dismissal.

57. RMdI, decree of June 11, 1934, "Akten der Reichskanzlei," pt. 1 (1933–34), 2:1321–22. According to Renate Lichtenegger, this decree was later extended to "also include civil servants who personally were not IBSA members, but whose wives belonged to the Bible Students Association" (Lichtenegger, "Die Bibelforscher im Widerstand gegen das NS-Regime," 182). Renate Lichtenegger does not provide evidence for the existence of such a decree, which, apparently, did not actually exist. Lichtenegger's conclusion was probably based on the fact that, in divorce proceedings, the IBSA membership of the wife of a civil servant was considered to be unacceptable for her husband because it undermined his position in public life and could result in economic hardship; see *JW* 66 (1937): 1308. In such cases, an employee in the civil service was coerced into divorcing his wife if she adhered to Bible Student teachings. At their places of employment, these civil servants were exposed to all kinds of difficulties and were not given any opportunity for advancement. However, it is not known that any civil servants were dismissed for such reasons.

58. *Amtliches Schulblatt für den Regierungsbezirk Hildesheim* 31 (1934): 211.

59. Even prior to the June 11, 1934, decree by the RMdI, civil servants were dismissed because they refused to give the Hitler salute or because they were IBSA members. For instance, at the end of 1933, a watchman and a court officer in Friedrichstadt were forced into retirement (see Kühl, "Friedrichstadt," 176). In 1933, in Hamburg, three civil servants were dismissed (a city hall clerk, a health administration official, and a social welfare service official). See VVN HH (Hamburg Association of Persecution Victims of the National Socialist Regime), Komiteeakten B 27, 3.

60. BA, R 22/4277, Bl. 187, notations of the June 18, 1937, discussion held at the RJM with the Higher Regional Court senior judges and the chief public prosecutors.

61. BA, Z Sg. 134/28, no page numbers (regarding Heinrich H.), Reich Disciplinary Division in Liegnitz, Pr.L.6/34/5, decision of Dec. 21, 1934.

62. The third DVO of the Law for the Re-establishment of the Civil Service with Tenure states that "politically unreliable civil servants" who were dismissed were supposed to receive three quarters of the legally required pension (*RGBl.* 1933 I, 245).

63. *ZBB* 7 (1936/37): 176, Reich Court of Disciplinary Hearings, F 25/35, decision of May 6, 1935.

64. Personal documents of J. E. Straßer ("Sammlung zur historischen Dokumentation"), Reich Court of Disciplinary Hearings, F. 74/35, decision of Oct. 29, 1935.

65. Reich Court of Disciplinary Hearings, F 212/35; correspondence involving these court proceedings is included in SLG HH, HSG 11 Js. Sond. 1617/34, vol. 2, Bl. 193; SLG HH, HSG 11 Js. Sond. 127/35. In this case, the Reich Court of Disciplinary Hearings granted the defendant to receive half of his pension for five years.

66. *ZBB* 7 (1936/37): 104, Reich Court of Disciplinary Hearings, F 199/35, decision of Feb. 11, 1936.

67. Ibid., 258–60 (259), Reich Court of Disciplinary Hearings, F 47/35, decision of June 4, 1935.

68. Statements cited in VVN HH, Komiteeakten M 20; LA SH, Abt. 352 Altona no. 9201, Bl. 46, Reich Post Administration in Hamburg, letter of Sept. 10, 1936.

69. During the Sept. 24, 1936, proceedings at the Schleswig-Holstein Special Court in Altona, an acquittal was pronounced "because of lack of evidence" (LA SH, Abt. 352 Altona no. 9201, Bl. 65–71). On the proceedings, see this book, pt. 4, ch. 12, pp. 264–66.

70. *DJ* 99 (1937): 245, PrOVG, decision of Nov. 17, 1936; see also *RVerwBl.* 58 (1937): 245.

71. Cited in Echterhölter, *Recht,* 197.

72. Appropriately, Klaus J. Volkmann acknowledges that, by means of this decision, the PrOVG made "an infringement on the *forum internum*" that would have far-reaching consequences: "There was no such law that put officials or people in general under obligation to acquire political information, or, in particular, to subscribe to a newspaper" (Volkmann, *Rechtsprechung,* 28).

73. *JW* 66 (1937): 1368, OVG of Saxony, 101 I 35, decision of Dec. 4, 1936.

74. Apr. 4, 1933, Law Regarding Works Counsels [Gesetz über Betriebsvertretungen], *RGBl.* 1933 I, 161.

75. Cited in Zürcher, *Kreuzzug,* 89.

76. Not only did the DAF take action against Jehovah's Witnesses who refused to join this trade union, it also took action against those of Jehovah's Witnesses who joined the DAF but continued their IBSA activities. For instance, legal punishment generally resulted in an expulsion from the DAF. While the people concerned had no problem accepting such expulsions, they now faced the danger of losing their jobs because the DAF tried to dismiss them from

their places of employment. Quotation from a letter directed to a company owner requesting him to dismiss one of his employees who was a Jehovah's Witness, cited in *Awake!*, June 22, 1985, 10–11. Apparently, even the "institution that had been entrusted" by the NS state "with maintaining peace at the places of employment" considered the Bible Students as "disturbing elements." In July 1935 Stiehler, the Reich trustee of employment in the state of Saxony, attributed disputes at work and disruption of peace in the company to the fact that there were "people forming cliques, fault-finders, incorrigible social reformists, but also religious extremists and sectarians, such as the Earnest Bible Students." See *Deutschland-Berichte* 2 (1935): 777.

77. *Deutschland-Berichte* 3 (1936): 504.

78. Ibid., 923.

79. See Zürcher, *Kreuzzug*, 90.

80. See *Deutschland-Berichte* 3 (1936): 1177.

81. See VVN HH, Komiteeakten K 37; Garbe, "'Gott mehr gehorchen als den Menschen,'" 201. In ibid., 199–207, the persecution of Karl Zietlow, who worked as a fireman for his company, is described in the form of an extensive biography. In 1938 Zietlow, who was one of the four Hamburg IBSA group leaders since the beginning of 1936, was sentenced to three years in prison. He died during the "evacuation" of the Neuengamme concentration camp at the beginning of May 1945. After the war the company refused to provide Karl Zietlow's widow with a statement for retribution purposes indicating that her husband had been dismissed from work for his refusal to give the Hitler salute. Instead, the company tried to dispose of its responsibility by stating: "We had to dismiss Karl Zietlow since he persistently refused, because of his religious convictions, to follow the instructions of our company security service provided by the Fire Brigade office" (May 18, 1946, statement by Company Blohm & Voss; a copy of this statement is in the possession of the author). Four years later, the company merely stated: "We had to dismiss your late husband on Feb. 28, 1934, because he refused to follow the instructions provided by the company's fire department" (statement of Dec. 11, 1950).

82. Cited in Zürcher, *Kreuzzug*, 133.

83. Ibid.

84. See *Yearbook* 1974, 126; *Yearbook* 1989, 115; VVN HH, Komiteeakten O 4.

85. June 5, 1984, recollections by Heinrich Markert. For evidence of Robert Bosch's repeated assistance in protecting people who were persecuted by the National Socialist authorities, see Treue, "Widerstand von Unternehmern," 930–31. Bosch died in 1942.

86. See this book, pt. 3, ch. 8, p. 153.

87. Personal documents of Straßer ("Sammlung zur historischen Dokumentation"), Jan. 30, 1947 letter by the tax auditor to the Internal Revenue Service.

88. See VVN HH, Komiteeakten Z 4.

89. Straßer ("Sammlung zur historischen Dokumentation"), mayor of Leipzig, Trade Office, notice of Jan. 9, 1937.

90. *RGBl.* 1934 I, 566.

91. BHStA, Reichsstatthalter 638, BPP, interoffice decree of Jan. 28, 1936.

92. See *Der Hoheitsträger,* series 1, Jan. 1938, 34; Nov. 23, 1987, recollections by Bruno Knöller; VVN HH, Komiteeakten B 30. Sometimes, business licenses were even withdrawn by the State Police authorities. For instance, the Kiel Gestapo withdrew the business license from the owner of a manufacturing business in Hochdonn "because he was strongly suspected of using his business trips to promote IBSA activities" (SLG HH, SH SG 11 Son KMs 149/36, Bl. 140, Oct. 30, 1936, file remark of the Kiel State Police office).

93. Reger 56 (1936): 533–535, Bavarian Administrative Court, 12 II 36, decision of May 8, 1936.

94. PrOVG, III C 152.53, decision of Jan. 16, 1936, cited in Frege, "Preußisches Oberverwaltungsgericht," 151.

95. PrOVG, III C 99.36, decision of Aug. 13, 1936, cited in Frege.

96. Ibid., decision of Apr. 21, 1938.

97. Reger 58 (1938): 470, decree of Aug. 28, 1937.

98. Ibid., Saxony Higher Administrative Court, decision of Feb. 28, 1938.

99. VVN HH, Komiteeakten A 12. The fate of the Appel family is published in Burmeister et al., "Verfolgung der Zeugen Jehovas in Kiel," 36–50; Philipsen, "Für den Glauben in den Tod." On Oct. 11, 1941, Rolf Appel was beheaded at the Brandenburg-Görden penitentiary. In Oct. 1944 the SS also executed one of Appel's sons.

100. VVN HH, Komiteeakten S 55, copy of Jan. 4, 1939, decision of the appeal proceedings at the Landeserbhofgericht in Celle.

101. See VVN HH, Komiteeakten Sch 24.

102. See Zürcher, *Kreuzzug,* 117, 129.

103. AfW HH, 280891, Bl. 18, Feb. 2, 1954 statement by Dorothea G.

104. Knöller, "Erinnerungen," 19.

105. This July 14, 1933, Law on the Reversion of Property Inimical to Nation and State (*RGBl.* 1933 I, 479) determined that the regulations of the May 26, 1933, Law on the Confiscation of Communist Property (Gesetz über die Einziehung kommunistischen Vermögens) (*RGBl.* 1933 I, 293) can be applied even to property of the Social Democratic Party of Germany, as well as to property, which, "according to the RMdI," was used to promote "anti-national and anti-state purposes." Consequently, it merely required a police decree to declare the property of IBSA groups as property "used for anti-national and anti-state purposes."

106. See Billstein, *Krefeld,* 304.

107. See Burmeister et al., "Verfolgung der Zeugen Jehovas in Kiel," 45; VVN HH, Komiteeakten A 12.

108. See Kühl, "Friedrichstadt," 181.

109. SLG HH, SH SG 11 Son KMs 149/36, Bl. 34, Sept. 3, 1936, file remark by the Kiel State Police office. See also the *Hamburger Tageblatt* of Aug. 13, 1937 ("Staatsfeinde nicht ans Steuer").

110. VVN HH, Komiteeakten J 5, Mar. 18, 1946, biography of Otto J.

111. An extensive description of the following events is published in Thévoz et al., *Pommern 1934/35*, 2:409–13; see also the explanations of the companion volume, *Pommern 1934/35*, 1:161–62.

112. Quotation from "Geheimes Staatspolizeiamt," Oct. 15, 1934, report by the Prussian prime minister, cited in Thévoz et al., *Pommern 1934/35*, 2:409.

113. Jan. 15, 1934, letter by Reinhard Lemke to the RMdI, cited in Thévoz et al., *Pommern 1934/35*, 2:410.

114. Secretary of State Pfundtner, RMdI, Jan. 22, 1934 letter to the Prussian Prime Minister, cited in Thévoz et al., *Pommern 1934/35*, 2:411.

115. See United States Court of Restitution Appeals, 697–700, Court of Restitution Appeals (U.S. zone), decision of Nov. 13, 1952.

116. Ibid., 698.

117. See Zürcher, *Kreuzzug*, 91.

118. See Garbe, "'Gott mehr gehorchen als den Menschen,'" 187; 215n106.

119. SLG HH, HSG 11 Js. Sond. 1675/36, Bl. 12, Hamburg Secret State Police office, letter of Aug. 30, 1937.

120. Personal documents of Margot Seidewitz, "Der Reichs- und Preußische Arbeitsminister," letter of Apr. 27, 1938.

121. See Echterhölter, *Recht*, 199.

122. *DV* [*Deutsche Verwaltung*] 18 (1941): 184, Reichsdienststrafhof III D 64.39, decision of July 9, 1940.

123. See *Watchtower*, Sept. 1, 1985, 12.

124. See Echterhölter, *Recht*, 196–97.

125. According to Ernst Fraenkel's analysis in *The Dual State*, a prerogative state and normative state existed side by side in the Third Reich. Consequently, the NS "Dual State" continued to subject certain areas, such as contracts under private law, to the formal judiciousness of law. In these areas (at least during the initial period of NS rule), the state maintained the formal elements of traditional rule of law. At the same time, other social areas, especially those related to the prosecution of opponents of the regime, were removed from its attachment to the normative system and declared to be no longer subject to any legal procedures. In my opinion, Fraenkel's theory explains, at least to a certain extent, the disparate administration of justice in Bible Student proceedings. DR 10 (1940): 516–17, Reich Labor Court, 88/39, decision of Nov. 29, 1939.

126. On Nov. 10, 1934, the Altona Hospital administration dismissed a head nurse because she refused to give the "Hitler salute" (AfW HH, 260488, Bl. 1).

127. In 1935 a thirty-seven-year-old Hamburg office clerk was dismissed from her place of employment (VVN HH, Komiteeakten O 4). See also *Yearbook* 1974, 117.

128. A mailman was dismissed from the post office and denied permission to start his own business of delivering newspapers (VVN HH, Komiteeakten B 30).

129. In 1934 a thirty-two-year-old metalworker was dismissed from his place of employment. According to his own statement, he incurred the disfavor of the official handling his paper work even for the simple fact that he did not greet with "Heil Hitler" upon entering the room (VVN HH, Komiteeakten H 34).

130. See Zürcher, *Kreuzzug*, 91. In Hamburg, a similar case resulted in court proceedings according to the Law against Insidious Attacks on State and a Party and for the Protection of the Party Uniforms, on the charge of "disparagement of the Reich government" (SLG HH, HSG 11 Sond. 1545/34).

131. See Zürcher, *Kreuzzug*, 88.

132. BA, Sammlung Schumacher/267 I, cited in the Feb. 7, 1938, memo of the Regensburg State Police office.

133. The president of the Rhineland employment office, Aug. 8, 1937, letter to the chairman of the Wuppertal employment office, cited in *Duisburg im Nationalsozialismus*, 108.

134. BA Sammlung Schumacher/267 I, Regensburg State Police office, memo of Feb. 7, 1938.

135. RuPrMdI, May 30, 1938, letter to the Düsseldorf district president, cited in *Duisburg im Nationalsozialismus*, 108. The letter of the RFSS was probably written on Apr. 8, 1937; see the respective quotation in BA, Sammlung Schumacher/267 I, Regensburg State Police office, memo of Feb. 7, 1938.

136. RuPrMdI, May 30, 1938, letter to the Düsseldorf district president, cited in *Duisburg im Nationalsozialismus*, 108.

137. *Yearbook* 1974, 212.

138. Ibid. According to the Watch Tower Society's records, "in 30 cases, marriages had been dissolved due to pressure by political officials, and in 108 cases divorces had been granted when requested by mates."

139. *JW* 66 (1937): 1308–9, Rudolstadt Regional Court, 1 R 63/36, decision of Jan. 11, 1937.

140. BA, Sammlung Schumacher/267 I, commentary on a court decision that was received at the Rosenheim NSDAP district office on May 4, 1938.

141. On the changes in the daily school routine as well as external aspects of school education in the course of National Socialist consolidation of power, see Breyvogel and Lohmann, "Schulalltag," 199–21. On the consequences involving the contents of educational subjects, see Flessau, *Schule;* Rossmeissl, *Erziehung.*

142. In the state of Prussia, specific regulations became compulsory on Jan. 20, 1934, based on the "Leitgedanken zur Schulordnung." See *Zentralblatt für die gesamte Unterrichts-Verwaltung in Preussen* 76 (1934): 128.

143. Aug. 11, 1933, instructions by the Hamburg school authorities, cited in Lehberger, "'Umbau' der Hamburger Volksschule," 20.

144. See Lehberger, "'Umbau' der Hamburger Volksschule," 19.

145. See *Zentralblatt für die gesamte Unterrichts-Verwaltung in Preussen* 76 (1934): 128; Jan. 20, 1934, "Leitgedanken zur Schulordnung."

146. On the function of commemorations in the daily routine of school in the Third Reich, see W. Müller, "Sprechchöre, Goebbels-Reden und Flaggenappelle," 34ff.; Rossmeissl, *Erziehung*, 89ff.

147. The report of Helmut Knöller is published in *Yearbook* 1974, 117–18.

148. Jan. 25, 1986, recollections by Karl-Heinz Zietlow.

149. Nov. 23, 1987, recollections by Elise Kühnle.

150. *ZJJ* [*Zentralblatt für Jugendrecht und Jugendwohlfahrt*] 28 (1937): 281.

151. In 1938 the central European office of Jehovah's Witnesses in Switzerland published the book *Kreuzzug gegen das Christentum*. Its documentation includes reports that had been smuggled from Germany to Switzerland, according to which children of Bible Students were mistreated by their teachers because they refused to give the Hitler salute or perform similar acts. See Zürcher, *Kreuzzug*, 159, 162, 164–65, and 167–68.

152. See *Yearbook* 1974, 119–21.

153. Nov. 23, 1987, recollections by Elise Kühnle. The report by Mrs. Kühnle refers to an incident involving her sister. Zürcher describes a case in which fellow students seriously mistreated a child with violent kicks at the teacher's request. Even after a careful search, the father could not find a doctor who was willing to certify the injuries. See Zürcher, *Kreuzzug*, 167–68.

154. See also Günther Pape's report about his school experiences during the NS period, cited in Pape, *Zeuge Jehovas*, 9–12.

155. Willi Seitz wrote his report after his expulsion from school on Jan. 22, 1937, and his move to a neighboring country. See recollections by Willi Seitz; Zürcher, *Kreuzzug*, 164.

156. Magdalena Reuter, "My Family's Love for God Despite Prison and Death," *Watchtower*, Sept. 1, 1985, 10–15 (12).

157. The report about Horst Henschel is published in *Yearbook* 1974, 122–23.

158. Only students with foreign citizenship were exempt from attending such group events. Jewish students were unwelcome. In fact, they were even ordered not to attend (see W. Müller, "Sprechchöre, Goebbels-Reden und Flaggenappelle," 46.) If, on the other hand, children of Jehovah's Witnesses failed to attend these NS school ceremonies, their parents had to pay fines. See *DJ* 99 (1937): 1857, Waldenburg municipal court, 8. 195, decision of Sept. 2, 1937.

159. Klauß, *Feierstunden*, 7.

160. Nov. 23, 1987, recollections by Elise Kühnle.

161. See Garbe, "'Gott mehr gehorchen als den Menschen,'" 192.

162. Knöller, "Erinnerungen," 19.

163. Nov. 23, 1987, recollections by Bruno Knöller.

164. AfW HH, 070319, Bl. 38, June 19, 1946, statement from the *Oberrealschule* in Eilbeck

165. The choice of schools for Jehovah's Witnesses was also limited because they generally refused to send their children to schools that were sponsored by the churches.

166. Reich Ministry for Science, Art, and National Education, decree of Mar. 27, 1935, cited in Benze, *Erziehung*, 13.

167. Knöller, "Erinnerungen," 20.

168. BA, R 58/405, Bl. 3, Secret State Police office, memorandum of Aug. 8, 1934. A copy of this memo is included in the Aug. 13, 1934, interoffice decree of the State Police office for the administrative district of Cologne.

169. IfZ, MA 554, 936279–87 (82), memo, "Die Internationale Bibelforscher-Vereinigung," encl. to the Dec. 24, 1936, interoffice decree of the central State Police office in Munich.

170. BA, R 58/264, Bl. 201, "Weisung des Politischen Polizeikommandeurs der Länder." A copy of this order is included in the Mar. 21, 1936, interoffice decree of the BPP.

171. See Garbe, "'Gott mehr gehorchen als den Menschen,'" 202–3; VVN HH, Komiteeakten L 2 and M 8; Nov. 23, 1987, recollections by Bruno Knöller. The children of arrested Jehovah's Witnesses were housed with other Jehovah's Witnesses, which emphasizes the close relationships within the Bible Student community. Even under difficult circumstances, they tried to be of assistance. For instance, in addition to her own two children, a farmer in Gruibingen (the Swabian Mountains), whose husband had been executed for his refusal to perform military service, took in the three children of a fellow believer from Augsburg, whose husband had been executed for the same reason (Nov. 23, 1987, recollections by Elise Kühnle).

172. An expression borrowed from Michael H. Kater. See Kater, "Bibelforscher," 200. Even Jehovah's Witnesses used the term "child robbery" during the National Socialist period. See Zürcher, *Kreuzzug*, 154; *ZJJ* 28 (1936/37): 281, Hamburg Regional Court, 1. T 284/36, decision of June 5, 1936.

173. Saxony Ministry for Cultural Affairs, Nov. 13, 1936, interoffice decree to the school authorities of the various districts regarding "children from Bible Student groups." Cited in Zürcher, *Kreuzzug*, 157.

174. See July 9, 1922, Reich Law Regarding Youth Welfare Services, *RGBl.* 1922 I, 633–48 (articles 56–61 include the instructions regarding "protective supervision"). On the legal conditions of youth welfare services during the NS period, see Hasenclever, *Jugendhilfe*, 127ff.; Kraus, "Fürsorgeerziehung," 161ff.

175. In addition to government officials, such protective supervision was also carried out by members of the NS Women's Association and the NSV. They carried out unannounced visits on a weekly basis and, if there were any grounds for suspicion, the police conducted official house searches. Because of their direct access to the individual families of "Volksgenossen" (national comrades) the

National Socialists used the NSV for "surveillance purposes," i.e., the NSV became an organization of informers. See *Ermittlungshilfe*, 19ff.

176. See Otto and Sünker, *Soziale Arbeit*.

177. According to the RJWG, art. 60, para. 3, the youth welfare offices were allowed to perform so-called unofficial protective supervision without obtaining a court order. This, however, required the approval of the legal guardians.

178. More detailed excerpts of the decision are published in *HRGZ* 19 (1936): cols. 353–54, as well as *ZJJ* 28 (1937): 281–82. The versions are not completely identical in wording.

179. *ZJJ* 28 (1936/37): 281, Hamburg Regional Court, 1. T 284/36, decision of June 5, 1936 (the statement, which emphasizes the important role played by the representative of the Hamburg youth welfare office, is not included in the *Hanseatische Rechts- und Gerichts-Zeitschrift* [*HZ*]). According to Zürcher's explanations, which most certainly apply to this case, the principal at the orphanage beat the boys with a club. See Zürcher, *Kreuzzug*, 162.

180. Cited in *HRGZ* 19 (1936): col. 353. In Oct. 1935 the HSG sentenced both parents to two months of imprisonment because of their involvement in prohibited IBSA activities.

181. *ZJJ* 28 (1936/37): 281.

182. *HRGZ* 19 (1936): col. 353.

183. VVN HH, Komiteeakten S 37, Hamburg Municipal Court, 116 VIII S 86.

184. Ibid., decision of Mar. 12, 1937.

185. According to the mother, the assessment is included in the court decision because of the objection raised by the representative of the youth welfare office. During an entire year (within the context of the imposed protective supervision), the official had to examine whether the mother had a subversive influence on her children and so was quite familiar with the family situation. During the court proceedings, this official specifically asked the judge to include in his decision that the mother was a morally upright person. At first, the judge refused to follow this request because it would have required him to pronounce an "ignominious judgment." But the representative of the youth welfare office insisted that this statement should be included because he did "not want to take responsibility for the removal of the children" (Jan. 29, 1985, and Feb. 14, 1986, recollections by Ella S). It cannot be ignored that in her memory, Ella S. idealizes the picture of the youth welfare office official. However, since the wording of the 1937 court decision is available, her report is certainly trustworthy.

186. VVN HH, Komiteeakten S 37, Hamburg municipal court, decision of Mar. 12, 1937. After the custody withdrawal, the ten- and eleven-year-old sons were placed in custody of various NS families. Toward the end of the war, they

did their military service and even became prisoners of war. The imposed separation from their mother lasted almost ten years.

187. Cited in Zürcher, *Kreuzzug*, 155. Franz Zürcher's book was published in German and French by Europa-Verlag in 1938. Zürcher, one of the leading officials at the central European office of Jehovah's Witnesses in Bern, generally refrained from mentioning names and places so as not to increase the danger of the people concerned in Germany. Therefore, it is not possible to name the municipal court that made that decision.

188. Cited in Zürcher, *Kreuzzug*, 160–61.

189. Personal documents of Straßer ("Sammlung zur historischen Dokumentation"), June 21, 1937, interoffice decree by the Gestapa. A copy of this decree is included in the July 6, 1937, interoffice decree by the local State Police office in Stuttgart.

190. IfZ, MA 554, 936263, central State Police office in Munich, interoffice decree of July 2, 1937.

191. Personal documents of Straßer ("Sammlung zur historischen Dokumentation"), central State Police office in Stuttgart, interoffice decree of July 6, 1937.

192. Kiel State Police office, decree of July 14, 1937. A copy of this decree is included in the July 16, 1937, interoffice decree that the Schleswig district administrator sent to the local police offices. Cited in Kühl, "Friedrichstadt," 185.

193. Municipal police in Eutin, letter of July 30, 1937, cited in Stokes, *Eutin*, 710.

194. In the following years, corrective training was generally ordered along with custody withdrawal. However, protective supervision for Jehovah's Witnesses was ordered only in a few cases.

195. *JW* 67 (1938): 2145, Zwickau Regional Court, 5 T 179/37, decision of Apr. 14, 1937.

196. See Fraenkel, *Dual State*, 56.

197. Dec. 1, 1936, Hitler Youth Law, *RGBl.* 1936 I, 993.

198. See Stachura, "Jugenderziehung," 233. The second DVO to the Hitler Youth Law issued on Mar. 25, 1939 states in article 1: "It is an honor to serve the German people in the Hitler Youth. All youths between ten and eighteen years of age are required to serve in the Hitler Youth" (*RGBl.* 1939 I, 710).

199. According to the absolute numbers mentioned by Klönne, *Jugend*, 34, of the 8.87 million ten- to eighteen-year-olds, a total of 8.7 million were enrolled in the Hitler Youth at the beginning of 1939.

200. According to BGB, article 1626, and article 1631, paragraph 1, child education was a right reserved principally for parents. In the Third Reich, however, the guardianship courts continued to violate this right by placing the state's claim to child education above the parents' right to child education.

201. See Klönne, *Jugend*, 50.

202. Benze, *Erziehung*, 15; on the NS "state-controlled education" [Erziehungsstaat] and its objectives, see U. Herrmann, *Formung des Volksgenossen.*

203. *JW* 67 (1938): 1264, Wilster Municipal Court, VIII B 229/38, decision of Feb. 26, 1938.

204. At the time of the court proceedings, both parents were in prison on the charge of involvement in IBSA activities. On May 5, 1938, the mother was released from prison. On Feb. 24, 1940, the father died in the Sachsenhausen concentration camp. See VVN HH, Komiteeakten B 28; Möller, "Steinburg," 217.

205. Nov. 23, 1987, recollections by Bruno Knöller; Apr. 30, 1983, recollections by Egon Knöller.

206. This regulation, which was subsequently added into the Youth Welfare Law, in the context of an amendment of article 63, in 1936, states that corrective training could not be ordered "if there is no potential for success." This amendment of article 63 was made in the context of the Nov. 4, 1932, Reich president's decree regarding youth welfare services (*RGBl.* 1932 I, 522–23). This amendment to the law was closely related to the policy of economic measures of the Reich government: it had no educational objectives but was made for economic reasons.

207. Cited in Zürcher, *Kreuzzug*, 161; this judgment was made in the second half of 1937.

208. Nov. 23, 1987, recollections by Elise Kühnle.

209. Zürcher, *Kreuzzug*, 154.

210. *DJ* 100 (1938): 954–55, Munich Higher Regional Court, 8 WX 478/37, decision of Dec. 3, 1937.

211. Ibid., 955.

212. Extensive excerpts of the judgment are included in the journals *Deutsche Justiz, Höchstrichterliche Rechtsprechung,* and *Ministerialblatt des RMdI,* which were published by the RJM as *Amtliches Blatt der deutschen Rechtspflege.* See *DJ* 100 (1938): 954–55; *HRR* 14 (1938): 545; *RMBliV* [*Ministerialblatt des Reichs- und Preußischen Ministeriums des Innern*] 99 (1938): cols. 317–20.

213. *Kriminalistik* 12 (1938): 68.

214. IfZ, MA 603, 20198; significantly, the statement of the RMdI is titled "No permission for 'Earnest Bible Students' to educate children."

215. The children were picked up by police officers and two deaconesses from Stuttgart. This caused quite a stir in the town. Elise Kühnle reports: "All of a sudden, a car pulled up in front of the school in Alfdorf. . . . We fought not to be pulled into this car. And there were tears and struggling until they finally overpowered us. Naturally, they were stronger. Even the police and the teachers helped to push us into the car" (Nov. 23, 1987, recollections by Elise Kühnle). The following descriptions are also based on Kühnle's recollections.

216. The father's arrest took place in the late autumn of 1938. The Gestapo sent him to the Welzheim concentration camp. In Jan. 1951 he died as a

result of his imprisonment. Dire experiences were reported in other accounts about Jehovah's Witnesses who were sent as children to reformatories. A female Jehovah's Witness who was sent to the Wessenberg reformatory in Konstanz in July 1943 remembers "the icy and harsh atmosphere in the reform school" (*Watchtower*, Oct. 1, 1978, 20–21).

217. These three sentences are the complete wording of a guardianship court decision. See personal documents of Straßer ("Sammlung zur historischen Dokumentation"), Leipzig municipal court, 18 X Gro 7/38, decision of Apr. 14, 1938.

218. *ZJJ* 27 (1935/36): 232, Berlin-Lichterfelde Municipal Court, 6 X 126, decision of Apr. 15, 1935.

219. *ZJJ* 28 (1936/37): 139–40, Torgau Regional Court, 6 T 527/35, decision of Nov. 27, 1935.

220. DR 7 (1937): 466, Frankfurt/Main-Höchst Municipal Court, decision of May 4, 1937.

221. See *Watchtower*, Feb. 1, 1976, 82; *Yearbook* 1974, 125. The *Yearbook* also emphasizes that "the exact number may be quite a bit higher." On the methods used by the Watch Tower Society to collect information, the circumstances of the investigation, and the inevitably resulting incorrect numbers, see this book, p. 734, n.11.

222. VVN HH, Komiteeakten B 10, Apr. 23, 1946, recollections by B. According to the court records (SLG HH, HSG 44/38), the father of the girl did not compromise despite the fact that he was prohibited from practicing his profession and was punished with imprisonment for many years.

223. VVN HH, Komiteeakten Z 4; AfW HH, 310300.

224. Cited in Philipsen, "Für den Glauben in den Tod," 41.

225. The mayor of Süderbrarup, letter of June 30, 1941, cited in Burmeister et al., "Verfolgung der Zeugen Jehovas in Kiel," 50. On June 18, 1941, the Kappeln Municipal Court ordered temporary corrective training.

226. The recollections by Marie Appel are published in *Yearbook* 1974, 186–90 (188), under the title "Parents and Children Put Jehovah First." On the persecution of the Appel family, see Philipsen's essay, "Für den Glauben in den Tod"; and Imberger, *Widerstand*, 370–73.

227. See "Ehrenbuch Brandenburg-Görden," 2:52; Oct. 15, 1941, statement of the Oberrreichskriegsanwalt (senior Reich military attorney), St.P.L. (RKA) I 175/41, cited in Burmeister et al., "Verfolgung der Zeugen Jehovas in Kiel," 49. In 1944 the oldest son of the Appel family was also executed (see this book, pp. 676–77, n.177).

228. BA, R 22/4002, Bl. 12, *Richterbriefe*, Dec. 1, 1942, Mitteilungen des RJM, Nr. 3, case no. 14 (recorded in *Richterbriefe*, 48–51). If not otherwise indicated, the following descriptions are based on this source.

229. In his Apr. 26, 1942, speech before the Reichstag, Hitler threatened to remove from office any "judges who obviously do not recognize the present

requirements." This speech is cited in *Völkischer Beobachter* of Apr. 27, 1942. It is also cited in Staff, *Justiz*, 95–99.

230. Oct. 1, 1942, statements by Thierack on the occasion of introducing the *Richterbriefe*, cited in Staff, *Justiz*, 68.

231. On the question of selecting the court decisions to be denounced in the *Richterbriefe*, Thierack states: "These *Richterbriefe* will especially include court decisions that I consider noteworthy, particularly with regard to their results or the reasons given for the judgment. By means of these decisions, I want to demonstrate how a better decision could have been made and, actually, should have been made" (Staff, *Justiz*, 68).

232. See *Richterbriefe*, 49. This case probably involves Margot M. Oberhausen, born in 1931. In 1942 custody was withdrawn from her parents, and she was sent to a reformatory. She was also not allowed to have "a proper apprenticeship." Her fate is briefly mentioned in Stern, *Wir "Hoch- und Landesverräter,"* 291.

233. However, in Weinkauff, *Justiz*, 165, we read: "In *Richterbrief,* no. 3 custody withdrawal was requested (and finally achieved)." The wording of former BGH president Hermann Weinkauff suggests that custody withdrawals came about only as a result of the ministerial intervention. In reality, the Appellate Court had revoked the decision of the previous court even before this case was included in the *Richterbriefe*. Such "apportioning of blame" reflects the general tendency of this standard work, which tried to move responsibility for the corruption of administration of justice during the NS period to the "brutal terrorization methods" of the "Thierack regime" (ibid., 164). In this way, the publication sought to minimize the extent to which the generally conservative national judges contributed to the legal degradation in the National Socialist state. See *Der Unrechts-Staat*, 123ff.

234. *DJ* 100 (1938): 829–30; RG, 5 D 599/37, decision of Feb. 17, 1938.

235. Ibid., 830, Herbert Klemm, comments on the court decision.

236. In some recollections, it is mentioned that parents were legally punished on the charge of child education (see Zürcher, *Kreuzzug*, 167). This perception could be based on the reproach to which these Jehovah's Witnesses were exposed during interrogations or court proceedings. This perception is incorrect because there was no special regulation that put child education contrary to NS ideology under threat of punishment. Nevertheless, in numerous court proceedings, anti-state child education aggravated the accusations and could therefore increase the penalty. Sometimes, the Gestapo took Jehovah's Witnesses, whose children attracted attention at school because of their refusal to give the Hitler salute or because of similar offenses, into protective detention.

237. *DJ* 101 (1939): 182, RMdI, interoffice decree of Dec. 27, 1938. With reference to the Apr. 17, 1939, Gestapa decree, the Düsseldorf State Police office stated, in its Apr. 30, 1939, decree, that the group of "politically unreliable families" also included the Bible Students (cited in Kater, "Bibelforscher," 201).

238. The first confrontation with NS educational requirements took place when children started school. Children of preschool age were usually protected from outside influences by their parents. Problems began when, as first graders, they followed the instructions of their parents and refused to give the Hitler salute. In these cases, the school authorities immediately insisted on custody withdrawal. For instance, in a case involving three seven- and eight-year-old children, the Besigheim Municipal Court quickly ordered temporary corrective training merely five days after the district schools inspector had submitted a request in this regard. See personal documents of Rolf Zehender, Besigheim Municipal Court, GR. 43–45/40, decision of Feb. 5, 1940; Hildebrandt and Hoffmann, *Streiflichter*, 43–45.

239. Hans Neumann, "I Grew Up In Nazi Germany," cited in *Awake*, May 22, 1983, 23–27 (23).

240. Some of the children in the reformatories who persistently refused to give the Hitler salute were severely abused. For instance, Zürcher reports about a boy who escaped from a reformatory because he was repeatedly beaten (Zürcher, *Kreuzzug*, 158). However, the youths in the reformatories were protected from one particular problem: they were not forced to join the Hitler Youth. According to the law, a youth was considered to be "unworthy" of joining the Hitler Youth as long as he was held in custody (second DVO to the Hitler Youth Law, article 3, paragraph 2, *RGBl.* 1939 I, 710).

241. This statement was made by the sister of the boy during an interview on Jan. 21, 1983, cited in Burmeister et al., "Verfolgung der Zeugen Jehovas in Kiel," 40. According to her statement, the "foster father" reported her brother (Walter Appel) to the police because he openly spoke his mind and expressed his abhorrence for the NS regime. On the further fate of Walter Appel, who was executed in Oct. 1944 for his refusal to perform labor service, see the description in Garbe, "'Gott mehr gehorchen als den Menschen,'" 210. StA HH, Jugendbehörde I, 343b, office in Walddörfer (Hamburg-Volksdorf), department for youth training, Mar. 31, 1944.

242. See Burmeister et al., "Verfolgung der Zeugen Jehovas in Kiel," 38.

243. *Yearbook* 1974, 122.

244. Personal documents of Zehender, head of the Württembergischer Landesfürsorgeverband (youth welfare offices for corrective training), decision of Dec. 12, 1942.

245. In this way, the authorities wanted to prevent parents who strongly resisted the orders of corrective training from trying to hide their children, for instance, by sending them abroad to fellow believers. A letter written to the Gestapo in Detmold in July 1939 mentions a different reason. Even though the NSV district administration had already made the necessary arrangements for accommodation, the mother was not supposed to be informed because the authorities feared that the Bible Student "would commit suicide with her children if she learned about these arrangements" (cited in Hopster and Moll, *Lage*, 37).

246. See VVN HH, Komiteeakten A 11.

247. Report of Elisabeth Reuter, *Watchtower,* Sept. 1, 1985, 12.

248. See *Yearbook* 1974, 120; *Watchtower,* Oct. 1, 1978, 23; *Watchtower,* Sept. 1, 1985, 12.

249. See recollections by Willi Seitz; Zürcher, *Kreuzzug,* 163–64. There, the report is cited under the title "Flucht ins Ausland als einziger Ausweg."

250. See *Yearbook* 1974, 122.

251. On the determining factors for corrective training during the NS period, see Lampert, "Sozialpolitik," 198. Accordingly, the youth welfare offices placed children "with a potential to be reformed" into NSV youth homes, the "partially reformable" into reformatories, and the "incorrigible ones" into concentration camps for the youth.

252. *RMBliV* 6 (1941): 1773, RMdI, interoffice decree of Oct. 3, 1941, regarding admission into the Moringen youth concentration camp. This camp for male minors between sixteen and twenty-one years of age had been established during the previous year in the small town of Moringen, in the south of Lower Saxony.

253. There is evidence that a small number of Bible Students were imprisoned in the Moringen youth concentration camp. See Guse and Kohrs, "'Bewahrung' Jugendlicher," 145, 310–11. Concerning the results of this thesis, which is available only in typewritten form, see Guse et al., "Das Jugendschutzlager Moringen"; Guse and Kohrs, "Entpädagogisierung." On the history of the Uckermark concentration camp for female minors, see Hepp, "'Jugendschutzlager' Uckermark." It is not known whether children of Jehovah's Witnesses were imprisoned in this concentration camp.

254. The Volpriehausen army ammunition factory was located approximately sixteen miles (twenty-five kilometers) away from the concentration camp. There, the prisoners of the Moringen youth concentration camp had to mount ignition switches on grenades in an abandoned mine.

255. Cited in Guse and Kohrs, "'Bewahrung' Jugendlicher," 310.

256. Cited in ibid., 311. Another publication makes the statement that, in the Volpriehausen army ammunition factory, a Jehovah's Witness was "beaten to death" because he refused to participate in the production of military equipment for the war. See *Heimatgeschichtlicher Wegweiser, Niedersachsen I,* 38. Based on the available reports, it is not possible to determine whether this statement refers to the above-mentioned case.

257. In its Nov. 28, 1942, decree, the RSHA determined that the age for youths to be sent to Litzmannstadt (Lodz) concentration camp for youth in Poland should be between eight and sixteen years (BA, R 22/1191). Roman Hrabar indicates that, in reality, children younger than eight were sent to this concentration camp. See Hrabar, "Osadzanie," 53.

258. "Der Landrat des Kreises Teschen," letter of July 13, 1943, Hrabar, "Osadzanie," 60.

259. Because of a permanent lack of supplies and countless abuses, there was an extremely high mortality rate in Litzmannstadt (Lodz). See Hepp, "'Polenverwahrlager Litzmannstadt.'"

260. The Sept. 15, 1935, decree regarding children's allowance for large families (*RGBl.* 1935 I, 1160) initially provided for only a one-time payment. The decree regarding children's allowance issued on Dec. 9, 1940, provided for a continuous monthly payment (*RGBl.* 1940 I, 1571–72). Generally, this children's allowance was granted to families with at least three children. See also Lampert, "Sozialpolitik," 195–96.

261. Reichssteuerblatt 31 (1941): 105, Reich minister of financial affairs, interoffice decree of Jan. 30, 1941. According to the guidelines issued three months later, the objective of this children's allowance was "a policy to support the strength of the German nation. The decision of granting or refusing children's allowance" was therefore not based on any intentions of "providing charitable assistance and social welfare" (ibid., 313).

262. Ibid., 313, guidelines for the purpose of objecting to the granting of children's allowance. These guidelines were issued by the Reich minister of finance, the RMdI, and the representative of the Führer (for the NSDAP).

263. VVN HH, Komiteeakten G 21, Aug. 8, 1946, statement of Helmut H.

264. If the authorities refused to grant the legal children's allowance, the people concerned could only request an examination of this decision by submitting a "petition" or a "complaint." The Sept. 28, 1939, decree by the "Führer and Reich chancellor" (*RGBl.* 1939 I, 1535) restricted the possibility of instituting administrative court proceedings to only a few cases that do not belong to the subject under discussion. Consequently, the people concerned were able to file only an administrative complaint.

265. StA HH Senatskanzlei-Präsidialabteilung, 1942 S III/1706, "Der Reichsstatthalter in Hamburg, Einspruchsstelle," Nov. 11, 1942, letter to the chief of police.

266. Ibid., central State Police office in Hamburg, letter of Dec. 19, 1942 (the author changed the initials in the letter). During 1935 both parents spent several months in concentration camps. The father was imprisoned in Esterwegen and the mother in Fuhlsbüttel. In 1937 the mother lost custody of her oldest child. See VVN HH Komiteeakten; AfW HH, 160299.

267. StA HH, Senatskanzlei-Präsidialabteilung, 1942 S III/1706, "Der Reichsstatthalter in Hamburg, Einspruchsstelle," Jan. 6, 1943, letter to the leader of the NSDAP district Hamburg 1.

268. Ibid., "Der Kreisleiter des NSDAP-Kreises Hamburg 1," letter of Feb. 19, 1943.

269. StA HH, Senatskanzlei-Präsisialabteilung, 1942 S III/1706, Reich governor, decision of Mar. 10, 1943.

270. Ibid., Reich governor of Hamburg, office responsible for dealing with complaints, Mar. 8, 1943, letter to the central State Police office in Hamburg.

Part 4. Self-Assertion of Jehovah's Witnesses until 1939

1. At first, the police authorities knew nothing about this religious denomination. At the beginning of 1935, in order to increase their knowledge, the Lübeck State Police office requested an IBSA district overseer who was imprisoned there to provide some explanations about the "teachings and [religious] rites" of the Bible Students (SLG HH, HSG 11 Js. Sond. 1617/34, vol. 3, Bl. 345, Lübeck State Police office, Feb. 4, 1935, letter to the Hamburg police authorities; the explanations, ibid., Bl. 348ff.).

2. See *Yearbook* 1935 [German edition], 86; EZA, 1/C3 No. 309, Kurt G., Oct. 16, 1934, memo to the Reich chancellor. One week later, the Gestapo realized (probably because of the resolutions of protest they had received in the meantime) that they had dealt with a "prohibited meeting" of the IBSA. The list of names they had been able to obtain enabled the Gestapo subsequently to arrest the people who had attended this meeting.

3. SLG HH, HSG 11 Js. Sond. 1617/34, vol. 1, Bl. I, police headquarters of Dresden, letter of Oct. 23, 1934.

4. SLG HH, HSG 11 Js. Sond. 1617/34, vol. 1, enclosure to Bl. 12a.

5. See the statements included in SLG HH, HSG 11 Js. Sond. 1617/34. See also the statements included in the subsequent proceedings: 1617/34a–34/35.

6. SLG HH, HSG 11 Js. Sond. 1617/34, vol. 2, Bl. 212, Feb. 7, 1935, remarks of the State Police.

7. Personal documents of Rolf Schwarz, Altona State Police office for the administrative district of Schleswig, interoffice decree of Oct. 24, 1934. On Oct. 27, 1934, the Rendsburg district administrator sent a copy of this interoffice decree to the local police authorities.

8. Rolf Schwarz, interoffice decree of Jan. 12, 1935. On Jan. 17, 1935, the Rendsburg district administrator sent a copy of this interoffice decree to the local police authorities.

9. See BA, R 43 II/179, Bl. 268–72, Hans Dollinger, memo of Jan. 5, 1935.

10. Lichtenegger ("Die Bibelforscher im Widerstand gegen das NS-Regime," 182) and Pingel (*Häftlinge*, 88) make the assumption that there was a direct connection between the introduction of compulsory military service and the increasing number of arrests or admissions of Bible Students into concentration camps. However, this does not exactly correspond with the facts. This increasing number of protective detentions imposed on Jehovah's Witnesses by the Gestapo can be attributed to the fact that in accordance with the resolution at the Basel general assembly, Jehovah's Witnesses completely resumed their preaching activity in Oct. 1934, despite the ban. Even though the Mar. 16, 1935, restoration of military sovereignty of the German Reich presented further challenges for conscientious objectors, it did not have a direct influence on the seriousness of the controversy, at least not at that point.

11. See *Yearbook* 1974, 141.

12. Doyon, *Hirten*, 230.

13. In the NS press, respective requests were made and informers were commended for their "exemplary behavior": "Fortunately, this perceptive national comrade had the boldness to report the false preacher [to the authorities] so that he could be immediately arrested" (*VB*, July 25, 1936).

14. SLG HH, HSG 11 Js. Sond. 1617/34, vol. 1, Bl. 10, Hamburg police authorities, police station 58, report of Dec. 5, 1934.

15. SLG HH, HSG 11 Js. Sond. 298/38, Gestapo 2 B 1, 2052/37, Hamburg State Police office, July 23, 1937, records of interrogation.

16. Quite frequently the literature also includes statements that Jehovah's Witnesses were not sent to the concentration camps until 1936/37. For example, Dieter Kolbe makes the inaccurate assumption that, until the nationwide actions against criminals and so-called asocials in 1937, protective detention was imposed only on political opponents. In this regard, Kolbe further compounded his error by adding "besides homosexuals and alcoholics, the 'asocials' particularly included members of the 'International Bible Students'" (Kolbe, *Bumke*, 281). During the summer of 1935, in the Sachsenburg and Esterwegen concentration camps, there were supposedly about 400 and 120 Jehovah's Witnesses, respectively, under the control of the SS (see *Awake!*, Nov. 22, 1992, 18; Zürcher, *Kreuzzug*, 150–51). In Jan. 1935 the first Bible Students were sent to the Moringen concentration camp for women. Soon, they made up 22 percent of the prisoners and represented, after the Communists, the second largest group of prisoners. By the end of 1937 more than three hundred Bible Students were imprisoned there (statement of the KZ Gedenkstätte Moringen). During 1935/36 the majority of Jehovah's Witnesses were generally still released from concentration camp imprisonment after several months.

17. See this book, pt. 4, ch. 11, pp. 224–25. On Nov. 29, 1934, because of their defiance of the IBSA ban, the Schöffengericht 3 in Dortmund sentenced one male Jehovah's Witness to two years, one female Jehovah's Witness to one year, and another female Jehovah's Witness to nine months of imprisonment (cited in LA SH, Abt. 352 Altona no. 8869). According to the records of Legal Counsel Dollinger, this was the maximum penalty imposed on the Bible Students during that period (see BA, R 43 II/179, Bl. 271).

18. EZA, 7/Generalia 12 No. 161, no page numbers, press release of Nov. 4, 1935.

19. SLG HH, HSG 11 Js. Sond. 100/37, no page numbers; *Bibelstudien*, substitute publication for the *Watchtower*, undated [Nov. 1934], reprint of the article "Zulassung der Christenvervolgung," published in *Der Wachtturm*, Oct. 15, 1934 [*Watchtower*, Nov. 1, 1934].

20. See *Yearbook* 1935, 116.

21. Personal documents of Rolf Schwarz, duplication of *Der Wachtturm* (titled "Verräter," probably 1935).

22. Zürcher, *Kreuzzug*, 31. The attitude at headquarters of the Watch Tower Society unquestionably increased the confrontation. Therefore, some authors consider this to show that the Brooklyn leaders deliberately exposed Jehovah's Witnesses in Germany to this persecution to advance their own interests. On the one hand, Dietrich Hellmund makes the restricting statement that "there is some quite significant evidence" that, in his opinion, indicates "that the psychologically very inappropriate and unrealistic direction of the Brooklyn leaders forced many a Jehovah's Witness unnecessarily into martyrdom" (Hellmund, "Zeugen Jehovas," pt. 4, ch. 2, n.535). Rolf Nobel, on the other hand, assumes that the Brooklyn leaders pursued a deliberate strategy: their actions supposedly were based on "definite, even murderous, calculations." According to his opinion, only "one word of the sectarian leadership" would have been able "to prevent the bloodbath. But they remained silent. As a result, 2,000 members of this sect died in the concentration camps, useful martyrs for the 'divine channel' in the security of far away New York, martyrs that provided 'evidence of the uncompromising attitude of Jehovah's Witnesses'" (Nobel, *Falschspieler Gottes*, 192–93). Perhaps it is still possible to debate whether the Brooklyn leaders sought a confrontation to be able to interpret the beginning persecution as a fulfillment of their predictions. At the same time, one cannot ignore the fact that as early as 1933, during the period in which the IBSA leaders were still relying on a course of negotiations, the leaders of the local IBSA groups, that is, at the base, often pleaded with their fellow believers to show more determination and decisiveness. The wholehearted resistance and martyrdom of many Jehovah's Witnesses, even in later years, did not require any instructions from Brooklyn. Rather, the maxims were already so strongly internalized that it was their faith that moved the Bible Students to action.

23. Knöller, "Erinnerungen," 18, 22.

24. See Möller, "Steinburg," 209.

25. BA, R 58/1128, Bl. 375, Kiel State Police office for the administrative district of Schleswig. Mar. 5, 1935, general survey of the political situation in Feb. 1935.

26. See BA, R 58/1074, Bl. 28.

27. BA, Sammlung Schumacher/267 I, BPP, interoffice decree of Apr. 8, 1935.

28. See Imberger, *Widerstand*, 278–79.

29. See *Yearbook* 1974, 143.

30. Hannover State Police office, May 4, 1935, situation report for Apr. 1935, *Gestapo Hannover*, 358.

31. GStAPrK, Rep. 90 P/80, Kiel State Police office for the administrative district of Schleswig, general survey of the political situation in Apr. 1935. During the following month, the Kiel State Police office reported that a total of sixty-nine people "had been reported to the police" in Flensburg, Glücksburg, Schleswig, and the surrounding areas (BA, R 58/480, Bl. 53).

32. Balzereit was officially dismissed from office by means of an article titled "Diener," published in *Der Wachtturm* in 1936. See also this book, pt. 2, ch. 5, pp. 117–18.

33. See Gebhard, *Zeugen Jehovas*, 140–41; Hetzer, "Augsburg," 627.

34. The service or activity reports indicate the number of Kingdom proclaimers and the number of hours these Kingdom proclaimers spent in their preaching activity during a certain period of time. They also include the number of distributed Bibles, books, and booklets. Winkler compiled these reports into one general report and submitted it to Harbeck. This practice of compiling reports was not a new arrangement as the Gestapo assumed (see, for instance, SLG HH, SH SG 11 Son KMs 149/36, Bl. 1). It represented the continuance of a practice that is common among Jehovah's Witnesses.

35. See *Yearbook* 1974, 151–52; John, *Wewelsburg* (1996), 147; M. Koch, "Die kleinen Glaubensgemeinschaften," 421.

36. IfZ, MA 554, 936279–87 (85), memo, "Die Internationale Bibelforscher-Vereinigung," encl. to the Dec. 24, 1936, interoffice decree of the central State Police office in Munich. Two weeks earlier, in its Dec. 12, 1936, interoffice decree, the Gestapa had sent this decree, which did not mention the names of the writers, to the regional State Police offices. Most likely, it was written by employees of Department 2 B 1 of the Secret State Police office responsible for IBSA affairs (see the "concise collection of decrees regarding sectarian affairs" at the RSHA. In this collection, the Dec. 12, 1936, interoffice decree by the Gestapa is listed under reference no. 16/IBV, BA, R 58/1074, Bl. 29. The Gestapa decree itself is not available).

37. Elke Fröhlich reports that in Bavaria the State Police offices discontinued the practice of filing separate petitions for Jehovah's Witnesses as well as former prisoners, for reasons of work relief. Instead, they proceeded to file collective petitions and carry out group-related mail surveillance. (Previously, the State Police offices were required to file a separate petition at the regional district office for every person under surveillance.) The other German states probably proceeded in a similar way. See Fröhlich, *Herausforderung*, 138–39.

38. See Kühl, "Friedrichstadt," 175; *Yearbook* 1986, 150; June 5, 1984, recollections by Heinrich Markert.

39. Cited in Kühl, "Friedrichstadt," 175.

40. See BA, R 43 II/179, Bl. 263; SLG HH, HSG 11 Js. Sond. 1617/34, vol. 1, Bl. 1–2, Dresden police headquarters, letter of Oct. 23, 1934.

41. The description is based on a report by Ernst Wiesner, published in *Yearbook* 1974, 141–42; recollections by Johannes Rauthe, "Geschichtsbericht," 39; and the May 31, 1986, recollections by Richard Rudolph. See also the Apr. 2, 1937, Gestapo records, cited in Gebhard, *Zeugen Jehovas*, 178. These records mention that, during an unspecified period of time, a total of 40,000 books and booklets of the IBSA were smuggled from Czechoslovakia into Germany.

42. *Yearbook* 1987, 142.

43. See Hetzer, "Augsburg," 629; StA M, Staatsanwaltschaften 8551, Munich Special Court 16 KMs So 45–47, 37 (37), vol. 1; June 6, 1984, recollections by B. Maurer.

44. See Imberger, *Widerstand*, 320–21; *Yearbook* 1974, 139–40; Möller, "Steinburg," 212; BDC, VGH, 8 J 20/38, Bl. 22–33, Hamburg State Police office, report of Dec. 21, 1937.

45. See Marßolek and Ott, *Bremen*, 305–6; SLG HH, HSG 11 Js. Sond. 399/37.

46. See SLG HH, HSG 11 Js. Sond. 298/38, Gestapo 2 B 1, 2052/37.

47. Gebhard, *Zeugen Jehovas*, 175; *Yearbook* 1974, 113; M. Koch, "Die kleinen Glaubensgemeinschaften," 424.

48. See SLG HH, SH SG 11 Son KMs 149/36, Bl. 1, Kiel State Police office, file remarks of Sept. 2, 1936.

49. See Garbe, "Kompromißlose Bekennerinnen," 61ff.; Wickert, "Frauen," 214ff.

50. See *Yearbook* 1968 [German edition], 17.

51. See SLG HH, SH SG 11 Son KMs 149/36, Bl. 25.

52. See the description about Georg Klohe, cited in John, *Wewelsburg* (1996), 145; see also recollections by Addi Klohe, who supported his father in producing the records.

53. BA, R 58/405, Bl. 58, Reich minister of financial affairs, memo of Nov. 4, 1936.

54. See SLG HH, SG 11 Son KMs 149/36, Bl. 11. The Aug. 1936 *Deutschland Berichte* includes a remark according to which "quite a number" of Bible Students, who had conducted their religious services on a large sailboat on Lake Constance, had been betrayed and were arrested. See *Deutschland Berichte* 3 (1936): 1049.

55. See also Wickert, "Frauen," 202. At times, people of different ideological backgrounds also joined Jehovah's Witnesses. In Oct. 1934 in Holzgerlingen, a village near Stuttgart, a "Nazi Zealot," who used to wear the golden party badge, and an SA-Scharführer (platoon leader) resigned from the NSDAP to perform a "service for the truth." See Willi Wanner, "From Nazi Zealot to Christian Overseer," published in *Awake!*, Apr. 22, 1986, 13–16.

56. See Fahle, *Verweigern*, 156.

57. VVN HH, Komiteeakten P 4, Jan. 20, 1947, biography of Walter.

58. AfW HH, K 250702, Bl. 83, July 17, 1964, report of the widow.

59. Statement by Frieda Christiansen, regional service director of Schleswig-Holstein, according to the Sept. 20, 1937, interrogation records. Cited in Imberger, *Widerstand*, 329.

60. *Deutschland Berichte* 3 (1936): 922–23. The Prague editorial office, in particular, received reports about IBSA activities in Saxony. These reports especially mention the uncompromising attitude of the Bible Students that neither the persecution by the Gestapo nor the large number of court cases were able

to change. The description of the methods that the IBSA used in their under-ground activities reflects great respect and high regard for their logistical skills.

61. See this book, pt. 6, ch. 18, p. 493.

62. In 1938 Ernst Fraenkel, a legal counsel of the German Association of Metal Workers, emigrated to the United States. Three years later, in his work *The Dual State*, Fraenkel makes the statement that "the sectarian movement of Jehovah's Witnesses experienced such an astonishing growth during the last seven years" (117). This statement demonstrates how the extensive and, in view of the circumstances of that period, especially obvious advertising activity of Jehovah's Witnesses could cause people to draw incorrect conclusions regard-ing their actual effectiveness.

63. BA, R 58/233, Bl. 20, RFSS, special report, "Die Lage in der protes-tantischen Kirche und in den verschiedenen Sekten und deren staatsfeindliche Auswirkung." Feb./Mar. 1935, 18.

64. Cited in Diamant, *Gestapo Frankfurt*, 85.

65. Hannover State Police office, Mar. 4, 1936, situation report for the month of Feb. 1936, *Gestapo Hannover*, 522.

66. BHStA, Reichsstatthalter 638, BPP, interoffice decree of Feb. 1, 1936. Gerhard Hetzer reports that, after this decree had been issued, an organized wave of persecution began in Bavaria. As a result, during the second week of Feb., the homes of all Bible Students in Augsburg who were known to the au-thorities were searched. Consequently, the police authorities discovered ap-proximately 6,000 to 7,000 pounds (between 3,000 and 3,500 kilograms) of publications that were stored in a hollow space in the floor of an attic. During this police action, still more publications were discovered and a number of people were arrested. See Hetzer, "Augsburg," 628.

67. IfZ, MA 554, 936279–87 (83), memo, "Die Internationale Bibelforscher-Vereinigung," encl. to the Dec. 24, 1936, interoffice decree of the central State Police office in Munich.

68. BA, R 58/405, Bl. 55, Prussian Secret State Police, "Der Politische Po-lizeikommandeur der Länder," interoffice decree of July 7, 1936.

69. "Der Oberstaatsanwalt beim SG Breslau," indictment of Oct. 1, 1935. Cited in Zürcher, *Kreuzzug*, 94.

70. See VVN HH, Komiteeakten R 10; AfW HH 121189; *Deutsche Frauen-schicksale*, 202. In 1937 a group of male and female German anti-fascists who were living in exile in Prague published the book *Deutsche Frauenschicksale*. In its appendix, the book includes "incomplete statistical records" (196–209) and lists political court decisions that had been imposed on women in Germany between 1935 and 1936. These records indicate how much more extensive the persecution of Jehovah's Witnesses was in comparison to other opponents of the regime during that period. The records list 319 convicted people who were tried in 290 court cases. A total of 41 of these female Bible Students (12.9%) were tried in 32 court cases.

71. See this book, pt. 6, ch. 18, p. 494. In Hamburg, during the period of the police investigations, the people who were taken into protective detention were sent to the Fuhlsbüttel concentration camp, which served as a police prison. Therefore, the number of Jehovah's Witnesses who were exposed to concentration camp conditions, generally for a few weeks or months, corresponded almost directly to the number of people who were taken into custody. This number by far exceeded the number of five admissions into concentration camps. With regard to Hamburg, this study makes a general distinction between imprisonment at the Fuhlsbüttel concentration camp for the purpose of "preliminary pretrial detention," which was followed by pretrial detention if a judicial arrest warrant was issued, and an officially ordered transfer to a concentration camp. This distinction has been made for reasons of analytic clarity and not in an effort to diminish the severity of the conditions of imprisonment. In cases in which people were sent to concentration camps for the purpose of prevention, this imprisonment was a completely independent instrument of punishment by the Gestapo. In other cases, the imprisonment in the Fuhlsbüttel concentration camp preceded legal prosecution and, consequently, allowances were also made for the time spent in pretrial detention.

72. See Mammach, *Widerstand 1933–1939*, 146.

73. Dec. 20, 1934, Law against Insidious Attacks on State and Party and for the Protection of the Party Uniform, *RGBl.* 1934 I, 1269. However, in only a few cases, judgments were actually based on this law. From among the 408 Bible Students who were sentenced by the Munich Special Court between 1933 and 1938, the people were charged with a violation of the Law against Insidious Attacks in only two cases (see Kalous, "Bibelforscher," 40). With regard to Jehovah's Witnesses from Hamburg, as far as can be determined, 383 of the special court decisions (apart from acquittals and dismissals of court cases) were based on a violation of the Feb. 28, 1933, VOSchVuS. In only five cases, the judgment was based on the Law against Insidious Attacks. Consequently, in the majority of cases, Kater's statement that the "various offenses" of the Bible Students were punished according to the Law against Insidious Attacks is incorrect (Kater, "Bibelforscher," 197).

74. On May 6, 1933, a decree was issued that regulated the jurisdiction of the special courts (*RGBl.* 1933 I, 259). According to this decree, the special courts were assigned to deal with cases involving offenses that, according to the Feb. 28, 1933, VOSchVuS, were subject to punishment. They also were assigned to handle offenses that, according to the Mar. 21, 1933, Decree by the Reich President for the Resistance of Insidious Attacks against the Government of the National Uprising [VO des Reichspräsidenten zur Abwehr heimtückischer Angriffe gegen die Regierung der nationalen Erhebung] (*RGBl.* 1933 I, 135), were subject to punishment. This decree was later replaced by the Law against Insidious Attacks.

75. See SLG HH, HSG 11 Js. Sond. 449/35, decision of Aug. 2, 1935.

76. The description is based on the subsequently instituted preliminary investigations (SLG HH, HSG 11 Js. Sond. 698/35).

77. SLG HH, HSG 11 Js. Sond. 698/35, Bl. 5, arrest warrant of Aug. 3, 1935.

78. *Hamburger Tageblatt*, Aug. 3, 1935 ("'Weird Saint' on Trial").

79. On prohibitions of conducting funerals or restrictions on their performance, see also *Yearbook* 1989, 120–21; Zürcher, *Kreuzzug*, 176, 182.

80. SLG HH, HSG 11 Js. Sond. 774/34. For additional information, see Garbe, "'Gott mehr gehorchen als den Menschen,'" 187–88.

81. SLG HH, HSG Js. Sond. 1617/34, vol. 4, enclosure, no page numbers, Aug. 9, 1948, statements of the son.

82. See the accounts of people who were exposed to these methods of persecution mentioned in Zürcher's report (Zürcher, *Kreuzzug*, 114–15, 138–49, 169–83). Michael H. Kater points out that the mistreatment was "actually unnecessary because, in the majority of cases, Jehovah's Witnesses immediately confessed, as long as they did not run the risk of betraying their fellow believers" (Kater, "Bibelforscher," 204). Kater's statements are correct to the extent that the Gestapo records indicate that Jehovah's Witnesses usually admitted their participation in Bible Student activities of which they were accused during the initial interrogations. They also openly declared being Jehovah's Witnesses and adhering to their principles (such as the refusal to give the Hitler salute, refusal to perform military service, etc.). However, they usually persistently refused to give the names of fellow believers or to provide details involving the organization or their preaching activity. Since, however, they refused to provide the Gestapo with information on which to base their further investigations, the Gestapo officials tried to obtain this information by force. Such mistreatment of Jehovah's Witnesses was not only the result of excessive sadistic actions on the part of particular Gestapo officials. The arrangements made between the RJM and the Gestapa regarding "the degree to which methods of police interrogations were permissible" show that such mistreatment was part of the interrogation methods of the police (see this book, pt. 4, ch. 12, pp. 267–68).

83. Zürcher, *Kreuzzug*, 139–40.

84. Ibid., 140.

85. Ibid., 142. Soon, the interrogation methods of the Dortmund Gestapo resulted in the death of individual Jehovah's Witnesses. In Dec. 1936 thirty-year-old Stanislaus Schwarz from Ahlen (Westphalia) was arrested and taken to Steinwache, the location of the Dortmund Gestapo office, for interrogations. In the police prison, Theiß saw Schwarz slip a secret message to a fellow believer to deny knowing each other. Several days later, his relatives received a letter indicating that Schwarz had supposedly hanged himself in his prison cell (ibid., 179–80).

86. See ibid., 140, 142; VVN HH, Komiteeakten J 6.

87. See Milton, "Deutsche und deutsch-jüdische Frauen," 4; Zürcher, *Kreuzzug*, 139.

88. See *Yearbook* 1974, 117.

89. See Zürcher, *Kreuzzug*, 153.

90. Corresponding evidence is included in the records of the special courts. See, for instance, SLG HH, SH SG 11 Son KMs 19/37; SLG HH, HSG 11 Js. Sond. 298/38; StA M, Staatsanwaltschaften 8551, Munich Special Court 16 KMs So 70–71, 37 (71), vol. 2, Bl. 326 hh.

91. See M. Koch, "Die kleinen Glaubensgemeinschaften," 428; Kühl, "Friedrichstadt," 187–88.

92. Zürcher, *Kreuzzug*, 118.

93. StA M, Staatsanwaltschaften 8551, Munich Special Court 16 KMs So 70–71, 37 (71), vol. 1, Bl. 65–66, Police District 5 (Munich), Dec. 15, record of interrogation.

94. Ibid., Bl. 76, Mar. 23, 1937, psychiatric report by the medical expert of the regional court.

95. Lange also made his own extensive examinations regarding the question of the extent to which Jehovah's Witnesses could be made responsible under penal law (see Lange, "Dienstverweigerung"). Lange and his pupils, Sollmann and Wagner, established the thesis that in most cases, the religiously based refusal of Jehovah's Witnesses to perform military service cannot be judged according to StGB, article 51. However, with regard to the handling of cases of conscientious objection during World War II, this thesis proved to result in serious consequences. For additional information, see this book, pt. 5, ch. 14, pp. 369–70.

96. Sollmann and Wagner, "Bibelforscher," 437.

97. Ibid., 444.

98. See ibid., 433, 436–37.

99. AfW HH, 181109, medical opinion of Feb. 4, 1936; see also Garbe, "'Gott mehr gehorchen als den Menschen,'" 208–9.

100. See personal documents of Günther Pape, "Geheime Staatspolizei Darmstadt," records of Sept. 9, 1936. Excerpts published in Gebhard, *Zeugen Jehovas*, 188–90, and 193.

101. For unknown reasons, Fritz Winkler made "a full confession" even during the first Gestapo interrogation. In subsequent interrogations, Gestapo officials were able to persuade him even to betray the names of several leaders and numerous other details. The Gestapo persuaded him to send a letter to the various regional service directors requesting them to give up their resistance and "tell the whole truth," since the police authorities had already been informed about their activities. Winkler was later sent to Sachsenhausen. See SLG HH, SH SG 11 Son KMs 149/36, Bl. 1, Sept. 2, 1936, remarks of the Kiel State Police Office; StA M, Staatsanwaltschaften 8551, Munich Special Court 16 KMs So 45–47, 37 (37), vol. 1, Bl. 1.

102. Secret State Police office, decree of Aug. 28, 1936, cited in Gebhard, *Zeugen Jehovas*, 171–72.

103. See SLG HH, SH SG 11 Son KMs 149/36, Bl. 134. In Apr. 1936 district overseer Hermann Schlömer (mentioned in this book, pt. 4, ch. 10, p. 214), turned the responsibility of caring for the district of Schleswig-Holstein over to Georg Bär. Schlömer, in turn, accepted responsibility as subordinate regional service director for the Rhineland district in support of Albert Wandres. In addition to the Rhineland, Wandres was also responsible for Saar and southern Hessen but was not able to fulfill the organizational responsibilities for these large areas. Bär, who had previously been in Czechoslovakia, received his assignment as district overseer of Schleswig-Holstein from the central European office in Bern.

104. Cited in Stokes, *Eutin*, 709; see also Möller, "Steinburg," 209.

105. Secret State Police office, decree of Aug. 28, 1936, cited in Gebhard, *Zeugen Jehovas*, 171–72.

106. *DKBl.* [*Deutsches Kriminalpolizeiblatt*] 9 (1936), no. 2643 (Dec. 23, 1936): 1599. Friese was able to remain in hiding for more than one year. In the autumn of 1937 he was arrested. The *DKBl.* also announced the searches for IBSA functionaries Arthur Nawroth (eastern Silesia and Grenzmark) and August Fehst (western Silesia and parts of Saxony; he was one of the main organizers of the smuggling of the literature). Nawroth was arrested in the spring of 1937, and Fehst probably in the summer of 1939. See *DKBl.* 9 (1936), no. 2638 (issue of Dec. 17, 1936): 1571; Gebhard, *Zeugen Jehovas*, 174.

107. BA, Sammlung Schumacher/267 I, BPP, interoffice decree of Aug. 20, 1936.

108. In the Free City of Danzig, which was under the protection of the League of Nations, the NSDAP gained an absolute majority for the first time in the May 28, 1933, *Volkstag* elections. From then on, the city-state of 330,000 inhabitants was under the authority of the NSDAP. On Mar. 28/29, 1935, the police authorities seized the local branch office of the Watch Tower Society. Three months later, on July 6, 1935, the IBSA was dissolved, by means of a police decree. This resulted in dismissals, house searches, and abuses during police interrogations. The Watch Tower Society sent several petitions to the High Commissioner of the League of Nations protesting the ban, as well as the increasing persecution of the Danzig Jehovah's Witnesses. On the persecution of Jehovah's Witnesses in Danzig, see *Yearbook* 1936, 132–33; *Yearbook* 1938, 129–31; Zürcher, *Kreuzzug*, 197–210. From the beginning of the 1920s on, the Austrian branch office of the Watch Tower Society was confronted with serious opposition from the Catholic Church. In Mar. 1933, after Dollfuß's Christian Socialist government had repealed the constitution, the publications of the Watch Tower Society were also subjected to censorship. On Sept. 10, 1934, the Federal Security Commissioner of Vienna issued a dissolution decree against the Watch Tower Society. Initially, the Austrian branch office of the Watch Tower

Society was able to get a withdrawal of this dissolution decree from the Austrian Federal chancellery. Nine months later, on June 17, 1935, another ban was issued. This time, the appeal proceedings against the ban remained unsuccessful. On Feb. 7, 1936, the Federal Supreme Court pronounced the ban lawful. See Maislinger, "Die Zeugen Jehovas," 369; Neugebauer, "'Ernste Bibelforscher,'" 161.

109. Resolution adopted at the general assembly of Jehovah's Witnesses in central Europe, Sept. 4–7, 1936, published in Zipfel, *Kirchenkampf,* 363–66.

110. See *Yearbook* 1974, 155; see also the reference to this resolution made in the Oct. 30, 1936, situation report of the Karlsruhe public prosecutor's office: "At the beginning of Sept. of this year, the [Watch Tower Society's] branch office in Switzerland sent a copy of the resolution to a large number of public prosecutors in Baden, including myself" (BA, R 22/3133, Bl. 184).

111. See Zürcher, "Die Verschwörung," in *Kreuzzug,* 37–58. Franz Zürcher was the editor responsible for the German issue of the *Golden Age* and published his book in 1938. In this book, Zürcher tries to substantiate the alleged complicity between the Catholic Church and the NS regime. In this regard, the references, to the position taken by the bishop of Osnabrück and Prussian Counsel Wilhelm Berning indicate that the accusations made in the book are not completely unfounded.

112. *Yearbook* 1937, 151; "Alltägliches aus Deutschland," excerpt from *Das Goldene Zeitalter,* Feb. 1, 1937, published in Zipfel, *Kirchenkampf,* 412–17 (412), 415.

113. Rutherford, *Enemies,* 72.

114. Ibid., 164. During the following years, this polemic was further intensified. The booklet "Conspiracy against Democracy," which Jehovah's Witnesses distributed during 1942/43, argues that the "Nazi-fascist dictators [were] all products of the Catholic Church."

115. See Rutherford, *Facts,* passim; Rutherford, *Fascism or Freedom,* 12ff.

116. See *Yearbook* 1987, 147.

117. On the restructuring of the IBSA during 1936/37, see Imberger, *Widerstand,* 308–18.

118. With reference to the IBSA organizational structure and activities, some literary works have suggested that these show "remarkable similarities" to the forms of resistance practiced by the KPD as, for instance, the concept of agitation in groups of five, practiced by the KPD until 1935 (see Imberger, *Widerstand,* 318, 375; Mann, *Protest,* 222; Marßolek and Ott, *Bremen,* 308). In his comparative study about the "religious and political resistance of the working class" in the Steinburg district, Reimer Möller emphasizes that the organizational characteristics of resistance of the IBSA "remarkably" resemble "the concept of Communist resistance until 1935." In this regard, Möller refers to the method of dividing the organization into various small groups, the hierarchical management of the organization, and the propaganda performed by means of pamphlet campaigns (Möller, "Steinburg," 227).

119. See *Yearbook* 1937, 151; Nov. 23, 1987, recollections by Elise Kühnle. *Yearbook* 1987, 147, reports that "Nazi agents secretly photographed German conventioneers."

120. *VB*, June 2, 1937.

121. *VB*, Apr. 25, 1937.

122. After the general suppression of the resistance of the workers' parties during the middle of the 1930s, the Gestapo had a large police force at its disposal. And, not the least, for the justification of their overblown staff plan during 1933/34, they required another "opponent."

123. The total number of protective detentions imposed in Bavaria between Mar. 30 and Nov. 2, 1936, is not available. According to these records, the Bavarian Political Police took a total of 1,791 people into protective detention, 137 (7.0%) of whom were arrested on the charge of involvement in the prohibited activities of the "Earnest Bible Students." During the same period, they arrested 252 people (14.0%) "for preparation or suspicion of preparation of *high treason*." They also arrested 156 people (8.0%) "for activity on behalf of, or propaganda for, *the KPD or SPD*." A comparison of these numbers reveals the importance that the State Police authorities attached, at that time, to the resistance of the IBSA. The remaining number involved people who were arrested on the charge of "behavior harmful to the State"" or "hostile to the State," committing offenses against StGB, paragraph 175, and other reasons that cannot be specifically classified. Cited in Broszat, *Anatomy of the SS State*, 169.

124. See Zürcher, *Kreuzzug*, 201–2.

125. According to Constitution, article 76, paragraph 3, a citizen of Danzig cannot be extradited to a foreign government.

126. These petitions are recorded in Zürcher, *Kreuzzug*, 197–203, and 207–9. On Jan. 15, 1938, the Watch Tower Society submitted a petition to Carl Jacob Burckhardt of the League of Nations. In this petition, they requested that the League of Nations take action against the persecution of Jehovah's Witnesses in Danzig, and to take effective measures for their protection (see *Yearbook* 1938, 130). The Watch Tower Society apparently no longer entertained the hope that the League of Nations would still be able to improve matters. The fact that the extensive petition was submitted anyway had the objective "that the League of Nations and its representing nations would not have any excuse" (Zürcher, *Kreuzzug*, 197).

127. According to the service report of the Watch Tower Society, the number of believers decreased by approximately 2,300 during the last quarter of 1936, in comparison to the monthly service report of May/June 1936. See *Yearbook* 1974, 156.

128. See Garbe, "'Gott mehr gehorchen als den Menschen,'" 193, 203. In Hamburg a considerable part of the restructuring had already been carried out nine months prior to the Lucerne general assembly, in response to a suggestion by Heinrich Dietschi, the regional service director of northern Germany (see

BDC, VGH, 8 J 20/38, Bl. 22–33, Hamburg State Police office, concluding report of Dec. 21, 1937; VVN HH, Komiteeakten Z 4).

129. IfZ, MA 554, 936279–87 (87), memo, "Die Internationale Bibelforscher-Vereinigung," enclosure to the Dec. 24, 1936, memo of the central State Police office in Munich.

130. See Hetzer, "Augsburg," 631.

131. Based on their service reports and subsequently performed calculations, the Watch Tower Society states that a total of 3,450 Jehovah's Witnesses had been involved in the distribution campaign. See *Yearbook* 1974, 155; Bergman, *Jehovah's Witnesses*, 21.

132. If, as anticipated, every person that was involved in the campaign distributed between twenty and forty copies of the resolution in his assigned area, we can assume that approximately 100,000 pamphlets were directly distributed. In addition, quite a number of resolutions were also sent by mail. The Watch Tower Society's publications mention the number of 300,000 distributed resolutions (see *Jehovah's Witnesses in God's Purpose*, 164; *Yearbook* 1974, 155–56). Hetzer calls this number into question. He considers the number of 300,000 to be an overstatement (see Hetzer, "Augsburg," 631n60). The numbers that the Gestapo had determined in various locations (in Augsburg, 1,500–2,000; in Hamburg, 1,800–3,000; and in Munich, 1,800–2,400) indicate that the campaign was not carried out to the anticipated extent.

133. See Imberger, *Widerstand*, 334–35.

134. See StA M, Staatsanwaltschaften 8551, Munich Special Court 16 KMs So 70–71, 37 (71), vol. 3, Bl. 1–2, police district Munich 9, station 1, court order of Dec. 12, 1936. Only one month earlier, Martin Pötzinger had been assigned as group servant for the "metropolitan area of Munich." Until 1936 he had been active as a "pioneer" of Jehovah's Witnesses in Prague, Sofia, and Budapest. After the war, he was appointed to high leadership positions within the Watch Tower Society. In 1978 he became the first German member of the eighteen-member "governing body." He remained a member of this governing body until his death in 1988.

135. Ibid., vol. 4, Bl. 1. According to Bergman, *Jehovah's Witnesses*, 12, at 6:15 p.m., a warning about the distribution of the pamphlets was supposedly given on German radio stations.

136. BA, Sammlung Schumacher/267 I, telex by the Würzburg Secret State Police office.

137. Cited in *Yearbook* 1974, 155.

138. LA SH, Apt. 358 no. 409, public prosecutor's office at the Schleswig-Holstein Special Court, indictment of Nov. 13, 1937.

139. *Jehovah's Witnesses in God's Purpose*, 164–65. See also *Jehovah's Witnesses: Proclaimers of God's Kingdom*, 449.

140. See the attachment to the records of the court proceedings against the Flensburg IBSA group, which includes a list of all "resolutions submitted at the

police office." SLG HH, Kiel Special Court, 11 Son KMs 19/37. According to Reinhard Mann, nine "responsible citizens" from Düsseldorf sent letters with information about the distribution of the resolution to the Political Police office (Mann, *Protest*, 222).

141. SLG HH, SH SG 11 Son KMs 19/37, no page numbers, Dec. 12, 1936 letter of the Flensburg veterinarian.

142. IfZ, MA 554, 936288–91, "Der Regierungspräsident von Oberbayern," Dec. 14, 1936, telegram to the Friedberg district authorities.

143. See Kammler, *Kasseler Soldaten*, 138–41 (139).

144. StA M, Staatsanwaltschaften 8551, Munich Special Court 16 KMs So 70–71, 37 (71), vol. 1, Bl. 27, Munich State Police office, report of Feb. 19, 1937.

145. BA, R 22/3133, Bl. 209–10, Karlsruhe chief public prosecutor, situation report of Dec. 20, 1936.

146. In Apr./May 1937, in eight cases at the Munich Special Court, a total of sixty people who had been involved in the pamphlet distribution were sentenced to prison sentences of between three weeks and twenty-one months (see StA M, Staatsanwaltschaften 8551). In Feb. 1937 the Schleswig-Holstein Special Court imposed an average of 10.8 months of imprisonment on the Bible Students who had distributed the pamphlet in Flensburg. In Düsseldorf the prison sentences usually amounted to approximately one year (Mann, *Protest*, 222). On May 5, 1937, the Kassel Special Court pronounced a prison sentence of two years (Kammler, *Kasseler Soldaten*, 136).

147. SLG HH, SH SC 11 Son KMs 19/37, Bl. 120–32 (129), decision of Feb. 27, 1937.

148. IfZ, MA 554, 936279–87 (82), memo, "Die Internationale Bibelforscher-Vereinigung," enclosure to the Dec. 24, 1936, interoffice decree of the central State Police office in Munich.

149. See Zürcher, *Kreuzzug*, 138ff., esp. 177ff.

150. The following list is based on the statements by Zürcher, *Kreuzzug*, 114, 169ff. After referring to the "legal" death penalty the SS press (*Das Schwarze Korps*) was asking for Jehovah's Witnesses, Zürcher states: "Up until that time, the murderers will hide behind the lie: 'suicides committed by hanging'" (Zürcher, *Kreuzzug*, 170).

151. The studies by Kuno Bludau and Hans-Josef Steinberg mention the case of Ignatz Lesniewski, which is not included in the list of the Bern IBSA central European Office. On June 23, 1937, in the Duisburg police prison, this Jehovah's Witness "took his life after the Gestapo had subjected him to the most terrible acts of torture" (Bludau, *Gestapo-geheim!*, 224). One of the prison doctors took the initiative to write a report about the autopsy. The photographs he made provide evidence that Lesniewski had been exposed to severe mistreatment. In this exceptional case, the records also include the motives for the suicide. See Steinberg, *Essen*, 22.

152. See Hetzer, "Augsburg," 631. Manfred Koch reports that, in the spring

of 1937, in Mannheim, a male Bible Student, who disguised himself as a woman, distributed 500 pamphlets (see M. Koch, "Die kleinen Glaubensgemeinschaften," 426.)

153. See Wickert, "Frauen," 219.

154. See Ziegler, *Die kirchliche Lage in Bayern* (Niederbayern and Oberpfalz), 118.

155. See SLG HH, HSG 11 Js. Sond. 173/38, decision of Apr. 11, 1938, 18; BDC, VGH, 8 J 20/38, Bl. 31. Even in other locations, Bible Students had reservations about the pamphlet campaigns. In June 1937, Jehovah's Witnesses in neighboring Hamborn distributed the open letter in the metropolitan area of Duisburg because the Bible Students in Duisburg refused to participate in this campaign. See Bludau, *Gestapo-geheim!*, 292.

156. StA M, Staatsanwaltschaften 8551, Munich Special Court 16 KMs So 70–71, 37 (71), vol. 1, Bl. 10, Munich State Police office, report of Feb. 19, 1937.

157. See Gebhard, *Zeugen Jehovas*, 173–87; Cole, *Jehovah's Witnesses* (German edition), 192; FGN, NHS 13-7-0-4, Erich Frost, letter of July 15, 1969; *Der Spiegel*, July 19, 1961, 38–39 ("Väterchen Frost"). On Oct. 29, 1937, the Berlin Special Court sentenced Erich Frost to three years and six months of imprisonment. After his release from prison, he was sent to Sachsenhausen. On May 5, 1945, he was released from this camp.

158. SD (SS Security Service), file remark of Apr. 2, 1937, cited in Gebhard, *Zeugen Jehovas*, 174; see also Imberger, *Widerstand*, 305.

159. BA, R 22/4277, Bl. 186.

160. Staecker, the chief public prosecutor, also reports that the State Police authorities requested "solitary confinement for every [prisoner]." Apparently, this arrangement had the objective of preventing Jehovah's Witnesses from having conversations with one another and from preaching to other prisoners. However, it was not possible to "put this arrangement into practice."

161. In the majority of cases, the searches went on for extended periods of time. For instance, the Dortmund Gestapo had put Heinrich Dietschi on the most-wanted list as early as May 23, 1936 (SLG HH, HSG 11 Js. Sond. 88/37, Bl. 20–21). Albert Wandres, the regional service director of the Rhineland, was hunted by the Gestapo as early as 1934 (see *Yearbook 1974*, 146–48). Repeated searches were made, for instance, for the subordinate regional service director, Hermann Schlömer, and IBSA functionary Michael Hilgers who had "escaped from prison" during the night of Feb. 7, 1937. See *DKBl.* 10 (1937), no. 2707 (issue of Mar. 12, 1937); *DKBl.* 10 (1937), no. 2699 (issue of Mar. 3, 1937): 255–56.

162. The Watch Tower Society's history report gives the following description: "Since the majority of the regional service directors had been arrested, sisters were called on to fill the breaches." Consequently, the "sisters joyfully filled up the places left open by the arrests of the brothers" (*Yearbook 1974*, 160, 179).

163. See Garbe, "Kompromißlose Bekennerinnen"; Lichtenegger, "Wiens Bibelforscherinnen," 166ff. An examination of the legal proceedings also

showed the increasing involvement of female Bible Students in the resistance activities. Erika Kalous points out, in her study regarding Bible Student cases that took place at the Munich Special Court and the Munich Court of Appeals, that between 1935 and 1945 an increasing number of cases involved women. At the Munich Special Court (between 1933 and 1938), 52.7 percent of the sentences were imposed on men. At the Munich Higher Regional Court (between 1943 and 1945), on the other hand, the majority of sentences were imposed on women (114 women compared to 41 men, that is, 73.5%, compared to 26.5%). Between 1935 and 1937, at the Munich Special Court, "women were also given considerably more lenient sentences" than men. However, between 1943 and 1945, at the Munich Higher Regional Court, "women received the same amount of punishment" as the men.

164. Based on the information that had been collected up to the early summer of 1937, the Bern "IBSA central European office" wrote a comprehensive study about the recent occurrences. In 1938 Europa-Verlag (Zurich) published this study, entitled *Kreuzzug gegen das Christentum* (see also this book, p. 553, n.84). During the next year, a French translation of this study was published in Paris. Its introduction includes editorial commentaries and statements that people in public life had made about the first edition. For example, Thomas Mann expressed his deep sorrow and "appealed to the consciences of people throughout the world" (retranslation from Zürcher, *Croisade*, no page numbers). Even though this publication did not have the anticipated effect on the international public and did not result in expressions of solidarity, the Watch Tower Society's message was recognized. Especially in the United States, France, and Switzerland, a number of press reports covered the persecution of Jehovah's Witnesses in Germany. See, for instance, *Humanité Paris,* May 20, 1937 ("Hitler persécute les Protestants"). Additional press reports from French and Swiss newspapers are published in Zürcher, *Kreuzzug,* 107, 111, 124.

165. An unabridged edition of this letter is published in Zürcher, *Kreuzzug,* 192ff.

166. See (Strafabteilungsvorsteher) Liesche, "Der Bibelforscher im Strafvollzug."

167. "Offener Brief—An das bibelgläubige und Christus liebende Volk Deutschlands," cited in Bludau, *Gestapo-geheim!,* 289–90.

168. On Oct. 9, 1936, two days after his arrest, thirty-four-year-old Heinen was interrogated at the Gelsenkirchen Town Hall, which, at that time, also included the police prison. There, officials of the Gelsenkirchen Gestapo outpost beat him to death. See Zürcher, *Kreuzzug,* 180–83.

169. In some locations, the open letter was apparently not distributed on June 20, 1937. The distribution rather took place either one day before, or after, this date. For instance, Hans-Josef Steinberg reports that the distribution of three hundred copies in Essen took place on June 19, 1937 (see Steinberg, *Essen,* 165). In some areas of the district of the Augsburg State Police office, the open

letter was distributed during the evening hours on Monday, June 21, 1937. See IfZ, MA 554, 936260, Augsburg State Police office, letter of July 9, 1937.

170. BDC, VGH, 8 J 20/38, Bl. 32, Hamburg State Police office, concluding report of Dec. 21, 1937.

171. Zürcher, *Kreuzzug,* 194.

172. SLG HH, HSG 11 Js. Sond. 173/38, decision of Apr. 11, 1938, 19.

173. The report of *Yearbook* 1938, 188, does not provide any information about the subjects discussed at the Paris general assembly. Also in other publications, this Paris assembly is not specifically mentioned.

174. BA, Sammlung Schumacher/267 I, Darmstadt State Police office, memo of July 16, 1937. Three months prior to the general assembly in Paris, the local State Police office in Munich had given instructions that "no passports should be issued to people who are known to be Bible Students." All passports already issued were supposed to be confiscated (BA, Sammlung Schumacher/267 I, local State Police office in Munich, interoffice decree of May 19, 1937). These passport restrictions by the central State Police office in Munich were probably based on the Apr. 28, 1937, interoffice decree by the Gestapa (see BA, R 58/1074, Bl. 29).

175. IfZ, MA 554, 936259, central State Police office in Munich, interoffice decree of Aug. 14, 1937. On Aug. 20, 1937, the central State Police office in Stuttgart, on the other hand, gave instructions that its subordinate police offices should "merely" determine discreetly whether any people known to be IBSA members had planned to leave the area during the period of the "general assembly" (personal documents of J. E. Straßer ["Sammlung zur historischen Dokumentation"], central State Police office in Stuttgart, interoffice decree of Aug. 20, 1937).

176. See also the report of Albert Wandres, *Watchtower,* Sept. 1, 1965, 537–42.

177. At times, Wandres was responsible for the entire southwestern and western districts of Germany (the Rhineland, southern Hessen, Palatinate-Baden, Württemberg, and the Saarland). During this period, he supervised sixty-five IBSA groups. See Billstein, *Krefeld,* 306; M. Koch, "Die kleinen Glaubensgemeinschaften," 422; Steinberg, *Essen,* 164.

178. BDC, VGH, 8 J 20/38, Bl. 22–33 (26), Hamburg State Police office, concluding report of Dec. 21, 1937.

179. Ibid. In its July 8, 1937, interoffice decree, the Darmstadt State Police office had already informed its subordinate police offices about the way in which Wandres arranged his meetings with the group leaders: "He determines his meeting places with the local IBSA leaders in the following way: He writes a postcard with inconspicuous contents, signing it with a different name. On the postcard, he mentions a date on which he will meet the recipient of the postcard at a pre-determined place. However, this is only a false [!] date. In reality, the meeting takes place one week earlier" (BA, Sammlung Schumacher/267 I). The meeting-place for the monthly meetings between the female district

overseer and the IBSA leader on the Reich level, or his substitute, was the Hamburg train station. See Imberger, *Widerstand*, 308.

180. See *Yearbook* 1974, 162.

181. BDC, VGH, 8 J 20/38, Bl. 25.

182. On Apr. 11, 1938, the HSG sentenced Max Grote to four years of imprisonment. He died on Oct. 21, 1940, at the age of fifty-eight, during his imprisonment at the Wolfenbüttel penal institution (personal documents of Walter Tod). On Feb. 18, 1938, the SH SG also sentenced Frieda Christiansen to four years of imprisonment.

183. By comparing the names on the lists of the Fuhlsbüttel police prison (Sta HH, Justizverwaltung 1, Verzeichnis der entstandenen Schutzhaftkosten, Generalakte 451 a E, Bd. 1, continuation on Bd. 1c) to the names of Jehovah's Witnesses he already knew, the author of this report has been able to determine the respective above-mentioned minimum numbers of imprisoned Jehovah's Witnesses. Since the lists of names do not mention the reasons for imprisonment, it is possible that the number of Jehovah's Witnesses imprisoned in Fuhlsbüttel was considerably higher.

184. SLG HH, HSG 11 Js. Sond. 173/38; 179/38; 279/38; 298/38; 369/38; 373/38; 385/38; another record of court proceedings has been removed.

185. SLG HH, HSG 11 Js. Sond. 298/38, GnH [records of act of pardon] 3659/42, central State Police office in Hamburg, report of Nov. 21. 1938.

186. In some locations, the IBSA groups were not discovered around the turn of 1937/38. In his study regarding the district of Steinburg, Reimer Möller gives a detailed description of the stages of the destruction of the IBSA groups (see Möller, "Steinburg," 215–17). Between Dec. 10, 1937, and Mar. 2, 1938, one by one, the groups in Neuenkirchen, Itzehoe, Wilster, Glückstadt, and Kellinghusen were closed. The local police offices received their orders for these actions from Gestapo officials in Kiel and Neumünster. In the course of this "destruction of the IBSA groups" in Schleswig-Holstein, around the turn of 1937/38, at least 267 Jehovah's Witnesses were taken into custody. See Imberger, *Widerstand*, 349.

187. Without exception, it is possible to substantiate this information by means of local studies. See, for instance, Hetzer, "Augsburg," 640; M. Koch, "Die kleinen Glaubensgemeinschaften," 423; Mann, *Protest*, 222; Steinberg, *Essen*, 165.

188. The chief public prosecutor in Karlsruhe, situation report of Oct. 18, 1937, cited in *Verfolgung und Widerstand unter dem Nationalsozialismus in Baden*, 260.

189. Situation report for Jan. 1938 of the Central Department II 1 of the Security Main Office of the RFSS, "Berichte des SD und der Gestapo," 278.

190. 1938 annual situation report of the Security Main Office, *Meldungen aus dem Reich*, 2:7–214 (52).

191. SS, situation report for the first quarter of 1939, *Meldungen aus dem Reich*, 2:237.

192. The Feb. 28, 1933, VOSchVuS repealed Reich Constitution article 114 that had guaranteed the inviolability of personal freedom. This opened up the possibility of issuing protective detention. Consequently, the National Socialists had finally removed the legal barrier that had prevented them from persecuting opponents of the regime during the initial period of their seizure of power.

193. BA, R 58/264, Bl. 16, RMdI, Jan. 9, 1934, letter to the governments of the various German states. Three months later, the RMdI issued a major Decree Regarding the Imposition and Execution of Protective Detention [Erlass des Reichsinnenministeriums über die Verhängung und Vollstreckung der Schutzhaft] that established this regulation. Under point 3, paragraph 3, it states: "Furthermore, it is not permissible to impose protective detention as a penalty for punishable . . . offenses. Punishable offenses are subject to legal proceedings" (BA, Sammlung Schumacher/271, RMdI, interoffice decree of Apr. 12, 1934). Four years later, the RMdI sent out new regulations regarding protective detention. However, it still included the earlier regulation. Article 1, para. 1 states that protective detention cannot be used "for the purpose of punishment or as a substitute for legally imposed imprisonment" (BA, R 58/1027, Bl. 2, RMdI, interoffice decree of Jan. 25, 1938).

194. Rolf Schwarz, Altona State Police office, interoffice decree of Jan. 12, 1935. A copy of this decree is included in the interoffice decree that the Rendsburg district administrator sent to the local police authorities on Jan. 17, 1935.

195. VVN HH, Komiteeakten B 19, H 9, M 6.

196. In May 1937 the central State Police office in Munich issued an important decree regarding the imposition of protective detention on Bible Students. This decree confirmed the procedure that had already been in use for a considerable period of time; it determined that Bible Students who were taken into protective detention be "immediately handed over to the legal authorities for the purpose of obtaining a judicial arrest warrant." However, in cases in which the legal authorities "did not issue an arrest warrant or later withdrew the warrant," the Gestapo offices "had to take steps to transfer [the people] to a concentration camp" (BA, R 58/264, Bl. 306, central State Police office in Munich, interoffice decree of May 19, 1937).

197. The Code of Penal Procedure [Strafprozeßordnung] regulated that the accused had to be immediately brought before a judge, at the latest on the day following the arrest (StPO [Code of Penal Procedure], article 114 b). Contrary to these regulations, the Gestapo took those arrested into protective detention during the period of police investigations. In this way, they exceeded the authority of the legal authorities with regard to prosecution procedures. Often, this preliminary pretrial detention was extended over a period of several months before the cases were finally transferred to the legal authorities with a request for issuing a judicial arrest warrant.

198. The district president of Hildesheim, June 1, 1935, situation report for the months of Apr./May 1935 to the Reich minister of the interior, *Gestapo Hannover*, 381.

199. BA, R 58/264, Bl. 162, BPP, interoffice decree of Sept. 23, 1935.

200. BHStA, Reichsstatthalter 638, BPP, interoffice decree of June 26, 1935.

201. Secret State Police office, interoffice decree of Apr. 26, 1935, Cited in Rürup, *Topographie*, 98.

202. See Zürcher, *Kreuzzug*, 96–97; with regard to further "lenient" penalties, see also ibid., 99–100.

203. Frankfurt (am Main) State Police office, Nov. 30, 1935, general summary of the development of the internal political situation during Nov. 1935, cited in *Die Lageberichte der Geheimen Staatspolizei über die Provinz Hessen-Nassau*, 516.

204. LA SH, Apt. 352 Altona no. 8869, enclosure, Dortmund Regional Court, 10 M 69/34, decision of Jan. 16, 1935.

205. Cited in Warmbrunn, "Strafgerichtsbarkeit," 374.

206. BA 22/3136, Bl. 63, Der Generalstaatsanwalt in Karlsruhe, situation report of Mar. 27, 1937. The RMdI did not accept the proposal of the chief public prosecutor. Court proceedings involving offenses against the IBSA ban remained exclusively under the jurisdiction of the special courts. There is no evidence of any cases being transferred to other courts of law.

207. BHStA, Reichsstatthalter 638, BPP, interoffice decree of Feb. 1, 1936.

208. StA M, Staatsanwaltschaften 8551, Munich Special Court 16 KMs So 45–47, 37 (37), vol. 1, Bl. 55, central State Police office in Munich, report of Nov. 17, 1936.

209. IfZ, MA 554, 936279–87 (79), memo, "Die Internationale Bibelforscher-Vereinigung," encl. to the Dec. 24, 1936, interoffice decree of the central State Police office in Munich.

210. This includes the Gestapa memo "Die Internationale Bibelforscher-Vereinigung," which has been repeatedly quoted (see this book, p. 621, n.36). Further, it includes the article "Die 'Internationale Ernste Bibelforschervereinigung' (IBV), deren Grundsätze und Organisation" that Kriminalkommissar [Detective Superintendent] Müller probably also wrote at the end of 1936. This article mainly describes the IBSA organizational structure (StA M, Staatsanwaltschaften 8551, Munich Special Court 16 KMs So 70–71, 37 [71], vol. 7, encl., no page numbers). Moreover, it includes an article about "sectarianism," written by SS-Hauptsturmführer Kolrep as part of the training materials for the purpose of resisting opponents, which extensively discussed the IBSA (BA, R 58/779, Bl. 141–47).

211. IfZ, MA 554, 936277, central State Police office in Munich, interoffice decree of Dec. 24, 1936.

212. IfZ, MA 554, 936269, central State Police office in Munich, interoffice decree of May 22, 1937.

213. Ibid. The article is titled "Alltägliches aus Deutschland." The Gestapo probably considered this article especially disgraceful because it contrasted the actual economic and social situation in Germany with NS promises. The various paragraphs include subjects such as Pressure to Perform, Compulsory Services, Wage Cuts, "Happiness Produces Power" Propaganda or Party Leader

System. It also includes typical Bible Student subjects, such as Child Education, Compulsory Hitler Salutes, and Elections. Each of these paragraphs ended with a taunting "Heil Hitler!" (IfZ, MA 554, 936271–74; also published in Zipfel, *Kirchenkampf*, 412–17).

214. IfZ, MA 603, 20474–204080, "Mitteilungen zur weltanschaulichen Lage," no. 34 (second year), Oct. 2, 1936.

215. Since the Catholic Church belonged to the anti-republican forces (and Jehovah's Witnesses were executed for their refusal to support Franco's troops during the Spanish Civil War), the Watch Tower Society took a strong position against Spanish Fascism in their publications. (For additional information, see *Yearbook* 1934 and following years; Zürcher, *Kreuzzug*, 44ff.) As a result, some scholars state that Jehovah's Witnesses were "taking sides with the republic" (M. Koch, "Die kleinen Glaubensgemeinschaften," 419). Others even place them on the side of "anti-National Socialist, anti-fascist forces of the world" (Struve, "Zeugen Jehovas," 293). These scholars fail to recognize the true character of the commitment of Jehovah's Witnesses.

216. See Ernst Ludwig Illinger, "Die Ernsten Bibelforscher"; [anon.], "'Verblendete' Volksgenossen und 'harmlose' Menschen." The reports are published in the series *Hoheitsträger, kennst du diese?* By means of these reports, "background knowledge" based on specific information provided by the SS or the Gestapo was transmitted for the purpose of resisting opponents.

217. Anon., "'Verblendete' Volkgenossen," 16.

218. BA, R 58/779, Bl. 147, training materials, "Das Sektenwesen," 13.

219. Some press reports involving Bible Student cases are published in Zürcher, *Kreuzzug*, 95–110. Press coverage as a whole emphasized that Jehovah's Witnesses were not merely "innocent, religious fanatics." The reports tried to counteract such opinions among the general public that were apparently prevalent despite the NS propaganda. The *Völkische Beobachter*, for example, states (regarding religious Bible Student meetings): "In reality, however, their 'Bible discussions' have nothing to do with our Lord God or with religious faith. Rather, they serve the purpose of disseminating defeatism" ("Narren! 'Ernste Bibelforscher' vor dem Gericht," *VB*, Mar. 4, 1937).

220. *VB*, Jan. 16, 1937 ("Energische Maßnahmen gegen Staatsfeinde: Zwei Jahre Gefängnis für einen aufhetzenden Ernsten Bibelforscher").

221. *Das schwarze Korps*, Feb. 11, 1937, 14 ("Besuch beim Sondergericht: Die Kleinen lässt man laufen").

222. E. Rings, "Die Ernsten Bibelforscher: Sendboten des jüdischen Bolschewismus. Das nationale Denken ist für sie eine 'Versündigung gegenüber Jehova,'" cited in *Westdeutscher Beobachter*, Aug. 21, 1938.

223. Meyer, *Meyers Lexikon*, cols. 297–98.

224. See *Hamburger Tageblatt*, May 14, 1938; further evidence published in Zürcher, *Kreuzzug*, 63–65.

225. IfZ, MA 554, 936279–87 (83), memo, "Die Internationale

Bibelforscher-Vereinigung," encl. to the Dec. 24, 1936, interoffice decree of the central State Police office in Munich. In Mar. 1937 the Bern central European office published a statement in sixty-eight newspapers of Switzerland. According to this statement, the press reports that indicated that Jehovah's Witnesses had connections with Communism were "lies of the Nazis." To make such a statement about Stalin would be "completely incompatible with the teachings and beliefs of the Bible Students" (Zürcher, *Kreuzzug*, 64). The Brooklyn headquarters of the Watch Tower Society gave instructions to examine the origin of the letter. As a result, in Aug. of 1936 a letter from Winnipeg, Canada, was indeed sent to the Magdeburg branch office, but the person sending the letter had absolutely no connections with Jehovah's Witnesses. According to the Watch Tower Society, this letter provided the Gestapo with a "convenient and most welcome instrument to carry out the most atrocious persecution" (ibid., 65).

226. *Hamburger Tageblatt*, Apr. 13, 1938 ("200 staatsfeindliche 'Bibelforscher' gefasst—Stalin als 'Jehovas Stellvertreter'").

227. See Jonak von Freyenwald, *Bibelforscher*, 69–70.

228. In this context, it is also appropriate to mention the *Handbuch der Judenfrage*, which also includes explanations about the IBSA, and which, at that time, was considered to be a "scholarly study" (see Fritsch, *Handbuch der Judenfrage* [1933], 264ff.). In the Third Reich, this book had a circulation of more than a quarter of a million copies. After the death of the author, Theodor Fritsch (1933), the book was revised. This revised version specifically mentions that "in the struggle against Judaizing . . . the 'Association of Earnest Bible Students,' which proclaims world domination for the 'chosen people,' [was] also banned" (cited in the 49th ed. [Leipzig, 1943], 543.)

229. After the distribution of large numbers of anti-Semitic defamatory literature in Bern, the Association of the Jewish Community in Switzerland instituted court proceedings. In May 1935 the Bern judges completely supported the experts who disputed the authenticity of the protocols. They considered the contents of the protocols to be "complete nonsense." According to the experts, the protocols were counterfeit documents that probably had been written by members of the Russian Secret Police around the turn of the century. They provided "evidence "for a Jewish conspiracy in order to increase the hatred against the Jews.

230. Fleischhauer states that "the authenticity of the protocols could be substantiated also by means of the Bible Student publications." He further states that "they are not merely polemical writings that have been falsely attributed to the Jews. They reflect the same ideas as the Bible Student teachings" (Fleischhauer, *Protokolle*, 119). The central European office of Jehovah's Witnesses brought charges against Fleischhauer on the grounds of false assessment and defamation. Since the accused refused to confront the charges, court proceedings were never instituted. See Zürcher, *Kreuzzug*, 68.

231. Fleischhauer, *Protokolle*, 117.

232. IfZ, MA 554, 936279–87 (83), memo, "Die Internationale Bibelforscher-Vereinigung," encl. to the Dec. 24, 1936, interoffice decree of the central State Police office in Munich.

233. Jonak von Freyenwald, *Zeugen Jehovas*, 96. See also the explanations about the IBSA in Jonak von Freyenwald's study *Jüdische Bekenntnisse aus allen Zeiten und Ländern* (250ff.), which he published five years later. In Mar. 1937, under the pseudonym Dr. Hans von Jonak, Jonak von Freyenwald also wrote an article in a paper of the Austrian Catholic clergy, published in Vienna. In this article, he also circulated his theses to his Catholic readership in neighboring Austria. See Jonak von Freyenwald, "Bibelforscher," 69–70.

234. See, for instance, the Apr. 11, 1938, judgment of the Hanseatic Special Court against members of the IBSA group Hamburg I in which main group leader Grote was the principal defendant. These records include an eight-page explanation of the Bible Student teachings, in which the name Jonak von Freyenwald is used at least six times. See SLG HH, HSG 11 Js. Sond. 173/38.

235. IfZ, Fa 119/2, Bl. 204, BPP, memo of Dec. 17, 1935. The court proceedings at the Weimar Special Court against seven Jehovah's Witnesses took place in Zella-Mehlis and resulted in a court decision that completely confirmed the legality of the IBSA ban. As a result, the defendants were sentenced to imprisonment of between three months and two years (IfZ, Fa 119/2, Bl. 186–93, Weimar Special Court, So. G. 40/35, decision of Aug. 27, 1935).

236. BA, R 58/405, Bl. 24, Der Politische Polizeikommandeur der Länder, memo of Apr. 1, 1936.

237. BA, R 58/405, Bl. 25–38 (32), Weimar Special Court, So. G. 4/36, decision of Jan. 24, 1936; an almost unabridged copy of this judgment is published in Zipfel, *Kirchenkampf*, 352–58.

238. BA, R 22/4277, Bl. 128–29, the records of the Sept. 23, 1935, discussion between the senior Reich attorney and the chief public prosecutors at the RJM. See also Angermund, *Richterschaft*, 153.

239. The numbers mentioned by the RJM regarding the average amount of punishment imposed on the Bible Students actually misrepresent the situation. The administration of justice at the court that imposed the highest amount of punishment (an average of fifteen months, functionaries up to three years and three months) can, in reference to 1935, be considered as completely atypical. The court was probably used as an example to emphasize the expectations of the ministry. According to the 1936 Gestapa memo on the IBSA, the punishment generally amounted only "to prison sentences of between four and six months, even for functionaries." Only in exceptional, especially serious cases, punishments of between one and two years of imprisonment were imposed (IfZ, MA 554, 936286). Even though we need to consider that the Gestapa was probably interested in underestimating their numbers in order to establish a basis for criticizing the errors of the legal authorities, these numbers

are still more realistic. For instance, during 1935 the Hanseatic Special Court imposed an average of 3.1 months of imprisonment against Hamburg Jehovah's Witnesses. The Altona Special Court imposed an average of 2.2 months of imprisonment (see this book, pt. 4, ch. 12, p. 264). The Munich Special Court sentenced Bible Students generally to four months of imprisonment during 1935 (see Kalous, "Bibelforscher," 35, and appendix 4).

240. RJM, interoffice decree of Dec. 5, 1936, cited in Johe, *Justiz*, 122.

241. According to the Feb. 28, 1933, VOSchuS, article 4, defiance of the IBSA bans had to be punished with fines or imprisonment (in other words, the scope of the punishment could range from a minimum fine of 150 Reichsmark and the maximum penalty of five years of imprisonment).

242. Also during the following years, higher court officials made repeated requests indicating the need to provide the courts with additional information about the Bible Students. In Sept. 1938 Burczek, the director of the Berlin Regional Court, published an article in the *Juristische Wochenschrift* in which he warned the judiciary about the generally underestimated "subversive" nature of the Bible Students. Even though their "actions are based on supposedly idealistic motives," it would still be required to take a determined stand against them: "In these cases it is inappropriate to show compassion. . . . Even though otherwise this old woman leads a blameless life, she commits a serious offense against state and people simply by being a member of the IBSA. By participating in the activities of this association, she contributes to the fact that this association is able to continue to exist with detrimental consequences for the State. People still generally fail to recognize this fact. However, it is an important factor in assessing the apparently harmless, but from a viewpoint of national policy and penal law, subversive actions [of members of this association]" (Burczek, "Staatsbürgerpflichten," 2378; see also a similar argumentation in Crohne, "Strafrechtspflege," 9, and in Freisler, "Strafrechtspflege," 367).

243. RJM, interoffice decree of Mar. 2, 1937; Johe, *Justiz*, 122.

244. On June 2, 1933, in the context of court proceedings involving the events of the "Altona Bloodbath" [Blutsonntag], the Altona Special Court imposed the first death penalties for political offences in the Third Reich. The judges sentenced four Communists to be executed on the scaffold on the charge of assassination attempts, even though their guilt could not be substantiated. See Meyer, *Nacht über Hamburg*, 34ff.

245. See this book, pt. 2, ch. 6, p. 132.

246. Further evidence for the refusal of the Altona Special Court to impose serious sentences on Bible Students is included in Imberger, *Widerstand*, 292–93; Möller, "Steinburg," 214, 224–25. In this regard, Möller points out that the special court used specific forms of argumentation to justify the relatively short prison sentences they imposed on first offenders. To this end, the court argued that the respective defendant was "not fully aware" of the "subversive nature"

of the IBSA. His attitude toward the state was "misguided by means of questionable interpretations from abroad with regard to the Bible's commandment of having 'to obey God rather than men.'"

247. In the spring of 1937 the Schleswig-Holstein Special Court was transferred to Kiel. After this transfer, the court adjusted its assessment of punishment to the general tendency in the Reich. In fact, it even exceeded the generally accepted standards. Klaus Bästlein reports that this court "imposed extremely high prison sentences of up to four years" in Bible Student proceedings (Bästlein, "Sondergericht Kiel," 166).

248. BA, R 58/570, Bl. 47–54 (54), Kiel State Police office for the administrative district of Schleswig, General survey about the political situation in Jan. 1936.

249. See LA SH, Abt. 352 Altona no. 8928, SH SG, 11 Son KMs 70/35, decision of Nov. 11, 1935.

250. During the spring of 1937 the Schleswig-Holstein Special Court (11 Son KMs 3/37) sentenced a Jehovah's Witness from Wewelsfleth, who was accused of receiving Bible Students from other areas into his home and upholding contacts with his fellow believers in Wilster, to a fine of "only" 300 Reichsmark. According to the Wewelsfleth head official, the court imposed this minimal punishment despite the fact that the accused was an incorrigible opponent of National Socialism. See Möller, "Steinburg," 214.

251. See, for instance, SLG HH, SH SG 11 Son KMs 19/37. The court proceedings involved eight members of the Flensburg IBSA group who, among other things, were accused of involvement in the Dec. 12, 1936, pamphlet distribution (distribution of the Lucerne resolution). Three of the accused were acquitted on Feb. 27, 1937.

252. See, for example, SLG HH, SH SG 11 Son KMs 149/36. These court proceedings involved five members of the Itzehoe IBSA group. In four cases, the punishment imposed by the court corresponded to "only" half of the penalty that the State Attorney had requested.

253. The fines were always converted analogous to the imposed alternative prison sentence (five Reichsmark corresponding to one day of imprisonment). Acquittals were also taken into account. However, dismissals of court proceedings were disregarded. These statements are based on court cases involving Jehovah's Witnesses from Hamburg (main IBSA groups Altona and Hamburg).

254. See LA SH, Abt. 352 Altona no. 9194, Bl. 70–79, SH SG, 11 Son KMs 130/36, decision of Sept. 3, 1936; SLG HH, SH SG 11 Son KMs 139/36, reference files, no page numbers, Oct. 14, 1936 interrogation records of Willy T.

255. LA SH, Abt. 352 Altona no. 9201, Bl. 59, Altona outpost of the Secret State Police office, concluding report of Sept. 21, 1936.

256. LA SH, Abt. 352 Altona no. 9201, Bl. 65–71 (70), SH SG, 11 Son KMs 138/36, decision of Sept. 24, 1936; the following quotations from the same source. In this application for recognition as a former victim of NS persecution,

a Jehovah's Witness who had been imprisoned from Aug. 28 to Sept. 29, 1936, states that he was not merely threatened as indicated in the judgment but that the Gestapo official T. mistreated him during the interrogations. See VVN HH, Komiteeakten M 20, Paul M., application of Mar. 18, 1946.

257. Willy T., the criminal investigator, owed his position to a party career typical for a Gestapo official of his rank. He joined the SA in 1930, at the age of seventeen. On Oct. 1, 1931, he became an NSDAP member. During the following year, he became an SS member, and on Apr. 20, 1933, he became an assistant policeman. This, in turn, qualified him for his later acceptance as a regular police officer.

258. SLG HH, SH SG 11 Son KMs 139/36, reference files, Bl. 9–10, Der Oberstaatsanwalt beim Sondergericht in Hamburg, Aug. 5, 1937, letter to the RJM.

259. SLG HH, SH SG 11 Son KMs 139/36, subsequently connected to HSG 11 Js. Sond. 298/38.

260. SLG HH, SH SG 11 Son KMs 149/36, reference files, Bl. 25, Kiel State Police office, Oct. 22, 1936, letter to the Kiel chief public prosecutor.

261. LA SH, Abt. 352 Altona no. 9201, reference files, Bl. 1–2, Kiel State Police office, letter of Oct. 15, 1936.

262. StA HH, Hanseatic Higher Regional Court in Hamburg, presidential office, 461–3a/1, Bl. 40. This statement is included in a correction list of court decisions made by the police that higher regional court senior judge Rothenberger had compiled at the end of 1938 (the correspondence between the RJM and the RFSS is not available).

263. SH SG 5 Js 166/36, cited in SLG HH, SH SG 11 Son KMs 139/36, reference files, Bl. 5.

264. The Düsseldorf senior public prosecutor wrote a report about the discussion (enclosed in the June 8, 1937, letter to the Düsseldorf chief public prosecutor), which is published in *Beweisdokumente für die Spruchgerichte*, 279–80, document G.J. 144.

265. Four years later, the chief of the Security Police and Security Service issued another decree on Oct. 6, 1941, which referred back to a regulation made on July 1, 1937. This decree indicates that the Gestapo representatives successfully insisted on their position, and states with regard to Reich Germans that intensified interrogations should *continue* to be "restricted to Communist or Marxist leading officials, Bible Students and saboteurs" (BA R 58/243, Bl. 326–28, chief of the Security Police and Security Service, decree of Oct. 6, 1941). The wording of the July 1, 1937, decree is not available and was substituted through the June 12, 1942, regulations. It had to be "destroyed according to security regulations." See Gruchmann, *Justiz,* 718n98.

266. The June 4, 1937, discussion determined that, in cases that raised the suspicion of undue "extortion of statements by duress," the public prosecutor's office should, first of all, inquire whether the Gestapo had permission for

"intensified interrogations." If this was the case, the proceedings had to be abolished. Lothar Gruchmann states correctly that the Gestapo leaders were therefore "able to cover up even 'illegal' mistreatment performed by subordinate police authorities. They simply provided permissions subsequently" (Gruchmann, *Justiz*, 717).

267. BA, R 58/243, Bl. 337–40, the chief of the Security Police and Security Service, decree of June 12, 1942.

268. IfZ, MA 554, 936279–87 (86), memo, "Die Internationale Bibelforscher-Vereinigung," encl. to the Dec. 24, 1936, interoffice decree of the central State Police office in Munich.

269. SLG HH, HSG 11 Js. Sond. 96/37, Bl. 8, Hamburg Gestapo, file remarks of Mar. 25, 1937.

270. Ibid., Bl. 10.

271. Ibid., decision of Aug. 17, 1937.

272. BA, R 22/4277, Bl. 185, records of the June 18, 1937, discussion with the higher regional court senior judges and the RJM chief public prosecutors.

273. Liesche, "Bibelforscher."

274. Brandstätter, "Strafvollzug," 53.

275. Ibid., 48. According to Brandstätter, "only a little more than one third" of the Bible Students listened to the ideas presented and "gradually accepted them." Only two out of sixteen Jehovah's Witnesses exposed to especially "intensive instructions" supposedly disassociated completely from the IBSA and two were "especially stubborn." The others, according to the prison warden, had lost their confidence and could still be persuaded to accept to the Third Reich. According to Brandstätter, these people should, however, not be placed under "all kinds of restrictions" after they had been released from prison: "They should receive an opportunity to march along, even if in the beginning this would be in the very last row."

276. Brandstätter, "Strafvollzug," 52.

277. Cited in BA, R 22/1422, Bl. 29.

278. BA, R 22/1422, Bl. 29, RJM, letter of Nov. 21, 1935. The suggestion of providing Jehovah's Witnesses "only with the New Testament" was probably based on the reasoning that "Jehovah" is generally regarded as the God of the Old Testament. Therefore, it was not considered "dangerous" to provide Jehovah's Witnesses with the New Testament. At the same time, this gives evidence of the general rejection of the Old Testament during the NS period. As a religious document from a Jewish source, it was only reluctantly accepted as part of the Christian faith.

279. Liesche, "Bibelforscher."

280. Herr, "Bibelforscher," 87–88.

281. BA, R 22/4371, no page numbers, RJM, decree of Nov. 21, 1940.

282. See *Yearbook* 1974, 128–29.

283. These explanations are based on the following court records: SLG HH, HSG 11 Js. Sond. 298/38.

284. On July 18, 1937, in a meeting of the SS Security Service, the question was discussed how "religious opponents" and "sectarianism" could be resisted in the future by using the intelligence service. As a result, the "heads of the superior and subordinate departments" were provided with "regulations for the resistance of sectarianism." These regulations requested an increasing use of "police informers." See Neuhäusler, *Kreuz und Hakenkreuz*, 1:376.

285. Several reports substantiate the fact that the SS and the Gestapo used police informers for the purpose of spying on IBSA groups. They even re-cruited Bible Students for this purpose and promised to suspend their sentences in exchange for turning their fellow believers over to the police (see Imberger, *Widerstand*, 351; *Yearbook* 1974, 150–51, 178–79; *Yearbook* 1986, 128; Steinberg, *Essen*, 165–66; Wickert, "Frauen," 218–19). This also disproves Weyrauch's the-ory (*Gestapo V-Leute*, 64–66, 78–79), that the Gestapo counted Jehovah's Wit-nesses among the group of people who was generally "uncooperative."

286. The explanations are based on: SLG HH, HSG 11 Js. Sond. 298/38, GnH 3659/42; VVN HH, Komiteeakten XZ 1; AfW HH R 231191. After 1945, in their application for recognition as former victims of NS persecution, several Jehovah's Witnesses from Hamburg state that their condemnation was the result of a denunciation by Erwin Z., the former leader of the IBSA youth group. To a great extent, these accusations are based on the fact that Erwin Z. renounced his IBSA membership in 1940 and did not return to the IBSA after 1945. There-fore, Jehovah's Witnesses consider him to be an "apostate" and to be respon-sible for the betrayal at that time. According to discussions with people who were members of the Hamburg IBSA group at that time, Jehovah's Witnesses were apparently not sure who provided the Gestapo with the information about the Hamburg IBSA activities after the end of 1938. Therefore, no personal in-formation is provided and, in addition to changing data regarding time and lo-cations, the initial of that particular person has been substituted with X.

287. IfZ, MA 554, 936279–87 (86), memo, "Die Internationale Bibelforscher-Vereinigung," encl. to the Dec. 24, 1936, interoffice decree of the central State Police office in Munich.

288. Secret State Police office, situation report for the period between Oct. 1, 1936, and Feb. 28, 1937, cited in Steinberg, *Essen*, 160n8.

289. Ibid.

290. Niedersächsisches Hauptstaatsarchiv Hannover, Lower Saxony, Hann 80, Lün. II-94b, Secret State Police office, interoffice decree of Apr. 22, 1937.

291. BA, R 22/1467, Bl. 286, central State Police office in Stettin, letter of May 13, 1937.

292. Several months earlier, on Jan. 18, 1937, the RJM had issued a decree according to which the penal institutions were instructed to inform the regional State Police offices immediately of any anticipated releases from prison of "people who were guilty of acts of treason and high treason." See *Dokumente zur Gleichschaltung*, 228.

293. See BA, R 22/1467, Bl. 286, "Der Generalstaatsanwalt in Stettin," letter of June 4, 1937. The discussion in the ministry took place two days earlier, on June 2, 1937. See Gruchmann, *Justiz*, 620–22.

294. SLG HH, SH SG 11 Son KMs 19/37, Bl. 160, "Aussendienststelle Flensburg der Staatspolizeistelle für den Regierungsbezirk Schleswig," letter of June 4, 1937. The dates for the releases from prison in the four cases concerned are as follows: Oct. 13, 1937; Oct. 26, 1937; Nov. 5, 1937; and Apr. 25, 1938.

295. The Karlsruhe chief public prosecutor stated that he considered it "inappropriate to impose protective detention as a general measure on all Earnest Bible Students after they had served their sentence" (BA, R 22/3136, Bl. 131, the Karlsruhe chief public prosecutor, situation report of Oct. 18, 1937).

296. BA, R 22/3136, Bl. 157, cited in the Dec. 16, 1937, situation report of the Karlsruhe chief public prosecutor.

297. Brandstätter, "Strafvollzug," 55.

298. Herr, "Bibelforscher," 88. From May 1938, Rudi Herr, senior instructor at the Ichtershausen prison, followed the concept of selecting from among the Bible Students those who had a "potential of being reintegrated into society" in order to reclaim them to the "people's community." In this way, he separated them from the Bible Students whom he considered to be "incorrigible," and who "lacked the potential for re-integration." According to Herr, these Bible Students should be "placed into a concentration camp." The senior instructor used certain categories according to which he "selected the available Bible Students."

299. BA, R 22/1467, Bl. 285, cited in the May 21, 1937, letter sent to the RJM from the senior judge of the higher regional court in Frankfurt am Main. The RJM's files include a copy of this report, which the presiding judge of the Frankfurt Special Court had submitted to the local regional court senior judge on May 10, 1937. According to this copy, the quotation in which the author made an omission reads as follows: The Gestapo official "gave orders to arrest the defendant again, right there in the courthouse, even though the special court had *not* ordered a release from prison." In consideration of the context in its entirety, both with regard to the report as well as the subsequent development, this was probably a simple error in transcription as a result of repeated copying.

300. The writ of protective detention for the purpose of preventing imminent danger gave the Gestapo considerable power, which was extensively used to correct judgments made by the legal authorities: The Gestapo imposed protective detention prior to, or instead of, legally imposed penalties. In cases in which the Gestapo considered the amount of punishment inadequate, they imposed protective detention even after prison sentences had been served. These violations of their authority became even more apparent in cases in which protective detention was imposed after the legal authorities had pronounced an acquittal or had granted a pardon. On the practice of "judgment reversals" by

means of imposition of protective detention, see Gruchmann, *Justiz*, 583–631; Johe, *Justiz*, 138–43, 155–66.

301. BA, R 22/4277, Bl. 145, RJM, letter of June 12, 1937.

302. BA, R 22/4277, Bl. 149–91, records of the June 18, 1937, discussion with the higher regional court senior judges and the chief public prosecutors at the RJM. The following statements are included in these records.

303. Six months earlier, in the journal *Deutsche Justiz*, Crohne had made similar comments on the IBSA activities. See Crohne, "Strafrechtspflege," 9.

304. As early as Jan. 13, 1937, the RJM informed the Darmstadt Special Court that "this problem of connections between the KPD and the IBSA had caused [the ministry] to work closely together with the Secret State Police office" (in Warmbrunn, "Strafgerichtsbarkeit," 375n195).

305. In 1938 SS-Hauptsturmführer (chief Storm leader) Kolrep wrote an article on "sectarianism" (possibly as part of the training materials of the Security Service for the "resistance of opponents") stating that the membership of the IBSA was estimated to be 350,000. Kolrep estimated that the total number of adherents of sectarian movements in Germany "currently amounted to . . . several million" (BA, R 58/779, Bl. 143 Rs).

306. The interoffice decree is probably the same as the decree issued by the RJM on Mar. 2, 1937 (see this book, pt. 4, ch. 12, p. 263).

307. The documentary of the central European Office of the Watch Tower Society confirms Crohne's statements regarding the pronouncement of judgments against Bible Students in the higher regional court districts. According to the reports included in Zürcher (*Kreuzzug*, 93ff.), the maximum punishment of five years of imprisonment was imposed by the Saxony Special Court in Leipzig (jurisdictional district of the Dresden Higher Regional Court), the Thuringia Special Court in Rudolfstadt (jurisdictional district of the Jena Higher Regional Court), as well as the special courts in Königsberg, Dresden, and Darmstadt. The press reports and individual reports of victims, on which this documentation is based, reach as far back as the middle of 1937 and, consequently, cover approximately the same period.

308. In Nov. 1933, under leadership of RJM Gürtner, an "official committee dealing with penal law" was appointed for the purpose of establishing a new German Penal Code. In the context of a fundamental penal reform, this new Penal Code was to replace the Penal Code of 1871 criticized by the National Socialists for its "liberalism." At the end of Oct. 1936 this committee had completed the draft for the new Penal Code. At the beginning of Dec. 1936 the draft was submitted to the Cabinet for adoption. Despite several discussions in the Cabinet, this new German Penal Code was not approved. Martin Broszat states about the reasons for this nonapproval: "Without a doubt, at least for a considerable period of time, Hitler rejected the idea of being restricted to a codified penal law provided with detailed explanations. He especially rejected this idea in the context of a so-called 'National Socialist Law,' which could no

longer be disregarded by referring to it as an 'outdated, liberal, legal norm'" (Broszat, "Strafjustiz," 393).

309. In May 1934 Ministerialrat (ministerial counsel) Fritz Grau at the RJM submitted the suggestions for the section "disparagement of the Wehrmacht," which the official penal law committee had developed. These suggestions included penal regulations regarding "involvement in anti-military associations." According to Grau, these penal regulations were directed against "pacifist associations that had the objective of undermining or ridiculing the willingness of the [German] nation to perform military service" (BA, R 22/962). A slightly amended version of these regulations is included under article 147 in the new German Penal Code. Since, however, this Penal Code was not adopted, appropriate penal regulations were enacted after the beginning of the war by means of article 3 of the Nov. 25, 1939, Protective Regulations for the Armed Forces [Wehrkraftschutzordnung]. These regulations enabled the courts to punish any "involvement in anti-military associations" with severe prison sentences. See this book, pt. 5, ch. 13, pp. 341–42.

310. StA HH, Gefängnisverwaltung II, Abt. 7, RJM, interoffice decree of July 2, 1937.

311. In a letter that the RFSS sent to the RJM on Feb. 8, 1939, it is stated that the ministry, by means of its July 6, 1937, letter, "generally agrees with this way of handling matters" (BA, R 22/1467, Bl. 326).

312. BA, R 22/4371, no page numbers, RJM, July 7, 1937 interoffice decree to all chief public prosecutors.

313. BA, R 22/1261, Bl. 93, cited in the Jan. 22, 1938, letter by the chief public prosecutors in Naumburg/Saale to the RJM.

314. Secret State Police office, interoffice decree of Aug. 5, 1937, cited in *Der Prozeß gegen die Hauptkriegsverbrecher*, 31:13–14, document 084-D.

315. The Jan. 25, 1938, Decree Regarding Protective Detention [Schutzhafterlass] by the RMdI (BA, R 58/1027) further centralized the authority of imposing and withdrawing protective detention. Afterwards, this authority rested *exclusively* with the Gestapa in Berlin, meaning that only the Gestapa was allowed to impose protective detention. The other regional State Police offices were authorized only to issue orders for a "temporary arrest." For additional information, see Broszat, *Anatomy of the SS State*, 190–91.

316. DdW, protective detention records of Julius R., Kislau convict camp; see also Concentration Camp Memorial Breitenau, Guxhagen, Akte/Schutzhäftling, no. 1120.

317. In the literature, it is often not taken into consideration that, after a prison sentence had been served, the Gestapo first of all examined whether the prisoner had "changed his attitude," or whether he was an "incorrigible" Bible Student. With reference to the Apr. 22, 1937, Gestapa decree, Möller ("Steinburg," 217) makes the assumption that "all IBSA members who had received prison sentences" were generally "transferred to a concentration camp after they had served their [legally imposed] prison sentence."

318. The Apr. 12, 1934, decree by the RMdI involving the "imposition and execution of protective detention" prescribed quarterly appointments for a review of the detention order (BA, Sammlung Schumacher/271). These reviews had the objective of determining whether there was still a basis for further imprisonment. Subsequent revisions of the decree for protective detention did not affect this regulation.

319. See, Imberger, *Widerstand*, 299; Zipfel, *Kirchenkampf*, 193.

320. In the literature, the reverse statements were often mentioned only in the context of releases from concentration camps and were taken to be an "offer for release from imprisonment" (see, for instance, Kater, "Bibelforscher," 190). In addition to the concentration camps, the Gestapo used these statements for various other purposes also. For instance, they presented the statement for preventive purposes at Gestapo interrogations, requiring people to manifest their loyalty to the state. The Gestapo presented the statements prior to an imposition of "supplementary detention," which became the usual practice in 1937. In such cases, the decision of whether those concerned were taken into protective detention after they had served their legally imposed prison sentence also depended on their willingness to sign the statement.

321. SLG HH, HSG 11 Js. Sond. 298/38, Verpflichtungserklärung.

322. See, Zipfel, *Kirchenkampf*, 193.

323. *Yearbook* 1974, 170–71. Therefore, the NS representatives accused Jehovah's Witnesses of adopting the "principle of a relative obligation to speak the truth" (*VB*, Apr. 25, 1937). In this regard, the Gestapo stated: "The IBSA ban in Germany has led to a situation in which its members are even allowed to lie. In order to salve their consciences, they have been told: You are not obligated to tell the truth to the police or the courts because these institutions were not established by God. On the contrary, they are part of Satan's organization, and it is not necessary to tell Satan the truth" (BDC, VGH, 8 J 20/38, Bl. 24, Hamburg State Police office, concluding report of Dec. 21, 1937).

324. See *Yearbook* 1974, 170–71. During the initial period of the NS regime, Jehovah's Witnesses frequently adopted this position during interrogations. In such cases, the records state: "I am not a member of the IBSA. I am a Jehovah's Witness" (SLG HH, SH SG 11 Son KMs 149/36, Bl. 63, Sept. 28, 1936, statement at the local police authorities in Itzehoe). Since the new 1931 arrangement, the IBSA members considered themselves to be Jehovah's appointed witnesses. Therefore, they did not object to denying a Bible Student membership; they denied *only in exceptional cases* that they were Jehovah's Witnesses.

325. See, for instance, the statement that a Bible Student from Krefeld made to the Gestapo on Sept. 20, 1938: "I served my second prison sentence and promise that I will no longer be involved in prohibited IBSA activities. I will, however, keep my religious convictions. In the event of war, I will do any kind of work. But I will not take up arms" (cited in Billstein, *Krefeld*, 307).

326. SLG HH, HSG 11 Js. Sond. 298/38. It is possible to make these statements because, apart from two exceptions, the public prosecutor's records of

investigation also include the respective personal records from the Gestapo. In general, records were returned to the State Police office after court proceedings were concluded. Besides the accusation records, personal identification records, interrogation records, and so forth, the records include also the reverse statement.

327. Christl Wickert analyzed the Düsseldorf Gestapo records of cases involving female Bible Students. According to her statements, "more than half of the number of suspects and accused succumbed to the coercion and signed the statement of renouncing membership in their religious association" (Wickert, "Frauen," 218).

328. Even in the concentration camps, the number of Bible Students who signed the statement was initially significantly higher than in later years. In 1935, 13 of the 120 Bible Student prisoners at the Esterwegen concentration camp (approximately 1 in every 10) supposedly signed the statement. See, *Awake!*, Nov. 22, 1992, 18–19.

329. See Lichtenegger, "Wiens Bibelforscherinnen," 172. Even though a comparatively high number of people signed the statement during "pretrial detention," it might not be appropriate to speak of the "'negative aspects' of the Bible Students' resistance." In my opinion, this questionable viewpoint is the result of a naive idealizing retrospective that had the objective of transforming the history of resistance activities into a heroic epic. Such representations ignore the reality of human behavior.

330. Apr. 30, 1938, Law Regarding the Guarantee of Exemption from Punishment [Gesetz über die Gewährung von Straffreiheit], *RGBl.* 1938 I, 433.

331. BA, Sammlung Schumacher/267 I, Secret State Police office, decree of May 4, 1938, cited in the May 14, 1938, interoffice decree by the central State Police office in Munich.

332. BA, Sammlung Schumacher/267 I, central State Police office in Munich, interoffice decree of May 14, 1938.

333. In the "concise collection of decrees regarding sectarian affairs" that the RSHA compiled until the end of 1942, the Gestapa decree is recorded under reference no. 25/IBSA (BA, R 58/1074, Bl. 30). The wording of this Gestapa decree is included in the Jan. 6, 1939, interoffice decree by the Düsseldorf State Police office, cited in Steinberg, *Essen*, 282.

334. As far as can be determined, apart from a few particularly exceptional cases, until new regulations were instituted in 1943/44, Bible Student prisoners were released from concentration camp imprisonment without giving the required signature on only one occasion. These releases were the result of an amnesty that was issued on the occasion of Hitler's fiftieth birthday on Apr. 20, 1939. This was the last time that a relatively large number of prisoners of different categories were released from the concentration camps. In consultation with the State Police offices, the chief of the Security Police determined who would be considered for this release. In the regulations that were issued to the

State Police offices by means of the Apr. 5, 1939, interoffice decree, Heydrich gave the following instructions under Point 5: "Prisoners 60 years and older, including the incorrigible Bible Students who persistently refuse to sign the statement that would show their loyalty [to the State], if they had no previous convictions" (BA, R 58/264, Bl. 376–78, chief of the Security Police, interoffice decree of Apr. 5, 1939). On Apr. 20/21, 1939, a total of fifty-three Jehovah's Witnesses were released from the Buchenwald concentration camp, most likely as a result of the "amnesty on the occasion of [Hitler's] birthday." See, BA, NS 4 Bu/vorl. 137, Buchenwald concentration camp, records of the prisoner head count.

335. BA, Sammlung Schumacher/267 I, central State Police office in Munich, interoffice decree of Jan. 23, 1939.

336. AfW HH, 260488, Bl. 29, Apr. 15, 1941, arrest warrant. In some cases, the people who refused to sign the statement had to provide the State Police offices with a confirmation of their refusal. On Apr. 3, 1944, after serving a prison sentence of two years, thirty-six-year-old Eleonore Müller was taken into protective detention by the police. At the Düsseldorf State Police office, she refused to sign the statement presented to her. Therefore, she was requested to confirm her refusal by signing the following statement for the interrogation records: "I am not able to sign the requested 'statement . . . ' First of all, I do not think that the IBSA is distributing false teachings. Secondly, I still adhere to these teachings. I calmly anticipate my impending transfer to a concentration camp" (records of Apr. 3, 1944, cited in Steinberg, *Essen*, 283).

337. District administration of Waldenburg, letter of Apr. 5, 1937, reprinted in Zürcher, *Kreuzzug*, no page numbers (following 192).

338. As early as 1939, the regional State Police office in Hamburg—and probably also other State Police offices—began in some cases to simplify administrative procedures. For this purpose, they sent copies of the reverse statement to the administration offices of the penal institutions with the request for further action (see SLG HH, HSG 11 Js. Sond. 298/38). The Gestapo was not concerned about this procedure since they still made the final decision in every case.

339. Herr, "Bibelforscher," 88.

340. Apr. 15, 1971, recollections by Willi Lehmbecker.

341. See Hartmann, "Kriegsdienstverweigerung" (1982), 93.

342. The following excerpt gives some insight into such a meeting: "My wife cried and my little daughter threw her arms around my neck and begged: 'Please, daddy, come home!' I gave in and said that I would sign the statement on the next day. However, when I was taken back to my cell, I realized the consequences of my decision. In tears, I regretted my wrong decision and prayed to Jehovah to forgive me" (cited in Menzinger, "Jugend," 120).

343. On Rothenberger's protest note against "judgment reversals," see also Gruchmann, *Justiz*, 623–26; Johe, *Justiz*, 156–60.

344. StA HH, Hanseatic Higher Regional Court in Hamburg, presidential office, 461-3a/1, Bl. 75.

345. From Fuhlsbüttel, this Jehovah's Witness was transferred to Sachsenhausen. He was released a broken man and later had a fatal accident; his wife was murdered at Auschwitz. See "Zeitzeugen aus Schleswig-Holstein. Ergänzung zur Ausstellung 'Standhaft trotz Verfogung,'" Kiel, 1997 (plaque regarding Ruth H).

346. StA HH, Hanseatic Higher Regional Court in Hamburg, presidential office, 461-3a/1, Bl. 79.

347. BA, R 22/1467, RJM, Dec. 13, 1938, letter to the chief of the Security Police.

348. Cited in BA, R 22/1467, Bl. 349, the senior judge of the Hanseatic Higher Regional Court, letter of Jan. 30, 1939.

349. StA HH, Hanseatic Higher Regional Court in Hamburg, presidential office, 461-3a/1, Bl. 87, records of the Feb. 1, 1939, discussion with the senior judges.

350. BA, R 22/1467, Bl. 325–27, RFSS, Feb. 8, 1939, letter to the RJM (italics in the original).

351. In the literature, it is generally stated that Jehovah's Witnesses, as the "only group," could "avoid being admitted" into a concentration camp by merely signing the reverse statement. It has also been asserted that they could "determine the final outcome of their imprisonment through specific actions on their part." However, both statements have to be considered incorrect (Pingel, *Häftlinge*, 87). On the contrary, the State Police offices and "political departments" at the concentration camps examined, first of all, the "trustworthiness" of a submitted signature. To this end, in its Apr. 27, 1939, interoffice decree, the Düsseldorf State Police office provided the police authorities with specific instructions. The decree states that even "if Bible Students would make a trustworthy statement to the effect that they would no longer be involved in [IBSA activities], or if they signed the statement," a release could take place only on orders by the Gestapa. The "right to release prisoners was exclusively reserved for the Gestapa" (*Der Prozeß gegen die Hauptkriegsverbrecher*, 31:15–16, document 084-D). Such examinations took place during a police detention of generally several days at the local State Police office, immediately following the release from legally imposed imprisonment. In some cases, they were also performed during periods of intermediate imprisonment in police prisons or convict camps (pt. 4, ch. 12, pp. 284–85). In the concentration camps, Jehovah's Witnesses who had signed the statement were subjected to extended "periods of surveillance." This practice was based on the experience that many Jehovah's Witnesses later withdrew their signature and "corrected" their decision because they had generally signed the statement under extreme coercion (pt. 5, ch. 15, pp. 416–17). As a result of these examinations of trustworthiness, quite a number of people were not released, even if they had signed the statement (or had

not withdrawn their signature). After 1942, in the course of improving conditions for Jehovah's Witnesses in the concentration camps (pt. 5, ch. 15, pp. 439–47), a change took place. Subsequently, the commandant's headquarters no longer required a special period of surveillance. Prisoners who signed the declaration were immediately released from the concentration camp. Toward the end of the war, some of the releases were even based merely on a "handshake" (pt. 5, ch. 15, pp. 449–52).

352. BA, R 22/1467, Bl. 328, RJM, file remarks of Mar. 27, 1939.

353. BA, R 22/1467, Bl. 329–30, RJM, Mar. 27, 1939, letter to the senior judge of the Hanseatic Higher Regional Court.

354. In some cases, acquittals were pronounced not because of lack of evidence but rather because the defendant had been found innocent. In such cases, the RMdI categorically rejected an imposition of protective detention. See Gruchmann, *Justiz*, 601–2.

355. From the beginning of this controversy, the legal authorities did not question the fact that protective detention that the "State Police offices imposed for purposes of prevention" would come under the exclusive authority of the Gestapo. Protective detention was considered to be a political measure and, therefore, belonged to an area in the Führer state that had to remain outside of the control and examination by the legal authorities. Article 7 of the Feb. 10, 1936, Prussian Law Regarding the Secret State Police [Preußisches Gesetz über die Geheime Staatspolizei] determined that Gestapo decrees were not subject to due process of law. It states: "Decrees and affairs of the Secret State Police are not subject to legal procedure" (*PrGS* 1936, 21–22).

356. SLG HH, HSG 11 Js. Sond. 173/38, decision of Apr. 11, 1938, 81–82.

357. 1938 annual situation report of the RSHA, *Meldungen aus dem Reich*, 2: 7–214 (126).

358. See the charts about the average assessment of punishment in Zipfel, *Kirchenkampf*, 188 (based on Berlin compensation records; various court decisions). See also the charts in Kalous, "Bibelforscher," 35, and appendix 4 (Bible Student proceedings at the Munich Special Court between 1933 and 1938).

359. To this end, the courts could refer to the Feb. 17, 1938, decision by the highest court. The Reich Court viewed the gathering for "family worship" as a prohibited activity since it involved the danger that, in this way, the family would continue to uphold the close relationship that existed between the former members of this denomination. The family, in turn, would become the center "for a future reorganization of the sect" (*DJ* 100 [1938]: 829–30, RG, 5D 599/37, decision of Feb. 17, 1938).

360. SLG HH, HSG 11 Js. Sond. 608/40, decision of May 20, 1940. (At the place "continued to talk about the Bible," the judgment included the following handwritten remark: "according to their interpretation.") In 1934 the Reich Court still supported the view that the continuation of a "friendship between two people" did not signify that "an organizational arrangement was maintained."

361. Two years earlier, the Hamburg Special Court defined "involvement in Bible Student activities" in the following way (this definition was also used as a basis for the above-mentioned court proceedings): "To be liable to prosecution, it is required, from an objective point of view, that at least two people form or maintain connections based on the teachings of the International Bible Students. From a subjective point of view, these connections have to be maintained voluntarily and deliberately" (FGN, NHS 13-7-3-3, HSG, 11 Js. Sond. 279/38, decision of Apr. 23, 1938, 32). The court adopted this legal opinion in acknowledgment of the fact that it is impossible to separate the activities of Jehovah's Witnesses into activities subject to punishment and personal faith exempt from punishment since "the proclamation of their teachings [is] an essential part of their faith:" "In other words: Every Bible Student is under obligation to 'proclaim the Kingdom' if he does not want to run the risk of being expelled and, consequently, lose his prospect of life in the Kingdom. (The Bible Students themselves also consider this 'proclamation' to be an integral part of their faith and not merely a religious activity.)" (SLG HH, EHSG 11 Js. Sond. 173/38, decision of Apr. 11, 1938, 13).

362. SLG HH, Hamburg Municipal Court 131 Ds 1432/40, including HSG 11 Js. Sond. 956/40, decision of Mar. 25, 1941.

363. BDC, VGH, 8 J 20/38, Bl. 1–20 (19), "Der Generalstaatsanwalt bei dem Hanseatischen Oberlandesgericht," letter of Jan. 5, 1938.

364. BDC, VGH, 8 J 20/38, Bl. 35, "Der Oberreichsanwalt beim VGH," decree of Jan. 19, 1938.

365. SLG HH, HSG 11 Js. Sond. 173/38, decision of Apr. 11, 1938, 75. In other court proceedings involving the same offense it was specifically stated that a connection between the Bible Students and Communism cannot be substantiated: "To protect the National Socialist state against the International Bible Students it is necessary that the accused receive serious punishment. Such punishment is required despite the fact that people in general do not fully appreciate the danger [of this association]. It is required despite the fact that there is no evidence that any of the defendants were formerly Communists or presently sympathize with the Communists in Soviet Russia" (SLG HH, HSG 11 Js. Sond. 179/38, decision of May 4, 1938, 32).

366. Ibid., decision of Apr. 11, 1938.

367. BA, R 22/3390, Bl. 20, "Der Oberreichsanwalt beim VGH," situation report of Jan. 31, 1940.

368. See the court case of Lothar Schirmacher documented in Kammler, *Kasseler Soldaten*, 138–41. In this case, involvement in IBSA activities coincided with political resistance activities. Schirmacher was born in 1916. His parents became IBSA members in 1922. Shortly before the NS takeover, Schirmacher had joined the "International Socialist Combat Federation." On May 5, 1937, because of his involvement in the distribution of the IBSA "Resolution" pamphlet, the Kassel Special Court sentenced him to two years of imprisonment.

According to his statements, his judgment was based on an offense against the VOSchuS in concurrence with "preparation for high treason."

369. It must be emphasized that it was not the Gestapo's involvement in acts of pardon, which took place as early as 1937, that had a bearing on the fact that in only a few cases a pardon was granted. Instead, it was the legal authorities' own practices that proved to be extremely restrictive. For instance, in the spring of 1937, twenty court proceedings took place at the Munich Special Court, resulting in the punishment of 103 Jehovah's Witnesses with various periods of imprisonment (StA M, Staatsanwaltschaften 8551). According to an analysis of the corresponding execution records and acts of pardon, the practice of granting a pardon is represented as follows: In 101 cases, records of execution were available. In almost half (47.5%) of these cases, petitions for an act of pardon were submitted. Twenty-one of these forty-eight petitions were submitted by the condemned people themselves. In the majority of the other cases, the petitioners were marriage mates or close relatives. In a few cases, even employers or defense attorneys submitted the petitions. Forty-two of these forty-eight petitions for an act of pardon were rejected. In only six cases, the petitions were approved. Seventeen of the people rejected filed an appeal against this rejection. In eight of these cases, a pardon was granted. Consequently, a total of fourteen petitions (29.2%) resulted in an act of pardon. In these cases, the remainder of the sentence was suspended on probation. The other eighty-seven people had to serve their full sentences.

370. SLG HH, HSG 11 Js. Sond. 298/38, GnH 1256/41, Bl. 5, central State Police office in Hamburg, Nov. 11, 1939, letter to the chief public prosecutor at the Hanseatic Court of Appeals.

371. Ibid., Bl. 13, central State Police office in Hamburg, letter of Mar. 16, 1940.

372. SLG HH, HSG 11 Js. Sond. 298/38, GnH 1256/41, Bl. 15, central State Police office in Hamburg, letter of Mar. 28, 1940.

Part 5. Jehovah's Witnesses during the War Years

1. BA, Sammlung Schumacher/267 I, Würzburg State Police office, interoffice decree of Mar. 16, 1938.

2. The persecution of the Austrian Jehovah's Witnesses under the Austrofascist government of Dr. Kurt Schuschnigg was restricted mainly to the confiscation of publications, house searches, and short periods of imprisonment. On this persecution, see *Yearbook* 1939, 140; *Yearbook* 1989, 92–98. See also this book, p. 627, n.108.

3. On the persecution and resistance of Austrian Jehovah's Witnesses between 1938 and 1945, see especially the country report of *Yearbook* 1989, 98–134. This report also includes a number of documents. See also the various publications of the DÖW, which are included in the bibliography (listed under

the main editor). See also Lichtenegger, "Wiens Bibelforscherinnen," 138–65; and Luza, *Austria*, 62–64.

4. On the Prague convention, see *Yearbook* 1938, 129; *Yearbook* 1989, 97–98; Neugebauer, "'Ernste Bibelforscher,'" 166–67.

5. The annual service report of the Watch Tower Society mentions a total of 467 Kingdom proclaimers who were active in Austria during the year prior to the ban (*Yearbook* 1936, 89). In 1937 this number amounted to 549 Kingdom proclaimers (*Yearbook* 1989, 134). In Germany, there were between 25,000 and 30,000 Jehovah's Witnesses, about 0.38 percent of the total population. The total number of Jehovah's Witnesses in Austria amounted to 700 at the most, corresponding to only 0.1 percent of the total population. Consequently, regarding the successes in their preaching activity, there was a ratio of four to one between Jehovah's Witnesses in the German Reich and in Austria.

6. See *Yearbook* 1989, 99–100.

7. See this book, pt. 4, ch. 10, p. 218; pt. 4, ch. 11, pp. 243–44.

8. Between 1938 and 1945, at least 445 Austrian Jehovah's Witnesses were arrested for various periods of time (see this book, pt. 5, ch. 13, pp. 323–24.) Taking into consideration that in 1937 the number of Kingdom proclaimers amounted to 549, we can assume that more than 80 percent of the Austrian Jehovah's Witnesses participated in the underground activities.

9. See *Yearbook* 1989, 112–13; May 23, 1986, recollections by Alois Moser.

10. BA Sammlung Schumacher/267 I, no page numbers, cited in the Mar. 27, 1939, interoffice decree by the Würzburg State Police office.

11. The so-called Decree Concerning the Division of Functions [Funktionstrennungserlass], issued on July 1, 1937, regulated which responsibilities the Gestapo and the SS had in monitoring the activities of opponents of the regime. With regard to the surveillance of activities of the churches, sectarian groups, and other religious and ideological associations, the Gestapo handled "all individual cases." The SS, on the other hand, had the responsibility of handling "all general and fundamental questions." See *Meldungen aus dem Reich*, 1:14.

12. See Zinnhobler, "Zeugen Jehovas," 199, 204–6.

13. The book was first published in New York in 1939 and had wide circulation. It is directed against all "totalitarian forces" (including the pope, Hitler, Stalin, Franco, and Mussolini), and describes fascism under Hitler as the cruelest component. However, the title *Fascism or Freedom* does not refer to the difference between an authoritarian regime and a democratic form of society. Consequently, it should also not be considered as a politically polemical document. It rather addresses the central issue of the Bible Student teachings, which Rutherford proclaimed as follows: "Shall the world be ruled in righteousness by Christ the enthroned King of Jehovah? or shall it be ruled by selfish, arbitrary dictators? To be sure, men cannot settle that issue; but soon the Lord will settle it, and every person must choose to take one side or the other and to receive the consequences" (Rutherford, *Fascism or Freedom*, 3).

14. Gestapo Vienna, report of Nov. 2, 1939, cited in *Yearbook* 1989, 105.

15. Vienna Special Court, 1 KLs 29/40, decision of Jan. 28, 1941, cited in *Yearbook* 1989, 110.

16. Gestapo decree of June 8, 1940, cited in *Yearbook* 1989, 108–9

17. See Neugebauer, "'Ernste Bibelforscher,'" 166–67; *Yearbook* 1989, 109. The court proceedings against Jehovah's Witnesses who had been taken into custody during the wave of arrests in June 1940 took place at the Vienna Special Court. During these proceedings, the court demanded the death penalty for Peter Gölles on the charge of "demoralization of the armed forces." However, the special court sentenced him to ten years of imprisonment.

18. See Neugebauer, "'Ernste Bibelforscher,'" 168ff.

19. The Mauthausen concentration camp, located near Linz, records an extremely high number of deaths. In 1940 the death rate amounted to 76 percent (see Pingel, *Häftlinge*, 82). During the initial period, the Bible Student prisoners at this concentration camp, the majority of whom were Austrians, were systematically destroyed. At the end of Feb. 1940 a recruiting board was set up at the concentration camp. According to reports, thirty-five Jehovah's Witnesses refused to sign the military identification card. Consequently, they were gradually worked to death in the Mauthausen quarry. The severe winter of 1939/40, with temperatures between 10 and 25 degrees below zero Fahrenheit (20 and 30 degrees below zero Celsius), hunger, and lack of clothing, increased the suffering. In just four months, between Jan. and Apr. 1940, a total of 52, according to other sources 53 (36.37%), of the 143 Jehovah's Witnesses (number of prisoners on Jan. 1, 1940) died. In this context, it must be taken into consideration that on Feb. 18, 1940, twenty-five Jehovah's Witnesses were "fortunate" to be transferred to the Dachau concentration camp. Cited in Chêne, *Mauthausen*, 182; Gostner, *1000 Tage im KZ*, 96; Maršálek, *Mauthausen*, 273; May 27, 1986, recollections by Hubert Mattischek; May 23, 1986, recollections by Alois Moser.

20. Numerical data cited in *Yearbook* 1989, 133–34; Cole, *Jehovah's Witnesses* [German edition], 199. Radomir Luza mentions slightly different numbers. According to his report, 131 Austrian Jehovah's Witnesses "died at the hands of the Nazis" and twenty-five were executed. See Luza, *Austria*, 63.

21. See *Yearbook* 1938, 143; Nov. 24, 1987, recollections by Karl Hanl.

22. SS, first quarterly report of 1939, *Meldungen aus dem Reich*, 2:237.

23. See *Yearbook* 1986, 130–31.

24. See *Yearbook* 1987, 145.

25. With regard to the persecution of the Bible Students Association in Czechoslovakia, see *Yearbook* 1972, 134–36.

26. For the following explanations, see M. Koch, "Engelhard," 95ff.; BA, R 60 II/99-3.

27. See Steinberg, *Essen*, 165.

28. Personal documents of Richard Singelenberg, records of interrogation of Ludwig Cyranek, II B 1–69/40.

29. From the beginning of 1940 on, Robert Arthur Winkler, a Jehovah's Witness from Germany, directed IBSA activities in the Netherlands. After his arrest on Oct. 21, 1941, he was first sent to the Vught concentration camp. He was later transferred to the Sachsenhausen concentration camp. He survived both concentration camps as well as the Apr. 1945 death march. For personal information about Winkler and his activities, see Graffard and Tristan, *Bibelforscher*, 148–49, 211; *Yearbook 1986*, 134–35, 154ff.; *Watchtower*, Mar. 1, 1972, 143.

30. Some of the statements made in the literature in this regard have to be considered incorrect. For instance, Steinberg states that during the war "the former [IBSA] leader on the Reich level Winkler lived in the Netherlands" and that Ludwig Cyranek was his "leader on the state level" (Steinberg, *Essen*, 165). Koch considered Engelhard to be the IBSA "leader on the Reich level" (Koch, "Die kleinen Glaubensgemeinschaften," 423). Steinberg misinterprets some of the information included in the Gestapo records. A chart of the Dresden Gestapo about the "prohibited IBSA in Germany and Austria according to its state on Mar. 15, 1940," which was partially based on information from the interrogations of Ludwig Cyranek (included in Steinberg, *Essen*, 284), mentions as IBSA leader on the Reich level for Germany and Austria "Winkler, in the Netherlands." However, this is not the former IBSA leader on the Reich level Fritz Winkler. It is the previously mentioned Robert Arthur Winkler.

31. According to the instructions by Winkler, Hans Müller was responsible for the eastern part of Germany and, at least temporarily, Ernst Bojanowski for the northern part of Germany. However, as far as can be determined, compared to nationwide results, the activities in these parts of the country were not very effective.

32. See Garbe, "'Gott mehr gehorchen als den Menschen,'" 199; Kühl, "Friedrichstadt," 187; Marßolek and Ott, *Bremen*, 307.

33. SS, report no. 55 of Feb. 19, 1940; *Meldungen aus dem Reich*, 3:776.

34. See SS, report no. 26 of Dec. 8, 1939; report no. 30 of Dec. 18, 1939; report no. 57 of Feb. 23, 1940; *Meldungen aus dem Reich*, 3:547, 581–82, 797.

35. The chief of the Secret State Police office and the Security Service, report about the current political attitude of churches and sects, submitted to the head of the Reich chancellery with the letter of Oct. 20, 1939, cited in Poliakov and Wulf, *Das Dritte Reich*, 194–98 (195).

36. See *Watchtower*, Oct. 1, 1978, 22.

37. See, for instance, *Der Wachtturm*, "Erkenntnis," n.d. [1941], personal documents of Günther Pape; *Der Wachtturm*, "Fürchtet Euch Nicht," n.d. (report about the persecution of August Dickmann, a Jehovah's Witness who was shot to death because "he did not follow the call to murder his fellow humans"), cited in Neugebauer, "'Ernste Bibelforscher,'" 173.

38. Dan. 11:40ff.

39. See Hetzer, "Augsburg," 642.

40. For the aging Watch Tower Society's president, Joseph Franklin Rutherford, the beginning of World War II unmistakably confirmed that the end of the world was approaching. Consequently, he was firmly convinced that Armageddon was near and did not expect another postwar period. He died on Jan. 8, 1942. To a certain extent, Nathan H. Knorr, Rutherford's successor, was able to help the members of the denomination understand that the end of the world was not coming. The Brooklyn leaders came to realize that there was still a tremendous work ahead of them with regard to the preaching activity before this system of things would come to an end.

41. The various publications are difficult to identify. Because of the intensity of persecution, the mimeographed copies are usually not particularly specific (title, date, etc.). Therefore, it is often almost impossible to distinguish them. The [German] *Watchtower* is generally marked with the abbreviation "W. T.," while the "Mitteilungsblatt der deutschen Verbreitungsstelle des W. T." is marked with the abbreviation "M."

42. "Mitteilungsblatt der deutschen Verbreitungsstelle des W. T. an alle treuen Zeugen Jehovas in Deutschland," undated [beginning of 1942], cited in Kalous, "Bibelforscher," appendix 26a.

43. BDC, "Mitteilungsblatt der deutschen Verbreitungsstelle des W. T.," Sept. 1942, quotation according to the Aug. 3, 1943, indictment of the senior Reich attorney at the People's Court, 8 J 131/43. The following quotations are also taken from this indictment.

44. Several recollections indicate that the Wehrmacht or the military courts offered Jehovah's Witnesses the option of not having to take the military oath. In one case, a person who had served as a military officer during World War I became an active Bible Student during the early 1920s. Since he also had several influential connections, when he was drafted into the Wehrmacht he was allowed to serve in his homeland without being required to take the oath (see Nov. 23, 1987, recollections by Bruno Knöller). From a legal standpoint, such an option actually did not exist. By means of the Aug. 20, 1934, Law Regarding the Swearing in of Civil Servants and Soldiers of the [German] Wehrmacht, the (military) oath in acknowledgement of the Führer (*RGBl.* 1934 I, 785) had become compulsory for all members of the Wehrmacht. Only the Mennonites had been granted an exemption from taking the oath and, instead, performed a vow associated with a handshake (Sept. 20, 1935, Regulations Regarding the Swearing in of Army and Air Force Personnel, cited in Dade, "Fahneneid," 50; Heckel, *Wehrverfassung*, 182n2). This possibility was exclusively provided for members of this religious denomination (see also this book, pp. 601–2, n.54). Statements in the literature to the contrary (e.g., in Fauck, "Fahneneid," 472) have to be considered incorrect.

45. "Beantwortung einiger Fragen: Mitteilungsblatt der deutschen Verbreitungsstelle des W. T.," July 1942. (A copy of this paper is in the possession of

the author; italics in the original.) The following statements are taken from this Mitteilungsblatt.

46. With regard to attempts on the part of the military courts to persuade defendants to change their mind, see this book, pt. 5, ch. 14, pp. 376–79.

47. Personal documents of Günther Pape, *Der Wachtturm*, titled "Trost für die Verfolgten," undated [1942], *Watchtower*, July 15, 1942. In this regard, Jehovah's Witnesses refer to Jesus's statement in the Sermon on the Mount that says of "those who are persecuted in the cause of uprightness: the kingdom of Heaven is theirs" (Matt. 5:2ff. [10]).

48. The persecution of non-German Jehovah's Witnesses and the reasons for such persecution has occasionally caused historians to be baffled. For instance, Polish historian Andrej J. Kamiński mentions the "strange reasoning of the Nazis" who even sent Polish Bible Students to the concentration camps "instead of honoring them as the only Poles who refused to take up arms against Hitler" (Kamiński, *Konzentrationslager*, 205). With this statement, Kamiński points to the general paradox of the persecution of conscientious objectors in "enemy territory." However, such contemplations would restrict the conflict between National Socialism and the Bible Student teachings to the question of performing military service and, therefore, fail to recognize the deeper reasons for the conflict. These actions against non-German Jehovah's Witnesses were taken to stop their activities in support of a religious association that vehemently advocated its disapproval of the NS movement, especially from the time that the German fellow believers were persecuted. To confirm this viewpoint, reference can also be made to the statements Arthur Seyß-Inquart made before the International Military Court in Nuremberg, on June 12, 1946. According to the statements by this former Reich Commissioner, the property of the Bible Students in the Netherlands was "confiscated because of their refusal to perform military service." The public prosecutor asked whether this would mean that they took actions against foreigners because they refused to support the "military efforts of Germany." Seyß-Inquart responded to this question by stating that the Bible Students in the Netherlands were not banned "because they refused to serve in the German Armed Forces. They were banned because [the Nazis], as a general rule, opposed the Bible Students" (*Der Prozeß gegen die Hauptkriegsverbrecher*, 16:1127).

49. Apparently, the situation proved to be different in Denmark. Even during the war, Jehovah's Witnesses there were able to publicly distribute publications of the Watch Tower Society and even hold conventions (see country report of Denmark in *Yearbook* 1993, 99–106). Afterwards, on Aug. 29, 1943, when the Danish government refused to cooperate further with the Germans and resigned from office, Jehovah's Witnesses experienced some restrictions in their activities. In general, however, there "was no noticeable opposition from the German occupational forces" (ibid., 101). Some of the countries that ultimately

came under German occupation had already taken official measures against Jehovah's Witnesses before they were under occupation: In Poland, where Jehovah's Witnesses were seriously opposed by the Catholic Action prior to the war, the RMdI imposed a ban on the printing and distribution of the *Watchtower*, as early as 1937. In 1938 the branch office of the Watch Tower Society in Lodz was closed (see *Yearbook* 1994, 198ff.). On July 4, 1940, ten months after the Germans had occupied Poland, the local Gestapo office in Kattowitz issued a dissolution decree against the IBSA. See Majer, *Fremdvölkische*, 388n5. In France, the branch office of the Watch Tower Society was also closed eight months before coming under German occupation, on Oct. 18, 1939. This was still during the Daladier government (see Knorr, *Be Glad, Ye Nations!*, 50. On the persecution of Jehovah's Witnesses in France, see *Watchtower*, Aug. 15, 1980, 5–10).

50. On the persecution of Jehovah's Witnesses in the Netherlands during German occupation, see *Yearbook* 1986, 135–69. Other statements are based on the June 25, 1986, recollections by Johan Wildschut; AfW HH, 220305; VVN, Kommitteeakten K 14.

51. See *Yearbook* 1986, 169. Dietrich Hellmund mentions different numbers, but these numbers show a similar rate of increase. According to his statements, the number of "active Jehovah's Witnesses" during the five-year period of occupation of the Netherlands increased from 317 to 2,166. See Hellmund, "Zeugen Jehovas," no page numbers (chap. 4, subhead 3, n.521).

52. See *Yearbook* 1986, 171.

53. Jehovah's Witnesses were also seriously persecuted in Japan. There, the conflict was based on the issue that Jehovah's Witnesses in Japan refused to accept the divinity of the Tenno, or emperor. In June 1939 there was an extensive wave of arrests. In retrospect, several publications stated that the "complete" membership of this denomination was arrested and confined to prison for several years. See Matsue Ishii, "Jehovah Does Not Forsake His Servants," cited in *Watchtower*, May 1, 1988, 21–25.

54. See *Yearbook* 1938, 135–39; Knorr, *Be Glad, Ye Nations!*, 51.

55. On the persecution of Jehovah's Witnesses in Italy up until 1945, see Graffard and Tristan, *Bibelforscher*, 92ff.; *Yearbook* 1982, 156–79; Pierro, "Testimoni di Geova"; Rogerson, *Millions Now Living Will Never Die*, 58.

56. See *Weckruf*, Jan. 6, 1938, "Hungary against the 'International Bible Students'"; *Yearbook* 1938, 135–39; *Watchtower*, July 15, 1993, 9–12; as well as the country report of Hungary in *Yearbook* 1996, 67–115 (concerning the period between 1933 and 1945, see 76–95).

57. See *Yearbook* 1996, 94–95.

58. See *Watchtower*, Mar. 1, 1987, 21ff.; *Watchtower*, Apr. 1, 1989, 27; *Awake!*, May 8, 1993, 3–6; Solzhenitsyn, *GULAG*, 325; Zürcher, *Kreuzzug*, 44ff.; as well as references in the appropriate country reports in the yearbooks of Jehovah's Witnesses.

59. According to reports of the Watch Tower Society, Jehovah's Witnesses or their literature had been banned in twenty-three nations of the British Commonwealth. See *Jehovah's Witnesses: Proclaimers of God's Kingdom*, 676, 721.

60. See Lahrtz, "Zeugen Jehovas," 44.

61. See *Yearbook* 1974, 178–79; Steinberg, *Essen*, 165–66. For the same purpose, the Gestapo also used an IBSA functionary in the Netherlands whom they had probably coerced into this collaboration. The Gestapo records refer to this informer as the "familiar Bible Student." Apparently, this informer was not able to provide the Gestapo with any useful information. See *Yearbook* 1986, 128; personal documents of Richard Singelenberg, interrogation records of Ludwig Cyranek, II B 1–69/40.

62. Besides Cyranek, severe sentences were also imposed on five other accused Jehovah's Witnesses. For instance, Ernst Bojanowski and Anna Voll were sentenced, respectively, to twelve and four years of imprisonment. Excerpts from the judgment are published in Neugebauer, "'Ernste Bibelforscher,'" 170–73. On July 3, 1941, the evening prior to his execution, Cyranek wrote a farewell letter. This letter is published in Gollwitzer, Kuhn, and Schneider, *Du hast mich heimgesucht*, 341.

63. See *Yearbook* 1974, 200–201. Himmler intended to undertake a gigantic reconstruction of the Wewelsburg to transform it into a model center of the SS. In his efforts to cut down on costs for employees, he planned to use prisoners for this building project. For this purpose, in 1939 Himmler set up a subcamp of the Sachsenhausen concentration camp. As far as can be determined, 302 Jehovah's Witnesses were sent to this subcamp until the spring of 1941. In the beginning, Jehovah's Witnesses actually represented the largest number of prisoners. In 1942, however, the situation changed when large numbers of prisoners, especially from the Soviet Union, were sent to this concentration camp, which, on Sept. 1, 1941, was designated to be the independent "Niederhagen concentration camp." See Brebeck, "Wewelsburg," 154, 157; Hüser, *Wewelsburg*, especially 73ff.; John, *Wewelsburg* (1996), 37ff., 70–71.

64. See John, *Wewelsburg* (1996), 128.

65. The Mar. 29, 1943, report of the Gestapo branch office in Essen includes information about the arrest of a forty-three-year-old disabled mineworker, twelve days earlier. With regard to the results of the police investigations, which probably had been obtained by means of beatings during the interrogations, the report makes the cynical statement: "After a period of stubborn refusal, he finally condescended to give the names of the Bible Students with whom he had recently conducted his Bible discussions" (Gestapo branch office in Essen, letter of Mar. 29, 1943, cited in *Widerstand und Verfolgung in Essen*, document no. 25).

66. See Steinberg, *Essen*, 166, 374–75.

67. BA, R 60 II/99–3, VHG, 7 (8) J 191/43, decision of June 2, 1944. On Aug. 11, 1944, Auguste Hetkamp and Klara Stoffels were executed in

Berlin-Plötzensee. Three days later, on Aug. 14, 1944, Friedrich Stoffels, Paul Weseler, Johann Hörstgen, and Wilhelm Bischoff, the four men who had also been sentenced to death on June 2, 1944, were guillotined in Brandenburg-Görden. The place or date of execution of Julius Engelhard, the principal defendant, cannot be determined. In one case, based on the Nov. 29, 1944, decree by the RJM, an act of pardon was granted and the death penalty was changed to ten years of imprisonment. See *Ehrenbuch Plötzensee,* 133; "Ehrenbuch Brandenburg-Görden," 6:236–37; Gebhard, *Zeugen Jehovas,* 196–98; M. Koch, "Engelhard," 103; Steinberg, *Essen,* 166; BDC, card files of the Berlin-Plötzensee prison.

68. Between May 1943 and Aug. 1944, as a result of a few transfers of prisoners, the remaining command was further reduced to a total of forty-two prisoners (forty Bible Student prisoners and two political prisoners). These prisoners remained in Wewelsburg until their liberation by the American forces on Apr. 2, 1945. They were assigned to perform maintenance and repair work, and to camouflage-paint the building. The prisoners had comparatively good working and living conditions: They had enough food; they were allowed to go to their respective places of work without supervision. Even the SS guard, consisting of twelve SS officers, was eventually reduced to four officers. This remaining command was formed during the final two years of the war. During this time, none of the prisoners at the Wewelsburg concentration camp lost their lives. There are also no records about any mistreatment. See Hüser, *Wewelsburg,* 82, 99–106; John, *Wewelsburg* (1996), 128ff.

69. See *Yearbook* 1974, 201; John, *Wewelsburg* (1996), 128–29.

70. The following descriptions are based on *Yearbook* 1982, 175–79; *Yearbook* 1989, 104–5; BDC, VGH, 6 J 91/44, decision of Nov. 9, 1944.

71. See this book, pt. 5, ch. 15, pp. 434–36.

72. IfZ, MA 442/2, 5491527, Apr. 21, 1944, RSHA report regarding important State Police events. Narciso Riet was sent to the Dachau concentration camp, put in chains, confined to a cell, and subjected to severe torture. For further investigation, he was transferred to the Berlin-Plötzensee prison and later to the Brandenburg-Görden penitentiary (see USHRI [U.S. Holocaust Research Institute], RG-02.058.01, biography by Johannes Schindler, 44–45). As far as can be determined, Riet, who had been sentenced to death in Nov. 1944, died in prison at the beginning of 1945 (see Pierro, "Testimoni di Geova," 6).

73. See Hetzer, "Augsburg," 641–43; Kalous, "Bibelforscher," appendix 26.

74. IfZ, MA 442/2, 5490990, RSHA report of June 26, 1943. On Feb. 18, 1944, the Munich Higher Regional Court sentenced Georg Halder to death on the charge of "demoralization of the armed forces." On Apr. 4, 1944, he was executed in Munich-Stadelheim.

75. BA, R 22/3390, Bl. 130, senior Reich attorney at the People's Court, situation report of June 1, 1943.

76. IfZ, MA 442/2, 5491527, RSHA report of Apr. 21, 1944.

77. Nov. 23, 1987, recollections by Elise Kühnl; Nov. 23, 1987, recollections by Bruno Knöller. According to the records, one death penalty was pronounced against a female Jehovah's Witness. However, it was not carried out.

78. See Struckmeier, "Eickhorst," 23; Zipfel, *Kirchenkampf,* 197n53; Neugebauer, "'Ernste Bibelforscher,'" 183.

79. The following descriptions are based on IfZ, MA 442/2, 5490990, RSHA report of Feb. 26, 1943; BDC, chief public prosecutor at the [Berlin] Court of Appeals, 12 OJs 549/44 (A), indictment of Nov. 16, 1944; BDC, Ersatz-Vollstreckungsband Emmi Zehden, People's Court, 1 J 56/43; "Ehrenbuch Brandenburg-Görden," 3:54, 65; Haase, "Praxis des Reichskriegsgerichts," 395; Zipfel, *Kirchenkampf,* 199–200, 527–33.

80. The death penalties that the Reich Military Court imposed on Werner Gaßner and Gerhard Liebold were carried out on Apr. 9, 1943 (Gaßner), and on May 6, 1943 (Liebold), in Brandenburg-Görden (see "Ehrenbuch Brandenburg-Görden," 3:54, 65). Only Horst-Günter Schmidt, who had been sentenced to death by the People's Court (Az. 7 J 110/44), survived. After a long period of imprisonment in the death cell, his execution was suspended.

81. On the activities of Wilhelm Schumann, see also Gebhard, *Zeugen Jehovas,* 199–200.

82. *Yearbook* 1974, 201–2; see also ibid., 199.

83. The records of the court proceedings are kept at the Berlin Court of Appeals, under the collective file no. 12 OJs 549/44. The Nov. 18, 1944, indictment, 12 OJs 549/44 (B), is published in Zipfel, *Kirchenkampf,* 527–33.

84. Johannes Schindler spent an extended period of time in the death cell at the Brandenburg-Görden penitentiary. He was later transferred to the prison in Halle from which American soldiers liberated him in Apr. 1945. Six years later, this time through DDR authorities, he was again imprisoned because of his activities as a Jehovah's Witness. His extensive memoirs are presently preserved at the United States Holocaust Memorial Museum in Washington (USHMM, RG-02.058.01).

85. The records of the proceedings, which took place at the People's Court, under file no. 7 J 79/44, are not available. According to Zipfel, the execution of the death penalties was suspended because the prisoners "were still needed as witnesses for other pending court proceedings" (Zipfel, *Kirchenkampf,* 199–200. Gebhard's statement [*Zeugen Jehovas,* 199], according to which Franz Fritsche was executed, is incorrect).

86. *Yearbook* 1974, 182 (emphasis in the German edition of the yearbook).

87. See VVN HH, Komiteeakten K 16; June 6, 1984, recollections by Luise Polsterer; Hetzer, "Augsburg," 640.

88. Brigitte Oleschinski makes a historical comparison between the activities of the IBSA and the Quakers in the Third Reich. Rightly, she emphasizes that, in contrast to the Quakers who "did not expect from the recipients of

their charitable assistance any specific religious activity in advance," Jehovah's Witnesses did not "specifically arrange for assisting" people outside of their religious association. However, considering the "relentless pressure from the state," it was inevitable for Jehovah's Witnesses to turn their attention primarily to "the survival of their fellow believers" (Oleschinski, "Religiöse Gemeinschaften," 100).

89. Nov. 23, 1987, recollections by Elise Kühnle. Schlotterbeck, who published his memoirs immediately after the end of the war, states: "I was not afraid to tell him why I came. He filled my backpack with bread, bacon, and butter and accompanied me a short distance through the forest. When I left, he told me that I could come back and stay" (Schlotterbeck, *Erinnerungen*, 298). See also this book, p. 598, n.9.

90. VVN HH, Komiteeakten M 8. (Pauline Matschke offered this assistance probably because she was related by marriage to a member of the Bästlein-Jacob-Abshagen-Group.) On July 18, 1944, Jonny Stüve was arrested. Seven days later, he died as a result of mistreatment at the Fuhlsbüttel police prison. On Stüve and the resistance activities of the Bästlein-Jacob-Abshagen-Group, see Bästlein, "Hitlers Niederlage"; Hochmuth and Meyer, *Streiflichter*, 363, 377ff., 601.

91. Herr, "Bibelforscher," 87. National Socialist propaganda emphasized that Jehovah's Witnesses "did not understand the racial policy" (*Hamburger Tageblatt*, May 14, 1938). The Weimar Special Court complained: "They are not interested in the welfare of the German nation. They are concerned only about the welfare of Jehovah's Witnesses; regardless of whether they are German or non-German, Negro or Mongolian. . . . They have no national pride. To them all people are equal" (BA, R 58/405, Bl. 31, Weimar Special Court, So. G. 4/36, decision of Jan. 24, 1936).

92. See VVN HH, Kommiteeakten G 21; Dec. 30, 1982, recollections by Bruno Knöller.

93. See Kammler, *Kasseler Soldaten*, 138–41.

94. Aug. 17, 1938, Special Penal Regulations during War and a State of Emergency (KSSVO/Special Penal Regulations during War), *RGBl.* 1939 I, 1455. The KSSVO, which had been issued in Aug. 1938, was published in the *RGBl.* on Aug. 26, 1939. However, "for special reasons," it was sent out on Aug. 31, 1939 (BA, R 22/2290, Bl. 328, OKW [High Command of the Armed Forces], express letter of Aug. 31, 1939). Initially, the military judges were responsible only for court cases dealing with offenses that fell under the KSSVO. They probably knew of this decree, since it had already been issued in Aug. 1938 to give the military courts an opportunity to "get acquainted with these regulations in peacetime." Until the seventh implementing regulation was issued on May 18, 1940, civilians who were guilty of "demoralization of the armed forces" also came under military jurisdiction (BA, R 22/2296, Bl. 461, OKW, Apr. 19, 1940, letter to the Reich RMdI).

95. Kohlrausch and Lange, *Strafgesetzbuch*, 798.

96. Schwinge, *Militärstrafgesetzbuch* (1943), 397.

97. *ZAkDR* [*Zeitschrift der Akademie für Deutsches Recht*] 2 (1935): 174–76 (175), report of the committee for military law on its Feb. 28, 1935, meeting.

98. *Verhandlungen des Reichstags, Anlagen zu den stenographischen Berichten*, vol. 440, application no. IV/1741.

99. BA, R 22/962, no page numbers, May 14, 1934, suggestions by the commentator, Vice President Grau, regarding the subject "Agitation against the Wehrmacht."

100. BA, R 22/962, no page numbers, June 4, 1934, suggestions by the subcommittee 21. One year later, the committee for criminal justice suggested changing this paragraph so that not only was the *act* of "demoralizing the armed forces" placed under threat of punishment, but also any *attempt* at such demoralization (BA, R 22/962, no page numbers, committee for criminal justice, "Protokoll der 78. Sitzung am 26. 6. 1935," 3–4). Consequently, art. 5 of the subsequently issued KSSVO was already preformulated in all its essential parts.

101. *RGBl.* 1939 I, 2319.

102. Nüse, *Kriegsstrafrecht*, 33.

103. In a remarkable way, the second paragraph of this regulation took into account the operational requirements of the Gestapo. According to this clause, people "who were able to prevent the continuation of this association or reported it to the authorities" were exempt from punishment (VOSchdW [Amendments Involving Punishment Regulations for the Protection of Military Strength of the German Nation], art. 3, para. 2). It can be assumed that the authorities responsible for the persecution anticipated that this Special Regulation Involving Voluntary Self-Denunciation [Besondere Vorschrift über tätige Reue] would achieve long-term results in their struggle against the IBSA. Besides rewarding denunciation, this regulation also emphasized "the idea of a *Willensstrafrecht*," that is, according to the new legal thinking, a penalty was no longer based only on the elements of the offense but also on the attitude of the offender: "A person who provides evidence of a change of mind and abandons his former course of action shall be rewarded with exemption from punishment" (Rietsch, *Wehrkraft*, 79).

104. *Deutsches Strafrecht*, 1:172.

105. Nüse, *Kriegsstrafrecht*, 33; see also *Deutsches Strafrecht*, 1:172–73. Between 1943 and 1945, court proceedings against 155 Jehovah's Witnesses took place at the Munich Higher Regional Court. An evaluation of these court cases provides information regarding the numerical proportion of the two above-mentioned types of offense. According to Kalous's statements ("Bibelforscher," 41), seventy-six Jehovah's Witnesses were sentenced according to VOSchdW, art. 3 (support of an anti-military association) and twenty Jehovah's Witnesses according to KSSVO, art. 5, no. 1 (demoralization of the armed forces). In fifty-nine cases the elements of the offense are not available.

106. Jan. 29, 1943, "Verordnung zur Ergänzung und Änderung der Zuständigkeitsverordnung," *RGBl.* 1943 I, 76.

107. BA, R 22/3390, Bl. 134, the senior Reich attorney at the People's Court, situation report of Oct. 8, 1943.

108. BDC, VGH, 8 J 131/43, decision of Oct. 4, 1943. Excerpts of the judgment are published in Maislinger, "Die Zeugen Jehovas," 375–78.

109. BA, R 60 I/342, VGH, 2 J 637/43, decision of Nov. 30, 1943.

110. BA, R 60 II/108–4, VGH, 7J. 58/44, decision of Aug. 4, 1944.

111. Statements according to BDC, card files of the Berlin-Plötzensee prison; *Ehrenbuch Plötzensee,* 100, 104, 118, 121, 139; "Ehrenbuch Brandenburg-Görden," 6:401; personal documents of Frank Braßel, "Jehovas Zeugen, Gruppe Herne," report of Jan. 22, 1946.

112. BDC, VGH, 5a J 405/44, decision of Aug. 30, 1944.

113. BDC, VGH, 6 J 91/44, decision of Nov. 9, 1944.

114. Two days earlier, other court proceedings took place against a Jehovah's Witness from the protectorates. In 1941 she had translated several Bible Student publications into the Czech language. Until her arrest, she had also attended IBSA meetings. Even so, the People's Court assumed a "less serious case," since the accused was so "absorbed in these false teachings" that she did not recognize "the favoritism of the enemy" resulting from her actions. Consequently, she was sentenced to four years of imprisonment. See BDC, VGH, 6 J 134/44, decision of Nov. 7, 1944; Wagner, *Volksgerichtshof,* 385, 630.

115. BDC, VGH, 1 J 56/43, decision of Nov. 19, 1943; regarding the occurrence, see this book, pt. 5, ch. 13, p. 338. Copies from excerpts of the "Ersatz-Vollstreckungsband" are published in Füllberg-Stolberg, *Für immer ehrlos: Aus der Praxis des Volksgerichtshofes,* 22–32 (the following citations are taken from documents included in this publication).

116. RJM, decree of May 31, 1944, cited in Füllberg-Stolberg, *Für immer ehrlos,* 27.

117. With regard to death penalties pronounced against Jehovah's Witnesses in the Third Reich, the Watch Tower Society's history report about Jehovah's Witnesses does not make a specific distinction between general court decisions (special court, higher regional court, People's Court) and military court decisions (almost always the Reich Military Court). According to the incomplete statements in these reports, 253 Jehovah's Witnesses were sentenced to death. A total of 203 sentences were also carried out (see *Yearbook* 1974, 182, 212). We can assume that approximately 80 percent of these death penalties were imposed on conscientious objectors by the military courts of the Wehrmacht. Consequently, approximately 50 Jehovah's Witnesses were sentenced to death by general courts.

118. In at least fifteen cases, the death penalties were carried out. In four cases, a pardon was granted. Regarding the remaining six sentences, it cannot be determined whether they were carried out. In view of the generally high

proportion with regard to the execution of death penalties (see Wagner, *Volksgerichtshof,* 279), presumably only half, or perhaps only one third, of these cases were granted a pardon.

119. See this book, pt. 5, ch. 15, pp. 439–47.

120. *Der Prozeß gegen die Hauptkriegsverbrecher,* 11:323.

121. The order by RJM Thierack to which Kaltenbrunner refers is not available. If, in fact, this order actually was given, it was probably issued during the final months of the war. However, since written records of this period are especially scarce, it is also difficult to determine from the court records whether such an order had ever been issued. There is substantial evidence that, during the second half of 1944, in at least nineteen court proceedings against Jehovah's Witnesses death penalties were imposed and carried out. The last death penalty on record imposed on a Bible Student by the People's Court was to be carried out on Jan. 12, 1945 (regarding the execution of thirty-two-year-old Mathilde Hengeveld in Plötzensee, see BA, R 60 II/108–4, VGH, 7 J. 58/44, decision of Aug. 4, 1944; *Ehrenbuch Plötzensee,* 104.) On Mar. 8, 1945, the OKW sent a letter to the chief of the Central Office SS Court [Hautamt SS-Gericht]; with regard to military court jurisdiction, at least at the beginning of Mar. 1945, we can assume that the Regulations Involving Penal Proceedings against Earnest Bible Students, etc. [Richtlinien für Strafverfahren gegen ernste Bibelforscher usw.], issued six months earlier, were still in force (IfZ, MA, 333, 657686; see 392–93). According to these regulations, the death penalty had to be imposed, without exception, in all cases in which the refusal to perform military service was *not* withdrawn. The last death penalty on record was a court martial decision that was pronounced against a Jehovah's Witness only a few days before the end of the war. It was imposed and carried out under the jurisdiction of Generalfeldmarschall [general of the Army] Ferdinand Schörner, the commander in chief of the Heeresgruppe Mitte [Army Group Center] (Johannes Rauthe, "Geschichtsbericht," 40). At best, Kaltenbrunner's statement can be supported by the fact that, toward the end of the war, there was a more liberal handling of acts of pardon. And, during the final days of the war, some Jehovah's Witnesses who refused military service received only prison sentences. See, for instance, Kammler, *Soldaten,* 55. For example, the special court responsible for the military operation zone Alpenvorland changed a death penalty that had been pronounced on Apr. 9, 1945, on the charge of "refusal to comply with the draft for the *Volkssturm* [unit of old men and boys]," to a five-year prison sentence. See Hartmann, *Kriegsdienstverweigerung* (1986), 60. During the final months of the war, a few court proceedings were even dismissed (see Maislinger, "Andere religiöse Gruppen," 331). For example, at the Hanseatic Special Court, court proceedings on the charge of "refusal to comply with the draft for the *Volkssturm*" according to KSSVO, art. 5, para. 1, clause 3, were in progress. The hearing scheduled for Jan. 16, 1945, was dismissed because "the file had been requested by the RJM" (SLG HH, HSG, 11 Js. Sond.

464/44, Bl. 16). The accused remained in prison for another three months, without any further court proceedings (AfW HH, 080789). Without additional examination of the records, it is not possible to determine whether this previously mentioned case substantiates Kaltenbrunner's statement. Nevertheless, the truthfulness of his statement remains questionable. There are certainly no indications that court proceedings against Jehovah's Witnesses were generally dismissed.

122. May 21, 1935, Military Service Law, art. 1, para. 2, and art. 4, *RGBl.* 1935 I, 609. The Military Service Law (art. 14) made only two exceptions with regard to an exemption from military service: (1) those who were "liable for military service but were completely unfit" and (2) "Roman Catholics liable for military service who had been consecrated as subordinate deacons" were exempt from military service during peace time ("Jews, gypsies, and people who were considered to be unworthy of serving in the armed forces" were not even allowed to perform military service).

123. Only one reference is available that indicates that the question of granting exemption from military service was even considered. In the context of pronouncing the Military Service Law, superintendent dean Max Diestel from Berlin, acting chairman of the Deutsche Vereinigung des Weltbundes für internationale Freundschaftsarbeit der Kirchen, had discussed the question of religiously motivated conscientious objection with the respective advisor of the Ministry of War (RKM), "especially with regard to the Quakers and the Mennonites." He stated that the RKM had promised him "to show consideration in their dealings with such cases" (Max Diestel, Oct. 19, 1939, letter to the Gericht des 2. Admirals der Ostseestation [military court], cited in Röhm, *Sterben für den Frieden*, 147). According to Röhm, this letter was "the only statement regarding conscientious objection of a leading church official during World War II that became publicly known" (ibid., 206).

124. Preamble of the Military Service Law (art. 1, para. 1).

125. Heckel, *Wehrverfassung*, 96.

126. In principle, Jehovah's Witnesses did not change their position regarding the refusal to perform military service, even after the war. In the Federal Republic of Germany, the right of conscientious objection is constitutionally guaranteed (GG, art. 4, para. 3). Despite this, the members of this religious denomination again came into conflict with the state. Since the government requires recognized conscientious objectors to perform civil service, which is considered to be a fulfillment of one's duty of performing military service, Jehovah's Witnesses also refused this kind of service. With the requirement of performing civil service as a form of alternative military service, the state assumes the right to subject Jehovah's Witnesses to liability for military service, a right to which, according to their understanding, the state is not authorized. In this "world doomed to destruction," Jehovah's Witnesses are required to remain "neutral" (see Burski, "Die Zeugen Jehovas," 33–35; Hannover,

"Ersatzdienstverweigerung," 33ff.). As a result, during the 1950s and 1960s, hundreds of Jehovah's Witnesses in the Federal Republic of Germany were imprisoned for their "complete refusal." In Aug. 1969 a change in law regarding alternative military service took into account the conscientious objection of Jehovah's Witnesses. "In consultation with the German branch office of the Watch Tower Society," a new regulation was included in the Constitution (Krölls, *Kriegsdienstverweigerung*, 211). This new regulation, Alternative Military Law [Ersatzdienstgesetz], art. 15a, decreed that, under certain conditions, a recognized conscientious objector "who is prevented from performing alternative military service for reasons of conscience" can be exempt from alternative military service. Such exemption can be granted if the person concerned works for at least two and a half years, on a voluntary basis, in a hospital, mental institution, or nursing home before reaching the age of twenty-four. Recently, the Watch Tower Society started to abandon the rejection of liability to civil service. In the process of these gradual changes in attitude (see also this book, pt. 5, ch. 15, pp. 530–31), it is now left to the discretion of the individual believer whether he will agree to perform civil service or whether he will choose the alternative of working in a health-care facility on a voluntary basis. See *Watchtower*, May 1, 1996, 15–16).

127. On the reasons for Jehovah's Witnesses' conscientious objection, see *"Let God be True,"* 240ff.; Cole, *Jehovah's Witnesses*, 93–94; Lichtenegger, "Wiens Bibelforscherinnen," 36–42. Outsiders frequently describe Jehovah's Witnesses as pacifists. They, however, consider themselves to be "conscientious objector[s], yes; . . . pacifist[s], no" (Cole, *Jehovah's Witnesses*, 128). Jehovah's Witnesses do not want the large number of IBSA members who refused military service in the Third Reich to be represented, in retrospect, as "forerunners of the peace movement." It is necessary to make such a distinction in order to show respect for the motives of those Jehovah's Witnesses who died for their religious conviction. This distinction also has to be made from an objective point of view because Jehovah's Witnesses are not concerned about worldly affairs. They did not refuse military service because they objected to the use of force as a means for resolving a political controversy. They also did not pursue the goals of establishing international peace or achieving radical disarmament. Therefore, their objectives had nothing to do with pacifism in the sense of taking an active stand for nonviolence. Jehovah's Witnesses based their conscientious objection on the Christian obligation of remaining "strictly neutral" (see this book, pt. 1, ch. 2, p. 40). This conscientious objection of Jehovah's Witnesses was a sign of their faithfulness toward God. It was not a sign for the world. See *Watchtower*, Nov. 1, 1979, 3–8 ("Neutrality in a Mixed-up World").

128. Knöller, "Erinnerungen," 21–22.

129. Wording of the military oath according to the version issued on July 20, 1935, *RGBl.* 1935, I, 1035. With his Mar. 29, 1936, decree, the RKM emphasized that the military oath required by the Wehrmacht was a "religious oath,"

even though it was not based on a Christian confession (RKM, decree of Mar. 29, 1936; cited in Dade, "Fahneneid," 50).

130. MStGB [Military Service Law], art. 48, states: "The fact that a person bases his actions, or lack of actions, on reasons of conscience or on his religious conviction does not exempt him from punishment."

131. Schwinge, *Militärstrafgesetzbuch* (1936), 115–16.

132. Dörken and Scherer, *Militärstrafgesetzbuch*, 40.

133. May 12, 1933, Law for the Reestablishment of Military Court Jurisdiction [Gesetz zur Wiedereinführung der Militärgerichtsbarkeit], *RGBl.* 1933, 264.

134. *RGBl.* 1936 I, 517. According to Kater, the RKG sentenced Jehovah's Witnesses on the charge of refusal to take the military oath as early as 1935 (see Kater, "Bibelforscher," 199). This, however, is incorrect. According to military penal law [*Militärstrafgerichtsordnung*], such cases came under the jurisdiction of the military courts or, in cases of appeal proceedings, under jurisdiction of the higher military courts. They were not under jurisdiction of the RKG (which was not established until 1936). On the day of mobilization, the War Penal Code [KStVO, Kriegsstrafverfahrensordnung] was issued. On the basis of this decree, the offense of "demoralization of the armed forces," which had been newly introduced by means of the KSSVO, came to be under RKG jurisdiction (KStVO, art. 14, para. 1, clause 9). Only after this decree had been enacted did proceedings against Jehovah's Witnesses become the responsibility of this highest military court. (See also this book, pt. 5, ch. 14, p. 360.)

135. *RGBl.* 1936 I, 1165; *RGBl.* 1935 I, 1021. During World War II, by means of the regulations issued on Oct. 10, 1940 (*RGBl.* 1940 I, 1347), several rules of the Military Service Law (MStGB) were again amended and intensified.

136. At the same time as a new German penal code was prepared, preparations were also made for the drafting of a new military penal code. However, neither code ever passed. The draft for a new military penal code also did not include any specific regulations with regard to conscientious objection (see BA, R 43 II/1284, Bl. 18ff.; report by the committee responsible for military law regarding the revision of the military penal code). The draft of the penal code for the German Wehrmacht that Reich minister of war Blomberg submitted for passage in Dec. 1936 included only the following punishable offenses of evading military duties: "desertion" (arts. 52–54), "rendering unfit for military service" (art. 55), and "evading of military service by means of deception" (art. 56). The legal and military experts could probably not comprehend the idea that people liable for military service would, with reference to reasons of conscience, evade military service, a priori, and accept the consequences without taking steps to avoid subsequent prosecution. This thought was so far removed from their viewpoint that they did not even take this element of offense into consideration. Prior to the war, the question of conscientious objection remained legally unregulated.

137. The term "conscientious objection" refers to the openly demonstrated refusal of a person to comply with the draft for military service, or service under arms, regardless of whether the person had already been drafted or expected to be drafted: "Conscientious objection is the openly stated, or otherwise openly expressed, refusal toward the State to participate in any military action or training for such action" (Hartmann, *Kriegsdienstverweigerung* [1986], 4; see also Bredemeier, *Kriegsdienstverweigerung,* 7). In this restricted sense, only people who were actually required to perform military service, that is, people liable for military service, could also perform an act of conscientious objection. Other forms of refusal would, however, not come under this definition. For the purpose of clarity of definition or reasons of subsumption, the following explanations are based on this restricted understanding of the term "conscientious objection." It should at least be pointed out that in a broader sense, this term includes the refusal of all actions that serve to support warfare. For example, based on this broader sense of understanding, the refusal of the Bible Students—male and female—to support the production of military equipment can also be considered as a "refusal to perform military service" (see this book, pt. 5, ch. 15, pp. 417–22).

138. BA-MA, RW 15/76, Reich minister of war, memo of Oct. 14, 1936.

139. MStGB, art. 69. In peacetime, desertion was punished with imprisonment of between six months and two years. The second offense of desertion was punished with imprisonment of between one and five years. Repetition of the offense ("subsequent offenses") was punished with five to ten years of imprisonment.

140. June 28, 1935, Law Regarding the Amendment of the Penal Code [Gesetz zur Änderung des Strafgesetzbuches], *RGBl.* 1935 I, 839. The obviously intensified threats of punishment had the objective of punishing the following offenses: evading military service by means of escaping from the German Reich (art. 140), persuading and assisting in desertion (art. 141), performing self-mutilation (art. 142), evading military service by means of deception (art. 143).

141. Schäfer, "Änderung des Strafgesetzbuchs," 2478–79.

142. Previously, such offenses were punished with fines or imprisonment of up to one year. From midnight onward of the day the draft was issued, the draftee was considered to be a soldier (WG [Military Service Law], art. 21). As a result, he was subject to the military laws of the Wehrmacht and to military jurisdiction.

143. Friedrich Zipfel assumes that the NS state tried to resist the "serious danger" the Bible Students supposedly represented by means of an intensification of the penal laws (see Zipfel, *Kirchenkampf,* 198). However, Penal Code articles 140–43 did not deal with an openly expressed refusal of military service as was expressed by the majority of Jehovah's Witnesses. The articles dealt with other forms of evading compulsory service. These penal regulations did not

apply to people eligible for military service who came under military jurisdiction on the day they were drafted. There was no direct relationship between the intensification of punishment as regulated in Penal Code articles 140–43 and the actions taken against Jehovah's Witnesses. According to the records, the conscientious objection of Jehovah's Witnesses did not have any bearing on the discussions regarding an intensification of penal laws (see BA, R 22/962; see also "Veröffentlichungen der Strafrechtskommission," published by Franz Gürtner in 1935–36).

144. "Der Politische Polizeikommandeur der Länder," letter of May 13, 1935, to the Gestapo in Frankfurt, cited in Diamant, *Frankfurt*, 84; see also BHStA, Reichsstatthalter 638, BPP, interoffice decree of May 24, 1935.

145. BHStA, Reichsstatthalter 638, BPP, interoffice decree of Jan. 28, 1936.

146. BA-MA, RW 6/v.2, RKM, interoffice decree of Jan. 18, 1937.

147. IfZ, MA 554, 936279–87 (80), memo, "Die Internationale Bibelforscher-Vereinigung," encl. to the Dec. 24, 1936, interoffice decree by the central State Police office in Munich.

148. The statement continues as follows: "In this way, I promised God that I would prove to be faithful and obedient to his word under all circumstance and during any trial. My failure to obey [God] would be like breaking my oath and would result in death, that is, eternal destruction" (BA, R 58/779, Bl. 145).

149. IfZ, MA 554, 936280. On deliberate acts of causing "unworthiness of serving in the armed forces," see Klausch, *Bewährungsbataillone*, 23; Zipfel, *Kirchenkampf*, 197n54.

150. See Heuzeroth and Wille, "Lila Winkel," 203 (report regarding J. Harms). Using this particular argument, people who had been legally punished or were released from the concentration camp tried to evade the draft. For instance, one Jehovah's Witness who had been imprisoned in Esterwegen during the mid-1930s was drafted at the beginning of the war. He returned the draft to the military authorities with the remark that he thought that former concentration camp prisoners were considered to be "unworthy of serving in the armed forces." See Fahle, *Verweigern*, 157.

151. WG, art. 13, para. 1e. People on whom prison sentences had been imposed or who had lost their worthiness of serving in the armed forces because of a military court decision were also considered to be unworthy of serving in the armed forces and, consequently, were exempt from the duty of performing military service. The same applied to people who had lost their civil rights or who had been taken into protective detention according to German Penal Code, art. 42a.

152. Right from the beginning, the military judges were displeased with the regulation of art. 13 of the MStGB, according to which "unworthiness of serving in the armed forces" resulted in an exemption from "fulfilling one's liability for military service." In 1936 Heinrich Dietz, a prudent counselor regarding

German Military Law, stated that people who were considered "unworthy of serving in the armed forces" lost a "right." However, they were not deprived of their responsibility: "Liability for military service never stops, even if it is not being discharged. During wartime and national states of emergency, that is, even during peacetime, people unworthy of serving in the armed forces can be drafted for military service in the Wehrmacht, without being freed from their unworthiness of serving in the armed forces" (Dietz, "Wehrunwürdigkeit," 174). This laid the basis for recruiting people "unworthy of serving in the armed forces" into Probation Battalions [Bewährungsbatallione], a practice performed from 1942 on.

153. Cited in *Entscheidungen des Reichskriegsgerichts*, vol. 2, book 1, 33. The July 21, 1936, general decree by the RJM (*DJ* 98 [1936]: 1168) stated that these regulations also became binding for the legal authorities.

154. Explanations of the concept of "subversive activities" (encl. 2 to art. 17, para. 1e, of the Apr. 17, 1937, Regulations Regarding Examination Before Enlistment and Recruitment [VO über die Musterung und Aushebung] [*RGBl.* 1937, 469]); see also Otto and Güldenpfennig, *Ersatzwesen*, 131. In the explanations, it is stated that the specification had the objective of "counteracting attempts of people who try to evade liability for military service by committing less serious political offenses."

155. The list of punishable offenses that resulted, or had the potential of resulting, in "unworthiness of serving in the armed forces" did not include offenses against VOSchVuS. Jehovah's Witnesses who were sentenced to upwards of nine months of imprisonment on the charge of an offense against the Law of Malicious Intent were usually considered to be "unworthy of serving in the armed forces." Now, after the enactment of the Nov. 25, 1939, Decree for the Protection of Military Strength, Jehovah's Witnesses who had been sentenced to imprisonment of more than one year on the charge of "supporting an antimilitary association" were also considered to be unworthy of serving in the armed forces.

156. See, for instance, Hetkamp, "Du sollst nicht töten," 188; VVN HH, Komiteeakten Z4.

157. According to the Nov. 25, 1935, Decree Regarding a Draft for Military Training in the Wehrmacht [Verordnung über die Einberufung zu Übungen der Wehrmacht] (*RGBl.* 1935 I, 1358, new Mar. 28, 1936, edition, *RGBl.* 1936 I, 326), people liable for military service who were on leave of absence could also be drafted for military training. This is also the reason why the number of court proceedings against Jehovah's Witnesses who refused military service prior to the war is considerably higher than previously assumed in the literature (Zipfel, *Kirchenkampf*, 198).

158. See "Regierung von Unterfranken," monthly report (Mar. 1937) of Apr. 8, 1937; Wittstadt, *Die kirchliche Lage in Bayern* (Unterfranken), 110. Contrary to Gestapo practices, art. 8, para. 5, of the Apr. 17, 1937, Regulations Regarding

Examination before Enlistment and Recruitment (*RGBl.* 1937, 469) required that the police authorities should hand over to the appropriate local military district command any people liable for compulsory services who "were guilty of refusing to respond to the draft, examination before enlistment, or recruitment." If these people liable for compulsory services already "fulfilled their duty of labor service," they should be "immediately" drafted "to a special division in the Wehrmacht."

159. BA, R 58/264, Bl. 178, "Der Politische Polizeikommandeur der Länder," interoffice decree of Nov. 14, 1935, cited in BPP, interoffice decree of Nov. 26, 1935.

160. BA, R 58/267, Bl. 43–50 (45), Prussian Secret State Police, May 28, 1936, Regulations Regarding Police Measures against Members of the Wehrmacht and People Liable for Military Service [Polizeiliche Maßnahmen gegen Wehrmachtsangehörige und Wehrpflichtige].

161. Recollections by Johannes Rauthe, "Geschichtsbericht," 40–55.

162. The Gestapo practice of taking people into protective detention after they had served a military prison sentence corresponded to their practice of taking people into protective detention after they had served a prison sentence imposed by the legal authorities. Even after the beginning of the war, the Gestapo took such actions against Jehovah's Witnesses who were liable for military service. For instance, during the summer of 1939, the Luftwaffengericht [military court] in Munich imposed a nine-month prison sentence on an IBSA member from Ludwigsburg. In the spring of 1940, after he had served his prison sentence, the Gestapo sent this Jehovah's Witness to the Sachsenhausen concentration camp (June 7, 1984, recollections by Otto Wulle). To a certain extent, the admission into a concentration camp "saved the life" of this man. It protected him from a repeated draft and a subsequent, almost inevitable, death penalty if he would have continued to refuse military service.

163. The description is based on the documents of the military court proceedings concerned, which are in the possession of his son (personal documents of Rolf Zehender).

164. Three months after his release from prison, on Mar. 15, 1941, Zehender was drafted again. Since he did not respond, on Dec. 10, 1941, the RKG sentenced him to death on the charge of "demoralization of the armed forces." On Jan. 17, 1942, at the age of thirty-two, Zehender was guillotined at the Brandenburg-Görden penitentiary. The RKG decision is published in Hartmann, *Kriegsdienstverweigerung* (1986), 74–77.

165. The description is based on AfW HH, 130313; VVN HH, Komiteeakten K1; SLG HH, HSG 11 Js. Sond. 1617d/34. In 1935 this previously convicted man, born in 1913, was sentenced to two months of imprisonment on the charge of defiance of the IBSA ban. As a person liable for military service on leave of absence, he was no longer drafted for regular military service. Instead, he was drafted only for abbreviated military training.

166. In this case, the Gestapo did not take the man into protective detention after his release from prison. On July 28, 1943, after a period of five years of "freedom," this Jehovah's Witness was again drafted into the Wehrmacht. Under pressure, he gave up his resistance and complied with the draft.

167. The June 26, 1935, Reich Labor Service Law [Reichsarbeitsdienstgesetz] (*RGBl.* 1935 I, 769) introduced compulsory labor service for men. During the introductory period of compulsory military service—that is, the period required to establish the Wehrmacht as a draft army—some people were exempt from their labor service duties. Instead, they were directly drafted for military service. At the beginning of the war, matters were handled in a similar way. Those born in 1921 were drafted immediately into the Wehrmacht. They did not have to fulfill their Reich Labor Service duty first.

168. In 1935 a twenty-year-old Jehovah's Witness was drafted to the Reich Labor Service. In retrospect, he states that he did not refuse this service because he assumed that it was a community service. See John, *Wewelsburg* (1996), 159.

169. According to art. 13, para. 1, of the second implementation regulation of the Oct. 1, 1935, Reich Labor Service Law (*RGBl.* 1935 I, 1215), the act of taking an oath was compulsory.

170. The description is based on the June 1984 recollections by Erwin Rinker; the Feb. 28, 1985, recollections by Erwin Knöller; personal documents of Norbert Weiß, "Landesstelle für die Betreuung der Opfer des Nationalsozialismus," statement of Jan. 29, 1949.

171. Sollmann and Wagner, "Bibelforscher," 437.

172. Ibid.

173. VVN HH, Kommiteeakten K 12, statement included in the Apr. 3, 1946, biography.

174. With reference to art. 3 of the Mar. 12, 1940, Decree for the Protection of Reich Labor Service [Verordnung zum Schutze des Reichsarbeitsdienstes] (*RGBl.* 1940 I, 485), which specified the punishment for evading compulsory service for the Reich Labor Service, legal penalties were also imposed. For instance, in 1940 twenty-year-old Kurt Auschner was sentenced to eight months of imprisonment on the charge of refusing labor service. In Oct. 1941, shortly after his release from prison, he received his draft for the Wehrmacht. Since he refused to take the oath and perform military service, the Reich Military Court sentenced him to death on Jan. 27, 1942. One month later, on Feb. 28, 1942, he was executed in Brandenburg-Görden (VVN HH, Kommiteeakten A 11; see also *Yearbook* 1989, 118).

175. See Knaut, *Propheten*, 134.

176. Apr. 30, 1983, recollections by Egon Knöller.

177. See Leber, *Lebensbilder*, 20; *Yearbook* 1974, 183. A well-documented case in this regard is that of seventeen-year-old Walter Appel. In Oct. 1944, after he had been drafted for Reich Labor Service, the SS in Königsberg executed him

"on the charge of his refusal to perform labor service and military service." See Garbe, "'Gott mehr gehorchen als den Menschen,'" 210; Imberger, *Widerstand*, 372–73; *Yearbook* 1974, 189; Philipsen, "Für den Glauben in den Tod," 43; Burmeister et al., "Verfolgung der Zeugen Jehovas in Kiel," 50.

178. Hans Joachim H., biography of Mar. 8, 1948, cited in Kammler, *Kasseler Soldaten*, 55–56. H. allowed himself to be pressured into performing military service against his convictions. However, in the summer of 1944, while serving on the eastern front, he had an opportunity to escape. He made his way to his hometown of Kassel. There, he was arrested by the military police. In the summer of 1945 the military court sentenced him to four years and four months of imprisonment.

179. See this book, pt. 5, ch. 13, pp. 344–42. The KSSVO was not a "military law" but was part of "general penal law." It applied "to all people who were subject to German Penal Law, military people as well as civilians." This made it possible to subject all people who refused military service to prosecution. Consequently, art. 5, para. 1, clause 3, replaced German Penal Code articles 140–43, which restricted the penal regulations regarding evasion of military service to specific cases. See Heyne, "KSSVO," 258–60.

180. OKW [Wehrmachtrechtsabteilung, legal department of the Wehrmacht High Command], Aug. 17, 1938, explanations regarding the KSSVO and a State of Emergency [Verordnung über das Sonderstrafrecht im Kriege und bei besonderem Einsatz], cited in Absolon, *Wehrmachtstrafrecht*, 51–56 (54). On art. 48 of the MStGB, see this book, pt. 5, ch. 14, p. 350.

181. "Rechtsgrundsätze des Reichskriegsgerichts," 4.

182. Ibid., 5.

183. This penalty was imposed on Dr. Hermann Stöhr, former secretary of the International Reconciliation Federation. Subsequently, he also refused to take the military oath, which had been required of him during his period of imprisonment. Therefore, he was again subjected to military court proceedings, this time on the charge of an "offense according to KSSVO, art. 5, para. 1, clause 3." On Mar. 16, 1940, the RKG sentenced him to death. On June 21, 1940, he was executed. Stöhr was the only known Christian from the Evangelical churches who was sentenced to death on the charge of conscientious objection for religious reasons. See Röhm, *Sterben für den Frieden;* on the military court proceedings, ibid., 186ff.

184. BA, R 60 II/131, "'Totenregister' des Generalstaatsanwaltes beim Kammergericht"; see also Hartmann, "Kriegsdienstverweigerung" (1982), 87–89.

185. During the initial period, after the imposition of martial law, the "legal situation" with regard to the prosecution of conscientious objectors was still uncertain. Therefore, several court proceedings involving conscientious objection still took place at other military courts. See *Yearbook* 1989, 119–20; Poliakov and Wulf, *Das Dritte Reich*, 195; *RzW* 15 (1964): 501–5.

186. Aug. 17, 1938, KSSVO, *RGBl.* 1939 I, 1457. According to KStVO regulations, all such cases came under military court jurisdiction. Especially serious cases were handled at the RKG. According to KSSVO, art. 5, all cases of "demoralization of the armed forces" also came under RKG jurisdiction (KStVO, art. 14, para. 1, clause 9).

187. The KStVO provided the military judicial convening authority with almost unrestricted power. The military commanders of the various high commands, who were entrusted with the duty of acting as judicial convening authority, had to arrange for the preliminary investigations, issue the bill of indictment, and confirm the judgment. At the RKG, the senior judge had the duty of acting as judicial convening authority, in addition to his administrative responsibilities. Consequently, he also exercised the right of confirming or withdrawing a judgment (KStVO, art. 80). Only in cases in which death penalties were imposed on military officers did Hitler himself act as "highest judicial convening authority." In the various RKG divisions, on the other hand, the judicial convening authority was exercised by judges.

188. May 18, 1940, seventh implementing regulation for the KSSVO, *RGBl.* I, 787; see Hülle, "Kriegsstrafverfahrensordnung," 153ff.; see also this book, p. 000, n.95.

189. BA, R 22/2296, Bl. 442, OKW, decree of May 18, 1940. During the initial period of the war, the expression "Jünger Jehovas" (disciples of Jehovah) was included in several OKW decrees. There was, however, no religious denomination by that name. This could have been a reference to the Menschenfreundliche Versammlung/Engel Jehovas, a group that had separated from the IBSA. It could also have been a misrepresentation of the name "Zeugen Jehovas" (Jehovah's Witnesses), based on a lack of knowledge regarding sectarian affairs on the part of the Wehrmacht's legal department.

190. According to the military criminal statistics of the Wehrmacht, 159 court proceedings on the charge of "demoralization of the armed forces" (including all groups of offenses mentioned in KSSVO, art. 5) took place during the initial four months of the war (between Aug. 26 and Dec. 12, 1939). In forty cases, a death penalty was pronounced (see BA-MA, RW 6/v. 129 D). At least thirty-nine of these death penalties—that is, almost all of them—were imposed on Jehovah's Witnesses. See also this book, p. 000, n.216.

191. See Garbe, *Einzelfall*, 47ff.; Messerschmidt and Wüllner, *Wehrmachtjustiz*, 26ff. and 133ff.; see this book, pt. 5, ch. 13, p. 341–42.

192. According to MStGB, arts. 31 and 32, in addition to the death penalty, the accused were also sentenced to "loss of civil rights." This was to signify the special "disgrace" of the committed offense. According to art. 13, para. 1, of the Military Service Law, the withdrawal of the "civil rights" generally resulted in "loss of the right to serve in the armed forces." This, in turn, resulted in an expulsion from the Wehrmacht. Therefore, people who were sentenced to "death and loss of civil rights" on the charge of conscientious objection were

not executed through a firing squad ("death by means of a comrade"), as directed by the KStVO, art. 103. They were executed by the "dishonorable" and "disgraceful" method of beheading (see Schmidt, *Straftat*, 28).

193. According to various recollections, some Jehovah's Witnesses who were sentenced to death by a military court were shot to death (see *Yearbook* 1989, 119ff.; *Watchtower*, Sept. 1, 1985, 14). A considerable number of Jehovah's Witnesses were shot by firing squads at the military training area in Heuberg (members of the Probation Battalions 999), as well as at the Torgau military prison. See Haase, *Deserteure*, 101; Klausch, *Bewährungsbataillone*, 234.

194. In 1939 nearly every second person executed in Berlin-Plötzensee was a Jehovah's Witness: From ninety-four listed executions (BA, R 22/1315, Bl. 22), forty-seven of which were issued by the RKG, at least thirty-nine were carried out against Jehovah's Witnesses (see this book, p. 000, n.192). Altogether, approximately 100 Jehovah's Witnesses who had been sentenced to death on the charge of conscientious objection by the RKG were executed in Plötzensee. On July 3, 1940, the RJM ordered that, in the future, death penalties imposed by the RKG should be carried out at the newly established "place of execution" at the Brandenburg-Görden penitentiary (BA, R 22/1315, Bl. 234). The first recorded executions of Jehovah's Witnesses in Brandenburg took place in Sept. 1940. Walter Hammer estimates the total number of these executed Jehovah's Witnesses to be between fifty and sixty (Hammer, *Brandenburg*, 2; Weisenborn, *Aufstand*, 87). However, the number is probably even higher. In the autumn of 1943 the RKG was transferred from Berlin to Torgau. From then on, death penalties imposed by this court were carried out in nearby Halle. It cannot be determined how many Jehovah's Witnesses were executed there in 1944/45.

195. See Heuzeroth and Wille, "Lila Winkel," 199ff.

196. BA, R 60 II/131, "'Totenregister' des Generalstaatsanwaltes beim Kammergericht"; BDC, records of the Berlin-Plötzensee prison and Charlottenburg public health department.

197. See Garbe, "Im Namen des Volkes," 104ff.

198. Max Bastian, May 30, 1940, activity report, cited in Haase, "Praxis des Reichskriegsgerichts," 391.

199. BA-MA, RH 53-6/76, Bl. 139, OKH/BdE (High Command of the Army/Commander of the Reserve Army), decree of Oct. 17, 1939 (see introduction, p. 21). The OKH controlled only military forces operating from land.

200. In 1938 the RKG pronounced fifteen death penalties (on the charge of treason, etc.). Twelve of these death penalties were carried out (see BA-MA, RW 2/v. 258, statistics regarding military penal law of 1938; BA, R 22/1315, Bl. 229). According to an incomplete compilation by the author (Garbe), 130 Jehovah's Witnesses were sentenced by the military courts during World War II. In Nov. 1939 at least thirteen of these sentences were death penalties imposed by the RKG (twelve of these death penalties were carried out). However,

it can be assumed almost certainly that the actual number of death penalties imposed on Jehovah's Witnesses during that particular month clearly exceeded the total number of fifteen death penalties imposed during the previous year.

201. See Schorn, *Richter*, 170ff.; Schweling, *Militärjustiz*, 117ff., 212ff.; Schwinge, *Verfälschung und Wahrheit*, 57ff. According to Schorn (*Richter*, 170), particularly during the establishment of military jurisdiction (between 1934 and 1938), "many of the judges who had problems with the party, or who were expecting such problems because of their attitude" chose to become judges at the military courts. Granted that, because of the obviously apologetic objectives of the study by Schorn, and especially the studies by the former military judges Schweling and Schwinge, these studies have to be considered with special skepticism. At the same time, it cannot be denied that several judges who had certain reservations toward the NSDAP resorted to the military courts of the Wehrmacht, which, during the middle of the 1930s, were still relatively free from the party's influence. These judges also had their reservations about the "developing new legal thinking." However, apart from a few exceptions, these ideological differences are not reflected in the military court decisions (see Haase, "Praxis des Reichskriegsgerichts," 411).

202. RKG, Rev. L. 158/37 I, decision of Jan. 20, 1938, *Entscheidungen des Reichskriegsgerichts*, 1:123–28 (127). This case does not involve Bible Student proceedings.

203. Schwinge, *Entwicklung der Mannszucht*, 54.

204. See Garbe, "Im Namen des Volkes," 101ff.; Messerschmidt and Wüllner, *Wehrmachtjustiz*, 63ff.; Wüllner, *NS-Militärjustiz*, 192ff.

205. BA-MA, N 192/1, Max Bastian, "Lebenserinnerungen" (1956), 55–56. (The appendix of Schweling's study, *Militärjustiz*, 399–402, includes almost the complete account of Bastian's explanations regarding the "problem" of the Bible Student proceedings.) However, not until Oct. 1, 1944, one month before his resignation, did Bastian approach the OKW with the suggestion "of suspending the execution of death penalties against so-called 'Bible Students'" (see Haase, "Torgau und das Reichskriegsgericht," 55). Recognized sources also confirm the insecurity of the RKG judges with regard to Bible Student cases. For instance, the resistance fighter and Plötzensee prison chaplain, Harald Poelchau, reports that "during the initial period of the war, between 1939 and 1940," the RKG was "very reluctant in carrying out the death penalties imposed on Bible Students" (Poelchau, *Die letzten Stunden*, 34). Like Poelchau, Kurt Scharf was a member of the "Bekennende Kirche." During the 1960s, he was the chairman of the Council of the Evangelical churches in Germany. He too reports that the military judges who imposed the death penalties on these conscientious objectors "generally were very sensitive people, most of whom were imbued with Christian principles" (Scharf, "Gespräche mit Kurt Scharf," 24).

206. BA-MA, N 192/1, 56; see also Haase, "Praxis des Reichskriegsgerichts," 392.

207. BA-MA, RH 53–6/76, Bl. 168, the chief of the OKW, letter of Dec. 1, 1939.

208. Picker, *Hitlers Tischgespräche*, 360. His statement that the executions were performed through "shooting" is incorrect; also the number of "130" Jehovah's Witnesses executed up until the middle of 1942 is underestimated.

209. Jochmann, *Monologe*, 320.

210. See "Sicherheitsdienst der SS," report no. 30 of Dec. 18, 1939; report no. 43 of Jan. 22, 1940; report no. 44 of Jan. 24, 1940; report no. 46 of Jan. 29, 1940; report no. 57 of Feb. 23, 1940; *Meldungen aus dem Reich*, 3:581–82, 669, 679, 700, 797.

211. "Sicherheitsdienst der SS," report no. 50 of Feb. 7, 1940; *Meldungen aus dem Reich*, 3:732.

212. See Haase, "Praxis des Reichskriegsgerichts," 390–91.

213. "Kriegs-Kriminalistik für die Wehrmacht," 9 (recorded in BA-MA, RW 6/v. 129 D, pt. 1).

214. At least four of the five death penalties not imposed on Witnesses were also pronounced on the charge of conscientious objection. (Consequently, almost all death penalties were based on KSSVO, art. 5, clause 3.) They were imposed on the Adventist Gustav Psyrembel (RKG decision made at the beginning of Mar. 1940, execution on Mar. 30, 1940); the Protestant Dr. Hermann Stöhr (RKG decision made on Mar. 16, 1940, execution on June 21, 1940); as well as the members of the Catholic Christkönigsgesellschaft, Michael Lerpscher (RKG decision made on Aug. 2, 1940, execution on Sept. 5, 1940) and Josef Ruf (RKG decision made on Sept. 14, 1940, execution on Oct. 10, 1940).

215. See Haase, "Praxis des Reichskriegsgerichts," 390–91.

216. The chief of the OKW, letter of June 1, 1940, cited in Haase, "Praxis des Reichskriegsgerichts," 392.

217. BA-MA, RH 15/221, Bl. 27, OKW, decree of Nov. 8, 1940. In his study (*Kriegsdienstverweigerung* [1982], 88), Hartmann includes the Jan. 15, 1952, letter by the Württemberg-Hohenzollern "Landesamt für Wiedergutmachung." According to this letter, as early as the beginning of the war, the Gestapo instructed the military registration offices to perform a "special draft for potential conscientious objectors, especially the Bible Students." It is not possible to find any further evidence in support of this statement. At the period of mobilization, there was a general increase in the number of draftees. Therefore, it cannot be stated with certainty whether the relatively high number of RKG proceedings regarding conscientious objection in the autumn of 1939 would justify the assumption of such a "special draft." Some literary studies mention a "special action" directed against the Bible Students "at the beginning of the World War II" (see Billstein, *Krefeld*, 302). However, this Gestapo action did not involve a draft of Bible Students into the Wehrmacht, but had different objectives. (For additional information, see this book, pp. 694–95, n.335.)

218. Subsequent military statistics of the Wehrmacht do not have different statements regarding the Bible Student cases. Based on these statistics, we can conclude that during the following years, the number of death penalties imposed on Jehovah's Witnesses who refused military service was considerably lower than during the first year of the war: During the second year of the war (between Oct. 1, 1940, and Sept. 30, 1941), the number of death penalties according to KSSVO, art. 5, dropped to a total of 54; thereafter it increased again. Between Oct. 1, 1941, and June 30, 1942 (there are no records for the third quarter of 1942), a total of 167 death penalties according to KSSVO, art. 5, were pronounced. During the following period, this number increased even more. This increase is exclusively the result of death penalties involving other groups of offenses against KSSVO, art. 5—primarily an offense of evading military service for other reasons. For the first time, these numbers have been analyzed according to the various offenses recorded in book 13 of the "Kriegs-Kriminalstatistik." According to these analyses, during the fourth quarter of 1942 (between Oct. 1, 1942, and Dec. 31, 1942), the majority of the 171 death penalties on the charge of "demoralization of the armed forces" were cases of self-mutilation (112), as well as evading military service by means of deception (35). The number of death penalties for other offenses is not specified. These death penalties are summarized under the term "Other Offenses [KSSVO, art. 5] para. 1, clauses 1–3." According to this summary, during the fourth quarter of 1942, a total of twenty-four death penalties were pronounced on the charge of "demoralizing statements," offenses involving KSSVO, art. 5, para. 1, clause 2 (persuasion toward a refusal to fulfill duties of compulsory service, or persuasion toward insubordination, etc.), and the refusal to perform military service. Of these twenty-four death penalties, ten were pronounced against "legionaries." Available statistical records for the following years show a corresponding development regarding cases according to KSSVO, art. 5 (cited in BA-MA, RW 6/v. 129D and v.130 D, H 25/39, H 25/40; Hennicke, "Wehrmachtkriminalstatistik," 444). In comparison to the beginning years of the war, obvious changes can be observed: During the first year of the war, the majority of death penalties on the charge of "demoralization of the armed forces" was imposed on people who refused to perform military service (at least 116 out of 117 cases). In the following war years, the number of death penalties for this reason decreased in comparison to the number of death penalties imposed for other reasons of evading military service. These tendencies can also be observed with regard to the 130 substantiated cases of military court proceedings against Jehovah's Witnesses that have been compiled for this study. Accordingly, the court cases, for which it is possible to determine the date of the pronouncement of the penalty and the amount of punishment, took place as follows: in 1939, a total of 36 cases took place; in 1940, 30 cases; 1941, 14; 1942, 10; 1943, 13; 1945, 3.

219. According to the numbers published by Seidler in 1993, the death penalty was imposed in 62 percent of the cases against conscientious objectors

that took place during the entire period of the war. Consequently, it can be assumed that, in comparison to the first year of the war (73.7%), an increasing number of military court cases involving conscientious objection did not result in death penalties. See Seidler, *Fahnenflucht*, 128–29.

220. For a considerable period of time, incorrect statements were made in the literature with regard to the pronouncement of judgments in Bible Student cases at the RKG. For instance, the apologetic study of Schweling and Schwinge speaks of a "humanitarian solution" to which the RKG had turned because the court referred to the possibility of making use of the mitigation clause of KSSVO, art. 5, para. 2, in cases that involved Jehovah's Witnesses: "By means of such judgments, they were generally able to protect the 'Earnest Bible Students' against the death penalty. As a result, in the majority of cases, they were subjected only to prison sentences" (Schweling, *Militärjustiz*, 193). However, statements that the RKG judges displayed a certain graciousness and reluctance in imposing death penalties are made not only by former military judges and postwar authors advocating similar ideological ideas—foremost among them the chairman of the association of German soldiers, Brigadier General Dr. Jürgen Schreiber (see Schreiber, "Wehrmachtjustiz und Kriegsdienstverweigerung," 145–46). Such statements have also been made in scientifically recognized studies. For instance, Zipfel states that "even during the war," the RKG "tried, as far as possible, to avoid imposing death penalties on the Bible Students" (Zipfel, *Kirchenkampf*, 198–99; likewise Hellmund, "Zeugen Jehovas," no page numbers, chap. 4, 3). Fauck bases his assumption on a document that addresses a different problem (actions that were taken against people from occupied western territories who refused to take the [military] oath). Accordingly, he states that, "at least in a considerable number of cases, the military authorities were able to avoid having to impose death penalties" (Fauck, "Fahneneid," 473).

221. From the numbers included in the Watch Tower Society's publications, it can be determined that acts of pardon were granted in 19.8 percent of the cases (*Yearbook* 1974, 212). However, these numbers also include penalties imposed on people by non-military courts. (With regard to acts of pardon granted after People's Court decisions, see this book, pp. 667–68, n.118.) Therefore, the number of people who were granted a pardon by military court jurisdiction is probably much smaller. Based on the military criminal statistics during the second quarter of 1942, a pardon was granted in 23.2 precent of all court cases according to KSSVO, art. 5. See BA-MA, H 25/39.

222. In 1991 Norbert Haase published "a summary of the death penalties that the RKG had imposed and carried out between Aug. 26, 1939, and Feb. 7, 1945." This summary is based on an analysis of the (incomplete) lists of criminal cases and executions of the RKG that had been discovered at the historical military archives in Prague (Haase, "Praxis des Reichskriegsgerichts," 390). According to this summary, this court pronounced a total of 1,189 death penalties.

Of these death penalties, 251 were imposed on the charge of "demoralization of the armed forces." The vast majority of these death penalties were imposed and carried out on Jehovah's Witnesses who refused to perform military service. With reference to the same source, Franz W. Seidler mentions in his 1993 publication that the RKG imposed 196 death penalties on the charge of conscientious objection (Seidler, *Fahnenflucht,* 128–29). In consideration of the high proportion of executions carried out, the number of RKG decisions that is not included in the above-mentioned summary, as well as the death penalties imposed on Jehovah's Witnesses by other military courts, the numbers published by Haase and Seidler support my quantitative assessment. This assessment has also been confirmed by means of an exhibition catalogue published in 1992, which refers to an "incomplete collection of data from 1948," according to which the RKG imposed and carried out death penalties "on the charge of conscientious objection on 236 Jehovah's Witnesses" (see Knobelsdorf et al., *"Das Recht wurzelt im Volk,"* 59, 73). In 1991 Wüllner (by misquoting the author) mentions the number of "approximately 1,000 executions of Earnest Bible Students" (Wüllner, *NS-Militärjustiz,* 517). This number is not supported by other sources and has to be considered considerably overstated. Even more so, this applies to the incorrect projection that Karsten Bredemeier performed in his 1991 dissertation. He bases his estimation on a total of "10,500 court cases" performed "on the charge of conscientious objection." With reference to the military criminal statistics, Bredemeier assumes that, between Aug. 26, 1940 (actually Aug. 26, 1939!), and Sept. 28, 1940, a total of 152 Bible Student cases took place—per month. He simply multiplies this number by the 69 months of the war. See Bredemeier, *Kriegsdienstverweigerung,* 84–85.

223. The total number of conscientious objectors in the Third Reich who were sentenced and executed as a result of a military court decision is probably not much higher than the number of executed Jehovah's Witnesses (see Garbe, "'Du sollst nicht töten,'" 93ff.). In almost all cases, the refusal was (purely) based on religious reasons. There are only a few cases in which the conscientious objection was based on pacifist and political considerations. The literature includes specific biographies of six Catholic conscientious objectors, five members of the Seventh-day Adventists Reformation Movement, one Baptist, and one member of the "Bekennende Kirche" who were sentenced by a military court and died for their convictions. See Bredemeier, *Kriegsdienstverweigerung,* 109ff.; Hartmann, *Kriegsdienstverweigerung* (1986); Röhm, *Sterben für den Frieden,* 212ff.

224. The total number of conscientious objectors from among Jehovah's Witnesses is considerably higher than the number of those who were sentenced by the military courts. This number also includes the 1,500 male Bible Student prisoners in the concentration camps who refused to follow the request to perform military service after the beginning of the war. Some studies include statements that more than 6,000 to 7,000 Jehovah's Witnesses refused to perform military service during World War II (Röhm, *Sterben für den Frieden,* 213; Hartmann,

"Kriegsdienstverweigerung" [1982], 78). Such statements include the entire number of persecuted Jehovah's Witnesses, including those who, mainly during the mid-1930s, were "only" imprisoned for short periods of time. From an objective point of view, to include these in the number of conscientious objectors cannot be justified. To do so would obscure the term "conscientious objection."

225. Among the victims of military jurisdiction, those who did not comply with the draft and who refused to take the (military) oath represented only a relatively small number. Considerably larger is the number of soldiers who used other methods to evade (further) military service. According to recent estimates, 22,750 death penalties were imposed on the charge of "desertion." Approximately 5,000 to 6,000 death penalties were imposed on the charge of "demoralization of the armed forces," in most cases as a result of self-mutilation and evading of one's duty by means of deception. It can be assumed that between 60 percent and 70 percent of these death penalties were also carried out (Messerschmidt and Wüllner, *Wehrmachtjustiz*, 90 and 138).

226. See Schreiber, "Wehrmachtjustiz und Kriegsdienstverweigerung," 145–46.

227. *Entscheidungen des Reichskriegsgerichts*, vol. 2, book 1, 63ff., RKG, StPL (HLS) III 25/40, decision of May 3, 1940.

228. RKG, StPL (HLS) III 79/41, decision of Dec. 10, 1941, cited in Hartmann, *Kriegsdienstverweigerung* (1986), 74–77 (76).

229. RKG, StPL (RKA) III 349/41, indictment of July 31, 1941, 72–73.

230. *Entscheidungen des Reichskriegsgerichts*, vol. 2, book 1, 44–45, RKG, StPL (HLS) II 63/39, decision of Dec. 6, 1939; see also *ZWR* [*Zeitschrift für Wehrrecht*] 5 (1940/41): 290.

231. Ibid., 58–59, RKG, StPL (HLS) II 18/40, decision of Feb. 20, 1940.

232. "Rechtsgrundsätze des Reichskriegsgerichts," 13.

233. KSSVO, art. 5, para. 2, does not mention any requirements that would justify the assumption that this was a matter of a "less serious case." Consequently, based on the seriousness of the offense and in accordance with the personal degree of guilt, the judges had to determine the question of whether it was even possible to use this mitigation clause. With regard to cases involving Jehovah's Witnesses and other conscientious objectors, even Schweling and Schwinge acknowledge that the RKG judges "always [had] the option of turning to KSSVO, art. 5, para. 2, and assuming a 'less serious case.' However, for reasons of deterrence, the judges of the various court divisions did not consider this to be acceptable" (Schweling, *Militärjustiz*, 195).

234. This is often described as a general practice of the RKG (see Schweling, *Militärjustiz*, 194; Schreiber, "Wehrmachtjustiz und Kriegsdienstverweigerung," 146.) There were certainly cases in which the RKG judges requested expert opinions confirming the appropriateness of referring to art. 51. However, this does not prove that it was a general practice of the RKG.

235. See Ziemann, "Psychopathen," 41.

236. See Lange, "Dienstverweigerung"; see also this book, pt. 5, ch. 13, pp. 228–30.

237. See Lange, "Dienstverweigerung," 15.

238. See Zipfel, *Kirchenkampf,* 199; Garbe, "'Gott mehr gehorchen als den Menschen,'" 208–9.

239. *Entscheidungen des Reichskriegsgerichts,* vol. 2, book 2, 65–66, RKG, StPL (HLS) II 4/40, decision of Jan. 24, 1940; see also *DJ* 102 (1940): 939.

240. Ibid., 63–64, RKG, StPL (HLS) III 25/40, decision of May 3, 1940.

241. Schmidt, "Entscheidungen," 325; on Schmidt's criticism of RKG jurisdiction, which is often overemphasized, see the assessment in Messerschmidt and Wüllner's study of this work made by Garbe, cited in *Kritische Justiz* 21 (1988): 352–58, here 356–57.

242. Schmauser, "Minder schwerer Fall," 132–41 (133).

243. Ibid., 137 (italics in the original).

244. Ibid., 139 (italics in the original).

245. *Entscheidungen des Reichskriegsgerichts,* vol. 2, book 3, 144–55 (155), RKG, StPL (HLS) III 122/41, decision of Mar. 10, 1942.

246. In 1944 the RKG senior judge provided the OKW with the Regulations Regarding Court Proceedings Involving "Earnest Bible Students" [Grundsätze über Strafverfahren gegen "Ernste Bibelforscher"]. These regulations clearly required that, in order to base a judgment on KSSVO, art. 5, para. 1, clause 3, it did not make "any difference whether the accused refused any kind of military service or whether he merely refused service under arms and otherwise was willing to fulfill his duties of military service." Even in such cases a death penalty should be imposed. Also, a previously imposed death penalty could be withdrawn only in cases in which the conscientious objector indicated his willingness "to perform military service in the requested form" (IfZ, MA 333, 657694–96, the president of the RKG, Aug. 3, 1944, letter to OKW).

247. It was not uncommon for Jehovah's Witnesses to reconsider their decision and then refuse military service again. This clearly indicates the pangs of conscience and inner struggle to which they were exposed. Schweling (*Militärjustiz,* 194–95) reports of other Bible Student cases in which the court proceedings had to be repeated three times because the defendant repeatedly withdrew his decision.

248. *Entscheidungen des Reichskriegsgerichts,* vol. 2, book 3, 147 (anonymity even in the original).

249. Schweling, *Militärjustiz,* 194. The numerous death penalties that the military courts imposed on people who refused to perform military service for religious reasons diminish the image of strict yet "reasonable" military jurisdiction, which former military judges have disseminated to this day. They tried to justify or find excuses for those judgments. In defending themselves, they used the following arguments: the continuous efforts made by the judges to "persuade the defendants to change their mind"; the "opportunity" provided for

the conscientious objectors "to be able to change their attitude" up until the time immediately prior to executing the judgment; the inability to counteract a "decision from the Führer." During that period, they also referred to the fact that conscientious objectors were also subjected to military court proceedings in democratic countries. With regard to this argument, however, the judges fail to mention that these countries restricted the punishment exclusively to prison sentences. See also Haase, "Praxis des Reichskriegsgerichts," 381, 392–93.

250. "Der Präsident des Reichskriegsgerichts," Aug. 17, 1942, letter to the heads of the various court divisions. Cited in Haase, "Praxis des Reichskriegsgerichts," 393 (italics in the original).

251. See Schweling, *Militärjustiz*, 195; Weisenborn, *Aufstand*, 88; BA-MA, N 192/1, 39, 57–58. According to KStVO, art. 91, para. 1, in cases where "new factual material or evidence" was submitted, it was possible to reopen proceedings, even after the court decision had been pronounced and confirmed by the judicial convening authority. The various RKG divisions that had to approve of such applications always considered a withdrawal of the refusal to perform military service to be an adequate basis for reopening the court proceedings. This "extended interpretation of the regulations" was legally established in the Regulations Involving Court Proceedings against Earnest Bible Students, etc., which the OKW had issued in 1944 (IfZ, MA 333, 657687–89).

252. Without exception, the military courts rejected the offer of Jehovah's Witnesses to perform alternative civilian service outside of the armed forces. See *Entscheidungen des Reichskriegsgerichts*, vol. 2, book 3, 145.

253. BA-MA, N 192/1, Max Bastian, "Lebenserinnerungen" (1956), 57.

254. Poelchau, *Die letzten Stunden*, 34.

255. Poelchau, *Ordnung der Bedrängten*, 76–77.

256. Poelchau, *Die letzten Stunden*, 35.

257. Poelchau, *Ordnung der Bedrängten*, 77.

258. Reports about discussions that prison chaplains had with Jehovah's Witnesses who refused to perform military service are, for instance, included in the following studies: Müller and Weckerling, "Protestantismus," 297; Scharf, *Widerstehen*, 42–45; Scharf, "Gespräche mit Kurt Scharf," 24–25. But not all prison chaplains who were asked to give pastoral care to people awaiting execution also considered the assistance and support of "delinquents" to be part of their pastoral duties. Dr. Max Schultz, who, at that time, was the pastor of the Breslau prison for pretrial detention, which was used as place of execution, indicates that he had a different concept of his responsibilities. See Schultz, "Seelsorge," 52ff.

259. Bruno Knöller, Rudolf Daur, Feb. 20, 1942, letter to Emma Stange.

260. Bruno Knöller, Rudolf Daur, letter of Dec. 15, 1942.

261. Contrary to the statements included in his 1952 report, in his 1992 autobiography Jentsch makes the incorrect assumption that the "delinquent" by the name Bernhard was not a Bible Student but a Protestant Christian

(Jentsch, *Ernstfälle,* 183, and 557n12). However, his previous statement is correct. It is the Jehovah's Witness Bernhard Grimm, born on May 14, 1923. On July 14, 1942, the RKG sentenced him to death on the charge of conscientious objection. The penalty was carried out at the Brandenburg-Görden penitentiary, on Aug. 21, 1942. He was beheaded along with Father Franz Reinisch, among others. See "Ehrenbuch Brandenburg-Görden," 2:106.

262. Jentsch, *Wehrdienstfrage,* 182.

263. On Sept. 26, 1942, on Hitler's order, Rottka was suspended from office. Apparently, this action was based on the fact that Rottka "showed more than the required consideration," especially with regard to Bible Student cases (see Haase, "Praxis des Reichskriegsgerichts," 411; Haase, *Reichskriegsgericht,* 72). Consequently, Rottka belongs to a small minority of judges who refused, for reasons of conscience, to continue supporting an increasingly criminal administration of justice.

264. See Jentsch, *Ernstfälle,* 191ff.; Bredemeier, *Kriegsdienstverweigerung,* 165–66.

265. According to Jentsch's report, this brochure had to be prepared "more or less in secret since the whole action could have been considered as a revolt against the 'order of the Führer'" (Jentsch, *Wehrdienstfrage,* 13). After the second draft of the brochure was completed in the summer of 1944, it was "secretly passed from cell to cell in the prison bunkers." Jentsch presents the judges of the RKG in a very positive light ("men who could not just watch without taking any action") and presented their actions almost as acts of resistance. This resulted in the fact that these statements are repeatedly used, in the pertinent literature, for exonerating the RKG. In 1988 Jürgen Schreiber used Jentsch's report to contradict "Messerschmidt and Wüllner's accusations regarding the brutality and mercilessness of the military courts" (Schreiber, "Wehrmachtjustiz—Anmerkungen," 104).

266. Jentsch, *Wehrdienstfrage,* 13.

267. Ibid. See the annotated edition of a collection of excerpts in Jentsch, *Ernstfälle,* 240ff. In 1952 Werner Jentsch, who later became professor for practical theology, published a book on "the question of military service." This publication includes an article (17–84) about "the question of military service in the light of the New Testament," based on the 1943 brochure. By stating these explanations, Jentsch had tried to save Jehovah's Witnesses who refused to perform military service from execution. However, his explanations also indicate that Jentsch was still deeply rooted in the traditional viewpoint of the churches that Christians were obligated to comply with the request by the authorities to perform military service.

268. BA-MA, N 192/1, Max Bastian, "Lebenserinnerungen" (1956), 57.

269. See Zipfel, *Kirchenkampf,* 199n58.

270. See the description of the persecution of the Appel family from Süderbarup in this book, pt. 3, ch. 9, pp. 192–93.

271. Reports about such attempts at persuasion are included in *Yearbook* 1974, 123–24; *Yearbook* 1989, 119–20; *Watchtower,* Mar. 1, 1987, 22.

272. BA-MA, N 192/1, Max Bastian, "Lebenserinnerungen" (1956), 57. Efforts to support prisoners in their resolve to remain steadfast could result in punishment on the charge of "demoralization of the armed forces." On Aug. 11, 1941, the Vienna Special Court sentenced Wilhelm Blaschek to four years of imprisonment; six days prior to RKG proceedings involving his friend Franz Zeiner, Blaschek had written him a letter. He encouraged Zeiner to "be strong in the faith because Jesus Christ will help us." The special court considered this as an act of supporting a person in his refusal to perform military service. See Neugebauer, "'Ernste Bibelforscher,'" 182; *Yearbook* 1989, 122–23.

273. Elise Harms, "Enduring After a Tragic Loss," cited in *Watchtower,* Oct. 15, 1981, 26–28 (27). A well-documented biography of Johannes Harms, born in Wilhelmshaven, is included in Fahle, *Verweigern,* 154–55; Heuzeroth and Wille, "Lila Winkel," 203–7.

274. See Hartmann, *Kriegsdienstverweigerung* (1986), 79; Heuzeroth and Wille, "Lila Winkel," 203; Scharf, *Widerstehen,* 42–43. The "offers" that some military court judges made were not in agreement with the OKW Regulations Regarding Court Proceedings Involving Earnest Bible Students, etc. (IfZ, MA 333, 657687–89). These regulations state that the resumption of proceedings required the submission of a "convincing" statement in which the person concerned indicated his willingness "to perform military service without reservation."

275. On the motives, see *Yearbook* 1974, 182–91 (reports of conscientious objectors from Germany); *Yearbook* 1989, 119–23 (reports of conscientious objectors from Austria).

276. "Beantwortung einiger Fragen: Mitteilungsblatt der deutchen Verbreitungsstelle des W. T.," July 1942 (a copy of this Mitteilungsblatt is in my possession). See also this book, pt. 5, ch. 13, pp. 330–31.

277. Johannes Harms, Nov. 9, 1940, letter to his father, Martin Harms, cited in Heuzeroth and Wille, "Lila Winkel," 204–5.

278. The farewell letter is published in Steiner, *Österreich,* 127–30. On the persecution of Franz Mattischek, who was sentenced to death by the RKG on Nov. 10, 1939, see Vogl, *Widerstand,* 172; Zinnhobler, "Zeugen Jehovas," 202–3.

279. Cited in Gollwitzer, Kuhn, and Schneider, *Du hast mich heimgesucht,* 342.

280. Hanns Lilje came in contact with Jehovah's Witnesses at the end of 1944, during his imprisonment at the Berlin Gestapo prison. Regarding their attitude, he reports that they "faced death truly without fear" (Lilje, *Im finstern Tal,* 59). Werner Jentsch states: "Here death was a serious matter. And especially for this reason they have my deepest respect! If those hundreds of Bible Students who died during those years had been just blatantly afraid, they would have soon given up. However, the fact that they even stood up straight in the face of the scaffold, approaching death with contented faces, proved, and still

proves, that these were people who had the support of Christ" (Jentsch, *Wehr-dienstfrage*, 183).

281. In cases where the decision to refuse military service was withdrawn, the military courts generally suspended the sentence and gave the conscientious objector the opportunity to "prove his adjusted attitude in direct contact with the enemy." With reference to this practice, the chief of the OKW states in his Aug. 15, 1944, letter that the "suspensions of sentences are well received" by the Bible Students (IfZ, MA 333, 657692).

282. The Sept. 30, 1939, Regulations Regarding the Execution of a Sentence during War and a State of Emergency [Richtlinien für die Strafvollstreckung im Kriege und bei besonderem Einsatz] (BA-MA, RH 14/22, Bl. 70–71) required that in cases in which a military court imposed prison sentences, no allowance should be made for periods of imprisonment served during the war, since the actual sentence would be served after the war. Therefore, according to the Nov. 3, 1939, implementing regulations, the authorities of the Reich Administration of Justice had to admit those people into special penal camps "for detention without counting the detention period as part of the imposed penalty." See Wüllner, *NS-Militärjustiz*, 780–81.

283. From the autumn of 1939 on, the RJM used Esterwegen for the purpose of detaining people who had been sentenced by military courts. In the summer of 1940 other Emsland penal camps were used for such purposes. In 1942 the newly built camps of Bernau (Bavaria), Elberregulierung (Coswig), Rodgau (Dieburg), and Zweibrücken were also used (see Ausländer, "Militärstrafgefangene," 165ff.; Kosthorst and Walter, *Konzentrations- und Strafgefangenenlager*, 234–40; Suhr, *Emslandlager*, 50–54, 167–68).

284. Quite a number of soldiers who had been expelled from the Wehrmacht because they were considered to be "unworthy of serving in the armed forces" were drafted again after they were granted a "conditional" status of "worthiness of serving in the armed forces." For these soldiers, the Probation Battalion 500 (with the Führer decree of Dec. 21, 1940, for delinquent soldiers) was established. In the autumn of 1944 special prison battalions were also formed for military convict units. However, for Jehovah's Witnesses who were sentenced by a military court, the only possibility of surviving the war without having to serve in the armed forces was a prison sentence and, consequently, detention in a penal camp.

285. See Frese, *Bremsklötze*, 79–80.

286. IfZ, MA 333, 657694–96, "Der Präsident des Reichskriegsgerichts," Aug. 3, 1944, letter to the chief of the OKW.

287. IfZ, MA 333, 657692, letter from the chief of the OKW, Aug. 15, 1944.

288. See Bredemeier, *Kriegsdienstverweigerung*, 78.

289. IfZ, MA 333, 657690, RSHA, Sept. 30, 1944, telex to the SS judge at the Reichsführer SS.

290. IfZ, MA 333, 657687–89, Regulations Regarding Court Proceedings Involving Earnest Bible Students, etc. See also Messerschmidt and Wüllner, *Wehrmachtjustiz*, 110–11.

291. See Klausch, *Bewährungsbataillone*, 67ff.; *Die Sondereinheiten*, 29–32.

292. See Burkhardt et al., *Die mit dem blauen Schein*, 50–51; Hartmann, *Kriegs-dienstverweigerung* (1986), 64–67; Vogl, *Widerstand*, 160–61.

293. The exact number of Bible Students who were shot to death at the Probation Battalion 999 is unknown. According to a list of executions that took place at the Heuberg military training area, a total of thirty-seven were shot to death between Dec. 12, 1942, and Nov. 17, 1943 (Klausch, *Bewährungsbataillone*, 220). Hans-Peter Klausch assumes "that during the training period in Germany, at least during the first year of the existence of the 999-units, the Bible Students had the highest number of deaths from among the groups of ideological opponents of National Socialism" (ibid., 234). Only a small number of people were shot to death because of "ideological" reasons for refusing to perform military service. Therefore, the total number of Jehovah's Witnesses who were executed at the Heuberg is probably also very small.

294. Jan. 26, 1986, recollections by Herbert Baade. According to the Gospel accounts, while in Capernaum, Jesus made the eschatological promise to his followers that he would sit down with the patriarchs of Israel at the table in the Kingdom of Heaven (Matt. 8:11–12).

295. This attitude was taken to such an extreme that some Jehovah's Witnesses expressed their refusal to perform military service even when this was not directly required of them. For example, Johann Oswald from Thürnthal, the younger brother of Franz Oswald, had been rejected as unfit for military service at his medical examination and was therefore exempt from military service. However, when he was later arrested because of his IBSA activities, he told the custodial judge that he would refuse to perform military service. As a result of this statement he received a more serious penalty. In the autumn of 1940 the St. Pölten Special Court sentenced him to two years of imprisonment. See Mitterrutzner, "Internationale Bibelforscher-Vereinigung," 276, 285–86.

296. See this book, pt. 5, ch. 13, pp. 330–31.

297. Struckmeier, "Eickhorst," 23.

298. See Lichtenegger, "Die Bibelforscher im Widerstand gegen das NS-Regime," 188; Neugebauer, "'Ernste Bibelforscher,'" 183.

299. See Fahle, *Verweigern*, 156–58.

300. See Hartmann, *Kriegsdienstverweigerung* (1986), 60; BA, Z Sg. 134/28, no page numbers (regarding Horst H.). One recorded case from 1941 involves a Jehovah's Witness who signed the statement before the Gestapo and, as a result, was released from protective detention. However, later he still openly refused military service. After he had been drafted in Sept. 1943, he reported, as ordered, to the appropriate division. There, he submitted a statement indicating

his refusal of military service. To this end, he stated that he had put himself under obligation "to follow the divine laws" and "remain neutral with regard to the affairs of this world." On Jan. 4, 1944, the RKG sentenced the forty-four-year-old miner to death. See BA-MA, RW 11 II/v.27, RKG, StPL (RKA) I 359/43, decision of Jan. 4, 1944.

301. See Marßolek and Ott, *Bremen*, 308; FGN, NHS, 13-7-9-8.

302. Recollections by Bruno Knöller from May 6, 1981, and Nov. 23, 1987; Knöller, "Erinnerungen," 21.

303. AfW HH, 070319, Bl. 33.

304. See Kammler, *Kasseler Soldaten*, 138; R. Zehender, report by Gerhard Oltmann regarding Jehovah's Witnesses from the area of Unterweser/Ems who were executed because of their refusal to perform military service.

305. See Grünewald, *Geschichte der Kriegsdienstverweigerung*, 33.

306. SLG HH, HSG 11 Js. Sond. 464/44, Bl. 4, letter of Oct. 22, 1944.

307. Ibid., Bl. 8, records of interrogation of Nov. 11, 1944.

308. Ibid., Bl. 2, "Der Oberstaatsanwalt beim Hanseatischen Sonderge-richt," Nov. 25, 1944, letter to the RJM.

309. The records do not contain any details about the reasons for aban-doning the court proceedings. The last entry into the records was made on Nov. 8, 1945[!]: "Discontinued, since proceedings are pointless" (SLG HH, HSG 11 Js. Sond. 464/44, Bl.23). On the question of whether the legal authorities made any changes in their dealings with Bible Student proceedings toward the end of the war, see this book, p. 669, n.122.

310. Apr. 4, 1945, indictment of the special court for the operation zone Al-penvorland, cited in Maislinger, "Andere religiöse Gruppen," 349. The death penalty was not carried out. Instead, by an act of pardon, the sentence was changed to five years of imprisonment. See Hartmann, *Kriegsdienstverweigerung* (1986), 60.

311. See Zipfel, *Kirchenkampf*, 197n53; *Awake!*, Nov. 22, 1992, 19. There are also a few references to cases of self-mutilation (see Hartmann, "Kriegsdienst-verweigerung" [1982], 75, 126). To this end, the Gestapa memo about the IBSA, probably written at the end of 1936, states that "in their fanaticism, some adherents to these false teachings . . . mutilated themselves to evade military service" (IfZ, MA 554, 936280). Klausch reports about a member of the Proba-tion Battalion 999 who was sentenced to death on the charge of "demoraliza-tion of the armed forces" in 1942/43 and subsequently executed at the Heu-berg military training area. "Most certainly," this was a Bible Student who had "swallowed thumbtacks (according to a different report, a spoonful) to evade military service" (Klausch, *Bewährungsbataillone*, 234).

312. See Minninger, "Bielefeld," 67–68; Kammler, *Kasseler Soldaten*, 138, 141.

313. VVN HH, Komitteeakten B 15, biography of Sept. 12, 1946.

314. Ibid., L 27, biography of Feb. 27, 1946; see also Möller, "Steinburg," 217.

315. Nov. 23, 1987, recollections by Bruno Knöller.

316. Recollections by Johannes Rauthe, "Geschichtsbericht," 39.

317. See this book, pp. 652–53, n.351.

318. See Ziebold et al., "Das Schicksal der Freiburger Zeugen Jehovas," no page numbers; June 1984 recollections by Wilhem Molsich; Nov. 23, 1987, recollections by Elise Kühnle; VVN HH, Kommiteeakten, 37.

319. May 31, 1986, recollections by Richard Rudolph.

320. Report by Karl Schild, cited in Klausch, *Bewährungsbataillone*, 235–36. On the service of other Jehovah's Witnesses in Probation Battalions, see Burkhardt et al., *Die mit dem blauen Schein*, 239; Schmiedgen, "Partisanen," 145–46.

321. June 1984 recollections by Paul Marszałek.

322. May 23, 1986, recollections by Alois Moser.

323. BA-MA, RH 15/209, Bl. 100, RKM, Mar. 27, 1936, Decree Involving the Draft of Political Prisoners for Active Military Service [Erlass zur Heranziehung der politischen Schutzhäftlinge zum aktiven Wehrdienst].

324. Periodically, the military registration offices inquired at the concentration camp commandant's headquarters requesting information about anticipated releases from protective detention (see also Kammler, *Kasseler Soldaten*, 144–46). In the context of those requests, the concentration camp commanders or other responsible SS leaders asked the Bible Student prisoners if they would agree to perform military service without reservations. Apart from a few exceptions, it was possible to be released from the concentration camps by submitting a certain statement confirming the willingness to perform military service and by signing the reverse statement. Frequently, such interrogations regarding a Bible Student's willingness to perform military service resulted in beatings. In other cases, they resulted in submission of a complaint or the transfer to a punishment battalion. See, for instance, Poel, *Neuengamme*, 107ff.

325. See Apr. 17, 1937, Regulations Regarding Examinations before Enlistment and Recruitment, art. 2, para. 4, *RGBl.* 1937 I, 469.

326. In 1941 a decree was issued to discontinue "examinations before enlistment of prisoners in protective detention." With its Aug. 30, 1941, decree, the OKW ordered that in the future, concentration camp prisoners "should not be subjected to examinations before enlistment until they were released from protective detention" (BA-MA, RH 15/226, Bl. 41).

327. These descriptions are based on KmW [Wewelsburg District Museum], investigation results of the 1971 Wewelsburg trial at the Paderborn *Schwurgericht* [jury court]; KmW, KW D 87, Buder, "Wewelsburg"; Hüser, *Wewelsburg*, 88–89; May 16, 1992, recollections by Klingenberg; May 23, 1986, recollections by Alois Moser.

328. After their return to Wewelsburg in Mar. and Apr., the twenty-six Bible Students were repeatedly subjected to serious mistreatment. According to the reports by former fellow prisoners, the SS stated that they would now get the treatment "that the Wehrmacht was too cowardly to give." The commandant's

headquarters submitted a request for execution to the Reichsführer SS. Contrary to expectation, the request was denied. As a result, the SS in Wewelsburg put the conscientious objectors together into a special punishment battalion. There, the prisoners first of all had to perform all work at double pace. They were given reduced food rations and were denied any medical treatment during the entire period. As a special act of persecution, SS officials forced the group to do "sports" in the roll-call area—under terrible conditions and to the point of exhaustion. The prisoners had to perform punishment drills: rolling over, crawling, and jumping. If the SS was not satisfied with the speed, they abused the prisoners with clubs and kicks with their boots. During this particularly difficult situation of their fellow believers, the solidarity among the Bible Students proved to be especially valuable. Despite prohibitions, the other prisoners supported them to the best of their ability; only after several months did conditions improve. In Aug. 1941 such terrible treatment was completely discontinued.

329. In the autumn of 1944 an increasing number of people were drafted into the SS-Sonderformation [special SS division] of General Dirlewanger. As early as the summer of 1943, asocials and criminals from among the German concentration camp prisoners, as well as prisoners from the group of opponents of the regime, were drafted into this unit. As far as can be determined, these drafts did not include any Jehovah's Witnesses. See Auerbach, "Konzentrationslagerhäftlinge"; *Yearbook* 1974, 204.

330. See Bredemeier, *Kriegsdienstverweigerung*, 86.

331. Zentrumspartei [Center Part] was a German political party represented in the German Reichstag after 1871 as the party of organized Catholicism. Under the pressure of the Nazi regime, it dissolved in 1933.

332. See Günter and Wille, "Lila Winkel"; John, *Wewelsburg* (1996), 136ff.

333. See Broszat, *Anatomy of the SS State*, 188–89.

334. Based on the prisoners' number assignments, it can be assumed that a total of 1,416 women were sent to the Lichtenburg concentration camp during the eighteen months of its existence. The number of prisoners varied considerably. In May 1939, at the time of its dissolution, almost 1,000 prisoners were at this concentration camp. According to statistical records, this number includes 386 (40.3%) Bible Students, 240 (25.1%) described as "asocials," 119 (12.4%) "criminals," and 114 (11.9%) "political prisoners." It also includes 98 (10.2%) people who were persecuted because of so-called Rasseschande [the defilement of the German race through relations between Germans and Jews]. Cited in Arndt, "Ravensbrück," 100; Drobisch, "Frauenkonzentrationslager," 103; also Drobisch, "Frauen-KZ Lichtenburg."

335. As a result of the "special action" against Jehovah's Witnesses "at the beginning of World War II" (see Billstein, *Krefeld*, 302), the number of Bible Student prisoners increased only insignificantly. This special action, which was not specifically directed against the IBSA but involved all groups of opponents

of the regime, was based on instructions that Heydrich had given to the State Police offices as early as the beginning of 1936. According to these instructions, "all opponents of the state" that "were to be taken into protective detention in the event of war" had to be "registered immediately in files (= A files)." Besides "all left-wing extremists" and "leaders of oppositional or reactionary movements," Heydrich also counted "all leaders of the Bible Students Association among the opponents of the state mentioned in these instructions" (BA, R 58/264, Bl. 195–97, Prussian Secret State Police office, interoffice decree of Feb. 5, 1936). Because of these prepared files, several members of the left-wing parties were sent to concentration camps at the beginning of the war. However, the number of Bible Students sent to the concentration camps in the autumn of 1939 increased only insignificantly. This is probably due to the fact that the majority of leaders had already been arrested during the previous years. For instance, between Sept. 1, 1939, and Jan. 1, 1940, the total number of prisoners at the Buchenwald concentration camp (5,397) increased by 6,377 to a total of 11,774 (an increase of 118.0%). During the same period, the number of Bible Students only increased from 386 to 405 (an increase of 5.0%). See BA, NS 4 Bu/vorl. 137.

336. By the beginning of WWII, the total number of prisoners in all concentration camps had increased to about 25,000 prisoners. This increase was especially a result of the high numbers of nonpolitical prisoners (the "action against the asocials" during Apr. and June 1938, and the "Nov. 1938 action against the Jews") who were sent to the camps, as well as the numbers of opponents of the regime from the "annexed" areas (Austria, Sudetenland). During the war, the number of prisoners increased considerably because of the admission of prisoners of non-German nationality, even though there was also a considerable increase in the death rate (Dec. 1942: 718,000; Aug. 1943: 224,000; Aug. 1944: 524,000; middle of Jan. 1945: 718,000; cited in Broszat, *Anatomy of the SS State*, 196–97; Pingel, *Häftlinge*, 129–30; BA, NS 3/439).

337. The total number of prisoners at the Mauthausen concentration camp on Dec. 1, 1939: 143 Bible Students compared to a total of 2,772 prisoners; on Dec. 31, 1944: 85 Bible Students compared to a total of 72,426 prisoners. The total number of prisoners at the Buchenwald concentration camp on Dec. 1, 1939: 405 Bible Students compared to a total of 12,341; in Sept. 1944: approximately 260 Bible Students compared to a total of 82,239 prisoners. Figures cited in Chêne, *Mauthausen*, 178–90; Pingel, *Häftlinge*, 282n47; BA, NS 4 Bu/vorl., 143, "Schutzhaftlagerrapport Buchenwald." The diagram is also based on the "daily reports of prisoner numbers" at the Buchenwald concentration camp between July 29, 1937, and Dec. 31, 1942, which are preserved at the Federal archives (BA, NS 4 Bu/vorl. 137–39).

338. To the greatest extent possible, the prisoners at the concentration camps were placed into separate blocks, according to the respective groups to which they belonged. With regard to Jehovah's Witnesses, special importance

was attached to this separation since the authorities were determined to isolate them from all other prisoners. At the Moringen Provinzialwerkhaus (a factory building), which, from Oct. 1933 on, served as a central concentration camp for women in Prussia and into which the first IBSA members were admitted in Jan. 1935, there was a separate "dormitory for the Bible Students" as early as 1936/37. See Distel, "Schatten," 30; *Deutschland-Berichte* 4 (1937): 713.

339. Cited in Pingel, *Häftlinge,* 90. (The reference to the concentration camp in Sachsenhausen instead of Sachsenburg at this place is a spelling mistake. See the correct statement, ibid., 76.)

340. See Drobisch, *Konzentrationslager,* 36.

341. During this period, the Bible Student prisoners in Buchenwald were identified by means of large blue patches (approximately 4 inches [10 centimeters] in diameter). Therefore, according to a report by Otto Horn, an Austrian union official, the Bible Students were also called *Blaupunkte* [blue spots] (DÖW, no. 1458, Otto Horn, report about the Buchenwald concentration camp).

342. During this period, the groups of Bible Student prisoners in the concentration camps were assigned to the punishment battalions (see this book, pt. 5, ch. 15, pp. 402–4). Therefore, they also had to wear the penalty patch that identified the members of the punishment battalions. The Bible Student prisoners of Jewish origin had to wear the purple triangle identifying them as Bible Students and underneath that patch, like other Jews, a yellow triangle with the tip pointing upward. As a result, the two triangular patches resembled the Star of David. There was only a small number of Bible Students of Jewish origin. (In the SS records they are referred to as "Bible Student, Jew.") See Chêne, *Mauthausen,* 40; Kautsky, *Teufel und Verdammte,* 125; Kogon, *Theory and Practice of Hell,* 44–45.

343. During the following years, other special categories were added (for instance, the special division of the Wehrmacht). Other classifications were made in conjunction with the original category (Jews, "Rasseschänder" [Germans who defiled the race by having relations with Jews], "second offenders").

344. Even in some of the penal institutions used by the legal authorities, Jehovah's Witnesses were distinguished by means of special marks of identification. At the Emsland penal camps (at least during 1938/39), they were identified with white armbands. In this way, the guards were able to notice right away if Bible Students tried to establish contact with fellow prisoners. If they saw several prisoners with white armbands involved in conversation, the guards assumed that they were possibly organizing their preaching activity. According to the camp instructions, they had to take immediate action against such efforts (Apr. 15, 1971, recollections by Willi Lehmbecker).

345. In the recollections of IBSA members, with regard to prisoners who wore the purple patch of the Bible Students, a clear distinction is made between "true Jehovah's Witnesses," "false brothers" (those who abandoned their faith during their imprisonment), "apostates" (those who left the Bible Students

and formed their own groups, as, for instance, Engel Jehovas), as well as the Adventists.

346. It can be estimated that a total of fifty members of the Seventh-day Adventists (Reformation movement) were sent to the concentration camps. As far as can be determined, twelve of these people lost their lives during their imprisonment in the concentration camps. See Fleschutz, *Gedenkbuch*, 8–9.

347. *Deutschland-Berichte* 4 (1937): 707. The assumption that Jehovah's Witnesses rejected a release from the concentration camps probably alludes to the fact that they refused to sign a statement (which was different from the standardized statements introduced two years later) that the Gestapo presented to them during their review of the detention order, as a requirement for release. It indicated that the person concerned would no longer participate in Bible Student activities. It also indicated that the person accepted the legality of the IBSA ban.

348. *Deutschland-Berichte* 4 (1937): 714.

349. GBu [Memorial Buchenwald], 36-1/2, Sachsenburg concentration camp, report of Apr. 24, 1935.

350. GBu, 36-1/2, Apr. 25, 1935, letter of the commanding officer of the Sachsenburg concentration camp to the inspection office of the concentration camps.

351. In the literature, several unfounded generalizing statements have been made on the basis of individual occurrences. Erika Weinzierl makes the following statement regarding the female Bible Students: "They refused to greet the SS officers in the required form. They attended the roll calls only under force" (Weinzierl, "Österreichische Frauen," 182).

352. Höß, *Kommandant in Auschwitz*, 96. Both Jehovah's Witnesses were later executed because of their refusal to report to the recruiting board (see this book, p. 000, n.410).

353. *Todeslager Sachsenhausen*, 42.

354. Richard Rudolph was sent to Sachsenhausen in Jan. 1939. He reports that the (more moderate) Bible Student group there discouraged fellow believers from adopting a rigorous attitude. When he considered refusing to greet the SS guards in the required form, he was told that such refusal was not necessary and not requested by the Bible. The greeting would also not be an act of idolatry. The refusal to greet would only needlessly provoke the SS. The Sachsenhausen Jehovah's Witnesses did not condemn their fellow believers who refused the greeting for reasons of conscience. However, they also did not encourage such conduct as an act worthy of imitation (May 31, 1986, and Sept. 9, 1986, recollections by Richard Rudolph).

355. In 1935, after his escape to Switzerland, Wolfgang Langhoff published his report, *Die Moorsoldaten*. In this book, he describes how SS officers at the Lichtenburg concentration camp repeatedly abused a Bible Student prisoner because he refused to give the "Hitler salute." Fellow political prisoners tried to

persuade him to use clever tactics ("we also only pretend"). According to the report, after weeks of torment, the man was so weakened that he was no longer able to keep up his resistance. See Langhoff, *Moorsoldaten,* 311ff.

356. FGN, NHS 13-4-2-1, "Aufzeichnungen von Alfred Hübsch," 8.

357. Ibid., 5.

358. Kupfer-Koberwitz, *Mächtigen,* 215; see also ibid., 243.

359. This description is based on Drobisch, "Frauenkonzentrationslager," 107–8; Elling, *Frauen,* 30; Haag, *Staub,* 151–52; MGRa [Memorial Ravensbrück], RA, Bd. 25, no. 332, Berta Hartmann, "Erlebnisse der Zeugen Jehovas in den Frauen-Konzentrationslagern," unpublished manuscript (1948).

360. Report by Charlotte Groß, cited in Elling, *Frauen,* 104.

361. Cited in Maur, *Lichtenburg,* 26.

362. Report by Maria Zeh, cited in Elling, *Frauen,* 171. In his study "Frauenkonzentrationslager," Drobisch makes the following statement: "The Communist prisoners provided the Bible Students also with bread when they were denied their food rations because of their refusal to listen to the Hitler speech. They did this even though, as experienced fighters, they considered this to be an 'unnecessary demonstration and futile sacrifice'" (112).

363. "Der Politische Polizeikommandeur der Länder," Mar. 23, 1936, letter to the concentration camps' inspector, SS-Gruppenführer [SS group leader] Theodor Eicke. In this letter he commanded the forming of these "special battalions," published in Rürup, *Topographie,* 98.

364. See Kogon, *SS-Staat,* 264; *Konzentrationslager Buchenwald, Post Weimar,* 34–35; Zahnwetzer, *Buchenwald,* 27–28. Only a small number of particularly skilled specialists whom the SS intended to use at other labor details were exempt from the general deployment of newly arriving concentration camp prisoners at punishment battalions.

365. According to the statements of the union official Otto Horn, the punishment battalion in Buchenwald was composed "primarily of 'blue spots' for an extended period of time" (DÖW, no. 1458, Otto Horn, report about the Buchenwald concentration camp).

366. Karl Siebeneichler, report of Apr. 24, 1945, Gbu, 31–826. A revised version of this report is also included in the so-called Buchenwald report. However, this version does not include the quoted passage (see Hackett, *Buchenwald-Report,* 214–15).

367. USHRI, RG-32.008.01, Franz Josef Seitz, "Meine Erlebnisse im Dritten Reich," 5–6.

368. See Gostner, *1000 Tage im KZ,* 40; Matthias Lex, "Eidesstattliche Versicherung, Der Prozeß gegen die Hauptkriegsverbrecher," vol. 31, 300, document 2928-PS; May 23, 1986, recollections by Alois Moser.

369. In several recollections, Hermann Baranowski is called "Foursquare." The prisoners gave him this designation because of his rude manners and husky build. According to Alfred Hübsch's report, he had chosen the Bible Students in

Dachau as his special "targets" (FGN, NHS 13-4-2-1, "Aufzeichnungen von Alfred Hübsch," 6; see also *Yearbook* 1974, 69).

370. See Graffard and Tristan, *Bibelforscher*, 69. The so-called *SK-Isolierung* [special command isolation blocks] was established after the construction of the barracks was completed on June 1, 1938. The Bible Students were assigned to barracks 35 and 36. In the following years, the SS also assigned other especially despised groups to these isolation blocks: the homosexuals, the "special division Wehrmacht," and, temporarily, the "Rasseschänder." (With regard to the conditions at the special command isolation blocks in Sachsenhausen and the cruel acts of atrocity committed there, see *KZ-Verbrechen vor deutschen Gerichten*, 295ff.; Lienau, *Zwölf Jahre Nacht*, 110ff.; Naujoks, *Sachsenhausen*, 109–10, 179ff.) The use of isolation blocks in Sachsenhausen was discontinued in the autumn of 1941. Not all Jehovah's Witnesses were kept in them until the camp was dissolved. A small number, approximately between forty and fifty, had already been transferred over the previous years, little by little, to the main camp. See DdW, AN 707, "Herbert Baron: Jahre des Grauens."

371. ETG [Ernst Thälmann Memorial], biography of the Bible Student Erich Mundt, n.d.

372. See *Yearbook* 1974, 165; recollections by Johannes Rauthe, "Geschichtsbericht," 56.

373. In the beginning, the text for the letters was prepared and usually read: "Dear . . . , Your letter has been received, thank you very much. I am safe and sound. Greetings." See Garbe, "'Gott mehr gehorchen als den Menschen,'" 172.

374. At the majority of concentration camps, stamps were used for this purpose. However, at Buchenwald, hectographic copies were used with the same wording. The Buchenwald commandant's headquarters sent such letters to relatives of Jehovah's Witnesses as late as Apr. 1945 (BA, NS 4 Bu/32). For Jehovah's Witnesses at Buchenwald, the restrictions of letter writing were not withdrawn. This could have been due to the fact that the majority of the Bible Student group there belonged to the "radical faction" of the IBSA (see this book, pt. 5, ch. 15, pp. 418–20).

375. *Jehovah's Witnesses in the Divine Purpose*, 168.

376. See Kogon, *SS-Staat*, 264; Zahnwetzer, *Buchenwald*, 28. See also DÖW, no. 1458, Otto Horn, report about the Buchenwald concentration camp; USHRI, RG-32.008.01, Franz Josef Seitz, "Meine Erlebnisse im Dritten Reich," 12; May 23, 1986, recollections by Alois Moser.

377. May 31, 1986, recollections by Richard Rudolph; Jan. 29, 1985, recollections by Alfred Knegendorf. In 1940 Trenkle was, for a certain period of time, in command of reporting in Neuengamme.

378. Apr. 15, 1971, recollections by Willi Lehmbecker.

379. Ibid. Other reports about such procedures and rituals at the time of admission are published in *Jehovah's Witnesses in the Divine Purpose*, 166–67.

380. Rolf Zehender, account about Gerhard Oltmanns.

381. Alexander Joseph, Nov. 24, 1958, statement at the Bonn Regional Court during proceedings against Schubert and Sorge (Sachsenhausen); *KZ-Verbrechen vor deutschen Gerichten*, 209.

382. Some SS officers supposedly even made bets about the outcome of such power struggles with Jehovah's Witnesses; see Langhoff, *Moorsoldaten*, 313.

383. May 31, 1986, and Sept. 9, 1986, recollections by Richard Rudolph.

384. W. Koch, *Leben im Widerstand*, 218.

385. Willy Henschel, Nov. 23, 1958, statement at the Bonn Regional Court during proceedings against Schubert and Sorge (Sachsenhausen); *KZ-Verbrechen vor deutschen Gerichten*, 197.

386. On the biography of Rachuba, see also John, *Wewelsburg* (1996), 141–43.

387. *KZ-Verbrechen vor deutschen Gerichten*, 391–92. According to some reports, during camp inspections, Himmler frequently requested that Bible Student prisoners be brought to him in order to ask them personally to renounce their faith. See *Yearbook* 1974, 174; Langbein, *Against All Hope*, 178; *Der Prozeß gegen die Hauptkriegsverbrecher*, 11:563; MGRa, RA, Bd.25, no. 332, Berta Hartmann, "Erlebnisse der Zeugen Jehovas in den Frauen-Konzentrationslagern," unpublished manuscript (1948), 3.

388. In his publication, Buder includes a copy of the punishment records, which had the following entries: "Aug. 13, 1935: Locking in a crooked position, because of not following orders; July 1, 1936: Ten days of severe detention and twenty-five strokes with a club for his refusal to work; Nov. 5, 1936: Ten days of detention and twenty-five strokes with a club for propagating Jehovah in the camp; Jan. 11, 1937: Twenty-one days of severe detention for repeated refusal to work; May 1, 1937: Eighteen days of severe detention for refusal to work and undisciplined behavior; May 3, 1937: Twenty-one days of severe detention and three months of service in the punishment battalion for inciting other prisoners and denouncing the government during a speech; Mar. 7, 1938: Thirty days of severe detention and twenty-five strokes with a club for laughing at the first concentration camp commander while he was giving a lecture; Apr. 6, 1938: Five days of severe detention and fifteen strokes with a club for refusal to sign the arrest order; Aug. 12, 1938: Eight days of severe detention and fifteen strokes with a club for remaining seated and not taking off the cap during the singing of the "Deutschlandlied"; Oct. 12, 1938: Twice for two hours hanging on a stake for laziness [the Nazi practice of tying a prisoner's hands on his back and hanging him on a pole, thus preventing his feet from touching the ground]. Oct. 18, 1938: Eight days of standing at the gate without supper; Sept. 13, 1940: Four hours of punitive drill for extensive discussions with other prisoners during working hours without working; Sept. 3, 1942: Died as a result of physical weakness" (KmW, KW D 87, Buder, "Wewelsburg," 91).

389. Ibid., 92.

390. Karl Block, Nov. 23, 1958, statements at the Bonn Regional Court during the proceedings against Schubert and Sorge (Sachsenhausen); *KZ-Verbrechen vor deutschen Gerichten,* 197.

391. Otto Gede, statements at the Soviet Military Tribunal held in Berlin-Pankow between Oct. 23 and Nov. 1, 1947; *Todeslager Sachsenhausen,* 43 (the spelling of the names of Rachuba and Bugdalle was corrected; with regard to the designation of the Bible Students as "sectarians" in these court records, see this book, p. 549, n.46). The same incident was also discussed during the proceedings against Schubert and Sorge held at the Bonn Regional Court between Oct. 13, 1958, and Feb. 6, 1959. See *KZ-Verbrechen vor deutschen Gerichten,* 196–97. Statements by witnesses as well as the investigations of the public prosecutor's office confirm the incident. At the Soviet Military Tribunal in 1947, Sorge had already admitted that he "had personally given orders to bury one of the sectarians" during forest clearing in the autumn of 1938 (see *Todeslager Sachsenhausen,* 43; Sorge further stated, "that is how we dealt with sectarians"). Now, however, he claimed that this order actually came from the concentration camp administration. In addition, when he came before the legal authorities of the Federal Republic of Germany, he denied determinedly that he "relieved himself on the head of the buried prisoner" (*KZ-Verbrechen vor deutschen Gerichten,* 392–93). The Bonn Regional Court declared Sorge guilty of murder in sixty-seven cases and sentenced him to lifelong imprisonment. Under recognition of the "particular seriousness of the crime," the court sentenced him to twelve years of imprisonment only for his "participation in the attempt to murder the Bible Student Rachuba."

392. KmW, KW D 87, Buder, "Wewelsburg," 94.

393. See Naujoks, *Sachsenhausen,* 166; Pingel, *Häftlinge,* 260n81.

394. Sept. 9, 1986, recollections by Richard Rudolph.

395. To support the concentration camp organization, the SS arranged for the prisoners' self-administration. This self-administration was organized according to traditional prison and military structures. The SS assigned camp leaders, block leaders, and room seniors, who were held responsible for an orderly routine of life in the concentration camp. For the labor details, supervisors and foremen were assigned to support the supervision of the guards. These so-called functionary prisoners received a special status within the camp. In this way, the SS tried to sow seeds of dissention, envy, and resentment among the concentration camp prisoners. In return, the SS anticipated willing cooperation from these functionary prisoners who had a considerable measure of influence. Depending on their individual personalities, they were able to use this influence to the advantage or disadvantage of other prisoners.

396. See *Yearbook* 1974, 164–65; May 31, 1986, recollections by Richard Rudolph; May 23, 1986, recollections by Alois Moser; VVN, Komiteeakten H 34, Emil Horn, report of Aug. 28, 1949.

397. According to reports from Jehovah's Witnesses, mostly some of the

political functionary prisoners in the isolation blocks at Sachsenhausen tried to improve their status with the SS officers by actively opposing the Bible Student activities. In this way, they tried to direct the attention of the SS away from themselves to the Bible Students. The reports of Jehovah's Witnesses sometimes reflect certain resentment toward these functionary prisoners, but this is not always the case. Some reports also recognize the solidarity extended toward people from other prisoner groups. One of these functionary prisoners was the Communist Albin Lüdke who was imprisoned at the Esterwegen concentration camp from 1933 on. Later, he was imprisoned as a political second offender in Sachsenhausen and Neuengamme. In his recollections, Paul Buder makes the following statements about him: "One evening, ten o'clock. Everybody out of bed! Strip naked! Out in the snow! The snow turned red from the blood of those who were beaten!—Even Albin Lüdke participated in the beatings! What is wrong with him, I thought! They were searching for the Bible! But they could not find it! Lüdke had it in his pocket! 'Well, Paul, I had to beat, at least a little. Otherwise, they would have suspected something'" (KmW, KW D 87, Buder, "Wewelsburg," 97). A similar act of support at Sachsenhausen resulted in Lüdke losing his position as block leader. However, Jehovah's Witnesses always appreciated his spirit of solidarity. In 1949 one of them, Alfons Kupka, sent a letter of appreciation to "my dear fellow Albin," for the solidarity he showed toward the Bible Students, especially for the acts of loyalty in Sachsenhausen "where you often took the blame upon yourself in order to protect us" (VVN HH, Komiteeakten K 41, Alfons Kupka, letter of Nov. 30, 1949).

398. *Jehovah's Witnesses in the Divine Purpose,* 167; see also Geschonneck, *Meine unruhigen Jahre,* 90; *Sachsenhausen, Dokumente,* 51.

399. See Wolff, *Sachsenhausen,* 17.

400. BHStA, OMGUS, Dachau trial of war criminals, Microfilm 1a/1, no. 182f, Paul Wauer, statement of May 21, 1945.

401. Apr. 15, 1971, recollections by Willi Lehmbecker.

402. See Kater, "Bibelforscher," 210. Numerous acts of cruelty were performed in the context of ridiculing the act of baptism. In Sachsenhausen, Johann Wrobel had been deployed as foreman for the prisoners at the labor detail Garagenbau (construction of storage places for vehicles and trucks of the SS). He reports that, at one time, SS-Oberscharführer [staff sergeant] Wilhelm Schubert requested Jehovah's Witnesses to baptize an old Jewish prisoner whom he held over a barrel of water. In view of the difficult situation, the Bible Students agreed to comply with this request, even though it was supposed to ridicule their faith. However, they would not participate in mistreating a fellow prisoner: "In a symbolic act, we splashed water on his forehead. Schubert was furious about our resistance and submerged him in the water. When he let go, the Jewish prisoner collapsed. Schubert had strangled and drowned him" (Johann Wrobel, statement of Nov. 23, 1958, "KZ-Verbrechen vor deutschen Gerichten," 196; see also the statement Wrobel made about this incident on Feb. 1,

1965, during the Düsseldorf Treblinka proceedings, cited in Langbein, *Against All Hope,* 181).

403. BHStA, OMGUS, Dachau trial of war criminals, Microfilm 1a/1, no. 182, Paul Wauer, statement of May 21, 1945; see also *Todeslager Sachsenhausen,* 43.

404. See this book, p. 657, n.19.

405. BA, R 58/243, Bl. 278–80 (278), the chief of the Security Police, decree of Sept. 3, 1939. On Sept. 9, 1939, to "rule out all misunderstandings," Heydrich explained that a distinction had to be made between cases "that could be handled in the usual way and cases that warrant special treatment," using, for the first time, this euphemistic *terminus technicus.* "Special treatment would be appropriate in cases that, because of their reprehensibility, dangerousness, or propagandistic effect, required ruthless elimination (that is, execution), without regard for the person" (BA, R 58/243, Bl. 213–14, the chief of the Security Police, telex of Sept. 20, 1939).

406. Prior to Dickmann's execution, several executions ordered by the RFSS had already taken place at Sachsenhausen. However, they were not carried out publicly.

407. Naujoks, *Sachsenhausen,* 142.

408. On admission of people into a concentration camp even after they signed the statement, see this book, pt. 4, ch. 12, pp. 296–97.

409. The political offices at the various concentration camps were offices occupied by the Gestapo. These offices handled all issues related to admission and release of the prisoners in protective detention and also kept the prisoner records.

410. Naujoks, *Sachsenhausen,* 142. In Aug. 1938 Baranowski, the former Dachau concentration camp commander, had requested the transfer of Rudolf Höß from Dachau to Sachsenhausen. Various sources confirm that Höß was directly involved in the execution of Dickmann. During his pretrial detention in Krakow after the war, Höß wrote his memoirs in which he also extensively describes executions of Jehovah's Witnesses at Sachsenhausen (see Höß, *Kommandant in Auschwitz,* 95–99). According to these memoirs, at the concentration camp two "especially fanatical Bible Students" refused to submit to the examination before enlistment. As a result, the commandant's headquarters obtained permission for their execution from the RFSS. According to Höß's exaggerated report, these two Jehovah's Witnesses "went almost mad for joy and ecstasy, and could hardly wait for the day of execution. They wrung their hands, gazed enraptured up at the sky, and constantly cried: 'Soon we will be with Jehovah. How happy we are to have been chosen.'" Höß continues: "A few days earlier, they had witnessed an execution of some of their fellow believers, and they could hardly be kept under control, so great was their desire to be shot with them. . . . Transformed by ecstasy, they stood in front of the wooden wall of the rifle range, seemingly no longer of this world. . . . All who saw them die were deeply moved, and even the execution squad itself was affected" (ibid., 95–96).

411. Arthur Schinnagel, report published in *Niemand und nichts vergessen,* 142; see also Naujoks, *Sachsenhausen,* 143. Wolfgang Szepansly asserts: "The SS leaders wanted to set a precedent and hoped their victims would surrender. However, they remained steadfast in their faith and died as martyrs. This was a defeat for the SS and was generally also considered as such" (Szepansky, *Weg,* 173).

412. Report by Gustav Auschner, cited in *Awake!,* Apr. 8, 1989, 14.

413. The command to execute August Dickmann was one of the last official actions of this concentration camp commander. From Sept. 1939 on, because of serious illness, fifty-five-year-old Hermann Baranowski was no longer able to carry out his official responsibilities. At the beginning of 1940, he died. Since Jehovah's Witnesses had long been annoyed by the commanding officer "Foursquare" Baranowski, the rumor circulated throughout the camp and among the SS officers (most of whom were quite superstitious) that "the Bible Students prayed Baranowski to death." According to Paul Buder, the Sachsenhausen Bible Student group included in their prayers the request: "If you are alive, Jehovah God, teach him a lesson" (see *Yearbook* 1974, 169; KmW, KW D 87, Buder, "Wewelsburg," 12; Sept. 9, 1986, recollections by Richard Rudolph). Rudolph, who was himself a Jehovah's Witness, considers this and similar incidents described in the literature to be evidence of the fact that sometimes the strangest "figments of imagination" circulated in the concentration camps.

414. See *Watchtower,* Aug. 1, 1991, 28 (report by Ernst Wauer).

415. Cited in Graffard and Tristan, *Bibelforscher,* 85.

416. According to a report by Gustav Auschner, about 16 to 18 of the approximately 450 Bible Students imprisoned at Sachsenhausen during that period signed the statement. The SS presented the statements separately to each prisoner hoping, in this way, to be able to isolate them from the group (FGN, NHS 13-7-0-1, Auschner, report of July 8, 1969). Harry Naujoks, the first camp leader, mentions in his recollections that after the execution of August Dickmann, ninety Jehovah's Witnesses willingly signed the statement. Naujoks adds: "Many of them later withdrew their signature" (Naujoks, *Sachsenhausen,* 143).

417. Also in other concentration camps, Himmler subsequently ordered no further public executions of Jehovah's Witnesses on the charge of conscientious objection and for the purpose of deterrence. It can therefore be concluded that this course of ordering executions if Bible Student prisoners refused to perform military service was discontinued after the execution of August Dickmann. Most likely this was the case; otherwise the SS would have had to execute almost all Jehovah's Witnesses in the concentration camps.

418. Different statements are available about the number of Jehovah's Witnesses executed at Sachsenhausen. Some of these statements could possibly refer to one and the same case: several reports mention that, at the end of 1939, two Jehovah's Witnesses were executed in addition to August Dickmann (see Szepansky, *Weg,* 173; Apr. 15, 1986, recollections by Harry Dubinsky.) The Bible Students Weiß and Zibold were probably executed at the beginning of 1940

(see Sept. 9, 1986, recollections by Richard Rudolph). During the proceedings against Schubert at the Bonn Regional Court, it was stated that four Jehovah's Witnesses were executed in the industrial area of the camp in 1939/40 (see *KZ-Verbrechen vor deutschen Gerichten*, 198). According to Höß, during his period as commanding officer at Sachsenhausen, "a great number" of executions took place (Höß, *Kommandant in Auschwitz*, 95). In his study (*Erinnerungen*, 154), Grüber reports on another execution that took place in 1941. It was the execution of a Jehovah's Witness who had withdrawn his signature from the "statement." At the end of 1943 seventeen-year-old Jonathan Stark was hanged (see Leber, *Lebensbilder*, 20). Dickmann's execution (which was carried out in front of all other prisoners), the threat of mass executions, the steadfast resistance of Jehovah's Witnesses, their separation from the prisoners of the major camp by being placed in an isolated area, as well as subsequent executions laid the foundation for exaggerated misrepresentations. For instance, Martin Niemöller, who was detained in solitary confinement in the punishment block at Sachsenhausen, reports that, "for a certain period of time, at every morning roll call, the SS picked out one Jehovah's Witness." They asked him "whether he would agree to military service. If he answered, 'No,' he was hanged in front of everybody. Without exception, they all answered, 'No'" (see Hutten, *Seher, Grübler, Enthusiasten*, 119; see also Bredemeier, *Kriegsdienstverweigerung*, 85). Also, Kogon's statement in this regard has to be considered as incorrect. According to his statement, at the beginning of the war, at Sachsenhausen, "each refusal was followed by the shooting of ten men from their ranks. After forty victims had been killed, the SS desisted" (see Kogon, *Theory and Practice of Hell*, 42). Kogon wrote his study during a very short period of time in 1945. Since he was a prisoner at Buchenwald, he relied on the reports of other people for information from other concentration camps. In the literature, Kogon's statement has often been used as basis for other studies about the resistance of Jehovah's Witnesses (see, for instance, Langbein, *Against All Hope*, 178). With reference to Kogon and to parallel reports "from the entire spectrum of concentration camp literature," which are not specifically mentioned by name, Zipfel even speaks of "actual mass executions" of Jehovah's Witnesses that took place at Sachsenhausen during the beginning of the war (see Zipfel, *Kirchenkampf*, 195).

419. Cited in the Sept. 28, 1939, file remarks by RJM Gürtner, Broszat, "Strafjustiz," 408.

420. For the following explanations, see Broszat, "Strafjustiz," 390ff.; Gruchmann, *Justiz*, 675–80.

421. Sept. 28, 1939, recordings by RJM Gürtner, cited in Broszat, "Strafjustiz," 408.

422. Cited in Gruchmann, *Justiz*, 678.

423. Sept. 28, 1939, recordings by RJM Gürtner, cited in Broszat, "Strafjustiz," 408–9.

424. Oct. 14, 1939, file remarks by Gürtner that included Hitler's statement

as transmitted by Lammers, cited in Broszat, "Strafjustiz," 411. Gruchmann (*Justiz*, 679) assumes that possibly Hitler "accepted" responsibility for the three executions only subsequently.

425. See this book, pt. 5, ch. 14, pp. 353–56.

426. See Zahnwetter, *Buchenwald*, 28.

427. See Kogon, *Theory and Practice of Hell*, 42.

428. Regarding Buchenwald, the following dates have been recorded: Jan. 6, 1938, Easter Sunday 1939, Pentecost 1939, Sept. 6, 1939; see Freund, *Buchenwald*, 128–29; Grünewald, *Geschichte der Kriegsdienstverweigerung*, 30–33; Menzinger, "Jugend," 119; DÖW, no. 1458, Otto Horn, report about the Buchenwald concentration camp.

429. It is not possible to provide the exact number of Jehovah's Witnesses who signed the statement during their imprisonment at the concentration camps. But it can certainly be assumed that the number of those who signed the statement during concentration camp imprisonment is considerably smaller than the number of those who signed the statement during Gestapo detention or after they served their sentences. (See this book, pt. 4, ch. 12, pp. 287–89.) According to the few available reports, only 2 of the 140 to 150 prisoners at Neuengamme signed the statement (see Suchowiak, *Mai 1945*, 14; Nov. 24, 1987, recollections by Karl Hanl). At Mauthausen, which had a total of 200 Bible Student prisoners, one was released in 1939, three in 1940, and two in 1942, apparently after signing the statement (see Maršálek, *Mauthausen*, 273; Mauthausen Memorial, June 18, 1986, letter to the author). Larger numbers were recorded for the concentration camps in Buchenwald (30 signed statements; Kautsky, *Teufel und Verdammte*, 139), Sachsenhausen (up to 90, many of which were later withdrawn; Naujoks, *Sachsenhausen*, 143), and Ravensbrück. The letters secretly written in 1943 mention the number of 50 who made "compromises with the devil" (Gerhard Kaiser, "Briefe. Nachrichten für die Zeugen Jehovas und ihre Gefährten," 5; see also Buber-Neumann, *Under Two Dictators*, 227). The unspecified numbers of the Watch Tower Society ("a large number of the brothers"; *Yearbook* 1974, 178) indicates that even though the total number of signed statements is comparatively small, it is still higher than the numbers mentioned at times in the literature and in reports by fellow prisoners of other groups (see, for instance, Maislinger, "Die Zeugen Jehovas," 370; Wiechert, "Totenwald," 150).

430. Report by H. Mattischek, cited in Hartmann, "Kriegsdienstverweigerung" (1982), 92–95 (94). Even fellow prisoners who were favorably disposed to Jehovah's Witnesses tried to persuade them to sign the statements for their own benefit (see Buber-Neumann, *Under Two Dictators*, 226–28ff.; Buber-Neumann, *Milena*, 172–73). In the opinion of these fellow prisoners, the Bible Students should make use of the possibility offered by the SS to ease their difficult situation in the camp. These fellow prisoners considered this action only as a matter of formality and, therefore, advised the Bible Students to use tactics. Block

leader Albin Lüdke made the suggestion that they should not take the signature so seriously. It was enough if the SS took it seriously. If they would not attach any further importance to the signature, it would not hinder them from maintaining their convictions. Even though such a choice failed to recognize the importance Jehovah's Witnesses attach to the "question of loyalty," as well as the fact that they consider such an argumentation as a temptation coming from "Satan," Lüdke was one of the political functionary prisoners whom they highly appreciated (see this book, pp. 701–2, n.397).

431. Such occasions could also have been letters from relatives. See, for instance, the extensive report of Albert van de Poel regarding the interrogation of Jehovah's Witness Ernst Raddatz (see Poel, *Neuengamme*, 105–9). According to this report, in 1942 Raddatz was called to the commanding officer where he was shown a letter from his wife. In this letter, his wife asked him to sign the statement since she was no longer able to carry the responsibility for the farm alone and did not know what to do. The description of the following dialogue between the commanding officer and Raddatz clearly indicates the paradoxical situation: the commanding officer is shocked about the hard-heartedness of this Jehovah's Witness, not comprehending, even remotely, that Raddatz is not able to see for himself any alternative to his actions without disowning his faith.

432. See Garbe, "'Gott mehr gehorchen als den Menschen,'" 206.

433. Recollections by Thieme, n.d.

434. Such periods of surveillance often lasted "more than a year"; see *Yearbook* 1974, 177.

435. Höß, *Kommandant in Auschwitz*, 96 (English edition differs).

436. Kautsky, *Teufel und Verdammte*, 139.

437. See Grüber, *Erinnerungen*, 154; *Yearbook* 1974, 170–71, 178; Naujoks, *Sachsenhausen*, 143.

438. Höß, *Kommandant in Auschwitz*, 96.

439. On the refusal of Bible Student prisoners to work in armament production, see also Langbein, *Against All Hope*, 180; Pechel, *Widerstand*, 107; *Watchtower*, Aug. 15, 1980, 6; DhN, Ng. 2.8, report by Jan van Bork.

440. Statement written by Jehovah's Witnesses after their liberation from the Buchenwald concentration camp, cited in Grünewald, *Geschichte der Kriegsdienstverweigerung*, 30–33 (32).

441. R. Weißenborn, report about life in a concentration camp, GBu, 32/IX-70.

442. See *Yearbook* 1974, 195.

443. The following explanations about Jehovah's Witnesses at Buchenwald are based on *Yearbook* 1974, 174–75; Nov. 23, 1987, recollections by Bruno Knöller; May 23, 1986, recollections by Alois Moser; recollections by Johannes Rauthe, "Geschichtsbericht," 56–65.

444. Freund, *Buchenwald*, 128. The Austrian Socialist Julius Freund provides a detailed report about a dispute between a representative of the Bible Students

and an SS officer at a special roll call on Easter 1939. Even though Freund does not mention Töllner by name, according to other reports, the representative was indeed Töllner (see "Bericht Wanner," cited in Menzinger, "Jugend," 119). According to Freund, the "representative of the Bible Students had arranged a program . . . as if he was in freedom. He openly explained his opinions to the SS officer and thus to all the Nazis, without making any concession in his viewpoint. I had never before heard anything like that. I would have never imagined that a prisoner at a concentration camp would speak up so courageously, despite the dangers and punishments" (Freund, *Buchenwald*, 128).

445. *Yearbook* 1974, 174.

446. Report by Wilhelm Bathen, published in *Yearbook* 1974, 175.

447. See *Die Frauen von Ravensbrück*, 147; May 19, 1986, recollections by Günther Pape; Sept. 21, 1986, and Oct. 3, 1986, recollections by Charlotte Tetzner.

448. DÖW, Maria Herfort, report about the situation of the Bible Students in Ravensbrück.

449. See *Die Frauen von Ravensbrück*, 147; Höß, *Kommandant in Auschwitz*, 97; Langbein, *Against All Hope*, 180.

450. Herbermann, *Abgrund*, 125.

451. *Die Frauen von Ravensbrück*, 146–47.

452. *Angora-Zucht* were breeding plants for Angora rabbits that existed at the concentration camps in Buchenwald, Dachau, Ravensbrück, Neuengamme, and several other concentration camps. In 1943 a total of 25,000 rabbits was kept at those plants (see "Konzentrationslager: Hasen im Buch," cited in *Der Spiegel*, Jan. 22, 1968, 36). This action of refusal took place at the end of 1941. For Oct. 22, 1941, the deployment list for the labor detail *Angora-Zucht* still mentions twenty Bible Student prisoners (see Füllberg-Stolberg, "Gertrud Pötzinger," 328). However, the Jan. 4, 1942, deployment list no longer includes any Bible Student prisoners (see C. Müller, *Klempnerkolonne*, documents chapter following 112).

453. See Buber-Neumann, *Under Two Dictators*, 248. Buber-Neumann reports that in the autumn of 1942, "all 'extremist' Bible Students" were transported to the Auschwitz concentration camp. However, "a little later . . . I recognized about a dozen of the 'extremist' Bible Students who had been sent to Auschwitz and had now returned. . . . The next day all the extremist Bible Students were taken away in a prison wagon and the day after that all their things came back, complete with triangle and number." Consequently, Margarete Buber-Neumann assumes that the SS had "put them to death because of their 'laziness'" (ibid., 299).

454. May 23, 1986, recollections by Alois Moser.

455. See *Watchtower*, Oct. 1, 1978, 23; a similar case is described in Höß, *Kommandant in Auschwitz*, 97.

456. Szepansky, *Weg*, 176.

457. See Kogon, *Theory and Practice of Hell*, 121–22; Grünewald, *Geschichte der Kriegsdienstverweigerung*, 30–33; DÖW, no. 1458, Otto Horn, "Keeping Integrity in Nazi Germany," *Awake!*, June 22, 1985, 10–13.

458. Report of Viktor Bruch, *Yearbook* 1976, 39.

459. Ibid.

460. In his recollections, Rudolf Höß, the former commanding officer of the Auschwitz concentration camp, reports that the Bible Students would appear for roll call "only in a chaotic crowd" (*Kommandant in Auschwitz*, 97).

461. Buber-Neumann, *Under Two Dictators*, 248. See also the (slightly different) description of C. Müller, *Klempnerkolonne*, 271–72; Langbein, *Against All Hope*, 180 (report by Hermine Jursa).

462. Buber-Neumann divides the Bible Student group at Ravensbrück into three "factions": the extremists, the wavering middle, and the moderates. These factions fought each other fiercely, every bit as fiercely as political factions struggling for control do. They "accused each other of treachery and abused their rivals with rude names culled from the Bible" (Buber-Neumann, *Under Two Dictators*, 236).

463. Nov. 23, 1987, recollections by Bruno Knöller.

464. See Buber-Neumann, *Under Two Dictators*, 236; Kater, "Bibelforscher," 215; Lev. 17:12; see also Gen. 9:3–4: "Every living thing that moves will be yours to eat . . . you must not eat flesh with life, that is to say blood, in it," and Acts 15: 29: "You are to abstain . . . from blood."

465. Buber-Neumann, *Under Two Dictators*, 236.

466. Interview with Herta Brünen-Niederhellmann, cited in Elling, *Frauen*, 79. Sybil Milton considers this action to be evidence of the fact that strong religious convictions, which generally increased the possibilities for self-assertion in the concentration camps (faith that provides inner strength), could also have a negative effect on the chances for survival (Milton, "Deutsche und deutsch-jüdische Frauen," 15).

467. See *Arbeit und Vernichtung*, 113, 116; DhN, Ng. 5.6.1; FGN, NHS 13-7-4-1.

468. Sept. 9, 1986, recollections by Richard Rudolph.

469. W. Koch, *Leben im Widerstand*, 219. On disputes among Jehovah's Witnesses in the concentration camps that were based on dogmatic reasoning, see also Doyon, *Hirten*, 232–33; *Yearbook* 1974, 174–75; Nov. 23, 1987, recollections by Bruno Knöller.

470. See, for instance, Buber-Neumann, *Under Two Dictators*, 220–38; Gostner, *1000 Tage im KZ*, 46; Herbermann, *Abgrund*, 126; Kautzky, *Teufel und Verdammte*, 139, 178; Meier, *Neuengamme*, 31–32.

471. Zahnwetzer, *Buchenwald*, 29.

472. Buber-Neumann, *Under Two Dictators*, 224.

473. See *Awake!*, June 22, 1985, 12; Sept. 9, 1986, recollections by Richard Rudolph.

474. The following descriptions are mainly based on the Nov. 24, 1987, recollections by Karl Hanl; May 23, 1986, recollections by Alois Moser; and May 31, 1986, recollections by Richard Rudolph.

475. Oct. 29, 1942, decree by Himmler, BA, NS 3–425. As early as the autumn of 1941, the prisoners were allowed to receive packages with clothing.

476. Sept. 9, 1986, recollections by Richard Rudolph; see also Meier, *Neuengamme*, 31–32.

477. Kerstin John provides a description about the meticulous rules followed in the Bible Student blocks at the Niederhagen concentration camp: "Before going to bed, they took off their prisoners' clothing, folded it neatly, and laid it on their clean shoes in the day-room. Then, they entered the dormitory only in their underwear" (John, *Wewelsburg*, 137).

478. See Buber-Neumann, *Under Two Dictators*, 224.

479. Ibid., 250ff.; Füllberg-Stolberg, "Gertrud Pötzinger," 330; Pingel, *Häftlinge*, 91.

480. See Maršálek, *Mauthausen*, 274; Pingel, *Häftlinge*, 91. Jehovah's Witnesses did not show any interest in participating in the self-administration of the prisoners. But their relationship with the prisoner groups that organized the camp resistance was not without conflicts. Often, this resulted from the difficulties of everyday life in the camp. On the one hand, the Bible Student groups certainly tried to pursue their own interests, which could easily cause problems with other groups of prisoners. In Buchenwald, a serious dispute arose over the right to move into a new brick building, a right asserted by the prisoners used for the prisoners' (self-) administration who belonged to the nucleus of the prisoners. Jehovah's Witnesses who had also been imprisoned for many years at the Buchenwald concentration camp claimed the same right. On the other hand, the strained relationship between the two groups of prisoners also resulted from the behavior of particular functionary prisoners from the group of political prisoners, who considered it their duty to take actions against the illegal Bible Student activities.

481. This is a characteristic that, at times, gave reason to question generally the integrity of the Bible Student prisoners, even though this cannot be applied to all Bible Student prisoners. (Fellow prisoners report that the camp was, at times, surprised at the "unkind and stubborn way in which the Bible Students remained silent or lied" [Meier, *Neuengamme*, 31–32].) In this regard, Hanns Lilje, later bishop of Hanover, states that the Bible Students were frequently used for special privileges because of the fact that their love of truth would even disregard friendships. Therefore, it was often easy for the Gestapo "to supervise other prisoners with their assistance" (Lilje, *Im finstern Tal*, 58–59). With reference to this source, Kater ("Bibelforscher," 215) even reports of "Jehovah's Witnesses" who supposedly "acted as informers." Pingel also circulates the assumption that the SS "deployed the Bible Students even to spy on other prisoners." However, I have not been able to find any further evidence confirming that

Jehovah's Witnesses were actually used as informers for the purpose of undermining the camp resistance. Since Jehovah's Witnesses did not get involved with the camp resistance and also refrained from participating in the struggle involving the prisoners' self-administration, it can almost certainly be assumed that the number of those willing to act as police informers for the political office was considerably smaller than that of other prisoner groups.

482. See Winzierl, *Österreichische Frauen*, 182.

483. See this book, pt. 5, ch. 16, pp. 464–65.

484. Kupfer-Koberwitz, *Mächtigen*, 286.

485. See Buber-Neumann, *Under Two Dictators*, 237–38; Meier, *Neuengamme*, 31–32; Kautsky, *Teufel und Verdammte*, 138; Wiechert, "Totenwald," 148–49; Zahnwetzer, *Buchenwald*, 27.

486. In addition to Ernst Schneider's diary entry, this incident has also been confirmed by a number of other reports. See Schön, *Ostsee '45*, 531–33; VVN HH, Komiteeakten H 34; recollections by Alfred Knegendorf (Jan, 29, 1985) and Karl Hanl (Nov. 24, 1987). These two Jehovah's Witnesses had also been able to save themselves by hanging onto the capsized wreck of the ship.

487. Personal documents of Günther Schwarberg, diary of Ernst Schneider (Apr. 20–May 20, 1945). After about five hours, a lifeboat took the prisoners on board. The report does not indicate to what extent the discussions with the two Russians who, according to Ernst Schneider, spoke some German, were successful.

488. Only a few reports include statements regarding the number of conversions. A resolution from May 1945 indicates that 36 "men of good will" were also among the 230 Bible Students who formed one of the marching columns during the evacuation of the Sachsenhausen concentration camp (see this book, pt. 5, ch. 16, pp. 454–58.) With regard to the Ravensbrück concentration camp, 70 conversions are reported (Weinzierl, "Österreichische Frauen," 182; Lichtenegger, "Wiens Bibelforscherinnen," 221, 278). According to other reports, 300 young female Russians joined the ranks of Jehovah's Witnesses (Gebhard, *Zeugen Jehovas*, 209; *Jehovah's Witnesses in the Divine Purpose*, 168–69). "Several baptisms" took place at the Mauthausen concentration camp. Reports for the neighboring Gusen concentration camp indicated that "five Poles" were baptized (*Yearbook* 1989, 132–33).

489. See Max Liebster, "Deliverance! Proving Ourselves Grateful," *Watchtower*, Oct. 1, 1978, 20–24; *Yearbook* 1974, 174; Nov. 1, 1987, recollections by Marco Max Feingold.

490. Based on July 5, 1986, Aug. 18, 1986, Sept. 21, 1986, Oct. 3, 1986, recollections by Charlotte Tetzner. Her memoirs are also included in an anthology about female prisoners at Auschwitz, published in the United States in 1992. See Charlotte Tetzner, "Temporary Stabsgebaeudlerin," in Shelley, *Auschwitz*, 247–56.

491. On a list of Dachau prisoners, July 7, 1941, is mentioned as the date of

death of Charlotte Tetzner's father. According to this list, her father, Anton Decker, died only one month after his registered arrival at the concentration camp, on June 6, 1941 (Feb. 2, 1987, letter of the Dachau Concentration Camp Memorial to the author). Details about the cause for the death of Anton Decker cannot be determined.

492. I do not have any information about which prisoners other than those who were Bible Students at the time of their admission or were baptized as Jehovah's Witnesses in the camp were requested to sign the statement. We can assume that this was done on the initiative of this particular SS concentration camp administration and not upon specific instructions from the Gestapo or the RSHA.

493. See Czech, *Auschwitz-Birkenau*, 54.

494. Several other reports also include descriptions of such occurrences. See Buber-Neumann, *Under Two Dictators*, 238; May 23, 1986, recollections by Alois Moser; May 31, 1986, and Sept. 9, 1986, recollections by Richard Rudolph. Rudolph remembers a political prisoner who worked with Jehovah's Witnesses in the *Entkrautungskommando* (drainage ditch detail). He discontinued wearing his red patch and made for himself a purple triangle. Because of this exchange, the SS punished him with twenty-five strokes with a club.

495. During the following years, Charlotte Tetzner was used as an office worker for the concentration camp commander Maria Mandel, where she was exposed to the horrors of this extermination camp. She also worked as a shorthand typist at the SS military hospital. During the evacuation of the camps, she encountered four more locations of persecution: Groß-Rosen, Mauthausen, Bergen-Belsen, and Mittelbau-Dora. During her activity at the Auschwitz SS military hospital, Tetzner became acquainted with Hermann Langbein, who worked at the office of Dr. Eduard Wirth, the medical doctor of the camp. At that time, Langbein was one of the highest leaders of the concentration camp resistance (Kampfgruppe Auschwitz). In his Jan. 22, 1985, letter to the author, Langbein acknowledges the "exemplary conduct" of Charlotte Tetzner.

496. See John, *Wewelsburg* (1996), 140; Kater, "Bibelforscher," 216; Zürcher, *Kreuzzug*, 105.

497. See Durand, *Buchenwald*, 57.

498. See *Yearbook* 1989, 132; KmW, KW D 87, Buder, "Wewelsburg," 96.

499. This description is based on reports from Richard Rudolph (Feb. 18, 1986, Sept. 9, 1986, and Aug. 5, 1987), which were confirmed through a comparison with documents from the DhN; with regard to Ahrend, see Glienke, "Curio-Haus-Prozeß," 2:455.

500. It cannot be determined whether such an order for execution had been issued or whether it was "only" a repetition of the threat that Strippel, the commanding officer of this camp, had made months earlier.

501. Richard Rudolph, "Bericht über besondere Erfahrungen aus der Nazizeit," Heidelberg, n.d. (copy in the possession of the author). Rudolph

maintained sporadic contact with Ahrend, who was later released from imprisonment at the British internment camp in Neumünster.

502. See this book, pt. 5, ch. 15, pp. 439–47.

503. At times, up to fifteen Jehovah's Witnesses worked at the "sculpture's workshop" in Buchenwald (see this book, pp. 719–20, n.564). There, they felt relatively secure, since they were among fellow believers and did not have to fear any betrayal from other prisoners. Even SS officers were allowed to visit the sculpture's workshop, a special hobby of commanding officer Karl Koch, but only with Koch's permission. Jehovah's Witnesses used this situation to print considerable amounts of Bible Student publications, for instance, copies of the book *Justification*, which was smuggled out of the camp, and handwritten copies of the *Daily Text*. They were also able to obtain a Bible during this period. See recollections by Johannes Rauthe, "Geschichtsbericht," 56–65.

504. See John, *Wewelsburg* (1996), 128–29; see also this book, pt. 5, ch. 13, pp. 335–36.

505. The following descriptions are based on May 23, 1986, recollections by Alois Moser; Sept. 10, 1986, recollections by Richard Rudolph; *Awake!*, June 22, 1985, 10–13; VVN HH, Komiteeakten M 25 and T1. Regarding the central role Jehovah's witnesses played at the Hartzwalde estate with regard to smuggling literature, see this book, p. 724, n.591.

506. On the IBSA groups around Engelhard, Riet, and Fritsche, see this book, pt. 5, ch. 13, pp. 334–40.

507. Besides Erich Frost, two other former leaders of the IBSA branch in Germany, Paul Balzereit and Fritz Winkler, were imprisoned at Sachsenhausen. The SS used the disagreements and conflicts attached to these leaders regarding the IBSA course to trigger divisions in the Bible Student group. For example, the SS used the former leader of the Watch Tower Society's branch office in Germany, Paul Balzereit, who had been imprisoned in 1937, to present him to the Bible Students as an example worth following because he had abandoned his faith. Even though Balzereit had signed the statement, he was not released from Sachsenhausen until more than one year later. The Bible Student group generally avoided him. Erich Frost, however, who had been transferred to Sachsenhausen at the beginning of 1941 after having served a prison sentence of three and a half years, maintained his position of authority in the camp. He was one of the spokesmen of the group of Bible Student prisoners. Once, as a result of Bible discourses he gave at the Bible Student barracks, he was sent to the punishment battalion and given twenty-five strokes with a club on the infamous "rack." Eventually, however, Frost's situation, as well as that of his fellow believers, improved considerably. The SS used the former music director from Leipzig to provide the musical background for their "sociable evenings." Statements according to *Yearbook* 1974, 150, 198; *Der Wachtturm*, Apr. 15, 1956, 247; FGN, NHS 13-7-0-4, Erich Frost, letter of July 15, 1969; Feb. 7, 1987, recollections by Willi Lehmbecker; June 24, 1984, recollections by Alfred Skoda.

508. After their liberation in 1945, the Buchenwald Bible Student group laid claim to the leadership of the German IBSA branch office. In the end they finally came to a friendly agreement. The divisions were resolved and both parties continued to work shoulder to shoulder in the preaching activity, although, according to one person, "some of the wounds remained."

509. G. Kaiser, "Briefe. Nachrichten für die Zeugen Jehovas und ihre Gefährten" (italics in the original).

510. BA, NS 3/426, WVHA, interoffice decree of Sept. 10, 1943, regarding "subversive propaganda from the Bible Students at the concentration camps and at their places of work." At approximately the same time that Pohl issued this decree reprimanding the concentration camp administrations for neglecting their responsibilities, similar occurrences took place right in front of his eyes, as it were. Oswald Pohl had received the fiefdom Comthurey estate (near Fürstenberg/Mecklenburg and not far from the Ravensbrück concentration camp). During the war, his family lived on the estate. There, the daily contact with Jehovah's Witnesses, who were highly regarded as workers, resulted in the same "carelessness." To this end, Ilse Unterdörfer, who occupied a position as a supervisory prisoner, reports: "Some of us [Bible Students] even slept there and did not have to go to the camp [Ravensbrück] at all anymore. It was thus possible for me, according to arrangements made in a letter delivered by a sister, to get in touch with Franz Fritsche from Berlin, whom I met one evening in a wooded section of the farm. He always supplied me with a number of *Watchtowers*" (report by Ilse Unterdörfer, *Yearbook* 1974, 199).

511. At Ravensbrück, the communal housing of the Bible Students had already been temporarily discontinued in 1942. See Buber-Neumann, *Under Two Dictators*, 236–37, 268. During 1939/40, at Dachau, the experiment was made to put individual Bible Students into the barracks with other prisoner groups. See, in this regard, this book, pt. 5, ch. 15, pp. 437–38.

512. *Jehovah's Witnesses in the Divine Purpose*, 171.

513. In mid-1942, at Ravensbrück, the SS put 100 prisoners whom they considered to be asocial into the block of the Bible Students. This action, by means of which the SS tried to spy on the Bible Students, produced similar results. These asocial prisoners had been instructed to report any cases in which they observed Jehovah's Witnesses to be involved in religious discussions. However, even this action proved to be a failure for the SS. Margarete Buber-Neumann reports that the Bible Students "kindly [cared] for these 'gems.'" Their kindness and missionary zeal did not remain without results: "In quite a short space of time, there were quite a number of asocials—a gypsy, a Pole, a Jewess, and a Political—who presented themselves at the S.S. office, declaring that henceforth they wished to be regarded as Jehovah's Witnesses and demanding the lilac triangle for their sleeves. When it got too bad, the S.S. just stormed and raved at the converts and threw them out. In the end the S.S. got

so fed-up that they removed the asocials from our block and peace descended again" (Buber-Neumann, *Under Two Dictators*, 237–38).

514. Pingel, *Häftlinge*, 90.

515. May 23, 1986, recollections by Alois Moser.

516. Ibid.

517. See Gostner, *1000 Tage im KZ*, 46.

518. See *Yearbook* 1989, 133. In 1943 the Bible Students in Ravensbrück celebrated the Lord's Supper in the same way. According to the report, 172 Jehovah's Witnesses took the emblems at that occasion (G. Kaiser, "Briefe. Nachrichten für die Zeugen Jehovas und ihre Gefährten," 7).

519. Ibid., 5.

520. See this book, pt. 5, ch. 16, pp. 473–74.

521. See Doyon, *Hirten*, 231; Zahnwetzer, *Buchenwald*, 28; May 23, 1986, recollections by Alois Moser.

522. Recollections by Johannes Rauthe, "Geschichtsbericht," 59.

523. The following descriptions are based on a report by Gustav Auschner (July 8, 1969, FGN, NHS 13-7-0-1; excerpts of this report are published in *Arbeit und Vernichtung*, 197). They are also based on the reports by Karl Hanl (Nov. 24, 1987), Richard Rudolph (May 31, 1986, and Sept. 9, 1986), and Ernst Wauer (May 29, 1986; *Watchtower*, Aug. 1, 1991, 25–29). The date of the Gestapo action in Neuengamme cannot be determined.

524. Prisoners on whom the SS imposed "gate restrictions" were not allowed to work at the labor details outside of the camp.

525. Nansen, *Tagebuch*, 158–59. The Gestapo arrived at the outside labor detail Berlin-Lichterfelde as early as Apr. 26, 1944. But also in Lichterfelde, the Bible Students were threatened and "put back to work" (*Yearbook* 1974, 203–4).

526. Kogon, *Theory and Practice of Hell*, 43.

527. MGRa, RA, Bd. 25, no. 332, Berta Hartmann, "Erlebnisse der Zeugen Jehovas in den Frauen-Konzentrationslagern," unpublished manuscript (1948). After seven weeks of detention in the punishment block, the fifteen Bible Students were transferred back to the punishment section at the concentration camp. The courageous conviction of Jehovah's Witnesses remained undiminished until the very end. This was confirmed by means of one of the last reports, which Suhren, the commanding officer of the Ravensbrück concentration camp, made to the WVHA. On Apr. 6, 1945, he reported that, "in comparison with former reports, the Bible Students . . . have not changed their behavior with regard to subversive propaganda" (MGRa [Memorial Ravensbrück], RA, Bd. 36, no. 710).

528. *Yearbook* 1974, 204.

529. See also the data analysis regarding the living and working conditions of the Bible Students at the Neuengamme concentration camp in this book, pt. 5, ch. 16, pp. 472–73.

530. On the social structure of the community of prisoners and the development of a hierarchical order of individual national and social groups, see Botz, "Überleben," 22ff.; Pawelczyńska, "Differenzierung."

531. In 1942 structural changes took place in the camps. These changes had the objective of making extensive use of the potential of human labor in the concentration camps for armament production, war economy, and other military purposes. At the beginning of Mar. 1942, an organizational restructuring of the concentration camp administration also took place (effective from Feb. 1, 1942, on, camp inspections came to be under the supervision of the newly introduced SS Central Office of Economy and Administration). See Broszat, *Anatomy of the SS State*, 217–18; Pingel, *Häftlinge*, 123ff.

532. See Pingel, *Häftlinge*, 151ff.

533. See Bettelheim, *The Informed Heart*, 123. This accuracy and diligence of Jehovah's Witnesses did not always win the full approval of the political prisoners. By means of slow work and low-quality production, these prisoners rather tried, if possible, to damage the economic system of the concentration camps. Therefore, they did not appreciate the fact that Jehovah's Witnesses in foremen positions "often endeavored to carry out the assignments of the SS even before schedule" (Kautsky, *Teufel und Verdammte*, 138–39).

534. See King, *Nazi State and the New Religions*, 169.

535. At Buchenwald, during a special roll call, the SS promised to release Jehovah's Witnesses if they signed the statement. According to a report by the Austrian Socialist and political prisoner Julius Freund, a "spokesman of the Bible Students" told an SS Oberscharführer: "We will stay here because the hour is coming soon when all mankind will be punished. We will patiently wait for a sign from Jehovah. Only then will we leave the camp" (Freund, *Buchenwald*, 129).

536. A few cases of escapes by Bible Student prisoners are known. Most of these escapes took place during the final weeks of the war, obviously to avoid being killed during the dissolution of the camps or during the evacuation marches. A remarkable exception is the case of one Jehovah's Witness who had been released after years of imprisonment at a penal camp in the spring of 1943 as "unfit to be kept in prison" due to a serious illness. When he was arrested again, on Dec. 12, 1944, he was able to flee on the way to the police office. He barely escaped the hail of bullets the pursuing police officer fired at him. The following day he was arrested again, and again he was lucky. The Chemnitz prison was severely damaged during a major attack from the Allies. As a result, the prisoners were able to escape. See June 24, 1984, recollections by Alfred Skoda.

537. See Pingel, *Häftlinge*, 91. Jehovah's Witnesses were also used primarily for the construction of concentration camps before security equipment was installed. At the beginning of 1940 the SS used "BV-prisoners" (the National Socialists' expression for "habitual criminals") for the construction of the

Wewelsburg concentration camp. After several attempts of escape, they were transferred back to the main camp in Sachsenhausen. The SS now began to use Bible Student prisoners exclusively. The change was ordered because the brutal outcome of such escape attempts (in a neighboring village, one habitual criminal was shot from behind) caused quite a commotion among the rural population. Therefore, the SS withdrew the criminals and replaced them with Bible Students, hoping that such instances would no longer occur. Besides reducing considerably the danger of escape attempts, the SS had another important reason for using the Bible Students in reconstructing the Wewelsburg into an SS-Ordensburg. The construction required a considerable number of skilled workers with the necessary qualifications. Not until the late summer of 1940, when a new concentration camp complex was established in the area of Niederhagen, were prisoners from non–Bible Student groups also sent to Wewelsburg. Even during the following years, Jehovah's Witnesses formed the nucleus of prisoners at this concentration camp. See Hüser, *Wewelsburg*, 72ff.; John, *Wewelsburg* (1996), 37ff. and 76ff.

538. June 17, 1987, and Nov. 24, 1987, recollections by Karl Hanl; May 31, 1986, recollections by Richard Rudolph.

539. Whether it was possible that the prisoners at these labor details could use the opportunities in order to gather additional food always depended on the disposition of the particular SS guards. For instance, gathering windfalls (fruit), herbs, or other plants for themselves always involved the risk that the guards decided to beat the prisoners or to file an "incident report."

540. See May 29, 1986, recollections by Ernst Wauer.

541. In Sept. 1941 even SS-Hauptsturmführer [chief Storm leader] Otto Söldner, the commanding officer responsible for questions involving the labor details, who had been sent to Neuengamme for the supervision of the camp administration, used Bible Students to build a small boathouse in the neighboring village of Kirchwerder. See May 31, 1986, recollections by Richard Rudolph; DhN, Ng. 5.1.1.

542. See June 17, 1987, recollections by Karl Hanl; DhN, Ng. 9.2.5.

543. See KZGDa [Concentration Camp Memorial Dachau], archive no. 481, Heinrich Lutterbach, Oct. 26, 1963, report regarding the labor detail at Lake Wolfgang; *Yearbook* 1974, 198.

544. See BHStA, OMGUS, Dachau trial of war criminals, Microfilm 1a/1, no. 184, May 21, 1945, statements by Paul Wauer; *Yearbook* 1974, 198–99; Lienau, *Zwölf Jahre Nacht*, 181. In Aug. 1942 Loritz was removed from office because of misusing his position for "profiteering." See Höhne, *Orden*, 355.

545. See BHStA, OMGUS, Dachau trial of war criminals, Microfilm 1a/1, no. 184, May 21, 1945, statements by Paul Wauer.

546. See June 17, 1987, and Nov. 24, 1987, recollections by Karl Hanl; May 23, 1986, recollections by Alois Moser; Apr. 15, 1971, and Feb. 7, 1987, recollections by Willi Lehmbecker.

547. Apr. 15, 1971, recollections by Willi Lehmbecker.

548. May 23, 1986, recollections by Alois Moser.

549. See *Yearbook* 1974, 203–4; Szepansky, *Weg*, 154; AfW 310504; VVN HH, Komiteeakten W 9; Apr. 15, 1971, recollections by Willi Lehmbecker.

550. Sven Anders Hedin was a Swedish scientist performing genealogical research. See Kater, *"Ahnenerbe,"* 214, 416; Kater, "Bibelforscher," 217. From Sept. 1, 1944, to Mar. 31, 1945, one female Bible Student was also deployed at the household of Ernst Schäfer, the head of the department for Inner-Asia Research of the Ahnenerbe [genealogical research]. This privilege was also accorded to SS-Standartenführer [standard leader] Wolfram Sievers, head of the Berlin SS Office Ahnenerbe. Bible Student Hedwig Patzer from Ravensbrück camp was assigned to work at his home.

551. Hartzwalde was one of the first private estates at which Bible Student prisoners were deployed. The "Jan. 4, 1942, list of work assignments" compiled at Ravensbrück had already included assignments of Jehovah's Witnesses to the Hartzwalde estate. See C. Müller, *Klempnerkolonne*, no page numbers (documents chapter following 112). In 1943, in addition to the women, a labor detail of approximately ten men was also sent to the Hartzwalde estate for agricultural work assignments (cultivation of rutabaga and potatoes). These men were also sent to Hartzwalde for the purpose of building a hunting lodge. See Jan. 31, 1971, recollections by Franz Birk; May 16, 1992, recollections by Klingenberg.

552. The widow of SS-Obergruppenführer Reinhard Heydrich, who had been the Deputy Reich Patron of Moravia and Bohemia from Sept. 1941 on, had received from the Reich authorities ownership of the Jungfern-Breschan estate near Odolenswasser (Bohemia). For the first eighteen months, a labor detail of Jewish prisoners from Theresienstadt was assigned to work there. On Feb. 11, 1944, these prisoners were replaced with a labor detail consisting of fifteen Bible Students (ten German and three Dutch prisoners, one Czech prisoner, and one Polish prisoner) from the Flossenbürg concentration camp. The prisoners were housed in the barns and stables. They had to perform repair work and cultivate the ground (cited in BA, NS 19/18; *Yearbook* 1974, 198).

553. May 23, 1986, recollections by Alois Moser; see also the report by Gertrud Pötzinger, cited in Füllberg-Stolberg, "Gertrud Pötzinger," 330, as well as the report by Ilse Unterdörfer, published in *Yearbook* 1974, 199.

554. See Heiber, *Reichsführer!*, 218; see also this book, pp. 724–25, n.595.

555. MAu, WVHA, June 2, 1943. Requests were also made "for Bible Student prisoners who were able to work as foremen at sawmills or who were trained to work at sawmills."

556. By means of the Deutsche Versuchsanstalt für Ernährung und Verpflegung, the SS leaders intended to make Germany independent from food imports. For example, planting herbs and spices in Dachau and Buchenwald had the objective of substituting foreign herbs with those cultivated in Germany. Ultimately, more than fifty agricultural, forestry, and fish farming estates

were established that were also used for research and breeding purposes. See Georg, *Unternehmungen der SS*, 62–66.

557. See Buszko et al., *Auschwitz. Geschichte und Wirklichkeit*, 25–26; Höß, *Kommandant in Auschwitz*, 116–17.

558. The Harmense poultry farm, an outside labor detail of Auschwitz, produced pure-bred poultry (chicken, geese, pheasants, etc.). From June 1942 on, approximately ten female Bible Students, who were housed separately from the other 100 prisoners, were deployed at this outside labor detail. These Bible Students were in charge of the kitchen, worked at the "laboratory," and sometimes even became block leaders. See Zieba, "Geflügelfarm Harmense," 41ff.

559. See Chêne, *Mauthausen*, 131.

560. The Jan. 4, 1942, list of work assignments at Ravensbrück provides an overview of the deployment of 212 Bible Students. It also shows the high percentage of privileged positions assigned to them. According to this list (see C. Müller, *Klempnerkolonne*, documents chapter following 112), 51 female Bible Students were deployed at agricultural estates (labor details *Kellerbruch, Gutshof,* and *Hühnerfarm*), which were under the direct administration of the WVHA. Ten female Bible Students were deployed at the Hartzwalde estate of Dr. Kersten; 6 at the concentration camp greenhouse, and 12 at the barns and stables (total number of Bible Students working at farming estates: 79). Of the four commands that were listed under the section "SS office and settlements," three consisted only of Bible Students: 16 Bible Students worked at the "personnel department," 7 at the "homes of leading officials," and another 16 at the homes of "subordinate officials." Four Bible Students worked at the children's home, 7 Jehovah's Witnesses worked at the construction office, 5 had cleaning assignments there, 10 worked at the worker's dining hall, and 4 had cleaning assignments at the office for textile and leather processing (total number of Bible Students working for SS officers: 69). Eighteen Bible Students were deployed at the commandant's headquarters for "shoveling snow," 16 for "carrying and stacking wood" (total number of unskilled workers: 34). At the labor details, which were listed under the section "armaments factory," the IBSA was mentioned only once, i.e., 30 Bible Students worked at the navy warehouse.

561. In 1943/44 Richard Rudolph was deployed to the SS kitchen at Neuengamme. He even received training as a dietician in order to cook for the thirteen SS officers at the camp according to the conceptions of a healthy diet that had been developed by Max Pauly, the commanding officer of the camp. Pauly was as committed to a healthy diet as was the Reichsführer SS and certified farmer, Himmler. See Sept. 9, 1986, recollections by Richard Rudolph.

562. Zürcher, *Kreuzzug*, 105; see also Chêne, *Mauthausen*, 130; *Yearbook* 1974, 198; King, *Nazi State and the New Religions*, 169.

563. See GBu, 31–826, Karl Siebeneichler, report of Apr. 24, 1945.

564. Recollections by Johannes Rauthe, "Geschichtsbericht," 58. Rauthe was a sculptor by profession. He reports that he had been especially assigned

for this activity at Buchenwald. He received special tools and materials as equipment for the sculptor's workshop. As a supervisor, he was even allowed to select other qualified fellow prisoners to assist him with preparatory work (stonemasons, experts in pottery, carpenters, lathe workers, etc.). He selected only Bible Students for these jobs.

565. See Buber-Neumann, *Under Two Dictators,* 259; C. Müller, *Klempnerkolonne,* 131-32.

566. See *Jehovah's Witnesses in the Divine Purpose,* 170; Kogon, *Theory and Practice of Hell,* 51. In 1943, after the Italian Badoglio Government and the Royal Family had been able to escape to the Allies, Princess Mafalda of Hessen was taken hostage. She died as a result of the injuries she sustained during the air raid on Buchenwald on Aug. 24, 1944. See Bartel and Trostorff, *Buchenwald: Mahnung und Verpflichtung,* 349.

567. See John, *Wewelsburg* (1996), 162.

568. Höß, *Kommandant in Auschwitz,* 150. This can also be confirmed by a report from a Jehovah's Witness. Charlotte Tetzner was deployed as a shorthand typist at the SS military hospital at Auschwitz and was greatly appreciated as a reliable and accurate worker. She reports that several SS officers requested her as a worker at their private households. However, she was not released for these purposes. One of these SS officers who had unsuccessfully requested Tetzner to be employed at his home was Dr. Werner Rhode, the medical doctor of the SS camp. In 1943, when Charlotte Tetzner suffered from typhoid fever, he personally looked after her and, contrary to his usual practices, visited her on a daily basis at the section of the hospital that was reserved for the so-called commanders. See Aug. 18, 1986, recollections by Charlotte Tetzner.

569. Oct. 6, 1944, deployment list for the prisoners at the Auschwitz I concentration camp for women, cited in Friedman and Holuj, *Oświęcim,* 217.

570. Höß, *Kommandant in Auschwitz,* 150.

571. Ibid.

572. Gertrud Pötzinger worked in Oranienburg as a nursemaid at the household of an SS-Sturmbannführer (Storm battalion leader). (Probably Max Kiefer, head of the Amt C II/Sonderbauaufgaben im WVHA [Office C II/ Special Building Projects of the WVHA].) She also accompanied the family during their escape in Apr. 1945. Several reports about Gertrud Pötzinger are published in Füllberg-Stolberg, "Gertrud Pötzinger," 325-32; Graffard and Tristan, *Bibelforscher,* 164, 212; *Watchtower,* Aug. 1, 1984, 25-31. With regard to the biography of Gertrud Pötzinger, see also Jacobeit, *Ravensbrückerinnen,* 60ff.

573. If the statements by Oswald Pohl to the widow of Reinhard Heydrich can be considered to be reliable, the SS leaders had to give a small donation to the Reich treasury (which the widow was reluctant to pay): "Every one of us, even the Reichsführer SS, has to pay, in addition to board and lodging, a predetermined wage for the prisoner who works at his household" (Pohl, Aug. 26, 1944, letter to Lina Heydrich, BA, NS 19/18, no page numbers).

574. Paul Buder reports that a Bible Student was also deployed as a house-keeper at the home of Heinrich Himmler (KmW, KW D 87, Buder, "Wewels-burg," 74).

575. The Niederhagen concentration camp represented an exception in this regard. During the construction of Wewelsburg, between Feb. and Sept. 1940, Jehovah's Witnesses were the only group of prisoners there. Even during the following years, after the admission of several hundred Germans from other groups of prisoners as well as several thousand foreigners (mostly Russian prisoners), Jehovah's Witnesses formed the nucleus of the prisoners and accepted several functions (see Hüser, *Wewelsburg*, 81). In Wewelsburg, Jehovah's Witnesses were deployed, for instance, at positions as camp leaders (G. Klohe, O. Martens, W. Wilke), camp clerks (W. Müller, B. Draht), block leaders (G. Früchtl, H. Dickmann, and others), and caretakers (P. Buder, J. Schmook, and others). They also occupied positions as supervisors and foremen at several labor details (cited in KmW; DdW, AN 707, Herbert Baron, "Jahre des Grauens"; May 16, 1992, recollections by Klingenberg; May 23, 1986, recollections by Alois Moser; *Yearbook* 1974, 175–76; John, *Wewelsburg* [1996], 78, 147).

576. See, for instance, *Einer muß überleben*, 25; Langbein, *Auschwitz*, 243–44. Apparently, there were only very few cases where Jehovah's Witnesses misused their positions to the disadvantage of fellow prisoners, or where they misused their positions as foremen to beat other prisoners. One camp senior and a few other functionary prisoners at the Wewelsburg concentration camp were accused of such behavior (*Yearbook* 1974, 175–76; May 23, 1986, recollections by Alois Moser; G. Kaiser, "Briefe. Nachrichten für die Zeugen Jehovas und ihre Gefährten," 9). A foreman at the outside labor detail Alderney was also accused of such behavior (FGN, NHS 13-7-5-5; Sept. 27, 1986, recollections by Otto Spehr).

577. Sept. 23, 1986, recollections by Lauritz G. Damgaard.

578. Bettelheim, *The Informed Heart*, 123. Cases in which Jehovah's Witnesses worked as foremen raised the question of how a Jehovah's Witness would respond if somebody in his command did not work in a way required to fulfill the assignment. In this regard, one Jehovah's Witness states: "The brother assigned as supervisor went to the prisoner and wrote down his prisoner's number. The next day, he put this prisoner into a command supervised by a political foreman. That was his punishment! . . . The prisoners came to feel that life was much easier and more peaceful if nobody pushed and screamed" (May 23, 1986, recollections by Alois Moser).

579. RFSS, order of Jan. 6, 1943 (RF/Dr. I 37/43), cited in the July 15, 1943, letter of the chief of the Security Police and the Security Service to the RFSS, published in Friedman and Holuj, *Oświęcim*, 183–86.

580. Kersten had provided medical treatment for Himmler since 1939 and knew how to gain his trust. According to Besgen, Kersten first heard about the real state of conditions in the concentration camps through conversations with

Jehovah's Witnesses (Besgen, *Der stille Befehl*, 146). As a result, the medical officer exerted his influence on Himmler in the way of repeatedly requesting better working and living conditions for the prisoners in the German concentration camps (see Kersten, *Totenkopf und Treue*). In the spring of 1945 Kersten also played an important part in the rescue operation of concentration camp prisoners (Bernadotte-Action of the Swedish Red Cross). During the latter period of the war, upon Kersten's request, Himmler even ordered the release from concentration camp imprisonment of one of the women who worked at the Hartzwalde estate, so that she could work as a housekeeper at Kersten's second home in Sweden. From his visits to Sweden, Kersten also brought Bible Student publications back to his Hartzwalde estate. See Gebhard, *Zeugen Jehovas*, 209; *Yearbook* 1974, 196, 198–99.

581. Himmler's letter to Müller and Pohl is published in *Yearbook* 1974, 196–97. It is not possible to locate this undated letter in the archives. However, it can be assumed almost certainly that it is the Jan. 6, 1943, order Himmler mentions and briefly describes in his July 15, 1943, letter. See also Gebhard, *Zeugen Jehovas*, 206; Hutten, *Seher, Grübler, Enthusiasten*, 120.

582. Himmler's changing attitude regarding the Bible Student question did not remain unnoticed by Jehovah's Witnesses. For instance, as early as 1943/44, they circulated the news in the concentration camps that Himmler had started to change his opinion about the Bible Students. This change probably resulted from the impression Himmler gained from his encounters with the Bible Student prisoners at the Hartzwalde estate of Felix Kersten. See Gebhard, *Zeugen Jehovas*, 206; *Yearbook* 1974, 195–97; May 16, 1992, recollections by Klingenberg.

583. Apr. 16, 1946, statements by Alfred Rosenberg at the International Military Court in Nuremberg, cited in *Der Prozeß gegen die Hauptkriegsverbrecher*, 11:563.

584. Cited in *Yearbook* 1974, 196–97 (see note 581 above).

585. Ibid., 197. Himmler's suggestion of using Bible Students for the "Lebensborn" homes was accepted and put into practice (see Friedman and Holuj, *Oświęcim*, 184; *Yearbook* 1974, 197). For instance, in July 1943 the name of Mathilde Stuhlmüller-Legenstein from Amsterdam, who had been arrested because of her IBSA activities and sent to Ravensbrück in 1941, was removed from the "transport list to Auschwitz." Instead, she was sent to the "Lebensborn" home Taunus in Wiesbaden, which was, since the previous month, one of the outside labor details of Ravensbrück. See Bembenek, "Außenkommando Lebensbornheim Taunus," 82; Kater, "Bibelforscher," 217.

586. Cited in *Yearbook* 1974, 197. The July 15, 1943, response of Kaltenbrunner to the RFSS (published in Friedman and Holuj, *Oświęcim*, 183–86) indicates that, based on requests made in the Oct. 29, 1942, report, "two new drafts for the reverse statement" had been "presented." However, the report, according to which Himmler had made the suggestion to revise the statement, is not

available in the archives. (This also applies to an interoffice decree issued by the Gestapa shortly before, on Sept. 10, 1942. The subject matter indicates that the issue of the statement had also been discussed there: "Handling after release from prison and before admission into a concentration camp. Instructions according to guidelines.") Since Kaltenbrunner's response made extensive references to the Oct. 29, 1942, report, it is possible to state the reasons and objectives for a revised version of the statement. Accordingly, a new wording of the statement should take into account the fact that "individual Bible Students often objected to the wording of the statement, in particular to the fact that they had to declare their own convictions to be false teachings. Otherwise, they agreed to follow the requirements of the state and to carry out any work they were assigned to do." With the two new drafts of the statement, an approach was intended that took into account the respective situations. One of the statements should "be used for Bible Students who had completely abandoned the Bible Student teachings and were willing to perform military service." The second, "considerably more moderate draft" should be presented only to Bible Students "who had not yet completely changed their attitude. Based on an extensive period of surveillance in the camp, they gave reason to anticipate that, after their release, they would conduct themselves in a respectable way and would not give any cause for complaint." It had also been decided to present this "more moderate statement" only to "female Bible Students and male Bible Students who were no longer liable for military service." At the time of Kaltenbrunner's response (July 15, 1943), a decision regarding the use of the drafts for these new statements "had not yet been made." It cannot be determined whether this "differentiated" new approach was later put into practice on a large scale.

587. The chief of the Security Police and the Security Service, letter of July 15, 1943, cited in Friedman and Holuj, *Oświęcim*, 183–86 (185). Regarding the procedure of "releasing prisoners without requiring their signatures," this letter indicates that the particular female Bible Students had to accept, by means of a handshake, certain obligations toward the concentration camp commanding officer that were not specifically mentioned in the letter. The commanding officer had to explain to these prisoners that they would be "immediately arrested again" if they violated "the obligations they had accepted." The acceptance of these obligations had to be recorded. The records had to be submitted to the RSHA, which, according to the letter of Kaltenbrunner, "would then order the immediate release" (Friedman and Holuj, 185–86).

588. This extensive letter, which reflects an attitude of reservation, even rejection, of the suggestions made, clearly contradicts Kaltenbrunner's Apr. 12, 1946, statements at the International Military Court in Nuremberg. There, he stated that the Bible Students were placed under "undue hardship for an attitude based on religious convictions." He even asserted that it was due to his interventions with Thierack and Himmler that the Bible Students were treated

with more consideration during the final period of the war. See this book, pt. 5, ch. 13, p. 348.

589. The chief of the Security Police and the Security Service, letter of July 15, 1943, cited in Friedman and Holuj, *Oświęcim*, 186.

590. See Buber-Neumann, *Under Two Dictators*, 227; Langbein, *Auschwitz*, 243–44. During the middle of 1944 the Bible Student Viktor Bruch, from Esch (Luxemburg), was "evacuated" from Majdanek to Auschwitz. He reports that "several sisters were allowed to walk to the city without a guard to make purchases for their mistresses." They used these opportunities to contact Jehovah's Witnesses on the outside (*Yearbook* 1976, 40).

591. Jan. 31, 1971, recollections by Franz Birk. With the approval of Dr. Kersten, Jehovah's Witnesses deployed at the Hartzwalde estate were allowed to supply their fellow believers at nearby Ravensbrück and Sachsenhausen with food. This allowed them to establish contact and exchange information. Because of the relative freedom of movement granted to Jehovah's Witnesses in Hartzwalde, the estate became a center of the IBSA underground activities, as it were. It was the center from which they organized the smuggling of publications and letters in and out of the neighboring concentration camps. See Gebhard, *Zeugen Jehovas*, 209; May 16, 1992, recollections by Friedrich Klingenberg; May 19, 1986, recollections by Günther Pape.

592. Heydrich, *Leben*, 128.

593. BA, NS 19/18, no page numbers, RFSS, letter of Jan. 14, 1945.

594. Heydrich, *Leben*, 128. During the middle of Apr. 1945, Lina Heydrich escaped together with the rest of her personnel and Jehovah's Witnesses. In Oct. 1946 Lina Heydrich's father sent a letter to a Jehovah's Witness who had been deployed at the Jungfern-Breschan estate, requesting this Jehovah's Witness to put in a good word for his daughter. After some initial hesitation, the Jehovah's Witness sent a reply to the father; he described the conditions to which Jehovah's Witnesses were exposed at the estate: "During the first week of our working for your daughter, the commanding officer of our command once told your daughter that she would need to feed the prisoners better, since, otherwise, they would break down during work. Her reply: 'You just take care that nobody dies here. Inform me early enough that we can exchange them. We can always request others.' She did not dream of giving us more food. If Jehovah would not have provided us by moving the hearts of the Czech people, we would have starved right there on her estate. . . . If your daughter truly regrets the sorrow inflicted on God's people with her knowledge and consent she would ask Jehovah for forgiveness instead of asking people for rehabilitation. After all, she also used and misused these people to enrich herself unjustly" (Heinrich Vieker, undated letter, cited in Struckmeier, "Heinel," 179).

595. Heinrich Himmler, June 26, 1943, letter to Johann Marx, cited in Heiber, *Reichsführer!*, 218. Himmler used this description when he suggested to a farmer from Upper Bavaria that he could provide him with a Bible Student

prisoner to help him with his harvest since his son (who was probably in the service of the SS) was not granted leave for the harvest: "I can appreciate your difficult situation. Therefore, I will send you a concentration camp prisoner. He is a Bible Student belonging to a crazy sect. He believes that Jehovah prohibited him from taking the oath in acknowledgement of the Führer and from fighting for his fatherland. The Bible Students are people who believe that Jehovah subjected them to fifteen or more years of imprisonment and various other difficulties. In general, however, they are good workers. But in this one area they are crazy [*die spinnen*], as we say here in Bavaria. To be of some assistance, I would like to send you such a Bible Student from the camp."

596. Höß, *Kommandant in Auschwitz*, 99.

597. On *Wehrbauern*, see Kersten, *Kersten Memoirs*, 132–40; for additional literature references, see Kater, "Bibelforscher," 191n52.

598. Any of the peoples speaking Turkish languages and living in a region extending from the Balkans to east Siberia.

599. KZGDa, file folder "Bible Students," RFSS, Feldkommandantur [District Military Administrative Headquarters], letter of July 21, 1944. Various versions or stages of revision of this letter, which had the letter heading of the Reichsführer SS, have been preserved. The original, which was sent to Kaltenbrunner, is not available. In 1968 Heiber (*Reichsführer!*, 272–74), published a copy without signature. Excerpts of this copy had been published three years earlier by Zipfel (*Kirchenkampf*, 200–201). This copy is divided into four sections and, in a few places, includes variations in terminology. Another copy with the stamp of the chief of the SS Rasse- und Siedlungshauptamt [SS Central Office involving matters of race and settlement], dated Sept. 22, 1944, includes an additional (fifth) section. In 1954 Ritter ("Wunschträume Heinrich Himmlers," 162–68) published the uncorrected dictation of this letter, which corresponds in length with the Sept. 22, 1944, version. In contrast, this letter was divided into six sections. The letter quoted above represents the version sent to the chief of the SS Rasse- und Siedlungshauptamt. This selection was made because the uncorrected dictation of the letter published by Ritter clearly reflects the linguistic and stylistic character of a draft. The most recently revised version (the version published by Heiber and Zipfel includes the handwritten postscript "Sept. 28"), on the other hand, is incomplete. This letter was typed on a machine with large characters. Therefore, Zipfel (*Kirchenkampf*, 201) assumes that the nonpreserved original of this copy was the version intended to be presented to Hitler. Hitler usually requested documents to be presented to him in this form. According to Zipfel, this would also explain why the last section was not included in the letter. Himmler probably did not want Hitler to know of the "concessions" he had made regarding the issue of the Bible Students.

600. Kater, "Bibelforscher," 190. On the change in attitude of NS ideologists toward the Mennonites that Himmler mentions also in his letter, see Götz, *Schwarzmeerdeutschtum;* see also this book, p. 584, n.131.

601. Erdmann, *Die Zeit der Weltkriege,* 401.

602. See this book, pt. 5, ch. 16, p. 467.

603. Personal documents of Johan Wildschut, memo regarding the evacuation march of Jehovah's Witnesses from the Sachsenhausen concentration camp, May 1945. If not mentioned otherwise, the following quotations were taken from this source. Important information about the fate of the Bible Student prisoners during the evacuation of Sachsenhausen is included in Graffard and Tristan, *Bibelforscher,* 210ff.; *Yearbook* 1974, 207–10; Louis Piéchota, "I Survived the 'Death March,'" cited in *Watchtower,* Aug. 15, 1980, 5–10; June 25, 1986, recollections by Johan Wildschut.

604. On the death camp in the Below forest, see *Sachsenhausen, Dokumente,* 125–27.

605. Piéchota, "I Survived the 'Death March,'" cited in *Watchtower,* Aug. 15, 1980, 5–10.

606. Wildschut, resolution of 230 Jehovah's Witnesses from ten different nationalities gathered in a forest near Schwerin, May 1945.

607. See *Awake!,* June 22, 1985, 13.

608. Wildschut, memo regarding the evacuation march of Jehovah's Witnesses from the Sachsenhausen concentration camp, undated [May 1945].

609. A statistical data collection regarding concentration camp imprisonment of Bible Students for the purpose of comparison was performed in the context of a research study about the persecution of homosexuals (see Lautmann, Grikschat, and Schmidt, "Der rosa Winkel," 325–65; besides the Bible Students, a comparison was also made with the group of political prisoners). This study, which was presented in 1997, is based primarily on prisoners' files from Buchenwald, Dachau, Flossenbürg, and Mauthausen (personal identity cards, security and transportation lists, labor detail records, medical report cards, reports of death, etc.). These prisoners' files are preserved at the "Internationaler Suchdienst" in Arolsen (Hessen), which, at that time, was still accessible for historians. Data from a total of 751 Bible Student prisoners is included in the study.

610. This study is based on the total number of Jehovah's Witnesses sent to Neuengamme between 1940 and 1945. At the end of Apr. 1945, shortly before the camp was evacuated, the SS ordered the burning of the prisoners' files and indexes that were kept in the commandant's headquarters, the orderly room, and the political office. It is not possible to determine the exact number of prisoners who had to wear the purple patch of the Bible Students.

611. Poel, *Neuengamme,* 105.

612. Eiber, "Arbeitssklaven," 559.

613. Meyer, *Nacht über Hamburg,* 60.

614. Nov. 24, 1987, recollections by Karl Hanl, "approximately 80"; May 30, 1986, recollections by Richard Rudolph, "close to 80"; May 29, 1986, recollections by Ernst Wauer, "approximately 70"; Willi Seidel, letter of Jan. 3, 1985,

"more than 70." See also the statement in *Yearbook* 1974, 192, of "about 70," which is based on reports from prisoners. In a written report from 1969 by Jehovah's Witness Gustav Auschner, this number is estimated to be only "approximately 50–60" (FGN, NHS 13-7-0-1).

615. Sources from various provenances were employed for the data collection. Such sources were, for instance, verbal and written statements from former prisoners, documents from the Hamburg VVN (applications for certificates identifying the former prisoner as a victim of persecution, records, and letters). Data was also obtained from the Document Center of the Neuengamme Concentration Camp Memorial (transportation and security lists, laboratory records, records of deaths, documents from the registry office, prisoners' reports, and court records). Additional data was obtained from the Amicale Internationale de Neuenegamme/Nachlass of Hans Schwarz at the FGN (number and name files based on information provided by survivors, correspondence). Information was also obtained from the Office for Compensation.

616. Statements regarding eleven additional Bible Student prisoners from the Neuengamme concentration camp had to be disregarded since, apart from their names, there is only insufficient information or the information cannot be adequately substantiated. Also disregarded is the data from seventeen Bible Students who were imprisoned at the outside camp Alderney. The first SS construction brigade is not included in this study. In Sept./Oct. 1942 this construction brigade consisted of prisoners from the Sachsenhausen concentration camp. Initially, these prisoners were deployed for the purpose of performing salvage work after bomb attacks on Düsseldorf and Duisburg. In Mar. 1943, after its transfer to the occupied English Channel island of Alderney, the brigade was placed under the supervision of the Neuengamme concentration camp. However, this command was only under administrative supervision of the Neuengamme concentration camp. The prisoners themselves did not have any connections with Neuengamme. Therefore, it did not seem appropriate to include the Alderney command in this study, not least because of the numerous special features of this labor detail. With regard to Jehovah's Witnesses included in the first SS construction brigade, see *Ein KZ-Außenlager in Düsseldorf-Stoffeln*, 71, 82–83, 97; *Yearbook* 1974, 118.

617. At the end of 1940 the number of prisoners at the main camp of Neuengamme amounted to approximately 2,850–2,900; at the end of 1941, about 4,500–4,800 (including 1,000 Soviet prisoners of war who, in Oct. 1941, were placed into a separate area of the concentration camp designated as "labor camp for prisoners of war." Within a few months, 652 of these prisoners died of hunger or were killed by gasoline injections). In mid-1942 the number of prisoners at the main camp was 2,800–3,300; in mid-1943, 5,500–6,000; in mid-1944, 8,000–10,000; toward the end of the war, 13,000–14,000. Numerical data according to Kaienburg, *Vernichtung durch Arbeit*, 155–56, 339.

618. Since it can be generally established that the majority of Bible Students

were imprisoned between 1935 and 1939, the number of Bible Student prisoners in the concentration camps changed only insignificantly during the war. The number of new admissions of Jehovah's Witnesses (especially non-German ones) made up only for the losses that the SS bookkeeping department recorded as deaths, transfers, or releases. In view of these explanations, the statements by Kater according to which "after the beginning of the war . . . the number of Bible Students in the concentration camps continued to increase" can no longer be maintained (Kater, "Bibelforscher," 208).

619. On May 3, 1945, at almost sixty years of age, Franz Pawelka was released from more than ten years of imprisonment. In Neuengamme, he had worked for some time in the orderly room. He had also worked for about two and a half years for SS officers. Since he was a barber by occupation and had the trust of the SS officers, he was allowed to cut their hair and trim their beards.

620. This statement corresponds almost exactly to the statement made by Lautmann, Grikschat, and Schmidt (forty-one years). See "Der rosa Winkel," 331.

621. In her study, Kirsten John analyzes the dates of birth of 198 Jehovah's Witnesses who were imprisoned at the Niederhagen (Wewelsburg) concentration camp. According to her analysis, only 5.5 percent of the Bible Student prisoners at this concentration camp were younger than thirty. See John, *Wewelsburg* (1996), 42.

622. BA, NS 4 Bu/vorl. 141. An examination based on other dates (June 29, 1940/Nov. 29, 1940/Sept. 30, 1941), did not produce any significant differences.

623. Initially, probably for a couple of months, this "block for Jews and Bible Students" also included prisoners from the punishment battalion and other prisoners. Subsequently, with the exception of the block leader, it included only Jehovah's Witnesses and Jewish prisoners. Until the autumn of 1942 (transfers to Auschwitz), only several hundred Jews were imprisoned in Neuengamme. See Garbe and Homann, "Jüdische Gefangene."

624. Those Jehovah's Witnesses who worked as so-called *Kommandierte* (prisoners in command) and had to carry out assignments in the SS section of the camp (SS kitchen, services at the SS casino, barber shops, motor vehicle park, stable, etc.), or who worked as clerks for SS officers, were housed in "Block I," which accommodated a smaller number of prisoners and had better sanitary conditions. Other *Kommandierte* and superior functionary prisoners were also housed there. On the living quarters of these "prominent ones" or as they were also called, the living quarters "Läusefreien" [without lice], see Kaienburg, *Vernichtung durch Arbeit*, 366; Meier, *Frühwind*, 160–60, 164–65.

625. WVHA, interoffice decree of Sept. 10, 1943, BA, NS 3/426; see also this book, pt. 5, ch. 15, p. 436.

626. According to reports, at the Mauthausen concentration camp, there was "apparently not one Bible Student who held a position as functionary

prisoner" during the entire time this camp was in existence (Maršálek, *Mauthausen*, 274).

627. Pingel, *Häftlinge*, 89; see also this book, pt. 5, ch. 15, p. 446.

628. See Meier, *Frühwind*, 392.

629. The Neuengamme concentration camp and its subsidiary camps included 106,000 prisoners. Of these prisoners, 9.1 percent were Germans. The largest national groups consisted of Russians (18.7%), Poles (16.7%), French (11.4%), Ukrainians (10.4%), Dutch (6.9%), Belgians and Danes (4.75% each), and Latvians (4.1%).

630. See Maršálek, *Mauthausen*, 274.

631. These data are based primarily on an analysis of death certificates that had been issued by the Neuengamme concentration camp registry office. They are also based on the death records preserved from the camp infirmary (subsidiary camp only until Dec. 29, 1944) between May 1, 1942, and Mar. 15, 1945. Both sources are incomplete and include several deficiencies. Until the autumn of 1944, with regard to the main camp (not the subsidiary camps, for which only an extremely small number of deaths are registered) these sources can be considered relatively complete (with certain exceptions as the executions and the 1942 typhus fever epidemic). Because of the considerable number of subsidiary camps (more than eighty of them; in 1944/45 these subsidiary camps included three times as many prisoners as the main camp), as well as the more than 10,000 people who died during the evacuation, the names (16,956) recorded in both sources represent only about one third of all the prisoners who died at the Neuengamme concentration camp.

632. According to one report, more than sixty Jehovah's Witnesses were supposedly on these prisoners' ships (personal documents of Helmut Lasarcyk: Konrad Franke, "Geschichte der Zeugen Jehovas in Deutschland," discourse [transcript], Bad Hersfeld, 1976, 38). Twenty-two of these prisoners survived the British bomb attack. Because of a lack of other sources, this statement cannot be confirmed. However, it is possible that this number includes at least some of the Bible Student prisoners from the Neuengamme concentration camp for whom no other data is available (see this book, pt. 5, ch. 16, p. 459).

633. A number of other Bible Students also became seriously ill during this time and recovered only after several months. To a certain extent, these illnesses were the result of the forced labor, the provisional housing at the old brickworks, and the severe cold in Mar. 1940. However, the personality of the commanding officer at that time also contributed to these illnesses. This commanding officer, SS-Sturmbannführer Walter Eisfeld, had already singled out the Bible Students for special harassment at the Sachsenhausen concentration camp. It also has to be taken into consideration that the Bible Students were already exhausted and emaciated when they arrived in Neuengamme: the fact that, in Sachsenhausen, they had been housed at the isolation blocks and repeatedly deployed in the

punishment battalion, did not remain without consequences (see this book, pt. 5, ch. 15, pp. 402–3).

634. The records at the registry office recorded this death, which occurred on June 13, 1940, as: "died because he was run over by a truck, accident." This prisoner had arrived in Neuengamme only nine days earlier with the June 4, 1940, transport. The SS refused to assign him to a labor detail with fellow believers. Therefore, according to the report by a fellow prisoner, he threw himself in despair before a truck (see May 31, 1986, recollections by Richard Rudolph). According to Kupfer-Koberwitz (*Mächtigen*, 401), there was another case of suicide at the Neuengamme concentration camp. He reports of a Bible Student who "ran into the barbed wire fence" on Easter Saturday of 1941 (a death certificate regarding this case is not available). There were several cases of Bible Students committing suicide because they were not able to deal with the severe difficulties of concentration camp imprisonment and the distress caused by the conflict between the requirements of their faith and the threats of the SS (see Schlotterbeck, *Erinnerungen*, 169–80, which describes the case of a demoralized Jehovah's Witness who tried to kill himself with a razor blade in order to escape the persecution at the Welzheim concentration camp). In 1937 the *Deutschland-Berichte* stated in this regard that, in the concentration camps, "the majority of suicides and suicide attempts occurred among the Earnest Bible Students" (707). However, at least for the later period, this assessment cannot be substantiated. To the contrary, the suicide rate among Jehovah's Witnesses was rather comparatively low. See also John, *Wewelsburg* (1996), 138.

635. However, during the first quarter of 1941, a sick fifty-one-year-old Bible Student from Vienna was transported to the Dachau concentration camp. Several months later, in a "transport for the disabled," the SS removed a fifty-year-old blind Bible Student from the camp.

636. The death certificate states as cause of death "eight shots in the chest" (DhN, Ng. 4.8.1). Shortly after his arrival in Neuengamme, Trausner (from St. Johann in Austria), strictly refused to comply with any orders that, in his opinion, involved actions that Jehovah's Witnesses could not perform because of their religious beliefs. According to reports from fellow prisoners, he supposedly complained to the camp administration about the acts of persecution. Several times, he conspicuously refused to do any service for the SS, considering it to be an act of idolatry. See Maislinger, "Andere religiöse Gruppen," 325; Poel, *Neuengamme*, 106; Nov. 24, 1987, recollections by Karl Hanl; May 31, 1986, recollections by Richard Rudolph; FGN, NHS 13-7-0-1, Gustav Auschner, report of July 8, 1969.

637. Probably this number would have been even higher if a considerable number of Bible Student prisoners from Neuengamme (statements vary between thirty and forty-eight) had not been sent to a labor detail on the Baltic Peninsula Darß to cut reed. These prisoners were transferred back to Neuengamme only after the end of the quarantine period. They considered their

deployment at this labor detail and, consequently, their protection during the epidemic, as divine providence.

638. Because of the small number of foreign Jehovah's Witnesses, it is not possible to make a detailed comparative analysis. It can still be concluded that there was also at least the tendency of a higher death rate even among the group of foreign Bible Students. Based on the available data (without taking into consideration the people who died during the shipwreck of the *Cap Arcona*), the death rate among the foreign Jehovah's Witnesses was 35 percent (7 out of 20). At the same time, the death rate among the (Reich) German prisoners was 17.4 percent.

639. A forty-nine-year-old IBSA member from Herne/Westphalia died on Sept. 21, 1944. Six months earlier, on Mar. 13, 1944, a fifty-eight-year-old Jehovah's Witness from Upper Silesia had been transported to the Majdanek extermination camp.

640. Based on the documents from the registry office as well as the (incomplete) death records from the camp infirmary, the following development with regard to the death rate at the Neuengamme concentration camp can be established: 430 (1940), 434 (1941), 3,140 (1942), 3,985 (1943), 5,527 (1944), 3,440 (Jan. 1–Mar. 15, 1945).

641. See Pingel, *Häftlinge*, 186.

642. A Jehovah's Witness from the Netherlands was transferred to the Drütte subsidiary camp. Only the remaining four cases involved Bible Students who belonged to the "nucleus of concentration camp prisoners" who had been admitted in 1940/41. Apparently, as a result of the 1944 Gestapo action (see this book, pt. 5, ch. 15, pp. 438–39), two of them were transferred to a subsidiary camp as punishment. Transfers that took place during the final weeks of the war due to evacuations from the camps have not been taken into consideration.

643. For instance, a report by Werner Kahn, the former executive engineer of the brickworks in Neuengamme, indicates the reasons behind such acts of protection. According to this report, a Bible Student prisoner who worked as cook at the factory kitchen but was a mineworker by occupation had been selected for an outside labor detail. Together with other specialists, he had the assignment of constructing underground facilities for the production of armaments. Kahn reports that, as soon as he heard of the plan, he went to the concentration camp commanding officer. He informed the commanding officer that he could use only prisoners who could be trusted not to commit any acts of fraud in the factory kitchen. Therefore, his present cook was the perfect person for this position. As a result of this intervention, the Bible Student was taken off the transport list. See Dec. 20, 1984, recollections by Werner H. Kahn.

644. The examples involve, without exception, labor details at which Jehovah's Witnesses were deployed. On the conditions at these labor details, see also Kaienburg, *Vernichtung durch Arbeit*, 198, 219–20.

645. Albert van de Poel, a prisoner from the Netherlands, worked at the political office of the Neuengamme concentration camp. According to his statements, the Bible Students began to have comparatively better conditions at their labor details in 1942. From that point onward, the IBSA prisoners were even given positions of trust. See Poel, *Neuengamme*, 106.

646. See this book, pt. 5, ch. 3, pp. 439–40. Pingel assumes that, during the final period of existence of the concentration camps, approximately 15 to 20 percent of all German prisoners were deployed at "relatively secure, privileged labor details" (Pingel, *Häftlinge*, 168).

647. For the following explanations, see *Jehovah's Witnesses in the Divine Purpose*, 171; Ernst Wauer, "What a Joy to Sit at Jehovah's Table!," cited in *Watchtower*, Aug. 1, 1991, 25–29; May 31, 1986, recollections by Richard Rudolph; Nov. 24, 1987, recollections by Karl Hanl; May 29, 1986, recollections by Ernst Wauer.

648. The "Luther Bible" was found during salvage work after a bomb attack. During his deployment at a labor detail involving salvage work, one Jehovah's Witness discovered the Bible in the ruins of a destroyed house. On his way back, he smuggled it into the concentration camp.

649. Kater states that, "during certain periods," the Bible Students in Neuengamme and Buchenwald "even wrote and circulated . . . journals for the camp community" (Kater, "Bibelforscher," 214). However, this can be considered as a typical example of the lack of familiarity of historians with the religious expressions of Jehovah's Witnesses. The Bible Students had not produced just any kind of journal. They produced the "testimony cards" in several languages. By means of these cards, the "Kingdom proclaimers" were also able to contact people with different languages. The Bible Students had used such cards even in their preaching activity outside of the camps, prior to their imprisonment.

650. The description is based on the May 29, 1986, recollections by Ernst Wauer; Nov. 24, 1987, recollections by Karl Hanl; FGN NHS 13-7-0-1, Gustav Auschner, report of July 8, 1969; *Yearbook* 1974, 192–93.

651. See interview with Ernst Wauer, Nov. 14, 1982, broadcast by the SDR III/Südwestfunk Baden-Baden (Programme *Schaufenster*); Nov.24, 1987, recollections by Karl Hanl; Sept. 9, 1986, recollections by Richard Rudolph.

Part 6. Conclusion

1. Leber, *Lebensbilder*, 20. Three years earlier, in his "report about the resistance movement of the German nation between 1933 and 1945," Günther Weisenborn wrote an acknowledgment about Jehovah's Witnesses. With regard to the number of victims among Jehovah's Witnesses, he states: "According to the Bible Students' estimation, a total of ten thousand of them were imprisoned between 1933 and 1945. One thousand of these were sentenced to death and

executed. Another one thousand were killed in the concentration camps or lost their lives in other ways." Weisenborn, *Aufstand*, 87.

2. See this book, pt. 1, ch. 3, pp. 63–64. The source of the figures used by Annedore Leber cannot be determined. Since she mentions "exact" figures, we can assume that she bases them on information received from the Watch Tower Society with regard to the number of Jehovah's Witnesses who were active during the period of the ban. For instance, the monthly report to the central European office in Bern mentions that 5,930 Kingdom proclaimers were active in the preaching activity in the period between May 16 and June 15, 1936. See *Yearbook* 1974, 156.

3. Zipfel, *Kirchenkampf*, 176.

4. In her 1978 study, Barbara Grizzuti Harrison tries to expose Jehovah's Witnesses and draws attention to a contradiction between the statements made in research studies and the official statements of the Watch Tower Society (see Harrison, *Visions of Glory*, 283). She points out that, according to Conway's statement (*Nazi Persecution of the Churches*, 196), which he based on Zipfel's study, "no less than a third of the whole following" lost their lives. Consequently, in consideration of the actual membership of the IBSA, "over 8,000 were killed in the camps." This, however, would be ten times the number mentioned by the Watch Tower Society.

5. See, for instance, Conway, *Nazi Persecution of the Churches*, 196; Roon, *Widerstand*, 24.

6. This number of 19,268 corresponds to the number of Jehovah's Witnesses who participated in the preaching activity during their "testimony period" between Apr. 4 and 16, 1933. However, it does not represent the total number of members in this religious denomination (see this book, p. 571, n.162).

7. Kater, "Bibelforscher," 181. Kater bases this statement on two pieces of evidence. First is a discussion he had with Franz Wohlfahrt, whose family was seriously affected by National Socialist persecution: his father and brother were both executed because of their refusal to perform military service. One of his brothers-in-law lost his life in the Sachsenhausen concentration camp. One of his uncles lost his life in the gas chambers in Auschwitz-Birkenau. Concerning the biography of Wohlfahrt, see *Frankfurter Rundschau* of Sept. 15, 1983, insert, "Dietzenbach-Rodgau," II. Probably because of this family tragedy, Kater makes the exaggerated statement: "Wohlfahrt estimates now that four to five thousand Bible Students were killed in the Third Reich. This includes the number of Bible Students who died after the liberation in 1945 in consequence of their imprisonment" (IfZ, ZS 1909, recollection records, discussion of Franz Wohlfahrt and Michael H. Kater in Toronto, Feb. 11, 1967). See also Kater's statements in his intermediate manuscript, archived in FGN, NHS 13-7-3-3. Second, Kater bases his statements on the publication *Jehovah's Witnesses in the Divine Purpose* (163), which was published in English in 1959. This source can be

used as evidence only for the number of imprisonments ("about 10,000"). It does not mention the number of deaths. Therefore, Kater's "new estimation" is basically supported only by a statement from a contemporary witness. This, however, is a very meager basis for making such far-reaching conclusions.

8. See, for instance, Aleff, "Mobilmachung," 98; M. Koch, "Die kleinen Glaubensgemeinschaften," 434. Even in *Ploetz,* a 1983 publication about the Third Reich, the indicative is used when mentioning the number—estimated by Kater—of Jehovah's Witnesses that were killed in the Third Reich ("four to five thousand lost their lives"). Correct statements are made with regard to the number of prisoners, according to which "approximately 50% of the almost 20,000 Bible Students (in 1933) . . . had been taken *into custody* in the period between 1933 and 1945" (Mehringer and Röder, "Gegner," 173). In his 1990 publication, Wolfgang Benz mentions the same number of deaths as is mentioned in *Ploetz.* Benz, however, makes the additional statement that "*a total of approximately 20,000* of the Earnest Bible Students were *in the concentration camps* because of their religious convictions. Four to five thousand of them lost their lives" (Benz, "Deutsche gegen Hitler," 188 [my emphasis]).

9. King, *Nazi State and the New Religions,* 169.

10. *Watchtower,* Oct. 1, 1984, 8.

11. On the one hand, the report in *Yearbook* 1974 is based on records of Jehovah's Witnesses who submitted accounts of the persecution they experienced to the Watch Tower Society's branch office (which was, until 1950, in Magdeburg and later in Wiesbaden) during the postwar period. On the other hand, the report is based on research studies conducted by the "department for historical research" under the leadership of Konrad Franke, the German branch leader from 1971 to 1973. The actual number of victims is most certainly much higher than the figures mentioned in this report. This is probably the case because several Jehovah's Witnesses, for various reasons, did not report to the German branch of the Watch Tower Society after 1945. Some of these people, for example, had moved to other countries. Other Bible Students who had been persecuted in the Third Reich had subsequently left the Bible Students Association. This considerably large number is not included in the statistics of *Yearbook* 1974, simply because both sides are no longer interested in any kind of association. In 1993 the Watch Tower Society published another study dealing with this subject. Based on an analysis of additional information, this comprehensive study slightly raises the number of imprisonments: Accordingly, a total of 6,262 Jehovah's Witnesses were arrested. Together, they spent a total of 14,332 years in prison. All told, 2,074 of these spent a total of 8,332 years behind the barbed-wire fences of the concentration camps. See *Jehovah's Witnesses: Proclaimers of God's Kingdom,* 720.

12. *Yearbook* 1974, 212. Prior to this publication, the Watch Tower Society stated that approximately two thousand Jehovah's Witnesses had been killed during NS rule (see *Then is Finished the Mystery of God,* 121). This figure corresponds to the number of deaths mentioned by Weisenborn and Leber.

13. Struve, "Zeugen Jehovas," 266, 286, 289, 292, presents an overview of all numbers mentioned in the literature regarding Jehovah's Witnesses who were imprisoned, sent to concentration camps, and killed in the Third Reich. A 1998 publication clearly demonstrates the consequences that result from a superficial reception of figures in this regard. In this publication, the membership numbers mentioned by Leber and Zipfel (6,034) are associated with the number of arrests (6,019) mentioned in *Yearbook* 1974. Consequently, it is stated that there was a persecution ratio of 99.75 percent (see Lechner, *KZ Oberer Kuhberg*, 89). Such conclusions do not merely reflect a thoughtless reception of certain figures. They attribute to the Gestapo and other coercive NS authorities an effectiveness that would have made their dreams come true.

14. Hellmund, "Zeugen Jehovas," no page numbers (ch. 4, 3). This statement in Hellmund's dissertation is based on a comparison between the persecution of Jehovah's Witnesses and that of the Jews: "Therefore, despite the high mortality rate in the concentration camps, the statistics mention, at the most, 'only' 2,000 deaths among Jehovah's Witnesses. And this, regarding a group that had been imprisoned since 1934!"

15. Some studies try to address the subject of "coming to terms with the past" by exaggerating the suffering. This is especially the case in studies about groups of victims of persecution whose sufferings have been denied for decades, such as those of homosexuals. In a study conducted at the University of Bremen, the authors make an assessment about this kind of approach. These authors were not seeking the approval of historians who try to "draw the curtain over events of the past." At the same time, they could not be accused of showing a lack of empathy. However, they make the truthful statement: "Without appropriate examinations, the impression is given that homosexuals were more seriously persecuted than any other group and were systematically eliminated in the concentration camps. This is, however, a misconception" (Lautmann, Grikschat, and Schmidt, "Der rosa Winkel," 327). After careful data collection, they estimated that a total of 10,000 homosexuals were imprisoned in the concentration camps. Considering the many years of refusal to accept the NS atrocities against homosexuals, it would be appropriate for the public to take into account the fate of these people as well.

16. Compensation law took these considerations into account by counting Jehovah's Witnesses among the so-called group-related victims of persecution (see introduction, p. 5).

17. *Jehovah's Witnesses: Proclaimers of God's Kingdom*, 720 (I determined the average number here).

18. Concentration camp literature includes a large number of statements, according to which "all *Jehovah's Witnesses*" had been sent to the concentration camps (see, e.g., Bettelheim, *Informed Heart*, 122 [italics in original]). Other publications mention that, among the concentration camp prisoners, there were "several tens of thousands" of members of the Bible Students Association (see Meier, *Neuengamme*, 18). However, these statements are as incorrect as the

statement in the Watch Tower Society's publications according to which there were 8,000 Bible Student prisoners "who came forth from concentration camps" (*Then is Finished the Mystery of God*, 121).

19. Statements regarding the year 1944; see Langbein, *Auschwitz*, 243; Langbein, *Against All Hope*, 179; *Jehovah's Witnesses in the Divine Purpose*, 169.

20. Statement regarding 1938; see BA, NS 4, Bu/vorl. 137, strength report of Nov. 1, 1938; Kogon, *Theory and Practice of Hell*, 41–42; Zahnwetter, *Buchenwald*, 27.

21. Statements regarding the year 1939; see Matthias Lex, "Eidesstattl. Versicherung, Der Prozeß gegen die Hauptkriegsverbrecher," vol. 31, 300, document 2928-PS; Maršálek, *Mauthausen*, 273.

22. BA, NS 4 Fl/15, July 18, 1942, list regarding the number of available beds and the number of prisoners in the concentration camps.

23. The following statements should demonstrate the difficulty of providing definite "statistical" figures regarding the number of prisoners. During the entire period of its existence, a total of 250 Jehovah's Witnesses were imprisoned in the Mauthausen concentration camp. On Sept. 29, 1939, a total of 144 Bible Students were transferred to Mauthausen from the Dachau concentration camp, which had been temporarily dissolved. During the following year, more than 60 of these transferred prisoners were killed. During the subsequent years, the number of Bible Student prisoners dropped considerably. On Dec. 1, 1943, the number of Bible Student prisoners in Mauthausen had decreased to 22. Toward the end of the war, as a result of further transfers, this number, once again, reached 1939 levels. On Mar. 31, 1945, a total of 104 Bible Students were recorded. On Mar. 31, 1945, a total of 43 Bible Students were among the female prisoners at the Mauthausen concentration camp. Statements according to Maršálek, *Mauthausen*, 273–74; Pingel, *Häftlinge*, 302n182; Milton, "Deutsche und deutsch-jüdische Frauen," 10; Ministry of the Interior, Mauthausen Memorial, letters of Feb. 22, 1985, and June 18, 1986.

24. Statement regarding the year 1941; see this book, pt. 5, ch. 15, pp. 460–61.

25. Statement regarding the year 1940; see Buber-Neumann, *Under Two Dictators*, 222; *Jehovah's Witnesses in the Divine Purpose*, 168–69. The number did not include the "300 young Russian Jonadabs [newly converted believers who were not yet baptized] who learned of the truth in the camp itself," as mentioned in the previous source.

26. Statement regarding the year 1939; see *Awake!*, Apr. 8, 1989, 14; *Todeslager Sachsenhausen*, 42.

27. Statement regarding the year 1941; see Hüser, *Wewelsburg*, 81, 91.

28. Statement regarding Majdanek, see Marszałek, *Majdanek*, 81; regarding Natzweiler and Schirmeck, *Watchtower*, Oct. 1, 1978, 20–24; Apr. 30, 1983, recollections by Egon Knöller; regarding Stutthof, *Watchtower*, Mar. 1, 1987, 21–24; regarding Rudolph H., VVN HH, Komiteeakten N 3; BA, Z Sg. 134/28, no

page numbers; regarding Vught, *Watchtower,* Aug. 15, 1980, 5–10; June 25, 1986, recollections by Johan Wildschut.

29. Because of the cooperation of Johannes Wrobel, who obtained the appropriate information from various branch offices of Jehovah's Witnesses, I am able to include the exact numbers for the various countries. Regarding the number of foreign Jehovah's Witnesses who were imprisoned in the concentration camps, see also *Yearbook* 1974, 164ff.; *Yearbook* 1976, 39; *Yearbook* 1986, 153, 170–71; *Yearbook* 1989, 133–34; *Jehovah's Witnesses in the Divine Purpose,* 169, Cole, *Jehovah's Witnesses* (German edition), 199; Maršálek, *Mauthausen,* 274.

30. The figure of 700 to 800 foreign Bible Student prisoners mentioned in the first edition of this study is probably an underestimation. However, it is certainly also incorrect to state that, "in the course of National Socialist occupation, thousands of foreign Bible Students were arrested in their homelands and transported to the concentration camps" (Kater, "Bibelforscher," 208). In this regard, Pingel makes the statement that the Bible Students, "in the various concentration camps, formed small groups of several hundred, primarily German, prisoners" (Pingel, *Häftlinge,* 262n99).

31. The records of the coercive NS authorities or those of compensation offices usually include only statements regarding people who had been imprisoned. Based on such information, calculations that mention a persecution ratio of 97 percent seem to be reasonable. In other words, if the number of defendants during court proceedings or the number of people who requested compensation is used as a basis for calculations regarding the group as a whole, it follows (just to demonstrate the obvious flaw in reasoning) that even *the* Catholic Church or *the* German Social Democratic Party, as a whole, had a considerably high degree of persecution.

32. See this book, p. 734, n.11.

33. In this regard, the following aspect should also be taken into consideration: The available reports of the coercive authorities (Gestapo, special courts, etc.), as well as the recollections of the persecuted people and, consequently, the most important sources for examinations about resistance and persecution, show a tendency to exaggerate the extent and organizational structure of IBSA underground activities. Both sides had obvious reasons for overemphasizing the actual extent of the Bible Students' resistance. On the part of the Gestapo, it was ideological prejudice and legitimation of their overblown system of institutions even after eliminating the majority of political opponents of the regime during the mid-1930s. On the part of the Watch Tower Society, it was concern for their preaching activity with the objective of drawing attention to the fact that they continued to fulfill "their assignment from Jehovah," despite the most serious persecution.

34. The Gestapo was not able to detect every instance in which Jehovah's Witnesses participated in pamphlet campaigns and other resistance activities (VVN HH, Komiteeakten K 16; June 6, 1984, recollections by Luise Polsterer).

However, the statement according to which the number of those who were "undetected" was as high as the number of those who were arrested made in the 1959 publication of the Watch Tower Society, *Jehovah's Witnesses in the Divine Purpose* (163), can certainly be considered as incorrect: "Hitler's dragnet attempts from 1933 to 1945 succeeded only in imprisoning or banishing about half the Witnesses at any one time. This meant that about 10,000 were incarcerated while thousands of others were free on the outside to maintain underground activity and an energetic, though cautious, witness work." However, while this exaggeration was motivated by special interests, other more reliable descriptions of the Watch Tower Society, such as *Yearbook* 1974, presented a more realistic picture of the extent of participation in "underground activities."

35. Ziebold et al., "Das Schicksal der Freiburger Zeugen Jehovas," appendix. The Freiburg IBSA group included eighty-two people. Two of these were killed in the concentration camps.

36. Monika Minninger estimates that the IBSA group in Bielefeld had approximately sixty to eighty adult members. She states that her estimation of two Jehovah's Witnesses being killed in Bielefeld does not confirm Kater's assessment of "deaths at the Reich level (one out of every four Bible Students)." However, she further states that her findings confirm the "degree of persecution, which, with regard to Bielefeld, could be compared only to [the persecution of] the Jews and the Communists" (Minninger, "Bielefeld," 68).

37. According to Manfred Koch, during the period prior to the ban, Mannheim had an IBSA membership of between sixty and sixty-five people. Six of these died as a result of persecution (see M. Koch, "Die kleinen Glaubensgemeinschaften," 420, 428–31).

38. Hetzer ("Augsburg," 633–34) was able to determine data regarding seventy-eight Jehovah's Witnesses from Augsburg. He mentions four deaths (three in concentration camps, one as a result of mistreatment during imprisonment).

39. Friedrich Zipfel was able to determine data regarding the persecution of almost 400 Jehovah's Witnesses. At least 21 of these died as a result of NS persecution. (As many as ten death penalties were pronounced in military courts.) Zipfel, *Kirchenkampf*, 195, and 199n59.

40. Werner (*Karlsruhe*, 183) states that forty-seven Jehovah's Witnesses from Karlsruhe were sentenced to imprisonment in penal institutions. Fourteen of these were subsequently admitted into concentration camps. Five did not survive the concentration camp imprisonment.

41. Bludau (*Gestapo-geheim!*, 224) mentions fifty-one Bible Students from Duisburg and Hamborn who were active during the period of the ban. Seven of these died in concentration camps. On June 23, 1937, one of these Bible Students supposedly committed suicide after being tortured by the Gestapo.

42. Stern, *Wir "Hoch- und Landesverräter,"* 29ff. This publication mentions six deaths from among a group of forty-one Jehovah's Witnesses, four of whom

were sentenced to death as a result of the detection of the local congregation in 1943.

43. A number of publications suggest even higher death rates. In 1987, with reference to the dissertation by Renate Lichtenegger, which was written under Weinzierl's supervision, Erika Weinzierl states: "Fifty percent of the 1,000 Bible Students who lived in Vienna prior to 1938 survived" (Weinzierl, "Österreichische Frauen," 182). This statement indicates that one out of two Vienna Bible Students did not survive the NS era. However, a closer examination of the dissertation provides a different picture. It presents a completely new "definition of victims: The number of approximately five hundred victims includes not only Jehovah's Witnesses who received death penalties or who died as a result of persecution in the concentration camps or in a penal institution. It also includes those who disassociated from the Bible Student movement because of fear of persecution after National Socialism became established in Austria, as well as those who abandoned their faith during a period of pretrial detention." Lichtenegger, "Wiens Bibelforscherinnen," 286.

44. Statements according to Maršálek, *Mauthausen*, 273–74; May 27, 1986, recollections by Hubert Mattischek; May 23, 1986, recollections by Alois Moser.

45. See *Todeslager Sachsenhausen*, 43.

46. Among other things, Lautmann determines a death rate of 35 percent from his analysis of data of 751 Bible Student prisoners in various concentration camps (see "Der rosa Winkel," 350–51). With regard to Mauthausen, the death rate is considerably higher than 50 percent, which resulted from the severe conditions in this camp (see this book, p. 657, n.19). Also the death rate in Sachsenhausen and Flossenbürg is probably above average. In other cases, the death rate corresponds to the figures determined by Lautmann, Grikschat, and Schmidt. Because of exceptionally favorable conditions (for the Bible Students) at the Niederhagen (Wewelsburg) concentration camp, the death rate is considerably lower. Of the 306 IBSA members imprisoned in Wewelsburg, a total of 19 died (6.2%; however, among the German prisoners of other prisoner categories the death rate was 39.5%). Hüser, *Wewelsburg*, 81, 85.

47. See this book, pt. 5, ch. 13, p. 324 and p. 332.

48. In addition to their religious persecution, Jehovah's Witnesses from Eastern European countries were also persecuted for racial reasons. Therefore, compared to their German and Western European fellow believers, they had to deal with even more severe circumstances. Although from 1942 on, conditions for these Jehovah's Witnesses improved, they benefited only to some degree from this improvement (additional food supplies from fellow believers who had better conditions). They were usually not withdrawn from labor details with harsh conditions.

49. The number of Bible Students who died in the women's concentration camps has been estimated as 120 (see *Verfolgung, Widerstand, Neubeginn in Freiburg*, 138).

50. See *Yearbook* 1974, 212; *Watchtower,* July 1, 1979, 8.

51. See *Yearbook* 1974, 182, 212. According to statements by the Watch Tower Society, forty-eight IBSA members from Austria were executed (see *Yearbook* 1989, 133–34).

52. With regard to the numbers of executions that were pronounced by military courts, see this book, p. 667, n.117.

53. See *Statistisches Jahrbuch Hamburg 1932/33,* 237. In the statistical yearbook for 1933, published in 1934, the Bible Students were removed from the list of Christian religious denominations.

54. See *Die Religionszugehörigkeit/Hamburg,* 156; *Die Volks-, Berufs- und Betriebszählung in Hamburg/1933,* 13 (the numbers mentioned in these publications include all surrounding districts of Hamburg).

55. The statistical records for the Prussian states do not mention the membership of the Bible Students separately. The IBSA is included in the category of other religious denominations under the section "members of other evangelical religious denominations." The respective statements, regarding Altona (1.0%) and Harburg-Wilhelmsburg (1.3%), correspond almost exactly to the percentage mentioned regarding Hamburg (1.0%). See *Die Bevölkerung des Deutschen Reiches/1933,* 36ff.

56. The information is based on the following sources: The individual records (requests for recognition as victims of National Socialism) of the "Committee of Former Political Prisoners in Hamburg;" compensation files (AfW HH), special court records (HSG, SLG HH; SH SG, LA SH), various individual documents (VGH, BDC; concentration camp memorials) and extensive questioning of contemporary witnesses.

57. The following studies about the resistance of local IBSA congregations also include a data analysis: Hetzer, "Augsburg," 634–35 (data from the records of the Munich special court regarding 78 IBSA members of Augsburg); Imberger, *Widerstand,* 246ff. (data from the records of the Kiel special court regarding 388 people who were persecuted because of their IBSA activities in Schleswig-Holstein); M. Koch, "Die kleinen Glaubensgemeinschaften," 429–30 (general data regarding a total of 70 people; about 65 of these were members of the IBSA, a few belonged to the religious denomination of Engel Jehovas, and some were Adventists); Möller, "Steinburg," 155–56, 218–20 (data from the records of the Committee of Former Political Prisoners and from the SH SG regarding twenty-six persecuted Bible Students. Möller specifically emphasizes that it is impossible, "on this small basis, to make generalizing statements," see 218n392); Struve, "Zeugen Jehovas," 271ff. (By comparing data regarding twelve Jehovah's Witnesses with the statistical results of other studies, Stuve tries to describe the social structure and persecution of Jehovah's Witnesses in the small town of Osterode. This, however, is an extremely meager basis, since the data of only one person reflected almost 10 percent of the analysis.); Zipfel, *Kirchenkampf,* 176–77 (data regarding almost 400 Jehovah's Witnesses from the compensation files of the PrV-Office of the Berlin Senate).

58. See also Hetzer, "Augsburg," 634; Imberger, *Widerstand*, 248–49; M. Koch, "Die kleinen Glaubensgemeinschaften," 434; Minninger, "Bielefeld," 68; Zipfel, *Kirchenkampf,* 178.

59. An examination of groups who participated in Austrian resistance activities produced similar results. Regarding age distribution, it can be established that Jehovah's Witnesses born in 1910 and later represent only 8.6 percent (to a certain extent, this corresponds to the number in Hamburg, 10.9%). In all other resistance groups, this age group is represented with a total of 34.1 percent. In the total population, it is represented with 31 percent; see Luza, *Austria*, 297.

60. See *Totenliste Hamburger Widerstandskämpfer,* 103.

61. The comparative numbers (52.2% men, 47.8% women) mentioned in figure 8 refer to the percentage of men and women in the Hamburg population as reflected in the national census of 1933.

62. Studies regarding other cities confirm this high percentage of women among the persecuted Jehovah's Witnesses (see, e.g., Kalous, "Bibelforscher," 37; Möller, "Steinburg," 97; Zipfel, *Kirchenkampf,* 181). Christl Wickert assumes that "one out of five persecuted Bible Students were women" (Wickert, "Frauen," 215). However, this percentage certainly has to be considered as understated.

63. *Die Volks-, Berufs- und Betriebszählung in Hamburg/1933,* 13, chart 8, "The population of the city of Hamburg and its surrounding districts, according to religious groups."

64. Ibid., 10, chart 5, "The population of the city state of Hamburg, according to age groups and family status." The statistics do not include information regarding divorced people. For a calculation of the percentages mentioned, only age groups from twenty years and up were taken into consideration.

65. In contrast to these statements, with regard to Berlin and Mannheim, Zipfel (*Kirchenkampf,* 178) and M. Koch ("Die kleinen Glaubensgemeinschaften," 434) mention an unusually high percentage of single and widowed Bible Students. Hetzer ("Augsburg," 634), Imberger (*Widerstand,* 249), Minninger ("Bielefeld," 68), and Möller ("Steinburg," 219), on the other hand, mention a high number of married people, similar to the percentages determined for Hamburg. They speak of a majority of Jehovah's Witnesses living in "secure marital relationships."

66. *Die Volks-, Berufs- und Betriebszählung in Hamburg/1933,* 32, chart 21.

67. With regard to the number of children in Bible Student families, the available data analyses provide a variety of different statements. The respective statements made in this regard do not take into consideration any comparative numbers of the total population. For example, Zipfel's study states that "a considerable number of married couples" from among the Bible Students in Berlin "were without children" (46 of the 135 married couples were without children). He further states that a "relatively high number" of married couples had only a small number of children. On this circumstantial evidence, Zipfel bases

his theory that the Bible Students were "thought to be disadvantaged in life" (Zipfel, *Kirchenkampf*, 178). Also Manfred Koch ("Die kleinen Glaubensgemeinschaften," 434) reports that more than one-third of married couples from among the Bible Students in Mannheim had no children. Minninger ("Bielefeld," 68), on the other hand, states that Bible Student families had an "almost average" number of children. Hetzer ("Augsburg," 635) mentions an average of 2.8 children. The ratio between married couples with children and "married couples without children" is approximately five to one.

68. A comparatively high number of Bible Students in Augsburg were people who had moved to the city from rural areas. This caused Gerhard Hetzer to conclude that, in comparison to the total population, "the Bible Students included an especially high number of people coming from rural areas" (Hetzer, "Augsburg," 636). According to Hetzer, this was one of the reasons, "for a number of Bible Students, that it was difficult to adapt to the structure of a big city." This, in turn, led him to the conclusion that the difficulty many Bible Students experienced integrating into the social environment was a crucial factor in their decision to join this excluded religious minority. In view of these uncharacteristic results with regard to mobility, origin, and degree of social adaptability and, consequently, with regard to integration or disintegration of Jehovah's Witnesses, Hetzer's interpretation seems inappropriate, to say the least. It is certainly not based on empirical evidence. See also Möller, "Steinburg," 219.

69. For a consideration of Zipfel's characterization of Jehovah's Witnesses as a "religion of the poor," see this book, p. 563, n.74.

70. Other analyses of data provide similar results (see Minninger, "Bielefeld," 68; Möller, "Steinburg," 218). Hetzer makes the following statement: "In the majority of cases in which previous memberships of Bible Students in political associations could be determined, these were memberships in Left-wing parties." In this regard, there was an obvious "preference for social democratic parties" (Hetzer, "Augsburg," 637–38).

71. See this book, pt. 4, ch. 10, pp. 220–21.

72. Regarding the development of historiographic resistance studies and research, see Langewiesche, "Widerstand"; Mommsen, "Geschichte des deutschen Widerstands"; Müller and Mommsen, "Der Deutsche Widerstand"; Plum, "Widerstand und Resistenz"; Steinbach, "Widerstandsforschung"; Steinbach, "Widerstand."

73. Schulz, "Entscheidungen," 89.

74. Ibid., 89.

75. Langewiesche, "Widerstand," 147.

76. Broszat, "Resistenz und Widerstand," 692.

77. Hüttenberger, "Vorüberlegungen," 130.

78. I explain this particular term, which has no real equivalent in the English language that adequately describes the scope of meaning of the term, later in this chapter, pp. 503–8, 526–28.

79. Löwenthal, "Widerstand im totalen Staat," 14. The category of "political opposition" most closely corresponded to the meaning of the former concept of resistance. But even in this regard, Löwenthal argued against a reduction of political resistance to plans for coup d'états and preparations for subversion for which there was actually no requirement if the regime did not face an acute political crisis. Therefore, according to Löwenthal, within the field of political opposition the conclusion had been reached "that the main objectives of political resistance were the preservation of a close relationship within the oppositional groups, acts of solidarity toward victims of persecution and their families, and the development of the state of political information within their inner circle by means of education and reporting, including communication with offices in other countries" (ibid., 15). Apart from people who, because of their occupation, had exposed positions of influence or had at their disposal possibilities to perform acts of conspiracy, for the majority of opponents to the regime, these actions were the most realistic forms of resistance during the "successful stages" of the NS regime. From this point of view, the activities of Jehovah's Witnesses did not substantially differ from the actions of the political opposition during the Third Reich.

80. Ibid., 19.

81. See Peukert, *Volksgenossen*, 97–98.

82. See Norden, "Teilwiderstand," 227–39.

83. Mommsen, "Geschichte des deutschen Widerstands," 16.

84. Kershaw, "Dissens," 785.

85. Broszat and Fröhlich, *Alltag*, 61.

86. Broszat, "Resistenz und Widerstand," 697.

87. See Plum, "Widerstand und Resistenz," 265.

88. Broszat and Fröhlich, *Alltag*, 61.

89. See Broszat, "Resistenz und Widerstand," 697.

90. Ibid., 73.

91. See Garbe, "Ausgrenzung," 210–11; Kershaw, "Dissens," 783; Ritscher, "Widerstandskampf," 130.

92. See Löwenthal, "Widerstand im totalen Staat," 14n1.

93. See Plum, "Widerstand und Resistenz," 264.

94. In contrast to the interim analysis of 1981, which was not completely clear in this respect, the 1987 comprehensive analysis of the Bavarian research study emphasizes that the behavior patterns of social refusal, protest, dissent, and nonconformity subsumed under the concept of *Resistenz* can be characterized as segments of acts of resistance. Therefore, *Resistenz* can be considered as "one of the major forms of resistance in the Third Reich" (see Broszat and Fröhlich, *Alltag*, 61).

95. Löwenthal, "Widerstand im totalen Staat," 14n1.

96. Rothfels, *Opposition*, 44. Despite the fact that it is still necessary to examine the question of whether their resistance could be classified as "passive

resistance," we should also consider the Quakers in this context. (See Oleschinski, "Religiöse Gemeinschaften," 198ff.; Otto, *Quäkertum*, 297–373.) However, the Mennonites can hardly be associated with resistance movements. (See Lichdi, *Mennoniten*.) Only a few Mennonites offered resistance to the regime, while their leaders and the majority of believers largely adapted to the circumstances. In 1934 the Mennonite groups abandoned their position of conscientious objection. However, even though their initial approval of National Socialism later gave way to an increasingly reserved attitude, this was not expressed publicly. See also this book, p. 584, n.131.

97. Pingel, *Häftlinge*, 89.

98. Benz, "Deutsche gegen Hitler," 188.

99. *Zeugen des Widerstandes*, 5 (in this publication, the statement is applied to all victims of NS persecution).

100. M. Koch, "Die kleinen Glaubensgemeinschaften," 434.

101. Zipfel, *Kirchenkampf*, 179–80.

102. Kater, "Bibelforscher," 182.

103. Erdmann, *Zeit der Weltkriege*, 443.

104. M. Koch, "Die kleinen Glaubensgemeinschaften," 434.

105. Ibid., 417.

106. Kater, "Bibelforscher," 182.

107. Aleff, "Mobilmachung," 98.

108. Struve, "Zeugen Jehovas," 274, 295.

109. Struve, *Aufstieg und Herrschaft*, 273. With regard to objections against characterizing Jehovah's Witnesses as belonging to the working class, see this book, p. 563, n.74.

110. Broszat, "Resistenz und Widerstand," 705.

111. Ibid., 698. Broszat includes two forms of oppositional behavior in this resistance type: First and foremost, the Communist underground activities in 1933 and 1935, which resulted in an especially high number of victims, and also the Bible Student activities, which resulted in an equally high number of victims. Both groups can be characterized by an eschatological conception of the world and a deliberate self-sacrificing, irrational fanaticism. From an effect-historical perspective, Broszat considers "the active, fundamental resistance against the National Socialist regime, in almost every case, as futile" and characterizes strategies that allow for the possibility of a large number of victims as irresponsible actions. However, he does recognize that, on an individual basis, "even though their resistance was futile, their main objective was to set an example and follow the dictates of self-respect among masses of people who gave in to conformity" (ibid., 705.)

112. *Deutschland-Berichte* 4 (1937): 707.

113. VVN HH, Komiteeakten A 11, farewell letter by Rudi Auschner to his aunt (Halle, Sept. 22, 1944).

114. Ibid., concluding sentence in the Sept. 22, 1944, farewell letter by Rudi Auschner to his mother.

115. M. Koch, "Engelhard," 98.

116. Erdmann, *Zeit der Weltkriege*, 443.

117. Kammler, *Kasseler Soldaten*, 137.

118. Halle, "'Alle Menschen sind unsere Brüder,'" 132.

119. Marßolek and Ott, *Bremen*, 304.

120. Kater, "Bibelforscher," 193.

121. *Deutschland-Berichte* 3 (1936): 922.

122. This is the title selected by Günther Weisenborn for his 1953 "report about the resistance movement of the German nation in the period between 1933 and 1945."

123. Regarding the pamphlet campaign, which the IBSA carried out in 1936/37, Imberger (*Widerstand*, 345) states that, "during the period of National Socialism, [there was] no other resistance organization that carried out a comparable mission."

124. Marßolek and Ott, *Bremen*, 308.

125. The 1937 "Regulations to Resist Sectarian Movements" of the SS Security Service (published in Neuhäusler, *Kreuz und Hakenkreuz*, 1:36ff.) mention ten points to summarize the danger of sectarian movements: "(1) teaching adherents to accept egocentric opinions and being indifferent toward issues involving state and people; (2) an infiltration of Marxist and Communist [elements]; (3) maintaining freemasonic, Jewish, and international connections; (4) refusal to take oaths and to give the Hitler salute; (5) rejection of compulsory military service; (6) refusal to accept positions in governmental organizations and the [NS] movement (DAF, air-raid protection, NSV, WHW, etc.); (7) refusal to participate in company parades and refusal to work in the armaments industry; (8) faith-healings; (9) exploitation and brainwashing people; (10) rejection of the NS race theory."

126. See Maršálek, *Mauthausen*, 273; Steinberg, *Essen*, 159. Even though the NS regime took serious actions against the propagation and practice of Jehovah's Witnesses to refuse military service, there is no direct connection between the beginning of the persecution of Jehovah's Witnesses and the introduction of compulsory military service, a connection that frequently has been suggested. See also this book, p. 618, n.10.

127. See Pingel, *Häftlinge*, 87; Steinberg, *Essen*, 159.

128. Pingel, *Häftlinge*, 87. Inge Marßolek and René Ott question that any top-level NS leaders actually believed in the "insinuations regarding supposed connections between the Bible Students and 'worldwide Judaism,'" which were disseminated for propaganda purposes and for the instruction of subordinate officials (*Bremen*, 304). According to Marßolek and Ott, the NS leadership was certainly aware of "the ultimately nonpolitical character of this religious denomination." However, in view of contrary statements on the part of prominent NS politicians (such as Freisler, Kaltenbrunner, Rosenberg, and even Hitler; Himmler, on the other hand, apparently had a "change of mind" in 1943/44; see this book, pt. 5, ch. 15, pp. 447–57), as well as an IBSA assessment in

internal Gestapo memoranda, this assumption by Marßolek and Ott cannot be supported.

129. Conway, *Nazi Persecution of the Churches,* 197.

130. Ibid. Previously, Zipfel suggested that the intensity of the persecution might also be attributed to the fact that the NS leadership was reminded of the start-up period of its party, which also began in form of a "sect," a small group of "idealists." Within a short period of time, the NS party had developed into a mass organization: "Why should the Bible Students not be able to accomplish a similar [phenomenon]?" (Zipfel, *Kirchenkampf,* 202).

131. Kater, "Bibelforscher," 187.

132. Besides the authors mentioned at other places in this chapter, the thesis of "similarities in structure" has also been discussed in the following studies: King, *Nazi State and the New Religions,* 176; M. Koch, "Engelhard," 98; M. Koch, "Die kleinen Glaubensgemeinschaften," 417; Kühl, "Friedrichstadt," 165; Minninger, "Bielefeld," 65; Rothfels, *Opposition gegen Hitler,* 53; Steinberg, *Essen,* 159.

133. Neugebauer, "'Ernste Bibelforscher,'" 161.

134. Sandvoß, *Wedding,* 76.

135. Hetzer, "Augsburg," 638.

136. Ibid., 639.

137. In this context, Hetzer referred to a supposed involvement of the Watch Tower Society in the "affairs of the Republic" during the period of the Spanish Civil War (639). Contrary to Hetzer's implication, the rejection of Spanish fascism in the Watch Tower Society's publications (see Zürcher, *Kreuzzug,* 44–49) cannot be considered as involvement in "political conflicts." Primarily, these explanations in the Watch Tower Society's publications were a response to the persecution that the Spanish Falange (a fascist party, founded in Madrid in 1933) carried on against Jehovah's Witnesses who refused to perform military service. The Falange received support from prominent circles of the Catholic Church. Moreover, the Watch Tower Society considered Spanish fascism, as well as the fascism of other European countries, as a "conspiracy" instigated by the Vatican against "true Christianity." Consequently, the response of the Watch Tower Society was a continuance of the Bible Students' polemic against the "forces of Satan," which became manifest through the clergy, big business, and politics (see Zürcher, *Kreuzzug,* 37ff.) To interpret these actions as involvement in the "affairs of the Republic," therefore, completely fails to recognize the true intentions of Jehovah's Witnesses (see also this book, p. 638, n.215.)

138. Apart from historical studies in the stricter sense, and a long time before Kater, Hetzer, and other protagonists propagated the "thesis of analogy," critics referred to the "totalitarian character" of Jehovah's Witnesses. An example is Werner Cohn according to whom the structure of the Watch Tower Society shows typical characteristics of totalitarian systems: an unquestioned dictatorship of the president of the religious denomination, executive committees

that completely submit to the leadership of their president, and subjects that are required to show unconditional obedience. For this reason, Cohn suggests structural similarities to National Socialism as well as Communism. In this regard, he indicates that the similarities involve not only organizational and membership structures but also ideologies. Supposedly, there are extensive similarities regarding the claim of possessing the monopoly of truth and the proclamation of a monocausal and dichotomous worldview, the rejection of scientific findings and the determination of reality according to ideological allegations, an exclusive application of promises to their own following and the threat of destruction for all opponents or even outsiders in general, and a reference to real social deprivations and the mobilization of salvation prospects. According to Cohn, there are even similarities in the pursuit of ultimate goals. He mentions with regard to the National Socialists the pursuit of the "Thousand-Year Reich," with regard to the Communists, "socialism," and with regard to Jehovah's Witnesses, expectations of the "New World." Without further substantial analysis of content, Cohn, who summarizes all three groups under the term "proletarian movements," derives their similarity from a comparison with the democratic and pluralistic community, i.e., the American model of society. In contrast to Cohn, William Cumberland can be considered as a more balanced critic. In his dissertation he also refers to the "totalitarian structure" of the Watch Tower Society. But he recognizes a more obvious similarity in structure: "In destroying the democracy of the ecclesias, Rutherford's organization had taken on the appearance of totalitarian and hierarchial structure not dissimilar to that of the Roman Catholic Church, which the Judge [Rutherford] so often referred to as the 'Beast of Revelation'" (Cumberland, "History of Jehovah's Witnesses," 198; see also Imberger, *Widerstand*, 253).

139. Throughout history, repeated efforts have been made to motivate the masses by means of the vision of an imminent "Thousand-Year Reign" (or chiliasm) that will bring salvation. In this regard, the study of the British medievalist Norman Cohn is of special interest. He makes reference to the millennialist elements in modern totalitarian movements (National Socialism, Soviet Communism, etc.) and tries, by way of a historical analogy, to gather information regarding their structure and origin. On the one hand, Cohn sees analogies between medieval millennialism and modern totalitarianism, especially in the correlation made between an anticipation of salvation and a desire of the disadvantaged for a change of circumstances. On the other hand, he recognizes a disturbed relationship to "normality," epidemic fear, and increasing radicalism. Regarding the results of Cohn's considerations and their limitations, see Achatz von Müller's explanations, cited in Cohn, *Pursuit of the Millennium*, 385ff.

140. For additional information, see Garbe, "'Sendboten des jüdischen Bolschewismus.'"

141. Zipfel, *Kirchenkampf*, 176.

142. Poppitz, *Staatskirchenrecht*, 14.

143. Pingel, *Häftlinge*, 88.

144. Ibid.

145. Regarding interpretations of the apocalyptic predictions of the IBSA in nationalist and NS literature of the 1920s, see this book, pt. 1, ch. 3, pp. 50–54; Garbe, "'Sendboten des jüdischen Bolschewismus,'" 149–53.

146. Cited in Hildebrandt and Hoffmann, *Streiflichter*, 40.

147. See Hetzer, "Augsburg," 639.

148. Dietrich Hellmund rightly emphasizes that the coercive authorities certainly tried to undermine the Bible Student teachings. However, their primary objective was to remove, if possible, the IBSA members from the close relationship to their religious denomination: "This was their goal! Once a Jehovah's Witness stopped being a Jehovah's Witness, the pressure from the authorities also stopped" (Hellmund, "Zeugen Jehovas," no page numbers, ch. 4, 2).

149. BHStA, Reichsstatthalter 638, BPP, interoffice decree of Jan. 31, 1936.

150. RFSS, letter to Müller and Pohl, cited in *Yearbook* 1974, 197. On the instructions by Himmler and the reasons for these instructions, see the extensive descriptions in this book, pt. 5, ch. 15, pp. 447–49.

151. See King, *Nazi State and the New Religions*, 173ff. After stating that the threats of the NS regime intimidated other minor religious denominations to the extent that they were willing to make compromises, Christine Elizabeth King makes the appropriate, though idealizing and heroic statement: "Only against the Witnesses was the government unsuccessful, for although they had killed thousands, the work went on and in May 1945 the Jehovah's Witness movement was still alive, whilst National Socialism was not. The Witnesses' numbers had increased and no compromises had been made. The movement had gained martyrs and had successfully waged one more battle in Jehovah-God's war" (193). The author's statement that the number of Jehovah's Witnesses "had increased" during NS rule can certainly be called into question. Most probably, the "successes of their preaching activity," which were even recorded in the concentration camps, could not make up for, or exceed, the considerable number of Bible Students who withdrew from the IBSA during the early period of the Third Reich or who separated themselves from the denomination. However, a different picture presents itself by looking at the period following May 1945 and by taking into consideration the medium-term and long-term results. From this perspective, King's statements are justified. The steadfastness shown by many Jehovah's Witnesses resulted in an improved reputation of their religious denomination in large parts of the population (see Algermissen, *Zeugen Jehovas*, 10). Consequently, especially during the postwar period in which people were generally more responsive toward religion, people responded more favorably to the preaching activity of Jehovah's Witnesses. During this period, there was an enormous increase in numbers. Even many people who had abandoned the denomination under the pressure of the NS

regime returned to the association. As a result, in Aug. 1947 the Watch Tower Society was able to report, with the number of 36,526 Kingdom proclaimers, a new peak of Jehovah's Witnesses in Germany. See Hutten, *Seher, Grübler, Enthusiasten*, 117.

152. Kogon, *Theory and Practice of Hell*, 43.

153. See King, *Jehovah's Witnesses under Nazism*, 191.

154. Even in the Watch Tower Society's publications, it is emphasized that Jehovah's Witnesses did not "perform any active resistance." In this regard, the appropriate statement is made: "They did not, at any period, make plans to overthrow the government or to kill Hitler" (*Jehovas Zeugen: Menschen aus der Nachbarschaft*, 16).

155. Hüttenberger, "Vorüberlegungen," 130.

156. Broszat and Fröhlich, *Alltag*, 61.

Epilogue

1. See Gebhard, *Zeugen Jehovas*, 75, 203, 158, 171; see also introduction, pp. 11–12.

2. In order to have a closer look at the denomination, the Hamburg journalist Rolf Nobel converted pro forma to Jehovah's Witnesses and stayed with them undercover for two years. He later wrote a report in the magazine *Stern* (no. 11, Mar. 1984) informing the public about his experiences. Initially, his "disclosures" caused quite an uproar. But a closer look at his chapter "Von Märtyrern und Verrätern" [About Martyrs and Traitors] (185–211) regarding Jehovah's Witnesses in the Third Reich showed that his information was nothing but a warm-up of the "facts" published fourteen years earlier by Gebhard. For example, Nobel copied from Gebhard's "documentation" the Apr. 2, 1937, records of a Gestapo interrogation of Erich Frost, the former leader of Jehovah's Witnesses on the Reich level. To his embarrassment, Nobel included in six instances Gebhard's personal comments in the interrogation records (see Nobel, 196–99; Gebhard, 175–81). Similar to Nobel, the journalist Horst Knaut "disclosed" statements that Konrad Franke (German WTG branch leader during the period of 1955 and 1969) made to the Gestapo in Sept. 1936 (the respective Gestapo protocol of Sept. 9, 1936, had already been published in Gebhard's documentation, 188–90). Knaut considered Franke's conduct to be evidence of his assumption that IBSA leaders understood how to improve their situation while ordinary members were exposed to severe persecution as a result of loyally adhering to their faith (see Knaut, *Propheten*, 128ff.). In an effort to discredit Jehovah's Witnesses, both authors tried to exploit so-called failures of certain IBSA members in positions of responsibility during the NS period in order to represent the activities of Jehovah's Witnesses today. As a result, their accounts prevented an open-minded assessment of the historical facts.

3. In recent years, this increasing openness of the Watch Tower Society

can also be observed with regard to other issues. Since May 1996, the teachings of Jehovah's Witnesses allow performance of civil service. Previously, because of its close relationship to military service, this was considered to be a violation of the Christian commandment of neutrality. For additional information, see this book, pp. 669–70, n.126.

4. See this book, p. 554, n.93.

5. *Awake!*, May 8, 1993, 4.

6. *Awake!*, Aug. 22, 1995; see also the acknowledgement of the 1995 commemoration of the fiftieth anniversary of the liberation, held throughout Europe, and its message "May we never forget," *Awake!*, June 8, 1996, 16–17.

7. *Awake!*, Aug. 22, 1995, 15.

8. *Awake!*, Apr. 22, 1996, 30.

9. See *Jehovas Zeugen: Menschen aus der Nachbarschaft. Wer sind sie?*

10. *Jehovas Zeugen: Antworten auf häufig gestellte Fragen. Informationsdienst der Zeugen Jehovas*, 3. As evidence for the increased public interest, the information service makes reference to the extensive press response toward the court decisions in favor of the denomination's claim for recognition as a corporation under public law (see epilogue, pp. 534–36).

11. See *A Witness Testimony, 1933–1945.*

12. *Purple Triangles*, produced and directed by Martin Smith, a Starlock Pictures Production for TVS, 1991.

13. Manfred Stolpe, letter of Oct. 30, 1996. The Watch Tower Society kindly provided me with a copy of this letter.

14. Statements based on the information service and the *Fürther Nachrichten* of Feb. 25, 1997.

15. Watch Tower Society (German Branch), letter of Nov. 29, 1996.

16. *Fear Not: Persecution and Resistance of Jehovah's Witnesses Under the Nazi Regime*, a ninety-two-minute film documentary by Stefanie Krug and Fritz Poppenberg, Drei Linden Film, 1997. The film was produced in German, English, and Spanish editions.

17. The following excerpt from the text on the video cassette cover indicates this intended objective: "For over fifty years, the history of Jehovah's Witnesses' unequaled resistance under the Nazi regime has been suppressed. . . . In stark contrast with the state churches, which supported Hitler's campaign of destruction, Jehovah's Witnesses were the ones to preserve the original Christian heritage."

18. Nov. 6, 1996, press statement of the information service, 3–4.

19. Ibid., 4.

20. This name was adopted after the reunification of Germany in Mar. 1990.

21. Both courts rejected the allegation that Jehovah's Witnesses had already received its legal status as a corporation under public law on Sept. 29, 1990, the date on which the Church Tax Law had become effective. The court

further stated that they had the right to "request this legal status . . . from the accused Land Berlin" (OVG Berlin, decision of Dec. 14, 1995, Az. OVG 5 B 20.94, 14).

22. For decades, with reference to the prophecy of Jesus recorded in Matt. 24:34, the Watch Tower Society proclaimed "that the end of this wicked world would come *before* that generation passed away in death." Therefore, "the years left before the foretold end comes cannot be many" (*Awake!*, Oct. 8, 1968, 13–14; see also this book, pt. 1, ch. 2, p. 36). With increasing distance from 1914, the year (according to the teachings of Jehovah's Witnesses) Jesus began ruling in the Heavens, and the unavoidable decrease in the number of people who belong to "the generation of 1914" due to old age, an adjustment became necessary. On this adjustment, see the critical discussion of Franz, *Crisis of Conscience*, 212–22; Twisselmann, *Wachtturm-Konzern*, 253–65.

23. See the change regarding this subject in the semimonthly journal *Awake!* The last reference to the generation of 1914 was made in the issue of Oct. 22, 1995 (see also the corresponding article in *Watchtower*, Nov. 1, 1995).

24. In representations involving groups of victims of persecution, Jehovah's Witnesses are no longer excluded but receive appropriate recognition. See the revised edition of the extensively distributed booklet "Deutscher Widerstand 1933–1945" (*Informationen zur politischen Bildung* 243 [1994]: 21). See also *Lexikon des deutschen Widerstandes* (s.v. "Zeugen Jehovas," 321–25), published by Wolfgang Benz and Walter H. Pehle in 1994.

25. See Friedman, *Other Victims*; Berenbaum, *Mosaic of Victims*.

26. See, for example, the exhibition catalogue *The World Must Know* by Michael Berenbaum, 51–52, 129–30; see also "The Holocaust: A Historical Summary" at www.ushmm.org/museum. Five percent of the text discusses the persecution of Jehovah's Witnesses.

27. The Watch Tower Society published the introductory slide presentation for this event. See *The Spirit and the Sword: Jehovah's Witnesses Expose the Third Reich*.

28. On Emmi Zehden, see this book, pt. 5, ch. 13, pp. 346–47.

29. See *Esslinger Zeitung*, Jan. 9/10, 1993. On the occasion of the fiftieth anniversary of the execution, by request of *Die Grünen*, the municipal council decided on this street name. On Bernhard Grimm, see this book, pp. 687–88, n.261.

30. See the reviews by Francis L. Carsten, *German Historical Institute London, Bulletin* 16, no. 4 (1994): 29–31; Klaus Drobisch, 1999: *Zeitschrift für Sozialgeschichte des 20. und 21. Jahrhunderts* 11, bk. 1 (1996): 115–17; Heinz Hürten, *Militärgeschichtliche Mitteilungen* 53 (1994); Kirsten John, *Niedersächsisches Jahrbuch für Landesgeschichte* 66 (1994): 468–70; Christine E. King, German History 13, no. 1 (1995): 143–44; and Hans Otte, *Internationale Wissenschaftliche Korrespondenz* 31, bk. 2 (1995). A critical discussion of this subject has been presented by Franz Graf-Stuhlhofer in *Materialdienst der Evangelischen Zentralstelle für Weltanschauungsfragen* 58 (1995): 31–32. Stuhlhofer's thesis that Jehovah's Witnesses, in their entirety,

fought the NS coercion still requires a critical analysis. The critical study of Richard Singelenberg is published in *Sociology of Religion*, Apr. 24, 1995. Singelenberg presents a poor evaluation of the anti-Jewish tendencies in Rutherford's agitation during the 1930s. He also underestimates the social peer pressure regarding the actions of resistance of Jehovah's Witnesses.

31. See, for instance, the extensive discussion of Thomas Rahe in *Süddeutsche Zeitung*, Apr. 5, 1994 ("Die Zeugen Jehovas im Hitler-Reich" [Jehovah's Witnesses during the Hitler Regime]). See also the annotation in *Spiegel*, Dec. 20, 1993, no. 51, 68–69, under the title "Vergessene Opfer" (Forgotten Victims).

32. Watch Tower Society (German Branch), letter of May 18, 1994.

33. Lecture of Eberhard Fabian, WTG board member, recorded in the Nov. 6, 1996, "Pressemappe zu der Pressekonferenz" in Berlin, information service of Jehovah's Witnesses.

34. See Baumgärtel, *Kirchenkampf-Legenden*.

35. Even today the requirement for obedience of the believers has changed. Jehovah's Witnesses are still requested to show absolute and unconditional loyalty toward their governing body. This includes cases in which the believers do not understand certain information or are not in agreement with their leaders. In these instances, *Watchtower* makes the suggestion: "Loyalty includes waiting patiently until further understanding is published by the faithful and discreet slave" (Watchtower, Mar. 15, 1996, 15–16).

36. On these sources, see this book, pt. 2, ch. 4, pp. 87–91.

37. Drobisch, Review of Garbe, *Zwischen Widerstand und Martyrium*, 117.

38. Even in more recent publications of the Watch Tower Society, Jehovah's Witnesses emphasize that they "never [performed] any active resistance at all."

39. On the measures of prohibition and persecution introduced against Jehovah's Witnesses in almost all European countries during the 1930s and 1940s, see this book, pt. 5, ch. 13, pp. 332–34. On measures taken against Jehovah's Witnesses in free countries, see ibid., p. 334. Even after the war ended, Jehovah's Witnesses were exposed to measures of repression in quite a number of countries. Between 1945 and the beginning of the 1990s, they were banned in twenty-three African countries, nine Asian, eight European, three Latin American, and four island nations. See *Jehovah's Witnesses: Proclaimers of God's Kingdom*, 676.

40. For additional information, see this book, pt 1, ch. 2, pp. 39–40.

41. See this book, pp. 560–61, n.54.

BIBLIOGRAPHY

Unpublished Sources

ARCHIVES

1. Amt für Wiedergutmachung, Hamburg (AfW HH)
Individualakten (Wiedergutmachungsakten, Rentenakten, ggf. Klagehefte)

2. Amtsgericht Hamburg (AG HH)
Vereinsregister ("Altregister")

3. Bayerisches Hauptstaatsarchiv, Munich (BHStA)
Bayerisches Staatsministerium des Äußeren (MA), Bayerisches Staatsministerium des Innern (MInn), Reichsstatthalter in Bayern, OMGUS, Kriegsverbrecherprozeß U.S./Weiß (KZ Dachau)

4. Bundesarchiv, Koblenz (BA)
Reichsinnenministerium (R 18), Reichsjustizministerium (R 22), Reichskanzlei (R 43), Reichssicherheitshauptamt (R 58), Volksgerichtshof und Oberreichsanwalt beim VGH (R 60), SS-Wirtschafts-Verwaltungshauptamt (NS 3), Konzentrationslager (NS 4), Persönlicher Stab des Reichsführers-SS (NS 19), Presseausschnitt-Sammlung Deutsche Glaubensbewegung (Z Sg. 107), Presseausschnitt-Sammlung Bauer (Z Sg. 124), Sammlung Bauch betr. Widerstand und Verfolgung von Angehörigen des öffentlichen Dienstes im NS-Staat (Z Sg. 134), Sammlung Schumacher zur Geschichte des Nationalsozialismus

5. Bundesarchiv—Militärarchiv, Freiburg (BA-MA)
Chef der Heeresrüstung und Befehlshaber des Ersatzheeres, Amtsgruppe Heeresrechtswesen (RH 14), Oberkommando des Heeres/Allgemeines Heeresamt (RH 15), Wehrkreiskommando VI (RH 53-6), Chef des Oberkommandos der Wehrmacht and directly subsidiary offices (RW 2), Oberkommando der Wehrmacht/Allgemeines Wehrmachtamt (RW 6), Oberste Wehrmachtgerichte (RW 11), Wehrbezirkskommandos and Wehrmeldeämter (RW 15), Druckschriften (H 25), Nachlass Max Bastian, 1939-1944 Präsident des Reichskriegsgerichts (N 192)

6. Document Center Berlin (DCB)
Karteikarten Gefängnis Berlin-Plötzensee, Karteikarten Gesundheitsamt Charlottenburg (Todesmeldungen Plötzensee), Volksgerichtshofprozeße

7. Dokumentationsarchiv des deutschen Widerstandes, Frankfurt am Main (DdW)

Dokumenten- und Erlasssammlungen, Häftlingsberichte

8. Dokumentationsarchiv des Österreichischen Widerstandes, Vienna (DÖW)

Häftlingsberichte

9. Dokumentenhaus der KZ-Gedenkstätte Neuengamme, Hamburg (DhN)

Bestände "Hamburg im Nationalsozialismus," "Das System der Konzentrationslager," "Konzentrationslager Neuengamme und Außenlager"

10. Evangelisches Zentralarchiv, Berlin (EZA)

Previous institution of EKD: Deutscher Evangelischer Kirchenausschuß, Deutsche Evangelische Kirche, Kirchenkanzlei, Sekretariat des Reichsbischofs (1/A u. 1/C), Evangelischer Oberkirchenrat der Altpreußischen Union (7/Generalia), Konsistorium Berlin-Brandenburg, files regarding. "Sektenwesen" (14/808–811)

11. Forschungsstelle für die Geschichte des Nationalsozialismus in Hamburg (FGN)

Nachlass Hans Schwarz, Generalsekretär der Amicale Internationale de Neuengamme (NHS)

12. Ernst Thälmann-Gedenkstätte, Hamburg (ETG)

Biographiensammlung

13. Gedenkstätte Breitenau, Guxhagen (GBr)

Individual files of "Landesarbeitsanstalt Breitenau"

14. Gedenkstätte Buchenwald, Weimar (NMGBu)

Prisoner reports, files of the camp commanding office of KZ Sachsenburg

15. Geheimes Staatsarchiv Preußischer Kulturbesitz, Berlin (GStAPrK)

Preußisches Ministerium des Innern (Rep. 77), Preußisches Justizministerium (Rep. 84a), Geheimes Staatspolizeiamt (Rep. 90 P)

16. Institut für Zeitgeschichte, Munich (IfZ)

Fa 119/1, Fa 119/2, Fa 183/1, Fa 506/12, MA 333, MA 414, MA 442/2, MA 554, MA 603, ZS 1909

17. Körber-Stiftung, Archiv "Schülerwettbewerb Deutsche Geschichte," Hamburg (KS AS)

Student contest "Deutsche Geschichte" regarding the prize of the Federal President 1981/82 ("Alltag im Nationalsozialismus—Vom Ende der Weimarer Republik bis zum Zweiten Weltkrieg") and 1982/83 ("Die Kriegsjahre in Deutschland, 1939 bis 1945")

18. Kreismuseum Wewelsburg (KmW)

Paul Buder, "O Wewelsburg, ich kann dich nicht vergessen," unpublished manuscript. Lipperode 1976 (KW D 87), witness literature KZ Wewelsburg, interview transcriptions

19. KZ-Gedenkstätte Dachau (KZGDa)
National Archives, Microcopy No. T-175, Roll No. 218, various documents
20. Landesarchiv Schleswig-Holstein, Schleswig (LA SH)
Land- und Sondergericht Altona (Abteilung 352 Altona)
21. Mahn- und Gedenkstätte Ravensbrück (MGRa)
Prisoner reports
22. Museum Auschwitz, Oświęcim (MAu)
Various documents
23. Staatsanwaltschaft bei dem Landgericht Hamburg (SLG HH)
Hanseatisches Sondergericht
24. Staatsarchiv Hamburg (StA HH)
Amtsgericht Hamburg, Gefängnisverwaltung II, Hanseatisches Oberlandes-
gericht Hamburg, Jugendbehörde I, Justizverwaltung I, Polizeibehörde II,
Senatskanzlei—Präsidialabteilung, Senatskanzlei—Verwaltungsbeschwerden
25. Staatsarchiv Munich (StA M)
Sondergericht Munich (Staatsanwaltschaften 8551)
26. United States Holocaust Memorial Museum—Archives (USHMM)
Survivor Testimonies (RG-02), Jehovah's Witnesses (RG-32)
**27. Vereinigung der Verfolgten des Naziregimes /
Bund der Antifaschisten, Landesverband Hamburg (VVN HH)**
Komiteeakten: Unterlagen des "Komitees ehemaliger politischer Gefangener
in Hamburg"

PRIVATE DOCUMENTS

Braßel, Frank. Jehovah's Witnesses, Herne group, report of Jan. 22, 1946.
Fahle, Günter. Records about the fate of two IBSA members from Nesse
(Landkreis Oldenburg) who refused military service.
Kaiser, Gerhard. Copies from "Briefe. Nachrichten für die Zeugen Jehovas und
ihre Gefährten" from the Ravensbrück concentration camp circulating in
the underground.
Knöller, Bruno. Compensation proceedings, letters, and documents.
Kraushaar, Erich. Documents about the persecution of Dorothea and Erich
Golly, IBSA Hamburg.
Lasarcyk, Helmut. Documents about the history of Jehovah's Witnesses in
Germany.
Möller, Reimer. Documents about the history of the Bible Students in the dis-
trict of Steinburg.
Pape, Günther. Documents about the persecution of his family; Bible Student
publication and memoranda from the early 1940s.
Pohl, Willi K. Various documents about the reception of the persecution his-
tory of Jehovah's Witnesses in the DDR.
Renner, M. Documents about the persecution of her parents Paula and Josef
Himmen, IBSA group Hamburg-Finkenwerder.

Schwarberg, Günther. Diary of Ernst Schneider (Apr. 20 to May 20, 1945) about the evacuation of the Neuengamme concentration camp and the sinking of the *Cap Arcona.*

Schwarz, Rolf. Documents about the fate of the Bible Students in the district of Rendsburg; copies of *Watchtower* articles from the 1930s circulating in the underground.

Seidewitz, Margot. Documents from the persecution of her parents, Alfred and Emilie Knegendorf.

Singelenberg, Richard. Documents about IBSA organizer Ludwig Cyranek.

Straßer, Josef Ernst. "Sammlung zur historischen Dokumentation, Jehovas Zeugen/Bereich Süddeutschland" (reports, correspondence, documents, also from the StA Ludwigsburg and local sources).

Todt, Walter. Compensation proceedings; documents about his father-in-law, the main group servant of the Hamburg IBSA, Max Grote.

Wildschut, Johan. Memorandum about the exodus of Jehovah's Witnesses from the Sachsenhausen concentration camp.

Wrobel, Johannes. Reports and documents about the persecution of Jehovah's Witnesses, in particular with regard to the position of the WTG in 1933.

Zehender, Rolf. Compensation proceedings; documents from the Reich Military Court proceedings against his father, Ernst Wilhelm Zehender; documents about Guardianship Court proceedings (custody withdrawal); records of Gerhard Oltmanns (conscientious objection of Jehovah's Witnesses).

RECOLLECTIONS

Information on recollections that are not available in the archives are listed according to the following pattern: kind of report/date of compilation (interviews: date of discussion), name of interviewer, in cases in which the discussion was not performed by the author. The following abbreviations are used to identify the kind of recollections: Gp = discussion protocol; K = correspondence; sB = written report; mA = verbal statements; Ti = tape-recorded interview.

Rolf Appel (K/Feb. 10, 1985; mA/May 17, 1988), Herbert Baade (Gp/Jan. 26, 1986), Helmuth Brembach (K/Apr. 8, 1986), Fritz Bringmann (K/Feb. 7, 1986; mA/Feb. 14, 1986), Lauritz G. Damgaard (sB/Sept. 23, 1986), Harry Dubinsky (mA/Apr. 15, 1986), Marco Max Feingold (mA/Nov. 1, 1987), Manfred Gebhard (K/May 29, 1994), Max von der Grün (mA/Dec. 3, 1986), Karl Hanl (Gp/June 17, 1987/interview by H. Kaienburg; Gp/Nov. 24, 1987), Werner H. Kahn (Gp/Dec. 20, 1984/interview by H. Kaienburg), Hellmut Kalbitzer (K/Mar. 26, 1986), Friedrich Klingenberg (Gp/May 16, 1992/interview by H. Scholz), Addi Klohe (K/1995; K/Mar. 12, 1997), Alfred Knegendorf/Margot Seidewitz (mA/Jan. 29, 1985; mA/Feb. 7, 1985; K/April 3, 1986), Bruno Knöller (sB/May 6, 1981; Ti/Dec. 30, 1982/interview by N. Weiss; K/Feb. 28, 1985; K/Feb. 3, 1987; Gp/Nov. 23, 1987), Egon Knöller (Ti/Apr. 30, 1983/interview by

N. Weiss), Dr. Werner Koch (mA/Dec. 14/15, 1985), Elise Kühnle (Gp/Nov. 23, 1987), Erich Kulka (Gp/Aug. 12, 1988/interview by L. Eiber), Willi Lehmbecker (sB/Apr. 15, 1971; Gp/Feb. 7, 1987; K/Oct. 15, 1987), Klaus Maase (K/Jan. 3, 1986), Hubert Mattischek (sB/May 27, 1986), Alois Moser (sB/May 23, 1986), Günther Pape (mA/May 19, 1986), Jan Pupek (Gp/July 1984/interview by H. Kaienburg), Gertrud Rast (mA/Feb. 23, 1986), Hermann Reineck (K/Feb. 27, 1986), Richard Rudolph (sB/Feb. 18, 1986; Gp/May 30/31, 1986; Gp/Sept. 9, 1986), Ella S. (mA/Jan. 29, 1985; Gp/Feb. 14, 1986), Willi Seidel (K/Jan. 3, 1985), Willi Seitz (K/Feb. 26, 1995), Frantisek Setina (Gp/Dec. 9, 1984/interview by H. Kaienburg), Otto Spehr (Ti/Aug. 17, 1982/interview by L. Eiber; mA/Sep. 27, 1986), Charlotte Tetzner (sB/July 5, 1986; sB/Aug. 18, 1986; Gp/Sep. 21, 1986; K/Oct. 3, 1986), Friedel Thron (K/April 14, 1986), Hans-Jürgen Twisselmann (mA/Jan. 20, 1987), Frantisek Vala (Gp/Oct. 21, 1985/interview by L. Eiber/recorded by H. Kaienburg), Günther Wackernagel (Gp/Sept. 1, 1985/interview by H. Kaienburg), Ernst Wauer (K/May 19, 1986; Gp May 29, 1986; K/Dec. 31, 1986), Johan Wildschut (sB/June 25, 1986), Karl-Heinz Zietlow (Gp/Jan. 25, 1986; sB/July 11, 1986)

"Sammlung zur historischen Dokumentation, Jehovas Zeugen / Bereich Süddeutschland" (personal documents of J. E. Straßer):
Emma Ammann (sB/June 1984), Liesel Baroni (sB/June 8, 1984), Josef Barta (sB/June 5, 1984), Franz Birk (sB/Jan. 31, 1971), Hanna Bläse (sB/June 1984), Hedwig Ehmann (sB/May 3, 1984), Ferdinand Frey (sB/June 15, 1984), Willi Groß (sB/June 8, 1984), Maria Herdtfelder (sB/June 3, 1984), Julie Kanderer (sB/June 1984), Martha Klenk (sB/June 3, 1984), Minna Knöller (sB/June 8, 1984), Elfriede Kühne (sB/June 7, 1984), Heinrich Markert (sB/June 5, 1984), Paul Marszałek (sB/June 1984), B. Maurer (sB/June 6, 1984), Wilhelm Molsich (sB/June 1984), Helene Parsiegla (sB/June 7, 1984), Luise Polsterer (sB/June 6, 1984), Johannes Rauthe (sB/"Geschichtsbericht," beginning of the 1970s), Erwin Rinker (sB/June 1984), Charlotte Rottner (sB/June 3, 1984), Helene Schiemann (sB/June 4, 1984), Paul Scholz (sB/June 6, 1984), Gertrud Semmler (sB/June 2, 1984), Alfred Skoda (sB/June 24, 1984), Betty Sontopski (sB/May 31, 1984), Friedrich Speidel (sB/June 9, 1984), Walter Spengler (sB/June 1984), Emma Stange (sB/June 3, 1984), Herr Thieme (sB/n.d.), Gustav Widmaier (sB/June 1984), Otto Wulle (sB/June 7, 1984), Eva Zimmermann (sB/June 8, 1984)

Periodicals

Archiv für Polizeirecht. Beilage zur Zeitschrift "Die Polizei." Berlin.
Brücke zum Menschen. Ein Bruderdienst an Sektenopfern, Suchenden und Angefochtenen, sowie allen, die ihnen helfen möchten. Itzehoe.
Bundesgesetzblatt. Bonn.
Das Evangelische Deutschland. Kirchliche Rundschau für das Gesamtgebiet des Deutschen Evangelischen Kirchenbundes. Berlin.

Der Gerichtssaal. Zeitschrift für Zivil- und Militär-Strafrecht und Strafprozeß-recht. H. Dietz, A. Schoetensack, and J. Nagler. Stuttgart.

Der Hoheitsträger. Dienstliches Informationsorgan. Reichsorganisationsleiter der NSDAP, Reichsleiter Dr. Robert Ley; Schriftleitung: Reichsamtsleiter F. H. Woweries, Amt für Schulungsbriefe im Hauptschulungsamt. Berlin.

Der Spiegel. Hamburg.

Deutsche Juristenzeitung. Otto Liebmann. Berlin.

Deutsche Justiz. Rechtspflege und Rechtspolitik. Amtliches Blatt der deutschen Rechtspflege. Franz Gürtner, Reichsminister der Justiz. Berlin.

Deutsche Rechtswissenschaft. Vierteljahresschrift der Akademie für Deutsches Recht. Published by Abteilung für Rechtsforschung der Akademie für Deutsches Recht. Hamburg.

Deutsche Richterzeitung. Zeitschrift der Reichsfachgruppe Richter und Staatsan-wälte des Bundes Nationalsozialistischer Deutscher Juristen. Berlin.

Deutsche Verwaltung. Organ der Verwaltungsrechtswahrer des Nationalsozialis-tischen Rechtswahrerbundes. Berlin.

Deutsche Verwaltungsblätter. Berlin.

Deutsches Kriminalpolizeiblatt. Preußisches Landeskriminalpolizeiamt. Berlin.

Deutsches Pfarrarchiv. Zeitschrift für die Rechtspraxis der Deutschen Evange-lischen Kirche und der Preußischen Landeskirchen. Kurt von Rohrscheidt. Berlin.

Deutsches Recht. Hans Frank. Berlin.

Deutsches Strafrecht. Strafrechtswissenschaftliches Ergänzungsblatt der "Deut-schen Justiz." Staatssekretär Dr. Roland Freisler. Berlin.

Entscheidungen des Ehrengerichtshofs der Reichs-Rechtsanwalts-Kammer. Berlin. Edited by the board of the Reichs-Rechtsanwalts-Kammer. (See also p. 000, n.248.)

Entscheidungen der Gerichte und Verwaltungsbehörden aus dem Rechtsgebiete der inneren Ver-waltung. Established by Anton Reger. Rudolf Oeschen. Berlin.

Entscheidungen des Reichskriegsgerichts. Vol. 1, 1938/40; vol. 2, 1, 1940; vol. 2, 2, 1942; vol. 2, 3, 1943. Edited by members of the Reichskriegsgericht.

Entscheidungen des Reichsgerichts in Strafsachen. 77 vols. Edited by members of the Gerichtshof and the Reichsanwaltschaft. (See also p. 000, n.283.)

Entscheidungen des Reichsgerichts in Zivilsachen. 172 vols. Edited by members of the Gerichtshof and the Reichsanwaltschaft.

Evangelium im Dritten Reich. Kirchenzeitung für Christentum und Nationalsozia-lismus. Berlin.

Hanseatische Rechts- und Gerichts-Zeitschrift. Supervised by Oberlandesgerichtsrat Prof. Dr. A. Bertram et al. Berlin/Hamburg.

Höchstrichterliche Rechtsprechung. Ergänzungsblatt zur "Deutschen Justiz" und zur "Amtlichen Sammlung der Reichsgerichtsentscheidungen." Eugen Fried-richs, Hans Gündel, and Eberhard Staud. Berlin.

Juristische Wochenschrift. Organ der Reichsfachgruppe Rechtsanwälte des Bundes Nationalsozialistischer Deutscher Juristen. Leipzig/Berlin.

Kirchliches Jahrbuch für die evangelischen Landeskirchen Deutschlands. Ein Hilfsbuch zur Kirchenkunde der Gegenwart. Johannes Schneider; continued by Hermann Sasse. Gütersloh.

Materialdienst. Evangelischen Presseverband für Württemberg; Schriftleitung: Dr. Kurt Hutten. Stuttgart.

Ministerialblatt des Reichs- und Preußischen Ministeriums des Innern. Reichsministerium des Innern. Berlin.

Ministerialblatt für die Preußische innere Verwaltung. Preußischen Ministerium des Innern. Berlin.

Monatsschrift für Kriminalbiologie und Strafrechtsreform. Organ der Kriminalbiologischen Gesellschaft. Munich/Berlin.

Neue Pfälzische Landeszeitung. Ludwigshafen.

Preußische Gesetzessammlung. Berlin.

Rechtsprechung zum Wiedergutmachungsrecht, als monatliche Beilage herausgegeben durch die *Neue Juristische Wochenschrift.* Munich/Berlin.

Reichsgesetzblatt. Berlin.

Reichsverwaltungsblatt. Hans-Heinrich Lammers (Staatssekretär und Chef der Reichskanzlei). Berlin.

Sächsisches Verwaltungsblatt. Dresden.

Statistisches Jahrbuch für die Freie und Hansestadt Hamburg. Hamburg.

Süddeutsche Zeitung. Munich.

Völkischer Beobachter (various regional issues).

Wort und Tat. Zeitschrift für volksmissionarische Arbeit. Central-Außchuss für Innere Mission. Berlin.

Zeitschrift der Akademie für Deutsches Recht. Reichsminister Dr. Hans Frank, Präsident der Akademie für Deutsches Recht. Berlin.

Zeitschrift für Beamten- und Behördenangestelltenrecht nebst der gesamten höchstrichterlichen Rechtsprechung. Carl Heyland. Berlin.

Zeitschrift für die gesamte Strafrechtswissenschaft. Wilhelm Gallas, Wenzeslaus Graf Gleispach, Eduard Kohlrausch, and Friedrich Schaffstein. Berlin.

Zeitschrift für Wehrrecht. Akademie für Deutsches Recht und geleitet von Heinrich Dietz. Berlin.

Zentralblatt für Jugendrecht und Jugendwohlfahrt. Hermann Althaus, Fritz Ruppert, Dr. Georg Usadel, and Dr. Ralf Zeitler. Berlin.

Publications of the Watch Tower Bible and Tract Society/ Wachtturm Bibel- und Traktat-Gesellschaft

Awake! Brooklyn (published since Aug. 1946 as successor of *Golden Age* and *Consolation*).

Byington, Steven. *The Bible in Living English*. Brooklyn, 1972.

Frieden und Sicherheit: Wie wirklich zu finden? Brooklyn, 1986.

Gesänge zum Preise Jehovas. Magdeburg, 1928.

The Golden Age: A Journal Based on Fact, Hope, and Conviction. Brooklyn, 1922/23 (*Das Goldene Zeitalter;* first issue in English, 1919).

Jahrbuch der Zeugen Jehovas (Yearbook of Jehovah's Witnesses). Brooklyn/ Magdeburg: Internationale Bibelforscher-Vereinigung, 1933; Brooklyn: Wachtturm Bibel- und Traktat-Gesellschaft, Volkskanzel-Vereinigung, International Bible Students Association, 1933; Bern: Wachtturm Bibel- und Traktat-Gesellschaft, Volkskanzel-Vereinigung, Internationale Bibelforscher-Vereinigung, 1934–; Wiesbaden: Wachtturm Bibel- und Traktat-Gesellschaft, 1948–; Selters (Taunus): Wachtturm Bibel- und Traktat-Gesellschaft, 1984–.

Jehovah's Witnesses in the Divine Purpose. Brooklyn, 1959.

Jehovah's Witnesses: Proclaimers of God's Kingdom. Brooklyn, 1993.

Jehovah's Witnesses: Unitedly Doing God's Will Worldwide. Brooklyn, 1986.

Jehovas Zeugen: Antworten auf häufig gestellte Fragen; Informationsdienst der Zeugen Jehovas. Selters/Taunus, 1996.

Jehovas Zeugen: Menschen aus der Nachbarschaft. Wer sind sie? Selters/Taunus, 1995.

Knorr, Nathan H. *Be Glad, Ye Nations!* Brooklyn, 1946.

"Let God Be True." Brooklyn, 1946.

New World Translation of the Bible. Rev. ed. Brooklyn, 1984.

Russell, Charles Taze. *The New Creation*. Vol. 6 of *Studies in the Scriptures*. Brooklyn, 1904. (German issue: *Die Neue Schöpfung*. Magdeburg, 1926.)

Rutherford, Joseph Franklin. *Deliverance*. Brooklyn, 1926.

———. *Comfort for the Jews*. Brooklyn, 1925.

———. *Enemies: The Proof That Definitely Identifies All Enemies, Exposes Their Methods of Operation, and Points Out the Way of Complete Protection for Those Who Love Righteousness*. Brooklyn, 1937.

———. *Face the Facts*. Brooklyn, 1938.

———. *Fascism or Freedom*. Brooklyn, 1939.

———. *Freedom for the Peoples*. Brooklyn, 1927.

———. *Government: The Indisputable Evidence Showing That the Peoples on Earth Shall Have a Righteous Government and Explaining the Manner of Its Establishment*. Brooklyn, 1928.

———. *Millions Now Living Will Never Die*. Brooklyn, 1920.

———. *The Peoples Friend*. Brooklyn, 1928.

School and Jehovah's Witnesses. Brooklyn, 1983.

The Spirit and the Sword: Jehovah's Witnesses Expose the Third Reich. Watch Tower Bible and Tract Society of Pennsylvania, 1995. (Text and photos of the Sept. 29, 1994, slide presentation at the U.S. Holocaust Memorial Museum by James N. Pellechia, the editor of *Awake!*)

Then Is Finished the Mystery of God. Brooklyn, 1969.

The Truth Shall Make You Free. Brooklyn, 1943.

Watchtower. See *Zion's Watch Tower and Herald of Christ's Presence.*

Zion's Watch Tower and Herald of Christ's Presence. Brooklyn, 1935 (from Apr. 15, 1957, as *The Watchtower Announcing Jehovah's Kingdom;* all variations are referred to in this book as *Watchtower;* in Germany the equivalent publication is referred to in this book as *Der Wachtturm*).

Printed Sources and Literature References

Absolon, Rudolf. *Wehrgesetz und Wehrdienst, 1935–1945: Das Personalwesen in der Wehrmacht.* Boppard am Rhein, 1960.

——. *Das Wehrmachtstrafrecht im 2. Weltkrieg.* Collection of the basic laws, orders, and decrees. Kornelimünster, 1958.

Akten Deutscher Bischöfe über die Lage der Kirche, 1933–1945. Vol. 1, *1933–1934.* Edited by Bernhard Stasiewski. Mainz, 1968.

Akten Kardinal Michael von Faulhabers 1917–1945. Vol. 1, *1917–1934.* Edited by Ludwig Volk. Mainz, 1975.

Aleff, Eberhard. "Mobilmachung." In *Das Dritte Reich,* edited by Eberhard Aleff. Hannover, 1970.

Algermissen, Konrad. "Bibelforscher." In *Lexikon für Theologie und Kirche,* edited by Michael Buchberger, cols. 279–80. First published as *Kirchliches Handlexikons.* Freiburg im Breisgau, 1931.

——. *Christliche Sekten und Kirche Christi.* 2nd and 3rd rev. ed. Hannover, 1925.

——. *Die Internationale Vereinigung Ernster Bibelforscher.* Hannover, 1928.

——. *Konfessionskunde.* Hannover, 1930.

——. *Konfessionskunde.* 8th ed., revised by Heinrich Fries. Paderborn, 1969.

——. *Die Zeugen Jehovas.* Celle, 1949.

Angermund, Ralph. *Deutsche Richterschaft 1919–1945.* Frankfurt am Main, 1990.

Anon. "'Verblendete' Volksgenossen und 'harmlose' Menschen." *Der Hoheitsträger* 8 (Aug. 1938): 12–16.

Anschütz, Gerhard. *Die Verfassung des Deutschen Reichs vom 11. August 1919.* 14th ed. Berlin, 1933.

Arbeit und Vernichtung: Das Konzentrationslager Neuengamme, 1938–1945. Katalog zur ständigen Ausstellung im Dokumentenhaus der KZ-Gedenkstätte Neuengamme. Edited by Ulrich Bauche, Heinz Brüdigam, Ludwig Eiber, and Wolfgang Wiedey. 2nd ed. Hamburg, 1991.

Arndt, Ino. "Das Frauenkonzentrationslager Ravensbrück." In *Studien zur Geschichte der Konzentrationslager,* edited by Martin Broszat, 93–129. Stuttgart, 1970.

Asmussen, Nils. *Der kurze Traum von der Gerechtigkeit: "Wiedergutmachung" und NS-Verfolgte in Hamburg nach 1945.* Hamburg, 1987.

Auerbach, Hellmuth. "Konzentrationslagerhäftlinge im Fronteinsatz." In *Miscellanea: Festschrift für Helmut Krausnick zum 75. Geburtstag*, edited by Wolfgang Benz, with Ino Arndt et al., 63–83. Munich, 1980.

Ausländer, Fietje. "Vom Wehrmacht- zum Moorsoldaten: Militärstrafgefangene in den Emslandlagern 1939 bis 1945." In *Bremsklötze am Siegeswagen der Nation: Erinnerungen eines Deserteurs an Militärgefängnisse, Zuchthäuser und Moorlager in den Jahren 1941–1945*, edited by Hans Frese, with additional comments by Fietje Ausländer and Norbert Haase, 165–93. Bremen, 1989.

Ayass, Wolfgang, Reimar Gilsenbach, Ursula Körber et al. *Feindererklärung und Prävention: Kriminalbiologie, Zigeunerforschung und Asozialenpolitik*. Vol. 6. Berlin, 1988.

Ballmann, Hans. *Im KZ: Ein Tatsachenbericht aus dem Konzentrationslager*. Backnang, 1945.

Bartel, Walter, and Klaus Trostorff, eds. *Buchenwald: Mahnung und Verpflichtung. Dokumente und Berichte*. Berlin, 1983.

Bästlein, Klaus. "Die Akten des ehemaligen Sondergerichts Kiel als zeitgeschichtliche Quelle." *Zeitschrift für Schleswig-Holsteinische Geschichte* 113 (1988): 157–211.

———. "'Hitlers Niederlage ist nicht unsere Niederlage, sondern unser Sieg!' Die Bästlein-Organisation. Zum Widerstand aus der Arbeiterbewegung in Hamburg und Nordwestdeutschland während des Krieges (1939–1945)." In *Vom Zweifeln und Weitermachen: Fragmente der Hamburger KPD-Geschichte*, edited by Beate Meyer and Joachim Szodrzynski, 44–89. Hamburg, 1988.

———. "Zum Erkenntniswert von Justizakten aus der NS-Zeit. Erfahrungen in der konkreten Forschung." In *Datenschutz und Forschungsfreiheit. Die Archivgesetzgebung des Bundes auf dem Prüfstand*, edited and with an introduction by Jürgen Weber, 85–102. Munich, 1986.

Bauernfeind, Otto. *Eid und Frieden: Fragen zur Anwendung und zum Wesen des Eides*. Stuttgart, 1956.

Baumgärtel, Friedrich. *Wider die Kirchenkampf-Legenden*. Neuendettelsau, 1958.

Beckford, James A. *The Trumpet of Prophecy: A Sociological Study of Jehovah's Witnesses*. Oxford, 1975.

Bembenek, Lothar. "Außenkommando Lebensbornheim Taunus Wiesbaden." In *Hessen hinter Stacheldraht: Verdrängt und vergessen, KZs, Lager, Außenkommandos*, edited by Lothar Bembenek and Frank Schwalba-Hoth, 77–82. Frankfurt am Main, 1984.

Bembenek, Lothar, and Axel Ulrich. *Widerstand und Verfolgung in Wiesbaden 1933–1945: Eine Dokumentation*. Gießen, 1990.

Benz, Wolfgang. "Deutsche gegen Hitler: Widerstand, Verweigerung, Kampf gegen die nationalsozialistische Herrschaft." In his *Herrschaft und Gesellschaft im nationalsozialistischen Staat: Studien zur Struktur- und Mentalitätsgeschichte*, 180–96. Frankfurt am Main, 1990.

Benz, Wolfgang, and Barbara Distel, eds. *Frauen-Verfolgung und Widerstand*. Dachau, 1987.

Benze, Rudolf. *Erziehung im Großdeutschen Reich: Eine Überschau über ihre Ziele, Wege und Einrichtungen.* 3rd ed. Frankfurt am Main, 1943.

Berenbaum, Michael. *A Mosaic of Victims: Non-Jews Persecuted and Murdered by the Nazis.* New York, 1990.

———. *The World Must Know: The History of the Holocaust as Told in the United States Holocaust Memorial Museum.* Boston, 1993.

Bergman, Jerry. *Jehovah's Witnesses and Kindred Groups: A Historical Compendium and Bibliography.* New York, 1984.

Besgen, Achim. *Der stille Befehl: Medizinalrat Kersten, Himmler und das Dritte Reich.* Munich, 1960.

Besier, Gerhard, and Stephan Wolf. *"Pfarrer, Christen und Katholiken": Das Ministerium für Staatssicherheit der ehemaligen DDR und die Kirchen.* 2nd ed. Neukirchen-Vluyn, 1992.

Bettelheim, Bruno. *The Informed Heart: Autonomy in a Mass Age.* Glencoe, IL, 1960.

———. "Die psychische Korruption durch den Totalitarismus." In his *Erziehung zum Überleben: Zur Psychologie der Extremsituation,* 331–47. Stuttgart, 1980.

Die Bevölkerung des Deutschen Reichs nach den Ergebnissen der Volkszählung 1925. Statistik des Deutschen Reichs, vol. 401. Berlin, 1930.

Die Bevölkerung des Deutschen Reichs nach den Ergebnissen der Volkszählung 1933. Book 3: *Die Bevölkerung des Deutschen Reichs nach der Religionszugehörigkeit.* Statistik des Deutschen Reichs, vol. 451. Revised by the Statistischen Reichsamt. Berlin, 1936.

Beweisdokumente für die Spruchgerichte in der Britischen Zone. Hamburg, 1947.

Die Bibel: Altes und Neues Testament. Einheitsübersetzung [standard version]. Stuttgart, 1980.

Die Bibel: Die Heilige Schrift des Alten und Neuen Bundes. 17th German edition with explanations of the Jerusalem Bible. Freiburg, 1968.

Billstein, Aurel. *Der eine fällt, die anderen rücken nach . . . : Dokumente des Widerstandes und der Verfolgung in Krefeld 1933–1945.* Frankfurt am Main, 1973.

Blessin, Georg. *Bundesentschädigungsgesetze: Kommentar.* 3rd rev. ed. by Hans-Georg Ehrig and Hans Wilden. Munich, 1960.

Block, Just. "Die Ausschaltung und Beschränkung der deutschen ordentlichen Militärgerichtsbarkeit während des Zweiten Weltkrieges." Jur. diss., Würzburg, 1967.

Bludau, Kuno. *Gestapo-geheim!: Widerstand und Verfolgung in Duisburg, 1933–1945.* Bonn, 1973.

Boberach, Heinz. *Berichte des SD und der Gestapo über Kirchen und Kirchenvolk in Deutschland 1933–1944.* Mainz, 1971.

———, ed. "Das Schriftgut der staatlichen Verwaltung, der Wehrmacht und der NSDAP aus der Zeit von 1933–1945." *Der Archivar, Mitteilungsblatt für deutsches Archivwesen* 22 (1969): cols. 137–52.

Bosch, Manfred. *Als die Freiheit unterging: Eine Dokumentation über Verweigerung, Widerstand und Verfolgung im Dritten Reich in Südbaden.* Konstanz, 1985.

Botz, Gerhard. "Überleben im Holocaust." In *Ich will reden: Tragik und Banalität des Überlebens in Theresienstadt und Auschwitz,* by Margareta Glas-Larsson, 9–74. Vienna, 1981.

Botz, Gerhard, and Josef Weidenholzer. *Mündliche Geschichte und Arbeiterbewegung: Eine Einführung in Arbeitsweisen und Themenbereiche der Geschichte "geschichtsloser" Sozial-gruppen.* Vienna, 1984.

Bracher, Karl Dietrich. "Stufen der Machtergreifung." In *Die nationalsozialistische Machtergreifung: Studien zur Errichtung des totalitären Herrschaftssystems in Deutschland 1933/34,* by Von Karl Dietrich Bracher, Wolfgang Sauer, and Gerhard Schulz, 31–368. Cologne, 1960.

Braeunlich, Paul. *Die Ernsten Bibelforscher als Opfer bolschewistischer Religionsspötter.* 2nd ed. Leipzig, 1926.

Brandstätter, H. "Erfahrungen im Strafvollzug an Gefangenen, die wegen Verstosses gegen das Verbot der Internationalen Bibelforscher bestraft worden sind." *Blätter für Gefängniskunde* 70 (1939): 48–55.

Brebeck, Wulff E. "Wie Wewelsburg zu einer Gedenkstätte kam." In *Die vergessenen KZs?: Gedenkstätten für die Opfer des NS-Terrors in der Bundesrepublik,* by Detlef Garbe, 153–76. Bornheim-Merten, 1983.

Bredemeier, Karsten. *Kriegsdienstverweigerung im Dritten Reich: Ausgewählte Beispiele.* Baden-Baden, 1991.

Breyvogel, Wilfried, and Thomas Lohmann. "Schulalltag im Nationalsozialismus." In *Die Reihen fast geschlossen: Beiträge zur Geschichte des Alltags im Nationalsozialismus,* edited by Detlev Peukert and Jürgen Reulecke, 199–221. Wuppertal, 1981.

Bringmann, Fritz. *KZ Neuengamme: Berichte, Erinnerungen, Dokumente.* Frankfurt am Main, 1981.

Broszat, Martin. *Anatomy of the SS State.* London, 1968.

———. "Resistenz und Widerstand: Eine Zwischenbilanz des Forschungsprojekts." In *Bayern in der NS-Zeit,* vol. 4, *Herrschaft und Gesellschaft im Konflikt,* edited by Martin Broszat et al., 691–709. Munich, 1981.

———. "Zur Perversion der Strafjustiz im Dritten Reich." *Vierteljahrshefte für Zeitgeschichte* 6 (1958): 390–419.

Broszat, Martin, and Elke Fröhlich. *Alltag und Widerstand: Bayern im Nationalsozialismus.* Munich, 1987.

Brüning, Heinrich. *Memoiren 1918–1934.* Stuttgart, 1970.

Brunotte, Heinz. *Bekenntnis und Kirchenverfassung: Aufsätze zur kirchlichen Zeitgeschichte.* Göttingen, 1977.

Buber-Neumann, Margarete. *Als Gefangene bei Stalin und Hitler.* Munich, 1949.

———. *Milena.* New York, 1988.

———. *Under Two Dictators.* Translated by Edward Fitzgerald. London, 1950.

Buchheim, Hans. *Glaubenskrise im Dritten Reich: Drei Kapitel nationalsozialistischer Religionspolitik.* Stuttgart, 1953.

————. "Verbot religiöser Sekten im Dritten Reich." In *Gutachten des Instituts für Zeitgeschichte*, 45–49. Munich, 1958.

Burczek (Landgerichtsdirektor). "Staatsbürgerpflichten bei der Bekämpfung von Staatsfeinden." *Juristische Wochenschrift* 66 (1937): 2377–80.

Burkhardt, Hans, Günter Erxleben, and Kurt Nettball. *Die mit dem blauen Schein: Über den antifaschistischen Widerstand in den 999er Formationen der faschistischen deutschen Wehrmacht (1942 bis 1945)*. 2nd ed. Berlin, 1986.

Burmeister, Andreas, Torsten Karschulin, Dörtlis Schultze, Cerstin Spinger, and Sabine Triebwasser. "Verfolgung der Zeugen Jehovas in Kiel und Umgebung (1933–1945)." Kiel, n.d. [1983]. (Results and suggestions from the student competition "German History" for a reward by the Federal president, 1982–83, archives of the Körber-Stiftung NS II/0584.)

Burski, Ulrich von. "Die Zeugen Jehovas: Die Gewissensfreiheit und das Strafrecht." Jur. diss., Freiburg im Breisgau, 1970.

Busch, Johannes. *Das Sektenwesen unter besonderer Berücksichtigung der Ernsten Bibelforscher: Entstehung, Ausbreitung und Hauptirrtümer, sowie Widerlegung und Abwehr der modernen Sektiererei*. Hildesheim, 1929.

Buszko, Jósef, Danuta Czech, Tadeusz Iwaszko et al. *Auschwitz. Geschichte und Wirklichkeit des Vernichtungslagers*. Reprint, Reinbek bei Hamburg, 1980.

Büttner, Ursula, and Werner Jochmann. *Hamburg auf dem Weg ins Dritte Reich: Entwicklungsjahre 1931–1933*. Hamburg, 1983.

Chêne, Evelyn Le. *Mauthausen: The History of a Death Camp*. London, 1971.

Christen, Kuno. *Kirche und Sekten*. Interlaken, 1937.

Christoffel, Udo, ed. *Berlin Wilmersdorf: Die Jahre 1920 bis 1945*. Berlin, 1985.

Cohn, Norman. *The Pursuit of the Millennium: Revolutionary Millenarians and Mystical Anarchists of the Middle Ages*. London, 1993.

Cohn, Werner. "Jehovah's Witnesses as a Proletarian Movement." *American Scholar* 24, no. 3 (1955): 281–98.

Cole, Marley. *Jehovah's Witnesses: The New World Society*. New York, 1955.

Conway, John S. *The Nazi Persecution of the Churches, 1933–45: Their Goals, Contradictions and Failures*. New York, 1968.

Crohne, Wilhelm. "Die Strafrechtspflege 1936." *Deutsche Justiz* 99 (1937): 7–12.

————. "Die Verbote der Internationalen Bibelforschervereinigung sind rechtsgültig." *Deutsche Justiz* 97 (1935): 1144ff.

Cumberland, William. "A History of Jehovah's Witnesses." PhD diss., University of Iowa, 1958.

Czech, Danuta. *Auschwitz Chronicle, 1939–1945*. New York, 1990.

Dade, Peter. "Fahneneid und feierliches Gelöbnis: Zur militärischen Verpflichtungsform in der deutschen Wehrgeschichte, insbesondere zur geltenden Regelung für die Soldaten der Bundeswehr." Jur. diss., Kiel, 1970.

Debus, Karl Heinz. "Kirchen und Religionsgesellschaften in Speyer seit 1918." In *Geschichte der Stadt Speyer*, edited by Wolfgang Eger, 465–523. 2nd ed. Stuttgart, 1983.

Denzler, Georg, and Volker Fabricius. *Die Kirchen im Dritten Reich: Christen und Nazis Hand in Hand?* Vol. 2, *Dokumente*. Frankfurt am Main, 1984.

Deutsch, Martin. *Die Sekte der Ernsten Bibelforscher im Lichte der Vernunft und der Heiligen Schrift.* Heidelberg, 1925.

Deutsche Frauenschicksale. Edited by Union für Recht und Freiheit. London, 1937.

Deutsches Strafrecht. Vol. 1, *Erläuterungen zu den seit dem 1.9.1939 ergangenen strafrechtlichen und strafverfahrensrechtlichen Vorschriften,* compiled by Fritz Grau, Karl Krug and Otto Rietzsch. Berlin, 1943.

Deutschland-Berichte der Sozialdemokratischen Partei Deutschlands (Sopade) 1934–1940. 6 vols. 1934. Reprint, Salzhausen, 1980.

Diamant, Adolf. *Gestapo Frankfurt am Main: Zur Geschichte einer verbrecherischen Organisation in den Jahren 1933–1945.* Frankfurt am Main, 1988.

Dibelius, Otto. *Friede auf Erden.* Berlin, 1930.

Dietz, Heinrich. "Zum Begriff der Wehrunwürdigkeit: Ausländer in der deutschen Wehrmacht." *Zeitschrift für Wehrrecht* 1 (1936/37): 167–77.

Dirksen, Hans-Hermann. "Jehovah's Witnesses in the German Democratic Republic." In *Persecution and Resistance of Jehovah's Witnesses During the Nazi Regime, 1933–1945,* edited by Hans Hesse, 210–28. Bremen, 2001.

Distel, Barbara. "Im Schatten der Helden: Kampf und Überleben von Centa Beimler-Herker und Lina Haag." In Benz and Distel, *Frauen-Verfolgung und Widerstand,* 21–57.

Dokumente zur Gleichschaltung des Landes Hamburg 1933. Edited by Henning Timpke. Frankfurt am Main, 1964.

Dörken, Georg, and Werner Scherer, eds. *Das Militärstrafgesetzbuch und die Kriegssonderstrafrechtsverordnung.* 4th ed. Berlin, 1943.

Doyon, Josy. *Hirten ohne Erbarmen.* Stuttgart, 1966.

———. *Ich war eine Zeugin Jehovas: Bericht über einen Irrweg.* Hamburg, 1971.

Drobisch, Klaus. "Frauenkonzentrationslager im Schloß Lichtenburg." In Benz and Distel, *Frauen-Verfolgung und Widerstand,* 101–15.

———. "Frauen-KZ Lichtenburg." Referat [Presentation]. Berlin, 1993.

———. *Konzentrationslager im Schloß Lichtenburg.* Cottbus, 1987.

———. Review of Garbe, *Zwischen Widerstand und Martyrium. 1999: Zeitschrift für Sozialgeschichte des 20. und 21. Jahrhunderts* 11, bk. 1 (1996): 115–17.

Duisburg im Nationalsozialismus. Eine Dokumentation zur Ausstellung des Stadtarchivs Duisburg. Edited by J. Milz, H. Raschkewitz, K. Ebbers, and H. G. Kraume. Duisburg, 1983.

Durand, Pierre. *Die Bestie von Buchenwald.* Berlin, 1985.

Echterhölter, Rudolf. *Das öffentliche Recht im nationalsozialistischen Staat.* Stuttgart, 1970.

Eckart, Dietrich. *Der Bolschewismus von Moses bis Lenin: Zwiegespräch zwischen Adolf Hitler und mir.* Munich, 1924.

Eggenberger, Oswald. *Die Kirchen, Sondergruppen und religiösen Vereinigungen. Ein Handbuch.* 3rd ed. Zurich, 1983.

Ehrenbuch der Opfer von Berlin-Plötzensee. Edited by Willy Perk and Willi Desch. Berlin, 1974.

"Ehrenbuch für die im Zuchthaus Brandenburg-Görden ermordeten Antifaschisten." 7 vols. Edited by Rudolf Zimmermann on behalf of the Arbeitsausschuß der ehemaligen politischen Gefangenen des faschistischen Zuchthauses Brandenburg-Görden. Printed manuscript, 1986.

Eiber, Ludwig. "Arbeitssklaven für SS und Kriegswirtschaft: Häftlingsarbeit im KZ Neuengamme 1940–1945." In *Arbeiter in Hamburg,* edited by Arno Herzig, Dieter Langewiesche, and Arnold Sywottek, 559–68. Hamburg, 1983.

Einer muß überleben: Gespräche mit Auschwitzhäftlingen 40 Jahre danach. Edited by Jörn-Erik Gutheil et al. Düsseldorf, 1984.

Elling, Hanna. *Frauen im deutschen Widerstand, 1933–45.* 3rd ed. Frankfurt am Main, 1981.

Das Ende einer Legende: Die Wachtturm-Gesellschaft und das "Dritte Reich." Vom Anpassungskurs zur Konfrontation. Special edition of *Brücke zum Menschen,* no. 122 (2nd quarter 1995).

Engelland, Hans. *Die Zeugen Jehovas: Die Neuapostolischen.* 2nd ed. Hamburg, 1969.

Erdmann, Karl Dietrich. *Die Zeit der Weltkriege.* 9th rev. ed. Stuttgart, 1976.

Ermittlungshilfe und Straffälligenbetreuung: Kameradschaftsarbeit von Mitgliedern der Reichsjustizverwaltung und des Hauptamtes für Volkswohlfahrt (Reichsleitung NSDAP). Edited by Roland Freisler. Berlin, 1937.

Ernst, Christoph, and Ulrike Jensen. *Als letztes starb die Hoffnung: Berichte von Überlebenden aus dem KZ Neuengamme.* Hamburg, 1989.

Es gab nicht nur den 20. Juli–: Dokumente aus einer Sendereihe im Westdeutschen Fernsehen. Edited by Michael Schmid-Ospach. Wuppertal, 1980.

Fahle, Günter. *Verweigern, Weglaufen, Zersetzen: Deutsche Militärjustiz und ungehorsame Soldaten 1939–1945.* Bremen, 1990.

Fauck, S. "Konnten Angehörige von Sekten den Fahneneid verweigern?" In *Gutachten des Instituts für Zeitgeschichte,* 2:472–73. Stuttgart, 1966.

Fetz, August. *Der grosse Volks- und Weltbetrug durch die "Ernsten Bibelforscher!"* 4th ed. Hamburg, 1924.

———. *Weltvernichtung durch Bibelforscher und Juden.* Munich, 1925.

Fiebig, Paul. *Die Bibelauslegung der "Internationalen Vereinigung Ernster Bibelforscher."* 2nd ed. Berlin-Dahlem, 1925.

Fleischhauer, Ulrich. *Die echten Protokolle der Weisen von Zion: Sachverständigengutachten, erstattet im Auftrage des Richteramtes V in Bern.* Erfurt, 1935.

Fleschutz, Hans. *Und folget ihrem Glauben nach!: Gedenkbuch für die Blutzeugen der Siebenten-Tags-Adventisten Reformationsbewegung. Zeugnisse der Treue und Standhaftigkeit aus Deutschlands dunklen Tagen.* Reprint, Jagsthausen, 1985.

Flessau, Kurt Ingo. *Schule der Diktatur: Lehrpläne und Schulbücher des Nationalsozialismus.* Frankfurt am Main, 1979.

Foitzik, Jan. *Zwischen den Fronten: Zur Politik, Organisation und Funktion linker politischer Kleinorganisationen im Widerstand 1933 bis 1939/40 unter besonderer Berücksichtigung des Exils.* Bonn, 1986.

Foreign Relations of the United States: Diplomatic Papers, 1933. Vol. 2, *The British Commonwealth, Europe, Near East, and Africa.* Washington, D.C., 1949.

Fraenkel, Ernst. *The Dual State: A Contribution to the Theory of Dictatorship.* New York, 1969.

Franz, Raymond. *Crisis of Conscience: The Struggle between Loyalty to God and Loyalty to One's Religion.* Atlanta, 1983.

Frauen-KZ Ravensbrück. Prepared by the Komitee der Antifaschistischen Widerstandskämpfer der Deutschen Demokratischen Republik and edited by Guste Zörner. 1973. Reprint, Berlin/Frankfurt am Main, 1982.

Die Frauen von Ravensbrück. Prepared by the Komitee der Antifaschistischen Widerstandskämpfer in der Deutschen Demokratischen Republik and edited by Erika Buchmann. Berlin, 1960.

Frege, Ludwig. "Der Status des Preußischen Oberverwaltungsgerichtes und die Standhaftigkeit seiner Rechtsprechung auf politischem Gebiet." In *Staatsbürger und Staatsgewalt: Verwaltungsrecht und Verwaltungsgerichtsbarkeit in Geschichte und Gegenwart,* edited by Helmut R. Külz and Richard Naumann, 131–55. Anniversary publication. Karlsruhe, 1963.

Freisler, Roland. "Vom Schutzzweck der Strafrechtspflege gegenüber Volksschädlingen." *Deutsche Justiz* 100 (1938): 365–67.

Frese, Hans. *Bremsklötze am Siegeswagen der Nation: Erinnerungen eines Deserteurs an Militärgefängnisse, Zuchthäuser und Moorlager in den Jahren 1941–1945.* Edited with additional information by Fietje Ausländer and Norbert Haase. Bremen, 1989.

Freund, Julius. *O Buchenwald!* Klagenfurt, n.d. [1945].

Friedman, Filip, and Tadeusz Holuj. *Oświęcim.* Warsaw, 1946.

Friedman, Ina R. *Other Victims: First-Person Stories of Non-Jews Persecuted by the Nazis.* Boston, 1990.

Friedman, Philip. *Das andere Deutschland: Die Kirchen.* Berlin, 1960.

Fritsch, Theodor. *Handbuch der Judenfrage: Die wichtigsten Tatsachen zur Beurteilung des jüdischen Volkes.* Leipzig, 1933.

———. *Handbuch der Judenfrage: Die wichtigsten Tatsachen zur Beurteilung des jüdischen Volkes.* 49th ed. Leipzig, 1943.

Fröhlich, Elke. *Die Herausforderung des Einzelnen: Geschichten über Widerstand und Verfolgung.* Vol. 6, *Bayern in der NS-Zeit,* edited by Martin Broszat. Munich, 1983.

Füllberg-Stolberg, Claus. "'Bedrängt, aber nicht völlig eingeengt—verfolgt, aber nicht verlassen': Gertrud Pötzinger, Zeugin Jehovas." In *Frauen in Konzentrationslagern: Bergen-Belsen, Ravensbrück,* edited by Claus Füllberg-Stolberg et al., 321–32. Bremen, 1994.

———, ed. *Für immer ehrlos: Aus der Praxis des Volksgerichtshofes.* 3rd ed. Berlin, 1981.

Gamm, Hans-Jochen. *Führung und Verführung: Pädagogik des Nationalsozialismus.* Frankfurt am Main, 1984.

Garbe, Detlef. "Ausgrenzung und Verfolgung im Nationalsozialismus." In *Norddeutschland im Nationalsozialismus*, edited by Frank Bajohr, 186–217. Hamburg, 1993.

———. "'Du sollst nicht töten'. Kriegsdienstverweigerer 1939–1945." In *Die anderen Soldaten: Wehrkraftzersetzung, Gehorsamsverweigerung und Fahnenflucht im Zweiten Weltkrieg*, edited by Norbert Haase and Gerhard Paul, 85–104. Frankfurt am Main, 1995.

———. "'Gott mehr gehorchen als den Menschen'. Neuzeitliche Christenverfolgung im nationalsozialistischen Hamburg." In *Verachtet, Verfolgt, Vernichtet: Zu den vergessenen Opfern des NS-Regimes*, 2nd ed., edited by Klaus Frahm, 172–219. Hamburg, 1988.

———. "Im Namen des Volkes?!: Die rechtlichen Grundlagen der Militärjustiz im NS-Staat und ihre 'Bewältigung' nach 1945." In *Verräter oder Vorbilder?: Deserteure und ungehorsame Soldaten im Nationalsozialismus*, edited by Fietje Ausländer, 90–129. Bremen, 1990.

———. *In jedem Einzelfall—bis zur Todesstrafe: Der Militärstrafrechtler Erich Schwinge. Ein deutsches Juristenleben.* Hamburg, 1989.

———. "Kompromißlose Bekennerinnen: Selbstbehauptung und Verweigerung von Bibelforscherinnen." In *Frauen gegen die Diktatur: Widerstand und Verfolgung im nationalsozialistischen Deutschland*, edited by Christl Wickert, 52–73. Berlin, 1995.

———. "The Purple Triangle—Die 'Bibelforscher' (Jehovah's Witnesses in the Concentration Camps." In *Dachau and the Nazi Terror 1933–1945*, edited by Wolfgang Benz and Barbara Distel, 87–114. Dachau, 2002.

———. "'Sendboten des jüdischen Bolschewismus'. Antisemitismus als Motiv nationalsozialistischer Verfolgung der Zeugen Jehovas." In *Nationalsozialismus aus heutiger Perspektive*, edited by Dan Diner and Frank Stern, 145–71. Gerlingen, 1994.

———. "Die 'vergessenen' Opfer." *Verachtet, Verfolgt, Vernichtet: Zu den vergessenen Opfern des NS-Regimes*, 2nd ed., edited by Klaus Frahm, 5–13. Hamburg, 1988.

Garbe, Detlef, and Sabine Homann. "Jüdische Gefangene in Hamburger Konzentrationslagern." In *Die Juden in Hamburg 1590 bis 1990: Wissenschaftliche Beiträge der Universität Hamburg zur Ausstellung "Vierhundert Jahre Juden in Hamburg,"* edited by Arno Herzig, 545–59. Hamburg, 1991.

Gasper, Hans, Joachim Müller, and Friedericke Valentin, eds. *Lexikon der Sekten, Sondergruppen und Weltanschauungen: Fakten, Hintergründe, Klärungen.* Freiburg im Breisgau, 1990.

Gaupp, R. "Die gerichtsärztliche Beurteilung der militärischen Dienstverweigerung aus religiösen Gründen." *Münchener Medizinische Wochenschrift, Organ für amtliche und praktische Ärzte* 64 (1917): 950–51.

Gebhard, Manfred, ed. *Die Zeugen Jehovas: Eine Dokumentation über die Wachtturm-gesellschaft.* Leipzig, 1970. Reprint, Schwerte (Ruhr), 1971.

Gedenkbuch "Kola-Fu": Für die Opfer aus dem Konzentrationslager, Gestapogefängnis und KZ-Außenlager Fuhlsbüttel. Edited by Herbert Diercks. Hamburg, 1987.

Geigenmüller, Otto. *Die politische Schutzhaft im nationalsozialistischen Deutschland.* Würzburg, 1937.

Georg, Enno. *Die wirtschaftlichen Unternehmungen der SS.* Stuttgart, 1963.

Gerecke, Karl. *Deutschkritischer Gottesgeist: Abraham der Fluch der Kirche und der Völker.* Leipzig, 1931.

———. *Die Gotteslästerungen der "Ernsten 'Bibel'-Forscher."* Leipzig, 1931.

Gerhardt, Martin. *Ein Jahrhundert Innere Mission: Die Geschichte des Central-Ausschußes für die Innere Mission der Deutschen Evangelischen Kirche.* Vol. 2, *Hüter und Mehrer des Erbes.* Gütersloh, 1948.

Geschonneck, Erwin. *Meine unruhigen Jahre.* Berlin, 1984.

Gestapo Hannover meldet—: Polizei- und Regierungspräsidentenberichte für das mittlere und südliche Niedersachsen zwischen 1933 und 1937. Rev. ed. with introduction by Klaus Mlynek. Hildesheim, 1986.

Glienke, Franz, ed. "Curio-Haus-Prozeß: Protokoll des in der Zeit vom 18. März bis 3. Mai 1946 vor dem britischen Militärgericht abgehandelten Prozeßes gegen die 14 Hauptverantwortlichen des Konzentrationslagers Neuengamme." Unauthorized copy. Hamburg, 1969.

Gostner, Erwin. *1000 Tage im KZ: Ein Erlebnisbericht aus den Konzentrationslagern Dachau, Mauthausen und Gusen.* Mannheim, 1946.

Gotthilf, P. B. *Die grösste Geheimmacht der Welt: Die Ursache aller Kriege sowie aller nationalen und internationalen Zerwürfnisse. Ein Jahrhunderte alter Betrug aufgedeckt.* Leipzig, 1924.

Gollwitzer, Helmut, Käthe Kuhn, and Reinhold Schneider, eds. *Du hast mich heimgesucht bei Nacht: Abschiedsbriefe und Aufzeichnungen des Widerstandes 1933–1945.* Munich, 1954.

Gotto, Klaus, Hans Günter Hockerts, and Konrad Repgen. "Nationalsozialistische Herausforderung und kirchliche Antwort: Eine Bilanz." In *Kirche, Katholiken und Nationalsozialismus,* edited by Klaus Gotto and Konrad Repgen, 101–18. Mainz, 1980.

Götz, Karl. *Das Schwarzmeerdeutschtum.* Posen, 1944.

Graf, Christoph. *Politische Polizei zwischen Demokratie und Diktatur: Die Entwicklung der preußischen Politischen Polizei vom Staatsschutzorgan der Weimarer Republik zum Geheimen Staatspolizeiamt des Dritten Reiches.* Berlin, 1983.

Graffard, Sylvie, and Léo Tristan. *Les Bibelforscher et le nazisme, 1933–1945: Ces oubliés de l'Histoire.* 2nd ed. Paris, 1991.

Graf-Stuhlhofer. Review of Garbe, *Zwischen Widerstand und Martyrium.* *Material-dienst der Evangelischen Zentralstelle für Weltanschauungsfragen* 58 (1995): 31–32.

Grüber, Heinrich. *Erinnerungen aus sieben Jahrzehnten.* Cologne, 1968.

Gruchmann, Lothar. *Justiz im Dritten Reich 1933–1940: Anpassung und Unterwerfung in der Ära Gürtner.* Munich, 1988.

Gründler, Johannes. *Lexikon der christlichen Kirchen und Sekten unter Berücksichtigung der Missionsgesellschaften und zwischenkirchlichen Organisationen.* Vienna, 1961.

Grünewald, Guido. *Geschichte der Kriegsdienstverweigerung: Ein Beitrag zur Friedenspolitik? Mit einer kommentierten Dokumentation Deutsche Kriegsdienstverweigerer 1650 bis 1945.* Essen, 1979.

Günzl, Maria. "Freiheit, wann wirst du auferstehen . . ." In *Frauen leisten Widerstand, 1933–1945: Lebensgeschichten nach Interviews und Dokumenten,* edited by Gerda Szepansky, 250–75. Frankfurt am Main, 1983.

Guse, Martin, and Andreas Kohrs. "Die 'Bewahrung' Jugendlicher im NS-Staat: Ausgrenzung und Internierung am Beispiel der Jugendkonzentrationslager Moringen und Uckermark." Manuscript (thesis), Fachhochschule Hildesheim, 1985.

———. "Zur Entpädagogisierung der Jugendfürsorge in den Jahren 1922 bis 1945." In Otto and Sünker, *Soziale Arbeit und Faschismus,* 228–49.

Guse, Martin, Andreas Kohrs, and Friedhelm Vahsen. "Das Jugendschutzlager Moringen — Ein Jugendkonzentrationslager: Der Bewahrungsgedanke im Übergang von Weimar zur NS-Zeit." In Otto and Sünker, *Soziale Arbeit und Faschismus,* 321–44.

Haack, Friedrich-Wilhelm. *Jehovas Zeugen.* 6th ed. Munich, 1977.

Haag, Lina. *Eine Handvoll Staub.* Halle, 1948.

Haase, Norbert. "Aus der Praxis des Reichskriegsgerichts: Neue Dokumente zur Militärgerichtsbarkeit im Zweiten Weltkrieg." *Vierteljahrshefte für Zeitgeschichte* 39 (1991): 379–411.

———. *Deutsche Deserteure.* Berlin, 1987.

———. "' . . . dem Gebot der Stunde Rechnung tragen': Torgau und das Reichskriegsgericht (1943–1945)." In *Das Torgau-Tabu: Wehrmachtstrafsystem, NKWD-Speziallager, DDR-Strafvollzug,* edited by Bernward Dörner, 45–60. Leipzig, 1993.

———. *Das Reichskriegsgericht und der Widerstand gegen die nationalsozialistische Herrschaft: Katalog zur Sonderausstellung der Gedenkstätte Deutscher Widerstand in Zusammenarbeit mit der Neuen Richtervereinigung.* Berlin, 1993.

Hackett, David A. *Der Buchenwald-Report: Bericht über das Konzentrationslager Buchenwald bei Weimar.* Munich, 1996.

Hahnenfeld, Günter. *Kriegsdienstverweigerung.* Hamburg, 1966.

Halle, Anna Sabine. "'Alle Menschen sind unsere Brüder. . . . ': Nahezu unbekannter religiöser Widerstand im 'Dritten Reich.'" In *Widerstand und Exil, 1933–1945,* edited by Otto R. Romberg et al., 127–33. Bonn, 1985.

———. "*Die Gedanken sind frei* — ": Eine Jugendgruppe der Berliner Quäker, 1935–1941. 2nd ed. Berlin, 1982.

Hammer, Walter. *Brandenburg: Das deutsche Sing-Sing.* Hamburg, n.d. [1952].

Handbuch religiöse Gemeinschaften: Freikirchen, Sondergemeinschaften, Sekten, Weltanschauungsgemeinschaften. 2nd ed. Gütersloh, 1979.

Hannover, Heinrich. "Ist die Bestrafung der Ersatzdienstverweigerung der Zeugen Jehovas mit dem Grundrecht der Glaubens- und Gewissensfreiheit vereinbar?" *Goltdammer's Archiv für Strafrecht* (1964): 33–46.

Hannover, Heinrich, and Elisabeth Hannover-Drück. *Politische Justiz, 1918–1933.* 1966. Reprint, Bornheim-Merten, 1987.

Harrison, Barbara Grizzuti. *Visions of Glory: A History and a Memory of Jehovah's Witnesses.* New York, 1978.

Hartmann, Albrecht. "Kriegsdienstverweigerung im Dritten Reich." Master's thesis, Universität Stuttgart, 1982.

Hartmann, Albrecht, and Heidi Hartmann. *Kriegsdienstverweigerung im Dritten Reich.* Frankfurt am Main, 1986.

Hasenclever, Christa. *Jugendhilfe und Jugendgesetzgebung seit 1900.* Göttingen, 1978.

Heckel, Johannes. *Wehrverfassung und Wehrrecht des Großdeutschen Reiches.* Pt. 1, *Gestalt und Recht der Wehrmacht: Der Waffendienst.* Hamburg, 1939.

Hecker, Hellmuth. *Die Kriegsdienstverweigerung im deutschen und ausländischen Recht.* Frankfurt am Main, 1954.

Heiber, Helmut, ed. *Reichsführer!* Letters to and from Heinrich Himmler. Stuttgart, 1968.

Heimatgeschichtlicher Wegweiser zu Stätten des Widerstandes und der Verfolgung 1933–1945. Vol. 2, *Niedersachsen I. Regierungsbezirke Braunschweig und Lüneburg,* edited by Ursula Krause-Schmitt et al. Cologne, 1985.

Heimbucher, Max. *Was sind denn die "Ernsten Bibelforscher" für Leute?: Zugleich eine Aufklärung über das "tausendjährige Reich" Christi.* Regensburg, 1923.

Heinz, Daniel. "Kriegsdienstverweigerer und religiöser Pazifist: Der Fall Anton Brugger und die Haltung der Siebententags-Adventisten im Dritten Reich." In *Jahrbuch 1996,* edited by Siegwald Ganglmair, 41–56. Vienna, 1996.

Hellmund, Dietrich. "Geschichte der Zeugen Jehovas in der Zeit von 1870 bis 1920. Mit einem An hang: Geschichte der Zeugen Jehovas in Deutschland bis 1970." Theol. diss., Hamburg, 1972.

Helmreich, Ernst Christian. *The German Churches under Hitler: Background, Struggle and Epilogue.* Detroit, 1979.

Hennicke, Otto. "Auszüge aus der Wehrmachtkriminalstatistik." *Zeitschrift für Militärgeschichte* 5 (1966): 438–56.

———. "Über den Justizterror in der deutschen Wehrmacht am Ende des zweiten Welt krieges." *Zeitschrift für Militärgeschichte* 4 (1965): 715–20.

Hepp, Michael. "Denn ihrer ward die Hölle. Kinder und Jugendliche im 'Polenverwahrlager Litzmannstadt.'" *Mitteilungen der Dokumentationsstelle zur NS-Sozialpolitik* 2, no. 11/12 (1986): 49–71.

———. "Vorhof zur Hölle. Mädchen im 'Jugendschutzlager' Uckermark." In *Opfer und Täterinnen: Frauenbiographien des Nationalsozialismus,* edited by Angelika Ebbinghaus, 191–216. Nördlingen, 1987.

Herbermann, Nanda. *Der gesegnete Abgrund: Schutzhäftling Nr. 6582 im Frauenkon-zentrationslager Ravensbrück.* Nürnberg, 1946.

Herr, Rudi. "Die Bibelforscher in Strafhaft." *Monatsblätter für Straffälligenbetreuung und Ermittlungshilfe* 15, no. 11/12 (1940): 87–88.

Herrmann, Friedrich Wilhelm. *Bibelforscher oder Bibelfälscher.* Kassel, 1925.

Herrmann, Ulrich, ed. *"Die Formung des Volksgenossen": Der "Erziehungsstaat" des Dritten Reiches.* Weinheim, 1985.

Hetkamp, Elise. "Du sollst nicht töten." In Stern, *Wir "Hoch- und Landesverräter,"* 186–91.

Hetzer, Gerhard. "Ernste Bibelforscher in Augsburg." In *Bayern in der NS-Zeit,* vol. 4, *Herrschaft und Gesellschaft im Konflikt,* edited by Martin Broszat et al., 621–43. Munich, 1981.

Heuzeroth, Günter, and Sylvia Wille. "Die unter dem lila Winkel litten: Die Verweigerung der Zeugen Jehovas und ihre Verfolgung." In *Verfolgte aus religiösen Gründen,* edited by Franz-Josef Ensel, 3:167–210 (see under "der Gewaltherrschaft des Nationalsozialismus 1933–1945"). Oldenburg, 1985.

Heydrich, Lina. *Leben mit einem Kriegsverbrecher.* Pfaffenhofen, 1976.

Heyne. "Ist § 5 KSSVO ein militärisches oder ein allgemeines Strafgesetz?" *Zeitschrift für Wehrrecht* 6 (1941/42): 258–60.

Hildebrandt, Reinhard, and Werner Hoffmann. *Streiflichter aus Verfolgung und Widerstand 1933–45.* Vol. 5. Ludwigsburg, 1993.

Hillermeier, Heinz, ed. *"Im Namen des Deutschen Volkes!": Todesurteile des Volksgerichtshofes.* Darmstadt-Neuwied, 1982.

Hirsch, Martin, Diemut Majer, and Jürgen Meinck, eds. *Recht, Verwaltung und Justiz im Nationalsozialismus: Ausgewählte Schriften, Gesetze und Gerichtsentscheidungen von 1933 bis 1945.* Cologne, 1984.

Hitler, Adolf. *Mein Kampf.* Vol. 2, *Die nationalsozialistische Bewegung.* Munich, 1934.

Hochmuth, Ursel, and Gertrud Meyer. *Streiflichter aus dem Hamburger Widerstand 1933–1945: Berichte und Dokumente.* 1969. Reprint, Frankfurt am Main, 1980.

Höhne, Heinz. *Der Orden unter dem Totenkopf: Die Geschichte der SS.* Munich, n.d. [1967?].

Holzapfel, Heribert. *Die Sekten in Deutschland: Dargestellt für das katholische Volk.* Regensburg, 1925.

Hoppe, Adolf. "Militärischer Ungehorsam aus religiöser Überzeugung." *Zeitschrift für die gesamte Neurologie und Psychiatrie, Originalien* 45 (1919): 393–412.

Hopster, Norbert, and Alex Moll. *Träume und Trümmer: Der Nationalsozialismus von 1933 bis 1945. Ausstellung der Stadt Lage/Lippe von November 1984.* Lage, 1984.

Horstmann, W. "Religiosität oder Wahn." *Zeitschrift für die gesamte Neurologie und Psychiatrie, Originalien* 49 (1919): 218–42.

Höß, Rudolf. *Kommandant in Auschwitz.* Autobiographical notes, introduction, and comments by Martin Broszat. Munich, 1983.

Hrabar, Roman. "Osadzanie Małoletnich z TZW. Prowincji Górnośląskiej w Obozach." *Biuletyn Głównej Komisji Badania Zbrodni Hitlerowskich w Polsce* 19 (1968): 51–79.

Huber, Ernst Rudolf. *Verfassungsrecht des Großdeutschen Reiches.* 2nd ed. Hamburg, 1939.

Hülle, Werner. "Die Änderungen der Kriegsstrafverfahrensordnung durch die 7: DurchfVO. vom 18. Mai 1940." *Zeitschrift für Wehrrecht* 5 (1940/41): 153–61.

Hüser, Karl. *Dokumentation: Wewelsburg 1933–1945. Kult- und Terrorstätte der SS: Eine Einführung.* Paderborn, 1982.

Hutten, Kurt. *Seher, Grübler, Enthusiasten: Das Buch der traditionellen Sekten und religiösen Sonderbewegungen.* Rev. ed. Stuttgart, 1982.

———. *Vorwort zu Alan Rogerson: Viele von uns werden niemals sterben. Geschichte und Geheimnis der Zeugen Jehovas.* Hamburg, 1971.

Hüttenberger, Peter. "Dimensionen des Widerstandsbegriffs." In *Widerstand: Ein Problem zwischen Theorie und Geschichte,* edited by Peter Steinbach, 80–95. Cologne, 1987.

———. "Heimtückefälle vor dem Sondergericht München 1933–1939." In *Bayern in der NS-Zeit,* vol. 4, *Herrschaft und Gesellschaft im Konflikt,* edited by Martin Broszat et al., 435–526. Munich, 1981.

———. "Vorüberlegungen zum 'Widerstandsbegriff.'" In *Theorien in der Praxis des Historikers: Forschungsbeispiele und ihre Diskussion,* edited by Jürgen Kocka, 117–39. Göttingen, 1977.

Idel, Wolfgang. "Die Sondergerichte für politische Strafsachen: Eine Gesamtdarstellung ihres Wesens, ihrer Entwicklung und ihrer rechtlichen Besonderheiten im Anschluß an die Verordnung der Reichsregierung über die Bildung von Sondergerichten vom 21.3.1933 und unter Berücksichtigung des Volksgerichtshofes und seiner Verfahren." Jur. diss., Freiburg im Breisgau, Schramberg, 1935.

Illinger, Ernst Ludwig. "Die Ernsten Bibelforscher als Sendboten des jüdischen Bolschewismus." *Der Hoheitsträger* 6 (June 1938): 12–15.

Imberger, Elke. *Widerstand "von unten": Widerstand und Dissens aus den Reihen der Arbeiterbewegung und der Zeugen Jehovas in Lübeck und Schleswig-Holstein 1933–1945.* Neumünster, 1991.

Inventar archivalischer Quellen des NS-Staates: Die Überlieferung von Behörden und Einrichtungen des Reichs, der Länder und der NSDAP. Part 1, *Reichszentralbehörden, regionale Behörden und wissenschaftliche Hochschulen für die zehn westdeutschen Länder sowie Berlin.* Edited by Heinz Boberach on behalf of the Institut für Zeitgeschichte. Munich, 1991.

Jacobeit, Sigrid, ed. *Ravensbrückerinnen: Biographien, Zeugnisse, Lebensdaten.* Berlin, 1995.

Jacobi, Gerhard. "Sekten." In *Das religiöse Deutschland der Gegenwart,* vol. 2, *Der christliche Kreis,* edited by Carl Schweitzer, 69–97. Berlin, 1929.

Jentsch, Werner. *Christliche Stimmen zur Wehrdienstfrage.* Kassel, n.d. [1952].

————. *Ernstfälle: Erlebtes und Bedachtes.* Moers, 1992.

Jochmann, Werner, ed. *Monologe im Führer-Hauptquartier 1941–1944.* By Adolf Hitler, based on the recordings by Heinrich Heims. Hamburg, 1980.

Johe, Werner. *Die gleichgeschaltete Justiz: Organisation des Rechtswesens und Politisierung der Rechtsprechung 1933–1945 dargestellt am Beispiel des Oberlandesgerichtsbezirks Hamburg.* Frankfurt am Main, 1967. Reprint, Hamburg, 1983.

————. *Neuengamme: Zur Geschichte der Konzentrationslager in Hamburg.* Hamburg, 1984.

John, Kirsten. "Häftlinge im Konzentrationslager in Wewelsburg unter besonderer Berücksichtigung der Ernsten Bibelforscher." Master's thesis, Universität Münster, 1992.

————. *"Mein Vater wird gesucht—":Häftlinge des Konzentrationslagers in Wewelsburg.* Essen, 1996.

Jonak von Freyenwald, Hans. "Die Ernsten Bibelforscher—eine politische Kampforganisation." *Korrespondenzblatt für den katholischen Klerus* 56 (1937): 69–70.

————. *Jüdische Bekenntnisse aus allen Zeiten und Ländern.* Nürnberg, 1941.

————. *Die Zeugen Jehovas: Pioniere für ein jüdisches Weltreich. Die politischen Ziele der Internationalen Vereinigung Ernster Bibelforscher.* Berlin, 1936.

Joos, Joseph. *Leben auf Widerruf: Begegnungen und Beobachtungen im K.Z. Dachau 1941–1945.* Olten, 1946.

Kaienburg, Hermann. *Vernichtung durch Arbeit: Der Fall Neuengamme: Die Wirtschaftsbestrebungen der SS und ihre Auswirkungen auf die Existenzbedingungen der KZ-Gefangenen.* Bonn, 1990.

Kaiser, Fritz. *Wer sind die sogenannten "Ernsten Bibelforscher?": Die verderblichen Irrlehren der "Internationalen Vereinigung Ernster Bibelforscher" (IVEB)—auch Millenniums-Tagesanbruchleute genannt—biblisch beleuchtet.* 2nd ed. Witten (Ruhr), 1924.

Kalb, Ernst, ed. *Kirchen und Sekten der Gegenwart: Unter Mitarbeit verschiedener evangelischer Theologen.* Stuttgart, 1905.

Kalous, Erika. "Widerstand der Ernsten Bibelforscher im Dritten Reich." Licensed manuscript; archived at the IfZ. Heidelberg, n.d.

Kamiński, Andrzej J. *Konzentrationslager 1896 bis heute: Analyses.* Stuttgart, 1982.

Kammler, Jörg. *Ich habe die Metzelei satt und laufe über: Kasseler Soldaten zwischen Verweigerung und Widerstand 1939–1945: Eine Dokumentation.* Fuldabrück, 1985.

Kater, Michael H. *Das "Ahnenerbe" der SS, 1935–1945: Ein Beitrag zur Kulturpolitik des Dritten Reiches.* Stuttgart, 1974. Reprint, Munich, 2006.

————. "Die Ernsten Bibelforscher im Dritten Reich." *Vierteljahrshefte für Zeitgeschichte* 17 (1969): 181–218.

Kaul, Friedrich Karl. *Geschichte des Reichsgerichts.* Vol. 4, *1933–1945.* Glashütten, 1971.

Kautsky, Benedikt. *Teufel und Verdammte: Erfahrungen und Erkenntnisse aus sieben Jahren in deutschen Konzentrationslagern.* Zurich, 1946.

KDV im Dritten Reich. Special edition of *zdl-Informationen* (second quarter 1987).

Kershaw, Ian. "'Widerstand ohne Volk?': Dissens und Widerstand im Dritten Reich." In Schmädeke and Steinbach, *Der Widerstand gegen den Nationalsozialismus*, 779–98.

Kersten, Felix. *The Kersten Memoirs, 1940–1945*. London, 1956. Reprint, Alexandria, VA, 1992.

———. *Totenkopf und Treue: Heinrich Himmler ohne Uniform: Aus den Tagebuchblättern des finnischen Medizinalrats*. Hamburg, 1952.

King, Christine Elizabeth. "Jehovah's Witnesses under Nazism." In Berenbaum, *A Mosaic of Victims*, 188–93.

———. *The Nazi State and the New Religions: Five Case Studies in Non-Conformity*. New York, 1982.

———."Strategies for Survial: An Examination of the History of Five Christian Sects in Germany 1933–1945." *Journal of Contemporary History* 14, no. 1 (1979): 211–33.

Kirchberg, Christian. "Die Kontrolle von Maßnahmen der 'politischen Polizei' durch die Verwaltungsgerichte." In *Verwaltung contra Menschenführung im Staat Hitlers: Studien zum politisch-administrativen System*, edited by Dieter Rebentisch and Karl Teppe, 141–52. Göttingen, 1986.

Klaus, Andreas. *Gewalt und Widerstand in Hamburg-Nord während der NS-Zeit*. Hamburg, 1986.

Klausch, Hans-Peter. *Die Geschichte der Bewährungsbataillone 999 unter besonderer Berücksichtigung des antifaschistischen Widerstandes*. Cologne, 1987.

Klauß, Hermann. *Feierstunden der deutschen Schule*. Stuttgart, 1941.

Klöckner, Adolf. "Das Grundrecht der Religionsfreiheit im nationalsozialistischen Staat." Jur. diss., Hamburg, 1937.

Klönne, Arno. *Jugend im Dritten Reich: Die Hitler-Jugend und ihre Gegner: Dokumente und Analysen*. Düsseldorf, 1982.

Knaut, Horst. *Propheten der Angst: Berichte zu psychopathologischen Trends der Gegenwart: Eine kritische Analyse*. Percha/Kempfenhausen, 1975.

Knobelsdorf, Andreas, Monika Minninger, and Bärbel Sunderbrink. *"Das Recht wurzelt im Volk": NS-Justiz im Landgerichtsbezirk Bielefeld; Katalog zur Ausstellung des Stadtarchivs Bielefeld vom 17. September bis 31. Oktober 1992*. Bielefeld, 1992.

Knöller, Bruno. "Erinnerungen." Protokolldienst "Das Vermächtnis der Opfer des Nationalsozialismus" der Evangelischen Akademie Bad Boll 32/84, May 18–20, 1984, 18–22.

Koch, Manfred. "Julius Engelhard: Drucker, Kurier und Organisator der Zeugen Jehovas." In *Der Widerstand im deutschen Südwesten*, edited by Michael Bosch and Wolfgang Niess, 95–103. Stuttgart, 1984.

——— "Die kleinen Glaubensgemeinschaften." In *Widerstand gegen den Nationalsozialismus in Mannheim*, edited by Erich Matthias and Hermann Weber, 415–34. Mannheim, 1984.

Koch, Werner. *"Sollen wir K. weiter beobachten?":* Ein Leben im Widerstand. Stuttgart, 1982.

Kogon, Eugen. *The Theory and Practice of Hell: The German Concentration Camps.* New York, 1949.

Köhler, Walther. *Wesen und Recht der Sekte im religiösen Leben Deutschlands.* Gießen, 1930.

Kohlrausch, Eduard, and Richard Lange. *Strafgesetzbuch mit Nebengesetzen und Erläuterungen.* 38th ed. Berlin, 1944.

Kolbe, Dieter. *Reichsgerichtspräsident Dr. Erwin Bumke: Studien zum Niedergang des Reichsgerichts und der deutschen Rechtspflege.* Karlsruhe, 1975.

König, Stefan. *Vom Dienst am Recht: Rechtsanwälte als Strafverteidiger im Nationalsozialismus.* Berlin, 1987.

Konzentrationslager Buchenwald, Post Weimar / Thür. Catalogue for the exhibition from the Deutschen Demokratischen Republik at the Martin-Gropius-Bau Berlin (West). Nationale Mahn- und Gedenkstätte Buchenwald. N.p., n.d. [1990].

Köppl, Elmar. *Die Zeugen Jehovas: Eine psychologische Analyse.* Munich, 1985.

Kortzfleisch, Siegfried von. "Sekten." In *Evangelisches Staatslexikon,* 2nd ed., edited by Hermann Kunst, Roman Herzog, and Wilhelm Schneemelcher, cols. 2278–80. Stuttgart, 1975.

Kösling, Günther. "Die deutschen Baptisten 1933/1934: Ihr Denken und Handeln zu Beginn des Dritten Reiches." Theol. diss., Marburg (Lahn), 1980.

Kosthorst, Erich, and Bernd Walter. *Konzentrations- und Strafgefangenenlager im Emsland 1933–1945: Zum Verhältnis von NS-Regime und Justiz: Darstellung und Dokumentation.* Düsseldorf, 1985.

Kraus, R. "Die Fürsorgeerziehung im Dritten Reich (1933–1945)." *Archiv für Wissenschaft und Praxis der sozialen Arbeit* 5 (1974): 161–210.

"Kriegs-Kriminalstatistik für die Wehrmacht. Zusammenfassung der kriminalstatistischen Ergebnisse des ersten Kriegsjahres." Government document, published by Oberkommando der Wehrmacht. Berlin, 1941.

Krölls, Albert. *Kriegsdienstverweigerung: Das unbequeme Grundrecht.* Frankfurt am Main, 1980.

Kühl, Reiner W. "Widerstand im Dritten Reich: Die ernsten Bibelforscher in Friedrichstadt." *Unterhaltung für Friedrichstadt und die angränzende Gegend, Mitteilungsblatt der Gesellschaft für Friedrichstädter Stadtgeschichte* 27 (1985): 165–90.

Künneth, Walter, and Carl Schweitzer, eds. *Freidenkertum und Kirche.* Berlin, 1932.

Kupfer-Koberwitz, Edgar. *Die Mächtigen und die Hilflosen: Als Häftling in Dachau.* Vol. 1, *Wie es begann.* Stuttgart, 1957.

Kuptsch, Julius. *Aufklärung über die "Ernsten Bibelforscher."* Tilsit, 1927.

Ein KZ-Außenlager in Düsseldorf-Stoffeln. Scientific editing by Andreas Kussmann. Düsseldorf, 1988.

KZ-Verbrechen vor deutschen Gerichten: Dokumente aus den Prozeßen gegen Sommer (KZ

Buchenwald), Sorge, Schubert (KZ Sachsenhausen), Unkelbach (Ghetto in Czenstochau). Edited by H.G. van Dam and Ralph Giordano. Frankfurt am Main, 1962.

Die Lageberichte der Geheimen Staatspolizei über die Provinz Hessen-Nassau 1933–1936. Edited by Thomas Klein, with additional evidence and introduction. Cologne, 1986.

Lahrtz, Jens-Uwe. "Die Zeugen Jehovas während des Zweiten Weltkrieges in Großbritannien, Kanada und den USA." *Beiträge zur Geschichte der Arbeiterbewegung* 37, no. 3 (1995): 44–54.

Lampert, Heinz. "Staatliche Sozialpolitik im Dritten Reich." In *Nationalsozialistische Diktatur, 1933–1945: Eine Bilanz,* edited by Karl Dietrich Bracher, Manfred Funke, and Hans-Adolf Jacobsen, 177–205. Bonn, 1983.

Langbein, Hermann. *Against All Hope: Resistance in the Nazi Concentration Camps, 1938–1945.* New York, 1994.

———. *People in Auschwitz.* Chapel Hill, 2004.

Lange, Johannes. "Dienstverweigerung aus religiösen Gründen." *Münchener Medizinische Wochenschrift* 84 (1937): 13–16.

Langewiesche, Dieter. "Was heißt Widerstand gegen den Nationalsozialismus?" In *1933 in Gesellschaft und Wissenschaft,* part 1, *Gesellschaft.* Hamburg, 1983.

Langhoff, Wolfgang. *Die Moorsoldaten: 13 Monate Konzentrationslager.* Zurich, 1935.

Lasch, Gustav. *Die Internationale Vereinigung Ernster Bibelforscher und die evangelische Kirche.* Straßburg, 1921.

Lautmann, Rüdiger, Winfried Grikschat, and Egbert Schmidt. "Der rosa Winkel in den nationalsozialistischen Konzentrationslagern." In *Seminar Gesellschaft und Homosexualität,* edited by Rüdiger Lautmann, 325–65. Frankfurt am Main, 1977.

Leber, Annedore. *Das Gewissen steht auf: 64 Lebensbilder aus dem deutschen Widerstand 1933–1945.* Berlin, 1956.

Lechner, Silvester. *Das KZ Oberer Kuhberg und die NS-Zeit in der Region Ulm, Neu-Ulm.* Stuttgart, 1988.

Lehberger, Rainer. "Der 'Umbau' der Hamburger Volksschule: Eine Dokumentation schulpolitischer Maßnahmen in der Frühphase der NS-Zeit." In *Die Fahne hoch: Schulpolitik und Schulalltag in Hamburg unterm Hakenkreu,* edited by Ranier Lehberger and Hans-Peter de Lorent, 15–33. Hamburg, 1986.

Lengemann, Rolf. "Höchstrichterliche Strafgerichtsbarkeit unter der Herrschaft des Nationalsozialismus." Jur. diss., Marburg, 1984.

Lichdi, Diether Götz. *Mennoniten im Dritten Reich: Dokumentation und Deutung.* Heilbronn, 1977.

Lichtenegger, Renate. "Die Bibelforscher im Widerstand gegen das NS-Regime unter besonderer Berücksichtigung des weiblichen Bibelforscherwiderstandes aus Wien." *Zeitgeschichte* 13, no. 5 (1986): 179–91.

———. "Wiens Bibelforscherinnen im Widerstand gegen den Nationalsozialismus 1938–1945." PhD diss., Vienna, 1984.

Lienau, Heinrich. *Zwölf Jahre Nacht: Mein Weg durch das "Tausendjährige Reich."* Flensburg, 1949.

Lienhardt, Hans. *Ein Riesenverbrechen am deutschen Volke und die Ernsten Bibelforscher.* 2nd ed. Weißenburg, 1921.

Liesche (Strafabteilungsvorsteher). "Der Bibelforscher im Strafvollzug." *Der deutsche Justizbeamte* 21, no. 3 (1937): 140.

Lilje, Hanns. *Im finstern Tal.* Nürnberg, 1947.

Loeb, S. "Dienstverweigerung aus religiösen Gründen und ihre gerichtsärztliche Beurteilung." *Psychiatrisch-Neurologische Wochenschrift* 20 (1918/19): 191–99.

Lohse, Eduard. *Die Offenbarung des Johannes.* 12th ed. Göttingen, 1979.

Loofs, Friedrich. *Die "Internationale Vereinigung Ernster Bibelforscher."* 2nd ed. Leipzig, 1921.

Löwenthal, Richard. "Widerstand im totalen Staat." In Löwenthal and Mühlen, *Widerstand und Verweigerung,* 11–24.

Löwenthal, Richard, and Patrik von zur Mühlen, eds. *Widerstand und Verweigerung in Deutschland 1933 bis 1945.* Berlin, 1982.

Luza, Radomir V. *The Resistance in Austria, 1938–1945.* Minneapolis, 1984.

Mai, Gunther. "'Warum steht der deutsche Arbeiter zu Hitler?': Zur Rolle der Deutschen Arbeitsfront im Herrschaftssystem des Dritten Reichs." *Geschichte und Gesellschaft* 12 (1986): 212–34.

Maislinger, Andreas. "Andere religiöse Gruppen." In *Widerstand und Verfolgung in Salzburg 1934–1945: Eine Dokumentation,* edited by Christa Mitterrutzner et al., 2:323–51. Vienna, 1991.

———. "Die Zeugen Jehovas (Ernste Bibelforscher)." In *Widerstand und Verfolgung in Tirol 1934–1945: Eine Dokumentation,* edited by Peter Eppel et al., 2: 369–83. Vienna, 1984.

Majer, Diemut. *"Fremdvölkische" im Dritten Reich: Ein Beitrag zur nationalsozialistischen Rechtssetzung und Rechtspraxis in Verwaltung und Justiz unter besonderer Berücksichtigung der eingegliederten Ostgebiete und des Generalgouvernements.* Boppard am Rhein, 1981.

Mammach, Klaus. *Widerstand 1933–1939: Geschichte der deutschen antifaschistischen Widerstandsbewegung im Inland und in der Emigration.* Cologne, 1984.

———. *Widerstand 1939–1945: Geschichte der deutschen antifaschistischen Widerstandsbewegung im Inland und in der Emigration.* Cologne, 1987.

Mann, Reinhard. *Protest und Kontrolle im Dritten Reich: Nationalsozialistische Herrschaft im Alltag einer rheinischen Großstadt.* Frankfurt am Main, 1987.

———. "Validitätsprobleme retrospektiver Interviews." In *Mündliche Geschichte und Arbeiterbewegung. Eine Einführung in Arbeitsweisen und Themenbereiche der Geschichte "geschichtsloser" Sozialgruppen,* edited by Gerhard Botz and Josef Weidenholzer, 355–70. Vienna, 1984.

Maršálek, Hans. *Die Geschichte des Konzentrationslagers Mauthausen: Dokumentation.* 2nd ed. Vienna, 1980.

Marßolek, Inge, and René Ott. *Bremen im Dritten Reich: Anpassung, Widerstand, Verfolgung.* Bremen, 1986.

Marszałek, Józef. *Majdanek: Geschichte und Wirklichkeit des Vernichtungslagers.* Reinbek bei Hamburg, 1982.

Marxen, Klaus. *Der Kampf gegen das liberale Strafrecht: Eine Studie zum Antiliberalismus in der Strafrechtswissenschaft der zwanziger und dreissiger Jahre.* Berlin, 1975.

Mason, Timothy W. *Sozialpolitik im Dritten Reich: Arbeiterklasse und Volksgemeinschaft.* Opladen, 1977.

Matthias, Erich, and Hermann Weber, eds. *Widerstand gegen den Nationalsozialismus in Mannheim.* Mannheim, 1984.

Maur, Hans. *Antifaschistische Mahn- und Gedenkstätte Lichtenburg.* Jessen, n.d. [1981].

Meffert, Franz. "Bibelforscher" und Bibelforschung über das Weltende: Fünf Vorträge über die sog. Ernsten Bibelforscher. Freiburg im Breisgau, 1925.

Mehringer, Hartmut, and Werner Röder. "Gegner, Widerstand, Emigration." In *Ploetz, Das Dritte Reich: Ursprünge, Ereignisse, Wirkungen,* edited by Martin Broszat and Norbert Frei, 173–84. Freiburg, 1983.

Meier, Heinrich Christian. *Im Frühwind der Freiheit.* Hamburg, 1949.

———. *So war es: Das Leben im KZ Neuengamme.* Hamburg, 1946.

Meldungen aus dem Reich, 1938–1945: Die geheimen Lageberichte des Sicherheitsdienstes der SS. 17 vols. Edited and with an introduction by Heinz Boberach. Herrsching, 1984.

Menter, Leo. "Himmlers Auferstehung." *Die Weltbühne* 5 (1950): 1283–87.

Menzinger, Stefanie. "Jugend im NS-Staat." Wiesbaden, n.d. (Beitrag zum Schülerwettbewerb Deutsche Geschichte um den Preis des Bundespräsidenten 1981/82, Archiv der Körber-Stiftung NS I/1860.)

Messerschmidt, Manfred. "Deutsche Militärgerichtsbarkeit im Zweiten Weltkrieg." In *Die Freiheit des Anderen: Festschrift für Martin Hirsch,* edited by Adalbert Podlech, Helmut Simon, and Hans Jochen Vogel, 111–42. Baden-Baden, 1981.

Messerschmidt, Manfred, and Fritz Wüllner. *Die Wehrmachtjustiz im Dienste des Nationalsozialismus: Zerstörung einer Legende.* Baden-Baden, 1987.

Meyenberg, A. *Über die sogenannten "Ernsten Bibelforscher": Geschichte, Lehre und Kritik.* Lucerne, 1924.

Meyer, Gertrud. *Nacht über Hamburg: Berichte und Dokumente.* Frankfurt am Main, 1971.

Meyer, Hermann Julius, ed. *Meyers lexikon.* Vol. 6. 8th ed. Leipzig, 1939.

Miksch, Leonhard. *Die Ernsten Bibelforscher.* With appendix "Die Gerichtsverhandlung in St. Gallen wegen der Frage: Werden die 'Ernsten Bibelforscher' mit amerikanischem Judengeld für ihre Zersetzungsarbeit bezahlt?" Lorch (Württemberg), 1925.

Milton, Sybil. "Deutsche und deutsch-jüdische Frauen als Verfolgte des NS-Staats." In Benz and Distel, *Frauen-Verfolgung und Widerstand,* 3–20.

Minninger, Monika. "Politisch und religiös Verfolgte in Stadt und Kreis Bielefeld: Ein Überblick." In *Verdrängte Geschichte: Verfolgung und Vernichtung in Ostwestfalen 1933–1945*, edited by Joachim Meynert and Arno Klönne, 39–75. Bielefeld, 1986.

———. "Staatsfeind Bibelforscher." In *"Das Recht wurzelt im Volk": NS-Justiz im Landgerichtsbezirk Bielefeld*, by Andreas Knobelsdorf, Monika Minninger, and Bärbel Sunderbrink. Catalogue for the September 17–October 31, 1992, exhibition of the Bielefeld Archives. Bielefeld, 1992.

Minuth, Karl-Heinz, ed. *Die Regierung Hitler: Teil 1, 1933/34.* Vol. 2 (Sept. 12, 1933–Aug. 27, 1934). Boppard am Rhein, 1983.

Mirkes, Adolf, and Karl Schild. *Zeugnisse, Offenbach 1933–1945: Verfolgung und Widerstand in Stadt und Landkreis Offenbach.* Cologne, 1988.

Mitterrutzner, Christa. "Internationale Bibelforscher-Vereinigung (Zeugen Jehovas)." In *Widerstand und Verfolgung in Niederösterreich, 1934–1945: Eine Dokumentation*, vol. 3, *1938–1945*, edited by Heinz Arnberger et al., 275–302. Vienna, 1984.

Möller, Reimer. "Widerstand und Verfolgung in einer agrarisch-kleinstädtischen Region: SPD, KPD und 'Bibelforscher' im Kreis Steinburg 1933–1945." *Zeitschrift für Schleswig-Holsteinische Geschichte* 114 (1988): 125–228.

Mommsen, Hans. "Die Geschichte des deutschen Widerstands im Lichte der neueren Forschung." *Aus Politik und Zeitgeschichte* B50 (1986): 3–18.

Mosse, George L. *Der nationalsozialistische Alltag: So lebte man unter Hitler.* 2nd ed. Königstein (Taunus), 1979.

———. *Rassismus: Ein Krankheitssymptom in der europäischen Geschichte des 19. und 20. Jahrhunderts.* Königstein (Taunus), 1978.

Müller, Charlotte. *Die Klempnerkolonne in Ravensbrück: Erinnerungen des Häftlings Nr. 10787.* 3rd ed. Berlin, 1983.

Müller, Ingo. *Furchtbare Juristen: Die unbewältigte Vergangenheit unserer Justiz.* Munich, 1987.

Müller, Johannes, and Rudolf Weckerling. "Die Mehrheit des deutschen Protestantismus hatte einen Januskopf." In *1933: Wie die Deutschen Hitler zur Macht verhalfen: Eine Lesebuch für Demokraten*, edited by Ingke Brodersen, Klaus Humann, and Susanne von Paczensky, 266–303. Reinbek bei Hamburg, 1983.

Müller, Klaus-Jürgen, and Hans Mommsen. "Der deutsche Widerstand gegen das NS-Regime: Zur Historiographie des Widerstandes." In *Der deutsche Widerstand 1933–1945*, edited by Klaus-Jürgen Müller, 13–21. Paderborn, 1986.

Müller, Wolfram. "Sprechchöre, Goebbels-Reden und Flaggenappelle. Die 'Feierpraxis' in den höheren Schulen Hamburgs 1933–1939." In *Die Fahne hoch: Schulpolitik und Schulalltag in Hamburg unterm Hakenkreuz*, edited by Reiner Lehberger and Hans-Peter de Lorent, 34–48. Hamburg, 1986.

Münch, Ingo von. *Staat und Verwaltung in der NS-Zeit.* Hamburg, 1984.

München, Theo. *Das Volk als Wehrgemeinschaft.* Berlin, 1942.

Nansen, Odd. *Von Tag zu Tag: Ein Tagebuch.* Hamburg, 1949.

Der Nationalsozialismus: Dokumente 1933–1945. Rev. ed. Edited by Walther Hofer. Frankfurt am Main, 1982.

Naujoks, Harry. *Mein Leben in Sachsenhausen, 1936–1942: Erinnerungen eines ehemaligen Lagerältesten.* Edited by Ursel Hochmuth. Cologne, 1987.

Neugebauer, Wolfgang. "'Ernste Bibelforscher' (Internationale Bibelforscher-Vereinigung)." In *Widerstand und Verfolgung in Wien, 1934–1945: Eine Dokumentation,* edited by DÖW, 3:161–183. Vienna, 1984.

Neuhäusler, Johann. *Kreuz und Hakenkreuz: Der Kampf des Nationalsozialismus gegen die katholische Kirche und der kirchliche Widerstand.* 2 vols. Munich, 1946.

Neumann, Franz. *Behemoth: Struktur und Praxis des Nationalsozialismus 1933–1944.* 1977. Reprint, Frankfurt am Main, 1984.

Neumann, Volker. "Vom Entscheidungs- zum Ordnungsdenken: Carl Schmitts Rechts- und Staatstheorie in der nationalsozialistischen Herausforderung." In *Recht, Rechtsphilosophie und Nationalsozialismus,* edited by Hubert Rottleuthner, 152–62. Wiesbaden, 1983.

Niemand und nichts vergessen: Ehemalige Häftlinge aus verschiedenen Ländern berichten über das KZ Sachsenhausen. Edited by Wolfgang Szepansky and Gabriele Schnorrenberg. Berlin, 1984.

Niethammer, Lutz, ed. *Lebenserfahrung und kollektives Gedächtnis: Die Praxis der "Oral History."* Frankfurt am Main, 1980.

Nobel, Rolf. *Falschspieler Gottes: Die Wahrheit über Jehovas Zeugen.* Hamburg, 1985.

Nolte, Ernst. *Three Faces of Fascism: Action Française, Italian Facisism, National Socialism.* New York, 1966.

Norden, Günther van. "Zwischen Kooperation und Teilwiderstand: Die Rolle der Kirchen und Konfessionen: Ein Überblick über Forschungspositionen." In Schmädeke and Steinbach, *Der Widerstand gegen den Nationalsozialismus,* 227–39.

Nüse, Karl-Heinz. *Das Kriegsstrafrecht und Kriegsstrafverfahren mit Erläuterungen und Durchführungsbestimmungen.* Berlin, 1940.

——. "Die sachliche Zuständigkeit der Strafgerichte." *Deutsche Justiz* 98 (1936): 898–99.

Obst, Helmut. "Reich-Gottes-Erwartungen christlicher 'Sondergemeinschaften' nordamerikanischen Ursprungs (Mormonen, Adventisten, Zeugen Jehovas)—Symptome der Krise christlicher Eschatologie." In *Traditio, Krise, Renovatio aus theologischer Sicht: Festschrift Winfried Zeller,* edited by Bernd Jaspert and Rudolf Mohr, 357–69. Marburg, 1976.

Ohrtmann, Johann. *Die Kriegsdienstgegnerbewegung.* Heide (Holstein), 1932.

Oleschinski, Brigitte. "Religiöse Gemeinschaften im Widerstand." In *Widerstand gegen den Nationalsozialismus,* edited by Peter Steinbach and Johannes Tuchel, 193–201. Berlin, 1994.

Otto, Hans-Uwe, and Heinz Sünker, eds. *Soziale Arbeit und Faschismus: Volkspflege und Pädagogik im Nationalsozialismus.* Bielefeld, 1986.

Otto, Heinrich. *Werden und Wesen des Quäkertums und seine Entwicklung in Deutschland.* Vienna, 1972.

Otto, Karl, and W. Güldenpfennig, eds. *Ersatzwesen: Textausgabe zu den Erfassungs-, Musterungs- und Aushebungsvorschriften einschl. VO über das Wehrersatzwesen bei besonderem Einsatz.* 2nd ed. Berlin, 1943.

Paffrath, Tharsicius. *Die Sekte der Ernsten Bibelforscher.* Paderborn, 1925.

Pape, Günther. *Ich war Zeuge Jehovas.* 6th ed. Aschaffenburg, 1978.

———. *Die Wahrheit über Jehovas Zeugen: Problematik, Dokumentation.* Rottweil/Neckar, 1970.

Partei-Justiz: Eine vergleichende Dokumentation über den nationalsozialistischen und kommunistischen Rechtsmißbrauch in Deutschland 1933–1963. Edited by Bundesministerium für gesamtdeutsche Fragen. Berlin, 1964.

Pawelczyńska, Anna. "Differenzierung der Häftlingsgemeinschaft und Überlebenschancen im KZ Auschwitz." In *Zweiter Weltkrieg und sozialer Wandel,* edited by Waclaw Długoborski, 171–83. Göttingen, 1981.

Pechel, Rudolf. *Deutscher Widerstand.* Erlenbach/Zurich, 1947.

Penton, James. *Apocalypse Delayed: The Story of Jehovah's Witnesses.* Toronto, 1985.

———. "Jehovah's Witnesses and the Secular State: A Historical Analysis of Doctrine." *Journal of Church and State* 21, no. 1 (1979): 55–71.

———. "A Story of Attempted Compromise: Jehovah's Witnesses, Anti-Semitism and the Third Reich." *Christian Quest* 3, no. 1 (1990): 33–45.

Peters, Fritz. *Zwölf Jahre Bremen, 1933–1945: Eine Chronik.* Bremen, 1951.

Peters, Karl. "Abschließende Bemerkungen zu den Zeugen-Jehovas-Prozeßen." In *Festschrift für Karl Engisch zum 70. Geburtstag,* edited by Paul Bockelmann, Arthur Kaufmann, and Ulrich Klug, 468–89. Frankfurt am Main, 1969.

Petrich, Hermann. *Unsere Sekten, Freikirchen und Weltanschauungsgesellschaften.* Berlin, 1928.

Peukert, Detlev. *Die KPD im Widerstand: Verfolgung und Untergrundarbeit an Rhein und Ruhr 1933 bis 1945.* Wuppertal, 1980.

———. *Volksgenossen und Gemeinschaftsfremde: Anpassung, Ausmerze und Aufbegehren unter dem Nationalsozialismus.* Cologne, 1982.

Philipsen, Bernd. "Für den Glauben in den Tod: Martyrium einer Süderbraruper Familie in der NS-Zeit." In *Kreis-Chronik: Handbook for the District of Schleswig-Flensburg 1993/94,* edited by Spagat Kulturmagazin, 39–43. Schleswig, 1994.

Picker, Henry. *Hitlers Tischgespräche im Führerhauptquartier.* Rev ed. Stuttgart, 1976.

Pierro, Matteo. "La repressione fascista dei Testimoni di Geova." *Informando,* April 1996, 6–7.

Pingel, Falk. *Häftlinge unter SS-Herrschaft: Widerstand, Selbstbehauptung und Vernichtung im Konzentrationslager.* Hamburg, 1978.

―――. "Jehovah's Witnesses." In *Encyclopedia of the Holocaust,* edited by Israel Gutman, 2:742–43. New York, 1990.

Plum, Günter. "Widerstand und Resistenz." In *Das Dritte Reich: Herrschaftsstruktur und Geschichte: Vorträge aus dem Institut für Zeitgeschichte,* edited by Martin Broszat and Horst Möller, 248–73. Munich, 1983.

Poel, Albert van de. *Ich sah hinter den Vorhang: Ein Holländer erlebt Neuengamme.* Hamburg, 1948.

Poelchau, Harald. *Die letzten Stunden: Erinnerungen eines Gefängnispfarrers, aufgezeichnet von Graf Alexander Stenbock-Fermor.* 1949. Reprint, Cologne, 1987.

―――. *Die Ordnung der Bedrängten: Autobiographisches und Zeitgeschichtliches seit den zwanziger Jahren.* Berlin, 1963.

Poliakov, Léon, and Joseph Wulf. *Das Dritte Reich und seine Denker.* 1959. Reprint, Frankfurt am Main, 1983.

Poppitz, Johannes. *Die Grundfrage des Staatskirchenrechts: Der Anspruch des Staates und das geistliche Wesen der Kirche.* Leipzig, 1938.

Prolingheuer, Hans. *Kleine politische Kirchengeschichte: Fünfzig Jahre Evangelischer Kirchenkampf von 1919 bis 1969.* Cologne, 1984.

Der Prozeß gegen die Hauptkriegsverbrecher vor dem Internationalen Militärgerichtshof, Nürnberg, 14 November 1945–1 Oktober 1946. Vols. 1–23 (interrogation records) and 24–42 (documents). Nürnberg, 1947–49.

Ramm, Thilo. "Familien- und Jugendrecht im Nationalsozialismus." In *Recht, Rechtsphilosophie und Nationalsozialismus,* edited by Hubert Rottleuthner, 75–81. Wiesbaden, 1983.

―――. *Das nationalsozialistische Familien- und Jugendrecht.* Heidelberg, 1984.

Rast, Gertrud. *Allein bist Du nicht: Kämpfe und Schicksale in schwerer Zeit.* Frankfurt am Main, 1972.

"Rechtsgrundsätze des Reichskriegsgerichts zu § 5 KSSVO." In *Gesetzesdienst für die Wehrmachtgerichte: Sonderheft.* Berlin, 1940.

Reimer, Hans-Diether, ed. *Stichwort "Sekten": Glaubensgemeinschaften außerhalb der Kirchen.* Stuttgart, 1977.

Reintjes, Theo. "Die religiösen Glaubensgemeinschaften im Strafrecht und in der Strafrechtsreform." Jur. diss., Cologne, Emsdetten, 1935.

Die Religion in Geschichte und Gegenwart: Handwörterbuch für Theologie und Religionswissenschaft. 2nd ed. Edited by Hermann Gunkel and Leopold Zscharnack. Tübingen, 1927.

Die Religion in Geschichte und Gegenwart: Handwörterbuch für Theologie und Religionswissenschaft. 3rd ed. Edited by Kurt Galling. Tübingen, 1962.

"Die Religionszugehörigkeit der Wohnbevölkerung in der Stadt Hamburg im Jahre 1933, in Aus Hamburgs Verwaltung und Wirtschaft." *Monatsschrift des Statistischen Landesamtes* 11, no. 7 (1934).

Renker, Z. *Unsere Brüder in den Sekten: Die Zeugen Jehovas.* Limburg, 1963.

Richterbriefe: Dokumente zur Beeinflussung der deutschen Rechtsprechung, 1942–1944. Edited by Heinz Boberach. Boppard am Rhein, 1975.

Rietzsch, Otto. "Die Verordnung zur Ergänzung der Strafvorschriften zum Schutz der Wehrkraft des deutschen Volkes vom 25. November 1933." *Deutsche Justiz* 102 (1940): 77–80.

Ritscher, Bodo. "Zum organisierten Widerstandskampf deutscher Antifaschisten im KZ Buchenwald." In *Verfolgung, Ausbeutung, Vernichtung: Die Lebens- und Arbeitsbedingungen der Häftlinge in deutschen Konzentrationslagern 1933–1945,* edited by Ludwig Eiber, 130–48. Hannover, 1985.

Rittau, Martin. *Militärstrafgesetzbuch mit Einführungsgesetz und Kriegssonderstrafrechtsverordnung.* 4th ed. Berlin, 1943.

Ritter, Gerhard. "Wunschträume Heinrich Himmlers am 21. Juli 1944." *Geschichte in Wissenschaft und Unterricht* 5 (1954): 162–68.

Rogerson, Alan. *Millions Now Living Will Never Die: A Study of Jehovah's Witnesses.* London, 1969.

Röhm, Eberhard. *Sterben für den Frieden: Spurensicherung: Hermann Stöhr (1898–1940) und die ökumenische Friedensbewegung.* Stuttgart, 1985.

Romey, Stefan. "Zu Recht verfolgt? Zur Geschichte der ausgebliebenen Entschädigung." In *Verachtet, Verfolgt, Vernichtet: Zu den vergessenen Opfern des NS-Regimes,* edited by Klaus Frahm et al., 220–45. 2nd rev. ed. Hamburg, 1988.

Roon, Ger van. *Widerstand im Dritten Reich: Ein Überblick.* 2nd ed. Munich, 1981.

Rosenberg, Alfred. *Der mythus des 20. jahrhunderts: Eine wertung der seelischgeistigen gestaltenkämpfe unserer zeit.* Munich, 1930.

———. "Die Protokolle der Weisen von Zion und die jüdische Weltpolitik (1923)." In his *Schriften und Reden,* vol. 2, *Schriften aus den Jahren 1921–1923,* 249–428. Munich, 1943.

Rosmus-Wenninger, Anja. *Widerstand und Verfolgung am Beispiel Passaus 1933–1939.* Passau, 1983.

Rossmeissl, Dieter. *"Ganz Deutschland wird zum Führer halten—": Zur politischen Erziehung in den Schulen des Dritten Reiches.* Frankfurt am Main, 1985.

Rothfels, Hans. *Die deutsche Opposition gegen Hitler: Eine Würdigung.* New expanded edition, with an introduction by Hermann Graml. Frankfurt am Main, 1986.

Rüping, Hinrich. *Bibliographie zum Strafrecht im Nationalsozialismus: Literatur zum Straf-, Strafverfahrens- und Strafvollzugsrecht mit ihren Grundlagen und einem Anhang: Verzeichnis der veröffentlichten Entscheidungen der Sondergerichte.* Munich, 1985.

Rürup, Reinhard, ed. *Topographie des Terrors: Gestapo, SS und Reichssicherheitshauptamt auf dem "Prinz-Albrecht-Gelände": Eine Dokumentation.* 2nd ed. Berlin, 1987.

Rüthers, Bernd. *Die unbegrenzte Auslegung: Zum Wandel der Privatrechtsordnung im Nationalsozialismus.* Tübingen, 1968.

Sachsenhausen. Dokumente, Aussagen, Forschungsergebnisse und Erlebnisberichte über das ehemalige Konzentrationslager Sachsenhausen. Edited by Zentralleitung des Komitees der Antifaschistischen Widerstandskämpfer der Deutschen Demokratischen Republik. Berlin, 1982.

Sandvoß, Hans-Rainer. *Widerstand in einem Arbeiterbezirk (Wedding)*. Berlin, 1983.

Schäfer, Ernst, and Hans von Dohnanyi, eds. *Die Strafgesetzgebung der Jahre 1931 bis 1935*. Appendix to the 18th ed. by Reinhard Frank. Tübingen, 1936.

Schäfer, Gerhard, ed. *Die Evangelische Landeskirche in Württemberg und der National-sozialismus: Eine Dokumentation zum Kirchenkampf.* Vol. 1, *Um das politische Engagement der Kirche, 1932–1933*. Stuttgart, 1971. Vol. 2, *Um eine deutsche Reichs-kirche, 1933*. Stuttgart, 1972.

Schäfer, Karl. "Das Gesetz zur Änderung des Strafgesetzbuchs vom 28. Juni 1935." *Juristische Wochenschrift* 64 (1935): 2478–85.

Scharf, Kurt. "Gespräche mit Kurt Scharf." In *Zumutungen des Friedens: Kurt Scharf zum 80. Geburtstag,* edited by Volkmar Deile, 17–42. Reinbek bei Hamburg, 1982.

———. *Widerstehen und Versöhnen: Rückblicke und Ausblicke*. Stuttgart, 1987.

Scherer, Werner. "Zur Kriegssonderstrafrechtsverordnung." *Zeitschrift für Wehrrecht* 4 (1939/40): 226–30.

Scheurlen, Paul. *Die Sekten der Gegenwart*. 2nd ed. Stuttgart, 1921.

Schimmler, Bernd. *Recht ohne Gerechtigkeit: Zur Tätigkeit der Berliner Sondergerichte im Nationalsozialismus*. Berlin, 1984.

Schirach, Baldur von. *Die Hitler-Jugend: Idee und Gestalt*. Leipzig, 1934.

Schlegel, Fritz. *Die Teufelsmaske der "Ernsten Bibelforscher."* Vol. 2, *Propheten und Pioniere gewaltsamen Umsturzes*. Neckargemünd, 1925.

———. *Die Wahrheit über die "Ernsten Bibelforscher."* Freiburg im Breisgau, 1922.

Schlotterbeck, Friedrich. *Je dunkler die Nacht: Erinnerungen eines deutschen Arbeiters, 1933–1945*. Stuttgart, 1986.

Schmädeke, Jürgen, and Peter Steinbach, eds. *Der Widerstand gegen den National-sozialismus: Die deutsche Gesellschaft und der Widerstand gegen Hitler*. Munich, 1985.

Schmauser, Karl. "Minder schwerer Fall und verminderte Zurechnungsfähig-keit bei Verweigerung des Wehrdienstes nach § 5 Abs. 1 Nr. 3 KSSVO." *Zeitschrift für Wehrrecht* 7 (1942/43): 132–41.

Schmid, Heinrich. *Apokalyptisches Wetterleuchten: Ein Beitrag der Evangelischen Kirche zum Kampf im "Dritten Reich."* Munich, 1947.

Schmidt, Eberhard. "Die materiellrechtlichen Entscheidungen des Reichs-kriegsgerichts." *Zeitschrift für Wehrrecht* 6 (1941/42): 308–27.

———. *Die militärische Straftat und ihr Täter*. Berlin, 1936.

Schmidt, Ernst. *Lichter in der Finsternis: Widerstand und Verfolgung in Essen 1933–1945: Erlebnisse, Berichte, Forschungen, Gespräche*. 2nd rev. ed. Frankfurt am Main, 1980.

Schmidt, Wolf-Dietrich. "'Wir sind die Verfolgten geblieben': Zur Geschichte der Vereinigung der Verfolgten des Naziregimes (VVN) in Hamburg 1945–1951." In *Das andere Hamburg: Freiheitliche Bestrebungen in der Hansestadt seit dem Spätmittelalter,* edited by Jörg Berlin, 329–56. Cologne, 1981.

Schmiedgen, Werner. "Mit den ELAS-Partisanen nach Saloniki." In *Strafdivision 999: Erlebnisse und Berichte aus dem antifaschistischen Widerstandskampf.* Berlin, 1966.

Schnell, William J. *Thirty Years a Watch Tower Slave: Confessions of a Converted Jehovah's Witness.* Grand Rapids, MI, 1956.

Schön, Heinz. *Ostsee '45: Menschen, Schiffe, Schicksale.* Stuttgart, 1984.

Schorn, Hubert. *Der Richter im Dritten Reich: Geschichte und Dokumente.* Frankfurt am Main, 1959.

Schreiber, Jürgen. "Kriegsdienstverweigerung: Eine historische und rechtsvergleichende Untersuchung." Jur. diss., Bad Godesberg, 1952.

———. "Wehrmachtjustiz—Anmerkungen zu den 'Enthüllungen' von Messerschmidt-Wüllner." *Neue Zeitschrift für Wehrrecht* 30, no. 3 (1988): 100–106.

———. "Wehrmachtjustiz und Kriegsdienstverweigerung." *Wehrwissenschaftliche Rundschau* 31 (1982): 145–46.

Schultz, Max. "Seelsorge bei der Vollstreckung von Todesurteilen." *Monatsschrift für Kriminalbiologie und Strafrechtsreform* 33 (1942): 52–57.

Schulz, Gerhard. "Über Entscheidungen und Formen des politischen Widerstandes in Deutschland." In *Faktoren der politischen Entscheidung: Festgabe für Ernst Fraenkel zum 65. Geburtstag,* edited by Gerhard A. Ritter and Gilbert Ziebura, 73–114. Berlin, 1963.

Schwarz, Walter. *Rückerstattung nach den Gesetzen der Alliierten Mächte.* Munich, 1974.

Schweitzer, Carl, ed. *Antwort des Glaubens: Handbuch der neuen Apologetik.* Schwerin, 1928.

Schweling, Otto Peter. *Die deutsche Militärjustiz in der Zeit des Nationalsozialismus.* 2nd rev. ed. Edited by Erich Schwinge. Marburg, 1978.

Schwind, Hans-Dieter. *Kurze Geschichte der deutschen Kriegsgerichte.* Munich 1966.

———. "Umfang und Träger der Wehrstrafgerichtsbarkeit: Historische, rechtsvergleichende und rechtstaatsächliche Untersuchungen." Jur. diss., Hamburg, 1966.

Schwinge, Erich. *Die Entwicklung der Mannszucht in der deutschen, britischen und französischen Wehrmacht seit 1914.* Berlin, 1940.

———. *Militärstrafgesetzbuch.* Berlin, 1936.

———. *Militärstrafgesetzbuch nebst Kriegssonderstrafrechtsverordnung.* 5th ed. Berlin, 1943.

———. *Verfälschung und Wahrheit: Das Bild der Wehrmachtgerichtsbarkeit.* Tübingen, 1988.

Scott, Richenda C. *Die Quäker.* Vol. 14 of *Die Kirchen der Welt.* Stuttgart, 1974.

Seidler, Franz W. *Fahnenflucht: Soldat zwischen Eid und Gewissen.* Munich, 1993.

Shelley, Lore, ed. *Auschwitz—The Nazi Civilization: Twenty-Three Women Prisoners' Accounts.* New York, 1992.

Siedenschnur, Günther. *Wer sind die Zeugen Jehovas?* Gütersloh, 1956.

So ging es zu Ende, Neuengamme. Documents and reports edited by Lagergemeinschaft Neuengamme. Hamburg, 1960.

Sollmann, H., and W. Wagner. "Ernste Bibelforscher." *Deutsche Zeitschrift für die gesamte gerichtliche Medizin, Organ der Deutschen Gesellschaft für gerichtliche und soziale Medizin* 28 (1937): 433–44.

Solzhenitsyn, Alexander. *Der Archipel GULAG.* Bern, 1976.

Die Sondereinheiten in der früheren deutschen Wehrmacht (Straf-, Bewährungs- und Erziehungseinrichtungen). Rev. ed. Kornelimünster, n.d. [1952].

Spohr, Werner. *Das Recht der Schutzhaft.* Berlin, 1937.

Stachura, Peter D. "Das Dritte Reich und die Jugenderziehung: Die Rolle der Hitlerjugend 1933–1939." In *Nationalsozialistische Diktatur, 1933–1945: Eine Bilanz,* edited by Karl Dietrich Bracher, Manfred Funke, and Hans-Adolf Jacobsen, 224–44. Bonn, 1983.

Staehelin, Ernst. *Was haben wir von den "ernsten Bibelforschern" zu halten?* Basel, 1925.

Staff, Ilse. *Justiz im Dritten Reich: Eine Dokumentation.* 1964. Reprint, Frankfurt am Main, 1978.

Steinbach, Peter. "Einführung." In his *Widerstand: Ein Problem zwischen Theorie und Geschichte,* 9–27. Cologne, 1987.

——. "Der Widerstand als Thema der politischen Zeitgeschichte—Ordnungsversuche vergangener Wirklichkeit und politischer Reflexion." In *Bekenntnis, Widerstand, Martyrium: Von Barmen 1934 bis Plötzensee 1944,* edited by Gerhard Besier and Gerhard Ringshausen, 11–74. Göttingen, 1986.

——. "Widerstandsforschung im politischen Spannungsfeld." *Aus Politik und Zeitgeschichte* B 28/88 (1988): 3–21.

Steinberg, Hans-Josef. *Widerstand und Verfolgung in Essen, 1933–1945.* Hannover, 1969.

Steiner, Herbert. *Gestorben für Österreich: Widerstand gegen Hitler.* Vienna, 1968.

Stern, Annemarie, ed. *Wir "Hoch- und Landesverräter": Antifaschistischer Widerstand in Oberhausen, eine Lesebuch.* Oberhausen, 1983.

Stevenson, William Charles. *The Inside Story of Jehovah's Witnesses.* New York, 1968.

Stobwasser, Albin. *Die den roten Winkel trugen: Zur Geschichte der VVN–Bund der Antifaschisten.* Hamburg, 1983.

Stödter, Rolf. "Verfassungsproblematik und Rechtspraxis: Die Rechtsprechung zum Bibelforscherverbot." *Archiv des öffentlichen Rechts* NF 27 (1936): 166–226.

Stokes, Lawrence D. *Kleinstadt und Nationalsozialismus: Ausgewählte Dokumente zur Geschichte von Eutin, 1918–1945.* Neumünster, 1984.

Stolleis, Michael. "Die Verwaltungsgerichtsbarkeit im Nationalsozialismus." In *System des verwaltungsgerichtlichen Rechtsschutzes: Festschrift für Christian-Friedrich Menger zum 70. Geburtstag,* edited by Hans-Uwe Erichsen et al., 57–80. Cologne, 1985.

Strafdivision 999: Erlebnisse und Berichte aus dem antifaschistischen Widerstandskampf.
Berlin, 1966.

Streiflichter: Hamburger Widerstand. Compiled by VVN Hamburg. Hamburg, n.d.
[1948].

Struckmeier, Ingo. "Die Verfolgung der Zeugen Jehovas: Martin Heinel aus
Eickhorst." In *Die Kriegsjahre in Deutschland, 1939 bis 1945,* edited by Dieter
Galinski and Wolf Schmidt, 159–79. Hamburg, 1985.

———. "Verfolgung von Jehovas Zeugen aus Eickhorst und Umgebung: Eine
Dokumentation über Einzelschicksale der Verfolgung von Jehovas Zeugen
aus Eickhorst und Umgebung während der NS-Zeit." From the student
competition "German History" with an award by the Federal president,
1982–83, archives of the Körber-Stiftung NS II/0215.

Struve, Walter. *Aufstieg und Herrschaft des Nationalsozialismus in einer industriellen
Kleinstadt: Osterode am Harz 1918–1945.* Essen, 1992.

———. "Die Zeugen Jehovas in Osterode am Harz: Eine Fallstudie über Widerstand und Unterdrückung in einer kleinen Industriestadt im Dritten
Reich." *Niedersächsisches Jahrbuch für Landesgeschichte* 62 (1990): 265–95.

Stuhlhofer, Franz. *Charles T. Russell und die Zeugen Jehovas: Der unbelehrbare Prophet.*
3rd ed. Berneck, 1994.

Suchowiak, Bogdan. *Mai 1945: Die Tragödie der Häftlinge von Neuengamme.* Reinbek
bei Hamburg, 1985.

Suhr, Elke. *Die Emslandlager: Die politische und wirtschaftliche Bedeutung der
emsländischen Konzentrations- und Strafgefangenenlager 1933–1945.* Bremen, 1985.

Süsskind, Eckhard von. *Zeugen Jehovas: Anspruch und Wirklichkeit der Wachtturm-
Gesellschaft.* Neuhausen-Stuttgart, 1985.

Szepansky, Wolfgang. *Dennoch ging ich diesen Weg.* Berlin, 1985.

Teetzmann, Otto A. *Der Luftschutz-Leitfaden für alle.* Berlin, n.d. [1935].

Thamer, Hans-Ulrich. *Verführung und Gewalt: Deutschland 1933–1945.* Berlin, 1986.

Theek, Bruno. "KZ Dachau: Erlebnisbericht." Lecture held on May 13, 1945,
in Ludwigslust.

Thévoz, Robert, Hans Branig, and Cécile Lowenthal-Hensel. *Pommern 1934/35
im Spiegel von Gestapo-Lageberichten und Sachakten.* Vol. 1, *Darstellung.* Vol. 2, *Quellen.* Cologne, 1974.

Timpke, Henning. "Das KL Fuhlsbüttel." In *Studien zur Geschichte der Konzentrationslager,* edited by Martin Broszat, 11–28. Stuttgart, 1970.

Todeslager Sachsenhausen: Ein Dokumentarbericht vom Sachsenhausen-Prozeß. Compiled
by Fritz Sigl. Berlin, 1948.

Totenbuch Neuengamme. Edited by Franz Glienke et al. Wiesbaden, n.d. [1967].

Totenliste Hamburger Widerstandskämpfer und Verfolgter. 1933–1945. Edited by Willi
Sander et al. Hamburg, 1968.

Treue, Wilhelm. "Widerstand von Unternehmern und Nationalökonomen."
In Schmädeke and Steinbach, *Der Widerstand gegen den Nationalsozialismus,*
917–37.

Twisselmann, Hans-Jürgen. *Vom Frieden mit Gott und auf Erden.* Special issue, *Bruderdienst* 13 (n.d.).

—— *Vom "Zeugen Jehovas" zum Zeugen Jesu Christi.* 6th ed. Gießen, 1983.

—— *Der Wachtturm-Konzern der Zeugen Jehovas: Anspruch und Wirklichkeit.* Gießen, 1995.

—— *Die Wahrheit, die frei macht: Zum Thema "Jehovas Zeugen": Anfragen, Antworten, Alternativen.* Gießen, 1985.

—— *Die "Zeugen Jehovas": Erwählte oder Verführte?* 6th ed. Witten, 1985.

United States Court of Restitution Appeals of the Allied High Commission for Germany. *Reports,* vol. 3. Nürnberg, 1953.

Der Unrechts-Staat: Recht und Justiz im Nationalsozialismus. Special edition, *Kritische Justiz* (1979).

Verfolgung und Widerstand unter dem Nationalsozialismus in Baden: Die Lageberichte der Gestapo und des Generalstaatsanwalts Karlsruhe, 1933–1940. Edited by Jörg Schadt. Stuttgart, 1976.

Verfolgung, Widerstand, Neubeginn in Freiburg, 1933–1945. Edited by Henri Büttner et al. Freiburg, n.d. [1981].

Verhandlungen des Deutschen Bundestages, Anlagen zu den stenographischen Berichten. Vol. 341. Bonn, 1986

Verhandlungen des Reichstags, Anlagen zu den stenographischen Berichten. Vol. 440. Berlin, 1930.

Vogl, Friedrich. *Widerstand im Waffenrock: Österreichische Freiheitskämpfer in der Deutschen Wehrmacht 1938–1945.* Vienna, 1977.

Volkmann, Klaus J. *Die Rechtsprechung staatlicher Gerichte in Kirchensachen: 1933–1945.* Mainz, 1978.

Die Volks-, Berufs- und Betriebszählung in Hamburg am 16. Juni 1933. Compiled by Statistisches Landesamt. Hamburg, 1935.

Vollmer, Bernhard. *Volksopposition im Polizeistaat: Gestapo- und Regierungsberichte 1934–1936.* Stuttgart, 1957.

Vultejus, Ulrich. *Kampfanzug unter der Robe: Kriegsgerichtsbarkeit des zweiten und dritten Weltkrieges.* Hamburg, 1984.

Wagner, Walter. *Der Volksgerichtshof im nationalsozialistischen Staat.* Stuttgart, 1974.

Warmbrunn, Paul. "Strafgerichtsbarkeit in der Pfalz und in Rheinhessen im Dritten Reich." In *Justiz im Dritten Reich: Justizverwaltung, Rechtsprechung und Strafvollzug auf dem Gebiet des heutigen Landes Rheinland-Pfalz,* 1:337–500. Frankfurt am Main, 1995.

Weber, Hermann. "Die Ambivalenz der kommunistischen Widerstandsstrategie bis zur 'Brüsseler' Parteikonferenz." In Schmädeke and Steinbach, *Der Widerstand gegen den Nationalsozialismus,* 73–85.

Weber, Werner. *Die Dienst- und Leistungspflichten der Deutschen.* Vol. 2, *Idee und Ordnung des Reiches.* Hamburg, 1943.

——. "Die kleinen Religionsgemeinschaften im Staatskirchenrecht des nationalsozialistischen Regimes." In *Forschungen und Berichte aus dem*

Öffentlichen Recht: Gedächtnisschrift für Walter Jellinek, edited by Otto Bachof et al., 101–12. Munich, 1955.

Weinkauff, Hermann. *Die deutsche Justiz und der Nationalsozialismus: Ein Überblick.* Stuttgart, 1968.

Weinzierl, Erika. "Österreichische Frauen in nationalsozialistischen Konzentrationslagern." In Benz and Distel, *Frauen-Verfolgung und Widerstand*, 166–204.

Weis, Christian. *Zeugen Jehovas, Zeugen Gottes?: Eine Hilfe zur kritischen Auseinandersetzung mit der Lehre der Wachtturm-Gesellschaft.* Salzburg, 1984.

Weisenborn, Günther. *Der lautlose Aufstand: Bericht über die Widerstandsbewegung des deutschen Volkes 1933–1945.* 1953. Reprint, Frankfurt am Main, 1974.

Werner, Josef. *Karlsruhe 1945: Unter Hakenkreuz, Trikolore und Sternenbanner.* 2nd ed. Karlsruhe, 1986.

Weyrauch, Walter Otto. *Gestapo V-Leute: Tatsachen und Theorie des Geheimdienstes. Untersuchungen zur Geheimen Staatspolizei während der nationalsozialistischen Herrschaft.* Frankfurt am Main, 1989.

Wickert, Christl. "Frauen im Hintergrund — das Beispiel von Kommunistinnen und Bibelforscherinnen." In *Das "andere Deutschland" im Widerstand gegen den Nationalsozialismus: Beiträge zur politischen Überwindung der nationalsozialistischen Diktatur im Exil und im Deutschen Reich*, edited by Helga Grebing and Christl Wickert, 199–224. Essen, 1994.

Widerstand und Verfolgung in Essen, 1933–1945: Dokumentennachdrucke zur Ausstellung. Reprint of documents for the exhibition. Essen, 1983.

Wiechert, Ernst. "Der Totenwald." Report. Munich, n.d. [1946].

Wiedergutmachung und Entschädigung für nationalsozialistisches Unrecht. Öffentliche Anhörung des Innenausschußes des Deutschen Bundestages am 24. Juni 1987. Bonn, 1987.

A Witness Testimony, 1933–1945. Edited by Cercle Européen des Témoins de Jéhoval anciens déportés et internés. Louviers, 1996. Originally published as *Mémoire de Témoins, 1933–1945* (Paris, 1994).

Wittstadt, Klaus, ed. *Die kirchliche Lage in Bayern nach den Regierungspräsidentenberichten 1933–1943.* Vol. 6, *Regierungsbezirk Unterfranken 1933–1944.* Mainz, 1981.

Wolff, Georg. *Kalendarium der Geschichte des KZ Sachsenhausen.* Oranienburg, 1987.

Wrobel, Johannes. "Einige Grundwerte und Glaubensinhalte der Zeugen Jehovas und ihr Verhalten während der Haft." Typewritten manuscript. Selters/Taunus, 1994.

Wüllner, Fritz. *Die NS-Militärjustiz und das Elend der Geschichtsschreibung: Ein grundlegender Forschungsbericht.* Baden-Baden, 1991.

Zahnwetzer, Moritz. *KZ Buchenwald: Erlebnisbericht.* Kassel, 1946.

Zehnter, Annette. *Widerstand und Verfolgung in Bochum und Wattenscheid, 1933–1945.* Essen, 1992.

Zehrer, Karl. *Evangelische Freikirchen und das "Dritte Reich."* Göttingen, 1986.

Zeugen des Widerstandes: Eine Dokumentation über die Opfer des Nationalsozialismus in Nord-, Ost- und Südtirol von 1938 bis 1945. Revised by Johann Holzner, Anton Pinsker, Johann Reiter, and Helmut Tschol. Innsbruck, 1977.

Zieba, Anna. "Die Geflügelfarm Harmense." *Hefte von Auschwitz* 11 (1970): 41–72.

Ziebold, Irmi, et al. "Das Schicksal der Freiburger Zeugen Jehovas während der NS-Zeit." Manuscript. Freiburg im Breisgau, n.d. (Beitrag zum Schülerwettbewerb Deutsche Geschichte um den Preis des Bundespräsidenten 1981/82, Archiv der Körber-Stiftung NS I/1186).

Ziegler, Walter, ed. *Die kirchliche Lage in Bayern nach den Regierungspräsidentenberichten 1933–1943.* Vol. 4, *Regierungsbezirk Niederbayern und Oberpfalz: 1933–1945.* Mainz, 1973.

Ziemann, Helmut. "Die Stellung der Psychopathen im Militärstrafrecht." Jur. diss., University of Marburg, Rheinhausen, 1941.

Zimmermann, Josef Franz. *Die NS-Volkswohlfahrt und das Winterhilfswerk des deutschen Volkes.* Würzburg, 1938.

Zimmermann, Michael. "Die Ernsten Bibelforscher." In *Widerstand gegen den Nazismus in Oberhausen,* edited by Joseph C. Rossaint and Michael Zimmermann, 67–69. Frankfurt am Main, 1983.

Zinnhobler, Rudolf. "Die Zeugen Jehovas (Ernste Bibelforscher)." In *Widerstand und Verfolgung in Oberösterreich, 1934–1945: Eine DoKumentation,* edited by Brigitte Galanda et al., 2:199–210. Vienna, 1982.

Zipfel, Friedrich. *Kirchenkampf in Deutschland 1933–1945: Religionsverfolgung und Selbstbehauptung der Kirchen in der nationalsozialistischen Zeit.* Berlin, 1965.

Zur Neugestaltung des Militärstrafgesetzbuches: Bericht des Wehrrechtsausschußes der Akademie für Deutsches Recht. Berlin, 1936.

Zürcher, Franz. *Croisade contre le Christianisme: Persécution moderne des chrétiens. Une documentation.* Paris, 1939.

——— *Kreuzzug gegen das Christentum.* Zurich, 1938.

Films

Fear Not: Persecution and Resitance of Jehovah's Witnesses Under the Nazi Regime. Documentation by Stefanie Krug and Fritz Poppenberg, Drei Linden Media. Berlin, 1997. 92 minutes.

Jehovah's Witnesses Stand Firm against Nazi Assault. Produced by Watch Tower Bible and Tract Society of New York, Inc. Brooklyn, NY, 1996. 78 minutes.

Purple Triangles. Produced and directed by Martin Smith. A Starlock Pictures Production for TVS. 1991. 25 minutes.

INDEX

Numbers in italics refer to figures.